ENGLISH HISTORICAL DOCUMENTS

General Editor
DAVID C. DOUGLAS
M.A., F.B.A.

ENGLISH HISTORICAL DOCUMENTS

General Editor: DAVID C. DOUGLAS, M.A., F.B.A.

*The following is a complete list of volumes in preparation; those marked * are already published, and those marked † are expected shortly.*

*Vol. I. *c.* 500–1042. DOROTHY WHITELOCK, M.A., LITT.D., F.S.A.

*Vol. II. 1042–1189. DAVID DOUGLAS, M.A., F.B.A., and G. W. GREENAWAY, M.A.

†Vol. III. 1189–1327. HARRY ROTHWELL, M.A., PH.D.

Vol. IV. 1327–1485. ALEC R. MYERS, M.A., F.S.A.

†Vol. V. 1485–1558. C. H. WILLIAMS, M.A.

Vol. VI. 1558–1603. DOUGLAS PRICE, M.A., B.LITT., F.S.A.

Vol. VII. 1603–1660. MARY COATE, M.A.

*Vol. VIII. 1660–1714. ANDREW BROWNING, M.A., D.LITT.

*Vol. IX. American Colonial Documents to 1776. MERRILL JENSEN, M.A., PH.D.

*Vol. X. 1714–1783. D. B. HORN, M.A., D.LITT., and MARY RANSOME, M.A.

*Vol. XI. 1783–1832. A. ASPINALL, M.A., LITT.D.

*Vol. XII(1). 1833–1874. G. M. YOUNG, M.A.,D.LITT. and W. D.HANDCOCK, M.A., B.LITT.

Vol. XII(2). 1874–1914. G. M. YOUNG, M.A., D.LITT. and W. D. HANDCOCK, M.A., B.LITT.

GENERAL PREFACE

ENGLISH HISTORICAL DOCUMENTS is a work designed to meet a present need. Its purpose is to make generally accessible a wide selection of the fundamental sources of English history.

During the past half-century there has been an immense accumulation of historical material, but only a fraction of this has been made readily available to the majority of those who teach or who study history. The transcendent importance of the original authorities is recognized, but direct approach to them remains difficult, and even some of the basic texts (which are frequently quoted) are hard to consult. A gulf has thus opened between the work of the specialist scholar and those students, both at schools and universities, who best can profit by his labours. Historical studies tend too often today to consist of a commentary on documents which are not included in the available books; and, in the absence of any representative and accessible collection of the sources, the formation of opinion proceeds without that direct study of the evidence which alone can give validity to historical judgment. Correspondingly, the reading public outside schools and universities, has no adequate means of checking, by reference to the evidence itself, tendentious or partial interpretations of the past.

The editors of these volumes consider that this situation now calls for a remedy. They have striven to supply one by providing what they hope can be regarded as an authoritative work in primary reference.

An enterprise of this nature could only be effective if planned on a large scale. In scope and content, therefore, these volumes differ materially from the conventional "source-books" which usually contain only a restricted number of selected extracts. Here, within much wider limits, each editor has sought to produce a comprehensive *corpus* of evidence relating generally to the period with which he deals. His aim, in each case, has been to present the material with scholarly accuracy, and without bias. Editorial comment has thus been directed in the main towards making the evidence intelligible, and not to drawing conclusions from it. Full account has been taken of modern textual criticism to compile a reliable collection of authentic testimony, but the reader has in general been left to pass his own judgment upon this, and to appraise for himself the value of current historical verdicts. For this reason, everything in this work has been presented in such a manner as to be comprehensible by readers of English, and critical bibliographies have been added to assist further investigation.

The present volume is one of two which will be devoted to the Victorian age. In it the aim has been to illustrate, chiefly from the public records, the main movement in English history between 1833 and 1874: namely the transformation of the political, social and economic structure of England during these years as a result of the growth of industrialism and democracy. So important was this development, and so enduring were its consequences, that it has been thought fit to consecrate an entire volume to its documentation. The history of the Empire and of foreign policy (both of which have been treated elsewhere in authoritative documentary collections) is not therefore here represented, and the direct documentation of Irish affairs has been postponed to a subsequent volume in the series. The scope of the present volume, the unity of the period with which it deals, and the wide ramifications of the central theme which it seeks to display, are explained by the editors in their general introduction. They have drawn their material from a very wide variety of sources, some of which are little known, and it is hoped that their work provides essential contemporary evidence of an historical process whose consequences are still to be felt not only in England but in many other countries in the world.

All concerned in this series are fully aware of the magnitude of the undertaking to which they have addressed themselves. They are conscious of the hazards of selecting from the inexhaustible store of historical material. They realize also the difficulties involved in editing so large a mass of very varied texts in accordance with the exigent demands of modern scholarship. They believe, however, that the essential prerequisite for the healthy development of English historical studies is wider acquaintance with the original authorities for English history. And they are content that their work should be judged by the degree to which they have succeeded in promoting this object.

DAVID DOUGLAS

VOLUME XII(1)

ENGLISH HISTORICAL DOCUMENTS

1833–1874

ENGLISH HISTORICAL DOCUMENTS

1833–1874

Edited by

G. M. YOUNG, M.A., D.Litt.

Fellow of All Souls College, Oxford

and

W. D. HANDCOCK, M.A., B.Litt.

Senior Lecturer in History, University of Exeter

1970

OXFORD UNIVERSITY PRESS

New York

First Published 1956
Reprinted 1964, 1970

Reprinted in Great Britain

ACKNOWLEDGEMENTS

THE editors wish to offer their most grateful thanks to the Warden and Fellows of All Souls College, Oxford, and the Senate and Council of University College, Exeter (now the University of Exeter), to the Board of the Faculty of History, the Librarian and staff of the Bodleian Library and of the Codrington Library, All Souls College, in the University of Oxford, and to the Librarian and staff of the Roborough Library of the University of Exeter, for the facilities they provided for the work necessary to the compilation of this volume, and for their unvarying helpfulness and kindness during its course. Mr. A. B. Rodger, of Balliol College, Oxford, Mr. G. W. Greenaway and Mr. B. W. Clapp, of the University of Exeter, have read different Parts of the work, and have given assistance and advice for which the editors are deeply grateful. The general editor of the series, Professor David Douglas, has been unwearying in encouragement and help, particularly in the difficult task of keeping the volume within the limits of space permitted by the series. Miss Kathleen M. Dexter, of the University of Exeter, has given the most devoted help in the ungrateful and laborious tasks of the preparation of the final copy, the reading and correction of the proofs, and the compilation of the index. The editors' debt to her generous assistance can hardly be measured.

For the use of material still under copyright, the editors' thanks are due, in the first place, to the Controller of H.M. Stationery Office, without whose permission to make free use of official papers the compilation of the volume would have been impossible; to Sir John Murray, for the *Letters of Queen Victoria*, and also for letters from the *Life of Disraeli* and the *Life and Letters of Sir James Graham*; to Messrs. Methuen, for tables from Porter's *Progress of the Nation*, and material from Sir W. Holdsworth's *History of English Law*; to Messrs. Constable, for tables from William Page's *Commerce and Industry*; to Professor Albert H. Imlah, of the Fletcher School of Law and Diplomacy, Massachusetts, and to the *Economic History Review*, for the table at No. 89, and again to Professor Imlah, for supplying, with permission to make use of them, his revised calculations of some of the figures in the table.

G. M. YOUNG
W. D. HANDCOCK

CONTENTS

PAGE

Part II. PARLIAMENT

Part III. NATIONAL RESOURCES: ECONOMIC STRUCTURE AND DEVELOPMENT

A. TABLES

B. DOCUMENTS

PART IV. THE CHURCHES

Part V. CHARTISM AND FREE TRADE

Part VI. LAW, PENAL SYSTEM, AND COURTS

Part VII. CENTRAL ADMINISTRATION

Part VIII. LOCAL GOVERNMENT

Part IX. THE POOR LAW

Part X. PUBLIC HEALTH

PAGE

Part XI. EDUCATION

Part XII. INDUSTRIAL CONDITIONS AND LEGISLATION

INTRODUCTION

INTRODUCTION

THE Victorian period witnessed a profound transformation of English society. It saw the decisive shift from agriculture to industry and trade as the bases of the national livelihood,[1] the growth of a predominantly urban society of a sort, and on a scale, new in the experience of mankind, while in the political sphere it saw the engrafting first of middle-class and then of large popular elements on to a predominantly aristocratic constitution that had just recently, in the Napoleonic Wars, given the world a singular demonstration of its stability and strength. From the wider than national point of view it may not without reason be regarded as the epoch of Britain's greatest influence in the world. For a brief while, before America had developed the full strength of her continental frame, and while Europe was still beset with political division and economic backwardness, Britain's pioneer industrial vigour and her political stability enabled her to play the part of the leading power of the world. Her commerce and her naval might penetrated its uttermost seas; her example was felt wherever men's minds turned to newer ways of life; British business and political methods were equated with progress wherever progress was discussed, except perhaps in America. Even after the period of unquestioned leadership had passed, the character and temper of the renovated English society remained a matter of world interest and importance. For it had provided the prototype of the industrial civilization that was gradually to spread over the world. Problems that had been Britain's alone became those also of other nations and continents. Britain's attitudes towards them–still more, perhaps, the somewhat summary interpretations of those attitudes that gained currency–had a considerable influence on the world's behaviour in face of them. Thus the central theme of Victorian history, which can be described as that of the response of the institutions and traditions of an old, vigorous, and highly integrated society to the twin impacts of industrialism and democracy, has more than a national, even something of an oecumenical significance. To illustrate this theme by contemporary evidence, between the years 1833 and 1874, to provide original testimony of its complexity and development, is the object of this volume.

In one respect the student of Victorian history is in a fortunate position today. Its issues are near enough to us to be readily intelligible, while they may be said to have receded just sufficiently into the past to be grasped in their connected significance, as the expression of the total spirit and circumstances of their age. If this means that a good deal of earlier secondary material written,

[1] Part III.

very often, under pressure of the immediate controversies of the age is sometimes, in some respects, an inadequate or even an untrustworthy guide, the documentary sources, on the other hand, have a ready intelligibility, lacking, on occasion, to those of remoter periods. But against this is to be set their enormous bulk. The volumes of the Statutes of the Realm increase in size, in an age which began to regard legislation as the primary function of Parliament; the Parliamentary Debates are officially recorded in the volumes of Hansard from 1820 onwards; and, above all, in 1836 begins the publication of Parliamentary Papers, or Blue Books, running into an increasing number of closely printed folios each year, and into many hundreds for the period. To these must be added the biographies consecrated by contemporaries or immediate successors to almost every Victorian figure of any public eminence, containing, in many cases, a great deal of contemporary correspondence, and constituting an almost unparalleled documentation of the more personal aspects of public and social life. Further, as was natural in an age in which public libraries grew in number and size, and in which the importance of records and of historical study in all its forms won increasing public recognition, a vast array of newspapers, magazines, pamphlets, and works of research and imagination bearing on public problems provide ancillary evidence on every aspect of social life. These are the printed sources alone, and do not include the unprinted sources available in the British Museum, the Public Record Office, and other collections, public and private.

To distil even the essence of such overflowing testimony into a single volume would be manifestly impossible, if rigid exclusions were not made. The editors took the view that priority must be given to the public records which constitute the foundation of a knowledge of the period. They have further concentrated their attention on those social and political transformations which constitute the central thread of Victorian history, and give their character to its every theme. Indeed the present state of the documentary presentation of Victorian history would of itself have indicated this course. The history of the Empire, and of Foreign Policy in the nineteenth century have already been made the subjects of volumes of selected documents which are of the highest authority,[1] and to trench further on this ground in the present volume would seem to be unnecessary. Moreover, foreign and imperial relations, however important in themselves, play relatively little part in the period of this volume in shaping its central theme; they impinge from time to time on its story, rather than are of its essence. The same may be said in a lesser degree of Irish affairs in the earlier half of the Victorian period. Irish history,

[1] A. Berriedale Keith, *Selected Speeches and Documents on Colonial Policy* (2 vols., Oxford, 1918) and H. Temperley and Lilian M. Penson, *Foundations of British Foreign Policy from Pitt to Salisbury* (Cambridge, 1938).

in the period from 1833 to 1874, is that of a distinct and imperfectly assimilated part of the society whose development is here to be considered. Its problems constitute a frequent concern of the common government and Parliament, as will be illustrated in the succeeding pages of this essay, but they are not the same problems as those of the larger society. They require a distinct documentation, and it has been thought better to postpone this to the volume dealing with the succeeding period, when Irish questions command the political stage, and are the continuous and dominant preoccupation of both islands.

It will not be out of place, at this stage, to say something of the plan upon which this volume proceeds. The monarchy, as the symbol of unity and continuity in the society and in its vigorous response to the challenge of new conditions, is first considered. Parliament, the chief organ of the national will in the new conditions created for it by the act of energetic statesmanship which drove through the reform of 1832, in its response to the problems of a changing society, and in the movements which led up to the Reform Act of 1867 and prepared a new age of politics, is treated next. The economic changes which meanwhile were transforming the bases of society are illustrated in Part III. The history of the churches in the Victorian period is the record not only of the contemporary consciousness of values beyond the contingencies of time and place, but also of the active source of much of the growing conscientiousness with which social problems are regarded–of an influence of the profoundest significance for the whole temper and outlook of the society. This occupies Part IV. The twin and contemporary movements of Chartism and Free Trade, rising to their peaks in the unhappiest years of the period, express the discontents and demands of classes outside the political country, and supply the main external impulse–*i.e.* outside the development of opinion in Parliament and among the enfranchised classes–to political movement in the period. They are the subject of Part V. Reforms in the law and in its administration affecting the daily life of citizens are dealt with in Part VI. The processes and controversies as a result of which the character and efficiency of central administration were revolutionized occupy Part VII. The not dissimilar changes in the machinery and in the spirit of local government form the theme of Part VIII. The beginnings and the continuation of the system set up by the Poor Law Amendment Act of 1834–of central importance both as the primary expression of the new temper of administrative efficiency of the period and as the confirmation and enforcement of its insistence on the individual's economic responsibility for himself–is the subject of Part IX. The Public Health movement, so tense a trial, in the circumstances of the time, of the temper and courage of men, so vital to the health and happiness of the masses, and even to the survival of industrial civilization, as it found its pioneers and its earliest opportunities within the framework of the Poor Law, follows naturally in Part X. The perplexed and yet determined drive by which, in spite of divisions not only of prejudice but of deepest principle, the efforts of churchmen, statesmen, administrators, and innumerable individuals acting in a private capacity achieved the foundations of the national system of education demanded by the new circumstances of society, follows in Part XI. Finally, in Part XII, working conditions in the industries of the country, the movements for their regulation by the State, and the aims and activities, and also the difficulties, of trade unionism are illustrated. The complexity of these topics, and the mass of the documentary material from which the illustration of them has had to be drawn, has necessitated the writing of separate and somewhat lengthy Introductions to each Part. But the total story is something more than the sum of its parts, and in the following pages, though necessarily very briefly, the attempt is made to indicate the interconnection of these, and to sketch the broad phasing of the story as a whole.

By the eighteen-thirties it was clear that the economic transformations of the preceding half-century had made Britain a wealthier and more powerful country; it was by no means so clear that they had made her a happier or a more united one. The difficulty of the time was connected not only with economic change, but as much with the fact that twenty of its central years had been years of critical and exhausting conflict with Revolutionary and Napoleonic France. This had absorbed the energies of government and Parliament, leaving little to spare for more than cursory consideration of domestic problems; had saddled the country with an immense debt; disturbed the currency; wrested the economy to its own purposes, giving a particular stimulus to agriculture and to war industries; and had created the utmost confusion in foreign markets by its vicissitudes. It had thus left as a legacy a problem of its own, that of the adjustment of the economy to peace conditions, in addition to those which the novelty of the economy itself had created. Politically, its results were unpropitious. On its ideological side, the French Revolution arose from intellectual sources largely common to this country and to France. It resulted, therefore, in England, in the stimulation of native radicalism, and in the easy assimilation, in some quarters, of its own extravagant expectations and hopes. But amongst the governing classes and in wide circles outside, the effect of the war, and of revulsion from the course of development which the Revolution took, was to create an attachment to the constitution, as settled in Church and State, and to traditional modes of action and of thought, which attained the rigidity of a fixed idea. Burke had been the prophet of this change of mind, and, in Professor

Trevelyan's phrase, "had heard the fall of civilisation in the falling stones of the Bastille". Understandable, not ungenerous in many of its phases, the temper was not a happy one in which to confront the problems of a new age. Both the material and the psychological effects referred to endured for a generation. It was not till the mid-'forties or the 'fifties that the economy may be said to have begun to find a balance;[1] and for the remaining active lifetime of many of those who had witnessed the crisis of the struggle, the cycle of disorder, concession, revolution, which had brought to birth, in their view, the monster against which they had struggled, remained, despite the effect of the more moderate French Revolution of 1830, the bottom of their political feeling and thought. The sense of living on top of a volcano never quite left them.

The Tory governments which inherited the prestige of victory and the problems of peace are no longer considered the incompetent and frightened reactionaries that they used to be painted. In the resettlement of Europe they followed a moderate and far-sighted policy, and performed the greatest service possible in their generation, not least, indirectly, to the solution of Britain's domestic problems, in laying foundations which made possible the preservation of European peace, without major war, for forty years. They followed a policy of strict governmental economy; they carried out, at some expense of deflation, the restoration of gold payments; they effected valuable tariff reforms. Even the measures for which they have been most criticized–the abandonment of the income tax and the protective corn tariff of 1815–were measures rather of Parliament than of the Government. They were harsh in their treatment of popular agitation, but police for preventing it from getting out of hand was virtually non-existent, and the agitations were not, after all, rose-water storms. Probably their greatest responsibility before history is their failure, Peel's legal reforms and institution of the Metropolitan Police apart, to show initiative in the wide field of administrative reform, and their refusal to entertain any proposal of reform of the representation at a time when measures involving no vital change in its principles might well have satisfied opinion. In the whole political field the paralysis of the fear of revolution lay upon them.

There was little in the circumstances in which Lord Grey took office in 1830 to presage a decade of Whig government and of fruitful reform. The Whigs had recently split in two over the question of co-operation with Canning. Grey himself, since his salad days, as one of Fox's young men and a Friend of the People, had shown considerable moderation in politics. But in his constant care for the preservation of the Whig Party, his obvious indifference to office for its own sake, in the very responsibility of his attitudes there were hints, though they were not generally perceived, that he would use office for serious

[1] Part III.

purposes, if it should come his way. The groups from which he drew support were the two sections of the Whigs, the Canningites, and a few Tories sufficiently disgusted by Wellington's and Peel's passing of Catholic Emancipation, despite a lifetime of opposition to it, to join Grey, who had spent a lifetime in supporting it. Grey's Cabinet was one of the most aristocratic of the century. It was nevertheless a very able one: Melbourne, Russell, Stanley, and Palmerston were future prime ministers; Brougham, though erratic and untrustworthy, was the most brilliant man of his generation, with a flair for what needed doing politically; Althorp, Durham, and Graham, in diverse ways, were men of outstanding ability.

Whiggism, at its core, was perhaps little more than the devotion of a handful of aristocratic families to the parliamentary constitution which they had largely nursed into effective being–the sense that it was safest in their hands, and perhaps never fully safe out of them. Associated with this central devotion was a feeling for monarchy as an institution, but jealousy of its playing any very active role; loyalty to the Church, but a refusal to regard its affairs as the business only of its spiritual leaders; sympathy with popular causes, provided they submitted to aristocratic leadership; most important of all, perhaps, at the moment, the sense that aristocracy owed leadership–the belief, expressed by Locke, that revolution rarely comes from below unless the leadership from above has been such as to invite it. During a long political exile the party leadership had several times been in close contact with popular Radicalism, without being prepared to yield the political initiative to it, and individual Whigs had developed, on different points, Radical ideas. There had been times, too, of what were regarded as dangerous sympathies, on the Whig part, with the Revolution and with Napoleon. It was this readiness, partly intrinsic and partly fortuitous, to look at things with a fresh and unjaundiced eye, this preference for meeting popular clamour with reform rather than with repression, combined with political touch and a sense of tradition, that was the source of the eminent contribution that Whiggism was able to make to the problems of the generation.

Political Radicalism was inchoate, a temper of impatience and scorn, rather than a party, or a philosophy. There was the radicalism of Cobbett, which was the nostalgia for an older rural England, never, perhaps, quite as Cobbett's imagination painted it, combined with a hatred of humbug and corruption, consorting, a little uneasily, in Cobbett's own make-up, with considerable self-satisfaction in the role of publicist and demagogue. There was the London radicalism, nursed in the battles of Westminster elections, represented by Francis Place, the tailor and political wire-puller of Charing Cross, friend of Hume and Roebuck, and of James Mill and Bentham, and behind this the extremer radicalism, verging into socialism, of the Rotunda, which it gave Place so much difficulty to handle during the Reform Bill struggles. There was the radicalism of Attwood and Birmingham and the political unions, representing on the one hand the common denominator of the political aspirations of middle and working classes in a vigorous industrial city where classes shaded into each other, rather than were sharply marked off, and on the other the inflationary currency radicalism that was Attwood's personal gospel. There was the radicalism of the factory masses in Yorkshire and Lancashire clamouring, in vast meetings and with a formidable organization,[1] for a Ten Hours Act, under a largely Tory upper leadership. Throughout the country there was the radicalism of merchants opposed, after the example of the petitioning London merchants of 1821, to the Corn Laws; the radicalism of Dissent; and the radicalism of manufacturers, merchants, tradesmen, here and there independent farmers and craftsmen, conscious of a place in the economic and social life of the country, and of exclusion from its political life.

Within political Radicalism, but initially the mode of thought only of an intellectual *élite* of leaders, was Philosophical Radicalism, the Utilitarianism of Jeremy Bentham. Neither particularly original, nor particularly profound, it was particularly apt for its time, and its influence within the period was to be profound and widespread. It represented a confident attempt to apply the scientific spirit–*la méthode Newtonienne*, as Elie Halévy has aptly called it–to the less tractable sphere of human affairs. It was based on the two principles of psychological and ethical hedonism–the doctrine, in the first place, that human action is governed by a calculation of its consequences in terms of pleasure and pain, and that "man, by the very constitution of his being, prefers his own happiness to that of all other people put together", and the apparently inconsistent further teaching that the proper end of human action is the greatest happiness of the greatest number. These propositions were linked together by the assumption, shared by Benthamism and the classical economics, and a commonplace of this confident morning of sociological rationalism, that "Society is so constituted that in labouring for our particular good we labour for the good of the whole". It was not so much in these broad propositions, but in the deductions that he drew from them and the practical exemplification he gave of their bearings, in voluminous writings, that Bentham showed his strength. There was, in the first place, the hedonistic calculus, which, on the assumption that one sort of pleasure is as good as another–"pushpin as good as poetry"–and that pleasures could be reckoned in 'lots', under the headings of 'intensity', 'duration', 'certainty', 'proximity', 'productiveness', and 'purity', and, for general calculations, of 'extent', proffered itself to strike the

[1] Part XII.

balance-sheet of any proposed course of action, whether in private or public affairs. As an ethical teaching, Benthamism became more than a doctrine; it became an attitude of mind. It taught no morals, as morals were traditionally conceived, but, instead, 'enlightened self-interest', into which much of the irrepressible moral impulses of its more generous votaries had to learn to compress themselves. If it bred some of its own, it was thus a corrosive solvent of much conventionally accepted humbug. It became, too, more even than an attitude of mind–it served as the flag of the intellectual independence of a class, for through it the business man learned that the high matters of politics, of whose understanding the older governing classes had claimed a monopoly, and the even higher matters of morals, on which parsons and church dignitaries claimed to pronounce, were, in sober fact, reducible to the intellectual operations of his counting-house.

The relevance of Bentham's doctrines to politics arose from the fact that the "natural identity of interests"–i.e. of individual interests with the general interest–was not quite complete, and required to be made so by political action. Bentham began his career as a legal reformer, with the view that the business of law was to render this identification complete by attaching as much 'pain' –and no more–to anti-social courses of action as was required to deter from them individuals to whom they might offer themselves. He spent a mountain of labour in legal 'codifying' to this effect. But when he found that the intrinsic reasonableness of his proposals was not enough to secure their acceptance, he passed over to the view that 'sinister interests' of privileged minorities were obstructing them, and in particular to the opinion that "the most hopeless of reforms would be to raise a thorough-paced English lawyer to the moral level of an average man". This led him to extreme Radical democracy, as the "last step in the artificial identification of interests"–the conception of representative government, based on universal suffrage, annual parliaments, vote by ballot, elaborate measures to secure that Members of Parliaments functioned solely as the conduits of their constituents' views–as the means of securing the political sovereignty of the greatest good of the greatest number from the dominance of sinister interests. Bentham's influence was probably not any very great reinforcement to older radicalism in this particular field, though he claimed to be the grandfather of the Reform Act, through his disciple, James Mill, whose *Encyclopaedia Britannica* articles on government had a considerable circulation and vogue.

It was in his ruthless examination of the whole field of law from the standpoint of public utility, his determined attempt to reduce what the great Coke had called the "artificial reason of the law" to the plain reason of every day, that Bentham's first great influence lay. The impulse persisted through the century.[1] Of more immediate importance for the 'thirties was the extension of his inquiry into the field of what we should nowadays call social administration. With all its strong prejudice in favour of individualism, Benthamism accepted no absolute rights–"natural rights were simple nonsense, natural and imprescriptible rights rhetorical nonsense–nonsense on stilts". Wherever the play of private interests produced socially unacceptable results was an appropriate sphere, on its principles, for the intervention of law. Here lay the root of much of the working philosophy of the New Poor Law, of factory legislation and administration, and later of the campaign for sanitary reform. Finally, the structure of administration itself was brought under the searchlight, and the claim can not unreasonably be made that, as a result, Bentham became the founder of the science of public administration. Just as representative government was conceived as machinery for the precise formulation of what the greatest number themselves thought to be their greatest good, so administration was conceived as machinery for the precise and punctual translation of these views into effect. Hence an insistence on logical structure and clearly defined chains of responsibility. But the passion for scientific accuracy was greater in Bentham than the passion for democracy, and led him to emphasize the importance of expert gathering and reporting of knowledge and facts, and expert interpretation of them where necessary. Hence the strong bureaucratic tendencies of Benthamism, which make it in many ways the anticipation and inspiration of Fabian Socialism. The attitude to social problems was summed up in the formula: inquiry, legislation, execution, inspection, and report. Bentham's proposals were elaborated in his *Constitutional Code*, written in an almost impenetrable jargon, which nevertheless became the *lingua franca* of his sect. They included the setting up of Ministries of Interior Communications, Indigence Relief, Education, and Health, and the assignment to Central Departments of "inspective, statistic, requisitive, officially-informative, information-elucidative, and melioration-suggestive" functions in relation to local administration. Others of them were summarized in a pamphlet gaily and optimistically entitled *Official Aptitude maximised: Expense minimised.*

The Reform Act is Grey's political monument. How striking an initiative it represented in terms of contemporary expectation may be measured by the fact that Brougham, with the laurels of his recent election for Yorkshire fresh upon him, proposed, in the Resolutions he had announced his intention to move in the House on the very eve of the formation of Grey's Government, to disfranchise only six rotten boroughs, as against the Reform Bill's sixty. Durham and Russell may have influenced Grey to put forward a large proposal, but the responsibility for it was his, as his was the authority that imposed it on

[1] Part VI.

a Cabinet by no means uniformly enthusiastic for it, and his the firmness and sagacity that steered the successive Bills, with a still united Cabinet and increasing popular support, through the perils that beset them. No other member of his Cabinet could have filled his place with like success. The Reform Act may not have achieved the permanent settlement of the constitution that Grey professed to have in mind; it may even have contained within itself the seeds of its own decay.[1] But it undoubtedly raised the authority of Parliament and of government at a time when this was sorely needed, and in the course of time the constitutional balance that it created came to command almost universal consent. The constitutional consequences of the Act are more fully discussed in Parts I and II. The political results of its passage were just as far-reaching. The Whig party healed its own dissensions, absorbed the Canningites, and emerged permanently enlarged and strengthened. For the purposes of the struggle virtually the whole political forces of Radicalism had rallied behind it. Whiggism secured, as a result, an initiative in the politics of reform, which Radicals sought often, indeed, to dispute, but which their lack of leadership, of standing with the more moderate part of the electorate, and their own divisions, prevented them more than occasionally capturing from it. Finally, the Act broke the *tabu* which since the war with France had lain upon measures of major political and social reconstruction. So sudden a thaw, after so long a frost, was not without its dangers; there was a risk lest the Whigs should be unable to control the rage to reconstruct. But it was a situation which Peel perceived, and during the decade his efforts, as well, were bent towards its control.

The election of 1832 returned some 320 of Grey's supporters, of varying degrees of attachment, some 190 Radicals and Irish Repealers, and only about 150 Tories. It was a resounding vote of confidence in the Ministry, although it could still be put in a minority by a coalition of extremes against it. The legislation of the decade, though it is often of Radical inspiration, bears the unmistakable Whig stamp upon it: Radicalism might have initiated it, but could not have carried it through; Conservatism, under the guidance of Peel, might support it in principle, but could not, as yet, have initiated it. While the struggle over the Reform Bill was still in progress, the Whigs had offered its first opportunity to Benthamite social science in setting up a Royal Commission on the administration of the Poor Laws – the unhappiest of the problems that were the legacy of haphazard domestic policies during the wars. The accession of Chadwick to the Commission secured a report at once thorough in its examination of the facts, consistent in the principles inspiring it, and fearless in its recommendations – a classic of applied Benthamism, and a continuing

[1] Part II.

influence upon opinion throughout the period.[1] The upshot was the Poor Law Amendment Act of 1834, setting firmly the economic note of the century; providing drastic, if painful, surgery for an admitted evil; and setting up an administrative machinery which at once challenged political preconceptions and set a new standard of efficiency. Next to the Reform Act it was the most far-reaching of the measures of the Whig governments in its effects. Radicals were among its warmest supporters and its bitterest critics.

In the interval between the two Acts, the problem of the hours and conditions of employment of children in factories was put on the administrative road to solution. The inquiries of the Select Committee of the preceding Parliament had been terminated when only the agitators' evidence had been heard; the renewal of proposed legislation in the new House threatened to lead to an embittered and uninforming slanging match between workers and owners, which would have afforded no satisfactory basis for legislation. The knot was cut by the Government's appointment of a Commission of Inquiry, whose recommendations included the appointment of full-time factory inspectors, the administrative clue, as it proved, to the hitherto insoluble problem of enforcement, and to the no less vital difficulty of providing – through the regular reports of the inspectors – a continuous supply of further expert and unbiased opinion on which amending legislation, in an intricate administrative problem, could be based in the future. The Factories Act of 1833, incorporating these provisions, limited the hours of work in textile factories for children to eight per day, and for young persons to twelve. It also required that factory children should attend school, without taking any steps, however, to ensure that schools should be available for them.[2] But in the same year the first State grant – of £20,000 – was made to the philanthropic religious societies which, in the preceding quarter of a century, had taken on their shoulders the principal part of the burden of providing for popular education. The grant was increased, year after year, and in 1839 Russell set up the Committee of Council for Education to oversee its administration, and in the following year appointed the first school inspectors. Arrangements were worked out between the religious bodies and Kay-Shuttleworth – the Clerk to the Committee of Council – which laid foundations on which the whole not unimpressive structure of the voluntary system of popular education was reared in the succeeding generation.[3] The same *annus mirabilis* of 1833 saw the Act for the Abolition of Slavery – a triumph, primarily, of Evangelical agitation, but one in which the Whigs had had a creditable part in the past.

The Municipal Corporations Act, of 1835, based on the recommendations of another Commission, was, in Whig and Radical views, the complement of

[1] Part IX. [2] Part XII. [3] Part XI.

the Reform Act, extending to the oligarchies of town government the treatment that had been applied to rotten boroughs. It did not open immediately a golden age of town government, but it achieved its immediate end of strengthening authority by substituting open election for prescriptive titles whose validity was no longer generally recognized; it identified the middle classes more closely with government in general; it led to the organization of an effective police, hitherto hardly found outside the metropolis, in many of the principal towns of the country; and it created a machinery through which, ultimately, policies of constructive town government found the means to operate.

In other fields Brougham, as Grey's Lord Chancellor, had initiated a vigorous movement of law reform;[1] an Act of 1835 had set up a system of prison inspection;[1] an Act of 1836 provided for the licensing of Dissenters' places of worship for marriages and baptisms, and set up a system of State registration of births, marriages, and deaths, which, as an incidental result, made possible the scientific study of vital statistics.[2] A County and District Constabulary Act, in 1839–following a further Commission of Inquiry–gave counties powers to set up police forces on models similar to those of the metropolitan and new municipal forces.[3] In virtually every field of political and administrative life the Whig governments born of the Reform Act set their mark, acting largely on Radical and, indeed, Benthamite inspiration, but with a political moderation and realism that made their work, even where incomplete in itself, a foundation on which the future could build.

Irish and Church questions were the great stumbling-blocks of the Whigs. Catholic Emancipation had come too late and too ungraciously to effect any reconciliation of Irish feeling, nor was there much evidence in the immediately following years that it was intended to; O'Connell's machinery of agitation was the strongest force in the country; there were grievances of the tithe and the Church cess, paid by the vast majority to the Church of the tiny minority; behind this, the deep social distress of the country and the looming threat of a Repeal agitation O'Connell had faithfully supported the Reform Bill, but he and his immediate followers–his 'tail'–were unpopular and mistrusted in the House; Dissenting and Radical support could be commanded for an attack on the Established Church, but Anglican feeling, though conscious of its weakness and unpopularity, looked on it as a beleagured fortress, and was bound in faith to hope that its garrison might one day issue forth to the conquest of the land. Any weakening of it was therefore regarded as treason. To English Protestantism, even to the early Oxford Movement, Irish Catholicism was the religion of an ignorant and benighted peasantry, and, even to Dissenters,

[1] Part VI. [2] Parts VI and X. [3] Part VIII.

measures that wore the air of favour to it were suspect. In the industrial towns the Irish were chiefly known through the immigrants who clustered in the most lawless and squalid districts, and tended to undercut wages. There was little of that readiness to understand the unfortunate plight of Ireland which grew up later in the century. For an Irish policy, then, little in the way of support could be looked for, except from the sense of its political advantage and from the jealousies and irritations of Radicals and Dissenters. Yet pursuit of an active Irish policy was imposed on Grey by Whig tradition, by regard for O'Connell and the support he could command, and, imperatively, by the situation in Ireland itself, where a tithe war had virtually brought law and order to an end.

Whig policies had thus to combine a swingeing Coercion Act with reorganization of the finances of the Church in Ireland, a redistribution of its bishoprics, relief from the Church cess and a commutation of tithe. The first, when the question of renewal came up, led to intrigues and dissensions in the Cabinet, resulting in Grey's own resignation in 1834; the second occasioned Keble's Assize Sermon of 1833, which touched off the Oxford Movement, and wide Anglican opposition;[1] the third, on the question of the 'appropriation' of Church revenues for secular purposes, raised by Russell, brought about the resignation from Melbourne's Cabinet, the successor of Grey's, of Stanley and Graham and several of their supporters. The reform of the Church in Ireland made it more defensible, but not more palatable to the Irish, and on the other questions, nothing that the Whigs dared suggest went far enough for O'Connell. Grey initiated similar policies of reform as regards the Church in England, and these, though they had the cautious support of moderates among the Church leaders, deepened, in other circles, the impression that reform was a surrender to Dissent, if not to Atheism.[1] A Bill to open Oxford and Cambridge to Dissenters passed the Commons but was thrown out by the Lords in 1834.[2] The Act of 1836 to license Dissenters' places of worship for baptism and marriages, referred to above, met some of the Dissenters' grievances, but a proposal to substitute a payment by the Treasury for the Church rate, to which they were legally liable, infuriated them. A Bill to transfer the liability to the Ecclesiastical Commission[3] was lost in 1837. Meanwhile, in 1834, Melbourne's Government had resigned, or been dismissed,[4] and Peel, in his brief government, had endorsed policies of moderate reform and had appealed to the country with a large measure of success. The alliance of Irish Catholics, Protestant Dissenters, and Radicals, which had dominated a brief period, had been neither markedly successful nor outstandingly happy. But it was this alliance that threw Peel out, and Melbourne's Government returned on a vote in favour of the

[1] Part IV. [2] Part XI. [3] Part IV. [4] Part I.

appropriation of Irish Church surpluses. Church reform proceeded, but its pace and character were dictated, thereafter, largely by Peel's proposals, and, as regards Ireland, Melbourne found himself compelled to the treadmill of a policy which the House of Lords constantly delayed and frustrated, without his being in a position to appeal to the country against it. By persistence he carried parts of his policy, but the prestige of his Government necessarily declined. The political conditions for a successful Irish policy did not exist; the tragedy, from the Whig point of view, was that they were compelled, by their responsibility as a government, and by political necessity, to seek and pursue one.

Even at the height of the Reform crisis the interests of the factory workers had not been wholly with the Whigs, and at Leeds, in 1832, Michael Sadler, the Tory Factory Reformer, had fought unsuccessfully against Macaulay, representing Whiggism and Reform. Nevertheless, on the whole, the Reform agitation had commanded popular support, and this was an element in the collapse of Toryism in the election of 1832. But the voting powers of working people were decreased, rather than increased, by the Reform Act.[1] The realization of this, after the crisis had passed, caused disillusionment in working-class circles, and the break of events and the conduct of the Government increased the feeling. The appointment of the Factory Commissioners in 1832, which was looked on as an attempt to delay or evade legislation, and the passing of an Act based on its recommendations, instead of on the popular demands, caused resentment. The Poor Law Amendment Act was also bitterly opposed by popular Radicalism. From 1829 a growing interest in trade unionism had been manifesting itself in the industrial parts of the country. In 1833–1834, fed by political disillusionment, this took on an enormous extension, and fell under the influence of Robert Owen, successful factory owner, pioneer of factory reform and of a socialism which, impracticable as it proved itself in the instance, had an enduring influence on working-class movements.[2] The attempt at comprehensive trade unions broke down in an orgy of strikes and counter-action on the part of the employers, but not before the case of the Dorchester Labourers[2] had made the Government the target of immense hostile demonstrations in London and elsewhere. In 1836 the Factory agitation was stung into fresh life by Poulett Thomson's proposal to modify the Act of 1833, and in that and the following year popular opposition to the introduction of the New Poor Law into industrial England took, in many places, violent form, while in Parliament a continuous attack on it from Radical and Tory sources began.[3]

After the brush with William IV, in 1834–1835, which had threatened the revival in the party of the anti-monarchical sentiments of the days of Fox, the Whigs, in 1837, had become the party of the Crown. The duke of Kent had

[1] Part II. [2] Part XII. [3] Part IX.

professed liberal sentiments, in opposition to his father and his eldest brother, and his daughter, on her accession, remained loyal to them. But more important was the personal relation that sprang up between her and Melbourne. The fresh yet disciplined vigour of the queen's nature and the perplexities, almost the pathos of her position, made an irresistible appeal to the chivalry which was the finest side of Melbourne's nature, and the country was treated to the sight of the consummate worldling and sophisticated cynic devoting himself in all sincerity to the political tuition of the girl queen. The country shared the sense of refreshment at the personality of the new monarch, but the experience it had had of an ageing voluptuary and a well-meaning buffoon as the occupants of the throne had eroded monarchical sentiment, and the partisanship of the queen, and the unhappy incident of Lady Flora Hastings, prevented its rise, as yet, to the heights afterwards attained. In the election of 1837 the influence of the Crown, not yet entirely negligible, was cast firmly on the side of the Whigs. It did not check the drift to Peel, which was manifesting itself particularly in the counties, but it may have helped the Whigs to the exiguous majority that they obtained. A further feature of the elections was the weakening of Radicalism, which emboldened Russell to pronounce firmly against further constitutional reform.[1] The Bedchamber Incident of 1839[2] emphasized once more the Crown's identification of itself with the Whigs. The constitutional role was not yet learned, but it was of some importance for the future that the queen's relations with Whig ministers should have begun on the footing of friendly and confidential loyalty.

Meanwhile, in the autumn of 1836, the economic skies darkened, and the country was in the throes of a crisis which hardly lifted till 1843.[3] Two parallel movements took their rise in the distress: Chartism and the Anti-Corn Law League–the one an amalgamation of all the working-class discontents into a demand for a complete renovation of the form of government; the other the claim of the industrial middle class, now becoming conscious of its power in the political country, for a step to which both the traditions and the economic interests of the older governing classes, as they were then regarded, were opposed. Chartism, despite its formidable spread, and the apprehensions of revolution that it roused in 1839, was largely, as the large Irish element in the leadership suggested, a movement of the sections of the population left behind by industrial progress–the unhappy hand-loom weavers and their like.[4] The factory workers and trade unions gave it only intermittent support. But its rise placed the Whig Government in clear opposition to working-class claims. Nevertheless Russell refused to seek extraordinary legislation to deal with it,[5] confiding in the strengthened constitution to ride out the storm. The Anti-Corn

[1] Part II. [2] Part I. [3] Part III. [4] Part XII. [5] Part V.

Law League was to impinge otherwise on government policy. Finance was the mortal wound of the Whig régime, in its later days. Since Althorp's half-hearted efforts to follow a Free Trade policy, Whig budgets had been timid and uninspiring. The end of the decade found their chancellors resorting to percentage additions to taxation to fill a deficit which refused to be satisfied. It was in these circumstances that the Whigs turned again to a Free Trade policy.[1] The institution of the Penny Post in 1839, popular, if financially risky, and the brilliant, if equally risky carrying through of his policy on Mehement Ali by Palmerston in face of the wrathful opposition of France shed a dying lustre on the Government. But its position in parliamentary confidence, as in public confidence, had been sapped, and it failed to defend its financial policy against the scepticism of the House and the onslaught of Peel. Defeated in a House elected only in 1837, it used its credit with the Crown to obtain what was regarded, in the conventions of the time, as a dissolution of favour. But the appeal to the country did it no good; against the disillusionment of its one-time supporters, the attacks of Tory critics both of its social and of its fiscal policy, and the enhanced reputation of Peel, its position crumbled, and a Conservative majority of over eighty was the result.

Whiggism absorbed the whole loyalty of men like Grey and Russell; the preservation of the Whig party and of Whig principles was the sum of public duty to them. Peel's Conservatism, on the other hand, was conceived rather as an instrument to national ends. At the opening of the Reform crisis Peel was a lonely and a somewhat embittered figure on his party benches. The criticism to which he had been exposed for his change of front on Catholic Emancipation, and the loss of his Oxford University seat which it had entailed, had deeply wounded a nature which under its mask of reserve was deeply sensitive to attack. It is to the combination of these feelings with the seriousness of the Reform crisis that would seem to be owing the deeper sense of direction, even of mission, which Peel shows from 1830 onwards, and which divides his new career from his old. Peel's was essentially a governing mind. The established institutions and recognized governing cadres of the nation were the bases, to him, of the order which it was his deepest instinct to defend, to impose, if necessary; an order, moreover, in which his family had won an honoured place. It has sometimes been suggested that Peel had joined the wrong party. But he could not have led a popular cause; nor would there easily have been place for him, without such credentials, in the close governing caste of the Whigs. The party which Liverpool, a political parvenu, had led so long, whose primacy Peel himself had disputed with Canning, the actress's son, was the only possible one for him. But, on the other hand, he had paid his scot, both in

[1] Part V.

praise and dispraise, both in the recognized services he had rendered and in the condemnations he had incurred, to party loyalties in the ordinary sense. In the Reformed Parliament of 1833 he was easily the outstanding man on the Tory side, and shortly the outstanding man in the House. The situation that his pride demanded came about; party came to him, instead of his having to make concessions to party. In his deeply felt view the Whig craving for change, their vulnerability to Radical pressure, created a situation of great danger. The need was to rebuild the party of order on new bases; the old foundations of land and Church were no longer wide enough.

But in the meanwhile it was necessary to uphold the Whigs against the Radicals. The immediate and the longer-ranged aims could be combined by frank acceptance both of the Reform Act and of the need for further reforms, while insisting on giving the latter a practical and moderate stamp. Above all, it was necessary to prevent the hotheads of the Tory party from headlong collision with the Whigs on issues on which the latter could rally the country against them. The Whig strength lay in the alliance between them and the middle classes they had enfranchised. An hereditary understanding, perhaps, told Peel that the stabler part of this class could be detached for the party of order, and this is the long-range strategy that he pursued. Over the Poor Law, in 1833 and 1837, the Municipal Corporations Act, even over Church reform and over the Factory Bill of 1836, Peel avoided opposition in principle, and was, in many ways, helpful to the Government. On poor law and factory legislation many Tories felt strongly, and there was an opportunity of out-Whigging the Whigs in a bid for popular support. This was the strategy which Disraeli was already revolving. But it was not Peel's line, though he had an hereditary qualification to lead on factory questions. When, in forming his Government in 1841, he offered a Household, rather than a Cabinet, post to Ashley, the offer, though couched in flattering terms, was regarded by the latter as an attempt to exploit the popularity that his name commanded to buttress a different policy.

William IV's call, in 1834, to take over the Government was an interruption to Peel's plans, but he came without hesitation to the monarch's aid, and converted embarrassment into opportunity, without formal concession of any of the monarchy's rights.[1] The Tamworth Manifesto[2] put his policy before the country, and the elections strengthened his party in the House. In the conduct of business he showed himself supreme. "There is nobody who approaches him," wrote Greville, contrasting his attitude with the feverish partisanship of Russell, "and every day he displays more and more his capacity for government, and undoubted fitness for the situation he is in." Stanley and

[1] Part I. [2] Part II.

Graham, the Whig dissidents, had refused to join him, so soon after their resignation, and there was even an attempt by Stanley to head a new middle party. That the attempt should have been made illustrated the prescience of Peel's strategy; that it failed, that strategy's success. For within a couple of years the dissidents were members of the Carlton. The violent Whiggism of the queen embarrassed Peel for a time, particularly in 1839, but he could afford to wait, and preferred to do so rather than risk a collision with the Crown, dangerous both to itself and to him. Only in 1841, when the Whigs sought to turn to their profit the rising Free Trade feeling in the country, was the initiative that they still, as a government, possessed dangerous again, and Peel put forth his strength to crush them. A couple of years earlier, and the initiative might have transformed the political situation.

But not for nothing had Peel's apprenticeship to the highest office been passed under the duke of Wellington, whose ultimate of political duty was the fact that he had taken his sovereign's shilling. As Peel had consistently refused to allow his party's strategy to be dictated to him, so, in the crucial debates of the Whig Government's fall, and in his election address, he refused to disclose a fiscal policy. On other matters his attitude was known; on this he must mature his plans under sanction of responsibility, and with access to government information. Unpledged he entered the election; unpledged, in September 1841, he took up power. The party behind him was the instrument he would use as 'Minister of England'–a phrase he later applied to himself–in the service of the nation and of the queen whose hand he had just kissed, and whose relations with him had just been smoothed over by the tactful intervention of her husband. It was a conception of party that had more in common with that of Chatham and Pitt than with that of Fox and Grey and Russell, and it is the key to the political history of the next five years.

The first year of Peel's ministry was one of deep and widespread distress, of mounting Chartist and Anti-Corn Law League agitation, and of great bitterness of feeling, both in Parliament and in the country. Perhaps the most serious symptom was the indication–slight but ominous–of the readiness of some of the Anti-Corn Law League employers to play with revolution by provoking industrial strife.[1] Even in Peel's own party the triple plan that he produced–the abolition and lowering of many duties, the lowering of the sliding scale on corn, and the reintroduction of the income tax–occasioned many murmurs, and not a little open discontent. But the prime minister's firmness and abilities enabled him to dominate them. The sequence of steps that the Cabinet took, the gradual recovery of the country, assisted by good harvests, by the natural resilience of trade, and by the employment and stimulus provided by large-scale railway

[1] Part V.

building, but animated by the consistent policy and wide-ranging measures of government are matters more fitly dealt with in the parts devoted to Economic Structure and Organization, and Chartism and Free Trade.[1] So far as the fortunes of Peel and Conservatism are concerned, they were in a steady though not unchequered ascendant until 1846.

Nemesis was preparing for both, however, and, not inappropriately, it came from Ireland. On matters affecting the larger island Peel's opposition, in the 'thirties, had always been conducted under a strong sense of responsibility for the event; on Ireland his record is not so clear. But when he came to power the Irish problem came on to his own plate, and an embittered O'Connell, expecting nothing from him, reopened the campaign for the repeal of the Act of Union. In the contest between the two men–for it was almost that–Peel emerged the victor. O'Connell's culminating mass meeting of protest at Clontarf was proclaimed by the Irish Government. After a week in which he announced his intention of holding it, O'Connell, in face of the prospect of serious bloodshed, gave way and abandoned it. He was subsequently tried in Ireland on charges of conspiracy and sedition, convicted, and the verdict, on appeal to the House of Lords, reversed, substantially on the ground that the trial had not been a fair one. But his prestige in Ireland did not recover. Nor, however, was Peel's victory more than a Pyrrhic one; the more violent symptoms of Irish *malaise* might have been suppressed, but the disease remained. It was an index, perhaps, of what a more considered and extended attention to Ireland's needs might have enabled Peel to achieve that in his appointment of the Devon Commission to inquire into Irish land tenure, in 1843, he put his finger on the root of the trouble. But the Commission was not able to report for a couple of years, and when it did, the modest Bill based on its recommendations, put forward by Stanley on the Government's behalf, foundered in the Lords. A row of minor, if valuable, concessions to the Catholics culminated in Peel's proposal, in 1845, to increase the meagre grant, made since 1795, to the Maynooth College for the training of priests. Peel carried the Bill, but in face of bitter objurgations from many of his own party, and of caustic attacks on his earlier record in Irish affairs from Whigs who supported the Bill. Macaulay's speech, in the bitterness of its personal attack, might well have passed for one of Disraeli's. The feeling in Peel's party perhaps measures the difficulty he would have had, in opposition, in taking any other course than he did. On the other hand, a more sympathetic attitude then would have facilitated enormously his problems in power. As it was, time was not to be allowed him to achieve anything solid in Ireland. In the late summer of 1845 the Irish potato crop failed, and Peel was faced with the problem of national starvation in Ireland which

[1] Parts III and V.

drove him, in the following year, to the Repeal of the Corn Laws. The bitter struggle this entailed drove him from office, split irrevocably in two the great Conservative party it had been his life work to build up, but, ironically, proved the prelude to a period of unexampled social stability, and, by its very bitterness imparted a sort of consecration to the principle over which it was fought. Russell succeeded Peel, though the stability of his ministry depended on the support of the fallen minister and the hundred or so of his followers whose great aim was to keep the Protectionists from power. Russell had therefore to deal with the lamentable *sequelae* of famine in Ireland, for which he needed a Coercion Act not very different from the one he had refused Peel. On him fell the responsibility of the first suspension of Peel's Bank Act, rendered necessary by the commercial crisis that famine and railway speculation engendered in 1847.[1] He also had to deal with the much-heralded, much-dreaded Chartist demonstration of 1848, to which the circumstances of the year of revolution lent terror, but which proved, in fact, much less formidable than its predecessors.[2] His repeal of the Navigation Acts in 1849 announced that the policy of Free Trade, born of Peel's budgets and of 1846, had hardened into a doctrine.

Not only in the fiscal field was there important progress, in the 'forties, towards the settlement of the institutions and policies of the country. One of Peel's early steps had been to renew the powers of the Poor Law Commissioners for another five years. The principles and outlook of the Act of 1834 were too necessary to the economic rehabilitation of the country that he had in view for Peel to dispense with the Act. The hopes that some Tories had encouraged that the end of Whig power might bring the end of the Act, or at least its substantial modification, proved delusive, and the country had to settle down to acceptance of it. But its administration now lacked the animating zeal and fecundity of resource of Chadwick; though he was still nominally secretary, his relations with the Commissioners virtually prevented him from exercising his functions. This situation, and scandals arising from laxity in administration, led, in 1847, under Russell, to the supercession of the Commission by a board, under a parliamentary chief, subject to the normal rules and responsibilities of departmental administration. But so far as the working of the system was concerned, the change was little more than formal, save, perhaps, that the prospects of realization of the wider and more generous hopes of the Report of 1834 were diminished.[3]

The success of Free Trade, the comparative failure of Chartism, and the educative influence of the Anti-Corn Law League campaigns up and down the country, drilling their audiences in the principles of individualist economics, prepared the way for their substantial assimilation by the working classes

[1] Part III. [2] Part V. [3] Part IX.

during the subsequent decade of prosperity. It resulted also in something of a change in the character of Radicalism. Westminster Radicalism, Philosophic Radicalism, the Radicalism of the whole gospel of Bentham, yielded to the leadership of the Manchester men, Cobden and Bright, whose outlook was much more that of the factory office than of the study or the administrator's chair. Bright had desired the League to turn its attention to franchise questions, but Cobden and his associates demurred, and the League was suspended, virtually wound up, though the influence of its principal figures was not thereby diminished–possibly the reverse. The conception of the State administrator, actively intervening in fields where the need for regulation could be demonstrated, made little appeal to the new men and the new temper; their prejudices were indiscriminately against any extension of State action. It is to this influence, added to that of the interests that stood to lose, that may probably be ascribed the evisceration of Gladstone's Railway Bill of 1844, the downfall of the Railway Department, as administered by Dalhousie, and the general defeat of those who sought to bring the activities of railway promoters under some plan and control.[1] The overtones, the emotional idealism, of Manchester Radicalism were directed rather to the conception of Free Trade as the basis of a universal society, devoted only to unarmed rivalries, and renouncing the politics of power. This was responsible for a strain of pacifism in English politics, reaching its apotheosis in some of the greater orations of Bright, which was not without its influence both on foreign and domestic politics, though it never wholly succeeded in mastering the belligerency inherent in the temper of English Radicalism. It was also not without its business aspect–dislike of the cost of war, and of paying taxes for military preparedness.

But before the new temper reached its zenith, the principle of regulation had consolidated its hold on one field, and advanced into another of supreme importance. These successes were by no means wholly the work of Philosophical Radicalism; Tory paternalism, the growing sense of responsibility in the governing classes, the religious sense of responsibility for the neighbour, played their parts, and refused to be satisfied with what Carlyle contemptuously called the political philosophy of buttoning the breeches pockets and sitting still. But Philosophical Radicalism may be said to have instructed these sentiments how to make themselves effective. The inquiries of the Commission on the Labour of Women and Children in Mines, which Ashley had secured, shocked the conscience of the nation and enabled him, with much less delay and fewer frustrations than the hard path he had chosen in politics had accustomed him to expect, to secure legislation prohibiting their employment underground. The further inquiries of the Commission into conditions in non-textile factories

[1] Part III.

and in agriculture, at least exposed the wide spread of evils, comparable, if not so gross. The 1844 Factories Act, the product of Ashley's perseverance and of Peel's and Graham's administrative conscientiousness, increased the scope of protection afforded by the 1833 Act, and put it on sound administrative foundations. Peel and Graham themselves prevented the writing into it of the Ten Hours' clause that the House demanded. But in 1847, in different political and economic circumstances, came Fielden's Ten Hours Act, securing to textile workers what, by Victorian standards of work, was their charter of leisure.[1] The feature of the decade was the wide rallying of opinion to this principle. The great Whig lords, Russell and Palmerston, swung into its support, and Macaulay, in 1846, pronounced a classic oration in favour of it.

Meanwhile, before the 'forties had started, the indomitable Chadwick had opened his campaign for public health. Even under the roar of Chartist and Free Trade controversy, the noise of the series of inquiries by select committees and royal commissions made itself heard. The appeal was to much the same dispositions as in the case of factory legislation; support came chiefly from the upper and professional classes; there was no widespread popular agitation behind the movement; and it ran counter to powerful private interests, to entrenched bumbledom and the ratepayer democracy in the towns, and to the prejudice against bureaucracy which was attaining the status of a fixed idea in the country. Chadwick's handling of it was not to prove disarming. The political leaders gave it, on the whole, a tepid support, Russell and Palmerston rather less so, perhaps, and it was to the Whigs that Chadwick owed his chance, as it was from them that he deserved it. The Acts setting up the General Health Board and the Metropolitan Sewers Commission came in 1848, and Disraeli–even at this early stage a paladin of *sanitas*–said that but for the personality of Morpeth, Russell's Commissioner of Woods and Forests, to whose sylvan cares that of drains was added, the Commons could not have been persuaded to accept the Public Health Act.[2] On the education front, sectarian jealousies ruined the prospect of a national system of popular education contained in Graham's Factory Bill of 1843, but in partial compensation Russell's Education Minutes of 1846 founded a teaching profession, with essential State aid, put an end to the sorry monitorial system, and immensely strengthened the whole fabric of the voluntary system. The growth of the Oxford Movement had been largely responsible for the storms that had beaten round the devoted Graham's head in 1843; the attention which its varying phases attracted and the storm over the Disruption in Scotland in 1843,[3] evidenced, at least, the increasing place which religion was occupying in the national consciousness. The temper of Victorianism, as it settled down, was to be positive, aggressive, the temper

[1] Part XII. [2] Part X. [3] Part IV.

of industrial and scientific achievement, lacking somewhat in the wider and profounder ranges of imaginative sympathy, however, and in the comprehensions and charities that can come with them. But if sectarian spirit intensified, the threat of a secularist issue, which had momentarily raised its head in the mid-'thirties, died away, except in remoter corners of the educational controversy, where it was to be important again.[1]

Peel presides over the 'forties, whether in office or not, its dominant political figure. Few careers have been more variously assessed. In Disraeli's view he was the "burglar of other men's intellects", incapable himself of initiating extensive policies, but only of appreciating the immediate political profit to be made out of them, and his fall was the nemesis attending the effort to construct a party without a principle. Disraeli's own career is an ironic comment on his judgment. It is echoed, however, by a contemporary of very different stamp. "This statesman's career is without precedent in the history of politicians; he has begun by opposing, and ended by carrying (not simply supporting) almost every great question of the day. . . . Cunning, I fear, has ruled him. . . . Peel must retire, having reduced Parliament, party, and men's minds to original chaos." So wrote Shaftesbury in his diary. Bagehot departed from the general run of Liberal opinion of his day, and treats Peel, in a famous essay, as the supreme type of the run of constitutional statesmen–"the powers of a first-rate man, and the creed of a second-rate man". Yet a number of the most eminent men of the day, members of his Cabinet, passed, in some cases, the rest of their political lives in fidelity to his memory and example. On two things, at any rate, Peel was rarely mistaken – the political methods and measures that conduced to order, and the opinion of the central mass of responsible Englishmen on whom its preservation ultimately depended. No statesman won a more undisputed popular fame. Few can claim a greater record of achievement. In opposition he built up the party of order from a handful to a handsome majority; in power he used his authority over it to make it the instrument of measures which consolidated and ordered the economic revolution through which the country was passing. More than anyone else, he can be regarded as the architect of the Victorian Compromise, of the body of adjustments between ancient institutions and the self-expression of a developing society; between tradition and innovation; between regulation and liberty, which provided solid foundations for the life of the country for the rest of the century. They were so solidly laid that the half generation of political instability that followed his fall did little to disturb them.

The 'fifties was a decade of unstable governments, but of increasing social stability and a growing measure of broad political agreement. It opened

[1] Part XI.

auspiciously with the Great Exhibition of 1851, planned and largely organized by Prince Albert, to celebrate the triumphs of British industry, and the inauguration, it was hoped, of an age of commerce in which rivalry in the arts of peace should take the place of war. It was indeed a landmark of social peace. The elaborate precautions taken to have police and military in readiness to deal with possible disorders proved wholly unnecessary. The trainloads of excursionists from the north–coming, often, in part, or wholly, at their employers' expense–behaved with notable restraint and decorum; the two nations of Disraeli's earlier description jostled each other in the streets and in the Exhibition Hall, drawn together by a common pride in their country's achievements. The holding of the exhibition five years after the repeal of the Corn Laws, three after the Chartist collapse of 1848, and while the major European countries were still rocking in the ground-swell of revolution, was both a mark of the national self-confidence, not to say complacency, that succeeds, in the 'fifties, to the fears and forebodings of the 'forties, and a contribution to it.

Of the national achievement that lay behind this mood, the middle classes felt themselves the symbols and the representatives. After the Chartist fiasco, with their Ten Hours Act, made watertight by legislation early in the decade,[1] with food prices stable or falling, and employment responding to the rapid expansion of the nation's industries,[2] the working classes turned either to their individual affairs, or, the more active spirits, to co-operation, or the building up of a New Model trade unionism[1]–cautious in policy, sound in organization, breeding a race of working-class leaders whose outlook and aspirations led them towards the middle classes. Russell, in 1851, lifted the veto he had laid in 1837 on further reform, and himself introduced Reform Bills in 1852 and 1854. But not till the mid-'sixties did the issue wake any wide response, either in Parliament or in the country.[3] Free Trade was secured beyond dispute by the Protectionists' renunciation of their own *raison d'être* in 1852.[4] The great issues of the previous two decades had been settled, on the whole to the country's satisfaction, or at any rate acceptance–and even Ireland, exhausted, for the time, by the terrible sufferings of the famine, and emptying by emigration, ceased from troubling. No great domestic issues arose to take the place of the old ones. Enough effect remained of the class struggles that had lain behind the Anti-Corn Law and Chartist agitations to edge independence very often with acerbity, to provide fire for industrial and political issues as they arose. Under a parliamentary constitution, issues must be created, and the public mind given food, or politicians and journalists have none. But none arose in the 'fifties of the scope and continuing character of the previous decades–those that stir public feeling

[1] Part XII. [2] Part III. [3] Part II. [4] Part V.

for the moment are as stubble fire compared to what had been before. It is in this decade that is to be marked the growth of that 'deferentialness'–that respect of class for class, and particularly for the class above it, that general indisposition to tamper drastically with existing institutions, which Bagehot later noted as a characteristic of the English society of his time. On the other hand, it is to be noted as a not altogether auspicious foreshadowing of the age of democracy that for the first time since the Reform Act, issues of national prestige and prejudice are among those that stir popular feeling, often irrelevantly enough, and that in the decade consecrated by the prince consort to Peace, what later would have been called popular jingoism makes a not infrequent appearance.

The elections of 1847 slightly increased Whig and Radical strength, which was approximately 320, and left the two wings of Conservatism correspondingly weakened, with about 200 Protectionists and 100 Peelites. Radical and Peelite support was generally available for Russell, but he could rely fully on neither. Neither Conservative wing was fully effective. Peel refused to assume the responsibilities of leadership, but behaved as a private member with whom friends are associated, and his principal colleagues took up the same attitude after his death in 1850, though they referred constantly to each other on important issues. Lord Stanley led the Protectionists in the Lords, and Bentinck in the Commons, until his resignation, and tragic and unexpected death in 1848. Virtual leadership was then in Disraeli's hands, though prejudice against him and his race deprived him until 1849 of formal power and recognition. In 1845 one of the difficulties alleged by Russell as a reason for his inability to form a Cabinet to repeal the Corn Laws was the objection of some of his party to Palmerston's resumption of the Foreign Office. In 1846 nothing was heard of this. Russell's preoccupations and the uncertainty of his position gave the Foreign Minister increasing personal scope, and his turbulent genius played a vigorous if not wholly helpful part in the pre-revolutionary situation in Europe, and also in defining and defending British interests in the completely fluid situation that the revolutions for the moment created.

The same factors brought another influence to the fore. The queen and Prince Albert had gained both in political experience and in confidence from the close and friendly association with Peel and with his foreign minister, Aberdeen, whose cautious and pacific policies they had warmly seconded. The Crown, too, had grown in popular strength. The decorum of the royal household, the rapidly filling nursery, the obvious devotion of the queen and of the prince to their public duties and responsibilities had won it a new respect. Prince Albert's lack of popularity with the aristocracy was not a discommendation to the middle classes, while his known sympathy with Free Trade and appearance in the gallery of the House during the third reading debate of the Bill for repeal and the queen's acceptance, at Shaftesbury's hands, of the medal struck by the Ten Hours Movement in commemoration of the Act of 1847, were instances of steps that exposed the Crown to some criticism, but betokened both a keen interest in the welfare of the people at large, and a certain independence of view. In foreign affairs both queen and prince were largely identified in sympathy with much of the royal order in Europe which Palmerston saw toppling over in 1848 with so much equanimity, and were resentful both of his casual consideration for kings, and of the vigour of his policies, which often threatened, in their view, both order and peace. Russell respected his mistress's views, and knew that Palmerston's insistence on making his voice heard in Europe was mistrusted by many responsible statesmen, though popular with the people. He had already promised to place him elsewhere in the Cabinet, when the Don Pacifico crisis, in June 1850, exposed the Minister to a combined attack from Peelites, Protectionists, and Radicals, from which, in the House of Commons, he extricated himself by his famous "dusk till dawn" speech, in vindication of his whole record as a minister.

The change had to be deferred. In September 1850, Pius IX issued his brief reconstituting a territorial Roman hierarchy in England. Popular anti-Roman feeling, sensitized by the recent course of the Oxford Movement, was set ablaze, and Russell, injudiciously and inconsistently with his record of support of religious toleration, fanned the blaze with his Durham Letter and Ecclesiastical Titles Bill.[1] But his impetuousness estranged the Peelite leaders, and the temporary popularity he gained was offset by the difficulties into which his legislation plunged him. The weakening of his position was demonstrated by the narrow success of the Government in defeating a motion of Disraeli's upon agricultural distress. Then a blow fell upon him from the camp of those he reckoned his friends. Radicals, resentful of his slowness in carrying out a pledge given in 1848 to introduce a Reform Bill,[2] carried a vote against him on the subject in a House which the Protectionists had deliberately deserted. Russell resigned, but Stanley was conscious that he had neither a majority nor an acceptable policy, and negotiations to bring in the Peelites to strengthen Russell's forces split primarily on the rock of the Peelite disapproval of Russell's anti-Roman policy.[3] Russell had therefore to resume office. At the end of the year Palmerston's nonchalant approval of Louis Napoleon's *coup d'état* of December[3] both unwhigged the minister, for the moment, and brought his conflict with the Crown to a head. Russell cut the Gordian knot by dismissing Palmerston. The incident settled, for the rest of the reign, the question whether the queen was to be a 'mandarin figure' or a real political influence.[3] But the

[1] Part IV. [2] Part II. [3] Part I.

loss of its strongest and most popular figure also irreparably weakened the ministry. In the following February, Palmerston was able to take his revenge, and forced Russell to resign. Russell–or Palmerston–had also weakened Whiggism; its authority was not fully recovered until 1860, and Russell himself was not to be prime minister again in Palmerston's lifetime.

Spurred on by Disraeli, Derby–as Stanley had now become–on this occasion accepted office, and formed a ministry no member of which except himself, Disraeli, and the duke of Wellington, now in his last year of life, was known to the wider public. It nevertheless faced its duties with ability. But it could not stand in the existing House of Commons, and Derby obtained a dissolution from the queen. An equal dilemma faced the Conservatives in the election, however. They could not put forward a Protectionist policy with any hope of electoral success, and they could not decently disavow it. Ambiguous tactics were adopted, and the elections improved Derby's position, a number of Peelites, in particular, returning to the official fold. But he still confronted a Free Trade majority in the House, which was determined to obtain a recantation of Protection from him. The attitude of Palmerston, to whom, in the meantime, the leadership of Conservatism in the House of Commons was being offered by Disraeli, enabled the Government to surmount this ordeal with dignity.[1] But its prospects still depended on some accession of strength, or, negatively, on the combination of groups and personalities in the House. Disraeli's budget, at the end of the year, provoking Gladstone's violent attack,[1] was the occasion rather than the cause of its fall.

There now came into being that combination of Whigs and Peelites which had been discussed in 1851 and which the logic of events, the predispositions of the party leaders, and the anxious desires of the Crown all called for. Aberdeen became prime minister, but it was understood that he would shortly retire in favour of Russell; Russell provisionally took both the Foreign Office–with Clarendon as his destined successor–and the lead in the House; Gladstone was chancellor of the exchequer; and Palmerston cheerfully accepted the Home Office, in which he took the opportunity of passing a valuable Youthful Offenders Act, introduced the ticket-of-leave system for convicts, and gave steady support to Chadwick. The Ministry started brilliantly with Gladstone's budget of 1853, in which were laid down plans for seven years ahead. But it was not happy politically; Russell, leader of the vast majority of its supporters, fretted at his subordination, and Aberdeen's resignation–for one reason or another–was delayed. Russell's insistence on a Reform Bill which the Cabinet did not want,[2] imposed strains on its unity. The dispute between Russia and Turkey, over the Holy Places in Palestine, involving France and engaging

[1] Part V. [2] Part II.

3

Britain's historic susceptibilities in this area, imposed more. Not even the briefest account of the steps that led to the Crimean War can be attempted, but it is germane to the theme of this essay that frantic popular dislike for Russia, the reputation of some of the Cabinet for pacifism verging on complaisancy to the autocrat of the East, and that of Palmerston for a fearless vindication of Liberal interests in Europe–which were identified with hostility to the Tsar–played no small part in the mingled hesitancy and precipitation that marked the handling of the issues. But a still-united Cabinet entered upon the war. In a generation of peace, the machinery of war had been allowed to run down, and the early phases of the fighting were marked by disgraceful administrative and military muddles and mistakes. Public passions, already inflamed, now turned vindictively against political leaders, and the whole upper class which supplied the leading military and administrative positions. The Radical, J. A. Roebuck, demanded an inquiry into the conduct of the war by a select committee of the House. The Cabinet prepared to resist this as a motion of lack of confidence, but on the eve of the debate Russell suddenly resigned. He had been a critic of war administration in the Cabinet, but he had not made his criticism effective, and he shared responsibility for what had been done and left undone. His action was deeply resented. Roebuck carried his motion by a large majority, and Aberdeen resigned.

The post of danger and opportunity reverted naturally to Derby, as the leader of the largest opposition party. After attempting in vain to enlist Peelites and Palmerston he resigned the queen's commission, to the infinite distress of Disraeli. The leadership of England was going for the man who had courage to pick it up, and Derby left it lying. Russell, next applied to, could not get anyone to serve with him. It was the nadir of his political fortunes. Palmerston was next asked, and accepted. His Government included, at first, the Peelites, Graham, Gladstone, and Herbert. But Roebuck, and indeed the majority of the House, made it clear that they did not intend to be balked of their inquiry by the fall of the Government against which it had originally been directed. The duke of Newcastle, a Peelite, as Aberdeen's secretary of state for war, was in the front line of those likely to be attacked, and the Peelites rated their loyalty to him and to Aberdeen's Government higher than their new obligations, and resigned–Gladstone to an increasingly querulous criticism of the conduct of affairs. His immense conscientiousness was henceforth, in periods of opposition, to have difficulty with his subconscious sense of vast unemployed powers, and his instinctive dissatisfaction with what he did not himself do. To a man of less robust courage than Palmerston's these defections might have been fatal. Palmerston, however, replaced the resigning ministers, rode out the political storms which continued to assail government and the governing classes,[1] and carried on the war to a successful, if not to a wholly triumphant, conclusion.

War, and his own courage, had carried him to the top, but his position was still an unstable one. Russell–who in the interval had joined Palmerston's Cabinet and then resigned–was far from reconciled to Palmerston's leadership of the Whigs; the Radicals, especially Cobden and Bright, mistrusted him, and so did the Peelites. In 1857 occurred the incident of the *lorcha Arrow*, in which the British representative in Hong Kong, the Benthamite, Sir John Bowring, took drastic reprisal for what he regarded as an insult offered to the British flag. Derby in the Lords, and Cobden in the Commons, moved a vote of censure on the Government which upheld him. Defeated in the Commons, Palmerston determined to dissolve, and was returned by the country in triumph. Cobden and Bright, and Cardwell, the ablest of the younger Peelites, lost their seats. One use which Palmerston made of his renewed authority was to force the Divorce Act[1] through the House. But the political situation was not, in fact, much changed; until Palmerston could bind Russell, the Peelites, and the Radicals to him, he remained at the mercy of any issue that might swing unattached opinion in the House against him. In 1858 such an incident occurred. The Italian, Orsini, attempted to assassinate Napoleon III. There was evidence that the conspiracy had been hatched in England, and Palmerston proposed to meet French protests by legislation making such conspiracy an offence. Milner Gibson, a Manchester Radical, was put up by the prime minister's foes to accuse him of truckling to France. On a snap division, and on this issue, Palmerston was defeated–by those who should have rejoiced at his change of heart–and, unexpectedly, resigned.

Derby found himself again called on to form a minority government. The situation was as it had been before; his tenure of power depended principally on the dissensions of his opponents, but there was this time the favouring factor that, until they could agree, the only alternative on the horizon was the return of the old Palmerston Government. Two factors clarified the situation. Disraeli brought forward a Reform Bill, and defended it with great ability. But Russell and Bright, specialists in the subject, regarded it as a mockery, and even Palmerston, who might have accepted the rest of it, objected to its assimilation of the borough and county franchises. A union of Whigs and Radicals defeated it, Gladstone, however, voting to keep it alive.[2] He had accepted a mission to the Ionian Isles at the Government's hands, and Disraeli, before and after his acceptance, with his leader's authorization, had made generous offers to him to induce him to join the Cabinet, which Gladstone had not irrevocably refused. In face of parliamentary defeat, Derby obtained a dissolution.[3] Again

[1] Part VI. [2] Part II. [3] Part I.

he improved his position, but again not enough. Meanwhile Napoleon III's obvious alliance with Cavour and his anti-Austrian manœuvres had produced deep anxiety in the country. In his efforts to preserve the peace, Malmesbury, the Conservative foreign secretary, appeared to incline to the side of Austria, which in any case was defending its treaty rights. At the critical moment Austrian patience gave way, and she took steps which her enemies could construe as provocation. War broke out, and English opinion swung to the French and Italian side. On the undesirability of Austrian power south of the Alps, Palmerston, Russell, and Gladstone were agreed; the latter, in 1851, had risked the disapproval of his friend Aberdeen in publishing an attack on the Government of Naples. The returning Derby Government faced a vote of no confidence in the House. Gladstone voted in the lobbies with it, although already his mind was "deeply perplexed" at the situation abroad. Derby was nevertheless defeated; the queen, after a first invitation to Granville, called on Palmerston to form a government; Russell accepted the new premier-designate's invitation to the Foreign Office, and Gladstone became chancellor of the exchequer.

Thus, for the first time since Peel, government was in the hands of a Cabinet resting on the foundations of a solid parliamentary majority. Despite the political spread of the Government–it went as far to the left as Milner Gibson–Palmerston's hand in managing it never seriously faltered. Opinion in the country–not least that of his political opponents–settled now into affectionate admiration of his resilience and courage, of the political good temper he had shown throughout his career, and of his readiness, despite a Conservative bias to call a spade a spade, and to right obvious wrongs when he saw them. The common interest in Italy–to whose unification the Government made an important contribution–provided ground for co-operation with Russell and Gladstone. But it was Gladstone who showed himself, very soon, unmistakably the man of destiny of the Cabinet. His series of budgets, carrying to a logical conclusion the gospel of Free Trade; his Commercial Treaty with France;[1] his rigid sense of economy, which brought him into conflict with the prime minister over the necessities of defence; the improvement of audit machinery;[2] the setting up of the Post Office Savings Bank,[3] gave him an ascendancy in the field of finance such as only Pitt and Peel had had before him. His relations with Palmerston were never easy, and it was Palmerston's well-known remark that the chimneys of Downing Street smoked regularly with the letters of resignation from Mr. Gladstone that he put on the fire. These are the years of Gladstone's political approximation to the Manchester Radicals–over Free Trade, over the Commercial Treaty, over the Paper Duties and the quarrel

[1] Part V. [2] Part VI. [3] Part III.

with the House of Lords,[1] and even, in 1864, over the franchise.[1] Political reasons offer sufficient explanation of this, but it is difficult, perhaps, not to see in it psychological change–the release, with power, of the dynamism of his nature, a shedding of inhibitions, and, with this, a delectation in the moral approval of others, added to the need he had always had of his own, which inclined him to those who thought of themselves as pre-eminently the party of principle.

Outside the sphere of finance, the great series of educational inquiries[2] mark the most important initiative of the Government in domestic affairs. Lowe's handling of the Newcastle Report and the Revised Code was politically, as well as educationally, unhappy, but schoolmasters and their friends have never been very potent politically, and the coating of Free Trade principles which Lowe gave to his proposals lent them a specious commendation to the time. If Palmerston had learned aptness in domestic politics, the Europe of Bismarck contained hazards for which he had no gauge, and his handling of the Schleswig-Holstein dispute between Denmark and Prussia damaged his prestige. That of his Government was not improved by the resignation, in succession, of his lord chancellor, Westbury; a junior lord of the Admiralty, Stansfeld; and finally of Lowe, the vice-president of the Council, for personal reasons ranging from the improper to the indiscreet. But when an election became due in 1865, the nation was still happy with the administration of Lord Palmerston, and the veteran statesman received the remarkable tribute of a further lease of power.

The consequences of Lord Palmerston's death; the accession of Earl Russell, as he had then become, to his place; the introduction of the Reform Bill of 1866; the struggles that resulted in its defeat; Disraeli's success in carrying a much more drastic Bill; and Gladstone's turning of the tables on him in the House and in the country fall more properly to be narrated in the part dealing with Parliament.[3] With the passing of Palmerston, and then of Russell and Derby, new times had come, and new conditions of politics conformable to the ambitions and rivalries that inspired the new men. Moreover the spectre of the Irish problem, in the grim shape of Fenianism, had come knocking again at the door, threatening the domestic cosinesses of English politics. It is to be noted as the fruit of a generation's assiduous reform in the charitableness and comprehensiveness of the English political outlook that in the new period the political advantage was to lie with a positive Irish policy–the initiative that Gladstone grasped–rather than with its obstruction. In the long run the dynamism of newly invigorated party was to transform the issues of politics beyond the recognition of an earlier generation. But the newly acclaimed head

[1] Part II. [2] Part XI. [3] Part II.

of the party of progress was not himself, except as regards Ireland, an innovator, and played little part in the process. The Liberal Government of 1868–1874 left a deeper mark on the statute book than any of its predecessors since the Whig governments of the 'thirties. But most of its measures were the delayed fulfilment of Radical hopes, or the achievement of Peelite initiatives. The Ballot;[1] the opening of the Civil Service to competition,[2] and of the universities to Dissenters;[3] Forster's Education Act, for which the enthusiasm of the prime minister was not high;[3] Cardwell's Army reforms;[4] the great Judicature Act of 1873[5] were measures that, in appropriate circumstances, Peel might have carried himself. Except again for Peel's neglected subject of Ireland, his greatest pupil systematized rather than transcended his master's inspiration.

Thus the years from 1833 to 1874 have a considerable measure of unity. They may also claim a not inconsiderable achievement. The popularity and prestige of the central institutions of government had been notably enhanced, and the political country considerably enlarged without, as yet, any apparent threat to the quality of political life. The dominant middle-class had merged at one extreme with the gentry and the aristocracy, and at the other was drawing the working classes after it. The advantage of an early start in industrialization had been so consolidated as to secure to the country reserves of capital, prestige, and business experience that were to be of the utmost value in the strenuous international competition and the grave trials to the country's position that the future was to bring. State paternalism had been strictly eschewed, yet policy had co-operated with circumstances to make the working classes sharers, not on terms of political favour or power, but of personal achievement, in the material and social advance of the time.

Despite the dominance of the personality and policies of a great Conservative statesman in the period, it may be regarded as the zenith of British liberalism. International peace, the increase of free economic co-operation, both nationally and internationally, the development of self-government, and the social progress that were regarded as the natural concomitants of these, were looked upon as the only political objects worthy of adult and serious consideration. National power was thought of not as the object or product of policy but as a function of the vigour and quality of the national life itself. The flood of American wheat descending on Europe in the 'seventies, the intensification of national rivalries consequent upon the rise of Germany, and the social strains resulting from keener economic competition were to weaken very seriously the authority of these assumptions. The first was to put an end to the brief movement for Free Trade in Europe which had marked the middle years of the century, though the hold of the doctrine in England itself was not to be shaken for

[1] Part II. [2] Part VI. [3] Part XI. [4] Part VII. [5] Part VI.

another fifty years. The second brought into the forefront of politics a conception of national power rather than personal freedom as the primary object of national policy, which was to lead on to imperialist rivalries and contribute, in no small measure, to the catastrophe of 1914. The third was to afford opportunities for the popularization of ideas of class war – also of German origin – as opposed to the class co-operation of Liberalism, which were to have even profounder consequences for the stability of the industrial civilization which it had been the primary business of the period we have been considering to consolidate.

SELECT GENERAL BIBLIOGRAPHY

The third series of Hansard covers the period, and will be cited in the following form–Hansard 3/xxvi/76–82, *i.e. Parliamentary Debates, Third Series,* vol. xxvi, cols. 76–82. Parliamentary Papers include House of Lords Papers, published in a single numerical sequence, Command Papers, also forming a single numerical sequence, marked by the number 1 to 4222 enclosed in square brackets up to 1868–1869, and thereafter by the letter C. and the number, also enclosed in square brackets, and Sessional Papers, numbered consecutively for each session. Each session's Papers were also issued in a series of bound volumes at the conclusion of the session. This is the form in which most libraries have them, and in which reference is most commonly made to them, and it is the mode of reference adopted here–*e.g. Report of the Commissioners on the St Albans Election, 1852* (*Parlty. Papers,* 1852/xxvii–*i.e.* the twenty-seventh volume of the bound series issued for 1852). The *Parliamentary Papers* include Reports of Royal Commissions and Select Committees of either House, and numerous Returns or Statements asked for by the House of Commons or issued by the Government for its information and the information of the country. *Reports* nearly always print evidence in full, and the more important of them are equipped with full indexes. Lists and indexes to each year's series of volumes were printed with the series, and indexes covering a series of years at irregular intervals. H. Vernon Jones, *Catalogue of Parliamentary Papers, 1800–1901* (London, 1901), lists the more important *Papers,* with short descriptive summaries of many of them, and is of great value, but refers to *Papers* by numbers and not by their place in the annual series. The more recent *Select List of British Parliamentary Papers, 1833–99,* by P. G. Ford (Oxford, 1953), and the *London Bibliography of the Social Sciences* (the Catalogue of the Library of the London School of Economics and Political Science) listing *Parliamentary Papers* among its references, constitute easy and reliable guides, the latter to secondary sources as well.

The *Annual Register* gives a short summary of the year's political and parliamentary events, of increasing value as the period goes on, analyses of important Bills and biographical and social detail. Files of newspapers are of considerable, but variable, value. Unfortunately Palmer's *Index to the Times* did not begin publication till 1866. The more serious quarterly and monthly magazines contain discussions of political and social events and problems which are often extremely valuable; reference may especially be made to the *Edinburgh* and *Quarterly Reviews,* which run throughout the whole period and maintained a high standard of information and interest. Early editions of the *Encyclopaedia Britannica* are often of considerable documentary and historical value. The *Dictionary of National Biography* is indispensable for reference; the Institute of Historical Research publishes, from time to time, in the *Bulletin of the Institute of Historical Research,* corrections of fact which later research has revealed.

The volumes of the *Oxford History of England* covering the period, E. L. Woodward, *The Age of Reform, 1815–1870,* and R. C. K. Ensor, *England, 1870–1914* (Oxford, 1939 and 1936), are now the standard works on the subject. Each is equipped with an excellent bibliography. Two volumes of Elie Halévy's great *Histoire du Peuple Anglais* refer to the period–vol. iii, *De la Crise du Reform Bill a l'Avènement de Sir Robert Peel, 1830–41* (Paris, 1936), and *Le Milieu du Siècle, 1841–52* (Paris, 1946). The latter was put together from the author's papers after his death and has many gaps, but is still indispensable. G. M. Trevelyan, *British History in the Nineteenth Century and After* (London, 1938), conserves its value. H. W. C. Davis, *The Age of Grey and Peel* (Oxford, 1929), though dealing primarily with an earlier period, has much in it of value to the student of this. Of the earlier histories, J. A. R. Marriott, *England since Waterloo* (Oxford, 1913); G. C. Broderick and J. K. Fotheringham, *England, 1801–37* (London, 1906); and S. Low and L. C. Sandars, *England, 1837–1901* (London, 1907), are still valuable. G. Slater,

Growth of Modern England (London, 1932), and C. R. FAY, *Adam Smith to the Present Day* (Cambridge, 1936), deal more with social and economic aspects. SPENCER WALPOLE, *History of England from the Conclusion of the Great War in 1815 to 1858* (5 vols., London, 1886), and his *History of Twenty Years* (4 vols., London, 1903–1908), continuing the narrative from 1856 to 1881, are probably still the best narratives for general purposes. G. M. YOUNG's *Portrait of an Age* (Oxford, 1936) is an essay in interpretation.

Among the more important biographies of statesmen are LORD STANMORE, *Earl of Aberdeen* (London, 1893); LADY FRANCES BALFOUR, *Life of George, 4th Earl of Aberdeen* (2 vols., London, 1923); D. LE MARCHANT, *Memoirs of Lord Althorp* (London, 1876); INA, DUCHESS OF ARGYLE, *Autobiography and Correspondence of 8th Duke of Argyle* (2 vols., 1896); D. HUDSON, *Thomas Barnes and the Times* (Cambridge, 1943); B. DISRAELI, *Lord George Bentinck: A Political Biography* (London, 1852); G. M. TREVELYAN, *John Bright* (London, 1913); A. A. ASPINALL, *Lord Brougham and the Whig Party* (Manchester, 1927); G. T. GARRATT, *Lord Brougham* (London, 1932); J. L. GARVIN, *Life of Joseph Chamberlain*, vol. I, 1836–1885 (London, 1932); SIR H. MAXWELL, *Life of the 4th Earl of Clarendon* (2 vols., London, 1913); A. L. DASENT, *John Delane, 1817–79* (2 vols., London, 1908); GEORGE SAINTSBURY, *The Earl of Derby* (London, 1892); B. HOLLAND, *Life of Spencer Compton, Eighth Duke of Devonshire*, vol. I (London, 1911); S. GWYNN and G. TUCKWELL, *Life of Rt. Hon. Sir C. W. Dilke*, vol. I (London, 1917); W. F. MONYPENNY and G. BUCKLE, *Life of Disraeli* (2 vols., London, 1929); C. W. NEW, *Life of Lord Durham* (Oxford, 1929); T. WEMYSS REID, *Life of W. E. Forster* (2 vols., London, 1888); JOHN MORLEY, *Gladstone* (3 vols., London, 1903); F. W. HIRST, *Gladstone as Financier and Economist* (London, 1931); F. E. HYDE, *Gladstone at the Board of Trade* (London, 1934); W. E. WILLIAMS, *Rise of Gladstone to Leadership of the Liberal Party* (Cambridge, 1934); P. GUEDALLA, *Gladstone and Palmerston* (London, 1928); G. T. GARRATT, *The Two Mr Gladstones* (London, 1936); A. TILNEY BASSETT, *Speeches of W. E. Gladstone* (London, 1936); ERICH EYCK, *Gladstone* (tr. B. Miall, London, 1938); SIR PHILLIP MAGNUS, *Gladstone* (London, 1954); C. S. PARKER, *Life and Letters of Sir James Graham* (2 vols., London, 1907); A. B. ERIKSON, *Public Career of Sir James Graham* (Oxford, 1952); LORD E. FITZMAURICE, *Life of Earl Granville* (2 vols., London, 1905); G. M. TREVELYAN, *Lord Grey of the Reform Bill*, 2nd edn. (London, 1953); A. P. MARTIN, *Life and Letters of Robert Lowe, Viscount Sherbroke* (2 vols., London, 1893); SIR G. O. TREVELYAN, *Life and Letters of Lord Macaulay* (2 vols., London, 1876); C. WHIBLEY, *Life of Lord John Manners and his Friends* (2 vols., London, 1925); EARL OF MALMESBURY, *Memoirs of an ex-Minister* (2 vols., London, 1884); LORD DAVID CECIL, *The Young Melbourne* (London, 1929), and *Lord M.* (London, 1954); W. M. TORRENS, *Memoirs of Melbourne* (London, 1890); L. C. SANDARS, *The Melbourne Papers* (London, 1889); ANDREW LANG, *Sir Stafford Northcote* (2 vols., Edinburgh, 1890); F. PODMORE, *Life of Robert Owen* (London, 1906); G. D. H. COLE, *Life of Robert Owen* (London, 1925); EVELYN ASHLEY, *Life of Viscount Palmerston* (2 vols., London, 1879); SIR H. L. BULWER, *Life of Viscount Palmerston* (3 vols., London, 1870–1874); P. GUEDALLA, *Palmerston* (London, 1926); KINGSLEY MARTIN, *Triumph of Lord Palmerston* (London, 1926); H. C. F. BELL, *Lord Palmerston* (2 vols., London, 1936); C. S. PARKER, *Sir R. Peel from his Private Papers* (3 vols., London, 1891–1899); E. CARDWELL, LORD STANHOPE, *Memoirs of Sir R. Peel* (2 vols., London, 1857); G. PEEL, *Private Letters of Sir R. Peel* (London, 1920); A. H. RAMSAY, *Peel* (London, 1928); G. KITSON CLARK, *Peel and the Conservative Party* (London, 1929); GRAHAM WALLAS, *Life of Francis Place* (London, 1898); SIR T. MARTIN, *Life of the Prince Consort* (5 vols., London, 1875–1880); ROGER FULFORD, *The Prince Consort* (London, 1949); R. E. LEADER, *Autobiography and Life of J. A. Roebuck* (London, 1897); SPENCER WALPOLE, *Life of Lord John Russell* (2 vols., London, 1899); ROLLO RUSSELL (ed.), *Early Correspondence of Lord John Russell, 1805–1840* (2 vols., London, 1913); G. P. GOOCH (ed.), *Later Correspondence of Lord John Russell, 1840–1878*

(2 vols., London, 1930); LORD JOHN RUSSELL, *Recollections and Suggestions* (London, 1875); LADY GWENDOLEN CECIL, *Life of Robert, Marquis of Salisbury* (2 vols., London, 1921); EARL OF SELBORNE, *Personal and Political Memoirs* (4 vols., London, 1898); E. HODDER, *Life and Work of Lord Shaftesbury* (3 vols., London, 1886); J. L. and B. HAMMOND, *Lord Shaftesbury* (London, 1923); A. C. BENSON and VISCOUNT ESHER, *Letters of Queen Victoria, 1837–1861*, (3 vols., London, 1908); G. E. BUCKLE, *Letters of Queen Victoria, 1862–1878* (2 vols., London, 1926); P. GUEDALLA, *The Queen and Mr Gladstone* (2 vols., vol. I, 1845–1879, London, 1933); LYTTON STRACHEY, *Queen Victoria* (London, 1921); DORMER CRESTON, *The Youthful Queen Victoria* (London, 1952); P. GUEDALLA, *The Duke* (Wellington) (London, 1931); E. L. BARRINGTON, *The Servant of All: Life of James Wilson* (London, 1927).

Collections of Biographical Studies: W. BAGEHOT, *Biographical Studies* (London, 1881); JAMES BRYCE, *Studies in Contemporary Biography* (London, 1903); J. B. ATLAY, *The Victorian Chancellors* (London, 1906–1908); LYTTON STRACHEY, *Eminent Victorians* (London, 1922); K. FEILING, *Sketches in Nineteenth Century Biography* (London, 1930); F. J. C. HEARNSHAW, *Political Principles of Some Prime Ministers of the Nineteenth Century* (London, 1926); CHESTER KIRBY, *The English Country Gentleman: a Study of some Nineteenth Century Types* (London, n.d.); H. J. and H. MASSINGHAM (eds.), *The Great Victorians* (London, 1933); ALGERNON CECIL, *Queen Victoria and her Prime Ministers* (London, 1953); ASA BRIGGS, *Victorian People* (London, 1954). LORD ROSEBERY, *Miscellanies* (London, 1921), contains some valuable studies in biography, and the Introduction to the Cabinet Edition of W. E. H. LECKY, *Democracy and Liberty* (2 vols., London, 1898), contains a study of Gladstone.

Of diaries published as such, SIR HERBERT MAXWELL, *The Creevey Papers, ii* (London, 1904); L. JENNINGS, *Croker's Correspondence and Diaries* (3 vols., London, 1884); LYTTON STRACHEY and ROGER FULFORD, *The Greville Diaries* (8 vols., 1939), and P. BRIGHT (ed.), *Diaries of John Bright* (London, 1930), are the most valuable. Works dealing with aspects or periods of political history are R. L. HILL, *Toryism and the People, 1832–46* (London, 1929); F. E. GILLESPIE, *Labour and Politics in England, 1850–1867* (London, 1927); S. MACOBY, *History of Radicalism, 1832–52 and 1858–86* (2 vols., London, 1935 and 1938); and G. D. H. COLE, *British Working Class Politics, 1832–1914* (London, 1941); A. ASPINALL, *Politicians and the Press, 1700–1850* (London, 1949); *The History of the Times*, vol. I, *The Thunderer in the Making, 1765–1841*, vol. II, *The Tradition Established, 1841–1884* (London, 1945–1948), and the *Economist Centenary Book, 1843–1943* (Oxford, 1943). Social history may be best approached through G. M. YOUNG (ed.), *Early Victorian England* (2 vols., Oxford, 1934), to which may be added LORD DAVID CECIL, *Early Victorian Novelists* (London, 1934); HUMPHRY HOUSE, *The Dickens World* (Cambridge, 1941); AMY CRUSE, *The Victorians and their Books* (London, 1936); BASIL WILLEY, *Nineteenth Century Studies* (London, 1949); A. V. DICEY, *Law and Public Opinion in England* (London, 1914); C. BRINTON *English Political Thought in the Nineteenth Century* (London, 1949); and D. C. SOMERVELL, *English Thought in the Nineteenth Century* (London, 1929). LESLIE STEPHEN, *English Utilitarians* (3 vols., London, 1900, reprinted 1950); ELIE HALÉVY, *Growth of Philosophical Radicalism* (trans. M. Morris, London, 1928).

Historical periodicals to be consulted include *English Historical Review* (which publishes in its last number each year a note of important articles appearing in other periodicals); *History*; *Transactions of the Royal Historical Society*; *Bulletin of the Institute of Historical Research*; *Economic History Review* (which publishes each year a list of important articles appearing in local periodicals); *Journal of Modern History*; *Cambridge Historical Journal*; *Economic History*; *Economica*; *Politica*; *Birmingham University Historical Journal*; *American Historical Review*.

Select Bibliographies of the subjects of the various Parts of this volume are appended to the Introductions of these Parts.

ADDITIONAL BIBLIOGRAPHY

Advantage is taken of the re-printing of this volume to add to the bibliography some items which have appeared since publication.

GENERAL

W. E. HOUGHTON, *The Victorian Frame of Mind* (1957); ASA BRIGGS, *The Age of Improvement* (1959), covering the period from 1784 to 1867; G. KITSON CLARK, *The Making of Victorian England* (1962); The Ford Lectures for 1960, *An Expanding Society: Britain 1830–1900;* W. L. BURN, *The Age of Equipoise* (1964), concentrating on the years between 1852 and 1867; NORMAN GASH, *Reaction and Reconstruction in English Politics, 1832–1852* (1965); the Ford Lectures for 1964, constitute an important group of reconsideration and re-interpretation; ROBERT ROBSON (ed.), *Ideas and Institutions of Victorian Britain, Essays in honour of George Kitson Clark* (1957), on themes cognate with those considered in Kitson Clark, above; D. C. M. PLATT, *Finance, Trade and Politics, British Foreign Policy 1815–1914* (1968) cannot be ignored by the student of internal politics.

Other books of general interest for the period include RICHARD D. ALLTICK, *The English Common Reader* (1957); CHRISTOPHER BARTLETT, *Great Britain and Sea Power, 1815–1853* (1963); NICHOLAS BENTLEY, *Russell's Dispatches from the Crimea 1854–5* (1965); D. S. L. CARDWELL, *Organisation of Science in England* (1957); SIR GAVIN DE BEER, *Darwin* (1963); JOHN HOLLOWAY, *The Victorian Sage* (1953), penetrating studies of the language and thought of the great Victorian writers; BASIL WILLEY, *More Nineteenth Century Studies, A Group of Honest Doubters* (1956).

To the list of biographies originally cited should now be added:

A. BUCHAN, *The Spare Chancellor: Life of Walter Bagehot,* (1959); N. A. F. ST. JOHN STEVAS, *Walter Bagehot* (1959) includes extracts from his works; H. AUSUBEL, *John Bright, Victorian Reformer, 1842–1889* (1966); D. READ, *Cobden and Bright* (1967); W. D. JONES, *Lord Derby and Victorian Conservatism* (1957); ROBERT BLAKE, *Disraeli* (1966); HILARY DUNN, *James Anthony Froude* (2 vols., 1961 and 1964); GEORGINA BATTISCOMBE, *Mrs. Gladstone* (1956); AGATHA RAMM, *Correspondence of Gladstone and Lord Granville, 1868–1876* (1952); J. T. WARD, *Sir James Graham* (1967); GORDON WATERFIELD, *Layard of Ninevah* (1963); R. K. WEBB, *Harriet Martineau* (1960); MAURICE COWLING, *Mill and Liberalism* (1963); DONALD SOUTHGATE, *The Most English Minister–Palmerston* (1966); G. F. A. BEST, *Shaftesbury* (1964); SIR CHARLES PETRIE, *The Victorians* (1967).

Part I
THE MONARCHY

THE MONARCHY

Introduction

THE history of the monarchy, in the period of this volume, is conditioned in the main by three factors: the working out of the political and constitutional implications of the Reform Act of 1832, the circumstances under which the Corn Laws were repealed in 1846, and the renaissance of affection and respect for the Crown. The last was initially based on chivalrous feeling for the young queen, and became something more as the strength and integrity of her character, and the quality of her patriotism, were revealed. The Reform Act made it inevitable that party should ultimately replace the Crown as the basis and centre of working government. But in 1846 the structure of party was shattered. Till it was restored–and the character and abilities of the Peelites made the process of realignment a lengthy one–it was inevitable that a larger initiative and responsibility should fall back on the Crown. The insight and sense of public duty of the queen and of her consort secured that in the interim the opportunities afforded the Crown should be fully accepted, and discharged in the spirit of the post-1832 constitution. As a result a subtler and more intimate synthesis of the monarchical and popular elements in our constitution emerged than could easily have been foreseen in the reigns of the predecessors of the queen.

The power of the Crown had, on balance, been declining since 1782. But George IV had still looked on ministers as his personal nominees, though circumstances might restrict his choice, and on policy as concerning him as much as them. A considerable, if declining, influence of the Crown in Parliament and in the constituencies provided a practical sanction for these claims. When, in 1830, Grey came into office, he was as much the nominee of the new king as the man indicated by the state of feeling of the new Parliament. In framing a Reform Bill drastic enough to command the vehement support of the country, and at the same time sufficiently on historic lines to retain that of his Cabinet and of his motley parliamentary following–reunited Whigs, Canningites, Radicals, Irish, and a few dissident Tories–and in steering the Bill successfully through the resultant crises, Grey achieved three major results–a triumph of opinion in the country over the opposition of the Lords and the ultimate reluctance of the Crown, a reframing of the representation making it more responsive to opinion in the country, and a considerable reduction of the influence of the Crown and the Lords in the constituencies. This is his claim to have initiated a new epoch in the history of Parliament and the Crown. But the fruits of these changes did not reveal themselves at once. The discipline imposed on Grey's following by the crisis of the Bill relaxed, and what had functioned as a party for a time, became again much more of an agglomeration of groups. Irish and Radical pressure on the Government stiffened; difficulties in his Cabinet over Irish policy, involving the resignations of Stanley and Graham, and later of Althorp, caused Grey himself to throw in his hand in the summer of 1834; the Ministry was reconstituted under Melbourne, with

Althorp back in his place as leader in the Commons; and finally, in November 1834, Earl Spencer died, and Althorp was called to the Lords. In the admission of the Whig leaders themselves, the keystone of the Whig arch was removed. Meanwhile, under Peel's astute and masterful leadership, the Tories were recovering from the disarray into which the Reform struggle had cast them, and already were shaping the policy with which they were to appeal to the new constituencies.

These were the circumstances in which William IV, irritated with his ministers and taking advantage of an unguarded expression of Melbourne's, chose to reassert the older conception of the political role of the Crown by dismissing Melbourne, and calling upon the duke of Wellington to advise him as to a successor. Wellington refused the premiership himself, and advised calling on Peel, who was in Rome at the time. While Peel was hurrying back, Wellington took over himself the principal offices of state, which gave an additional handle to the Whig view that the Crown's action was a reversion to arbitrary government.[1] Peel formed a Ministry on his return, and without presenting it to the House obtained a dissolution. The Conservatives came back from the country very much strengthened, but still without a majority unless they could get the support of the recent Whig dissidents, and of lightly attached moderates who might rally to the view that ministers of the king's choice deserved, at any rate, a fair trial. This explains Peel's persistence in office after a defeat by seven votes on the Address in February 1835. But a series of defeats on Irish Church questions in April convinced him both of the solidity of the Opposition and of its determination to bring him down, and on the 8th he resigned.

Peel's brief ministry is of primary constitutional significance. Its leader had clearly neither expected nor desired royal intervention on his behalf. But devotion to the institutions of the country, to their re-establishment in national affection and esteem after the shock of Reform, was the one unqualified loyalty of Peel's later political life, and forms the guiding thread of his career. The Whigs had condemned the royal action out of hand; for them the parallel with 1784 was too uncomfortably close. Peel's attitude showed the limits to which the new Conservatism was prepared to go. He neither defended nor excused what the king had done, but he took full responsibility for it.[2] He thus avoided subscribing to the Whig doctrine of royal passivity in politics, and to their view–which he would never have accepted–that political initiative and power should be the monopoly of party leaders and Parliament. But he made it clear that royal action must be covered by ministers prepared to stake their political lives in its defence, and thus made sure that in any but very exceptional circumstances it would, in future, take place behind the scenes, and not be of a nature to incur public controversy. The refusal to compromise the theoretical rights of the Crown, while indicating that their exercise must be in conformity with the parliamentary constitution, was important not only in forecasting the future role of the Victorian monarchy but more permanently in its assertion, against the rigour of the representative theory, that in this country government is the king's government, not only in form but in spirit, serving ends to which party itself is only an instrument.

The political consequences of William's action were also far-reaching. Peel was given the opportunity of stating the doctrines of post-Reform Conservatism to the country, in the classic Tamworth Manifesto,[3] and to Parliament, in the measures that he proposed to it. His party was reinvigorated, and Peel himself was enabled to

[1] No. 2. [2] No. 4. [3] Part II, No. 52.

dominate the Parliaments of the later 'thirties. In Opposition, he was able to prevent the Radical and Irish tail from wagging the Whig dog, while supporting the Whigs in what he regarded as constructive measures. Almost he may be said to have laid down, in these years, the role of her Majesty's Opposition in a parliamentary state. His brief period of government laid the foundations of that steady growth in public favour and esteem which led to his triumphant return in 1841.

What is known as the Bedchamber Incident provided an interlude to this process. In May 1839 the Whigs succeeded in carrying a Bill to suspend the constitution of Jamaica by only five votes, and in consequence resigned. Peel was called upon to form a government. Queen Victoria had ascended the throne a couple of years earlier as a girl of eighteen, and Melbourne had set himself, with great tact and charm, to act as her political mentor. The queen, with a robust partisanship which was partly youth and partly a temperamental trait that she never wholly outgrew, had surrounded herself with the wives and daughters of her ministers, and made her court virtually a Whig stronghold. Peel was not in a strong political position, and as a mark of the royal confidence he asked that in addition to the usual changes in the household some Tory ladies should be appointed to places about the queen's person. Wellington once said that Peel had no manners. Shy and awkward, giving an impression of icy rigour that really belied his nature, he managed the proposal tactlessly, and alarmed the queen into thinking that he required from her the sacrifice of private friendships, and an alteration in her way of life. In consequence she refused Peel's request, and Peel in turn declined to take office.[1] The upshot was that Melbourne returned. The incident belongs to the years before the queen's sense of the responsibilities of her office had fully matured; it is interesting as illustrating the importance that was still attached to royal support of a government; and, so far as concerns the Whigs, for their readiness, excused by a sense of chivalrous loyalty to the queen, themselves to benefit, on this occasion, from the partiality of the Crown.

The queen's marriage, developing her character, and maturing, in particular, her wilfulness into a deep sense of the responsibilities of her office, the abilities and seriousness of character of her husband, and the coming into power of Peel, provide the keys of the next phase of development. Albert conducted the negotiations which bridged the past between Peel and the queen, and, the barriers of his shyness once overcome, the commanding qualities of the prime minister soon won the entire confidence of the royal couple. It became Peel's turn to conduct the queen's political education. It has been sufficiently seen what respect he possessed for the monarchy. Other influences helped to strengthen in the royal minds the sense of their responsibilities and duties: Albert's deep need of a vocation, nurtured, however, in a land of less qualified monarchical traditions than England; and the influence of Baron Stockmar, the Coburg family counsellor, a liberal, indeed, but understandably indisposed to any view that would reduce the role and importance of his princely protégé. His letter of 22 January 1854 to Prince Albert was written to brace his pupil's mind at a crisis of his popularity in England. It is unlikely that the expositions of constitutional doctrine reproduced[2] represent the day-to-day advice that the baron had given in the past. The baron was nothing if not a student of opportunity and occasion, and by 1854 what may not inaptly be called the Albertine monarchy had already reached a considerable degree of stability on far other lines. But the revelation of the background of his thought is of considerable significance, and the idea that the

[1] No. 5 [2] No. 6.

Crown possessed a sort of superintending responsibility for the country, that because it stood apart from parties it stood, in a sense, over them, does, in fact, play a considerable part in the thought of the queen and the prince. The queen's predecessors, as we have seen, had not been in the habit of playing a purely passive political role. But they had been active as partisans. In the post-Reform constitution this was no longer possible. If the monarchy was not to become what Stockmar calls a mandarin figure, the part of a moderator and mediator in party government was the only active political role open to it. It did not necessarily involve any encroachment on the parliamentary constitution, any derogation from ministerial responsibility such as Peel, for one, would neither have counselled nor accepted. On the contrary it might well prove a reinforcement of the constitution, a safeguard against the shortcomings of party and parliamentary politics, and a standing monition to party chiefs of their responsibility to the permanent interests of the nation.

While Peel was prime minister, his authority, both personal and as the leader of a great majority, confined the play between monarchy and ministry within narrow limits, and bonds of reciprocal amity and confidence. But the situation created by his fall, in the vote in which Lord John Russell combined with the Protectionists to bring down the minister who had just carried a great measure which the majority in Parliament and in the nation supported, was a totally different one. Protectionists and Peelites, the fragments of the once mighty Conservative Party, were divided by the bitterness which the vitriolic tongue of Disraeli,[1] and the long martyrdom of Peel under it had created, and by the determination of Peel and his supporters to uphold Russell's hands in the cause of Free Trade, despite the blow he had just dealt them. This determination ceased, in the efflux of time, with the death of Peel, and with the renunciation of Protection in 1852,[2] to supply the principal motive of political division, but the memory of their chief persisted among the Peelites, and for many years the uncertainty of their action and allegiance, combined with the weight that their abilities gave to them, created a state of affairs in politics in which no man could foretell what the morrow would bring forth. In a memorandum of 17 April 1856, Gladstone went so far as to describe the Peelites as "a main cause of disunion and weakness in the executive government so long as we were not absolutely incorporated into one or other of the two great parties".[3] This was the state of affairs that made the assumption of an active political role by the Crown possible, and at times essential.

The modes and nature of that action are sufficiently indicated in the documents printed below. The patient effort to find by consultation with representative persons the government that would be most effective politically and parliamentarily is best illustrated in the Cabinet crisis of 1851.[4] The Aberdeen coalition of 1852 was largely the deferred fruit of these negotiations, and a similar careful series of soundings preceded the setting up of the Palmerston Government of 1855, when its incompetent handling of the Crimean War had brought the Aberdeen Government down. The queen's care to guard the prerogative of dissolution, that ultimate sanction of ministerial control over the House of Commons, is illustrated both in 1851 and in 1858.[5] Her aim is to prevent its action from becoming mechanical, to ensure that its mode and moment should require a genuine consent of the sovereign, acting in the spirit of the constitution of which she was guardian. The right to veto the appointment of

[1] Part V, No. 146. [2] Part V, Nos. 148–150. [3] Morley, *Gladstone*, ed. 1905, I, pp. 551–552.
[4] Nos. 7–11. [5] Nos. 8, 9, 22, 23, 24.

particular ministers had been freely exercised by the queen's predecessors, though it may be questioned, perhaps, whether it had any real place in the post-Reform constitution. The queen clung to it tenaciously, long after the period of the present volume. The instance in 1851[1] gains piquancy from the fact that it is Disraeli who is under consideration. Of more consequence was the struggle with Palmerston.[2] Palmerston offended in two ways. Himself a masterful spirit, he was accustomed to run the Foreign Office without overmuch consultation even with his colleagues. He tended to look on the necessity for obtaining the queen's consent to the dispatches sent out in her name as a tiresome formality which added unnecessarily to the burdens of an already overloaded man. But to the queen and the prince consultation was vital. If they were not told, they could not advise, and the keystone of the whole system of royal influence was subtracted. Secondly, in foreign policy, the queen had feelings, views, and sources of information of her own. A monarch, she did not share Palmerston's rather lofty Whig superciliousness about monarchy, which he qualified as regards herself on the almost equally injurious assumption that monarchy in England was different. Through her connexions abroad, and those of her husband–through Leopold of Belgium, Louis Philippe in France, and the vast cousinage of the Coburgs–she was able to size up situations as shrewdly as Palmerston himself, and from an independent angle. Finally, to Palmerston's blatant and perhaps rather shallow Liberalism in foreign policy she opposed a strong sense for legal rights, and for the freedom of foreigners to run their affairs, if they chose, in foreign ways. On the right to be consulted she won, and the lesson was not lost on future ministers. As her experience accumulated, it became no light matter for ministers to overrule her. Even on the issue of substance between her and Palmerston it may be permitted to doubt whether she was wrong, whether much of permanent value has come from the influence among the European nations of the British constitutional pattern, which the Whigs so assiduously tendered to them.

With the death of the Prince Consort, and the redrawing of party lines in the 'sixties, something of the energy, and something also of the effect, of her influence departed. It was the queen's pathetic, and indeed profoundly praiseworthy, attempt still to do everything that her 'dear one' would have done. But what two heads and hearts had accomplished, not without labour, indeed, but in fullness of energy and spirit, was now a task done out of duty and piety. From 1859, when Gladstone, the greatest of the Peelites still actively in the political ring, joined Palmerston's Government, a two-party system rapidly developed. Ministers more securely based, and with their eyes rather on party tactics in the country than on the possibilities of shifting allegiance in the House, became more self-confident and less ready to defer to advice. The extension of the franchise in 1867 accentuated this tendency. Relations with Gladstone and Disraeli, the leaders of the newer time, constitute a chapter in themselves. The impetus is not exhausted; the monarchy can still play a part in policy, and perform valuable services, as the queen's intervention over Reform in 1866-1867[3] and the Irish Church[4] indicate. But the creative phase of the Albertine monarchy is over.

The monarchy has been the matrix of English political institutions. The Courts, the Council, Parliament, the Cabinet, have all grown up under its wing, and within the ambit of its fostering and disciplining influence. It is this fact, more than any other, that gives to English political institutions their distinctive character. In this proud

[1] No. 9. [2] Nos. 12–21. [3] Nos. 26–30. [4] Nos. 31–38.

pageant of history the monarchy of Queen Victoria takes its place. In a utilitarian and increasingly practical age, it preserved the spirit of a higher and more exacting devotion; to an age becoming sceptical, it imparted the touch of romantic faith. The creation of exceptional circumstances and of an exceptional pair of personalities, flawed and flecked, no doubt, by the inevitable limitations of personalities, it could not survive unchanged. But it is not to be judged wholly by the canons of an *a priori* constitutional propriety, though even of these it may claim to have been justified in its time. Constitutions are spirit, as well as convention and law; and the thought of the queen labouring daily at her desk, early and late, as it came to dominate the imagination of her subjects, despite some ill-conditioned Radical criticism,[1] so, to politicians, it served as a reminder that they served a mistress, who, if sometimes querulous and harsh, claimed by titles both of descent and of labour to stand for the dignity, the greatness, and the permanent interests of her realms. No 'mandarin figure' could have served these ends. To have enhanced the moral status of monarchy within the framework of democracy, to have found a new function for it as the *vis medicatrix* of a popular constitution, to have made it effective in terms of daily political life as the symbol of the forbearances, the sacrifices, the devotion exacted by the affairs of a great empire, was to have renewed its mighty youth, to have demonstrated in changed times its continued creative vitality. This ranges the Victorian Age among the great epochs of our monarchy.

[1] Nos. 39–41.

SELECT BIBLIOGRAPHY

The primary source for the history of the monarchy is the *Letters of Queen Victoria, First Series*, edited by A. C. BENSON and VISCOUNT ESHER (3 vols., London, 1907), *Second Series* edited by G. E. BUCKLE (3 vols., London, 1926–1928). LYTTON STRACHEY, *Queen Victoria* (London, 1921), holds the field as the best life of the queen. SIR THEODORE MARTIN, *Life of the Prince Consort* (5 vols., London, 1875–1880), is a quarry rather than a biography, but a quarry in which it is still profitable to dig. H. BOLITHO, *The Prince Consort and his Brother* (London, 1933), and ROGER FULFORD, *The Prince Consort* (London, 1949), offer more discriminating material on his personal character, and the latter an appreciation of his political role. Gladstone's review of MARTIN'S *Prince Consort*, in vol. I of his *Gleanings of Past Years* (London, 1879), gives an authoritative criticism of some of Stockmar's and the prince's views on the place of the monarchy. *The Memoirs of Baron Stockmar*, by BARON E. STOCKMAR (2 vols., London, 1872), should also be consulted. P. GUEDALLA, *The Queen and Mr Gladstone* (2 vols., London, 1933), presents a continuous picture of the relations of two potent and often uncongenial spirits; the first volume covers the period of this work. F. HARDIE, *The Political Influence of Queen Victoria* (London, 1935), should be used with caution. Further detailed information on political issues on which the queen was active must be sought in the biographies of leading statesmen (see *General Bibliography*).

Further reference must chiefly be had to works on the constitution. WALTER BAGEHOT, *The English Constitution* (London, 1867), was never wholly correct, but has never been wholly superseded. T. ERSKINE MAY, *Constitutional History of England since 1760*, edited by F. HOLLAND (3 vols., London, 1912), is still valuable, flanked by W. R. ANSON, *The Law and Custom of the Constitution*, 5th edn., M. L. GWYER (3 vols., Oxford, 1922; vol. 2, *The Crown*, ed. A. B. Keith, Oxford, 1935), the one primarily narrative, the other analytical in form. D. L. KEIR, *The Constitutional History of Modern Britain 1485–1937* (London, 1938), and K. B. SMELLIE, *A Hundred Years of English Government* (London, 1937), dealing with the century of the Reform Act, and A. B. KEITH, *The Constitution of England from Queen Victoria to George VI* (2 vols., London, 1940), are the standard modern constitutional histories. R. H. GRETTON, *The King's Majesty* (London, 1930), is a perceptive small essay. W. I. JENNINGS, *Cabinet Government* (Cambridge, 1937), though primarily concerned with modern working of the constitution, discusses the major problems of the period of this book. A. B. KEITH, *The British Cabinet System*, revised by M. H. GIBBS (London, 1953), should also be consulted. Of the many smaller books L. S. AMERY, *Thoughts on the Constitution* (London, 1948), is the most penetrating.

SIR LEWIS NAMIER'S Romanes Lecture, *Monarchy and the Party System* (Oxford, 1952), though dealing primarily with an earlier period, should not be missed. Among articles may be cited GAVIN HENDERSON, "The Influence of the Crown 1854–6" in *Juridical Review* (December 1936); N. GASH, "The Influence of the Crown at Windsor and Brighton, 1832, 1835, and 1837" in *English Historical Review*, vol. LXIV (1948); C. K. WEBSTER, "The Accession of Queen Victoria" in *History*, vol. XXII (1937); W. E. MORSE, "The Crown and Foreign Policy, March–May 1866; Queen Victoria and the Austro-Prussian Conflict", in *Cambridge Historical Journal*, vol. II (1951), and C. H. STUART, "The Coalition Cabinet of 1852", in *Transactions of the Royal Historical Society, Fifth Series*, vol. IV (1954).

ELIZABETH LONGFORD, *Victoria R.I.* (1964) is now the most satisfactory life of Queen Victoria; R. FULFORD (ed.), *Dearest Child, Letters between Queen Victoria and the Princess Royal 1858–61* throws valuable light on the relations between the two; H. BOLITHO, *Albert Prince Consort* (1959); F. EYCK, *The Prince Consort* (1959) dealing especially with his interest in foreign affairs.

(*a*) DEBATE ON THE ADDRESS IN THE LORDS AND COMMONS, 24 FEBRUARY 1835

1. Speech of Viscount Melbourne

Hansard, 3/xxvi/76–82.

VISCOUNT MELBOURNE: ... With respect to the change of the Administration, I have nothing more to say than has already been said in public on many occasions. That step was determined upon by his Majesty, and approved, adopted, sanctioned, and carried into effect by the counsel and advice of the noble Duke opposite, the Secretary of State for Foreign Affairs. For that change, therefore, that noble Duke is undoubtedly responsible. He advised it, and I apprehend that it is a constitutional doctrine which will not admit of doubt, that he is responsible for it. Whether that change were prudent or wise, it is certainly not for me or my colleagues to determine. It is for the country – it is for your Lordships – it is for the other House of Parliament to decide that question. But when I consider the situation in which we are placed – when I consider the position in which the noble Lords opposite have placed themselves – when I consider the position in which they have placed the country – when I consider our actual state, and our prospects for the future, I must say that I do not see any thing that justifies the prudence or the discretion of that determination.... But the Ministry having been dissolved, the present Prime Minister in course of time returned from the Continent, and on his arrival the Ministry was constituted as it now stands. They shortly came to a decision, which, in my mind, presents the strongest grounds of charge against noble Lords opposite, *viz*., the decision of dissolving the late Parliament. Your Lordships will be pleased to observe, that all this took place while the country was in an admitted state of peace and prosperity. . . . The present Prime Minister, at a dinner given to him and others of his colleagues, at the Mansion-house, shortly after the formation of the Ministry, said, "It is impossible to deny, that since the occurrence of the important events that have taken place within the last six weeks, there has been calm and tranquillity in this country, which, after the political excitement in which we have lived for some time past, could not have been anticipated." ... The right hon. Baronet after some eloquent sentences, proceeded to state. "Gentlemen, I believe, if the public feeling of this country could be embodied into expressions, it would speak in words, to some such purport as this: – We are tired of agitation; we are tired of that state of excitement which, in private life, withdraws men from their proper stations, and which, in public life, exercises the energies of public men in any other matters than their moral duties. We will not yield to the pressure from without; we will not have this domination; we are content that the public opinion and the public will should be expressed through the authorized public channels, and by authorized public means." Now, I ask your Lordships, how it is possible that, any man holding these opinions, having these feelings in his heart, with these expressions in his mouth, could at that time have contemplated the dissolution of Parliament?

Why, we have here the strongest argument against such a step I ever heard in my life. Here is the exact statement of every evil that can arise from a dissolution of Parliament, of all the misfortunes which such a public contest as follows that act must produce. What tends to agitation, and takes men from their proper business so much as a dissolution of Parliament? What is a pressure from without if it be not a general election? Is it not bringing the influence of the people to bear immediately upon their recognized and constituted organs? If ever there were reasons for not dissolving Parliament, here they are in the speech of Sir Robert Peel, at the Mansion-house. But in what course are you embarking?–you have had one dissolution, and you menace us with another ["Cries of No, no"]. . . . Your Lordships will recollect that it is admitted, that the dissolution took place when the public mind was in a state of calm and tranquillity–when the country was approaching to that state of quiet and repose which, it is to be hoped, we are some day or other to enjoy. If so the Parliament which has been just elected must be taken fairly to represent the opinions of the people. You cannot appeal from it with success. I recollect that the noble Lord, the Keeper of the Privy Seal, said, that the Parliament of 1831 was elected under excitement, and that the people were deluded by the name and authority of the King. Now that last topic has been employed pretty liberally upon the present occasion, but it has been employed on the side of the Government, and that Government cannot pretend to allege that the present Parliament does not represent the will of the people. Now what is the character of the House of Commons? Under what banners have its members obtained their seats? Every one of them under the banners of Reform. Some have said, that they are willing to go further than others; but all have Reform in their mouths. Must we not conclude, therefore, that the country is in favour of the principle thus recognized? The King's Speech is also, we are told, a Reforming Speech. Why then was it not pronounced to the former House? Former dissolutions had definite and important objects in view. That of 1784 prevented the meditated change in the government of the East Indies; that of 1807 changed the policy of the country, most unfortunately, with respect to the Roman Catholics, and measures which we are ruing to this day were adopted. The dissolution of 1831 carried the Reform Bill. But what is the object of this dissolution, if the same measures are to be pursued, the same language held, as would have been held without a dissolution? There has been no object in view but a change of men, by a wanton act of power. No reason can be seen for the act, except the introduction of a certain number of Tory supporters of the Ministry into the House of Commons, dragging them through the dirt, making them desert their old principles, and act against all the professions of their former lives. I can imagine no other motive for the conduct of the Government unless it be embarking us in dissolution upon dissolution–a desperate and fearful game, of which I see no end unless it be the fulfilment of the predictions of which you were so lavish at the passing of the Reform Bill, that it would be impossible for the Government of the country to be carried on under that dispensation. . . . The noble Viscount concluded by moving the following Amendment:–"That we acknowledge with grateful recollection, that the Act for Amending the Representation of the people was submitted to Parliament with Your Majesty's sanction, and carried into law by your Majesty's assent. That, confidently expecting to derive further advantages from that wise and necessary measure, we trust that your Majesty's Councils will be directed in the spirit of well-considered and effective Reform; and, that the liberal and comprehensive policy which restored to the people the right of choosing their Representatives, and which provided for the emancipation of all persons held in slavery in your Majesty's Colonies and possessions abroad, will, with the same enlarged view, place without delay our Municipal Corporations under vigilant popular control, remove all the well-founded grievances of the Protestant Dissenters, and correct those abuses in the Church which impair its efficiency in England, disturb the peace of society in Ireland, and lower the character of the Establishment in both countries. That we beg leave submissively to add, that we cannot but lament that the progress of these Reforms should have been interrupted and endangered by the dissolution of a Parliament earnestly intent upon the vigorous prosecution of measures to which the wishes of the people were most anxiously and justly directed.

2. Speech of the duke of Wellington

Hansard, 3/XXVI/82–87.

DUKE OF WELLINGTON said, their Lordships would admit, that, after having been personally called on as he was by the noble Viscount who had just sat down, he should feel anxious to take the first opportunity which was open to him to offer a few remarks on what the noble Viscount had stated. The noble Viscount had directed a great part of his speech to show that the dissolution of Parliament was not necessary; and that he (the Duke of Wellington) was responsible for the dissolution of the late Government. He must beg the noble Viscount's pardon, and deny that he was responsible for those measures which caused the dissolution of the late Government and led to the formation of the present. That which led to the dissolution of the late Government was the absolute impossibility that it could go on longer without a noble Lord, who had ceased to be a Member of the House of Commons, by his removal from that to be a Member of their Lordships' House. He would beg to call to the recollection of their Lordships what had been stated by a noble Earl, who had for nearly four years been at the head of the Government, when Lord Althorp had resigned his office of Chancellor of the Exchequer and leader of the House of Commons. The noble Earl stated, that he could not, under such circumstances, continue at the head of the Government; for, by the resignation of his noble Friend, he had lost his right hand; and it would be impossible to carry on the Government with advantage from the time that that noble Lord had quitted power. But that was not all. The noble Viscount (Melbourne) had himself stated to their Lordships, as one of the grounds on which he had been induced to take office, that he had been assured that his noble Friend was willing to go on in office with him, and, therefore, that, with his assistance, he would consent to undertake to carry on the Government. But even that was not all, for he happened to know that, when the noble Viscount felt that he was likely to lose the aid of Lord Althorp, he declared that he should feel himself placed in great difficulty, for that the noble Lord was the very foundation on which the Government stood, and when that was removed, it was impossible to go on. When, then, the question of the Government came before his Majesty, he found it fairly put to him whether he would seek for other councils, and whether he would consent to other arrangements for the formation of a Government, or whether he would be content to abide by the particular administration which at that moment existed. Let their Lordships only observe the situation in which the King was placed, and ask themselves, what he was to think in the new position in which he found himself. The noble Earl had been under the necessity of resigning when the noble Lord, then Chancellor of the Exchequer, had sent in his resignation. The noble Viscount, too, had declared that he considered the noble Lord's assistance essentially necessary to him. But when his Majesty was left by the noble Earl, and when Lord Althorp was removed from the other House, his Majesty, forsooth, was not to be permitted to consider whether his position was not materially altered by these events, and whether it would not be expedient for him to make some other arrangements for carrying on the public service. Everybody, indeed, but his Majesty was to be allowed to take into consideration the alterations which had taken place in the power of the Government by the loss of Lord Althorp in the House of Commons! Their Lordships, however, he was convinced, would not acquiesce in such a decision. They would see and declare that the Sovereign was fully entitled to take into consideration his own peculiar position, and the state of public affairs, and to deliberate whether it would be advisable for him to make other arrangements with respect to the existing Administration, or, if not, whether it would not be better for him to form a new Government altogether. Under the circumstances in which his Majesty was placed, he had thought proper to send to him (the Duke of Wellington); and he was happy to find that all those histories and stories which were propagated respecting Court intrigues–[Viscount *Melbourne*: "Not by me".]–He was quite certain of that. But all those idle stories were now entirely laid aside. It was now fully admitted on all hands that there never was any such thing. For his own part, he had had no communication of any description with the Court for two–ay, he might say, for three, months previous to the communication from his Majesty. He was then at his house in Hampshire; and it was as much a matter of surprise to him at the moment as it possibly could be to any of their Lordships. Certainly, he was previously satisfied that some great change in the Administration must be the consequence of the removal of Lord Althorp from the House of Commons; but when the communication reached him, it was as much a matter of surprise to him as it could be to many of their Lordships, if they were to receive a similar summons to-morrow. When his Majesty sent for him, he might have accepted the offer his Majesty was graciously pleased to make to him. He might have come down to their Lordships in a higher situation; but he did not recommend that course to his Majesty, which would have been accessory to the gratification of his own ambition. He did not act as if he had a personal object to serve. He recommended to his Majesty that line of proceeding which he conceived would be most advantageous for his service, which was, that he should send for the right hon. Gentleman then in the other House of Parliament as the individual in the present times most fit and capable of discharging the duties of the King's first Minister. That right hon. Gentleman was then in another part of the world, at a considerable distance from England; and it appeared advisable to his Majesty, and to him that he should take possession of the Government for Sir Robert Peel; and absolutely necessary, at the same time, whoever might carry on the Government until the right hon. Gentleman's arrival, that he should exercise no patronage, and take no step whatever which should in the least tend to diminish the full and free authority of the right hon. Gentleman when he might come to act. His advice to his Majesty, accordingly, had been to put him provisionally at the head of affairs as Secretary for the Home Department and First Lord of the Treasury. But the noble Viscount (Melbourne) accused him of holding the Seals of the three principal Secretaryships of State at the same time. But this, although gravely urged, was not a very serious charge. Having been appointed to any one of the Secretaryships, a man was competent to hold the Seals of the other two, in the absence of those to whom they might be confided. It was true, that he had, as Secretary for the Home Department, held the Seals of the three Secretaryships; but he had exercised no more authority than he should have done if he had been one of the three principal Secretaries, and his colleagues were absent. And was there, he would ask, no precedent for such a proceeding? Why, Mr. Canning, while he was yet Secretary for the Foreign Department, was on the 12th of April appointed First Lord of the Treasury, and he did not resign the Seals of the Foreign Department until the 30th of the same month; consequently, during the whole of the intervening time, he was both Secretary for Foreign Affairs and First Lord of the Treasury. He knew very well the difference that there was between the two cases. There were two Secretaries who had resigned their offices but had not given up the Seals. But before the noble Viscount proceeded to blame a transaction of this description, he should have shown that some inconvenience had arisen from it. He said that no inconvenience had resulted from it. He might say, too, that during the whole time he held the Seals, there was not a single office disposed of, nor an act done, which was not essentially necessary for the service of the King and of the country. Moreover, he might add, that Sir Robert Peel on his arrival found all things, as nearly as possible, in the same situation as upon the 15th of November. The noble Viscount (Melbourne), however, had observed, that the office of First Lord of the Treasury was incompatible with the other offices which he held. It might be true, if those offices were held for any length of time by the same individual. But, in the first place, he only occupied them provisionally; and, secondly, he would remark that constitutionally the First Lord of the Treasury had no more power than any other Lord at the Board. It was perfectly understood, too, by all men, that the arrangement was not permanent, and that he only held the Government for another individual, who had been sent for by his Sovereign. Next, the noble Viscount (Melbourne) blamed him highly for having attended his Majesty, and facilitated his arrangements for the formation of a new Administration; and yet, strange to say, the noble Viscount himself it was, if he were not mistaken, who brought to town the order in consequence of which he had waited upon his Majesty. If there were anything criminal in attending his Sovereign, and assisting in carrying into execution the plan for the formation of a new Administration, what should be said of that Minister who brought a letter to town the object of which was to secure that attendance and co-operation, that Minister well knowing at the time what were the contents of that letter? Was the noble Viscount, then, the man to bring him forward as a criminal for having attended to the wishes of his Sovereign, when he himself was the bearer of those commands which carried him into the presence of his Majesty, and to the performance of those services which the noble Viscount now repudiated? If he were disposed so to argue, he might contend that the fact of the noble Viscount being the bearer of this letter showed the *animus* with which the noble Viscount had waited upon his Majesty, and the *animus* of the transactions between them, and also the *animus* of the communications between himself and his Majesty; but it was not necessary. He would only repeat that he never was more surprised than at the mode in which he had understood the arrangement was afterwards received by the noble Viscount. He trusted that he had stated enough to justify him in assisting to form a new Ministry. The next charge to which he had to advert was, that the Ministers had dissolved the late Parliament. With respect to this, it was true, that whatever Ministry advised the dissolution of a Parliament was liable to be called on for some reason which might have induced them so to do; but he had seldom heard of such a course of proceeding as that Ministers should be called upon on the first day of the assembling of Parliament, and told, "Give me some reason why you thought fit to dissolve; and justify your dissolution of Parliament, by showing that the effort you have made has been a successful one." But the noble Viscount, after heaping his censure upon them for dissolving, added, that in all cases where Parliament was dissolved it was success which justified the measure. If, then, they had made an experiment which was to depend upon so peremptory a criterion, surely he ought, at least, to allow them a short time to wait and see fairly what had been the result. The noble Lord and his friends had dismissed in June a Parliament which was chosen in November. Their experiment he acknowledged was perfectly successful. He hoped, that the present experiment would also prove perfectly successful. At all events, it would be but fair to give them some little time for the prescribed justification, and not to assail them on the first day of the Session. And now as to this success, he wanted to know, after all, how great was that measure of success which the late Ministry enjoyed in the late Parliament, when it appeared to rest solely and exclusively on the shoulders of a single individual; so, that when he was removed to the upper House, the Government to which he belonged had found it impossible to go on. As to himself, he was convinced that the course he had pursued was correct, and by it he was ready to stand or fall. He believed that a great number of persons was disposed and determined to support the Administration, and he hoped the House would have the patience to wait and see what were the measures the Ministers had to propose. He was not aware that there were any other topics on which it was necessary for him to speak. He had, he should think, said enough to show that there was no reason why their Lordships should see it expedient to adopt the Amendment of the noble Viscount. He ought, perhaps, to say, as to the Municipal Corporations, that it was not the intention of Ministers in any way to thwart the Commissioners, and they were unwilling to pledge themselves to any particular system of legislation without knowing what the Report of those Commissioners would be. In that mode of proceeding, their Lordships must he was sure, be disposed to acquiesce, as his Majesty informed them that the Report would be laid before them in a short time.

3. Personal explanation of Viscount Melbourne

Hansard, 3/xxvi/87–88.

I rise to explain the fact to which the noble Duke has alluded, of my bringing from Brighton the letter which led the noble Duke to the presence of his Majesty. After I had had my audience of his Majesty on the 14th of November, I went into the room of Sir Herbert Taylor, and he requested me, as I was going to London immediately, to convey a letter from him to Sir Henry Wheatley, at St. James's Palace. I will not deny that I knew that that letter enclosed a letter to the noble Duke; but when so requested, would it not have been the most captious, churlish, ungracious conduct, if I had refused to allow my servant to carry it, and if I had said, "No! send a messenger of your own?" and can any approbation of the act of sending for the Duke be implied from the manner in which I acted upon that occasion?

4. Speech of Sir Robert Peel

Hansard, 3/xxvi/215–227.

Chancellor of the Exchequer (Sir R. Peel, Tamworth): . . . I shall in the first place, refer to the circumstances under which the present Government was constituted; I shall defend the course which I thought it my duty to advise the King to pursue at the period of its formation; and give accurate delineations of the measures which it is the intention of his Majesty's Government to introduce; those explanations the House has a right to require, and I should shrink from that duty which is imposed upon me if I did not avow a willing disposition to afford them. I stand here as the Minister of the Crown–placed in this situation by no act of my own–in consequence of no dexterous combination with those to whose principles I have been uniformly opposed, and with whom I might frequently have made, had I been so inclined, a temporary alliance for the purpose of embarrassing the former Government. I stand here in fulfilment of a public duty, shrinking from no responsibility, with no arrogant pretensions of defying or disregarding the opinions of the majority of this House, yet still resolved to persevere to the last, so far as is consistent with the honour of a public man, in maintaining the prerogative of the Crown, and in fulfilling those duties which I owe to my King and to my country.

In vindication of the course which I have pursued, it is necessary that I should refer to the circumstances which preceded the dissolution of the last Government. I have been asked whether I would impose on the King in his personal capacity, the responsibility of the dismissal of that Government? In answer to this question, I will at once declare, that I claim all the responsibility which properly belongs to me as a public man; I am responsible for the assumption of the duty which I have undertaken, and, if you please, I am, by my acceptance of office, responsible for the removal of the late Government. God forbid that I should endeavour to transfer any responsibility which ought properly to devolve upon me to that high and sacred authority which the constitution of this country recognizes as incapable of error, and every act of which it imputes to the advice of responsible counsellors. But whilst I disclaim all intention of shrinking from that responsibility, which one situated as I am, must necessarily incur; I must at the same time unhesitatingly assert, what is perfectly consistent with the truth, and what is due to respect for my own character, – namely, that I was not, and under no circumstances would I have been a party to any secret counselling or instigating the removal of any Government. But although I have not taken any part in procuring the dismissal of the late Government, although I could not from circumstances which are notorious to the world, hold communication with any of those with whom I have now the honour to act, much less with the highest authority in the State, as to the propriety or policy of that dismissal, still I do conceive that by the assumption of office, the responsibility of the change which has taken place is transferred from the Crown to its advisers; and I am ready – be the majority against me what it may – to take all the responsibility which constitutionally belongs to me and to submit to any consequences to which the assumption of that responsibility may expose me. . . . I now come to the subject of the dissolution of the late Parliament. I have been asked whether I take upon myself the responsibility of that proceeding, and without a moment's hesitation I answer that I do take upon myself the responsibility of the dissolution. The moment I returned to this country to undertake the arduous duties now imposed upon me, I did determine that I would leave no constitutional effort untried to enable me satisfactorily to discharge the trust reposed in me. I did fear that if I had met the late Parliament, I should have been obstructed in my course, and obstructed in a manner, and at a season, which might have precluded an appeal to the people. But it is unnecessary for me to assign reasons for this opinion. Was it not the constant boast that the late Parliament had unbounded confidence in the late Government? And why should those who declare they are ready to condemn me without a hearing, be surprised at my appeal to the judgment of another, and a higher, and a fairer tribunal – the public sense of the people? Notwithstanding the specious reasons which have been usually assigned for the dissolution I believe it will be found, that whenever there has occurred an extensive change of Government, a dissolution of Parliament has followed. In the year 1784, a change took place in the Government, Mr. Pitt was appointed to the office of Prime Minister, and in the same year a dissolution took place. Again, in 1806, when the Administration of Lords Grey and Grenville was formed, the Parliament, which had only sat four years, was shortly after the assumption of power by those Noblemen dissolved. It was on that occasion urged, that a negotiation with France having failed, it became necessary to refer to the sense of the country, but I never will admit that the failure of the negotiation with France could constitute any sufficient grounds for the dissolution of a Parliament which there was not the slightest reason to believe was adverse to the continuance of the war, or dissatisfied with the conduct of the negotiation. In the year 1807, another change took place in the Government by the accession of Mr. Perceval to power, and then again a dissolution immediately took place. In the year

1830, Earl Grey was called into office as Prime Minister, and shortly after the vote in committee on the Reform Bill, the Parliament which had been elected in 1830, was dissolved in 1831. Hence it appears that in the case of the four last extensive changes in the Government, those changes have been followed by a dissolution of the then existing Parliament. The present, however, is I believe to be the first occasion upon which the House of Commons has ever proceeded to record its dissatisfaction at the exercise of the prerogative of dissolution.[1]

(*b*) THE BEDCHAMBER CRISIS 7–10 MAY 1839

5. Speech of Sir Robert Peel in the Commons (13 May 1839)

Hansard, 3/XLVII/979–986.

The debate arose on the occasion of Russell's reappearance as Minister, and Leader of the House of Commons on Peel's giving up his effort to form a ministry. Russell spoke very briefly, Peel with some embarrassment, but with the express intention of confining himself to the bare facts. He also took the opportunity of denying exaggerated rumours of his proposals to the queen, and of reiterating the view he had taken that the state of public affairs had made it necessary for him to ask "the fullest and most unequivocal proof" that he "possessed the confidence of her Majesty". Russell made an elaborate reply, from which it became clear that the queen had feared a general assimilation of the position of her ladies to that of the great court officers, and cited a number of precedents against this, not all precisely in point. Peel did not avail himself of the opportunity Russell offered him of further explanation, and the debate closed. A debate in the Lords ran a similar course, with Wellington and Melbourne as the speakers.

Sir Robert Peel:* Mr. Speaker, I have reserved for this place, and for this occasion, the explanations which I feel it my duty to offer with regard to the circumstances which have induced me to relinquish the attempt to form an administration for the conduct of the public service. Sir, I need scarcely say that I disclaim any sanction for any other statements which may have appeared in these circumstances; that for them I am wholly irresponsible; and that they have been made without my authority, and contrary to my wishes, if those wishes could have prevailed. . . .

On the Wednesday evening–that is, the day I saw her Majesty on this particular point–I had the opportunity of conferring with all those whom I proposed to submit to her Majesty as Ministers. I saw them on Wednesday night at my own house about ten o'clock. I then stated to them–and there are four of them now present who heard the communication, and can give their evidence upon it–my right hon. Friend, the Member for the University of Cambridge (Mr. Goulburn), the Member for Launceston (Sir H. Hardinge), the Member for Pembroke (Sir James Graham), and my noble Friend the Member for North Lancashire (Lord Stanley); I stated to them, and to the Peers whom I have before named, the course which I meant to pursue with respect to the household. I had very little information with respect to the household,

* From a corrected report.

[1] The House divided on the original question: Ayes 302, Noes 309. Majority for the Amendment: 7.

and had very little considered the matter (I am speaking of the female part of it): I really scarcely knew of whom it consisted. I took the "Red Book" into my hand, and saw there the different appointments of the household. I said to those who were intended to be my future colleagues, that, with respect to all the subordinate appointments – meaning every appointment, without exception, below the rank of a Lady of the Bedchamber – I should propose to her Majesty no change whatever with respect to those. With respect to the superior class, I stated, that those Ladies who hold offices of that class, and who were immediate relatives of our political opponents, would, I took it for granted, relieve us from any difficulty, by at once relinquishing their offices. But I stated, at the same time, that I did think it of great importance, as conveying an indication of her Majesty's entire support and confidence, that certain offices in the household, of the higher rank, if not voluntarily relinquished by the Ladies holding them, should be subject to some change. Even with respect to the higher offices, namely, the Ladies of the Bedchamber, I did state, however, that there were some instances in which, from the absence of any strong party or political connexion, I thought it would be wholly unnecessary to propose a change. My noble and right hon. Friends will confirm what I assert. This passed on the evening of Wednesday; and I mention it only in complete proof of my intentions, being perfectly willing, as I before observed, to have transferred exclusively to me whatever blame may attach to the imperfect explanation of my views. I saw her Majesty on Thursday, and verbal communications took place on this subject. As I stated before, into the nature of those communications I shall not now enter in the slightest degree. I shall merely read the two letters which passed; one conveying the impressions of her Majesty, and the other my own. The letter which I had the honour of receiving from her Majesty is dated May 10, 1839. I received it at an early hour on Friday morning, and it is as follows:

"Buckingham Palace, May 10, 1839.

"The Queen, having considered the proposal made to her yesterday by Sir Robert Peel, to remove the Ladies of her Bedchamber, cannot consent to adopt a course which she conceives to be contrary to usage, and which is repugnant to her feelings."

Immediately – that is, in two or three hours after having received the letter from her Majesty, I addressed to her Majesty a letter, of which this is a copy, dated Whitehall, May 10:

"Whitehall, May 10, 1839.

"Sir Robert Peel presents his humble duty to your Majesty, and has had the honour of receiving your Majesty's note of this morning.

"In respectfully submitting to your Majesty's pleasure, and humbly returning into your Majesty's hands the important trust which your Majesty had been graciously pleased to commit to him, Sir Robert Peel trusts that your Majesty will permit him to state to your Majesty his impression with respect to the circumstances which have led to the termination of his attempt to form an Administration for the conduct of your Majesty's service.

"In the interview with which your Majesty honoured Sir Robert Peel yesterday morning, after he had submitted to your Majesty the names of those whom he proposed to recommend to your Majesty for the principal executive appointments, he mentioned to your Majesty his earnest wish to be enabled, with your Majesty's sanction, so to constitute your Majesty's household that your Majesty's confidential servants might have the advantage of a public demonstration of your Majesty's full support and confidence; and that at the same time, as far as possible consistently with that demonstration, each individual appointment in the household should be entirely acceptable to your Majesty's personal feelings.

"On your Majesty's expressing a desire that the Earl of Liverpool should hold an office in the household, Sir Robert Peel requested your Majesty's permission at once to offer to Lord Liverpool the office of Lord Steward, or any other which he might prefer.

"Sir Robert Peel then observed, that he should have every wish to apply a similar principle to the chief appointments which are filled by the Ladies of your Majesty's household; upon which your Majesty was pleased to remark, that you must reserve the whole of those appointments, and that it was your Majesty's pleasure that the whole should continue as at present, without any change.

"The Duke of Wellington, in the interview to which your Majesty subsequently admitted him, understood also that this was your Majesty's determination, and concurred with Sir Robert Peel in opinion that, considering the great difficulties of the present crisis, and the expediency of making every effort in the first instance to conduct the public business of the country with the aid of the present Parliament, it was essential to the success of the commission with which your Majesty had honoured Sir Robert Peel, that he should have that public proof of your Majesty's entire support and confidence, which would be afforded by the permission to make some changes in that part of your Majesty's household, which your Majesty resolved on maintaining entirely without change.

"Having had the opportunity, through your Majesty's gracious consideration of reflecting upon this point, he humbly submits to your Majesty that he is reluctantly compelled, by a sense of public duty, and of the interest of your Majesty's service, to adhere to the opinion which he ventured to express to your Majesty.

"He trusts he may be permitted at the same time to express to your Majesty his grateful acknowledgements for the distinction which your Majesty conferred upon him, by requiring his advice and assistance in the attempt to form an administration, and his earnest prayers that whatever arrangements your Majesty may be enabled to make for that purpose, may be most conducive to your Majesty's personal comfort and happiness, and to the promotion of the public welfare."

These are the letters that passed, and I add nothing to the simple reading of them.

(c) BARON STOCKMAR'S VIEW ON THE PLACE OF THE MONARCHY IN THE CONSTITUTION

6. Letter from Stockmar to the Prince Albert (22 January 1854)

T. Martin, *Prince Consort*, 1875–80, II, pp. 545–557.

In December 1853 and January 1854, partly in consequence of the temporary resignation of Palmerston from Aberdeen's Coalition Ministry, and the popular excitement as to the policy towards Russia, there was a series of scurrilous newspaper attacks on the prince, on the ground of his supposed Russian sympathies, and his influence. Rumour even got so far as to say that he had been sent to the Tower. The calumny soon died down, and on the opening of Parliament was put in its proper place by a few dignified sentences from Lord John Russell. In the meantime Stockmar had written the prince a long letter from Germany, dealing largely with the prince's duties, more particularly in so far as he was virtually the queen's secretary, and with the object of bracing him to their more disagreeable aspects. From this are here extracted the passages bearing more directly upon the position of the Crown.

. . . The old Tories, who, before the Reform Bill, were in power for fifty years, had a direct interest in upholding the prerogatives of the Crown, and they did uphold them manfully, although the Hanoverian Kings, by their immoral, politically exceptionable, dynastic or private wishes and interests, made the task anything but an easy one. As a race, these Tories have died out, and the race, which in the present day bears their name, are simply degenerate bastards. Our Whigs, again, are nothing but partly conscious, partly unconscious Republicans, who stand in the same relation to the Throne as the wolf does to the lamb. And these Whigs must have a natural inclination to push to extremity the constitutional fiction–which, although undoubtedly of old standing, is fraught with danger–that it is unconstitutional to introduce and make use of the name and person of the irresponsible Sovereign in the public debates on matters bearing on the Constitution. But if the English Crown permit a Whig Ministry to follow this rule in practice, without exception, you must not wonder, if in a little time you find the majority of the people impressed with the belief, *that the King, in the view of the law, is nothing but a mandarin figure, which has to nod its head in assent, or shake it in denial, as his Minister pleases.*

Now, in our time, since Reform, the extinction of the genuine Tories, and the growth of those politicians of the Aberdeen school, who treat the existing Constitution merely as a bridge to a Republic, it is of extreme importance, that this fiction should be *countenanced only provisionally, and that no opportunity should be let slip of vindicating the legitimate position of the Crown.* And this is not hard to do, *and can never embarrass a Minister, where such straightforward loyal personages as the Queen and the Prince are concerned.* For the most jealous and distrustful Liberalism, in any discussion about the definite interpretation of the law of Royal prerogative, must be satisfied, if *this be placed no higher than a right on the part of the King to be the permanent President of his Ministerial Council.* Now the most stupid of Englishmen knows, that, up to the present hour at least, his country is always governed by only one party, and that consequently the Premier of the Cabinet for the time is and can be nothing else but *the Chief of the Party then in power.* Out of the very character of this Party Chief it ought to be demonstrable to the narrowest capacity, that every Premier, even were he a patriot of the most far-seeing views, and absolutely exempt from prejudice, must suffer from two drawbacks inherent in his office, which demand a constitutional corrective, and for which none can be sought or found, except in the true position of the Crown towards the Cabinet, and in the way it deals with it in the exercise of its prerogative. The first of these drawbacks consists in the temptation, to which the Premier is directly exposed by the obvious insecurity and brief duration of his tenure of office, to give to the personal, selfish, and transitory tendencies of the dominant majority precedence over the substantial interests of the country. The second arises from the instinctive struggle of party (without reference to whether, so far as the State is concerned, they are in the right or not), to strengthen their majority, and to weaken the minority by every possible official resource. . . .

Prior to 1831, the centre of gravity of the combined forces of the State in their relation to each other had lain in the Upper House, where the Tories for sixty years had commanded the majority. Although the Oppositions of those days sometimes spoke "of an overgrown power in the Crown," nothing more was seriously meant by this than the identity of principle and interest which was assumed to exist between the Crown and the majority of the Upper House. This notion the dominant majority could afford to encourage, and in its own interest to protect a Crown, which was making itself every day more unpopular and weak by its folly and immorality.

The Reform Act, while it gave to the democratic element a preponderance in the Constitution over the aristocratic, removed its centre of gravity from the Upper to the Lower House, and thereby threw all political life into a state of feverish excitement and oscillation, which was very apt to have proved fatal to it. In this conjuncture the healing force of the self-adjusting principle was demonstrated, all the more that Peel proved himself an honest and skilful physician. By successfully allaying the dangerous excitement of the one organ, which had now gained the preponderance, it was for the first time brought into harmonious action with the others, and the dangers were averted, which most imminently threatened the entire fabric.

A happy change, which placed a moral Sovereign upon the throne, came powerfully and palpably in aid of the self-adjusting principle and of Peel's endeavours. Whether the Minister, whether the Upper House was ever consciously aware, what a safeguard for them against the wild power of democracy had grown up in the moral purity of the Queen, I do not know. The Ministry, however, could hardly fail to know, even although they did not openly acknowledge, how greatly the popularity of the throne operated to the advantage and security of their administration ; and just as little could the Lords fail to be struck by the reflection, that, instead of the time when they had to support an unpopular Sovereign, another time had come, in which a popular Sovereign was able to support them, and disposed to do so, on the assumption, that the part which they were entitled to take in legislation would be performed with intelligence, with sympathetic feeling suited to the spirit of the age (zeitmässiger Humanität), with industry and with courage. . . .

The feverish crisis into which the life of the Constitution has been thrown by the Reform, in consequence of the very material alterations of the reciprocal relations between the individual forces of the State which had previously existed, is not yet past; although the self-adjusting principle and Peel's statesmanship have averted serious danger, and brought about a healthier state of things . . . Still, much remains to be done. The task which is especially incumbent on the Minister, and is his foremost duty is manfully to defend the present well-deserved popularity of the Sovereign, while yours is to lend all the aid in your power towards the assumption by the Lords of their rightful position in the Legislature, and the fulfilment of their vocation as sagacious, liberally-minded, and honourable men. . . .

(*d*) THE CABINET CRISIS OF 21 FEBRUARY–3 MARCH 1851

On 21 February 1851 Lord John Russell's Government was defeated in the House of Commons by 100 votes to 52 on a motion of Locke King's for equalizing the county and borough occupying franchises. Locke King and many of his supporters were Radicals–*i.e.* normally supporters of the Government, and the motion was an incident in the Radical pressure to force Russell to implement the hopes he had held out in 1848 of another Reform Bill (see Part III, Introduction). The documents printed emphasize the political instability resulting from the split in the Conservative Party, and from Radical and Irish unreliability. These negotiations though, for reasons made clear in the documents, they did not succeed, paved the way for Lord Aberdeen's Coalition Government in 1852, which, but for the strains of the Crimean War, and in part the uncertainty of Russell's own conduct, might have given the queen the stable government she was looking for. As things fell out in 1855, the Peelites remained unattached until the end of the decade–when most of them were passing from the political scene–and Palmerston, not Russell, inherited the Whig leadership, which he held till his death in 1865.

7. Memorandum by the Prince Albert (22 February 1851)

Letters of Queen Victoria, First Series, II, pp. 289–293.

Lord John Russell having been for a few minutes with the Queen, in order to prepare her for the possibility of the Government's resignation (yesterday, at two o'clock), went to Downing Street to meet the Cabinet, and promised to return at four in order to communicate the decision the Cabinet might have arrived at. On his return he explained that after the vote at the beginning of the Session on the Orders of the Day, which went directly against the Government, after the small majority (only fourteen) which they had had on the motion of Mr. Disraeli on the landed interest, and now the defeat on the Franchise it was clear that the Government did not possess the confidence of the House of Commons. He complained of the Protectionists staying away in a body on Mr. King's motion, and he (Lord John) himself being left without a supporter even amongst his colleagues in the debate, but most of all of the conduct of the Radicals; for when Mr. King, hearing Lord John's promise to bring in a measure next Session, wanted to withdraw his Motion, as he ought to have done on such a declaration by the head of the Government, Mr. Hume insisted upon his going on, "else Lord John would withdraw his promise again in a fortnight"; and when the result of the vote was made known the shouting and the triumph of the hundred was immense.

Lord John had declared to the Cabinet that he could not go on, that the Income Tax would have to be voted the next day, and a defeat was probable; it were much better therefore not to hesitate, and to resign at once. The Cabinet agreed, although some members thought with Lord Palmerston that the occasion was hardly sufficient.

Lord John begged to be allowed till to-day, in order to see Lord Lansdowne, whom he had sent for from the country, and to be able to tender then his resignation; he would go down to the House to adjourn it, promising explanations on Monday.

We agreed with Lord John that he owed to his station personally, and as the Queen's Minister, not to put up with ignominious treatment, praised his speech on the Suffrage, which is admirable, and regretted that his colleagues had prevented him from bringing in a measure this year. We talked of the difficulty of forming any Government, but agreed that Lord Stanley and the Protection party ought to be appealed to; they longed for office and would not rest quiet till they had had it if for ever so short a time only.

We further went over the ground of a possible demand for a Dissolution, which might bring on a general commotion in the country. Lord John agreed in this; but thought the responsibility to be very great for the Crown to refuse an appeal to the country to the new Government; he thought a decision on that point ought to depend on the peculiar circumstances of the case.

Lord Lansdowne, who had come from Bowood by the express train, arrived at twelve o'clock, and came at once to meet Lord John Russell here at the Palace.

In the audience which the Queen gave him he expressed his entire concurrence with the decision the Cabinet had come to, as the resignation could at any rate only have been delayed. It was clear that the Cabinet had lost the confidence of the House of Commons; what had happened the other night was only the last drop which made the cup flow over, and that it was much more dignified not to let the Government die a lingering and ignominious death; he (thought) that Lord Stanley would have great difficulties, but would be able to form a Government; at least the Protectionist Party gave out that they had a Cabinet prepared.

We then saw Lord John Russell, who formally tendered his resignation, and was very much moved on taking leave; he said that considering Lord Stanley's principles, it would not be possible for him to hold out any hope of support to that Government, except on the estimates, for which he felt responsible, but he would at all times be ready vigorously to defend the Crown, which was in need of every support in these days.

At three o'clock came Lord Stanley, whom the Queen had summoned.

The Queen informed him of the resignation of the Government, in consequence of the late vote, which had been the result of the Protectionists staying away, of the small majority which the Government had had upon Mr. Disraeli's Motion, and of the many symptoms of want of confidence exhibited towards the Government in the House of Commons. The Queen had accepted their resignation, and had sent for him as the head of that Party, which was now the most numerous in Opposition, in order to ask him whether he could undertake to form a Government.

Lord Stanley expressed great surprise. The impression had been that the Government were not in earnest in their opposition to Mr. L. King's Motion; in the minority had voted only twenty-seven members of the Government side, the rest had been of his Party. He asked if the whole Cabinet had resigned, or whether there had been dissension in the Cabinet upon it? The Queen replied that the resignation had been unanimously agreed upon in the Cabinet, and that Lord Lansdowne, who had only come up from Bowood this morning, had given his entire approval to it. Lord Stanley then asked whether anybody else had been consulted or applied to, to which the Queen replied that she had written to him a few minutes after Lord John's resignation, and had communicated with no one else. Lord Stanley then said that he hoped that the Queen's acceptance had only been a conditional one; that he felt very much honoured by the Queen's confidence; that he hoped he might be able to tender advice which would contribute to the Queen's comfort, and might relieve the present embarrassment.

In order to do so he must enter most freely and openly into his own position, and that of his Party . . . that he should have great difficulties in presenting to the Queen a Government fit to be accepted, unless he could join with some of the late Sir Robert Peel's followers; . . . As to his principles, he would frankly state that he thought that the landed interest was much depressed by the low state of prices; that an import duty on corn would be absolutely necessary, which, however, would be low, and only a revenue duty; . . . He thought the present House of Commons could hardly be expected to reverse its decision upon the financial and commercial policy of the country, and that accordingly a Dissolution of Parliament would become necessary. . . . He hoped . . . that the Queen would try to obtain a Government by a coalition of the Whigs and the Peelites, but that this failing, if the Queen should send again for him, and it was clear no other Government could be formed, he would feel it his duty as a loyal subject to risk everything, except his principles and his honour, to carry on the Government; and he hoped that in such a case the Queen would look leniently on the composition of the Cabinet which he could offer, and that the country would, from the consideration of the circumstances, give it a fair trial. He begged, however, that he might not be called upon to take office except as a *dernier ressort*, a *necessity*. . . .

. . . Before taking leave, he repeated over and over again his advice that the Coalition Ministry should be tried.

8. Memorandum by the Prince Albert (25 February 1851)

Letters of Queen Victoria, First Series, II, pp. 300–301.

Lord Aberdeen and Sir James Graham came yesterday evening at nine o'clock; the Queen put it to them whether *they* could form a Government, to which they replied that they had turned it in their heads a hundred times, that there was nothing they would not do to show their readiness to serve the Queen, but that they did not see a possibility of forming an Administration which could stand a day. They were most likely at that moment the two most unpopular men in England, having declared that nothing should be done in Parliament against the Papal Aggression, which the whole country clamoured for; the Whigs would be very angry with them for their having broken up the new combination; they might find favour with the Radicals, but that was a support upon which no reliance could be placed. There was a growing opinion that Lord Stanley ought to have a chance of bringing forward his measures;

that it was perilous, but that it was an evil which must be gone through; that this opinion had been strongly expressed by Lord Lansdowne, whose moderation nobody could doubt; that it was shared by the Duke of Newcastle, Mr. Sidney Herbert, and others of Sir James's friends whom he had had time to consult.

Upon the Queen's expression of her great apprehension as to the consequence of such a step on the country, they said there would no doubt spring up a most violent opposition, that there would be attempts to stop the supplies and dissolve the Army, but that Lord John Russell and Sir James Graham together would do their utmost to preach moderation, and would refer the House of Commons to the Queen's example, who had taken strictly the Constitutional course throughout the crisis, whose opinions on Free Trade were well known (as far as subjects could allow themselves to pretend to know their Sovereign's *private* opinions) from the hearty support she had given to Sir Robert Peel's and Lord John's Governments. That upon the first proposition of a Stanley Government the junction of Parties would be completed, and there would be only *one* strong opposition. After having fought together, there would be no longer any difficulty about forming a strong Government out of their joint ranks, whilst now it was impossible not to see that every Minister displaced would feel personally aggrieved, that then they stood on a footing of perfect equality. Sir James had seen Lord John since he had tendered his second resignation and found him quite altered; whilst he was embarrassed and *boutonné* before, he was open and unreserved now, and they could speak on terms of private friendship. Lord Aberdeen would save his influence in the House of Lords, which he would probably have lost if he had joined the Whigs in office; in future all this would be different.

Lord John Russell's letter with the Memoranda came and interrupted us. From these papers, and what Sir James and Lord Aberdeen said, it is clear that all parties are relieved by the failure of their attempt to form a Coalition Government, but determined to form a positive junction, which will be most salutary to the country. The Queen will therefore send for Lord Stanley.

We discussed further the means Lord Stanley would have to form an Administration, for which the material was certainly sad. Disraeli's last scene in the House of Commons would render the publication of Lord Stanley's letter necessary. Mr. Gladstone might possibly join him; at least no pains would be spared to bring him in. Lord Palmerston had often so much secret understanding with Disraeli that he might be tempted with the bait of keeping the Foreign Office, particularly if personally offended.

Whether the Queen should allow or refuse a Dissolution was debated: the latter declared a most heavy responsibility for the Sovereign to undertake, but a subject upon which the decision should only be taken at the time, and on a due consideration of the circumstances.

ALBERT

9. Memorandum by the Prince Albert (25 February 1851)

Letters of Queen Victoria, First Series, II, pp. 302–304.

Lord Stanley obeyed the Queen's summons at eleven o'clock, and seemed very much concerned when she informed him that Lord John Russell had given up his task, as differences of opinion, particularly on the Papal Bill, had prevented a junction between him, Lord Aberdeen, and Sir James Graham; that an appeal to Lord Aberdeen had been equally unsuccessful from the same cause, *viz.* their difficulty in dealing with the Papal question; that consequently the contingency had arisen under which Lord Stanley had promised to undertake the formation of a Government.

Lord Stanley said his difficulties were immense, and he could not venture to approach them unless he was sure of every support on the part of the Crown: that he would have arrayed against him a formidable opposition of all the talent in the country.

The Queen assured him that he should have every Constitutional support on her part, of which Lord Stanley said he had felt sure, although the total change must be very trying to the Queen.

On his question, whether there was any hope of Lord Aberdeen joining him and taking the Foreign Office, we had to tell him that he must quite discard that idea. He replied, with a sigh, that he would still try and see him; he had thought of the Duke of Wellington taking the Foreign Office *ad interim*, but felt that he could hardly propose that, considering the Duke's age and infirmity; he would make the attempt to see Lord Canning with the Queen's permission and that failing could only think of Sir Stratford Canning, now at Constantinople, which the Queen approved.

He still hoped he might get Mr. Gladstone to take the lead in the House of Commons, without which assistance he must not conceal it would be impossible for him to go on. Mr. Gladstone was on his way home from Paris, and he had written to him to see him as soon as he arrived; till then he could not promise that he would succeed to form an Administration, and he only undertook it for the good of his country, he was afraid of ruining his reputation.

To this I rejoined that who tried to do his best by his country need never be afraid for his reputation. . . .

. . . Returning to the offices to be filled, Lord Stanley said he should have to propose Mr. Disraeli as one of the Secretaries of State. The Queen interrupted him by saying that she had not a very good opinion of Mr. Disraeli, on account of his conduct to poor Sir R. Peel, and what had just happened did not tend to diminish that feeling; but that she felt for Lord Stanley's difficulties, that she would not aggravate them by passing a sentence of exclusion on him. She must, however, make Lord Stanley responsible for his conduct, and should she have cause to be displeased with him when in office, she would remind Lord Stanley of what now passed. Lord Stanley promised to be responsible, and excused his friend for his former bitterness by his desire to establish his reputation for cleverness and sharpness; nobody had gained so much by Parliamentary schooling, and he had of late quite changed his tone. . . .

. . . At the conclusion of the interview he broached the important question of Dissolution, and said that a Dissolution would anyhow become necessary; and that if it was thought that the Queen would withhold from him the privilege of dissolving, he would not have the slightest chance in the House of Commons; he would be opposed and beat, and then his adversaries would come in and dissolve. He avowed that it could not be said that the Queen had refused him the power of dissolving, but he required some assurance.

On the Queen's objecting to give him a contingent positive promise, but declaring her readiness fairly to discuss the question when the emergency arose, he contented himself with the permission to deny, if necessary, that she would *not* consent to it, putting entire confidence in the Queen's intention to deal fairly with him.

I tried to convince Lord Stanley, and I hope not without effect, of the advantage, both to the Queen and Lord Stanley himself, that they should not be hampered by a positive engagement on that point, which might become very inconvenient if circumstances arose which made a Dissolution dangerous to the country. ALBERT

10. Memorandum by the Prince Albert (28 February 1851)

Letters of Queen Victoria, First Series, II, p. 309.

FRIDAY, 28th February 1851. Lord Lansdowne, who arrived at twelve o'clock, was asked by the Queen what advice he could offer her in the present complication. His answer was: "I wish indeed I had any good advice to offer to your Majesty." He expressed his delight at the Queen having sent for the Duke of Wellington. We talked generally of the state of affairs; he agreed in a remark of mine, that I thought the Queen should be entirely guided in her choice of the person to construct a Government, by the consideration which Party would now appear to be the strongest in the House of Commons. On my asking, however, whether he knew if, on the failure of Lord Stanley to form a Government, part of his followers would now give up Protection as past hope, and be prepared in future to support the Peelite section of the Conservative Party, Lord Lansdowne said he had heard nothing on the subject, nor could he give us more information on the chance of the Radicals and Irish members now being more willing to support Lord John Russell in future. He liked Lord Stanley's plan of dealing with the Papal Question, of which the Queen communicated to him the outlines, was afraid of Sir J. Graham's excessive leaning towards economy, shook his head at Lord John Russell's letter to the Bishop of Durham which had been instrumental in bringing on the present crisis, and confessed that he had been amongst those in the Cabinet who had prevented the bringing forward of a measure of reform in the present Session. He offered to do whatever might be most conducive to the Queen's comfort–stay out of office, or come into office–as might be thought the most useful. ALBERT

11. Memorandum by the Prince Albert (3 March 1851)

Letters of Queen Victoria, First Series, II, p. 312.

The Queen now asked whether Lord John proposed a modification of his own Cabinet, to which Lord John replied, None, except perhaps an exchange of Office between Sir C. Wood and Sir F. Baring, if Sir Charles were to refuse bringing in a different budget from the one he had already propounded; he was for maintaining the Income Tax, whilst Sir Francis was for repealing it by degrees. The Queen then reminded Lord John of her objections to Lord Palmerston, and his promise that Lord Palmerston should not again be thrust upon her as Foreign Secretary. Lord John admitted to the promise, but said he could not think for a moment of resuming office and either expel Lord Palmerston or quarrel with him. He (Lord John) was in fact the weakness and Lord Palmerston the strength of the Government from his popularity with the Radicals. . . . He said he was very anxious that he and Lord Lansdowne should bear the responsibility of removing Lord Palmerston from the Foreign Office and not the Queen; her refusal now could only go to the country as a personal objection on her part, and the country would be left without a Government in consequence. On the Queen's reiterating that she wanted to keep Lord John and get rid of Lord Palmerston, and that it was too painful to her to be put into the situation of having actually to *wish* the fall of her own Government, Lord John promised to move Lord Palmerston in the Easter recess, or to resign then himself if he should meet with difficulties; in the meantime he must apprise Lord Palmerston of this intention which he could explain to him as a wish to make a general modification of his Government. He would offer him the Lieutenancy of Ireland or the Presidency or lead in the House of Lords, which Lord Lansdowne would be ready to resign. He might at that period perhaps get some of the Radicals into office or some Peelites. The Queen finally entrusted Lord John with the Government on these conditions. ALBERT

(*e*) THE CONTEST WITH PALMERSTON

Differences between the queen and Palmerston on foreign affairs, and complaints as to his failure fully to consult her, can be traced, in the queen's letters, as far back as 1846 (17 August 1846, *Letters*, 1/2/96, and 28 November 1846, *Letters*, 1/2/111). Russell felt bound to support the queen on the constitutional question, though he urged the danger to the Government of alienating Palmerston, in view of his strength in the country, and pleaded that in all else he was an ideal colleague. By the beginning of 1849 he was discussing with the queen the possibility of transferring Palmerston to some other office, and, in principle, Palmerston had agreed. In June 1850 occurred the 'Don Pacifico' crisis, in which Palmerston defended himself against the assembled talent of the House in his famous 'dusk till dawn' speech. After this triumph Palmerston was no longer ready to be moved, as "it would be loss of character to him . . . those who had wished to injure him had been beat, and now, it would be giving them a triumph after all" (Memo. by the Prince Albert, 8 August 1850, *Letters*, 1/2/263). The queen therefore sent him, through Russell, the memorandum at No. 12. It was probably influenced by a memorandum of Stockmar's of 12 March (*Letters*, 1/2/238). The mildness of Palmerston's reply to Russell, at No. 13, was due to the same determination not to give a triumph to his enemies, and, as he later explained, to reluctance to bring his sovereign's name into discussion, "and the Sovereign a lady". The queen hoped that the Cabinet crisis of February 1851 might end her difficulties, but her hopes were disappointed (No. 11). In November there was a prolonged struggle to prevent the Foreign Minister receiving the Hungarian patriot, and Austrian rebel, Kossuth, in which Palmerston gave way, but almost immediately he offended the queen's sense of propriety by receiving an address from a meeting of Finsbury Radicals in which the emperors of Russia and Austria were referred to in very violent terms. So far as both Russell and the queen were concerned, therefore, the cup was already full when the incidents which form the subject of No. 16, and subsequent documents, occurred. The queen's view of matters was largely shaped by letters from the marchioness of Normanby to Colonel Phipps, the prince's secretary. These letters are printed in *Letters of Queen Victoria*, First Series, II, pp. 336–340. In a letter to Russell on 20 December the queen said that "in view of the sad experience she has just had she must reserve to herself the unfettered right to approve or disapprove of the choice of Minister for this office", and asked that Lord Granville, the successor agreed upon, should draw up a memorandum on the principles of foreign policy, to be submitted to her. Granville's tact was equal to the double task of satisfying the queen and preserving the independence of his office.

12. Memorandum from the queen to Lord John Russell (12 August 1850)

Letters of Queen Victoria, First Series, II, p. 264.

With reference to the conversation which the Queen had with Lord John Russell the other day, and Lord Palmerston's disavowal that he ever intended any disrespect to her by the various neglects of which she has had so long and so often to complain, she thinks it right, in order *to prevent any mistake* for the *future*, shortly to explain *what it is she expects from her Foreign Secretary*. She requires: (1) That he will distinctly state what he proposes in a given case, in order that the Queen may know as distinctly to *what* she has given her Royal sanction; (2) Having *once given* her sanction to a measure, that it be not arbitrarily altered or modified by the Minister; such an act she must consider as failing in sincerity towards the Crown, and justly to be visited by the exercise of her Constitutional right of dismissing that Minister. She expects to be kept informed of what passes between him and the Foreign Ministers before important decisions are taken, based upon that intercourse; to receive the Foreign Despatches in good time, and to have the drafts for her approval sent to her in sufficient time to make herself acquainted with their contents before they must be sent off. The Queen thinks it best that Lord John Russell should show this letter to Lord Palmerston.

13. Letter from Lord Palmerston to Lord John Russell (13 August 1850)

Letters of Queen Victoria, First Series, II, pp. 264–265.

FOREIGN OFFICE, 13th August 1850. MY DEAR JOHN RUSSELL, – I have taken a copy of this memorandum of the Queen and will not fail to attend to the directions which it contains. With regard to the sending of despatches to the Queen, they have sometimes been delayed longer than should have been the case, in consequence of my having been prevented by great pressure of business, and by the many interruptions of interviews, etc., to which I am liable, from reading and sending them back into the Office so soon as I could have wished. But I will give orders that the old practice shall be reverted to, of making copies of all important despatches as soon as they reach the Office, so that there may be no delay in sending the despatches to the Queen; this practice was gradually left off as the business of the Office increased, and if it shall require an additional clerk or two you must be liberal and allow me that assistance. – Yours sincerely, PALMERSTON

14. Letter from the queen to Lord John Russell (4 December 1851)

Letters of Queen Victoria, First Series, II, p. 334.

OSBORNE, 4th. December, 1851. The Queen has learnt with surprise and concern the events which have taken place at Paris.[1] She thinks it is of great importance that

[1] On the 3rd the tidings of the *coup d'état* reached London. Count Walewski announced it to Lord Palmerston, who expressed his approval of it, and wrote to Lord Normanby the letter printed in his *Life*, disavowing surprise that the President had struck the blow when he did, "for it is now well known here that the duchess of Orleans was preparing to be called to Paris this week with her younger son to commence a new period of Orleans dynasty". – BENSON and ESHER.

Lord Normanby should be instructed to remain entirely passive, and to take no part whatever in what is passing. Any word from him might be misconstrued at such a moment.

15. Letter from Lord John Russell to the queen (4 December 1851)

Letters of Queen Victoria, First Series, II, pp. 334–335.

DOWNING STREET, 4th December 1851 (6 P.M.) Lord John Russell presents his humble duty to your Majesty. Your Majesty's directions respecting the state of affairs in Paris shall be followed. Lord Normanby[1] has asked whether he should suspend his diplomatic functions; but the Cabinet were unanimously of opinion that he should not do so.

The result is very uncertain; at present the power is likely to rest in the Army, to whose memory of victories and defeats the President has so strongly appealed.

16. Letter from the queen to Lord John Russell (13 December 1851)

Letters of Queen Victoria, First Series, II, p. 340.

OSBORNE, 13th. December 1851. The Queen sends the enclosed despatch[2] from Lord Normanby to Lord John Russell from which it appears that the French Government *pretend to have received* the entire approval of the late *coup d'état* by the British Government, as conveyed by Lord Palmerston to Count Walewski. The Queen cannot believe in the truth of the assertion, as such an approval given by Lord Palmerston would have been in complete *contradiction* to the line of strict neutrality and passiveness which the Queen had expressed her desire to see followed with regard to the late convulsion at Paris, and which was approved by the Cabinet, as stated in Lord John Russell's letter of the 6th inst. Does Lord John know anything about the alleged approval, which, if true, would *again* expose the honesty and dignity of the Queen's Government in the eyes of the world?

17. Letter from the marquis of Normanby to Lord Palmerston (15 December 1851)

Ashley, *Palmerston*, 1879, II, pp. 205–206.

PARIS, December 15. 1851. My Lord,–In my despatch of the 6th instant, notifying my communication of my instructions to M. Turgot, I reported that his Excellency had mentioned that M. Walewski had written a despatch in which he stated that your Lordship had expressed your complete approbation of the course taken by the President in the recent *coup d'état*. *I also reported* that I had conveyed to M. Turgot

[1] Lord Normanby, having applied for instructions as to his future conduct, was desired to make no change in his relations with the French Government, and to abstain from even the appearance of interference in her internal affairs. Having made a communication to this effect to M. Turgot, the latter replied that M. Walewski had notified to him that Lord Palmerston had already expressed to him his "entire approbation of the act of the President", and his "conviction that he could not have acted otherwise".

[2] This is Normanby's dispatch of 6 December to which reference is made in No. 17.—BENSON and ESHER.

my belief *that there must be some mistake in this statement, and my reasons for that belief.*

But as a week has now elapsed without any explanation from your Lordship on this point, I must conclude M. Walewski's report to have been substantially correct.

That being the case, I am perfectly aware that it is beyond the sphere of my present duties to make any remark upon the acts of your Lordship, except inasmuch as they affect my own position. But within these limits I must, with due deference, be permitted to observe, that if your Lordship, as Foreign Minister, holds one language on such a delicate point in Downing Street, without giving me any intimation you had done so–prescribing afterwards a different course to me, namely, the avoidance of any appearance of interference of any kind in the internal affairs of France–I am placed thereby in a very awkward position.

If the language held in Downing Street is more favourable to the existing order of things in France than the instructions on which I am directed to guide myself upon the spot, it must be obvious that by that act of your Lordship's I become subject to misrepresentation and suspicion in merely doing my duty according to the official orders received through your Lordship from Her Majesty.

All this is of more importance to me, because, as I stated before, several of my diplomatic colleagues had had the despatch read to them, and had derived from it the conviction that, if accurately reported, your expressions had been those of unqualified satisfaction.

I have, &c.,
NORMANBY

18. Letter from Lord Palmerston to the marquis of Normanby (16 December 1851)

Ashley, *Palmerston*, 1879, II, pp. 206–207.

FOREIGN OFFICE: December 16, 1851. My Lord,–I have received your Excellency's despatch of the 15th instant, referring to the statement made to you by the French Minister for Foreign Affairs on the occasion of your communicating to his Excellency the instructions with which you have been furnished by Her Majesty's Government for your guidance in the present state of affairs in France, and I have to state to your Excellency that there has been nothing in the language which I have held, nor in the opinions which I have at any time expressed on the recent events in France, which has been in any way inconsistent with the instructions addressed to your Excellency, to abstain from anything which could bear the appearance of any interference in the internal affairs of France. The instructions contained in my despatch of the 5th instant to which your Excellency refers, were sent to you, not in reply to a question as to what opinions your Excellency should express, but in reply to a question which I understood to be, whether your Excellency should continue your usual diplomatic relations with the President during the interval which was to elapse between the date of your Excellency's despatch of the 3rd instant and the voting by the French nation on the question to be proposed to them by the President.

As to approving or condemning the step taken by the President in dissolving the Assembly, I conceive that it is for the French nation, and not for the British Secretary of State or for the British Ambassador, to pronounce judgment upon that event; but if your Excellency wishes to know my own opinion on the change which has taken place in France, it is that such a state of antagonism had arisen between the President and the Assembly that it was becoming every day more clear that their co-existence could not be of long duration; and it seemed to me better for the interests of France, and, through them, for the interests of the rest of Europe, that the power of the President should prevail, inasmuch as the continuance of his authority might afford a prospect of the maintenance of social order in France, whereas the divisions of opinions and parties in the Assembly appeared to betoken that their victory over the President would only be the starting-point for disastrous civil strife.

Whether my opinion was right or wrong, it seems to be shared by persons interested in property in France, as far at least as the great and sudden rise in the Funds and in other investments may be assumed to be indications of increasing confidence in the improved prospect of internal tranquillity in France.

I am, &c.,
PALMERSTON

19. Letter from Lord John Russell to the queen (18 December 1851)

Letters of Queen Victoria, First Series, II, p. 341.

WOBURN ABBEY, 18th December 1851. Lord John Russell presents his humble duty to your Majesty. He received from Lord Palmerston yesterday an explanation of his declaration of opinion to Mr. Walewski, which Lord John Russell regrets to state, was quite unsatisfactory.

He thought himself compelled to write to Lord Palmerston in the most decisive terms.

Lord Palmerston requested that his letter might be returned to be copied.

The whole correspondence shall be submitted to your Majesty.

Your Majesty will find in the box a despatch of Lord Normanby of the 15th, and an answer of Lord Palmerston of the 16th,[1] which has been sent without your Majesty's sanction, or the knowledge of Lord John Russell.

20. Letter from Lord John Russell to Lord Palmerston (19 December 1851)

Ashley, *Palmerston*, 1879, II, p. 211.

WOBURN ABBEY: Dec. 19, 1851. My dear Palmerston,–I have just received your letter of yesterday. No other course is left to me than to submit the correspondence to the Queen, and to ask Her Majesty to appoint a successor to you in the Foreign Office.

[1] Nos 17 and 18.

Although I have often had the misfortune to differ from you in minor questions, I am deeply convinced that the policy which has been pursued has maintained the interests and the honour of the country.

I remain, yours truly,
J. RUSSELL

21. Lord Palmerston's defence of himself in the House of Commons (3 February 1852)

Hansard, 3/CXIX/104–113.

VISCOUNT PALMERSTON: Sir, I am sure the House will feel that after what has passed on the part of my hon. Friend behind me (Sir B. Hall), and the noble Lord who has just sat down, it is absolutely incumbent on me to make some observations to the House. I should be sorry, indeed, Sir, that this House and the country should run away with the impression which the speech of the noble Lord has been too well calculated to make, that I have abandoned principles I have ever entertained – that I have changed opinions, and which, I trust, I never shall alter – that I have been the advocate of absolute power – and that I have been in favour of the abolition of constitutional government; but I shall come to that immediately. The noble Lord at the head of the Government began the remarks he made to the House by stating his opinion of the relations which ought to subsist between the Foreign Secretary and the Crown on the one hand, and the Foreign Secretary and Prime Minister on the other. In that definition I most entirely concur, and I flatter myself I have done nothing which is inconsistent with either of those relations. Sir, the practice that prevails in the Foreign Office was that which the noble Lord has described as laid down in the Memorandum of 1850; but the practice did not begin at that time, but was in existence before – namely, that no important political instruction is ever sent to any British Minister abroad, and no note addressed to any Foreign diplomatic agent, without the draught being first submitted to the head of the Government, in order that the pleasure of the Crown might be taken upon it; and if either the higher authority or the Prime Minister suggested alterations, those alterations were made, or the despatch was withheld. It has, I know, sometimes been said, that though the general tenor of the policy pursued by me had met with the approval of Her Majesty's Government and was right, yet there was, notwithstanding, something in the manner of conducting it calculated to excite irritation on the part of foreign Governments. Now, the manner of conducting that business consisted in the framing of despatches or notes; and I have stated that these despatches and notes were never sent unless they had obtained the previous sanction of the noble Lord at the head of the Government. The noble Lord has commented upon an incident which I am ready to admit excited some degree of regret on my part – namely, the interview which took place between me and a certain deputation from Finsbury and Islington on the subject of the efforts made by Her Majesty's Government to obtain the release of the Hungarian refugees detained in the Turkish dominions. I was asked by letter to receive a deputation, instructed to express the acknowledgements of a certain meeting to me, as a member of the Government, and the organ of its foreign policy, for the efforts made to obtain the liberation of those refugees. I thought it was my duty, being thus applied to by respectable persons, to receive this deputation from a meeting of Her Majesty's subjects. I certainly did not expect, not being so much in the habit of receiving deputations as my noble Friend probably is, I did not expect that what passed in conversation with those persons was to appear in a newspaper paragraph next day as "an important declaration on the part of Her Majesty's Government." But nothing was said to that deputation by me which I had not stated previously in my place in this House, and elsewhere, and which has not been perfectly well known to the Government. I certainly regret that the meeting should have mixed up with their acknowledgments to Her Majesty's Government expressions with respect to foreign Sovereigns, which it was entirely unfitting to be addressed to a person in my situation. If I had taken the precaution, which I certainly might, to see the address previously, I might have objected to such parts, and they might have been expunged; but being taken by surprise, and the address being read to me on the spot, all I could do was to repudiate those expressions, and to disclaim any participation in the opinions which they expressed. I do not think that what passed on that occasion was reasonably calculated to impair the friendly relations between Her Majesty's Government and any Continental Power. I will now come to the particular transaction to which the noble Lord has referred as the ground-work of my removal from office. The event which is commonly called the *coup d'état* happened in Paris on the 2nd December. On the 3rd the French Ambassador, with whom I was in the habit of almost daily communication, called on me at my house to inform me of the news which he had received, and to talk over the events of the preceding day; and I stated conversationally the opinion I entertained of the events which had taken place. That opinion was exactly the opinion expressed in the latter part of the despatch to Lord Normanby, which the noble Lord has read; and the French Ambassador, as I am informed, communicated the result of that conversation in a private letter to his Minister. On that day, the 3rd of December, Her Majesty's Ambassador at Paris, wrote a despatch to ask what instructions he should receive for his guidance during the interval which must elapse before the vote of the French nation upon the questions to be proposed to them by the President was known; and whether in that interval he should infuse into his relations with the French Government any greater degree of reserve than usual. I took the opinion of the Cabinet on that question, and a draught of answer was prepared and sent for Her Majesty's approbation. The answer could only be one, in consistence with the course we had pursued from the very beginning of the events in 1848, and was such as the noble Lord has read. Her Majesty's Ambassador was instructed to make no change in his relations with the French Government, and to do nothing that should wear the appearance of an interference of any kind in the internal affairs of France. There was no instruction to communicate that document to the French Government; it simply contained instructions, not, in fact, what the English Ambassador was to do, but what he was to abstain from doing. The noble Lord, however (the Marquess of Normanby), thought it right to communicate to the

French Minister for Foreign Affairs the substance of that instruction, accompanying his communication with certain excuses for delay. Delay, however, there had been none, because his despatch was dated the 3rd, the answer was sent off on the 5th, and he communicated the reply on the 6th. The French Minister stated that he had nothing to say with respect to the delay, and the less, indeed, because two days before he had received from the French Ambassador in London, a statement which the noble Lord (Lord J. Russell) has read, namely, that I had entirely approved of what had been done, and thought the President of the French could not have acted otherwise. That was a some-what highly-coloured explanation of the result of a rather long conversation. Those particular words I never used, and probably the French Ambassador never would have conceived it consistent with the dignity of his country to ask the approval of a Foreign Secretary of State. Consequently, the approval was not given, and was not asked. When the Marquess of Normanby's despatch reached my noble Friend (Lord J. Russell), he wrote to say he trusted that I would contradict that report. There was, as he has stated, an interval between the receipt of the noble Lord's letter and my answer. The noble Lord's letter was dated on the 14th, and my answer the 16th. I was at the time labouring under a heavy pressure of business, and, wishing fully to explain the opinion I had expressed, it was not until late in the evening of the 16th, that I was able to write my answer. The noble Lord got it early next morning, on the 17th. My answer was, that the words quoted by the Marquess of Normanby gave a high colouring to anything I could have said in my conversation with the French Ambassador on the 3rd of December; but that my opinion was, and that opinion, no doubt, I expressed, that such was the antagonism which had arisen between the French Assembly and the President of the Republic, that their long co-existence had become impossible, and that it was my opinion that if one or the other were to prevail, it would be better for France, and, through the interests of France, better for the interests of Europe, that the President should prevail than the Assembly. My reason was, that the Assembly had nothing to offer as a substitute for the President, but alternatives ending obviously in civil war or anarchy; whereas the President, on the other hand, had to offer unity of purpose and unity of authority, and if he were inclined to do so, he might give to France internal tranquillity with permanent good government. This was the opinion I expressed on the 3rd, the day after the *coup d'état*. I will not trouble the House with all the arguments in my letter of the 16th to the noble Lord at the head of the Government, or with all the illustrations it contained. My noble Friend replied to that letter, that he had come to the reluctant conclusion that it would not be consistent with the interests of the country to allow the management of the Foreign Affairs of the country to remain any longer in my hands. He said that the question between us was not whether the President was justified or not in what he had done, but whether I was justified or not in having expressed any opinion on the subject. To that I replied, that of course I should be ready to give up the Seals whenever my successor was appointed; but I added that there is in diplomatic intercourse a well-known and perfectly understood distinction between official conversations, by which Governments are bound, and which represent the opinions of Governments, and those non-official conversations by which

Governments are not bound, and in which the speakers do not express the opinion of Governments, but simply the opinions they may themselves for the moment entertain. I said, that in my conversation with Count Walewski, on the 3rd December, nothing passed which could in the slightest degree fetter the action of the Government, and that if the doctrine of the noble Lord were established, and if the Foreign Secretary were to be precluded from expressing on passing events any opinion to a Foreign Minister, except in the capacity of an organ of a previously consulted Cabinet, there would be an end to that freedom of intercourse between Secretaries of State for Foreign Affairs and Foreign Ministers, which tends so much to good understanding and to the facility of public business. To this my noble Friend replied that my letter left him no other course than to ask Her Majesty to appoint a successor to me. Now, it is my humble opinion that my doctrine is right, and that of my noble Friend is wrong; because it is obvious that if the Secretary of State for Foreign Affairs were never allowed in easy and familiar conversation with Foreign Ministers to express an opinion on foreign events, whether important or not, not as the opinion of the Government, but as an opinion which he had formed himself at the moment, then such a restriction on his intercourse with Foreign Ministers would be extremely injurious and very prejudicial to the public service. Now be it remembered that I expressed this opinion to which the noble Lord has referred, to the French Ambassador, on the 3rd of December, the day immediately after the *coup d'état*; but was I the only Member of the Cabinet who did thus express an opinion on that event? I am informed that on the evening of that very day, and under the same roof, the noble Lord at the head of the Government, in conversation with the same Ambassador, expressed his opinion. It is not, perhaps, for me to say what that opinion was, but from what has just now fallen from the noble Lord this evening, it may be assumed that that opinion was not very different even from the reported opinion which I am supposed to have expressed. Was that all? On the Friday, and in the noble Lord's own house, I have been informed that the French Ambassador met the noble Lord the President of the Council and the right hon. Gentleman the Chancellor of the Exchequer. The noble Lord at the head of the Government again expressed an opinion, and the President of the Council and the Chancellor of the Exchequer also expressed an opinion. I believe their opinions were similar to mine; but, be it remembered, the charge against me was not the nature of the opinion I had expressed, but the fact that I had expressed an opinion, for the noble Lord distinctly told me, "You mistake the question between us; it is not whether the President was justified or not, but whether you were justified in expressing an opinion on the matter at all." I believe that the noble Lord the Secretary of State for the Colonies did also in those few days express an opinion on those events; and I have been informed also that the Vice-President of the Board of Trade, and now the Secretary of State for Foreign Affairs, also expressed his opinion. Then it follows that every Member of the Cabinet, whatever his official avocations may have been–however much his attention may have been devoted to other matters–is at liberty to express an opinion on passing events abroad; but the Secretary of State for Foreign Affairs, whose peculiar duty it is to watch over those events and to form an opinion–who is unfit for his office if he has not an opinion on them–is the only man not permitted to express any opinion at all; and when a foreign Minister comes and tells him news, he is to remain speechless, like a gaping dolt, or as silent as the mute of some Eastern Pasha? Why, Sir, I say such a course would not be consistent with the position of a Minister; it would not be consistent with the interests of the country. But I am told now, "It is not your conversation with Count Walewski that is complained of, but your despatch to the Marquess of Normanby." What did I state in that despatch, in reference to which a great parade is made, as if I had been guilty of breach of duty to the Crown, and of my obligations to the Prime Minister, in sending it without previously communicating with the noble Lord? No man can lay down the matter more strongly than I have as to the obligations of the Secretary of State for Foreign Affairs. I have always admitted that if the Secretary of State for Foreign Affairs sends a despatch of importance to an Ambassador abroad, without ascertaining the opinion of the Prime Minister, or Crown, he is guilty of a breach of duty. But there are many cases in which he perfectly well knows that he is only expressing the opinion of the Government, and when inconvenience might arise from delay. There are many cases in which a sedulous and careful observance of the strict rule on my part has been attended with inconvenience to the public service, and has exposed me to imputations of neglect and delay in answering despatches received. But what was the despatch from the Marquess of Normanby, and what was my answer? Lord Normanby, in his despatch of the 6th Dec., had said that the French Minister had reported that I used certain expressions which Lord Normanby represents as inconsistent with the instructions not to interfere in the internal affairs of France. I cannot see, even if I had used the language ascribed to me, that it would have been in any way inconsistent with the instructions to him to make no alteration in the nature of his relations with the Government of France, and not to interfere in the internal affairs of France. But what does he report in that despatch of the 6th as having been done? He says, that after making that communication to M. Turgot to which the noble Lord has alluded, namely, that he had been instructed to do nothing which should have the appearance of interfering in any way in the internal affairs of France, he proceeded to tell M. Turgot that he was quite sure that if the Government had known the events of Paris on the Thursday and Friday they would have joined their congratulations to his. Surely that was a greater apparent interference in the internal affairs of the French nation than any conversation of mine with Count Walewski. However, Lord Normanby having reported the expressions of the French Minister to me, I did not think it necessary to go into any argument on the subject; but ten days afterwards, on the 15th of December, the Ambassador at Paris, rather inverting, I think, the positions of Ambassador and Secretary of State, calls on the Secretary of State to give him an explanation as to the language the Secretary of State was supposed to have used to Count Walewski on the 3rd. I repeated in my despatch to him, that neither the Secretary of State nor the Ambassador were entitled to pronounce a judgment on the events which had taken place in France and I told him shortly what was the nature of the opinion to which I had given expression in conversation with the French Ambassador. Therefore it is a misrepresentation of the facts of the case to say that, in answering Lord Normanby's letter, I was giving instructions inconsistent with the nature of our relations with the French Government. It was no instruction at all. I did not give the opinion of the Government or of England. It was my own opinion; which I had expressed ten days before; and, whether right or wrong; it was shared by numbers in France. Therefore the charge which the noble Lord (Lord J. Russell) has brought against me, founded on that despatch, has no foundation in justice or in fact. That is the state of the case as between the noble Lord and myself. As for the noble Lord advising the Queen to appoint a successor to me, that was a step which it was perfectly competent for the noble Lord to take without assigning any reason to me. But he chose to assign a reason, and that reason was, that I did, in conversation with Count Walewski, that which he and other divers Members of the Cabinet appear also to have done in conversation with the same person. I do not, however, dispute the right of the noble Lord to remove any Member of the Government whom he may think it better to remove than to retain in the Cabinet. With respect to myself, the noble Lord has done me justice by saying that the course of foreign policy of which I was the instrument had received the constant approbation and support of the rest of the Government. I think that course of foreign policy was the proper one for this country to pursue. I always thought it was the duty of the Government of this country to make the interests of England the polar star to guide our course; and that it was my duty to be – as the noble Lord described me in 1850, neither the Minister of Austria, of Russia, nor of Prussia, but the Minister of England. I have felt it my duty to maintain the interests of England, to afford protection to British subjects abroad in all parts of the world, to protect their commerce, their persons, and their property. It is not to be expected that, in pursuing that course, and in giving that encouragement which our own disposition and the wishes of the country stimulated us to give to the progressive diffusion of constitutional government in other countries – it is not to be expected, I repeat, that such a course could be pursued without meeting with opposition from persons and Governments who entertained opposite opinions, or who have happened to be wrongdoers, and from whom redress might be demanded. But I am happy to say – and my statement is confirmed by what has just fallen from the noble Lord – that after having for a considerable time had the good fortune and honour to be the instrument to guide the foreign relations of this country, I have left the country in a state of friendly relations with respect to every country in the world, and that there is no question, no political question of any importance, creating a difference between this and any foreign State. It is not always that that could have been said. There have been periods when, unfortunately, differences have existed; but at all events, that "firebrand of revolutions," as I have been called, that individual who has been accused of having embroiled the relations of England with all other countries, after having found the country involved in difficulties, has left office with no question of serious difference between this and other nations, but with amity subsisting between this and all other countries.

(*f*) THE PREROGATIVE OF DISSOLUTION, 1858

On 19 February 1858, Palmerston's Government, recently triumphantly returned after the Dissolution of 1857, was defeated on Milner Gibson's motion on the Conspiracy to Murder Bill, introduced after the Orsini plot to assassinate the Emperor Napoleon III, which had been planned in this country. Palmerston resigned, and Derby was called on to form a Ministry, though he had not a majority in the House. He was speedily in difficulties over India; both over his Bill to take over the government of India from the East India Company, and over the publication by Lord Ellenborough, president of the Board of Control, of a stinging disavowal of the proclamation to the rebels of Oudh issued by Lord Canning, the governor-general. Ellenborough had acted without consulting his colleagues, but his resignation did not, at first, clear up the situation. The Government did, however, emerge from its immediate difficulties, and when it was defeated on its Reform Bill in April 1859,[1] the queen made no difficulty in granting a Dissolution.

22. Memorandum by the Prince Albert (11 May 1858)

Letters of Queen Victoria, First Series, III, p. 283.

BUCKINGHAM PALACE, 11th. May, 1858. Lord Derby had an audience at twelve o'clock. He said he had received a copy of Lord Ellenborough's letter, and had told him that should the Queen consult him (Lord Derby) he should advise her to accept the resignation, Lord Ellenborough had behaved in the handsomest manner, and expressed his belief that he brought bad luck to the Government, for this was now the second difficulty into which they had got by his instrumentality, the first having been the Election Clause in the India Bill. Lord Derby hoped that this resignation would stop the vote of censure in the House of Commons, as the House could not hold responsible and punish the Cabinet for that with which they had had no concern. If the House persisted, it was clear that the motives were factious, and he hoped the Queen would allow him to threaten a Dissolution of Parliament, which he was certain would stop it. The Queen refused to give that permission; she said he might leave it quite undecided whether the Queen would grant a Dissolution or not, and take the benefit of the doubt in talking to others on the subject; but she must be left quite free to act as she thought the good of the country might require at the time when the Government should have been beat; there had been a Dissolution within the year, and if a Reform Bill was passed there must be another immediately upon it; in the meantime most violent pledges would be taken as to Reform if a general election were to take place now. Lord Derby concurred in all this, and said he advised the threat particularly in order to render the reality unnecessary; when she persisted in her refusal, however, on the ground that she could not threaten what she was not prepared to do, he appeared very much disappointed and mortified.

We then discussed the state of the question itself, and urged the necessity of something being done to do away with the injurious impression which the publication of the despatch must produce in India, as the resignation of Lord Ellenborough left this quite untouched, and Parliament might with justice demand this. He agreed, after much difficulty, to send a telegraphic despatch, which might overtake and mitigate the other. On my remark that the public were under the impression that there had been collusion, and that Mr. Bright had seen the despatch before he asked his question

[1] Part II, Introduction and Nos. 61–63.

for its production, he denied this stoutly, but let us understand that Mr. Bright had known of the existence of such a despatch, and had wished to put his question before, but had been asked to defer it until Lord Canning's Proclamation should have appeared in the newspapers! (This is nearly as bad!!) The Queen could not have pledged herself to dissolve Parliament in order to support such tricks!

ALBERT

It was arranged that Lord Derby should accept Lord Ellenborough's resignation in the Queen's name.

23. Memorandum by Sir Charles Phipps (? 15 May 1858)

Letters of Queen Victoria, First Series, III, pp. 286–289.

[Undated. ? 15th May 1858.] Upon being admitted to Lord Aberdeen, I informed him that the Queen, and Prince were anxious to hear his opinion upon the present most unfortunate state of affairs, but that, knowing how easily every event was perverted in such times as the present, Her Majesty and His Royal Highness had thought that it might have been subject to misapprehension had he been known to have been at Buckingham Palace, and that I had been therefore directed to call upon him, with a view of obtaining his opinion and advice upon certain important points.

The first was the question of a Dissolution of Parliament in the event of the Government being defeated upon the question which was at present pending. I told him that I was permitted to communicate to him in the strictest confidence, that in a late Audience which Lord Derby had with the Queen, he had asked her permission to be allowed to announce that, in the event of an adverse majority, he had Her Majesty's sanction to a Dissolution of Parliament.

That the Queen had declined to give such sanction, or even such a pledge, and equally guarded herself against being supposed to have made up her mind to refuse her sanction to a Dissolution, had told Lord Derby that she could not then make any prospective decision upon the subject. I told him that in point of fact Her Majesty was disinclined to grant to Lord Derby her authority for a Dissolution, but that the Queen had at once refused to grant to Lord Derby her sanction for making the announcement he wished, as she considered that it would be a very unconstitutional threat for him to hold over the head of the Parliament, with her authority, by way of biassing their decision.

Lord Aberdeen interrupted me by saying that the Queen had done quite right–that he never heard of such a request being made, or authority for such an announcement being sought–and he could not at all understand Lord Derby making such an application. He knew that the Government had threatened a Dissolution, that he thought that they had a perfect right to do so, but that they would have been quite wrong in joining the Queen's name with it.

He said that he had never entertained the slightest doubt that if the Minister advised the Queen to dissolve, she would, as a matter of course, do so. The Minister who advised the Dissolution took upon himself the heavy responsibility of doing so, but that the Sovereign was bound to suppose that the person whom she had appointed as a Minister was a gentleman and an honest man, and that he would not advise Her Majesty to take such a step unless he thought that it was for the good of the country. There was no doubt of the power and prerogative of the Sovereign to refuse a Dissolution–it was one of the very few acts which the Queen of England could do without responsible advice at the moment; but even in this case whoever was sent for to succeed, must, with his appointment, assume the responsibility of this act, and be prepared to defend it in Parliament.

He could not remember a single instance in which the undoubted power of the Sovereign had been exercised upon this point, and the advice of the Minister to dissolve Parliament had been rejected–for it was to be remembered that Lord Derby would be still at this time her Minister–and that the result of such refusal would be that the Queen would take upon herself the act of dismissing Lord Derby from office, instead of his resigning from being unable longer to carry on the Government.

The Queen had during her reign, and throughout the numerous changes of Government, maintained an unassailable position of constitutional impartiality, and he had no hesitation in saying that he thought it would be more right, and certainly more safe, for her to follow the usual course, than to take this dangerous time for exercising an unusual and, he believed he might say, an unprecedented, course, though the power to exercise the authority was undoubted.

He said that he did not conceive that any reasons of expediency as to public business, or the possible effects of frequent general elections, would be sufficient grounds for refusing a Dissolution (and reasons would have to be given by the new Minister in Parliament), and, as he conceived, the only possible ground that could be maintained as foundation for such an exercise of authority would be the fearful danger to the existence of our power in India, which might arise from the intemperate discussion upon every hustings of the proceedings of the Government with respect to that country–as the question proposed to the country would certainly be considered to be severity or mercy to the people of India.

Upon the second point, as to a successor to Lord Derby in the event of his resignation, he said that the Queen would, he thought, have no alternative but to send for Lord Palmerston. The only other person who could be suggested would be Lord John Russell, and he was neither the mover of the Resolutions which displaced the Government, nor the ostensible head of the Opposition, which the late meeting at Cambridge House pointed out Lord Palmerston to be. That he was not very fond of Lord Palmerston, though he had forgiven him all, and he had had *much* to forgive; and that in the last few days it had appeared that he had less following than Lord John; but the Queen could not act upon such daily changing circumstances, and it was evident that Lord Palmerston was the ostensible man for the Queen to send for.

Lord Aberdeen seemed very low upon the state of public affairs. He said that the extreme Liberals were the only Party that appeared to gain strength. Not only was the Whig Party divided within itself, hated by the Radicals, and having a very doubtful support from the independent Liberals, but even the little band called the Peelites had entirely crumbled to pieces. In the House of Lords, whilst the Duke of Newcastle voted with the Opposition, he (Lord Aberdeen) had purposely abstained from voting, whilst, in the House of Commons, Cardwell moved the Resolution, and Mr. Sidney Herbert would, he believed, vote for it: Gladstone would speak on the other side, and Sir J. Graham would also vote with the Government.

He concluded by saying that if the majority against the Government was a very large one, he thought that Lord Derby ought not to ask to dissolve; but that he knew that the members of the Government had said that the present Parliament was elected upon a momentary Palmerstonian cry, and was quite an exceptional case, and that they would not consent to be driven from office upon its verdict.

24. Memorandum by the Prince Albert (16 May 1858)

Letters of Queen Victoria, First Series, III, p. 289.

BUCKINGHAM PALACE, 16th May 1858. We saw Lord Derby after church. . . .

. . . Lord Derby spoke much of the Debate, which he expects to go on for another week. He expects to be beaten by from 15 to 35 votes under present circumstances, but thinks still that he could be saved if it were known that the Queen had not refused a Dissolution, which was stoutly maintained by Lord Palmerston's friends. He begged again to be empowered to contradict the assertion. The Queen maintained that it would be quite unconstitutional to threaten Parliament, and to use her name for that purpose. Lord Derby quite agreed, and disclaimed any such intention, but said there were modes of letting the fact be known without any risk. We agreed that we could not enter into such details. The Queen allowed him (Lord Derby) to know that a Dissolution would not be refused to him, and trusted that her honour would be safe in his hands as to the use he made of that knowledge. He seemed greatly relieved, and stated that had he had to resign, he would have withdrawn from public business, and the Conservative Party would have been entirely, and he feared for ever, broken up. On a Dissolution he felt certain of a large gain, as the country was in fact tired of the "Whig Family Clique"; the Radicals, like Mr. Milner Gibson, Bright, etc., would willingly support a Conservative Government. ALBERT

(g) REFUSAL TO ACCEPT THE RESIGNATION OF THE CABINET

On 18 June 1866, Russell's Government was defeated by eleven votes in the House of Commons on the Dunkellin Amendment to its Reform Bill. As the climax to a long campaign against the Bill (Part II), and as involving a not inconsiderable raising of the level of the new franchise proposed, the Government took the defeat as implying that it no longer had the confidence of the House, and resigned. A week earlier fighting had started in the Austro-Prussian War. This is the circumstance on which the queen based her refusal to accept the resignation of the Cabinet. She had constantly insisted that the Reform question should be settled by mutual concession between the parties (Nos. 26–29, and Introduction to Part II), and urged this view now, not only impressing it on Russell and Gladstone, but insisting that it be put before the Cabinet, and authorizing the leaders of the Government to state publicly her reluctance to accept its resignation, and the reason. The disarray of its own parliamentary forces, and the uncertainty of public opinion, made a Dissolution inadvisable for the Government, and the Cabinet could find no alternative course that it felt it could accept with dignity, but not till 26 June did the queen accept the position and the Government's resignation.

25. Letter from the queen to Lord John Russell (19 June 1866)

Letters of Queen Victoria, Second Series, I, pp. 334–335.

BALMORAL, 18th. June, 1866. The Queen considers it the bounden duty of her Government, in the present state of the Continent, to set aside all personal considerations, and to continue at their posts. In fact, knowing the impossibility of forming another Government, the Queen could not accept their resignations.

(*h*) THE ROYAL INITIATIVE IN POLITICS: THE QUEEN AND REFORM

The foreign background is, again, the situation arising out of the Austro-Prussian War. The queen's letter of 28 October 1866 to Lord Derby[1] was probably decisive in determining the Government to grapple with this question.

26. Letter from the queen to the earl of Derby (26 May 1866)

Letter of Queen Victoria, Second Series, I, pp. 331–332.

The Queen had hoped to have seen Lord Derby before this time, but was prevented by the alarming illness of his dear little grandson, at whose recovery she so truly rejoices. She, however, cannot refrain from writing him a few confidential lines to express her great anxiety at the present state of affairs. The Queen has known Lord Derby long and well, and has had so many proofs of his loyalty and devotion to her person and service, that she does not think she will appeal to him in vain, when she expresses her earnest hope that no violent or factious opposition will be pursued on this important question of Reform, which has for so many years been the cause of so much difficulty to succeeding Governments. However unpopular the question of Reform may be in itself it is one, the calm and dispassionate discussion of which is of the utmost importance.

To raise agitation in the country, which is now, thank God, so quiet, in the present state of foreign affairs, would be most unfortunate, not to say alarming. She does ask Lord Derby to try and use his influence with his Party to treat this question *not* as a mere Party one, but with a view of settling it and trying to come to some agreement upon it, so that it may not become the cause of agitation and excitement in the country, the results of which might be very serious.

The Queen will not repeat what she has often said to Lord Derby, *viz.* how worn, shaken, and shattered she feels, but she may say, how peculiarly unfit she feels at the present moment to meet a crisis, which can lead to no permanent good. She has gone through such anxiety and worry this winter and spring, and Dr. Jenner thinks it absolutely necessary that she should have some complete change of air and scene; she is therefore going on the 13th June for *ten* days only to Balmoral, the loss of her usual spring visit being considered so very detrimental to her health. Hitherto that short change has kept her from suffering *seriously* from the constant wear and tear of anxiety which since December 1861 she has been exposed to.

[1] No. 29 and Part II.

The Queen writes this letter without the knowledge of anyone. She hopes to see Lord and Lady Derby at Windsor.[1]

27. Letter from the queen to Earl Russell (31 May 1866)

Letters of Queen Victoria, Second Series, I, p. 331.

CLIVEDEN, 31st May 1866. The Queen grows so alarmed at the present aspect of public affairs, and at the prospect of a Ministerial crisis, while negotiations and discussions, on which the peace of the world may depend, are just about to take place, that she must appeal strongly to Lord Russell and Mr. Gladstone to endeavour to avert the danger which now again seems imminent.

From the nature of the amendments moved, from the quarters from which they proceed, and from the tone of the debates in which they are discussed, it seems to the Queen *absolutely* hopeless to expect the Reform measure to pass during the present Session, or that changes will not be carried in it, which the Government might think it inconsistent with their pledges to accept. At the same time it is so evidently the interest of the Opposition to have the question settled, that the Queen cannot but hope, were *more time* given for deliberation, that such changes might be made in the measure, as would conciliate the support of those parties who now oppose it so vehemently. It is certain that the Redistribution of Seats Bill was brought in somewhat hastily, in compliance with the pressure of the House of Commons. If the Government should think it inconsistent with their honour, that the Session should terminate without the settlement of the question, might not a long adjournment take place, with a view to the removal of some of the objections which have been made to the Bill in its present shape, and the discussion be resumed in October with better prospects of success? *Any* change at the Foreign Office at the *present* moment would be most unfortunate, indeed *most* serious; and it seems to the Queen that not only it would not be inconsistent with the honour of Government to postpone the further discussion of the Reform Bill at *this* moment, on *that* ground; but that it would be their *duty* towards *herself* and the *Country* to take *this* or *any* other step which may avert a crisis which cannot but have a *most injurious* influence on the conduct of *those* negotiations on which the *Peace of the world* depends!

The Queen hopes Lord Russell will communicate this urgent appeal from her to his colleagues in the Cabinet.

28. Letter from Earl Russell to the queen (2 June 1866)

Letters of Queen Victoria, Second Series, I, p. 332.

DOWNING STREET, 2nd June 1866. Lord Russell presents his humble duty to your Majesty; he has sent word to his colleagues and also read in the Cabinet your Majesty's letter of the 31st May. Your Majesty's confidential servants are very sensible of the

[1] Lord Derby, in his exhaustive reply (which would occupy *in extenso* about 5½ pages), deprecated a change of government at the moment, and especially a change at the Foreign Office; attributed the existing difficulties to the course pursued by Ministers since Lord Palmerston's death; and trusted that they would even now withdraw their Reform Bill for the present session. But he considered that Bill so fatal to the Constitution that he must resist it to the utmost of his ability. If a crisis came, he would do his best to facilitate the formation of a safe and constitutional government. – G. E. BUCKLE.

difficulty of the present crisis, and of the inconvenience of a change of Government. They will therefore anxiously consider their position, before offering to your Majesty their resignations, in case of a defeat in the House of Commons.

The course of obstruction so openly followed by the Opposition makes it, however, very difficult to yield to them on any point without incurring just reproach on the part of the public as having abandoned their principles and forsaken their measure on light and insufficient grounds.

29. Letter from the queen to the earl of Derby (28 October 1866)

Monypenny and Buckle, *Disraeli*, ed. 1929, II pp. 191–192.

BALMORAL, Oct. 28. 1866. The Queen has been thinking a great deal, ever since Lord Derby left Balmoral, of the subject on which she had some conversation with him while he was here. As she then told him, she is convinced that, if the question of Reform be not taken up in earnest by her Ministers, with a view to its settlement, very serious consequences may ensue.

The Queen is well aware of the great difficulties which her Government must be prepared to meet, in any attempt to effect this object, and if she can in any way help in surmounting them, Lord Derby and his colleagues may reckon confidently on her best support and assistance.

It seems evident to the Queen, after the failure of so many successive Administrations, which have all been overthrown in their attempts to settle this question, that it never can be settled unless adverse parties are prepared to concede something, and to meet each other in a spirit of mutual conciliation. Nothing would gratify the Queen more than to be instrumental in bringing about such a dispostion; and if Lord Derby thinks there is any chance of its doing good–indeed, she views the matter so seriously that she hardly thinks she would be justified in not making the attempt under any circumstances–she is ready to make a personal appeal to Lord Russell and Mr. Gladstone, and other leading members of both Houses of Parliament, and to urge them, by every consideration of loyalty and patriotism, to meet her present Ministers fairly, in an honest endeavour to find out terms of agreement as might lead to a measure of Reform being proposed which would conciliate the support of all moderate men, and afford at least a chance of setting a question at rest, which, while it continues to be made a subject of agitation, must act injuriously upon the best interests of the country, and may even threaten the disturbance of its pace and tranquillity.

Lord Derby need not answer this letter at once. He is quite at liberty to consult his colleagues upon it previously, and the Queen relies with confidence upon their patriotism not to allow any feelings of a mere party nature to interfere with their candid consideration of her suggestions.

30. Letter from the earl of Derby to the queen (1 November 1866)

Letters of Queen Victoria, Second Series, I, pp. 371–372.

ST. JAMES'S SQUARE, 1st. Nov. 1866. Lord Derby, with his humble duty, begs that your Majesty will accept his grateful thanks for your Majesty's most gracious letter of the 28th ult., to which, by your Majesty's permission, he has deferred returning an answer, till he had had an opportunity of conferring with his colleagues on the subject to which it refers. The first meeting of the Cabinet took place on Wednesday last; and the first question which he brought under the consideration of his colleagues was the course to be pursued in reference to the question of Parliamentary Reform. He did not think it expedient to lay before any of your Majesty's servants, except the Chancellor of the Exchequer, your Majesty's letter *in extenso*; but he did not conceal from the Cabinet your Majesty's earnest desire for an early settlement of the question, and, if possible, by your Majesty's present servants: nor the gracious offer which your Majesty made, of the exercise of any personal influence towards coming to an understanding with the principal Members of the late Government, which might lead to a final and amicable settlement of this great question. It will, Lord Derby thinks, be satisfactory to your Majesty to know that it was the *unanimous* opinion of the Cabinet, that whatever might be the difficulties surrounding the question, it could not be ignored, but must be resolutely grappled with. The mode of doing so is under the anxious consideration of your Majesty's servants; and to give time for the matured deliberation the farther discussion has been postponed for a week; but while Lord Derby's colleagues were equally grateful with himself for the offer of interposition so graciously made by your Majesty, and for the proof it afforded of your Majesty's confidence, they were also of opinion that any private communication with any members of the late Government *at the present moment* might be more prejudicial than advantageous; and, without pledging himself as to the ultimate advice which it may be his duty to tender to your Majesty, he thinks he may venture to say that the course likely to be recommended will give ample time for the exercise of any influence which your Majesty may be pleased to exert, towards the settlement of the question, *after* a proposal may have been submitted to Parliament, and when, consequently, there can be no ground for a charge of collusion between the Heads of rival Parties.

(*i*) ROYAL MEDIATION BETWEEN THE PARTIES, AND BETWEEN THE LORDS AND COMMONS: THE QUEEN AND THE IRISH CHURCH BILL

Between March and May 1868, Gladstone had carried in the House of Commons, against Disraeli's Government, Resolutions in favour of the Disestablishment and Disendowment of the Irish Church. Parliament was dissolved, and a large Liberal majority returned at the General Election. On 1 March 1869, Gladstone introduced his Bill, in one of his greatest orations, and it was carried, on the Second Reading, by a majority of 118, and on the Third, after little serious change in Committee, by 114. Its real crisis–and, as the queen's action indicated, a crisis for more than the Bill–came in the House of Lords. Thanks largely to the action of the queen, aided by Lord Granville, the Liberal Leader in the Lords, Lord Cairns, the Conservative Leader, and the newly appointed archbishop of Canterbury, A. C. Tait, the Second Reading was carried, in one of the fullest houses in living memory, by a majority of thirty-three. The Lords then proceeded, as their intention had been, to modify the financial settlement of the Bill substantially in favour of the Church, and to modify phraseology in its preamble designed to exclude any use of the proceeds of Disendowment for religious purposes with the object of leaving the way open for the 'concurrent endowment' of the Roman Catholic and Presbyterian Churches, a policy which had strong supporters in the House, including the archbishop, though the Government was strongly opposed to it. The Lords' amendments were at first curtly rejected by the Government and the House of Commons, but on the Lords' insistence, and after complicated and anxious negotiations, an agreement between Cairns and Granville formed the basis of a settlement. Better financial terms were secured for the Church, and the final form of the preamble neither affirmed nor excluded the principle of concurrent endowment.

Lord Derby's reference in No. 33 is to his resignation from Lord Grey's Government, in 1834, on the proposed appropriation of revenues of the Irish Church to lay purposes.

31. Letter from the queen to the earl of Derby (7 June 1869)

Letters of Queen Victoria, Second Series, I, pp. 603–604.

BALMORAL, 7th June 1869. The Queen writes to Lord Derby to-day upon a subject which causes her the deepest anxiety, and, she must add, considerable surprise.

She *hears* that it is proposed to throw out the Irish Church Bill by opposing the second reading.

The Queen has never concealed her opinion as to this measure–which remains unaltered; but, after the Dissolution last autumn, and the large majorities with which the Bill has been passed in the House of Commons, for the House of Lords to throw it out, and thus place itself in collision with the House of Commons, would be most dangerous, if not *disastrous*.

The Queen knows too well how loyal, and how devoted to her person and Throne, Lord Derby is; and she cannot therefore doubt, that he will pause before he concurs in pursuing a course fraught with such danger to the country and constitution.

If the House of Lords does not oppose the second reading, it will be in its power to make important and useful amendments, which it is hoped the House of Commons may be disposed to adopt.

This would raise the House of Lords in the country; but to put itself into collision with the other House would–above all at this moment when alas! the aristocracy is lowered by the conduct of so many who bear the oldest, proudest names–she must repeat it, lead to *most disastrous results*.

Most earnestly does the Queen appeal to Lord Derby to try and prevent this dangerous course from being pursued.

She would ask him to show this letter in confidence to Lord Cairns.[1]

32. Letter from Gladstone to the queen (8 June 1869)

Letters of Queen Victoria, Second Series, I, pp. 604–605.

11 CARLTON H. TERRACE, 8th June 1869. Mr. Gladstone learns from General Grey that your Majesty has in your goodness addressed a letter to the Earl of Derby, on the subject of the Second Reading of the Irish Church Bill. It is probable that Lord Derby may have gone too far in committing himself so far as his own personal vote is concerned. But the main question is the influence which the leaders of the party may exercise on other Peers: and it is quite possible that in regard to this influence your Majesty's representation may have beneficial and important consequences.

[1] During this session Leader of the Opposition in the Lords. – G. E. BUCKLE.

Mr. Gladstone would humbly repeat that the rejection of the Bill, though probable, is by no means, as yet, to be considered certain.

Meantime, as was to be expected, the majority of the House of Commons begin to show signs of susceptibility. Suggestions have been made to Mr. Gladstone with reference to public meetings, and to a meeting of the party at Willis's Rooms, for the purpose of declaring confidence in the Government. These suggestions have been discouraged by Mr. Gladstone, and it will, he is sure, be the desire and endeavour of the Cabinet to prevent agitation in the country as long as it may be possible, notwithstanding the pertinacious efforts on the other side. But the essential condition of their power to be useful in this respect is that the confidence of their supporters should continue unimpaired.

Without doubt the Archbishop of Canterbury will inform your Majesty what he considers to be the upshot of his correspondence with Mr. Gladstone, growing out of your Majesty's letter to his Grace.

Mr. Gladstone's reply to the Archbishop was in substance this: that in his opinion the House of Commons would adhere to disendowment as a rule, though as a rule with exceptions for marked and special cause; and that the Bill might still admit of changes which would be material as improvements, though not material as deviations from its principle. Mr. Gladstone also signified that in his opinion the main interest involved in the acceptance of the Bill on the Second Reading, is the interest of the House of Lords itself, with the interest of the country in the dignity, efficiency, and permanence of that Assembly.

33. Letter from the earl of Derby to the queen (9 June 1869)

Letters of Queen Victoria, Second Series, I, pp. 606–608.

St. James's Square, 9th June 1869. Lord Derby, with his humble duty, submits to your Majesty the expression of his deep regret at finding by the letter with which he was honoured yesterday evening, that the course which he has felt himself bound to take with regard to the Irish Church Bill, has caused your Majesty the deepest anxiety, and even surprise. It is, however, a great satisfaction to Lord Derby to be assured that your Majesty does not doubt his loyalty and devotion to your Majesty's person and Throne. He ventures to assure your Majesty that there is no sacrifice that he would not be prepared to make for your Majesty's ease and comfort, except that of his own personal honour and character, which would be involved in his abstaining from opposing such a measure as has been brought forward by your Majesty's Ministers. At the same time Lord Derby must beg your Majesty to believe that the prominent part which has been assigned to him on this occasion is not one of his own seeking. From the moment at which broken health compelled him to retire from your Majesty's service, it has been his anxious wish to place himself as much as possible in the background, and to leave to those on whom official responsibility *may* devolve, the duty of conducting the course of the Conservative party. But in the present crisis the views which he is known to have entertained for nearly half a century have naturally made him the medium of communication with those throughout the country who share his principles; and he ventures to think that your Majesty can form no adequate conception of the amount of discontent which will universally be produced by the passing of the present measure.

Lord Derby does not affect to conceal from himself the serious peril of a collision with the House of Commons, especially under the guidance of the present head of your Majesty's administration; but on the other hand he sees in the passing of this measure consequences so infinitely more serious, that he will not venture to contemplate them, still less to hint at them to your Majesty. It would not be consistent with the deference which Lord Derby owes to your Majesty, to enter into anything which might have the appearance of an argument; but he may be permitted to observe that, though it is undoubtedly true that at the late Election the Liberal party, from a combination of circumstances, obtained a large majority, and that the Irish Church question was prominent among the subjects placed before the Constituencies, yet that the country has had no opportunity of judging of the merits of the proposition by which the principle is carried out; and there is every reason to believe that already there is a considerable reaction in the public, and even in the popular mind. Lord Derby therefore is humbly of opinion that in a matter of such deep moment, and when a step once taken cannot be retraced, some farther time should be allowed for the deliberate judgment of the country, and that the House of Lords should not be called upon to give a vote on so vital a question in opposition to their known opinions, with more haste than ever attended any measure, within his recollection, of importance at all comparable.

Having, however, submitted to your Majesty, with that frankness which your Majesty has always graciously allowed him to use, his own individual opinion, he may add, from a conversation which he has had with Lord Cairns (to whom he has communicated your Majesty's letter, in obedience to your Majesty's command), that there is a great probability that a majority of the House of Lords may support the Second Reading of the Bill, in hopes that some substantial amendments may be introduced in Committee; and that this probability would be greatly increased if any assurances were given by your Majesty's Ministers that such amendments would be favourably, or even fairly considered. But the House of Lords have at present no reason to anticipate such a conclusion. Every amendment proposed in the Commons tending to mitigate the severity of the enactment has been summarily, and even contemptuously rejected by Mr. Gladstone, and the majority which blindly follows him; and the organs of the Government in the Press have not hesitated to say that any amendment of importance would be tantamount to a rejection of the Bill, and to menace the House of Lords with the most serious consequences, to which they venture to assume your Majesty's consent. Lord Derby is bound to say that no amendments would remove his individual objections to the whole principle of the Bill; but he ventures to add that if there be one way more certain than another to ensure its rejection, it is the language of menace and coercion which is sought to be applied to the House of Lords; and to which if they were to submit, their influence in the State would be for ever and deservedly lost.

Lord Derby humbly entreats your Majesty to forgive this long and full exposition of his views, and to accept the sincere regret of Lord Cairns and himself, that, however anxious they are in every possible way to meet your Majesty's wishes, it would be destruction to their own character and honour, now to recede from the position which they have so publicly, and so recently, announced themselves to have taken up, on deliberate consideration of all the conflicting difficulties.

34. Letter from Gladstone to the queen (19 July 1869)

Letters of Queen Victoria, Second Series, I, pp. 618–619.

11 CARLTON H. TERRACE, 19th July 1869. Mr. Gladstone presents his humble duty to your Majesty; and, having had the advantage of seeing the Dean of Windsor this afternoon, who will have reported to your Majesty as from him before the hour at which this letter is written, he need not trouble your Majesty with many details.

Both yesterday and to-day, some intimations were conveyed to Lord Granville and to Mr. Gladstone of the views entertained by the leading Peers of the Opposition. They did not afford much hope of a settlement, inasmuch as they proceeded upon the assumption that, of the many questions at issue between the two Houses of Parliament, the greater part was to be yielded by the House of Commons. The answer made was to the effect that the Government had already done all that they could do consistently with the principle and basis of the Bill: and that all which remained for them was to recommend out of simple deference to the House of Lords, and not as on its merits, some further and necessarily very moderate concession.

The interview which your Majesty was so gracious as to procure for Mr. Gladstone with the Archbishop of Canterbury, and which without doubt had been well prepared by the judicious action of the Dean of Windsor, was much more satisfactory. Mr. Gladstone went through a variety of particulars, none of which did the Archbishop seem decisively to contest; and altogether the Archbishop both showed a conciliatory temper in general, and used language which might be considered as implying that some one substantial yet moderate concession might settle the affair. On the whole therefore there is some improvement in the prospect, though great uncertainty still prevails, and no confidence can yet be felt as to the issue.

35. Letter from Gladstone to the queen (20–21 July 1869)

Letters of Queen Victoria, Second Series, I, pp. 619–620.

11 CARLTON H. TERRACE, 20th–21st July 1869. The crisis apprehended in the House of Lords arrived about eleven o'clock, when the House by a majority of 175 to 93 re-excluded from the preamble the words which the House of Commons had placed and replaced there in order to declare solemnly the policy of Parliament for matters ecclesiastical in Ireland. This amendment, independently of all those which were announced as about to follow, contained matter, or rather involved a meaning which no power could induce the present House of Commons to accept. Lord Granville thereupon moved the adjournment of the debate. The Cabinet is summoned for

tomorrow: and will very probably find itself unable with advantage to carry the Bill further forwards.[1]

Mr. Gladstone regrets to report that the Archbishop of Canterbury, together with every Prelate present except the Bishop of Oxford, voted in the majority.

He is apprehensive that feeling will be much excited in the country: but he may safely assure your Majesty that it will be the constant desire and endeavour of the Government to keep the controversy upon its present ground, that of the Irish Church, and to prevent any widening of its field, which they would regard as a great calamity.

36. Letter from the queen to Gladstone (22 July 1869)

Letters of Queen Victoria, Second Series, I, pp. 620–621.

OSBORNE, 22nd July 1869. The Queen has to thank Mr. Gladstone for all his letters received yesterday, as well as for the telegram, and the communication received this morning with a full account of the deliberations of the Cabinet. She was deeply grieved to see that the hopes of an amicable settlement between both Houses, which we had good reason to entertain on Monday, were all frustrated on Tuesday night. The Queen, however, rejoices to see that the most moderate counsels have prevailed in the Cabinet, and she still hopes that if a conciliatory spirit is shown in the House of Commons, and attempts to coerce and override the House of Lords are abstained from, that the House of Lords will also meet them in a spirit of conciliation, and then this most unhappy question may be settled this Session.

37. Letter from Earl Granville to the queen (22 July 1869)

Letters of Queen Victoria, Second Series, I, pp. 621–622.

COLONIAL OFFICE, 22nd July 1869. Lord Granville presents his humble duty to your Majesty. He had great pleasure in announcing to your Majesty by telegraph a result to which your majesty has so much contributed both before the second reading of the Bill, and at the last stage.[2]

Your Majesty will see by the newspapers the course of the debate. Lord Cairns' statement was clear, fair, and very skilful. The Archbishop of Canterbury supported him, but in a speech which was calculated to injure the compromise exceedingly in the House of Commons. The unanimous chorus in favour of moderation was almost ridiculous, particularly after the discussion on Tuesday. Lord Russell ended by great praise of the Bill, which settled in a satisfactory way a question which he had had at heart for thirty-five years. Even Lord Grey admitted that the Ministers were not as bad as he had supposed them to be. Lord Derby, however, was indignant. When Lord Cairns had finished, he said, loud enough for the Government to hear, "I shall

[1] The Cabinet rejected this extreme course, and determined to proceed at any rate with the endowment amendments. In consequence of this moderation, Lord Cairns communicated with Lord Granville, and a settlement was effected. – G. E. BUCKLE.

[2] On receipt of the telegram from Lord Granville and a similar one from Mr. Gladstone, the queen wrote in her Journal: "What a wonderful change and *dénouement*! Truly thankful do I feel."– G. E. BUCKLE.

go away". He then whispered something to Lord Salisbury, and on passing Lord Cairns said, "I have nothing left but to go away".

Lord Salisbury did not succeed in regaining the ground he had lost. Although he said that it was necessary to support Lord Cairns, and that he believed he had acted according to his conscience, he suggested that he, Lord Salisbury, should have tried, and should have succeeded in getting better terms. The House would not laugh at the only joke he made. The division that took place was a surprise, and was disapproved by all the leaders in the House. The account from the Commons is excellent; everybody in favour of the compromise.

Lord Granville ventures to suggest to your Majesty to send a line to Mr. Gladstone to approve the conciliatory line which he sanctioned.

38. Letter from the queen to Gladstone (23 July 1869)

Letters of Queen Victoria, Second Series, I, p. 622.

OSBORNE, 23rd July 1869. The Queen has received Mr. Gladstone's in cypher, as well as Lord Granville's telegrams, and Mr. Gladstone's letter this morning, with the greatest satisfaction and relief.

Lord Granville seems indeed to have displayed more than his ordinary tact and conciliatoriness on this occasion; and, on his side, Lord Cairns seems to have met him in a conciliatory spirit.

The Queen is sorry, but not surprised, to hear of Mr. Gladstone's indisposition, which she trusts will not be of long duration.

(*j*) CRITICISM OF THE MONARCHY: DILKE'S MOTION OF 3 MARCH 1872

The queen's long seclusion after the death of Prince Albert, and the establishment of a Republic in France, created, for a brief while, a Republican movement in England, of which Charles Bradlaugh and George Odger were the popular tribunes, and Sir Charles Dilke and Auberon Herbert the parliamentary representatives. Joseph Chamberlain–mayor of Birmingham, but not yet in Parliament–was also a sympathizer. Dilke initiated a Republican campaign in a speech at Newcastle-on-Tyne on 6 November 1871, associating his cause with accusations of extravagance against the monarchy. The sudden serious illness and recovery of the Prince of Wales, December 1871 to February 1872, caused an outburst of loyal feeling in the country, and provided a more than expectedly unfavourable atmosphere for Dilke's motion, the aim of which was to give Republicanism the benefit of the parliamentary platform. Dilke's speech was long, detailed, and dull; Gladstone replied professing an entire readiness to meet Dilke's inquiries in another context than that of a Republican motion. Herbert was an anarchist by intellectual conviction. Dilke ceased his campaign shortly afterwards; on 3 November 1874 the Prince and Princess of Wales lunched at Birmingham as the guests of the mayor–still Joseph Chamberlain–and in 1882 Dilke publicly recanted.

39. Speaker's ruling on the motion of Sir Charles Dilke

Hansard, 3/CCX/251–253.

Civil List: Motion for Returns.

SIR CHARLES W. DILKE rose according to Notice, to move that there be laid before the House certain returns relating to the Civil List, when–

Viscount *Bury* rose and said: Mr. Speaker, I rise to speak to a Question of Privilege. I hold in my hand a copy of the oath to be taken by every hon. Member of this House. It is in the following terms:–

> "I do swear that I will be faithful and bear true allegiance to Her Majesty Queen Victoria, her heirs and successors according to law. So help me God."

Now, on the 21st of November last the hon. Member for Chelsea, is reported to have said that he would make no concealment of the fact that he was a Republican. He is reported as speaking exactly to the same effect in several newspapers. The Question that I have put to you, Mr. Speaker, as a point of Order, is whether these two statements are not irreconcilable; and whether, if, the statement of the hon. Baronet is not explained and repudiated, he will not have been guilty of an infringement of the solemn declaration taken at the Table of the House? I am fortified in my reasons for asking the question by the fact that every item of the Returns which the hon. Baronet wishes to move for can be found in the Library of this House, and are within the reach of every hon. Member. The Motion of the hon. Baronet, therefore, as it seems to me, can only be regarded as a colourable method of repeating, under the authority of the House, the statements to which I have referred. [*Loud cries of* "Hear, hear!"]

Mr. *Auberon Herbert*: Mr. Speaker, I rise to Order. [*Cries of* "Order!"]

Mr. *Speaker*: Viscount Bury is in possession of the House.

Mr. *Auberon Herbert* again rose, but being met with loud cries of "Order!" sat down.

Viscount *Bury*: I therefore ask you, Sir, whether it would not be for the honour of the House, and within its power, before hearing the hon. Member for Chelsea, if you ask him whether he repudiates or acknowledges the accuracy of the statements which he is reported to have made on the 21st of November?

Mr. *Speaker*: The noble Lord has called my attention to the Oath of Allegiance taken by the Members of this House. I apprehend that it is no part of my duty to say what is consistent or what is not consistent with that oath. Looking at the terms of the Motion of the hon. Baronet the Member for Chelsea, I see in them no violation of the Rules of this House.

40. Sir Charles Dilke's motion

Hansard, 3/ccx/290–291.

Motion made, and Question proposed,

"That there be laid before this House, Returns showing the duties of the auditor (or deputy auditor) of the Civil List, to whom he makes his Reports, and a Copy of such Reports for each year since the accession of Her Majesty:

Of the Directions or Warrants issued by the Treasury under section 9 of the Civil List Act, specifying the classes from which the savings arose, and the classes to which they were transferred, for each year since the accession of Her Majesty:

Showing the income and expenditure of the Civil List from the accession of Her Majesty to the present time:

Of all offices held in connection with the Court which have been abolished since the date of the Report of the Committee of 1837–8:

List of all charges formerly borne by the Civil List or hereditary Revenues which have been transferred to the Consolidated Fund or yearly Estimates since the accession of Her Majesty:

Returns showing the amounts charged on Estimates since the commencement of the present reign for fees on installation, robes, collars, and badges, royal presents, passages or conveyance of 'distinguished personages,' funerals of members of the Royal Family, the coronation, journeys of Her Majesty, building, draining, repairing, furnishing, and fitting up of Palaces, ceremonials connected with the Court, allowances and clothing for trumpeters, fees to watermen, payments to the Marshal of the Ceremonies and to the Lord Chamberlain:

Of the services of the Royal Yachts during the last ten years:

Showing, for each year since the accession of Her Majesty, the gross amount of the income arising from the Duchy of Lancaster, and also the amount in each year paid over to the Keeper of Her Majesty's Privy Purse:

And, showing, for each year since the accession of Her Majesty, the gross amount of the income arising from the Duchy of Cornwall, and also the amount in each year paid over for the use of His Royal Highness the Prince of Wales."

41. Division on Sir Charles Dilke's motion

Hansard, 3/CCX/317.

Original Question put.

The Houses *divided*:–Ayes 2; Noes 276; Majority 274.

AYES.

Anderson, G.	Lawson, Sir. W.

TELLERS.

Dilke, Sir. C. W.	Herbert, H. A.

(*k*) RESPONSIBILITY OF PARTY LEADERS TO THE CROWN: THE CABINET CRISIS OF 1873

Gladstone's resignation was in consequence of his defeat by three votes on his Irish University Bill, on 10 March 1873. Disraeli was sent for. No. 43, below, is the queen's account of his audience with her. On being notified by the queen of Disraeli's attitude, Gladstone asked that it might be put in writing. No. 44 is Ponsonby's official record of the interview with Disraeli at which this request was made. No. 45 is his private record of the same business. No. 46 is the memorandum which Disraeli prepared. Gladstone remained in office until 23 January 1874, when Parliament was dissolved. In the ensuing General Election he was defeated.

42. Letter from the queen to Disraeli (13 March 1873)

Monypenny and Buckle, *Disraeli*, ed. 1929, II, p. 548.

BUCKINGHAM PALACE, March 13, 1873–Mr. Gladstone has just been here and has tendered his resignation and that of his colleagues in consequence of the vote of the

House of Commons on Tuesday night–which the Queen has accepted. She therefore writes to Mr. Disraeli to ask him whether he will undertake to form a Government.

The Queen would like to see Mr. Disraeli at 6 or as soon after as possible.

She sends this letter by her private secretary, Colonel Ponsonby, who can be the bearer of any written or verbal answer from Mr. Disraeli.

43. Memorandum by the queen of interview with Disraeli (13 March 1873)

Monypenny and Buckle, *Disraeli*, ed. 1929, II, pp. 548–9.

BUCKINGHAM PALACE, March 13, 1873.–Mr. Disraeli came at a little after 6. After expressing my feeling for him in his sorrow and shaking hands with him, I said I had sent for him in consequence of last night's vote; and he asked whether I wished him to give a categorical answer, or to say a few words on the present state of affairs. I said I should willingly hear what he had to say.

He then went on to say that he had not expected the vote; he had thought, after Mr. Cardwell's speech, the Government would have a majority. That the Conservative party never was more compact or more united; that there was the most perfect understanding between him and all those who had served with him, and especially named Ld. Derby, Ld. Cairns, Mr. Hardy, and Sir S. Northcote. That he was perfectly able to form a Government at once, perfectly fit to carry on the administration of the country to my entire satisfaction; that he could command 280 votes; that since, as he said, "I had left your Majesty's *immediate* service, for I never consider myself out of your Majesty's service," the party had gained considerably, about thirty seats; that he had laboured to keep the party as much together and in as efficient a state as possible; but that it would be useless to attempt to carry on the Government with a minority in the House of Commons, and that he must therefore state his inability to undertake to form a Government in the present Parliament.

What was then to be done? I asked. "Mr. Gladstone ought to remain in and continue to carry on the Government." This, I said, I thought he very likely would object to, having declared his views so strongly on this measure. This was a mistake, Mr. Disraeli replied, and he ought never to have done so. That might be so or not, I said, but anyhow Mr. Gladstone *did* feel this, and did not ask for a dissolution, therefore I thought it doubtful whether he would consent to resume or continue in office, feeling he could not submit to this vote. "But he has *condoned* for it by his resignation and readiness to give up power," was the answer; that he should not throw up office merely for this vote; it would not be a good return to the present Parliament, which had supported him so warmly, and in which he had carried 3 great measures, for so he must call them, though he might not agree with them. I again asked him what I was to say to Mr. Gladstone, and he repeated that "I decline to form a Government in the present Parliament, and I do not ask for a dissolution."

Of course, he said, there were instances where a Sovereign had been left without a Government, and in such a case he would, of course, be ready to serve me. I said that I would at once let Mr. Gladstone know, but that I might have to call upon him again.

44. Memorandum in Colonel Ponsonby's handwriting (13 March 1873)

Monypenny and Buckle, *Disraeli*, ed. 1929, II, p. 550.

March 13, 1873.-Colonel Ponsonby called on Mr. Disraeli in the evening with a message from the Queen, asking him to give Her Majesty, in writing, the substance of his conversation with the Queen.

Mr. Disraeli willingly complied with Her Majesty's wishes, and wrote down roughly the chief points on which he had spoken.

Colonel Ponsonby asked Mr. Disraeli if he might assume that this meant an unconditional refusal. Mr. Disraeli replied that such was the meaning in the present state of affairs.

Colonel Ponsonby asked, if the Queen was ready to sanction a dissolution as soon as possible, whether Mr. Disraeli could then accept office, taking, of course, the responsibility of giving the advice to Her Majesty to dissolve.

Mr. Disraeli replied that he could not accept office with such an understanding, and that his refusal was absolute.

He hoped in some future day, when another Parliament assembled, to find an opportunity of serving the Queen, but with the present House of Commons with a large majority opposed to him, he could not undertake the Government.

45. Memorandum by Colonel Ponsonby of interview with Disraeli (13 March 1873)

Monypenny and Buckle, *Disraeli*, ed. 1929, II, pp. 551, 552.

Her Majesty sent me to see Mr. Disraeli in Edwards's Hotel, George Street, Hanover Square. He at once acceded to the Queen's wish, and getting pens and ink said, "There, let me see, I can easily put down what is wanted; that is very nearly what I said." I observed that I did not quite understand it, and hoped he would forgive me if I asked him whether he meant it as a refusal to take office while this Parliament sat, or whether he refused entirely, whether the Queen consented to dissolve or not. He said he meant it as a refusal, that he could not carry on the Government in a Parliament where there were 80 votes of majority against him. "But," I said, "would you take office and dissolve?" He said, "I thought the Queen would not agree to this." I replied I thought she would not object, in fact, I felt certain she would not. "But," he said, "there is an idea that this, being my Parliament, cannot be dissolved by me." "But," I remarked, "the Queen could offer you a dissolution, though, of course, you would be responsible for advising her to do so." "Of course," he said, "I well understand that; but I decline altogether to accept office."

He went on, "How could I proceed? For two months at least Parliament must continue, while the regular estimates, Mutiny Act, etc., are passed. The Conservatives are gaining favour in the country, but these two months would ruin them. They would be exposed in a hostile House to every insult which the Opposition might choose to fling at them, and the party would be seriously damaged, while the business of the country would suffer. The only possibility of carrying any measure would be by allying myself to the Irish lot, whom I detest and disagree with, and who would throw me over whenever it suited their purpose." I said, "You have defeated the Government; ought you not therefore to undertake the responsibility of forming one?" "No," he replied; "we did not defeat the Government. We threw out a stupid, blundering Bill, which Gladstone, in his *tête montée* way, tried to make a vote of confidence. It was a foolish mistake of his; but he has condoned for it by resigning. He can now resume office with perfect freedom."

During the first part of the interview Disraeli sat at a table, and as he spoke with eagerness, there was something in his over-civil expressions about the Queen or "my dear Colonel," which made me think he was playing with me, and I felt once or twice a difficulty in not laughing; but when he developed the reasons of his policy he rose and stood much more upright than I have ever seen him, spoke in a most frank and straightforward manner, and with a sharpness and decision which was different from his early words. Yet probably he had measured the length of my foot, and had been more sincere and honest in his message to the Queen than when he made me believe in his frank exposition of policy.

He was far easier to speak to than Gladstone, who forces you into his groove, while Disraeli apparently follows yours and is genial, almost too genial, in his sentiments. . . .

46. Memorandum by Disraeli to the queen (13 March 1873)

Monypenny and Buckle, *Disraeli*, ed. 1929, II, p. 552.

In answer to the gracious inquiry, whether he would undertake to form a Government, Mr. Disraeli said he was prepared to form an Administration which he believed would carry on Her Majesty's affairs with efficiency, and would possess her confidence, but he could not undertake to carry on Her Majesty's Government in the present House of Commons.

Subsequently, Her Majesty having remarked that Mr. Gladstone was not inclined to recommend a dissolution of Parliament, Mr. Disraeli stated, that he himself would not advise Her Majesty to take that step.

47. Memorandum by Gladstone to the queen (15 March 1873)

Morley, *Gladstone*, ed. 1906, II, p. 58; App. p. 831.

March 15.–Not being aware that there can be a question of any intermediate party or combination of parties which would be available at the present juncture, he presumes that your Majesty, if denied the assistance of the conservative or opposition party, might be disposed to recur to the services of a liberal government. He is of opinion, however, that either his late colleagues, or any statesman or statesmen of the liberal party on whom your Majesty might call, would with propriety at once observe that it is still for the consideration of your Majesty whether the proceeding which has taken place between your Majesty and Mr. Disraeli can as yet be regarded as complete. The vote of the House of Commons on Wednesday morning was due to the deliberate and concerted action of the opposition, with a limited amount of adventitious numerical aid. The division was a party division, and carried the well-known symbol of such divisions in the appointment of tellers of the opposition and government respectively. The vote was given in the full knowledge, avowed in the speech of the leader of the opposition, that the government had formally declared the measure on which the vote was impending to be vital to its existence. Mr. Gladstone humbly conceives that, according to the well-known principles of our parliamentary government, an opposition which has in this manner and degree contributed to bring about what we term a crisis, is bound to use and to show that it has used its utmost efforts of counsel and inquiry to exhaust all practicable means of bringing its resources to the aid of the country in its exigency. He is aware that his opinion on such a subject can only be of slight value, but the same observation will not hold good with regard to the force of a well-established party usage. To show what that usage has been, Mr. Gladstone is obliged to trouble your Majesty with the following recital of facts from the history of the last half century. There have been within that period [1830–1873] twelve of what may be properly called parliamentary crises involving the question of a change of government. In nine of the twelve cases (*viz.* those of 1830, 1835, 1841, 1846, 1852, 1858, 1859, 1866, and 1868) the party which had been in opposition was ready to take, and did take, office. In the other three it failed to do this (*viz.* in 1832, 1851, 1855), and the old ministry or a modification of it returned to power. But in each of these three cases the attempt of the opposition to form a government was not relinquished until after such efforts had been made by its leaders as to carry the conviction to the world that all its available means of action were exhausted; and there is no instance on record during the whole period (or indeed so far as Mr. Gladstone remembers at an earlier date) in which a summary refusal given on the instant by the leader was tendered as sufficient to release the opposition from the obligations it had incurred. This is the more remarkable because in two of the three instances the opposition had not, in the same mode or degree as on Wednesday morning last, contributed by concerted action to bring about the crisis. On the 7th of May 1832 the opposition of the day carried in the House of Lords a motion which went only to alter the order of the opening (and doubtless very important) clauses of the Reform Bill, but which the government of Lord Grey deemed fatal to the integrity of the measure. Their resignation was announced, and Lord Lyndhurst was summoned to advise King William IV, on the 9th of May. On the 12th the Duke of Wellington was called to take a share in the proceedings, the details of which are matters of history. It was only on the 15th that the Duke and Lord Lyndhurst found their resources at an end, when Lord Grey was again sent for, and on the 17th the Duke announced in the House of Lords his abandonment of the task he had strenuously endeavoured to fulfil. On the 20th February 1851 the government of Lord Russell was defeated in the House of Commons on Mr. Locke King's bill for the enlargement of the county franchise by a majority composed of its own supporters. Lord Derby, then Lord Stanley, being sent for by your Majesty on the 22nd, observed that there were at the time three parties in the House of

Commons and that the ministry had never yet been defeated by his political friends. He therefore counselled your Majesty to ascertain whether the government of Lord Russell could not be strengthened by a partial reconstruction, and failing that measure he engaged to use his own best efforts to form an administration. That attempt at reconstruction (to which nothing similar is now in question) did fail, and Lord Derby was therefore summoned by your Majesty on the 25th, and at once applied himself, as is well known, to every measure which seemed to give him a hope of success in constructing a government. On the 27th he apprised your Majesty of his failure in these efforts; and on March 3rd the cabinet of Lord Russell returned to office. (This recital is founded on Lord Derby's statement in the House of Lords, Feb. 28, 1851.) On Jan. 29, 1855, the government of Lord Aberdeen was defeated in the House of Commons on a motion made by an independent member of their own party and supported by twenty-five of the liberal members present. Though this defeat resembles the one last named in that it cannot be said to be due to the concerted action of the opposition as a party, Lord Derby, being summoned by your Majesty on the 1st. of Feb., proceeded to examine and ascertain in every quarter the means likely to be at his disposal for rendering assistance in the exigency, and it was not until Feb. 3 that he receded from his endeavours. There is, therefore, a very wide difference between the manner in which the call of your Majesty has been met on this occasion by the leader of the opposition, and the manner which has been observed at every former juncture, including even those when the share taken by the opposition in bringing about the exigency was comparatively slight or none at all. It is, in Mr. Gladstone's view, of the utmost importance to the public welfare that the nation should be constantly aware that the parliamentary action certain or likely to take effect in the overthrow of a government; the reception and treatment of a summons from your Majesty to meet the necessity which such action has powerfully aided in creating; and again the resumption of office by those who have deliberately laid it down,—are uniformly viewed as matters of the utmost gravity, requiring time, counsel, and deliberation among those who are parties to them, and attended with serious responsibilities. Mr. Gladstone will not and does not suppose that the efforts of the opposition to defeat the government on Wednesday morning were made with a previously formed intention on their part to refuse any aid to your Majesty, if the need should arise, in providing for the government of the country; and the summary refusal, which is the only fact before him, he takes to be not in full correspondence either with the exigencies of the case, or as he has shown, with the parliamentary usage. In humbly submitting this representation to your Majesty, Mr. Gladstone's wish is to point out the difficulty in which he would find himself placed were he to ask your Majesty for authority to inquire from his late colleagues whether they or any of them were prepared, if your Majesty should call on them, to resume their offices; for they would certainly, he is persuaded, call on him, for their own honour, and in order to the usefulness of their further service if it should be rendered, to prove to them that according to usage every means had been exhausted on the part of the opposition for providing for the government of the country, or at least that nothing more was to be expected from that quarter.

48. Memorandum in Colonel Ponsonby's handwriting (15 March 1873)

Monypenny and Buckle, *Disraeli*, ed. 1929, II, pp. 553, 554.

BUCKINGHAM PALACE, March 15.–The unusual course followed by Mr. Gladstone of asking the Queen for further explanations before he could call the Cabinet together, made it necessary for Her Majesty to consider how she could meet his request.

The Queen could not refuse to take any notice of it, as this would have retarded the progress of the negotiations, which Her Majesty was anxious to bring to a satisfactory termination. Besides which, Her Majesty desired there should be no misunderstanding.

The Queen could not assure Mr. Gladstone that Mr. Disraeli's refusal to accept office was complete, as Her Majesty would then have undertaken the responsibility of answering for the Opposition party.

The Queen could not herself have called on Mr. Disraeli for further explanations, as Her Majesty would then have assumed the view taken by Mr. Gladstone of Mr. Disraeli's conduct.

The Queen therefore, with Mr. Gladstone's knowledge and consent, forwarded his letter entire to Mr. Disraeli.

49. Memorandum by the queen (15 March 1873)

Monypenny and Buckle, *Disraeli*, ed. 1929, II, p. 554.

BUCKINGHAM PALACE, March 15, '73.–The Queen communicated, as Mr. Disraeli is aware, the substance of his refusal to undertake to form a Government in the present Parliament, to Mr. Gladstone, and she thinks it due to Mr. Disraeli to send him the accompanying letter (with Mr. Gladstone's knowledge), and will be glad to receive a reply from Mr. Disraeli which she can show Mr. Gladstone.

The Queen allows this communication to be made through her in order to prevent as much as possible any misunderstanding.

50. Memorandum by Disraeli to the queen (16 March 1873)

Monypenny and Buckle, *Disraeli*, ed. 1929, II, pp. 554–557.

GEORGE STREET, HANOVER SQUARE, March 16, 1873.–Mr. Disraeli with his humble duty to your Majesty.

He thanks your Majesty for communicating to him Mr. Gladstone's letter, with Mr. Gladstone's knowledge.

He is grateful to your Majesty for deigning to allow these communications to be made through your Majesty, and humbly agrees with your Majesty that it is a mode which may tend to prevent misunderstanding.

The observations of Mr. Gladstone, generally considered, may be ranged under two heads: an impeachment of the conduct of the Opposition in contributing to the vote against the Government measure, when they were not prepared, in the event of success, to take office; and a charge against the Leader of the Opposition, that, when honored by the commands of your Majesty, he gave a 'summary refusal' to undertake your Majesty's Government, without exhausting all practicable means of aiding the country in its exigency.

The argument of Mr. Gladstone, in the first instance, is that the Opposition, having, by 'deliberate and concerted action' thrown out a Bill, which the Government had declared to be 'vital to their existence,' is bound to use all means to form a Government of its own, in order to replace that which it must be held to have intentionally overthrown.

It is humbly submitted to your Majesty, that though, as a general rule, this doctrine may be sound, it cannot be laid down unconditionally, nor otherwise than subject to many exceptions.

It is undoubtedly sound so far as this: that for an Opposition to use its strength for the express purpose of throwing out a Government, which it is at the time aware that it cannot replace–having that object in view, and no other–would be an act of recklessness and faction, which could not be too strongly condemned. But it may be safely affirmed that no conduct of this kind can be imputed to the Conservative Opposition of 1873.

If the doctrine in question is carried further; if it be contended that, whenever, from any circumstance, a Minister is so situated that it is in his power to prevent any other Parliamentary leader from forming an Administration which is likely to stand, he acquires, thereby, the right to call upon Parliament to pass whatever measures he and his colleagues think fit, and is entitled to denounce as factious the resistance to such measures–then the claim is one not warranted by usage, or reconcilable with the freedom of the Legislature.

It amounts to this: that he tells the House of Commons, "Unless you are prepared to put some one in my place, your duty is to do whatever I bid you."

To no House of Commons has language of this kind ever been addressed: by no House of Commons would it be tolerated.

In the present instance, the Bill which has been the cause of the crisis, was, from the first, strongly objected to by a large section of the Liberal party, and that on the same grounds which led the Conservative Opposition to resist it, namely, that it seemed calculated to sacrifice the interests of Irish education to those of the Roman Catholic hierarchy.

A protracted discussion strengthened the general feeling of the House of Commons as to the defects of the measure: the party whom it was, apparently, intended to propitiate, rejected it as inadequate; and, probably, if the sense of the House had been taken on the Bill, irrespective of considerations as to the political result of the division, not one-fourth of the House would have voted for it. From first to last, it was unpopular, both inside and outside Parliament, and was disliked quite as much by Liberals as by Conservatives.

It is humbly submitted to your Majesty that no Minister has a right to say to Parliament, "You must take such a Bill, whether you think it a good one or not, because, without passing it, I will not hold office, and my numerical strength in the present House is too great to allow of any other effective Administration being formed."

The charge against the Leader of the Opposition personally, that, by his 'summary refusal' to undertake your Majesty's Government, he was failing in his duty to your Majesty and the country, is founded altogether on a gratuitous assumption by Mr. Gladstone, which pervades his letter, that the means of Mr. Disraeli to carry on the Government were not 'exhausted.' A brief statement of facts will at once dispose of this charge.

Before Mr. Disraeli, with due deference, offered his decision to your Majesty, he had enjoyed the opportunity of consulting those gentlemen, with whom he acts in public life; and they were unanimously of opinion, that it would be prejudicial to the interests of the country for a Conservative Administration to attempt to conduct your Majesty's affairs, in the present House of Commons. What other means were at Mr. Disraeli's disposal? Was he to open negotiations with a section of the late Ministry, and waste days in barren interviews, vain applications, and the device of impossible combinations? Was he to make overtures to the considerable section of the Liberal party who had voted against the Government, namely, the Irish Roman Catholic gentlemen? Surely Mr. Gladstone is not serious in such a suggestion. Impressed by experience, obtained in those very instances to which Mr. Gladstone refers, of the detrimental influence upon Government of a 'crisis' unnecessarily prolonged by hollow negotiations, Mr. Disraeli humbly conceived that he was taking a course at once advantageous to the public interests and tending to spare your Majesty unnecessary anxiety, by at once laying before your Majesty the real position of affairs.

There are many observations in Mr. Gladstone's letter which Mr. Disraeli, for convenience, refrains from noticing. Some of them are involved in an ambiguity not easy to encounter in a brief space: some of them, with reference to Mr. Disraeli's conduct in the House of Commons, Mr. Disraeli would fain hope are not entirely divested of some degree of exaggeration. "The deliberate and concerted action of the Opposition" would subside, Mr. Disraeli believes, on impartial investigation, into the exercise of that ordinary, and even daily, discipline of a political party, without which a popular assembly would soon degenerate into a mob, and become divested of all practical influence. In the present instance, Mr. Disraeli believes he is correct in affirming, that his friends were not even formally summoned to vote against the Government measure, but to support an amendment by an honourable gentleman, which was seconded from the Liberal benches, and which could only by a violent abuse of terms be described as a party move.

Then, again, much is made of the circumstance that the existence of the Government was staked on this measure. Mr. Disraeli has already treated of this subject generally. But what are the particular facts? No doubt, more than a month ago, the Prime Minister, in a devoted House of Commons, had, in an unusual, not to say unprecedented, manner, commenced his exposition of an abstruse measure by stating that the existence of the Government was staked on its success. But inasmuch as, in the course of time, it was understood that the Government were prepared to modify, or even to withdraw, most of the clauses of this measure, these words were forgotten or condoned, and could not be seriously held as exercising a practical influence on the ultimate decision.

51. The Queen's reply to Disraeli (16 March 1873)

Monypenny and Buckle, *Disraeli*, ed. 1929, II, p. 557.

WINDSOR CASTLE, March 16, 1873.–The Queen thanks Mr. Disraeli for his letter. She has sent it to Mr. Gladstone, and asked him whether he will undertake to resume office.

Part II
PARLIAMENT

PARLIAMENT

Introduction

THE struggle over the Reform Act had convulsed the whole political life of the country. To the Tory opponents of the Act the accompanying popular disturbances had seemed the presages of imminent revolution and the breaking up of laws. The Act accomplished a revolution, indeed, but not the one the Tories had feared. It was to prove the prelude to one of the stablest and most brilliant parliamentary epochs. Disraeli, who had been the principal critic of the middle-class power that it had created, looking back on it after nearly thirty years, paid an impressive tribute to the increase in the energy and public spirit of the House of Commons in which it had resulted, a tribute the more remarkable for being coupled with a recognition of the reforming work of Liverpool's Cabinets, to which he had not always rendered justice.[1]

But this does not necessarily mean that the Tory fears had been unfounded. To many of its Radical supporters the Act had mattered less for itself than as the prelude to the further reforms that they envisaged, in the representative system, in the Church, and in the law; nor is it likely that if they had been able to have their way the monarchy and the House of Lords would have been exempted. This would have been revolution indeed; the pouring of more new wine into the old bottles than the bottles could have stood. But Radical political anticipations were not to be fulfilled. Radicalism was to win important triumphs, not least the legislative implementation of the Benthamite conception of the State as administrator, which was to prove a revolution in itself, the importance of which is exhibited in every subsequent Part of this book. But the triumphs were to be under Whig leadership, and with Whig modifications. For this the reasons were several. The individualism inherent in the Radical temperament made it difficult for its representatives in Parliament to work effectively together as a group. The skill with which Peel rallied disconcerted Toryism under the Conservative banner confronted them with a formidable opposition. The popular interest which the Reform struggles had roused was not maintained when the political issues were less clear-cut and momentous. Above all, popular attention shifted to new questions on which Radicalism itself was deeply divided–the Poor Law and Factory Legislation. Radicalism had no coherent social programme to offer the country, and it was bread and butter, life and labour issues that really concerned its masses. The elections of 1837–the first of the queen's–registered a sharp check to political radicalism, and Russell was emboldened to dig in his toes over the issue of further constitutional reform, in the speech which won him, in reforming circles, the nickname of 'Finality Jack'.[2]

The House of Lords suffered a double blow from Reform. The influence which its members had exercised in the House of Commons through their control of

[1] No. 61. [2] No. 54.

constituencies underwent a sharp decline, and the collective authority and prestige of the House was weakened through its enforced acceptance of the Act. Nothing in the political history of the decade is more remarkable than its rapid recovery of power. Under Peel's remote control, exercised through Wellington and Lyndhurst, it amended Government legislation freely, slowed down the tempo of reform, and finally forced Melbourne's second Government to abandon the principle of lay appropriation of the surplus revenues of the Irish Church on which it had been founded. In 1836 Russell suggested to Melbourne that the Government should resort, piecemeal, to the creation of peers.[1] Melbourne did not accept the suggestion, but the incident measures both the exasperation caused by the Upper House and the revival of its prestige.

The situation of the 'thirties does not recur for a generation. Thanks mainly to Wellington's lapidary statement to the Lords of their position,[2] the Corn Law crisis passed off without any renewal of conflict between the Houses. Free Trade peers provided thenceforth a middle party; long periods of power increased the Whig strength; and a more evenly balanced House had less temptation to play a party role. Its more tranquil self-assurance is indicated by its unhesitating rejection, largely at Lyndhurst's instigation, of Palmerston's proposal, in 1856, to make Sir James Parke a peer for life. In the form in which the Government had put it, this would undoubtedly have compromised the independence of the House. When the plan was revived in 1876, it was with rigorous safeguards.[3] In 1860 a sharp controversy arose over Gladstone's proposal to carry out the old Radical demand for the remission of the remainder of the Paper Duties. The cost was £125,000, or the equivalent of a penny on the income-tax. Though part of his financial scheme for the year, it was embodied in a separate Bill. It was opposed both in the Cabinet and in the House, and Gladstone only just succeeded in carrying the third reading in the Commons. The Lords rejected it, as involving issues of policy as well as of finance. Palmerston could not avoid taking up the cudgels on behalf of the Commons financial privilege, but both the resolutions that he moved, and the speech in which he moved them, were markedly temperate in tone. The debate, notably Horsman's speech, showed that the Lords now commanded considerable sympathy in Whig circles. Gladstone's speech, on the other hand, heralded the rise of a stern and uncompromising Liberalism, and described the Lords' action as a "gigantic innovation, the most gigantic and dangerous that has been attempted in our time". Two years after the great divide of 1867, Gladstone's Bill for the Disestablishment of the Irish Church once more presented the Lords with the issue on which they had triumphed over Melbourne, and in its most extreme and unpalatable form. For the first time since 1832 they had again to face a strong and determined Ministry, with the Commons and the country behind it. On this occasion, thanks, in the first place, to the initiative of the queen,[4] prudence prevailed, and the leaders of the majority in the House decided to meet trouble half-way. As a result, they were able not only to preserve the constitutional position of the House intact, but to win substantial concessions from the Government on the Bill itself.

The Reform Act disfranchised fifty-six English boroughs completely, and took part of their representation away from thirty-one more. It created twenty-two new parliamentary boroughs with the traditional two members apiece, and twenty with one, mainly in industrial areas. It added sixty-two members to the county representation,

[1] No. 53. [2] No. 58. [3] Part VI, No. 168. [4] Part I, Nos. 31–38.

in some cases dividing counties in two, in others giving them a third member. In addition it created a uniform £10 householder franchise in boroughs. These were the major changes; they aimed firstly at cutting out anomalies and excrescences that invited attack, and secondly at safeguarding the constitution, and property itself, by bringing within the political country the mass of middle-class wealth that economic change had created, together with its dependants.

The place of property in Victorian political thought requires a special word. In spite of the challenge of the British Socialist school, from Godwin and Paine to Hodgskin and Owen, its credit as an economic institution had not been seriously shaken. The course of economic development seemed too clearly on its side. New wealth and new wealthy classes – the latter recruited largely from below – were multiplying year by year before men's eyes, and visibly as the outcome of individual energy and enterprise. It was not easy, therefore, for contemporaries to conceive what other basis there could be for the common economic endeavour than the freedom of property which gave these qualities their scope. The categories of owner and worker, master and man, though they were by no means rigid or exclusive, tended to be looked upon as natural and necessary concomitants of the economic process. On the level of responsible thought, therefore, property could be appealed to as a unifying and not a dividing principle; its security was put forward as the guarantee of the poor man's independence and hopes of rising in the world, as much as it was of his richer neighbour's status and wealth. The age of Chartism and of the Corn Law controversy, of Christian Socialism and the Co-operative Movement, was as familiar as any other with the crude facts, and indeed with the idea of the class war. But the country that gave asylum to Marx had not yet been seriously influenced by the harsh Teutonic scholasticism that found in this elemental clash the key to the whole of man's history, and incidentally took the economic chaos that Victorianism inherited as the creation of its spirit, ignoring its upsurge against it. The corroding effect that this doctrine was to have on confidence and kindliness was reserved for later generations to experience. The Victorian analysis was a different one, and not necessarily less realistic. It did not expect perfection of institutions, though it believed that they were indefinitely reformable.[1] It accepted self-interest as the specific motive-power of the economic machine, but because, by and large, it was believed to work for the general good. It assumed that expanding prosperity was in the interests of everyone. Clashes over the division of the spoils, some justifiable, some based largely on envy, were inevitable, and must be adjusted in the light of the overriding general interest. Self-interest must be brought under rule, and in the meanwhile a just and kindly use of economic power should mitigate the asperities of inequality. Confidence – in the amenability of the economic institutions which had achieved so much to reasonable human needs – and kindliness, expressing itself in the determination to make them thus amenable, and to supplement their immediate deficiences – were the keynotes of its better mind; the taint of original sin lay not in institutions, which could never outstrip the human nature on which they were founded, but in the human nature which neglected or blinded itself to its duties.

This combination of realism and idealism – which its defenders might claim that Marx found standing on its feet and stood on its head – had its corollaries, *mutatis mutandis*, in the political sphere. It was assumed that those who were on the bread-and-butter line economically would think in bread-and-butter terms politically. The

[1] Part III, Introduction.

essence of the political art was to co-ordinate and conciliate conflicting interests, to resolve them in an enduring harmony. Economic independence, on the other hand, carried with it the assumption of gentle birth and education, or at any rate of exceptional ability in the field of all men's primary endeavour. Its possessors had margins which enabled, and in part compelled them to think in longer and wider terms than the personal and immediate ones, and, in fact, the social outlook of the time expected this effort of them, as the responsibility attaching to their possessions. In this view, property was the primary enfranchisement, almost the *sine qua non* of the genuinely political animal. That it should be accepted as a relevant factor in determining the franchise was therefore natural. It was also very widely regarded as an almost indispensable qualification for the disinterested execution of public offices. Most constituencies accepted these assumptions. What they looked for in a representative was knowledge of the constituency itself, sympathy with its needs and problems, combined with sufficient knowledge of the wider world, and status in it, to command attention. In a country constituency a neighbouring landowner, combining, if possible, wealth and family with acceptable views and personality, was generally looked on as the ideal member. Even in industrial constituencies, less feudally minded and more modern in outlook, such candidates, or, failing them, a well-established local manufacturer, were acceptable. To be of no position was an almost insuperable obstacle.

Even Radicals hardly challenged this outlook, though they might be critical of the special deference accorded to landed wealth. The Whigs, in any case, were almost as much of a landed party as their Tory opponents, and there had been no intention, on their part, in the Reform Act, to subvert the territorial constitution. The influence of station and wealth continued, therefore, to play a large part in elections. One form of influence which the eighteenth century had known disappeared, indeed, in the course of the nineteenth–the influence by which governments in the past had been virtually able to 'make' elections. A long course of legislation since Burke's Economical Reform Bill of 1782, the growth of new standards of purity in administration,[1] and of a higher standard of public responsibility in members of Parliament, reflecting the increasing responsibilities of Parliament itself, and accentuated by the Reform Act, had practically swept it away. There was still a good deal of patronage of the smaller kind, and the patronage secretary of the Treasury went through all the motions of doling out favours to members and candidates of the right political colour. Leading statesmen had to spend time that they often grudged in dealing with applications, and members might be criticized if they failed to get a share of what was going for their constituency. But the amount and value of what was available was very limited, and the granting of applications hemmed round with conventions and restrictions. Subject to the growing independence of members, patronage still, perhaps, served its eighteenth-century function of stabilizing, in the House, the relations between members and parties, and in the constituencies, those between members and their supporters. But its total effect was probably little more than to slow down the rate of political change. The possession of patronage did not save the Tories from decline in 1830, nor the Whigs in the ensuing decade. Similarly, there still survived a few 'government boroughs', but government control in them was weakening, and in 1845 Queen Victoria made a significant and symbolic renunciation of royal interest in elections at Windsor. Nomination and 'close' boroughs, of the type which in the past had afforded a secure basis for a deal with the administration, had been swept

[1] Part VII.

away by the Act. But in counties elections continued to be settled largely between the leading landowners, with serene confidence in the amenability of the electorate, and little reference to party leaders or headquarters. Many boroughs were still small enough for a single influence to dominate them, and most had their local personalities of standing and weight, whose favour or disfavour was a primary element in the election. Professor Gash has recently calculated, for the period just after the Reform Act, that in 5 boroughs the electorate was under 200; in 26, between 200 and 300; in 92, between 300 and 1,000; in 35, between 1,000 and 2,000; and in 29, over 2,000. The electorate grew from 652,777 in 1832 to 1,056,659 in 1866, modifying this state of affairs to some extent, but unequally as between constituencies. Local influences were frequently so strong that, once their balance had been decided, it was not worth while contesting a seat. In counties and larger boroughs not infrequently the seats would be divided, a couple of representative moderates being put forward to avoid the expense and ill-feeling incidental to a party fight. In the five general elections between 1832 and 1841 nearly half the seats were not contested. But the political traffic was not all one-way, and electors were more easily led than driven. On large issues, particularly, they would assert themselves; thus nearly all the counties had swung round to Reform, and Mr. Kitson Clark has recently suggested that protectionist farmers drove their landlords into opposition to Free Trade, at the time of the Repeal of the Corn Laws. Sanctions were sometimes used to vindicate what was looked on as a proper influence; tenants might be given notice, employees dismissed, or custom withdrawn from tradesmen. But their too harsh use engendered resentment. In spite of all, popular feeling made itself felt, and constituencies developed their own colour and outlook. Few seats were unchallengeable unless sensitively handled, and the surrender or compromise of seats was itself the outcome of expert assessment of political strength and feeling.

If electors were generally prepared to regard themselves as politically infeudated to their social and economic betters, reciprocal services were expected. Where influence was old and solidly established, these might be no more than the services which well-to-do and well-placed persons can always render to their poorer neighbours, and which the social outlook of the time regarded as in any case within the ambit of normal neighbourly duty. But it became a usual practice for candidates, as a sort of retaining fee, to pay the registration fees required of electors under the new registration machinery of the 1832 Act, and admission fees in freeman boroughs. At election times treating and entertainment were a matter of course, and the expense of bringing out-voters to the poll fell on candidates. They also paid the legal and administrative expenses of the election, and though these were largely prescribed by law, they were paid direct to the local officials, and too close a scrutiny of the bills was inadvisable. Thus even in the quietest and most respectable of constituencies, politics were an expensive business, and generally only for the well-to-do. These were the normal incidents of the operation of influence, and aroused little real criticism, though political purists might object to them. The case was different with outright corruption and intimidation. Something of this went on in most places, though it might affect only a few voters. In some, the not ungenial practice prevailed of paying voters 'head money'.[1] In others, such as Sudbury,[2] St. Albans, and Lancaster–in the last, in a notorious instance, as late as 1865–outright venality, the competitive auction of votes, established itself. Constituencies varied a great deal in their records, some remaining

[1] No. 59, § VI. [2] No. 56.

little affected by corruption, others, through some accident of their electoral history, becoming infected, and virtue, once lost, was rarely regained. Small boroughs were not necessarily the worst; the most flagrant examples came from the middle range; and the largest were not necessarily exempt. Freemen, and 'ancient right' voters, *i.e.* those voting in boroughs in virtue of pre-Reform Act qualifications which were continued for their lives, had the worst contemporary reputation. But the £10 householders were often as frail, though they sold their honour dearer. County electorates were usually free from the grosser forms of corruption, whether, as on the one hand had been alleged, because they were more respectable, or, as Radical critics said, because they were already firmly in hand. Generally elections were rowdy; with beer and perhaps money flowing they had everything to make them so. The candidates' opening speeches on the hustings, and the open voting, were occasions for demonstrations in which the unenfranchised took full part, sometimes for pay, sometimes as a genuine means of expressing their political preferences, sometimes out of mere love of a contest. In the worst instances election brawls degenerated into pitched battles between rival gangs of hired toughs, and kidnapping or 'cooping' of voters was freely resorted to. Again, political traffic was not wholly one-way; the less respectable electors felt cheated if they were not offered something for their votes. St. Albans had a party which made it its business to see that no election in the borough was compromised; its symbol was a key, which unlocked the door through which money flowed into the town. Election petitions were not necessarily the fruits of outraged purity; more often they were part of the regular tactics of the game, or arose out of spite and vindictiveness. Till 1842 their withdrawal by the petitioning party ended the inquiry, and party agents often arranged balancing withdrawals. Disraeli's unchallenged retention of his Shrewsbury seat in 1841 was the result of such a bargain. Constituency bargains gained special notoriety in 1842, and led to legislation.[1] Radicals were the special critics of other people's electoral practices, which they blamed for their permanent minority, but in many of the northern towns mass intimidation was regularly practised in the Radical interest. There were few distinctions between parties in these matters, save of opportunity and method.

A stream of legislation sought to lessen these abuses. It was still the practice for election petitions to be tried by committees of the House. To get greater impartiality and experience on the committees, an Act of 1839 arranged for panels to be drawn up at the beginning of each session, from which committees were drawn. Acts of 1841 and 1842[2] stopped up some of the loopholes through which offenders had escaped. Special commissions to conduct inquiries on the spot were set up in the cases of the flagrantly corrupt elections at Sudbury in 1841[3] and St. Albans in 1852, and in both cases the boroughs were disfranchised. An Act of 1852[4] provided for the regular use of this way of inquiry. In 1854 the first comprehensive legislative definition of bribery was provided,[5] and the Act also required the publication of election expenses. Later, this was to prove a useful check, but the Lancaster Report of 1865 proved that a coach and horses could be driven through the provisions as they then existed. In 1868, after much protest from the judges, who feared that their impartiality might be imperilled or impugned, jurisdiction in election petitions was transferred to the courts.[6] The Radical specific against corruption had always been the ballot. Its opponents had insisted that the vote was a public function, which should be publicly exercised, and that secrecy was likely to encourage corruption rather than diminish

[1] Nos. 55, 57. [2] No. 55. [3] No. 56. [4] No. 59. [5] No. 60. [6] No. 71.

it. The passing of the Ballot Act[1] in 1872 did not, in fact, very greatly alter the situation. The factors of change, when change came, as slowly it did, were more general ones. The increasing stringency of legislation played its part, no doubt; but more important were the increased size of the electorate after 1867, the march of Respectability, and, most important of all, the growth of party, which, by processes which may be variously described as the spread of political consciousness, the democratization of policy, or the substitution of public for private inducements to vote, put an end to it as it had been historically known. Thus, while for the older political country, the period was one of the absorption of new blood and new ideas, for the mass of the voters it was one of transition from the older disciplines of class and economic subordination to the new discipline of party; or, as Professor Smellie has put it, the period saw "the transformation of the conflicting cliques within a governing class into the party organisation of a democratic state".

Radical theories of representation, which provided the major dynamic of change, went back, in the main, to Benthamism. Benthamite theory assumed that in every issue that came before him, the voter would address his mind to the discovery of the course most effectively conducing to the greatest good of the greatest number, and would vote accordingly. The theory assured him that this would coincide with his own ultimate good. On this view most of what had been written and said on the finer problems of representative government was otiose–the problems were, in fact, simple questions of arithmetic and administrative mechanics. Thus Radical reforming ideas tended to be singularly uninhibited. But their practical validity depended on the assumption that each elector would exercise an intelligent, independent, and conscientious vote. Radicalism had the honour of breeding much independence of this sort, though less, perhaps, than it claimed. But its view of the average voter, as the extensive literature of election petitions amply evidences, flattered both his interest in political matters and his intelligence. He required, in fact, to be stimulated into interest, and supplied with intelligent opinions, though he might exercise a consumer's choice of what was offered to him. In popular government, the means of thus interesting him and instructing him is party. The development of party organization and machinery was therefore in the logic of Reform. The struggle over the Act produced some forward steps: an increased use was made of party funds; in 1832 the Tories founded the Carlton Club, as a political centre and rallying point, the first professedly political club; and a few years later Radicals and Whigs followed with the Reform Club. More permanent party organizations grew out of this; for the Conservatives, Francis Bonham acted virtually as chief party agent, and played a valuable part, by his labours, in the Conservative victory of 1841; and Joseph Parkes and James Coppock regularly managed Whig elections. The Reform Act had contained provisions setting up a system for the registering of electors. The electoral rolls were placed under the final control of revising barristers, sitting at regular intervals, in a judicial capacity. Electoral law was complicated; the barristers' practice not always uniform; the power of lodging objections was widely vested, and an undefended objection had the automatic result of removing the name objected to from the register. Electors would not take the trouble to enforce or defend their claims themselves. It came to be realized that a 'good registration' might be half the battle in a constituency, and constituency organizations grew up to get favourable voters on the roll, and keep off others. In Peel's words, registration became a new political power. The largest

[1] No. 72.

scale exploitation of the technicalities of the situation was by the Anti-Corn Law League, which, by lodging mass objections at the last minute, and by the creation of forty-shilling freeholds, aimed at carrying several of the more industrialized counties. Out of registration needs constituency political machines thus developed. Their natural managers were local solicitors, and equally it was natural for these, in complicated and technical registration matters, to seek expert advice at the Carlton or the Reform, as the case might be. Thus, in Ostrogorski's words, "registration became the gap through which the central parties, hitherto confined to Parliament, made their way into the constituencies, and gradually covered the whole country with the network of their organisation". But constituency machines remained for long under local control, serving primarily local purposes. The territorial constitution preserved creeks and backwaters of local interest and feeling into which the full tide of party for long hardly penetrated. Constituencies might seek central help and advice, but party managers and leaders moved charily, if they dared move at all, in interfering with them. For long years after the great crisis of Reform, the movement of politics did little to disturb this situation. The issues which stirred the country profoundly–Poor Laws, Factory Legislation, Public Health, the Corn Laws–were ones on which parties themselves were divided, and, as has been seen,[1] Peel's handling of the Corn Laws blurred party lines for nearly half a generation. In part this state of affairs preserved the territorial constitution; in part it resulted from it. Elections, depending so much on local issues, swung slowly; only two, between 1832 and 1868, were directly decisive of the fate of a government, those of 1841 and 1857. Members came up representing a locality, owing their election to local as much as national support, having commended themselves to their constituents, very often, by proclaiming their independence of views. They did not abandon their characters the moment they got to Westminster. Between the two Reforms, and especially between 1846 and 1859, the fate of governments depended on the swing of individual opinion in the House; small margins of votes, the accession of this or that individual or group, the failure of the Government to judge correctly the temper of the House, decided the issue. England was nearer parliamentary government than ever before or since–the form of government, that is, in which the policy and composition of the Government is determined by the independent views of the members of the House of Commons. Hence, in part, the long dominance in these years of the great parliamentary middlemen, Peel and Palmerston. How little the activities of party organization belonged to the forefront of politics is illustrated by the fact that in 1868 Glyn, the new Liberal Whip, had to explain to his new leader, Gladstone, who had been forty years in the House, the purposes for which party organization and funds were required.

In 1837 Russell had closed the issue of further Reform; in 1852 he reopened it. Already, in 1848, just after the Chartist threat had been triumphantly dispelled,[2] he had promised Joseph Hume that when a quieter season came round he would give consideration to the subject, and in the session of 1851 he had been under heavy Radical pressure to carry out his pledge.[3] The Bill that he introduced in 1852 was lost shortly afterwards in the fall of his Government. In 1854, as a member of Aberdeen's Coalition Government, he put forward another, but was compelled to abandon it, with very visible distress, in the face of imminent war. In 1857 Palmerston pledged his Government to tackle the problem, but his Government fell before he could be called upon to carry out his promise. Disraeli had always been determined not to

[1] Part I, Introduction. [2] Part V. [3] Part I, Nos. 7–11.

allow the Whigs a monopoly of the subject, and in the Derby Government that succeeded Palmerston's brought forward a measure[1] which was defeated, however, on a motion of Russell's[2] condemning its failure to lower the borough suffrage. Palmerston succeeded Derby, and Russell, under the implied obligation created by his attack on Disraeli, made his third attempt to solve the problem. But in a parliamentary time-table crowded with Gladstone's financial proposals[3] and foreign affairs, Reform was forced to the wall, and the Bill was abandoned, on this occasion without any very visible regret on the part of Russell or of anyone else. A summary of the proposals of these Bills is appended to this Introduction.

Of more interest than the details are the theories and considerations that shaped the proposals. Russell based his case for reopening the subject on the stability of British institutions, particularly as amended by the Act of 1832, during the storms that swept Europe in 1848, on the improvements in education and social conditions, and the increased intelligence and responsibility they had brought with them, making an extension of the measure of 1832 desirable, and on the advantage of considering this before there was popular excitement on the subject. But he repudiated the idea that every individual had a claim to a vote, emphasized the gravity and the complexity of the responsibilities falling on the British Parliament, as compared with other assemblies, and insisted that the first consideration about reform must be the contribution it could make to better government. His reservations on the subject made, perhaps, more impression than his positive case; particularly, through the decade and a half of debate that followed, it was emphasized again and again, in the context of the responsibilities of Parliament, that the personal calibre of the members it sends up must be regarded as a primary criterion of a representative system. It was on the ground that they exercised a more personal and discriminating choice in this regard that many members, notably Gladstone,[4] defended the smaller borough constituencies. On the franchise question, the operative Whig ideal was that rare animal, the independent voter, and Whig speeches abound with defences of the 'worthiness' of this or that section of the population, on the score of their increasing education and responsibility, to enjoy the privilege, and undertake the responsibility, of the franchise. This brought the Whigs on to ground adjoining the Radicals, whose view was that everyone not *prima facie* disqualified ought to vote. Tory emphasis, on the other hand, was more often placed on the desirability of securing that the social and occupational groups which made up the articulated life of the nation should have their distinct voices and appropriate weight. This went with an understandable emphasis on the importance of the land. Tories had criticized the Reform Act on the ground that it deprived the working classes of the distinct representation that the wide suffrage of some of the scot and lot boroughs had given them; and it is not too much to say that the whole series of Bills was largely an effort to give the working classes an equivalent of what they had thus lost, without giving them supremacy in Parliament. This might have been a hopeful line to follow in the pre-1832 constitution, but the introduction of the uniform borough suffrage had made success in it virtually impossible. The principle of uniformity had itself been an object of Tory attack in 1832. Disraeli had been the most vocal critic of the middle-class ascendancy that had been founded on it, but when, in 1859, in the difficult circumstances of minority government, it fell to him to introduce his own Bill, he proposed to assimilate the county and borough occupying franchises, while securing, under cover of this, an object of

[1] No. 61. [2] No. 62. [3] Part V, No. 151. [4] No. 63.

long-standing Tory endeavour, the provision that forty-shilling freeholders in boroughs should vote in their boroughs, and not in the county, as hitherto.[1] This was ostensibly to preserve the purity of county representation from urban defilement. Henley and Walpole resigned from the Cabinet on the issue, and attacked him for espousing the most unhistoric and the most dangerous of the Whig principles of 1832. Both sides to the debate shared, in varying measure, the fear of the preponderance of numbers, the domination of a mass vote, which it was feared might flatten out independence, and thus destroy the reality of discussion. When it came to questions of redistribution, both also repudiated the idea of 'electoral districts', the view that the equalization of numbers of electors in constituencies was of primary importance, and both showed a desire to retain, as far as possible, the historic structure of representation, in which a community of interest and a habit of working together had given constituencies something of a common mind and an articulated political tradition. Both, in fact, mistrusted the Radical conception of representative government as a delegation of power from a people conceived primarily as a mathematical expression; they thought in vital, rather than in mathematical or mechanical terms; constitutional government was primarily government by discussion, in which it was important that distinct interests and points of view should have their representation, but in which, above all, voices should be weighed, and representatives be prepared to allow the ultimate decision to be governed by the common sense of the national interest and duty, as it took shape in the discussion. These were ideals, no doubt, by no means fully answered in practice, but nor were they without substantial efficacy. There was agreement that some advance on 1832 was desirable; the difficulty was to advance on the lines it had laid down without some sacrifice of these ideals, and of values which the success of parliamentary government in the meantime had vindicated.

None of the Bills we have been discussing evoked much enthusiasm, or even much interest in the country. But the repetition of proposals of reform built up an expectation of it. Democratic influences were gaining ground; Bright, in 1858, opened a vigorous campaign for household suffrage; and foreign influences and events, the liberation of Italy, the triumph of the Northern States in the American Civil War, which was regarded as a vindication of democratic against aristocratic society, the visit of Garibaldi to this country in 1864, contributed to them. Meanwhile, in the politics of the country, party lines were clearing up. The junction of Gladstone with Palmerston, shortly after his speech and vote in favour of keeping alive Disraeli's Reform Bill,[2] marked the virtual extinction of the great Peelite schism. His Budget, the Commercial Treaty with France,[3] and his struggle with the Lords brought him closer to the Radicals, and his speech on Baines' Bill, in 1864,[4] marked his virtual espousal, with the reservations that his dialectical ingenuity could emphasize or abolish at will, of the Radical position on Reform. There was little talk of Reform, however, in the election of 1865, which returned Palmerston again triumphantly. A few weeks later Palmerston was dead. Russell succeeded him as prime minister, and Gladstone, who had been turned out of his Oxford University seat and had come in 'unmuzzled' for South Lancashire, became chancellor of the exchequer. Russell, now in the House of Lords, was nearing the end of his political tether, and Gladstone was his destined successor. In the Conservative ranks Derby was preparing to give way to Disraeli. The ring was clearing, leaving in it these two stripped and deadly antagonists, a political Tom Sayers and Heenan, each anxious to leave his mark on

[1] No. 61 [2] No. 63. [3] Part V, No. 152. [4] No. 64.

history, each readier and apter in the game of democratic politics than most of his followers, sharply contrasted in temperament and outlook, and divided by a mutual mistrust that went back to the political grave of Peel. Russell was determined, if possible, to round off his career by giving his name to a second Reform. The Bill that Gladstone, in 1866, brought into the House of Commons was not immoderate in itself, but a Palmerstonian House fretted at the imposition upon it of a measure for which the enthusiasm of their chief, so lately triumphantly returned, and so lately dead, had notoriously been qualified. Moreover, Gladstone's parliamentary tactics were dangerous; he separated franchise reform and redistribution, reserving the latter subject for a separate Bill. The effect was of a contingent sentence of parliamentary death upon the Whig members for the smaller boroughs, not the most enthusiastic for Reform, to be executed or not as the Government might decide, or as the conduct of individuals might deserve. Robert Lowe made himself the mouthpiece of the resentment and mistrust that was felt, in a series of speeches which turned the ensuing debates into the greatest parliamentary tourney of the century. Caustic, powerful, and impetuous,[1] Lowe dominated the House and the session, but angered the country, where Bright and Gladstone exploited his indiscretions, opening the organ stops of their oratory in a manner quite out of keeping with the modesty of the Bill and the conventions of such debates. The rising popular agitation stimulated rather than reassured the parliamentary critics; a partial surrender and the introduction of a new Bill, combining franchise and redistribution proposals, failed to save the Government. Derby found himself called on to form a Cabinet, and appealed vainly to the Adullamites, as Bright had christened the dissident Whigs, to come to his aid. Disraeli, his lieutenant in the Commons, could not therefore hope to command the House. The Cabinet would have been glad not to embark on the troubled sea of Reform, but representations from the queen that the question ought not to be left in an unsettled state[2] tipped the scales of its decision. Disraeli tried first to get an agreed plan by laying resolutions before the House, but in its disorganized state, the House called for a lead and a Bill. A household suffrage plan, qualified by plural voting and 'fancy franchises', was provisionally adopted by the Cabinet. But a later examination by Cranborne–the future Lord Salisbury–convinced him that while, as Derby had argued, the 'safeguards' balanced the accession to the working-class vote in the country as a whole, in 60 per cent of the boroughs they would leave it supreme. Faced with the prospect of the resignation of Cranborne and others, the Cabinet hurriedly reverted to a £6 rating plan, and this–the 'Ten Minutes Bill'–was presented to Parliament. But the news had leaked out that a larger plan had been in contemplation, and Conservative back-benchers disliked what seemed to them no more than repetition of the old Whig measures. After a day or two's hesitation, Derby decided to revert to his larger scheme, and face the resignations. In the Commons, Gladstone attacked on principle the plural voting and 'fancy franchise' safeguards, and tried to rally his party down the trodden ways of a £5 rental amendment. But his party preferred the household suffrage flag which Disraeli had hung out, and the net result of Gladstone's exertions was to emphasize the democratic aspects of the Bill. Lowe fulminated in vain,[3] and deservedly in vain, for he had not shouldered the responsibilities he had incurred in destroying the previous Government. A major difficulty cropped up in the course of debate, which the haste of its preparations had prevented the Government from measuring. In many, but not in all, of the large towns, the

[1] No. 65. [2] Part I, Nos. 26–30. [3] No. 67.

practice had grown up of landlords who owned considerable working-class property paying the rates themselves, receiving a discount from the authorities for the trouble they saved them, and recovering from their tenants in rent. This was known as 'compounding'. Disraeli had based his Bill, in accordance with Conservative principles, on ratepayer suffrage, and it followed from this that the 'compound householders'–indistinguishable in all else from other working-class householders–would not be enfranchised. There were half a million of them, and the Opposition pressed their case. But Disraeli, flexible till now, refused to surrender his principle, and the situation and the Bill were only saved by his acceptance, at the Opposition's hands, and on his personal responsibility, for his principal colleagues were away from the House, of the Hodgkinson amendment, which abolished compound householding. The 'compounders' got their vote, but in many cases at the expense of increased rates. Gladstone's Bill had proposed to add 400,000 to the electorate. The Act of 1867 added 938,427 to an existing electorate of 1,056,659. Disraeli had scored an outstanding political success over the discomfited Gladstone. He defended his policy[1] on the ground that once the settlement of 1832 was seriously disturbed, no final or logical resting-place could be found, short of household suffrage. But the principle that survived the debates was John Bright's, not the Tory one.

Thus the system of 1832 was overthrown, and replaced by another, the logical consequence of which was democracy. It cannot be said that the principal actors in the change–Lowe, Gladstone, and Disraeli–unless we credit Disraeli with deliberate Machiavellianism rather than opportunism–fully intended this result, or that it represented a deliberate judgment of Parliament or of the nation. The rising tension of party feeling made it possible. Lack of measure, excessive self-will, on the part of the chief protagonists, brought it about. Gladstone's attempts to bully the House and his indulgence of his oratorical powers in the country, Lowe's vehement bitterness in the House, Disraeli's determination to emerge at any cost victor from the struggle, created a situation of which none of them could guarantee the outcome. In comparing the debates with those of 1846, it cannot be said that the partisan exaggeration was any greater, but what is lacking is the continued effort on the part of independent members in the earlier debates to evaluate the issues for themselves. It is this which gives to the 1846 debates the character of a continuous intellectual evolution and makes them, even in their entirety, enthralling reading today. The writing is on the wall, so far as the independent member is concerned, though his disappearance is gradual. With so large an element of accident in its demise it is impossible to say whether the Act of 1832 could have survived intact, in a rapidly developing country; whether the self-adjusting elements in it to which Lowe had drawn attention[2] would have sufficed to preserve it, or whether it could have been amended in a way more consonant with the historic constitution, which, in 1832, Russell had professed to save, and which subsequently, by his obsession with Reform, he had done so much to disturb. The Tory Reform was in many ways more revolutionary than the Whig had been. Gladstone soon found, in Irish Church Disestablishment, a cause which rallied to him all the elements of his disrupted following–Whigs, Radicals, and Nonconformists. At the election of 1868 he turned the tables on his opponent, and entered upon his great reforming ministry of 1868–1874. The spotlight of popular attention focused henceforth on him and his antagonist; the playing to the popular gallery which had hurried the last stages of Reform over the brink of

[1] No. 69. [2] No. 65. [3] No. 67.

action became a central and recognized feature of politics; the new voters found in the party clash, and in the 'programmes', framed for their delectation, which now became fashionable, matter for their interest and understanding. General elections are henceforth the moments of political change. In our complex and flexible constitution, relative weights were silently adjusted; parliamentary government, as it had been practised in the generation that was gone, slips into the background; the new determinant of the character of government is organized party, dominating, with its discipline, opinion both in Parliament and in the country. The age of machine politics begins. The Birmingham caucus, successful in the 1868 election, provided the model for Liberalism; Disraeli had initiated a reform of party organization in the same year, and between then and 1874 Gorst, under his direction, carried it to a completion which was vindicated in the 1874 election. Re-invigorated party spirit began to flood up the creeks and backwaters of the territorial constitution. These were to be the politics of the rising generation. To this newer time, the age of parliamentary government had bequeathed no inconsiderable inheritance: an economy balanced and vigorous, a country healed of the bitterest of its social dissensions, a mass of valuable reform and legislation, high and exacting conceptions of probity and patriotism in members and ministers. To critics like Bagehot and Lecky the period between the two Reforms represented a golden age of constitutionalism, setting standards of wisdom and self-restraint, of far-sightedness, and public spirit, which they did not expect to see maintained.

In the course of the 1866 debates Lowe had urged that the working classes, once in a majority, would desert the older political parties, and set up shop for themselves. Gladstone, on the other hand, had insisted that they would range themselves, like everyone else, as Liberals or Conservatives, following what seemed to him, no doubt, a dichotomy of nature. Disraeli, pausing on the brink of the Leap in the Dark, had assured himself and his hearers that the spirit of the constitution would be strong enough to assimilate the larger numbers to whom he was preparing to give the vote. Cranborne, who, as Lord Salisbury, was to hold office under a popular constitution, as Conservative prime minister, for longer than anyone since Liverpool, predicted that the working classes would use their power to enrich themselves. Politicians, even the greatest of them, the lords of our earthly destinies, seem not to be exempted from the rule that 'we know in part, and we prophesy in part'.

NOTE ON PRINCIPAL REFORM BILLS, 1852–1866

RUSSELL'S BILL, 1852

Franchise: borough occupation franchise reduced from £10 clear annual value to £5 rateable value; county occupation franchise (Chandos clause) reduced from £50 to £20 clear annual value, copyhold and long leasehold franchises from £10 to £5, new borough and county franchise for persons paying 40*s.* a year taxes.

Redistribution: boroughs with fewer than 500 electors to have fresh districts added to them.

RUSSELL'S BILL, 1854

Franchise: borough occupation franchise reduced to £6 annual rateable value, with 2½ years' residential qualification, as against 1 year of £10 voters under 1832 Act. Provision that rates and taxes must have been paid repealed. Freeman qualification to expire with existing possessors.

County occupation franchise reduced to £10 clear annual value, subject to including a building worth £5. New borough and county qualifications–receipt of £100 annual salary, £10 annual dividend from funds, Bank or East India Co. stock, payment of 40*s.* income tax or assessed taxes, possession of £50 in savings bank for not less than three years, possession of a university degree.

Redistribution: Disfranchisement of 19 boroughs, returning 29 members, where number of electors less than 300 and/or population did not exceed 5,000; one member taken away from 23 boroughs with less than 500 electors and population not in excess of 10,000[1] West Riding of Yorkshire, and Lancashire to be divided, and each division of each to return 3 members. Thirty-eight counties and 9 towns with population in excess of 100,000 to have 3 members each, in place of 2. Birkenhead, Staleybridge, and Burnley to be given a member apiece; new division of Kensington and Chelsea to have 2 members, Inns of Court 2, London University 1, Scotland 3.

In interests of minority representation electors in three-member constituencies to have only two votes apiece.

Disraeli's Bill of 1859

Franchise: borough occupation franchise unaltered; 40*s.* freeholders in boroughs to vote in boroughs; county occupation franchise reduced to £10. New franchises for borough and county–persons possessing £10 in funds, Bank of East India Co. stock, £60 in savings bank, in receipt of £20 annual military, naval, or civil service pension, dwellers in part of dwelling-house aggregate rent of which is £20, graduates of universities, ministers of religion, members of legal profession, of medical body, and certain schoolmasters.

Redistribution: Fifteen smaller boroughs to lose 1 member each; 4 members added to West Riding, 2 to South Lancashire, 2 to Middlesex, 1 member each to Hartlepool, Birkenhead, West Bromwich and Wednesbury, Bromley and Staleybridge, Croydon, and Gravesend. Boundary Commissioners to rearrange borough boundaries so as to bring urban areas properly belonging to them within constituencies.

Russell's 1860 Bill

Franchise: borough occupation franchise to £6 clear annual value; county occupation to £10 rental.

Redistribution: Twenty-five smaller boroughs to lose 1 seat apiece; West Riding to have 2 additional members, 15 other counties to have extra member apiece, Kensington and Chelsea 2 members, Birkenhead, Staleybridge, and Burnley 1 member, Manchester, Leeds, Liverpool, and Birmingham additional member each, making 3, London University 1.

Voters in three-member constituencies to have two votes.

Gladstone's 1866 Bill

Franchise: borough occupation £7 clear annual value, lodger qualification of £10 annual value, provisions that rates, etc., must have been paid, and that voters must be ratepayers (cf. compound householders) to be repealed. County occupation franchise £14 clear annual value.

Redistribution (Bill of 7 May): Boroughs with population under 8,000 to surrender 1 seat, or be grouped with other boroughs, with 1 or 2 seats as joint representation, so as to provide 49 seats. South Lancashire to be divided and each division to have 3 members, 26 seats to go to counties with population over 50,000 to give them 3 members apiece, Manchester, Liverpool, Leeds, and Birmingham to have 3 members apiece, Salford to have extra member, Tower Hamlets to be split into two with 2 members to each division, Kensington and Chelsea 2 members, 6 towns with population over 18,000 to have member apiece, University of London 1, Scotland 7 extra members.

Boundary revision to equate municipal and parliamentary boundaries.

[1] Four further seats from Sudbury and St. Albans were also to be distributed.

Reform Act of 1867

The Representation of the People Act, 30 & 31 Vict. c. 102, provided as follows:

Franchise: Boroughs, householders having paid rates, lodgers having occupied, for at least a year, rooms of clear annual value, unfurnished, of £10, qualified to vote. Occupiers, and not owners, to be responsible for rates. Counties – freehold, or life tenure, or long lease, of clear annual value of £5; occupation of rateable value of £12, and payment of rates, to qualify.

In three-member constituencies voter to have two votes only.

Redistribution: Totnes, Reigate, Yarmouth, and Lancaster to cease to return members. Thirty-eight boroughs to return 1 member instead of 2. Manchester, Leeds, Birmingham, and Liverpool to return 3 members. Ten new boroughs created, of which Chelsea to return 2 members, the others 1. Merthyr Tydfil and Salford to return 2 members. Tower Hamlets to be divided into two 2-member constituencies, Hackney, and Tower Hamlets. A number of counties divided, each division returning 2 members. University of London to return 1 member.

Boundary Commissioners to be appointed to undertake precise delimitation of new constituencies.

SELECT BIBLIOGRAPHY

The primary authority is Hansard's *Parliamentary Debates.* Only familiarity with it, and not merely with the principal debates but with the course of day-to-day business, yields the clue to much of parliamentary history.

Parliamentary Papers throw a great deal of light on conditions in the constituencies; a few, which may be specially mentioned, are the *Report of the Select Committee on Bribery at Elections* (1835/VIII); on *Election Proceedings* (1842/V); on the *Registration of County Electors* (1846/VIII); the *Returns relating to Election Petitions presented since 1833* (1852–1853/7/XXXIII); *Return of Election Petition alleging Bribery and Intimidation at Elections since 1865* (1868/9/L); on *Corrupt Practices in Parliamentary and Municipal Elections* (1868/LX and 1870/VI). Till 1868, election petitions were referred to Committees of the House, and their *Reports* constitute a considerable literature. Among the more striking are *Sudbury* (1843/V and 1844/XVIII); *St. Albans* (1851/XIII and 1852/XXVII); and *Lancaster* (1866/XI and 1867/XXVII). Important as this class of source is, it should be borne in mind that it represents rather the pathology than the health of the representative system.

The constitutional histories and biographies of statesmen listed in the Bibliography to Part I and the General Bibliography deal very largely with parliamentary history. W. I. JENNINGS, *Parliament* (Cambridge, 1938), though largely concerned with modern practice, is of great value for the period. CHARLES SEYMOUR, *Electoral Reform in England and Wales* (Yale and Oxford, 1915), is indispensable for the technical aspects of the representative system; HUGH FRASER, *The Law of Parliamentary Elections* (London, 1922), summarizes legislation dealing with corruption, and NORMAN GASH, *Politics in the Age of Peel* (London, 1953), is the first considerable effort to penetrate the realities of representation. J. KITSON CLARK, "The Politics of the Forties: the Electorate and the Repeal of the Corn Laws", in *Transactions of the Royal Historical Society, Fifth Series*, vol. I (1951), gives instances in which it worked more effectively than used to be supposed. DOD's *Parliamentary Companion*, published annually from 1833, gives personal information about members, and J. A. THOMAS, *The House of Commons 1832–1901* (Cardiff, 1947), H. R. G. GREAVES, "The Personal Origins and Interrelations of House of Parliament since 1832", in *Economica*, vol. IX (1929), and S. F. WOOLLEY, "The Personnel of the Parliament of 1833", in *English Historical Review*, vol. LIII (1938), discuss the economic and social affiliations of members. J. A. THOMAS, "The Repeal of the Corn Laws", in *Economica*, vol. IX (1929), analyses the voting in the light of the 'interests' of members. OSTROGORSKI, *Democracy and the Organisation of Parties* (2 vols., London, 1902), is still suggestive on its subject; the beginnings of a more complete investigation of it are found in A. ASPINALL, "English Parliamentary Organisation in the Early Nineteenth Century", in *English Historical Review*, vol. XLI (1926); A. ASPINALL, *Three Early Nineteenth Century Diaries* (London, 1952); N. GASH, "F. R. Bonham, Conservative Political Secretary 1832–47", in *English Historical Review*, vol. LXIII (1948); J. A. THOMAS, "Registration and the Development of Political Parties", in *History*, vol. 35 (1950); N. GASH, "Peel and the Party System", in *Transactions of the Royal Historical Society, Fifth Series*, vol. I (1951); W. G. WILLIAMS, *The Rise of Gladstone to the Leadership of the Liberal Party* (London, 1934); and A. F. THOMPSON, "Gladstone's Whips and the Election of 1868", in *English Historical Review*, vol. LXIII (1948). J. K. BUCKLEY, *Joseph Parkes of Birmingham* (London, 1926), records the life of one who played an important part as a political agent. H. JEPHSON, *The Platform; its Rise and Progress* (London, 1892), is still of primary importance. A. TEMPLE PATTERSON, *Radical Leicester, 1780–1850* (Leicester, 1954), pioneers in a field in which there is a great deal to be done. LORD JOHN RUSSELL, *Essay on the History of the English Government and Constitution*, 2nd edn. (London, 1865), EARL GREY, *Parliamentary Reform* (London, 1858), and WALTER BAGEHOT, *Parliamentary Reform* (London, 1883), give contemporary views of the function and working of Parliament; C. S. EMDEN, *The People and the Constitution*

(Oxford, 1930), and H. J. LASKI, *Parliamentary Government* (London, 1938), discuss similar topics from a more modern standpoint. G. F. M. CAMPION, *Introduction to the Procedure of the House of Commons* (London, 1929), J. REDLICH, *Parliamentary Procedure* (3 vols., translated London, 1908), and T. ERSKINE MAY, *Parliamentary Practice*, ed. CAMPION (London, 1946), are leading authorities, and F. CLIFFORD, *History of Private Bill Legislation* (2 vols., London, 1887), and C. ORLO WILLIAMS, *Private Bill Legislation* (2 vols., London, 1948), deal with a side of parliamentary procedure particularly important for social and economic history.

On the privilege of parliamentary printing, the various actions arising from Stockdale *v.* Hansard are reported in *State Trials, New Series*, vol. III (8 vols., London, 1888–1898). The *Report of the Select Committee on Printed Papers* (*Parlty. Papers*, 1839/XII) should also be seen, and the debates be consulted.

On the relations between Lords and Commons the debates should be consulted. On those in the 'thirties, G. KITSON CLARK, *Peel and the Conservative Party 1832–41* (London, 1929), provides an interpretation and guide. Those on the Second Reading of the Corn Law Repeal Bill in the Lords in 1846, on the Wensleydale Peerage Case in the Lords in 1856, in both Lords and Commons on the Paper Duty Controversy of 1860, and again in both Houses on the Irish Church Bill of 1869, are particularly illuminating. The Report of the Lords Committee on Privileges in the Wensleydale Case is 5/HLC/958. L. O. PIKE, *Constitutional History of the House of Lords* (London, 1894), and, especially, EMILY ALLYN, *Lords* v. *Commons 1830–1930* (New York, 1931), are valuable discussions.

DONALD READ, *Press and People 1790–1851* (1961) deals with the newspapers of the industrial towns; J. B. CONAGHER, *The Aberdeen Coalition 1852–55*; JOHN VINCENT, *The Formation of the Liberal Party 1857–68* (1966), studies the movements of popular opinion; DONALD SOUTHGATE, *The Passing of the Whigs 1832–1866* (1962); F. B. SMITH, *The Making of the Second Reform Bill* (1966); M. COWLING, *Disraeli, Gladstone and Revolution* (1968) new studies of the political crises of 1866 and 1867 which complement each other; H. J. HANHAM, *Elections and Party Management: Politics in the Time of Disraeli and Gladstone* (1959); REYDEN HARRISON, *Before the Socialists – Studies in Labour and Politics 1861–1881* (1965); W. D. GWYNN, *Democracy and the cost of Politics in Britain* (1962); A. L. KENNEDY, *My Dear Duchess, Letters to Duchess of Manchester 1858–1869, mainly from Lord Clarendon*; W. A. MUMFORD, *William Ewart, M.P.* (1960); Articles F. L. M. THOMPSON, *Land and Politics in Nineteenth Century England*, Tr.R.Hist.Soc. 5/xv, 1965; J. M. PREST, *Gladstone and Russell*, Tr.R.Hist.Soc. 5/xvi, 1966.

PARLIAMENT

52. The Tamworth Manifesto (January 1835)

Peel, *Memoirs*. II, 1857, pp. 58–67.

To the Electors of the Borough of Tamworth.
Gentlemen,

On the 26th. of November last, being then at Rome, I received from His Majesty a summons, wholly unforeseen and unexpected by me, to return to England without delay, for the purpose of assisting His Majesty in the formation of a new Government. I instantly obeyed the command for my return; and on my arrival, I did not hesitate, after an anxious review of the position of public affairs, to place at the disposal of my Sovereign any services which I might be thought capable of rendering.

My acceptance of the first office in the Government terminates, for the present, my political connection with you. In seeking the renewal of it, whenever you shall be called upon to perform the duty of electing a representative in Parliament, I feel it incumbent on me to enter into a declaration of my views of public policy, as full and unreserved as I can make it, consistently with my duty as a Minister of the Crown.

You are entitled to this, from the nature of the trust which I again solicit, from the long habits of friendly intercourse in which we have lived, and from your tried adherence to me in times of difficulty, when the demonstration of unabated confidence was of peculiar value. I gladly avail myself also of this, a legitimate opportunity, of making a more public appeal–of addressing myself, through you, to that great and intelligent class of society of which you are a portion, and a fair and unexceptionable representative–to that class which is much less interested in the contentions of party, than in the maintenance of order and the cause of good government, that frank exposition of general principles and views which appears to be anxiously expected, and which it ought not to be the inclination, and cannot be the interest, of a Minister of this country to withhold.

Gentlemen, the arduous duties in which I am engaged have been imposed on me through no act of mine. Whether they were an object of ambition coveted by me–whether I regard the power and distinction they confer as of any sufficient compensation for the heavy sacrifices they involve–are matters of mere personal concern, on which I will not waste a word. The King, in a crisis of great difficulty, required my services. The question I had to decide was this–Shall I obey the call? or shall I shrink from the responsibility, alleging as the reason, that I consider myself, in consequence of the Reform Bill, as labouring under a sort of moral disqualification, which must preclude me, and all who think with me, both now and for ever, from entering into the official service of the Crown? Would it, I ask, be becoming in any public man to act upon such a principle? Was it fit that I should assume that either the object or the effect of the Reform Bill has been to preclude all hope of a successful appeal to the good sense and calm judgment of the people, and so fetter the prerogative of the Crown, that the King has no free choice among his subjects, but must select his Ministers from one section, and from one section only, of public men?

I have taken another course, but I have not taken it without deep and anxious consideration as to the probability that my opinions are so far in unison with those of the constituent body of the United Kingdom as to enable me, and those with whom I am about to act, and whose sentiments are in entire concurrence with my own, to establish such a claim upon public confidence as shall enable us to conduct with vigour and success the Government of this country.

I have the firmest convictions that that confidence cannot be secured by any other course than that of a frank and explicit declaration of principle; that vague and unmeaning professions of popular opinion may quiet distrust for a time, may influence this or that election; but that such professions must ultimately and signally fail, if, being made, they are not adhered to, or if they are inconsistent with the honour and character of those who made them.

Now I say at once that I will not accept power on the condition of declaring myself an apostate from the principles on which I have heretofore acted. At the same time, I never will admit that I have been, either before or after the Reform Bill, the defender of abuses, or the enemy of judicious reforms. I appeal with confidence in denial of the charge, to the active part I took in the great question of the Currency–in the consolidation and amendment of the Criminal Law–in the revisal of the whole system of Trial by Jury–to the opinions I have professed, and uniformly acted on, with regard to other branches of the jurisprudence of the country–I appeal to this as a proof that I have not been disposed to acquiesce in acknowledged evils, either from the mere superstitious reverence for ancient usages, or from the dread of labour or responsibility in the application of a remedy.

But the Reform Bill, it is said, constitutes a new era, and it is the duty of a Minister to declare explicitly–first, whether he will maintain the Bill itself, secondly whether he will act on the spirit in which it was conceived.

With respect to the Reform Bill itself, I will repeat now the declaration I made when I entered the House of Commons as a Member of the Reformed Parliament –that I consider the Reform Bill a final and irrevocable settlement of a great Constitutional question–a settlement which no friend to the peace and welfare of this country would attempt to disturb, either by direct or by insidious means.

Then, as to the spirit of the Reform Bill, and the willingness to adopt and enforce it as a rule of government: if, by adopting the spirit of the Reform Bill, it be meant that we are to live in a perpetual vortex of agitation; that public men can only support themselves in public estimation by adopting every popular impression of the day,–by promising the instant redress of anything which anybody may call an abuse–by abandoning altogether that great aid of government–more powerful than either law or reason–the respect for ancient rights, and the deference to prescriptive authority; if this be the spirit of the Reform Bill, I will not undertake to adopt it. But if the spirit of the Reform Bill implies merely a careful review of institutions, civil and ecclesiastical, undertaken in a friendly temper, combining, with the firm maintenance of established rights, the correction of proved abuses and the redress of real grievances,

–in that case, I can for myself and colleagues undertake to act in such a spirit and with such intentions.

Such declarations of general principle are, I am aware, necessarily vague: but in order to be more explicit, I will endeavour to apply them practically to some of those questions which have of late attracted the greater share of public interest and attention.

I take first the inquiry into Municipal Corporations:

It is not my intention to advise the Crown to interrupt the process of that inquiry, nor to transfer the conduct of it from those to whom it was committed by the late Government. For myself, I gave the best proof that I was not unfriendly to the principle of inquiry, by consenting to be a member of that Committee of the House of Commons on which it was originally devolved. No report has yet been made by the Commissioners to whom the inquiry was afterwards referred: and until that report be made, I cannot be expected to give, on the part of the Government, any other pledge than that they will bestow on the suggestions it may contain, and the evidence on which they may be founded, a full and unprejudiced consideration.

I will, in the next place, address myself to the questions in which those of our fellow-countrymen who dissent from the doctrines of the Established Church take an especial interest.

Instead of making new professions, I will refer to the course which I took upon those subjects when out of power.

In the first place I supported the measure brought forward by Lord Althorp, the object of which was to exempt all classes from the payment of Church-rates, applying in lieu thereof, out of a branch of the revenue, a certain sum for the building and repair of churches. I never expressed, nor did I entertain, the slightest objection to the principle of a bill of which Lord John Russell was the author, intended to relieve the conscientious scruples of Dissenters in respect to the ceremony of marriage. I give no opinion now on the particular measures themselves: they were proposed by Ministers in whom the Dissenters had confidence; they were intended to give relief; and it is sufficient for my present purposes to state that I supported them.

I opposed–and I am bound to state that my opinions in that respect have undergone no change–the admission of Dissenters as a claim of right, into the universities; but I expressly declared that if regulations, enforced by public authorities superintending the professions of law and medicine, and the studies connected with them, had the effect of conferring advantages of the nature of civil privileges on one class of the King's subjects from which another was excluded–those regulations ought to undergo modification, with the view of placing all the King's subjects, whatever their religious creeds, upon a footing of perfect equality with respect to any civil privilege.

I appeal to the course which I pursued on those several questions, when office must have been out of contemplation; and I ask, with confidence, does that course imply that I was actuated by any illiberal or intolerant spirit towards the Dissenting body, or by an unwillingness to consider fairly the redress of any real grievances?

In the examination of other questions which excited the public interest, I will not omit the Pension List. I resisted–and, with the opinions I entertain I should again resist–a retrospective inquiry into pensions granted by the Crown at a time when the discretion of the Crown was neither fettered by law nor by the expression of any opinion on the part of the House of Commons; but I voted for the Resolution, moved by Lord Althorp, that pensions on the Civil List ought, for the future, to be confined to such persons only as have just claims to the Royal beneficence, or are entitled to consideration on account either of their personal services to the Crown, or of performance of duties to the public, or their scientific or literary eminence. On the Resolution which I thus supported as a private Member of Parliament, I shall scrupulously act as a Minister of the Crown, and shall advise the grant of no pension which is not in conformity with the spirit and intention of the vote to which I was a party.

Then, as to the great question of Church Reform. On that head I have no new professions to make. I cannot give my consent to the alienating of Church property, in any part of the United Kingdom, from strictly ecclesiastical purposes. But I repeat now the opinions that I have already expressed in Parliament in regard to the Church Establishment in Ireland–that if, by an improved distribution of the revenues of the Church, its just influence can be extended, and the true interests of the Established religion promoted, all other considerations should be made subordinate to the advancement of objects of such paramount importance.

As to Church property in this country, no person has expressed a more earnest wish than I have done that the question of tithe, complicated and difficult as I acknowledge it to be, should, if possible, be satisfactorily settled by means of a commutation, founded upon just principles, and proposed after mature consideration.

With regard to alterations in the laws which govern our Ecclesiastical Establishment, I have had no recent opportunity of giving that grave consideration to a subject of the deepest interest, which could alone justify me in making any public declaration of opinion. It is a subject which must undergo the fullest deliberation, and into that deliberation the Government will enter, with the sincerest desire to remove every abuse that can impair the efficiency of the Establishment, to extend the sphere of its usefulness, and to strengthen and confirm its just claims upon the respect and affection of the people.

It is unnecessary for my purpose to enter into any further details. I have said enough, with respect to general principles and their practical application to public measures, to indicate the spirit in which the King's Government is prepared to act. Our object will be–the maintenance of peace–the scrupulous and honourable fulfilment, without reference to their original policy, of all existing engagements with Foreign Powers–the support of public credit–the enforcement of strict economy–the just and impartial consideration of what is due to all interests–agricultural, manufacturing, and commercial.

Whatever may be the issue of the undertaking in which I am engaged, I feel assured that you will mark, by a renewal of your confidence, your approbation of the course I have pursued in accepting office. I enter upon the arduous duties assigned to me with the deepest sense of the responsibilities they involve, with great distrust of my own qualifications for their adequate discharge, but at the same time with a resolution to persevere, which nothing could inspire but the strong impulse of public duty, the consciousness of upright motives, and the firm belief that the people of this country will so far maintain the prerogative of the King, as to give to the Ministers of his choice, not an implicit confidence, but a fair trial.

I am, Gentlemen,
With affectionate regard,
Most faithfully yours,
Robert Peel.

53. Letter from Lord John Russell to Lord Melbourne, suggesting the creation of Whig peers (5 June 1836)

S. Walpole, *Lord John Russell*, 1889, I, pp. 266–267.

Important as indicating what were considered to be the relations between Lords and Commons.

I beg to call the attention of the Cabinet to the position in which the present conduct of the House of Lords may place the Ministry and the country. It is evident that a majority of that House are combined, not to stop or alter a particular measure, but to stop or alter all measures which may not be agreeable to the most powerful, or, in other words, the most violent, among their own body. Both the Tories and the Radicals have the advantage of a definite course with respect to this state of things. The Tories praise the wisdom of the Lords, and wish to maintain their power undiminished. The Radicals complain of a mischievous obstacle to good government, and propose an elective House of Lords. The Ministers stand in the position of confessing the evil and not consenting to the remedy. The influence of public opinion is, indeed, to be looked to as some check to the House of Lords; but, on Irish questions, it is a very imperfect one. It is certainly possible to wait till the beginning of next session before any definite course is taken. But I own it appears to me better to take every opportunity of increasing the strength of the Liberal party in the House of Lords, than to begin a struggle against a majority such as that which the Tory Peers now possess. It is possible, nay probable, that, if the Tories could see a steady and gradual creation of peers to meet this obstinate resistance, they would be disposed to yield. Before the passing of the Reform Bill they were coerced by [the threat of] a large creation and by that alone. It appears to me, therefore, that this opportunity should be taken for the creation of eight, ten, or twelve peers, and that the Ministry be prepared to advise a similar creation whenever it is *provoked*.

54. Lord John Russell's 'Finality' speech, in the House of Commons (20 November 1837)

Hansard, 3/XXXIX/68–71.

This speech was made on the Address at the meeting of Queen Victoria's first Parliament, and was in reply to amendments proposed by Thomas Wakley, Radical M.P. for Finsbury, in favour of the extension of the suffrage, the introduction of the ballot, and the repeal of the Septennial Act.

. . . The hon. Member[1] who moved the amendment has brought forward questions which have also been dwelt upon by other Members, and he has asked me whether I will support them. He has mentioned the question of the ballot–he has mentioned the question of the extension of the suffrage, and the question of triennial

[1] Wakley, Member for Finsbury.

parliaments. These he has brought forward in three separate amendments, all forming parts of the same measure. He has put his powders into three separate papers, as portions of the same medicine. I am not going now to enter into the reasons and arguments with which each of these measures may be supported or opposed, – I will not enter into the discussions of the question generally, but I am bound to give some explanation of my views with regard to the Reform Act in relation to my present position. I cannot conceal the disadvantages and the injuries to which the Reform Act is subject. I admit that at the late elections corruption and intimidation prevailed to a very lamentable extent. I admit that some parts of the Reform Act are the means of making it a source of great vexation to the real and *bona fide* voter. I admit that with respect to the registration of voters in particular, great amendments may be made. But these are questions upon which I consider Parliament should always feel bound to be alive and attentive to see that the Act suffers no essential injury, and that any errors in the details which might be made in the commencement might be afterwards remedied. But these are questions which are totally different from those now brought forward, such as the question of the ballot, the extension of the suffrage, and triennial parliaments, which are, taken together, nothing else, but a repeal of the Reform Act, and placing the representation on a different footing. Am I then prepared to do this? I say certainly not. With respect to the question of the registration, I am ready to bring forward some measures to amend it, or rather my hon. and learned Friend, the Attorney General, will bring forward such a measure. The matter has been frequently under discussion in this House. I proposed some amendments myself last year, and if any further facilities can be given by me I shall feel it my duty to afford them, and more particularly upon the subject on which I introduced the Bill of last year, namely, the payment of rates. But I do say that having now only five years ago reformed the representation, having placed it on a new basis, it would be a most unwise and unsound experiment now to begin the process again, to form a new suffrage, to make an alteration in the manner of voting, and to look for other and new securities for the representation of the people. I say at least for myself, that I can take no share in such an experiment, though I may be, and indeed must be, liable to the somewhat harsh term of the hon. Member for Kilkenny.[1] I must explain, however, in what sense I consider myself bound with regard to the Reform Act. When I brought forward that measure it will be recollected that the cry was that it was too large, that it was too extensive; and those who were Radical Reformers were upon the whole much better pleased with it than those who were moderate Reformers. But it was the opinion of Earl Grey, an opinion stated by him in the House of Lords, and an opinion stated repeatedly by Lord Althorp in the House of Commons, that it was safer to make a large and extensive measure of reform, than a small measure of reform, for this reason, that in bringing forward the extensive measure we might be assured that we were bringing forward one which might have a prospect of being a final measure. Do I then say that the measure is in all respects final? I say no such nonsense. Do I say that the people of England are deprived of the right of re-considering the provisions of that Act? I say no such folly. I maintain that the people of England are fully

[1] Joseph Hume.

entitled to do so, if to the people of England it shall so seem fit. But I am not myself going to do so. I think that the entering again into this question of the construction of the representation so soon would destroy the stability of our institutions. It is quite impossible for me, having been one who brought forward the measure of reform, who feel bound by the declarations then made, to take any part in these large measures of reconstruction, or to consent to the repeal of the Reform Act, without being guilty of what I think would be a breach of faith towards those with whom I was then acting. If the people of England are not of that mind they may reject me. They can prevent me from taking part either in the Legislature or in the councils of the Sovereign; they can place others there who may have wider and more extended, more enlarged, and enlightened views, but they must not expect me to entertain these views. They may place others in my situation, but they must not call upon me to do that which I do not only consider unwise, but which I should not feel myself justified, without a breach of faith and honour, in proposing. The hon. Member who moved the amendment has asked, among other questions, whether a coalition is intended? I am sure I can only say I know nothing of such a coalition; I have no such intention, and I know nothing of any such being intended. This is the only answer I can give. . . .

55. Election compromises in 1841

Select Committee of 1842 on Election Proceedings, *Parlty. Papers*, 1842/v.

The boroughs reported on were Bridport, Reading, Harwich, Falmouth, Nottingham, and Lewes. The passages printed are from the general report, and the report on Nottingham. The chairman of the committee was J. A. Roebuck.

. . . It appears by the concurrent testimony of witnesses most experienced in Election proceedings, that the two last Acts relating to the trial of Election Petitions, the one introduced by Sir Robert Peel, constituting an improved tribunal, the 4 & 5 of Vict. c. 58, the other by Lord John Russell, 4 & 5 of Vict. c. 57, enabling Committees to inquire into the general charge of Bribery, without the preliminary proof of agency, together with the greater stringency of the decisions of these Committees in charges of Bribery, directly led in many instances to Compromises between parties prosecuting or defending their individual rights, by which charges of gross Bribery and Corruption were entirely withdrawn from further investigation. These Compromises becoming matter of general notoriety were brought under the notice of The House by the Chairman of Your Committee.

Your Committee desire to call the attention of The House to a part of the law of Elections, which appears unsettled, if not defective. Two parties at an Election, both being equally guilty of Bribery, but one successful on the poll, and the other defeated, may experience a very different fate in consequence of the present state of the law. If the defeated candidate present a petition against the return of his successful opponent, and simply pray that the Election may be adjudged to be a void Election on the ground of Bribery and Corruption, but do not ask for the seat, he may unseat his opponent, and render him incapable of being again returned; but as he himself does not pray for the seat, it has in some instances been determined that a case of retaliation cannot be entered into as respects the Petitioner by the sitting Member.

Thus the Petitioner, though equally guilty, may again propose himself and be returned in consequence of the very Bribery practised at the preceding Election, and into which no inquiry was permitted. . . .

Your Committee also found that, in the case of

NOTTINGHAM,

at the last General Election, the Right honourable Sir John Cam Hobhouse and Sir George Larpent were returned as duly elected Members for that town; Mr. John Walter and Mr. Charlton being the opposing candidates.

That in consequence of the retirement of Mr. Walter and Mr. Charlton early on the day of the poll, a few only of the electors gave their votes. The state of the poll was as follows:–

Sir John Cam Hobhouse . . .	527
Sir George Larpent	529
Mr. Walter	144
Mr. Charlton	142

That two petitions were presented against the return of Sir John Cam Hobhouse and Sir George Larpent, by electors, on behalf of Mr. Walter. These two petitions, among other things, charged, in various forms, that Bribery, Corruption, Treating, Abduction of Voters, Riot, &c., had been practised at the Election by the sitting Members and their agents.

A third petition of electors was also presented, but this petition seems to have been presented by persons in the interest of the sitting Members, and apparently the object in view was to give, if possible, to the sitting Members, an opportunity of making a counter case against the petitioners. The two first-mentioned petitions prayed only that the Election should be declared void. It was apprehended that on the trial of such petitions no defence by way of retaliation would have been allowed: the third petition, therefore, seems to have been presented in order to let in such evidence. –(See Appendix B.)

That after the appointment of a Committee to try the case of the said Election, but before the trial thereof, a Compromise was entered into between the agents of Sir John Cam Hobhouse and Sir George Larpent, on the one part, and an agent, who signed as agent of the petitioners against the return, and of Mr. Walter, the defeated candidate, on the other.

The terms of this arrangement are set forth in a written agreement, as follows:–

Memorandum.–London, 4 May 1842.

NOTTINGHAM ELECTION PETITIONS.

It is expedient to settle the petitions now pending, and it is agreed that–

1. All the petitions shall be abandoned.

2. Within four days from this day, one seat shall be vacated.

3. The sum of One thousand pounds to be paid to Messrs. Clarke, Fynmore and Fladgate, within Seven days from this date, in consideration of the expenses incurred in the petition.

4. It is understood that Mr. Walter is to be returned at the election resulting from the above-mentioned vacancy; for security whereof, it is agreed that Lord Rancliffe, Mr. Wakefield, Mr. John Heard, Mr. Enfield, Mr. Biddle, Mr. Hurd, Mr. Birkin, Mr. Wells, Mr. Hart, Mr. Alfred Fellowes, Mr. Henry Leaver, Mr. Bean, Mr. Jonathan Burton, Mr. George Bacon and Mr. Aulton, shall not directly or indirectly oppose Mr. Walter at such an election, and that in addition Mr. Wakefield shall discourage all opposition on the part of the persons named in the list copied on the other side of this paper.

5. That a promissory note for Four thousand pounds, signed by Sir John Cam Hobhouse or Sir George G. De H. Larpent at one month from this date, shall be this day deposited with Messrs. Cocks, Biddulph & Co., bankers, London; and that James Bacon, esq., and Sutton Sharpe, esq., shall decide whether the above conditions have been honourably fulfilled; and if such referees (or, in case of their disagreement, an umpire appointed by them,) shall decide that such conditions have not been honourably fulfilled, then the promissory note in question shall be handed to Mr. Walter, or returned to Sir John Cam Hobhouse or Sir George G. de H. Larpent if such conditions have been honourably fulfilled.

The circumstances which induced the agents of the sitting Members to enter into this agreement are stated to have been, –

1. The fear that both sitting Members would have been unseated for Bribery and Treating, committed by their agents.

2. And also the dread of the enormous expense that must necessarily have been incurred, with small hopes of success.

That the number of electors were about 5,400.

That the sum expended in the election on the part of Sir John Cam Hobhouse and Sir George Larpent was £.12,000.

Of this sum a very large part was expended in an illegal manner; some in direct Bribery – some in Treating, and other unlawful proceedings – without the personal cognizance of the candidates. – *See* the whole evidence of Mr. Charles Parkes, Mr. Thomas Wakefield, as well as that of Mr. Fladgate.

The expenditure on the part of the opposing candidates appears to have been about £.4,000 or £.5,000.

The expense was thus comparatively small, because the poll was not taken, and it is stated that the Bribery of the voters and other illegal practises in this interest were thus rendered unnecessary. It is clear that the system on the one side and the other was the same, which system arose in some of the preceding Elections, and was particularly developed at that of April 1841.

56. Report of commissioners on bribery at Sudbury (1841)

Parlty. Papers, 1844/XVIII.

The allegations of bribery in the 1841 election at Sudbury led to an adverse report of the Election Committee, and to a Bill for the disfranchisement of the constituency, which passed the Commons in 1842, but lapsed at the end of the session in the Lords. It was revived in the following session, and again passed the Commons, but was lost in the Lords because the evidence forthcoming before the Lords was not sufficient to substantiate the charges of bribery contained in the Bill. In face of the threat of disfranchisement, the townsmen had refused to repeat before the Lords the evidence they had been ready enough to give before the Commons Committee, when the issue had appeared to be only that of invalidating the election. The Commons therefore set up a fresh committee to report on the situation, and on the basis of its findings passed a Bill to send commissioners down to Sudbury itself, to investigate what had happened at the election. The Lords agreed, and the passage printed is the more important part of the Commissioners' Report. On its publication the Bill for the disfranchisement of the borough was revived, and, after the defeat of an amendment to throw the borough into the Hundred of Bramber, was passed. A similar procedure was followed in the St. Albans case, and the Act of 1852[1] provided for its application in future cases.

. . . A short statement of the difficulties attending the investigation may be considered a proper introduction, and an essential part of our Report; and we regret to report to Your Majesty, in the first instance, that in the prosecution of the inquiry, we received no assistance from the electors or other inhabitants of the borough. Not only was no disposition manifested on their part to assist in carrying out the object and intent of the Legislature in appointing such a Commission, but there appeared on all sides a settled purpose to defeat that object, as far as it lay in their power, by preventing or discouraging such a disclosure of the practices which prevailed at the last election as would have enabled us to ascertain the precise extent of the bribery committed, and to report the names of all those persons who were guilty of giving or receiving money in the bargain and sale of votes which took place.

It appears from the recitals of the Act appointing the Sudbury Commission that "great difficulty hath been hitherto experienced in obtaining complete proof of the system of bribery believed to be practised and carried on there, by reason of the contrivance of certain parties more or less implicated in the same." At every stage of the inquiry we encountered the same difficulty, arising from the same cause.

One of the contrivances for rendering a complete proof more difficult, if not altogether impracticable, was this:–Three strangers were sent down to the borough, to carry into execution a system of bribery adopted by one of the parties. These strangers left a few hours after the election, and have never been seen there since; indeed it was admitted that any subsequent communication with them would have defeated the object of their mission. Their names and residence are equally unknown to the inhabitants; and after the most diligent inquiry we could obtain no clue to any of them.

From the secrecy with which bribery is generally conducted, the knowledge of specific acts is usually confined to the person giving and the person receiving a bribe; and where the persons giving and receiving are both equally privileged in refusing to make those disclosures which they alone can make, a complete proof of their guilt can hardly be expected.

In anticipation of the difficulties that were likely to arise from this privilege of guilt, the Legislature had invited disclosures by an offer of Indemnity to all those witnesses who made "a true discovery, to the best of his or her knowledge, touching all things to which he or she should be so examined;" but it will be seen in the course of the Report that this clause of the Act was rendered almost nugatory by a Special Provision, "that no person should be compellable to answer any question, or to produce any book, paper, deed, or writing, the answer to which, or the production

[1] No. 59.

of which, might criminate, or tend to criminate such person, or to expose such person to any pains or penalties."

The common law privilege of the witness being thus extended to all answers which might have a tendency to criminate, and the choice being left to himself whether he would confess his guilt, secure from penal consequences, or refuse to make a true discovery, and thereby co-operate in defeating the object of the inquiry, he chose the latter course. The indemnity was rejected, while the privilege was almost universally claimed.

The protection of those Burgesses who might be criminated by their answers was an object of solicitude with the municipal authorities of the borough. At the commencement of the inquiry, the Town Clerk wished to know, on behalf of the Corporation, "whether each individual witness was to have the protection of counsel; inasmuch," he observed, "as there might be many questions which it might not be proper for them to answer, particularly with regard to the lower grade of witness." The Commissioners informed him that, even if counsel did appear, the objection must proceed from the witness himself; that they would protect the witnesses, and, in their opinion, it was not necessary to have counsel for that purpose. The burgesses, however, did not require to be reminded by us of their privilege. The proviso of the Act was exhibited in a shop-window in the market-place from the time of our arrival in the borough. This was done by a tradesman, "for the benefit," he said, "of the freemen." "I put it there to show the freemen that they might not answer the questions without they pleased."

The first witness we examined, one of the most active agents at the election, had given material evidence before the House of Lords in support of the Disfranchisement Bill. When examined before us, he referred to the Proviso, and refused to answer any questions relating to the same matters. On a subsequent day, indeed, he withdrew this refusal, and expressed his readiness to answer; but the example he had set was generally followed, and continued to be so throughout the inquiry. The tradesmen and publicans of the town who were implicated in acts of bribery, one and all asserted their privilege and refused to make any disclosures.

These refusals by a large body of witnesses created the first and chief difficulty in the conduct of the inquiry. But this was not the only one; for almost all the evidence relating to the bribery, and to the persons engaged in it, was extracted from unwilling witnesses.

Professional agents endeavoured to shelter themselves under professional privilege, extending it so far beyond its legal limits as to include not only matters of confidential communication, but all acts arising out of such communications, however illegal those acts might be. Even where the privilege had been waived by his clients, it was urged and reluctantly abandoned by one of the leading agents, while another was compelled to admit, when a similar claim was overruled, that he was himself so far implicated in the scheme of bribery which was laid open, that he could not answer the questions proposed without criminating himself, or making disclosures which might have that tendency.

Where privilege could not be claimed, or had been claimed and disallowed, the answers were generally disingenuous and evasive, often contradictory, seldom fairly disclosing the whole truth. Knowledge was denied against all probability, and there was no recollection of matters which, in the ordinary course of affairs, and with the ordinary powers of memory, could scarcely be forgotten.

A merchant in the borough, who had himself urged the necessity of bribery, and had obtained at three successive periods of the polling large sums of money for that purpose, professed not to know what became of the money. He 'presumed' that it was distributed among the electors; it was only "probable or feasible to suppose" that it was so distributed; but he did not know by whom, nor could he name any of the electors who received it.

One of the professional agents, who had issued tickets during the election to a large body of voters, did not know the use and purport of the tickets he had issued, though they were known to other persons who were assisting him in the same room. He could remember the names of eighty persons to whom he had not given a ticket, but he could not remember the name of a single individual to whom he had given one.

Another agent of the same party had made out lists of the unpolled voters, who were supposed to be holding back for a higher bribe, and these lists he had delivered to certain active partizans; but he could not remember the names he had set down in the lists, nor any of the persons to whom he delivered them. The same witness had been retained as the legal adviser of one of the strangers before-mentioned, and had, during the polling, referred to his client certain voters who were open to bribes. He 'imagined' that his client would see them with a view to the purchase of their votes; but this, he said, was "a mere supposition." He presumed that person had come down to make arrangements of that nature, but he knew nothing of the arrangements.

Even among the witnesses who had been examined before the Election Committee in support of the petition, several pretended to have lost all recollection of the facts they had then sworn to. One of them, in contradicting his former statements, alleged, as an excuse, that his recollection was confused when he was examined before the Committee. He had been employed at a public house, where a great deal of bribery was proved to have been committed, and where he was stationed for the purpose of keeping order among the voters; he could not distinguish a single voter. Another, who had given distinct evidence of bribery at this public house, and elsewhere, could recollect nothing about it; he could not remember whether he received money at the election, nor what he had stated in his former examination, "it was so long ago." When he was pressed upon the subject, he answered, "What is the use of my coming here when I am not positive;" the thing "is so long gone by." A third, who had also made a full confession before the Committee, could not recollect whether he had received any money or not, and when he at length reluctantly admitted that he had received £6, he said that he had not received it as a bribe. In his former examination, he had mentioned the names of certain persons he had seen at one of the inns where bribery was carried on. When reminded of this, he said, "I will not swear it now. I was sworn then and I spoke the truth–I will not swear it now." A fourth witness of the same class, who had admitted his own bribery before the Committee, refused to answer, on the ground that his answer might tend to criminate him, the ground of refusal being suggested to him by one of the agents.

The disclosures before the Election Committee had in fact been obtained for party purposes, and were made with a view to a fresh election. Those purposes had been accomplished by unseating the members returned, and, during the inquiry under the Commission, all party feeling was merged in one common desire to preserve the franchise, which was supposed to be endangered by the investigation.

57. Act for better discovery of bribery and corruption (1842)

Statutes of the Realm. 5 & 6 Vict. c. 102.

"Whereas it has become notorious that extensive Bribery prevails in many places in the Election of Members to serve in Parliament, and that the Laws now "in force are insufficient for the Discovery thereof; and it is expedient that further "Powers be given for that Purpose, and for collecting Evidence on which to found "further Proceedings in regard to Places in which Bribery shall be found to have "been generally or extensively practised;" be it enacted by the Queen's most Excellent Majesty, by and with the Advice and Consent of the Lords Spiritual and Temporal, and Commons, in this present Parliament assembled, and by the Authority of the same, That if after a Committee shall have been nominated for the Trial of an Election Petition, in which Bribery shall be charged to have been committed, the Petition shall be withdrawn, or the Charges of Bribery therein contained, or any other Charge of Bribery which shall have been made or stated before such Committee, whether in support of any Petition complaining of the Return, or by way of Recrimination, or in answer to any Petition, shall be withdrawn, abandoned, or not *bona fide* prosecuted before the said Committee, it shall and may be lawful for such Committee in its Discretion to examine into and ascertain the Circumstances under which such Withdrawal, Abandonment, or Forbearance to prosecute such Charges as aforesaid shall have taken place, and whether the same has been the Matter of Compromise, Arrangement, or Understanding, covert or otherwise; in order to avoid the Discovery of Bribery at the said Election; and the said Committee shall be authorized, if it shall think fit, to state in their Report upon the Election Petition any special Matter relating to the Cause and Reason of the Abandonment or Forbearance to prosecute the said Charges; and for more effectual Discovery of the Truth of the Matters so to be inquired into full Power and Authority is hereby given to such Committee to examine (as Witnesses subject to the ordinary Rules of Evidence) the Sitting Member or Members, or Candidate or Candidates at the said Election, and their several and respective Agents, and all other Persons whomsoever, touching and concerning such Withdrawal, Abandonment, or Forbearance to prosecute such Charges. . . .

20. "And whereas a Practice has prevailed in certain Boroughs and Places of "making Payments by or on behalf of Candidates to the Voters in such Manner "that Doubts have been entertained whether such Payments are to be deemed "Bribery;" be it declared and enacted, That the Payment or Gift of any Sum of Money, or other valuable Consideration whatsoever, to any Voter, before, during,

or after any Election, or to any Person on his behalf, or to any Person related to him by Kindred or Affinity, and which shall be so paid or given on account of such Voter having voted or having refrained from voting, or being about to vote or refrain from voting, at the said Election, whether the same shall have been paid or given under the Name of Head Money, or any other Name whatsoever, and whether such Payment shall have been in compliance with any Usage or Practice, or not, shall be deemed Bribery. . . .

22. "And whereas the Provisions of an Act passed in the Seventh Year of the "Reign of King *William* the Third, intituled *An Act for preventing Charges and Expences "in Elections of Members to serve in Parliament*, have been found insufficient to prevent "corrupt Treating at Elections, and it is expedient to extend such Provisions;" be it enacted, That every Candidate or Person elected to serve in Parliament for any County, Riding or Division of a County, or for any City, Borough, or District of Boroughs, who shall, from and after the passing of this Act, by himself, or by or with any Person, or in any Manner, directly or indirectly, give or provide, or cause or knowingly allow to be given or provided, wholly or partly at his Expense, or pay wholly or in part any Expenses incurred for any Meat, Drink, Entertainment, or Provision to or for any Person, at any Time, either before, during, or after any such Election, for the Purpose of corruptly rewarding such Person, or any other Person, for having given or refrained from giving his Vote at any such Election, shall be incapable of being elected or sitting in Parliament for that County, Riding or Division of a County, or for that City, Borough, or District of Boroughs, during the Parliament for which such Election shall be holden.

58. Speech of the duke of Wellington on the second reading of the Bill for the repeal of the Corn Laws, House of Lords (28 May 1846)

Hansard, III/LXXXVI/1401–5.

My Lords, I cannot allow this question for the second reading of this Bill to be put to your Lordships, without addressing to you a few words on the vote you are about to give. I am aware, my Lords, that I address you on this occasion under many disadvantages. I address your Lordships under the disadvantage of appearing here, as a Minister of the Crown, to press this measure upon your adoption, knowing at the same time how disagreeable it is to many of you with whom I have constantly acted in political life, with whom I have long lived in intimacy and friendship with the utmost satisfaction to myself–on whose good opinion I have ever relied, and, I am happy to say, whose good opinion it has been my fortune hitherto to have enjoyed in no small degree. My Lords, I have already in this House adverted to the circumstances which gave rise to this measure. My Lords, in the month of December last, I felt myself bound, by my duty to my Sovereign, not to withhold my assistance from the Government–not to decline to resume my seat in Her Majesty's Councils –not to refuse to give my assistance to the Government of my right hon. Friend (Sir R. Peel)–knowing as I did, at the time, that my right hon. Friend could not do otherwise than propose to Parliament a measure of this description–nay, more, my

Lords, this very measure–for this is the very measure which my right hon. Friend stated to the Cabinet prior to their resignation in the month I have referred to. My Lords, it is not necessary that I should say more upon that subject. I am aware that I address your Lordships at present with all your prejudices against me for having adopted the course I then took–a course which, however little I may be able to justify it to your Lordships, I considered myself bound to take, and which, if it was to be again adopted to-morrow, I should take again. I am in Her Majesty's service–bound to Her Majesty and to the Sovereigns of this country by considerations of gratitude of which it is not necessary that I should say more to your Lordships. It may be true, my Lords, and it is true, that in such circumstances I ought to have no relation with party, and that party ought not to rely upon me. Be it so, my Lords–be it so, if you think proper: I have stated to you the motives on which I have acted–I am satisfied with those motives myself–and I should be exceedingly concerned if any dissatisfaction respecting them remained in the mind of any of your Lordships. I am aware that I have never had any claim to the confidence which you have all reposed in me for a considerable number of years. Circumstances have given it to me; in some cases the confidence of the Crown, and, in others, the zeal with which I have endeavoured to serve your Lordships, to promote your Lordships' views, and my desire to facilitate your business in this House; and I shall lament the breaking up of that confidence in public life. But, my Lords, I will not omit, even on this night–probably the last on which I shall ever venture to address to you any advice again–I will not omit to give you my counsel with respect to the vote you ought to give on this occasion. My noble Friend (Lord Stanley), whose absence on this occasion I much lament, urged you, and in the strongest manner, to vote against this measure; and he told you, in terms which I cannot attempt to imitate, that it was your duty to step in and protect the people of this country from rash and inconsiderate measures passed by the other House of Parliament, and which, in his opinion, were inconsistent with the views and opinions of the people themselves. My Lords, there is no doubt whatever that it is your duty to consider all the measures which are brought before you, and that it is your right to vote in regard to those measures as you think proper; and, most particularly, it is your duty to vote against those that appear to be rash and inconsiderate; but, my Lords, I beg leave to point out to your Lordships that it is also your duty to consider well the consequences of any vote you give on any subject–to consider well the situation in which you place this House–nay, my Lords, that it is the duty of every one of you to place himself in the situation of this House, to ponder well the consequences of his vote, and all the circumstances attending it, and the situation I repeat, in which this House would be placed if it should adopt the vote which he himself is about to give. This, indeed, has been the line of conduct pursued by this House before. I myself once prevailed upon this House to vote for a measure on which it had pronounced positive opinions by former votes; and persuaded it subsequently to take a course different from that which it had pursued on previous occasions, upon the same subject. My Lords, I now ask you to look a little at the measure in respect of which you are going to give your votes this night–to look at the way in which it comes before you, and to consider the consequences likely to follow your rejection–if you do reject it–of this Bill. This measure, my Lords, was recommended by the Speech from the Throne, and it has been passed by a majority of the House of Commons, consisting of more than half the Members of that House. But my noble Friend said that that vote is inconsistent with the original vote given by the same House of Commons on this same question, and inconsistent with the supposed views of the constituents by whom they were elected. But, my Lords, I think that is not a subject which this House can take into its consideration–for, first, we can have no accurate knowledge of the fact; and, secondly, whether it be the fact or not, this we know, that it is the House of Commons from which this Bill comes to us. We know by the Votes that it has been passed by a majority of the House of Commons; we know that is recommended by the Crown; and we know that, if we should reject this Bill, it is a Bill which has been agreed to by the other two branches of the Legislature; and that the House of Lords stands alone in rejecting this measure. Now that, my Lords, is a situation in which I beg to remind your Lordships, I have frequently stated you ought not to stand; it is a position in which you cannot stand, because you are entirely powerless; without the House of Commons and the Crown, the House of Lords can do nothing. You have vast influence on public opinion; you may have great confidence in your own principles; but without the Crown or the House of Commons you can do nothing–till the connexion with the Crown and the House of Commons is revived, there is an end of the functions of the House of Lords. But I will take your Lordships a step further, and let you see what will be the immediate consequences of rejecting this Bill. It appears very clear, that whatever may be the result of this Bill in this House, the object I had in view in resuming my seat in Her Majesty's Councils will not be attained. I conclude that another Government will be formed; but whether another government is formed or not, let me ask, do your Lordships suppose that you will not have this very same measure brought before you by the next Administration which can be formed? And do your Lordships mean to reject the measure a second time? Do you mean the country to go on in the discussion of this measure two or three months longer? But the object of the noble Duke and of the noble Lords who have addressed the House against this Bill is, that Parliament should be dissolved–that the country should have the opportunity of considering the question, and of returning other representatives; and that it may be seen whether or not the new House of Commons would agree to this measure or not. Now, really if your Lordships have so much confidence, as you appear to have, in the result of other elections, and in the exercise of public opinion on this question, I think that you might venture to rely upon the elections which must occur, according to the common course of law, in the course of a twelvemonth from this time; and that you might leave it to the Parliament thus elected to consider the course which it will take on the expiration of the term of the Bill now before you; for that Bill is to last only till the year 1849. I think your Lordships might trust to that Parliament to take the matter into consideration at that time, without interfering with the prerogative of the Crown, by compelling the Queen to dissolve Parliament as the immediate consequence of the rejection of the present measure. Your Lordships, therefore, have now the option of immediately accepting this Bill, reserving it to another Parliament to pass or reject it again, if again the question should be brought forward, or of rejecting the Bill now, and obtaining a fresh election, of which you are so desirous: your Lordships have that choice–you may reject the Bill now, or you may appeal again to the new Parliament to confirm or reject it, at the time when its operation will cease, in the year 1849.

59. Act for more effectual inquiry into corrupt practices (1852)

Statutes of the Realm, 15 & 16 Vict. c. 57.

I. Where by a joint Address of both Houses of Parliament it shall be represented to Her Majesty that a Committee of the House of Commons appointed to try an Election Petition, or a Committee of that House appointed to inquire into the Existence of corrupt Practices in any Election or Elections of a Member or Members to serve in Parliament, have reported to the House that corrupt Practices have, or that there is reason to believe that corrupt Practices have, extensively prevailed in any County, Division of a County, City, Borough, University, or Place in the United Kingdom electing or sharing in the Election of a Member or Members to serve in Parliament, at any Election or Elections of such Members or Member, and the said Houses shall thereupon pray Her Majesty to cause Inquiry to be made under this Act, by Persons named in such Address, such Persons being (where the Inquiry to be made relates to a Place in *England* or *Ireland*) Barristers-at-Law of not less than Seven Years Standing, or (where such Inquiry relates to a Place in *Scotland*) Advocates, of not less than Seven Years Standing, and not being Members of Parliament, or holding any Office or Place of Profit under the Crown, other than that of a Recorder of any City or Borough, it shall be lawful for Her Majesty, by Warrant under Her Royal Sign Manual, to appoint the said Persons to be Commissioners for the Purpose of making Inquiry into the Existence of such corrupt Practices; and in case any of the Commissioners so appointed die, resign, or become incapable to act, it shall be lawful for the surviving or continuing Commissioners or Commissioner to act in such Inquiry as if they or he had been solely appointed to be Commissioners or a sole Commissioner for the Purposes of such Inquiry, and (as to such sole Commissioner) as if this Act had authorized the Appointment of a sole Commissioner; and all the Provisions of this Act concerning the Commissioners appointed to make any such Inquiry shall be taken to apply to such surviving or continuing Commissioner or Commissioners.

. . . VI. Such Commissioners shall, by all such Lawful Means as to them appear best, with a view to the Discovery of the Truth, inquire into the Manner in which the Election in relation to which such Committee as aforesaid may have reported to the House of Commons, or where the Report of such Committee has referred to Two or more Elections, the latest of such Elections, has been conducted, and whether any corrupt Practices have been committed at such Election, and if so, whether by way of the Gift or Loan or the Promise of the Gift or Loan of any Sum of Money or other valuable Consideration to any Voter or Voters, or to any other Person or

Persons on his or her Behalf, for the Promise or the giving of his or their Vote or Votes, or for his or their refraining or promising to refrain from giving his or their Vote or Votes, at such Election, or for his or their procuring or undertaking to procure the Votes of other Electors at such Election, or whether by the Payment of any Sum of Money or Loan or other valuable Consideration whatsoever to any Voter, or to any other Person on his Behalf, before, during, or after the Termination of such Election, by way of Head Money, or in compliance with any Usage or Custom in the County, Division of a County, City, Borough, University, or Place to which the Inquiry relates, or how otherwise, or whether any Sum of Money or other valuable consideration whatsoever has been paid to any voter, or to any other Person on his Behalf, after the Termination of such Election, as a Reward for giving or for having refrained from giving his Vote at such Election; and in case such Commissioners find that corrupt Practices have been committed at the Election into which they are herein-before authorized to inquire, it shall be lawful for them to make the like Inquiries concerning the latest previous Election for the same County, Division of a County, City, Borough, University, or Place; and upon their finding corrupt Practices to have been committed at that Election it shall be lawful for them to make the like Inquiries concerning the Election immediately previous thereto for such County, Division of a County, City, Borough, University, or Place, and so in like Manner from Election to Election, as far back as they may think fit; but where upon Inquiry as aforesaid concerning any Election such Commissioners do not find that corrupt Practices have been committed thereat, they shall not inquire concerning any previous Election; and such Commissioners shall from time to time report to Her Majesty the Evidence taken by them, and what they find concerning the Premises, and especially such Commissioners shall report with respect to each Election the Names of all Persons whom they find to have been guilty of corrupt Practice at such Election, and as well of those who have given Bribes for the Purchase or the Purpose of purchasing the Votes of others as of those who have themselves received Money or any other valuable Consideration for having given or having refrained from giving their Votes at such Election, and also the Names of all Persons whom they find to have given to others, or to have received themselves, Payments by way of Head Money, or as a Reward for giving or refraining from giving their Votes at such Election, and all other things whereby in the Opinion of the said Commissioners the Truth may be better known touching the Premises.

. . . VIII. It shall be lawful for such Commissioners, by a Summons under their Hands and Seals, or under the Hand and Seal of any One of them, to require the Attendance before them, at a Place and Time to be mentioned in the Summons, which Time shall be a reasonable Time from the Date of such Summons, of any Persons whomsoever whose Evidence, in the Judgment of such Commissioners or Commissioner, may be material to the Subject Matter of the Inquiry to be made by such Commissioners, and to require all Persons to bring before them such Books, Papers, Deeds, and Writings as to such Commissioners or Commissioner appear necessary for arriving at the Truth of the Things to be inquired into by them under this Act; all which Persons shall attend such Commissioners, and shall answer all

Questions put to them by such Commissioners touching the Matters to be inquired into by them, and shall produce all Books, Papers, Deeds, and Writings required of them, and in their Custody or under their Control, according to the Tenor of the Summons: Provided always, that no Statement made by any Person in answer to any Question put by such Commissioner shall, except in Cases of Indictment for Perjury committed in such Answers, be admissable in Evidence in any Proceeding, civil or criminal.

60. Corrupt Practices Act (1854)

Statutes of the Realm, 17 & 18 Vict. c. 102.

II. The following Persons shall be deemed guilty of Bribery, and shall be punished accordingly:–

1. Every Person who shall, directly or indirectly, by himself, or by any other Person on his Behalf, give, lend, or agree to give or lend, or shall offer, promise, or promise to procure or to endeavour to procure, any Money, or valuable Consideration, to or for any Voter, or to or for any Person on behalf of any Voter, or to or for any other Person in order to induce any Voter to vote, or refrain from voting, or shall corruptly do any such Act as aforesaid, on account of such Voter having voted or refrained from voting at any Election.

2. Every Person who shall, directly or indirectly, by himself or by any other Person on his Behalf, give or procure, or agree to give or procure, or offer, promise, or promise to procure or to endeavour to procure, any Office, Place, or Employment to or for any Voter, or to or for any Person on behalf of any Voter, or to or for any other Person, in order to induce such Voter to vote, or refrain from voting, or shall corruptly do any such Act as aforesaid, on account of any Voter having voted or refrained from voting at any Election:

3. Every Person who shall, directly or indirectly, by himself, or by any other Person on his Behalf, make any such Gift, Loan, Offer, Promise, Procurement, or Agreement as aforesaid, to or for any Person, in order to induce such Person to procure, or endeavour to procure, the Return of any Person to serve in Parliament, or the Vote of any Voter at any Election:

4. Every Person who shall, upon or in consequence of any such Gift, Loan, Offer, Promise, Procurement, or Agreement, procure or engage, promise, or endeavour to procure the Return of any Person to Serve in Parliament, or the Vote of any Voter at any Election:

5. Every Person who shall advance or pay, or cause to be paid, any Money to or to the Use of any other Person with the Intent that such Money or any Part thereof shall be expended in Bribery at any Election, or who shall knowingly pay or cause to be paid any Money to any Person in Discharge or Repayment of any Money wholly or in part expended in Bribery at any Election:

And any Person so offending shall be guilty of a Misdeameanor, and in *Scotland* of an Offence punishable by Fine and Imprisonment, and shall also be liable to forfeit the Sum of One hundred Pounds to any Person who shall sue for the same, together with full Costs of Suit: Provided always, that the aforesaid Enactment shall not extend or be construed to extend to any Money paid or agreed to be paid for or on account of any legal Expenses *bona fide* incurred at or concerning any Election.

III. The following Persons shall also be deemed guilty of Bribery, and shall be punishable accordingly:

1. Every Voter who shall, before or during any Election, directly or indirectly by himself or by any other Person on his Behalf, receive, agree, or contract for any Money, Gift, Loan, or valuable Consideration, Office, Place or Employment, for himself or for any other Person, for voting or agreeing to vote, or for refraining or agreeing to refrain from voting, at any Election:

2. Every Person who shall, after any Election, directly or indirectly, by himself or by any other Person on his Behalf, receive any Money or valuable Consideration on account of any Person having voted or refrained from voting, or having induced any other Person to vote or to refrain from voting, at any Election.

And any Person so offending shall be guilty of a Misdemeanor, and in *Scotland* of an Offence punishable by Fine and Imprisonment, and shall also be liable to forfeit the Sum of Ten Pounds to any Person who shall sue for the same, together with full Costs of Suit.

IV. Every Candidate at an Election, who shall corruptly by himself, or by or with any Person, or by any other Ways or Means on his behalf, at any Time, either before, during, or after any Election, directly or indirectly give or provide, or cause to be given or provided, or shall be accessory to the giving or providing or shall pay, wholly or in part, any Expenses incurred for any Meat, Drink, Entertainment, or Provision to or for any Person, in order to be elected, or for being elected, or for the Purpose of corruptly influencing such Person or any other Person to give or refrain from giving his vote at such Election, or on account of such Person having voted or refrained from voting, or being about to vote or refrain from voting, at such Election, shall be deemed guilty of the Offence of Treating, and shall forfeit the sum of Fifty Pounds to any Person who shall sue for the same, with full Costs of Suit; and every Voter who shall corruptly accept or take any such Meat, Drink, Entertainment, or Provision, shall be incapable of voting at such Election, and his Vote, if given, shall be utterly void and of none effect.

V. Every Person who shall, directly or indirectly, by himself, or by any other Person on his Behalf, make use of, or threaten to make use of, any Force, Violence, or Restraint, or inflict or threaten the Infliction, by himself or by or through any other Person, of any Injury, Damage, Harm, or Loss, or in any other Manner practise Intimidation upon or against any Person in order to induce or compel such Person to vote or refrain from voting, or on account of such Person having voted or refrained from voting, at any Election, or who shall, by Abduction, Duress, or any fraudulent Device or Contrivance, impede, prevent, or otherwise interfere with the free Exercise of the Franchise of any Voter, or shall thereby compel, induce, or prevail upon any Voter, either to give or to refrain from giving his Vote at any Election, shall be deemed to have committed the Offence of undue Influence, and shall be guilty of a Misdemeanor, and in *Scotland* of an Offence punishable by Fine or Imprisonment, and shall also be liable to forfeit the Sum of Fifty Pounds to any Person who shall sue for the same, together with full Costs of Suit. . . .

XV. Whereas it is expedient to make further provision for preventing the Offences of Bribery, Treating, and undue Influence, and also for diminishing the Expenses of Elections: Be it enacted, That . . . *once* in every Year in the month of August, the Returning Officer of every County, City, and Borough shall appoint a fit and proper Person to be an Election Officer, to be called "Election Auditor, or Auditor of Election Expenses", to act at every Election or Elections for and during the Year then next ensuing and until another Appointment of Election Auditor shall be made; and such Returning Officer shall, in such Way as he shall think best, give public notice of such Appointment in each County, City, or Borough; provided that any Person appointed such Election Auditor may be reappointed as often as the Returning Officer for the Time being shall think fit; and that every Person who shall be an Election Auditor on the Day appointed for any Election shall continue to be the Election Auditor in respect of such Election until the whole Business of such Election shall be concluded notwithstanding the subsequent appointment of any other Person as Election Auditor; and every Election Auditor upon his Appointment shall make and sign before the Returning Officer the following Declaration:–

"I, A.B., do solemnly and sincerely promise and declare that I will well and truly and faithfully, to the best of my Ability in all Things, perform my duty as Election Auditor, according to the Provisions of the Corrupt Practices Prevention Act, 1854."

And any Election Auditor wilfully doing any Act whatever contrary to the true Intent and Meaning of such Declaration shall be deemed guilty of a Misdemeanour, and in Scotland of an Offence punishable with Fine and Imprisonment.

XVI. Bills to be sent in within One Month or right to recover barred.
XVII. Bills received within One Month to be sent to Election Auditor.
XVIII. No Payments to be made except through Election Auditor.

. . .

XXIII. Refreshment to Voters on days of Nomination or polling declared Illegal.
XXIV. No Person to pay Expenses except to Candidate or Election Auditor.

. . .

XXVI. The Election Auditor shall, as soon as he conveniently can, make out a full and true Account of all the Expenses incurred at the Election, specifying therein every Sum of Money paid to him or by him or by his Authority on behalf of each Candidate, and of all the Sums claimed, though the same shall not have been allowed or paid, and every Sum which has been paid into Court as aforesaid, or recovered by Judgement against such Candidate, and to whom, by Name, such payment was made, and what particular Debt or Liability; and the Elections Auditor shall include in such general Account the Amount of the Sums paid by each Candidate for Advertisements, and he shall specify thereon the total amount of Expenses incurred by each Candidate; and the Account, when so made out, shall be duly signed by him: Provided always that when it shall be found necessary the Election Auditor may from Time to Time make out a supplementary Account or Accounts, which shall be made and abstracted in the Manner herein provided with reference to the first general Account.

XXVII. The Election Auditor shall keep all Accounts which shall come into his Hands in some fit and convenient Place, and shall, at all reasonable and convenient Times, submit the same to the Inspection of the Candidates and their Agents, and permit them to take Copies of the same, or of any Part thereof, upon Request, and when such general Account as aforesaid shall be so made out and signed by him, he shall keep the same in some fit and convenient Place, and such general Accounts shall be open to the Inspection of any Persons, and Copies thereof, or of any Part thereof, shall be furnished to any Person at all reasonable and convenient Times upon Request, such Person paying a Fee at the Rate of One Shilling for every Two Hundred Words to a Copying Clerk for the same; and when the Election Auditor shall have concluded the Business of any Election he shall deliver over all Accounts in his Hands to the Clerk of the Peace in Counties, and to the Town Clerk or other Officer performing the Duties of Town Clerk in Cities and Boroughs.

. . .

61. Reform Bill of 1859: Disraeli's speech moving for leave to introduce (28 February)

Hansard, 3/CLII/967–99.

In his first speech on Reform as a minister responsible for a Bill on the subject, Disraeli gave what is, perhaps, a more considered view of the Act of 1832, and of the administrations of the 'Arch-Mediocrity' preceding it, than the better known ones expressed in *Coningsby*. Its main proposal was to assimilate borough and county franchises by making the £10 occupation and 40*s*. freehold franchises common to both. As a corollary, urban freeholders, who had hitherto voted in the counties, were to vote in their boroughs. The Chandos clause was the clause in the Act of 1832 giving £50 occupiers in the counties the vote. It was imposed on the Government by the House, under Tory leadership, and was later criticized by Russell as the first step in the confusion of the hitherto distinct county and borough qualifications.

. . . I do not doubt that our future records will acknowledge that, during some of the most important political events of modern history, those events were treated with the energy and the resource becoming British statesmen. If we judge of the Act of 1832 by its consequences, in the measures of this House and in the character of its Members, it must be admitted that that policy was equal to the emergency it controlled and directed. I cannot, indeed, agree with those who attribute to the legislation of 1832 every measure of public benefit that has been passed by this House during the last twenty-five years. I know well that before the reform of this House took place the administration of this country was distinguished by its ability and precision. I believe, indeed, that, especially in the latter part of the administration of Lord Liverpool, this House was rather in advance of the opinion of the country at large. But I think that the reform of the House of Commons in 1832 greatly added to the energy and public spirit in which we had then become somewhat deficient. . . .

. . . In the first place, voters under the Chandos clause at no time ever exceeded one-fifth of the constituent body of counties. Therefore, had they all voted the same way, they never could have exercised that influence upon public events which has been ascribed to them. But the proprietary of the soil does not rest alone with Tories and Conservatives. There are Whig landlords. The proprietary of the soil is distributed among proprietors of all opinions; and the consequence is, that if you look at the elections, you will find that those who voted under this Chandos clause were much divided–often equally divided. It is not true, therefore, that those who vote under this qualification have exercised any very great influence upon the legislation of this country, or that they are a class who have acted always without intent or meaning. But there is no doubt that dissatisfaction, followed by distrust and misrepresentation, did raise in the country an idea that the county representation was an exclusive representation; that it was animated only by one object; that it had a selfish interest always before it, and that it had not that sympathy with the community which we desire in that body to whom the privilege of election is intrusted. An effort was made by means of the 40s. freehold, which was retained in counties, to counteract the exaggerated influence of the £50 tenancy voters. A manufacture of votes–from the facts before me I am entitled so to call it–was carried on in the boroughs, by which it was supposed that the injurious influence of the tenants living upon the land, dwelling in the counties, might be counteracted. For the last fifteen years–for the last ten years at a very great rate–this has been going on, until it has really arrived at this point, that the number of county voters who do not dwell in the counties now exceeds the number of those who vote under the £50 clause. It was proclaimed with great triumph that when a gentleman stood for a county, his neighbours who dwelt in the county might vote for him, but some large town in the district would pour out its legions by railway, and on the nomination of some club in the metropolis would elect the representative for the county. The dwellers in the county found themselves not represented in many instances by those who lived among them. A sort of civil war was raised in this manner; and if hon. Gentlemen look into the statistics on this point, they will see that what I may call an unnatural state of things was brought about; because there is no doubt that a man should vote for the place where he resides, or for the locality in which he is really and substantially interested. A man who votes for a place where he resides, or in which he has an interest, votes with a greater sense of responsibility than a mere stranger. Where, then, when we are considering the condition of the constituency of the country; when we are endeavouring to reconstruct it on a broad basis, which will admit within its pale all those who are trustworthy,–shall we look for means by which we may terminate these heart-burnings, and restore the constituencies of England to what I will venture to call their natural elements? No doubt it is a labour of great difficulty. Are we to attempt to do it by restrictions?–by artificial arrangements? It might be possible to pass a law which would remove these strangers from the sphere of their political power. But, whether possible or not, who would be rash enough to propose it? How could we terminate these misunderstandings, how restore that good feeling,–that which Lord Clarendon called the "good-nature of the English people,"–if we took a course which would give occasion to a perpetual agitation for the removal of the restrictions which we had succeeded in establishing? Her Majesty's Government have given to this subject the most anxious consideration. I may say, that if labour, if thought, could assist us to arrive at a proper solution, neither labour nor thought has been spared. Is there any principle on which we can restore the county constituency to its natural state, and bring about that general and constant sympathy between the two portions of the constituent body which ought to exist? Her Majesty's Government are of opinion that some such solution does exist. We think there is a principle, the justness of which will be at once acknowledged, the logical consequences of which will be at once remedial, and which, if applied with due discretion, will effect all those objects which we anxiously desire with respect to the county constituency. We find that principle in recognizing the identity of suffrage between county and town. I will proceed to show the House what, in our opinion, would be the practical consequences of recognizing that identity. If the suffrages of the town are transferred to the county, and the suffrages of the county transferred to the town, all those voters who, dwelling in a town, exercise their suffrage in the county in virtue of a county suffrage, will record their votes in the town, and the free-holder, resident in a town–subject to provisions in the Bill which would prevent this constitutional instrument being turned to an improper use,–will have a right to vote for the borough in which he resides. This, as well as the franchise founded on savings-banks, will open another avenue to the mechanic, whose virtue, prudence, intelligence, and frugality entitle him to enter into the privileged pale of the constituent body of the country. If this principle be adopted, a man will vote for the place where he resides, and with which he is substantially connected. Therefore the first measure would embody this logical consequence–that it would transfer the free-holders of the town from the county to the town. But if this principle be adopted, there are other measures which, in our opinion, it would be the duty of Parliament in this respect to adopt. Since the year 1832 there has been a peculiar increase in the population of this country irrespective of the ratio of increase, with which we are acquainted. The creation of railways in particular districts has stimulated that increase; and this has come to pass in England, that in a great many of the boroughs there is a population residing, who, for all social and municipal purposes, are part and parcel of the community, but who for Parliamentary purposes are pariahs. A man votes for a municipality; he pays his parochial rates and taxes; he is called upon to contribute to all purposes of charity and philanthropy in the borough; but, because he lives in a part of the borough which exceeds the boundary that was formed in 1832, he is not, though he lives in a £10 house, permitted to vote for Members of Parliament. Now, all this extramural population in fact and in spirit consists of persons who ought to be electors in the boroughs in which they reside; and we therefore propose that Boundary Commissioners should visit all the boroughs of England, and re-arrange them according to the altered circumstances of the time. . . .

. . . But a complete representation does not depend merely upon the electoral body, however varied you may make its elements, however homogeneous its character. It also depends upon whether, in your system, the different interests of the country are adequately represented. Now, discarding for ever that principle of population upon which it has been my duty to make some remarks; accepting it as a truth that the function of this House is to represent not the views of a numerical majority–not merely the gross influence of a predominant property, but the varied interests of the country, we have felt that on this occasion it was incumbent on us diligently and even curiously to investigate the whole of England, and see whether there were interests not represented in this House whose views we should wish to be heard here; and whether the general representation of the country could be matured and completed. In undertaking this office, it must not be supposed that we have been animated by a feeling that we would only do that which the hard necessity of the case required. Had we been so influenced, it is possible we might have brought forward a measure that would have served the purpose of the moment, and yet left seeds behind us which might have germinated in future troubles, controversies, and anxieties. We have been sincerely desirous to adapt the scheme of 1832 to the England of 1859, and to induce the House to come to a general settlement, whether as regards the exercise of the franchise or the direct representation in this House of the various interests of the community which should take this question for a long period out of the agitating thoughts of men. We have sought to offer to the country, in the hope that it will meet with its calm and serious approval, what we believe to be a just and–I will not say a final, but–conclusive settlement. Finality, Sir, is not the language of politics. But it is our duty to propose an arrangement which, as far as the circumstances of the age in which we live can influence our opinion, will be a conclusive settlement. And we have laid it down as our task to consider, without any respect to persons, what we honestly think are the interests of the country that are not represented, but which we should at this moment counsel the House to add to their numbers. . . .

62. Reform Bill of 1859: Lord John Russell's motion on the second reading (2 March)

Hansard, 3/CLIII/405.

The motion was carried by 330 votes to 291. The Derby Government obtained a dissolution, and returned from the country strengthened, but not sufficiently so to avert defeat on a motion of confidence in June, as a sequel to which Palmerston formed his second Government, 1859–1865.

"This House is of opinion, that it is neither just nor politic to interfere, in the manner proposed in this Bill, with the Freehold Franchise as hitherto exercised in the Counties in England and Wales; and that no re-adjustment of the Franchise will satisfy this House or Country, which does not provide for a greater extension of the Suffrage in Cities and Boroughs than is contemplated in the present Measure."

63. Reform Bill of 1859: Gladstone's speech against Russell's motion (29 March)

Hansard, 3/CLIII/1054–59.

Gladstone had just returned from the Ionian Islands, where, at the invitation of the Conservative Government, he had been acting for four months as high commissioner. Several overtures had been made to him to join the Government, including Disraeli's well-known and generous appeal of May 1858, printed in Monypenny and Buckle. In his speech Gladstone deplored the constant breakdown of Reform proposals, and supported the second reading of Disraeli's Bill with a view to its amendment in committee. It was always his view that the Bill had offered an opportunity of settling the vexed question with a large measure of consent. The passage printed is in defence of its redistribution proposals. The occasion is notable as the last on which, on a major issue, Gladstone both spoke and voted on the Conservative side. In June 1859 he joined Palmerston's Government as chancellor of the exchequer.

. . . I must frankly own it appears to me that to proceed far in the disfranchisement of small boroughs is a course injurious to the efficiency of the House of Commons. You must not consider in this matter the question only of the electors. You must consider quite as much who are likely to be elected. And permit me to say that the time has come when, in the examination of any scheme of Reform, it is of vital and capital importance that this matter should be brought fully under the view of the House. Let me point out that the Reform Bill of 1832 has not, in this respect, been fairly and fully tried. For twenty-seven years, it is true, it has been in operation, and it has communicated great vigour to the working of the legislative machine. For the first ten or fifteen years of that period the working of the Reformed Parliament has exhibited a union of power, circumspection, and sagacity such as it would be difficult to find an equal to in the history of legislative assemblies. But look at the advantages which attended the first working of this change in our representation. It is true we had a new electoral system, but we had the old statesmen to work it. Read the admirable argument of Lord Macaulay in his *History of William III.* upon the state of the House of Commons at that time, before you had organized the system under which Ministries are constituted and maintained in this country. The House of Commons was then an assembly of units incapable of forming into one body and of working together. Why is it that, from that time to the present, they have become, instead of a mere aggregate of units, an organized whole, capable of conducting the affairs of this great empire? It has been because of the race of statesmen who have adorned this House, who have been reared from generation to generation under the operation of your improved Parliamentary system, and of that race I rejoice to say, notwithstanding the twenty-seven years that have elapsed since the Reform Bill, a very considerable number still remain to us. Now, how were these men introduced into the House of Commons? I am sure I may entreat the patience of the House. I need not trouble them with wearisome citations; but it is really worth our while to consider how this great provision for the exigencies of the country has been made. We have heard in the course of this debate some apology for small constituencies. Well, I am no great lover of small constituencies, and it never was my lot to sit for one. At the same time small constituencies undoubtedly tend to answer the great purpose of a representative system in securing its diversity and completeness. If you have nothing but large and populous bodies to return your Members of Parliament, there, as recent experience seems, I am sorry to say, in a great degree to prove, local interests and local influences will upon the whole prevail, and you will not find it possible to introduce adequately into this House the race of men by whom the Government of the country is to be carried on. By means of small boroughs, generally considered–I have no doubt there are objections to them, but I believe those objections are gradually disappearing under the action of improved laws and an improved state of public feeling–by means of small boroughs you introduce into this House the representatives of separate interests, who stand apart from the great and the paramount interests of the country. You introduce here the masters of civil wisdom, such as Mr. Burke above all, Sir James Mackintosh, and many others who might be named–a class of men with respect to whom nothing is less probable than that they should command to any great extent the suffrages of large and populous constituencies. You introduce those calm, sagacious, retired observers who are averse from the rough contact necessary in canvassing large bodies of electors, but who form no small part of the best *substrata* of this House, and contribute greatly to the efficiency of your representative system. Many, however, have spoken on behalf of small boroughs. I want to speak on behalf of a certain description of small boroughs–of those where, from kindly interest, from ancient affectionate recollections, from local and traditional respect, from the memory of services received, from the admiration of great men and great qualities, the constituencies are willing to take upon trust the recommendation of candidates for Parliament from noblemen or gentlemen who may stand in immediate connection with them. (Some cries of "Oh!") I do not complain at all of that interruption. I admit that there is something of paradox in such an argument upon such a question, if it is to be considered as an argument upon paper only; but practice has proved that the real paradox lies with those who will allow of no ingress into this House but one. If that one ingress is to be the suffrages of a large mass of voters, the consequence is a dead level of mediocrity which destroys not only the ornament but the force of this House, and which, as I think the history of other countries will show, is ultimately fatal to the liberties of the people. Allow me in explanation of my meaning to state the case of six men in one line each,–Mr. Pelham, Lord Chatham, Mr. Fox, Mr. Pitt, Mr. Canning, and Sir Robert Peel. Mr. Pelham entered this House for the borough of Seaford in 1719, at the age of twenty-two; Lord Chatham entered it in 1735, for Old Sarum, at the age of twenty-six; Mr. Fox in 1764, for Midhurst, at the age, I think, of twenty; Mr. Pitt in 1781, for Appleby, at the age of twenty-one; Mr. Canning in 1793, for Newport, at the age of twenty-two; and Sir Robert Peel in 1809, for the city of Cashel, at the age of twenty-one. Now, here are six men, every one of whom was a leader in this House. I take them because the youngest is older than the eldest of those Statesmen who now sit here, and because the mention of their names can give rise to no personal feeling. Here are six men whom I do not hesitate to say you cannot match out of the history of the British House of Commons for the hundred years which precede our own day. Every one of them was a leader in this House, almost every one was a Prime Minister, all of them entered Parliament for one of those boroughs where influence of different kinds prevailed. Every one of them might, if he had chosen, after giving proof of his powers in this House have sat for any of the open constituencies of the country, and many of them did so. Mr. Pelham, after sitting for Seaford in one Parliament, represented Sussex for all the rest of his life. Lord Chatham never, I think, represented an open constituency. Mr. Fox, after sitting for Midhurst, became the chosen of Westminster. Mr. Pitt went from Appleby at a very early age to the University of Cambridge. Mr. Canning, after representing Newport, was returned by Liverpool, and Sir Robert Peel from Cashel became the Member for the University of Oxford. Now, what was the case of Sir Robert Peel? The University, on account of a conscientious difference of opinion, refused the continuance of his services. Were it not for a small borough those services would have been lost to the British Parliament. ("Oh!") The hon. Member is right; it was an over statement. I should have said they would have been lost to the British Parliament at that moment. But in Westbury he found an immediate refuge–for so it must be called–and he continued to sit for a small borough for the remainder of his life. Mr. Canning, in the same way, not losing but resigning the representation of Liverpool, found it more conducive to the public business that he should become the representative of a small borough for the rest of his days. What does this show? It shows that small boroughs were the nursery-ground in which these men were elected–men who not only were destined to lead this House, to govern the country, to be the strength of England at home and its ornament abroad, but who likewise, when once they had an opportunity of proving their powers in this House, became the chosen of large constituencies and the favourites of the nation. It cannot be denied that, whatever advantages have attended our Parliamentary Reforms we have latterly, by what we have done, narrowed the means of ingress to the House of Commons. What chance would there be for any of the six men I have mentioned, at the age of twenty-one or twenty-two, under the present system? It is not too much to say that no one of these mere boys could have become a Member of Parliament if it had not been for the means of access to the House of Commons which then existed. You must recollect that they were nearly all chosen when they were about twenty-one or twenty-two. What is the case now? I fully grant that you have an answer as far as regards a very limited class of persons indeed. Take the heir to a dukedom or an earldom, or the son of a great territorial potentate, and there will be ready access to Parliament for such men; nor, I trust, shall we ever see any measures adopted which will exclude them. I rejoice to see that by so limited a class so much ability and so much promise is shown. If you look to the young men of this day–and, after all, it is to them we must look to carry on the business of the country in future years–the most distinguished persons in this House are the men who owe their seats here to territorial influence. The cases of Canning, Fox, Pitt and Peel carry a moral with them. What would have been Mr. Canning's chance had he been dependent on that influence. I do not know what would have been the chances of Mr. Fox or Mr. Pitt, or Sir Robert Peel at twenty-one or twenty-two if they had been dependent on territorial influence. You cannot expect of large and populous constituencies that they should return boys to Parliament; and yet if you want a succession of men trained to take part in the government of the country, you must have a great proportion of them returned to this House while they are boys. The conclusion to which this brings me is that the matter will be a more serious one if you are prepared to part with your whole system of small boroughs. I am not arguing this in the sense of one party or another; far less am I arguing it in a sense adverse to popular rights. For what, let me ask, have these men whose names I have just mentioned been? Have they been the enemies of popular rights? Is it not, upon the contrary, under Providence, in a great degree to be attributed to a succession of those distinguished statesmen, introduced at an early age into this House, and once made known in this House securing to themselves the general favour of their countrymen, that we enjoy our present extension of popular liberty, and, above all, the durable form which that liberty has assumed? I am aware that this has now become a rather antiquated subject. ("Hear, hear!" from the Opposition side of the House.) I thank the hon. Gentleman for his concurrence in the sentiment to which I have given expression, and let me remind him that there are many things which are old which are nevertheless good. But, Sir, we are called upon in this discussion to consider a subject which, as my noble Friend the Member for London has so well stated, involves, not only our own condition, but the condition of our children and of the latest posterity. In dealing with it I wish to ask myself the question how the benches of this House are to be filled; how all the diversities of powers and aptitudes which have formed this great nation are to find their way within those sacred precincts of the constitution after we shall have lost the guiding influence and authority of that race of statesmen who were reared under our ancient system, particularly if we should proceed by rash and unwise legislation to cut off from our representative system that class of constituencies through the medium of which alone, with the exception of the case of the eldest sons and heirs of great families, the energy and vigour of the nation can easily be introduced into the House of Commons at an age at which they may become available for the public service. . . .

64. Gladstone's speech on Baines' Bill for lowering borough franchise (11 May 1864)

Hansard, 3/CLXXV/321–27.

Edward Baines, M.P. for Leeds, 1859–1874, introduced Bills for lowering the borough franchise to £6 in 1861, 1864, and 1865. Gladstone's speech led to remonstrances from Palmerston, and Gladstone admitted that it required to be construed. In his introduction to the published version of the speech, he accomplished this with such effect that critics said he had explained himself away. Nevertheless, his standing in Radical circles went up.

. . . Again, Sir, let us look for a few moments at the altered, the happily altered, relations of the working classes to the Government, the laws, the institutions, and, above all, to the throne of this country. Let us go back–it is no long period in the history of a nation–to an epoch not very many years before the passing of the Reform Bill, and consider what was the state of things at a time when many of us were unborn, and when most of us were children–I mean, to the years which immediately succeeded the peace of 1815. We all know the history of those times; most of us recollect the atmosphere and the ideas, under the influence of which we were brought up. They were not ideas which belonged to the old current of English history; nor were they in conformity with the liberal sentiments which pervaded, at its best periods, the politics of the country, and which harmonized with the spirit of the old British Constitution. They were, on the contrary, ideas referable to those lamentable excesses of the first French Revolution, which produced here a terrible re-action, and went far to establish the doctrine that the masses of every community were in permanent antagonism with the laws under which they lived, and were disposed to regard those laws, and the persons by whom the laws were made and administered, as their natural enemies. Unhappily, there are but too many indications to prove that this is no vague or imaginary description. The time to which I now refer, was a time when deficiencies in the harvests were followed by riots, and when rioters did not hold sacred even the person of Majesty itself. In 1817, when the Prince Regent came down to open Parliament, his carriage was assailed by the populace of London; and what was the remedy provided for this state of things? Why, the remedy was sought in the suspension of the *Habeas Corpus* Act; or in the limitation of the action of the press, already restricted; or in the employment of spies and the deliberate defence of their employment, who, for the supposed security of the Government, were sent throughout the country to dog the course of private life, and to arrest persons, or to check them, in the formation of conspiracies real or supposed. And what, let me ask, is the state of things now? With truth, Sir, it may be said that the epoch I have named, removed from us, in mere chronological reckoning, by less than half a century, is in the political sphere separated from us by a distance almost immeasurable. For now it may be fearlessly asserted that the fixed traditional sentiment of the working man has begun to be confidence in the law, in Parliament, and even in the executive Government. Of this gratifying state of things it fell to my lot to receive a single, indeed, but a significant proof no later than yesterday. (Cries of "No, no!" and laughter.) The quick-witted character of hon. Gentlemen opposite outstrips, I am afraid, the tardy movement of my observations. Let them only have a very little patience, and they will, I believe, see cause for listening to what I shall say. I was about to proceed to say, in illustration of my argument, that only yesterday I had the satisfaction of receiving a deputation of working men from the Society of Amalgamated Engineers. That society consists of very large numbers of highly-skilled workmen, and has two hundred and sixty branches; it is a society representing the very class in which we should most be inclined to look for a spirit of even jealous independence of all direct relations with the Government. But the deputation came to state to me that the society had large balances of money open for investment, and that many of its members could not feel satisfied unless they were allowed to place their funds in the hands of the Government, by means of a modification in the rules of the Post Office savings banks. Now that, I think, I may say, without being liable to any expression of adverse feeling on the part of hon. Gentlemen opposite, was a very small but yet significant indication, among thousands of others, of the altered temper to which I have referred. Instead, however, of uttering on the point my own opinions, I should like to use the words of the working classes themselves. In an address which, in company with my right hon. Friend the Member for Staffordshire,[1] I heard read at a meeting which was held in the Potteries last autumn, they say, of their own spontaneous Motion, uninfluenced by the action of their employers, in relation to the legislation of late years—

> "The great measures that have been passed during the last twenty years by the British Legislature have conferred incalculable blessings on the whole community, and particularly on the working classes, by unfettering the trade and commerce of the country, cheapening the essentials of our daily sustenance,

[1] Orme Foster.

placing a large proportion of the comforts and luxuries of life within our reach, and rendering the obtainment of knowledge comparatively easy among the great mass of the sons of toil."

And this is the mode in which they then proceed to describe their view of the conduct of the upper classes towards them–

"Pardon us for alluding to the kindly conduct now so commonly evinced by the wealthier portions of the community to assist in the physical and moral improvement of the working classes. The well-being of the toiling mass is now generally admitted to be an essential to the national weal. This forms a pleasing contrast to the opinions cherished half a century ago. The humbler classes also are duly mindful of the happy change, and, without any abatement of manly independence, fully appreciate the benefits resulting therefrom, contentedly fostering a hopeful expectation of the future. May heaven favour and promote this happy mutuality! as we feel confident that all such kindly interchange materially contributes to the general good."

Now, such language does, in my opinion, the greatest credit to the parties from whom it proceeds. This is a point on which no difference of opinion can prevail. I think I may go a step further, and consider these statements as indicating not only the sentiments of a particular body at the particular place from which they proceeded, but the general sentiments of the best-conducted and most enlightened working men of the country. It may, however, be said, that such statements prove the existing state of things to be satisfactory. But surely this is no sufficient answer. Is it right, I ask, that in the face of such dispositions, the present law of almost entire exclusion should continue to prevail? Again, I call upon the adversary to show cause. And I venture to say that every man who is not presumably incapacitated by some consideration of personal unfitness or of political danger is morally entitled to come within the pale of the Constitution. Of course, in giving utterance to such a proposition, I do not recede from the protest I have previously made against sudden, or violent, or excessive, or intoxicating change; but I apply it with confidence to this effect, that fitness for the franchise, when it is shown to exist–as I say it is shown to exist in the case of a select portion of the working class–is not repelled on sufficient grounds from the portals of the Constitution by the allegation that things are well as they are. I contend, moreover, that persons who have prompted the expression of such sentiments as those to which I have referred, and whom I know to have been Members of the working class, are to be presumed worthy and fit to discharge the duties of citizenship, and that to admission to the discharge of those duties they are well and justly entitled. The present franchise, I may add, on the whole–subject, of course, to some exceptions–draws the line between the lower middle class and the upper order of the working class. As a general rule, the lower stratum of the middle class is admitted to the exercise of the franchise, while the upper stratum of the working class is excluded. That I believe to be a fair general description of the present formation of the constituencies in boroughs and towns. Is it a state of things, I would ask, recommended by clear principles of reason? Is the upper portion of the working classes inferior to the lowest portion of the middle? That is a question I should wish to be considered on both sides of the House. For my own part, it appears to me that the negative of the proposition may be held with the greatest confidence. Whenever this Question comes to be discussed, with the view to an immediate issue, the conduct of the general body of the operatives of Lancashire cannot be forgotten. What are the qualities which fit a man for the exercise of a privilege such as the franchise? Self-command, self-control, respect for order, patience under suffering, confidence in the law, regard for superiors; and when, I should like to ask, were all these great qualities exhibited in a manner more signal, I would even say more illustrious, than under the profound affliction of the winter of 1862? I admit the danger of dealing with enormous masses of men; but I am now speaking only of a limited portion of the working class, and I, for one, cannot admit that there is that special virtue in the nature of the middle class which ought to lead to our drawing a marked distinction, a distinction almost purporting to be one of principle, between them and a select portion of the working classes, so far as relates to the exercise of the franchise.

But, Sir, this Question has received a very remarkable illustration from the experience of the last few years. So far as Lancashire is concerned, we have the most extraordinary evidence–evidence amounting almost to mathematical demonstration–of the competency of the working man to discharge those duties of retail trade and the distribution of commodities, which are commonly intrusted to the lower part of the middle class. I allude to the evidence afforded by the marvellous success in that particular county (and I hope the example of that county may not be too eagerly followed elsewhere) of the co-operative system. For my own part, I am not ashamed to say that, if twenty or ten years ago anybody had prophesied to me the success of that system, as it has recently been exhibited in Rochdale and other towns of the north–if I had been told that labouring men would so associate together with mutual advantage, to the exclusion of the retail dealer who comes between the producer and the consumer of commodities, I should have regarded the prediction as absurd. There is, in my opinion, no greater social marvel at the present day than the manner in which these societies flourish in Lancashire, combined with a consideration of the apparent soundness of the financial basis on which they are built; for the bodies of men who have had recourse to the co-operative system have been, as it would appear, those who have stood out with the most manly resolution against the storms of adversity, who have been the last to throw themselves on the charity of their neighbours, and who have proved themselves to be best qualified for the discharge of the duties of independent citizens. And when we have before us considerable numbers of men answering to this description, it is, I think, well worth our while to consider what is the title which they advance to the generous notice of Parliament in regard to their appeal to be admitted in such measure as may upon consideration seem fit, to the exercise of the franchise. I, for myself, confess that I think the investigation will be far better conducted if we approach the question at an early date, in a calm frame of mind, and without having our doors besieged by crowds, or our table loaded with petitions; rather than if we postpone entering upon it until a great agitation has arisen.

And now, Sir, one word in conclusion. I believe that it has been given to us of this generation to witness, advancing as it were under our very eyes from day to day, the most blessed of all social processes; I mean the process which unites together not the interests only but the feelings of all the several classes of the community, and which throws back into the shadows of oblivion those discords by which they were kept apart from one another. I know of nothing which can contribute, in any degree comparable to that union, to the welfare of the commonwealth. It is well, Sir, that we should be suitably provided with armies, and fleets, and fortifications; it is well too that all these should rest upon and be sustained, as they ought to be, by a sound system of finance, and out of a revenue not wasted by a careless Parliament, or by a profligate Administration. But that which is better and more weighty still is that hearts should be bound together by a reasonable extension, at fitting times, and among selected portions of the people, of every benefit and every privilege that can justly be conferred upon them; and, for one, I am prepared to give my support to the Motion now made by my hon. Friend (Mr. Baines), because I believe, and am persuaded, that it will powerfully tend to that binding and blending and knitting of hearts together, and thus to the infusion of new vigour into the old, but in the best sense still young, and flourishing, and undecaying British Constitution.

65. Reform Bill of 1866: Robert Lowe's speech (13 March)

Hansard, 3/CLXXXII/144-63.

The queen's speech, at the opening of the session, had announced the Government's intention to have statistics of the electorate prepared, to serve as a basis for the consideration of Reform. In his speech on the first reading of the Reform Bill of 1866, Gladstone had admitted that they had not been available, in their full form, even to himself, until a day or two before the Government's Bill was presented. The proportion of working-class electors they revealed had surprised him, though it was, at the most, 26 per cent, and at the minimum 21 per cent, as against the 32 per cent of the 1832 constituency. The pre-Reform constituency had included 'scot and lot', and other 'ancient right' voters whose franchise was limited to their lives, as well as freemen, whose right it had been the intention of the Whig Government similarly to limit. Lowe's speech, on the second day of the debate, opened the Whig opposition to the Bill. Gladstone said he supplied its whole brains.

. . . Passing from that subject, I will state in a few words to the House all that I deem it to be necessary to address to them with respect to the Bill which the right hon. Gentleman asks leave to introduce. This Bill proposes, in short, to increase the whole electors of the country, whom he estimates at 900,000, by 400,000–that is to say, nearly one-third. (An hon. Member: One-half.) Yes, one-half of the present constituency, but only one-third of that which will exist if the Bill passes into law. That is, nearly one-half of the existing number, and one-third of what the number would be. He proposes to make in the counties 171,000 new electors, and in the boroughs 204,000, the latter being almost altogether derived from the single class of persons renting at £10, or under £10. It will be almost entirely so, but there may be some slight difference–144,000 are absolutely and the rest pretty nearly so. With regard to the county franchise, I have only one observation to make. The proposition of the Chancellor of the Exchequer will very much enlarge the electoral area, enormously increase the expense of elections, and create a great re-distribution of political power. That may be right, or it may be wrong, but before we pass it we should be told the reason why. Then coming to the boroughs, the case is much more serious. The right hon. Gentleman opposed the voters in counties as being of the middle class to the voters in boroughs as being of the working class; and, according to the right hon. Gentleman's showing, if this Bill pass, we are to have 330,000 voters in the constituencies belonging to the working class, and 360,000 in the constituencies not working men. That is the system he proposes for our adoption. This leads us to a very grave consideration, because not only the statement of the right hon. Gentleman, but the statistics laid before the House show that the number of persons belonging to the working class already admitted to the franchise is 126,000 or about one-fifth of the whole amount of electors. That is a most grave and momentous fact. Look what it proves. It proves in the first place that the Government were entirely mistaken as regards the main ground on which they introduced the present measure. The main ground they put forth for bringing in the Bill–until they came to bring it in, when they thought it expedient to put forth no ground at all–was that the best of the working class were excluded from the franchise. The authority on which I make this statement is an authority which no one can dispute–it is a work on the English Government and Constitution issued by Lord Russell twice in the course of last year–once in the spring, and again in the autumn. This is a passage from the Preface to the work–

"But may there not be still improvements?"

–in the Reform Bill, the noble Lord means; and this is the answer he gives–

> "Each of the last four Ministries have been willing to add as it were a supplement to the Reform Act. For my part, I should be glad to see the sound morals and clear intelligence of the working classes more fully represented. They are kept out of the franchise, which Ministers of the Crown have repeatedly asked for them, partly by the jealousy of the present holders of the suffrage, and partly by a vague fear that, by their greater numbers, they will swallow up all other classes. Both those obstacles may be removed by a judicious modification of the proposed suffrage."

That proves most clearly that, in the opinion of Lord Russell as expressed last autumn, the best of the working classes had not the franchise. Is that true? Take the right hon. Gentleman's own statistics in your hands, and compare them with that Preface. Can you reconcile them? No, for they are absolutely irreconcilable. It is quite clear that Earl Russell wrote under a delusion, which was shared in by every gentleman who used the argument, and that I believe comprehended almost every Gentleman on the Treasury Bench. He was under the delusion that we all more or less shared in and believe that the working classes were excluded from the franchise, and that there was a sharp line drawn at the £10 franchise, above which the working men could not penetrate. That being the whole proposition which the noble Lord put forward with respect to Reform, and that being proved to be founded upon a mistake–I want to know upon what principle it is that the Government, having received the statistics which my noble Friend the Member for Haddingtonshire (Lord Elcho) advised them to obtain, showing that these people, for the sake of whom they asked for a Reform Bill, were already represented–I want to know why they now go on at all with a Bill in respect of the representation of the people. Surely this was worth explaining. We could have perfectly understood it if these statistics had not been there; my right hon. Friend would have told us at once that it was to enfranchise the working men; but these facts being as they are, my right hon. Friend says absolutely nothing, but assumes that this House is going to entertain a proposition without knowing in the least what his adhesion to it in his own mind is based upon, or what reason there is for asking the House to accede to it. These statistics prove a little more. They prove a thing for saying which I have been greatly reproved–that the franchise was, in fact, in the power to a great extent of the working classes. I have been reviled in the best and in the worst of English for the statement, and nobody has taken me to task more severely than the noble Lord whose Preface I have read, because he has introduced a fresh series of paragraphs into his Preface to the last edition merely for the purpose of castigating me for saying anything so unkind and so untrue as that the franchise was in their power. All I can say is, if it is not in their power, how did they get there? These statistics prove something more still, and what is also very well worth the notice of the Government. It is this–I do not apprehend we have any statistics to show us when it was that this great increase in the constituencies took place, but I think no one who knows the history of this country can doubt that it is owing to the great expansion of everything during the last twenty or thirty years. We know the causes at work which produced the expansion, but are they permanent or are they transient? The first cause was undoubtedly the discovery of gold in California and Australia, and the consequent depreciation of the precious metals gave an apparent increase of prices both in wages and in commodities. This led to higher rents and to higher wages–though I do not wish to embarrass the subject by going into figures. Another cause which kept up the rate of wages was the great emigration which took place, and is still taking place, from Ireland. Another cause was the vast extension in our trade and commerce, making labour every day more and more in demand. Therefore, I am not wrong, I think, in considering that these causes which have existed hitherto have their efficacy by no means spent, and what we have a right to look at is, that the process of spontaneous enfranchisement that has been going on since the passing of the Reform Bill will go on hereafter and probably with redoubled vigour. We have to build upon an admission–I cannot extract many principles from the Chancellor of the Exchequer's speech, but it is impossible to manipulate figures and statements without implying something–and one thing that he laid down was that he did not wish to see the working classes in a majority in the constituencies in this country; at least, he said he did not much care himself, but for the sake of weaker brethren he would not like to see that. And, therefore, he rejected–with a bitter pang no doubt–the £6 franchise, and took the £7, because the £6 would have given 428,000, which would have been a clear majority of 362,000, whereas the £7 franchise gives 330,000, which leaves a very small majority the other way. But it must be remembered that we are not speaking for a year or two, but for the future, and I would ask the House what are the prospects of the constituencies–what are the chances that the principle which the Chancellor of the Exchequer could not screw his nerves up to face would remain inviolate? Is it not certain that in a few years from this the working men will be in a majority? Is it not certain that causes are at work which will have a tendency to multiply the franchise–that the £6 houses will become the £7 ones, and the £9 houses will expand to £10? There is no doubt an immense power of expansion; and therefore, without straining anything at all, it is certain that sooner or later we shall see the working classes in majority in the constituencies. Look at what that implies. I shall speak very frankly on this subject, for having lost my character by saying that the working man could get the franchise for himself, which has been proved to be true, and for saying which he and his friends will not hate me one bit the less, I shall say exactly what I think. Let any Gentleman consider–I have had such unhappy experiences, and many of us have–let any Gentleman consider the constituencies he has had the honour to be concerned with. If you want venality, if you want ignorance, if you want drunkenness, and facility for being intimidated; or if, on the other hand, you want impulsive, unreflecting, and violent people, where do you look for them in the constituencies? Do you go to the top or to the bottom? It is ridiculous for us to allege that since the Reform Bill the sins of the constituencies or the voters are mainly comprised between £20 and £10. But, then, it has been said the £10 shopkeepers, and lodging-house keepers, and beerhouse keepers, are an indifferent class of people; but get to the artizan, and there you will see the difference. It is the sort of theory the ancients had about the north wind. The ancients observed that as they went further to the north the wind got colder. Colder and colder it got the further they went, just as the constituencies get worse and worse the nearer you approach £10. They reasoned in this way–If it is so cold when you are in front of the north wind, how very warm it would be if you could only get behind it. And, therefore, they imagined for themselves a blessed land we have all read of, where the people, called the Hyperboreans, were always perfectly warm, happy, and virtuous, because they had got to the other side of the north wind. It is the same view that my right hon. Friend takes with respect to the £10 franchise–if you go a little lower you get into the virtuous stratum. We know what those persons are who live in small houses–we have had experience of them under the name of 'freemen'–and no better law, I think, could have been passed than that which disfranchised them altogether. The Government are proposing to enfranchise one class of men who have been disfranchised heretofore. This class, dying out under one name, the Government propose to bring back under another. That being so, I ask the House to consider what good we are to get for the country at large by this reduction of the franchise? The effect will manifestly be to add a large number of persons to our constituencies, of the class from which if there is to be anything wrong going on we may naturally expect to find it. It will increase the expenses of candidates –it will enormously increase the expenses of management of elections, even supposing that everything is conducted in a legitimate and fair manner–and it will very much increase the expenses of electioneering altogether. If experience proves that corruption varies inversely as the franchise, you must look for more bribery and corruption than you have hitherto had. This will be the first and instantaneous result. Then, there is another which I wish to point out to hon. Gentlemen on this side of the House–their own experience will bear me out if they would frankly admit it–and that is, that by a singular retribution of Providence the main mischief will fall on the promoters of this Bill. A great many of these new electors are addicted to Conservative opinions; I do believe the franchise of the Government, if carried, will displace a number of most excellent Gentlemen on this side, and replace them with an equal number of Gentlemen from the other side of the House. But all this is merely the first stage. The first stage, I have no doubt will be an increase of corruption, intimidation, and disorder, of all the evils that happen usually in elections. But what will be the second? The second will be that the working men of England, finding themselves in a full majority of the whole constituency, will awake to a full sense of their power. They will say, "We can do better for ourselves. Don't let us any longer be cajoled at elections. Let us set up shop for ourselves. We have objects to serve as well as our neighbours, and let us unite to carry those objects. We have machinery; we have our trades unions; we have our leaders all ready. We have the power of combination, as we have shown over and over again; and when we have a prize to fight for we will bring it to bear with tenfold more force than ever before." Well, when that is the case–when you have a Parliament appointed, as it will be, by such constituencies so deteriorated–with a pressure of that kind brought to bear, what is it you expect Parliament to stop at? Where is the line that can be drawn? The right hon. Gentleman has said to us that he does not pledge Government to any re-distribution of seats, but if the Government should bring it forward he thinks this Parliament might be kept alive in order to effect that re-distribution. I am very much obliged to my right hon. Friend; but for my part I think Parliamentary life would not be worth preserving on those terms. Look at the position Parliament will occupy. As long as we have not passed this Bill we are masters of the situation. Let us pass the Bill, and in what position are we? That of the Gibeonites–hewers of wood and drawers of water, rescued for a moment from the slaughter that fell on the other Canaanites in order that we may prepare the Bill for re-distribution, with a threat hanging over our heads that if we do not do the work we shall be sent about our business and make way for another Parliament.

. . . It has been said, indeed, that precisely the same arguments have been used now as were used in 1832; but you must remember that to make a good argument two things are requisite–first, that the principle itself be sound, and secondly that the fact corresponds to the fact which it assumes. Now, the arguments against Reform in 1832 were excellent, only they did not correspond to the facts of the case. The question which hon. Gentlemen beg in representing the two cases as parallel is–Are the facts of the case now the same as they were in 1832? Well, Sir, that is a question I am not going to enter into; but I may just point out this–that in 1832 the controversy was perfectly defined. The question was–Did the system then existing work well or not? One side maintained that it did work well, the other contended that it did not; and the country decided very rightly, as I, for one, think, that it did not. But that is not the controversy now. It is now admitted that the system does work well; and the controversy now is, ought we not still to alter it? Take, for instance, a very clever letter, signed "H.", which appeared in *The Times* of yesterday. In reply to the question what good a Reform Bill could be expected to accomplish, the writer said–

> "I am quite willing, for the sake of this argument, to answer 'none.' Nevertheless, I reply, even if that be so, the passing of a Reform Bill is a positive advantage,"

–simply, as I suppose, because gentlemen are, as they call themselves, 'committed.' That is, for the sake of preserving our consistency, we are to do that which we know to be injurious to the best interests of the country. You must also make this distinction between the present time and 1832. The grievances that were complained of in 1832 were practical grievances. Do not believe for a moment that the House of Commons was reformed simply on account of the anomalies of the system. The House of Commons was reformed because the public mind was revolted by things which they thought bad in the legislation and government of the country, and seized upon those anomalies as the weapons to abate the nuisance. That, being a practical grievance, has been redressed, and led for a certain time to a settlement of the question. But, Sir, nobody ever settles a question by remedying a mere theoretical grievance, and that is just the grievance we have now to deal with. My right hon. Friend the Chancellor of the Exchequer told us in his speech, as one great inducement to pass his Bill, that we should find in it a complete settlement of the question, and that he hoped that impracticable persons–I do not know whether I was one to whom he referred–if for no other reason, would be induced to give their assent to the Bill because it would be a settlement of the question. Settlement? What significance does the right hon. Gentleman attach to that word? He stated that you are to go on with this Bill for twelve nights in this Session, and if you cannot pass it in twelve nights, it is to be left to the charities of private Members, and those charities are, we know, very cold. Thus, probably, the measure might go over this year, and begin over again next year, and when we have disposed of it we are to be refreshed by a Franchise Bill for Scotland and a Franchise Bill for Ireland, about which we were told that the information was rather than not in a state of preparation. Then, when we have done with the three Franchise Bills, three Re-distribution Bills are to follow; and even then we shall not be out of the wood, because there is to be also a Boundaries Bill, one of the most difficult and irritating subjects which can be imagined–and after that we are to come to a Registration Bill, which is also a matter of great difficulty. We have now reckoned up eight measures, and there is one more yet, enough to make any man shudder to think of, and that is an anti-corruption Bill. So that the prospect of a settlement, which the right hon. Gentleman holds out, is that we are to begin *de novo* with the whole of our electoral system, and to go through the whole of it in measures which, according to his own enumeration, amount at least to nine; and that he holds out as a settlement, so that if we will pass this Bill we may possibly, if we behave well, employ ourselves in going through this amount of work. That, however, is not my idea of a settlement, and I am quite sure that in addition to that there are unsettling causes which the right hon. Gentleman did not tell us of. Supposing the Bills are passed–as they will be passed, if at all–in mere deference to numbers at the expense of property and intelligence, in deference to a love of sympathy and equality–I feel convinced that when you have given all the right hon. Gentleman asks you will still leave plenty of inequalities, enough to stir up this passion anew. The grievance being theoretical and not practical will survive as long as practice does not conform to theory; and practice will never conform to theory until you have got to universal suffrage and equal electoral districts. I say, therefore, that there is no element of finality in this measure, and though, as I have before said, I am perfectly willing to consider anything that may be brought forward, I crave leave to say that I shall consider the guidance of my own vote and conduct with reference to its influence on the good or bad working of the House of Commons, and not with reference to any theories about the ideal of good government, which, according to one great thinker, consists in everybody having a share in it–just as I suppose his ideal of a joint-stock company is one in which everybody is a director.

66. Reform Bill of 1866: Gladstone's speech on the second reading (12 April)

Hansard, 3/CLXXXII/1131–42.

Gladstone was followed by Lord Robert Grosvenor, a Whig, who moved that the House decline to proceed with the reduction of the franchise until it had before it the whole of the proposals of the Government–*i.e.* primarily the redistribution proposals, which had been announced for a separate and subsequent Bill. After eight nights' debate the motion was lost by five votes, and, as a result, the Government introduced on 7 May its Redistribution Bill, which, at the committee stage (28 May), was combined with the original Bill. But this move did not placate the Opposition, and, after a further series of stern fights–the whole debate constituting one of the greatest oratorical tourneys of the period–the Bill was lost on a motion of Lord Dunkellin to return to the rating basis for the franchise. Forty-four of the normal supporters of the Government voted with Dunkellin.

. . . Sir, the House will remember that on a former occasion I ventured to refer to the state of the constituency at the present moment as compared with what it was in 1832; and I endeavoured to show by a computation, of which I stated the grounds, that the proportion of the working classes included in the present constituency, although to our great satisfaction we had found it to be larger than we had supposed, yet was smaller than it had been in the year 1832. That statement has not been impugned in this House, and I do not think it can be impugned successfully. I do not think that any Gentleman who has examined the figures will venture to question my statement that at the present moment the quantitative proportion of the working men in the town constituencies is less than it was in 1832. But in order to obtain a full view of the importance of this fact, neither must the House forget that since 1832 every kind of beneficial change has been in operation in favour of the working classes. There never was a period in which religious influences were more active than in the period I now name. It is hardly an exaggeration to say that within that time the civilizing and training powers of education have for all practical purposes been not so much improved as, I might almost say, brought into existence as far as the mass of the people is concerned. As regards the press, an emancipation and an extension have taken place to which it would be difficult to find a parallel. I will not believe that the mass of Gentlemen opposite are really insensible to the enormous benefit that has been effected by that emancipation of the press, when for the humble sum of a penny, or for even less, newspapers are circulated from day to day by the million rather than by the thousand, in numbers almost defying the powers of statistics to follow, and carrying home to all classes of our fellow-countrymen accounts of public affairs, enabling them to feel a new interest in the transaction of those affairs, and containing articles which, I must say, are written in a spirit, with an ability, with a sound moral sense, and with a refinement, that have made the penny press of England the worthy companion–I may indeed say the worthy rival–of those dearer and older papers which have long secured for British journalism a renown perhaps without parallel in the world. By external and material, as well as by higher means, by measures relating to labour, to police, and to sanitary arrangements, Parliament has been labouring, has been striving to raise the level of the working community, and has been so striving with admitted success. And there is not a call which has been made upon the self-improving powers of the working community which has not been fully answered. Take, for instance, the Working Men's Free Libraries and Institutes throughout the country; take, as an example of the class, Liverpool; who are the frequenters of that institution? I believe that the majority of the careful, honest, painstaking students who crowd that library are men belonging to the working classes, a large number of whom cannot attend without making some considerable sacrifice. Then again, Sir, we called upon them to be provident, we instituted for them Post Office savings banks, which may now be said to have been in full operation for four years; and what has been the result? During these four years we have received these names at the rate of thousands by the week, and there are now 650,000 depositors in those savings banks. This, then, is the way in which Parliament has been acting towards the working classes. But what is the meaning of all this? Parliament has been striving to make the working classes progressively fitter and fitter for the franchise; and can anything be more unwise, not to say more senseless, than to persevere from year to year in this plan, and then blindly to refuse to recognize its legitimate upshot–namely, the increased fitness of the working classes for the exercise of political power? The proper exercise of that power depends upon the fitness of those who are to receive it. That fitness you increase from day to day, and yet you decline, when the growing fitness is admitted, to give the power. ("No, no!" from the back Opposition Benches.) You decline to give the working classes political power by lowering the borough franchise. ("No, no! from the back Opposition Benches.) I do not complain of the interruption–in fact, I am very glad to hear it. (Cheers and laughter.) I wish it were universal, I wish it came from the front Opposition Benches, and from my noble Friend behind me; for if our opponents were so prepared to proceed in what seems their natural sense, we should have little matter for controversy on the subject of this Bill. But I fear it is not so. I fear the intention is to resist the consummation of the process, of which the earlier stages have been favoured and approved. This course appears about as rational as the process of a man who incessantly pours water into a jug or bason, and wonders and complains that at last it overflows.

Now, what are the arguments that the busy brain of man has framed in opposition to this measure? It is one favourite plea of our opponents that we ought not to hand over the power to govern to those who do not pay the charges of Government. In the depository of wisdom to which I have referred that argument occupies a very prominent place, as it did in the speech of a noble Lord (Viscount Cranbourne), a very distinguished Member of this House, from which I am afraid the writers in the *Quarterly Review* have been guilty of gross plagiarism on more occasions than one. But is this the thing that we are really going to do? are we, indeed, going to hand over the power to those who do not pay the charges of Government? I will not at this moment go into the first portion of the proposition, although I say distinctly we are not going to hand over the power at all; but is it true that the working classes do not contribute fairly, fully, largely, to the expenses of Government? This question was put to me two days ago, in consequence of my statement that, according to the best estimate I could form, the working classes were possessed of an income forming not less than five-twelfths – that is, not very far short of one-half – of the entire income of the country. I repeat that statement in the presence of those who are able to correct me if I am wrong, and in the presence of the greatest economist of the day.[1] Others have made higher estimates. The hon. Member for Derby (Mr. Bass), who is no mean authority upon subjects connected with the earnings of the working classes, has placed their income at a much higher rate than I have done. This is a matter on which I may be confuted, but scarcely contradicted, because the question is not one of fact but of inquiry, argument, and inference. I repeat that, in my judgment, after the best examination I can make, it is a moderate estimate to put the income of the working classes at five-twelfths of the aggregate income of the country, whereas they are put off under the present law with, at the outside, only one-seventh of the electoral power. Now, on the very showing of our antagonists, and putting aside altogether the question how far the human element itself may weigh, apart from money, is not such a state of things absolutely unjust? (Loud cheers.) Perhaps I shall be told that I have based my estimate upon the income and not upon the property of the working classes. Probably that may be the answer to my statement. Yes, I hear a cheer. I admit I have spoken in reference to income, and not in reference to property. Well, anyone so inclined may take it on that ground if he chooses; but he must also take the consequence of having made that choice, and he must be prepared to change the whole system of your taxation. We now lay upon income the great bulk of your taxes, and to these taxes the working classes contribute, perhaps a larger proportion, looking at the amount of their earnings, than is paid by the proudest noble in the land. I, therefore, say to those Gentlemen who argue that the working classes are not entitled to the franchise because they do not possess property, but they must be prepared to join hands with the hon. Member for Birmingham (Mr. Bright), and with the financial reformers of Liverpool, and instead of raising a fourteenth part of the revenue, or some such proportion, as we now do, from property and the rest from income, we must raise a fourteenth part from income and the rest from property.

Again it is said, at least I believe it has been so said, that where the working classes have a majority they vote together as a class. Now, is there any shade or shadow, any rag of proof that such is the fact? I am going to trespass upon the patience of the

[1] J. S. Mill, elected for Westminster in 1865.

House by reading a letter which I received to-day from a working man, and which I shall venture to read for the especial benefit of the Gentlemen opposite. I believe the statements it contains to be perfectly true, and it is my sincere opinion that the writer's arguments are typical of the class to which he belongs. In any case their nature is such that I am confident hon. Gentlemen will not be sorry to hear them.

> "Dear Sir" (I do not know him personally, but he thus kindly addresses me)–"My motive in writing this is to remind you of the Tories who belong to the working classes, as you cannot think perhaps all you wish at the right time. We all know that there are the same variety of principles and opinions in all classes of society, I am a working man, and have an opportunity of knowing that the Tories in principle, especially the artizan class, who are very numerous, who are not now in possession of the franchise. The new Reform Bill, I think, will do about as much for the Tories as for the Liberals. It would for all we know. The love of country and constitution is confined to no particular class. A Liberal is as loyal as a Tory. Is there any evidence to show that these men which the Reform Bill or Franchise Bill would enfranchise are not fit to be trusted? They know well that the welfare and prosperity of the country and their masters is at the same time their welfare and prosperity. Please not to make my name public."

Well, Sir, in my opinion, the letter presents a true view of the question. There is in it that latent concentrated good sense which often comes from the mind, from the mouth, and from the pen of an uneducated man with a peculiar free meaning, perhaps because he is in a certain sense, as I may say, without any reproach or disparagement to education, so much nearer to the point at which nature originally placed him than are men with minds more refined and cultivated. Now, Sir, I maintain that there is no proof whatever that the working classes, if enfranchised, would act together as a class. Perhaps you ask for proofs to the contrary. It is exceedingly difficult to give a direct proof of that which has not happened: although in my opinion ample proof, substantial, even if indirect, of the correctness of my statement does exist. For example, I take this point. Municipal franchises are in a predominant degree working men's franchises. Those franchises, if they do not quite come up to universal suffrage, at all events nearly approach household suffrage. What has been the system followed by the working classes in municipal elections? In order to institute a comparison between the municipal and Parliamentary franchises we must select those towns in which the municipal and Parliamentary boundaries are the same. There are 346,000 municipal voters in that portion of the towns of this country, and, computing as well as the information in our hands will permit, I find that there are 163,000 of them on the Parliamentary register. I deduct from that number one-fourth or 41,000 as representing the maximum portion of working men, and the result is that there remain 122,000 as the number of non-working men in the municipal constituency. Thus the working men number 224,000. Is not this a dreadful state of things? Yet there has been no explosion, no antagonism between classes, no question has been raised about property, nor indeed has any, even the slightest attempt, been made to give a political character to municipal institutions. ("Oh, oh!") Yes, but when the municipal franchise was discussed in 1835 the party who occupied the seats of hon. Gentlemen opposite–(Mr. DISRAELI: Where were you sitting then?) If, however, such questions are relevant to the matter in hand, I was sitting on the Benches of that party; but I was not one of those who supported the argument. Where was the right hon. Gentleman sitting at that time? He was not sitting, indeed, for he did not sit at all, but he was standing somewhere or other in the interests of the 'Mountain' far above the Benches behind me. The material point, Sir, is this, that many of the Gentlemen who were then sitting opposite prophesied that great danger and mischief would spring from the municipal franchise, because it would give a political character to municipal elections, and imbue all our corporations with a similar spirit. That being the case, I think I am perfectly justified in standing upon an important and strictly relevant fact, that, as far as I am aware, we are not able to adduce a single instance in which this majority composed from the working class majority has given a democratic–I will not say a disloyal, but a democratic character–a character distinct from that which they bore under the influence of the middle classes to our municipal institutions.

Again, Sir, with respect to the Parliamentary constituency, let Gentlemen glance impervially at the present state of things. I have previously referred to the metropolitan boroughs, which return a large number of what are denominated 'advanced' politicians on this side of the House, and which have less than the usual proportion of voters of the working class. I pass now to the other end of the scale. I find that among the present town constituencies there are eight boroughs in which the working classes constitute a majority on the registers. These eight towns are–Beverley, Coventry, Greenwich, St. Ives, Maldon, Stafford, Pembroke, and Newcastle-under-Lyne. What is the revolutionary character of the Members whom they return? I find that these eight towns return five who bear the name of Liberal, and nine who claim to belong to the Opposition. This, then, is the result, as far as our narrow experience goes, of having the working classes in the majority.

But there is a much broader ground, to which, I think, no reference has yet been made, and that is the case of the boroughs which had open constituencies containing large majorities of the working classes before the Reform Act–constituencies much more popular than those of the present day. Upon examining the probable operation of the new Bill, I find that, according to our very large definitions of the working classes–a definition which I have employed rather for argument's sake, I mean in order to avoid contention, than because it was strictly and literally accurate–I find this as the result, that in sixty boroughs, returning 101 Members, the working classes will or may have majorities. In these sixty boroughs the electors form 8·4 per cent of the population. Now, let us compare with this state of things the state of things that existed in the popular boroughs before the Reform Act. Before 1830 there were sixty-five boroughs of a strictly popular character; more popular, indeed, than the sixty boroughs that are likely to have a majority of the labouring classes under the Bill now on the table, for the electors in them instead of being 8·4 per cent of the population, numbered nearly 10 per cent, and furthermore, the sixty-five boroughs returned Members for 130 seats. If it be true that the majority of the working classes in a constituency give the control of the seat, which, however, I entirely deny, you cannot show that, under our Bill, there would be more than 101 such seats; while, under the old Parliamentary system, that system which so scandalizes my right hon. Friend the Member for Calne (Mr. Lowe), they numbered 130. We now, therefore, stand, to a certain extent, upon the firm ground of history and experience for the purpose of comparison. Was there among those 130 Members at any period of our history developed a character in any degree dangerous to the institutions of the country? I doubt if any Gentleman will be found ready to affirm that there was.

. . . But, Sir, it is constantly alleged, and the argument is employed with confidence, that, if we would only let the matter take its course, the enfranchisement of the working classes is actually in course of being effected by a natural process, whereas we are endeavouring to stimulate and force onwards this enfranchisement by artificial means. This is a matter upon which I should be extremely slow to dogmatize; because it does not admit of being brought to a test with such precision as to warrant confidence. But I must say that the whole of the argument upon such facts as are known to us is the other way, and that I wait with anxiety, but without expectation, for the proof of this enlargement, of this natural and spontaneous enlargement, with which it is said we are rashly intermeddling. The number of working men on the register is, I think, undeniably less at present than it was in 1832; but, of course, there is the fact that since 1832 the working men belonging to the class of freemen have somewhat diminished. I do not think that the diminution in this direction is numerically of much importance, but there has been a great diminution in the scot and lot voters who are working men. This class is not, indeed, yet extinct; and therefore, in our computations respecting the future, we must allow for a continuance of this dwindling process, until the whole number of scot and lot voters in existence at the time of the Reform Bill has disappeared. It is said, however, that there is a rapid growth of the working classes among the £10 householders. But where is the proof of this assertion? I believe it to be undeniable that the rate of progress in the aggregate number of £10 householders has been very much less of late years than in the first few years after the passing of the Reform Bill. From 1832 to 1851, while the population increased at the rate of 43 per cent, the constituency grew more than twice as fast, but from 1851 to 1866 the constituency grew only 50 per cent faster than the aggregate population, thus showing a great slackening as compared with the earlier period. This, however, can in some degree be accounted for. There were persons not belonging to the working classes who were classed under other denominations at the time of the Reform Act, but whose successors, as they died off, have subsequently appeared as £10 householders. But it is a mistake, I believe, to imagine that some very extraordinary growth has taken place among the £10 householders; and a still greater mistake to imagine that such growth, as may have occurred, has taken place in the working portion of the population. Let us look at the economical facts of the case. If we take the case of the towns, we find that the increase of the constituencies since 1832 has been nearly the same for the entire period as that of the population. In the population it has been 79 per cent, and in the franchise 82 per cent; a variation so slight that it may be practically disregarded. It is said that there is a growth in the wealth of the working classes more than proportionate to that of the classes above them; but no attempt has been made to prove this. In my firm opinion, the largest share of the recent increase of wealth has taken place among the middle classes of the country. To put it shortly and intelligibly, the capital of the country has grown in a far greater degree than the income of the working classes. But other circumstances must be taken into view. We must not assume that the improvement in the dwellings of the artizans in towns has kept pace with the increase of their income, nor even that they are in as great a degree as formerly the occupiers of houses so as to obtain the franchise. Again, we must remember that in the large towns, where the area is limited, the growth in the value of land and rents has been much more rapid than the growth of wealth. If we inquire what is the value of land in the City of London, and compare it with what it was twenty years ago, we shall find that its growth is entirely out of proportion to the growth in the wealth of the City, great as that has been. This constant pressure of growing rents and limitation of area may drive the working man into lodgings, or may send him to such a dwelling beyond the limits of a represented town instead of within them. I shall not be going too far if I assert–in fact, I may say that it is notorious–that there are large masses of the labouring people, especially in London, who, as compared with their position twenty years ago, are better clothed and better fed, but who live in worse houses than they did, although enjoying a larger income. And this arises from the fact that there is not the same limitation in the supply of food and clothing as exists in the supply of houses, because of the contraction of area. I state my own opinions with the reserve that the nature of the question requires; but I must say that I have heard no good argument to the contrary. And I stand finally upon this general statement of the case. For a man to occupy a house of £10 clear annual value, setting aside only the class of men who receive lodgers into their houses, he must, all things considered, have an income from £90 to £100 a year. That clear annual value is minus rates and taxes, and it is minus the cost and the depreciation of furniture also. It is vain then to stand in the face of your working population and say, "We have a law which will enfranchise all the careful, diligent, and respectable men among you; but no working man is intelligent, or industrious, or respectable unless he can earn 35s. a week." That is too severe a test; and my general statement of the facts is enough, therefore, to show that it is vain to speak of a £10 franchise, taking the country all over, as one which is capable of admitting, by the natural or spontaneous process which has been set up in argument against us, all the industrious and diligent among the lower classes. . . .

67. Reform in 1867: Robert Lowe's speech on the Derby Government's household suffrage proposals (5 March)

Hansard, 3/CLXXXV/1358–60.

Derby had failed to induce the Whig rebels who had brought their own Government down to join his Cabinet, and, in his minority position in the House, might not have touched Reform, but for the queen's insistence that the problem should be got out of the way.[1] A plan of household suffrage, with safeguards against working-class ascendancy in the shape of 'fancy franchises' and provisions for plural voting, was considered by the Cabinet, but was abandoned in the face of the

[1] Part I, Nos. 29 and 30.

opposition of Cranborne, Carnarvon, and General Peel, after Cranborne had shown, by analysis of the figures, that in 60 per cent of the boroughs the proposals would give a working-class majority. A £6 rating plan was hurriedly substituted–the 'Ten Minutes Bill'–and was presented to the House. But the news that a larger scheme had been in contemplation had leaked out, and the House, the Tory back-benchers leading, demanded its production. Derby decided to face the resignation of his malcontents, and on 4 March Disraeli announced the intention of the Government to "recur to its original policy". On the following day, immediately after Cranborne's and Peel's resignation speeches, Lowe pronounced the great philippic against the Government which follows. It is not, however, altogether free of indications of his desire to preserve his communications with his party, and after the Bill was passed, and the Derby Government defeated at the 1868 election, Lowe joined Gladstone's Government as chancellor of the exchequer.

There is one cause, Sir, which no one seems to have any interest in defending, and with respect to which I ask permission to say a few words. The right hon. Gentleman the Member for South Lancashire (Mr. Gladstone) naturally supports the £7 rental franchise of last year, and the Chancellor of the Exchequer as naturally supports one of the two franchises, between which he has divided his affections, –£6 rating or household suffrage. I want to point out to the House, as the Chancellor of the Exchequer states that there is a principle in his proposal of a £6 rating franchise, that this principle is only a translation of the £7 rental franchise of last year into a £6 rating franchise. The right hon. Gentleman the Chancellor of the Exchequer, therefore, by implication admits that there was a principle in the Government measure of last year. Such being the case, the right hon. Gentleman has the onus thrown on him of telling us on what principle he assisted those who laboured so hard and so successfully to destroy the measure of last year and the Government with it. I have no doubt that most of the supporters of the Government measure of last year supported it because they believed that the £7 rental franchise was a point at which they could rest, and that it carried with it a sufficient safeguard. I believed that it did not. I believed that it was only a stage on the road to that household suffrage which the Chancellor of the Exchequer has announced. I wish, therefore, Sir, on behalf of myself and of those who voted with me on such grounds, that we should not be confounded with those who suppose that a measure containing no principle at all in one form acquires it when stated in another, and that we should not be assumed to be turning round with the right hon. Gentleman the Chancellor of the Exchequer, and, after opposing the £7 rental franchise of last year, acquiesce in his view to-night, when, for the first time, the Minister of the Crown pronounces the fatal and ominous words, "household suffrage." If we wanted this household suffrage our way to it was very plain. We might have got it much more easily than by placing the right hon. Gentleman and his Colleagues in office, with much more facility and much less expenditure of time. Of course, there is no 'understanding' in such matters–no indenture drawn, no engagements interchanged, but I ask hon. Gentlemen opposite whether it was for the purpose of bringing forth household suffrage that we combined with the right hon. Gentleman last year to defeat the Government measure. And here I feel it my duty to pay a tribute to the hon. Member for Birmingham, who, at meetings called in favour of manhood suffrage, manfully resisted giving his adhesion to that principle, and always declared his opinion to be in favour of household suffrage. The hon. Member for Birmingham approached that point from below; the Chancellor of the Exchequer approached it from above: at last they have met. You might try in vain to draw any practical distinction between the policy of the right hon. Gentleman who leads the Conservative party and the policy of the hon. Member for Birmingham.

> "So like they were, no mortal
> Might one from other know."

The one resisting pressure approached household suffrage from below, and the other dropped down from above upon it without any compulsion at all, but from a natural attraction and affinity which exist between the two. We have now an alliance of a new kind.

> "These be the Great Twin Brethren
> To whom the Dorians pray.
> Home comes the Chief in triumph,
> Who, in the hour of fight,
> Has seen the Great Twin Brethren
> In harness on his right.
> Safe comes the ship to haven,
> Through tempests and through gales,
> If once the Great Twin Brethren
> Sit shining on its sails."

I ask hon. Gentlemen opposite, with whom it rests whether this alliance shall take effect or not, what they have to say to it. Are they consenting parties to it? Do they agree that the victory attained last year for the principle that the ancient constitution of the country should be preserved in its integrity, shall give way to the alliance between the hon. Member for Birmingham and the right hon. Gentleman the Chancellor of the Exchequer? The decision rests with them; the country and all of us pause to see what decision they will pronounce. I could not help saying this, because it appears that the majority of last year has now nobody to defend it. We cannot expect defence from those whom we defeated, while those whom we placed in office, those to whom in an evil hour we intrusted the destinies of the country, have underbid those whom they then opposed for going too far, and placed themselves in a position which differs from their opponents only in this–that it is infinitely more democratic. I have only one more word to say. We have heard a great deal about figures, and about the construction which noble Lords and right hon. Gentlemen, who sat up all Sunday night to read them, put upon them. We are told we are to have a Reform Bill on the 18th, that then the matter is to be hurried on with the greatest possible speed, and that after the next stage the House is to sit *de die in diem*. Sir, we have had delays enough for want of information on this matter, and I would suggest to the right hon. Gentleman that if he really wishes the House to form a decision on his Bill, the best thing he can possibly do is to place on the table, without loss of time, those very figures which have been the subject of discussion. At present we have them not. We have the book of last year, in which we find a number of statements in regard to the municipal franchise; but, as is shown by an excellent letter in *The Times* the other day, written by the hon. Member for Cheltenham (Mr. Schreiber), there are only seventy-three boroughs which have conterminously the municipal and Parliamentary franchise, and where we can make comparison between them. It would be a great service to the House, therefore, if the right hon. Gentleman would, without loss of time, furnish us with the opportunity of going through the process which three Secretaries of State have gone through in order to see the real effect of the measure proposed. If we are to have these figures after the Reform Bill is brought in we probably shall not be in a condition to go on with it as the right hon. Gentleman wishes. Therefore, I do hope that the right hon. Gentleman will give us some means of judging of the proposal he intends to submit, that we may not always be in the position of receiving communications, but unable to act upon them for want of information. I thank the House for allowing one evidently of a past generation – who represents that which was a power last year, but which has been taken over by the right hon. Gentleman to the other side – to say a few words on this subject. The truth is, what was a conflict last year has become a race this year, and two parties are trying not which shall attack or which shall stand up for existing institutions, but which shall pass the other in attempting to reach first the goal of a perfectly level democracy.

68. Reform Bill of 1867: Gladstone's speech on the second reading (25 March)

Hansard, 3/CLXXXVI/475–77.

This is the speech in which Gladstone sought to take the shaping of Disraeli's Bill into his own hands.

. . . Sir, it appears to me nothing can be more discouraging than the prospect, when we survey the main heads connected with the settlement of the question. Sketching them lightly, and not attempting artificially to multiply those difficulties, I find they amount to these ten; – A Bill on this subject must, I think, to be satisfactory, contain a lodger franchise; but this Bill contains no lodger franchise. It seems to me that a Bill of this kind, professing largely to enfranchise downwards, must provide some means of preventing the traffic in votes that would infallibly arise in a large scheme affecting the lowest class of householders. This Bill contains no such provisions. It seems to me we must do away with the vexatious distinctions that now exist between compound-householders in a condition of life and society that are recognised by law as fitting them for the franchise, and those persons of the very same condition not being compound-householders. This Bill does not do away with these distinctions; on the contrary, it introduces new ones. I think that the taxing franchise must be omitted. I think that the dual vote must be abandoned. I apprehend there is no doubt that the re-distribution of seats proposed by this Bill must be considerably enlarged. I also venture to take it for granted that the county franchise proposed by the Bill must be reduced. I doubt whether the feeling of the majority of the House will allow the Government to entertain the important provision for the optional use of voting-papers. And finally, with respect to the collateral or bye-franchises or special franchises

–that, perhaps, is the best term for them–my opinion, I confess is that, although on principle no objection can be made to those franchises, or some of them, yet, when we come to examine we shall find, as we obtain acquaintance with the conditions of each proposal, that the advantages continually dwindle, that the obstacles and difficulties continually multiply, and that there will remain finally either a thin and sterile residuum, or else they will altogether disappear. These are the ten main heads to which I referred. But in the discussion I shall confine myself to the subject of the borough franchise, and for this reason:–It is a subject which appears to me to be involved in the greatest–nay, I will say, by the provisions of the Bill as they now stand in hopeless intricacy and difficulty; and it must depend on the assurance which may be given us by the Government with respect to the borough franchise in the course of this debate whether, when we come to the question of your leaving the Chair, there will be any prospect of really gaining ground by going into Committee on the Bill.

Now, if I look at the 3rd clause of this Bill–the great enfranchising clause–I find that it presents to me these prominent features. In the first place, it appears to convey an impression that we are now going to abandon all attempts to distinguish between class and class–to recognise the universal fitness of all classes of the community; and I must confess it appears to me, with great submission, if we do recognise that universal fitness it is not so very important–as the right hon. Gentleman the Chancellor of the Exchequer thinks it is–whether we recognise it under the name of 'popular privileges' or 'democratic rights.' The clause begins with a statement, as if to give the public the impression that we were going to confer what is called 'household suffrage.' Now, without attempting to commit any man in the House, and certainly without having any exaggerated apprehension of the evil consequences that might result even from an error that we might commit in this direction–because I believe the good sense of the country and the strength of its institutions and traditions would effectually qualify and restrain the evil consequence of such an error–I must say, it does not appear to me that we are required either by the state of the population, by the wishes of the country at large, by the opinion of this House, by previous pledges, or by any single consideration that can be brought to bear on the question to assent to that very broad principle. Treating that assent as an assent that is needless, and as one that might produce in several particulars inconvenient consequences, the fact that I do not apprehend ruin and destruction from it is no reason at all for my adopting the proposal, if I thought that a better proposal could be devised. Therefore, for the present, I merely demur to that proposal–not as being one under all circumstances undesirable, but as being at the present moment needless, and therefore unwise. But when I go on further in the clause, I find that this immense concession is so qualified by restraints that they absolutely stultify the concession itself. The House is asked to enfranchise, by adopting this proposal, 750,000 people, in order immediately afterwards to introduce a condition which cuts off two-thirds, or as I think I can show more, of that number. But this disqualification is itself qualified; because in this barrier of personal rating which is set up by the clause, and which *prima facie* shuts out this 500,000 is introduced a little wicket through which, by a process which we will presently examine, it will be in the power of individuals to introduce themselves into the franchise. I think I shall be able to show that that portion of the clause which introduces this restraint is thereby rendered almost entirely nugatory. In this case you have household suffrage to deal with. It may be entirely nullified by the restraint, or it may be that the restraint itself is nugatory, and that the 500,000 persons apparently shut out will be brought into the qualification. But that which will be also easily shown is this, that if this Bill were to become law, it would depend upon the accidental political leanings of local authorities, or upon the exertions of registration agents, to determine whether we were or were not to be landed on the broad principle of household suffrage, or were to be restricted to the narrow ground by which only one-third of the householders below £10 are to be enfranchised. . . .

69. Reform Bill of 1867: Disraeli's speech on the third reading (15 July)

Hansard, 3/CLXXXVIII/1599-1610.

. . . It is very easy for the noble Lord the Member for Stamford,[1] while he treats of a question which has occupied the attention of Parliament for more than fifteen years, to quote some ambiguous expression which was used early in that period of fifteen years by Lord Derby, and then to cite some small passage in a speech made by myself in the year 1866. But I think that hon. Gentlemen on both sides of the House will admit that to arrive at a just judgment of the conduct of public men and of the character of the measures they propose, it is necessary to take larger and fuller views. Measures of this importance, and the conduct of those who may recommend them, are not to be decided by the quotation of a speech made in 1852 or of remarks made in 1866.

Now, Sir, I accept the challenge made by the noble Lord. I will take that very term which he has himself fixed upon as the test of our conduct and of our policy. I will throw my vision back over those fifteen years–to that very term of 1852 when we were called upon to undertake the responsibility of administration. The question of Parliamentary Reform was becoming very rife in 1849 and 1850 and 1851. If I recollect right, it occupied the attention of Parliament when it first met in 1852, when we were sitting in opposition, and therefore when we acceded to office, and to office for the first time, in the year 1852, although the question was not one which upon reflection men who were responsible for the conduct of affairs would have deemed necessary to treat, yet it was one upon which it was absolutely necessary that a Cabinet should have some definite conclusions, and one upon which it was quite certain the moment they acceded to office they would be called to express their opinion. It happened in that wise, for I think that within a month after we acceded to office, Mr. Hume brought forward, as he was accustomed to do, the whole question of Parliamentary Reform in a very comprehensive manner–referring not only to the franchise, but to the re-distribution of seats, and many other matters connected with it. The Cabinet had to meet and decide upon the spirit in which they would encounter

[1] Lord Cranborne.

the Motion of Mr. Hume, and I was the organ to express their opinions on the subject. The opinions which I expressed upon that occasion from this very place were such as do not justify the remarks of the noble Lord and the remarks of the right hon. Gentleman. They may not be fresh in the recollection of the House, but I will say only that upon that occasion, with the full authority of a unanimous Cabinet, expressing the opinion of Lord Derby's Government with regard to the question of Parliamentary Reform, I expressed our opinion that if that subject were again opened–and its immediate reopening we deprecated–that fault which had been committed in 1832 in neglecting to give a due share of the representation to the working classes ought to be remedied. That was in the year 1852, when, with the full authority of the Cabinet, I said that no measure of Parliamentary Reform could be deemed satisfactory which did not remedy the great fault of the settlement of 1832, and I then contended, as I have since, that before the settlement of 1832, franchises existed which were peculiar to the working classes, and that although the precise character of those franchises could not, perhaps, have been entirely defended, they should certainly not have been destroyed without the invention of fresh franchises more adapted to the times in which we live and to the requirements of the classes concerned. Therefore it is quite clear that in 1852 our opinions upon the subject of Parliamentary Reform–for many of the Members of that Cabinet are Members of the present–were such that the expressions of the right hon. Gentleman opposite and the noble Lord cannot for a moment be justified.

And what, Sir, occurred afterwards? When we were in opposition during several years this question was constantly brought under the consideration of Parliament, and it continued to be patronized and encouraged by the then Ministers of the Crown, who yet would not deal with it until the very last year of their existence as a Cabinet; and then, after an official life of some six or seven years, they did introduce the subject to the consideration of Parliament, and left a Bill upon the table when they resigned their Seals of Office. It therefore became necessary for us in 1858 to consider the subject, and we did not conceal from ourselves for a moment the difficulties in treating it that we should have to encounter. But such was the situation of the question, such the state of the country with regard to it, such even the private counsel and encouragement of the most influential of our predecessors in office, that we engaged to consider the question and to bring forward some measure which we hoped might remove the difficulties that stood in the way of general legislation, and so disembarrass political life. We had then to consider the great question of the borough franchise. It was proposed upon that occasion in the Cabinet of Lord Derby that the borough franchise should be founded upon the principle of household suffrage. It is very true that that proposition was not adopted, but it was not opposed, so far as I can charge my memory, on any political ground; it was not adopted by many Members of the Cabinet, because they believed that if a scheme of that kind were brought forward it would receive no support generally speaking in the country. That opinion of Lord Derby's Government I may say was ultimately formed on no mean knowledge; elaborate machinery was had recourse to in order to obtain the information necessary to form an accurate opinion on the subject, and the general tenor of the information which reached us certainly forced us to the conclusion that there was an insuperable objection on the part of the constituencies at that time against any reduction of the borough franchise whatever. That that was a true conclusion; and that the information which led to that conclusion was correct there can be no doubt; for although we were forced to quit office by a Resolution declaring that a reduction of the borough franchise was expedient, those who succeeded us failed in carrying any measure of that kind, and remained in office for years without at all departing from their inaction.

But there is another feature in the policy of the Government of 1859 with regard to this question which I have a right to refer to, and, indeed, am bound to refer to, in vindication of the conduct of that Government. Whatever difference of opinion might have existed in the Cabinet of Lord Derby in 1859 on the question of establishing the borough franchise on the principle of rated household suffrage, there was no difference upon one point; the Cabinet was unanimous, after the utmost deliberation and with the advantage of very large information upon the subject, that if we attempted to reduce the borough qualification which then existed we must have recourse to household suffrage whatever might be the condition. Upon that conclusion we acted, and I am at a loss to discover in the conduct of public men who have acted in the way I have described any foundation for the somewhat frantic attacks which have been made upon us by the right hon. Gentleman opposite, and for the bitter, though more temperately expressed, criticisms of the noble Lord the Member for Stamford. As probably the majority of the present House sat in the late Parliament, the House is well acquainted with the fortunes of the question of Parliamentary Reform during the years which followed the retirement of Lord Derby in 1859. The question was unsuccessfully treated by the most powerful and popular Minister this country has possessed for many years–by one, indeed, who at various times after 1859 apparently occupied a commanding position with reference to any question with which he proposed to deal; and it has so happened that every leading Statesman of the day, every Party representing any important section of power and opinion in the country, who approached this subject, have all of them equally failed. Lord Russell failed, Lord Aberdeen failed, Lord Palmerston failed, Lord Derby failed, and we were called upon to re-consider the question when we came into office after a fresh failure by Lord Russell.

It is said that we have brought forward a measure stronger than the one we opposed. If that be the case, it is no argument against our measure if it be one adapted to the requirements of the time. But, Sir, we who believe that there should be no reduction of the borough franchise other than what we propose, because there can be no sound resting place between it and the present qualification, were perfectly justified in hesitating to accept a reduction of the franchise which might have disturbed the machinery of the State, and have resulted in consequences far more perilous than we believe can ensue from the measure we ask you to adopt. There had been for a considerable time a much-favoured plan before the public; and the object, or rather, I should say, the consequence, of this plan, which may be described as a moderate reduction of the borough franchise, was the enfranchisement of a certain and favoured portion of the working classes, who are always treated in this House and everywhere else publicly in terms of great eulogium, who are–

"Fed by soft dedication all day long,"

and assured that they are very much superior to every other portion of the working classes. These were to be invested with the franchise on the implied condition that they were to form a certain Praetorial guard, and prevent every other portion of the working classes of this country from acquiring the privilege, and thus those other portions would be shut out from what is called the pale of the Constitution. This proposal, in different shapes and different degrees, was constantly before Parliament. We were greatly opposed to it since we believed it was a dangerous policy, and we saw greater peril to the institutions of the country in admitting a small and favoured section of that kind into the political arena than in appealing to the sympathies of the great body of the people. The working classes will now probably have a more extensive sympathy with our political institutions, which, if they are in a healthy state, ought to enlist popular feeling, because they should be embodiments of the popular requirements of the country. It appeared to us that if this great change were made in the constituent body, there would be a better chance of arriving at the more patriotic and national feelings of the country than by admitting only a favoured section, who, in consideration of the manner in which they were treated, and the spirit in which they were addressed, together with the peculiar qualities which were ascribed to them, would regard themselves as marked out, as it were, from the rest of their brethren and the country, and as raised up to be critics rather than supporters of the Constitution. These were our views, and we retain the conviction that guided us in 1859, and from which, if we had deviated, it was only for a moment, and because we thought that on this question it was impossible to come to any solution except in the spirit of compromise and mutual concession. We still adhered to the policy of 1859, and believed if you reduced the borough qualification–and some reduction was now inevitable–there was no resting place until you came to a rating household suffrage.

Well, Sir, under these circumstances, we acceded to power last year, and we found it was absolutely necessary to deal with this question; we came into power unpledged; and I have heard with some astonishment reproaches in regard to our change of opinion. I am not here to defend, to vindicate, or even to mitigate every expression I may have used on this subject during the course of many years; but I can appeal to the general tenour of the policy we have recommended. I have always said that the question of Parliamentary Reform was one which it was quite open to the Conservative party to deal with. I have said so in this House, and on the hustings, in the presence of my countrymen, a hundred times. I have always said, and I say so now, that when you come to a settlement of this question, you cannot be bound to any particular scheme, as if you were settling the duties on sugar; but dealing with the question on great constitutional principles, and which I hope to show have not been deviated from, you must deal with it also with a due regard to the spirit of the time and the requirements of the country. I will not dwell upon the excitement which then prevailed in the country; for I can say most sincerely that without treating that excitement with contempt, or in any spirit analogous to contempt, we considered this question only with reference to the fair requirements of the country. But having to deal with this question, and being in office with a large majority against us, and knowing that Ministers of all colours of party and politics, with great majorities, had failed to deal with it successfully, and believing that another failure would be fatal not merely to the Conservative party, but most dangerous to the country, we resolved to settle it if we could. Having accepted office unpledged, what was the course we adopted? Believing that it was a matter of the first State necessity that the question should be settled–knowing the majority was against us, and knowing the difficulties we had to deal with, being in a minority, and that even with a majority, our predecessors had not succeeded–after due deliberation, we were of opinion that the only mode of arriving at a settlement was to take the House into council with us, and by our united efforts, and the frank communication of ideas, to attain a satisfactory solution. I am in the recollection of the House, and I ask whether that is not a faithful account of the situation? It was in harmony with these views that I placed Resolutions on the table. It is very true that at that time–in the month of March or February it may be–you derided those Resolutions and ridiculed the appeal; but reflection proved the policy was just, and you have adopted it. We have pursued the course which we felt to be the only one to bring this question to a happy termination, and your own good sense, on reflection, has convinced you that the original sneers were not well-founded. You have all co-operated with us, and it is by that frank and cordial co-operation that we have arrived at the third reading.

The noble Lord the Member for Stamford says that the Bill is no longer our Bill –that it has been enormously changed in consequence of our having accepted the ten conditions of the right hon. Gentleman the Member for South Lancashire,[1] which he also informed the House the right hon. Gentleman had so imperiously dictated. At the time there was some complaint of the imperious dictation of the right hon. Gentleman; but it did not come from me; I can pardon those in opposition who are inclined to be imperious, but I have no fault to find with the conditions that the right hon. Gentleman insisted upon, and which the noble Lord says I obsequiously observed.

. . . Now, Sir, the noble Lord says that by yielding to these ten severe conditions I have virtually altered the whole character of the Bill. Now, is that true? Is the whole character of the Bill altered? I contend, on the contrary, that the Bill, though adapted of course to the requirements of the year in which we are legislating, is at the same time in harmony with the general policy which we have always maintained. (Laughter from the Opposition.) This is a question that cannot be settled by a jeer or a laugh, but by facts, and by facts and results which many of you deprecate and deplore at this moment, and in consequence of which you tell us that you mean to re-open the agitation–a thing which I defy you to do. I begin with what the hon. Gentleman who smiles so serenely may regard as the most difficult question for us–namely, that of the borough franchise–and I say that if we could not maintain the £10 borough franchise, which Members of the Liberal party seem now so much to deplore, but which they opposed in 1859, it was perfectly in harmony with the general expression

[1] W. E. Gladstone.

of our opinions, and certainly with our policy as a party, that we should accept such a franchise as we are now recommending to you by this Bill. You declined, the House of Commons declined, and especially the Liberal party declined, to take their stand upon the £10 franchise. You will not deny that; you will not carp at that. Well, but has there been no question since that time between the £10 franchise, upon the merits of which the right hon. Gentleman the Member for Calne[1] is always dilating, saying it has existed–as he told us to-night in a kind of rhetorical *crescendo* which becomes more and more surprising–for at least 200 years; has there, I say, been no question since the Government of 1859 between retaining that £10 borough franchise and accepting household suffrage? Have you not heard of a franchise to be fixed at £8, £7, £6, and all sorts of pounds? The question therefore for us practically to consider was–whether we were to accept this settlement of the borough franchise, we will say at £5, or whether we should adhere to the conviction at which we had arrived in 1859–namely, that if you reduced the qualification there was no safe resting place until you came to a household rating franchise? The noble Lord says that immense dangers are to arise to this country because we have departed from the £10 franchise. (Viscount CRANBORNE: No!) Well, it was something like that, or because you have reduced the franchise. The noble Lord is candid enough to see that if you had reduced it after what occurred in 1859, as you ought according to your pledges to have done, you would have had to reduce it again by this time. It is not likely that such a settlement of the difficulty would have been so statesmanlike that you could have allayed discontent or satisfied any great political demands by reducing the electoral qualification by 40s. or so. Then the question would arise–is there a greater danger from the number who would be admitted by a rating household franchise than from admitting the hundreds of thousands–the right hon. Gentleman the Member for South Lancashire calculated them at 300,000–who would come in under a £5 franchise? I think that the danger would be less, that the feeling of the larger numbers would be more national, than by only admitting what I call the Praetorian guard, a sort of class set aside, invested with peculiar privileges, looking with suspicion on their superiors, and with disdain on those beneath them, with no friendly feelings towards the institutions of their country and with great confidence in themselves. I think you would have a better chance of touching the popular heart, of evoking the national sentiment, by embracing the great body of those men who occupy houses and fulfil the duties of citizenship by the payment of rates, than by the more limited and in our opinion, more dangerous proposal. So much for the franchise. I say that if we could not carry out our policy of 1859, the logical conclusion was that in settling the question we should make the proposition which you, after due consideration, have accepted, and which I hope you will to-night pass. . . .

70. Representation of the People Act (1867)

Statutes of the Realm, 30 & 31 Vict. c. 102.

. . . Every Man shall, in and after the Year One thousand eight hundred and sixty-eight, be entitled to be registered as a Voter, and, when registered, to vote for a

[1] Robert Lowe.

Member or Members to serve in Parliament for a Borough, who is qualified as follows; (that is to say,)

1. Is of full Age, and not subject to any legal Incapacity; and
2. Is on the last Day of July in any Year, and has during the whole of the preceding Twelve Calendar Months been, an Inhabitant Occupier, as Owner or Tenant, of any Dwelling House within the Borough; and
3. Has during the Time of such Occupation been rated as an ordinary Occupier in respect of the Premises so occupied by him within the Borough to all Rates (if any) made for the Relief of the Poor in respect of such Premises; and
4. Has on or before the Twentieth Day of July in the same year *bona fide* paid an equal Amount in the Pound to that payable by other ordinary Occupiers in respect of all Poor Rates that have become payable by him in respect of the said Premises up to the preceding Fifth Day of January:

Provided that no Man shall under this Section be entitled to be registered as a Voter by reason of his being a joint Occupier of any Dwelling House.

4. Every Man shall, in and after the Year One thousand eight hundred and sixty-eight, be entitled to be registered as a Voter, and, when registered, to vote for a Member or Members to serve in Parliament for a Borough, who is qualified as follows; (that is to say,)

1. Is of full Age, and not subject to any legal Incapacity; and
2. As a Lodger has occupied in the same Borough separately and as sole Tenant for the Twelve Months preceding the last Day of July in any Year the same Lodgings, such Lodgings being part of one and the same Dwelling House, and of a clear yearly Value, if let unfurnished, of Ten Pounds or upwards; and
3. Has resided in such Lodgings during the Twelve Months immediately preceding the last day of July, and has claimed to be registered as a Voter at the next ensuing Registration of Voters.

5. Every Man shall, in and after the Year One thousand eight hundred and sixty-eight, be entitled to be registered as a Voter, and, when registered, to vote for a Member or Members to serve in Parliament for a County, who is qualified as follows; (that is to say,)

1. Is of full Age, and not subject to any legal Incapacity, and is seised at Law or in Equity of any Lands or Tenements of Freehold, Copyhold, or any other Tenure whatever, for his own Life, or for the Life of another, or for any Lives whatsoever, or for any larger Estate of the clear yearly Value of not less than Five Pounds over and above all Rents and Charges payable out of or in respect of the same, or who is entitled, either as Lessee or Assignee, to any Lands or Tenements of Freehold or of any other Tenure whatever, for the unexpired Residue, whatever it may be, of any Term originally created for a Period of not less than Sixty Years (whether determinable on a Life or Lives or not), of the clear yearly Value of not less than Five Pounds over and above all Rents and Charges payable out of or in respect of the same:

Provided that no Person shall be registered as a Voter under this Section unless he has complied with the Provisions of the Twenty-sixth Section of the Act of the Second Year of the Reign of His Majesty William the Fourth, Chapter Forty-five.

6. Every Man shall, in and after the Year One thousand eight hundred and sixty-eight, be entitled to be registered as a Voter, and, when registered, to vote for a Member or Members to serve in Parliament for a County, who is qualified as follows; (that is to say,)

1. Is of full Age, and not subject to any legal Incapacity; and
2. Is on the last Day of July in any Year, and has during the Twelve Months immediately preceding been the Occupier, as Owner or Tenant, of Lands or Tenements within the County of the rateable Value of Twelve Pounds or upwards; and
3. Has during the Time of such Occupation been rated in respect to the Premises so occupied by him to all Rates (if any) made for the Relief of the Poor in respect of the said Premises; and
4. Has on or before the Twentieth Day of July in the same Year paid all Poor Rates that have become payable by him in respect of the said Premises up to the preceding Fifth Day of January.

7. Where the Owner is rated at the Time of the passing of this Act to the Poor Rate in respect of a Dwelling House or other Tenement situate in a Parish wholly or partly in a Borough, instead of the Occupier, his Liability to be rated in any future Poor Rate shall cease, and the following Enactments shall take effect with respect to rating in all Boroughs:

1. After the passing of this Act no Owner of any Dwelling House or other Tenement situate in a Parish either wholly or partly within a Borough shall be rated to the Poor Rate instead of the Occupier, except as herein-after mentioned:
2. The full rateable Value of every Dwelling House or other separate Tenement, and the full Rate in the Pound payable by the Occupier, and the Name of the Occupier shall be entered in the Rate Book:

Where the Dwelling House or Tenement shall be wholly let out in Apartments or Lodgings not separately rated, the Owner of such Dwelling House or Tenement shall be rated in respect thereof to the Poor Rate:

Provided as follows:

(1) That nothing in this Act contained shall affect any Composition existing at the Time of the passing of this Act, so nevertheless that no such Composition shall remain in force beyond the Twenty-ninth Day of September next:

(2) That nothing herein contained shall affect any Rate made previously to the passing of this Act, and the Powers conferred by any subsisting Act for the Purpose of collecting and recovering a Poor Rate shall remain and continue in force for the Collection and Recovery of any such Rate or Composition:

(3) That where the Occupier under a Tenancy subsisting at the Time of the passing of this Act of any Dwelling House of other Tenement which has been let to him free from Rates is rated and has paid Rates in pursuance of this Act, he may deduct from any Rent due or accruing due from him in respect of the said Dwelling House or other Tenement any Amount paid by him on account of the Rates to which he may be rendered liable by this Act.

. . .

71. Parliamentary Elections Act (1868)

Statutes of the Realm, 31 & 32 Vict. c. 125.

The Following Enactments shall be made with respect to the Trial of Election Petitions under this Act:

1. The Trial of every Election Petition shall be conducted before a Puisne Judge of One of Her Majesty's Superior Courts of Common Law at *Westminster* or *Dublin*, according as the same shall have been presented to the Court at *Westminster* or *Dublin*, to be selected from a Rota to be formed as hereinafter mentioned.

2. The Members of each of the Courts of Queen's Bench, Common Pleas, and Exchequer in *England* and *Ireland* shall respectively, on or before the Third Day of *Michaelmas* Term in every Year, select, by a Majority of Votes, One of the Puisne Judges of such Court, not being a Member of the House of Lords, to be placed on the Rota for the Trial of Election Petitions during the ensuing Year.

3. If in any Case the Members of the said Court are equally divided in their Choice of a Puisne Judge to be placed on the Rota, the Chief Justice of such Court (including under that Expression the Chief Baron of the Exchequer) shall have a Second or Casting Vote.

4. Any Judge Placed on the Rota shall be re-eligible in the succeeding or any subsequent Year.

5. In the event of the Death or the Illness of any Judge for the Time being on the Rota, or his Inability to act for any reasonable Cause, the Court to which he belongs shall fill up the Vacancy by placing on the Rota another Puisne Judge of the same Court.

6. The Judges for the Time being on the Rota shall, according to their Seniority, respectively try the Election Petitions standing for Trial under this Act, unless they otherwise agree among themselves, in which Case the Trial of each Election Petition shall be taken in manner provided by such Agreement.

7. Where it appears to the Judges on the Rota, after due Consideration of the List of Petitions under this Act for the Time being at issue, that the Trial of such Election Petitions will be inconveniently delayed unless an additional Judge or Judges be appointed to assist the Judges on the Rota, each of the said Courts (that is to say), the Court of Exchequer, the Court of Common Pleas, and Court of Queen's Bench, in the Order named, shall on and according to the Requisition of such Judges on the Rota, select, in manner herein-before provided, One of the Puisne Judges of the

Court to try Election Petitions for the ensuing Year; and any Judge so selected shall, during that Year, be deemed to be on the Rota for the Trial of Election Petitions.

8. Her Majesty may, in manner heretofore in use, appoint an additional Puisne Judge to each of the Courts of Queen's Bench, the Common Pleas, and the Exchequer in *England*.

9. Every Election Petition shall, except where it raises a Question of Law for the Determination of the Court, as herein-after mentioned, be tried by One of the Judges herein-before in that Behalf mentioned, herein-after referred to as the Judge sitting in open Court without a Jury.

10. Notice of the Time and Place at which an Election Petition will be tried shall be given not less than Fourteen Days before the Day on which the Trial is held, in the prescribed Manner.

11. The Trial of an Election Petition in the Case of a Petition relating to a Borough Election shall take place in the Borough, and in the Case of a Petition relating to a County Election in the County: Provided always, that if it shall appear to the Court that special Circumstances exist which render it desirable that the Petition should be tried elsewhere than in the Borough or County, it shall be lawful for the Court to appoint such other Place for the Trial as shall appear most convenient: Provided also, that in the Case of a Petition relating to any of the Boroughs within the Metropolitan District, the Petition may be heard at such Place within the District as the Court may appoint.

12. The Judge presiding at the Trial may adjourn the same from Time to Time and from any one Place to any other Place within the County or Borough, as to him may seem expedient.

13. At the Conclusion of the Trial the Judge who tried the Petition shall determine whether the Member whose Return or Election is complained of, or any and what other Person, was duly returned or elected, or whether the Election was void, and shall forthwith certify in Writing such Determination to the Speaker, and upon such Certificate being given such Determination shall be final to all Intents and Purposes.

14. Where any Charge is made in an Election Petition of any corrupt Practice having been committed at the Election to which the Petition refers, the Judge shall, in addition to such Certificate, and at the same Time, report in Writing to the Speaker as follows:

(*a*) Whether any corrupt Practice has or has not been proved to have been committed by or with the Knowledge and Consent of any Candidate at such Election, and the Nature of such corrupt Practice:

(*b*) The Names of all Persons (if any) who have been proved at the Trial to have been guilty of any corrupt Practice:

(*c*) Whether corrupt Practices have, or whether there is Reason to believe that corrupt Practices have, extensively prevailed at the Election to which the Petition relates.

15. The Judge may at the same Time make a special Report to the Speaker as to any Matter arising in the course of the Trial an Account of which in his Judgment ought to be submitted to the House of Commons.

16. Where, upon the Application of any Party to a Petition made in the prescribed Manner to the Court, it appears to the Court that the Case raised by the Petition can be conveniently stated as a Special Case, the Court may direct the same to be stated accordingly, and any such Special Case shall, as far as may be, be heard before the Court, and the Decision of the Court shall be final; and the Court shall certify to the Speaker its Determination in reference to such Special Case.

72. Ballot Act (1872)

Statutes of the Realm, 35 & 36 Vict. c. 33.

. . .

2. In the case of a poll at an election the votes shall be given by ballot. The ballot of each voter shall consist of a paper (in this Act called a ballot paper) showing the names and description of the candidates. Each ballot paper shall have a number printed on the back, and shall have attached a counterfoil with the same number printed on the face. At the time of voting, the ballot paper shall be marked on both sides with an official mark, and delivered to the voter within the polling station, and the number of such voter on the register of voters shall be marked on the counterfoil, and the voter having secretly marked his vote on the paper, and folded it up so as to conceal his vote, shall place it in a closed box in the presence of the officer presiding at the polling station (in this Act called "the presiding officer") after having shown to him the official mark at the back.

Any ballot paper which has not on its back the official mark, or on which votes are given to more candidates than the voter is entitled to vote for, or on which anything, except the said number on the back, is written or marked by which the voter can be identified, shall be void and not counted.

After the close of the poll the ballot boxes shall be sealed up, so as to prevent the introduction of additional ballot papers, and shall be taken charge of by the returning officer, and that officer shall, in the presence of such agents, if any, of the candidates as may be in attendance, open the ballot boxes, and ascertain the result of the poll by counting the votes given to each candidate, and shall forthwith declare to be elected the candidates or candidate to whom the majority of votes have been given, and return their names to the Clerk of the Crown in Chancery. The decision of the returning officer as to any question arising in respect of any ballot paper shall be final, subject to reversal on petition questioning the election or return.

Where an equality of votes is found to exist between any candidates at an election for a county or borough, and the addition of a vote would entitle any of such candidates to be declared elected, the returning officer, if a registered elector of such county or borough, may give such additional vote, but shall not in any other case be entitled to vote at an election for which he is returning officer.

Part III

NATIONAL RESOURCES: ECONOMIC STRUCTURE AND DEVELOPMENT

NATIONAL RESOURCES: ECONOMIC STRUCTURE AND DEVELOPMENT

Introduction

THE period of this volume sees the consummation of changes that had been coming over British society in the preceding fifty years. The economy shifts from the agrarian basis on which it had hitherto primarily moved to a commercial one; foreign trade, which had long enriched its life-stream, now becomes essential to it. The repeal of the Corn Laws in 1846 was both the public recognition of this change, and a girding up of the nation's loins for its new destiny. The growth of manufacture and trade had already brought with it great accessions of wealth and resources, and was to bring more. But it meant also considerably enhanced vulnerability to the political and economic conditions of the outside world. At its full development, and in order to find the stability it required, the transformed British economy was to need the world as its base: its food and raw materials to fill its granaries and supply its manufactures, its markets to match its increased power of export. Later Victorian prosperity has tended to disguise the fact that these economic relationships did not come into being of themselves, but had to be made. They were the fruit of Victorian effort, and many factors contributed to their making and maintenance: the energies of merchants and manufacturers at the top of the line, but an economic policy that supported their efforts as well, the freedom of the country from major political upsets, domestic and foreign, and the fortunate chance of gold discoveries in California and Australia, creating a monetary climate in the world favourable to enterprise. But in the 'thirties and 'forties all this was in the future, and the present was one of economic and political uncertainty, deepening into the prolonged distress of the hungry 'forties. The country was still in the long ground-swell of the Napoleonic Wars; political and economic relationships had been disrupted and took long to repair; a prolonged price-fall had accompanied the post-war deflation; and commercial and financial institutions and policy were not adequate to their tasks. Furthermore, the population in England was increasing by a couple of millions a decade,[1] entailing each year more mouths to feed and more hands to set to work. To those who accepted the Malthusian correlation of good wages and steady employment with fresh stimulus to the population–and there were many–the task was a Sisyphean one. The climate of economic thought since Adam Smith made it certain that it would be looked on as one which could only be dealt with by industrialists, not one with which statesmen or politicians could advantageously meddle. It is this combination of circumstances that gives to Victorian industrialism its peculiar dynamism and self-confidence. The merchant breaking into new markets, the mill-owner adding to his factory, the iron-master sending down his shafts and putting up his foundries where before had been a bleak hill-side, was, in his own idea, and in the

[1] Nos. 73, 74.

estimation of contemporaries, doing more than seizing his chance in an epoch of opportunity for the adventurous: he was contributing as he alone could to the solution of the national problem, helping to push back the threat of destitution, with all its political and social consequences, that till the middle of the century brooded unceasingly over the industrial areas and populations. The urban society that grew up in Victorian England,[1] on a scale such as to constitute a new phenomenon in the history of the world, faced a range of problems such as have fallen to few communities to grapple with at one and the same time. But the first of them was the bread-and-butter problem–how to get the economy on an even enough keel to be sure of food and work for the industrial masses.

But the new polity was not made in a day. As Sir John Clapham has pointed out, more than half the families enumerated in the 1851 census lived in the country. Statistically, the average Englishman was still a countryman. The economy, as well, responded almost as much to the state of the harvest as to that of foreign trade. Bad harvests meant dearer food, which meant less money for people to spend on other things, which affected trade, and an outflow of gold to pay for increased food imports, which made credit tighter. According to the President of the Manchester Chamber of Commerce, "the originating cause" of the crisis of 1837–1839 was a couple of bad harvests; the importance of this factor in 1847 is indisputable;[2] and in 1854 Leone Levi based the case for better agricultural statistics on the ground of the desirability of letting not only farmers but the other interests in the country have a completer knowledge of their market prospects.[3]

Agriculture is in the doldrums in the 'thirties, and it hardly lifts its head for twenty years. Many of its difficulties, and still more the perspective in which they are seen, go back to the artificial prosperity of the wars. In 1833 a select committee inquired into its ills; in 1836 and 1837 a great deal more evidence was taken, but the diagnosis of 1833 is hardly improved on.[4] The weight of the burdens on the land, the Poor Rate, and the rising County Rate is recognized, and later reform did something to lighten it.[5] But the real burden is the price-fall, accentuated by the restoration of gold payments (1821), and no hope is held out of any effective measures to deal with this. The committee's final reflection is the unwisdom of parliamentary interference with the course of natural adjustment. It recognized, as well, that home agriculture could no longer feed the nation. In 1839, with the foundation of the Anti-Corn Law League, the full-scale attack on protection began; in 1842 came Peel's modification of the Sliding Scale, and then the accidents and incidents that led to Repeal in 1846. Farmers thought that they faced disaster. Cobden argued that an average 10*s.* 6*d.* freight and insurance on corn imported from Odessa constituted an adequate natural protection, and that the effect of Free Trade would be to stimulate agriculture by ruining the worst farmers and putting the best on their toes. Nothing in the next twenty years disproved the diagnosis, though there was a different tale when American prairie corn, aided by cut freights, flooded the markets in the 'seventies. Over the immediate post-Repeal years, the famine and bad harvest of 1847, the political disturbances of the following few years in Europe, and then the Crimean War, kept prices much as they had been.[6] The second lowest in the series of yearly averages is 1835, which is also the lowest for imports. Meanwhile railways put the markets of the country at the general disposal of farmers; farming profited from reviving general prosperity, as the Anti-Corn Law League had argued it must; and

[1] No. 76 [2] Nos. 94, 99. [3] No. 102. [4] No. 91. [5] Part VIII, No. 187, Part IX. [6] Nos. 81–82.

the stimulus of the gold discoveries benefited agriculture as it did every other interest in the country. Agriculture moved into the Victorian prosperity, though with less transformation of its methods, and less spectacular results than attended commerce and industry. Lord Stamp has calculated that between 1842 and 1878 agricultural rents rose by 30 per cent. Wages, which, in the south and west of the country had been very low in the 'forties, followed suit more slowly. Housing lagged even more and was the subject of strong comment by the commissioners of 1867–1868 on the Employment of Women and Children in Agriculture. Agriculture had started the period under the shadow of depression and of the old Poor Law; the drastic innovations of the New Poor Law and the repeal of the Corn Laws were its midway stage; the slump of the 'seventies and the Agricultural Union its postscript. It is not, perhaps, altogether to be wondered at that not much of the increased prosperity of the industry was passed on to the labourer.

The Whig governments of the 'thirties had done little directly for industry and trade, and their last years, and the first of the young queen, were marked by bad harvests, the commercial crises of 1836–1839,[1] and Budget deficits which undermined confidence, and seemed to call for measures of economic rehabilitation more drastic than those promised by the last-minute conversion of the Whigs, in 1840, to measures of Free Trade. A recent calculation by Albert H. Imlah has brought out that the 'thirties were, in fact, the decade of the highest protection since Pitt. British tariff duties were specific, and the effect of the continuous price-fall had been to make them progressively higher in terms of the cost of the imports themselves, notwithstanding the reductions that had been carried out by the Whigs and by Huskisson (1824–1825) before them. The British market was the main market of the world; her ports, at this time, handled between a quarter and a third of the world's trade. The effect of her high tariffs, in Professor Imlah's view, was to cause furious competition to break into her markets in times of slump, and so to drive prices unnaturally low, and to drive them correspondingly higher in years of boom; while, at the same time, the difficulties of trade to Britain, and the uncertainties of its returns, militated against the development of steady return markets for British exports. The crisis of 1836–1839 was due to speculation, insufficiently checked by the Bank, to bad harvests, and to a credit collapse in America, implicating British houses trading to the United States.[2] Its industrial repercussions were disastrous, and conditions of slump and of extreme distress, particularly in textile districts, persisted into the early 'forties. In the bitterness that this bred, the Chartist movement and the Anti-Corn Law League grew like gourds,[3] the latter gradually winning over not only merchants and manufacturers who had hitherto accepted protection, but large working-class sections as well. The Report of the Select Committee on Joint Stock Banks of 1836,[4] and that of the Select Committee on Banks of Issue of 1840,[5] emphasized the dangerous part that a banking system little regulated and widely dispersed, yet in the ultimate dependent on a single bank, might play in boom and distress; and inquiries into the legal forms of joint enterprise–the Bellenden Ker Report of 1837,[6] and the Report of the Select Committee on Joint Stock Companies of 1844,[7] illustrated the irresponsibility with which ruin might strike, and the failure of the law either to facilitate desirable enterprise, or to keep a check on fraud.

Peel came into power in 1841, with the task, in his own mind, of putting the country's economy on a sound basis, so far as political action could do so. In spite of

[1] No. 94. [2] No. 94. [3] Part V. [4] No. 92. [5] No. 94. [6] No. 93 [7] No. 95.

bitter and captious opposition at the start, the scope and consequence of his measures came slowly to command for him the confidence of the business classes. The political storms that beat round them are dealt with in Part V. His first step was to secure himself financial elbow-room by reimposing the income-tax at the rate of 7*d.* in the pound. His tariff of 1842 was a major reconstruction, repealing a number of prohibitions, relaxing prohibitory duties, and reducing import duties on raw materials to a general level of 5 per cent, and those on manufactured goods to 20 per cent. His revised Sliding Scale for corn pivoted round a price of 54*s.* to 56*s.*, as against the 66*s.* of the existing scale. In later years most of the taxes on raw materials were abolished or reduced to insignificant dimensions, the crucial ones on sugar and timber were considerably lowered, most export duties and a further number of import duties were abolished or reduced, and the tariff began to assume the simplicity and concentration on a few duties, mainly for revenue purposes, which was increasingly to characterize it. Contemporary opinion regarded Peel's work as the beginning of the turn towards prosperity,[1] and Professor Imlah has spoken of it as perhaps having saved the economy from "premature senescence" and as "fully as important" to its revival as the new supplies of gold. From 1843, despite the interruptions of the potato famine and bad harvests, the railway slump of 1846, and the commercial crisis of 1847, trade took an upward turn. Above all, after 1851, prices, both of exports and of imports, tended to find stabler levels, the decline that had been going on for a generation was steadied, and the wilder fluctuations ironed out.

Peel's second great task was the Bank Charter Act of 1844. He had been a member of the Select Committee on Banks of Issue of 1840,[2] and the evidence before it of Samuel Jones Loyd, afterwards Lord Overstone, had so impressed him that not only its argument but even some of its actual phraseology were reproduced in the great speech with which he introduced the Act.[3] The position he had to deal with was that the Bank of England, by a practice which had the force both of custom and of convenience, held the balances of most of the other banks, and had also the monopoly of the note issue in the area 65 miles round London. Joint Stock banks other than the Bank of England had been permitted outside the metropolitan area in 1826, and within it in 1833. But there were also many private banks–some individual enterprises, some partnerships–many of them solid and responsible, but others flimsier and limited in resources and outlook. Many issued their own notes, subject to the restriction, imposed in 1826, of a minimum £5 denomination, and much of the business of the country was conducted in such notes. Evidence before the 1840 committee had suggested that in times of boom country banks tended to expand their note issues unduly. Since he had presided over the Bullion Committee of 1819, which had recommended the restoration of gold payments, Peel had been a 'gold man'. The aim of the Bank Charter Act was therefore to tie note issues as strictly as possible to gold. To this end, among other provisions, it divided the issue from the banking department of the Bank of England, limited its uncovered issue to £14,000,000, and restricted the issues of other banks.[4] The Act was the target of a great deal of criticism, both at the time and later, but successive inquiries upheld it,[5] and it remained the basis of British banking and currency until the 1914 war. Perhaps some of the hopes founded upon it were excessive. In the evidence before the Secret Committee of 1847–1848[6] there are traces of an idea that, with the Issue Department off its shoulders, the Bank could behave like other banks in a crisis, consulting its own interests first.

[1] No. 104. [2] No. 94. [3] No. 97. [4] No. 97 [5] Nos. 99, 104 [6] No. 99.

Its overriding national responsibilities had to be reaffirmed. Nor did the tying of the note issue to gold provide an automatic check to speculative booms, as in some quarters had been hoped. In 1847, 1857, and 1866 the Act had to be suspended,[1] and the Bank authorized to issue notes in excess of its gold cover. But Peel had not himself supposed that occasion for emergency action would never arise, and had expressed the hope that in such circumstances "public men would be found to assume a grave responsibility". As Sir John Clapham has said, "he preferred a bracing law which might have to be suspended, to a law which, by providing ways out of difficulties, would encourage bankers to slide into them". A more fundamental criticism was that its action was likely to be restrictive, and to cramp the growth of the national economy. But accident supplemented design: the influx of new gold, the further expansion of joint-stock banking and of the cheque habit,[2] provided the necessary correctives. With these adventitious aids the effect of the Act was almost entirely beneficial. Confidence in the currency and in financial institutions is a primary requisite of the healthy expansion of a free economy. Peel's Act, in making the golden sovereign the basis of English finance, provided a tangible symbol for confidence in it, not without value at home, and even more potent, perhaps, in the growing world economy which British commerce and finance so largely promoted and sustained.

Railways provided a second stimulus to prosperity. In the first place they gave welcome employment in difficult years. It has been calculated that at peak in 1849 railway construction gave employment to 200,000 men, apart from those running existing lines, and the indirect employment given to the iron and engineering industries. Sir Stafford Northcote, in his *Twenty Years of Financial Policy* (1862), noted that the time saved in transit, by cutting the stocks that merchants and manufacturers needed to hold, was equivalent to a considerable increase in the stocks themselves, and refers to a calculation made with respect to an inland town, where the coming of the railway had cut the price of coal by 10*s*., that this was as good to the inhabitants as a gift of the total rent of the town. More than financial advantages came along the iron rails. Something of the social shock caused by the invasions of 'navvies', ripping their way through the countryside, is indicated in the Report of the Select Committee on Railway Labourers, and the railway boom and collapse of 1846 brought the uglier aspects of speculative greed into classes and districts hitherto little touched. The immense capital demands of railway promotion, and the collapse of 1846, played their part in the larger crisis of 1847.[3] The railway age marked the end of the canal and turnpike age. Primarily, railways beat canals because they were competitively superior; thanks to their differences in management, in size, and standards of maintenance, canals could not, in fact, provide an alternative and independent system of transportation in competition with railways. But both canals and railways found their profit, at times, in amalgamation or agreement, rather than in competition, to the concern of Parliament, which felt responsible because of the powers it had given them, and was still being asked to concede.[4] Turnpikes found the long-distance through-traffic, which had paid them best, being taken from them, and one by one, in the course of the period, the turnpike companies fall on hard times and are wound up. As railway 'feeders', roads played an increasing part in the national economy. But for reasons of poverty the standards of maintenance of turnpikes made little advance, and that of the remaining roads – the great bulk of the mileage – remained also

[1] Nos. 99, 104, 106. [2] No. 104. [3] No. 99. [4] Nos. 101, 109.

low. They were still for the most part left in parish hands, although under adoptive legislation larger units of control could be set up.

The British railway system is in the main the achievement of this period. Its growth can be seen in the table at No. 84. But it was not as a system that its growth was initiated. The context of early railway building is the fairly considerable history of pre-locomotive railways, and canals and turnpikes. The early railways were put forward as primarily local improvements, and the resulting Bills were therefore referred to Local Bill Committees, the main duties of which were to see that genuine local advantages were in prospect, and that local interests were fairly treated. Hence local opposition could easily be fatal, and had to be squared, often at great expense. This, and the high legal costs, helped to make the capital costs of British railways so heavy. The first railways were thought of as roads, over which different hauliers would ply, and the early Acts particularize maximum tolls. Not till the Select Committee of 1840 is it recognized that companies must be monopolists of the locomotive power, and not till the 1844 committee was it laid down that national, rather than local, interests were at stake in railway development. The 1844 committee recommended that an option of State purchase after a term of years should be a condition of new railway Bills, and that a special department of the Board of Trade should be set up to report on Bills to Parliament from the standpoint of the national interest in the system of communications.[1] Gladstone introduced a Bill on these lines, but the proposals with regard to purchase were whittled down, and the option, when, after twenty years, it began to materialize, was not exercised. The Railway Department was reorganized, however, and Gladstone's successor, Dalhousie, made a great effort to give substance to its powers. But it was unremittingly attacked by the railway and business interests in the House, and after Peel had virtually disowned it, it was deprived of many of its functions. But in each of the later railway reports its demise is regretted. Meanwhile, in the early 'forties, by purchase, amalgamation, and extension, the great companies were taking shape, the Midland under Hudson, the London and North-Western under Carr Glynn, and the public mind was much exercised at the degree of monopoly resulting, resting, as in large part it did, on the parliamentary grant of powers. Cardwell's Committee on Amalgamations of 1852–1853 threw a lurid light on railway politics and finance in the context of the vexed question of competition.[2] Proposals for 'districting', and even nationalization, were before it, as before the Royal Commission of 1867, and the Select Committee of 1872.[3] But nothing came of them; the Victorian mind had convinced itself that the State's hand was a deadening and destroying one, and in return for the grant of statutory powers preferred to rely on such statutory protection of the public interest as was possible, on the influence which rivalry and competition, though latent rather than active, could still exercise, and on the pride and sense of public duty of the railway administrators.

The growth of the great exporting industries does not lend itself easily to documentation. Nos. 87 and 88 present the general picture. Particularly in cotton and iron, volume and value of exports are irregularly related, and the drastic and fluctuating character of the price-fall is illustrated. Even the bare figures suggest that markets had often to be forced open by sacrificial cutting of prices, and that trade cannot always have been remunerative. Both in volume and value, textiles lead the way, but, as the century proceeds, coal, iron, and engineering rise in importance. The export of rails becomes considerable, and great contractors, like Brassey and Morton

[1] No. 96. [2] No. 101. [3] No. 109.

and Peto, begin building railways abroad, first on the Continent and then farther afield, equipping the world for world trade, and taking, quite often, not merely staffs and machines but labourers with them, sharers in the country's industrial supremacy. Railway-borne coal supplements sea-coal, and not only makes its use more general but makes the developing export possible. No. 86 shows the growth of shipping. In the days of sail, America, with its great New England tradition of shipbuilding, was a formidable rival, but when steam and iron ships came, Britain took and maintained a decisive lead. In spite of their enormous growth, visible exports never paid for the food and raw materials and luxuries that the country imported. It was shipping and foreign services that provided the positives in the balance of trade, and made possible the building up of that immense Victorian foreign investment which cushioned later adversities, and helped so largely to finance the wars of our own century.[1]

The tables at Nos. 77–80 suggest the variety of the occupational structure of the population. In the industrial field great industry is the exception rather than the rule. Families like the Durhams and the Londonderrys might own great mining estates in the north-east, but the one or two-mine enterprise is the more usual; iron foundries were usually large concerns, but in textiles, in engineering, and in most other branches of industry, units were still, in general, small. Precision engineering, the technical basis of large-scale industry, was substantially a creation of the second half of the century. Whitworth was its pioneer, and Sir John Clapham speaks of his stand at the 1851 exhibition as "still preaching largely to the unconverted". Merchant businesses, export and domestic, shopkeepers, the myriads of makers and purveyors of foodstuffs, clothing, and articles of domestic use and consumption, the vast army, male and female, engaged in personal service, make up the tables. On the employing side it is still a world not only of private but of personal enterprise; men financing themselves on the basis of savings or personal credit, and rising or falling in the scale according to their industry and acumen, or perhaps their luck. This class, at any rate, regards itself as representative, and both in its energy and self-reliance, and in its impatience of restraint, sets the temper of the transformation British society is undergoing.

At the beginning of the period the only way of incorporation for a business was by royal charter or by Act of Parliament. The Letters Patent Act of 1837 made the former process rather easier, but it was still expensive and formidable. Otherwise, joint enterprises were subject to the law of partnership. The difficulties this might occasion, where there were more than very few partners, are illustrated in Bellenden Ker's Report to the Board of Trade,[2] and they were accentuated by the fact that the court of reference was usually Chancery, where the delays and complexities of procedure were notorious.[3] The 'Bubble' Act of 1720 had prohibited joint stock companies. This was repealed in 1825, but companies, while no longer illegal, still had no legal status, or means of deciding legal questions other than as above. This did not prevent company activity from flourishing, often as the cloak for fraudulent designs. The Select Committee of 1844 on Joint Stock Companies[4] thought it possible to legalize companies, while exercising an administrative check on fraud, and the Joint Stock Companies Act of that year was the expression of this belief. It provided for two stages of registration for companies, the second depending on the satisfaction of a Registrar of Companies as to its structure and genuineness. His functions were modelled on those of the Registrar of Friendly Societies, of whom something will be

[1] No. 89. [2] No. 93. [3] Part VI, No. 157. [4] No. 95.

said below, and he exercised a wide discretion. But the differences between quasi-public trusts and profit-making companies, and between the fairly uniform pattern of organization of Friendly Societies, and the variety that came before the Registrar of Companies, was such that the latter could have dealt adequately with his job only if his office had grown to a size which Victorian prejudices against bureaucracy would never have allowed. The Act, moreover, had drafting defects. Meanwhile the principle of limited liability–not embodied in the 1844 Act–was coming more under discussion. Support came to it from unexpected quarters. Three different select committees–on the Savings of the Middle and Working Classes in 1851; on Partnership Law in 1851;[1] and on Mercantile Law in 1854–made cautious recommendations in favour of it. They were not so much interested in its application to normal business as in making it easier for people of substance to lend financial support and the benefit of their wider experience to co-operative societies–much in the public mind at the time, thanks to the Christian Socialists–and to schemes for improving working-class sanitary and housing conditions, for which a company form was often desirable. The prospect of such people losing all they had if anything went wrong acted as a deterrent to this. A temporary Act of 1855 prepared the way for Lowe's Act of 1856, under which companies could be formed, with limited or unlimited liability, by straightforward registration with a minimum of formalities. Lowe's speech[2] represented the triumph of the hard-headed school, which objected in principle to interference with people's right to use their money as they pleased, whether prudently or imprudently. But Lord Overstone's Protest in the House of Lords[3] expressed the view of a not inconsiderable school of thought, and a financial experience much wider than Lowe's. Company Law was consolidated in 1862, and in 1867 a select committee sat to consider the working of limited liability. It made no drastic recommendations for change, but the evidence of the Master of the Rolls,[4] guarded as it was, showed that apprehension still existed. A great deal of promotion of companies with limited liability took place, but until well on in the 'eighties the more conservative business sentiment preferred, in ordinary contexts, full personal liability.

The passage from the report of the select committee of 1857–1858 on the Bank Acts and Commercial Distress[5] illustrates the tremendous upsurge of the Victorian economy in the 'fifties, and in that aspect requires little comment. The flow of gold from California and Australia, the unobstructed field for enterprise resulting from free-trade legislation, the addition of joint stock banks and joint stock companies to the machinery for the collection of capital, the pressure for its employment, and the facility of credit, brought an immense response from manufacturers and merchants, which is illustrated in the export figures.[6] The Crimean War (1854–1856) was taken almost in the country's stride. But prescient minds had seen that the going was too good to last, and again the blow came from America, where, in September 1857, a railway slump and the collapse of the Ohio Life and Trust Co. caused widespread distress, with disastrous repercussions on British mercantile houses. Special interest lies in the conduct of the Bank. A committee on the Bank Acts had already been sitting, and had reported in July 1857, before the blow fell. In evidence before it, Lord Overstone–so keen a critic of the Bank ten and twenty years earlier–had given the Bank the highest possible praise for its handling of the already difficult situation of the preceding eighteen months. It had been managed "as nearly as human affairs can be, perfectly–if there had been the same firmness in 1845 it would very materially

[1] No. 100. [2] No. 103A. [3] No. 103B. [4] No. 107. [5] No. 104. [6] Nos. 87, 88.

have mitigated some of the evils of that crisis". The technique which won his praise, and which became standard for the century, was that of raising the bank rate at the first sign of over-trading, and so checking the use of credit except on the soundest of prospects. The later committee, holding its inquest after the storm, had also nothing but praise for the Bank. It had done all in its power for stricken firms, and its officers' evidence fully showed their realization of their national responsibilities. The somewhat rueful conclusion to which the committee came was that "no system of currency can secure a commercial community against the consequences of its own improvidence". The commercial crisis of 1866 was almost entirely domestic in its causes. The great house of Overend and Gurney, which for a generation had been known as the 'bankers' banker', and in the country enjoyed implicit credit, had been under suspicion in City circles for some years. In 1865 it was converted into a limited company. This neither rectified its weaknesses nor discovered them. Some sharp movements in the money market early in 1866 found the firm short of resources, and on 11 May it failed for over £10,000,000, bringing many other houses down with it.[1] The measures taken during the period had not secured the economy from liability to recurrent crisis. But looking over it as a whole, it might seem that their repercussions had been limited, that the major financial institutions of the country had learned to make themselves to some extent earthquake-proof, and that the damage tends, on the whole, to concentrate on those whose carelessness and improvidence had invited it.

Early foreign investment had been mainly in government or corporation stocks. Joint stock and limited liability widened the field that was open to investors. Against the great profits and growing total of foreign investments had, at all periods, to be set considerable losses. The most spectacular instances in which the greed and gullibility of investors combined with fraud and irresponsibility on the part of promoters and sponsoring governments were a series of loans to certain Central American governments which were the subject of investigations by the Select Committee of 1875 on Foreign Loans.[2] Little of what the committee recommended was carried into effect, but the notoriety of the loans contributed to the formation, in 1872, of the Council of Foreign Bondholders, with the object of watching over investors' interests.

Complementary to the reforms in commercial policy and law which the period saw–breathing a similar spirit, but a greater solicitude for the individual–was a body of legislation, based on eighteenth-century foundations, designed to help working-class thrift, and helpful, in fact, in wider spheres. Rose's Act, of 1793, had given special status and protection to Friendly Societies, and an Act of 1818 had done the same for savings banks, in both cases making deposit of their rules with Quarter Sessions obligatory. Acts of 1828 and 1829 had appointed a barrister to report on these rules to Quarter Sessions, and in 1846 he became the registrar of Friendly Societies, with the independent responsibility of approving their rules. From this date until 1870 the registrar was Tidd Pratt. An almost continuous stream of legislation and inquiry sought to perfect these institutions, to give their members the maximum of protection against ignorance, irresponsibility, and fraud, with the minimum of legal formality such as might repel those whom it was intended to assist. Sir John Clapham has estimated that the membership of Friendly Societies grew from a million in 1835 to a million and a half in 1847, out of a male population over twenty

[1] No. 106. [2] No. 110.

years of age, at the latter date, of five and a half million. Contributors were not necessarily all working class; tradesmen and professional men also joined, sometimes for convenience, more often to assist and encourage the movement. The Co-operative Movement and the 'New Model' Trade Unions[1] grew up under the protection of this legislation. The beginning of Post Office Savings Banks in 1861[2] offered still wider facilities for thrift. The secretary of the Royal Commission of 1872–1874 on Friendly Societies was J. M. Ludlow, the Christian Socialist, who had himself played a part in shaping this legislation. He afterwards became registrar. His picture of the registrar as a sort of presiding genius of the prudential side of working-class life[3] is not fanciful; it is doubtful if many names were better known for good than that of Tidd Pratt. It may not be unfair to say that Victorian economic ideas and legislation were middle-class. But so also were the solidest ambitions of many of the working class; and it must be said that there was a sustained effort on the part of the governing class to help them.

[1] Part XII. [2] No. 105. [3] No. 108.

SELECT BIBLIOGRAPHY

Primary evidence on this subject is very scattered. Apart from the *Parliamentary Papers*, the best single body of source material is probably the files of the *Economist* (London, 1843 onwards). Statistical material is provided in G. R. PORTER, *The Progress of the Nation*, ed. F. W. HIRST (London, 1851), WILLIAM PAGE, *Commerce and Industry* (2 vols., London, 1919), and in the series of *Statistical Abstracts*, covering the period from 1840, issued by H.M. Stationery Office. TOOKE and NEWMARCH, *A History of Prices*, ed. T. E. GREGORY (6 vols., London, 1928), is a mine of information and discussion.

Lack of a single main body of primary material is compensated, to some extent, however, by the publication, within recent years, of the authoritative and indispensable general narrative of the subject by J. H. CLAPHAM, the first two volumes of which cover the period–*An Economic History of Modern Britain*, vol. I, *The Early Railway Age, 1820–1850* (Cambridge, 1926), and vol. II, *Free Trade and Steel, 1850–86* (Cambridge, 1932). G. P. JONES and A. G. POOL, *A Hundred Years of Economic Development in Great Britain* (London, 1940), gives an able and up-to-date shorter account, and has a useful bibliography; L. C. A. KNOWLES, *The Industrial and Commercial Revolutions in Great Britain during the Nineteenth Century* (London, 1927), is a brilliant development of certain aspects; C. R. FAY, *Great Britain from Adam Smith to the Present Day* (Cambridge, 1928), is episodic but illuminating. W. W. ROSTOW, *British Economy of the Nineteenth Century* (Oxford, 1948), briefly, and A. D. GAYER, W. W. ROSTOW, and A. SCHWARTZ, *Growth and Fluctuations of the British Economy, 1750–1850* (London, 1953) at greater length, deal primarily with industrial and commercial fluctuations.

The Select Committees on Agricultural Distress of the 'thirties (*Parlty. Papers*, 1833/V, 1836/VIII, and 1837/V), assemble reports from all quarters and on all aspects of agriculture, and the *Report of the Royal Commission on the Employment of Women and Children in Agriculture* (*Parlty. Papers*, 1843/XII), presents, in effect, a pretty complete picture of the conditions of employment as a whole. The *Report of the Select Committee on Allotments* (*Parlty. Papers*, 1843/VII) throws much incidental light on employment conditions, and a *Report on Enclosures* (*Parlty. Papers*, 1844/V) discusses the fuller utilization of waste land with some recommendations as to the reservation of some of it for public purposes. It contains evidence dealing with the effect of past enclosures in some places. The public debate on the state of agriculture shifts, with the increasing intensity of the movement against the Corn Laws, from Committees of the House to the country and Parliament (see Part V), though the 12th *Report of the Poor Law Board* (*Parlty. Papers*, 1846/XIX) has an appendix by CARLETON TUFNELL on wages in the west of England, containing some instructive household budgets. JAMES CAIRD, *English Agriculture in 1850–51* (London, 1852), reports conditions in the early free-trade epoch county by county, as well as generally. The *Report of the Lords Committee on Agricultural Statistics* (*Parlty. Papers*, 1854–1855/VIII) is valuable, and some incidental information on the gang system of labour in Suffolk is contained in a report by J. A. BECKETT in the Poor Law Board's *Report on the Law of Settlement* (*Parlty. Papers*, 1850/XXVII). Further evidence on this subject is contained in the *Sixth Report of the Children's Employment Commission* of 1863–1867 (*Parlty. Papers*, 1867/XVI), and further reports in the following year deal with housing and the physical and moral condition of the agricultural population (*Parlty. Papers*, 1867–1868/XVII and 1868–1869/XIII). The *Seventh Report of the Medical Officer of the Privy Council* (*Parlty. Papers*, 1865/XXVI) should also be seen, and the *Report of the Royal Commission on Depression in Agriculture* (the Richmond Commission) (*Parlty. Papers*, 1881/XVI and 1882/XIV, Parts 1–4), though dealing primarily with conditions arising from the depression beginning in 1873, looks backwards also. The *Journal of the Royal Agricultural Society* (London, 1840 onwards) is the prime source of information on technical progress. Of secondary authorities, LORD ERNLE and SIR A. D. HALL, *English Farming Past and Present* (London, 1935), W. H. HASBACH, *A History of the English Agricultural Labourer* (London, 1908), and W. H. R. CURTLER, *A Short History of English Agriculture* (London, 1909), are the most valuable; J. A. Venn, *Foundations of Agricultural Economics* (Cambridge, 1933), though not, in form, historical, contains much information on historical problems. David Spring, "English Landed Estates in the Age of Coal and Iron, 1830–50", in *Journal of Economic History*, vol. x (1951), is a valuable discussion of an aspect of agrarian history on which much work remains to be done.

On communications a series of *Reports* deals with problems arising in connexion with turnpike trusts; the most important is the *Report of the Royal Commission on Roads* of 1840 (*Parlty. Papers*, 1840/xxvii, Parts 1 and 2). The principal early railway *Reports*, containing an immense mass of material, both of general and of local interest, are those of the Select Committees of 1839 (*Parlty. Papers*, 1839/x, two *Reports*), of 1840 (*Parlty. Papers*, 1840/xiii, five *Reports*), of 1844 (the Gladstone Committee) (*Parlty. Papers*, 1844/xi, six *Reports*), and two of 1846–that on the *Amalgamation of Railways and Canals* (*Parlty. Papers*, 1846/xlvi) and on *Railways* (*Parlty. Papers*, 1846/xiv). *Parliamentary Papers*, 1844/xli and 1845/xxxix, contain a number of *Reports* from the Railway Board set up under the 1844 Act. Debates in Parliament on the *Reports* and on the Railway Bill of 1844 are instructive, though they leave a good deal as to the Gladstone Bill unexplained. The *Report of the Select Committee on Commercial Distress* of 1847–1848 (*Parlty. Papers*, 1847–1848/viii, Parts 1–3) contains a good deal of evidence about the railway boom and crash of 1846. The sequence of further investigations into railway matters is continued with the Cardwell Committee on the Amalgamation of Railways and Canals (*Parlty. Papers*, 1852–1853/xxxviii), the Royal Commission on Railways of 1867 (*Parlty. Papers*, 1867/xxxviii, Parts 1 and 2), the first part of which summarizes railway history to date, and the Select Committee on Amalgamations of 1872 (*Parlty. Papers*, 1872/xiii, Parts 1 and 2), which may be said to sum up on the issues of competition, amalgamation, and nationalization, which had perplexed the public and parliamentary consciences.

Secondary works are S. and B. Webb, *The Story of the King's Highway* (London, 1920); W. T. Jackman, *The Development of Transportation in England* (London, 1916); Sir W. M. Acworth, *The Railways of Scotland* (London, 1890); *The Railways of England* (London, 1900); E. Cleveland-Stevens, *English Railways: Their Development and their Relation to the State* (London, 1912); C. E. R. Sherrington, *A Hundred Years of Inland Transport, 1830–1934* (London, 1934). Samuel Smiles, *Lives of the Engineers* (3 vols., London, 1861–1862), has the atmosphere of the heroic days; R. S. Lambert, *The Railway King: George Hudson, 1800–71* (London, 1935), deals with the career of the most spectacular practitioner of amalgamation. F. C. Mather, "Railways, the Electric Telegraph and Public Order during the Chartist Period, 1837–48", in *History*, 38 (1953), is a valuable article. A select committee of 1844 dealt with shipping (*Parlty. Papers*, 1844/vii), and another, of 1847, with the Navigation Laws, the evidence of the Board of Trade officials as to the working of the Acts being particularly valuable (*Parlty. Papers*, 1847/x). C. Jones, *British Merchant Shipping* (London, 1922), is a valuable secondary authority, and A. W. Kirkaldy and A. D. Evans, *The History and Economics of Transport* (London, 1927), deals with shipping and its place in the general system of transport.

The organization and privilege to be accorded to the Bank of England is discussed in the *Report of the Select Committee on the Bank of England* (*Parlty. Papers*, 1832/vi), and the problem of Joint Stock Banks in three *Reports* of slightly later date (*Parlty. Papers*, 1836/ix, 1837/xiv, and 1837–1838/vii). The Law of Partnership is the subject of a *Report* in 1837 (*Parlty. Papers*, 1837/xliv). An important *Report* of 1844 discusses Joint Stock Companies (*Parlty. Papers*, 1844/vii); a Select Committee discussed the position of Friendly Societies in 1849 (*Parlty. Papers*, 1849/xiv); and the discussion of the subject continues, in a single stream, in a *Report* of 1850 on the *Savings of the Middle and Working Classes* (*Parlty. Papers*, 1850/xix); one of 1851 on the *Law of Partnership* (*Parlty. Papers*, 1851/xviii); of 1852, on *Friendly Societies* again (*Parlty. Papers*, 1852/v); on *Assurance Associations* (*Parlty. Papers*, 1852–1853/xxi); in 1854 on *Friendly Societies* (*Parlty. Papers*, 1854/vii); and of a Royal Commission in 1854 on *Mercantile Law* (*Parlty. Papers*, 1854/xxvii). The Parliamentary Debate, in both Houses, on the Joint Stock (Limited Liability) Act of 1856, is important. A select committee in 1867 reported on the operation of the *Limited Liability Acts* (*Parlty. Papers*, 1867/x), and a Royal Commission in 1874 on the *Friendly Societies*, the first Part of the *Report* containing a summary of the history of legislation on the subject (*Parlty. Papers*, 1874/xxiii, Parts 1 and 2).

The *Reports on Banks of Issue* of 1840 and 1841 (*Parlty. Papers*, 1840/LV and 1841/V), deal with banking and currency questions, but especially in the context of the economic disturbances of 1836–1839, on which they are a primary authority. The Debates on Peel's Bank Charter Act of 1844 are also of primary importance. The *Reports of the Select Committees* of 1847–1848 – both Commons and Lords – on *Manufacturing Distress* (*Parlty. Papers*, 1847–1848/VIII, Parts 1–3), deals with the crisis of 1847 largely from the point of view of the effect of the Act. The Select Committee of 1857 on the Operation of the Bank Acts was set up before the crisis of 1857, with the object of reporting on the effect of the Crimean War on the financial system (*Parlty. Papers*, 1857/X, Parts 1 and 2). It was followed by a committee on the recent commercial Distress (*Parlty. Papers*, 1857–1858/V). No committee was set up to report on the crisis of 1866.

The secondary literature on banking and currency is vast, and often highly technical, but the historical student will probably find the best introduction to the range of subjects in WALTER BAGEHOT, *Lombard Street* (London, 1873), which has documentary as well as expository value. A. ANDREADES, *A History of the Bank of England* (London, 1924), and J. H. CLAPHAM, *The Bank of England* (London, 1944), are probably the standard authorities on the subject. W. F. CRICK and J. E. WADSWORTH, *A Century of Joint-Stock Banking* (London, 1936); A. E. FEAVERYEAR, *The Pound Sterling: A History of English Money* (London, 1931); R. G. HAWTREY, *A Century of the Bank Rate* (London, 1938); W. T. C. KING, *History of the London Discount Market* (London, 1936); E. J. POWELL, *The Evolution of the Money Market, 1385–1915* (London, 1916); and J. SYKES, *The Amalgamation Movement in English Banking, 1825–1924* (London, 1926), may also be mentioned. J. K. HORSFIELD, "A Retrospective View of the Bank Charter Act", in *Economica*, New Series, vol. X (1944), and "The Opinions of Horsley Palmer", in *Economica*, New Series, vol. XIV (1948), are recent articles. On legal forms of business organization, B. C. HUNT, *The Development of Business Corporation in England, 1800–1867* (Harvard, 1936), should be consulted, and on limited liability, H. A. SHANNON, "The Coming of General Limited Liability", in *Economic History*, vol. II (1931), "The first Five Thousand Limited Companies", in *Economic History*, vol. III (1932), and "The Limited Companies of 1866–1883", in *Economic History Review*, vol. IV (1933), have attained the status of classics. G. TODD, "Some aspects of Joint Stock Companies, 1844–1900", in *Economic History Review*, vol. II (1932), covers a rather larger field. On the Friendly Society movement there is a great deal of information and much valuable discussion in LORD BEVERIDGE's *Voluntary Action* (2 vols., London, 1948). On the Co-operative movement G. J. HOLYOAKE, *The History of the Rochdale Equitable Pioneers* (London, 1893) and *The History of Co-operation* (2 vols., London, 1906) are written with inside knowledge and information; B. POTTER, *The Co-operative Movement in Great Britain* (London, 1930), and C. R. FAY, *Co-operation at Home and Abroad*, vol. I (2 vols., Cambridge, 1936), are the standard modern works. On the commercial panics, D. M. EVANS, *The Commercial Crises, 1847–8* (London, 1848) and *The History of the Commercial Crises, 1857–8* (London, 1859), are valuable, and F. W. HIRST, *The Six Panics and Other Essays* (London, 1913), may be consulted.

Industrial history was relatively little the subject of parliamentary inquiry. Both Lords and Commons set up committees to inform them on the state of the coal trade in 1830 (*Parlty.* Papers, 1830/VIII), and certain aspects were further inquired into in 1838 (*Parlty. Papers*, 1838/VI). A Royal Commission was set up in 1871, under the chairmanship of the duke of Argyle, to report on the reserves of coal remaining to be mined, and the Report contains valuable statistics on production and trade (*Parlty. Papers*, 1871/XXVIII). The *Report of a Select Committee on Manufactures and Commerce* in 1833 (*Parlty. Papers*, 1833/VI) contains a good deal of miscellaneous information. A Select Committee reported, in 1836, on the *Port of London* (*Parlty. Papers*, 1836/XII). Much incidental information of great value is given, however, in the Annual Reports of Factory Inspectors and in those of the various Commissions and Committees dealing with factory legislation (see *Bibliography* to Part XII for references). EDWARD BAINES, *History of the Cotton Manufacture* (London, 1835), though dealing with an earlier period, is still of value; S. I. CHAPMAN, *The Lancashire Cotton Industry* (London, 1904), carries the story further. J. BURNLEY, *The History of Wool and Wool Combing* (London, 1889), and J. H. CLAPHAM, *The Woollen and Worsted Industries* (Cambridge, 1909), deal with the second of the great staple industries. R. L. GALLOWAY, *Annals of Coal Mining and the Coal Trade* (2 vols., London, 1889), is valuable, and an important recent article is A. J. TAYLOR, "Combination in the Coal Industry in the Mid-Nineteenth Century", in *Transactions of the Royal Historical Society, Fifth Series*, vol. III (1953). H. SCRIVENER, *A Comprehensive History of the Iron Trade* (London, 1841); J. S. JEANS, *The Iron Trade of Great Britain* (London, 1906); and A. P. M. FLEMING and H. J. BROCKLEHURST, *A History of Engineering* (London, 1925), deal with other industries. SAMUEL SMILES, *Industrial Biography* (London, 1878), contains much beyond personal information. H. L. BEALES, "Studies in Bibliography, iv. The 'Basic' Industries of England, 1850–1914", in *Economic History Review*, vol. VI (1935), is indispensable to the student of the subject. Regional studies, such as A. H. JOHN, *The Industrial Development of South Wales, 1750–1850* (Cardiff, 1950); W. H. CHALONER, *The Social and Economic Development of Crewe, 1780–1923* (Manchester, 1950); T. C. BARKER and J. R. HARRIS, *A Merseyside Town in the Industrial Revolution: St Helens, 1750–1900* (Liverpool, 1954), and S. MIDDLETON, *Newcastle on Tyne: its Growth and Achievement* (Newcastle, 1950), represent valuable recent work.

On population questions, A. REDFORD, *Labour Migration in England, 1800–1850* (Manchester, 1926), is the standard authority. The Annual and Decennial *Reports* of the registrar-general, and the *Census Reports* of 1831, 1841, 1851, 1861, and 1871, are the fundamental sources.

SIR JOSIAH STAMP, *British Incomes and Property* (London, 1916), analyses, from income-tax returns, the distribution of wealth from 1842 onwards. A series of important articles, by ALBERT M. IMLAH, "Real Values in British Foreign Trade", in *Journal of Economic History*, vol. VIII (1948), and "British Terms of Trade, 1798–1913", in *Journal of Economic History*, vol. IX (1950), and "The British Balance of Payments and Export of Capital", in *Economic History Review*, vol. II (1952), are indispensable to the understanding of the national balance-sheet during the period. A. L. BOWLEY, *England's Foreign Trade in the Nineteenth Century* (London, 1905), L. LEVI, *History of British Commerce* (London, 1872), are studies of the growth and development of foreign trade. W. O. HENDERSON, *Britain and Industrial Europe, 1750–1870* (Liverpool, 1954), studies the influence of a number of British industrial leaders on European economic development. L. H. JENKS, *The Migration of British Capital of 1875* (New York, 1927), is the leading secondary authority on the building up of the foreign balances whose growth PROFESSOR IMLAH tabulates, and also on the losses incidentally incurred, a subject on which the *Report of the Select Committee on Loans to Foreign States* (*Parlty. Papers*, 1875/XI), throws a perhaps over-lurid light.

J. D. CHAMBERS, *The Workshop of the World* (1961) – admirable sketch of economic development 1820–1880; S. G. CHECKLAND, *Rise of Industrial Society in England 1815–1885* (1964) – excellent study of economic and social history of period; B. R. MITCHELL and P. DEANE, *Abstract of British Historical Statistics* (1962); P. DEANE and W. A. COLE, *British Economic Growth 1688–1959* (1962); S. ORWELL and E. H. WHETHAM, *History of British Agriculture 1846–1914* (1964); F. M. L. THOMPSON, *English Landed Society in the Nineteenth Century* (1963); DAVID SPRING, *English Landed Estate in the Nineteenth Century: its administration* (1963); L. OXLEY-PARKER, *The Oxley-Parker Papers* (1964), papers of an estate agent; A. REDFORD, *Manchester Merchants and Foreign Trade* (2 vols., 1934 and 1956); B. W. CLAPP, *John Owen, Manchester Merchant* (1965); HENRY PARRIS, *Government and the Railways in Great Britain* (1965); M. C. READ (ed.) *Railways in the Victorian Economy* (1969); L. T. C. ROLT, *Isambard Brunel* (1957); E. G. BARNES, *Rise of the Midland Railway, 1844–74* (1969); T. C. BARKER and MICHAEL ROBBINS, *History of London Transport* (vol. I 1963); T. C. BARKER, *Pilkington Brothers and the Glass Industry* (1960); J. H. MORRIS and L. J. WILLIAMS, *South Wales Coal Industry 1841–75* (1958); ROBERT MIDDLEMASS, *The Master Builders* (1963) – civil engineering contractors; R. S. SAYERS, *Lloyds Bank in the History of English Banking* (1957); J. M. PREST, *Industrial Revolution in Coventry* (1961); C. S. DAVIES, *History of Macclesfield* (1961); R. A. CHURCH, *Economic and Social Change in a Midland Town: Victorian Nottingham* (1966); SHEILA MARRINER, *Rathbones of Liverpool 1845–73* (1961) – fortunes of a merchant house; W. G. RIMMER, *Marshalls of Leeds, flax spinners, 1788–1886* (1969); P. H. GOSDEN, *Friendly Societies in England 1815–75* (1961); N. MASTERMAN, *John Malcolm Ludlow, Builder of Christian Socialism.* (1963) Articles: E. H. JONES, "Changing Basis of English Agricultural Prosperity 1853–73". *Agricultural History Review*, 1963; PHILIP S. BAGWELL, "The Railway Interest, its Organisation and Influence, 1839–1940" *Journal Transport History*, vii, 1965.

A. TABLES

73. Total population at censuses of 1831, 1841, 1851, 1861, and 1871

William Page, *Commerce and Industry*, vol. II, Table I.

Years	*England and Wales*	*Scotland*	*Ireland*	*Total for United Kingdom*		
				Males	*Females*	*Total*
1831	13,896,797	2,264,386	7,767,401	11,680,532	12,348,052	24,028,584
1841	15,914,148	2,620,184	8,196,597	13,060,497	13,670,432	26,730,929
1851	17,927,609	2,888,742	6,574,278	13,369,227	14,021,402	27,390,629
1861	20,066,224	3,062,294	5,798,967	14,063,477	14,864,008	28,927,485
1871	22,712,266	3,360,018	5,412,377	15,301,830	16,182,831	31,484,661

74. Birth rate, death rate, rate of increase of population for years from 1838 to 1875

Porter, *Progress of the Nation*, ed Hirst, Table VI.

Period	*Per 1,000 of population*		
	Average annual birth-rate	*Average annual death-rate*	*Average annual natural increase*
1838 . .	30·32	22·41	7·91
1839 . .	31·77	21·86	9·91
1840 . .	31·96	22·89	9·13
1841–1845 .	32·36	21·40	10·96
1846–1850 .	32·83	23·34	9·36
1851–1855 .	33·9	22·7	11·2
1856–1860 .	34·4	21·8	12·6
1861–1865 .	35·1	22·6	12·5
1866–1870 .	35·3	22·4	12·9
1871–1875 .	35·5	22·0	13·5

75. Emigration from the United Kingdom, from 1833 to 1875

Page, *Commerce and Industry*, vol. II, Table 5.

Years	*Australia and New Zealand*	*Cape of Good Hope and Natal*	*British North America*	*United States of America*	*Destination not stated*	*Total Emigrants*
1833	4,093	—	28,808	29,109	517	62,527
1834	2,800	—	40,060	33,074	288	76,222
1835	1,860	—	15,573	26,720	325	44,478
1836	3,124	—	34,226	37,774	293	75,417
1837	5,054	—	29,884	36,770	326	72,034
1838	14,021	—	4,577	14,332	292	33,222
1839	15,786	—	12,658	33,536	227	62,207
1840	15,850	—	32,293	40,642	1,958	90,743
1841	32,625	—	38,164	45,017	2,786	118,592
1842	8,534	—	54,123	63,852	1,835	128,344
1843	3,478	—	23,518	28,335	1,881	57,212
1844	2,229	—	22,924	43,660	1,873	70,686
1845	830	—	31,803	58,538	2,330	93,501
1846	2,347	—	43,439	82,239	1,826	129,851
1847	4,949	—	109,680	142,154	1,487	258,270
1848	23,904	—	31,065	188,233	4,887	248,089
1849	32,191	—	41,367	219,450	6,490	299,498
1850	16,037	—	32,961	223,078	8,773	280,849
1851	21,532	—	42,605	267,357	4,472	335,966
1852	87,881	—	32,873	244,261	3,749	368,764
1853	61,401	—	34,522	230,885	3,129	329,937
1854	83,237	—	43,761	193,065	3,366	323,429
1855	52,309	—	17,966	103,414	3,118	176,807
1856	44,584	—	16,378	111,837	3,755	176,554
1857	61,248	—	21,001	126,905	3,721	212,875
1858	39,295	—	9,704	59,716	5,257	113,972
1859	31,013	—	6,689	70,303	12,427	120,432
1860	24,302	—	9,786	87,500	6,881	128,469
1861	23,738	—	12,707	49,764	5,561	91,770
1862	41,843	—	15,522	58,706	5,143	121,214
1863	53,054	—	18,083	146,813	5,808	223,758
1864	40,942	—	12,721	147,042	8,195	208,900
1865	37,283	—	17,211	147,258	8,049	209,801
1866	24,097	—	13,255	161,000	6,530	204,882
1867	14,023	—	12,160	126,051	4,748	156,982
1868	12,332	—	12,332	108,490	5,033	138,187
1869	14,457	—	20,921	146,737	4,185	186,300
1870	16,526	—	27,168	153,466	5,351	202,511
1871	11,695	—	24,954	150,788	5,314	192,751
1872	15,248	—	24,382	161,782	9,082	210,494
1873	25,137	—	29,045	166,730	7,433	228,345
1874	52,581	—	20,728	113,774	10,189	197,272
1875	34,750	—	12,306	81,193	12,426	140,675

76. Note on population of town and country

Census Report of 1863 – *Parlty. Papers*, 1863/LIII/I, pp. 11–13.

The population of England consists of several thousands of small communities; which are associated together more or less intimately by vicinity, and by common interests, duties, or rights.

The populations of parishes or places are distinguished in the volume; and a certain number of these places are parts of cities, or constitute municipal boroughs which have legally defined boundaries. Many of them are market towns, others are such aggregations of houses as are commonly called on that account towns, without having yet any other elements of union, except the ordinary parish organization. It is difficult to distinguish these small growing towns from villages and hamlets; and the line of separation cannot be drawn between them by any definite rule.

The area of the small towns can only be determined approximately; but the density of population is so distinguishing a feature of towns, that, in the absence of better methods, the rules in the note to Table 45 were followed in a certain number of cases.

781 towns, of which the names are given at the foot of the table, contained 10,960,998 inhabitants; while the villages and country parishes contained 9,105,226, a large population in itself, and exceeding indeed in number the whole population of England and Wales in 1801, but less by 1,855,772 than the population of the towns in 1861.

The English nation then, without losing its hold on the country, and still largely diffused over 37 million acres of territory, has assumed the character of a preponderating city population. It enjoys the advantages of the cities of the ancient world in the proximity of its citizens for intercourse, for defence, for counsel, for production, and for the interchange of commodities; for rapidly as the population has increased, it has not kept pace with the progress of industry and wealth.

The area which the 781 towns covered was 2,991 square miles; while the area of the rest of the country was 55,330 square miles. [The area of the 781 towns was equivalent to 7,745 square kilometers. The average area of each town was 9·9, nearly 10 square kilometers, or 992 hectars.]

There were 10,960,998 people living on 2,991 square miles, and 9,105,226 people living on 55,330 square miles.

The average population of a town is 14,023; and the average size is represented by a square of two miles (1·957) to the side, or a circle of 1·1 mile to the radius. The people are distributed unequally, but the mean town density is expressed by 3,665 persons to a square mile, 5·73 persons to an acre. And upon the hypothesis of equal distribution the people live at a mean distance of three quarters of a mile (·736 mile) from the centre.

In the country around the towns the people are scattered; there are nearly 4 acres (3·89) to a person, 165 persons to a square mile.

But the towns are so distributed over the kingdom that every part of the country enjoys some of their advantages. Thus the kingdom is divided into 781 portions, in each of which there is a town. And the mean area of the districts of which the town is the centre is 75 square miles; so they are equal to circles of a radius of 4·875 miles; and on an average the distance of districts from centre to centre is 9·286 miles. The mean distance of the population of such a district from the centre is upon the hypothesis of equal distribution 3¼ miles.

580 towns were distinguished in 1851, and the population in them and in the surrounding country was nearly equal. But in the subsequent ten years, while the population in the villages and the country around increased by half a million (584,548), the population in the 580 towns increased by a million and half (1,554,067). The increase of the population of the country parishes is 6·5 per cent., and of the towns 17·3 per cent. The difference in the rates of increase is due to migration from country to town.

Three-fourths of the total increase of population has taken place in the towns.

There are seventy-two towns in England of an average population of 106,495, none of them having less than twenty thousand inhabitants. Their population in 1801 was 2,221,753, 4,225,958 in 1831, and 7,667,622 in 1861. The rates of increase varied to a great extent; thus Birkenhead on the south side of the Mersey had 667 inhabitants at the beginning of the century, and 51,649 in 1861. Canterbury had at the same dates 9,000 and 21,324 inhabitants. The population of York grew from 16,846 to 40,433; of Bradford from 13,264 to 106,218.

In population, next to London stands Liverpool (443,938), and Manchester (357,979) in the north-west; Birmingham (296,076) in the Midland counties; Leeds (207,165), and Sheffield (185,172) in Yorkshire; and Bristol in the west (154,093). In the vicinity of these large cities, and beyond their boundaries, are often towns and populous districts which are in constant relation with them. Thus Salford is almost as closely associated with Manchester as Southwark is with London. London still maintains its pre-eminence as the metropolis of the empire, of which it amply expresses the growth. Its population was 958,863 in 1801, and 2,803,989 in 1861.

The increase in the population of London during this century was 1,845,126, and the increase in the other seventy-one large towns and cities was 3,600,743; making the aggregate increase of the population of the great towns 5,445,869.

The increase in the towns of less than twenty thousand inhabitants as well as in villages and in the country was 5,727,819.

While the actual increase was greater, the annual rate of increase (1·039 per cent.) was less in the country and in the small towns than it was in the great towns (2·085). The velocity at which the great towns increase is double the rate at which the rest of the population increases.

77. Occupations (1841 Census)

Porter, *Progress of the Nation*, ed. Hurst, chap. 2, Table XIII.

	ENGLAND AND WALES				TOTAL
	Males		*Females*		
	20 years and over	*Under 20*	*20 years and over*	*Under 20*	
Persons engaged in commerce, trade, and manufacture	1,750,128	318,434	391,261	159,383	2,619,206
Agriculture	1,041,980	161,697	48,450	9,321	1,261,448
Labour–not agricultural	482,683	85,182	98,828	7,229	673,922
Army at home and abroad, including half-pay and East India Company:					
At home	30,460	6,303	—	—	36,763
Abroad and in Ireland	89,215	15	—	—	89,230
Navy and merchant service, fishermen, etc.:					
At home	87,843	7,350	—	—	95,193
Afloat	79,619	17,180	—	—	96,799
Professions: clerical	20,450	—	—	—	20,450
Professions: legal	14,155	—	—	—	14,155
Professions: medical	17,666	—	770	—	18,436
Other pursuits requiring education	81,372	10,637	30,060	1,809	123,878
Government and civil service	13,340	219	515	14	14,088
Municipal and parochial officers	19,955	321	1,896	13	22,125
Domestic servants	150,005	83,524	476,081	289,438	999,048
Living on means	118,688	5,092	308,061	14,132	445,973
In institutions	64,924	28,051	60,019	23,212	176,206
Total occupied	4,062,483	724,005	1,415,881	504,551	6,706,920
Unoccupied (including women and children)	239,013	2,935,752	3,059,350	3,156,751	9,390,866
Total population	4,301,497	3,659,757	4,475,231	3,661,302	16,097,786

78. Occupations (1851 Census)

Parlty. Papers, 1852–3/LXXXVIII/I, Intro. p. c.

Occupations	*Persons*
Agricultural Labourer, Farm Servant, Shepherd	1,460,896
Domestic Servant	1,038,791
Cotton Calico, manufacture, printing and dyeing	501,565
Labourer (branch undefined)	376,551
Farmer, Grazier	306,767
Boot and Shoe maker	274,451
Milliner, Dressmaker	267,791
Coal-miner	219,015
Carpenter, Joiner	182,696
Army and Navy	178,773
Tailor	152,672
Washerwomen, Mangler, Laundry-keeper	146,091
Woollen Cloth manufacture	137,814
Silk manufacture	114,570
Blacksmith	112,776
Worsted manufacture	104,061
Mason, Pavior	101,442
Messenger, Porter, and Errand Boy	101,425
Linen, Flax manufacture	98,860
Seaman (Merchant Service), on shore or in British Ports	89,206
Grocer	85,913
Gardener	80,946
Iron manufacture, moulder, founder	80,032
Innkeeper, Licensed Victualler, Beershop keeper	75,721
Seamstress, Shirtmaker	73,068
Bricklayer	67,989
Butcher, Meat Salesman	67,691
Hose (Stocking) manufacture	65,499
School-master, mistress	65,376
Lace manufacture	63,660
Plumber, Painter, Glazier	62,808
Baker	62,472
Carman, Carrier, Carter, Drayman	56,981
Charwoman	55,423
Draper (Linen and Woollen)	49,184
Engine and Machine Maker	48,082
Commercial Clerk	43,760
Cabinet maker, Upholsterer	40,897
Teacher (various), Governess	40,575
Fisherman, Woman	38,294
Boat, Barge, Man, Woman	37,683
Miller	37,268
Earthenware manufacture	36,512
Sawyer	35,443
Railway Labourer	34,306
Straw-plait manufacture	32,062

Occupations	*Persons*
Brick maker, dealer	31,168
Government Civil Service	30,963
Hawker, Pedlar	30,553
Wheelwright	30,244
Glover	29,882
Shopkeeper (branch undefined)	29,800
Horsekeeper, Groom (not Domestic), Jockey	29,408
Nail manufacture	28,533
Iron-miner	28,088
Printer	26,024
Nurse (not Domestic Servant)	25,518
Shipwright, Shipbuilder	25,201
Stone Quarrier	23,489
Lodging-house Keeper	23,089
Lead-miner	22,530
Copper-miner	22,386
Straw Hat and Bonnet maker	21,902
Cooper	20,245
Watch and Clock maker	19,159
Brewer	18,620
Dock Labourer, Dock and Harbour Service	18,462
Clergyman of Estab. Church	18,587 }
Protestant Dissenting Minister	9,644 }
Police	18,348
Plasterer	17,980
Warehouse-man, woman	17,861
Saddler, Harness maker	17,583
Hatter, Hat manufacture	16,975
Coachman (not Domestic Servant), Guard, Postboy	16,836
Law Clerk	16,626
Coachmaker	16,590
Cowkeeper, Milkseller	16,526
Ropemaker	15,966
Druggist	15,643
Surgeon, Apothecary	15,163
Tin-miner	15,050
Paper manufacture	14,501
Coalheaver, Coal Labourer	14,426
Greengrocer, Fruiterer	14,320
Muslin manufacture	14,098
Confectioner	13,865
Tinman, Tinker, Tin-plate worker	13,770
Staymaker	13,699
Solicitor, Attorney, Writer to the Signet	13,256
Dyer, Scourer, Calenderer	12,964
Currier	12,920
Builder	12,818
Farm Bailiff	12,805
Hair-dresser, Wig-maker	12,173
Coal merchant, dealer	12,092

Occupations	*Persons*
Glass manufacture	12,005
Carpet and Rug manufacture	11,457
Goldsmith, Silversmith	11,242
Brass founder, Moulder, manufacture	11,230
Maltster	11,150
Railway Officer, Clerk, Station Master	10,948
Book-binder	10,953
Road Labourer	10,923
Wine and Spirit Merchant	10,467
Fishmonger	10,439
Merchant	10,256
Ribbon manufacture	10,074

79. Occupations (1861 Census)

Parlty. Papers, 1863/LIII/1, p. 132.

Occupations	*Persons*
Agricultural Labourer, Farm Servant, Shepherd	1,188,789
Domestic Servant	1,106,974
Cotton, Calico, -manufacture, Printing and Dyeing	456,646
Labourer (Branch undefined)	309,883
Dressmaker and Milliner	287,101
Boot and Shoe Maker	250,581
Farmer, Grazier	249,745
Coal-miner	246,613
Army and Navy	199,905
Army (137,106)	
Navy and Marines (62,799)	
Carpenter, Joiner	177,969
Laundry-keeper, Mangler, Washerwoman	167,607
Seaman (Merchant Service)	159,469
Tailor	136,390
Woollen cloth manufacture	130,034
Iron manufacture, Moulder, Founder	125,771
Blacksmith	108,165
Satin, Silk, -manufacture	101,678
Grocer, Tea Dealer	93,483
Mason, Pavior	84,434
Bricklayer	79,458
Worsted manufacture	79,242
Gardener (not Domestic)	78,533
Seamstress, Shirtmaker	76,493
Messenger, Porter (not Government), Errand Boy, Girl	75,629
Glazier, Painter, Plumber	74,619
Butcher, Meat Salesman	68,114
Carman, Carrier, Carter, Drayman	67,651

Occupations	Persons
Charwoman	65,273
Engine and Machine Maker	60,862
Draper, Linen Draper, Mercer	57,653
School-master, -mistress	56,139
Commercial Clerk	55,931
Baker	54,140
Lace manufacture	53,987
Hose (Stocking) manufacture	45,869
Cabinet-maker, Upholsterer	41,037
Brick Maker, Dealer	39,620
Earthenware manufacture	38,072
Licensed Victualler, Publican	37,946
Groom (not Domestic), Horsekeeper	36,600
House Proprietor	36,082
Dock Labourer, Dock and Harbour Service	32,487
Miller	32,103
Sawyer	31,647
Bargeman, -woman, Lighterman	31,428
Civil Service	31,346
Shipbuilder, Shipwright	31,294
Land Proprietor	30,766
Printer	30,590
Wheelwright	30,070
Straw Plait manufacture	29,867
Hotel, Inn, -Keeper	28,314
Railway Labourer	27,773
Railway Company's Servant, Porter, Attendant	26,846
Nail manufacture	26,130
Glover (not other. des.), and Leather Glover	25,300
Teacher (General)	24,973
Nurse (not Domestic)	24,821
Governess	24,770
Flax, Linen, -manufacture	22,050
Police	21,938
Warehouseman, -woman (not Manchester)	21,798
Hawker, Pedlar	21,792
Stone Quarrier	21,004
Clockmaker, Watchmaker	20,757
Lodging, Boarding, House Keeper	20,700
Iron-miner	20,626
Brewer	20,352
Clergyman of Established Church	19,195 }
Protestant and Dissenting Minister	7,840 }
Coachmaker	18,870
Lead-miner	18,552
Plasterer	18,550
Saddler, Harness-maker	18,229
Straw Hat and Bonnet Maker	18,176
Fruiterer, Greengrocer	18,045
Cooper	17,821

Occupations	*Persons*
Copper-miner	17,727
Cowkeeper, Milkseller	17,694
Coalheaver, Labourer	17,410
Coachman (not Domestic)	17,251
Fisherman, -woman	17,227
Law Clerk	16,605
Chemist, Druggist	16,414
Brass manufacture, Moulder, Founder . . .	16,284
Goldsmith, Silversmith, Jeweller	15,893
Costermonger, General Dealer, Huckster . . .	15,879
Beerseller	15,767
Builder	15,757
Farm Bailiff	15,698
Glass manufacture	15,046
Shopkeeper (branch undefined)	14,580
Railway Officer, Clerk, Station Master . . .	14,559
Confectioner, Pastrycook	14,526
Tin-miner	14,314
Dockyards (H.M.) Artificers, Labourer in . . .	14,026
Hatter, Hat manufacture	13,814
Cord, Rope, -Maker	13,486
Paper manufacture	13,357
Currier	13,109
Boiler-maker	13,020
Merchant	12,982
Coal Merchant, Dealer	12,266
Apothecary, Surgeon	12,030
Bookbinder	11,920
Gunsmith, Gun manufacture	11,873
Manufacturer, Mechanic	11,639
Stay and Corset Maker	11,482
Attorney, Solicitor	11,386
Chelsea Pensioner	11,342
Fishmonger, Seller, Dealer	11,305
Brush, Broom, Maker, Seller	11,178
Hair-dresser, Wig-maker	11,064
Provision Curer, Dealer	11,052
Commercial Traveller	10,779
Maltster	10,677
Railway Engine Driver, Stoker	10,414

80. Occupations (1871 Census)

Parlty. Papers, 1873/LXXI/II, p. 111.

Occupations	*Persons*
Domestic Servant	1,237,149
Agricultural Labourer, Farm Servant, Shepherd	980,178
Labourer (Branch undefined)	516,605
Cotton manufacture	468,142
Milliner, Dressmaker	301,109
Coal Miner	268,091
Farmer, Grazier	249,907
Shoemaker, Bootmaker	223,365
Carpenter, Joiner	205,833
Iron Manufacture	180,207
Army and Navy	175,217
Army (126,074)	
Navy and Marines (49,143)	
Washerwoman, Laundry Keeper, Mangler	170,598
Seamen (Merchant Service)	169,933
Tailor	149,864
Woollen Cloth Manufacture	128,464
Blacksmith	112,471
Grocer, Tea Dealer	111,094
Engine and Machine Maker	106,680
Painter, Plumber, Glazier	103,912
Bricklayer	99,984
Gardener (not Domestic Servant)	98,069
Mason, Pavior	95,243
Worsted Manufacture	94,766
Messenger (not Government,), Porter	93,182
Commercial Clerk	91,042
Shirtmaker, Seamstress	80,730
Charwoman	77,650
Publican, Inn, Hotel, -Keeper	77,049
Butcher, Meat Salesman	75,847
Silk, Satin, -Manufacturer	75,180
Draper, Linen Draper, Mercer	74,337
Carman, Carrier, Carter, Drayman	74,244
Teacher, Governess &c.	68,595
Baker (see also Confectioner)	59,066
Schoolmaster, Mistress	58,152
Cabinet Maker, Upholsterer	56,945
Lace Manufacture	49,370
Railway Attendant, Servant	49,102
Straw Plait Manufacture	48,863
Earthenware Manufacture	45,122
Railway Labourer, Platelayer, Navvy	45,070
Printer	44,814
Hawker, Pedlar	44,617
Warehouseman, -Woman	44,013

Occupations	*Persons*
Horsekeeper, Groom (not Domestic Servant), Jockey .	42,682
Hosiery Manufacture	42,038
Shipbuilder, Shipwright, Boatbuilder	40,626
Cabman, Flyman, Coachman (not Domestic Servant) .	39,999
Shopkeeper (Branch undefined)	39,991
Brickmaker, Dealer	38,779
Miner (Branch undefined)	38,712
Engine Driver, Stoker (Branch undefined) . . .	31,026
Wheelwright	30,394
Miller	30,060
Bargeman, -Woman	29,864
Dock Labourer, Dock and Harbour Service . .	28,794
Civil Service	28,644
Nurse (not Domestic Servant)	28,417
Police	28,330
Coal-heaver, Labourer	27,998
Sawyer	27,965
Lodging-house, Boarding-house, -Keeper . . .	25,932
Brewer and others engaged in Brewing . .	25,831
Greengrocer, Fruiterer	25,819
Stone Quarrier	25,681
Plasterer	24,587
Government Messengers and Workmen . . .	24,582
Machininst, Machine Worker (Branch undefined) .	23,421
Builder	23,300
Nail Manufacture	23,231
Coachmaker	23,034
Saddler, Harness, Whip, -Maker	23,011
Land Proprietor	22,964
Agent, Broker, Factor	22,962
Railway Officer, Clerk, Station Master . . .	22,083
Goldsmith, Silversmith, Jeweller	22,031
Hatter, Hat Manufacture	21,778
Brass Manufacture, Brazier	21,421
Clock, Watch, -Maker	21,273
Fisherman, -Woman	21,043
Iron Miner	20,931
Clergyman	20,694
Cowkeeper, Milkseller	20,558
Glass Manufacture	20,081
Chemist, Druggist	19,684
Cooper; Hoop-Maker, Bender	19,330
Law Clerk	18,886
Musician, Music Master	18,631
Tinplate Worker	18,324
Flax, Linen, -Manufacture	17,993
Commercial Traveller	17,922
Cutler	17,903
Mechanic, Artizan (Branch undefined)	17,530
Ironmonger, Hardware Dealer	17,368

Occupations	*Persons*
House Proprietor	17,086
Confectioner, Pastry Cook	16,988
Leather Glover	16,811
Paper Manufacture	16,772
Farm Bailiff	16,476
Beerseller	16,361
Coal Merchant, Dealer	16,250
Merchant	15,936
Bookbinder	15,474
Fishmonger, Dealer	14,880
Currier	14,710
Physician, Surgeon	14,692
Lead Miner	14,563
Tobacco, Cigar, Snuff, -Manufacture	14,367
Weaver (not otherwise described)	14,260
Railway Engine Driver, Stoker	13,715
Gasworks Service	13,570
Municipal, Parish, Union, -Officer	13,423
Institution Service	13,304
Provision Curer, Dealer	13,236
Hairdresser, Wig Maker	13,125
Dyer, Scourer, Calenderer	12,882
Wood, Timber, -Merchant, Dealer	12,859
Corn, Flour, Seed, -Merchant, Dealer	12,765
Gamekeeper	12,431
Solicitor, Attorney	12,314
Brush, Broom Maker	11,708
Rope, Cord, -Maker	11,695
Gunsmith, Gun Manufacture	11,576
Carpet, Rug, -Manufacture	11,568
Manufacturing Chemist, Labourer	11,328
Wine and Spirit Merchant	10,969
Stationer (not Law)	10,889
Bank Service	10,887
Tin Miner	10,617
Box and Packing Case Maker	10,570
Maltster	10,356
Coal Mine Service	10,346

81. Quantities of grain and flour imported

Parlty. Papers, 1878–9/LXV, p. 437.

Years	Wheat	Barley	Oats	Maize	Other kinds of grain	Flour of wheat	Flour of other kinds	TOTAL
	Cwts.	Cwts.	Cwts.	Cwts.	Cwts.	Cwts.	Cwts.	Cwts.
1833	1,075,407	304,360	64,168	30	173,014	172,877	474	1,790,330
1834	576,727	316,289	481,181	3,655	495,634	151,306	304	2,025,096
1835	184,721	242,128	310,934	3,162	253,834	84,969	262	1,080,010
1836	730,803	298,153	360,404	7,620	764,918	255,830	680	2,418,408
1837	1,975,445	313,535	1,145,166	17,250	1,307,691	364,248	4,721	5,128,056
1838	5,379,660	7,864	147,246	17,323	411,373	456,739	3,149	6,423,354
1839	11,416,430	2,069,303	1,842,821	50,798	1,738,117	843,046	762	17,961,277
1840	8,637,993	2,233,707	1,487,024	99,703	1,252,615	1,537,858	8,707	15,257,607
1841	10,442,267	945,193	336,317	17,730	1,962,240	1,263,126	12,530	14,979,403
1842	11,775,634	261,911	828,498	153,454	1,001,991	1,129,852	21,003	15,172,343
1843	4,073,853	640,286	231,888	2,216	343,040	436,878	5,585	5,824,746
1844	4,762,667	3,640,518	823,902	158,846	397,993	980,645	4,056	10,768,627
1845	3,777,411	1,315,550	1,623,784	241,667	1,160,601	945,864	3,052	9,067,929
1846	6,207,894	1,324,432	2,170,682	3,024,883	2,110,170	3,190,429	157,136	18,185,626
1847	11,511,305	2,759,582	4,690,697	15,464,194	2,972,224	6,329,058	2,304,932	46,031,992
1848	11,184,156	3,765,264	2,659,404	6,752,233	3,290,065	1,754,449	275,788	29,681,359
1849	16,663,305	4,932,172	3,484,541	9,533,396	4,002,878	3,349,839	162,001	42,128,132
1850	16,202,312	3,699,653	3,174,801	5,473,161	3,061,800	3,819,440	18,568	35,449,735
1851	16,518,701	2,962,729	3,295,955	7,747,011	1,909,915	5,314,414	19,955	37,768,680
1852	13,261,161	2,234,071	2,720,539	6,305,472	2,122,960	3,865,173	1,546	30,510,922
1853	21,300,197	2,943,110	2,828,125	6,619,213	2,293,795	4,621,506	16,504	40,622,450
1854	14,868,650	1,974,900	2,791 110	5,784,420	2,149,934	3,646,505	58,656	31,274,175
1855	11,560,042	1,246,822	2,842,749	5,208,570	1,985,867	1,904,224	18,094	24,766,368
1856	17,648,943	2,612,186	3,153,832	7,619,199	2,007,201	3,970,100	21,267	37,032,728
1857	14,897,814	6,076,679	4,703,322	4,931,927	2,355,607	2,178,148	21,726	35,165,223
1858	18,380,782	5,933,543	5,104,773	7,503,536	2,921,752	3,856,127	38,389	43,738,902
1859	17,337,329	6,170,910	4,613,358	5,632,727	2,573,088	3,328,324	8,380	39,664,116
1860	25,484,151	7,546,185	6,300,115	7,936,123	3,768,722	5,086,220	84,122	56,205,638
1861	29,955,532	5,001,518	5,114,398	13,244,366	4,430,079	6,152,938	104,678	64,003,509
1862	41,033,503	6,625,143	4,426,994	11,694,818	3,096,122	7,207,113	21,668	74,105,361
1863	24,364,171	7,383,753	6,495,585	12,736,594	3,617,262	5,218,977	15,703	59,832,045
1864	23,196,714	4,921,486	5,562,959	6,285,938	2,530,018	4,512,391	9,216	47,018,722
1865	20,962,963	7,818,570	7,714,230	7,096,033	1,981,878	3,904,471	13,966	49,492,111
1866	23,156,329	8,434,323	8,844,586	14,322,863	3,132,623	4,972,280	88,105	62,951,109
1867	34,645,569	5,684,956	9,407,136	8,540,429	4,020,957	3,592,969	132,577	66,024,593
1868	32,639,768	7,476,490	8,112,563	11,472,226	4,150,657	3,093,022	62,643	67,007,369
1869	37,695,828	8,053,769	7,916,870	17,664,113	3,168,119	5,401,555	21,682	79,921,936
1870	30,901,229	7,217,369	10,830,630	16,756,783	3,559,898	4,803,909	33,695	74,103,513
1871	39,389,803	8,569,012	10,914,186	16,825,023	4,262,636	3,977,939	19,390	83,957,989
1872	42,127,726	15,046,566	11,537,325	24,532,670	4,521,011	4,388,136	42,800	102,196,234
1873	43,863,098	9,241,063	11,907,702	18,823,431	4,272,135	6,214,479	79,439	94,401,347
1874	41,527,638	11,335,396	11,387,768	17,693,625	4,724,235	6,236,044	93,130	92,997,836

YEARS	WHEAT			BARLEY			OATS			RYE		
	Highest weekly average	*Lowest weekly average*	*Average for the year*	*Highest weekly average*	*Lowest weekly average*	*Average for the year*	*Highest weekly average*	*Lowest weekly average*	*Average for the year*	*Highest weekly average*	*Lowest weekly average*	*Average for the year*
	s. d.	*s. d.*	*s. d.*	*s. d.*	*s. d.*	*s. d.*	*s. d.*	*s. d.*	*s. d.*	*s. d.*	*s. d.*	*s. d.*
1833	56 5	49 2	52 11	31 4	24 5	37 6	20 2	16 6	18 5	36 9	29 0	32 11
1834	49 6	40 6	46 2	33 3	26 8	29 0	24 6	17 11	20 11	35 8	29 9	32 9
1835	44 0	36 0	39 4	33 0	26 10	29 11	25 3	18 6	22 0	35 0	26 4	30 4
1836	61 9	36 0	48 6	39 10	27 4	32 10	27 6	18 7	23 1	44 11	25 8	33 4
1837	60 1	51 0	55 10	36 1	27 5	30 4	25 6	20 2	23 1	44 6	26 10	34 9
1838	78 4	52 4	64 7	37 5	28 6	31 5	26 3	19 11	22 5	52 6	27 6	35 1
1839	81 6	65 6	70 8	43 1	37 4	39 6	28 10	23 8	25 11	52 4	36 1	42 0
1840	72 10	58 10	66 4	40 9	31 6	36 5	30 7	21 4	25 8	40 0	32 10	37 0
1841	76 1	60 7	64 4	39 10	29 7	32 10	24 7	20 7	22 5	44 8	28 11	36 9
1842	65 8	46 10	57 3	29 7	25 11	27 6	22 4	17 2	19 3	43 0	28 1	33 0
1843	61 2	45 5	50 1	33 11	26 5	29 6	21 9	16 9	18 4	38 7	26 10	30 7
1844	56 5	45 1	51 3	36 1	30 7	33 8	22 11	18 3	20 7	39 3	30 8	33 11
1845	60 1	45 0	50 10	35 1	29 0	31 8	26 3	20 9	22 6	38 2	29 6	32 6
1846	62 3	45 1	54 8	44 6	26 9	32 8	27 3	21 5	23 8	44 2	28 2	35 0
1847	102 5	49 6	69 9	56 5	30 5	44 2	36 3	21 3	28 8	76 11	28 11	49 0
1848	56 10	46 10	50 6	34 1	29 0	31 6	22 10	18 0	20 6	33 8	28 0	30 5
1849	49 1	38 9	44 3	30 8	25 3	27 9	19 6	15 6	17 6	28 11	22 4	25 8
1850	44 1	36 11	40 3	26 4	21 5	23 5	18 4	14 7	16 5	29 6	19 1	23 3
1851	43 6	35 6	38 6	27 1	22 7	24 9	22 7	15 11	18 7	32 5	22 1	25 6
1852	45 11	37 2	40 9	31 0	26 3	28 6	20 8	17 4	19 1	33 6	24 10	29 10
1853	73 7	43 3	53 3	42 3	28 11	33 2	26 3	17 9	21 0	47 5	27 3	35 0
1854	83 3	52 5	72 5	43 0	29 2	36 0	30 8	24 7	27 11	63 0	34 8	45 10
1855	83 1	66 6	74 8	42 5	29 9	34 9	29 3	24 10	27 5	35 4	38 0	45 8
1856	77 10	59 8	69 2	47 6	35 6	41 1	27 11	22 9	25 2	54 8	38 11	45 0
1857	63 10	47 5	56 4	47 3	35 9	42 1	28 7	22 8	25 0	44 4	31 6	38 3
1858	48 8	40 0	44 2	37 6	29 9	34 8	28 5	21 9	24 6	35 10	26 0	32 3
1859	54 4	39 10	43 9	36 5	29 0	33 6	26 3	20 10	23 2	41 9	27 6	32 4
1860	62 11	43 6	53 3	41 4	32 5	36 7	28 2	21 0	24 5	45 6	28 11	36 3
1861	61 6	50 0	55 4	40 7	28 3	36 1	26 10	21 6	23 9	41 2	29 0	35 9
1862	62 1	45 7	55 5	37 3	31 6	35 1	26 3	20 4	22 7	43 6	31 0	36 4
1863	48 4	39 10	44 9	36 10	28 10	33 11	23 11	18 7	21 2	41 6	25 0	32 5
1864	44 1	37 10	40 2	32 5	27 2	29 11	22 11	18 8	20 1	40 0	26 7	30 11
1865	46 11	38 2	41 10	34 0	27 3	29 9	24 0	19 0	21 10	—	—	—
1866	61 7	44 5	49 11	46 2	32 6	37 5	27 7	22 8	24 7	—	—	—
1867	70 5	59 3	64 5	45 9	34 9	40 0	29 7	23 4	26 0	—	—	—
1868	74 7	49 5	63 9	47 3	35 8	43 0	31 4	25 5	28 1	—	—	—
1869	54 2	43 5	48 2	49 7	30 3	39 5	29 0	21 6	26 0	—	—	—
1870	54 11	40 7	46 11	36 11	30 3	34 7	28 8	19 10	22 10	—	—	—
1871	60 0	52 6	56 8	38 6	32 7	36 2	28 3	22 0	25 2	—	—	—
1872	60 3	53 11	57 0	44 1	30 3	37 4	26 7	21 8	23 2	—	—	—
1873	64 7	54 7	58 8	45 1	34 11	40 5	30 10	21 7	25 5	—	—	—
1874	63 9	43 5	55 9	49 11	39 1	44 11	32 0	25 5	28 10	—	—	—

83. Cultivated acreage and output (1851)

Caird, *English Agriculture in 1851*, p. 522.

	Acres in grass	*Acres in Tillage*
Assuming the Midland and Western counties to be two-thirds in grass, and one-third in tillage, we have of 13,000,000 acres of cultivated land	8,666,000	4,333,000
And assuming the Eastern division to be one-third in grass and two-thirds tillage, we have of 14,000,000 acres of cultivated land	4,666,000	9,334,000
	13,332,000	13,667,000

		Acres		*Produce per acre bush.*		*Total produce Qrs.*	*Deduct seed per acre Bush.*	*Seed Qrs.*		*Produce under deduction of seed Qrs.*
The 13,667,000 acres in tillage is divided thus:–										
One fourth in wheat . . .		3,416,750	×	27	=	11,531,531	3	1,281,281	=	10,250,250
One fourth in barley, oats, and rye, *viz.*:–										
Barley	1,416,750		×	38	=	6,729,562	4	708,375	=	6,021,187
Oats and rye	2,000,000		×	44	=	11,000,000	5	1,250,000	=	9,750,000
		3,416,750								
One-fourth in clover, "seeds," beans and pease, *viz.*:–										
One-sixth of whole area in clover and "seeds"	2,277,750									
One-twelfth beans and pease .	1,139,000		×	30	=	4,271,250	4	569,500	=	3,701,750
		3,416,750								
One-fourth in turnips, mangold, potatoes, rape and fallow, *viz.*:–										
In turnips, mangold, and potatoes	2,116,750									
In rape and fallow . . .	1,300,000									
		3,416,750								
		13,667,000				33,532,343		3,809,156		29,723,187

Railway returns (1842–1874)

Statistical Abstracts.

Years	Length of lines open on 31 Dec.	Total capital paid up (shares, loans, &c.) to 31 Dec.	Number of passengers conveyed (INcluding season ticket holders): Total	Number of passengers: Per mile	Total of Traffic receipts: Total	Total of Traffic receipts: Per mile	Total of working expenses	Net receipts
			In the years ended 30 June					
	Miles	£	No.	No.	£	£	£	£
1842	1,857	—	18,453,504	—	3,820,522[1]	—	Cannot be given previous to 1854	
1843	1,952	65,530,792	23,466,896	—	4,535,189	—		
1844	2,148	72,351,567	27,763,602	—	5,074,674	—		
1845	2,441	88,481,376	33,791,253	—	6,209,714	—		
1846	3,036	126,296,369	43,790,983	—	7,565,569	—		
1847	3,945	167,321,856	51,352,163	—	8,510,886	—		
1848	5,127	200,173,059	57,965,070	—	9,933,552	—		
			In the years ended 31 December					
1849	6,031	229,747,778	63,841,539	10,585	11,806,498	1,957		
1850	6,621	240,270,745	72,854,422	11,003	13,204,668	1,994		
1851	6,890	248,240,896	85,391,095	12,309	14,997,459	2,176		
1852	7,336	264,165,672	89,135,729	12,150	15,710,554	2,141		
1853	7,686	273,324,514	102,286,660	13,318	18,035,879	2,346		
1854	8,054	286,068,794	111,206,707	13,807	20,215,724	2,510	9,206,205	11,009,519
1855	8,280	297,584,709	118,595,135	14,323	21,507,599	2,597	10,299,709	11,207,890
1856	8,707	307,595,086	129,347,592	14,855	23,165,491	2,660	10,837,456	12,328,035
1857	9,094	315,157,258	139,008,888	15,395	24,174,610	2,659	11,240,239	12,934,371
1858	9,542	325,375,507	139,193,699	14,587	23,956,749	2,516	11,668,225	12,288,524
1859	10,002	334,362,928	149,807,148	14,980	25,743,502	2,573	(Not ascertained.)	

[1] Five railway companies did not make any returns in this year.

Years	Length of lines open at the end of each year	Total capital paid up (shares, loans, &c.) at the end of each year	Number of passengers conveyed (INcluding season ticket holders)		Total of traffic receipts		Total of working expenses	Net receipts
			Total	Per mile	Total	Per mile		
	Miles	£	No.	No.	£	£	£	£
1860	10,433	348,130,127	163,483,572	15,669	27,766,622	2,661	13,187,368	14,579,254
1861	10,869	362,327,338	173,773,218	15,988	28,565,355	2,628	13,843,337	14,722,018
1862	11,551	385,218,438	180,485,727	15,625	29,128,558	2,522	14,268,409	14,860,149
1863	12,322	404,215,802	204,699,466	16,612	31,156,397	2,528	15,027,234	16,129,163
1864	12,789	425,719,613	229,348,664	17,933	33,911,547	2,651	16,000,308	17,911,239
1865	13,289	455,478,143	251,959,862	18,960	35,751,655	2,691	17,149,073	18,602,582
1866	13,854	481,872,184	274,403,895	19,734	38,164,354	2,754	18,811,673	19,352,681
1867	14,247	502,262,887	287,807,904	20,201	39,479,999	2,771	19,848,952	19,631,047

UNITED KINGDOM

Years	Length of line open at the end of each year	Paid up capital at the end of each year Ordinary, guaranteed, preferential and loans and debenture stock	Number of passengers conveyed (EXclusive of season-ticket holders)	Weight of goods and minerals conveyed	Total of receipts	Working expenditure	Net receipts	Proportion of working expenditure to gross receipts
		Total						
	Miles	£	No.	Tons	£	£	£	Per cent
*1869	15,145	518,779,761	312,631,812	—	42,695,247	20,789,078	21,915,169	49
1870	15,537	529,908,673	336,545,397	—	45,078,143	21,715,525	23,362,618	48
1871	15,376	552,680,107	375,220,754	169,364,698	48,892,780	23,152,860	25,739,920	47
1872	15,814	569,047,346	422,874,822	179,302,121	53,235,510	26,277,640	26,957,870	49
1873	16,082	588,320,308	455,320,188	190,953,457	57,742,000	30,752,848	26,989,152	53
1874	16,449	609,895,931	477,840,411	188,538,852	59,255,715	32,612,712	26,643,003	55

* Returns for the year 1868 incomplete and not made up.

85. Coal and pig iron production (1854–1874)

Statistical Abstracts.

Years	*Coal*	*Pig iron*
	Tons	*Tons*
1854	64,661,401	3,069,838
1855	61,453,079	3,218,154
1856	66,645,450	3,586,377
1857	65,394,707	3,659,447
1858	65,008,649	3,456,064
1859	71,979,765	3,712,904
1860	80,042,698	3,826,752
1861	83,635,214	3,712,390
1862	81,638,338	3,943,469
1863	86,292,215	4,510,040
1864	92,787,873	4,767,951
1865	98,150,587	4,819,254
1866	101,630,544	4,523,897
1867	104,500,480	4,761,023
1868	103,141,157	4,970,206
1869	107,427,557	5,445,757
1870	110,431,192	5,963,515
1871	117,352,028	6,627,179
1872	123,497,316	6,741,929
1873	127,016,747	6,566,451
1874	125,067,916	5,991,408

86. Shipping registered as belonging to the United Kingdom (1840–1874)

Statistical Abstracts.

YEARS	SAILING VESSELS		STEAM VESSELS		TOTAL		YEARS
	Vessels	*Tons*	*Vessels*	*Tons*	*Vessels*	*Tons*	
1840	21,883	2,680,334	771	87,928	22,654	2,768,262	1840
1841	22,668	2,839,332	793	96,067	23,461	2,935,399	1841
1842	23,121	2,932,906	833	108,514	23,954	3,041,420	1842
1843	23,040	2,897,848	858	109,733	23,898	3,007,581	1843
1844	23,116	3,930,715	900	113,677	24,016	3,044,392	1844
1845	23,471	3,004,398	917	118,782	24,388	3,123,180	1845
1846	23,808	3,068,529	963	131,256	24,771	3,199,785	1846
1847	24,167	3,166,913	1,033	141,008	25,200	3,307,921	1847
1848	24,520	3,249,380	1,118	151,429	25,638	3,400,809	1848
1849	24,753	3,326,274	1,149	159,684	25,902	3,485,958	1849
1850	24,797	3,396,659	1,187	168,474	25,984	3,565,133	1850
1851	24,816	3,475,657	1,227	186,687	26,043	3,662,344	1851
1852	24,814	3,549,968	1,272	209,310	26,086	3,759,278	1852
1853	25,224	3,780,092	1,385	250,112	26,609	4,030,204	1853
1854	25,335	3,942,513	1,524	306,237	26,859	4,248,750	1854
1855	24,274	3,968,699	1,674	380,635	25,948	4,349,334	1855
1856	24,480	3,980,494	1,697	386,462	26,177	4,366,956	1856
1857	25,273	4,141,274	1,824	417,466	27,097	4,558,740	1857
1858	25,615	4,205,270	1,926	452,468	27,541	4,657,738	1858
1859	25,784	4,226,355	1,918	436,836	27,702	4,663,191	1859
1860	25,663	4,204,360	2,000	454,327	27,663	4,658,687	1860
1861	25,905	4,300,518	2,133	506,308	28,038	4,806,826	1861
1862	26,212	4,396,509	2,228	537,891	28,440	4,934,400	1862
1863	26,339	4,731,217	2,298	596,856	28,637	5,328,073	1863
1864	26,142	4,930,219	2,490	697,281	28,632	5,627,500	1864
1865	26,069	4,936,776	2,718	823,533	28,787	5,760,309	1865
1866	26,140	4,903,652	2,831	875,685	28,971	5,779,337	1866
1867	25,842	4,852,911	2,931	901,062	28,773	5,753,973	1867
1868	25,500	4,878,233	2,944	902,297	28,444	5,780,530	1868
1869	24,187	4,765,304	2,972	948,367	27,159	5,713,671	1869
1870	23,189	4,577,855	3,178	1,112,934	26,367	5,690,789	1870
1871	22,510	4,374,511	3,382	1,319,612	25,892	5,694,123	1871
1872	22,103	4,213,295	3,673	1,538,032	25,776	5,751,327	1872
1873	21,698	4,091,379	3,863	1,713,783	25,561	5,805,162	1873
1874	21,464	4,108,220	4,033	1,870,611	25,497	5,978,831	1874

87. Principal exports by quantity (1840–1874).

Statistical Abstracts.

Principal Articles		1840	1841	1842	1843	1844	1845	1846	1847	1848
Coals, Cinders, and Culm .	Tons	1,606,313	1,848,294	1,999,504	1,866,211	1,754,171	2,531,282	2,531,108	2,483,161	2,785,301
Cotton Yarn . . .	Lbs.	118,470,223	123,226,519	137,466,892	140,321,176	138,540,079	135,144,865	161,892,750	120,270,741	135,831,162
Cotton Piece Goods . .	Yds.	790,631,997	751,125,624	734,098,809	918,640,205	1,046.670,823	1,091,686,069	1,065,460,589	942,540,160	1,096,751,823
Linen Yarn . . .	Lbs.	17,733,575	25,220,290	29,490,987	23,358,352	25,970,569	23,288,725	19,484,203	12,688,915	11,722,182
Linen Manufactures:										
Total Piece Goods .	Yds.	89,373,431	90,321,761	69,232,682	84,172,585	91,283,754	88,401,670	84,799,369	89,329,310	89,002,431
Iron, Bar, Angle, Bolt and Rod } Iron, Railroad, of all sorts .	Tons } Tons	144,719	189,250	191,302	198,774	249,916	164,023	157,991	228,294	338,688
Total of Iron and Steel .	Tons	268,327	360,875	369,398	448,925	458,745	351,978	433,325	549,709	626,141
Woollen and Worsted Yarn.	Lbs.	3,796,645	4,903,291	5,962,401	7,410,313	8,271,906	9,405,928	8,630,608	10,065,231	8,429,152
Woollen and Worsted Manufactures:										
Cloths, Coatings, &c. Unmixed and Mixed .	Yds.	10,876,404	10,363,374	8,088,150	11,579,232	14,688,660	14,163,954	11,250,246	11,128,866	10,194,786
Flannels, Blankets, Blanketing, and Baizes .	Yds.	5,289,978	5,568,293	4,056,921	4,373,129	6,311,345	5,875,275	4,993,459	6,161,794	6,053,051
Worsted Stuffs, Unmixed and Mixed . .	Yds.	51,750,150	61,221,335	62,375,786	79,614,363	90,443,335	85,792,385	70,765,686	80,442,678	67,437,748
Carpets and Druggets .	Yds.	758,639	809,315	763,762	747,346	924,326	1,006,970	939,791	1,219,156	1,106,261

Principal Articles		1849	1850	1851	1852	1853	1854	1855	1856	1857
Coals, Cinders, and Culm .	Tons	2,828,039	3,351,880	3,468,545	3,640,194	3,935,062	4,309,255	4,976,902	5,879,779	6,737,718
Cotton Yarn . . .	Lbs.	149,502,281	131,370,368	143,966,106	145,478,302	147,539,302	147,128,498	165,493,598	181,495,805	176,821,338
Cotton Piece Goods . .	Yds.	1,337,536,116	1,358,182,941	1,543,161,789	1,524,256,914	1,594,592,659	1,692,899,122	1,937,734,025	2,035,274,969	1,979,270,780
Linen Yarn . . .	Lbs.	17,264,033	18,220,688	18,841,326	23,928,592	22,893,586	17,696,567	18,177,484	25,118,349	28,847,811
Linen Manufactures:										
Total Piece Goods. .	Yds.	111,259,183	122,342,516	129,106,753	133,192,627	134,165,291	111,648,657	118,039,721	146,410,188	133,839,593
Iron, Bar, Angle, Bolt and Rod	Tons	} 402,200	469,434	538,411	567,692	653,902	616,718	540,992 {	297,649	301,871
Iron, Railroad, of all Sorts .	Tons								461,870	457,660
Total of Iron and Steel .	Tons	709,492	783,424	919,479	1,035,884	1,261,272	1,196,663	1,092,735	1,438,900	1,532,386
Woollen and Worsted Yarn.	Lbs.	11,773,020	13,794,225	14,670,880	14,220,192	13,964,944	15,733,200	20,408,304	27,340,208	24,654,448
Woollen and Worsted Manufactures:										
Cloths, Coatings, &c. Unmixed and Mixed .	Yds.	16,278,738	27,355,188	25,051,740	26,406,828	27,105,624	30,516,318	21,930,384	27,352,332	30,036,006
Flannels, Blankets, Blanketing, and Baizes .	Yds.	7,974,984	9,295,122	9,068,549	9,046,677	13,788,258	12,767,186	7,699,819	11,641,426	13,011.038
Worsted Stuffs, Unmixed and Mixed . .	Yds.	98,216,048	112,000,812	115,296,580	127,798,552	123,632,208	105,989,380	100,061,472	112,916,692	129,632,748
Carpets and Druggets .	Yds.	1,565,745	1,868,675	1,814,284	2,280,373	4,035,268	4,052,588	3,351,098	4,550,666	4 452,428

Principal Articles		1858	1859	1860	1861	1862	1863	1864	1865	1866
Coals, Cinders, and Culm .	Tons	6,529,483	7,006,949	7,321,832	7,855,115	8,301,852	8,275,212	8,809,908	9,170,477	9,916,244
Cotton Yarn . . .	Lbs.	200,016,902	192,206,643	197,343,655	177,848,353	93,225,890	74,398,264	75,677,521	103,533,609	139,005,221
Cotton Piece Goods . .	Yds.	2,324,139,085	2,562,545,476	2,776,218,427	2,563,459,007	1,681,394,600	1,710,962,072	1,751,989,300	2,014,303,716	2,575,967,256
Linen Yarn . . .	Lbs.	32,047,492	27,290,387	31,210,612	27,981,042	32,559,244	38,452,030	40,177,150	36,796,673	33,666,338
Linen Manufactures:										
Total Piece Goods . .	Yds.	121,940,291	138,120,498	143,996,773	116,322,469	156,894,813	181,637,300	210,468,702	247,006,491	254,943,531
Iron, Bar, Angle, Bolt and Rod	Tons	254,061	300,786	311,459	258,074	308,061	330,653	279,758	254,257	269,419
Iron, Railroad of all Sorts .	Tons	433,250	528,927	453,445	377,565	400,765	446,440	408,215	434,300	498,021
Total of Iron and Steel .	Tons	1,349,058	1,465,191	1,442,045	1,322,694	1,501,451	1,640,949	1,502,964	1,617,509	1,683,390
Woollen and Worsted Yarn.	Lbs.	24,069,808	22,849,344	27,533,968	27,512,352	27,821,378	32,542,609	31,824,296	31,671,254	27,351,705
Woollen and Worsted Manufactures:										
Cloths, Coatings, &c. Unmixed and Mixed .	Yds.	23,759,778	24,118,080	23,968,182	24,371,340	35,400,976	27,762,256	29,615,556	25,615,689	34,520,340
Flannels, Blankets, Blanketing, and Baizes .	Yds.	10,478,787	14,526,320	12,641,689	13,403,882	17,874,264	17,311,400	18,128,421	14,769,397	14,519,298
Worsted Stuffs, Unmixed and Mixed . .	Yds.	127,397,116	150,433,360	148,685,124	122,155,508	118,812,137	165,835,142	187,305,448	233,078,142	224,343,474
Carpets and Druggets .	Yds.	4,506,064	4,609,919	5,076,542	4,067,351	5,378,562	6,257,992	5,992,832	5,743,090	7,613,609

Principal Articles		1867	1868	1869	1870	1871	1872	1873	1874
Coals, Cinders, and Culm .	Tons	10,415,778	10,837,513	10,744,945	11,702,649	12,747,989	13,198,494	12,617,566	13,927,205
Cotton Yarn . . .	Lbs.	169,096,708	174,537,970	168,841,075	186,078,060	193,695,156	212,327,972	214,778,827	220,682,919
Cotton Piece Goods . .	Yds.	2,832,023,707	2,966,706,542	2,868,630,125	3,266,998,366	3,417,405,811	3,537,985,311	3,483,735,585	3,606,639,044
Linen Yarn . . .	Lbs.	34,002,479	32,857,117	34,570,316	37,239,314	36,235,625	31,187,051	28,734,212	27,154,906
Linen Manufactures:									
Total Piece Goods . .	Yds.	211,275,196	209,380,250	214,792,554	226,470,696	220,467,476	245,019,404	208,123,476	194,682,464
Iron, Bar, Angle, Bolt and Rod	Tons	301,428	302,624	358,865	321,455	349,084	313,600	286,845	258,953
Iron, Railroad, of all Sorts .	Tons	580,571	583,488	888,010	1,059,392	981,197	945,420	785,014	782,665
Total of Iron and Steel .	Tons	1,882,650	2,041,852	2,675,331	2,825,575	3,169,219	3,382,762	2,957,813	2,487,522
Woollen and Worsted Yarn.	Lbs.	37,434,020	43,657,842	37,185,740	35,536,848	43,725,577	39,734,934	34,744,507	34,981,008
Woollen and Worsted Manufactures:									
Cloths, Coatings, &c. Unmixed and Mixed .	Yds.	31,189,209	24,630,978	28,218,489	32,404,719	35,583,697	40,734,224	38,633,833	40,331,686
Flannels, Blankets, Blanketing, and Baizes .	Yds.	11,126,055	12,785,623	14,925,716	14,985,389	14,091,282	15,022,122	14,447,313	16,004,436
Worsted Stuffs, Unmixed and Mixed . .	Yds.	200,469,996	224,621,434	250,062,934	235,936,604	307,237,042	344,968,689	282,884,692	261,135,081
Carpets and Druggets .	Yds.	6,673,951	7,385,769	9,656,404	9,374,173	10,957,453	11,815,900	9,921,100	9,208,271

88. Principal exports by value (1840–1874)

Statistical Abstracts.

Principal Articles	*1840*	*1841*	*1842*	*1843*	*1844*	*1845*	*1846*	*1847*	*1848*
	£	£	£	£	£	£	£	£	£
Coals, Cinders and Culm	576,519	675,287	734,000	690,424	672,056	973,635	971,175	968,502	1,088,221
Cotton Yarn	7,101,308	7,266,968	7,771,464	7,193,971	6,988,584	6,963,235	7,882,048	5,957,980	5,927,831
Cotton Piece Goods	17,567,010	16,232,510	13,907,884	16,254,000	18,816,764	19,156,096	17,717,778	17,375,245	16,753,369
Linen Yarn	822,876	972,466	1,025,551	898,829	1,050,676	1,060,567	875,405	649,893	493,449
Linen Manufactures	3,306,088	3,347,555	2,346,749	2,803,223	3,024,800	3,036,370	2,830,808	2,958,851	2,802,789
Iron, Bar, Angle, Bolt and Rod Iron, Railroad, of all Sorts	} 1,142,895	1,345,359	1,131,865	1,084,159	1,498,653	1,447,560	1,584,119	2,218,178	2,615,554
Total of Iron and Steel	2,524,859	2,877,278	2,457,717	2,590,833	3,193,368	3,501,895	4,178,026	5,265,779	4,777,966
Woollen and Worsted Yarn	452,957	552,148	637,305	742,888	958,217	1,066,925	908,270	1,001,364	776,975
Cloths, Coatings, &c. Mixed and Unmixed	1,465,328	1,372,396	1,044,710	1,506,367	1,997,090	2,037,535	1,536,101	1,560,385	1,322,167
Flannels, Blankets, Blanketing, Baizes	346,321	383,074	264,137	276,545	439,859	425,176	369,958	416,235	442,207
Worsted Stuffs, Unmixed and Mixed	3,196,254	3,656,598	3,556,963	4,644,414	5,363,961	4,802,288	4,054,253	4,492,705	3,656,808
Carpets and Druggets	104,784	108,215	101,557	101,156	128,594	138,808	132,450	175,055	147,872

Principal Articles	*1849*	*1850*	*1851*	*1852*	*1853*	*1854*	*1855*	*1856*	*1857*
	£	£	£	£	£	£	£	£	£
Coals, Cinders and Culm	1,087,122	1,284,224	1,302,473	1,372,114	1,604,591	2,127,156	2,446,341	2,826,582	3,210,661
Cotton Yarn	6,704,089	6,383,704	6,634,026	6,654,655	6,895,653	6,691,330	7,200,395	8,028,575	8,700,589
Cotton Piece Goods	20,071,046	21,873,697	23,454,810	23,223,432	25,817,249	25,054,527	27,578,746	30,204,166	30,372,831
Linen Yarn	732,065	881,312	951,426	1,140,565	1,154,977	944,502	932,981	1,365,980	1,647,953
Linen Manufactures	3,493,829	3,947,682	4,107,396	4,231,786	4,758,432	4,108,457	4,118,013	4,887,780	4,516,880
Iron, Bar, Angle, Bolt and Rod	} 2,605,247	2,801,043	3,116,345	3,406,360	5,647,773	5,731,671	4,628,399	{ 2,799,679	2,773,166
Iron, Railroad, of all Sorts								4,095,309	4,000,515
Total of Iron and Steel	4,986,508	5,350,056	5,830,370	6,684,276	10,845,422	11,674,675	9,465,642	12,966,109	13,603,337
Woollen and Worsted Yarn	1,090,223	1,451,642	1,484,544	1,430,140	1,456,786	1,557,612	2,026,095	2,889,642	2,941,800
Cloths, Coatings, &c. Mixed and Unmixed	1,814,649	2,692,492	2,572,181	2,683,395	2,923,515	3,089,334	2,371,324	2,762,622	3,030,788
Flannels, Blankets, Blanketing, Baizes	518,054	604,653	586,376	571,465	882,132	739,301	539,002	751,132	911,256
Worsted Stuffs, Unmixed and Mixed	4,592,813	4,794,610	4,720,775	4,933,090	5,418,737	4,441,165	3,961,824	4,737,799	5,551,403
Carpets and Druggets	204,127	248,019	266,706	309,417	497,753	490,179	426,130	610,848	613,246

Principal Articles	1858	1859	1860	1861	1862	1863	1864	1865	1866
	£	£	£	£	£	£	£	£	£
Coals, Cinders and Culm	3,045,434	3,270,013	3,316,281	3,604,790	3,750,867	3,713,798	4,165,773	4,427,177	5,102,805
Cotton Yarn	9,579,479	9,458,112	9,870,875	9,292,761	6,202,240	8,063,128	9,083,239	10,342,737	13,685,627
Cotton Piece Goods	33,421,843	38,744,113	42,141,505	37,579,728	30,548,731	39,524,060	45,799,090	46,923,384	60,927,419
Linen Yarn	1,746,340	1,674,602	1,801,272	1,622,216	1,852,451	2,530,404	2,991,969	2,535,321	2,374,132
Linen Manufactures	4,124,356	4,604,587	4,804,803	3,852,341	5,133,936	6,508,973	8,172,813	9,156,990	9,576,245
Iron, Bar, Angle, Bolt and Rod	2,059,163	2,373,910	2,385,871	1,882,275	2,250,964	2,568,034	2,568,049	2,199,837	2,328,695
Iron, Railroad of all Sorts	3,565,224	4,124,208	3,408,759	2,906,359	2,817,877	3,278,504	3,305,086	3,550,563	4,183,198
Total of Iron and Steel	11,197,072	12,314,437	12,154,997	10,326,646	11,365,150	13,150,936	13,310,484	13,471,359	14,842,417
Woollen and Worsted Yarn	2,966,923	3,084,061	3,843,450	3,552,976	3,852,998	5,087,293	5,417,377	5,429,504	4,742,162
Cloths, Coatings, &c. Mixed and Unmixed	2,548,394	2,905,756	2,996,091	2,998,465	4,425,122	3,964,910	4,533,519	4,023,954	5,303,602
Flannels, Blankets, Blanketing, Baizes	693,206	952,026	848,186	1,031,455	1,388,592	1,413,399	1,504,384	1,203,127	1,161,615
Worsted Stuffs, Unmixed and Mixed	5,530,722	6,910,214	7,012,793	6,121,616	5,881,789	8,336,957	10,800,521	13,360,527	13,294,059
Carpets and Druggets	525,773	593,110	667,370	508,652	671,215	810,783	861,499	861,453	1,217 682

Principal Articles	1867	1868	1869	1870	1871	1872	1873	1874
	£	£	£	£	£	£	£	£
Coals, Cinders and Culm	5,392,452	5,437,922	5,165,668	5,638,371	6,246,133	10,442,321	13,188,511	11,984,621
Cotton Yarn	14,871,617	14,714,899	14,095,449	14,671,135	15,061,204	16,697,426	15,895,440	14,517,425
Cotton Piece Goods	55,965,366	52,971,873	53,021,505	56,745,210	57,760,207	63,466,729	61,458,172	59,730,200
Linen Yarn	2,449,394	2,308,434	2,332,088	2,237,492	2,218,129	2,131,071	1,976,830	1,716,231
Linen Manufactures	7,438,382	7,113,873	6,800,141	7,248,345	7,503,816	8,225,690	7,306,153	7,116,302
Iron, Bar, Angle, Bolt and Rod	2,344,549	2,285,187	2,698,696	2,615,245	2,921,777	3,632,818	3,755,980	3,054,547
Iron, Railroad of all Sorts	4,861,129	4,660,612	7,238,170	8,756,552	8,084,619	10,225,492	10,418,852	9,638,236
Total of Iron and Steel	15,050,391	17,634,395	22,342,080	24,038,090	26,124,134	35,996,167	37,731,239	31,190,256
Woollen and Worsted Yarn	5,822,996	6,203,174	5,538,295	4,994,249	6,100,727	6,110,138	5,393,493	5,558,560
Cloths, Coatings, &c. Mixed and Unmixed	5,327,375	3,760,961	4,275,858	4,749,165	5,563,037	6,991,718	6,599,635	6,642,222
Flannels, Blankets, Blanketing, Baizes	859,519	963,866	1,099,299	1,078,983	1,030,302	1,104,835	1,089,864	1,318,007
Worsted Stuffs, Unmixed and Mixed	12,144,998	13,075,773	15,130,340	13,788,798	17,953,209	20,905,163	14,277,382	11,888,072
Carpets and Druggets	1,101,986	1,099,882	1,466,758	1,393,279	1,648,411	1,916,774	1,597,383	1,480,892

89. Balance of payments and export of capital

Albert H. Imlah, *Economic History Review*, v, II, 1952.[1]

ANNUAL AVERAGES BY QUINQUENNIAL PERIODS

All Values in millions of pounds

Years	Balance of Visible Trade			Balance of Business Services			Balance of other Current Items					
	A Merchandise	B Gold, silver bullion and specie	C Ship sales	D Profit on foreign trade and services	E Insurance brokerage commissions, etc.	F Net earnings of shipping	G Emigrant funds	H Tourists smuggling, etc.	Total of trade and services A–H	I Balance of interest and dividends	J Net income available for foreign investment	K Accumulating balance of credit abroad*
1831–35	−13·12	+0·60	—	+5·46	+2·72	+10·14	−1·08	−2·42	+2·30	+4·50	+6·80	145·0
1836–40	−23·96	+0·96	—	+7·16	+3·56	+12·90	−1·00	−2·98	−3·36	+6·80	+3·44	162·2
1841–45	−17·04	−2·30	—	+7·14	+3·54	+13·92	−1·42	−3·22	+0·62	+5·80	+6·42	194·3
1846–50	−26·82	+0·98	—	+8·50	+4·26	+15·90	−2·88	−3·16	−3·22	+9·16	+5·94	224·0
1851–55	−27·54	−5·38	+0·18	+11·90	+5·94	+18·68	−3·08	−4·44	−3·74	+11·74	+8·00	264·0
1856–60	−33·84	−0·84	+0·96	+16·60	+8·32	+26·26	−1·34	−6·22	+9·90	+15·62	+25·52	391.6
1861–65	−56·82	−2·94	+0·72	+21·94	+10·94	+34·54	−1·44	−6·28	+0·66	+21·24	+21·90	501·1
1866–70	−58·12	−8·28	+1·26	+26·36	+13·20	+43·92	−1·72	−7·52	+9·10	+29·28	+38·39	693·0
1871–75	−62·50	−4·30	+2·76	+32·90	+16·44	+49·68	−1·94	−9·58	+23·46	+49·54	+73·00	1058·1

* Estimated balance at end of quinquennium.

[1] Figures are according to Professor Imlah's latest revision, kindly supplied by him.

90. Trade cycle, depression and boom (1830–1879)

Poor Law Report, 1909, *Parlty. Papers*, 1909/xxxvii.

1830	Culmination of Distress (international)
1831	———————
1832	Depression
1833	Extreme Distress
1834	Revival
1835	Prosperity (depression of agriculture)
1836	———————
1837	Reaction ———————
1838	Distress
1839	Universal Distress
1840	———————
1841	———————
1842	"The lowest ebb"
1843	Revival
1844	Prosperity
1845	Prosperity and speculation
1846	Potato famine
1847	Crisis and depression
1848	Distress
1849	Revival
1850	Revival
1851	Prosperity
1852	Prosperity
1853	Pause
1854	Depression
1855	Distress
1856	Distress
1857	Distress and commercial collapse
1858	Revival
1859	Prosperity
1860	Prosperity
1861	Cotton famine
1862	Distress
1863	Revival
1864	Prosperity
1865	Wild speculation
1866	Crash (Overend and Gurney)
1867	Depression
1868	———————
1869	———————
1870	Revival
1871	General Prosperity
1872	"By leaps and bounds"
1873	Never more prosperous
1874	Highest point of prosperity
1875	Declining prosperity
1876	Depression
1877	———————
1878	Distress
1879	Culmination of Distress

B. DOCUMENTS

91. Select Committee of 1833 on Agriculture

Parlty. Papers, 1833/v/pp. 3–13.

On looking back at the Report of the Committee in 1821, to whom the Petitions complaining of the depressed State of the Agriculture of the United Kingdom were referred, it will be found that the Report commences by stating "that the complaints of the Petitioners are founded in fact, in so far as they represent that *at the present price* of Corn, the returns to the Occupier of an Arable Farm, after allowing for the Interest of his Investment, are by no means adequate to the charges and outgoings, of which a considerable proportion can be paid only out of the Capitals, and not from the Profits of the Tenantry."

The Average Price of Wheat for the Year 1821 was 54s. 5d. per Quarter. The Average Price of the present Year is 53s. 1d.; and although some of the charges connected with general Taxation have been reduced since 1821, yet the local burthens, such as Poor-rate and County-rate, have, in most parts of England, been grievously augmented. The Committee of 1821 arrived at the conclusion, "that the returns of farming Capital were at that time considerably below the ordinary rate of Profit;" and no Evidence adduced before Your Committee of diminished outgoings contrasted with the change of Prices in the interval, would warrant, at this moment, a different conclusion.

The Committee of 1821 expressed a hope "that the great body of the Occupiers of the Soil, either from the Savings of more prosperous times, or from the Credit which punctuality commands in this Country, possess resources which will enable them to surmount the difficulties under which they now labour." Your Committee with deep regret, are bound rather to express a fear that the difficulties alone remain unchanged, but that the Savings are either gone or greatly diminished, the Credit failing, and the resources being generally exhausted; and this opinion is formed not on the Evidence of Rent-payers, but of many most respectable Witnesses, as well Owners of Land as Surveyors and Land-agents.

The Committee of 1821 assumed "what they believed to be then true, that the Annual Produce of Corn, the growth of the United Kingdom, was upon an Average Crop about equal to the Annual Consumption." Your Committee, on the contrary, is satisfied by the strongest concurrent testimony from different parts of Great Britain, that the Occupiers of the inferior Soils, especially of heavy Clay Land, have of late expended less Capital and Labour in their cultivation. This neglect arising from low Profit and Prices inadequate to the Cost of Production, combined with a series of wet seasons, peculiarly disadvantageous to Land of this description, has caused a diminution in the gross amount of Produce, and the discontinuance of the use of artificial Manures, together with a system of over-cropping, has impaired the productive power of these inferior Soils; and in some cases where the Poor-rate is heavy, their cultivation has been entirely abandoned. Moreover, it is not unworthy of observation, that these Clay Lands are in many instances proved to be ancient Corn Land, on which Wheat has been grown from time immemorial; and in the Weald of Sussex a remarkable instance was adduced, where Rent and Poor-rate together amounted now to the same charge per Acre as before the War of 1792; but these burthens had changed places, the 8s. an Acre, which was Rent in 1792, is now Poor-rate; the 4s. per Acre, which was the Poor-rate then, is now the Rent.

But the diminished annual growth of Wheat cannot be considered apart from the amount of Stock on hand; and the Evidence of Mr. Jacob,[1] on this subject, is no less striking than important, especially since his general view is confirmed by the local experience of occupying Farmers throughout England.

Mr. Jacob's Evidence

Q. 38. Do you conceive, taking the dealers from the great dealers in sea-port towns to the small dealers in market towns, there is a lessening in the stocks such persons hold?–A. Certainly, of English wheat.

Q. 39. Could you state in what proportion to the time the stocks were considered high?–A. I did suppose at one time, when we had a harvest in 1816 which was so very deficient, we had then six months' consumption in the country; I do not think there has been a month's consumption in the country at the time of the harvest since 1829.

Q. 64. Can you form any opinion of what was the cause of the reduced stock in the hands of the farmers?–A. I suppose, in some measure, the reduction of capital; they have been paying a great deal of rent out of their capital.

Q. 51. You say that, in 1816, preceding the bad harvest of that year, you think there were six month's consumption in store, and recently not more than one month; supposing the harvest of 1816 was to come over again, from whence do you contemplate the supply?–A. It could not be supplied from all the world. My opinion is, that if we were to diminish the growth of English wheat by one-tenth part of that now produced, we should not be in a safe state in case of a deficient harvest, for all the world could not make up the deficiency. We are now about four weeks in the year deficient in our growth on the average; last year the harvest was one month earlier than the year previous, so that we were enabled to get to the end of the year. The harvest of 1832 ought to supply 13 months, and I dare say it will do so; but if we have a deficient harvest, and the next harvest gives us but 11 months' supply, and owing to bad weather it be deficient one-tenth more, there would then be such a deficiency as all the world could not easily supply at any price, for wheat is not the food of man in any other country to the same extent as in England.

In France even, where wheat is much more used than in the north and east of Europe, Chaptal states that there are only about 17,000,000 of quarters a year grown, of which near 3,000,000 are wanted for seed, and that for a population of 30,000,000 persons, whilst we require nearly as much for half that number of persons.

On this branch of the subject, after the most full enquiry and the most careful

[1] Controller of Corn Returns, 1822–42.

consideration of the Evidence, Your Committee have formed a decided opinion, that the Stocks of home-grown Wheat in the hands of the Farmer and of the Dealer at the time of Harvest have gradually diminished; that the Produce of Great Britain is in the average of years unequal to the Consumption; that the increased Supply from Ireland does not cover the deficiency; and that in the present state of Agriculture, the United Kingdom is in years of ordinary production partially dependent on the supply of Wheat from Foreign Countries. . . .

It is also worthy of consideration, whether in Parishes where the supply of Labour is greater than the demand, the Law of Settlement, as it now exists, may not aggravate the evil. Its tendency is to prevent the free circulation of Labour, to chain it to the spot where it is not wanted, and to check its natural flow to the place where it is required. The Labour of the Poor Man is his only commodity, and the reasons should be cogent indeed which justify any legal impediment to his carrying it to the best market he can discover.

Dr. Adam Smith, in the Wealth of Nations, has dwelt with peculiar force on this particular subject; he has laid down with his accustomed accuracy the general principle, that "the property which every man has in his own labour, as it is the original foundation of all other property, so it is the most sacred and inviolable." After stating the law, he points out the evil as it still exists in England, in these emphatic words: "The scarcity of hands in one parish cannot always be relieved by their superabundance in another, as it is constantly in Scotland, and I believe in all other countries where there is no difficulty of Settlement;" and he sums up the statement with this remarkable expression, which is true to the present day, "There is scarce a poor man in England of 40 years of age, I will venture to say, who has not in some part of his life felt himself most cruelly oppressed by this ill-contrived Law of Settlement."

Amidst the numerous difficulties to which the Agriculture in this Country is exposed, and amidst the distress which unhappily exists, it is a consolation to Your Committee to find that the general condition of the Agricultural Labourer in full Employment is better now than at any former period, his Money Wages giving him a greater command over the necessaries and conveniences of life. . . .

Emigration has taken place from all parts of the United Kingdom, and continues increasing from year to year; in some instances, local contributions have been raised to defray the Expense of the Passage of Pauper Families, and the Parishes where this measure has been adopted with due precautions, have experienced some relief; but in many cases, without such assistance, the poorest and least able remain, while the more efficient and richer depart, taking with them small accumulations of capital, and thus rather impoverishing than benefiting the district which they leave.

In the counties of England, where Yeomen heretofore abounded, occupying their own Estates, which Estates in many cases had been transmitted from Father to Son, a great change of Property has recently taken place. The high Prices of the last War led to Speculation in the purchase, improvement and inclosure of Land; Money was borrowed on the paternal Estate for Speculations of this nature, which, at the time, were not considered improvident. Prices have fallen, the Debt still remains, or the

Estate has changed Owners, and the interval between the fall of Prices and the adjustment of Charge and of Expenditure to the altered value of Money, has been most pernicious to this body of men.

In rural Districts, from the absence of competition, the small Tradesmen have been enabled to keep up their Prices, although perhaps bad Debts and diminished Custom have not added to their Profits; but the means of the Yeoman have diminished more rapidly than the fixed demands on his Income, and on him have fallen all the evils of an Income progressively decreasing, without a corresponding reduction of Charge.

The Landlords in every part of the United Kingdom, though in different degrees, have met the fall of Price by a reduction of Rent, except where during the War the Rents on their Estates had not been raised, or where by a large expenditure of Capital permanent Improvements have enriched the nature of the Soil itself.

The spread of the Drill System of Husbandry, a better rotation of Cropping, a more judicious use of Manures, especially of Bones, extensive Draining, improvement in the Breed both of Cattle and of Sheep, have all contributed to counterbalance the fall of Price, and to sustain that surplus Profit in the culture of the Soil on which Rent depends.

Where the fixed Incumbrances are heavy, and the family Settlements founded on the War rentals are still in operation, large reductions of Rent must necessarily occasion the most serious embarrassments, and the effect produced has already been an extensive change of Proprietors throughout the Kingdom.

It is impossible to overlook, and it would be criminal to disguise the fact, that the depreciation and restoration of the value of Money consequent on the Bank Restriction of 1797, have unsettled the habits, disturbed the fixed engagements, and injured alternately the interests of large classes of the community. . . .

The Committee of 1821 declared, "That they were not insensible to the importance of securing this Country from a state of dependence on other and possibly hostile Countries for the Subsistence of its Population." At that time the annual growth of Wheat was by them considered equal to the annual Consumption. Your Committee have come to an opposite conclusion with respect to the present time, and find that a diminished supply of Home-grown Corn, with an increasing demand, has rendered this Nation now annually dependent for a portion of its Supply on Importations from abroad.

The political considerations which weighed with the Committee of 1821 remain unchanged; and if it be not prudent to run the risk of rendering the dense Population of these Islands in a great degree dependent on the Supply of Bread-corn from abroad, the protection now given to Corn, the growth of the United Kingdom, may be justly regarded as an insurance against Famine, and against the danger of that reliance on Foreign Countries for the Staff of Life, which might be found inconsistent with the safety and permanent interests of the People, and ultimately fatal to our National Independence.

In the century prior to 1793, according to the Returns which it is admitted are imperfect, 50s. a quarter was the Average Price of Wheat, and England for a great part of that century was an exporting country. At this moment the Average

Price does not exceed 54s. a quarter; and in the last five years ending on the 1st January 1833, the importation of Wheat from abroad annually averages 1,145,000 quarters.

The present Price of Meat as compared with Corn is high; but this has been in a great measure attributed to an extensive loss in the flocks of Sheep, occasioned by rot, which recently prevailed among them for two or three years consecutively.

On the whole, it must be admitted that the difficulties are great and the burthens heavy which oppress the Landed Interests; but Contracts, Prices and Labour have a strong natural tendency to adjust themselves to the value of Money once established, and it is hoped that the balance may be restored which will give to Farming Capital its fair return.

Your Committee has endeavoured to trace the injurious effects of past Legislation; and to prove the caution necessary in future Measures, it may be urged, that they have stated many evils but have failed to suggest remedies; it should, however, be remembered, that Legislative Measures once taken and long established can rarely be abandoned without danger, and that to retreat is occasionally more dangerous than to advance.

In conclusion, Your Committee avow their opinion, that hopes of melioration in the condition of the Landed Interest rest rather on the cautious forbearance than on the active interposition of Parliament.

92. Select Committee of 1836 on Joint Stock Banks

Parlty. Papers, 1836/IX/pp. 418–19.

Subject to the local restrictions imposed for the protection of the privilege of the Bank of England, it is open to any number of persons to form a Company for Joint Stock Banking, whether for the purpose of deposit, or of issue, or of both:

1. The Law imposes on the Joint Stock Banks no preliminary obligation beyond the payment of a license duty, and the registration of the names of Shareholders at the Stamp Office.

2. The Law does not require that the Deed of Settlement shall be considered or revised by any competent authority whatever, and no precaution is taken to enforce the insertion in such Deeds of clauses the most obvious and necessary.

3. The Law does not impose any restrictions upon the amount of nominal Capital. This will be found to vary from 5,000,000 *l.* to 100,000 *l.*, and in one instance an unlimited power is reserved of issuing shares to any extent.

4. The Law does not impose any obligation that the whole or any certain amount of shares shall be subscribed for before banking operations commence. In many instances Banks commence their business before one-half of the shares are subscribed for, and 10,000, 20,000, and 30,000 shares are reserved to be issued at the discretion of the Directors.

5. The Law does not enforce any rule with respect to the nominal amount of shares. These will be found to vary from 1,000 *l.* to 5 *l.* The effects of this variation are strongly stated in the Evidence.

6. The Law does not enforce any rule with respect to the amount of Capital paid up before the commencement of business. This will be found to vary from 105 *l.* to 5 *l.*

7. The Law does not provide for any publication of the liabilities and assets of these Banks, nor does it enforce the communication of any balance sheet to the Proprietors at large.

8. The Law does not impose any restrictions by which care shall be taken that dividends are paid out of banking profits only, and that bad or doubtful debts are first written off.

9. The Law does not prohibit purchases, sales and speculative traffic on the part of these Companies in their own stock, nor advances to be made on the credit of their own shares.

10. The Law does not provide that the Guarantee Fund shall be kept apart and invested in Government or other securities.

11. The Law does not limit the number of branches or the distance of such branches from the Central Bank.

12. The Law is not sufficiently stringent to insure to the Public that the names registered at the Stamp Office are the names of persons *bona fide* Proprietors, who have signed the Deed of Settlement, and who are responsible to the Public.

13. The provisions of the Law appear inadequate, or at least are disregarded, so far as they impose upon Banks the obligation of making their notes payable at the places of issue.

All these separate questions appear to Your Committee deserving of the most serious considerations, with a view to the future stability of the Banks throughout the United Kingdom, the maintenance of Commercial Credit, and the preservation of the Currency in a sound state.

The most important facts which have come under the consideration of Your Committee, are connected with the operation of the Joint Stock Banks on Credit and Circulation. It appears that a great extension has been given to both, and that if the operations of all Banks, whether private, or formed on Joint Stock principles, are not conducted with prudence and with caution, measures adopted by the Bank of England with a view to the state of the Foreign Exchanges, and of the consequent demand for Bullion, may be counteracted by the advances and increased issues of Country Banks.

93. Bellenden Ker's report on Law of Partnership (1837)

Parlty. Papers, 1837/CLIV/pp. 406–408.

It is advisable to give a short statement of the law of partnership, before proceeding to advert to its defects, and the difficulties which occur in its practical application.

The law of partnership appears to have been derived from various sources, and consists partly of what is termed the common law, is partly borrowed from the civil, and is partly grounded on what has been considered the custom of merchants. It is without system, and is only to be collected from the decisions in particular cases.

From these decisions it is difficult, in many instances, to extract the rules of the law, and in many cases the rules established are not adapted to the circumstances of the present time, more especially as regards large partnerships or joint stock companies; and hence the evils and inconveniences which are experienced in this branch of our law.

By the present law, any number of persons may become partners in any specific adventure, or generally in any trade, &c.; no contract in writing is necessary to constitute such partnership. Nor is it necessary that all should bring in capital; this may be furnished by one, and labour and skill by another. It is not essential that the name of the partner should appear, nor that he should interfere in the management of the concern; and it may be stated as a general rule, that any one interested in the profits becomes a partner, and thereby liable to the whole engagements of the partnership: some cases exist, however, which may be considered as a modification of this rule. Partners whose names do not appear, are usually termed 'dormant partners.' A person may become liable as partner, as regards the creditors of a partnership, (though not interested in the profits,) by holding himself out as partner, either by allowing his name to appear in the firm, or by acting so as to induce a belief that he is a partner. The general rule applicable to all partnerships is, that each partner is liable as regards third parties, for the whole debts and engagements of the partnership, not only to the extent of his share in the partnership stock, but to the whole amount of his separate property. No private agreement amongst the partners can prevent this liability, though the partners, as between themselves, may engage to indemnify or limit the responsibility of any particular partner, or class of partners.

The general rule as to the liability of each partner can only be modified by the Crown, or by an Act of Parliament. Charters of incorporation are occasionally granted by the Crown to partnerships formed to carry on such undertakings as are considered deserving of encouragement on grounds of public policy; and on incorporation the personals liability of the partner ceases, and the claims of the creditor are confined to the corporate property; a similar exemption is occasionally, on the same grounds, conferred by Act of Parliament. This part of the subject will be subsequently noticed, in considering whether, in order to remove any impediments which may deter capitalists from engaging in trade, it may be expedient, under certain modifications and conditions, to introduce some restriction of the rule as to general liability

The principal difficulty in the present law arises in legal proceedings taken by or against partners, or in suits *inter se*, where the partners are numerous.

In suits between the partners and others, and in those between members of the same partnership, the general rule is, that all partners must be joined as parties. Exceptions to this, however, have been made both at law and equity, as in the case of nominal or dormant partners, or of contracts made with some only of the partners, acting as directors, committees, or trustees, and in some other instances; but notwithstanding these exceptions, where the partners are numerous, relief is often unattainable.

Another difficulty in the law arises from the want of adequate remedies between the partners *inter se*, and which equally exists whether the partners are numerous or not. Although actions are permitted to be brought by partners against their copartners in particular cases, yet the general rule at law is, that where no account has been settled between the partners, no action lies between them in respect of a partnership transaction, but that resort must be had to equity. The rule is founded on the relation subsisting between the parties, the difficulty of taking accounts at law, and the necessity of the examination of the parties themselves, which can only be done in equity.

The benefits of a resort to equity are however in many cases greatly, and it is submitted, injuriously narrowed by a rule (which however cannot be considered as absolutely established), *viz.*–that equity will not interfere in the concerns of a partnership, unless a dissolution is prayed.

The consequences of this latter rule are, not only that any dissatisfied partner is often enabled to put an end to the partnership, but that partners are disabled from obtaining a decision upon any dispute between them, without dissolving the partnership.

To avoid these difficulties, partners usually insert an agreement in their partnership deed, for a reference of all future disputes to arbitration. But though the award when made in consequence of such an agreement can be enforced, yet there are no effectual means of enforcing the performance of an agreement if in case of dispute either party refuses to refer. The courts of law hold that nominal damages only can be recovered for a breach of an agreement to refer disputes. And the courts of equity (although against the opinion expressed by Lord Kenyon) refuse to enforce them, and will themselves take cognizance of the matter in dispute, without regarding such an agreement, except in a very few instances.

The rule by which any person taking an interest in the profits incurs the liability of partner, is also attended with some difficulties.

An exception to this rule has been allowed where the interest in the profits is in the nature of a compensation for services, as in the case of captains of trading vessels, factors, agents, clerks, and others; but this exception has been thought (in consequence of some observations of Lord Eldon) to be narrowed to the case of a stipulation for a sum *equal in amount* to a share of the profits, and not to extend to a share of the profits themselves. This distinction was not considered by Lord Eldon himself to be satisfactory; and an attempt has lately been made to support the exception on the ground of the character and relation of the partners, and without resorting to the terms of the agreement. At present, however, it does not seem to rest on a satisfactory foundation. Another exception has been allowed in the case of annuities out of the profits of a partnership to retiring partners, widows and others; but doubts have been thrown on the security of these provisions, by a clause, as it seems, unnecessarily introduced into a late Act of Parliament.

The principal evils, therefore, of the existing law may be classed under three heads:

1. Those arising from the difficulties of suing and being sued.

2. Those arising from the difficulties which occur to partners in suing *inter se*, more especially as regards a resort to a court of equity in partnership disputes, and agreements to refer to arbitration.

And, lastly, those arising from the rule, that any person taking an interest in the profits becomes liable as a partner.

1. As to the difficulty of suing and being sued, these apply principally to the case of joint stock companies not having a special power by Act or Charter; although much of the evil is applicable to all partnerships; but as regards joint stock companies, it often amounts to an absolute denial of justice. It will be seen from the Appendix that there is no one person that has given evidence on the subject who has not fully admitted the evil, and urged the necessity of change. The slightest consideration of the present law will show that it is absolutely inapplicable to the case of large partnerships, or joint stock companies. And here it may be observed, that little has been done by the judges to correct the evils which exist in this branch of the law, or to adapt it to the changes of times and circumstances, as has usually been their practice where the Legislature was silent.

To account for the neglected and (until repeal of the Bubble Act) the mischievous state of the law relating to joint stock companies, it is necessary to advert shortly to their origin.

The utility of this kind of partnership, in accomplishing undertakings to which individual capital and enterprise are inadequate, or where the risk is beyond that usually incurred in private trade, as in mining adventures, canals, &c., has been admitted in all times. In order to give effect to joint stock companies, it was necessary that means should be afforded to individuals of withdrawing their capital, and to others of investing it. Hence the necessity of permitting the transfer of shares. But here an abuse arose, the enormity of which, when at its height, had nearly proved fatal to joint stock companies, and under the effects of which they are suffering at the present time. Members of companies, not content with the ordinary and legitimate profits of their capital, sought a further profit by the sale of their shares. The transfer of shares (or what is called stock-jobbing) became itself a trade, and was embarked in with all the energy with which trading speculations are followed up in this country. In order to supply the market for shares, it was necessary that companies should be multiplied—not with a view to the *bona fide* employment of capital or industry, but merely to enable the trader in shares to speculate in their rise and fall, to effect sales at a premium, and to shift the ultimate loss upon the last purchaser.

The Legislature was borne down by clamour, and directed its vengeance, not against the abuse merely, but against joint stock companies generally. The Bubble Act was passed, by which those concerned in speculations of this sort (with the exception of two companies) were subjected to the almost obsolete, but highly penal consequences of a *praemunire*. The severity of this enactment had the usual effect of excessive penal legislation. The Act remained nearly a dead letter in the statute book until a recent period, when the superabundance of unemployed capital revived the mania for this fraudulent trading, and again attracted the attention of the Legislature.

Lord Eldon, in the House of Lords, gave notice of his intention to bring in a Bill, the object of which he afterwards explained was to prevent the transfer of shares in companies, before they had obtained the sanction of a charter or Act of Parliament. But he subsequently apologised to the House for not having proceeded with it, on the ground that it would have involved questions which were pending before him judicially.

In the House of Commons, a Bill was brought in for the repeal of the Bubble Act; and after debates, in which its mischievous tendency was fully exposed, the repeal was ultimately carried.

In the course of the debates, Mr. Hudson Gurney observed, that "something certainly ought to be done, either by merely introducing a system of registration, and thus enabling any one to judge of the parties to be trusted, or by introducing the continental system of authorizing parties on actual deposits, and registered, to limit their responsibility"; and he stated that he was much inclined to think that the latter would be of very useful adoption. Mr. Huskisson expressed himself satisfied that the interests of commerce required the proper encouragement and protection of joint stock companies, and that the mere provision that partners should sue and be sued was not enough, as the inconveniences which every day's experience abundantly proved.

A considerable advance was undoubtedly made towards improvement, by the removal of a bad measure, but still no attempt was made for the introduction of a good one, although the importance and necessity of such a measure were generally admitted.

As regards the present law being a denial of justice where the parties are many, it is sufficient to refer to the case of *Van Sandau v. Moore* and others, Russell's Reports, 441. In that case, one of the shareholders of a joint stock company filed a bill against the directors and other shareholders, in order to have the partnership dissolved, and the proper accounts taken; 14 of the directors appeared, and filed 14 separate answers, with long schedules to each, the Court holding that the defendants could not be bound to answer jointly, and there was no reason, in fact, why the whole 300 shareholders might not have answered separately. The result was, that it became impossible to proceed with a suit in which the plaintiff might, as a preliminary measure, have had to take office-copies of 300 answers, each with a long schedule, and where on every alteration of the firm, by death, &c., he would have to revive his suit, &c. Lord Eldon's remark shows that he felt the jurisdiction of the Court was not suited to such partnerships. He observes, "Another consideration is this: ought the jurisdiction of the Court, which can be administered usefully only between a limited number of persons, to be employed for a purpose which it cannot by possibility accomplish? Here is a bill with nearly 300 defendants; how can such a cause ever be brought to a hearing? and if the plaintiff cannot show a probability of getting a decree, with what purpose, except that of oppression, can the proceeding have been instituted? In such a suit, the plaintiff can do nothing, except put himself and others to enormous expense."

Such being the state of the law, it became the practice with joint stock companies to apply to Parliament, to enable them to meet the inconveniences, without, however, absolving the members from their general responsibility. These were the Acts authorizing companies "to *sue and be sued by an officer*." Lord Eldon, in the case above mentioned, has given an account of the origin and progress of these Acts, which it may be important to insert, as showing the progress of legislation on this point, and the difficulties parties are exposed to.

"It is within my own memory," his Lordship observes, "that, when an application was made to Parliament to incorporate bodies, it was generally met with this short answer: 'Why have you not gone to the Crown with your request? why have you not obtained a charter?' However, that mode of thinking has gone by, and several Acts of Parliament have been passed, establishing companies similar to this one.

"There were not many of those Acts passed, before inconveniences were found to follow. If a man had occasion to bring an action against one of the bodies so constituted, he did not know how to proceed, or against whom to bring his suit; and if he brought it, naming the defendants who were known to him, he was treated with a plea in abatement, which was a checkmate to his action. To meet this inconvenience, it became necessary to introduce into those bills a clause, that the company should sue and be sued by their clerk or secretary. It was soon found that this provision did not set the matter right. The secretary, on behalf of the company, sued a man of opulence; and, if he succeeded, he recovered not only judgment, but payment of the demand. On the other hand, when the secretary was sued, the person suing found, that though he had gotten an individual with whom he could go into court of law or equity in order to enforce a claim against him as defendant, yet, after he had gone thither, he frequently found that it would have been better for him not to have stirred; for though the secretary, when he was plaintiff, got the money for which he sued, he was often unable, when made defendant, to pay what the plaintiff recovered.

"That state of things suggested to a learned lord the necessity of making all the members liable, as well as the secretary, for a demand against the company. Thus there arose a third class of Acts of Parliament establishing companies: Acts which made all the members, as well as the secretary, liable to answer demands recovered against the company. Still this was not enough; for, as these Acts did not provide the means of letting the world know who the members were, the consequence was, that though all the members were liable, nobody who had a claim against them could tell who the persons were that were thus liable.

"Another improvement was therefore made. A proviso was introduced, requiring that, before a Company was formed, or within a given time afterwards, there should be a register or enrolment of the individuals of whom the company was composed; and it was thought that thus, at last, the work had been done completely, and that all was safe. Unfortunately, however, it turned out, in consequence of sales and transfers of shares, that a person, who was a member of the company to-day, was not a member of it to-morrow; the constituent members of the body were constantly changing; and a plaintiff did not know against whom to proceed, whether against the present or against former members.

"A further alteration was then made; the effect of which was, that those who had been members should continue liable, although they had transferred their interest, and that those who became members should be also liable; an enrolment of the names, both of the one and of the other, being required. This had a very considerable operation; and it was wonderful to observe how much, after it was adopted, the passion for becoming members of these companies diminished.

"One thing was still wanting. If the members of these bodies happened to quarrel among themselves, (which, though they came harmoniously together, was very likely to happen,) how were they to sue one another? And it was not till the latest stage of improvement that that difficulty was provided for."

The inconvenience and expense of applying to Parliament to obtain these powers, has, in some degree, been obviated by the recent statute, which enables His Majesty, by letters patent, to grant to any trading company any of the privileges which it was competent to grant by any charter of incorporation, especially the privilege of suing and being sued in the name of an officer, upon such terms and conditions as His Majesty should think fit; but this statute has not removed, though it has mitigated the evil. For now, all partnerships are compelled to apply to the Crown for this privilege, and a responsibility is, in some degree, thrown on its advisers, who, whilst the right of suing and being sued is to be taken as a privilege, must of course be considered as in some degree judging of the propriety or expediency of the undertaking, and of the fitness of the parties, or of the capital subscribed by them, and of the provisions agreed on for attaining the object in view.

94A–B. Commercial crises of 1836–1839, from Select Committee of 1840–1841 on Banks of Issue

94A. Evidence of J. B. Smith, President of the Manchester Chamber of Commerce

Parlty. Papers, 1840/IV/ questions 4–14.

4. Towards the end of the year 1835, do you consider the trade and manufactures of the country to have been in a prosperous state?–I think that is what we state in the report of the Chamber of Commerce.

5. Was not that tranquil state of trade considerably disturbed early in 1836?–Yes.

6. Will you make any statement relative to that subject which you think it proper to put before the Committee?–We complain that the administration of the Bank is not founded on any fixed and settled principles, so that the public may be enabled at all times to estimate with some degree of certainty the value of their property, and that merchants and traders may also be enabled to calculate with some degree of certainty upon the success of their enterprises as regulated by the law of supply and demand. The operations of the Bank of England since 1835 afford a striking exemplification that calculations based upon the most enlarged experience afford no security against loss or failure from its forced expansions and contractions of the currency. Early in August of the year 1835, the Bank issued a notice, offering to make advances on Exchequer Bills, India Bonds, stock and other approved securities, at three-and-a-half per cent., her previous rate of interest for similar advances being four per cent. These notices were renewed, from time to time, during an uninterrupted period of eight months. The advances made by the Bank on securities, which in June 1835 amounted to £24,678,000 were increased to £31,954,000 in January 1836. This enormous addition to her loans in so short a period laid the foundation for that excessive stimulus to trade and speculation which prevailed in 1836, and which

manifested itself in the mania for the innumerable joint stock associations which were formed at that period. I regret that, having had only a short notice of the intentions of the Committee to call upon me, I have not had time to procure such facts as would have strikingly shown the inordinate spirit of speculation which then obtained. The following comparison of the number of railways, foreign loans and joint stock banks brought out in 1834, 1835, and 1836, will, however, be a sufficient illustration. In 1834, there was one railway, the London and Southampton; there were three foreign loans, the Spanish active five per cent., the Spanish deferred and the Spanish passive, and there were nine joint stock banks created. In 1835, there were three railways, the Great Western, the Croydon, and the Preston and Wyre; but in 1836 there were the Aylesbury; the Birmingham and Derby; the Birmingham and Gloucester; the Birmingham, Bristol and Thames Junction; the Bristol and Exeter; the Cheltenham and Great Western; the London and Blackwall; the Deptford Pier Junction; the Eastern Counties; the Edinburgh, Leith and Newhaven; the Great North of England; the Hull and Selby; the London Grand Junction; the Manchester and Leeds; the Midland Counties; the Northern and Eastern; the North Midland; the Sheffield and Rotherham; the South-eastern, the Taff Vale and the York and North Midland; making 21.

7. Mr. Pattison: Can you state the amount of capital invested in those concerns? –No, I have not got the amount of capital.

8. Mr. Philips: Nor of the calls made in that year?–No. The foreign loans in 1835 were the Portuguese Regency three per cent., and the Cuba Bonds six per cent.; the loans of 1836 were the Belgian four per cent. and the Portuguese five per cent.; the number of joint stock banks established in 1835 were nine, and in 1836 there were 47; the advance in the prices of commodities induced by the excessive loans of the Bank of England led to a demand for specie for exportation, and obliged the Bank to raise its rate of interest in July to four-and-a-half per cent., and in August to five per cent., and at the same time to reduce its loans by rejecting all bills drawn or indorsed by joint-stock banks of issue and bills drawn upon the Anglo-American houses; the result of these measures was great commercial embarrassment and general discredit, both in this and foreign countries; at the close of 1836 the stock of bullion in the Bank had fallen to little more than £4,000,000, whilst at the same time it was indebted to the world upwards of £30,000,000 for its circulation and deposits; and its loans, which in January 1836 amounted to £31,954,000, were reduced in December to £28,971,000; the effects of this sudden contraction of the currency were to produce alarm, panic and disastrous losses to the whole mercantile and trading community; the prices of most commodities fell to the lowest point to which they had been known to recede for a great number of years; the Manchester Chamber of Commerce estimate the amount of the losses incurred through the panic of 1836–7 on the five great articles of cotton, woollen, silk, linen and hardware, to be at least £40,000,000 sterling, independently of the moral and social evils inflicted upon the labouring classes by suddenly depriving them of employment, and subjecting them to the greatest privations.

9. Mr. Gisborne: You have referred to a time at which prices had reached their

lowest; what was that point?–Prices reached their lowest point in the course of the year 1837; according to a table compiled by Mr. Porter, of the Board of Trade, of the comparative prices of 50 articles at the beginning of each year, taking 1·000 to be the price in January 1833; it seems that in the month of September 1837, the prices of those 50 articles had attained their lowest point; the highest point to which prices had attained was in August 1836, when they were 1·3460; in September 1837 they had fallen to 1·1321.

10. Having been 1·000 in January 1833?–Yes; the originating causes of the more recent commercial pressure were the succession of two bad harvests; the present corn laws by preventing a regular and mutual exchange of corn for manufactures with other countries at all times, obliges us in periods of scarcity to export bullion as the only medium of payment for foreign grain; under a natural system of trade, no such sudden drain for specie would occur in payment for corn, any more than it is found to arise in exchange for tea, cotton or silk; the trade in grain becomes an exception to the ordinary rules of commerce, and all such sudden and extraordinary purchases are necessarily paid for in bullion. The directors of the Bank of England are supposed to be cognizant of the operation of our corn laws, and yet in the face of an ascertained failing harvest they offered advances in November 1838 at the low rate of three-and a-half per cent., repayable in January following, upon the usual securities, including stock; and notwithstanding the commercial crisis in Belgium and France, and the drain which had commenced upon its stock of bullion, the Bank in February 1839 again offered loans on all kinds of securities, including stock, at the low rate of three-and-a-half per cent., to be repaid in April following.

11. SIR J. R. REID: What stock do you mean?–I presume it means in the English funds. By means of this expansion of the currency, large sums were raised in this country on American bonds and other securities, which enabled the holders unnaturally to keep up the prices of cotton in the face of diminished consumption and bad trade; the additional supply of paper money thrown upon the market speedily produced the effects which might have been anticipated.

12. MR. GISBORNE: Does paper money mean Bank of England notes?–It means currency.

13. MR. O'CONNELL: It includes all?–Yes, it includes all. The Bank, alarmed at the drain for bullion, suddenly raised the rate of interest to 5 per cent.

14. MR. WARBURTON: When was that?–On the 16th of May 1839; on the 20th of June it was raised to 5½ per cent., and on the 1st of August it was fixed at the unprecedented rate of 6 per cent. Up to this period the Bank had constantly increased its loans; in December 1838, they amounted to £20,707,000; in September 1839, they reached £25,936,000, whilst, in the same period, its bullion had diminished from £9,362,000 to £2,816,000. From September, the Bank rapidly retraced her steps; and by December, a period of three months, she had reduced her loans by as great an amount as it had taken her seven months to increase them; thus aggravating, by these forced expansions and contractions of the currency, whilst a drain for gold to pay for imports of foreign grain was in operation, the natural evils entailed upon the community by the present corn law.

94B. Evidence of J. Horsley Palmer, Director of the Bank of England

Parlty. Papers, 1840/IV/ questions 1142 and 1272–1274.

1142. CHAIRMAN: As it was mainly your evidence given before the Bank Charter Committee in 1832, which contained the exposition of the principle by which in ordinary times the Bank is guided in the regulation of its issues, will you have the goodness to re-state that principle to the Committee?–I will re-state it in as nearly the same words as I can. The principle, with reference to the period of a full currency, and consequently par of exchange, by which the Bank has been guided in the regulation of its issues, always excepting special circumstances, has been to retain an investment in securities, bearing interest, to the extent of two-thirds of their liabilities, the remaining one-third being held in bullion and coin; the reduction of the circulation, so far as may be dependent upon the Bank, being subsequently solely affected by the foreign exchanges or by internal extra demands.

. . .

1272. Will you state generally what the circumstances affecting commercial credit were, which, in your opinion, justified the Bank in so wide a departure from the rule laid down in 1832?–The circumstances immediately arising out of that advance were a very great discredit upon the engagements for American account, in this country; that was the first cause of the advance; as that proceeded, towards the close of 1836, the northern and central bank and the agricultural bank of Ireland found themselves in great pecuniary difficulties; those were the two main causes which induced the Bank to make the advances they did, in aid, in the first instance, of the American Houses, from the discredit in which they were placed, and from the discredit that had attached to the northern and central Banks of England, the agricultural bank of Ireland, and other interests in London.

1273. Are there any peculiar circumstances to which you can attribute the discredit of the American houses?–I trace the American discredit to an early period, perhaps originating in America itself. The first effect of the American government determining not to renew the charter of the American bank, was to throw the deposits of the Bank into the hands of numerous other private banks in the States, which engendered a considerable extension of credit in America, and encouraged imports to an enormous extent, in excess of former years; the importations so arising were fostered by undue credits given by considerable American houses in this country, not furnished with adequate means to uphold such extensive engagements if discredited. The magnitude of those credits given in this country attracted general attention in the course of the autumn of 1836, and induced the Bank to conceive that there was greater credit given than the parties were able to maintain, and which proved in the end to be correct. Upon the Bank objecting to hold a considerable amount of those securities tendered for the East India Company's money, the securities themselves became discredited, and with that discredit arose the difficulty of circulating the bills of exchange that were passing to a very large amount between America and this country; and as the discredit proceeded, it became a necessary point of consideration in some cases (I beg to state only partially), whether those houses should be stopped, they not having capital of their own adequate to support their engagements, or whether they should be aided and assisted for the purpose of liquidation; and it was to accomplish that point of liquidation that the Bank were induced to give this extra aid.

1274. Do I understand you to state that the discredit of American houses arose, in your opinion, from their having engaged in transactions far beyond their means?– I do.

95. Select Committee of 1844 on Joint Stock Companies

Parlty. Papers, 1844/VII/pp. IV–XI.

From the evidence which has been taken on this head, it appears that bubble Companies may be divided into three classes:–

1st, Those which, being faulty in their nature, inasmuch as they are founded on unsound calculations, cannot succeed by any possibility.

2nd, Those which, let their objects be good or bad, are so ill constituted as to render it probable that the miscarriages or failures incident to mismanagement will attend them; and–

3rd, Those which are faulty, or fraudulent in their object, being started for no other purpose than to create shares for the purpose of jobbing in them, or to create, under pretence of carrying on a legitimate business, the opportunity and means of raising funds to be shared by the adventurers who start the Company.

All the Companies of the last class of course adopt, as far as possible, the outward characteristics common to those of the best kind. They exhibit an array of Directors and officers,–announce a large capital,–adopt the style and title of a company,–issue plausible statements, intimating excellent purposes,–declare that they are sanctioned or empowered by Act of Parliament,–use some conspicuous place of business, in a respectable situation,–and employ throughout the country respectable agents and bankers.

But many of these characteristics are fictitious. The Directors have either not sanctioned the use of their names, or they are not the persons they are supposed to be. Not only is there no capital, but neither subscribers nor deed of settlement. The style of the Company may be true, because any Company may adopt such style; but their purposes, though plausible, are often founded on calculations which do not admit of success, and they have not only not received the sanction or authority of Parliament, or of the Crown, but the very statutes which are cited as conferring the authority will be found to have a very different object.

Though their place of business may have all the indications of respectability, the persons employed there will not always be found to be of a corresponding character; and though good agents are employed, it will be found that they have been tricked into accepting the agency partly by the other indications of respectability employed by these Companies, and partly by tempting commissions; and the bankers are no further parties than that in the ordinary course of business they have permitted the concerns to open an account with them.

With this class the remedy is easy: publication of the Directors, of the Shareholders, of the Deed of Settlement, of the amount of the Capital, and whether subscribed or not subscribed, nominal or real, would baffle every case of fraud which has come under the notice of Your Committee. The public would have the means of knowing with whom they deal; and agents and bankers would be enabled to avoid participating in the discredit of such concerns, by giving the sanction of their names to questionable undertakings.

The difficulty is greater with the second class of Companies for good objects, but ill constituted. Companies of the third class, which are fraudulent in their objects, are commonly short lived; circumstances of suspicion soon arise, which, under the precautions already mentioned, would avail to counteract the projectors, but the character and credit of the persons engaged in Companies of this second class lull suspicion. The Directors themselves are often indifferent and careless, trusting too much to their officers; shareholders purchase on the strength of their names, without due inquiry, and thus confer factitious support; so that one set of persons relying upon another set, the delusion is sustained for a longer space of time.

Publication of the Directors and shareholders, of Deeds of Settlement and of the Capital, will not meet this class of cases; but it may be met by the periodical holding of meetings, by the periodical balancing, audit and publication of accounts, and by making the Directors and officers more immediately responsible to the shareholders, which may probably be accomplished by facilitating and improving the remedies available to Joint Stock Companies and their shareholders *inter se*. Periodical accounts, if honestly made and fairly audited, cannot fail to excite attention to the real state of a concern; and by means of improved remedies, parties to mismanagement may be made more amenable for acts of fraud and illegality.

The only class which is beyond certain cure by the Legislature is the first class,– Companies faulty in their nature. No antecedent check will avail; any authority appointed to act as censor would be as liable to be deceived as the promotors of the schemes, and it might sometimes sanction bad, and at other times prevent good, schemes.

THE MODES OF DECEPTION ADOPTED

These concerns continued to accomplish their frauds by the following modes of deception, from some of which, good concerns are not wholly free, and so far they sanction the adoption of them by the worst, and accustom the public not to regard them as a type or test of dishonesty.

By the use of the names of persons having no existence:

By the use of the names of distinguished persons, and persons of respectability and wealth, without their authority:

By the use of the names of such persons as patrons and honorary directors, with their consent, while such persons have been ignorant of the nature of the concern and of its transactions, and have exercised no control over its management:

By the issue of prospectuses and advertisements containing false statements as to the authority under which it exists, as to the amount of capital of the Company, or as to the period of its establishment, as well as to the Directors, &c. above mentioned:

By getting reports of pretended meetings, puffs relative thereto, inserted in the newspapers.

By prospectuses fraudulently varied from time to time:

By the employment throughout the country, on very tempting rates of commission, of respectable agents, whose character has cloaked the want of respectability of the Company. In one or two remarkable cases this appears to have been the most efficient means of success; it has procured business at a distance, where inquiries could not be readily made as to the character of the concern:

By opening banking accounts with the Bank of England and other respectable banks:

By the selection of offices in respectable situations, and fitted up in a respectable manner:

By the concoctors and managers living at great expense, entertaining their neighbours, and thereby endeavouring to fortify themselves against suspicion:

By the making up of fraudulent accounts, so as to deceive the Directors and the Shareholders, which has been facilitated sometimes by the accounts not being audited, or by the Accountant being a near kinsman of the Managing Director, the only party taking an active part in the concern:

By declaring dividends out of capital, on false representations of profits realized:

By concealing the names or preventing the meeting of the Shareholders, and falsifying the books containing transfers of shares; by the creation of fictitious votes, so as to secure the means of outvoting the *bona fide* Shareholders:

By the use of the names of respectable solicitors and counsel attached to the prospectuses and circulars of the Company, by which mercantile men and others are deceived into a belief of the *bona fide* character of the undertaking.

THE DURATION OF COMPANIES

One Insurance Company lasted two or three years, and another Loan Company three years. Both were stopped by the remarks of the press; but one commenced actions for libel, and was carrying them forward with success; but it became necessary to produce the deed of settlement, which exposed the character of the transaction. The parties, too, quarrelled about the spoil.

An Annuity Society lasted from 10 to 20 years, during which period the direction, which had commenced as a Pension Society, with the names of persons of great respectability, dwindled down to the Manager and one or two other persons, bankrupts.

In each of these cases the concern had good agents in the provinces.

Another society for effecting general life insurances existed for about two years, and then transferred its business to another Company under a new title.

Another existed for four years, the Manager having deluded the Directors by flourishing statements of accounts, until some of them became suspicious, and on examination found that they had no funds. They were obliged to pay the Manager £2,000 to induce him to remove, there being in the Deed of Settlement a provision that he was to have £1,000 a year.

A Mining Company remained in operation for two or three years, till the money paid for shares had been all expended. In the meantime it had declared dividends out of pretended profits, when none had been realized. One of these dividends was founded on a fictitious sale to the Auditor, a brother of the Manager, to sustain which a false entry was made in the books.

THE AMOUNT AND DISTRIBUTION OF THE PLUNDER

The amount of the plunder levied by Companies of this description is not so large probably as the amount of loss from Companies founded on good faith, but on bad calculations; but it falls with great weight on the sufferers, who are generally persons of limited means.

One of the least creditable of these concerns obtained in the course of two or three years from about £120,000 to £250,000; and another at least £100,000; by another the Shareholders lost about £100,000; by another £80,000 were lost in London, and £10,000 in Edinburgh. But it is impossible to estimate the full extent of the mischief. In two cases, where the chief actors have been bankrupts, no books or accounts were forthcoming. In another, the clue was the enrolment of annuities. In this case, too, property was discovered by the Registry of Deeds for the County of Middlesex.

The amount of these levies is determined by the duration of the Company; and this, if it be a Company for effecting insurances and granting annuities, is determined by the rapidity with which claims come in. The adventurers are eager to divide the spoil; hence their inability to meet their engagements is felt much earlier than by a concern which has simply founded its arrangements on bad calculations. The least hesitation in meeting demands provokes suspicion, and the concern is brought to an end.

The mode of distributing the plunder varies. Sometimes it is taken by one of the leaders, and shared among the others; sometimes it assumes the form of a high fixed payment, disproportionate to the service of the individual and to the means of the Company.

THE CIRCUMSTANCES OF THE VICTIMS

But the extent of the evil is to be measured rather by the circumstances of the victims than by the amount of the plunder. They are usually persons of very limited means, who invest their savings in order to obtain the tempting returns which are offered. Annuity Companies have proved the most dangerous in this respect. Old people, governesses, servants and persons of that description, are tempted to invest their little all, and when the concern stops, they are ruined. Sometimes persons of more property and better intelligence are tempted, but the greater number of sufferers are of the first-named descriptions.

In one case, a person who had effected an insurance in one of these offices fell into impaired health, and on its breaking up he could not succeed in renewing the insurance in any other office.

In one case the victims were the ordinary speculators in Companies, some of them merchants and men of business.

By one witness, a solicitor, it was stated that mercantile men of great sagacity neglect in such cases the most ordinary precautions; that they take more care in discounting a small bill than in forming a connexion with such companies, by which their fortunes may be wholly lost; and this neglect has been attributed to the fear of its being known that they are seeking an exorbitant return, or that they are embarking in undertakings of questionable character.

96. Select Committee of 1844 on Railways

Resolutions with regard to New Railways

Parlty. Papers, 1844/XI/pp. 9–11.

1. THAT the powers to be granted by any Act of the present or future Sessions of Parliament, for the construction of new Lines of Railway, whether Trunk, Branch, or Junction Lines, shall be subject to the following conditions:–

2. THAT if, at the end of a term of years to be fixed, the annual divisible Profits upon the paid-up Share Capital of any such Line of Railway shall be equal to a per-centage to be fixed, or so soon after the expiration of the said term as the said per-centage shall have been reached, it shall be in the option of the Government either, first, to purchase the Line at the rate of a number of years' purchase, to be fixed, of such divisible Profits; or, secondly, to revise the fares and charges on the Line, in such manner as shall, in the judgment of the Government, be calculated to reduce the said divisible Profits, assuming always the same quantity and kinds of annual traffic to continue, to the said per-centage: but with a guarantee, on the part of the Government, to subsist while such scale of fares and charges shall be in force, to make up the divisible Profits to the said per-centage.

3. AND also, that at or after the end of the said term of years, it shall be in the option of the Government to purchase the Line at the said number of years' purchase of the annual divisible Profits, whatever be the amount of such Profits.

4. THAT the term of years be Fifteen, to date from the next following first of January after the passing of the Act for the construction of the Railway.

5. THAT the rate of divisible Profits at which the right of revision shall accrue, shall be 10 per cent.

6. THAT the number of years' purchase at which the Railway may be bought for the public, shall be 25 years.

7. THAT the said annual divisible Profit shall be calculated upon the average of the three last preceeding years.

8. THAT the accounts of such Line, if a Branch or Junction Line, shall be kept separate from those of the main Lines with which they are connected, and shall be liable to inspection by the Government, and to be produced upon the demand of the Government.

9. THAT if any dispute shall arise as to what the actual amount of such divisible Profits in any given case may have been, the matter in question shall be referred to arbitration.

10. THAT power be taken by the Government, in the event of its exercising the right of revision, to provide for such regulations upon the Line as it shall deem necessary, in order to secure to the public the full advantages of the reduced rate of fares and charges fixed by the revising authority.

11. THAT the Companies may be required to provide upon such new Lines of Railway, as a *minimum* of third-class accommodation, one Train at least each way on every week-day, by which there shall be the ordinary obligation to convey such passengers as may present themselves at any of the ordinary stations, in carriages provided with seats and protected from the weather, at a speed not less than 12 miles an hour including stoppages, and at fares not exceeding a penny per mile; each Passenger by such Train being allowed not exceeding 56 lbs. of luggage without extra charge, and extra luggage being charged by weight at a rate not exceeding the lowest charge by other Trains: Children under Three years being conveyed without extra charge; and Children from Three to Twelve years at half-price.

12. THAT the tax upon the receipts from such conveyance of third-class passengers should not exceed one half of any duty that may be laid upon the general traffic of Railways.

13. THAT the Board of Trade have a discretionary power of dispensing with any of the above requirements, and of allowing alternative arrangements which shall appear to it to be better calculated to promote the public convenience upon any particular Railway; and that the Board of Trade have a discretionary control over the Train which satisfies the above *minimum* requirements, as regards times of starting, nature of accommodation, arrangements with connecting Lines, and other points of detail, subject to the above general principles, and to the understanding that such control is to be limited to the Train in question.

14. THAT the Companies shall be bound to convey upon such new Lines military and police forces, and public stores, baggage, and ammunition, on the requisition of the proper authorities, at fares not exceeding 1d. per mile for each private, and 2d. per mile for each officer, with the usual accommodation, and at charges not exceeding 2d. per ton per mile for stores and baggage; the same quantity of personal luggage being allowed free of charge to each officer and private as to each ordinary first and second-class passenger respectively; and the carriages in which such forces are conveyed being, whenever so required by the proper Authorities, provided with seats and protected against the weather.

15. THAT upon such new Lines the Post-office be empowered to require the transmission of the Mails (subject to the usual conditions as to payment for services performed by Railway Companies) at any rate of speed certified by the Inspector-general to be consistent with safety; and also to send a mail-guard with bags not exceeding the weight allowed for an ordinary passenger's luggage (or subject to the rules of the Company for any excess of that weight) by any of the ordinary Trains, upon the same terms and conditions as an ordinary passenger: it being understood,

that this power shall not authorize the Post-office to require the conversion of a regular Mail Train into an ordinary Train, nor to exercise any control over the Company in respect of any ordinary Train.

16. THAT it shall be open to the Government to determine what extensions of existing Lines of Railway are to be considered as New Lines, for the purposes of these Resolutions.

97. Speech of Sir Robert Peel on Bank Charter Acts (6 May 1844)

Hansard, 3/LXXIV/722–749.

My immediate proposition relates to Banking Concerns, and to the issue of Promissory Notes; but, considering that ten years have now elapsed since this subject was brought under consideration, I hope I shall be excused if I take a wider range than the immediate questions for decision might seem to justify, and if I advert at the outset to the great principles which govern, or ought to govern, the Measure of Value, and the Medium of Exchange. They lie, in truth, at the very foundation of our discussion. We cannot hope to agree on the Measure to be adopted with regard to Paper Currency, unless we are agreed on the principles which determine the value of that of which Paper is the representative, and on the nature of the obligation which is imposed upon the issuer of Promissory Notes. Now I fear there is not a general agreement on those fundamental principles–that there is still a very material difference of opinion as to the real nature and character of the Measure of Value in this country. My first question, therefore, is, what constitutes this Measure of Value? What is the signification of that word 'a Pound?' Unless we are agreed on the answer to these questions, it is in vain we attempt to legislate on the subject. If a 'Pound' is a mere visionary abstraction, a something which does not exist either in law or in practice, in that case one class of measures relating to Paper Currency may be adopted; but if the word 'Pound,' the common denomination of value, signifies something more than a mere fiction–if a 'Pound' means a quantity of the precious metals of certain weight and certain fineness–if that be the definition of a 'Pound,' in that case another class of measures relating to Paper Currency will be requisite. Now, the whole foundation of the proposal I am about to make rests upon the assumption that according to practice, according to law, according to the ancient monetary policy of this country, that which is implied by the word 'Pound' is a certain definite quantity of gold with a mark upon it to determine its weight and fineness, and that the engagement to pay a Pound means nothing, and can mean nothing else, than the promise to pay to the holder, when he demands it, that definite quantity of gold. . . .

These are the true doctrines as to the measure of value, doctrines delivered one hundred years before the Report of the Bullion Committee was made, but in precise conformity with that Report. The truth of them is not, I fear, even now admitted. Publications daily issue from the press contesting it. Here is a volume published at Birmingham since the commencement of the present year, not the production, I presume, of a single author, for it professes to be written by Gemini. I have no wish to withhold justice from writers who give that proof of their sincerity, which is implied by the publication of an octavo volume. And I admit at once, that I do not believe this work could have proceeded from any other town in the Queen's dominions than Birmingham, and that the efforts of no single writer are equal to the production of so much nonsense. This volume collects and repeats all the old exploded fallacies on the subject of the standard of value and currency. Its authors bewail the darkness of the age which adheres to a standard which was adopted in the reign of Queen Elizabeth, and which they consider wholly unsuitable as a measure of value now, considering the extent of our commerce, and the increase of all pecuniary transactions in number and amount. They might with equal justice complain, that since travelling has been increased by the completion of railways, the foot measure is still adhered to. There is no better reason for making the sovereign pass for twenty-five shillings instead of twenty, than for making the foot consist of sixteen inches instead of twelve. They consider it absurd that with the progress we have made in wealth and knowledge, we should still coin the ounce of gold into a sum represented by £3. 17s. 10½d. "Coin the ounce of gold," they say, "into £5, and we shall then have relief from our burthens, and encouragement to industry and trade."

. . . But to revert to the errors of those who are the advocates of some measure of value other than the precious metals. They object to the selection of gold as the standard of value, because gold is an article of commerce, – because there is a demand for it as bullion, affecting, therefore, its value as coin, and disqualifying it to be the measure of value. Now, no one contends that there is or can be an absolutely fixed and invariable standard of value. No one denies that the value of gold, with reference to all commodities, excepting gold itself, may be subject to slight variations. But what other substance is not more subject to variations in value than the precious metals? What other substance possessing intrinsic value will not also be in demand as an article of commerce? It is because gold is an article of commerce, because there are no restrictions upon its export or its import, that you can at all times depend upon such a supply of gold for the purposes of coin as may be sufficient for the wants of this country. The precious metals are distributed among the various countries of the world in proportion to their respective necessities, by laws of certain though not very obvious operation, which, without our interference, will allot to our share all that we require. Some entertain the apprehension that we may be drained of all our gold in consequence of a demand for gold from foreign countries, either for the payment of their armies in time of war, or in consequence of sudden and unforseen demand for foreign corn for our own internal consumption. It is supposed that gold, being an article in universal demand, and having at all times and in all places an ascertained value, is more subject to exportation than anything else. But the export of gold, whether coin or bullion, is governed by precisely the same laws by which the export of any other article is governed. Gold will not leave this country unless gold be dearer in some other country than it is in this. It will not leave this country, merely because it is gold, nor while there is any article of our produce or manufacture which can be exported in exchange for foreign produce with a more profitable return. If gold coin be in any country the common medium of exchange; or if the promissory notes, which perform in part the functions of gold coin, are at all times and under all circumstances of equal value with gold, and are instantly convertible into gold; there are causes in operation which, without any interference on our part, will confine within known and just limits the extent to which gold can be exported. There may no doubt be temporary pressure from the export of gold, even when it is confined within those limits; but none for which you may not provide, none to which you would not be subject, in a higher degree probably, were any other standard of value adopted in preference to gold. . . .

. . . We have a single standard, and that standard gold,–the metal which was practically the standard for many years previously to the suspension of cash payment. The silver coin is a mere token, auxiliary and subordinate to the gold coin; the ounce of silver being now coined into 66s. instead of 62s., and silver coin not being a legal tender for any greater sum than 40s. By the abolition, in this part of the United Kingdom, of the promissory notes below £5, you introduce the gold coin into general use for the purpose of effecting small payments; you enable the holder of the smallest note to demand payment in gold, and thus insure the maintenance of a very considerable quantity of gold as a part of the circulating medium. There is, no doubt, some expense in the maintenance of a metallic circulation, but none, in my opinion, sufficient to countervail the advantage of having gold coin generally distributed throughout the country, accessible to all, and the foundation of paper credit and currency. It is contended by some, that if you were to dispense with coin altogether, to adopt the principle of Mr. Ricardo's plan, and make bank notes not convertible into gold at the will of the holder, excepting when presented to the amount of a very considerable sum (£300 or £400 for instance), and then convertible into bullion and not coin, you would provide a security against the effects of a panic connected with political causes, causing a sudden demand for gold. I very much doubt the policy of taking such precautions against such a contingency, and consider that the most effectual measure for promoting permanent confidence in the paper circulation of the country, is to require that the gold coin shall be in general use for small payments, and that the promissory note shall be of equal value with the coin which it professes to represent. I shall here close my observations on the measure of value and the coinage, and proceed to the more immediate subject for consideration, namely, the state of the paper circulation of the country, and the principles which ought to regulate it. I must state, at the outset, that in using the word money, I mean to designate by that word the coin of the Realm, and promissory notes payable to bearer on demand. In using the words paper currency, I mean only such promissory notes. I do not include in those terms bills of exchange, or drafts on bankers, or other forms of paper credit. I will not weary the House with a discussion as to the precise nature of deposits, and whether they constitute a part of the currency of the country. There is a material distinction, in my opinion, between the character of a promissory note payable to bearer on demand, and other forms of paper credit, and between the effects which they respectively produce upon the prices of commodities and upon the exchanges. The one answers all the purposes of money, passes from hand to hand without endorsement, without examination, if there be no suspicion of forgery: and it is in fact, what its designations imply it to be, currency or circulating medium.

I do not deny that other forms of paper credit have some effects in common with Bank notes, that they all have a tendency to economise the use of metallic money, and have a common influence on the value of gold to the extent to which they dispense with the use of it, and thus leave a larger quantity available for the general purposes of the world than there would otherwise be. But I think experience shows that the paper currency, that is, the promissory notes payable to bearer on demand, stands in a certain relation to the gold coin and the foreign exchange in which other forms of paper credit do not stand. There are striking examples of this adduced in the Report of the Bullion Committee of 1810, in the case both of the Bank of England, and of the Irish and Scotch Banks. In the case of the Bank of England, shortly after its establishment there was a material depreciation of paper in consequence of its excessive issue. The notes of the Bank of England were at a discount of 17 per cent. There was no doubt as to the solvency of the Bank, for bank stock, on which 60 per cent. had been paid, was selling at 110 per cent. After trying various expedients, it was at length determined to reduce the amount of bank notes outstanding. The consequence was an immediate increase in the value of those which remained in circulation, the restoration of them to par, and a corresponding improvement in the foreign exchanges. . . .

(Paper Currency) is the substitute for and the immediate representative of coin, and with coin it constitutes 'money'. And if you will adhere to the standard of value, and will adopt such measures as shall ensure the uniform equivalency of Bank notes to coin, you may safely, in my opinion, leave untouched other forms of paper credit, and entrust the regulation and control of them to individual caution and discretion. There are some, however, who admit the validity of this distinction, and yet contend that no new legislative interference is required in the case of promissory notes. In their opinion the true principles which should govern the issue of such notes are, freedom of competition, and immediate convertibility into coin at the will of the holder. The combination of these principles will, in their opinion afford to the public a complete security against abuse of the privilege of issue. In support of that opinion they have, undoubtedly, the high authority of Adam Smith and of Ricardo. Both these eminent writers assume that immediate convertibility into coin is all that is requisite to prevent the excessive issue of paper. It is no impeachment of their sagacity, if, in the progress which this science, like all other sciences, is making, there be reason to doubt the soundness of any particular opinion which they may have delivered. And it is our duty to disregard their authority, and to act on the conclusions of our own judgment, if either reason or experience convinces us that they are safer guides. It appears to me that we have, from reasoning, from experience, from the admissions made by the issuers of paper money, abundant ground for the conclusion, that, under a system of unlimited competition, although it be controlled by convertibility into coin, there is not an adequate security against the excessive issue of promissory notes. We should infer, certainly from reasoning, that free competition in the supply of any given article will probably ensure us the most abundant supply of that article at the cheapest rate. But we do not want an abundant supply of cheap promissory paper. We want only a certain quantity of paper, not, indeed, fixed and definite in nominal amount, but just such a quantity of paper, and that only, as shall be equivalent in point of value to the coin which it represents. If the paper be cheaper than the coin, it is an evil and not an advantage. That system, therefore, which provides a constant supply of paper equal in value to coin, and so varying in amount as to insure at all times immediate convertibility into coin, together with perfect confidence in the solvency of the issuers of paper, is the system which ought to be preferred. Now, unless the issuers of paper conform to certain principles, unless they vigilantly observe the causes which influence the influx or efflux of coin, and regulate their issues of paper accordingly, there is danger that the value of the paper will not correspond with the value of coin. The difference may not be immediately perceived,–nay, the first effect of undue issue, by increasing prices, may be to encourage further issues; and as each issuer, where there is unlimited competition, feels the inutility of individual efforts of contraction, the evil proceeds, until the disparity between gold and paper becomes manifest, confidence in the paper is shaken, and it becomes necessary to restore its value by sudden and violent reductions in its amount, spreading ruin among the issuers of paper, and deranging the whole monetary transactions of the country. If we admit the principle of a metallic standard, and admit that the paper currency ought to be regulated by immediate reference to the foreign exchanges,–that there ought to be early contractions of paper on the efflux of gold,–we might, I think, infer from reasoning, without the aid of experience, that an unlimited competition in respect to issue will not afford a security for the proper regulation of the paper currency. Let us now refer to the admissions made by those who are the advocates for unlimited competition. Several country bankers were examined by the Select Committee, and their evidence is important: it demonstrates the absence of that controlling check upon issue which ought to be applied, if the principles for which I contend are just. Mr. Hobhouse a banker, in the south-west of England, (a brother of the right hon. Baronet the Member for Nottingham,) who spoke with some authority from his having been Chairman of the Committee of Private Bankers, and their selected organ, was examined before the Committee. What account did he give of the issues of private bankers? He was asked–

"With a rise of prices, would there be an increased paper issue by the country bankers?"

He answered–

"Yes, there will be an increase in the local circulation when prices rise. Gold is a commodity, of which there may be a glut as well as a scarcity; and I could never see any reason to be frightened at an export or drain of gold."

He was then asked–

"Ought not there to be a contraction of the circulation under such circumstances?"

He answers–

"Whether there ought or ought not, I cannot tell; but I am sure, that, in fact, there could not be. I am perfectly satisfied that it is quite impossible for these local currencies to be influenced by the price of gold or the foreign exchanges."

He is then asked–

"Does it not often happen that your circulation is increased in the beginning of a drain of gold?"

He answers–

"Yes; we do not pretend that our circulation is at all governed by it. It is governed by what I have stated already."

. . . It is now incumbent on me to detail and explain the practical measures which I propose for the regulation of the currency. I will state them consecutively, and without intermediate comment, in order that the House may be in full possession of the plan recommended by the Government. We think it of great importance to increase the controlling power of a single Bank of Issue. We think it the wisest course to select the Bank of England as that controlling and central body, rather than to appoint Commissioners acting under the authority of Parliament for the purpose of the issue of a Paper Currency. I therefore propose, with respect to the Bank of England, that it should continue in possession of its present privileges of Issue, but that there should be a complete separation of the business of banking from that of Issue; that there should be a department of Issue separate from the department of Banking, with separate officers and separate accounts. I propose that to the Issue department should be transferred the whole amount of bullion now in the possession of the Bank, and that the Issue of Bank Notes should hereafter take place on two foundations, and two foundations only:–first, on a definite amount of public securities; secondly, exclusively upon bullion. The action of the public will regulate the amount of that portion of the note circulation which is issued upon bullion. With respect to the banking business of the Bank, I propose that it should be governed on precisely the same principles as would regulate any other Body dealing with Bank of England notes. The fixed amount of securities on which I propose that the Bank of England should issue notes, is £14,000,000, the whole of the remainder of the circulation to be issued exclusively on the foundation of bullion. I propose that there should be a complete periodical publication of the accounts of the Bank of England, both of the Banking and Issue Department. Objections were urged in 1833, to frequent publications of these accounts; but, in my opinion, those objections are without foundation. I have the strongest impression that nothing will more conduce to the credit of the Bank itself, and to the prevention of needless alarm, than the complete and immediate disclosure of its transactions. I would, therefore, propose to enact by law that there should be returned to the Government a weekly account of the issue of notes by the Bank of England, of the amount of bullion, of the amount of deposits, of securities, in short, a general summary of every transaction both in the Issue department and the Banking department of the Bank of England; and that the Government should forthwith publish unreservedly, and weekly, the account which they receive from the Bank. It is desirable, in order to make the whole plan more clearly understood, that I should now state the regulations we propose to establish with respect to other banking establishments, and afterwards, that I should revert to the subject of the Bank of England, and state the terms which we have made with the Bank, subject to the ratification of Parliament. Our general rule is, to draw a distinction between the privilege of Issue and the conduct of the ordinary banking business. We think they stand on an entirely different footing. We think that the privilege of Issue is one which may be fairly and justly controlled by the State, and that the banking business, as distinguished from Issue, is a matter in respect to which there cannot be too unlimited and unrestricted a competition. The principle of competition, though unsafe in our opinion when applied to Issue, ought, we think, to govern the business of banking. After the issue of paper currency has once taken place, it is then important that the public should be enabled to obtain the use of that issue on as favourable terms as possible. With regard to banks in England and Wales other than the Bank of England, we propose, that from this time, no new bank of issue should be constituted. I have stated that our object is to effect the change we contemplate, with as little detriment as possible to individual interests. We, therefore, do not propose to deprive existing banking establishments, which are now actually banks of issue, of the privilege they possess. We do not wish to raise that alarm which we fear would be excited if there should be any sudden extinction of the power of issue now possessed by these banking establishments. Leaving, therefore, to the existing banks, which are actually banks of issue, their privilege of issue, we subject them to the condition that they shall not exceed the existing amount of their Issue; this amount to be determined by the average Issue of each Bank for a definite preceding period, of two or three years, for instance. The Bank of England will thus be acquainted with the extent of the Issue from all other establishments. I know I am liable to be told that the Issues of these Banks may be much larger, under particular circumstances and at particular periods, than at others: but I have obtained Returns, of a confidential nature, from ten of the best conducted banks in the country, six of them being in agricultural, and four in manufacturing districts; and the amount of their variation of Issue is much less than might be imagined. If, however, there should at any time be a demand for an increased Issue, there would always be the ready means of supplying it; as the Banks may, by investing a portion of their capital in public securities, command a given amount of Bank of England Notes by the sale of such securities, and, with those Notes, may supply any occasional demand for increased local issues. . . .

I interrupted my statement as to the Bank, because I can make our proposed relations to the Bank more intelligible by having first described the regulations applicable to other Banking Establishments. I have stated that the issues of the Bank are to be upon bullion and upon a fixed amount of securities. We propose that £14,000,000 should be that amount of securities. Seeing no advantage in a change, we propose to continue upon the present terms the existing loan of £11,000,000 made by the Bank to the Government, at 3 per cent. This debt of the Government to the Bank is to be assigned as part of the security on which the issues of the Bank are to take place. There will then remain £3,000,000 of additional securities, Exchequer bills or other securities, over which the Bank are to have entire control. We propose that the Bank should have a right, in case of necessity, to limit its issues upon that portion of the securities, *viz.* £3,000,000. Circumstances might possibly arise in which the

Bank might find it necessary to restrict its issues within the amount of £14,000,000. In that case the Bank will have full power to diminish the £3,000,000 of securities which are to be deposited in addition to the £11,000,000 of debt assigned. I can hardly conceive a case in which it would be advisable to limit the issues to less than £11,000,000. I have said that the Bank shall be restricted from issuing notes upon securities to any greater extent than £14,000,000. This restriction applies, however, to ordinary circumstances and the present state of the affairs of the Bank. The case may occur in which it would be reasonable, and indeed might be necessary, that there should be an increase of the issues of the Bank upon securities. Suppose the country circulation to amount to £8,000,000, and of this amount £2,000,000 to be withdrawn, either in consequence of the failure of banks, or in consequence of agreements with the Bank of England to issue Bank of England paper–in that case, in order to supply the void, it may be necessary that the Bank should make an increased issue. A part of this issue may fairly be made upon securities. Our proposal is, that the profit to be derived from such an issue shall be placed to the account of the Government; and that no increased issue upon securities shall take place without a communication from the Bank to the Government, and without the express sanction of three Members of the Government: the First Lord of the Treasury, the Chancellor of the Exchequer, and the President of the Board of Trade. We do not contemplate, and do not intend to provide for, an increased issue upon securities in any other case than to that which I have referred, namely, the supply of a void caused by the withdrawal of some considerable portion of the existing country circulation. Let me here advert to an Enactment which passed when the Bank Charter was last continued, which passes by the name of the Legal Tender Clause. It enabled other banks, than the Bank of England to pay their notes in notes of the Bank of England, and thus relieved them from the obligation of paying in coin. I opposed this Clause at the time, considering it to be at variance with the principle of immediate convertibility. I do not now propose to repeal it, seeing that it has been in operation for several years, and that it may facilitate the subsitution of Bank of England notes for the notes of other banks. It may serve to increase the controlling influence of the Bank, and to habituate the public to the use of its notes.

98. Second report of the Select Committee of 1846 on the Amalgamation of Railways and Canals

Parlty. Papers, 1846/XIII/pp. 95–96.

YOUR Committee have stated, in their former Report, that there are about 32 Bills before Parliament in which power is sought to effect the amalgamation of Canals with Railways. These may be classed under the following heads:

1st. Bills for the amalgamation, by lease, purchase, or otherwise, of entire lines of Canal with competing lines of Railway.

2dly. Bills for the amalgamation of some Canal forming a link in a chain of water communication with a line of Railway competing with the whole chain.

3dly. Bills for converting Canals into Railways.

The present extent of inland navigation in Great Britain, by means of Canals, is estimated to be about 2,500 miles. Up to a very recent period it afforded almost the exclusive means of conveyance of heavy goods and merchandize from one part of the country to the other, and especially from the principal manufacturing districts to the outports.

On the introduction of Railways, and in the early period of their development, when want of experience and the absence of information as to the capabilities of the new system, rendered it impossible for the Legislature to impose proper restrictions and limitations on the tolls and charges of the various Companies, the competition which they had to sustain with the Canals checked any great abuse of the powers delegated to them. As the Railway system extended itself, improvements in its organization and economy placed in turn a check upon Canals, and the consequent competition materially reduced the expense of conveyance. Instances have been adduced before Your Committee in which the charges for the conveyance of merchandize have been lowered by these means to one-seventh of their former amount; and there are now few parts of the country which have not derived material advantage from the competition between Railways and Canals.

It is obviously of importance that Parliament should not lightly sanction any arrangements which would tend to deprive the Public of this advantage; and it has been a subject of consideration with Your Committee, whether, inasmuch as the future maintenance of competition depends in some degree on the complete independence of the Canal system, and any interference with a link may greatly and prejudicially affect the whole chain, it might not be the duty of Parliament to refuse its assent to all Bills uniting the interests of the now rival parties.

Did Your Committee believe that the two systems could be preserved in entire independence one of the other, they might be disposed to recommend The House to adopt this course. But in the progress of their inquiry, several reasons have suggested themselves, showing the difficulty of securing the Canal interest altogether from the interference and control of Railway Companies, or of affording to the former a full opportunity of testing its capabilities as a rival system.

One great impediment has been found to exist, in the present disjointed state of the Canal interests and the varying systems under which they carry on their operations. Some of the existing Companies, possessing lines of Canal which form central links in a great chain, take advantage of their peculiar position, and establish a rate of charges so high as to secure to themselves a large return for their capital, even upon a small amount of traffic. This practice, while it obliges the other Companies, not so advantageously situated, to reduce their rates to such an extent that they are unable to conduct their business with a profit, at the same time prevents such a reduction in the general charges of the line as would enable the several Companies, as a body, to maintain a fair competition with the Railways.

Instances have also been brought under the notice of Your Committee in which Railway Companies have effected private arrangements with the proprietors of a portion only of a line of Canal, and thereafter, by raising the tolls of that portion to the utmost limit allowed by law, have rendered it impossible for the Companies in possession of the remainder of the line of Canal to maintain their traffic in competition with the Railway.

Another consideration which must not be overlooked is, that although it has been stated that with proper management Canals might maintain a successful competition with Railways in the carriage of heavy goods, still such competition has hitherto been carried on under a great disadvantage, owing to the large profits made by Railway Companies on passenger traffic, which enables them to submit in some instances even to a loss on the carriage of merchandize, with a view to withdraw the traffic from Canals.

Even, however, where effective competition has been for a time maintained, it has been attended with such a large reduction of profits, that it has become the interest of the rival Companies to combine for their mutual advantage, and hence have arisen private arrangements, under which a higher scale of tolls and charges has been re-established.

It has indeed been shown that in certain cases increased advantages might be obtained for the Public by the Union of a Canal and Railway through the same line of country, under one management, subject of course to proper check and control.

The general conclusion, therefore, to which Your Committee have come is, that it would not be politic altogether to refuse the sanction of Parliament to the amalgamation of Railways with Canals. They would, however, strongly impress upon the attention of the Committees to whom Bills, whether for the amalgamation of Canals with Railways, or for the conversion of Canals into Railways, may be referred, that a most searching inquiry should be instituted into the merits of each case; and that their sanction should be given only in those instances in which it shall have been clearly proved that the amalgamation can be effected without prejudice to the Public.

99. Commercial crisis of 1847 - Secret Committee of 1847-1848 on Commercial Distress

Parlty. Papers, 1847–1848/VIII, 1/pp. IV–VI.

There has been a general concurrence of opinion amongst the Witnesses examined before Your Committee, that the primary cause of the Distress was the deficient harvest, especially of the potato crop, in the year 1846, and the necessity of providing the means of payment in the year 1847, for the unprecedented importations of various descriptions of Food which took place in that year.

Among other causes, the deficient supply of Cotton, the diversion of Capital from its ordinary employment in commercial transactions to the construction of Railroads, the undue extension of credit, especially in our transactions with the East, and exaggerated expectations of enlarged trade, have been stated, by some of the Witnesses, as having contributed to the same result.

Your Committee see no reason to doubt that these causes have in different degrees, in different parts of the country, produced the effect thus ascribed to them.

For the further development of the views entertained on these various points by the gentlemen whom they have examined, they must refer to the Evidence.

With regard to some of the circumstances above referred to, provision has already been made by Parliament, and it must be obvious that others are beyond the control of Legislative enactment.

Many of the Witnesses, including the Governor and Deputy-Governor of the Bank of England, have expressed their belief that earlier steps in the Autumn of 1846 and the Spring of 1847, on the part of the Bank of England, might have obviated the necessity for the more stringent measures which circumstances compelled the Directors to adopt in April, and might thus have prevented the alarm which was caused by those measures. The grounds on which that belief is entertained, together with the considerations which influenced the proceedings of the Bank, are explained in the Evidence of those Witnesses who were examined on this branch of the subject. It is one, in respect to which a wide discretion must necessarily be left with those who are charged with the management of the business of the Bank, and Your Committee trust that this discretion will be exercised with due prudence, if similar circumstances should again occur.

An opinion appears to have been entertained by some persons, though not by the Governor and Deputy-Governor of the Bank of England, that the Bank is released by the Act of 1844 from any obligation, except that of consulting the pecuniary interests of its Proprietors.

It is true that there are no restrictions imposed by law upon the discretion of the Bank, in respect to the conduct of the Banking, as distinguished from the Issue Department. But the Bank is a public institution, possessed of special and exclusive privileges, standing in a peculiar relation to the Government, and exercising, from the magnitude of its resources, great influence over the general mercantile and monetary transactions of the country.

These Circumstances impose upon the Bank the duty of a consideration of the public interest, not indeed enacted or defined by Law, but which Parliament in its various transactions with the Bank has always recognized, and which the Bank has never disclaimed.

It is unnecessary to impose such duty by law, as there can be little doubt that the permanent interests of the Bank are identified with those of the Public at large.

That identity of interest gives both to the Public and to the Proprietors of Bank Stock a deep interest in every measure calculated to ensure an enlightened administration of the affairs of the Bank.

Your Committee have learnt, therefore, with satisfaction, that the attention of the Court of Directors has been given to this subject, and that a change has been made by them, as to the selection of the Governor and Deputy-Governor, calculated, in the opinion of Your Committee, to improve the constitution of the governing body of the Bank.

They feel confident that the effect of this change, and the experience which has been acquired during the events of the last two years, will ensure to the Public, in the future management of the Bank of England, greater benefits from this national establishment than it has hitherto been the means of conferring upon the country.

Your Committee have received, with deep regret, from many Witnesses, evidence of the extent of loss incurred by commercial houses in the course of last Autumn, from an unprecedented combination of the circumstances above referred to, and seriously aggravated by the want of confidence which prevailed in consequence of the numerous failures, and which induced Bankers and others to retain a reserve, both of Gold and of Bank-notes, to a very great extent. It is to be observed, that this took place with a very large amount of Notes in the hands of the Public, exceeding, in the opinion of a Witness most competent to form an opinion, by no less than £4,000,000, "the actual requirements of the public at the time."

The feeling of alarm which prevailed appears to have been immediately removed by the issue of the letter addressed to the Bank of England, on the 25th of October, by the First Lord of the Treasury and the Chancellor of the Exchequer.

The issue of that letter was, no doubt, an extraordinary exercise of power on the part of the Government; but The House has decided that, in the peculiar circumstances of the period, they were justified in taking that step. It will be seen from the evidence of Mr. Cotton, the Governor of the Bank in 1844, that the possibility of circumstances arising, in which some extraordinary measures might be called for in consequence of a state of monetary crisis, was not unforeseen by the Government at the time when the Act of 1844 was passed.

The Evidence which has been given as to the effects of the Act of 1844, has been contradictory. Its beneficial effects, as regards the issues of the Country Banks, have been admitted by many of the Witnesses, and although some have suggested an alteration of its provisions, very few have contested the general principles on which it is founded.

Your Committee have had under their consideration, whether it is advisable that powers should be conferred by Law upon the Government, to enable them to meet the occurrence of any circumstances which may call for extraordinary interference; but they have come to the conclusion that, looking to the impossibility of foreseeing what the precise character of the circumstances may be, and also what may be the measure best calculated to meet them, it is more expedient to leave to those with whom the responsibility of the Government may rest at the time, to adopt such measures as may appear to them best suited for the emergency.

Your Committee, therefore, after a careful review of all the Evidence, are of opinion that it is not expedient to make any alteration in the Bank Act of 1844.

100. Select Committee of 1851 on Law of Partnership

Parlty. Papers, 1851/XVIII/pp. IV–VII.

Your Committee also desire to record their conviction that if it be desired to promote association among the humbler classes for objects of mutual benefit, no measure will tend more directly to this end than one which will give a cheap and ready means of settling disputes of the partners, and enforcing the rules agreed to for mutual government.

Evidence of the increase of personal property of late years may be shortly stated. The Population Returns show an increase of the population of almost all of our largest towns (chiefly inhabited by persons dependent on personal property), at the rate of nearly 30 per cent. in every decennial period since the beginning of the century to the present time, whilst the rural inhabitants have augmented only at about one-third the same proportion.

A return of 10 February 1851 as to assessments to the property tax, shows that in Great Britain as a general result the annual value is as follows:

	1814–15	*1848*
	£	£
Of Lands	39,405,000	47,981,000
Messuages, or chiefly houses, &c. in towns	16,259,000	42,314,000
Railways, gas works, and other property, chiefly considered personal property .	636,000	8,885,000

The result in round numbers shows that in 33 years since the peace, whilst lands in Great Britain have increased in value to 1848 only 8½ millions in annual value, or a little more than five per cent., messuages (being chiefly houses and manufactories, and warehouses in and near towns, and inhabited by persons depending greatly on trade and commerce) have augmented in value above 26 millions in annual value, or about 130 per cent. in the same period.

From the same returns it appears that the value of railways, gas-works, and other property, chiefly held in shares as personal property, has increased above 12 fold in the same period.

The same results showing the increase of personal property, since the peace, in the United Kingdom, may be deduced from various Returns to Parliament, showing the increase of legacy duty to have been derived from a capital of 24 millions in 1815, and to have been paid on a capital increased to 45 millions in 1845; the increase of deposits in the saving banks, and from other undoubted sources of information.

Your Committee beg to state that in addition to the augmentation in the amount of personal property, is to be remarked its great division among large classes of the community, in the middle (or even the humbler) ranks of life, as is shown by the returns of amounts of public stock held by each person, and other sources of information.

Your Committee would observe that the course of modern legislation (the wisdom of which appears, in this particular, generally allowed) seems to have been gradually to remove restrictions on the power which every one has in the disposal of his property, and to remove those fetters on commercial freedom which long prevailed in this country.

The usury laws, and various laws against combinations, have been modified or repealed. General Acts to facilitate the formation of Joint Stock Associations and Building Societies, and other important Acts tending to the same result, have in late years been sanctioned by the Legislature.

Your Committee now proceed to consider whether any suggestions of a like nature ought to be made in reference to the laws of partnership, and especially the unlimited liability of partners, as it exists at present in this country.

By the existing law, no person can advance any capital to any undertaking, public or private, in the profits of which he is to participate, nor become partner or shareholder in any enterprise for profit, without becoming liable to the whole amount of his fortune, as expressed by a great legal authority, to his last shilling and his last acre.

Such general and unlimited liability can be restricted to any given sum or share only by Special Act of Parliament or Charter from the Crown; neither of which is obtained without much difficulty, expense and delay, and in many cases cannot be obtained at all.

It is contended, that however advantageous the law of unlimited liability of partners may be, as applied to the principal commercial transactions of this country, carried on for the most part by firms of few partners, that yet it would be of great advantage to the community to allow limited liability to be extended with greater facility to the shareholders in many useful enterprises, often promising at the same time public benefit and private profit, which are constantly called for by the increasing population and wants of our towns and populous districts; such as water works, gas works, roads, bridges, markets, piers, baths, wash-houses, workmen's lodging houses, reading rooms, clubs, and various other investments of a like nature, chiefly confined to spots in the immediate vicinity of the subscribers. Large stores for the sale of provisions and other necessaries in populous districts, and supported by the combined capital of small shareholders, may be considered as belonging to the same kind of enterprises.

Your Committee think it would be a subject of regret if cautious persons, of moderate capital, and esteemed for their intelligence and probity in their several neighbourhoods, should be now deterred from taking part in such undertakings by the heavy risk of unlimited liability; yet such persons would in many instances be the best guides for their humbler and less experienced neighbours, and their names would afford security that the enterprise had been well considered, and was likely to be well conducted.

Your Committee think that it would be desirable to remove any obstacles which may now prevent the middle and even the more thriving of the working classes from taking shares in such investments, under the sanction of and conjointly with their richer neighbours; as thereby their self-respect is upheld, their industry and intelligence encouraged, and an additional motive is given to them to preserve order and respect the laws of property.

Your Committee would therefore recommend that under the supervision of a competent authority, rules should be laid down and published for the guidance of persons applying for such charters, with requisite precautions to prevent fraud; and on compliance with such rules, that charters should be granted. Security for compliance with such rules might be given and enforced at the quarter sessions, or before some other local tribunal of requisite authority.

101A–F. Select Committee of 1852–1853 on Railway and Canal Amalgamation

Parlty. Papers, 1852–3/XXXVIII

101A. Evidence of Samuel Laing, M.P.

Questions 78–89.

78. CHAIRMAN: YOU have been Secretary to the Railway Department of the Board of Trade; you have had considerable practice as counsel before Committees of the Houses of Parliament upon railway subjects; you have been frequently examined as a witness before general Committees on the subject of railways, and you are now chairman of the Brighton Railway Company?–Yes, that is so.

79. Will you have the goodness to state to the Committee what is your opinion upon the subject of the past legislation of Parliament in reference to railways?–There can be no doubt that the railway legislation of this country has been exceedingly defective, and has entailed a very great loss, in the first instance, upon the railway proprietors, and ultimately upon the public; I may say, as the measure of the loss that has been sustained, to sum it up in round numbers, that I should think on the 7,000 miles of railway now in operation in this country, there has been an expenditure of about £10,000 a mile, upon the average, over and above the rate at which they might have been constructed under a different system of legislation, making a total of £70,000,000.

80. Will you explain how that great waste of capital has resulted from past legislation?–I think it has arisen mainly from the uncertainty of that legislation; from having no definite principle whatever laid down as to whether competition was or was not the rule. That circumstance during periods of excitement, such as 1845, has led to the multiplication of an immense number of schemes prosecuted at an almost reckless expense; in fact, I should say a company like the London and North Western Railway Company has been, for the last 10 or 15 years, almost perpetually in the position of carrying on a contested election, spread over half a dozen different counties.

81. Besides the waste of capital which you say has been raised in the creation of the lines which now exist, are you of opinion that the same number of miles of railway as now exist might, with more judicious legislation, have been made to render to the public much more efficient service than the present lines?–If they had been constructed, as I think they might have been, for £70,000,000 less than they have cost, there is no doubt the public might have had the advantage either by a reduction of fares, or by an increase of accommodation, or in both respects.

82. Might not lines of railway to the same amount in mileage have been more judiciously spread over the country, so as to render to the public a greater aggregate of service than is rendered by the present lines?–Certainly, in many cases it might have been so.

83. Could the same amount of population have been accommodated with railway communications more economically than they are at present?–I think so, decidedly.

84. What do you calculate the actual cost of the 7,000 miles of railway of which you speak, as now existing?–I think they will average about £40,000 a mile by the time they are fully completed; that would make £280,000,000 in round numbers.

85. Are you taking in your present estimate, the mere cost of construction, or are you including the additional expenditure which, as you think, has been needlessly thrown away?–That includes the additional expenditure of £70,000,000. Instead of costing £40,000 a mile, I think the railways might very well have been constructed for £30,000 a mile or less.

86. Therefore one-fourth part of all that has been expended on railways up to this time, has been absolutely wasted?–I think so.

87. Mr. Bright: In that estimate, do you include any unnecessary and increased expenditure from the extravagant price which has been paid for land?–That has been one very large item in the waste of capital.

88. In the £70,000,000?–Yes. When you have had two competing lines before a Committee, and a mere trifle, like the opposition of a single landowner, might turn the scale between two nearly evenly-balanced schemes, incredible sums have been paid for land.

89. Chairman: Are you of opinion that the same evil consequences may to any extent be expected to continue, unless Parliament, by some new plan of railway legislation, interferes to prevent them?–I think the only security against it now is, the reluctance of the public, after the losses of 1847 and 1848, to embark in new railway enterprises. But, assuming that there were a speculative disposition on the part of the public, I see nothing in the course of legislation, or in the constitution of Committees of this House, to prevent the recurrence of what took place in 1845.

101B. Evidence of Mark Huish, general manager of London and North Western Railway

Questions 1202–1207.

1202. What has been the effect upon cheapness and convenience to the public of making competing lines to the same places?–In the earlier history of the so-called competing lines, a very considerable temporary diminution took place in the fares and freights to the public, but in a very short time those lines coalesced and combined, and the result has been, I think, in almost every instance where the game has been played out, I may say in every instance, to raise the rates to a higher standard than they were at before the competition commenced.

1203. Will you be good enough to give us some examples?–There is no part of our system in which we are subject to so many rival, or, as they are called, competing lines, as between Liverpool and Manchester; the distance is only 30 miles, and there are between those two points three railways and two canals; making five means of communication between those large foci of commerce.

1204. The three railways being your own, the Lancashire and Yorkshire Railway and the East Lancashire Railway?–Yes; and the canals being the Bridgewater Canal and another canal, which has been recently purchased by the Bridgewater trustees, so that those now constitute only one.

1205. There is also a circuitous communication by means of the Leeds and Liverpool and Manchester Canal?–Yes; it scarcely comes into the category of competing lines between Manchester and Liverpool. The result has been what might have been anticipated; the first operation was, that the two canals combined; the one bought up the other. The next step in the process was, that the Lancashire and Yorkshire and the London and North Western Railway Companies threw their joint traffic into a common fund, dividing it in certain fixed proportions for a long period of years; and having thereby reduced the active forces to one combined railway and one combined canal, they immediately entered into an arrangement with the Duke of Bridgewater's trustees to prevent any competition between the canal and the railway by a reduction of rates. The effect of that was to throw the receipts of the combined railways and the combined canals into a joint fund, and divide it in a certain proportion. The result of the whole of this is, that the traffic between Liverpool and Manchester, where there were five means of competition, is charged a higher rate than the traffic upon many other parts of our system where we have no competition.

1206. To what do you attribute the circumstance that the rates are higher upon that part of your line than upon any other parts of your line?–The fact is, that a larger capital has been brought into the field, and that must have a return; none of the parties can afford to do for the same price that which we could afford to do, where the traffic was altogether in our hands. You have asked me for illustrations; that is one. The next I might quote is between Preston and Liverpool; there for a long period of years the only communication was by Parkside. On the map you will see a straight line from Preston to where it strikes the line of the Liverpool and Manchester Railway, and then by the Liverpool and Manchester Railway to Liverpool. After a time a straight line was projected between Preston and Liverpool, the short side of the triangle; it was opposed by the North Western Railway Company, on the ground that it would not effect what was proposed by it. However, the Bill passed, and the line was made; a short struggle, and a very short one, commenced, which was immediately put an end to by combination, and with the exception of the Parliamentary train, which could not be raised, because it was limited according to the distance, the rates from Preston to Liverpool generally are higher now than they were when there was but one line for the conveyance of the traffic.

1207. The result of that would be, that the Parliamentary limitation is effectual, and that the limitation produced by the competition of the lines is ineffectual?–Exactly. Then if I go to the east of the country, there is our great antagonist, the London and York Railway; that railway had a very severe Parliamentary contest, and obtained its Bill on the ground of shortening the distance to the north, and breaking down, as they stated at the time, the monopoly of the North Western and Midland Railway Companies combined, and they obtained their Act upon what was called the crow distance, that is, they were not allowed to charge according to the sinuous windings of the line, but on the actual distance; they got their Act, after a great struggle, upon that ground. Having got their Act, they came again to Parliament, and stated that they had made a mistake in asking for that, and they solicited and obtained from Parliament power to charge according to the actual distance of the railway. That was a step in advance. Of course we did not oppose them, as it was granting a higher rate. Their next was to come to Parliament to raise the tolls on the line, on the ground that the original calculations had been fallacious, and did not give the return which the proprietors had a right to expect. We did not of course oppose that either, and the result was that they obtained higher tolls. The line was made, and it was opened; a short struggle commenced there, as it has done in every other instance almost, but in a very short time the Great Northern Railway Company saw that combination was far more beneficial than competition, and we both came under an obligation to submit the division of the traffic at all the salient points to the decision of Mr. Gladstone. Mr. Gladstone very kindly undertook the office, which appeared to be a very difficult one; but in a short time he presented us with an award, which I believe both parties thought was not quite what it ought to have been as regards their company; both parties were dissatisfied with it at the time; but I am bound to admit, that the more I reflect upon the award, the more I am surprised at the result, and that a person of Mr. Gladstone's habits has been enabled to divide the whole country in a manner which I think ought to be reasonably satisfactory to both companies. The result of the whole of that is, that the prices which the West Riding are paying for their staple, such as wool, from London, and the prices which Sheffield is paying for its steel, and hardwares and plated goods, are considerably higher than they were when there was but one railway to perform the whole service.

101C. Evidence of Charles Russell, chairman of the Great Western Railway Company

Questions 1844–1845.

1844. Do you recollect making a speech at the half-yearly meeting of your company, in the month of August 1852?–Yes, I do.

1845. Do you recollect this paragraph: "If the legislature could be induced to adopt the views of the London and North Western, and to think that it would be wise to allow the complete amalgamation of these two great companies, and to rely for the protection of the public interests on careful restrictions and restraints, I, for one, should hail such an auspicious change in the public policy of the country as most advantageous both to the railways and to the public"?–I perfectly remember making those observations in the month of August 1852; I made them under a sense of the perpetual difficulty and distress that our differences with the North Western Company occasioned us. It is a state of such hateful warfare, that I should be happy to embrace any arrangement that would by possibility put an end to it; but, in the same speech, I stated distinctly that I did not believe the Legislature could, or would acquiesce in any such arrangement. I believe still further (and everything I have heard here confirms me in the opinion) that if the Legislature could be induced to give its consent to the arrangement, the railway companies, when they come to understand what it is they are to surrender for a mere nominal protection against competition, will almost universally decline it. That is my belief now, as it was, not erroneously, in 1844. But beyond this, an amalgamation between the London and North Western and the Great Western Companies is, practically, tantamount to an amalgamation of all the railways in the kingdom. Under such circumstances, I believe that it would become inevitable that the Government should assume not only the entire control, but the entire property in the railways. I think you have now to make your election; you must choose between the principle of private and Government enterprise. If you determine to continue the former, as you have hitherto done, you must leave to it the incitements and rewards that are proper to private enterprise, and which alone can make it successful and active. If you determine to take the railways into the hands of Government, take them at once and completely, and give to the system that energy and uniformity which belong to the centralization of Government administration. But do not palter between the two systems; I am satisfied if you seek to attempt any intermediate scheme you will fail. I look to the Amalgamation of the London and North Western and the Great Western as leading inevitably to the railways becoming, under Government control, Government property; and I am not at all prepared to say, that with the means which the Government will have the power to administer them, the interests of the public may not be promoted by such means.

101D. Evidence of E. E. P. Kelsey, mayor of Salisbury

Questions 3284–3285.

3284. Do you appear here for the purpose of explaining to the Committee certain general inconveniences which, in the opinion of the people of Salisbury, have resulted to them from past legislation on the subject of railways?–I do.

3285. Will you be so good as to explain the case which you wish to lay before the Committee?–Perhaps it might be convenient that I should state the facts generally, first of all, that the Great Western Company, or rather a company in alliance with them, under the title of the Wilts and Somerset Company, obtained in the year 1845 powers to make a system of railways, amounting to, I think, seven different lines; and in pursuance of those powers, which have been from time to time extended and increased, they have made a certain portion of that system; but the original scheme which they brought before the public, and upon which they obtained the support of the public of Salisbury and that neighbourhood, on whose behalf I now appear to complain, was to make a trunk line from Thingley, in the neighbourhood of Corsham, to Salisbury. That was the scheme which they propounded at Salisbury, representing that it would entail great advantages, as was undoubtedly the fact it would have done. After that, a change took place in the plan, and it was extended westward. The whole of the capital was raised, and, for all I know, may be expended. At any rate they have constructed the trunk portion of the line to Warminster only, there stopping, and although application has been made to them courteously to continue the line, they refuse to do so; at all events, they make no reply whatever. We then complain of the system by which railways are enabled to cover the country upon paper, and deprive other parties, who may be willing to afford the public means of communication, of the opportunity of doing so. The inhabitants of Salisbury, for all trading purposes, if desirous of travelling, or sending goods to Bristol, or backwards and forwards in that direction, have first to travel by coach to Warminster. They then go by a circuitous route over the Wilts and Somerset line to Thingley, and eventually they get deposited, by means of the Great Western line, at Bristol. But parties wishing to come from Bristol to Southampton or Portsmouth, are sent round usually by the Great Western Company all the way to Reading, and from thence to Basingstoke, and then on by the South Western to their destination. Thence arises, I believe, the true reason of the indisposition on the part of the Great Western Company to complete this link to Salisbury. If that link were complete, of course the traffic would be direct to Salisbury, which would be carrying them only 20 miles more over the Great Western Line, the Wilts and Somerset having merged in the Great Western Company, and really making the interests of the public entirely subservient to the private interest of the Great Western.

1011E. Evidence of John Hawkshaw, C.E.

Questions 3338–3341.

3338. What is your opinion as to past legislation on the subject of railways?–I am inclined to think, with reference to past legislation, that it has not been so bad as it has been represented to be. I think it is frequently argued, as if it would have been possible to have started with all the experience which it has taken us to the present time to attain. I think that is a fundamental mistake in a great many of the opinions which I see expressed in reference to past legislation. Gentlemen are too apt to say, if only we had started so and so, with such and such arrangements, to what a much better conclusion we might have arrived. Now, here is a fallacy. We could not have started with that experience, and, therefore, the argument is illegitimate. But, irrespective of that, I very much doubt whether any better system could be devised, even now, than the one which has been acted upon up to the present time. I think there is one change which ought to be made, and it might have been made earlier, because it is rather a financial mistake than otherwise; at all events, I think if it be permitted to continue now, it will be a very great error. I do not know that it is right to assume that it ought to have been discovered earlier, but it appears to me to have been a fundamental mistake in reference to railway legislation, that railways have been permitted to be projected on what, as it regards finance, I should call a boundless issue of paper currency. The fact is, that men were allowed, and are still allowed, to undertake and find any amount of paper money for the construction of railways, which paper money was, and is, of the most trashy description.

3339. By paper money, you mean scrip?–Yes; I think that is a fundamental mistake, and the remedy of that error is all that is wanted as a protection to railway property, and it is all, in my opinion, that can safely be done with reference to the future.

3340. That is, that no person should be allowed to obtain the sanction of Parliament to a Railway Bill without giving in hard money a sufficient security for the actual completion and opening of the line?–Certainly; with railways, as with other matters, if parties are prepared to find the money, I see no reason why they should not be allowed to construct a railway, supposing they can show that it will be of any public utility, just as readily as they would be allowed to construct a factory; but there should be a Standing Order of the House, that before any railway be granted, there should be a careful examination into the deed under which the parties proposed to find the money, and that you should ascertain the *bona fide* character of the subscribers to that deed, and that you should hold them to that deed until a very large proportion of that money is found. I do not think that the resolution that has been come to, merely binding parties to the extent of the 10 per cent. deposit, would be any great improvement; parties were always bound to that extent; men ran the risk of losing their deposits in former times; therefore supposing railway property were to improve, and you were to have another start of railways, the mere forfeiture of the deposits would be no security whatever against the former state of things. I cannot see any injustice to parties in saying, if you promise to make this line, you shall satisfy us that you can find the money for it, and you shall make it, and we will hold you, the promoters of the line, and the original proposers of it, liable till the line is made. I do not know that you should hold them to the whole extent, but certainly to 50 per cent. of the entire capital.

3341. Mr. Bright: If you carry your mind back 20 years, and apply that to any of the companies then started, do you think you would have had one-fourth of the railways made in the country that you now have?–Yes, I do; my opinion is, that you would have had, most likely, all the railways made that are now made. If you had adopted that rule at the outset, I think you would not have had so many wild schemes proposed; you would not have wasted quite so much money in Parliamentary warfare; you might not have had the many miles of railway sanctioned that have been abandoned; you would have induced parties to be more careful before they brought a scheme before Parliament, but I believe that every good scheme that is made would have been made under that principle.

101F. Evidence of R. Baxter, railway solicitor

Questions 3515, 3516.

3515. Mr. M. Milnes: In what point do you regard a system of amalgamation of railways to differ from the present system of voluntary combination which takes place, and seems to carry with it practically so much of the effect of amalgamation?–The voluntary combinations are merely another phase of competition; it is the peaceable phase of competition. You have the belligerent phase, where parties are running the rates down to the lowest point, and competing at full fight. You have the more peaceable phase when they have agreed upon equal rates, – which is one mode of doing it – or when they have agreed to divide the traffic, – which is another mode of doing it; but, even when that has taken place, the companies who have voluntarily made this arrangement are substantively and really competing with each other, because they know the voluntary arrangements must have an end, and according to the position in which each one of them stands when that arrangement comes to an end, will be the future division of the same traffic upon a renewed agreement, and therefore the voluntary arrangements, it appears to me, are not an end to competition, but merely a modification of it.

3516. Have you heard that it has been asserted before this Committee, that all the competition which is at present going on must soon come to a termination, that the competition will be worked out whether we will or not; and therefore the only question that we have to determine is, whether we should place certain conditions upon an inevitable system of amalgamation; do you agree with that view? – Not at all; if Parliament refuses to sanction the amalgamation of great companies, competition must and will continue. If Parliament could be induced to sanction the amalgamation of any two of the larger companies, the London and North Western and the Great Western, or the London and North Western and the Midland, they must then go on ultimately to amalgamate all the companies; but standing where they are, there will be a great deal of agreement, and a great deal of fighting; but still competition will continue to the end of the chapter. After you have a railway board, a public board, educated for the control of railways, it may then be practicable to take another view of the subject, and put them into another phase. But if you were to amalgamate all the railways, at present there is nobody to control them; Parliament cannot interpose – there is no public department which is competent to such a work, and it would require years of education to enable them to undertake it.

102. Evidence of Leone Levi before Lords' Committee of 1854 on Agricultural Statistics

Parlty. Papers, 1854–1855/VIII questions 820–857.

820. EARL OF HARROWBY: Was the question of the commercial importance of ascertaining annually, at an early period, returns of the agricultural prospects of the year considered in that congress?

No; I believe merchants consider it of very great importance to them to be as early as possible made acquainted with the probable wants of the country in matters of food; because I need not say that the prices of grain have a very great influence on the prices of all other articles, and the Mark Lane Journal is the barometer by which the value of all other articles is regulated. It is also of the utmost importance to merchants, in order to regulate their speculations and their orders abroad for other articles of consumption to be speedily informed whether we shall have abundance of grain at home, or whether we shall have to seek from foreign countries very large supplies. The influence of such uncertainty upon the funds is always remarkable, and upon the bullion in the Bank. The possibility of having to send a great deal of gold abroad has very considerable influence upon private credit, discounting bills, &c. &c. All those transactions are very considerably affected by the uncertainty which prevails as to the result of the crops in this country.

821. Therefore, the earlier intelligence can be procured upon this main governing element of the mercantile prospects of the year the better?

Certainly. Suppose at the very last moment we should find ourselves to be in want of about five or six millions of quarters to be imported into this country in two or three months, of course the price of grain would rise enormously. Let us calculate that, owing to the suddenness of the demand, the rise might be about 6s. a quarter; the natural rise beyond it would have taken place if it had been known before. Then to these 6s. there must be added, also, a very considerable rise in the rate of freights; for instance, I find that, during 1846 and 1847, the freight from Odessa to this country for tallow, ruled from 50s. to 110s. a ton; and from the Danube, from 9s. to 21s. per quarter; and from Alexandria, from 6s. to 12s. during 1846. Now, let it be admitted that, owing to the suddenness of the rise, as we must have the grain speedily brought in, the rate of freight also should rule 6s. per quarter higher than need be; that would make nearly 10s. a quarter, which, upon six millions, would prove a loss to the public of about £3,000,000 sterling. And this may actually be ascribed to our finding all at once to be in want of large supplies, and to the fact that for that reason speculation did not go on regularly from the commencement of the season to the last. There are other reasons besides in favour of obtaining such statistics as soon as possible: the later we are in foreign countries for our purchases, the less chance we have to obtain the grain. Our harvest here is about two months later than the harvest in Italy or France, and it is natural that, immediately as these countries find their crops to be very deficient, they should at once send for supplies, and as they are nearer to the Danube, from Marseilles for instance, than we are, they get their supplies provided for from the Danube, Alexandria, and other places, before almost we know ourselves that we also want them. This of course affects very materially the commerce of the country. The influence of such suddenness of rise in the price of grain, together with the rise of freight, has also great influence on the rise or on the decline of the prices of other articles of consumption here, because the more we have to pay for grain, the less we have to bestow upon other articles, and that affects the value of other articles, and our relations with such countries from whom we receive such articles of luxury; our exports are also affected from the same causes, and thus it acts and re-acts in many ways. I have thus contented myself in indicating what are the evils resulting from the present want of correct agricultural statistics. I know that estimates of the harvest are constantly made by private merchants and farmers, and these are abundantly published in the Mark Lane Express, and other papers; yet these estimates are generally uncertain, and are often made by interested parties. Indeed the conflicting nature of such information is often the source of extraordinary fluctuation of prices. I have not detailed the direct benefits of agricultural statistics, whether of those referring to the number of acres under cultivation, and under the several crops, to the estimate annual yield, or to periodical statistics of agriculture on an extensive plan. I believe they are likely to prevent great fluctuation of prices; to diminish the speculative character attached to all transactions in grain, and to enable us to obtain the necessary supplies for the year from foreign countries at lower rates, and with greater ease; and I believe, moreover, that such statistics will have a further important effect in calling forth greater energy among our farmers in the application of science into agriculture; in improving all the processes of cultivation, and in extending materially the agricultural resources of the country.

822. In fact, the prospects of the grain harvest are the great moving element of the whole of the mercantile prospects of the year, and the sooner they are ascertained the better for all classes?

Yes.

823. Have you ever considered this question as affecting the interest of the farmer himself?

I consider he stands upon the same level as the merchants, because, no doubt, whilst the merchants have often to pay dearer for grain on account of their ignorance, the farmer often sells a larger quantity in the first instance at lower prices than he was justified in doing; and this is especially the case with those who, being least acquainted with the general state of the country, go on selling; and, perhaps, after they have sold all they have, they find that those who have been fortunate enough to hold get double for their produce. If information was more general, they would only be disposed to sell such portions as they are under necessity of selling, and that would enable them all to participate in the rise when that rise happens.

824. Is it not thought a very important element in the manufacturing districts of Lancashire to ascertain, as early as possible, the prospect of the cotton crop; and is not the prospect of the grain crop, in fact, a similar question with respect to other classes in England?

Very similar; with respect to the cotton crop, it is by induction that the markets are regulated; that is, it is according to the number of bales sent to the shipping ports of the United States from the interior on certain days and certain months that calculations are made as to the possible results of the produce for the year. It is astonishing what an influence is produced upon the prices wherever, during any one week, there has been sent to the shipping ports any less number of bales than formerly. This at once gives a tone to the market in view of the possible scarcity of the cotton crops for the year; and immediately afterwards the prices of cotton manufactures rise, so that the slightest indication ascertained by facts of a possible abundance or scarcity in the cotton crop has very material influence upon the entire cotton trade and manufactures of the country. Let it be, moreover, remembered, with regard to the question of the probable supplies of grains, that our dependance upon foreign grain is yearly greater; for instance, from 1840 to 1846, we imported nearly 23,000,000 quarters of grain, giving an average importation of 3,000,000 quarters.

825. Including flour?

All grain and flour. From 1847 to 1853, in seven years, we imported 67,000,000 quarters, or 9,500,000 quarters of grain on an average per year, so that we are every year more dependent upon foreign supplies, and therefore we are the more interested in knowing early any extraordinary deficiency. As the returns for the last seven or eight years pretty well indicate what are the normal wants of the country, any extraordinary deficiency would increase the want from 10,000,000 to 15,000,000, and render it even more difficult to procure such supplies, and more necessary it is to be first in the market wherever it can be got from.

826. LORD COLCHESTER: Do those quantities increase regularly, year by year, or do they fluctuate?

The import in 1840 was 3,900,000; 1841, 3,600,000; 1842, 3,600,000; 1843, 1,400,000; 1844, 3,000,000; 1845, 2,500,000; 1846, 4,700,000; that is the first period of seven years. The second period of seven years is, 1847, 11,900,000; 1848, 7,500,000; 1849, 10,600,000; 1850, 9,000,000; 1851, 9,600,000; 1852, 7,700,000; 1853, 10,000,000: and in 1854 we imported 8,000,000 quarters.

827. It is not a regularly progressive increase, but has fluctuated from the season and other circumstances?

Yes; except that during those last seven years we never have had the importation go back to 2,000,000 or 3,000,000, as we used to do formerly.

828. There was a great change in the law about that period?

That may have affected it very much, but our consumption was greater.

829. EARL OF HARROWBY: During those seven years, what is the highest and what is the lowest importation?

The highest was in 1847, when we imported nearly 12,000,000; and the lowest in 1848, when it reached 7,500,000; and again in 1852, 7,700,000. It is very singular to observe how very little wheat is produced in Ireland and Scotland; from the last account of those two countries it appears that the produce of wheat in Ireland was only 1,133,585 quarters, and in Scotland, only 600,000 quarters. Now this suggests, also, our wants of foreign wheat, that must be always large: there were 10,000 quarters of oats produced in Ireland, and 4,000,000 produced in Scotland; but we require a considerable quantity of wheat from foreign countries.

830. Is there any record of the import of wheat and flour into Scotland?

I am not aware into Scotland. The consumption of wheat for the United Kingdom as given by M'Culloch was 16,000,000 of quarters of wheat. If 2,000,000 of quarters only are produced in those two countries, what is the quantity of wheat produced in England? I suppose that for wheat alone we must be very much dependent upon other sources.

831. What would appear to be about the monetary range of value of the grain imported between the highest and the lowest years?

The monetary value would result from prices. I find, from a list I made out of the highest and lowest prices for each year, that the highest price during this period from 1840 to 1854, was in 1847 when it was as high as 102s. 5d. a quarter; and the lowest during that same period of 15 years, was in 1851, when it was 35s. 11d. per quarter.

832. Are you speaking of weekly returns, or what?

The monthly average for 1847 was 92s. 10d. the highest, and 52s. 3d. the lowest;

but the highest weekly average in that same month was 102s. 5d. I find, taking the average of all the averages for the whole period together, that the highest would be 61s. 7d., and the lowest would be 46s. 10d. The highest and lowest from 1840 to 1854.

833. Have you added the highest of each week or each month?

The highest and lowest of each month.

834. The highest of each is 61s. 7d.; the lowest average of the same kind is 46s. 10d.?

Yes, the highest and lowest: the difference of prices in 1847 was 40s. a quarter, or £2 a quarter. And there is another curious observation out of these prices: it appears that the months when the highest prices ruled were mostly July and August; for this there may be two reasons. It may arise from sudden deficiency in the quantities of grain on hand of the old crop, from the non-arrival of foreign grain, or from the bad prospects of the next harvest. In many cases where a sudden rise in August takes place from a sudden want, it shows a want of agricultural statistics; because if we knew it sooner we should not be all on a sudden finding our rick-yards empty, and all on a sudden wanting extra supplies from abroad. I presume if we had agricultural statistics in time, the rise would not take place in August, but would take place in March or April, or earlier still, and so on progressively from the commencement of the year; immediately, in fact, as the harvest operations are over. In 1847, the highest was in June; in 1842, 1849 and 1851 the highest price was in July; in 1841, 1843 and 1859 the highest prices were in August. I am not now specifying what were the reasons, as I said it may have arisen from bad prospects of the crops in this or other countries, and again from the scanty remainder of the former years. As to the lowest prices in 1840, 1841, 1842, 1847, 1849 and 1852, the lowest prices ruled in December and January. If we had agricultural statistics after a bad harvest, prices would generally begin to rise in December and January, and yet those are the months when generally prices ruled the lowest.

835. Lord Portman: Why should they rise in December and January?

If the agricultural statistics obtainable in August or September were to tell us that we are likely to have a want of 10,000,000 quarters this year, immediately prices would rise accordingly, and speculation would sooner be set in motion; and whilst we would not experience a sudden and extraordinary rise, prices would be maintained on a high level.

836. You say that, for some reason or other, in December and January prices have been lowest?

Yes.

837. Looking at our present state of ignorance, are there any circumstances which would lead you to think, while we remain in the same ignorance, that those are probably the months in which the price would be the lowest?

Yes; there are reasons to believe that in those months prices under ordinary circumstances would rule the lowest, because farmers have then generally larger quantities on hand, and they bring it freely to market; at the same time, if agricultural statistics were to point out that prices during the whole year are likely to rule higher than immediately after the harvest, the farmer and speculator would at once become acquainted with it; and the one would keep the grain back, and the other would give higher prices, and so would prevent prices ruling very low up to a very considerably advanced period. As it is, all on a sudden, the harvest may be found to have been very deficient; and instead of having abundance at home, we are at the last moment reduced to the necessity of obtaining from abroad very large quantities at any prices it can be had.

838. Looking at the months of December and January, are there not circumstances that exist now which are very likely to continue to exist, namely, that it is a time of year most convenient for the farmers to thrash for the purpose of getting straw, and a time of year when they also think it expedient to thrash for the purpose of selling to pay their rent?

Yes; at the same time all those circumstances would be modified had they the knowledge I have indicated. Some sacrifices would be made in other ways in order not to sell their grain, which, if kept a month longer, would fetch a much higher price.

839. Earl of Harrowby: Would not persons be more willing to make advances upon the farmers' produce, having better data for knowing their prospective value?

Yes; if they knew the farmer was likely to get considerably more for his grain next month than now, they would say, we would rather give you any help you want just now, but keep the grain to sell at a better price.

840. You would put into the hands of the public as early as possible, including the grower, that information which at present is confined to a few enterprising corn merchants, who think it very important for their own interests?

Certainly.

841. Lord Colchester: Does not it appear that for the 14 years, prices have always risen as the month of June approached?

Not always; in 1854 the highest price was in February; in 1844 in March; in 1847 in June; in 1842, 1849 and 1851 in July; in 1840 August; in 1841 August; in 1843 August; in 1850 August; in 1848 September; in 1845 November; in 1846 November; in 1853 November; and in 1852 December. The lowest was in 1841 in January; 1852 in January; 1845 in March; 1843 in April; 1850 in April; 1853 in May; 1848 in June; 1846 in August; 1854 in September; 1851 in October; 1840 in December; 1842 in December; 1847 in December; 1849 in December. Those are just the lowest prices in those months.

842. Lord Portman: In one year, September is the highest?

One only, in 1848.

843. Would that arise from that being the seed time?

I am not aware.

844. Lord Colchester: Would not anybody speculating in corn be inclined to purchase in December for the purpose of holding back?

They would certainly, if they knew that much quantity was required; but as we are not acquainted with what are likely to be our wants, buyers do not come to markets so freely when the prices rule low; afterwards it is found that the farmers have not much on hand, and so prices rise.

845. Lord Portman: Is it your opinion, that there is at present as large a number

of gentlemen engaged in the corn trade as corn factors as in the early part of your recollection?

I am not aware. Another interesting observation may be made as to the time employed during the oscillation of prices; for instance, it appears that on an average, the time employed in the decline or rise of prices, whatever it may be during the year, was in the 15 years already alluded to, 1840 to 1854, 5½ months; so taking 1840 from August to December, the price declined 13s. 2d. a quarter in four months; in the next year, from January to August, it rose 12s. 1d. in seven months; the next year it declined, from July to December, 17s. 5d. in five months, and progressively. The average of the whole would be 5½ months.

846. LORD HARROWBY: What inference do you draw from that?

It is important for this reason, that it shows the suddenness in which profits and losses take place in the grain trade; and as the extent of the fluctuation is often 50 or 100 per cent., it is very important to see how soon such are realized, and how soon prices are expected to rise or go down.

847. You mean to say the oscillations are more rapid?

The average oscillation is 5½ months, that is, the average of the times employed in the oscillations of all the years.

848. That gives more of a speculative character to the trade than would be the case if more complete knowledge were acquired?

Certainly; for instance, in 1852, when there was not much oscillation, the difference was from the highest to the lowest only 4s. 11d. over 11 months, and in 1847 the decline was 40s. 7d. in six months, showing the steadiness of the rise in the one case, and in the other a very rapid decline.

849. Both these operations, the rapidity in the one case, and the slowness in the other, took place under the same amount of knowledge as to the conditions of our own harvest?

Certainly; in 1847 the price rose rapidly to 102s. and then as rapidly fell down, because there was a prospect of a good harvest next year.

850. EARL OF STRADBROKE: Was not that in consequence of there being an abundant harvest on the ground in the month of August?

Yes.

851. EARL OF HARROWBY: Would not an earlier knowledge of the real prospect of the harvest tend to mitigate those oscillations, and spread them over a wider surface?

That just refers to the previous question: the rise would commence earlier, and as soon as we knew that we should want a greater quantity; so that the rise would spread over longer periods than at present.

852. EARL OF STRADBROKE: Probably the price would not arrive at so high a pitch?

Certainly not; it would bring in additional supplies in time, and we should never be under the necessity of suddenly going to other markets, and fetching the grain at whatever price we can have it, and at whatever freight; when we are so pressed we can only have what we want by paying 20 per cent. or 40 per cent. higher than we should have paid had we sent our orders cautiously in due time.

853. EARL OF HARROWBY: Do not the very high prices, which are sometimes arrived at under the present circumstances, rather go to the profit of bold speculators than of the farmers?

I think so; in many cases speculators may happen to lose more, perhaps, than they have gained by the suddenness of the fall. Some who are fortunate enough to stop in time get enormous profits; and others, again, who are entering into speculation, perhaps too late, or hold the grain too long in their hands, lose, perhaps, far more; so that it is a very great speculation altogether.

854. LORD PORTMAN: With regard to the necessarily speculative character of the trade in wheat, have you observed the state of the trade in the year 1854, and up to the present time in 1855?

Not particularly.

855. Are you aware of the extraordinary sudden changes which during the summer of last year took place in the price of corn?

Not in connexion with this inquiry.

856. Supposing the fact to be, that during the last twelve months the fluctuations had been quite extraordinary, sometimes there being a large rise, at another time a large fall, and at other times, week by week, and in parts of weeks, the fluctuation has been 1s. up and 1s. down; are you of opinion that supplying agricultural statistics in the way which you suggest would tend to relieve all parties from the extraordinary hazard of speculation which is consequent upon such a state of things?

Partly. I do not think agricultural statistics would cure all the evils, because it would still be dependent upon other contingencies, such as the war with Russia, which would materially alter the circumstances. If we had the knowledge that we want 10,000,000 quarters, and we are likely to get it from foreign countries, and if other circumstances happen that we cannot get it, and it is uncertain how far we may be able to get it, that uncertainty would still cause the prices to fluctuate.

857. Would not the uncertainty be diminished if we knew the quantity of acres of wheat grown in this country?

To a certain extent.

103A–B. Debate on Limited Liability (1856)

Hansard, 3/CXL/123–138.

103A. Speech of Robert Lowe, vice-president of the council (1 February)

. . . It seems, then, upon the opinion of very competent witnesses, that these Acts, so far from having been a means of preventing fraud, have only afforded facilities for its commission, because fraudulent persons have availed themselves of the sort of *prestige* which is gained among ignorant people by a presumed association with the Government, and have announced companies as "established by Act of Parliament," or as "provisionally registered," and have thus given them a colour of respectability which their own merits would not obtain. It therefore appears to me that when the Government attempt, by a system of artificial restraints, to test the worth of any commercial undertaking, they endeavour to do what they are not able to accomplish. Indeed, they really have not the means of effecting such an object. The formal restraints which they devise will be complied with by the honest trader, who requires no coercion, and will be evaded by the fraudulent, who laughs at such restraints. But not only do these provisions prove nugatory–they serve as traps to the unwary. They give credit to unsound and unsubstantial concerns, and in a great degree facilitate those very frauds which they were intended to prevent.

Having now described the Acts which we propose to repeal–for the proposition of the Government is to repeal the Joint-Stock Companies Act and the Limited Liability Act of last Session–it may save time if, before I state the details of the measure which I shall ask leave to introduce, I explain as briefly as I can the principles upon which we believe that future legislation should be based. We entirely repudiate as the basis of legislation the principle upon which the present Joint-Stock Companies Act is founded–that it is in the power of the Government to prevent the institution of Fraudulent companies. We do not believe that it is in the power of the Government to supersede the vigilance of individuals, who are actuated by the strongest personal interests to detect these frauds; and, although I do not mean to say that many frauds will not still continue to occur, I believe that is a necessary incident of a large commercial society, and that it is an evil which cannot be met or cured by way of anticipation by any legal enactment whatever. I do not think it is a fair or right principle to embarrass, perhaps, a hundred honest, sound, *bona fide* concerns, in the vain and futile effort to correct the hundred-and-first, which may be of a contrary character. I think that, in such a case, with the view of doing a little good, you would do enormous harm, and you would set up a principle inimical to the well-being of civilised society: for, unless we deal with each other upon some presumption of confidence–unless we assume that a man is honest until he is proved to be a rogue–the disruption of human society must necessarily follow. Fraud and wickedness are not to be presumed in individuals. Why, then, when individuals are united together in society, should fraud and wickedness be presumed in those societies, which, after all, are but an aggregate of individuals, but individuals in the case of each of whom there is the presumption of innocence? We must base these laws upon the principle by which human transactions are guided, and the rule upon which men in business everywhere act is that persons are to be treated with confidence until something is proved against their character. The commercial intercourse of countries and of this great city and empire could not go on if a contrary rule were adopted. I may further observe that these restraints upon the creation or institution of commercial concerns tend very much to delay, and in such matters delay is fraught with danger. While a company is inchoate –before it is formed–the rights of parties are ill defined, and rest upon no strong or assured basis. That is, no doubt, the evil which was intended to be remedied by provisional registration, but I take it that such an evil is not to be cured by law. Rights in incipient companies are undefined, because men do not know what their rights are, and therefore cannot define them; and they, as in the case of provisional committee-men, often incur responsibilities unknowingly and are plunged into difficulties and embarrassments which they would have avoided had they been able to form their companies at once, and to proceed immediately to action. The condition of monetary affairs in which a company has been formed, perhaps, passes away, and it has to be organised in circumstances under which probably no one would have thought of establishing it; or those by whom the company has been projected are in a difficulty whether to abandon the undertaking and to return the money, or to attempt to carry it on. Every man of business must know that any delay in the formation of a company is frequently attended with such results. It is not for any fancied security, for any supposed advantage, that we ought to lay restrictions on the freedom of mankind in matters like these; and so far as we have yet gone, it would be impossible to show anything that comes near to a necessity for the imposition of such restrictions. The only ground on which you can defend such restriction is that it prevents fraud, which you have no right to assume; or that it secures stability, which it is impossible by any Government regulations whatever to secure. I shall now proceed to consider the nature of the restrictions imposed upon companies, and to show how little validity they have either in fact or in argument; and, in the first place, with respect to the paying up of a certain amount of capital. I admit that in the case of railway companies the principle of enforcing the paying up of a certain amount of capital is a good one, because it affords a protection to the public–it is in the nature of a deposit on the purchase of an estate; and the capital is ready for the purchase of property if required, and, if not, it is there to be returned to the depositors if the concern is not carried out; and it is only reasonable that men who come to Parliament, asking that powers to take the property of their neighbours, should give evidence of their sincerity by paying up a portion of the amount required. But the case is quite different with regard to other concerns. Taking the Limited Liability Act as it now stands, it is required that 20 per cent of the amount subscribed shall be paid up, and that the fact of such payment having been made shall be proved by a declaration made by two of the promoters. Now, in the case of *bona fide* companies I can imagine nothing more embarrassing than this. It involves such companies in a great deal of difficulty; and I have strong complaints from various quarters of the trouble and embarrassment which have been experienced in forming *bona fide* companies from this cause alone. This provision was not meant to hit the honest, but the fraudulent; but it is evident that fraudulent companies can easily evade it, for they have nothing more to do than to get two of their promoters to make a declaration to the effect that the amount of capital required by the Statute has been subscribed–it is, as Hamlet says, "as easy as lying,"–it is only required that the declaration shall be made, no power being given to inquire whether it really has been subscribed or not. So that while you are annoying and embarrassing *bona fide* concerns, you are not in the least degree placing a check upon those that are fraudulent. On the contrary, if they succeed in satisfying the Government requisitions, they obtain a spurious merit to which they are by no means entitled. By this enactment also you are taking the business of people out of their own hands. It is often a disadvantage to a concern to start with a great amount of paid-up capital. Sometimes, for example, the money may be wanted for the purchase of mines, but a long time may elapse before such a purchase can be concluded. What worse thing can you do for a company in such a case than to require that it should pay up a large portion of its capital? It is highly injurious in two ways. In the first place, it suggests to the directors a temptation to steal. They have got the money and do not know what to do with it, and in such cases it is apt to stick to people's fingers. In the second place, it very often perpetuates the existence of unsound and unwise concerns after the fallacies on which they may have been based have been found out; whereas, if it had had a small capital it would have been wound up at once: those who have the money and are, perhaps, making a good thing of it, think it would be sparing the Egyptians to return it, and thus they go on employing the capital of the shareholders, till it is entirely consumed. I shall say no more on the subject of capital being required to be paid up, as I think I have said sufficient to show that it gives no safety or security to the companies on whom it is imposed. But there is another point on which I have the misfortune to differ from some Gentlemen in this House, for whose opinions I entertain the greatest respect, to which I shall for a moment advert. There are many who would not require companies to pay up a certain amount of capital who yet think it necessary that this House should fix the amount of shares. Now the old Joint-Stock Companies Act, with all its faults, did not fix the amount of shares. Such an interference is wholly unnecessary, and would be productive of evil. I do not think it any part of the business of the Legislature to define whether shares shall be large or small. What presses strongly on my mind, and is with me one of the most powerful arguments against it, is that these small shares are much desired by the poor, and that there are many things in which they take an interest, and with regard to which it would be desirable to obtain their co-operation. There are various enterprises that they would be inclined to connect themselves with; but if you fix a large amount for shares, this natural wish it would be impossible to realise. I have in my possession letters from persons of that class who are desirous to establish, for example, a cotton-mill by means of a company with £1 shares. I do not say whether such a scheme as that will succeed or not. I am afraid these co-operative undertakings have not been, generally speaking, prosperous. But, whether that be so or not, can we imagine a more impolitic law than that which permits associations to be formed by the rich, but denies them to the poor? While we allow those who are possessed of capital to establish companies for their mutual benefit, when contests take place between capital and wages, shall we forbid the workmen to enter upon the formation of companies for themselves, because we think it right to fix as the amount of shares a sum larger than they can possibly raise? Let them try the experiment, or they never will be satisfied; and be assured that there can be no more unjustifiable law than that which gives facilities to the rich and excludes the poor from combining in any matter of trade, or for any legitimate object that they may demand. Take as another example the truck system. We have had many Committees of the House on the truck system. What can be a more natural remedy for people who find that at the only shop to which they have access they are cheated, that they should join together their small earnings, in order to save themselves from the overcharge and the adulteration and all the oppressions to which they are subjected by setting up an opposition establishment? I shall deeply regret if it is not the policy of this House to support the measure which we are prepared to lay before it on this matter–a measure which I believe to be cast in a spirit of comprehensive liberality; or if any difficulty should be felt as to giving facilities to poor persons in the conduct of affairs of which they themselves may be expected to be the best judges. The only argument which I have heard against those small share companies is, that they will lead to gambling in shares. It is not impossible that this may to some extent be so; but if we were to refrain from legislation on all matters that might possibly lead to gambling, the consequences would be more comprehensive than at first sight might be imagined. On this principle we should begin by burning haystacks lest people should draw straws out of them, and bet upon their lengths. If we are to take away one man's rights or property for fear another should make a bad use of them, we should not, indeed, check the bad, but despoil and plunder the good, and give an unnatural extension to the principle inseparable from human society, which already imposes on the good some part of the penalty incurred by the misconduct of the bad.

I come now to another subject, the liberty of incorporation. It is usual to say that, as these companies come to the Legislature for favours and for privileges, we have a right to impose upon them what terms we choose–that we can make them submit to whatever restrictive law we like. Now, I protest against the use of the word 'privilege' in such a case as this. In matters of commerce and exchange, of buying and selling, and of contract, it is impossible that under a just Government there can be any privileges. All associations ought to be equal before the law, and there can be no greater injustice than for a Government to ask for any undue exactions from any association on the one hand, or to give to any of them advantages above their fellows on the other. But there is no privilege. A partnership with many members ought to be considered in the light of an individual, and it is for the advantage of the public that the incorporation takes place. It is a sort of legal monster that cannot, without the aid of law, comply with the requisitions of the courts of justice, and it is therefore not only for its own convenience, but for that of the public, that it should be incorporated, so that it may both sue and be sued in one single name. It is a matter of procedure more than anything else–it should be encouraged wherever the mischief is likely to arise–that is, wherever such an association is likely to be party to any legal proceedings. It should be held as one single person; and for that reason we should throw no obstacle in the way of incorporation, as it is for the interest of the public as much as for that of the company itself that it should take place. It is no privilege, but a right to be conceded, a state of mischief to be corrected; and it is necessary, because such a company is so numerous that it would be difficult otherwise to proceed against it. I have already observed, that previous to the incorporation of a company, it was neither wise nor right to require any of those restraints and safeguards which had been demanded on behalf of the public. I now propose to show, that the fact of a company being established on the principle of limited liability, does not strengthen the case in favour of those restraints and safeguards. What I said of incorporations may be applied to companies with a limited liability. It is not a question of privilege; if anything, it is a right, and upon that ground we gave our assent to the Act of last Session. The principle is the freedom of contract, and the right of unlimited association–the right of people to make what contracts they please on behalf of themselves, whether those contracts may appear to the Legislature beneficial or not, as long as they do not commit fraud, or otherwise act contrary to the general policy of the law. It is easy to make anything a privilege. Any right, the exercise of which is denied, becomes a privilege, the very term privilege arising from the negation of a natural right. The process is this–it begins with prohibition, then becomes a privilege, and last of all a right. Till 1825, the law prohibited the formation of Joint-stock companies. From that time to the present it has been a privilege; but now we propose to recognise it as a right. So with limited liability; at first it was prohibited. Then came the Statute of the 1st Victoria, which gave the Board of Trade power to relax the law in certain cases; and, lastly, the Act of last Session, extended the privileges, but still imposes restrictions. Having thus gone through the first and second stages–prohibition and privilege–we propose now to take our stand upon the only firm foundation on which the law can be placed–the right of individuals to use their own property, and make such contracts as they please, to associate in whatever form they think best, and to deal with their neighbours upon such terms as may be satisfactory to both parties. The restrictions hitherto placed upon trading companies were intended to effect one of two objects–either to secure the stability of the company, or to prevent fraud. Is there anything in the nature of companies with limited liability that should make them less stable or more fraudulent than unlimited companies? I should say the contrary. Fraudulent people will never form a limited liability company. Their own liability, of course, is a mere bagatelle, unworthy of their notice. What they desire is a large credit; and to obtain that they endeavour to get as many persons as possible pledged to the utmost extent of their fortunes. It is plain that to such people an unlimited liability is a hundred times more advantageous than a limited liability. A company formed on the principle of limited liability carries on the face of it something like prudence and caution. Its shareholders seem to say, "we have entered into a partnership, but it is impossible to tell what may happen, and since the company may fail, we will not risk all we possess in the undertaking." Such is the nature and composition of a company which is supposed to offer such facilities for fraudulent practices, that it ought to be subject to restrictions which can be justified only on the ground that fraud is actually intended. Nor have we more reason to doubt the stability of a limited than that of an unlimited company. Nobody can tell *a priori* to which the preference in that respect may belong. The stability of a company depends upon two things–character and capital. But the character of a limited company may be quite as good as that of an unlimited company, and its capital may be as large. People confound unlimited with infinite, and think that the capital of an unlimited company must be large because it is all the shareholders have. There could not be a greater mistake. A limited company may have a capital of one or two millions; while an unlimited company may not be worth a thousand pounds. The capital of the latter is raised with difficulty; that of the former, owing to the terms of the subscription, will often be larger, and the temptation to borrow money less. Hence it follows that the limited may often be more stable than the unlimited company. My object at present is not to urge the adoption of limited liability. I am arguing in favour of human liberty–that people may be permitted to deal how, with whom they choose, without the officious interference of the State; and my opinion will not be shaken even though very few limited companies be established. Every man has a right to choose for himself between the two principles, and it is ill-advised legislation which steps in between him and the exercise of that right. It is right the experiment should be tried, and, in my judgment, the principle we should adopt is this,–not to throw the slightest obstacle in the way of limited companies being formed–because the effect of that would be to arrest ninety-nine good schemes in order that the bad hundredth might be prevented; but to allow them all to come into existence, and when difficulties arise to arm the courts of justice with sufficient powers to check extravagance or roguery in the management of companies, and to save them from the wreck in which they may be involved. That is the only way in which the Legislature should interfere, with the single exception–a very essential one–of giving the greatest publicity to the affairs of such companies, that everyone may know on what grounds he is dealing.

I now come to explain the provisions of the Bill which I propose to introduce. The Acts we propose to repeal are the Joint-Stock Companies Act, the Act amending the same, and the Winding-up Acts, the Limited Liability Act of last Session. The new Bill has a double principle–compulsory and permissive. The compulsory clauses provide that all partnerships consisting of more than twenty members, and established for purposes of gain or profit, shall be incorporated for the benefit of the public, and in order that any legal proceedings in which they may be engaged may not be unnecessarily embarrassed by the number of partners. By the second part of the Bill–the permissive clauses–all partnerships or associations consisting of more than six, and less than twenty members, having gain and profit for their object, and all associations not having gain or profit for their object, but consisting of upwards of six members, may avail themselves of the benefits of this Act. These last associations may adopt it or not as they please. So that the effect of what I propose is, that associations having gain or profit for their object, and consisting of more than twenty members, must adopt the provisions of the Bill; that associations not consisting of more than six members, and having gain or profit for their object, may adopt them or not; and that all other associations, whether of an educational or religious character, or for whatever purpose they may be formed, if they consist of more than six members, may have the same option. There are two classes of companies omitted from the Bill. I say so with regret, but it has been done in adherence to the principle on which the measure has been framed–to confine ourselves to the amendment of the Joint-Stock Companies Act, and to the application of limited liability to large and small partnerships in the most efficient manner, without interfering in difficult questions, such as those connected with banks. Banking companies have an act of their own, and therefore we do not propose to include them in the present Bill;

though, individually, I should have wished to apply the same law to all companies, and I hope the day will soon arrive when it will be so. The second exception, which I also regret, relates to insurance companies, which have been omitted in deference to opinions that we are bound to respect. I do not think that the provisions of the Bill will ever be applicable to companies established on the principle of mutual assurance, which are not Joint-stock companies at all; but I am convinced they might be applied with advantage to other kinds of assurance companies. We have omitted them, however, in deference to the opinion of a Select Committee of this House, which sat on the subject in 1853, and which declared in its report that the business of assurance companies differed so much from that of ordinary companies that it was desirable to repeal all the provisions of the Joint-Stock Companies Act, so far as they related to assurance societies, and to deal with them in a separate measure. Now, supposing a company to be in the course of formation under this Bill, I will now state how it is to obtain complete registration. We abolish the present system of registration, and every company affected by the Act is to sign a document which they call in America "a certificate of registration," but which we propose to call a "memorandum of association." That document is to be signed by at least seven shareholders; it is to contain the name of the proposed company; to state the object of the company; whether it is to be limited or unlimited as regards liability; the number of shares into which the capital is to be divided; and, if the company is limited, the word 'limited' is to appear. That document is to be filed with the Registrar; and upon its being filed the company is to be entitled to registration, from which it follows that it is incorporated and possesses all the privileges of a corporation, with the right of suing and being sued. The next step relates to the deed of settlement. We have prepared and appended, in the schedule of the Act, the by-laws of a company, which we call the "articles of association." We have taken them from the ordinary rules adopted in Joint-stock companies, and have applied to them the principles of the Railway Consolidation Act. When those articles appear to the persons who have signed the articles of association to be applicable to the company, they may be adopted bodily without any expense; but if it should turn out that those rules are not applicable to a particular company, the company will have the power of filing a document with their memorandum of association, either specifying the whole code which they have agreed upon, or enumerating such of the rules as they do not adopt, and giving those which they substitute for them. There is no compulsion, therefore, in the matter. We leave companies to form their constitutions as they please; but if the constitution provided by the Act be suitable to the promoters, they will have the advantage of being able to adopt it without expense. Next, as to the register of shareholders. The present mode of attempting to keep a register by means of the Public Registrar has, as hon. Gentlemen are no doubt aware, entirely failed. We propose, therefore, that the companies shall be compelled, themselves, under penalties, to keep a register of their own shareholders, which shall be accessible to the public at reasonable hours; and that that register shall be conclusive evidence as to who is a shareholder and who is not, together with the transfer of the shares to be signed by the transferee, much in the same manner as in railway companies. This will enable us to get rid of all those embarrassing questions as to what constitutes a contributor, which are frequently found to be so perplexing in winding-up cases. The clauses as to the management of the company I pass over, because the management we leave to the companies themselves. Having given them a pattern the State leaves them to manage their own affairs and has no desire to force on these little republics any particular constitution. One thing, indeed, will be required in reference to publicity, namely that a balance sheet, which shall contain certain items, shall be filed every year with the Registrar of Companies; this, I think, may be fairly demanded from companies who will be saved so much trouble and expense; and, as we prescribe a form, we shall at least succeed in obtaining an uniform sheet, so that the shareholders will be able to compare the accounts of succeeding years, and to gather information from them, which, from the practice too extensively prevailing of rendering a differently-framed balance-sheet every year, they are now unable to collect. I now come to a new clause, which I hope may be found to be of great benefit to companies in distress. It shall be lawful for shareholders holding one-fifth part of the shares of any company to apply to the Board of Trade, at their own expense, to have the affairs of the company inspected; and the Board of Trade may, according to their discretion, appoint inspectors to investigate the affairs of the company, and to make a report, which report shall be the property of the persons who pay for it. This proceeding will not necessarily be attended with any publicity. It is borrowed in some degree from the New York code; but there is this difference, that in New York the application is made to a court of justice, and therefore involves, as a matter of course, publicity and expense; whereas we propose that the application should be to the discretion of the Board of Trade, and it will not necessarily entail either the one or the other. This is a very important provision, and it will do more, I believe, to remove the real grievances under which shareholders labour than any restrictions that could be imposed upon the formation of companies. We propose to repeal the existing Winding-up Act, which has not worked very satisfactorily, and to replace that Act by a new one. The following are the terms upon which we propose by this Bill that a company may be wound up:–A company may be wound up by the Court whenever it is unable to pay its debts, or whenever such winding-up shall be for the benefit of the shareholders. It shall be taken to be "for the benefit of the shareholders" whenever three-fourths in number of the shareholders, holding half the capital, declare so in public meeting assembled; whenever the company does not commence or suspends its business for the space of a whole year; whenever the shareholders are reduced in number to less than seven; or whenever it is declared by the Court that it is for the interest of the shareholders, and not injurious to the public, that the company should be wound up; and a company shall be taken to be "unable to pay its debts" whenever it neglects for three weeks to pay a debt with respect to which a notice has been served, or whenever execution has issued upon a judgment obtained against it. The application for winding up is to be by petition. Both parties will appear before the Court in the first instance; and the Court will be empowered to order either that the company be wound up absolutely, or that it shall be wound up unless its debts be paid within a certain time.

This may appear to be a rather summary proceeding against companies; but it must be remembered that we propose to abolish the right of suing individual members of companies, and to require that suits shall be only brought against the companies themselves. In fact, we make these companies corporations, and we endow them with the attributes of corporations. The amount of debt which is fixed upon to warrant such a proceeding is £50. This is an alteration of the law of considerable importance, and I think that it is justified by these considerations: – Suppose a company of large capital – it is clearly for the interest of everybody that, if it cannot pay a debt of £50 it should be wound up, and I think that there can be no harm in winding up a company so summarily when we look at the analogy of the bankrupt laws. The fact of lying in prison for twenty-one days without paying a debt is an act of bankruptcy; and we propose that the non-payment of a debt for three weeks after notice shall be an act of bankruptcy in the case of a company. The principle on which the concerns of individuals are taken out of their own hands and placed in the hands of assignees is this – that when a man is unable to pay his creditors in full they have a kind of joint interest in him; the failure of their absolute rights sets up relative rights, and makes them a sort of *quasi* corporation. But in the case of a company not only the creditors, but the shareholders also become a *quasi* corporation – beside a dividend to be paid there may be also a call to be made – and the principle of the bankruptcy law would then require a double application. In the case of companies, with either limited or unlimited liability, it is desirable for the general good that a creditor should be prevented from the assertion of his private rights when the whole body of creditors have an equal interest in recovering from the company. Under the circumstances, therefore, I apprehend it would be wise to deprive parties of the power which they now possess of suing individual members of the corporation; but in order to compensate for that, we ought to give them a more summary and compulsory remedy against the companies in their corporate capacity, and to make the penalty of the non-payment of a debt to be nothing less than the extinction of the company itself. It is also proposed that a company should have the power of voluntarily winding up its affairs whenever three-fourths in number of the shareholders, assembled at any extraordinary meeting held for that purpose, and holding not less than one-half in the capital of the company, should pass a resolution for that purpose. And it is likewise proposed to give existing companies the power of bringing themselves under the operation of this Bill by means of a resolution agreed to by three-fourths of the shareholders, so that there shall be one uniform law with respect to such companies, whether formed before or subsequent to this Act.

I understand that the hon. Member for Paisley (Mr. Hastie), who was such a strenuous opponent of the Bill of last Session, has expressed a wish to know to what extent the Limited Liability Act has been made available in the commercial world. I am afraid I should find it difficult to satisfy the hon. Gentleman by any answer I may give him. Suppose I were to say that very few companies have taken the benefit of the Act, the reply of the hon. Gentleman, no doubt, would immediately be – "Yes, so I prophesied; your wretched principle has already broken down." If, on the other hand, I were to tell the hon. Gentleman that a great many parties have availed themselves of the provisions of that Act, he would, no doubt, with equal earnestness exclaim–"Here is the beginning of the end; here are the foundations laid of vast commercial ruin!" Therefore, Sir, I cannot give the hon. Gentleman any satisfaction as to the operation of that Act. But I will state to the House what has been done. The whole number of companies which have applied to be registered under the Act is not less than 142; of these eight have obtained limited liability; but the recent commercial crisis has prevented many of them from paying up their capital.

Having, Sir, now gone through the various provisions of this Bill, I would observe that, if any hon. Gentleman thinks that in this measure Her Majesty's Government has gone too far in leaving men to their own individual will and wishes, and has done in the way of Government interference too little, I hope he will remember this–that, among all the Governments that ever existed in the world, probably there has never been one which erred on the side of giving too much freedom to commerce. In the glorious reign of Louis XIV., when Racine, Corneille, Fenelon, and Boussuet flourished and adorned the age, the French Government were so grossly ignorant of the true principles of commerce that it actually prohibited the manufacture of goods, except of certain patterns–more especially of textile fabrics; and those things which were not made according to the prescribed form were nailed to the public gallows. That ought to teach us how cautious we should be in placing confidence in, or being led by, the authority of any man, apart from principle; it ought to teach us how much those matters which we have been in the habit of regarding as sure and certain are the effects only of prejudice; and it ought to make us more anxious to do honour to the principles on which all human transactions are founded. When the political economists say "*Laissez faire*," they do not mean to say, "Leave all matters to blind chance; let everything go on as it may." What they mean by *laissez faire* is, that we are not to interfere with human laws where other laws so much wiser already exist. Man, Sir, with his free will, his caprices, and his errors, is as much under the rule and government of a natural law as the planet in its orbit, or as water, which always seeks its level. Those laws, planned by Infinite sagacity, have the power of correcting and of compensating errors–one extreme invariably producing another–dearness producing cheapness and cheapness dearness; and thus the great machine of society is constantly kept oscillating to its centre. These laws are not made by a House of Commons; and before any Legislature steps in and attempts to correct them, it would be well that it should consider whether any Legislature can interfere and devise a better code than that which was framed before the first rude essays of mankind, to mould their collective will into a law. Who could have imagined it possible that a state of society resting on the most unlimited and unfettered liberty of action, where everything may be supposed to be subject to free will and arbitrary discretion–would tend more to the prosperity and happiness of man than the most mature decrees of senates and of States? These are the wonders of the science of political economy, and we should do well to profit by the lesson which that science has taught. That lesson is this–To interfere with and abridge men's liberty, and to undertake to do for them what they can do for themselves, is really lulling their vigilance to sleep, and depriving them of that safeguard which Providence intended for them, and helping fraudulent men to mislead and delude them. The right hon. Gentleman concluded by moving to resolve–

> "That the Chairman be directed to move the House, That leave be given to bring in a Bill to amend the Law of Partnership.
>
> "That the Chairman be directed to move the House, That leave be given to bring in a Bill for the incorporation and regulation of Joint-Stock Companies and other Associations."

103B. Protest of Lords Overstone and Mounteagle in the Lords

Hansard 3/CXLIII/1490-1493.

PROTEST

Die Lunae, 16 Junii, 1856. Against the Second Reading of the Joint-Stock Companies Bill

DISSENTIENT.–"1. Because the measure is wholly unnecessary; inasmuch as every concern has the means of limiting its liability by trading upon its own capital, and not upon the borrowed capital of others. Liability is not necessarily incident to trading or to the application of capital to the pursuits of industry; it is the result of taking credit or trading upon borrowed capital. Limited liability, therefore, is a measure of protection, not to the capitalist, great or small, but to the speculator, who wishes to trade for his own profit but with the capital, and at the risk of others.

"2. Because the principle of limited liability is antagonistic to, and will probably prove seriously destructive of, the sober and substantial virtues of the mercantile character. By weakening in the mind of the trader the sense of full responsibility for the consequences of all his actions, and limiting the obligation which now rests upon him to return in full all that he has borrowed from others, the general tone of commercial morality must be deteriorated. By limiting the unfortunate consequences of failure, while no corresponding limitation is placed upon the gains which may attend success, the due equipoise between the restraints and the stimulants to enterprise and speculation, upon which depend the solidity and safety of the commercial system, must be disturbed. By enabling parties to put a fixed limit to the amount of possible loss the chief incentive to caution or vigilance in the conduct of business will be taken away or seriously weakened, while by leaving the hope of gain unrestricted and indefinite, a gambling principle will be introduced into commercial transactions, and the risks of trade will assimilate themselves to the chances of the lottery-wheel rather than to what they now are, the legitimate results of hopeful industry and cautious enterprise.

"3. Because the measure in its present form, unaccompanied by safeguards or any attempt to obviate the clear and acknowledged danger of abuses to which the principle of limited liability must be exposed, is not only in opposition to the Report of the Royal Commission appointed to inquire into the subject, but is contradictory to the practice and experience of every country in the world which has admitted the principle of limited liability into its commercial code.

"In every other country the privilege of limited liability is surrounded by restrictions which are intended to guard against the danger–first, of excessive and reckless enterprise, naturally generated by the sense of strict limitation of risk; and, second, of fraudulent abstraction under the form of interest or profits, of that specific and fixed amount of capital which is alone appropriated as the security of the honest creditor.

"These restrictions indicate the universal conviction of all other countries that against these sources of abuse it is necessary that some proper safeguard be provided. If it be deemed impossible to render such safeguards efficient and satisfactory, the conclusion necessarily arises that a measure ought not to be persisted in which does not admit of effectual protection against injustice to the honest creditor and injury to the public interests.

"4. Because the effect of the Bill will be to give legal protection, and, therefore, to hold out moral encouragement, to dishonest practices in trade.

"Profits in trade consist of interest upon capital, remuneration for labour and skill, and premium of insurance on risk. In proportion as the risk in any business is great profits are usually high; but of these high profits a large share is by every honest trader set aside as the premium reserved against high risks. An unfortunate tradesman coming before the Bankruptcy Court would not be very leniently dealt with should it appear that, carrying on a very riskful business, he had year by year spent all the great apparent profits, making no reserve out of them to meet the high risks he was incurring. Now, this is the very practice which this Bill directly sanctions, and therefore encourages.

"The object of the measure is to enable concerns to limit their liability to a certain fixed sum, which has no reference to the varying magnitude of the risks which they incur, or to the high profits which, through those risks, they are appropriating to themselves, but not reserving for the honest protection of their creditors.

"They are, in fact, appropriating and misapplying the premium of insurance, which, under the form of high profits, they year by year receive; and in this immoral course they will have the authority and sanction of the Bill.

"5. Because the tendency of the measure must be to encourage and promote the transference of capital from trading concerns now constituted, and conducted with the caution and prudence which the sense of unlimited liability necessarily generates, to joint-stock companies, trading with small paid up capitals, and embarking, under the protection of limited liability, upon risks which no person would otherwise venture to encounter. When loss occurs a heavy portion of it will be made to fall upon the unfortunate creditor, who deserves our sympathy, whilst the adventurers who ought to be the victims of their own reckless speculations will remain comparatively safe under the aegis of limited liability. Meanwhile the sober calculations and legitimate transactions of real trade will give way to a general spirit of speculation, in hazardous enterprise, and jobbing in shares–a state of things of which the history of 1824 and 1825 affords a practical illustration, and, at the same time, holds out a warning example.

"6. Because many very important advantages arise from the high moral character and commercial credit founded upon the full and punctual discharge of all its obligations which this country at present enjoys throughout the world. If the effect of the measure shall be, as is predicted by its supporters, to restrict rather than to increase credit, by filling the community with a mass of concerns notoriously undeserving of public confidence, the consequence must be serious injury to our commercial character abroad–a diminution of the confidence which other countries repose in the engagements of our merchants and traders–an interruption to the ease and freedom with which all our trading intercourse with the world is at present conducted–and, in the end, absolute pecuniary loss to the country.

"7. Because the measure is singularly inappropriate to the present state of this country as regards capital and enterprise.

"There is abundance of capital in this country. We are the lenders of our surplus capital to every nation of the world. Any sudden demand, any new opening for speculation is at once supplied with inexhaustible funds; whilst we are subject to the frequent recurrence of periods of undue and dangerous inflation of credit and speculation. When these periods occur, the tendency of the measure must be to extend and intensify these evils, by giving facility for the widespread introduction of Joint-stock Companies, reckless in their procedure because protected by limited liability, and filling the community with the instruments of gambling in the form of shares upon which little or nothing has been paid up. The real want of the country is competent and duly qualified men (in whom confidence is duly blended with caution, and the spirit of mercantile enterprise is regulated by experience and the sense of responsibility) to wield successfully the vast resources of capital and credit which the country is prepared to place at their command.

"The evil to the correction of which the Bill is apparently directed–namely, insufficient supply of capital to meet the demands of industry and enterprise–does not, in fact, exist; whilst the real difficulty is one which legislation cannot effectually remedy.

"8. Because the period chosen for the introduction of this measure is peculiarly unfavourable to the safety of the experiment. After a long-continued heavy drain of the precious metals from this country, the reflux has apparently commenced; a great accumulation of bullion may be reasonably anticipated. Under such circumstances, credit and a blind spirit of speculation are always developed to a dangerous extent. On the present occasion this danger will be rendered more formidable by the effect, the character and extent of which is yet to be ascertained, of the recent extraordinary discoveries of gold. The time is therefore approaching, according to all probability, at which the prudence and firmness of the community will, through the natural course of events, be subjected to a severe trial.

"At such a moment it is eminently inexpedient and dangerous to introduce a change in the law seriously affecting the mutual relation of the debtor and creditor interest, and which must, in the first instance at least, exercise a powerful influence on credit and speculation. Important changes of the laws which affect our monetary or commercial system, however sound may be the principles on which they rest, are almost invariably followed by rapid and excessive development, leading to temporary, but serious embarrassment.

"The crisis of 1825 was preceded by, and was intimately connected with, the rapid development of the warehousing system which resulted from the Acts passed in 1822.

"The crisis of 1847 followed closely upon the extensive reduction of import duties introduced by Sir R. Peel and the sudden outburst of the railway system.

"Experience, therefore, compels us to anticipate a similar crisis as the necessary result of the first development of that great change in our monetary and commercial system which is involved in this abrupt and unqualified introduction of the principle of limited liability.

"If this crisis occurs simultaneously with the effect of a strong influx of the precious metals on the return of peace, and of the recent extraordinary addition to the total amount of the precious metals through the gold discoveries, the firmness and prudence of the country may be subjected to a trial too powerful to be withstood, and an artificial expansion of credit may ensue, causing monetary embarrassment and great mercantile disasters.

"OVERSTONE,
"MOUNTEAGLE OF BRANDON."

104. Commercial crisis of 1857: Select Committee of 1857–1858 on Bank Acts and Commercial Distress

Parlty. Papers, 1857–8/v/pp. III–XVI.

1. THE ten years which have elapsed since the last Committee sat under the same Order of Reference, *viz.*, the Committee on Commercial Distress, which reported in 1848, have been marked by many circumstances of peculiar interest and importance. The foreign trade of the United Kingdom has in that period increased with a development unprecedented, perhaps, by any other instance in the history of the world. The exports, which before 1848 had never exceeded £60,110,000,–the amount which they attained in 1845,–have risen with little variation and with great rapidity; and in 1857, notwithstanding the severe commercial pressure which marked the latter portion of that year, they stood at £122,155,000.

2. In the year 1849, the newly discovered mines of California began to add perceptibly to the arrivals of gold; and in 1851, the supply was increased by the still more fertile discoveries in Australia. The following figures, for which your Committee are indebted to the authorities of the Bank, will show how important an addition appears to have been made to the circulating medium of the world from these new sources of supply.

ESTIMATED INCREASE of the European Stock of BULLION in Seven Years 1851–1856

	Imports from Producing Countries		*Exports to the East from Great Britain and Mediterranean*	
	Gold	*Silver*	*Gold*	*Silver*
	£	£	£	£
1851	8,654,000	4,076,000	102,000	1,716,000
1852	15,194,000	4,712,000	922,000	2,630,000
1853	22,435,000	4,355,000	974,000	5,559,000
1854	22,077,000	4,199,000	1,222,000	4,583,000
1855	19,875,000	3,717,000	1,192,000	7,934,000
1856	21,275,000	4,761,000	479,000	14,108,000
1857	21,366,000	4,050,000	529,000	20,146,000
	£130,876,000	29,870,000	5,420,000	56,676,000

GOLD:

		£
The total import of gold in seven years has been, say . .		130,000,000
The exports of gold bullion and British gold coin to India, China, Australia, the Cape, Brazils, the West Indies, United States, &c., may be taken at		22,500,000
Which would leave as the increase to the European Stock of Gold		107,500,000

SILVER:

The exports of silver to India and China have been	£56,676,000	
The imports from the producing countries	£29,870,000	
Making the amount of silver abstracted from the European stock		26,800,000
And the estimated increase in the European stock of bullion		£80,700,000

3. The remission of duties upon articles of necessity, and upon the raw materials of industry, and the great increase of trade to which your Committee have referred, were naturally attended by a very remarkable improvement in the comforts and consuming power of the people, as exhibited in the imports; and especially in the vast increase in the clearances of those articles which enter most materially into the consumption of the working classes. It is probable that to this cause ought chiefly to be attributed the great increase which is believed to have taken place in the circulating medium of the United Kingdom. Mr. Weguelin, a Member of the Committee, and the Governor of the Bank, stated to the Committee of 1857, that this increase was estimated by those in whose judgment the Bank Directors placed the greatest reliance,

at 30 per cent. in the six years then last elapsed. The total gold circulation of notes, which under the Acts of 1844 and 1845 are permitted to circulate, without being represented by bullion, retained for that purpose in the coffers of those who issue the notes is £31,623,995, of which £14,475,000 are issued by the Bank of England; £7,707,292 by the English country bankers; £3,087,209 by the Scotch and £6,354,494 by the Irish bankers.

4. With regard to bank notes, it is interesting here to observe, that in the smaller denominations, those, namely, which enter most into the retail transactions of the country, the number has considerably increased, concurrently with the increase of the gold circulation above referred to. The £5 and £10 notes of the Bank of England, which in 1851 were £9,362,000, had risen in 1856 to £10,680,000.

5. At the same time, for a reason which will presently be noticed, a great diminution has been observable in the use of notes from £200 and upwards.

6. The silver currency has in the same time increased as follows, *viz.*

Silver coin issued to the Public in excess of Receipts from the Public:

	£
1851	26,307
1852	420,418
1853	554,442
1854	36,803
1855	47,754
1856	289,142
1857	242,273

7. While this expansion of trade was in progress, and the precious metals received this remarkable addition, a new feature in the banking business of the country was observable. The joint stock banks in London entered more and more into competition with the private banks, and by their practice of allowing interest on deposits, began to accumulate vast amounts. On the 8th of June 1854, the private bankers of London admitted the joint stock banks to the arrangements of the clearing-house, and shortly afterwards the final clearing was adjusted in the Bank of England. The daily clearances are now effected by transfers in the accounts which the several banks keep in that establishment. In consequence of the adoption of this system, the large notes which the bankers formerly employed for the purpose of adjusting their accounts are no longer necessary. The diminution in the use of these notes is shown by the following figures:

Bank Notes of £200 to £1,000:

	£
1852	5,856,000
1857	3,241,000

8. Meanwhile the joint stock banks of London, now nine in number, have increased their deposits from £8,850,774 in 1847 to £43,100,724 in 1867, as shown

in their published accounts. The evidence given to your Committee leads to the inference that of this vast amount, a large part has been derived from sources not heretofore made available for this purpose; and that the practice of opening accounts and depositing money with bankers has extended to numerous classes who did not formerly employ their capital in that way. It is stated by Mr. Rodwell, the chairman of the Association of Private Country Bankers, and delegated by them to give evidence to your Committee, that in the neighbourhood of Ipswich this practice has lately increased fourfold among the farmers and shopkeepers of that district; that almost every farmer, even those paying only £50 per annum rent, now keep deposits with bankers. The aggregate of these deposits of course finds its way to the employments of trade, and especially gravitates to London, the centre of commercial activity, where it is employed first in the discount of bills, or in other advances to the customers of the London bankers. That large portion, however, for which the bankers themselves have no immediate demand passes into the hands of the bill-brokers, who give to the banker in return commercial bills already discounted by them for persons in London and in different parts of the country, as a security for the sum advanced by the banker. The bill-broker is responsible to the banker for payment of this money at call; and such is the magnitude of these transactions, that Mr. Neave, the present Governor of the Bank, stated in evidence, "We know that one broker had 5 millions, and we were led to believe that another had between 8 and 10 millions; there was one with 4, another with 3½, and a third above 8. I speak of deposits with the brokers."

9. It thus appears that since 1847 three most important circumstances have arisen, affecting the question referred to your Committee, *viz.*:

1. An unprecedented extension of our foreign trade.
2. An importation of gold and silver on a scale unknown in history since the period which immediately succeeded the first discovery of America; and,
3. A most remarkable development of the economy afforded by the practice of banking for the use and distribution of capital.

10. In the years which immediately succeeded the great commercial crisis of 1847–8, the natural effect of such a crisis on the minds of persons engaged in trade was exhibited, and for a time prudence and caution were the marked characteristics of the commercial world. The bullion in the Bank meanwhile accumulated, increasing, with little variation, until in July 1852 it amounted to £22,232,000. At this time the notes in the hands of the public ran to the unusually large amount of £23,380,000, yet scarcely exceeded the amount of bullion, while the reserve of notes in the banking department of the Bank of England was 12½ millions, and the minimum rate of interest two per cent.

11. The consequence of such a state of things was manifested in the year 1853, when the exports, which in 1852 had amounted to £78,076,000, rose to £98,933,000. The bullion at the same time declined, and was on the 22d October of that year £14,358,000, while the reserve went down to £5,604,000, and the minimum rate of interest rose to five per cent.

12. In March 1854 war was declared against Russia, and an expenditure of nearly

90 millions is estimated to have been incurred by England on this account. The foreign payments were largely made in specie, which to a great extent was hoarded in the East. Foreign loans were also contracted in London for the purposes of the war. The aggregate trade of the United Kingdom varied little. The Bank rate of discount was raised in May 1854 from 5 to 5½ per cent., and continued at that rate till August 3, when it was again reduced to 5. On the 5th April 1855 it was reduced to 4½, the bullion then standing at £15,079,000, and the reserve at £8,580,000. The bullion continued to rise, until in June it amounted to £18,169,000, and the reserve to £11,887,000. Before the end, however, of that year a great change occurred, and on the 27th December the bullion stood at £10,275,000, the reserve at £6,993,000, while the minimum rate of interest had been raised on 18 October to 6 per cent., for 60 days, and 7 per cent. for 95 days, at which rate it stood till the following May. The changes in the rate of discount which took place from April 1855 to March 1857 are thus stated by Mr. Weguelin:

> "I have here a list of the various changes in the rates, beginning at April 5th, 1855, when the minimum rate of discount for bills having not more than 95 days to run was 4½ per cent. On May 3d, it was reduced to 4 per cent. On June 14th, it was reduced again to 3½ per cent. On September 6th, it was raised to 4 per cent. On September 13th, to 4½ per cent. On September 27th, to 5 per cent. On October 4th, to 5½ per cent. The Committee will remark that very rapid rise in the rate of interest which was caused by the commercial demand for accommodation, and for the export of bullion, occurring at the same time with a considerable demand for bullion to supply the armies in the East. On the 18th of October the rate was 6 per cent. for bills having 60 days to run, and for bills having 96 days to run it was 7 per cent. In 1856, on the 22d of May it was reduced to 6 per cent., and on the 29th of May to 5 per cent., and on the 26th of June to 4½ per cent., the minimum rate. There then occurred a great demand, and the rate was raised by order of the Governor on October the 1st to 5 per cent. That was not on the ordinary weekly court day, but in the interval of the court. On October the 6th (which was again not on a court day, but on a Monday) the rate was raised to 6 per cent. for 60 days' bills, and to 7 per cent. for bills not having more than 95 days to run. On November the 13th, the minimum rate for bills of all descriptions having not more than 95 days to run was raised to 7 per cent. On December the 4th, it was reduced to 6½ per cent., and on December the 18th to 6 per cent., at which it now stands. Here is also an account of the variations with regard to temporary advances upon stock. The first recent deviation from the practice that temporary advances on stock and Exchequer Bills should be made at the Bank minimum rate ordinarily, and at a half per cent. below the minimum during the shuttings, seems to have occurred in July 1854, when Exchequer Bond scrip was in the market. The Bank minimum rate was then 5½ per cent.; temporary advances were made at 5 per cent., and advances were made on Exchequer Bond scrip at 4 per cent. I believe that was an especial arrangement at the time which had not much reference to the state of the money market. The term of those advances varied from 14 to 31 days. During the shutting for the dividends due in January 1856 the allowance of a half per cent.

on advances on stock, &c., was withdrawn, and no such advances have since been made at a rate below the Bank minimum. On the 8th of January 1856, the demand for advances chiefly on Turkish scrip and bonds continuing beyond the payment of the dividends, the term was contracted to 14 days. During the shutting for the April dividends this restriction was removed. After the April payment the general term was 14 days; but there does not appear to have been any restriction to that period. After the October payment the term was contracted to seven days; and on the 16th of October the Bank refused to advance on any Government securities except Exchequer Bills. About the 11th of November the Bank declined to re-discount bills having more than 30 days to run; that is bills which had been advanced upon by brokers. During the shutting for January, the usual course was resumed, without restriction as to stock or term. On the 9th of January 1857 the rate for advances on Government stocks and Exchequer Bills was raised to 6½ per cent., the rate on bills of exchange remaining at 6 per cent.; and this restriction remained in force till the present shutting. It is now 6 per cent. In addition to those restrictions, I may state that the Governors have placed certain restriction upon the business conducted through the discount brokers. In their business with them, when it suited the convenience of the Bank to have only short bills, they have limited their advances to the discount brokers to 30 days, or have insisted upon their bringing in bills not having more than 30 days to run; the object being to obtain such a command of resources constantly returning to the Bank reserve as should keep the Bank safe in that respect."

13. Down, therefore, to the close of the inquiry of 1857, the Bank of England had continued, under the Act of 1844, to conduct its business without difficulty. The rate of discount had been raised, and the *échéance* of bills shortened, as the drain for bullion appeared to the Directors to render these measures necessary from time to time. But neither the failure of the silk crop in Italy, with the bad harvests in France and other parts of Europe, and the commercial drain thence arising, nor the requirements of specie for the military service, nor both these causes combined, had occasioned any important derangement of our monetary system.

The course of trade may be collected from the exports of the years referred to, *viz.*:-

	£
1852	78,076,000
1853	98,933,000
1854	97,184,000
1855	95,688,000
1856	115,826,000
1857	122,155,000

These exports do not include shipments of stores in Government transports.

14. In the earlier part of the autumn of last year, the trade of the United Kingdom was generally considered to be in a sound and healthy state, and in the words of the Governor of the Bank, in reply to the following question,-

"Was there, in the month of August, any circumstance which caused you to be apprehensive of any reason for raising the rate of discount?-Not in the month of

August; things were then pretty stationary; the prospects of harvest were very good; there was no apprehension that commerce at that time was otherwise than sound. There were more far-seeing persons who considered that the great stimulus given by the war expenditure, which had created a very large consumption of goods imported from the East and other places, must now occasion some collapse, and still more those who observed that the merchants, notwithstanding the enhanced prices of produce, were nevertheless importing, as they had done successfully in the previous years. But the public certainly viewed trade as sound, and were little aware that a crisis of any sort was impending, far less that it was so near at hand."

15. In this state of things, the bullion standing at £10,606,000, the reserve at £6,296,000, and the minimum rate of discount at 5½ per cent., the Bank, on the 17th of August 1857, commenced a negotiation with the East India Company, which ended in a shipment of £1,000,000 in specie for the East. The general aspect of affairs continued without change until the 15th September, when the first tidings arrived of the great depreciation of railway securities in the United States, and immediately afterwards of the failure of a very important corporation, called the Ohio Life and Trust Company. Before 8th October the tidings from America had become very serious; news of the suspension of cash payments by the banks in Philadelphia and Baltimore were received; cotton bills were reduced to par, and bankers' drafts to 105; railroad securities were depreciated from 10 to 20 per cent.; the artisans were getting out of employment; and discounts ranged from 18 to 24 per cent. The transactions between America and England are so intimate, and so large, the declared value of British and Irish produce exported in 1856 to the United States having been £21,918,000, while the amount of securities held by English capitalists in America was by some persons estimated at £80,000,000, that this serious state of commercial disorder there could not but produce in this country great alarm.

16. In New York, 62 out of 63 banks suspended their cash payments. In Boston, Philadelphia, and Baltimore, the banks generally did the same. The effect of the American calamity fell with the greatest weight upon the persons engaged in trade with that country, and Liverpool, Glasgow, and London naturally exhibited the first evidences of pressure. On the 27th October the Borough Bank of Liverpool closed its doors, and on the 7th November the great commercial house of Messrs. Dennistoun & Co. suspended payment. The Western Bank of Scotland failed on the 9th November, and on the 11th the City of Glasgow Bank suspended its payments, which it has since resumed. The Northumberland and Durham District Bank failed on the 26th, and on the 17th the Wolverhampton Bank for a time suspended payment.

17. Great alarm naturally prevailed in London, the centre of all the monetary transactions of the world. Vast sums deposited with the joint stock banks, at interests, and employed directly by themselves, or by the bill brokers, in addition to other monies deposited by their other customers, were chiefly held at call; and the bill brokers are stated to have carried on their enormous transactions without any cash reserve; relying on the run off of their bills falling due, or in extremity, on the power of obtaining advances from the Bank of England on the security of bills under

discount. The inevitable result of this system, at a time of commercial pressure and alarm, was, that the banks limited their discounts almost exclusively to their own customers, and began to add to their reserves both in their own tills and at the Bank of England. It is well known that a periodical disturbance in the reserve of notes at the Bank of England occurs regularly at the time when the dividends upon the National Debt are paid. Interesting information will be found in the evidence of 1857 as to the effect of this disturbance in aggravating the panic of 1847. It had no such effect last year. By the 24th October that periodical disturbance was at an end. The public deposits also were in a satisfactory state, amounting to £4,862,000. It is interesting to observe, with regard to the private deposits, that the causes to which your Committee have above referred, as affecting other bankers, tend to increase the balances in the Bank of England, the bank of last resort at a time of panic. Thus, for example, the deposits of the London bankers, which in ordinary times average about £3,000,000, continued to rise during the commercial pressure, and amounted on the 12th November to £5,458,000. The bill brokers were compelled to resort to that establishment for assistance; and that to so great an extent, that the principal house went to the Bank to ask whether they could obtain discount to an indefinite amount, and actually received, on one day, the day on which the Treasury Letter was issued, no less a sum than £700,000. Two discount houses failed. Speaking of the general discount market, the Governor of the Bank stated: "Discounts almost entirely ceased in London, except at the Bank of England."

18. It is manifest, therefore, that in this emergency everything depended on the Bank of England; and it appears to your Committee that the proceedings of that establishment were not characterised by any want of foresight or of vigour. On the 16th July, however, before any indications of the coming storm were visible in any quarter, the bullion read £11,242,000, the reserve £6,408,000, the discounts and advances £7,632,000, and the Directors reduced the rate of interest from 6 to 5½ per cent. On the 8th October, after the receipt of the American intelligence above referred to, the bullion was £9,751,000, the reserve £4,931,000, the discounts and advances £11,648,000, and the rate of interest was raised again to 6 per cent. Four days afterwards, the rate of interest was raised again to 7. The causes of this step are thus stated by the Governor:–

"Then four days afterwards there was another change?–Yes, on the 12th. After having raised the rate to 6 per cent. we thought it necessary to give a guarded caution to our agents, showing that we began to be a little uneasy. The rate at Hamburgh was 7¾; American discounts then were greatly higher. We also about that time were made aware that the East India Company would want £1,000,000 specie for shipment. The gold was then being taken for New York; we consequently raised the rate of interest under those circumstances to 7 per cent.

"The bullion which was wanted for the East, being silver, was to be purchased by the export of gold; that gold to be exchanged for silver upon the continent of Europe, which silver was to be sent to the East?–That was the effect of it; the exports to India were very large each month; but as they were in silver, of course that silver had to be purchased on the Continent or imported from America.

"I think it was about the 12th of October that you were first apprehensive about the Western Bank of Scotland?–Yes; we had no direct application at that time, but there were rumours, and we had intimations which made us aware that they were in difficulties."

19. On the 19th October, the news from America continuing still more unfavourable, there were numerous failures in this country. The bullion had gone down to £8,991,000 and the reserve to £4,115,000, and the rate of interest was raised to 8 per cent. At this time the Bank of France, which in one week had lost a million sterling, raised the rate to 7½, Hamburgh to 9. £.300,000 in gold had left Liverpool for America.

20. At this juncture negotiations took place for sustaining the Borough Bank of Liverpool and the Western Bank of Scotland, which eventually failed, under the circumstances related by the Governor of the Bank.

21. There was great uneasiness out of doors (*i.e.* in London), and the Bank had an application from the principal discount house for an assurance, that if it was necessary the Bank of England would give them any loans they might require. That application was made on the 28th October. There were also inquiries for assistance from other Scotch banks; and on the 30th October there was an express for 50,000 sovereigns for a bank in Scotland, part of £170,000, and £80,000 for Ireland. The first shipment of silver by the East India Company then took place. Under these circumstances the rate of discount was raised, on November 5th, to 9 per cent.

22. Between the 5th November and the 9th, an English bank received assistance from the Bank of England; the failure of Dennistoun's house for acceptance due upon nearly 2 millions occurred, and the Western Bank failed on the 9th. Failures in London were on the increase. At this time (as was natural) the purchases and sales of stock in the funds were enormous. The transfers were much beyond what they had ever been before. The bullion had sunk to £7,719,000, and the reserve to £2,834,000. On the 9th the rate was raised to 10 per cent.

23. On the 10th November, a leading discount house applied to the Bank of England for £400,000. The Bank of France raised its rate to 8, 9, and 10 per cent. for the three different months. There was another English bank assisted. The City of Glasgow Bank suspended payment. The discounts for that day at the Bank of England rose to £1,126,000. The demand for Ireland was recommencing, and on the 10th and 11th alone the gold sent to Scotland was upwards of £1,000,000. On the 11th, Sanderson & Co., the large bill brokers, stopped payment; their deposits were supposed to be £3,500,000. There was also an additional supply of gold required for the banks in Scotland. On the 12th, the discounts at the Bank exceeded two millions. The following figures sufficiently exhibit the result of the foregoing operations; *viz.*: –

	Bullion	*Reserve*	*Discounts and Advances*
	£m.	£m.	£m.
10.	7,411	2,420	14,803
11.	6,666	1,462	15,947
12.	6,524	581	18,044

24. The Government Letter was issued on the 12th, and was in the following terms:–

"Gentlemen, Downing-street, 12 November 1857.

"HER Majesty's Government have observed with great concern the serious consequences which have ensued from the recent failure of certain Joint Stock Banks in England and Scotland, as well as of certain large mercantile firms, chiefly connected with the American trade. The discredit and distrust which have resulted from these events, and the withdrawal of a large amount of the paper circulation authorised by the existing Bank Acts, appear to Her Majesty's Government to render it necessary for them to inform the Directors of the Bank of England, that if they should be unable in the present emergency to meet the demands for discounts and advances upon approved securities without exceeding the limits of their circulation prescribed by the Act of 1844, the Government will be prepared to propose to Parliament, upon its meeting, a Bill of Indemnity for any excess so issued.

"In order to prevent this temporary relaxation of the law being extended beyond the actual necessities of the occasion, Her Majesty's Government are of opinion that the Bank terms of discount should not be reduced below their present rate.

"Her Majesty's Government reserve for future consideration the appropriation of any profits which may arise upon issues in excess of the statutory amount.

"Her Majesty's Government are fully impressed with the importance of maintaining the letter of the law, even in a time of considerable mercantile difficulty; but they believe that, for the removal of apprehensions which have checked the course of monetary transactions, such a measure as is now contemplated has become necessary, and they rely upon the discretion and prudence of the Directors for confining its operation within the strict limits of the exigencies of the case.

"We have, &c.
(signed) Palmerston.
G. C. Lewis."

"To the Governor and Deputy-Governor
of the Bank of England."

25. Whatever effect this letter may have had in other ways in calming the public mind, and so tending to mitigate the severity of the pressure, it did not immediately diminish the demand for discounts and advances. This continued to increase until 21st November, on which day the Bank had advanced in discounts £21,600,000, a sum exceeding the whole amount of their deposits, both public and private; a sum nearly three-fold the amount of their advances in July, when the rate was reduced to 5½ per cent., and more than double what they had advanced on the 27th October, when the first bank failed. Half of these loans were made to the bill brokers, and were partly made upon securities which, under other circumstances, the Bank would have been unwilling to accept. They were made for the purpose of sustaining commercial credit in a period of extreme pressure.

26. The letter was issued on the 12th November, but whilst in 1847 it was not found necessary for the Bank Directors to avail themselves of the permission so given them to exceed the limits imposed by law, that necessity in this instance actually arose. An issue to the extent of £2,000,000 beyond the legal issue was made to the banking department. The following Account shows the sums actually issued from the Bank to the public:

An Account, showing the Extent to which the Bank of England availed itself of its Power, under the authority of Government, to issue Notes to the Public beyond the Limit allowed by the Act of 1844.

	Notes issued to the Public on Securities, beyond the Statutory Limit of £14,475,000
	£
1857, November 13	186,000
" 14–15	622,000
" 16	860,000
" 17	836,000
" 18	852,000
" 19	896,000
" 20	928,000
" 21–22	617,000
" 23	397,000
" 24	317,000
" 25	81,000
" 26	243,000
" 27	342,000
" 28–29	184,000
" 30	15,000

Average of 18 Days £488,830.

27. The causes which, in the judgment of the Bank Directors, immediately led to this result, are thus stated by them in their correspondence with the Treasury, laid before Parliament in December last:–

"On the 5th November the reserve was £2,944,000, the bullion in the Issue Department £7,919,000, and the deposits £17,265,000. The rate of discount was advanced to 9 per cent., and on the 9th November to 10 per cent.

"The continental drain for gold had ceased, the American demand had become unimportant, and there was at that time little apprehension that the Bank issues would be inadequate to meet the necessities of commerce within the legalised sphere of their circulation.

"Upon this state of things, however, supervened the failure of the Western Bank of Scotland, and the City of Glasgow Bank, and a renewed discredit in Ireland, causing an increased action upon the English circulation, by the abstraction in four weeks of upwards of two millions of gold, to supply the wants of Scotland and Ireland, of which amounts more than one million was sent to Scotland and £280,000 to Ireland, between the 5th and 12th November.

"This drain was in its nature sudden and irresistible, and acted necessarily in diminution of the reserve, which on the 11th had decreased to £1,462,000 and the bullion to £6,666,000.

"The public became alarmed, large deposits accumulated in the Bank of England, money-dealers having vast sums lent to them upon call were themselves obliged to resort to the Bank of England for increased supplies, and for some days nearly the whole of the requirements of commerce were thrown on the Bank. Thus, on the 12th, it discounted and advanced to the amount of £2,373,000, which still left a reserve at night of £581,000.

"Such was the state of the Bank of England accounts on the 12th, the day of the publication of the Letter from the Treasury. The demand for discounts and advances continued to increase till the 21st, when they reached their maximum of £21,616,000.

"The public have also required a much larger quantity of notes than usual at this season, the amount in their hands having risen on the 21st to £21,554,000." . . .

33. During the month of October there was a very great gloom in Glasgow, occasioned by the commercial panic in America, Glasgow being very intimately connected in trade with America, with New York particularly. Towards the end of October that feeling was much increased, from its being well known that the Western Bank were in difficulties from their connexion with the three houses which have been above referred to. The bank closed on the 9th November, at two o'clock. The Western Bank and the City of Glasgow Bank had establishments open at night for the purpose of receiving the savings of small depositors. During the evening of the 9th November, the Monday, there was a demand for gold by the savings bank depositors at the branches of the City Bank. On the Tuesday morning, when the doors of the banks were opened, a great number of parties appeared with deposit receipts, demanding gold; one witness, speaking of his own bank, says "The office of our own establishment was quite filled with parties within a quarter of an hour of the opening of the doors; I think at half-past nine." This run or panic increased, and the continued refusal of the notes of the Western Bank added very much to the excitement. These people who came for money would not take the notes of any bank; it did not matter what bank it was; they refused everything but gold. Two of the banks sent a deputation of the directors to Edinburgh to confer with the managers of the Edinburgh banks on the subject, and to induce them to rescind a decision at which they had arrived, not to take the notes of the Western Bank. They failed in that; the notes of the Western Bank were refused the whole day on the Tuesday. The streets of Glasgow were in a very excited state; crowds were walking about going from one bank to another to see what was going on; there was an immense crowd of people. At the National Securities Savings Bank the run was very great indeed. The National Savings Bank paid in notes, and then the depositors, having received their deposits in notes, went with those notes to the banks that had issued them to demand gold. The City of Glasgow Bank did not open on Wednesday the 11th. Troops were sent for by the authorities, who were afraid of some disturbance. The magistrates issued a proclamation either on the Tuesday night or on the Wednesday

morning, and it was circulated very extensively, advising the people not to press upon the banks for payment, and to take the notes of all banks. The magistrates held a meeting on the Wednesday morning, and they issued an order to all the rate collectors over the city to take all notes presented to them; they did all they could to allay the excitement. In accordance with the provisions of the Act of 1854 the banks held a considerable quantity of gold, but they were under the necessity of having more gold from London; upon two occasions, on the Wednesday and the Thursday mornings, the 11th and 12th, large remittances of gold from London arrived about 10 o'clock in the forenoon; it was taken down in waggons to the banks, and escorted by a strong police force, and no doubt, seeing such immense quantities of gold come, excited a great commotion in the town.

Mr. Robertson, the Manager of the Union Bank, is asked–

"What was the nature of that excitement; was it of a pleasurable character?–It was such a novelty; in the first place, a large bank stopping payment, and then such quantities of gold coming down from London; it was quite a new thing to the people altogether.

"Had it any effect in regard to the panic?–I should think it must have had an effect; the people saw there was gold there to pay them if they wanted it; but by the Thursday morning the panic was entirely allayed; it entirely ceased on the Wednesday afternoon about two o'clock; at half-past two I do not think there were half-a-dozen people in our establishment.

"To what do you attribute the cessation of the panic?–I cannot answer that question; whether the people thought better of it I cannot tell.

"When was it that it first became known that the other banks would take the Western Bank's notes?–I should like to speak of what I know positively; I understood that the Edinburgh banks on the Tuesday night, the 10th, had agreed to take the notes of the Western Bank among themselves. At the meeting it was announced to them that the City Bank had then failed; then there was an alteration again, and they agreed neither to take the notes of the Western Bank nor of the City Bank; and that was acted upon during the Wednesday by their agents in Glasgow, but not to the full extent after the Tuesday; they were partially taken.

"Had the notes of the Western Bank began to be taken in the course of the Wednesday?–Yes.

"And at two o'clock on the Wednesday afternoon you consider that the panic had come to an end?–Quite.

"And on the Thursday the Government letter was issued?–Yes, I believe so."

34. It has been observed that the panic in Glasgow had ceased before the Treasury Letter was issued, and that the demand at the Bank of England for advances and discounts did not cease with the publication of that letter; after which date it cannot of course be attributed to any fear that there was a limit to the quantity of bank notes. On the contrary, we have seen that the advances by discount kept rising continually, and though the rate of 10 per cent. was still maintained, they rose from £15,900,000, at which they stood on the day preceding the issue of that letter, to £21,600,000 the 21st November. It is obvious, therefore, that the principal causes of the

commercial crisis of 1857 must be sought elsewhere. That calamity cannot be attributed exclusively or chiefly to panic occasioned by the operation of the Act of 1844. Since, too, the difficulties here experienced took their origin from America, where no such law is in force; and that crisis was felt in still greater severity than here, by countries in the north of Europe, whose currency is regulated by laws widely different from ours, it remains for your Committee to inquire whether any cause or causes, common to all those countries, and sufficient to account for the occurrence of commercial disasters in them all respectively, have been disclosed by the evidence. . . .

38. Your Committee have before them the particulars of 30 houses which failed in 1857. The aggregate liability of these houses is £9,080,000, of this sum the liabilities which other parties ought to provide for amount to £5,215,000, and the estimated assets £2,317,000. Besides the failures which arose from the suspension of American remittances, another class of failures is disclosed. The nature of these transactions was the system of open credits which were granted; that is, by granting to persons abroad liberty to draw upon the house in England to such extent as had been agreed upon between them; those drafts were then negotiated upon the foreign exchanges, and found their way to England, with the understanding that they were to be provided for at maturity. They were principally provided for, not by staple commodities, but by other bills that were sent to take them up. There was no real basis to the transaction, but the whole affair was a means of raising a temporary command of capital for the convenience of the individuals concerned, merely a bare commission hanging upon it; a banker's commission was all that the houses in England got upon those transactions, with the exception of receiving the consignments probably of goods from certain parties, which brought them a merchant's commission upon them; but they formed a very small amount in comparison with the amount of credits which were granted. One house at the time of its suspension was under obligation to the world to the extent of about £900,000, its capital at the last time of taking stock was under £10,000. Its business was chiefly the granting of open credits, *i.e.*, the house permitted itself to be drawn upon by foreign houses without any remittance previously or contemporaneously made, but with an engagement that it should be made before the acceptance arrived at maturity. In these cases the inducement to give the acceptance is a commission, varying from ½ to 1½ per cent. The acceptances are rendered available by being discounted, as will appear hereafter, when the affairs of the banks which failed come under our notice.

39. The obvious effect of such a system is first unduly to enhance, and then, whilst it continues, to sustain the price of commodities. In 1857, that fall of prices which, according to Mr. Neave, far-seeing people had anticipated, actually occurred. Tables have been put in by more than one of the witnesses, exhibiting an average fall of 20 or 30 per cent., in many instances much more, upon the comparison of July 1857 with January 1858. It needs no argument to prove what effect such a fall must have upon houses which had accepted bills, on the security of produce consigned, to the extent of one hundred times the amount of their own capital. The witness says,

"In the case which you are now describing to the Committee, these transactions had gone on to the extent of £900,000. The real guarantee was partly produce and partly bills of exchange; to whatever extent that produce was depreciated, of course the liability of the firm to failure would arise, and the capital of that form to meet such depreciation of produce was about one hundredth part of the whole of their liabilities?–That is so.

"Do you consider that case to be a fair illustration of the recent commercial disasters which have occurred?–I think it is, though I should mention that in some cases the proportion of capital possessed was larger than that which I have mentioned.

"In some cases, also, perhaps it might be smaller?–In some cases considerably smaller. In some cases I have known houses come under very large obligations, who had really no capital at all."

40. This practice appears to have grown up of late, and to be principally connected with the trade of Sweden, Denmark and other countries in the north of Europe. One house at Newcastle is described as conducting before 1854 a regular trade in the Baltic. They were not great people, but were respectable people, and were doing a moderately profitable trade. They unfortunately entered upon this system of granting credits; and in the course of three years the following result ensued; *viz.* in 1854 their capital was between £2,000 and £3,000; in 1857 they failed for £100,000, with the prospect of paying about 2s. in the pound.

41. For other instances of this abuse of credit, your Committee refer to the evidence, concurring entirely in the opinions expressed by the witnesses, that the great abuse of credit is a feature common to the two years 1847 and 1857, and has been, in their judgement, the principal cause of the failures that took place in those years. Mr. Coleman says,–

"Speaking generally with regard to 1847, of which your experience is now complete, are you prepared to say that the failures which occurred in that year were owing to any imperfection of the law by which the facilities for obtaining credit were unduly curtailed?–No.

"With regard to the year 1857, what would your answer be to the same question?–That every house which applied and deserved assistance received it."

105. Debate on Gladstone's motion to set up Post Office Savings Banks (8 February 1861)

Hansard, 3/CLVI/262–267.

The Chancellor of the Exchequer said he would take occasion to state that, in submitting the Resolution to the notice of the Committee, he did not seek to pledge hon. Members to an approval of either the principle or the details of the Bill which it was his intention to found upon it. The object which he had in view in dealing with the question was to afford facilities for the deposit of savings of small amount to those who did not possess them, or possessed them but imperfectly, under the present system of savings banks. The establishment of savings banks had undoubtedly been of immense service to the humbler classes throughout the country;

but, while it was the wish of the Government so to improve their constitution as to render them still more advantageous, the mode of doing so was a problem which they found extremely difficult to solve. The main question, that of the liability of the trustees to the depositors, was one which had up to that time baffled the skill of those who had attempted to deal with it. Under those circumstances, they proposed to avail themselves of another description of machinery already in existence, simple in form, and recommended by its incomparable convenience, for the purpose of carrying out more effectually the objects for which savings banks had been set on foot. Of those institutions there were only about 600 scattered throughout the country, and of that number but a small proportion were open for a sufficient number of hours in the week. Looking, however, to the Post Office Department, he found that it comprised between 2,000 and 3,000 money order offices; that the number of postmasters was perfectly adequate to the transaction of increased money business; that they held their situations under pecuniary responsibility, and that every one of their offices was open six days in the week for not less then eight or ten hours each day. Now, there was a machinery ready to hand and admirably adapted for extending the usefulness of the savings bank system. The experience, he might add, of the present winter must have demonstrated to anybody who thought upon the subject that the resources of the labouring population of the country had not of late years increased in proportion to the increase in the rate of their wages and the improvement in their standard of living. A smaller proportion of their gross income was laid by at that moment than was laid by twenty years before. He did not, however, think he was indulging in too sanguine an expectation in supposing that if readier means of laying by their small savings were afforded them than they now possessed, those savings would become much larger in amount, and their ability to cope with periods of distress consequently greater. He did not, of course, intended [*sic*] to propose that the machinery of the Post Office should be applied at once and wholesale to the purpose of affording to the working classes the facilities of which he spoke. The scheme to which he was about to invite the assent of the Committee would, it was true, be worked through the agency of the Postmaster General and not that of the National Debt Commissioners, whose duty it would be simply to receive and hold the funds handed over to them by the Post Office for investment; but then the new arrangements would in no way interfere with the primary objects, for the attainment of which that important branch of the public service was established. He proposed that the Post Office should receive and return deposits with interest in the same way as money orders were now dealt with, charging merely a fair remunerative price for the work thus performed. He might further observe that the principle upon which his scheme was founded differed in some respects from that on which savings banks were based. Those institutions had been established with the notion that the State might very fairly offer to the labouring classes a certain premium by way of inducing them to make deposits; but, while he was far from desiring to cast any censure upon that principle, he did not deem it right in the present case to hold out to depositors the expectation of obtaining any high rate of interest. All, then, that he meant to do was to give a fair and moderate premium to the depositors of small savings, and that premium, he hoped to be able to pay them without imposing any additional burden on the State, by turning to account the very extensive and extremely economical machinery of the Post Office. The rate of interest which was now paid on deposits in savings banks stood at the somewhat high rate of £3 5s. per cent, and he proposed that under the operation of the scheme to which he was asking the assent of the Committee it should be fixed at £2 10s., with power to increase that amount within certain limits. Inasmuch as there were great difficulties in the way of dealing with the finances of savings banks and of attempting to alter their form of constitution, the Government proposed for the moment to pass over those difficulties, and to ask the assent of Parliament to a plan which, avoiding any competition with the existing savings banks, would greatly enlarge the facilities of making small deposits. The main difficulty in the present savings bank system was its imperfect organization in regard to the responsibility of the State. The State could only be responsible for the acts of its own officers, and as no plan had yet been devised by which the State could participate in all the proceedings of the savings banks, it was impossible to carry out the principle of a perfect Government guarantee. The State now only became responsible for the money of the depositors at the moment it received it from the savings banks' authorities. But as in this case the money would be received by the officers of the Government it would be inexcusable not to give a Government guarantee; and he proposed, therefore, to give a Government guarantee in the only effective technical form, by providing that if any difficulty arose in the means of meeting the demands of any lawful depositor it should be charged upon the Consolidated Fund. He hoped the notion of a Government guarantee would not cause any alarm in the minds of hon. Gentlemen, for he had expressly stated that the basis of this new arrangement was that it should be self-supporting. The right hon. Gentleman concluded by moving a Resolution:–

> "That it is expedient to charge upon the Consolidated Fund of the United Kingdom of Great Britain and Ireland the deficiency, if any such should arise, in the sums which may be held on account of Post Office Savings, to meet the lawful demands of depositors in such Banks, in the event of their being established by law."

Mr. Frank Crossley said, he thought it was impossible to overestimate the advantages that would accrue to certain classes in the country from the proposition of the right hon. Gentleman the Chancellor of the Exchequer. There were no less than fifteen counties in England without a savings bank. There were also many important towns containing a population of 10,000 to 30,000 without such a thing as a savings bank. Many of the savings banks in existence were only open about one or two hours a week, and at a period of the day when the working people could not visit them. A great deal of fault had been found with the improvidence of the working people in not saving money, but let them first see what was done by the Government. The State provided beer-shops in every street for working men to spend their money in as fast as they earned it; but hitherto it had not been sufficiently forward in giving them facilities for saving their money. Working men were often very much afraid to let their masters know that they were saving money from a notion that it would lead to a reduction of their wages, and under the present system the masters were very often concerned in the management of these banks and could know exactly how each man's account stood. By this new arrangement each account would be a secret between the depositor and the postmaster. He felt very much indebted to the attention which the right hon. Gentleman had given to the representations addressed to him on the subject by Mr. Sykes of Huddersfield. He did not think the Government ought to make a profit on the business, nor ought they to lose by it, for the working classes of this country did not want charity. All they wanted was a fair field and no favour, and he was glad to find they were to have it. He hoped that if it were found at any time that without putting a charge on the country, the rate of interest could be increased, it would be done.

Colonel Sykes said, that no praise could be too high for anything which tended to induce the working classes to lay by against a bad time. He wished, however, to point out what he thought would prove a drawback to the proposition just submitted. It would impose largely increased duties on officers who had already enormous functions to perform. Postmasters were generally shopkeepers who had their own business to attend to as well as the duties of the post-office. He would also suggest that each man's account should be kept in a book, as under the present system.

Mr. Arthur Kinnaird took an opposite view from that taken by his gallant Friend with respect to some of the points referred to by him. He saw brighter prospects in the future before them than his hon. Friend. No one accustomed to study the wants of the labouring population could fail to perceive that the Bill would supply a peculiar want. It was simple and practical, and would save the labouring classes from incalculable loss, entailed by their advancing money on all sorts of schemes because they had no place for depositing their savings with security. He heartily congratulated the Chancellor of the Exchequer on having at last succeeded in one of the fondest hopes of his heart, that of creating a $2\frac{1}{2}$ per cent. stock.

Mr. Ayrton expressed a hope that additional facilities would be afforded by the Post Office authorities for the transmission of small sums of money through the post. Threepence, or even twopence, would be a large sum to pay for the transmission of two or three shillings.

The Chancellor of the Exchequer, in reply, said, he must repudiate the notion that the Government, by this Bill, were about to establish a national bank. Whatever moneys came into the hands of Government under the Bill would be dealt with in precisely the same manner as the moneys which came into their hands under the existing savings banks' law. With regard to the proposal that increased facilities should be given for the transmission of money through the Post Office, he could only say that no proposal to that effect had ever been laid before him which had assumed a practical shape. He should, however, be very glad to see the machinery of the Post Office made available for the purpose to an extent consistent with the due performance of the important functions to be discharged by the department. He believed that when hon. Members came to examine the provisions of the Bill they would be found well adapted for their purpose. Let him add that he felt greatly indebted to Mr. Sykes, who had been already referred to, for the labour which he had devoted to this subject. At the same time the Bill did not altogether embody Mr. Sykes' plan. The plan adopted was not precisely a plan of interest notes, but that was a matter of detail on which he would not enter then, as the Bill would be on the table in two or three days.

Motion *agreed to.*

Resolved,–

"That it is expedient to charge upon the Consolidated Fund of the United Kingdom of Great Britain and Ireland the deficiency, if any should arise, in the sums which may be held on account of Post Office Savings Banks, to meet the lawful demands of depositors in such Banks, in the event of their being established by law."

Resolution to be reported on *Monday* next.

House adjourned at Eleven
o'clock, till *Monday* next.

106A–C. Failure of Overend and Gurney (11 May 1866)

The Economist, 19 May 1866.

106A. Letter from the Bank of England

Bank of England, May 11th, 1866

Sir,–We consider it to be our duty to lay before the Government the facts relating to the extraordinary demands for assistance which have been made upon the Bank of England today, in consequence of the failure of Messrs. Overend, Gurney and Co.

We have advanced to the bankers bill brokers, and merchants in London during the day upwards of four million sterling upon the security of Government stock and bills of exchange–an unprecedented sum to lend in one day, and which, therefore, we suppose would be sufficient to meet all their requirements, although the proportion of this sum which may have been sent to the country must materially affect the question.

We commenced this morning with a reserve of £5,727,000, which has been drawn upon so largely that we cannot calculate upon having so much as £3,000,000 this evening, making a fair allowance for what may be remaining at the branches.

We have not refused any legitimate application for assistance, and unless the money taken from the Bank is entirely withdrawn from circulation there is no reason to suppose that this reserve is insufficient.

We have the honour to be, Sir, your obedient servants,

(signed) H. L. Holland, Governor
(signed) Thos. Newman Hunt, Deputy Governor

The Rt. Hon. the Chancellor of the Exchequer, M.P., &c., &c.

106B. Letter suspending the Bank Act

To the Governor and the Deputy Governor of the
Bank of England.

Gentlemen,—We have the honour to acknowledge the receipt of your letter of this day to the Chancellor of the Exchequer, in which you state the course of action at the Bank of England, under the circumstances of sudden anxiety, which have arisen since the stoppage of Messrs. Overend, Gurney, and Co., Limited, yesterday.

We learn with regret that the Bank reserve, which stood so recently as last night as a sum of about five millions and three quarters, has been reduced in a single day by the liberal answer of the Bank to the demands of commerce during the hours of business and by its great anxiety to avert disaster, to little more than half that amount, or a sum (actual for London and estimated for the branches) not greatly exceeding three millions.

The accounts and representations which have reached Her Majesty's Government during the day exhibit the state of things in the City as one of extraordinary distress and apprehension. Indeed, deputations composed of persons of the greatest weight and influence, and representing alike the private and the joint stock banks of London, have presented themselves in Downing Street, and have urged with unanimity and with earnestness the necessity of some intervention on the part of the State to allay the anxiety which prevails and which appears to have amounted, through great part of the day, to absolute panic.

There are some important points in which the present crisis differs from those of 1847 and 1857. Those periods were periods of mercantile distress, but the vital consideration of banking credit does not appear to have been involved in them, as it is in the present crisis.

Again, the course of affairs was comparatively slow and measured; whereas the shock has in this instance arrived with an intense rapidity, and the opportunity for deliberation is narrowed in proportion. Lastly the reserve of the Bank has suffered a diminution without precedent relatively to the time in which it has been brought about, and in view especially of this circumstance Her Majesty's Government cannot doubt that it is their duty to adopt without delay the measures which seem best calculated to them to compose the public mind, and to arrest the course which may threaten trade and industry. If, then, the directors of the Bank of England, proceeding upon the prudent rules of action by which their administration is usually governed, shall find that in order to meet the wants of legitimate commerce, it be requisite to extend their discounts and advances upon approved securities, so as to require issues of notes beyond the limits fixed by law, Her Majesty's Government recommend that this necessity should be met immediately upon its occurrence, and in that event they will not fail to make application to Parliament for its sanction.

No such discount or advance, however, should be granted at a rate of interest of less than *ten per cent.*, and Her Majesty's Government reserve it to themselves to recommend, if they should see fit, the imposition of a higher one. After deduction by the Bank of whatever it may consider to be a fair charge for its risk, expense, and trouble, the profits of these advances will accrue to the public.

We have the honour to be, Gentlemen,
Your obedient servants,
(signed) Russell
(signed) W. E. Gladstone

Downing Street,
May 11th. 1866.

106C. Foreign Office Circular Letter of 12 May

Foreign Office, May 12th.

Sir,–The monetary crisis through which this country is now passing will naturally attract great attention in other countries, and it is therefore desirable that a clear conception should be formed, both of its nature and probable extent, but more particularly of the measures which Her Majesty's Government have adopted to enable the mercantile community to meet the difficulties of the present situation.

Long continued prosperity in commercial affairs, and the general wealth consequent on it, have produced their ordinary results in encouraging speculation, especially of a monetary or financial character, and fostering hopes of acquiring wealth by more speedy means than are presented by the ordinary methods of commercial industry. Again, the events which are taking place on the Continent have tended not only to produce immediate derangement in commercial transactions, but also to shake that confidence in the future without which a return to a sound state in monetary matters was not to be looked for.

The immediate cause, however, of the crisis lay in the stoppage of the great discount house of Overend, Gurney, and Co., in whose hands were lodged many millions sterling, which, in other times, would in great part have formed, and which, perhaps, ought to have formed, the reserves of the various private and joint-stock banks of the country. This failure directed the action of the panic against the banks in London, and it was to be apprehended that the movement in the capital would be followed by a similar agitation in the rest of the kingdom, where, in addition to the large deposits in the hands of the bankers, there are many millions of paper circulation resting only on the commercial credit of the nation.

In this state of things it could not be surprising that the reserve of the Bank of England was heavily affected yesterday, and it was the combined consideration of what had then actually happened, and of what might follow on subsequent days which induced Her Majesty's Government to adopt the measure on which, in the course of the evening, they decided. For the money drawn from the banks, having been withdrawn from circulation under the influence of panic, the Bank of England might, without some new resource, have been unable to continue its accustomed assistance. Thus the crisis, which had been anxiously apprehended from this combination of circumstances, has come at last, but with a suddenness in regard to its immediate consequences which could not have been anticipated.

The Bank of England is prepared to extend relief, to the utmost of its means, to all cases which are justly deserving of its support; while Her Majesty's Government, in full reliance on the eventual sanction of Parliament, if it should be necessary to go beyond the law as it now stands, have signified to the Bank of England their permission to hold itself free from the observance of the ordinary limitations on its issues, if the exigencies of the time require such an extraordinary measure. Her Majesty's Government trust that by this timely assistance all commercial establishments which are based on sound principles, and have been conducted with proper prudence, will be enabled to withstand the shock to which the panic occasioned by the recent great failure in the city will have exposed them. Her Majesty's Government have no reason to apprehend that there is any general want of soundness in the ordinary trade of this country which can give reasonable ground for anxiety or alarm either in this country or abroad; they are satisfied, on the contrary, that the present crisis, peculiar and unprecedented as it is, is one of a character essentially more favourable than others which have been successfully passed through; and that all that is required is that all classes should cooperate with the Government in endeavouring to allay needless alarm, and in acting with prudence and forbearance while so much agitation prevails.

It appears to Her Majesty's Government to be of great importance that the commercial interest abroad should be reassured as to what is passing in this country, and I have, therefore, lost no time in authorising you to make known to the Government to which you are accredited, and generally to those who have a direct interest in such matters, the view taken by Her Majesty's Government of the present state of affairs, the active measures which have been adopted to avert any evil consequences, and the confidence with which Her Majesty's Government feel that these measures will be attended with success.

The abatement of the panic in the city this morning is, Her Majesty's Government trust, an earnest of the good result likely to attend the measures which they have authorised the Bank of England to adopt.

I am, with great truth, your most obedient humble servant,

Clarendon.

107. Evidence of Lord Romilly, Master of the Rolls, before Select Committee of 1867, on Limited Liability Acts

Parlty. Papers, 1867/x/questions 1325–1329.

1325. Is there anything which your Lordship would like to state, bearing upon the general question of the improvement of the law?–I have felt very considerable difficulty about it, and I think it a very difficult subject. What I wish to know is (which I have no means of ascertaining) what are the benefits produced by the Act? They are of those things which do not come before the public, and which persons engaged in them may know; but that there is a good deal of profitable *bona fide* employment of capital to the great advantage of persons engaged in it, I do not entertain any doubt; I have seen something which makes me conclude that that must be the case; but, as I said before, those cases do not come before me, and unless I know exactly to what extent it operates, it is very difficult to know how one can introduce fetters upon the evil without introducing also impediments to the good.

1326. We have had before us many cases incidentally of great advantage in the operation of the law; we were told the other day by a witness, that the Atlantic Cable would never have been made without the Act of 1862, and we have had plenty of opportunities of seeing that there is a bright side in the operation of the law?–No doubt.

1327. MR. VANCE: Has not this law of limited liability been used to a great extent for the purposes of fraud?–To a very great extent.

1328. Does your Lordship think that, on the whole, the advantages which the public have gained by the operation of it have not been counterbalanced by the misfortunes which have been caused by the reckless frauds which have crept in?–To a great extent they have, unquestionably; but I am unable to draw the balance, because, as I said before, I see the evils and I do not see the good. The evil is really harrowing; the amount of calamity which is produced by it is quite extraordinary.

1329. Is it not the case that a great number of the limited liability companies which have been formed within the last few years are in difficulties, or in process of winding up?–I cannot tell; I could tell you how many there are in my chambers by referring to papers.

108. Royal Commission on Friendly Societies (1871–1874): Evidence of J. M. Ludlow, registrar

Parlty. Papers, 1874/XXIII: 1, App. I, pp. 243, 244.

From the above table it results that the various bodies the legal existence of which depends *prima facie* on the Registrar of Friendly Societies for England and Wales, with the Channel Islands, amount to over 25,000, comprising a membership of over 4½ millions at least, with £68,900,000 at least of funds; those whose legal existence depends in like manner upon the Registrar for Scotland, to 984, with over 374,000 members, and over £2,000,000 funds; and those whose legal existence depends in like manner on the Registrar for Ireland, to over 421, with over 88,000 members at least, and over £908,000 funds. That the above figures as to membership and funds are quite insufficient (except as to Savings Banks and Benefit Building Societies), is shown on the one hand by the immense number of Friendly and other societies which do not return the forms sent out, on the other by the large number of those which do not specify their membership, or in some cases their funds. And although a certain amount of double membership has to be allowed for, many persons being members of more than one Friendly, Building, or Co-operative society, or of two or more societies belonging to different classes, the probability is that any such deductions should fall very far short of the additions which would be required through the obscure or defective character of returns. If we estimated the total membership of registered bodies of all sorts at 5½ millions for England and Wales, with £72,000,000 funds, the total membership for Scotland at 500,000, with £2,200,000 funds, and the total membership for Ireland at 100,000, with £920,000, we should probably be within the mark, at all events as respects the two former countries. But to the above list should also be added Friendly Societies with deposited rules, the number of which in existence it is impossible to calculate; nor should Post Office Savings Banks be overlooked, with their million and a half of depositors, in respect to which the Registrar has to fulfil some important functions, nor yet the holders of Government annuities and insurance policies, amounting to several thousands more.

When we thus group together the various bodies of which the Registrar of Friendly Societies is the pivot, we perceive that they really form one whole, as representing the different modes in which the working of the spirit of self-help among what the Acts often term the 'industrious classes' has been recognised and deemed worthy of encouragement by the Legislature,–the various means by which that portion of the population which is most within the risk of pauperism endeavours to escape from it. And thus, although the enactments by which these bodies have been gathered together have been passed by the Legislature almost at haphazard, a true moral unity is to be discerned in the functions of the Registrar of Friendly Societies, whether exercised *eo nomine*, or as "barrister to certify the rules of Savings Banks." Mr. Tidd Pratt for many years was, Mr. Stephenson is, as it were a minister of self-help to the whole of the industrious classes. The first penny deposited by a school child in a penny savings bank finds its way still probably to a trustee savings bank, the rules of which are certified by Mr. Stephenson. When the boy begins to work for himself, if he has forethought and prudence, he very likely opens his own account, although still a minor, with a Savings Bank; towards the end of his apprenticeship he joins a benefit club or Odd Fellows lodge, certified by the same hand in a different capacity. If he desires to improve his mind he enters a Scientific or Literary institution, the rules of which have probably passed equally through the registrar's hand. If he become a member of a Trade Society, he learns that the only legal security for the funds is to be obtained by certification through the same hand. If he marry and have a family to provide for, he will seek to cheapen his living by entering a Co-operative Store, whose rules have received the same Registrar's sanction. As his capital accumulates, and he aspires to the possession of a house of his own, he subscribes to a Benefit Building Society, still certified by the same authority. On the other hand, if he has had difficulties to pass through, the Loan Society, certified by the same person, will frequently have proved his first resource, perhaps a fatal one. And if he has remained satisfied with the low rate of interest of the Post Office Savings Bank, he knows, or should know, that in case of dispute it is still Mr. Stephenson who will be the arbitrator. Thus, at every step in life, he will have been met by the authority of the same person, who has been for him, as it were, the embodiment of the goodwill and protection of the State, in all that goes beyond police, the poor law, justice, and the school.

109. Select Committee of 1872 on Railway Amalgamation

Parlty. Papers, 1872/XIII. 1/pp. XVIII–XXXII.

Summary of preceding history

From the above statement it appears:

1. That committees and commissions carefully chosen have for the last 30 years clung to one form of competition after another; that it has nevertheless become more

and more evident that competition must fail to do for railways what it does for ordinary trade, and that no means have yet been devised by which competition can be permanently maintained.

2. That in spite of the recommendations of these authorities, combination and amalgamation have proceeded at the instance of the companies without check and almost without regulation. United systems now exist, constituting by their magnitude and by their exclusive possession of whole districts monopolies to which the earlier authorities would have been most strongly opposed. Nor is there any reason to suppose that the progress of combination has ceased, or that it will cease until Great Britain is divided between a small number of great companies. It is therefore of the utmost importance that the actual facts should be clearly recognised, so that the public may become acquainted with the real alternatives which lie before them. With this view it appears desirable to consider fully the following questions, *viz.*:

> 1. To what extent does competition now exist, and to what extent can it be relied on?
>
> 2. If competition does not exist to a sufficient extent to regulate prices and accommodation, or if it is impracticable to maintain it, can the resulting monopolies be regulated, and, if so, in what manner?

. . .

Conclusions as to Competition

The answer to the questions, How far does competition exist, and how far can it be relied on? must then be as follows:–

There is real and effective competition between railways and the traffic by sea, especially in the carriage of heavy goods, and this competition is likely to continue, unless Parliament should give public harbours into the hands of the railway companies.

There is some competition between railways and canals, and it is desirable to make every effort to keep up and develop the system of inland water navigation, although it is improbable that that system can maintain a general or powerful competition with railways.

There is little real competition in point of charges between railway companies, and its continuance cannot be relied upon. There is at the present time considerable competition in points of facilities, but the security for its permanence is uncertain.

Interest of the Companies, how far that of the Public

Since, then, competition cannot be relied on to secure proper service and a fair price, the further questions arise–Can the self-interest of the companies be trusted? Is their interest the same as that of the public? And, if not, what is practicable in the way of regulation?

In the first place, it must not be too hastily assumed that self-interest will play the same part in these large undertakings which it plays in ordinary trading concerns. There is a powerful bureaucracy of directors and officers. The real managers are far removed from the influence of the shareholders, and the latter are to a great extent a fluctuating and helpless body. The history of railway enterprise shows how frequently their interests have been sacrificed to the policy, the speculations, or the passions of the real managers. On the other hand, the directors and principal officers of these great undertakings are often men of high standing, who feel that their position is something different from that of mere managers of a trading concern, and become in a certain sense amenable to public opinion, and especially to its expression in Parliament.

Thus, for good as well as evil, the management of railways differs from that of an ordinary trade or manufacture, and approximates in some degree to the business of a public department.

Self-interest, however, still is and will continue to be the leading motive of railway companies, and it is therefore important to see how far their interest coincides with that of the public. It is the interest of the companies to develop traffic whenever that traffic will produce them profit. It is their interest to encourage new and promising traffic, even though their immediate profit may be little or none; it is their interest to foster new routes, and to maintain them against existing competition; to develop new ports or harbours; and to promote competition between distant seats of trade or manufacture by neutralising the distances which nature has placed between these seats and the various markets for their products. In all these cases, the wealth and resources of the companies enable them to incur present loss for the sake of future advantage; and although in so doing they may be exposed to the charge of making some parts of their system pay for others, their action is probably, on the whole, advantageous to the public as well as to themselves.

But there are limits to this coincidence of interest. It is, as pointed out by the Committee of 1839–40, to the interest of the companies to make as large a profit with as little outlay as possible; it is, therefore to their interest to carry one passenger or one ton of goods for a shilling rather than to carry two passengers or two tons of goods for sixpence each, whilst the converse is clearly to the interest of the public. Again, it is to the interest of the companies to shut up rival routes by water; and according to some of the evidence they have in the case of canals sometimes succeeded in doing so. Again, it is or may be the interest of a company not to send passengers or goods by the shortest or most convenient route; but by the route which gives the company the greatest amount of profit, and with this object, to refuse to accept traffic from other railways at the nearest or most convenient points, in order to carry it round for longer distances on their own line; and to time passenger trains so as to make travelling on other lines difficult or impracticable; and, lastly, it is to the interest of the public that branch lines should be made, but it is not the interest of a company to make them unless they will pay good interest on the capital expended.

It is therefore clear that, both as regards the amount of charge and the accommodation afforded, the interest of the companies does not give any such complete or sufficient guarantee to the public as is given by competition, in cases where competition exists. Putting, therefore, aside the question of maintaining existing competition, which has been considered above, it becomes necessary to consider what can be done in the way of regulation.

It will be convenient to bear in mind that the questions which may thus arise between the railway companies and the public may be distinguished as follows, *viz.*:

1. Assuming that the profits of the companies continue to increase as they have recently done, are the whole of these profits to belong to the companies; and, if not, in what proportions, in what manner, and by what process are the increased profits to be divided between the shareholders and the public?
2. Is the discretion now exercised by the companies of charging different rates and fares on different parts of their systems for the public advantage; and, if not, how can it be controlled?
3. In what manner can the railway systems of the different companies, taken as a whole, be harmonised and extended so as to develop their several capacities to the utmost extent, and so as to secure to the public the full use of, and free choice between, the lines?

It will be found that the different suggestions we are about to consider all have relation to one or more of these three objects.

State Purchase

Another and a still greater question has been suggested which must be mentioned in this place, *viz.*, whether the progress of combination between railways may not lead at some future time to the creation of corporations so few, so large, and so powerful as to render it expedient, on political if not on commercial grounds, that a fundamental change should take place in the present relations between the railways and the State? The state of things so contemplated may possibly arise, and, so far as the evidence offered to the Committee has touched on the subject, the only remedy suggested for it is the acquisition of the railways by the Government. It does not, however, appear to us that any present necessity extends for entering upon the full and prolonged inquiry which so great and difficult a question would demand; and we therefore proceed to consider the Railway system as it at present exists with a view to ascertain what improvements can be made in Railway Legislation, consistently with the fair rights of the companies, which would protect the public against certain evils incident to the present system.

Opportunities afforded by Amalgamation

Before examining what terms, if any, can be imposed on railway companies, it may be well to consider what special occasion amalgamation presents for imposing such terms. Does amalgamation produce, or may it be expected to produce, any special evils against which it is desirable to provide special safeguards? Or supposing this not to be the case, and assuming that the present conditions imposed on railway companies are insufficient for the protection of the public interests, does amalgamation afford a fair opportunity for imposing satisfactory terms upon them?

The answer to the first of these questions must be doubtful. Few cases have been adduced in which amalgamations already effected have led to increased fares or reduced facilities, whilst, on the other hand, there is evidence that the most complete amalgamation which has hitherto taken place, *viz.*, that of the North Eastern, has been followed by a lowering of fares and rates and increase of facilities, as well as by increased dividends. Nor can it be doubted that some of the grievances complained of, especially in outlying districts, such as the want of system and power in the Welsh railways, and the failure to develop traffic on some of the Irish railways, would find their best remedy in amalgamation. What the case might be if amalgamations even more extensive than those now proposed should be allowed to take effect, and if the United Kingdom should be 'districted' between two or three companies, it is difficult to anticipate.

That the amalgamations proposed this Session would enable the companies to make harmonious and convenient arrangements seems evident.

On the other hand, amalgamation will no doubt diminish or destroy such motives for affording facilities as arise from the competition, actual or 'potential,' which now exists, and may strengthen the hands of the companies in resisting fresh competition.

The answer to the second question is much easier. It is admitted that amalgamation must prove a source of increased economy and profit to the shareholders, and that in order to effect it fresh powers must be obtained from Parliament. It is clear, therefore, that Parliament in granting such powers has a perfect right to insist on fresh conditions in favour of the public, whether such conditions have special reference to dangers apprehended from the amalgamations or to defects in the existing arrangements between the companies and the public.

It is important to make this point clear, because much of the evidence against the proposed amalgamations is directed against alleged general defects in the existing railway system, rather than against any new evils to arise from the extension of monopoly. And in dealing with the conditions which it has been proposed to impose on railway companies, it will be difficult, if not impossible, to distinguish between conditions having reference to amalgamations and conditions having reference to the railway system generally. In the following remarks, therefore, the various terms which Parliament is asked to impose on the companies now seeking amalgamation are considered as terms which for the most part it is believed to be desirable to impose on railways by general legislation, bearing in mind that applications for amalgamations, even if they do not render such terms specially necessary, afford a fair opportunity of requiring the companies so applying to adopt them.

110. Select Committee of 1875 on Loans to Foreign States

Parlty. Papers, 1875/XI/pp. XLIV–L.

Your Committee have thus endeavoured to place before the House the principal facts in connection with the several loans which have formed the subject of their inquiry.

Although the cases differ in many respects, there are incidents for the most part common to all the loans, which your Committee feel should be prominently referred to.

In respect of all these loans, those who introduced them to the public seem to have been regardless of the financial resources of the borrowing State; such resources, if inquired into, would have been found to have been totally inadequate to meet the liabilities incurred. In no case before your Committee, with one unimportant exception, has the borrowing Government repaid any portion of its indebtedness incurred in respect of these loans, except from the proceeds of the loans themselves.

By means of exaggerated statements in the prospectus the public have been induced to believe that the material wealth of the contracting State formed a sufficient security for the repayment of the money borrowed. Even if such were the case, the several Governments have taken no steps to apply the revenues of the State, or the other subjects of special hypothecation in discharge of their liabilities.

The whole of these loans were ostensibly raised for purposes of a similar character. An undertaking was given that the proceeds were to be spent on works calculated to develop the industrial resources of the different countries, and from such works a large return was promised. Your Committee have shown how small a proportion of each loan was applied to the above-mentioned purposes.

In order to induce the public to lend money upon a totally insufficient security, means have been resorted to which, in their nature and object, were flagrantly deceptive.

Conspicuous amongst them are the dealings in the stock by the contractors for the loan, before its allotment to the public.

In the opinion of your Committee these transactions are deserving of much censure. The buying and selling of the stock on behalf of the contractor created a fictitious market. The price at which the dealings took place in no way represented the value of the stock. It was fixed by the contractor or his agents at a premium, in order to induce the public to believe that the loan was a good investment, or that they would, if they obtained an allotment of the stock, realise that premium. The public had no means of learning that the contractor was the principal in these transactions; even the jobber was often ignorant of the fact. There was thus no apparent difference between a genuine and a fictitious market.

Great as the evils of this system are, they are increased when the money of the allottees is employed, as in some instances before your Committee, in paying for the stock purchased in excess of that sold. The contractor is then speculating with the proceeds of the loan itself, and not from his own resources; and if the speculation fails, the loss generally falls on the contracting Government or the public.

By these operations the contractor is placed in a position of unfair advantage. Where substantially the whole of the scrip has been purchased, and thereby is in the possession of the contractor, he has, by effecting further purchases of the stock, which no dealer has it in his power to deliver, the means of exacting large sums from the sellers.

That large portions of the loan by means of the repurchases in effect remained in the hands of the borrowing Government, was a fact most material to be known to those who lent their money in the belief that the proceeds of the whole loan would be applied in developing the resources of a State.

The methods by which these loans have been introduced to the public afforded opportunities for collusive action between those who issued them and the immediate agents of the contracting State, which it is difficult to detect.

When the money of the public had been received, its application to the alleged purposes of the loans depended upon the good faith of those issuing them. In some instances these funds have been flagrantly misapplied.

It is true that the credulity and cupidity of certain classes of the community have blinded them to the danger of embarking in speculations such as your Committee have described. They appear to have measured the value of the promises held out to them, not by any rule of experience, but by their own sanguine expectations; and thus they have fallen a prey to those who by trading on their credulity have obtained their money, and then betrayed their interests.

Your Committee feel that it is not their duty to apportion the blame to the different actors in these transactions; to a great extent they agree in the opinion of the Secretary to the Honduras Legation, that "the fault of the failure falls with equal force upon all who have interests, rights, claims, complaints or any participation whatever in these matters. It is a kind of *original sin*, which reaches even the most innocent who have anything to do with this undertaking."

Your Committee do not dwell on the transactions by which such enormous sums have been abstracted from the Honduras Loans, and appropriated among those who were entrusted with its management. Such acts have no more to do with foreign loans than with any other transaction by which the money of one person comes into the possession of another, and is converted to the use of the depositaries. A remedy for such proceedings ought to be found in the tribunals of the country.

It remains for your Committee to indicate the causes of the losses of which a more particular account has been given in the earlier part of this Report, in the hope that when these causes are clearly understood, some means of preventing the calamities which they have occasioned may be found.

Much evil has been caused by the misstatements and suppressions to be found in the prospectus.

Something may be attributed to the proceedings of the committee of the Stock Exchange, which gives, by granting a quotation, a certain prestige to a loan which neither the very slight and superficial investigation on which the grant of a quotation is founded, nor the nature of the tribunal seem to warrant. It appears from the evidence brought before your Committee that the committee of the Stock Exchange practically require nothing more than the production of documents showing the authority of the agent to issue the loan, of the prospectus, and of a certificate stating the amount subscribed for and allotted to the public. They receive notarial copies or official gazettes containing such of these documents as are not original, but they make no further inquiries into the circumstances or conditions of the proposed loan, nor into the truthfulness of the prospectus, nor into the solvency of the borrowing State. They require no amount of subscriptions before granting a settlement, and they accept the statement of the contractors for the loans, as to the *bona fides* and amount of allotment.

In respect of most of the loans quotations were obtained from the committee of the Stock Exchange on the faith of written statements made on behalf of the contractors, that the applications for allotment had been unconditionally made. It was, however, known to those on whose behalf such statements were made, that before any allotment, such contracts of purchase had been effected on behalf of the contractors or borrowing Government that as soon as the allotment took place, a large proportion of the stock would return into their hands, and therefore for the purposes of the loan was not allotted. In the St. Domingo Loan a quotation was given on a certificate that the total amount had been disposed of, a statement false in fact, and insufficient if true. In the first Honduras Loan the certificate only stated that £501,100 had been allotted in England, and that the rest was represented by French scrip.

But the principal cause, compared with which all others sink into relative insignificance, is undoubtedly the means employed in order to induce the public to apply for a loan. A clear and striking delineation of these proceedings may be found in the evidence of Mr. Scott, and the counter testimony of Baron Erlanger and Mr. Albert Grant.

This is the method of proceeding. In some cases it is certain, in others probable, that a loan if simply advertised and left to the judgment of the public will fail. The problem which the class of financiers to whose operations attention has been principally directed, have undertaken to solve, is, given such a loan, to provide that the whole of it shall be subscribed for. Before the loan is advertised, a secret agreement is entered into between the agent or contractor for the loan, and one or more persons of capital and influence, who if numerous are called a syndicate, to take such portion of the loan as is deemed necessary, on terms much more favourable than those on which it is to be offered to the public. Sometimes, a portion of the loan is taken 'firm,' that is, the transaction is final and complete; but sometimes terms are introduced by which the syndicate or contractors may throw back their liability on the borrowing state. When these arrangements are concluded the loan is advertised. The period between the advertisement and the allotment is the opportunity of the syndicate or contractors. Although no scrip is in existence, they contrive by purchases and concerted dealings on the Stock Exchange to raise the loan to a premium, and this premium is maintained at any cost till the period of allotment is over. As the loan is issued at a fixed rate, and is kept at a premium, there is a clear profit to the allottee, and many persons subscribe only with the view of realising this profit. Others less versed in the mysteries of the Stock Exchange, subscribe with a view to hold the loan, being influenced by the fact that it is above issue price, a fact which can only be accounted for, as they think, by the belief of the public that they will not be able to obtain any considerable allotment, that the price of the loan will consequently rise, and that it is better to make sure of obtaining what they want by a moderate sacrifice, than run the risk of having to pay more when the loan has once been allotted.

The next step is to forward a certificate to the Committee of the Stock Exchange, that the whole loan has been unconditionally allotted, and is in the hands of the public. By these means a quotation on the Stock Exchange is procured, and the operation of floating the loan is completed. Then comes the reverse of the process.

Those who have hitherto, as above described, been purchasers, now become sellers; if possible, the premium is maintained, and thereby a profit secured to them. But owing to the favourable terms on which the issuing of the loan has been contracted for, the stock may be sold at a discount, and yet yield a considerable profit. The position is still more favourable when, as in the case of the Paraguay and 2nd Costa Rica Loans, the agents of the respective Governments have authorised the buying back for their account any portion or even the whole of the loan at the issue price to the public.

Your Committee are informed that the essence of this operation is profound secrecy. Of course operations, the intention and effect of which are to tempt people to buy scrip by creating an artificial price, must be carefully concealed from those who may not unreasonably be called the victims.

It was stated to your Committee that if a law were passed making the action of syndicates public, it would drive all transactions in public loans to foreign countries. Your Committee do not hesitate to say that if these are the only terms on which the profits arising from such loans can be retained in England, they will be too dearly earned at such a price.

It remains for your Committee to inquire whether any remedy can be devised against a system such as they have described, that is, whether the profits and advantages of foreign loans can be retained by this country, on terms which an honourable community can accept.

. . . The Companies Act of 1867 affords a precedent for requiring certain things to be stated in the prospectus, and for making false statements or wilful omission a ground for a civil action.

Your Committee think this principle might be applied in the case of a prospectus for a foreign loan.

They think the prospectus should state (among other things)–

1. The authority from the borrowing State.
2. The public debt of the State.
3. The revenue of the State for the preceding three years.
4. In case of special hypothecation, a full statement of the revenues, lands, forests, public works, or other property upon which the proposed loan is secured, and of prior charges, if any, upon such security.
5. A statement that no part of the proceeds of the loan is to be applied in buying back any of the stock, or (as the case may be) the amount, if any, which the borrowing Government reserves to itself the right to re-purchase and cancel.
6. The funds out of which the interest is to be met during the next five years

Your Committee have been much impressed, in the course of their inquiry, with the great importance of the functions exercised by the agent or contractor for a foreign loan. Considering that in several of the cases which they have examined there has been something closely resembling repudiation, based upon the alleged misconduct of the agents in this country, they cannot escape the conviction that the proper discharge of these duties is a matter of importance, not only to the subscribers, but to the nation at large. They submit to the wisdom of Parliament, whether it is proper that an office, on the due exercise of which depends in no small degree our good understanding with the borrowing country, and our reputation for honesty and good faith, should be exercised by any person who may choose to undertake it, or, worse still, to whom the representative of some petty or insolvent state may choose to intrust it.

In conclusion, your Committee feel bound to express their conviction that the best security against the recurrence of such evils as they have above described will be found, not so much in legislative enactments as in the enlightenment of the public as to their real nature and origin. Your Committee hope that the history of the foreign loans embodied in this Report will tend to enlighten the public, and to render it more difficult for unscrupulous persons to carry out schemes such as those which, in the cases on which it has been the duty of your Committee to report, have ended in so much discredit and disaster.

Part IV
THE CHURCHES

THE CHURCHES

Introduction

AFTER their last flare-up in the reign of Queen Anne, the religious differences which had split the country from top to bottom in the seventeenth century tended to die away. The Hanoverian Succession settled the nation's way of life; the Church had played a leading part in the defence against Rome, and had thereby earned the gratitude of Dissent; and the Toleration Act had made it possible for Dissenters to worship in peace. George and pudding-time came in; and although the old nerves could still vibrate on occasion, on the whole, as the century wore on, both the disposition and the opportunity to make popular issues of religious matters underwent a decline. The influence of religion on the masses of the people was reduced to the intrinsic: to the effect on them of the continuance of the traditional worship, with undiminished outward prominence, and to the infection of personal faith and religious living, of which the examples were commoner in the century, according to recent historians, than used generally to be assumed. The intellectual tendencies of the time, under the influence of rationalism and science, were directed towards speculation and apologetics, and made it unlikely that among the upper and more self-conscious classes, the most exposed to these influences, any powerful movement of religious revival would be initiated. Humanism is the characteristic note of the age; developing into humanitarianism in those with a more active social conscience and leading to attacks on the more obvious social evils of the time; resulting in scepticism, and a good deal of relaxation of the traditional moral standards amongst others. Dissent remained relatively static and quiescent, except upon its Unitarian fringe, where there was considerable intellectual activity, resulting in the production of a stock of Radical political and social ideals. It was fully in accord with these general dispositions of the age that the Evangelical movement, the great religious movement of the century, should have found its earliest and greatest leaders in relatively obscure clergymen such as the Wesleys and Whitefield; that it should have contented itself with a minimum of dogmatic theology; and that it paid relatively little attention to the cultural tradition that had grown up within and alongside the Church, but laid its greatest stress on practical Christian belief and living, in forms that could appeal to the uncultivated as much as they challenged the cultivated.

In the latter part of the century the industrial revolution, and the consequent great shifts of population, had already begun. They were to constitute the principal challenge to organized religion in the immediate future. Their effect was to leave masses of the population without those ministrations of authorized priests and teachers, and opportunities of worship, which it was the profession of the Church to provide for the whole nation. The Church's episcopal and parochial organization was thrown out of gear. In these difficulties were to lie the great opportunity of Methodism, determined to act, and able to improvise, where the motions of the official Church were necessarily slower. Into a situation so developing came the catalytic shock of the French Revolution. The outcome of movements of thought similar to those which had characterized the century in this country, maturing across more articulated intellectual and harsher social and political backgrounds, its first effect was to stimulate Radical tendencies in this country. But then, as its more violent phases developed, as it became anti-religious and anti-monarchical, and as conflict broke out between it and England, the effect was to throw this country back on itself and its older traditions. Radical criticism came to be looked on as incipient revolution; the constitution, regarded not as a point of departure but as a peak of achievement, became the political rallying ground; and, particularly as the crisis deepened and challenged the whole national life, a new seriousness of religion developed. This was naturally primarily to the benefit of evangelicalism, as the religious movement possessing the public initiative: and Wilberforce and Hannah More became figures of national significance. As the party of Mr. Pitt wore into Toryism, a genuine, if not unadulterated, piety came to pervade its ranks, and found expression, for example, in the subsidies for church-building given under Liverpool. But for the major Church problem of the re-alignment of its forces to deal with the new industrial situation, this was not an unmixed advantage. The Church had become identified with Toryism, and was the object of Radical hostility after the war, typified in the acrimonious and exaggerated attacks on its wealth and pluralism of John Wade's *Black Book* of 1820. This was expanded, so far as the Church was concerned, and re-issued as the *Extraordinary Black Book* in 1831, when the bishops' opposition to the Reform Bill had made them particularly obnoxious to the Radicals. It was inevitable that with the triumph of Reform, Churchmen should feel themselves in an exposed position. The 'thirties had, indeed, the atmosphere of a delayed and muffled clash of Revolution and Romantic Revival, with the difference in development that may be ascribed to the dominance of the constitutional tradition in this country. Moreover, it was an added element of anxiety for the Church that while in the eighteenth century it had a political role to play from the point of view of the Government, in the nineteenth century conception of the State, there seemed little for it to do. 'Tuning the pulpits' was no longer effective as a means of controlling the masses, and the votes of the bishops were not of their old importance in a House of Lords which the creations of Pitt and of later prime ministers had considerably enlarged.

The Oxford Movement was born of this feeling of alienation from the dominant forces of the time. John Keble, whose Assize Sermon on National Apostasy of 14 July 1833 is regarded as its historical beginning, was a country clergyman, son of a country clergyman, Professor of Poetry, and a Fellow of Oriel, then the leading college in Oxford. He had been brought up in the old High Church tradition which still, in places, survived from the days of Queen Anne, and he possessed, it may fairly be said, a strong sense of the past and of eternity, but little of the present. The occasion of his sermon, Grey's not immoderate proposal to suppress certain of the Irish bishoprics, and to redistribute the revenues of the Irish Church, the Church of a tiny minority, must always shock by its inappropriateness. But the more general apprehensions to which the sermon gave expression were not exaggerated in relation to the temper of the time. Newman, who was to prove the compelling and dynamic figure of the movement, was a young Oriel don, of evangelical background, whom his Oxford teachers and seniors had brought to a sense of the continued corporate life of the Church, with a brooding and tender, almost masochistic piety, and a trenchant intellect. His initiative started, and his contributions set the temper of, the *Tracts for the Times*. The note of humble pride in a commission and an authority older and more august than that of the State is set from the start.[1] The body of the *Tracts*–ninety in number, and some of them considerable volumes–was devoted to the rediscovery and reaffirmation of central teachings of the Church. Much of them, to the Protestant temper of the times, savoured of Rome, but Church doctrine had undergone so much erosion that there was room for a great deal of restoration of Catholicism before the limits of historical Anglicanism were reached. And another note was equally emphatic, both in the lives and in the teachings of the Tractarians–a profound and unaffected concern for the daily living of the spiritual truths to which the Church was witness. Newman, since 1828, had been vicar of the university church of St. Mary's, and his sermons, week after week, came gradually to weave almost a spell round his university and undergraduate audiences. In the meantime, the delivery of the *Tracts*, sent singly or in bundles to parsons who were thought likely to be receptive, or to assist in their distribution, was re-invigorating, or re-creating, in parsonages all over the country, a specifically Anglican piety, distinct from Evangelicism, though not without its debts to it, or its points of contact with it. Bishop Bagot's *Charge* to his diocese in 1838[2] shows the better informed and more temperate leaders of the Church more grateful for these services than apprehensive of any dangerous results. In its earlier phases the movement, though Catholic, was anti-Roman, and was directed to the vindication of the position of the Anglican Church as the true Church, as not merely representative but as the most authentic representative of the Church Catholic. The claims were high, the grounds on which they were argued perhaps unduly narrow, and above all the instruments of historical research needed for their investigation not yet fully competent or tempered for the task. "The restless intellect of our common humanity"–typical of an academic movement not less among Newman's young men than with breeds outside the law–drove to newer and more paradoxical positions, and in the later phases the Romanism of many of his followers, and their contempt for Protestantism and the Reformation became undisguised. The clash of opinions aroused dominated university life and politics, and attracted considerable attention in the world outside. The climax was reached in Tract 90,[3] in which Newman, more to restrain his followers than for his own satisfaction, contended that the Thirty-Nine Articles, drawn up as the definition of the specific standing of the Anglican Church, were patient, none the less, of a Catholic, by which he had largely come to understand a Roman, interpretation. A hasty and unwise, if not positively unfair, condemnation of Newman by the University authorities, followed by the request of Bishop Bagot that the publication of the *Tracts* should cease–though, as his *Charge* of 1842[4] evidences, his sympathies were as much with the Tractarians as with their critics–brought this phase of the movement to an end. Newman now gradually withdrew into isolation. But in spite of the veil with which he deliberately shrouded his feelings and intentions, he remained the centre of the liveliest apprehensions and hopes. In 1845 the doubt was resolved; the over-freighted mind and sensibility found peace, if not always happiness, and the religious vocation its scope, in communion with Rome. His name sank into relative obscurity in England, to emerge into controversial prominence again in 1869, in the sustained and magnificent afterglow of the *Apologia*.

Meanwhile the task of making practical terms with a critical State had fallen largely on Bishop Blomfield, of London, upheld by the aged Archbishop Howley. His statesmanlike insight and capacity for business, his sense of the present, in marked contrast

[1] No. 111. [2] No. 114. [3] No. 115. [4] No. 116.

to Keble's, were chiefly responsible that the Church was reformed without sacrifice of its essential character. Peel's endorsement of the need for reform[1] and his practical proposals in his brief ministry of 1834–1835 also helped the cause of compromise. A dangerous grievance, lessened by a Bill brought in by the archbishop himself in 1831, was that of the still surviving tithe in kind. Where tithe had been commuted, its grievance was not felt, but where the parson's cart came round to bear off its quota of sheaves and so forth, the farmer felt he was being subjected to a special and unreasonable imposition, and not a few villages were in bitter feud on the subject. Legislation of 1836 (6 & 7 Wm. IV, c. 71), which Peel had helped to shape, set up the Tithe Commission, and provided a general machinery of commutation. The Whigs, meanwhile, had turned their favourite weapon of inquiry by Commission upon the Church–an Ecclesiastical Courts Commission in 1830, a Church Revenues Commission in 1832–and Peel, in 1835, set up a modified Ecclesiastical Duties and Revenues Commission, which the succeeding government continued. The Whigs had no intention of being stampeded by their Radical and dissenting allies into so unhistorical a measure as disestablishment. But the system of Church courts, the persistence of pluralism, the vast differences in the incomes of episcopal sees, from the £1,000 for Llandaff to the £17,000 for Canterbury, and the same, or more, for Durham, the inequalities of stipends[2] presented targets for criticism which it was difficult to meet. The Established Church Act of 1836[3] provided for some measure of equalization of the incomes and territorial responsibilities of bishoprics, and set up the permanent Ecclesiastical Commission, with the duty of managing the Church property transferred in these changes. Even more important was the power given to the Commission to recommend further changes. The Church benefited from a better management of much of its property, and gained a permanent instrument of reform, which commanded more of its confidence when all the bishops were made members of it in 1840 (3 & 4 Vict., c. 113). An Act of 1838 (1 & 2 Vict., c. 106) set limits of distance, population, and income to the holding of pluralities, and the Dean and Chapters Act of 1840 (3 & 4 Vict., c. 113) reformed cathedral bodies and provided fresh sources of income for the Ecclesiastical Commission. The Dissenters made less progress with the attempt–supported by the Government–to put right their ancient grievances–their dependance on the Church for baptism, marriage, and burial, their compulsory rating for the upkeep of Churches not their own, and the Anglican monopoly of the universities. Acts of 1836 (6 & 7 Wm. IV, cc. 85 & 86) met the first group of grievances but the resistance of the Lords frustrated attempts to deal with the others. It was not till 1868[4] and 1870[5] that they were satisfied on these points. In some dissenting quarters there was pressure for disestablishment, but on the whole the reforms and concessions made drew the fangs of the greater part of the opposition. Its disparate elements–Irish Catholics, Radical sceptics, and the more politically minded of the Dissenters, whom the body of their fellow-worshippers, and more particularly the Methodists, were not always ready to follow–resumed their separate courses. From 1837 the political tide set in the Conservative direction. The crisis was past, and there can be little doubt that the Church, if shaken at the time, emerged from it strengthened; little doubt, perhaps, that the threat of the rude hand of the State laid upon it had awakened its reforming energies, and perhaps had been necessary to awaken them.

On the whole, therefore, it was with strengthened organization, and a renewed

[1] Part II, No. 52. [2] No. 112. [3] No. 113 [4] No. 135. [5] Part XI, Introduction.

faith in its corporate commission, that the Church faced the 'forties. But there were losses, as well as gains, of contacts and sympathies. Thomas Arnold, "the representative of high, joyous, Lutheranism", as J. B. Mozeley called him, was nearer, perhaps, to the mean of the Churchmanship of the time than either Keble or Newman. Arnold's ideal of a comprehension of Dissenters in a still episcopal but eviscerated Church, on which should be founded a truly Christian state, was perhaps never practicable. In the new temper of the Church it was not to be thought of. Arnold's talents of inspiration and leadership were directed to schoolmastering,[1] where he bred a generation that took its Christian duties in the world with intense seriousness, but often found itself out of touch with the Church. A new energy of sectarianism is one of the less happy features of the time; and for this, the new temper of the Church was not wholly without responsibility. The search for catholicity of doctrine was not always matched with catholicity of sympathy and charity to those of different views, and social snobbishness envenomed religious differences.

While evangelicalism was the dominant piety of the Church, Methodist sympathies, so far as the main body was concerned, were still predominantly with it, rather than with Dissent. Their alienation in the 'forties is shown in the attitude to Sir James Graham's educational proposals,[2] when a prospect of Christian education for the nation was lost.[3] Methodism already had its problems of internal order and discipline. Secessions had begun almost with Wesley's death. By his Deed of Declaration, the great evangelist had handed over control of what, in his lifetime, had been an autocratic empire, to the care of a conference dominated by ministers. The connexional principle and ministerial control were the authentications, in his view, of the Church character of his work, to which he had attached the deepest importance. In 1835 the legal control of the conference over the churches and other property held by trustees up and down the land on behalf of the Connexion had been vindicated by an important decision of Lord Chancellor Lyndhurst. There were further secessions as a result; and the struggle between lay and clerical control, the individualist and the authoritarian principle, still went on, directed largely against Jabez Bunting, the incarnation, in the eyes of his enemies, of the Church and conservative principles which they attacked. Despite some concessions on his part, the disputes culminated, in 1849, in a spectacular secession. For some years the impressive numerical advance which Wesleyanism had been making since the beginning of the century was checked. When it was resumed, both the main and the seceding bodies bore a more markedly Dissenting character.

On the other wing, Newman's going over to Rome had led to others, and a famous case in 1850 produced a further crop. Bishop Phillpotts of Exeter had refused to institute an evangelically minded clergyman named Gorham to the living of Brampford Speke on the score of his denial of the doctrine of Baptismal Regeneration. The Court of Arches upheld the bishop; the Judicial Committee of the Privy Council, sitting with the archbishops and the bishop of London as assessors, held that Gorham's views did not disqualify from holding a living to which he was otherwise entitled. The Judicial Committee of the Privy Council had been constituted the supreme court of appeal in ecclesiastical cases in place of Henry VIII's High Court of Delegates, under legislation of 1832, which had not envisaged its dealing with this class of issue. Phillpotts refused to act on its decree, and broke off communion with his archbishop. To him, and to many high churchmen, the State was presuming to define doctrine,

[1] Part XI, Introduction. [2] No. 119. [3] Part XI, Introduction and Nos. 237–239.

which in fact it was not, except in the negative sense of determining what came within the doctrinal formularies. Among those who went over at this juncture was Archdeacon Manning, later to become cardinal archbishop of Westminster.

A similar issue had, meanwhile, been fought out in Scotland, with dissimilar results. The Presbyterian Church had always claimed complete autonomy from the State, so far as spiritual matters were concerned. The Revolution Settlement, which established the Presbyterian Church as the Church of Scotland, and the Act of Union, had both purported to secure this position, though an Act of 1712, re-establishing lay presentation to benefices, was held, in Church circles, to have infringed the claim. Protests were made against it, but no serious dispute arose till the eighteen-thirties, a period of religious revival associated particularly with the eminent name of Dr. Thomas Chalmers. In 1834, Lord Kinnoul nominated Thomas Young to the benefice of Auchterarder, and sought to overrule the protests of the congregation and the presbytery. The Court of Session upheld him. A series of disputes over Court of Session rulings succeeded, with mounting opposition from the Church and its General Assembly. The issue, so far as presentation was concerned, narrowed down to that of 'non-intrusion', the Church accepting the claim of the civil courts to determine the temporal incidents of disputes, *i.e.* the payment of stipends, but resolutely opposing attempts to 'intrude' a minister upon a congregation and church not prepared to accept him. Behind this lay the issue of Christ's headship of the Church, which was the formula in which the Church's claim for spiritual autonomy was enshrined. The General Assembly of 1842 summed up its view of the whole controversy in an elaborate 'Claim of Right'.[1] The Whig governments of the 'thirties had shown little sympathy with the Church's claim; mediatory efforts by the duke of Argyll had broken down; in a debate in the Tory House of Commons in March 1843, not only the Erastianism of Russell, but the deeply felt Churchmanship of Graham and Peel failed to comprehend the depth and acuity of the problem, the claims of an Establishment so markedly different, in its jealousy of the State, from that to which they belonged. The General Assembly of 1843 witnessed, therefore, the Disruption, more than four hundred of the Scottish clergy leaving St. Andrew's Church, and the panoply and perquisites of Establishment in procession for the hall of Canonmills, where they founded the Free Church of Scotland, claiming to preserve alone the primitive faith and authentic standards of Scotch churchmanship Pleasant homes were abandoned for bare cottages and odd rooms at inns; many cases of pitiful destitution occurred; and Scotch Presbyterians gathered again for their worship on the seashore and the hill-side. Church building and Sustentation Funds, early organized by the provident energy of Chalmers, to which the wealthier congregations and a public from all over the world made generous contributions, relieved the worst of the distress, and enabled the vast work of church building to be started almost at once. The greater part of the congregations rallied to the Free Church. The experiment which the outspoken vicar of Leeds was to commend to the English Church[2] seemed to have answered in Scotland; the vitality of the appeal to the world of a churchmanship that manifestly disdained the things of the world seemed triumphantly demonstrated. But the leaders of the Disruption had not become Voluntarists. The sacrifice of the official blessing of the State, and the automatic support of the upper and middle classes, was a real though a necessary sacrifice to them, the Disruption a weakening of the forces that, humanly speaking, had to be relied on for the slow

[1] No. 117. [2] No. 118.

building up of the City of God. Only its necessity and trust in God's providence to set all right in his way and his time justified it to them.

Rome, in the meantime, encouraged by the tide flowing apparently all in its favour, had been maturing the decision to reconstitute an English hierarchy on a territorial basis. In 1850 the decision was taken, and Nicholas Wiseman, known up till then as the Vicar Apostolic, was made a cardinal and given the title of archbishop of Westminster. The step itself, even more Cardinal Wiseman's jubilant but perhaps indiscreet announcement of it to his flock, in his *Letter out of the Flaminian Gate*,[1] gave widespread offence; even many who were against the proposals to legislate against it joined in the condemnation. The more ebullient English reaction, significant of the enduring sensitivity of the anti-Roman nerve, was typified in Lord John Russell's letter to the bishop of Durham.[2] His proposal to legislate was opposed by the Peelite leaders, and the difference over it was a principal cause of the postponement of the coalition between Peelites and Whigs from early 1851 to late 1852.[3] Nearly two years of consolidation of the coalition before the strains of the Near Eastern Question had to be taken, might have enabled the Crimean War to be averted, with incalculable consequences for England and for Europe. Though the Ecclesiastical Titles Bill,[4] when finally passed, was never acted upon, this incident, too, exacerbated all the differences between the Churches.

In the critical years that followed, the steadiness of the Church was due in the main to the loyalty of its body, less affected than might have seemed likely by the movements that constituted the surface stir of its history. Secessions continued to take place, but on a diminishing scale, and it became clear that the hopes and fears of a large-scale going-over, or of the breaking up of the Church, were without foundation. The unshaken loyalty of Keble and of Pusey, whose Anglicanism was of the bones and blood, as well as the head, was no unimportant factor. But qualities of ecclesiastical statesmanship were required in the leaders of the Church, and these were provided in the main by Samuel Wilberforce, bishop of Oxford, in 1848, family friend of Sumner, who succeeded to the archbishopric of Canterbury in 1848, and confidant of Longley, who followed. Third son of the great evangelical emancipator, a high churchman whose three brothers and only daughter and son-in-law went over to Rome, Wilberforce's own fidelity to a position he conceived as at once catholic and liberal, respectful of the Church's divine commission and of the authority of the State, was unshakeable. Both Tractarian and Protestant enthusiasm confronted him in his diocese, and he dealt firmly with what he regarded as Romanizing, in the saintly but formidable and obstinate Pusey, while firmly protecting as much of Tractarianism as he regarded as genuinely within the Anglican pale. The use of confession, the foundation of sisterhoods, ritualism, were among the problems which his policy in his diocese, and his influence outside, helped to reduce to proportion. His great work was in the organization of his diocese. Church societies, the building of churches and parsonages, constant visiting of his parishes, a standard of scrupulous care and pastoral solicitude in his confirmations and ordinations, an immense industry reinforced by eloquence in the pulpit, by social aptitude and charm, and by the power of getting the utmost out of his fellow-workers, set a new standard, thoroughly Victorian in its conscientiousness and industry, of episcopal care and leadership in the country. He found time, as well, for frequent preaching in other dioceses and assiduous attendance on general Church business in London, including attendance at the House

[1] No. 120. [2] No. 121. [3] Part I, Nos. 7–11. [4] No. 122.

of Lords. Wilberforce was the first bishop to exploit the full possibilities of the railway as a means to ubiquity, and it was entirely appropriate that the reply to a letter of his, directed to "Sam. Oxon, Esq., Great Western Railway, nr. Reading", should reach him without difficulty. He took a large share in the steps by which, from 1852 on, the meetings of Convocation, since 1740 purely formal in character, were gradually transformed. The Church acquired a deliberative organ distinct from the collective pronouncements of the bishops, which had no constitutional or corporate status. A later phase of Tractarianism, leading to the adoption of more elaborate ceremonial in services, brought about a series of bitter disputes which divided the sympathies of the bishops and the Church between zealous and often saintly, if headstrong, incumbents, and an opposition sometimes genuinely shocked by distasteful innovation and sometimes hounded on by sectarian antagonism. The principles at issue themselves, and still more the unhappy impression produced by lawsuits culminating in decisions by the Judicial Committee of the Privy Council, caused deep concern, and led finally to the Public Worship Regulation Act of 1874.[1] This increased the disciplinary authority of the bishops, but the disputes persisted still for a number of years. Archbishop Longley died in 1867, while Disraeli was in power, and Tait succeeded. Had Gladstone been in office it is probable Wilberforce would have been appointed. Though not fully in sympathy with the main body of high churchmen, Tait was a statesman and a reconciler of the highest order, whose honesty of purpose won him increasing authority. Not genius indeed, or overwhelming personal ascendancy, but patience, compromise, hard work, and the fidelity of different minds and temperaments to common standards and aims, had kept the Church together, and provided some solvent for its difficulties.

A different order of problems was raised by the growth of new knowledge, and the adjustments in the expression of belief made necessary thereby. Evangelicalism, in its emphasis on the Bible, and the Oxford Movement, in its revival of authoritarian religion, both exhibited a fundamentalist outlook, different from that of the eighteenth century. The Bible was still known throughout the length and breadth of the land, with a detail and thoroughness of which it is difficult to form a conception today. To the bulk of its readers it was still, at all points, and without any critical reservations, the Book of Truth. Habits of thought had hardened into articles of belief. Lyell's *Principles of Geology* (1833), the more popular though less authoritative *Vestiges of Creation* (1844), by Robert Chambers, and, above all, Darwin's *Origin of Species* (1859), presented a view of the origins of the world and of man which could not be reconciled with a literal acceptance of the scriptural account. A large part of the difficulty turned on the popular assumption that the keys possessed by religion and science were to the same kinds of truth. Not all religious leaders, and not all the eminent men of science, to whom the discipline of their studies had taught intellectual caution and modesty, shared this view; but enough did, on both sides, to make a quarrel; and for all religious leaders there was the difficulty that, unlike science, religion operates through generally accepted beliefs. Large and difficult adjustments of thought were necessary, therefore, and they could not be made in a moment. The temper of fundamentalism was not calculated to assist in them. On neither side can it be said that the problem was invariably faced with a proper equanimity of temper and mind. Bishop Wilberforce's intervention in the British Association discussion on the *Origin of Species* in 1860 was one of the least happy incidents in his career. In the

[1] No. 136.

same year appeared *Essays and Reviews*, an attempt on the part of a group of scholars and clergymen to embody a scientific approach to theology. The book contains little that would not nowadays be regarded as commonplace, but it represented a sharp breach with existing modes of theological discussion, and was looked upon as treason from within the beleaguered fortress. Nor was it altogether free from the desire to shock. The prosecution for heresy of one of the writers, and the subsequent condemnation of the book by Convocation, under heavy pressure from a large body of clergy, and the controversies over the writings of Bishop Colenso of Natal, beginning a little later, gave warning of the immense difficulties, in the realms both of corporate conduct and of thought, that were to face the Church, and indeed all the Churches, in the ensuing decades. The Clerical Subscription Act of 1865–promoted by Convocation[1]–represents a first legislative attempt to shorten sail in the storm, in its substitution of the relatively simple affirmations there imposed for the complicated and repetitive subscription hitherto required.

But the difficulties that begin to cloud the prospects of the Churches at the end of our period must not blind us to the immensity of their achievement in the course of it. England became, perhaps, more nearly a Christian country than she had ever been before, perhaps more nearly than any comparable community before or since. What had to be done to make possible such an achievement has been indicated in the opening paragraphs of this essay, and is illustrated in Dean Hook's letter to Samuel Wilberforce in 1843.[2] The earlier generation of Victorians looked mass infidelity in the face, as they did revolution, and much of the intense earnestness of their attitude to life is rooted in the vision. The measure of their achievement, even by the half-way mark of the century, which is also its climacteric, is indicated by the standard of religious accommodation and attendance accepted as their norm by the Census Commissioners of 1851–1853: that every man, woman, and child able to go to church or to chapel on Sunday should have somewhere within reach to go to, and should go there once at least on each Sunday. Nos. 124–132 show in cold figures how far this ideal was, and was not, attained. Nonconformist objections prevented the repetition of the count of 1851 at subsequent censuses, but there can be little doubt that as the end of our period approached progress towards the census-takers' ideal had been continued. The key tables are those that deal with the large towns. They show only slight improvement, perhaps, in the total situation between 1831 and 1851. But the years they cover are those of the rapidest growth in the population of the great towns, and of very rapid growth in the population generally. What is therefore implied is that a great deal of the work of tranquil centuries in the provision of religious accommodation had to be re-done in less than a generation. Provision in the villages and older towns became redundant; in the great new urban districts it had to be created from scratch. That there were still deficiencies in many of the towns, and in many rural areas, even with Methodists and Dissenters, a surplus, indicates the sort of motive force, apart from abstract Christian zeal, that fed much of the effort–the sense of duty to the neighbour, blended perhaps with the desire to be as an example before him, which is so much more easily effective where the neighbour is seen and known than in the acres of anonymous streets, rarely seen or visited, where he is one of hurrying thousands.

But it is not in brick or stone, or in figures of attendance at chapel or church, that the significance of this Christian endeavour is chiefly to be seen. It is one of the great

[1] No. 134. [2] No. 118.

underlying forces of the period; exhibited in the improvement of public and private morals and manners; in the work of the societies for education and the labours of countless parsons and others in schools (Part II) and working-class clubs; in the whole insurgence against the impersonality, the indifference, and the dehumanizing effect of the new civilization and of the socio-economic philosophy that went with it. It has often been remarked that evangelical and capitalist virtues had a great deal in common. It needs to be emphasized as well that the solid support and much of the personal initiative that lay behind the many-sided social reform of the period and maintained the vast charities that eased so many of its asperities, avoidable and inevitable, and much, also, of the sense of community that tempered its harsher tensions, had also Christian roots.

SELECT BIBLIOGRAPHY

For the reforms of the 'thirties the *Reports of the Commissioners on Ecclesiastical Revenues* (*Parlty. Papers*, 1834/XXIII, 1835/XXII), and the *Reports on the State of the Established Church* (First Report, *Parlty. Papers*, 1835/XXII; Second, Third, and Fourth, *ibid.*, 1836/XXXVI; draft of Fifth Report, *ibid.*, 1837–1838/XXVIII), are the capital public documents. HORACE MANN, *Report to the Registrar-General on Religious Worship* (*Parlty. Papers*, 1852–1853/LXXXIX), is an invaluable statistical survey of the position in the middle of the century.

There is no book covering religious history for the country as a whole, during the period. H. G. WOOD, *Belief and Unbelief since 1850* (Cambridge, 1953), discusses, however, the general position of religion. F. W. CORNISH, *History of the English Church in the Nineteenth Century* (2 vols., London, 1910), is the standard work on the subject. It has bibliographies. S. C. CARPENTER, *Church and People, 1789–1899* (London, 1933), is probably the most satisfactory single volume on the subject. W. L. MATHIESON, *English Church Reform, 1815–40* (London, 1923), is a useful summary of the crucial period. A. BLOMFIELD, *Memoir of Bishop Blomfield* (2 vols., London, 1863), deals with the most influential ecclesiastical statesman of the period. J. WELCH, "Bishop Blomfield and Church Extension", in *Journal of Ecclesiastical History*, vol. IV (1954), deals with one of the great achievements of his London episcopate. E. CHURTON, *Memoirs of Joshua Watson* (2 vols., London, 1861), covers the life of a prominent High Church layman surviving from earlier days through the Reform period. F. R. SALTER, "Political Nonconformity in the Eighteen-Thirties", in *Transactions of the Royal Historical Society, Fifth Series*, vol. III (1953), studies the attitude of responsible dissenting leaders to the question, and has valuable bibliographical material. The literature of the Oxford Movement is enormous. R. W. CHURCH, *The Oxford Movement, 1833–45* (London, 1891), is still, however, the starting-point for study of it. P. THUREAU DANGIN, *La renaissance catholique en Angleterre* (3 vols., Paris, 1906–1909), gives a French view; Y. BRILIOTH, *The Anglican Revival* (London, 1925), and *Three Lectures on Evangelicism and the Oxford Movement* (Oxford, 1933), together with *Northern Catholicism*, a volume of essays edited by N. P. WILLIAMS and CHARLES HARRIS (London, 1933), seek to set the movement in a wider setting. CHRISTOPHER DAWSON, *The Oxford Movement* (London, 1933), is a brilliant study from the angle of an imaginative and sympathetic Roman Catholicism; BISHOP KNOX, *History of the Oxford Movement* (London, 1933), looks at it from the Evangelical point of view, and GEOFFREY FABER, *Oxford Apostles* (London, 1933), is a somewhat astringent study of character. *Tracts for the Times* (London, 1833–1841) in the bound form run to ten volumes. *Tract Ninety* has been reprinted with an historical commentary by A. W. EVANS (London, 1933). R. D. MIDDLETON, "Tract 90", in *Journal of Ecclesiastical History*, vol. II (1951), deals with its reception in Oxford. The publication of the *Remains of the late Reverend Richard Hurrell Froude*, edited by J. H. NEWMAN and JOHN KETH (4 vols., London, 1838–1839), was one of the moments of the movement. R. W. GREAVES, "The Jerusalem Bishopric, 1841", in *English Historical Review*, 62 (1947), deals with an incident important in its effect on Newman. Contemporary views of men who were or became critical of Tractarianism are THOMAS ARNOLD, "The Oxford Malignants" (an unfortunate title not of Arnold's choice) in *Edinburgh Review*, vol. LXIII (1836), J. A. FROUDE, "The Oxford Counter Reformation", in *Short Studies on Great Subjects*, vol. IV (4 vols., London, 1893), and MARK PATTISON, *Memoirs* (London, 1885). ANNE MOZELEY, *Letters and Correspondence of John Henry Newman during his Life in the English Church* (2 vols., London, 1891), W. WARD, *Life of Cardinal Newman* (2 vols., London, 1912), J. T. COLERIDGE, *Memoirs of Rev. John Keble* (London, 1869), and H. P. LIDDEN, *Life of E. B. Pusey, D.D.* (4 vols., London, 1893–1897), deal with the three best-known figures of the movement. The best edition of NEWMAN'S *Apologia pro Vita Sua* is by W. WARD (Oxford, 1913 and 1931), which gives both the original and the later, revised, text.

A. P. STANLEY, *Life and Correspondence of Dr Arnold* (London, 1844), H. G. WOOD,

F. D. Maurice (Cambridge, 1950), W. R. W. STEPHENS, *Life of Dean Hook* (London, 1898), and UNA POPE-HENESSEY, *Canon Kingsley* (London, 1931), present other aspects of Church life and endeavour. C. E. RAVEN, *Christian Socialism* (London, 1939), is important in this connexion. G. HODDER, *Life and Work of the Earl of Shaftesbury* (3 vols., London, 1867), and J. L. and B. HAMMOND, *Shaftesbury* (London, 1923), present the great evangelical philanthropist. G. C. B. DAVIES, *Henry Phillpotts, Bishop of Exeter, 1778–1869* (London, 1954), gives a full-length picture of the redouted controversialist and central figure of the Gorham controversy. R. G. WILBERFORCE and A. R. ASHWELL, *Life of Bishop Wilberforce* (3 vols., London, 1880–1882), covers the central figure of Church history after the Oxford Movement. E. P. BATES has edited *Bishop Wilberforce's Visitation Returns for the Archdeaconry of Oxford in the Year 1854* (Oxfordshire Record Society, 1954). R. T. DAVIDSON and W. BENHAM, *Life of A. C. Tait, Archbishop of Canterbury* (2 vols., London, 1891), should be consulted. DUNCAN FORBES, *The Liberal Anglican Tradition in History* (Cambridge, 1952), is a searching study of fundamental Anglican attitudes.

W. WARD, *Life and Times of Cardinal Wiseman* (2 vols., London, 1897), *W. G. Ward and the Catholic Revival* (London, 1912), and E. S. PURCELL, *Life of Cardinal Manning* (2 vols., London, 1896), deal with Roman Catholicism in England and its relations with the Anglican Church. DENIS GWYER, *The Second Spring, 1818–52* (London, 1942), deals with Catholic expansion in these years. W. J. TOWNSEND, H. B. WORKMAN, and GEORGE EAYRS, *A New History of Methodism* (2 vols., London, 1909), deals with the whole Methodist movement, T. P. BUNTING, *Life of Jabez Bunting* (2 vols., London, 1859), with the champion of older Methodist attitudes in the first half of the century. R. F. WEARMOUTH, *Methodism and the Working Class Movement of England, 1800–1850* (London, 1937), emphasizes an important aspect of Methodist influence. A. PEEL, *History of the Congregational Union of England and Wales, 1831–1931* (London, 1931), and A. W. W. DALE, *Life of R. W. Dale* (London, 1899), deal with Nonconformity. A. W. BENN, *History of English Rationalism in the Nineteenth Century* (London, 1906), is wider in scope and importance than its title might suggest. W. HANNA, *Life and Writings of T. Chalmers* (4 vols., Edinburgh and London, 1849–1852), includes much documentary material, and, together with R. BUCHANNAN, *The Ten Years' Conflict* (2 vols., Edinburgh, 1879), provides a full account of the Disruption. Reference may also be made to the *Autobiography and Correspondence of the 8th Duke of Argyle*, ed. INA, DUCHESS OF ARGYLE (2 vols., London, 1896).

OWEN CHADWICK, *The Victorian Church, Part I* (1966), comprehensive and authoritative – goes down to 1860; *Victorian Miniature* (1960), local study of parson and squire. In Newman Studies, C. S. DESAIN, *Letters and Diaries of J. H. Newman*, 1961, in progress, vol. xviii, reaches 1858. LOUIS BOUYER, *Newman* (1958), M. TREVOR; *Newman, Pillar of the Cloud* (1962); *Newman, Light in Winter* (1962); WILLIAM ROBBINS, *The Newman Brothers* (1966); GEORGINA BATTISCOMBE, *John Keble* (1963); B. H. SMITH, *The Anglican Response to Newman: Dean Church* (1958); V. MCCLELLAND, *Cardinal Manning* (1962); A. O. J. COCKSHUT, *Anglican Attitudes* (1951), Study of Controversies; D. NEWSOME, *Godliness and Good Learning* (1961); *The Parting of Friends, The Wilberforces and Manning* (1966); G. F. A. BEST, *Temporal Pillars, Queen Anne's Bounty, The Ecclesiastical Commission and the Church of England*; O. J. BROSE, *Church and Parliament – the Reshaping of the Church of England, 1828–60* (1960); K. HEASMAN, *Evangelicals in Action* (1960) – social work; R. G. COWHERD, *Politics of English Dissent* (1957); K. S. INGLIS, *The Churches and the Working Classes* (1963); P. T. MARSH, *The Victorian Church in Decline* – the period of Archbishop Tait; STUART MACKIE, *The Church and Scottish Social Development* (1960); E. R. WICKHAM, *Church and Parish in Sheffield* (1957).

111. The first *Tract for the Times* (1833)

Tracts for the Times
By members of the University of Oxford, 9 September 1833 (ad Clerum)
No. 1, Price 1d.

[*Thoughts on the Ministerial Commission Respectfully addressed to the Clergy.*]

I am but one of yourselves,–a Presbyter; and therefore I conceal my name, lest I should take too much on myself by speaking in my own person. Yet speak I must; for the times are very evil, yet no one speaks against them.

Is not this so? Do not we "look one upon another," yet perform nothing? Do we not all confess the peril into which the Church is come, yet sit still each in his own retirement, as if mountains and seas cut off brother from brother? Therefore suffer me, while I try to draw you forth from those pleasant retreats, which it has been our blessedness hitherto to enjoy, to contemplate the condition and prospects of our Holy Mother in a practical way; so that one and all may unlearn that idle habit, which has grown upon us, of owning the state of things to be bad, yet doing nothing to remedy it.

Consider a moment. Is it fair, is it dutiful, to suffer our Bishops to stand the brunt of the battle without doing our part to support them? Upon them comes "the care of all the Churches." This cannot be helped; indeed it is their glory. Not one of us would wish in the least to deprive them of the duties, the toils, the responsibilities of their high office. And, black event as it would be for the country, yet, (as far as they are concerned,) we could not wish them a more blessed termination of their course, than the spoiling of their goods, and martyrdom.

To them then we willingly and affectionately relinquish their high privileges and honors; we encroach not upon the rights of the SUCCESSORS OF THE APOSTLES; we touch not their sword and crosier. Yet surely we may be their shield-bearers in the battle without offence; and by our voice and deeds be to them what Luke and Timothy were to St. Paul.

Now then let me come at once to the subject which leads me to address you. Should the Government and Country so far forget their GOD as to cast off the Church, to deprive it of its temporal honors and substance, *on what* will you rest the claim of respect and attention which you make upon your flocks? Hitherto you have been upheld by your birth, your education, your wealth, your connexions; should these secular advantages cease, on what must CHRIST's Ministers depend? Is not this a serious practical question? We know how miserable is the state of religious bodies not supported by the State. Look at the Dissenters on all sides of you and you will see at once that their Ministers, depending simply upon the people, become the *creatures* of the people. Are you content that this should be your case? Alas! can a greater evil befal Christians, than for their teachers to be guided by them, instead of guiding? How can we "hold fast the form of sound words," and "keep that which is committed to our trust," if our influence is to depend simply on our popularity? Is it not our very office to *oppose* the world, can we then allow ourselves to *court* it? to preach smooth things and prophesy deceits? to make the way of life easy to the rich and indolent, and to bribe the humbler classes by excitements and strong intoxicating doctrine? Surely it must not be so;–and the question recurs, on *what* are we to rest our authority, when the State deserts us?

CHRIST has not left His Church without claim of its own upon the attention of men. Surely not. Hard Master He cannot be, to bid us oppose the world, yet give us no credentials for so doing. There are some who rest their divine mission on their own unsupported assertion; others, who rest it upon their popularity; others, on their success; and others, who rest it upon their temporal distinctions. This last case has, perhaps, been too much our own; I fear we have neglected the real ground on which our authority is built,–OUR APOSTOLICAL DESCENT. . . .

112. First Report of the Commission on Ecclesiastical Revenues (1834)

Parlty. Papers, 1834/III/xxii.

. . . It would have been more satisfactory to us to have awaited the period when we could have completed our task by a final Report; but we are impressed with a conviction that it is expedient to lay before Your Majesty, without delay, a statement of the Total Income of the Church, and of the manner in which it is divided between the Archbishops, Bishops, Corporations aggregate and sole, and the Incumbents and Curates of Benefices.

The total amount of the gross Annual Revenues of the several Archiepiscopal and Episcopal Sees in England and Wales is One hundred and eighty thousand four hundred and sixty-two Pounds, affording an average of Six thousand six hundred and eighty-three Pounds; and the total amount of the net Annual Revenues of the same is One hundred and sixty thousand one hundred and fourteen Pounds, affording an average of Five thousand nine hundred and thirty Pounds.

The total amount of the gross Annual Revenues of the several Cathedral and Collegiate Churches in England and Wales, together with the separate gross Annual Revenues of the several Dignitaries and other Spiritual Persons, members of Cathedrals or Collegiate Churches, is Three hundred and fifty thousand eight hundred and sixty-one Pounds, and the total amount of the net Annual Revenues of the same is Two hundred and seventy-two thousand eight hundred and twenty-eight Pounds.

The total number of Benefices with and without Cure of Souls, the Incumbents whereof have made Returns to our Inquiries, omitting those which are permanently or accustomably annexed to superior preferments, and which are included in the statements respecting those preferments, is Ten thousand four hundred and ninety-eight; the total amount of the gross Annual Revenues of which Benefices is Three million one hundred and ninety-one thousand nine hundred and fifty Pounds, affording an average of Three hundred and four Pounds; and the total amount of the net Annual Revenues of the same is Three million three hundred and ninety-three Pounds, affording an average of Two hundred and eighty-five Pounds.

The total number of Benefices with and without Cure of Souls in England and Wales, including those not returned to us, is Ten thousand seven hundred and one; the total gross income of which, calculated from the average of those returned, will be Three million two hundred and fifty-three thousand six hundred and sixty-two Pounds, and the total net income thereof will be Three million fifty-eight thousand two hundred and forty-eight Pounds.

The total number of Curates employed both by resident and non-resident Incumbents returned to us is Five thousand two hundred and eighty-two, whose annual stipends in the aggregate amount to Four hundred and twenty-four thousand seven hundred and ninety-six Pounds, affording an average annual stipend of Eighty Pounds; and the total amount of the stipends of Curates, if one hundred and two be assumed as the proportionate number on the Benefices not returned, and the same be calculated on the average of those returned to us, will be Four hundred and thirty-two thousand nine hundred and fifty-six Pounds.

From a scale which we have prepared of the Benefices with Cure of Souls returned to us, it appears that there are Two hundred and ninety-four, the Incomes of which are respectively under Fifty Pounds; One thousand six hundred and twenty-one of Fifty Pounds, and under One hundred Pounds; One thousand five hundred and ninety-one of One hundred Pounds, and under One hundred and fifty Pounds; One thousand three hundred and fifty-five of One hundred and fifty Pounds, and under Two hundred Pounds; One thousand nine hundred and sixty-four of Two hundred Pounds, and under Three hundred Pounds; One thousand three hundred and seventeen of Three hundred Pounds, and under Four hundred Pounds; Eight hundred and thirty of Four hundred Pounds, and under Five hundred Pounds; Five hundred and four of Five hundred Pounds, and under Six hundred Pounds; Three hundred and thirty-seven of Six hundred Pounds, and under Seven hundred Pounds; Two hundred and seventeen of Seven hundred Pounds, and under Eight hundred Pounds; One hundred and twenty-nine of Eight hundred Pounds, and under Nine hundred Pounds; Ninety-one of Nine hundred Pounds, and under One thousand Pounds; One hundred and thirty-seven of One thousand Pounds, and under One thousand five hundred Pounds; Thirty-one of One thousand five hundred Pounds, and under Two thousand Pounds; and Eighteen of Two thousand Pounds and upwards.

The number of Sinecure Rectories returned to us, and which Sinecure Rectories are included in the number of Benefices above stated, is Sixty-two; the aggregate gross Annual Revenues of which amount to Eighteen thousand six hundred and twenty-two Pounds, affording an average of Three hundred Pounds, and the aggregate net Annual Revenues of the same amount to Seventeen thousand and ninety-five Pounds, affording an average of Two hundred and seventy-five Pounds.

We regret that it is not at present practicable to offer a full explanation of the various items which compose the difference between the gross and net amounts; but, to prevent misapprehension, we think it advisable to observe, that no deduction is made from income on account of payments to Curates, nor for the reparations of

Episcopal Residences, or of Glebe Houses and Offices, nor on account of payments of Rates and Taxes for the same, nor has any deduction been made on account of arrears due at the time of making the Returns, or of any payments not being of a compulsory nature.

The Returns of Income have been generally made upon an average of Three years, ending December the Thirty-first, One thousand eight hundred and Thirty-one.

Received this
day of June 1834

W. CANTUAR.	(L.S.)	CHARLES WATKIN WILLIAMS WYNN.	(L.S.)
E. EBOR.	(L.S.)	J. NICHOLL.	(L.S.)
LANSDOWNE.	(L.S.)	N. C. TINDAL.	(L.S.)
HARROWBY.	(L.S.)	E. J. LITTLETON.	(L.S.)
C. J. LONDON.	(L.S.)	STEPHEN LUSHINGTON.	(L.S.)
J. LINCOLN.	(L.S.)	GEORGE CHANDLER.	(L.S.)
C. BANGOR.	(L.S.)	CHR. WORDSWORTH.	(L.S.)
WYNFORD.	(L.S.)	JOSEPH ALLEN.	(L.S.)
W. S. BOURNE.	(L.S.)	CHAS. THORP.	(L.S.)
HENRY GOULBURN.	(L.S.)	HUGH C. JONES.	(L.S.)

Dated this
16th day of June 1834

113. Established Church Act (1836)

6 & 7 William IV, c. 77.

[*Recital of Commissions and Reports.*]

Whereas His Majesty was pleased, on the Fourth Day of *February* and on the Sixth Day of *June* in the Year One thousand eight hundred and thirty-five, to issue Two several Commissions to certain Persons therein respectively named, directing them to consider the State of the several Dioceses in England and Wales, with reference to the Amount of their Revenues, and the more equal Distribution of Episcopal Duties, and the Prevention of the Necessity of attaching by Commendam to Bishopricks Benefices with Cure of Souls, and to consider also the State of the several Cathedral and Collegiate Churches in *England* and *Wales*, with a view to the Suggestion of such Measures as may render them conducive to the Efficiency of the Established Church, and to devise the best Mode of providing for the Cure of Souls, with special Reference to the Residence of the Clergy on their respective Benefices: And whereas the said Commissioners have, in pursuance of such Directions, made Four several Reports to His Majesty, bearing Date respectively the Seventeenth Day of *March* One thousand eight hundred and thirty-five, and the Fourth Day of *March*, the Twentieth Day of *May*, and the Twenty-fourth Day of *June* One thousand eight hundred and thirty-six: And whereas the said Commissioners have, in their said

Reports, amongst other Things, recommended that Commissioners be appointed by Parliament for the Purpose of preparing and laying before His Majesty in Council such Schemes as shall appear to them to be best adapted for carrying into effect the following Recommendations; and that His Majesty in Council be empowered to make Orders ratifying such Schemes, and having the Full Force of Law. . . .

[*Commissions incorporated.*]

And whereas it is expedient that the said Recommendations should be carried into effect as soon as conveniently may be: Be it therefore enacted by the King's most Excellent Majesty, by and with the Advice and Consent of the Lords Spiritual and Temporal, and Commons, in this present Parliament assembled, and by the Authority of the same, That the Lord Archbishop of *Canterbury* for the Time being, the Lord Archbishop of *York* and the Lord Bishop of *London* for the Time being, *John* Lord Bishop of *Lincoln*, *James Henry* Lord Bishop of *Gloucester*, the Lord High Chancellor of *Great Britain*, the Lord President of the Council, the Lord High Treasurer or the First Lord of the Treasury, and the Chancellor of the Exchequer, for the Time being respectively, and such One of His Majesty's Principal Secretaries of State as shall be for that Purpose nominated by His Majesty under His Royal Sign Manual (such Lord Chancellor, Lord President, Lord High Treasurer or First Lord of the Treasury, Chancellor of the Exchequer, and Secretary of State being respectively Members of the United Church of *Great Britain* and *Ireland*,) the Right Honourable *Dudley* Earl of *Harrowby*, the Right Honourable *Henry Hobhouse*, and the Right Honourable Sir *Herbert Jenner* Knight, shall for the Purposes of this Act be One Body Politic and Corporate by the Name of "The Ecclesiastical Commissioners for *England*," and by that Name shall have perpetual Succession and a Common Seal, and by that Name shall and may sue and be sued, and shall have Power and Authority to take and purchase and hold Lands, Tenements, and Hereditaments, to them, their Successors and Assigns, for the Purposes of this Act, the Statutes of Mortmain, or any other Act or Acts, to the contrary hereof notwithstanding.

[*How Vacancies to be supplied.*]

II. And be it enacted, That the Two last-named Bishops and the Three last-named Lay Commissioners shall be at all Times removeable by His Majesty in Council by Warrant under the Sign Manual; and that when any Vacancy shall occur, by Death, Removal, Resignation, or otherwise, among the Two last-named Bishops and the Three last-named Lay Commissioners, or among such of the future Commissioners under this Act as shall not have become such Commissioners by virtue of any Dignity or Office, according to the Provisions of this Act, it shall be lawful for His Majesty to fill up such Vacancy by appointing under His Royal Sign Manual, instead of any such Commissioner being a Bishop some other Bishop of *England* or *Wales*, and instead of any such Commissioner being a Layman some other Layman, being a Member of the said Church, to be a Commissioner under this Act; and every such Bishop or Person so to be appointed shall accordingly become to all Intents and Purposes One of the Commissioners for the Purposes of this Act. . . .

[*Assent of Meeting of Episcopal Commissioners essential to Acts under Seal, &c.*]

V. Provided always, and be it enacted, That no Proceeding which requires to be ratified and confirmed by the Common Seal of the Corporation shall be finally concluded, nor the said Seal affixed to any Deed or Instrument, save at a Meeting whereof Notice shall have been in like Manner given, and whereat Two at least of the said Episcopal Commissioners shall be personally present: Provided also, that in case any Two Episcopal Commissioners, being the only Episcopal Commissioners present, shall object to the Ratification and Confirmation of any such Proceeding as aforesaid, or to the affixing of such Seal to any Deed or Instrument as aforesaid, such Ratification or affixing of the Seal shall not take place until a subsequent Meeting of the Commissioners shall have been held, after due Notice thereof shall have been given. . . .

[*Commissioners to lay Schemes before the King in Council for carrying into effect their Recommendations.*]

X. And be it enacted, That the said Commissioners shall from Time to Time prepare, and lay before His Majesty in Council, such Schemes as shall appear to the said Commissioners to be best adapted for carrying into effect the herein-before recited Recommendations, and shall in such Schemes recommend and propose such Measures as may, upon further Inquiry, which the said Commissioners are hereby authorized to make, appear to them to be necessary for carrying such Recommendations into full and perfect Effect: Provided always, that nothing herein contained shall be construed to prevent the said Commissioners from proposing in any such Scheme such Modifications or Variations as to Matters of Detail and Regulation as shall not be substantially repugnant to any or either of the said Recommendations, and in particular that it shall be competent to the said Commissioners to propose in any such Scheme that all Parishes, Churches, or Chapelries which are locally situate in any Diocese, but subject to any peculiar Jurisdiction other than the Jurisdiction of the Bishop of the Diocese in which the same are locally situate, shall be only subject to the Jurisdiction of the Bishop of the Diocese within which such Parishes, Churches, or Chapelries are locally situate. . . .

[*No Commendams to be held by Bishops.*]

XVIII. And be it enacted, That after the passing of this Act no Ecclesiastical Dignity, Office, or Benefice, shall be held in Commendam by any Bishop, unless he shall so hold the same at the Time of passing thereof; and that every Commendam thereafter granted, whether to retain or to receive, and whether temporary or perpetual, shall be absolutely void to all Intents and Purposes.

114. Bishop Bagot's charge of July–August 1838 to the Clergy of the Oxford Diocese on the Tractarian Movement

I have spoken of increased exertions among us, and of an increasing sense of our Christian responsibilities; and therefore you will probably expect that I should say something of that peculiar development of religious feeling in one part of the Diocese, of which so much has been said, and which has been *supposed* to *tend* immediately to a Revival of several of the Errors of Romanism. In point of fact, I have been continually (though anonymously) appealed to in my official capacity to check breaches both of doctrine and discipline, through the growth of Popery among us.

Now, as regards the latter point, breaches of discipline namely, on points connected with the public services of the Church, I really am unable, after diligent inquiry, to find any thing which can be so interpreted. I am given to understand, that an injudicious attempt was made in one instance, to adopt some forgotten portion of the ancient Clerical dress; but I believe it was speedily abandoned, and do not think it likely we shall hear of a repetition of this, or similar indiscretions. At the same time, so much of what has been objected to, has arisen from minute attention to the Rubric; and I esteem uniformity so highly, (and uniformity never can be obtained without strict attention to the Rubric,) that I confess I would rather follow an antiquated custom (even were it so designated) *with* the Rubric, than be entangled in the modern confusions which ensue from the neglect of it.

With reference to errors *in doctrine*, which have been imputed to the series of publications called the *Tracts for the Times*, it can hardly be expected that, on an occasion like the present, I should enter into, or give a handle to any thing, which might hereafter tend to controversial discussions. Into controversy I will not enter. But, generally speaking, I may say, that in these days of lax and spurious liberality, any thing which tends to recall forgotten truths, is *valuable*: and where these publications have directed men's minds to such important subjects as the union, the discipline, and the authority of the Church, I think they have done good service: but there may be some points in which, perhaps, from ambiguity of expression, or similar causes, it is not impossible, but that evil rather than the intended good, may be produced on minds of a peculiar temperament. I have more fear of the Disciples than of the Teachers. In speaking therefore of the Authors of the Tracts in question, I would say, that I think their desire to restore the ancient discipline of the Church most praiseworthy; I rejoice in their attempts to secure a stricter attention to the Rubrical directions in the Book of Common Prayer; and I heartily approve the spirit which would restore a due observance of the Fasts and Festivals of the Church: *but* I would implore them, by the purity of their intentions, to be cautious, both in their writings and actions, to take heed lest their good be evil spoken of; lest in their exertions to re-establish unity, they unhappily create fresh schism; lest in their admiration of antiquity they revert to practices which heretofore have ended in superstition.* . . .

* As I have been led to suppose that the above passage has been misunderstood, I take this opportunity of stating that it never was my intention therein to pass any *general censure* on the *Tracts for the Times*. There must always be allowable points of difference in the opinions of good men, and it is only where such opinions are carried into extremes, or are mooted in a spirit which tends to schism, that the interference of those in authority in the Church is called for. The authors of the *Tracts* in question have laid no such painful necessity on me, nor have I to fear that they will ever do so. I have the best reasons for knowing, that they would be the first to submit themselves to that authority, which it has been their constant exertion to uphold and defend. And I feel sure that they will receive my friendly suggestions in the spirit in which I have here offered them.

115. Remarks on certain passages in the Thirty-Nine Articles

Tracts for the Times, No. 90.

The passages printed are the Introduction and the Conclusion. The body of the work was devoted to an examination of the Articles in turn, to substantiate the thesis urged in the Introduction. The text is that of the first edition; in the second edition Newman modified some of the expressions in the penultimate paragraph of the Introduction, weakening the force of some of them, and substituting 'we' for 'the Church', to avoid the impression that he was sitting over in judgment upon it.

Introduction

It is often urged, and sometimes felt and granted, that there are in the Articles propositions or terms inconsistent with the Catholic faith; or, at least, when persons do not go so far as to feel the objection as of force, they are perplexed how best to reply to it, or how most simply to explain the passages on which it is made to rest. The following Tract is drawn up with the view of showing how groundless the object is, and further of approximating towards the argumentative answer to it, of which most men have an implicit apprehension, though they may have nothing more. That there are real difficulties to a Catholic Christian in the Ecclesiastical position of our Church at this day, no one can deny; but the statements of the Articles are not in the number; and it may be right at the present moment to insist upon this. If in any quarter it is supposed that persons who profess to be disciples of the early Church will silently concur with those of very opposite sentiments in furthering a relaxation of subscriptions, which, it is imagined, are galling to both parties, though for different reasons, and that they will do this against the wish of the great body of the Church, the writer of the following pages would raise one voice, at least, in protest against any such anticipation. Even in such points as he may think the English Church deficient, never can he, without a great alteration of sentiment, be party to forcing the opinion or project of one school upon another. Religious changes, to be beneficial, should be the act of the whole body; they are worth little if they are the mere act of a majority.* No good can come of any change which is not heartfelt, a development of feelings springing up freely and calmly within the bosom of the whole body itself. Moreover, a change in theological teaching involves either the commission or renunciation of erroneous doctrine, and if it does not succeed in proving the fact of past guilt, it, *ipso facto*, implies present. In other words, every change in religion carries with it its own condemnation, which is not attended by deep repentance. Even supposing then that any changes in contemplation, whatever they were, were good in themselves, they would cease to be good to a Church, in which they were the fruits not of the quiet conviction of all, but of the agitation, or tyranny, or intrigue of a few; nurtured not in mutual love, but in strife and envying; perfected not in humiliation and grief, but in pride, elation, and triumph. Moreover it is a very serious truth, that persons and bodies who put themselves into a disadvantageous state, cannot at their pleasure extricate themselves from it. They are unworthy of it; they are in prison, and CHRIST is the keeper. There is but one way towards a real reformation, – a return to Him in heart and spirit, whose sacred truth they have betrayed; all

* This is not meant to hinder acts of Catholic consent, such as occurred anciently, when the Catholic body aids one portion of a particular Church against another portion.

other methods, however fair they may promise, will prove to be but shadows and failures.

On these grounds, were there no others, the present writer, for one, will be no party to the ordinary political methods by which professed reforms are carried or compassed in this day. We can do nothing well till we act "with one accord;" we can have no accord in action till we agree together in heart; we cannot agree without a supernatural influence; we cannot have a supernatural influence unless we pray for it; we cannot pray acceptably without repentance and confession. Our Church's strength would be irresistible, humanly speaking, were it but at unity with itself: if it remains divided, part against part, we shall see the energy which was meant to subdue the world preying upon itself, according to our SAVIOUR's express assurance, that such a house "cannot stand". Till we feel this, till we seek one another as brethren, not lightly throwing aside our private opinions, which we seem to feel we have received from above, from an ill-regulated, untrue desire of unity, but returning to each other in heart, and coming together to God to do for us what we cannot do for ourselves, no change can be for the better. Till her members are stirred up to this religious course, let the Church sit still; let her be content to be in bondage; let her work in chains; let her submit to her imperfections as a punishment; let her go on teaching with the stammering lips of ambiguous formularies, and inconsistent precedents, and principles but partially developed. We are not better than our fathers; let us bear to be what Hammond was, or Andrews, or Hooker; let us not faint under that body of death which they bore about in patience; nor shrink from the penalty of sins, which they inherited from the age before them.*

But these remarks are beyond our present scope, which is merely to show that, while our Prayer Book is acknowledged on all hands to be of Catholic origin, our Articles also, the offspring of an uncatholic age, are, through God's good providence, to say the least, not uncatholic, and may be subscribed by those who aim at being catholic in heart and doctrine. . . .

Conclusion

One remark may be made in conclusion. It may be objected that the tenor of the above explanations is anti-Protestant, whereas it is notorious that the Articles were drawn up by Protestants, and intended for the establishment of Protestantism; accordingly, that it is an evasion of their meaning to give them any other than a Protestant drift, possible as it may be to do so grammatically, or in each separate part.

But the answer is simple:

1. In the first place, it is a *duty* which we owe both to the Catholic Church and to our own, to take our reformed confessions in the most Catholic sense they will admit; we have no duties towards their framers. [Nor do we receive the Articles from their original framers, but from several successive convocations after their time; in the last instance, from that of 1662.]

* "We, thy sinful creatures," says the Service for King Charles the Martyr, "here assembled before Thee, do, in behalf of all the people of this land, humbly confess, that they were the *crying sins* of this nation, which brought down this judgment upon us," *i.e.* King Charles's murder.

2. In giving the Articles a Catholic interpretation, we bring them into harmony with the Book of Common Prayer, an object of the most serious moment in those who have given their assent to both formularies.

3. Whatever be the authority of the [Ratification] prefixed to the Articles, so far as it has any weight at all, it sanctions the mode of interpreting them above given. For its injoining the "literal and grammatical sense," relieves us from the necessity of making the known opinions of their framers a comment upon their text; and its forbidding any person to "affix any *new* sense to any Article," was promulgated at a time when the leading men of our Church were especially noted for those Catholic views which have been here advocated.

4. It may be remarked, moreover, that such an interpretation is in accordance with the well-known general leaning of Melanchthon, from whose writings our Articles are principally drawn, and whose Catholic tendencies gained for him that same reproach of popery, which has ever been so freely bestowed upon members of our own reformed Church.

> "Melanchthon was of opinion," says Mosheim, "that, for the sake of peace and concord many things might be given up and tolerated in the Church of Rome, which Luther considered could by no means be endured . . . In the class of matters indifferent, this great man and his associates placed many things which had appeared of the highest importance to Luther, and could not of consequence be considered as indifferent by his true disciples. For he regarded as such, the doctrine of justification by faith alone; the necessity of good works to eternal salvation; the number of the sacraments, the jurisdiction claimed by the Pope and the Bishops; extreme unction; the observation of certain religious festivals, and several superstitious rites and ceremonies."–Cent. XVI. 3. part 2. 27, 28.

5. Further: the Articles are evidently framed on the principle of leaving open large questions, on which the controversy hinges. They state broadly extreme truths, and are silent about their adjustment. For instance, they say that all necessary faith must be proved from Scripture, but do not say *who* is to prove it. They say that the Church has authority in controversies, they do not say *what* authority. They say that it may enforce nothing beyond Scripture, but do not say *where* the remedy lies when it does. They say that works *before* grace *and* justification are worthless and worse, and that works *after* grace *and* justification are acceptable, but they do not speak at all of works *with* God's aid, *before* justification. They say that men are lawfully called and sent to minister and preach, who are chosen and called by men who have public authority *given* them in the congregation to call and send; but they do not add *by whom* the authority is to be given. They say that councils called *by princes* may err; they do not determine whether councils called *in the name of* Christ will err.

6. Lastly, their framers constructed them in such a way as best to comprehend

those who did not go so far in Protestantism as themselves. Anglo-Catholics then are but the successors and representatives of those moderate reformers; and their case has been directly anticipated in the wording of the Articles. It follows that they are not perverting, they are using them, for an express purpose for which among others their authors framed them. The interpretation they take was intended to be admissible; though not that which their authors took themselves. Had it not been provided for, possibly the Articles never would have been accepted by our Church at all. If, then, their framers have gained their side of the compact in effecting the reception of the Articles, let Catholics have theirs too in retaining their own Catholic interpretation of them.

An illustration of this occurs in the history of the 28th Article. In the beginning of Elizabeth's reign a paragraph formed part of it, much like that which is now appended to the Communion Service, but in which the Real Presence was *denied in words*. It was adopted by the clergy at the first convocation, but not published. Burnet observes on it thus:–

> "When these Articles were first prepared by the convocation in Queen Elizabeth's reign, this paragraph was made a part of them; for the original subscription by both houses of convocation, yet extant, shows this. But the *design of the government* was at that time much turned *to the drawing over the body of the nation to the Reformation*, in whom the old leaven had gone deep; and no part of it deeper than the belief of the corporeal presence of CHRIST in the Sacrament; therefore it was *thought not expedient to offend* them by so particular a definition in this matter; in which the very word Real Presence was rejected. It might, perhaps, be also suggested, that here a definition was made that went too much upon the principles of natural philosophy; which, how true soever, they might not be the proper subject of an article of religion. Therefore it was thought fit to suppress this paragraph; though it was a part of the Article that was subscribed, yet it was not published, but the paragraph that follows, 'The Body of CHRIST,' &c. was put in its stead, and was received and published by the next convocation; which upon the matter was a full explanation of the way of CHRIST's presence in this Sacrament; that 'He is present in a heavenly and spiritual manner, and that faith is the mean by which He is received.' This seemed to be more theological; and it does indeed amount to the same thing. But howsoever we see what was the sense of the first convocation in Queen Elizabeth's reign, it differed in nothing from that in King Edward's time; and therefore though this paragraph is now no part of our Articles, yet we are certain that the clergy at that time did not at all doubt of the truth of it; we are sure it was their opinion; since they subscribed it, though *they did not think fit* to publish it at first; and though it was afterwards changed for another, that was the same in sense."–*Burnet on Article XXVIII*, p. 416.

What has lately taken place in the political world will afford an illustration in point. A French minister, desirous of war, nevertheless, as a matter of policy, draws up his state papers in such moderate language, that his successor, who is for peace, can act up to them, without compromising his own principles. The world, observing this, has considered it a circumstance for congratulation; as if the former minister, who acted a double part, had been caught in his own snare. It is neither decorous, nor necessary, nor altogether fair, to urge the parallel rigidly; but it will explain what it is here meant to convey. The Protestant Confession was drawn up with the purpose of including Catholics; and Catholics now will not be excluded. What was an economy in the reformers, is a protection to us. What would have been a perplexity to us then, is a perplexity to Protestants now. We could not then have found fault with their words; they cannot now repudiate our meaning.

[J. H. N.]

OXFORD,
The Feast of the Conversion of St. Paul.
1841.

116. Bishop Bagot's charge of May 1842 to the Clergy of the Oxford Diocese, on Tractarianism and Tract 90

Since I last addressed you collectively from this chair, four years have elapsed, and, although it commonly happens, that men are disposed to exaggerate the importance of events occurring in their own time, and in which they are themselves more or less the actors,–still I cannot but think, that those four years will be hereafter looked upon as the commencement of one of the most eventful epochs in the history of the English Catholic Church.

Would to God, that he, who has been called to preside over you at so momentous a period, had been an abler and a better man,–one more fitted by learning, clear-sightedness, and experience, to cope with the emergencies of the times, and to guide you far better than I can hope to do, amid the daily increasing difficulties of our position!

My trust, however, is in that strength, which is made perfect in weakness,–my comfort in the assurance of your prayers.

But to proceed. The last four years have witnessed the rapid development of those principles, which the world (though untruly, for they are of no locality) has identified with Oxford, and to which I felt it my duty to advert at my last Visitation. Those principles have, during this short interval, spread and taken root,–not merely in our own neighbourhood, and in other parts of England, but have passed from shore to shore,–east and west,–north and south,–wherever members of our Church are to be found,–nay, are unquestionably the object to which, whether at home or abroad, the eyes of all are turned who have any interest or care for the concerns of religion. I am not now saying any thing about the tendency of those principles: I am simply asserting the fact of their existence and development. There they are, whether for good or evil; and they are forming at this moment the most remarkable movement, which, for three centuries at least, has taken place amongst us.

And now, in the next place, I would advert to the manner of their growth.

Certainly they have been fostered with no friendly hand. No adscititious aid of powerful patronage has helped them forward, - no gale of popular applause has urged them on. On the contrary, they seem to have been the single exception, which an age of latitudinarian liberality could discover, against the rule of tolerating any form of belief. And, while many, whose motives are above all suspicion, and whose honoured names need no praise of mine, have unhesitatingly and utterly condemned them, - while many more have looked on with caution and mistrust, - while many in authority (myself among the number) have felt it their duty to warn those committed to their trust of the possible tendencies of the doctrines in question, - they have likewise been exposed to a storm of abuse as violent as it has been unceasing, - to calumnies and misrepresentations of the most wanton and cruel description, and to attacks from the Dissenting, Democratic, and Infidel portions of the public press, clothed in language which I will not trust myself to characterize, but which, for the sake of our common humanity, (I say nothing of Christian charity,) it behoves us, as with one voice, to reprobate and condemn. I am not now saying, whether these principles deserved the chilling reception they have met with, - I am only stating an admitted fact, that such has been their reception.

Again, let us look at the character of the doctrines brought before the public. What has been their attraction? What have they to recommend them to general adoption? The system in question, instead of being an easy comfortable form of religion, adapting itself to modern habits and luxurious tastes, is uncompromisingly stern and severe, - laying the greatest stress upon self-discipline and self-denial, - encouraging fasting, and alms-deeds, and prayer, to an extent of which the present generation, at least, knows nothing, - and inculcating a deference to authority which is wholly opposed to the spirit of the age, - and uniformly upholding that minute attention to external religion, which our formularies, indeed, prescribe, but which the world has mostly cast aside as superfluous, or as shackling and interfering with the freedom which it loves.

Now, such being the character of the religious movement which has forced itself upon our notice, it must be obvious to every one, who thinks at all on the subject, that it has peculiarities about it, which render it quite unlike any thing which has hitherto been observed among us; - and, if this be the case, it is no less obvious, that a system, which has grown up under such disadvantages, and which professes, at least, to be that of the ancient Catholic Church, deserves at any rate to be treated with as much of prudence and circumspection, as Gamaliel prescribed in a not very dissimilar instance.*

But this is a sort of forbearance, of which I have seen no signs whatsoever. I do not mean, - God forbid! that, if the doctrines of which I am speaking are erroneous, they are not to be exposed and condemned, that high and low, rich and poor, are not in their several stations to be warned against adopting them; but what I say is this, that error is to be met with argument, not with clamour, and to be answered with painful care, and grave reverence, and firm (though kind) remonstrance; - not to be made the subject of rancorous declamation, - not to be treated with the rude,

* *Acts* v. 35-39.

coarse abuse, which party spirit is sure to elicit from ill-conditioned minds, and which is as opposite to the tone of Christian condemnation as darkness is to light. Persecution never has, never will, answer its object; – there is something in the very constitution of our common nature, which inclines men to side with those whom they think unfairly treated. And such, I am disposed to think, has been the case with respect to the opinions of which I am speaking. Whether those opinions are right or wrong, I verily believe, that the temper in which their advocates have been attacked has gained them more adherents than, perhaps, any other cause.

What can have been more lamentable than the tone, which (of course I am speaking generally) has been adopted by those who have set themselves (I hope conscientiously) to oppose the opinions in question, – what can be more offensive to Christian charity, than to hear men of blameless lives held up to public execration in the newspapers of the day, as "a synagogue of Satan," and branded as 'heretics' by persons, who yet hold back the grounds on which they make their charges? Above all, – and I cannot notice without grave reprehension the conduct of these individuals, – what can be more offensive than to see Clergymen, Ministers of the Gospel of Peace, so far forgetting themselves, their duties, and their position, as to appear at public meetings as speakers, or in the daily journals as correspondents, whose tone is rather that of personal opposition, than of grave objection to error, and who thereby almost compel us to think, that they are lamentably deficient in that spirit which is "pure, and peaceable, and gentle, and easy to be intreated, full of mercy and good fruits," – "thinking no evil," – "rejoicing not in iniquity, but rejoicing in the truth."

I would that such could see themselves as they appear to others, – and could think of themselves, as all good men, of whatever party, must think of them. I would that they would reflect, with whom they are leaguing themselves, and whether some of those with whom they act are not men whose hearts' desire, and ulterior object, is the total destruction of our National Church. And more than this, – I would that they should learn a lesson from the men, whose doctrines they repudiate, and whose persons they so bitterly assail. Whatever may have been the errors, whether of doctrine or of judgment, (and of these I am not at present speaking,) of which the Authors of the *Tracts for the Times* have been guilty, I will say this for them, that the moderation and forbearance they have shewn under insults the most galling and provoking that can be imagined, has been exemplary; and I am glad to avail myself of this public opportunity of expressing my admiration of the meek and Christian spirit they have invariably shewn, – not rendering railing for railing, and never tempted, by the frequent ignorance, and often immeasurable inferiority, of many of their adversaries, to retort upon them.

You will observe, that what I have now said has no reference whatever to the question, how far the doctrines promulgated by the Tract-writers are, or are not, erroneous: but I am desirous now to record my judgment, that, granting them to be ever so erroneous, ever so heretical, and ever so much to be condemned, they have been dealt with, for the most part, in that spirit of predetermined hostility, which is most apt to confound what is true with what is false, and which, from having so little of Christian charity in it (for charity, while it has no leaning to the error, is lenient to the erring), is on that very ground to be suspected.

I now proceed, in the discharge of the heavy responsibilities of my office, to offer some remarks and advice on the subject of the opinions of which we have been speaking.

Four years ago, when the principles in question were beginning to spread, men knew not how, and while there was more doubt than at present whereunto they would grow,–whether, like fire among the thorns they would blaze up for the moment, and then die away,–or whether the flame was kindled among such materials as would give forth no mean light, and not be readily extinguished, I took the opportunity to speak freely to you, of the good which, in my opinion, had actually resulted from the publication of the *Tracts for the Times*, of the tendencies in them which I considered dangerous; and I further stated to you, that my fears arose, for the most part, rather from the disciples than the teachers.

During the period which has intervened, I have, speaking generally, seen no reason to alter my sentiments.

The *Tracts for the Times* have indeed been brought to a close, and at my personal request. And I take this opportunity of repeating in public, what I have never been backward to acknowledge in private, my deep sense of the dutifulness, and ready submission, which was then shewn to the Bishop of the diocese, and of the affection and kind feeling displayed towards myself personally by the individuals most interested.

With respect to the 90th *Tract*, which was the immediate cause of my interference, I have already expressed my opinion, that it was objectionable, and likely to disturb the peace of the Church. I thought so last year, and I think so still. I deeply regret its publication, though I am quite ready to allow, that the explanations, with which it has been subsequently modified, or rather, I should say, by which the writer's original meaning has been made more clear, have in part relieved me from some of those most serious apprehensions, with which the first perusal of it filled my mind. I am aware, that the Articles of our Church were rather drawn up with the view of including, than of excluding men of various shades of opinion, and I am further aware, that, if a precedent were wanted for–I will not say stretching–but for contorting the meaning of those formularies, nothing can exceed the licence which has been assumed by Calvinistic interpreters of the Articles–a licence, which has often gone beyond what was attempted in the 90th *Tract*. Still, I cannot persuade myself, that any but the plain obvious meaning is the meaning which as members of the Church we are bound to receive; and I cannot reconcile myself to a system of interpretation which is so subtle, that by it the Articles may be made to mean anything or nothing.

Nevertheless, if within certain limits the Articles may be so construed as not to force persons of a Calvinistic bias to leave the Church, I do not see why a similar licence, within the same limits, is not to be conceded to those, whose opinions accord with those of our Divines who resisted the puritanical temper of the 16th and 17th centuries; or why such persons should be forced into communion with Rome. And I say this the more, because I am satisfied that the 90th *Tract* was written with the object of retaining persons within the bosom of our Church who might otherwise* have seceded, and further, because I think that few living men have written more ably upon the errors of the Romish Church, and the sin of leaving our own Church for her communion, than the author of that *Tract*. . . .

117. Claim of Right of the General Assembly of the Church of Scotland (May 1842)

Act XIX of the General Assembly: W. Hanna, *Memoirs of Dr. Chalmers*, vol. IV, Appendix C.

The General Assembly of the Church of Scotland, taking into consideration the solemn circumstances in which, in the inscrutable providence of God, this Church is now placed; and that, notwithstanding the securities for the government thereof by General Assemblies, Synods, Presbyteries, and Kirk-Sessions, and for the liberties, government, jurisdiction, discipline, rights, and privileges of the same, provided by the statutes of the realm, by the constitution of this country, as unalterably settled by the Treaty of Union, and by the oath "inviolably to maintain and preserve" the same, required to be taken by each Sovereign at accession, as a condition precedent to the exercise of the royal authority;–which securities might well seem, and had long been thought, to place the said liberties, government, jurisdiction, discipline, rights, and privileges, of this Church beyond the reach of danger or invasion;–these have been of late assailed by the very Court to which the Church was authorised to look for assistance and protection, to an extent which threatens their entire subversion, with all the grievous calamities to this Church and nation which would inevitably flow therefrom;–did and hereby do solemnly, and in reliance on the grace and power of the Most High, resolve and agree on the following Claim, Declaration, and Protest: That is to say:–

Whereas it is an essential doctrine of this Church, and a fundamental principle in its constitution, as set forth in the Confession of Faith thereof, in accordance with the Word and law of the most holy God, that "there is no other Head of the Church but the Lord Jesus Christ," (ch. xxv. sec. 6); and that, while "God, the supreme Lord and King of all the world, hath ordained civil magistrates to be under him over all the people, for his own glory, and to the public good, and to this end hath armed them with the power of the sword," (ch. xxiii. sec. 1); and while "it is the duty of the people to pray for magistrates, to honour their persons, to pay them tribute and other dues, to obey their lawful commands, and to be subject to their authority for conscience' sake," "from which ecclesiastical persons are not exempted," (ch. xxiii. sec. 4); and while the magistrate hath authority, and it is his duty, in the exercise of that power which alone is committed to him, namely, "the power of the sword", or civil rule, as distinct from the "power of the keys", or spiritual authority, expressly denied to him, to take order for the preservation of purity, peace, and unity in the Church, yet 'the Lord Jesus, as King and Head of his Church, hath therein appointed a government in the hand of Church officers distinct from the

* See pp. 28, 29 of Mr. Newman's letter to Dr. Jelf; also the introduction of Dr. Pusey's letter to Dr. Jelf.

civil magistrate," (ch. xxx. sec. 1); which government is ministerial, not lordly, and to be exercised in consonance with the laws of Christ, and with the liberties of his people:

And whereas, according to the said Confession, and to the other Standards of the Church, and agreeably to the Word of God, this government of the Church, thus appointed by the Lord Jesus, in the hand of Church officers, distinct from the civil magistrate or supreme power of the State, and flowing directly from the Head of the Church to the office-bearers thereof, to the exclusion of the civil magistrate, comprehends, as the object of it, the preaching of the Word, administration of the Sacraments, correction of manners, the admission of the office-bearers of the Church to their offices, their suspension and deprivation therefrom, the infliction and removal of Church censures, and, generally, the whole "power of the keys," which, by the said Confession, is declared, in conformity with Scripture, to have been "committed" (ch. xxx. sec. 2) to Church officers, and which, as well as the preaching of the Word and the administration of the Sacraments it is likewise thereby declared, that the "civil magistrate may not assume to himself," (ch. xxiii. sec. 3):

And whereas this jurisdiction and government, since it regards only spiritual conditions, rights, and privileges, doth not interfere with the jurisdiction of secular tribunals, whose determination as to all temporalities conferred by the State upon the Church, and as to all civil consequences attached by law to the decisions of Church Courts in matters spiritual, this Church hath ever admitted, and doth admit, to be exclusive and ultimate, as she hath ever given and inculcated implicit obedience thereto:

And whereas the above mentioned essential doctrine and fundamental principle in the government of the Church, and the government and exclusive jurisdiction flowing therefrom, founded on God's Word, and set forth in the Confession of Faith, and other standards of this Church, have been, by diverse and repeated Acts of Parliament, recognised, ratified, and confirmed; . . .

And whereas, not only was the exclusive and ultimate jurisdiction of the Church Courts, in the government of the Church, and especially in the particular matters, spiritual and ecclesiastical, above mentioned, recognised, ratified, and confirmed–thus necessarily implying the denial of power on the part of any secular tribunal, holding its authority from the Sovereign, to review the sentence of the Church Courts in regard to such matters, or coerce them in the exercise of such jurisdiction:–but all such power, and all claim on the part of the Sovereign, to be considered supreme governor over the subjects of this kingdom of Scotland, in causes *ecclesiastical and spiritual*, as he is in causes *civil and temporal*, was, after a long-continued struggle, finally and expressly *repudiated and cast out of the constitution* of Scotland, *as inconsistent with the Presbyterian Church government* established at the Revolution, and thereafter unalterably secured by the Treaty of Union with England; by the constitution of which latter kingdom, differing in this respect from that of Scotland, the Sovereign is recognised to be supreme governor "*as well* in all *spiritual and ecclesiastical things* and causes as *temporal*:" . . .

And whereas this Church protested against the passing of the above mentioned

Act of Queen Anne,[1] as "contrary to the constitution of the Church, as settled by the late Treaty of union, and solemnly ratified by Act of Parliament in both kingdoms", and for more than seventy years thereafter uninterruptedly sought for its repeal, she at the same time maintained, and practically exercised, without question or challenge from any quarter, the jurisdiction of her Courts to determine ultimately and exclusively, under what circumstances they would admit candidates into the office of the holy ministry, or constitute the pastoral relationship between minister and people, and, generally, to "order and conclude the entry of particular ministers":

And whereas, in particular, this Church required, as necessary to the admission of a minister to the charge of souls, that he should have received a call from the people to whom he was to be appointed, and did not authorise or permit any one so to be admitted till such call had been sustained by the Church Courts, and did, before and subsequent to the passing of the said Act of Queen Anne, declare it to be a fundamental principle of the Church, as set forth in her authorised standards, and particularly in the Second Book of Discipline, (ch. iii. sec. 5), repeated by Act of Assembly in 1638, that no pastor be intruded upon any congregation contrary to the will of the people:

And whereas, in especial, this fundamental principle was, by the 14th. Act of the General Assembly 1736, (c. 14), re-declared, and directed to be attended to in the settlement of vacant parishes, but having been, after some time, disregarded in the administration of the Church, it was once more re-declared by the General Assembly 1834, (c. 9), who established certain provisions and regulations for carrying it into effect in time to come:

And whereas, by a judgment pronounced by the House of Lords, in 1839, (Auchterarder Case, 1839), it was, for the first time, declared to be illegal to refuse to take on trial, and to reject the presentee of a patron, (although a layman, and merely a candidate for admission to the office of the ministry), in consideration of this fundamental principle of the Church, and in respect of the dissent of the congregation; to the authority of which judgment, so far as disposing of civil interests, this Church at once implicitly bowed, by at once abandoning all claim to the *jus devolutum*, – to the benefice, for any pastor to be settled by her, – and to all other civil right or privilege which might otherwise have been competent to the Church or her Courts; and anxiously desirous, at the same time, of avoiding collision with the Civil Courts, she so far suspended the operation of the above mentioned Act of Assembly, as to direct all cases, in which dissent should be lodged by a majority of the congregation, to be reported to the General Assembly, in the hope that a way might be opened up to her for reconciling with the civil rights declared by the House of Lords, adherence to the above-mentioned fundamental principle, which she could not violate or abandon, by admitting to the holy office of the ministry a party not having, in her conscientious judgment, a legitimate call thereto, or by intruding a pastor on a reclaiming congregation contrary to their will; and further, addressed herself to the Government and the Legislature for such an alteration of the law, (as for the first time now interpreted), touching the temporalities belonging to the Church, (which alone

[1] 10 Anne, c. 12, restoring the right of presentation of ministers to heritors and others; see Introduction.

she held the decision of the House of Lords to be capable of affecting or regulating), as might prevent a separation between the cure of souls and the benefice thereto attached: . . .

And whereas, pending the efforts of the Church to accomplish the desired alteration of the law, the Court of Sessions,–a tribunal instituted by special Act of Parliament for the specific and limited purpose of "doing and administration of justice in all *civil actions*," (1537, c. 36,) with judges appointed simply "to sit and decide upon all *actions civil*," (1532, c. 1,)–not confining themselves to the determination of "civil actions",–to the withholding of civil consequences from sentences of the Church Courts, which, in their judgment, were not warranted by the statutes recognising the jurisdiction of these Courts,–to the enforcing of the provision of the Act 1592, c. 117, for retention of the fruits of the benefice in case of wrongful refusal to admit a presentee, or the giving of other civil redress for any civil injury held by them to have been wrongfully sustained in consequence thereof,–have, in numerous and repeated instances, stepped beyond the province allotted to them by the Constitution, and within which alone their decisions can be held to declare the law, or to have the force of law, deciding not only "actions civil", but "causes spiritual and ecclesiastical,"–and that, too, even where these had no connexion with the exercise of the right of patronage,–and have invaded the jurisdiction, and encroached upon the spiritual privilege of the Courts of this Church, in violation of the constitution of the country–in defiance of the statutes above mentioned, and in contempt of the laws of this kingdom: as for instance–

By interdicting Presbyteries of the Church from admitting to a pastoral charge, (1st. Lethendy Case), when about to be done irrespective of the civil benefice attached thereto, or even when there was no benefice–no right of patronage–no stipend–no manse or glebe, and no place of worship, or any patrimonial right, connected therewith (Stewarton Case).

By issuing a decree, (Marnoch Case), requiring and ordaining a Church Court to take on trial and admit to the office of the holy ministry, in a particular charge, a probationer or unordained candidate for the ministry, and to intrude him also on the congregation, contrary to the will of the people;–both in this, and in the cases first mentioned, invading the Church's exclusive jurisdiction in the admission of ministers, the preaching of the Word, and administration of Sacraments–recognised by statute to have been "given by God" directly to the Church, and to be beyond the limits of the secular jurisdiction.

By prohibiting the communicants (Daviot Case) of the Church from intimating their dissent from a call proposed to be given to a candidate for the ministry to become their pastor.

By granting interdict against the establishment of additional ministers to meet the wants of an increasing population, (Stewarton Case), as uninterruptedly practised from the Reformation to this day; against constituting a new kirk-session in a parish, to exercise discipline; and against innovating on its existing state, "as regards pastoral superintendence, its kirk-session, and jurisdiction and discipline thereto belonging."

By interdicting the preaching of the gospel, and administration of ordinances,

(Strathbogie Case), throughout a whole district, by any minister of the Church under authority of the Church Courts; thus assuming to themselves the regulation of the "preaching of the Word" and "administration of the Sacraments", and at the same time invading the privilege, common to all the subjects of the realm, of having freedom to worship God according to their consciences, and under the guidance of the ministers of the communion to which they belong.

By holding the members of inferior Church judicatories liable in damages (2nd. Auchterarder Case) for refusing to break their ordination vows and oaths (sworn by them in compliance with the requirements of the statutes of the realm, and, in particular, of the Act of Security embodied in the Treaty of Union), by disobeying and setting at defiance the sentences, in matters spiritual and ecclesiastical, of their superior Church judicatories, to which, by the constitution of the Church and country, they are, in such matters, subordinate and subject, and which, by their said vows and oaths, they stand pledged to obey.

By interdicting the execution of the sentence of a Church judicatory, prohibiting a minister from preaching or administering ordinances within a particular parish (Culsalmond Case), pending the discussion of a cause in the Church courts as to the validity of his settlement therein.

By interdicting the General Assembly and inferior Church judicatories from inflicting Church censures; as in one case, where interdict was granted against the pronouncing of sentence of deposition upon a minister found guilty of theft, by a judgment acquiesced in by himself, (Cambusnethan Case); in another, where a Presbytery was interdicted from proceeding in the trial of a minister accused of fraud and swindling, (Stranraer Case); and in a third, where a Presbytery was interdicted from proceeding with a libel against a licentiate for drunkenness, obscenity, and profane swearing, (4th. Lethendy Case).

By suspending Church censures (1st. and 2nd. Strathbogie Cases), inflicted by Church judicatories in the exercise of discipline, (which, by special statute, all "judges and officers of justice" are ordered to give "due assistance" for making "to be obeyed, or otherwise effectual",) and so reponing ministers suspended from their office, to the power of preaching and administering ordinances; thus assuming to themselves the "power of the keys".

By interdicting the execution of a sentence of deposition from the office of the holy ministry, pronounced by the General Assembly of the Church, (3rd. Strathbogie Case); thereby also usurping the "power of the keys", and supporting the deposed ministers in the exercise of ministerial functions; which is declared by special statute to be a "high contempt of the authority of the Church, and of the laws of the kingdom establishing the same".

By assuming to judge of the right of individuals elected members of the General Assembly to sit therein, (5th. Strathbogie Case), and interdicting them from taking their seats; thus interfering with the constitution of the Supreme Court of the Church, and violating her freedom in the holding of General Assemblies, secured to her by statute.

By, in the greater number of instances above referred to, requiring the inferior judicatories of the Church to disobey the sentences, in matters spiritual and ecclesiastical, of the superior judicatories, to which, by the constitution in Church and State, they are subordinate and subject, and which, in compliance with the provisions of the statutes of the realm, their members have solemnly sworn to obey;–thus subverting "the government of the Church by Kirk-sessions, Presbyteries, Provincial Synods, and General Assemblies", settled by statute and the Treaty of Union, as "the only government of the Church within the kingdom of Scotland".

By which acts, the said Court of Session, apparently not adverting to the oath taken by the Sovereign, from whom they hold their commissions, have exercised powers not conferred on them by the Constitution, but by it excluded from the province of any secular tribunal,–have invaded the jurisdiction of the Courts of the Church,–have subverted its government,–have illegally attempted to coerce Church Courts in the exercise of their purely spiritual functions,–have usurped the "power of the keys",–have wrongfully acclaimed, as the subjects of their civil jurisdiction, to be regulated by their decrees, ordination of laymen to the office of the holy ministry, admission to the cure of souls, Church censures, the preaching of the Word, and the administration of the Sacraments,–and have employed the means entrusted to them for enforcing submission to their lawful authority, in compelling submission to that which they have usurped,–in opposition to the doctrines of God's Word set forth in the Confession of Faith, as ratified by statute,–in violation of the Constitution,–in breach of the Treaty of Union, and in disregard of diverse express enactments of the Legislature.

And whereas further encroachments are threatened on the government and discipline of the Church as by law established, (4th. Strathbogie Case), in actions now depending before the said Court, in which it is sought to have sentence of deposition from the office of the holy ministry reduced and set aside, (3rd. Auchterarder Case, 3rd. Lethendy Case), and minorities of inferior judicatories to take on trial, and admit to the office of the holy ministry, in disregard of, and in opposition to, the authority of the judicatories of which they are members, and of the superior judicatories to which they are subordinate and subject:

And whereas the government and discipline of Christ's Church cannot be carried on according to his laws and the constitution of his Church, subject to the exercise, by any secular tribunal, of such powers as have been assumed by the said Court of Session:

And whereas this Church, highly valuing, as she has ever done, her connexion on the terms contained in the statutes herein before recited, with the State, and her possession of the temporal benefits thereby secured to her for the advantage of the people, must, nevertheless, even at the risk and hazard of the loss of that connexion and of these benefits–deeply as she would deplore and deprecate such a result for herself and the nation–persevere in maintaining her liberties as a Church of Christ, and in carrying on her government thereof on her own constitutional principles, and must refuse to intrude ministers on her congregations, to obey the unlawful coercion attempted to be enforced against her in the exercise of her spiritual functions and jurisdiction, or to consent that her people be deprived of their rightful liberties:

Therefore the General Assembly, while, as above set forth, they fully recognise the absolute jurisdiction of the Civil Courts in relation to all matters whatsoever of a civil nature, and especially in relation to all the temporalities conferred by the State on the Church, and the civil consequences attached by law to the decisions, in matters spiritual, of the Church Courts,–DO, in name, and on behalf of this Church, and of the nation and people of Scotland, and under the sanction of the several statutes and the Treaty of Union herein before recited, CLAIM as of RIGHT, That she shall freely possess and enjoy her liberties, government, discipline, rights, and privileges, according to law, especially for the defence of the spiritual liberties of her people, and that she shall be protected therein from the foresaid unconstitutional and illegal encroachments of the said Court of Session, and her people secured in their Christian and constitutional rights and liberties.

And they declare, that they cannot, in accordance with the Word of God, the authorised and ratified standards of this Church, and the dictates of their consciences, intrude ministers on reclaiming congregations, or carry on the government of Christ's Church, subject to the coercion attempted by the Court of Session as above set forth; and, at the risk and hazard of suffering the loss of the secular benefits conferred by the State, and the public advantages of an Establishment, they must, as by God's grace, they will, refuse so to do; for, highly as they estimate these, they cannot put them in competition with the inalienable liberties of a Church of Christ, which, alike by their duty and allegiance to their Head and King, and by their ordination vows, they are bound to maintain, "notwithstanding of whatsoever trouble or persecution may arise".

And they protest, that all and whatsoever Acts of the Parliament of Great Britain, passed without the consent of this Church and nation, in alteration or derogation to the aforesaid government, discipline, right, and privileges of this Church, (which were not allowed to be treated of by the Commissioners for settling the terms of the union between the two kingdoms, but were secured by antecedent stipulation, provided to be inserted, and inserted in the Treaty of Union, as an unalterable and fundamental condition thereof, and so reserved from the cognizance and power of the federal Legislature created by the said Treaty), as also, all and whatever sentences of Courts in contravention of the same government, discipline, right, and privileges, are, and shall be, in themselves void and null, and of no legal force and effect; and that, while they will afford full submission to all such acts and sentences, in so far, –though in so far only–as these may regard civil rights and privileges, whatever may be their opinion of the justice and legality of the same, their said submission shall not be deemed an acquiescence therein, but it shall be free to the members of this Church, or their successors, at any time hereafter, when there shall be a prospect of obtaining justice, to claim the restitution of all such civil rights and privileges, and temporal benefits and endowments, as for the present they may be compelled to yield up, in order to preserve to their office-bearers the free exercise of their spiritual government and discipline, and to their people the liberties, of which respectively, it has been attempted, so contrary to law and justice, to deprive them.

And finally, the General Assembly call the Christian people of the kingdom, and all the Churches of the Reformation throughout the world, who hold the great doctrine of the sole Headship of the Lord Jesus over his Church, to witness, that it is for their adherence to that doctrine, as set forth in their Confession of Faith, and ratified by the laws of this kingdom, and for the maintenance by them of the jurisdiction of the office-bearers, and the freedom and privileges of the members of the Church from that doctrine flowing, that this Church is subjected to hardship, and that the rights so sacredly pledged and secured to her are put in peril; and they especially invite all the office-bearers and members of this Church, who are willing to suffer for their allegiance to their adorable King and Head, to stand by the Church, and by each other in defence of the doctrine aforesaid, and of the liberties and privileges, whether of office-bearers or people, which rest upon it; and to unite in supplication to Almighty God, that He would be pleased to turn the hearts of the rulers of this kingdom to keep unbroken the faith pledged to this Church, in former days, by statutes and solemn treaty, and the obligation, come under to God Himself, to preserve and maintain the government and discipline of this Church in accordance with His Word; or otherwise that He would give strength to this Church–office-bearers and people–to endure resignedly the loss of the temporal benefits of an Establishment, and the personal sufferings and sacrifices to which they may be called, and would also inspire them with zeal and energy to promote the advancement of His Son's Kingdom, in whatever condition it may be His will to place them; and that, in His own good time, He would restore to them those benefits, the fruits of the struggles and sufferings of their fathers in times past in the same cause; and, thereafter, give them grace to employ them more effectually than hitherto they have done for the manifestation of His glory.

118. Letter from Dr. W. F. Hook, Vicar of Leeds, to Archdeacon S. Wilberforce, on the Church and the Working Classes (July 1843)

A. R. Ashwell, *Life of Bishop Wilberforce*, 1880, I, p. 225.

Archdeacon Wilberforce, later bishop of Oxford, had written to Dr. Hook for facts for a speech which he was to deliver on the education proposals of Sir James Graham's Factory Bill of 1843.[1]

Vicarage, Leeds, July 5, 1843.

My dear Wilberforce,–I am not aware that I can help you to any facts beyond those that you will find in the public reports, only warning you that Lord Ashley's statements are one-sided and exaggerated.

As far as my opinion goes, it is a crying sin in the Church not to undertake the education of the people entirely into [*sic*] her own hands. And I really do not see how the Church can fairly ask the State to give money for the purposes of giving a Church education when the money is to be supplied by Dissenters and infidels, and all classes of the people, who according to the principles of the Constitution, have a right to control the expenditure. The State can only, if consistent, give an infidel education; it cannot employ public money to give a Church education because

[1] Part XI, Nos. 237–239.

of the Dissenters, nor a Protestant education because of the Papists; and have not Jews, Turks, and infidels as much right as heretics to demand that the education should not be Christian? In saying this, I do not, of course, mean to advocate the cause of infidel education, but I would have the Government see what the difficulty is, and not attempt to educate at all.

If we are to educate the people in Church principles, the education must be out of Church funds. I would not have the State take away the funds of the Church, but I would have the Church make an offer of them. We want not proud Lords, haughty Spiritual Peers, to be our Bishops. Offer four thousand out of their five thousand a year for the education of the people and call upon the more wealthy of the other clergy to do the same, and a fund is at once provided. Let Farnham Castle and Winchester House and Ripon Palace be sold, and we shall have funds to establish other Bishoprics. Let the Church do something like this, and *then* the Church will live in the hearts of the people who now detest her.

The people in agricultural districts are generally indifferent about the Church–lukewarmness is their sin; the upper and middle classes uphold her;–but in the manufacturing districts she is the object of detestation to the working classes. Among this class I have many friends, zealous and enlightened Churchmen; and from them, and the persecutions they endure, I know the feeling which exists. The working classes consider themselves to be an oppressed people. They think that they can only obtain the right and importance they desire by exhibiting their strength; they attend public meeting and rejoice in an occasional riot, not so much for the sake of any mischief to be immediately done, as to let their oppressors, they think their superiors, see their strength.

Such men as Lord Ashley, whom they laugh at and regard only as a fool for forsaking the policy of his order, only make them feel the more indignant at their wrongs. They consider themselves to be a Party in the State,–they, many of them, are noble and enthusiastic lovers of their Party. They place Party in the stead of the Church; and they consider the Church to belong to the Party of their oppressors; hence they hate it, and consider a man of the working-classes who is a Churchman to be a traitor to his Party or Order,–he is outlawed in the society in which he moves. Paupers and persons in need may go to church on the principle of living on the enemy; but woe to the young man in health and strength who proclaims himself a Churchman. I continually expatiate on the blessedness of being persecuted to keep my young men firm, for they have a sore trial of it.

Now, such being the case, the Church must try for God's sake to win the people by making a great sacrifice. We want not the State to take our funds and expend them, but the Church to use its own funds and to say, "We will educate the people in our own way out of our own funds." Till something like this is done, it is useless to invent a scheme of Factory improvement.

You see, I am almost a Radical, for I do not see why our Bishops should not become as poor as Ambrose or Augustine, &c. &c., that they may make the people truly rich.

Yours very truly

W. F. Hook.

119. Minutes of the Wesleyan Conference, Sheffield, on Sir James Graham's education proposals (26 July 1843)

Minutes, 1774–1843, IX, pub. John Mason, 1843.

There remains yet another subject to which we think it right to refer. In the commencement of the present session of Parliament, a measure[1] was introduced to promote the better education of the poor in the manufacturing districts, and, as it was generally supposed, with the intention of ultimately extending its application, substantially, to the entire kingdom. On a careful examination of this measure by the United Committees of Privileges and of Education, it was found to be based on unjust principles; to be defective in its provisions; and calculated to produce serious injury to many excellent schools now in existence, to sow the seeds of discord in every place in which it might come into operation, and to inflame, almost beyond the possibility of healing, those unhappy dissensions which at present exist in our land. They therefore recommended that our congregations and schools should petition Parliament against it; a recommendation which was very cheerfully and extensively complied with. The strong and general feeling of disapprobation which this measure excited, in various influential quarters, has led its proposers to withdraw it for the present; and we heartily congratulate you on this result. But we must not disguise or overlook the fact, that our recent proceedings, in reference to public education, have involved us in a most serious responsibility. The case stands thus: A large number of the youth of our country are found to be greatly in need of education. It is proposed to give them a certain amount of education upon certain terms; but we, in common with other bodies, object to the terms proposed, and are understood thus to prevent them from receiving the education offered. Unless, therefore, the education offered was itself an evil as great, or greater than absolute ignorance, or unless the terms proposed were such as to neutralise the benefit of education altogether, it is manifest that we must either exert ourselves to the utmost of our power for the instruction of the people on a better system, or we must incur the guilt of depriving them of instruction altogether; neither giving it ourselves, nor allowing it to be given by others. We would have you, dear brethren, deeply impressed with this conviction, and zealous to extend to the children of the poor in your several neighbourhoods the blessings of a truly Christian education. We do not suppose, indeed, that any private or denominational efforts can effect an amount of good equal to that which would result from a well-devised and equitable measure of national education; but we are sure that patient zeal, and self-denying liberality may find ample scope, and secure an ample reward, in almost any Circuit in our Connexion. The establishment and maintenance of efficient Week-Day and Infant Schools in large towns; and the further improvement of our valuable Sunday-schools everywhere, are objects which we once more earnestly commend to your kind and careful attention.

It has been publicly stated that *one* ground of our strenuous opposition to the lately-projected measure of public education was, its obvious tendency to give the Clergy of the Established Church, an unfair and undue control over the religious

[1] Education Clauses of Graham's Factory Bill, Part XI, Nos. 237–239.

teaching in the schools which it would have established. We think it right to confirm this statement, not out of any hostile feeling to the Established Church as such, for this has never been the feeling of our Body, but with a view to bear our distinct and solemn testimony against those grievous errors which are now tolerated within her pale. We have been hitherto accustomed to regard her as one of the main bulwarks of the Protestant faith; but her title to be so regarded has of late been grievously shaken. Opinions concerning the insufficiency of Scripture, as the sole authoritative and universal rule of faith and practice, the exclusive validity of Episcopal Ordination, and the necessarily saving efficacy of the Sacraments, which can only be distinguished from Popery by an acute and practised observer, and which in their necessary consequences lead directly to Popery, have been revived when they were almost extinct, have spread with fearful rapidity and are now held by a large number of the Established Clergy. As a natural result of such a state of opinion, an exclusive and persecuting spirit has appeared in many parts of the land. The influence of rank and station is arrayed in various forms of annoyance and intolerance against liberty of conscience; the common offices of good neighbourhood are often denied to all but strict Conformists; and every approach to Christian intercourse and co-operation for religious purposes with those beyond the pale of Episcopal jurisdiction is repudiated almost with indignation. A preference for Papists over their brethren of the Reformation is in some cases openly avowed; and feelings of tenderness, and even veneration, for the Church of Rome are carefully cultivated by this party. The simple worship hitherto practised in this country is depreciated by them in comparison with the gorgeous ritual of Rome; and the appliances of art are in constant and increasing requisition for the purposes of bringing Englishmen nearer to that standard of supposed perfection. Amidst all this zeal about externals the vital and essential doctrine of *Justification by Faith only* is awfully obscured or denied. We deeply condemn and deplore this alarming departure from the truth of the Gospel in doctrine, and from its godly simplicity in divine worship and ecclesiastical observance. Yet we are aware that there is a numerous and powerful body of holy and faithful men to be found in the ranks of the National Church; and we cherish the hope that they, and the authorities of that Church, may soon feel it to be a duty which they owe to Christ and to the souls of men, to stand forth, and, by a more vigorous, explicit, and united assertion of the doctrines of the Reformation, purify their branch of the Christian community from the evils which at present threaten its destruction.

120. Cardinal Wiseman's letter "Out of the Flaminian Gate" (October 1850)

Bernard Ward, *Sequel to Catholic Emancipation*, II, Appendix M.

Nicholas, by the Divine mercy, of the Holy Roman Church by the title of St. Pudentiana Cardinal Priest, Archbishop of Westminster, and Administrator Apostolic of the Diocese of Southwark:

To our dearly beloved in Christ, the Clergy secular and regular, and the Faithful of the said Archdiocese and Diocese:

Health and benediction in the Lord!–If this day we greet you under a new title, it is not, dearly beloved, with an altered affection. If in words we seem to divide those who till now have formed, under our rule, a single flock, our heart is as undivided as ever in your regard. For now truly do we feel closely bound to you by new and stronger ties of charity; now do we embrace you in our Lord Jesus Christ with more tender emotions of paternal love; now doth our soul yearn, and our mouth is open to you, though words must fail to express what we feel on being once again permitted to address you. For if our parting was in sorrow, and we durst not hope that we should again face to face behold you, our beloved flock, so much the greater is now our consolation and our joy, when we find ourselves not so much permitted as commissioned to return to you by the supreme ruler of the Church of Christ.

But how can we for one moment indulge in selfish feelings, when, through that loving Father's generous and wise counsels, the greatest of blessings has just been bestowed upon our country, by the restoration of its true Catholic hierarchical government, in communion with the see of Peter?

For on the twenty-ninth day of last month, on the Feast of the Archangel Saint Michael, prince of the heavenly host, his Holiness Pope Pius IX. was graciously pleased to issue his Letters Apostolic, under the Fisherman's Ring, conceived in terms of great weight and dignity, wherein he substituted for the eight Apostolic Vicariates heretofore existing, one archiepiscopal or metropolitan and twelve episcopal sees; repealing at the same time, and annulling all dispositions and enactments made for England by the Holy See with reference to its late form of ecclesiastical government.

And by a brief dated the same day his Holiness was further pleased to appoint us, though most unworthy, to the archiepiscopal see of Westminster, established by the above-mentioned Letters Apostolic, giving us at the same time the administration of the episcopal see of Southwark. So that at present, and till such time as the Holy See shall think fit otherwise to provide, we govern, and shall continue to govern, the counties of Middlesex, Hertford, and Essex as ordinary thereof, and those of Surrey, Sussex, Kent, Berkshire, and Hampshire, with the islands annexed, as administrator with ordinary jurisdiction.

Further, we have to announce to you, dearly beloved in Christ, that, as if still further to add solemnity and honour before the Church to this noble act of Apostolic authority, and to give an additional mark of paternal benevolence towards the Catholics of England, his Holiness was pleased to raise us, in the private consistory of Monday, the 30th of September, to the rank of Cardinal Priest of the holy Roman Church. And on the Thursday next ensuing, being the third day of this month of October, in public consistory, he delivered to us the insignia of this dignity, the cardinalitial hat; assigning us afterwards for our title in the private consistory which we attended, the Church of St. Pudentiana, in which St. Peter is groundedly believed to have enjoyed the hospitality of the noble and partly British family of the Senator Pudens.

In that same consistory we were enabled ourselves to ask for the archiepiscopal Pallium for our new see of Westminster; and this day we have been invested, by the hands of the Supreme Pastor and Pontiff himself, with this badge of metropolitan jurisdiction.

The great work, then, is complete; what you have long desired and prayed for is granted. Your beloved country has received a place among the fair Churches, which, normally constituted, form the splendid aggregate of Catholic Communion; Catholic England has been restored to its orbit in the ecclesiastical firmament, from which its light had long vanished, and begins now anew its course of regularly adjusted action round the centre of unity, the source of jurisdiction, of light and vigour. How wonderfully all this has been brought about, how clearly the hand of God has been shown in every step, we have not now leisure to relate, but we may hope soon to recount to you by word of mouth. In the meantime we will content ourselves with assuring you, that, if the concordant voice of those venerable and most eminent counsellors to whom the Holy See commits the regulation of ecclesiastical affairs in missionary countries, if the overruling of every variety of interests and designs, to the rendering of this measure almost necessary; if the earnest prayers of our holy Pontiff and his most sacred oblation of the divine sacrifice, added to his own deep and earnest reflection, can form to the Catholic heart an earnest of heavenly direction, an assurance that the Spirit of truth, who guides the Church, has here inspired its Supreme Head, we cannot desire stronger or more consoling evidence that this most important measure is from God, has His sanction and blessing, and will consequently prosper.

Then truly is this day to us a day of joy and exaltation of spirit, the crowning day of long hopes, and the opening day of bright prospects. How must the Saints of our country, whether Roman or British, Saxon or Norman, look down from their seats of bliss, with beaming glance, upon this new evidence of the faith and Church which led them to glory, sympathising with those who have faithfully adhered to them through centuries of ill repute for the truth's sake, and now reap the fruit of their patience and long-suffering. And all those blessed martyrs of these latter ages, who have fought the battles of the faith under such discouragement, who mourned, more than over their own fetters or their own pain, over the desolate ways of their own Sion, and the departure of England's religious glory; oh! how must they bless God, who hath again visited his people,–how take part in our joy, as they see the lamp of the temple again enkindled and rebrightening, as they behold the silver links of that chain which has connected their country with the see of Peter in its vicarial government changed into burnished gold; not stronger nor more closely knit, but more beautifully wrought and more brightly arrayed.

And in nothing will it be fairer or brighter than in this, that the glow of more fervent love will be upon it. Whatever our sincere attachment and unflinching devotion to the Holy see till now, there is a new ingredient cast into these feelings; a warmer gratitude, a tenderer affection, a profounder admiration, a boundless and endless sense of obligation, for so new, so great, so sublime a gift, will be added to past sentiments of loyalty and fidelity to the supreme see of Peter. Our venerable Pontiff has shown himself a true shepherd, a true father; and we cannot but express our gratitude to him in our most fervent language, in the language of prayer. For when we raise our voices, as is meet, in loud and fervent thanksgiving to the Almighty, for the precious gifts bestowed upon our portion of Christ's vineyard, we will also implore every choice blessing on him who has been so signally the divine instrument in procuring it. We will pray that his rule over the Church may be prolonged to many years, for its welfare; that health and strength may be preserved to him for the discharge of his arduous duties; that light and grace may be granted to him proportioned to the sublimity of his office; and that consolations, temporal and spiritual, may be poured out upon him abundantly, in compensation for past sorrows and past ingratitude. And of these consolations may one of the most sweet to his paternal heart be the propagation of holy religion in our country, the advancement of his spiritual children there in true piety and devotion, and our ever-increasing affection and attachment to the see of St. Peter.

In order, therefore, that our thanksgiving may be made with all becoming solemnity, we hereby enjoin as follows:–

1. This our Pastoral Letter shall be publicly read in all the churches and chapels of the archdiocese of Westminster and the diocese of Southwark on the Sunday after its being received.

2. On the following Sunday there shall be in every such church or chapel a solemn Benediction of the blessed Sacrament, at which shall be sung the *Te Deum*, with the usual versicles and prayers, with the prayer also *Deus omnium Fidelium Pastor et Rector* for the Pope.

3. The collect, *Pro Gratiarum Actione*, for thanksgiving, and that for the Pope, shall be recited in the Mass of that day, and for two days following.

4. Where Benediction is never given, the *Te Deum* with its prayers, shall be recited or sung after Mass, and the collects above-named shall be added as enjoined.

And at the same time, earnestly entreating for ourselves also a place in your fervent prayers, we lovingly implore for you, and bestow on you, the blessing of Almighty God, Father, Son, and Holy Ghost. Amen.

Given out of the Flaminian Gate of Rome, this seventh day of October, in the year of our Lord MDCCCL.

(Signed) NICHOLAS,
Cardinal Archbishop of Westminster.
By command of his Eminence,
FRANCIS SEARLE, *Secretary.*

121. Lord John Russell's letter to the bishop of Durham on papal aggression (November 1850)

Spencer Walpole, *Life of Lord John Russell*, 1889, II, p. 120.

Downing Street, November 4, 1850

MY DEAR LORD,–I agree with you in considering "the late aggression of the Pope upon our Protestantism" as "insolent and insidious", and I therefore feel as indignant as you can do upon the subject.

I not only promoted to the utmost of my power the claims of the Roman

Catholics to all civil rights, but I thought it right and even desirable that the ecclesiastical system of the Roman Catholics should be the means of giving instruction to the numerous Irish immigrants in London and elsewhere, who without such help would have been left in heathen ignorance.

This might have been done, however, without any such innovation as that which we have now seen.

It is impossible to confound the recent measures of the Pope with the division of Scotland into dioceses by the Episcopal Church, or the arrangement of districts in England by the Wesleyan Conference.

There is an assumption of power in all the documents which have come from Rome; a pretension of supremacy over the realm of England, and a claim to sole and undivided sway, which is inconsistent with the Queen's supremacy, with the rights of our bishops and clergy, and with the spiritual independence of the nation, as asserted even in Roman Catholic times.

I confess, however, that my alarm is not equal to my indignation.

Even if it shall appear that the ministers and servants of the Pope in this country have not transgressed the law, I feel persuaded that we are strong enough to repel any outward attacks. The liberty of Protestantism has been enjoyed too long in England to allow of any successful attempt to impose a foreign yoke upon our minds and consciences. No foreign prince or potentate will be at liberty to fasten his fetters upon a nation which has so long and so nobly vindicated its right to freedom of opinion, civil, political, and religious.

Upon this subject, then, I will only say that the present state of the law shall be carefully examined, and the propriety of adopting any proceedings with reference to the recent assumption of power, deliberately considered.

There is a danger, however, which alarms me much more than any aggression of a foreign sovereign.

Clergymen of our own Church, who have subscribed the Thirty-nine Articles and acknowledged in explicit terms the Queen's supremacy, have been most forward in leading their flocks "step by step to the very verge of the precipice". The honour paid to saints, the claim of infallibility for the Church, the superstitious use of the sign of the cross, the muttering of the liturgy so as to disguise the language in which it is written, the recommendation of auricular confession, and the administration of penance and absolution, all these things are pointed out by clergymen of the Church of England as worthy of adoption, and are now openly reprehended by the Bishop of London in his charge to the clergy of his diocese.

What then is the danger to be apprehended from a foreign prince of no great power compared to the danger within the gates from the unworthy sons of the Church of England herself?

I have little hope that the propounders and framers of these innovations will desist from their insidious course. But I rely with confidence on the people of England; and I will not bate a jot of heart or hope, so long as the glorious principles and the immortal martyrs of the Reformation shall be held in reverence by the great mass of a nation which looks with contempt on the mummeries of superstition, and with scorn at the laborious endeavours which are now making to confine the intellect and enslave the soul.–I remain, with great respect, &c.,

J. RUSSELL.

If you think it will be of any use, you have my full permission to publish this letter.

122. Ecclesiastical Titles Act (1851)

14 & 15 Vict. c. 60.

[10 *G.* 4. *c.* 7. *s.* 24.]

Whereas divers of Her Majesty's Roman Catholic Subjects have assumed to themselves the Titles of Archbishop and Bishops of a pretended Province, and of pretended Sees or Dioceses, within the United Kingdom, under colour of an alleged Authority given to them for that Purpose by certain Briefs, Rescripts, or Letters Apostolical from the See of *Rome*, and particularly by a certain Brief, Rescript, or Letters Apostolical purporting to have been given at *Rome* on the Twenty-ninth of *September* One thousand eight hundred and fifty: And whereas by the Act of the Tenth Year of King *George* the Fourth, Chapter Seven, after reciting that the Protestant Episcopal Church of *England* and *Ireland*, and the Doctrine, Discipline, and Government thereof, and likewise the Protestant Presbyterian Church of *Scotland*, and the Doctrine, Discipline, and Government thereof, were by the respective Acts of Union of *England* and *Scotland*, and of *Great Britain* and *Ireland*, established permanently and inviolably, and that the Right and Title of Archbishops to their respective Provinces, of Bishops to their Sees, and of Deans to their Deaneries, as well in *England* as in *Ireland*, had been settled and established by Law, it was enacted, that if any Person after the Commencement of that Act, other than the Person thereunto authorized by Law, should assume or use the Name, Style, or Title of Archbishop of any Province, Bishop of any Bishopric, or Dean of any Deanery, in *England* or *Ireland*, he should for every such Offence forfeit and pay the Sum of One hundred Pounds: And whereas it may be doubted whether the recited Enactment extends to the Assumption of the Title of Archbishop or Bishop of a pretended Province or Diocese, or Archbishop or Bishop of a City, Place, or Territory, or Dean of any pretended Deanery in *England* or *Ireland*, not being the See, Province, or Diocese of any Archbishop or Bishop or Deanery of any Dean recognized by Law; but the Attempt to establish, under colour of Authority from the See of *Rome* or otherwise, such pretended Sees, Provinces, Dioceses, or Deaneries, is illegal and void: And whereas it is expedient to prohibit the Assumption of such Titles in respect of any Places within the United Kingdom:" Be it therefore declared and enacted by the Queen's most Excellent Majesty, by and with the Advice and Consent of the Lords Spiritual and Temporal, and Commons, in this present Parliament assembled, and by the Authority of the same, That–

[*Briefs, Rescripts, or Letters Apostolical declared unlawful and void.*]

I. All such Briefs, Rescripts, or Letters Apostolical, and all and every the

Jurisdiction, Authority, Pre-eminence, or Title conferred or pretended to be conferred thereby, are and shall be and be deemed unlawful and void.

[*Persons procuring, publishing or putting in use any such Brief, &c. for constituting Archbishops, Bishops, &c. of pretended Provinces, Sees or Dioceses, liable to a Penalty of* 100*l. for every Offence.*]

[*Recovery of Penalties.*]

II. And be it enacted, That if, after the passing of this Act, any Person shall obtain or cause to be procured from the Bishop or See of *Rome*, or shall publish or put in use within any Part of the United Kingdom, any such Bull, Brief, Rescript, or Letters Apostolical, or any other Instrument or Writing, for the Purpose of constituting such Archbishops or Bishops of such pretended Provinces, Sees, or Dioceses, within the United Kingdom, or if any Person, other than a Person thereunto authorized by Law in respect of an Archbishopric, Bishopric, or Deanery of the United Church of *England* and *Ireland*, assume or use the Name, Style, or Title of Archbishop, Bishop, or Dean of any City, Town or Place, or of any Territory or District, (under any Designation or Description whatsoever,) in the United Kingdom, whether such City, Town, or Place, or such Territory or District, be or be not the See or the Province, or co-extensive with the Province, of any Archbishop, or the See or the Diocese, or co-extensive with the Diocese, of any Bishop, or the Seat or Place of the Church of any Dean, or co-extensive with any Deanery, of the said United Church, the Person so offending shall for every such Offence forfeit and pay the Sum of One hundred Pounds, to be recovered as Penalties imposed by the recited Act may be recovered under the Provisions thereof, or by Action of Debt at the Suit of any Person in One of Her Majesty's Superior Courts of Law, with the Consent of Her Majesty's Attorney General in *England* and *Ireland*, or Her Majesty's Advocate in Scotland, as the Case may be. . . .

123. Census Report of 1851–1853 on Religious Worship: Churchbuilding: Church of England

Parlty. Papers, 1852–1853/LXXXIX.

	Number of churches built	Estimated cost		
		Total	Contributed by	
			Public funds	Private benefaction
		£	£	£
1801 to 1831 . .	500	3,000,000	1,152,044	1,847,956
1831 to 1851 . .	2,029	6,087,000	511,385	5,575,615
1801 to 1851 . .	2,529	9,087,000	1,663,429	7,423,571

124. Census Report of 1851–1853 on Religious Worship: Accommodation for Worship: Basis for Calculations

Parlty. Papers, 1852–1853/LXXXIX.

[*Maximum of required accommodation in places of Worship.*]

If, by a happy miracle, on Sunday, March the 30th 1851, an universal feeling of devotion had impressed our population, and impelled towards the public sanctuaries all whom no impediment, of physical inability or needful occupation, hindered; if the morning or the evening invitation of the service-bell had called, no less from the crowded courts of populous towns and the cottages of scattered villages than from the city mansions and the rural halls, a perfect complement of worshippers; for what proportion of the 17,927,609 inhabitants of England would accommodation in religious buildings have been necessary?

The reply to this inquiry will determine mainly the extent by which our actual supply of spiritual ministration is inadequate to the demand.

[*Various estimates.*]

Various computations have been made respecting the number of sittings proper to be furnished for a given population. With respect to *towns*, it has been thought by some that accommodation for 50 per cent. would be sufficient; while others have considered that provision for not less than 75 per cent. should be afforded. Dr. Chalmers took the mean of these two estimates, and concluded that five eighths, or 62½ per cent., of the people of a town might attend religious services, and ought to have facilities for doing so.*

The maximum for rural districts is put lower than that for towns; the distance of the church from people's residences operating as an unavoidable check upon attendance. But, as, for the purpose of this estimate, the *rural* population will consist of only those who live remote as well from villages containing churches as from towns,–in fact, of only those who are remote from any place of worship,–the proportion deemed to be sufficient for a *town* may be applied, with very slight reduction, to the whole of England–town and country both together; and, according to the best authorities, this proportion seems to lie between 50 and 60 per cent. of the entire community.

[*Considerable deduction to be made from the total population. 1. Young children.*]

From many valid causes, there will always be a considerable number of persons absent from public worship. First, a large deduction from the total population must be made on account of *infants and young children*: of whom there were in England and Wales, in 1851, as many as 4,440,466 under ten years of age – 2,348,107 of this number being under five. Of course, opinions vary as to the earliest age at which a child, in order to acquire a habit of devotion, should be taken to a place of worship:

* *Christian and Economic Polity of a Nation*, I, p. 123. Mr. E. Baines (an excellent authority on subjects of this nature) assumes that accommodation for 50 per cent of the gross population would be ample. – *Letters on the Manufacturing Districts.*

some begin occasional attendance before they reach five years of age, while others are retained at home much later. Many parents too, no doubt, conceive that the attendance of their children at a Sunday-school is a sufficient tax upon their tender strength. Perhaps it will not, therefore, be unreasonable to assume that, either on account of immaturity or Sunday-school engagements, about 3,000,000 children will be always justifiably away from public worship.

[2. *Invalids and aged persons.*]

There will also always be in any large community a certain number kept at home by *sickness*. It is estimated that the proportion of persons constantly sick, or incapacitated by infirmities of age for active duties, is about five per cent. of the population; and, as the *degree* of indisposition which in general detains a prudent person from chapel or church is much slighter than that contemplated in this calculation, we shall probably not err in taking nearly seven per cent. of the 15,000,000 (which remain after deducting the 3,000,000 children who have already been supposed to be absent), and putting down 1,000,000 persons as the number usually and lawfully away from public worship on the ground of *sickness or debility*.*

[3. *Persons in charge of houses &c.*]

Another large deduction must be made for those who are necessarily left in charge of houses and in attendance upon the two preceding classes. There were, in 1851, in England and Wales, 3,278,039 inhabited houses. If some of these in country parishes were left untenanted, locked up, while the inmates were at service, others doubtless were in charge of more than one domestic; so that we may safely take the whole 3,278,039 houses as representing so many individuals legitimately absent from religious edifices on account of *household duties*. Many of these, no doubt, would discharge a double occupation, as guardians of the house and attendants upon children or invalids; but some addition must unquestionably be made for a distinct array of nurses, or of parents unavoidably detained at home, and also for the medical practitioners, whose Sunday services can scarcely be dispensed with.

[4. *Persons employed on public conveyances.*]

A fourth considerable class, of which a certain number will be always absent from religious worship, is the class employed in connexion with the various *public conveyances*; as railways, steamboats, omnibuses, coaches, barges on canals, &c.† It is impossible to form an estimate of the precise *extent* to which employment in this way may be admitted as an adequate excuse for non-attendance on religious ordinances; since opinions are extremely various as to the extent to which the use of conveyances upon the Sunday is to be considered a work of "necessity or mercy". It cannot, however, be doubted that, practically, whatever views are likely to prevail

* The number of persons in England and Wales in 1851, aged 70 years and upwards, was 503,305; aged 75 and upwards, there were 253,143; aged 80 and upwards, there were 107,041; aged 85 and upwards, there were 33,201; upwards of 90, there were 7,796; above 95 there were 1,545; and 215 were upwards of 100.

† It is estimated that the number of men engaged, in London alone, upon omnibuses, on the Sunday, is as many as 6,000.

upon the subject of Sabbath labour, very many persons will be constantly engaged in ministering to the public need of locomotion.

[*Result of these deductions.*]

Not attempting any numerical estimate of various minor classes, and designedly not making any deduction on account of Sunday traders, or the criminal population – since the object is to show the amount of accommodation needed for those who are *able*, not merely for those who are *willing*, to attend – it seems to follow from the previous computations that about 7,500,000 persons will, of necessity, be absent whenever divine service is celebrated; and, consequently, that sittings in religious buildings cannot be required for *more* than 10,427,609, being rather more than 58 per cent. of the entire community. It will be convenient for the subsequent calculations to deal with 58 per cent. exactly, and assume that the number always able to attend is 10,398,013.

[*Effect of double services.*]

It by no means results, from this, that the adult portion of the remaining 42 per cent. of the population (7,500,000 in round numbers) is entirely without opportunities of frequenting public worship; for, as there is generally more than one service on the Sunday, it is practicable, and in fact customary, to carry on a system of *relief* – some who attend service at one period of the day occupying at the other period the place of those who were before prevented; thus enabling these to attend a later service in their turn. This system is especially adopted in the case of domestic servants; consequently, though there is probably always about the *same number* (*viz.* 7,500,000) detained at home by lawful causes, this number will not always be composed of the *same persons*.

The custom of double, and sometimes treble, services each Sunday introduces an important element into the question of the number of sittings needful for a given population. It has been shown above, that sittings cannot be wanted for more than 10,398,013 persons (being the full number able to attend at one time). But does it therefore follow that there should be *as many* sittings as this number of persons? It is obvious that if attendance upon public worship *once a day* be thought sufficient for each individual, it is possible to conceive a case where, all the churches and chapels being open *twice* a day, the whole population could attend, though sittings should exist for only half their number. For instance; if in a district, with ten thousand persons able to attend, the places of worship (open twice upon the Sunday) should contain 5,000 sittings, it is possible for the whole ten thousand to attend them, simply by the one half going in the morning and the other in the evening: and if *three* services are held, a further diminution of the number of sittings might be made without depriving any person of the opportunity of attending *once*. This, though of course an extreme illustration, cannot fail to show the necessity of settling, ere a trusty calculation can be made of the accommodation needful for the country, whether it is to be assumed that a single sitting may be occupied by more than one person on one Sunday, or whether we must aim at a provision so extensive that every person may be able (if inclined) to attend each Sunday *twice* or oftener–in fact, at *every* service. Practically, I believe it will be found that very many persons think their duties as to Sabbath worship adequately discharged by *one* attendance; and most likely we may safely count upon the permanent continuance of a large class thus persuaded. Still, as no definite conception can be formed of the extent to which this practice is adopted–and as it might reasonably be contended that neglect of any opportunities for worship should not be *presumed*, but that such an extent of accommodation should be furnished as would utterly exclude excuse for non-attendance–it will be the better plan, if merely indicating the existence of the practice as an element in the question, I assume that the provision needful for the population should consist of at least as many sittings as there are individuals not incapacitated by the causes previously mentioned, *viz.*, 10,398,013, or 58 per cent. Indeed, whatever diminution in the estimate may be supposed to be allowable on account of double services will probably be more than counterbalanced by the absolute necessity there is that nearly every building should possess some *surplus* of accommodation; for as, practically, it is impossible that each religious body can compute so nicely its position and attractiveness as to provide exactly as many sittings as are wanted from it, and no more,–as some will naturally leave a margin for anticipated progress, which perhaps may not be realized, while others will miscalculate the other way, and grow beyond their utmost expectations,–there must needs be a certain excess of supply beyond demand, continuing as long as there exists a variety of churches, and the liberty for people to prefer one church before another. I am therefore inclined to consider that accommodation for 58 per cent. of the population is no more than would be absolutely needful if all persons able to attend were also willing.

[*The maximum of accommodation is affected by its distribution over the country.*]

But, of course, in order to be adequate to the wants of the community, the buildings which should contain these 10,398,013 sittings must be so located on the surface of the country as to bring the accommodation they afford within the reach of all by whom it is required. If many churches and chapels be clustered in a narrow compass, or if several thinly peopled parishes have each a church with more accommodation than is wanted, it will follow that in other portions of the country there must necessarily be some deficiency, unless the aggregate of sittings be raised *above* 10,398,013. So that what is wanted is, not merely such a number of sittings as shall equal the total number of persons capable of using them, but also such a *distribution* of these sittings as will render them *available* by all requiring them. A provision of 10,398,013 sittings for the whole of England would only be sufficient if *in every part* of England there should prove to be accommodation for as many as 58 per cent. It will presently be shown how far the actual distribution of religious buildings in this country affects the question of the adequacy or inadequacy of existing accommodation.

[*By what religious bodies should the necessary accommodation be provided?*]

Having advanced thus far, we meet a question much more difficult and delicate than any which has hitherto encountered us; this is, assuming that 10,398,013 sittings ought to be provided, would the provision be satisfactory supposing that that number could be furnished by the aid of *all the various churches and congregations in the aggregate*? or is it essential that they should belong to one particular church exclusively? or to a certain number of churches which agree upon particular fundamental doctrines? These are questions which are obviously beyond the range of this Report, and which must be discussed and settled for themselves by the different readers of the Tables. In the meantime, while endeavouring to estimate in some degree the actual extent of 'spiritual destitution', it may fairly be allowed, perhaps, to take the whole accommodation in the gross; since it is probable that yet for many years to come each church will continue to retain a hold upon the sympathies of a portion of our population, which then, of course, as now, will not require, as they would not accept, accommodation in the buildings of other denominations. The course of argument, however, will be of general applicability, and can easily be adapted to the Church of England or to any other body.

[*Actual provision according to the Census.*]

What, then, is the number of sittings actually furnished, by the agency of all the various churches, towards the accommodation of the 10,398,013 persons who, if only willing, would be able constantly to occupy them? The returns from 31,943 places of religious worship, many of them of course being simply rooms in houses, give an aggregate of sittings to the number of 9,467,738. But as 2,524 other places have omitted to return the number of their sittings, an estimate for these, computed from the average of complete returns,* will raise the total number of sittings reported to the Census Office to 10,212,563. This, when compared with the number calculated as desirable (10,398,013), shows a deficiency in the whole of England and Wales of 185,450.

[*Adequacy of existing accommodation if equally distributed.*]

The point, then, to which we have arrived is this: assuming that the joint provision made by all the sects together may be reckoned in the computation, the deficiency, upon the whole of England and Wales, will be only to the extent of 185,450 sittings (or for only 1·03 per cent. of the population), *if the entire provision now existing is found to be so well distributed over the country as that no part has too little and no part too much.* We must, therefore, now inquire how far this necessary distribution has been realized.

[*Effect of unequal distribution.*]

Every portion of the country, I assume, should have accommodation for 58 per cent. of the inhabitants.† It would clearly be of no avail that one part should have more

* In this calculation a separate average has been taken for each denomination; but it has not been thought essential to proceed so minutely as to distinguish whether the places of worship supplying defective returns are situate in town or country localities, nor how many of them are separate and entire buildings. It is not probable that any closer scrutiny would materially alter the estimate. Where, however, any reliable indication of the number of sittings has been furnished by a statement of the number of *attendants*, this has been adopted rather than the *average*.

† This may be taken as sufficiently near. In some parts, however, from peculiar circumstances, it is evident that this proportion will in some degree be varied. There may be a greater number of children or a greater number of servants, etc.–circumstances adequate to alter to a trifling extent the proportion of persons able to attend a place of worship.

than this percentage if another part had less; for since, according to the estimate, *no more* than 58 per cent. of the population could be present at one time at a religious service, it is evident that if in any place the number of sittings would accommodate a much *greater* proportion than 58 per cent., there would be in that locality a surplus of unused and useless sittings, generally inaccessible to residents in other neighbourhoods, and quite as unavailable as if they had never been provided. What is required is, not alone an *aggregate* percentage of 58 per cent. in an extensive area (such as the whole of England, or the whole of an English county); for this would not be any proof of adequate provision, since the rural portions might possess an unavailable abundance, while the urban portions suffered under an extreme deficiency; but that same percentage in localities of size so circumscribed that inequalities of distribution could but slightly operate. Then, what localities, of definite character, of this appropriate size, can be selected for comparison, by which to estimate more accurately our requirements? Of course, with regard to the Church of England, there should be accommodation for the 58 per cent. *in every parish*, since the very theory of a parochial arrangement is that the people of a parish should attend the parish church and none besides; but probably it is not needful to investigate so carefully as this. The Registration Districts, or Poor Law Unions, (of which there are in England and Wales 624), will afford convenient limits for comparison; and if in any of these we find a total amount of accommodation adequate for 58 per cent. of the inhabitants, we shall probably not err to any great extent, (although, no doubt, we shall to *some* extent), if we conclude that there is room for 58 per cent. within the reach of all dwellers in the District. The selection too of Districts as the standards of comparison will obviate the difficulty which, if *parishes* were taken, would arise with reference to the members of Dissenting Bodies, who, ignoring altogether the parochial system, often cross the limits of the parish where they dwell in order to attend a chapel situate beyond its boundaries. By taking the somewhat wider area of *Districts*, the disturbances to the calculations from this cause will be reduced to unimportance.

125. Census Report of 1851–1853 on Religious Worship: Total Accommodation for Worship

Parlty. Papers, 1852–1853/lxxxix.

Registration Divisions and Counties	Number of sittings already provided	Proportion per cent of the population already accommodated: In the gross	Proportion per cent of the population already accommodated: After deductions for unequal distribution	Number of additional sittings required in order to provide for 58% of the population
England and Wales	10,212,563	57·0	48·8	1,644,734
Div. I.–London	713,561	30·2	29·6	669,514
Div. II.–South Eastern Counties	940,418	58·0	52·4	91,431
Div. III.–South Midland Counties	800,688	64·8	55·5	30,892
Div. IV.–Eastern Counties	784,202	70·4	55·5	27,589
Div. V.–South Western Counties	1,301,847	72·2	57·3	13,715
Div. VI.–West Midland Counties	1,163,437	54·5	49·1	174,614
Div. VII.–North Midland Counties	852,003	70·1	55·5	29,818
Div. VIII.–North Western Counties	1,077,985	43·2	42·0	397,738
Div. IX.–Yorkshire	1,081,826	60·4	51·6	117,985
Div. X.–Northern Counties	491,186	50·7	48·7	91,438
Div. XI.–Welsh Counties	1,005,410	84·5	58·0	—

Registration Divisions and Counties	Number of sittings already provided	Proportion per cent of the population already accommodated: In the gross	Proportion per cent of the population already accommodated: After deductions for unequal distribution	Number of additional sittings required in order to provide for 58% of the population
Division I				
Middlesex (Metropolitan Portion)	523,183	29·9	29·2	502,243
Surrey (Metropolitan Portion)	143,655	29·7	29·7	136,158
Kent (Metropolitan Portion)	46,723	34·8	34·8	31,113
Division II				
Surrey (extra-Metropolitan)	99,288	49·0	48·9	18,547
Kent (extra-Metropolitan)	280,185	57·8	53·1	23,512
Sussex	192,135	56·5	51·1	23,503
Hampshire	238,481	59·3	52·7	21,371
Berkshire	130,329	65·4	55·7	4,498
Division III				
Middlesex (extra-Metropolitan)	68,602	45·6	45·6	18,749
Hertfordshire	106,041	61·0	55·7	4,069
Buckinghamshire	101,840	70·9	56·8	1,700
Oxfordshire	116,432	68·4	57·3	1,211
Northamptonshire	156,865	73·3	56·0	4,203

Registration Divisions and Counties	Number of sittings already provided	Proportion per cent of the population already accommodated: In the gross	Proportion per cent of the population already accommodated: After deductions for unequal distribution	Number of additional sittings required in order to provide for 58% of the population
Division III (*contd.*)				
Bedfordshire	91,987	70·8	58·0	—
Cambridgeshire	114,614	59·7	55·9	3,960
Huntingdonshire	44,307	73·4	58·0	—
Division IV				
Essex	223,679	65·0	54·6	11,532
Suffolk	248,702	73·7	57·1	3,151
Norfolk	311,821	72·0	55·0	12,906
Division V				
Wiltshire	185,254	76·8	58·0	—
Dorsetshire	138,995	78·5	58·0	—
Devonshire	382,556	66·9	55·9	12,308
Cornwall	279,627	78·3	58·0	—
Somersetshire	315,415	69·1	57·7	1,407
Division VI				
Gloucestershire	263,508	62·8	54·6	14,277
Herefordshire	62,116	62·7	58·0	—
Shropshire	164,331	67·1	57·3	1,542
Staffordshire	315,804	50·1	48·1	62,452
Worcestershire	133,602	51·6	48·9	23,428
Warwickshire	224,076	46·6	42·8	72,915

Registration Divisions and Counties	Number of sittings already provided	Proportion per cent of the population already accommodated: In the gross	Proportion per cent of the population already accommodated: After deductions for unequal distribution	Number of additional sittings required in order to provide for 58% of the population
Division VII				
Leicesterhire	170,334	72·5	53·7	10,164
Rutlandshire	20,483	84·4	58·0	—
Lincolnshire	309,658	77·3	58·0	—
Nottinghamshire	175,633	59·7	52·8	15,254
Derbyshire	175,895	67·5	56·3	4,400
Division VIII				
Cheshire	243,648	57·5	53·0	21,107
Lancashire	834,337	40·3	39·8	376,631
Division IX				
West Riding	724,537	54·0	49·8	109,987
East Riding	179,266	70·5	54·9	7,998
North Riding	177,923	91·4	58·0	—
Division X				
Durham	192,396	46·7	46·4	47,944
Northumberland	148,298	48·8	46·9	33,570
Cumberland	110,253	56·4	52·9	9,924
Westmorland	40,239	68·9	58·0	—
Division XI				
Monmouthshire	128,966	72·8	58·0	—
South Wales	507,432	83·5	58·0	—
North Wales	369,012	91·3	58·0	—

Where, in any district, the amount of accommodation exceeds 58 per cent of the inhabitants, the surplus has been deducted from the gross amount of the county; proceeding on the assumption that such surplus is not generally available by the inhabitants of other districts. – It has not been considered necessary to carry the

126. Census Report of 1851–1853 on Religious Worship: Religious Accommodation in Large Towns

Parlty. Papers, 1852–1853/LXXXIX.

Towns	Population, 1851	Number of sittings provided by all religious bodies	Proportion per cent of sittings to population	Additional number of sittings required to accommodate 58% of the population
Ashton-under-Lyne	30,676	11,828	38·6	5,964
Bath	54,240	33,149	61·1	—
Birmingham	232,841	66,812	28·7	68,236
Blackburn	46,536	18,483	39·7	8,508
Bolton	61,171	21,801	35·6	13,678
Bradford	103,778	32,827	31·6	27,364
*Brighton	69,673	24,098	34·6	16,312
Bristol	137,328	75,516	52·8	7,134
*Bury	31,262	13,434	43·0	4,698
Cambridge	27,815	14,807	53·2	1,326
Carlisle	26,310	11,407	43·4	3,853
*Chatham	28,424	13,089	46·0	3,397
*Cheltenham	35,051	19,819	56·5	511
Chester	27,766	14,176	51·1	1,928
Colchester	19,443	14,234	73·2	—
Coventry	36,208	15,537	42·9	5,464
Derby	40,609	20,338	50·1	3,215
*Devonport	50,159	23,372	46·6	5,720
*Dover	22,244	11,636	52·3	1,266
Dudley	37,962	15,911	41·9	6,107

Towns	Population, 1851	Number of sittings provided by all religious bodies	Proportion per cent of sittings to population	Additional number of sittings required to accommodate 58% of the population
Exeter	32,818	19,586	59·7	—
*Finsbury	323,772	94,165	29·1	93,623
Gateshead	25,568	9,081	35·5	5,748
Gravesend	16,633	6,532	39·3	3,115
Great Yarmouth	30,879	14,223	46·1	3,687
*Greenwich	105,784	35,497	33·6	25,858
Halifax	33,582	10,192	30·3	9,286
*Huddersfield	30,880	15,787	51·1	2,127
Hull	84,690	37,413	44·2	11,707
Ipswich	32,914	16,017	48·7	3,073
Kidderminster	18,462	9,829	53·2	879
King's Lynn	19,355	9,502	49·1	1,724
*Lambeth	251,345	62,307	24·8	83,473
Leeds	172,270	79,266	46·0	20,651
Leicester	60,584	25,008	41·3	10,131
Liverpool	375,955	125,002	31·4	93,052
§London (City)	127,869	68,330	53·4	18,706

Towns	Population, 1851	Number of sittings provided by all religious bodies	Proportion per cent of sittings to population	Additional number of sittings required to accommodate 58% of the population
†London (Metropolis)	2,362,236	713,561	29·7	669,514
Macclesfield	39,048	16,461	42·2	6,187
Maidstone	20,740	9,787	47·2	2,242
Manchester	303,382	95,929	31·6	80,033
*Marylebone	370,957	100,208	27·0	114,947
*Merthyr Tydfil	63,080	36,815	58·4	—
Newcastle	87,784	30,319	34·5	20,596
Newport (Mon.)	19,323	10,706	55·4	501
Northampton	26,657	14,268	53·5	1,193
Norwich	68,195	30,807	45·2	8,746
Nottingham	57,407	27,261	47·5	6,035
Oldham	52,820	16,976	32·1	13,660
Oxford	27,843	16,768	60·2	—
Plymouth	52,221	23,805	45·6	6,483
Portsmouth	72,096	26,608	36·9	15,208
Preston	69,542	24,642	35·4	15,692
Reading	21,456	11,401	53·1	1,043
Rochdale	29,195	13,533	46·4	3,400
Salford	63,850	24,772	38·8	12,261
Sheffield	135,310	45,889	33·9	32,591
Southampton	35,305	17,959	50·9	2,518
South Shields	28,974	14,198	49·0	2,607
*Southwark	172,863	50,237	29·1	50,024
Stockport	53,835	22,588	42·0	8,636
*Stoke-upon-Trent	84,027	40,723	48·5	8,013
Sunderland	63,897	31,264	48·9	5,796
Swansea	31,461	18,539	58·9	—
*Tower Hamlets	539,111	137,921	25·6	174,763
Tynemouth	29,170	12,854	44·1	4,065
Wakefield	22,065	15,649	70·9	—
Walsall	25,680	10,503	40·9	4,391
Warrington	22,894	10,083	44·0	3,196
*Westminster	241,611	76,181	31·5	63,953
Wigan	31,941	9,777	30·6	8,749
*Wolverhampton	119,748	48,455	40·5	20,999
Worcester	27,528	16,174	58·7	—
York	36,303	23,650	65·1	—
**Total	6,239,099	2,329,416	37·3	1,332,992

* The *Municipal* limits of the towns here mentioned have been generally taken: an asterisk (*) indicates the exceptions – where the *Parliamentary* boundaries have been followed. Estimates have been made of the number of sittings in those places of worship the returns for which omit to give this information. For other particulars relating to these towns, see *post*, SUMMARY TABLES, pp. cclii–cclxxii [not reprinted].

§ This is the Municipal and Parliamentary City of London; comprising the three Poor Law Unions of East London, West London, and City of London (within the walls). The latter union corresponds with the ancient City of London, and contains accommodation for 81 per cent of the inhabitants, or for 13,338 more than could at any one time attend.

† This proportion of sittings to population for the metropolis is calculated upon the number which remains after deducting 13,338 sittings, a surplus existing in the City of London (within the walls) over and above the number requisite for 58 per cent of the population of the district.

** In dealing with *London* in this total, the entire metropolis has been taken: the figures therefore which relate to the boroughs of *Finsbury*, *Greenwich*, *Lambeth*,

127. Census Report of 1851–1853 on Religious Worship: Amount of Accommodation, at different periods, in the whole of England and Wales

Parlty. Papers, 1852–1853/LXXXIX.

Periods	Population at each period	Number of places of worship at each period	Estimated number of sittings at each period	Rate of increase between the periods of population and sittings respectively: Population	Sittings	Number of sittings to 100 persons at each period
				Per cent	Per cent	
1801	8,892,536	15,080	5,171,123	—	—	58·1
1811	10,164,256	16,490	5,524,348	14·3	6·8	54·4
1821	12,000,236	18,796	6,094,486	18·0	10·3	50·8
1831	13,896,797	22,413	7,007,091	15·8	15·0	50·4
1841	15,914,148	28,017	8,554,636	14·5	22·5	53·8
1851	17,927,609	34,467	10,212,563	12·6	19·4	57·0

128. Census Report of 1851–1853 on Religious Worship: Increase of Accommodation, at different periods, in large town districts as compared with the residue of England and Wales

Parlty. Papers, 1852–1853/LXXXIX.

Large town districts							Residue of England						
Periods	Population at each period	Estimated number of places of worship and sittings at each period: Places of worship	Sittings	Rates of increase of population and sittings respectively: Population	Sittings	No. of sittings to 100 persons at each period	Periods	Population at each period	Estimated number of places of worship and sittings at each period: Places of worship	Sittings	Rates of increase of population and sittings respectively: Population	Sittings	No. of sittings to 100 persons at each period
				Per cent	Per cent						Per cent	Per cent	
1801	3,608,024	3,500	1,506,922	—	—	41·8	1801	5,284,512	11,580	3,664,201	—	—	69·3
1811	4,260,848	3,805	1,638,240	18·1	8·7	38·5	1811	5,903,408	12,685	3,886,108	11·7	6·1	65·8
1821	5,241,895	4,501	1,937,901	23·0	18·3	37·0	1821	6,758,341	14,295	4,156,585	14·5	7·0	61·5
1831	6,435,953	5,670	2,441,213	22·8	26·0	38·0	1831	7,460,844	16,743	4,565,878	10·4	9·8	61·2
1841	7,735,136	7,391	3,182,188	20·2	30·3	41·1	1841	8,179,012	20,626	5,372,448	9·6	17·7	65·7
1851	9,229,120	9,586	4,127,244	19·3	29·7	44·7	1851	8,698,489	24,881	6,085,319	6·3	13·3	70·0

129. Census Report of 1851–1853 on Religious Worship: rate of increase, in Decennial Periods, of Wesleyan Methodists, Independents, and Baptists, respectively, in the whole of England and Wales

Parlty. Papers, 1852–1853/LXXXIX.

Periods	WESLEYAN METHODISTS (*All branches*)			INDEPENDENTS			BAPTISTS (*All branches*)		
	Number of places of worship and sittings at each period		*Rate of increase per cent at each period*	*Number of places of worship and sittings at each period*		*Rate of increase per cent at each period*	*Number of places of worship and sittings at each period*		*Rate of increase per cent at each period*
	Places of worship	*Sittings*		*Places of worship*	*Sittings*		*Places of worship*	*Sittings*	
1801	825	165,000	—	914	299,792	—	652	176,692	—
1811	1,485	296,000	80·0	1,140	373,920	24·7	858	232,518	31·6
1821	2,748	549,600	85·0	1,478	484,784	29·2	1,170	317,070	36·4
1831	4,622	924,400	68·2	1,999	655,672	35·2	1,613	437,123	37·9
1841	7,819	1,563,800	69·2	2,606	854,768	30·4	2,174	589,154	34·7
1851	11,007	2,194,298	40·3	3,244	1,067,760	24·9	2,789	752,343	27·7

From this it appears that neither of these bodies is advancing at a rate so rapid as formerly. But then it must also be remembered that neither is there *room* for such a rapid increase, since the aggregate rate of increase during the half-century has been so much more rapid than the increase of the population that whereas, in 1801, the number of sittings provided for every 1,000 persons was–by Wesleyans 18, by Independents 34, and by Baptists 20; in 1851, the provision was–by Wesleyans 123, by Independents 59, and by Baptists 42.

130. Census Report of 1851–1853: comparative view of the Accommodation in rural and large town districts provided by the Wesleyan Methodists, Independents, and Baptists, respectively, in the whole of England and Wales

Parlty. papers, 1852–1853/LXXXIX.

	WESLEYAN METHODISTS			INDEPENDENTS			BAPTISTS		
	Number of places of worship and sittings		*Proportion per cent of sittings to population*	*Number of places of worship and sittings*		*Proportion per cent of sittings to population*	*Number of places of worship and sittings*		*Proportion per cent of sittings to population*
	Places of worship	*Sittings*		*Places of worship*	*Sittings*		*Places of worship*	*Sittings*	
Large town districts . .	3,050	896,372	9·7	936	454,729	4·9	839	318,013	3·5
Country districts . . .	7,957	1,297,926	14·9	2,308	613,031	7·1	1,950	434,330	5·0

131. Census Report of 1851–1853 on Religious Worship: Summary on Accommodation

Parlty. Papers, 1852–1853/LXXXIX.

[*General result as to accommodation.*]

The summary result of this inquiry with respect to accommodation is, that there are in England and Wales 10,398,013 persons able to be present at one time in buildings for religious worship. Accommodation, therefore, for that number (equal to 58 per cent. of the population) is required. The *actual* accommodation in 34,467 churches, chapels, and out-stations is enough for 10,212,563 persons. But this number, after a deduction, on account of ill-proportioned distribution, is reduced to 8,753,279, a provision equal to the wants of only 49 per cent. of the community. And further, out of these 8,753,279 sittings, a certain considerable number are rendered *unavailable* by being in churches or chapels which are *closed* throughout some portion of the day when services are usually held. There is therefore wanted an additional supply of 1,644,734 sittings, if the population is to have an extent of accommodation which shall be undoubtedly sufficient.* These sittings, too, must be provided *where* they are wanted; *i.e.* in the *large town districts* of the country,–more especially in London. To furnish this accommodation would probably require the erection of about 2,000 churches and chapels; which, in towns, would be of larger than the average size. This is assuming that all churches and sects may contribute their proportion to the work, and that the contributions of each may be regarded as by just so much diminishing the efforts necessary to be made by other churches. If, as is probable, this supposition be considered not altogether admissible, there will be required a further addition to these 2,000 structures; the extent of which addition must depend upon the views which may be entertained respecting what particular sects should be entirely disregarded.

Of the total existing number of 10,212,563 sittings, the Church of England contributes 5,317,915, and the other churches, together, 4,894,648.

132. Census Report of 1851–1853 on Religious Worship: attendance at Religious Worship

Parlty. Papers, 1852–1853/LXXXIX.

[*Attendance at religious services a better test of religious disposition than amount of accommodation.*]

Thus far, in considering the aspect of the English people towards religious institutions, our regard has been directed wholly to that proof of the existence or the absence of religious feeling, which is furnished by the ample or inadequate supply of the means of public worship. It is scarcely, however, with this evidence that one, desirous of obtaining a correct idea of the extent to which religious sentiments prevail among the masses of our population, would be satisfied. For, though the existence of a *small* provision only may be fairly taken as a proof of feeble spiritual life, since a people really governed by religious influences will not long remain without the

* It may be said that this contemplates an optimistic condition of society; but it has been thought better to take as a standard the actual *wants* of the people, rather than their probable conduct. Readers can make their own deductions.

means of outward worship; yet the converse of this proposition cannot be maintained, since much of the provision at the service of one generation may be owing to the piety of a former, whose religious zeal may not perhaps have been inherited by its posterity along with its rich legacy of churches. Even, too, a great *contemporary* addition to the number of religious edifices does not positively indicate the prevalence of a religious spirit in the body of the people: it may merely show the presence of a missionary spirit in a portion of the general Church. An inquirer, therefore, anxious to discover more precisely the extent to which religious sentiments pervade the nation, would desire to know not merely the amount of accommodation *offered* to the people, but also what proportion of the means at their command is actually *used*. A knowledge, therefore, of the number of ATTENDANTS on the various services of public worship is essential.

[*Number of attendants to be compared with accommodation and population.*]

We have seen that, in the gross, there are 34,467 places of worship in England and Wales, with 10,212,563 sittings. But, as many of these places of worship were closed upon each portion of the day, and the sittings in them consequently unavailable, it is with the provision in the *open* buildings that we must compare the number of attendants. In those open for the *morning* service there were (including an estimate for defective returns) 8,498,520 sittings; in those open in the afternoon, 6,267,928 sittings; in those open in the evening, 5,723,000 sittings. The total number of *attendants* (also including estimates for omissions) was, in the morning, 4,647,482; in the afternoon 3,184,135; in the evening, 3,064,449. From this it seems that, taking the three services together, less than half of the accommodation actually available is used. But here, again, the question of *distribution* is important. For if, in any locality, the amount of accommodation existing should be larger than that required, we cannot expect to find the number of attendants bearing there so large a proportion to the sittings as in other localities where the accommodation may be insufficient. There may really be a better attendance in a district where the churches are half empty than in one which they are completely filled: that is, a greater number out of a given population may attend in the former case than in the latter. Therefore, before we can assume a lax attendance in particular districts, the number of the *population* must be brought into account. To prove a disregard of spiritual ordinances, there must be exhibited not merely a considerable number of vacant sittings, but also a corresponding number of persons by whom, if so disposed, those sittings might be occupied. But if, according to the previous computation, 58 per cent. of the population is the utmost that can ever be attending a religious service at one time, it is evident that where, as in some districts, the available accommodation is sufficient for a *greater* number, there must *necessarily* exist, whatever the devotional spirit of the people, an excess of sittings over worshippers. If, for example, we refer to the City of London (within the walls), which, with a population of 55,932 has sittings for as many as 45,779–or for 13,338 more than could possibly, at any one time, attend–it is obvious that a great many sittings must inevitably be unoccupied; and this without regard to the question whether, in fulfilling their religious duties, the inhabitants be zealous or remiss. The best plan, therefore, seems to be, to compare the attendants, in the first place, with the population; and then, secondly, with the sittings. The former view will give us an approximate idea of the extent to which religion has a practical influence over the community–exhibiting the numbers who appreciate or neglect religious services; the latter view will show in what degree neglect, if proved, may be occasioned or excused by the supply of insufficient means of worship. If, for instance, in a certain district, the proportion of the population found attending some religious service should be small, while at the same time there should be within the district ample room for the remainder: this would show conclusively that in that district a considerable number of the people were without religious habits, and indifferent to public worship. And the same conclusion might be drawn, although the actual provision were inadequate, if even this inadequate accommodation were but sparely used.

[*Number of non-attendants.*]

Returning, then, to the total of England and Wales, and comparing the number of actual attendants with the number of persons *able* to attend, we find that out of 10,398,013 (58 per cent. of the total population) who would be at liberty to worship at one period of the day, there were actually worshipping but 4,647,482 in the morning, 3,184,135 in the afternoon, and 3,064,449 in the evening. So that, taking any one service of the day, there were actually attending public worship less than half the number who, as far as physical impediments prevented, *might* have been attending. In the *morning* there were absent, without physical hindrance, 5,750,531; in the afternoon, 7,213,878;* in the evening, 7,333,564. There exist no *data* for determining how many persons attended twice, and how many three times on the Sunday; nor, consequently, for deciding how many altogether attended on *some* service of the day; but if we suppose that half of those attending service in the afternoon had not been present in the morning, and that a third of those attending service in the evening had not been present at either of the previous services, we should obtain a total of 7,261,032 separate persons who attended service either once or oftener upon the Census-Sunday.† But as the number who would be able to attend at *some* time of the day is

* Many of these, no doubt, were teachers and scholars engaged in Sunday schools; which partake, indeed, of the character of religious services. The number of Sunday scholars on the Census-Sunday was about 2,280,000; and the number of teachers was about 302,000. Of these, a considerable proportion must have been engaged during the time for afternoon service.

† The calculations in the latter part of this paragraph are mainly conjectural. The extent to which the congregations meeting at different portions of the day are composed of the *same persons* can be ascertained only by a series of observations not yet made, so far as I am aware. We know, from the actual returns, that the number could not be less than 4,647,482 (the number of attendants in the morning), nor more than 10,896,066 (the aggregate of all the services); and these are the limits within which must lie the number of attendants at *some* service. The mean of these extremes is 7,771,774, which is not considerably different from the result of the previous estimates. Opinions have been expressed that the number of individual *attendants* is about *two-thirds* of the number of *attendances*. The latter number is, as above, 10,896,066; two-thirds of which are 7,264,044. Another supposition, is, that, taking the number attending at the most frequented service in each church or chapel, the addition of *one-third* would give the number of persons probably attending the other services of the day but not *that*. From Table N [not printed] we see that the former number (including Sunday scholars attending service) is 6,356,222, which, increased by a third, amounts to 8,474,693. From this of course a considerable deduction must be made on account of those places of worship in which only *one* service was held; the number of such places being as many as 9,915. So that there appears to be some ground for thinking that the computation hazarded above is not far from the fact.–I believe that 70 per cent of the total population may be taken as a fair estimate of the number able to worship at one period *or another* of the day.

more than 58 per cent. (which is the estimated number able to be present *at one and the same time*)–probably reaching 70 per cent.–it is with this latter number (12,549,326) that this 7,261,032 must be compared, and the result of such comparison would lead to the conclusion that, upon the Census-Sunday, 5,288,294 persons, able to attend religious worship once at least, neglected altogether so to do.*

[*Is there sufficient accommodation for the non-attendants?*]

This being then the number of persons failing to attend religious services, we now inquire how far this negligence may be ascribed to an inadequate accommodation. If there were not in all the various churches, chapels, and stations, *room* for more than those who actually attended, it is clear there would be no sufficient reason for imputing to the rest indifference to public ordinances: they might answer, they were quite inclined to worship, but were not provided with the means. Upon the other hand, if sittings, within reach of any given population, and available for their acceptance, were provided in sufficient number to accommodate (say) 58 per cent., it is no less manifest that absence in such case could only be attributed to non-appreciation of the service. In the latter case, however, the provision made must evidently be *within the reach* of the people and *open to their use*–accessible and available; for otherwise a portion of it might as well not be at all. As said before, a surplus of accommodation in one district cannot be regarded as supplying a deficiency in another. Therefore, before we can,–in order to compute the numbers who neglect religious worship, in spite of opportunities for doing so,–compare attendance with accommodation, we must, when dealing with the whole of England in the gross, deduct from the total number of sittings, the number which in any district may exist *above* the number requisite for 58 per cent. of the district-population;–the excess beyond that number being, if the supposition is correct, entirely unavailing both to the dwellers in the district and to the inhabitants of other districts: to the former, since no more than 58 per cent. could possibly attend; to the latter, because out of reach. The number thus assumed to be superfluous is 1,459,284: and this deducted from the total number (10,212,563) leaves a residue of 8,753,279. This will be the number of sittings which, *if all the churches and chapels were open*, might be occupied at once each Sunday if the people within reach of them were willing; and whatever deficiency is shown by a comparison between this number and the total number of attendants may be safely asserted to consist of persons who, possessing the facilities, are destitute of the inclination to attend religious worship. The gross number of attendants being 5,647,482 in the morning, 3,184,135 in the afternoon, and 3,064,449 in the evening, it would follow, if the places of worship were all open, that 4,105,797 persons were, without excuse of inability, absent from the morning, 5,569,144 from the afternoon, and 5,688,830 from the evening service. But, as the churches and chapels are *not* all open every Sunday at each period of the day; 10,798 with 1,714,043 sittings being closed in the morning, 13,096 with 3,944,635 sittings being closed in the afternoon, and

* It must not, however, be supposed that this 5,288,294 represents the number of *habitual* neglecters of religious services. This number is absent every Sunday; but it is not always composed of the *same persons*. Some may attend *occasionally* only; and if the number of such occasional attendants be considerable, there will always be a considerable number of absentees *on any given Sunday*. The number of *habitual* non-attendants cannot be precisely stated from these tables.

TABLE XXI

		1. *All places of worship*				2. *Places of worship* open			
		Morning	*Afternoon*	*Evening*	*Total*	*Morning*	*Afternoon*	*Evening*	*Total*
Total number of Sittings within reach.*		8,753,279	8,753,279	8,753,279	26,259,837	8,322,066	6,192,061	5,712,670	§20,226,797
Total number of Persons able to attend		10,398,013	10,398,013	10,398,013	12,549,326	10,398,013	10,398,013	10,398,013	12,549,326
Number of Sittings within reach	Occupied	4,647,482	3,184,135	3,064,449	10,896,066	4,647,482	3,184,135	3,064,449	10,896,066
	Unoccupied	4,105,797	5,569,144	5,688,830	15,363,711	3,674,584	3,007,926	2,648,221	9,330,731
Number of Persons unable to Attend	Attending	4,647,482	3,184,135	3,064,449	†7,261,032	4,647,482	3,184,135	3,064,449	†7,261,032
	Absent	5,750,531	7,213,878	7,333,564	†5,288,294	5,750,531	7,213,878	7,333,564	†5,288,294
Excess or Deficiency of unoccupied Sittings as compared with the Number of Persons absent	Excess	—	—	—	10,075,417	—	—	—	4,042,437
	Deficiency	1,644,734	1,644,734	1,644,734	—	2,075,947	4,205,952	4,685,343	—

* See *ante*, p. 450. § See *ante*, p. 449.

† These numbers are not the aggregate of the three preceding columns; but the computed number of separate persons who either attended at *some* service on the Census-Sunday, or were *altogether* absent.

16,412 with 4,489,563 sittings being closed in the evening; we are met by the question whether we should consider that the churches are closed because no congregations could be gathered, or that the people are absent because the churches are closed. If the former, the attendants may be properly compared with the total number of sittings in *all* places of worship (after making the deduction for unequal distribution) whether open or not; but, if the latter, the attendants cannot be compared with any but the number of sittings in the places of worship *open* at each period of the day. Perhaps as this is a question not to be decided here, the better course will be to make the comparison upon *both* hypotheses. The result will be observed in Table XXI.

This shows that if all who were absent from each service desired to attend that service, there would not be room for them on either supposition. On the first hypothesis (assuming that the buildings would all be open if the people wished to attend), there would be wanted 1,644,734 additional sittings; and the number of those who, in excuse for non-attendance, might plead absence of accommodation would be just that number; leaving, however, destitute of that excuse, 4,105,797 persons who neglected morning service, 5,569,144 who neglected afternoon service, and 5,688,830 who neglected evening service. On the second hypothesis (assuming that the churches closed are closed from necessary circumstances, and could not be opened even if it were desired), there would be wanted an additional supply of sittings to the extent of 2,575,947 in the morning, 4,205,952 in the afternoon, and 4,685,343 in the evening; and the number of persons who could plead the above excuse for non-attendance would be just as many. But this assumes that at *every* service 58 per cent. of the population would attend: a state of things which, however desirable, is scarcely likely to be realized. If we refer to the fourth and eighth columns of the Table, we shall see the computed number (7,261,032) who at the close of every Sunday can say that they have during the day attended a religious service; some thrice, some twice, but all at least *once*. As this would leave 5,288,295 *altogether absent* every Sunday, and as the aggregate of sittings is in the one case 26,259,837 and in the other 20,226,797, of which only 10,896,066 would be occupied; it is clear that, unless they should all select the *same service*, there is ample room for all the 70 per cent. who, according to the estimate, are able to attend at least *once* upon the Sunday. So that it is tolerably certain that the 5,288,294 who every Sunday, neglect religious ordinances, do so of their own free choice, and are not compelled to be absent on account of a deficiency of sittings.

Nor will this conclusion be invalidated by a reference to the portion of accommodation which is *free*. We have seen that out of a total of 10,212,563 sittings, 4,804,595 are thus described; and the very fact that the others are, in greatest measure, *paid* for (and therefore likely to be used), appears to indicate that it is principally these 'free' sittings that are thus unoccupied.

If therefore we were to measure the required additional supply of accommodation by the extent of the present demand for it, the use now made of our existing provision, as revealed by these few statements of attendance, would appear to indicate that very little more is wanted. The considerable number of available sittings which are every Sunday totally unoccupied, might be adduced as proof so manifest of unconcern for spiritual matters on the part of a great portion of the people, that, until they are impressed with more solicitude for their religious culture, it is useless to erect more churches. It will probably, however, be considered that, from various causes, many persons might attend new churches who would never attend the old; and that church and chapel extension is the surest means of acting on the neighbouring population – bringing into contact with it an additional supply of Christian agency, intent upon securing an increased observance of religious ordinances.

[*Most important result of this inquiry as to attendance.*]

The most important fact which this investigation as to attendance brings before us is, unquestionably, the alarming number of the non-attendants. Even in the least unfavourable aspect of the figures just presented, and assuming (as no doubt is right) that the 5,288,294 absent every Sunday are not always the same individuals, it must be apparent that a sadly formidable portion of the English people are habitual neglecters of the public ordinances of religion. Nor is it difficult to indicate to what particular class of the community this portion in the main belongs. The middle classes have augmented rather than diminished that devotional sentiment and strictness of attention to religious services by which, for several centuries, they have so eminently been distinguished. With the upper classes, too, the subject of religion has obtained of late a marked degree of notice, and a regular church-attendance is now ranked amongst the recognized proprieties of life. It is to satisfy the wants of these two classes that the number of religious structures has of late years so increased. But while the *labouring* myriads of our country have been multiplying with our multiplied material prosperity, it cannot, it is feared, be stated that a corresponding increase has occurred in the attendance of this class in our religious edifices. More especially in cities and large towns it is observable how absolutely insignificant a portion of the congregations is composed of artizans. They fill, perhaps, in youth, our National, British, and Sunday Schools, and there receive the elements of a religious education; but, no sooner do they mingle in the active world of labour than, subjected to the constant action of opposing influences, they soon become as utter strangers to religious ordinances as the people of a heathen country. From whatever cause, in them or in the manner of their treatment by religious bodies, it is sadly certain that this vast, intelligent, and growingly important section of our countrymen is thoroughly estranged from our religious institutions in their present aspect. Probably, indeed, the prevalence of *infidelity* has been exaggerated, if the word be taken in its popular meaning, as implying some degree of intellectual effort and decision; but, no doubt, a great extent of negative, inert difference prevails, the practical effects of which are much the same. There is a sect, originated recently, adherents to a system called 'Secularism'; the principal tenet being that, as the fact of a future life is (in their view) at all events susceptible of *some* degree of doubt, while the fact and the necessities of a present life are matters of direct sensation, it is therefore prudent to attend exclusively to the concerns of that existence which is certain and immediate – not wasting energies required for present duties by a preparation for remote, and merely possible, contingencies. This is the creed which probably with most exactness indicates the faith which, virtually though not professedly, is entertained by the masses of our working population; by the skilled and unskilled labourer alike–by hosts of minor shopkeepers and Sunday traders–and by miserable denizens of courts and crowded alleys. They are *unconscious Seculars*–engrossed by the demands, the trials, or the pleasures of the passing hour, and ignorant or careless of a future. These are never or but seldom seen in our religious congregations; and the melancholy fact is thus impressed upon our notice that the classes which are most in need of the restraints and consolations of religion are the classes which are most without them.

[*Causes of the neglect of religious Institutions.*]

As was to be expected, in an age so prone to self-inquiry and reform, this attitude of our increasing population towards religion and religious institutions has occasioned much solicitude and many questions; and the Christian church has not been backward to investigate the causes of her ill success with these the more especial objects of her mission. It is only purposed here to point out some of the more prominent results of this investigation.

[1. *Social distinctions.*]

1. One chief cause of the dislike which the labouring population entertain for religious services is thought to be the maintenance of those distinctions by which they are separated as a class from the class above them. Working men, it is contended, cannot enter our religious structures without having pressed upon their notice some memento of inferiority. The existence of pews and the position of the free seats are, it is said, alone sufficient to deter them from our churches; and religion has thus come to be regarded as a purely middle-class propriety or luxury. It is therefore, by some, proposed to abandon altogether the pew system, and to raise by voluntary contributions the amount now paid as seat rents. The objection and proposal come from churchmen and dissenters too; but from the former much more strenuously than from the latter; and with this addition in their case–that they point out the *offertory*, prescribed by the Rubric, as the specific mode in which the voluntary contributions should be gathered.–To other minds, the prevalence of social distinctions, while equally accepted as a potent cause of the absence of the working classes from religious worship, is suggestive of a different remedy. It is urged that the influence of that broad line of demarcation which on week days separates the workman from his master cannot be effaced on Sundays by the mere removal of a physical barrier. The labouring myriads, it is argued, forming to themselves a world apart, have no desire to mingle, even though ostensibly on equal terms, with persons of a higher grade. Their tastes and habits are so wholly uncongenial with the views and customs of the higher orders, that they feel an insuperable aversion to an intermixture which would bring them under an intolerable constraint. The same disposition, it is said, which hinders them from mixing in the scenes of recreation which the other classes favour, and induces their selection preferably of such amusements as can be exclusively confined to their own order, will for ever operate to hinder their attendance at religious services, unless such services can be devised as shall become exclusively

their own. An argument in favour of such measures is supposed to be discovered in the fact that the greatest success amongst these classes is obtained where, as amongst the Methodists, this course is (more perhaps from circumstances than design) pursued. If such a plan were carried out by the Church of England, and by the wealthier Dissenting bodies, it is thought that some considerable advantage would result. It has consequently been proposed to meet so far the prejudices of the working population; and to strive to get them gradually to establish places of worship for themselves. Experiments have been already put in operation with the persons lowest in the social scale; and RAGGED CHURCHES* are in several places making a successful start. In several places, too, among Dissenters, special services in halls and lecture rooms are being held, intended wholly for the working class; and the success of these proceedings seems to prove that multitudes will readily frequent such places, where of course there is a total absence of all class distinctions, who would never enter the exclusive-looking chapel.

[2. *Indifference of the churches to the social condition of the poor.*]

2. A second cause of the alienation of the poor from religious institutions is supposed to be an insufficient sympathy exhibited by professed Christians for the alleviation of their social burdens–poverty, disease and ignorance. It is argued that the various philanthropic schemes which are from time to time originated, though certainly the offspring of benevolent minds, are not associated with the Christian church in such a manner as to gain for it the gratitude of those who thus are benefited. This cause, however, of whatever force it may have been as yet, is certainly in process now of mitigation; for the clergy everywhere are foremost in all schemes for raising the condition of the poor, and the ministers and members of the other churches are not backward in the same good labour.

[3. *Misconceptions of the motives of ministers.*]

3. A third cause of the ill-success of Christianity among the labouring classes is supposed to be a misconception on their part of the motives by which Christian ministers are actuated in their efforts to extend the influence of the Gospel. From the fact that clergymen and other ministers receive in exchange for their services pecuniary support, a hasty inference is often drawn, that it is wholly by considerations of a secular and selfish kind that their activity and zeal are prompted.† Or, even if no sordid motives are imputed, an impression is not seldom felt that the exhortations and the pleadings of the ministry are matters merely of professional routine–the requisite fulfilment of official duty. It is obvious that these misapprehensions would be dissipated by a more familiar knowledge; so the evil of the case is that the influence of such misapprehensions is sufficient to prevent that closer intimacy between pastors

* The objections to this term are felt as much by the founders of these institutions as by others; but considerable difficulty is felt in providing any substitute.

† A very common objection taken against ministers by men of this [the labouring] class is that they would not preach or lecture if they were not paid for it; attributing the most sordid motives to all who call the attention of their fellow men to religious subjects. Absurd and untrue as is this objection, yet it is extensively entertained and avowed.–Twenty-seventh Annual Report of the Society for Promoting Christian Instruction.

and their flocks from which alone such better knowledge can arise. The ministers are distrusted–the poor keep stubbornly aloof; how shall access to them be obtained? The employment of LAY-AGENCY has been proposed as the best of many methods by which minds, indifferent or hostile to the regular clergy, can be reached. It is thought by some that that unfortunate suspicion, by the poor, of some concealed and secretly inimical design, by which the regular ministers are often baffled in their missionary enterprises, might be much allayed if those who introduced the message of Christianity were less removed in station and pursuits from those whom it is sought to influence.

[4. *Poverty and crowded dwellings.*]

4. Another and a potent reason why so many are forgetful of religious obligations is attributable to their *poverty*; or rather, probably, to certain conditions of life which seem to be inseparable from less than moderate incomes. The scenes and associates from which the poor, however well disposed, can never, apparently, escape; the vice and filth which riot in their crowded dwellings, and from which they cannot fly to any less degraded homes; what awfully effective teaching, it is said, do these supply in opposition to the few infrequent lessons which the Christian minister or missionary, after much exertion, may impart! How feeble, it is urged, the chance, according to the course of human probabilities, with which the intermittent voice of Christianity must strive against the fearful never-ceasing eloquence of such surrounding evil!–Better dwellings, therefore, for the labouring classes are suggested as a most essential aid and introduction to the labours of the Christian agent.* And, indeed, of secondary influences, few can be esteemed of greater power than this. Perhaps no slight degree of that religious character by which the English middle classes are distinguished is the consequence of their peculiar isolation in distinct and separate houses–thus acquiring almost of necessity, from frequent opportunities of solitude, those habits of reflection which cannot be exercised to the entire exclusion of religious sentiments; but, certainly, however this may be, no doubt can be admitted that a great obstruction to the progress of religion with the working class would be removed if that condition which forbids *all* solitude and *all* reflection were alleviated.

[*Inadequate supply of Christian agency.*]

Probably, however, the grand requirement of the case is, after all, a multiplication of the various *agents* by whose zeal religious truth is disseminated. Not chiefly an additional provision of *edifices*. The supply of these perhaps, will not much longer, if the present wonderful exertions of the Church of England (aided in but little less degree by other Churches) be sustained, prove very insufficient for the wants of the community. But what is eminently needed is, an agency to bring into the buildings thus provided those who are indifferent or hostile to religious services. The present rate of church-and-chapel-increase brings before our view the prospects, at no distant period, of a state of things in which there will be small deficiency of structures where to worship, but a lamentable lack of worshippers. There is indeed already, even in our present circumstances, too conspicuous a difference between accommodation and

* The "Metropolitan Association for Improving the Dwellings of the Industrious Classes" has already expended 60,000 *l.* in providing better residences for the poor, and has realized a dividend upon its capital.

attendants. Many districts might be indicated where, although the provision in religious buildings would suffice for barely half of those who might attend, yet scarcely more than half of even this inadequate provision is appropriated. Teeming populations often now surround half empty churches, which would probably remain half empty even if the sittings were all free.* The question then is mainly this: By what means are the multitudes thus absent to be brought into the buildings open for their use? Whatever impeding influence may be exerted by the prevalence of class distinctions, the constraints of poverty, or misconceptions of the character and motives of the ministers of religion, it is evident that absence from religious worship is attributable *mainly* to a genuine repugnance to religion itself. And, while this lasts, it is obvious that the stream of Christian liberality, now flowing in the channel of church-building, must produce comparatively small results. New churches and new chapels will arise, and services and sermons will be held and preached within them; but the masses of the population, careless or opposed, will not frequent them.

[*Necessity of aggressive measures.*]

It is not, perhaps, sufficiently remembered that the process by which men in general are to be brought to practical acceptance of Christianity is necessarily aggressive. There is no attractiveness, at first, to them in the proceedings which take place within a church or chapel: all is either unintelligible or disagreeable. We can never then, expect that, in response to the mute invitation which is offered by the open door of a religious edifice, the multitudes, all unprepared by previous appeal, will throng to join in what to them would be a mystic worship, and give ear to truths which, though unspeakably beneficent, are also, to such persons, on their first announcement, utterly distasteful. Something more, then, it is argued, must be done. The people who refuse to hear the gospel in the church must have it brought to them in their own haunts. If ministers, by standing every Sunday in the desk or pulpit, fail to attract the multitudes around, they must by some means make their invitations heard beyond

* Dr. Chalmers thus narrates the fate of an endeavour to induce, by the offer of sittings at a low rate, and even gratuitously, a better attendance of the working classes: "An experiment may often be as instructive by its failure as by its success. We have here to record the fate of a most laudable endeavour, made to recall a people alienated from Christian ordinances to the habit of attendance upon them. The scene of this enterprise was Calton and Bridgeton, two suburb districts of Glasgow which lie contiguous to each other, bearing together a population of above 29,000, and with only one chapel of ease for the whole provision which the establishment has rendered to them. It was thought that a regular evening sermon might be instituted in this chapel, and for the inducement of a seat-rent so moderate as from *6d.* to *2s. 6d.* a year, to each individual, many who attended nowhere through the day might be prevailed upon to become the regular attendance of such a congregation. The sermon was preached, not by one stated minister, but by a succession of such ministers as could be found; and as variety is one of the charms of a public exhibition, this also might have been thought a favourable circumstance. But besides, there were gentlemen who introduced the arrangement to the notice of the people, not merely by acting as their informants, but by going round among them with the offer of sittings; and in order to remove every objection on the score of inability they were authorized to offer seats gratuitously to those who were unable to pay for them. Had the experiment succeeded it would have been indeed the proudest and most pacific of all victories. But it is greatly easier to make war against the physical resistance of a people, than to make war against the resistance of an established moral habit. And, accordingly, out of 1,500 seats that were offered, not above fifty were let or occupied by those who before had been non-attendants on religious worship; and then about 150 more were let, not, however, to those whom it was warranted to reclaim, but to those who already went to church through the day, and in whom the taste for church-going had been already formed. And so the matter moved on, heavily and languidly, for some time, till, in six months after the commencement of the scheme, in September 1817, it was finally abandoned."–*Christian and Economic Polity*, I, p. 128.

the church or chapel walls. The myriads of our labouring population, really as ignorant of Christianity as were the heathen Saxons at Augustine's landing, are as much in need of missionary enterprise to bring them into practical acquaintance with its doctrines; and until the dingy territories of this alienated nation are invaded by *aggressive* Christian agency, we cannot reasonably look for that more general attendance on religious ordinances which, with many other blessings, would, it is anticipated, certainly succeed an active war of such benevolent hostilities.

[*The masses not inaccessible.*]

Nor, it is urged in further advocacy of these missionary efforts, are the people insusceptible of those impressions which it is the aim of Christian preachers to produce. Although by natural inclination adverse to the entertainment of religious sentiments, and fortified in this repugnance by the habits and associations of their daily life, there still remain within them that vague sense of some tremendous want, and those aspirings after some indefinite advancement, which afford to zealous preachers a firm hold upon the conscience even of the rudest multitude. Their native and acquired disinclination for religious truth is chiefly of a negative, inert description – strong enough to hinder their spontaneous seeking of the passive object of their dis-esteem – too feeble to present effectual resistance to the inroads of aggressive Christianity invading their own doors. In illustration, the conspicuous achievements of the patriarchs of Methodism are referred to; and a further proof is found in the success of Mormon emissaries. It is argued that the vast effect produced upon the populace by Wesley and Whitfield, in the course of their unceasing labours, shows that the masses are by no means inaccessible to earnest importunity; while the very progress of the Mormon faith reveals the presence in its votaries of certain dim, unsatisfied religious aspirations, which, to be attracted to an orthodox belief, need only the existence, on the part of orthodox evangelists, of zeal and perseverance similar to those displayed by Mormon 'prophets' and 'apostles'....

133. Census Report of 1851–1853 on Religious Worship: prominent facts elicited by the whole inquiry

Parlty. Papers, 1852–1853/LXXXIX.

The great facts which appear to me to have been elicited by this inquiry are, – that, even taking the accommodation provided by all the sects, including the most extravagant, unitedly, there are 1,644,734 inhabitants of England who, if all who might attend religious services were willing to attend, would not be able, on account of insufficient room, to join in public worship: that this deficiency prevails almost exclusively in *towns*, especially *large* towns: that, if these 1,644,734 persons are to be deprived of all excuse for non-attendance, there must be at least as many additional sittings furnished, equal to about 2,000 churches and chapels, and a certain number more if any of the present provision be regarded as of doubtful value; and that even such additional accommodation will fall short of the requirement if the edifices are so often, as at present, closed. Further, it appears that as many as 5,288,294 persons able to attend, are every Sunday absent from religious services, for all of whom there is accommodation for at least one service: that neglect like this, in spite of opportunities for worship, indicates the insufficiency of any mere addition to the number of religious *buildings*: that the greatest difficulty is to fill the churches when provided; and that this can only be accomplished by a great addition to the number of efficient, earnest, religious *teachers*, clerical or lay, by whose persuasions the reluctant population might be won. . . .

134. Clerical Subscription Act (1865)

28 & 29 Vict. c. 1222.

Whereas it is expedient that the Subscriptions, Declarations, and Oaths required to be made and taken by the Clergy of the United Church of *England* and *Ireland* should be altered and simplified: Be it enacted by the Queen's most Excellent Majesty, by and with the Advice and Consent of the Lords Spiritual and Temporal, and Commons, in this present Parliament assembled, and by the Authority of the same, as follows:

[*Declaration of Assent.*]

1. The following Declaration is herein-after referred to as "the Declaration of Assent."

"I A.B. do solemnly make the following Declaration:

"I assent to the Thirty-nine Articles of Religion, and to the book of Common Prayer and of the ordering of Bishops, Priests, and Deacons. I believe the Doctrine of the United Church of England and Ireland, as therein set forth, to be agreeable to the Word of God; and in Public Prayer and Administration of the Sacraments I will use the Form in the said Book prescribed, and none other, except so far as shall be ordered by lawful Authority." . . .

[*No other Declaration or Oaths than those required by Act to be enforced.*]

9. Subject as herein-after mentioned, no Person shall, on or as a Consequence of Ordination, or on or as a Consequence of being licensed to any Stipendiary Curacy, or on or as a Consequence of being presented, instituted, collated, elected, or licensed to any Benefice with Cure of Souls, Perpetual Curacy, Lectureship, or Preachership, be required to make any Subscription, or Declaration, or take any Oath, other than such Subscriptions, Declarations, and Oath as are required by this Act.

135. Compulsory Church Rates Abolition Act (1868)

31 & 32 Vict. c. 109.

Whereas Church Rates have for some Years ceased to be made or collected in many Parishes by reason of the Opposition thereto, and in many other Parishes where Church Rates have been made the levying thereof has given rise to Litigation and Ill-feeling:

And whereas it is expedient that the Power to compel Payment of Church Rates by any legal Process should be abolished:

Be it therefore enacted by the Queen's most Excellent Majesty, by and with the

Advice and Consent of the Lords Spiritual and Temporal, and Commons, in this present Parliament assembled, and by the Authority of the same, as follows:

[*Compulsory Church Rates abolished.*]

1. From and after the passing of this Act no Suit shall be instituted or Proceeding taken in any Ecclesiastical or other Court, or before any Justice or Magistrate, to enforce or compel the Payment of any Church Rate made in any Parish or Place in *England* or *Wales*. . . .

136. Public Worship Regulation Act (1874)

37 & 38 Vict. c. 85.

[*Appointment and duties of judge.*]

7. The Archbishop of Canterbury and the Archbishop of York may, but subject to the approval of Her Majesty to be signified under Her Sign Manual, appoint from time to time a barrister-at-law who has been in actual practice for ten years, or a person who has been a judge of one of the Superior Courts of Law or Equity, or of any court to which the jurisdiction of any such court has been or may hereafter be transferred by authority of Parliament, to be, during good behaviour, a judge of the Provincial Courts of Canterbury and York, herein-after called the judge.

If the said archbishops shall not, within six months after the passing of this Act, or within six months after the occurrence of any vacancy in the office, appoint the said judge, Her Majesty may by Letters Patent appoint some person, qualified as aforesaid, to be such judge.

Whensoever a vacancy shall occur in the office of official principal of the Arches Court of Canterbury, the judge shall become *ex officio* such official principal, and all proceedings thereafter taken before the judge in relation to matters arising within the province of Canterbury shall be deemed to be taken in the Arches Court of Canterbury; and whensoever a vacancy shall occur in the office of official principal or auditor of the Chancery Court of York, the judge shall become *ex officio* such official principal or auditor, and all proceedings thereafter taken before the judge in relation to matters arising within the province of York shall be deemed to be taken in the Chancery Court of York; and whensoever a vacancy shall occur in the office of Master of the Faculties to the Archbishop of Canterbury, such judge shall become *ex officio* such Master of the Faculties.

Every person appointed to be a judge under this Act shall be a member of the Church of England, and shall, before entering on his office, sign the declaration in Schedule (A.) to this Act; and if at any time any such judge shall cease to be a member of the Church, his office shall thereupon be vacant.

This section shall come into operation immediately after the passing of this Act.

[*Representation by archdeacon, churchwarden, parishioners, or inhabitants of diocese.*]

8. If the archdeacon of the archdeaconry, or a churchwarden of the parish, or any three parishioners of the parish, within which archdeaconry or parish any church or burial ground is situate, or for the use of any part of which any burial ground is

legally provided, or in case of cathedral or collegiate churches, any three inhabitants of the diocese, being male persons of full age, who have signed and transmitted to the bishop under their hands the declaration contained in Schedule (A.) under this Act, and who have, and for one year next before taking any proceeding under this Act have had, their usual place of abode in the diocese within which the cathedral or collegiate church is situated, shall be of opinion,-

(1) That in such church any alteration in or addition to the fabric, ornaments, or furniture thereof has been made without lawful authority, or that any decoration forbidden by law has been introduced into such church; or,

(2) That the incumbent has within the preceding twelve months used or permitted to be used in such church or burial ground any unlawful ornament of the minister of the church, or neglected to use any prescribed ornament or vesture; or

(3) That the incumbent has within the preceding twelve months failed to observe, or to cause to be observed, the directions contained in the Book of Common Prayer relating to the performance, in such church or burial ground, of the services, rites and ceremonies ordered by the said book, or has made or permitted to be made any unlawful addition to, alteration of, or omission from such services, rites, and ceremonies,-

such archdeacon, churchwarden, parishioners, or such inhabitants of the diocese, may, if he or they think fit, represent the same to the bishop, by sending to the bishop a form, as contained in Schedule (B.) to this Act, duly filled up and signed, and accompanied by a declaration made by him or them under the Act of the fifth and sixth year of the reign of King William the Fourth, chapter sixty-two, affirming the truth of the statements contained in the representation: Provided, that no proceedings shall be taken under this Act as regards any alteration in or addition to the fabric of a church if such alteration or addition has been completed five years before the commencement of such proceedings.

[*Proceedings on representation.*]

9. Unless the bishop shall be of opinion, after considering the whole circumstances of the case, that proceedings should not be taken on the representation, (in which case he shall state in writing the reason for his opinion, and such statement shall be deposited in the registry of the diocese, and a copy thereof shall forthwith be transmitted to the person or some one of the persons who shall have made the representation, and to the person complained of,) he shall within twenty-one days after receiving the representation transmit a copy thereof to the person complained of, and shall require such person, and also the person making the representation, to state in writing within twenty-one days whether they are willing to submit to the directions of the bishop touching the matter of the said representation, without appeal; and, if they shall state their willingness to submit to the directions of the bishop without appeal, the bishop shall forthwith proceed to hear the matter of the representation in such manner as he shall think fit, and shall pronounce such judgment and issue such monition (if any) as he may think proper, and no appeal shall lie from such judgment or monition

Provided, that no judgment so pronounced by the bishop shall be considered as finally deciding any question of law so that it may not be again raised by other parties.

The parties may, at any time after the making of a representation to the bishop, join in stating any questions arising in such proceedings in a special case signed by a barrister-at-law for the opinion of the judge, and the parties after signing and transmitting the same to the bishop may require it to be transmitted to the judge for hearing, and the judge shall hear and determine the question or questions arising thereon, and any judgment pronounced by the bishop shall be in conformity with such determination.

If the person making the representation and the person complained of shall not, within the time aforesaid, state their willingness to submit to the directions of the bishop, the bishop shall forthwith transmit the representation in the mode prescribed by the rules and orders to the archbishop of the province, and the archbishop shall forthwith require the judge to hear the matter of the representation at any place within the diocese or province, or in London or Westminster.

The judge shall give not less than twenth-eight days' notice to the parties of the time and place at which he will proceed to hear the matter of the said representation. The judge before proceeding to give such notice shall require from the person making the representation such security for costs as the judge may think proper, such security to be given in the manner prescribed by the rules and orders.

The person complained of shall within twenty-one days after such notice transmit to the judge, and to the person making the representation, a succinct answer to the representation, and in default of such answer he shall be deemed to have denied the truth or relevancy of the representation.

In all proceedings before the judge under this Act the evidence shall be given *vivâ voce*, in open court, and upon oath; and the judge shall have the powers of a court of record, and may require and enforce the attendance of witnesses, and the production of evidences, books, or writings, in the like manner as a judge of one of the superior courts of law or equity, or of any court to which the jurisdiction of any such court has been or may hereafter be transferred by authority of Parliament.

Unless the parties shall both agree that the evidence shall be taken down by a shorthand writer, and that a special case shall not be stated, the judge shall state the facts proved before him in the form of a special case, similar to a special case stated under the Common Law Procedure Acts, 1852–1854.

The judge shall pronounce judgment on the matter of the representation, and shall deliver to the parties, on application, and to the bishop, a copy of the special case, if any, and judgment.

The judge shall issue such monition (if any) and make such order as to costs as the judgment shall require.

Upon every judgment of the judge, or monition issued in accordance therewith, an appeal shall lie, in the form prescribed by rules and orders, to Her Majesty in Council.

The judge may, on application in any case, suspend the execution of such monition pending an appeal, if he shall think fit. . . .

Part V

CHARTISM AND FREE TRADE

CHARTISM AND FREE TRADE

Introduction

THE major impulses of English politics in the later 'thirties and the 'forties were supplied by two pressure groups, drawing their main strength from outside the political country, and organized to force on the attention of Parliament policies unacceptable to it. Popular agitation was no new thing in English politics. Whigs and Radicals had resorted to it against the government of George III; the years immediately after the war had seen the series of mass popular meetings that culminated in Peterloo; and the Short Time Movement,[1] the Reform agitation, and the movement against the New Poor Law in the north of the country[2] had provided further examples. But the distinction of the Chartist and Anti-Corn Law movements was their comprehensiveness and continuity; the first swept into its over-mastering current all the specifically working-class movements in the country; the second set a new standard in the thoroughness of its organization and propaganda; and both remained in being for virtually a decade, the Anti-Corn Law League dissolving on the attainment of its object in 1846, and Chartism dying down after its failure in 1848, though not before it had exercised a considerable influence in drawing attention to what became known as the 'condition of England' question. Both evidence the stimulus to popular politics, and the sense of the greater responsiveness of Parliament to public opinion, that the Reform Act had created. But both, though rooted further back, owe much of their dynamism to the deep economic distress that began in the autumn of 1836, brooded like a thundercloud over the ensuing years, lifted gradually as the 'forties went on, and disappeared decisively into the past only with the opening of the new decade.[3]

Chartism may be said to have had a triple origin; in the London Working Men's Association, which had been conducting a radical agitation for some years, under the leadership of William Lovett and Henry Hetherington; in the Birmingham Political Union, revived in May 1837 to promote political and currency reform as a cure for the distress of the town and the country; and in the agitation against the New Poor Law in the north and in the Midlands, to which, by 1836, the Poor Law Commissioners were seeking to extend their activities.[4] The London Working Men, in co-operation with that old Radical stalwart Francis Place, J. A. Roebuck, and others, had already, in 1837, drafted the People's Charter, which was to be the symbol of the movement. Birmingham, where members of the older Political Union, of the Reform Bill agitation, were shortly to grace the new corporation, provided a measure of middle-class countenance and leadership, and, in Attwood, the man who was to present the Chartist Petition to Parliament. The north, with its experience of mass agitation, provided the turbulent popular support on which demagogues like Feargus O'Connor relied for their influence; and it was this aspect of the movement–spreading over the whole of industrial England–that came, in the course of time, to dominate

[1] Part XII. [2] Part IX. [3] Part III. [4] Part IX.

the whole. It was agreed to elect delegates at mass meetings throughout the country to sit as a National Chartist Convention, and prepare and present to Parliament a petition embodying the Charter. The Convention met in London on 4 February 1839, the same day as Parliament, and the same day that delegates from Anti-Corn Law Associations in the country met to set up a common organization in the shape of the Anti-Corn Law League. Meanwhile signatures to the petition were being collected, not altogether on the scale that had been hoped. The Convention passed a resolution against the Anti-Corn Law League, and went on to prepare its petition, and to discuss the 'ulterior measures' that might be taken if Parliament failed to take proper notice of the petition. At this stage the distinction between Physical and Moral Force Chartists began to appear. Meanwhile a tumultuous agitation was going on in the country, partly at the instigation of emissaries of the Convention, and partly independently. But in London the Convention found relatively little popular support, and this, together with the increasing expense and difficulty of the Convention's long sojourn there, and the temporary fall of the Whig Government in May 1839,[1] dictated the decision to withdraw to Birmingham. The petition, with its million and a half signatures, was left in Attwood's London house, for him to present in due course. In April, Lord John Russell had appointed Sir Charles Napier to the Northern Command. Napier's diaries and letters show the atmosphere of disturbance, apprehension, and threat that pervaded the country, and illustrate the wisdom and humanity with which he carried out his duties, to which, in no small part, the ultimate peaceful issue from the crisis was due. Russell refused, in May, to ask the House for special powers, in accordance with the consistent Whig reluctance to go outside the normal powers of the constitution unless it was manifestly essential.[2] The petition was introduced into the House in June, and Attwood was allowed to speak in its favour.[3] The activities of the Convention in Birmingham, sporadic and discontinuous though they were, were causing anxiety to the corporation, which at this date had no police force at its disposal. The arrival of a detachment of Metropolitan Police, which the mayor had gone up to London to fetch, coincided with a meeting in the banned Bull Ring. The police attempted to break it up, and serious rioting ensued, with a number of casualties on both sides. Arrests followed, including that of Lovett, who had courageously insisted on being the sole signatory of a Chartist placard of protest. In other industrial centres movements of protest took place, and it was in the midst of a very tense situation that the debate on the motion to commit the Charter Petition began in the House on 12 July. Attwood and Fielden proposed and seconded; Russell argued that political changes were no cure for economic distress, and attacked Attwood's currency doctrines, which the Convention had just disowned. Disraeli, in a sympathetic speech, treated Chartism as a reflection of the *malaise* resulting from the middle-class rule that the Reform Act had initiated, a result of the narrowness of middle-class social sympathies. But after further desultory debate the motion was lost by 235 to 46. Serious riots in Birmingham followed on 15 July; the Convention decided on a general strike, or Chartist holiday, as an 'ulterior measure', then hesitated, and finally changed its mind; and meanwhile Chartist leaders up and down the country were being arrested on one charge or another. Almost certainly some of them were hoping to bring off a general rising. But nothing serious happened until, on the night of 3 November, miners from the valleys above Newport[4] began to move down in bodies on the town. Their plans went awry, and instead of arriving

[1] Part I, Introduction and No. 5. [2] No. 137. [3] No. 138. [4] Part XII, No. 255.

in the night they reached Newport in the broad daylight of nine o'clock, and after a sharp encounter with a small body of troops, as a result of which fourteen were killed and fifty wounded, dispersed. Over a hundred arrests followed, including that of Robert Frost, the chief leader; the trials began in December, and by February, Frost and his companions were on their way to Botany Bay. Amidst mutterings and threats and hesitations, and a few minor disturbances, Chartism died down in the country.

Before the 'forties, Free Trade had not been, to any considerable extent, a subject of party dispute. Pitt and Huskisson had been its pioneers; Liverpool had always inclined to it within the limits of what he thought to be politically practicable. On taking up the Chancellorship of the Exchequer in 1830, Althorp had professed himself a pupil of Sir Henry Parnell, whose recent 'Financial Reform' had called for a reduction and simplification of the tariff, coupled with a re-introduction of the income-tax to meet the initial revenue deficits. But the Whig Cabinet had refused to shoulder the unpopularity of the income-tax, and the House of Commons had rejected the alternative taxes that Althorp put forward. The political pressure to continue the policy of economy and tax reduction that Liverpool had initiated could not be resisted, but urban radicalism, at the time, was more interested in the house-tax and the paper-tax, which the Whigs were compelled to modify. The result was that they achieved little in the direction of Free Trade, and in the meanwhile the price-fall was increasing the relative weight of the tariffs.[1] In the bad years that began with 1837, the rigidities and lack of resource of the fiscal system began to make themselves felt. Spring Rice, who had succeeded Althorp as Chancellor, found himself facing deficits, and though his successor, Baring, imposed a 10 per cent increase in the assessed taxes, a 5 per cent increase in the Customs, and a new spirits tax, his position, in 1840, was even worse. Meanwhile the collapse of trade was driving the cotton manufacturers to despair. In 1838 the Manchester Anti-Corn Law Association was formed; in 1839 the Anti-Corn Law League. Business ability and thoroughness went into the organization; funds were ample; paid lecturers began to scour the country, and pamphlets to pour forth–taking advantage of the recent Whig boon of the penny post (1839). The complex social and economic issues involved were reduced to simple class and emotional and even religious terms. In the League the self-confident aggressiveness of the industrial middle class first found political expression; in Professor Fay's mordant words, it offered them "the satisfaction of their business instincts, the chastisement of their social superiors, the applause of the working man, and the undoubted blessing of God". In 1840 Joseph Hume succeeded in getting a Select Committee set up to inquire into import duties. It was largely dominated by Board of Trade officials appointed under Poulett Thomson (Vice-President and President, 1830–1839), and its Report[2] was little less than a Free Trade manifesto. It had a great deal of influence on opinion, though Peel, when he came into office, claimed not to have read it, and it did not reach the status of a classic on the subject until later. It was in these circumstances that Baring and Russell took the decision to attack the three great vested interests of protection, corn, sugar, and timber, with the proposal, in the case of corn, to substitute a fixed duty for the sliding scale of 1828, and in that of the other two, to lower the duties on foreign imports and raise them on those from the colonies. The Government was unwise enough to give the Opposition the opportunity of piecemeal attack. The Conservatives chose to

[1] Part III, Introduction. [2] No. 139.

concentrate on the sugar issue, which raised the question of slave competition with the emancipated labour of the West Indies, and, on 18 May, defeated the Government by thirty-six votes. In an effective speech in defence (12 May 1842) Palmerston covered the whole issue of Free Trade, with special reference to the difficulties of negotiating reciprocity treaties, of which he had official experience. Melbourne refused, however, to resign, in order to gain an opportunity of putting the whole of the Government's policy before the House, and, to defeat these tactics and bring matters to a crisis, Peel, on 27 May, moved a vote of 'no confidence'. This was carried in an extraordinarily full House by one vote–311 to 310. Melbourne then dissolved, and in the ensuing election Peel was triumphantly returned. Whigs always criticized Peel for opposing Free Trade at their hands in order, subsequently, to carry it through himself, with the aid of Protectionist votes. It is true that in the 1841 election many Conservatives fought under the Protectionist banner. But not Peel himself, nor had he declared himself in debate, except as in favour of the sliding scale for corn and protection against slave-grown sugar. Moreover, the Whig policy was open to the criticism that it was a partisan move, an attempt to inject the red blood of a newly popular issue into the arteries of a dying government, and to the still more decisive objection, from the point of view of Peel, that Baring's proposals offered no guarantee that the Budget deficits would be met. In the election, the Anti-Corn Law League, where it had no candidate of its own, had thrown its weight on the Whig side.

Peel had demanded an interval for consideration before he addressed himself to the connected problems of the Budget and of the nation. Meanwhile distress had shown no signs of abatement. Chartism had begun to revive in 1840; in the north under the aegis of Feargus O'Connor, whose *Northern Star*, by the influence, popular and financial, that it exercised, enabled him to dominate all but the most independent of his fellow-leaders. As an incidental outcome of a Manchester Free Trade Conference in November 1841, on the primary initiative of Joseph Sturge, a Birmingham banker and a Quaker, there grew up the Complete Suffrage movement, which Lovett and his fellows joined with the object of winning middle-class support for Chartism. No sort of fusion with the Anti-Corn Law League was implied, nor was there even a full fusion of Chartism and the Complete Suffrage movement. But Lovett, full of loyalty for the working-class symbol for which so many had worked and suffered, succeeded in giving a virtually Chartist complexion to a Complete Suffrage Convention, early in April 1842. The upshot was a petition to the House, and a motion by Sherman Crawford for its committal, which was lost by 226 to 67. Meanwhile the Chartist Convention had assembled, representative of all wings, and had persuaded Thomas Duncombe to undertake the task of presenting its petition. It had asked Crawford to defer the presentation of his, but he had refused. Peel had introduced his Corn Law, involving a lowering of the sliding scale, on 9 February, and Russell and the Leaguers had opened into full blast against it, Cobden's speech of 24 February illustrating the vigour and venom of the attack. Not till April was the committee stage concluded, Cobden protesting viciously even after his defeat.[1] The Budget was introduced on 11 March,[2] and was debated till the end of May, Leaguers attacking the income-tax as though Peel had proposed to pick their pockets. Gally Knight's speech on 11 April[3] illustrates the attitude of a high-minded and cultivated country member–the type of support which Peel valued particularly, and which was given him with unstinting generosity in these, the early and honeymoon days of his ministry, as Disraeli later

[1] No. 141. [2] No. 140. [3] No. 142.

bitterly called them. The Tariff Bill followed on 10 May, and was fought item by item–cattle, butter, cheese, timber, sugar, and the export duty on coal–every argument from principle, consistency, and the interest of the consumer being exploited to the full; Peel defending his scheme as one that had to answer budgetary requirements and to avoid too drastic change, as well as to give the greater freedom to trade which had now become the dominant theme of his statesmanship. The Bill passed on 28 June.

Into these debates was injected the issue of the Charter, introduced by Duncombe on 2 May,[1] and debated the following day. Roebuck's attack on O'Connell–coming from one who had helped to frame the original Charter–provided the key to the debate, but Cobden and Brotherton were in the minority of forty-nine, together with the expected rally of Radicals. Early in May came the Report of the Commission on the Labour of Women and Children in Mines,[2] which perhaps of all public documents of its kind most deeply shocked the country. In June, Ashley, in the most massive and searching speech of his career, introduced his Bill to prevent the labour of women and children underground.[3] Though the impetus given to the Bill was too great for it to be stopped, the debate was bitter at times, and gave rise to attacks and innuendoes which reverberated in the country. Cobden, hitherto the enemy of all Ashley's policies, had come over and shaken his hand after his speech, but if the cotton manufacturers felt an alleviation of the attacks, of which they had hitherto been the principal target, coal-owners, newly exposed, felt them the more intensely. Throughout July, tension in the House and in the country increased. A series of debates sought to prevent the adjournment of the House in view of the national distress. In a violent speech of the 8th, Cobden threatened the Government with every species of opposition. Later in the month J. L. Ricardo referred to disturbances in the Midland mining areas, and quoted arbitrary reductions of wages on the part of some owners as the cause. Peel, meanwhile, defended himself with restraint and dignity as doing all that he could to rectify a situation whose gravity he recognized as fully as his attackers. Once again talk of a general strike was in the mouths of Chartist agitators, and Chartist emissaries were speeding round the country. Distress of the bitterest kind, incendiary agitation, sporadic provocative action on the part of disgruntled coal-owners and cotton-masters, were inextricably mixed in the curious and sinister set of disturbances in the Midlands and Lancashire to which the name of the Plug Plot has been given. So, in confusion, recrimination, bitterness, and despair, the worst year of the decade drew to its troubled close.

The 1842 Budget did not produce a surplus, largely owing to Peel's having credited himself with a year's receipts from income-tax, whereas he only received, in fact, a half-year's. But the financial signs were favourable; industry began at last to pick up; harvest prognostications were good; and by the summer of 1843 recovery was definite. The 1843 Budget marked time; the major political struggle of the year was over the education proposals of Graham's Factory Bill,[4] on which most of the Free Traders were opposed to Peel. In 1844 a handsome surplus vindicated the measures of 1842. Some further remissions of tariff were made, including a reduction of the sugar duty which exposed Peel to the criticism that he was himself doing very much what he had refused to allow the Whigs to do. In committee a combination of some of his own followers with the Opposition voted for the lowering of the duty on free-labour sugar, but Peel, in a party meeting and subsequently in the House,

[1] No. 143. [2] Part XII, No. 258. [3] Part XII, Introduction. [4] Part XI, Nos. 237–239.

insisted in no very conciliatory fashion on the rescission of the vote. This followed similar conduct over the Ten Hours amendment to the Factory Bill of 1844.[1] But two great financial measures were safely carried through–the Bank Charter Act[2] and Goulburn's conversion of £250,000,000 of $3\frac{1}{2}$ per cent stock to $3\frac{1}{4}$ per cent, and after ten years to 3 per cent. This was itself a tribute to the recovered strength of the country's finances. Peel had wanted income-tax in 1842 for a five-year term, but had asked only for three. In 1845 he asked for its renewal for another three years, and made the request the occasion for another great Free Trade Budget. A number of the duties reduced in 1842 were now abolished, including most of those on raw materials and food; sugar was again reduced; and the total of remissions was nearly three times as great as in 1842. The foundations of a new fiscal system were definitively laid; Peel's prestige, damaged in 1844, stood higher than ever, and even the ranks of Tuscany, the Leaguers, though still insistent on total repeal, could scarce forbear to cheer.

The great crisis of Peel's career, and of Free Trade, was at hand. A rainy late summer in 1845 made it probable that the harvest would fail. From August, first from the Continent, then from England, and finally from Ireland, reports reached the Government of potato disease that threatened the whole of the crop. Between 1 and 6 November, Peel sought to persuade his Cabinet to suspend the Corn Duties, either by Order in Council or by summoning Parliament for the purpose. But only Graham, Herbert, and Aberdeen supported him: the attachment of a still largely Protectionist party to Protection was too strong; the extent of the disaster was not yet fully clear; and the benefit of a suspension of duties to Ireland, the most vulnerable part of the economy, was debatable, since the bulk of the Irish peasantry made what little money they needed by selling corn, and lived on potatoes. On 22 November, Russell issued his Edinburgh Letter to his constituents, abandoning the Whig policy of a fixed duty on corn in favour of total repeal. Peel's Cabinet met again on 26 November. Had it been ready to afford him unanimous support, Peel would still have carried on. But a minority, including Lord Stanley, were still recalcitrant, and Peel resigned. Russell was sent for to form a Cabinet, and by 20 December had thrown up his commission, his reasons for doing so being that Lord Howick refused to join his ministry if Palmerston went back to the Foreign Office, which Palmerston insisted on doing, and that Peel had not met Russell's full demands as to the support he would give him. Peel therefore returned to office with a reconstructed Cabinet. In January of the following year the great debates on the Corn Laws began. They constitute one of the most momentous and impassioned episodes in the modern history of Parliament. Every motive that can engage the various hearts of man was involved: pride of duty, tinged towards the end with something of the complacency of martyrdom, on the part of the greatest statesman of the day; the fine loyalty to him of some; and the furious resentment of others, who felt themselves betrayed; the almost diabolical malevolence of Disraeli; the somewhat self-conscious objectiveness of an Opposition knowing that the game was being delivered into its hands; the bewilderment of the paladins of the League at an almost too sudden realization of their hopes, and the necessity of blessing where they had schooled themselves to curse. The issues at stake–Ireland, accomplishing her destiny while men still spoke; food and jobs for the masses in factory and field; the shape of the fiscal polity, involving, it was felt, not altogether without reason,[3] the future structure of society itself, weighed with an

[1] Part XII. [2] Part III, No. 97. [3] Part III, Introduction.

almost palpable gravity. Peel made five great speeches, in the course of sustaining, almost daily, the burden of the debates. Those of 22 and 27 January, in which he introduced his policy, were long and elaborate, full of that complication of fact and distinction–statistic and sophistry, his enemies were wont to feel–with which the great parliamentarian was accustomed alternately to bludgeon and soothe his audience. But his old enchantments failed of their power in the fiercer air of this year's debates. His speech of 16 February,[1] curt, caustic, commanding, stripped of all unction and mellifluousness, reflects his consciousness of this. It is Peel at his greatest, and perhaps the nearest to his essential political self that his pride and shyness and caution ever allowed him to be. Disraeli, slighted in 1841 by not being taken into the ministry, still ignored after three years' patient correctitude in the House, had in 1844 proclaimed himself Peel's foe, and hunted to kill. The political opportunity was a rare one, and the political justification unexceptionable; the criticism of Disraeli's course is that it did not measure the gravity of the issue and the time, and by the heat that it generated, by making Peel the martyr of a cause, it condemned the policy which it sought to defend to a century of frustration. His speech of 15 May, on the third reading,[2] exhibits not only the merciless invective and satire which were his staple in the debates but also some considered vindication of that balance in the economy which was the live heart of the Protectionist case. Russell, on the same day, summed up the Whig case over the five years of debate. At the last, Peel ranged himself entirely with the League, and with the League case that the issue in Free Trade was that of cheap food for the people. His resignation speech, on 29 June, concluded with a warm and even a fulsome tribute to Cobden to which by no means all of his supporters, Gladstone among them, were fully assentient.

With whatever reserve long-sighted prudence might regard it, to the people at large the issue of the Corn Law debates was a vindication of Parliament and parliamentary statesmanship. The next year the Ten Hours Act[3] deepened the popular impression. But the economic consequences of the famine had still to be met; sharp fluctuations in the price of corn, heavy expenditure in the unavailing effort to lighten Ireland's tragedy, the economic collapse of 1847.[4] On the Continent similar causes produced revolution. In England they led to the last recrudescence of Chartism. Conventions had continued to be held in the intervening years, though they had not been well attended. In 1847 the demand for the ballot was dropped. In the same year O'Connor was elected M.P. for Nottingham, and some contacts were made between the Chartist leaders and foreign revolutionaries–Marx and Engels–at Brussels. The European revolutions stimulated a Chartist revival. In April a larger Convention determined to present a new petition. The plan was for Chartists from all over London to gather on Kennington Common, and carry the petition in procession to the House. In the light of recent happenings on the Continent these proposals caused the liveliest alarm; special constables were enrolled by the thousand, and the duke of Wellington, as Commander-in-Chief, posted considerable bodies of troops in concealment along strategic points of the route. But police action proved enough. The Metropolitan Commissioner, Sir Richard Mayne, met the procession at Waterloo Bridge and forbade it to proceed. O'Connell agreed to carry the petition to its destination in cabs, and the demonstrators dispersed through a pouring day. In the House, examination of the petition exposed the exaggeration of the Chartists' claims, and a number of ridiculous forgeries discredited it.[5] Some disturbances in the provinces, where parallel

[1] No. 145. [2] No. 146. [3] Part XII, No. 260. [4] Part III. [5] No. 147.

demonstrations had been planned, made the sum of the day's events. A few irreconcilables continued to meet and to fulminate, but the nation as a whole heaved a sigh of relief, and turned from continental heroics to the resumption of its island story. It is said that when the news of Louis Philippe's fall reached the House of Commons, Hume crossed the floor to carry the information to Peel. "This is what would have happened here," said Peel, pointing to the Protectionist benches, "if I had listened to them."

On Peel's fall, Russell had taken office, but his position depended more on the division of Peelites and Protectionists than on his own strength. Nominally, Lord George Bentinck led the Protectionists in the House of Commons, and Stanley in the Lords. Bentinck died in 1848; Disraeli, the real leader, was denied by racial and personal prejudice the recognition of his position for nearly two years longer. Brilliant as his performances were, nothing solid could be achieved while the incubus of Protection hung round his party's neck; the country would have none of it. But Peel's course could not be followed too blatantly, nor could Disraeli fully control Stanley's actions. In 1851 an opportunity of office occurred,[1] but Stanley rejected it. In 1852, when Palmerston turned Russell out, it could not be refused. Conservative reunion was called for by the circumstances, and Disraeli showed himself ready for personal sacrifices to achieve it. But he had grown too much in parliamentary stature to be relegated to a second place, nor could he persuade Stanley to go his own pace in the renunciation of Protection, the lion in the path of reunion. Stanley obtained a dissolution, and in the election he held one language on the burning subject, and his principal lieutenant another. The Conservatives returned in greater force, but still short of a majority. Very complicated political manœuvres followed, turning on the desire of the Free Trade majority to force a recantation upon the Protectionists, and on the personal positions of the Peelites and of Palmerston, standing somewhat unattached since his quarrel with Russell, and envisaged by the Conservatives as a potential recruit and leader in the House of Commons. The Government was compelled to a renunciation of Protection, but, thanks to Palmerston's intervention, in terms which it could with self-respect accept.[2] Meanwhile, and in these conditions, Disraeli, as Chancellor of the Exchequer, had to prepare his Budget. Peel's income-tax had expired in 1848. The heavy government expenditure, in Ireland, and the economic crisis, offered sound grounds for its renewal, but Russell had only obtained from the House its prolongation for three years at the old rate, instead of the five years for which he had asked, and a rate of 1*s.* for the first two years. In 1851 the House would accept renewal for a year only, and Hume obtained the appointment of a Select Committee to examine its operation. Many members were opposed to the tax altogether; others criticized its failure to discriminate between 'precarious' incomes, deriving from trade and salaries, and 'realized' incomes deriving from land or the funds, the criticism being that those with 'precarious' incomes had to save to insure their futures, and should therefore be taxed more lightly. Others thought that a reformed income-tax should increasingly take the budgetary strain, and make possible alleviations of indirect taxation. On coming into office, Disraeli had obtained, for his April Budget, necessary for the carrying on of public business, a year's extension of the existing tax. The Government's substantive financial proposals were promised for as soon after the election as possible, and were produced in December. Disraeli accepted, in his speech, the principle of unrestricted competition, as he

[1] Part I, Nos. 7–11. [2] Nos. 148–150.

preferred to call Free Trade. But his principal concessions were to the Protectionist interests: a reduction of the malt tax and the hop duty, permission to sugar refiners to refine in bond for the home market, and the reduction of certain duties payable by shipping. His troth was plighted to Free Trade, but his presents were for his Protectionist mistresses. Coupled with this was a proposal for the renewal of income-tax, with, however, a reduction to three-quarters rate for 'precarious' incomes, a lowering of the limit of taxation to £100 of 'precarious' and £50 of 'realized' income, a doubling of the house-tax, and its extension downwards to houses of £10 annual value. Disraeli's brilliant oratorical skill gave his proposals a flying start. But he had a galaxy of ex-chancellors and aspiring chancellors on the benches opposed to him, and defeat was probably certain before his closing speech, into which a good deal of acrimony and personal attack entered. Gladstone's attack on him in the small hours of the morning, after an exhausting debate, was one of his most powerful efforts, inspired above all by what he regarded as the irresponsibility with which Disraeli played politics with the nation's money, and by the craftsman's scorn of Disraeli's patent failure to unravel the complexities of income-tax schedules. It clenched the issue, and clenched, perhaps, the antagonism of the two greatest of the younger Conservatives. Derby resigned, and the next year, in the Aberdeen Government, it fell to Gladstone, as Chancellor of the Exchequer, to put forward his own proposals. The speech[1] in which they were introduced reverted to those principles of Sir Robert Peel which he had quoted with such effect against his antagonist. Income-tax was to be retained, but it was not to be reformed; it was to be retained for a purpose, and it was not to be reformed because its use was to be limited to that purpose, the carrying forward of the fiscal reforms which, as Gladstone sought to demonstrate, compensated the inequalities of the tax by the benefits they conferred. The only concession made to the claims of 'precarious' incomes was to remodel and extend Pitt's legacy duty, but this proposal achieved neither its financial nor its political aims. Duties on 123 articles were reduced; on 133 they were abolished. Gladstone's Budget decisively turned aside the current of feeling against the income-tax, and resumed as emphatically the march to Free Trade. A new Peel seemed to have come to light, and a new epoch of commercial reform to have been opened.

The Crimean War deferred these expectations for the whole of the seven years which Gladstone had given himself to meet them. He had himself to double the income-tax in the following year. Succeeding chancellors retained it at higher or lower levels, and the scale of national expenditure went up and remained up. Not till 1860 was Gladstone able to resume his task, and then no longer as a Conservative, but as a Liberal whose affiliations with Cobden and Bright were taking him more definitely to the left. The great feature of the Budget of that year[2] was the implementation of the commercial treaty which Cobden had negotiated with Napoleon III. It provided for the abolition of duties on manufactured goods, and the reduction of those on brandy and wine, in return for French reduction of their duties on coal and coke, iron, steel, machinery, and textiles. The British reductions were extended to all countries, though their benefits would be felt chiefly by France. Duties on butter, eggs, cheese, and tallow were also abolished. The price of all this was an income-tax of 10*d.* in the £. In succeeding Budgets the reductions were extended, and a series of surpluses enabled the Chancellor to bring the income-tax in 1865 to the low-water mark of 4*d.* The framework of Gladstonian finance was completed. Few taxes, chosen

[1] No. 151. [2] No. 152.

for their flexibility of yield and ease of collection; the cutting down of administrative costs; refusal to burden the State with any but the most essential duties; and the strictest attention to economy were its guiding principles. In a time of an expanding economy, and of the still unchallenged supremacy of Britain in manufactures and commerce, there could be, and there was, little challenge to them. Nor was the example of rigorous responsibility in the handling of public funds without its widespread and bracing moral influence. Free Trade was not seriously challenged till Joseph Chamberlain threw down his ill-starred glove in 1903. But the fight for economy proved in the long run a losing battle, and the presence of the 'mighty engine of taxation' which Gladstone, in 1853, had dedicated solely to reform, made it a difficult one to wage. In 1874, with an old war-horse's prescient sniff of the future, Gladstone went into electoral battle on the issue of abolishing the income-tax. He lost, and with his defeat it may be said that the doom of Gladstonian finance was inevitable.

SELECT BIBLIOGRAPHY

The *Parliamentary Debates* are of exceptional interest and value for the subject of this Part, especially those on the Chartist Petitions in 1839, 1842, and 1848; the series of interlocking debates on the Corn Law, the Tariff Bill, the Budget, and National Distress in 1842; the Budget debate of 1845; the debates on the Repeal of the Corn Laws (reprinted separately, under the title of *The Battle for Native Industry*, by the Society for the Protection of British Agriculture and Industry (London, 1846)), and the Budget debates of 1852, 1853, and 1860. Of *Parliamentary Papers*, the *Correspondence with Lords Lieutenants on the State of the Country* (*Parlty. Papers*, 1839/XXXVIII), the *List of Political Prisoners from Jan. 1839 to June 1840* (*Parlty. Papers*, 1840/XXXVIII) and the *Report of the Select Committee on Import Duties* (*Parlty. Papers*, 1840/V), are the most valuable. The *Report of the Select Committee on the Registration of County Electors* (*Parlty. Papers*, 1846/VIII), throws light on the relatively little-known electoral activities of the Anti-Corn Law League. Reports by Poor Law officers on *Pauperism in Birmingham etc.* (*Parlty. Papers*, 1840/XXXIX) and on *Distress in Bolton, Stockport and Rochdale* (*Parlty. Papers*, 1842/XXXV) reveal the appalling conditions to be found at the time. SIR W. NAPIER, *Life and Opinions of General Sir Charles Napier* (4 vols., London, 1857: vol. 2 refers), consisting largely of extracts from the General's diary for the period of his command in the North, gives an indispensable impression of the brooding anxiety and uncertainty of the time. THOMAS COOPER, *Life of Thomas Cooper* (London, 1872), THOMAS FROST, *Forty Years' Recollections* (2 vols., London, 1880), G. J. HOLYOAKE, *Sixty Years of an Agitator's Life* (London, 1906), WILLIAM LOVETT, *Life and Struggles of William Lovett* (London, 1876), may be mentioned among accounts by Chartist leaders of their activities. *State Trials, New Series*, vol. IV (8 vols., London, 1888–1898), gives accounts of the trials of Chartists, specially valuable being the trials of O'Connor and Thomas Cooper in connexion with the Plug Plot. An article in the *Quarterly Review*, vol. LXXI (December, 1842), "The Anti-Corn Law League, Chartism, and the Plug Plot", suggests connexions between the three. THOMAS CARLYLE, *Chartism* (London, 1839) and *Past and Present* (London, 1842), BENJAMIN DISRAELI'S historical novel *Sybil* (London, 1845), dealing with the period, and CHARLES KINGSLEY, *Yeast* (London, 1848–1851), and *Alton Locke* (London, 1850), are near enough to the time to have evidential value, at any rate as to the impression made by events. Accounts of the whole Chartist movement are R. G. GAMMAGE, *History of the Chartist Movement*, 2nd edn. (London, 1894); JULIUS WEST, *History of Chartism* (London, 1920); MARK HOVELL, *The Chartist Movement* (Manchester, 1919), with excellent bibliography; E. DOLLEANS, *Le Chartisme*, new edn. (Paris, 1949). Chartism is set in the general context of radical and working-class movements in S. MACOBY, *English Radicalism, 1832–52* (London, 1936), and G. D. H. COLE, *Short History of the British Working Class Movement, 1789–1947* (London, 1949), and *British Working Class Politics, 1832–1914* (London, 1941). M. BEER, *History of British Socialism* (2 vols., London, 1919–1920), should also be consulted. J. L. and B. HAMMOND, *The Age of the Chartists* (London, 1930), is a general picture of the age from the working-class angle. GRAHAM WALLAS, *Francis Place, 1771–1854* (London, 1898), G. D. H. COLE, *Chartist Portraits* (London, 1941), J. SAVILLE, *Ernest Jones, Chartist* (London, 1952), F. F. ROSENBLATT, *The Chartist Movement in its Social and Economic Aspects* (New York, 1916), PRESTON SLOSSON, *Decline of the Chartist Movement* (New York, 1916), and H. V. FAULKNER, *Chartism and the Churches* (New York, 1910), may also be consulted. S. J. CHECKLAND, "The Birmingham Economists, 1848–50" in *Economic History Review*, II, I (1948), is a study of Attwood and his associates from an economic standpoint less rigid than that of the Victorian orthodoxy in currency matters. G. D. H. COLE and A. W. FILSON, *British Working Class Movements: Select Documents, 1789–1875* (London, 1951), has valuable sections on Chartist and allied movements.

A. PRENTICE, *History of the Anti-Corn Law League* (2 vols., London, 1853), is the standard contemporary history of the League; D. G. BARNES, *A History of the English Corn Laws from*

1660–1846 (New York, 1930), is the best book on its subject, and C. R. FAY, *The Corn Laws and Social England* (Cambridge, 1932), is marked by the author's power of stimulating thought and imagination. B. DISRAELI, *Lord George Bentinck: A Political Biography* (London, 1852), is Disraeli's account of the political struggle, and his tribute to his ostensible leader. F. W. MONYPENNY and G. E. BUCKLE, *Life of Benjamin Disraeli, Earl of Beaconsfield* (2 vols., London, 1929), is indispensable. *Memoirs of Sir Robert Peel*, ed. STANHOPE and CARDWELL (2 vols., London, 1857), C. S. PARKER, *Sir Robert Peel* (3 vols., London, 1891–1899), H. A. RAMSAY, *Peel* (London, 1928), are among the many studies of his public personality. WALTER BAGEHOT, *Biographical Studies* (London, 1895), and LORD ROSEBERY, *Miscellanies, Literary and Historical* (2 vols., London, 1921: vol. I refers), are of fundamental importance. So also are JOHN MORLEY, *Life of Richard Cobden* (2 vols., London, 1881), and *Life of Gladstone* (3 vols., London, 1903). ERICH EYCH, *Gladstone*, tr. B. MIALL (London, 1938), is a more modern view by a distinguished Swiss scholar. F. E. HYDE, *Mr Gladstone at the Board of Trade* (London, 1934), may also be consulted. G. M. TREVELYAN, *John Bright* (London, 1913), is on the same plane of importance. COBDEN, *Speeches*, ed. JOHN BRIGHT and THOROLD ROGERS (London, 1903), and his *Political Writings*, edited by SIR LEWIS MALLET (London, 1878), should be studied, and W. H. DAWSON, *Richard Cobden and Foreign Policy* (London, 1926), and J. A. HOBSON, *Cobden; The International Man* (London, 1918), study the international aspects of Free Trade.

Recent articles of importance are DAVID SPRING, "Earl Fitzwilliam and the Corn Laws", *American Historical Review*, vol. LIX (1953–1954); G. L. MORSE, "The Anti-League, 1844–6", *Economic History Review*, vol. XVII (1947); G. KITSON CLARK, "The Electorate and the Repeal of the Corn Laws", *Transactions of the Royal Historical Society, Fifth Series*, vol. III (1951), "The Repeal of the Corn Laws and the Politics of the Forties", *Economic History Review*, vol. II, IV (1951), and "Hunger and Politics in 1842", *Journal of Modern History*, vol. XXV (1953); LUCY BROWN, "The Board of Trade and Tariff Problems, 1840–42", *English Historical Review*, vol. LXVIII (1953); and BETTY KEMP, "The General Election of 1841", *History*, vol. XXXVII (1952). On the comparatively neglected activities and arguments of the Anti-Corn Law Repeal League, G. G. DAY, *Speech at Huntingdon, June 17, 1843* (published as a pamphlet, London, 1843), and his *Speech at St Ives, Herts., Jan. 27th, 1844* (pamphlet, London, 1844), may be consulted.

On the further development of Free Trade the biographies, particularly those of Gladstone and Disraeli, should be consulted. SIR STAFFORD NORTHCOTE, *Twenty Years of Financial Policy* (London, 1862), is the best general book. S. BUXTON, *Finance and Politics, an historical study, 1783–1885* (2 vols., London, 1888), deals fully with the period in question. GLADSTONE, *Financial Statements, 1853–63* (London, 1864), are conveniently printed together; S. BUXTON published a study of *Gladstone as Chancellor of the Exchequer* (London, 1901), and SIR ROBERT GIFFERS, in *Essays in Finance* (2 vols., London, 1887), discusses "Mr Gladstone's Work in Finance". K. J. FUCHS, *The Trade Policy of Great Britain and her Colonies since 1860* (London, 1905), and H. L. DUNHAM, *The Anglo-French Treaty of Commerce of 1860 and the Progress of the Industrial Revolution in France* (ANN ARBOR, 1930), discuss the Treaty of 1860 and its repercussions.

LUCY BROWN, *The Board of Trade and the Free Trade Movement* (1951); NORMAN MCCORD, *The Anti-Corn Law League* (1957); L. G. JOHNSON, *General Perronet Thompson, 1783–1867* (1957); DAVID WILLIAMS, *The Rebbeca Riots* (1955); A. R. SCHOYER, *The Chartist Challenge: A Portrait of Julian Harney* (1958); F. C. MATHER, *Public Order in the Age of the Chartists* (1960); ASA BRIGGS (ed.), *Chartist Studies* (1959), essays emphasising the importance of local factors; D. READ and E. GLASGOW, *Feargus O'Connor* (1961).

137. Chartism in 1839: Lord John Russell's refusal to ask for special legislation (15 May)

Hansard, 3/XLVII/1025–1028.

MR. WILLIAM WYNN could not help expressing his surprise that so long an adjournment of the House should be proposed while the internal state of the country was so agitated. Six months had now elapsed since certain parties had recommended the people generally to procure arms. They knew that in different parts of the country those recommendations had been carried into effect, that fire arms had been provided, and that pikes had been made to a very great extent. Up to the present moment, they were publicly sold, and no steps had been taken to put an end to it. He had hoped that before that time the noble Lord who was charged with the care of internal affairs would have brought forward some measure on the subject, or, at all events, that he would have stated what the feelings of Government were upon the matter. Deadly weapons had been provided by a large number of people in the country, and it was no wonder that special constables should shew some reluctance in the discharge of their duties, they being armed only with the weapon provided by law for a constable. He was not afraid of the ultimate success of the parties who were misleading the people. What he was afraid of was, that if this arming continued unchecked, it would lead to a lamentable degree of bloodshed. In his opinion the House was not doing its duty by consenting to such a long adjournment without taking some measures for strengthening the hands of the magistrates, in the circumstances in which the country was now placed.

LORD JOHN RUSSELL had to state that throughout the period alluded to, which had been a most anxious one, the Government had not been unmindful of what was going on; but he had thought that it was better to rely on the existing law than to come down to that House for other measures, without a positive and imperious necessity for doing so, because the objects of the persons influencing the minds of the people, and inciting them to arm, were so clearly mischievous–so many of their acts so clearly exposed them to the penalties of the law, that it was impossible that they could meet with any general sympathy. He had always found, however, that when extraordinary measures were taken in Parliament in such a case, a sympathy was created, and a jealousy excited with regard to the constitution, which ought not to be suspended without absolute necessity. Still he was not prepared to say, that it might not be necessary to propose some measure to Parliament with regard to arms in the hands of evil-disposed persons. He was of opinion, however, that when the necessity arose it would be far better to introduce the measure at once, and to ask Parliament to direct its immediate and unceasing attention to the subject, than to give a long notice with respect to it; or, after having brought it forward, to postpone its further consideration for a considerable time. With regard to the measures already taken, he must say that on two occasions, when her Majesty's Ministers had advised her Majesty to issue proclamations regarding meetings of an illegal character, meetings held by night with torches under circumstances of danger and terror, and meetings which were attended by persons having pikes and bludgeons, each time those proclamations were issued the most salutary effects had been produced. He felt most undoubtedly that the responsibility was very great in taking measures to arrest, and if possible to repress, the disposition to disturbance that had been exhibited. The subject had been a frequent matter of consultation between himself and the Attorney-general, and he had likewise frequently brought the question before the Cabinet; and it appeared to him that the course adopted, and the views taken with respect to the general state of the country, were more likely ultimately to produce a return to peace, than if the Government had at once proposed measures of an extraordinary description.

Sir H. Verney wished, in reference to the subject which the noble Lord had now brought forward, to ask whether it was his intention in the course of the present session to introduce any measure for the establishment of a more effective rural police? He thought such a measure would be calculated to give great satisfaction to the country.

Mr. Attwood wished to know whether he understood the noble Lord right, when he supposed him to say that it was the intention of the Government to introduce further penal enactments. [No, no.] He thought the Government had done quite enough in putting in force the present law of the country. With regard to arms, he knew something about them, and he did not believe there had been fifty muskets or fifty pikes bought in England. He did not believe that the people of England had gone mad enough for that, or that they had ever thought of arming themselves. He was convinced they knew too well where their strength lay to take up arms. He was sure there had been a great deal of exaggeration on the subject, and he most earnestly urged upon her Majesty's Ministers and the House not to adopt any measure that would be calculated to excite the people to oppose the laws. If the people were outraged, the time might come when they might assume a far different appearance. These appeals to arms proceeded from the 'intense eloquence' of some Irish speakers, and had been used by Tories, Radicals, and Neutrals throughout the country, as all the papers testified.

Lord John Russell thought it might be necessary to take some measures for the restriction of that which was an abuse of the rights secured by the Bill of Rights. It was, undoubtedly, true that every person had a right to have arms in his own defence; but the arming of a portion of the population, exhibiting and brandishing those arms to the terror and alarm of Her Majesty's subjects, was an abuse of the right, and one which it might be necessary to meet by legislative enactment. The hon. Member said he did not believe there was any arming to any considerable extent. Certainly the information which he (Lord J. Russell) had from the town which the hon. Member represented, and other towns, would lead him to suppose there had been no very considerable quantity of arms made by the regular manufacturers, and the chief part of the sale which had taken place had been for exportation. But there had been weapons of a dangerous nature made by persons who were neither regular gun-makers nor manufacturers of arms. Whilst he wished, on one hand, to guard the

House against any exaggerated notion of there being large bodies of men regularly armed, on the other hand he believed there were a considerable number of persons in possession of very dangerous and offensive weapons.

138. Attwood's speech introducing the Charter (14 June 1839)

Hansard, 3/XLVIII/222.

MR. T. ATTWOOD said, in rising to present this very extraordinary and important petition, he was aware that the rules of the House would not allow him to enter upon any general statement on the subject to which it referred, nor to go into a defence of the great principles which were there set forth. He should, therefore, endeavour to keep strictly within the rules prescribed by the House, as the proper line of conduct to be observed by Members on presenting petitions, and confine himself to a statement of the substance and contents; and then, perhaps, the House would indulge him by permitting him to say a few words–a few words only–in explanation of the circumstances as regarded his own personal position in connection with the petition. The petition originated in the town of Birmingham. It was adopted there at a very numerous meeting on the 6th of August, last year. Having been so adopted, it was then forwarded to Glasgow, where, in a short time, it received no less a number than the signature of 90,000 honest, industrious men; and it afterwards received the signatures of nearly the same number at Birmingham and the neighbourhood of that town. He held in his hand a list of two hundred and fourteen towns and villages, in different parts of Great Britain, where the petition had been deliberately adopted and signed; and it was now presented to that House with 1,280,000 signatures, the result of not less than 500 public meetings, which had been held in support of the principles contained in this petition. At each of those meetings there had been one universal anxious cry of distress–distress, he must say, long disregarded by that House, yet existing for years–distress which had caused much discontent amongst the working people, and which discontent was created by the long sufferings and grievances which that class of the people had endured, and so long utterly disregarded by the people's representatives in that House. [Order, order.] He hoped the House would listen to what he said, and would afford due attention to a petition so universally signed; that the House would not say, because the petitioners were merely humble working men that their opinions should be disregarded, and that their grievances should not be considered and redressed. He sincerely trusted that such would not be the case. It would be a most serious grievance and offence to these people who signed the petition, if such were to be the result in the presence of their delegates, who had been allowed to be present to witness its presentation; and it would be most painful for him to have to state such a result, and to carry back a report to those who had intrusted the petition to his hands that it had been treated with any symptoms of disregard or disrespect by that House. The men who signed the petition were honest and industrious–of sober and unblemished character–men who have uniformly discharged the duties of good members of society and loyal subjects, and who had always obeyed the laws. Gentlemen enjoying the wealth handed down to them by hereditary descent, whose wants were provided for by the estates to which they succeeded from their forefathers, could have no idea of the privations suffered by the working men of this country. Yet at all the meetings which have been held, the persons attending them had confined themselves strictly to the legal pursuit of their constitutional rights, for the purpose of remedying the extreme sufferings which they had endured for so many years. They had seen no attempt to relieve their sufferings, whether they were hand-loom weavers, artisans, or agricultural labourers – no matter what they might be, still there was no relief. They met with no support, or even sympathy, from that House, and, therefore, they felt themselves bound to exercise every legal and constitutional effort within their power to recover the whole of their constitutional rights. All that these honest men said was, that the Members of that House by birth, parentage, habits of life, wealth, and education, had not shown that anxiety to relieve the sufferings and redress the wrongs of the working classes, which they believed to be their rights, as enjoying the privileges of British subjects. Therefore, they had adopted the extreme course of entering upon that separate path, with the view of endeavouring to recover those ancient privileges which they believed to form the original and constitutional right of the Commons of England. For many years they had hoped and trusted that such an effort on their part would not be needed. They hoped it might be spared, and they placed their confidence in that hope to the protection which they looked for, and which they were taught to expect they should receive at the hands of the gentlemen of England. He should now read a brief extract from the petition. It stated, that they only sought a fair day's wages for a fair day's work; and that if they could not give them that, and food and clothing for their families, then they said they would put forward every means which the law allowed, to change the representation of that House; that they would use every effort to act upon the electors, and that by these means ultimately, reason thus working upon influence, they should produce such a change as would enable them to succeed in the accomplishment of their views and wishes. He trusted in God they would succeed, and obtain all the objects sought for in the petition. The first thing sought for by these honest men, every one of whom produced by his labour four times more to the country than they asked for in exchange, was a fair subsistence – and yet their country refused them one-fourth of the value of their labours. Not only did the country do that, but some of them had only three days' wages in the week, and hundreds of them were paying 400 per cent. increase on debts and taxes. Such being the case, the House would not be surprised, that these honest men should have used rather strong language under trying circumstances. The first clause of the petition was for universal suffrage; that representations should be co-equal with taxation – the ancient constitutional law of England. It said, that they had been bowed down to the earth for a series of years. That capital of the master must not be deprived of due reward – that the labourer must have a return in wages for his labour – and that the laws which made money dear, and labour cheap, must be abolished. The petition next demanded universal suffrage, in the language of their forefathers, as expressed in the celebrated Petition of Right. Then it showed that the constitution guaranteed freedom of election, and contended, that to secure freedom of election, vote by ballot was absolutely necessary, and therefore vote by ballot was a constitutional right. It further declared, that agreeably to the acts of settlement, Parliaments were ordered to be triennial, or more frequent; and therefore the petition asked for annual Parliaments. Then it declared, that Members should be paid for their attendance in Parliament, as was the case in the days of Andrew Marvel, and as he might now easily establish, if he thought proper, in Birmingham. That was the ancient law. Members were paid by those who sent them to Parliament, and the petitioners were of opinion, until that right was restored, they should not have members who would properly feel and understand the wants, and real interests of the people. The fifth demand was, that the property qualification of Members should be abolished. In all these five points he most cordially agreed, and he most sincerely hoped that, by the progress of public opinion, the day might not be distant when the whole of those five points would be granted to the people; and that they would have them in full weight and measure, and no mistake about the matter.

Sir G. H. Smyth rose to order. The hon. Member had transgressed the rules of the House. It was a distinct rule of the House, that no Member should make a speech on presenting a petition, and he could not believe that any member, with that ridiculous piece of machinery (the immense petition had been rolled into the House), would be permitted to adopt a course that had been uniformly refused to himself and others.

The Speaker, as the hon. Member had appealed to him, must certainly say, that no Member had a right to speak at any length on presenting a petition. But when the House considered the circumstances of the case, and the position in which the hon. Member was placed, perhaps they would see that there were grounds for granting some indulgence in the matter.

Sir G. H. Smyth, as an individual, must enter his protest against the course adopted by the hon. Member for Birmingham.

Mr. Attwood was thankful for the indulgence extended to him, and would only trespass a few minutes longer upon the attention of the House. But he wished to say a few words in explanation of his own peculiar situation. Although he most cordially supported the petition, was ready to support every word contained in it, and was determined to use every means in his power in order to carry it out into a law, he must say, that many reports had gone abroad, in regard to arguments said to have been used in support of the petition on different occasions, which he distinctly disavowed. He never, in the whole course of his life, recommended any means, or inculcated any doctrine except peace, law, order, loyalty, and union, and always in good faith, not holding one face out of doors, and another in that House; but always in the same manner, and in the same feeling, fairly and openly doing all that he could as a man, a patriot, and a Christian, to work out the principles which he maintained, and to support the views of the petitioners. He washed his hands of any idea, of any appeal to physical force. He deprecated all such notions–he repudiated all talk of arms–he wished for no arms but the will of the people, legally, fairly, and constitutionally expressed–and if the people would only adopt his views, and respond to his voice–if they would send up similar petitions from every parish in England, and go on using every argument which justice, reason, and wisdom dictate, they would create such an action in the public mind, which would again act upon Members of that House–that giving due allowance for the prevalence of generous feeling among English gentlemen and the English people, if the people would act in that manner–if they proceeded wisely and discreetly, washing their hands of all insolence and violence –he was confident they would ultimately secure the attentive consideration of that House. Having said so much, he should now read the prayer of the petition, which was to the following effect:–

> "That it might please their honourable House to take the petition into their most serious consideration, and to use their utmost endeavour to pass a law, granting to every man of lawful age, sound mind, and uncontaminated by crime, the right of voting for Members to serve in Parliament; that they would cause a law also to be passed, giving the right to vote by the ballot; that the duration of Parliaments might in no case be of greater duration than one year; that they would abolish all property qualifications, to entitle persons to sit in their honourable House; and that all Members elected to sit in Parliament, should be paid for their services."

He would trespass no longer on their time, but move, that the petition be now brought up. This produced loud laughter, from the gigantic dimensions of the petition. The hon. Member unrolled a sufficient portion of it to enable him to place one extremity of it on the clerk's table.

Petition to be printed.

139. Select Committee on Import Duties (1840)

Parlty. Papers, 1840/v.

REPORT

THE SELECT COMMITTEE appointed to inquire into the several DUTIES levied on IMPORTS into the UNITED KINGDOM, and how far those Duties are for Protection to similar Articles, the Produce or Manufacture of this Country, or of the British Possessions abroad, or whether the Duties are for the purposes of Revenue alone; and to whom several Petitions were referred; and who were empowered to report the MINUTES OF EVIDENCE taken before them to The House;–HAVE considered the Matters to them referred, and agreed to the following REPORT:

The Evidence is of so valuable a character, that Your Committee could hardly do justice to it in detail, unless they were to proceed, step by step, to a complete analysis, which the advanced period of the Session will not allow them to do. They must, therefore, confine themselves to reporting the general impressions they have received, and submit the Evidence to the serious consideration of The House, persuaded that it cannot be attentively examined without producing a strong conviction that important changes are urgently required in our Custom-house legislation.

The Tariff of the United Kingdom presents neither congruity nor unity of purpose; no general principles seem to have been applied.

The Schedule to the Act 3 & 4 Will. 4, c. 56, for consolidating the Customs Duties, enumerates no fewer than 1,150 different rates of duty chargeable on imported articles, all other commodities paying duty as unenumerated; and very few of such rates appear to have been determined by any recognised standard; and it would be difficult for any person unacquainted with the details of the Tariff to estimate the probable amount of duty to which any given commodity would be found subjected. There are cases where the duties levied are simple and comprehensive; others, where they fall into details both vexatious and embarrassing.

The Tariff often aims at incompatible ends; the duties are sometimes meant to be both productive of revenue and for protective objects, which are frequently inconsistent with each other; hence they sometimes operate to the complete exclusion of foreign produce, and in so far no revenue can of course be received; and sometimes, when the duty is inordinately high, the amount of revenue becomes in consequence trifling. They do not make the receipt of revenue the main consideration, but allow that primary object of fiscal regulations to be thwarted by an attempt to protect a great variety of particular interests, at the expense of the revenue, and of the commercial intercourse with other countries.

Whilst the Tariff has been made subordinate to many small producing interests at home, by the sacrifice of Revenue in order to support these interests, the same principle of preference is largely applied, by the various discriminatory Duties, to the Produce of our Colonies, by which exclusive advantages are given to the Colonial Interests at the expense of the Mother Country. Your Committee would refer to the Evidence respecting the articles of Sugar and Coffee, as examples of the operation of these protective Duties.

Your Committee refer to a general Account prepared by the Inspector of Imports, of the several articles imported into the United Kingdom in 1838–39, stating in separate columns the quantity imported, exported, and retained for home consumption, with the rates of duty chargeable on each, and whether in a raw state, partially manufactured, or manufactured; by which it appears that 862 articles are divided into eight Schedules, which they submit to the serious consideration of The House: *viz.*

			Totals
Schedule 1, containing 349 articles, producing less than £100 each of Customs duty, and in the aggregate			£8,050
Schedule 2, containing 132 articles, producing from	£100 to	£500 each	31,629
Schedule 3, „ 45 „ „ „	£500 to	£1,000 each	32,056
Schedule 4, „ 107 „ „ „	£1,000 to	£5,000 each	244,733
Schedule 5, „ 63 „ „ „	£5,000 to	£100,000 each	1,397,324
Schedule 6, „ 10 „ „ „	£100,000 to	£500,000 each	1,838,630
Schedule 7, „ 9 „ „ „	£500,000 each and upwards		18,575,071
Schedule 8, „ 147 „ on which no duty has been received, but on which there has been an excess of drawback of			£5,398

It appears from the evidence of Mr. Porter, of the Board of Trade, that the total amount of Customs Revenue received in the United Kingdom in the year ending January 1840, was

£22,962,610, of which total amount, 17 articles, each producing more than £100,000, produced

94½ per cent., or	£	21,700,630
That 29 articles produced 3 9/10 per cent., or		898,661
And that these 46 articles produced 98 2/5 per cent., or		22,599,291
That all other articles, amounting to 144 in number, produced 1 3/5 per cent., or		363,319
Showing that 190 articles, exclusive of about £80,000 collected upon 531 other articles, and excluding 147 articles, upon which an excess of drawback of £5,398, was allowed, produced the total revenue of	£	22,962,610

It will be seen that 17 articles, affording the largest amount of Customs Revenue, are articles of the first necessity and importance to the community; *viz.* sugar, tea, tobacco, spirits, wine, timber, corn, coffee, butter, currants, tallow, seeds, raisins, cheese, cotton wool, sheep's wool, and silk manufactures; and that the interests of the Public Revenue have been by no means the primary consideration in levying the Import Duties, inasmuch as competing foreign produce is in some instances excluded, and in others checked by high differential duties, levied for the protection of British colonial interests; and, in many cases, such differential duties do not answer the object proposed, for it appears, in the case of foreign clayed sugars, where it was obviously intended they should be excluded from the British market, that the monopoly granted to British colonial sugars has so enormously raised the prices in our market, that they have lately come into consumption, though charged with a duty of 63s. per cwt., while our plantation sugars pay only 24s.

Another inconvenience which the differential duties create is, that they offer a premium for evading the intention of the Legislature; foreign coffees are charged 1s. 3d. per lb.; colonial coffees only 6d.; while coffees imported from the Cape of Good Hope, pay 9d. Now, as the cost of sending, in an unusual and indirect way, coffee from foreign countries to the Cape is only from ½d. to 1d. per lb., very large quantities are shipped from the Brazils and Hayti to the Cape, and thence re-shipped to England; the English consumer thus pays the increased duty, and the difference of freight, and the foreign coffee is not excluded from the British market, though it was obviously the purpose of the law to exclude it.

Your committee cannot refrain from impressing strongly on the attention of The House that the effect of prohibitory duties, while they are of course wholly unproductive to the revenue, is to impose an indirect tax on the consumer, often equal to the whole difference of price between the British article and the foreign article which the prohibition excludes. This fact has been strongly and emphatically urged on Your Committee by several witnesses; and the enormous extent of taxation so levied cannot fail to awaken the attention of The House. On articles of food alone, it is averred, according to the Testimony laid before the Committee, that the amount taken from the consumer exceeds the amount of all the other taxes which are levied by the Government. And the witnesses concur in the opinion that the sacrifices of the community are not confined to the loss of revenue, but that they are accompanied by injurious effects upon wages and capital; they diminish greatly the productive powers of the country, and limit our active trading relations.

Somewhat similar is the action of high and protective duties. These impose upon the consumer a tax equal to the amount of the duties levied upon the foreign article, whilst it also increases the price of all the competing home-produced articles to the same amount as the duty; but that increased price goes, not to the Treasury, but to the protected manufacturer. It is obvious that high protective duties check importation, and consequently, are unproductive to the revenue; and experience shows, that the profit to the trader, the benefit to the consumer, and the fiscal interests of the country, are all sacrificed when heavy import duties impede the interchange of commodities with other nations.

The inquiries of Your Committee have naturally led them to investigate the effects of the protective system on manufacture and labour. They find on the part of those who are connected with some of the most important of our manufactures, a conviction, and a growing conviction, that the protective system is not, on the whole, beneficial to the protected manufactures themselves. Several witnesses have expressed the utmost willingness to surrender any protection they have from the Tariffs, and disclaim any benefit resulting from that protection; and Your Committee, in investigating the subject as to the amount of duties levied on the plea of protection to British manufactures, have to report that the amount does not exceed half a million sterling; and some of the manufacturers, who are supposed to be most interested in retaining those duties, are quite willing they should be abolished, for the purpose of introducing a more liberal system into our commercial policy.

Your Committee gather from the evidence that has been laid before them, that while the prosperity of our own manufactures is not to be traced to benefits derived from the exclusion of foreign rival manufacturers, so neither is the competition of continental manufacturers to be traced to a protective system. They are told that the most vigorous and successful of the manufactures on the Continent have grown, not out of peculiar favour shown to them by legislation, but from those natural and spontaneous advantages which are associated with labour and capital in certain localities, and which cannot be transferred elsewhere at the mandate of the Legislature, or at the will of the manufacturer. Your Committee see reason to believe, that the most prosperous fabrics are those which flourish without the aid of special favours. It has been stated to Your Committee, that the Legislation of Great Britain, whenever it is hostile to the introduction of foreign commodities, is invariably urged by the foreign states that produce such commodities, as a ground and a sanction for laws being passed by them hostile to the introduction of products of British industry; and while on the one hand, there is reason to believe that the liberalizing the Tariffs of Great Britain would lead to similar favourable changes in the tariffs of other nations, so it is seriously to be apprehended that a persistence in our illiberal and exclusive policy will bring with it increased imposts on, if not prohibitions against, the products of British labour being admitted to other countries.

With reference to the influence of the protective system upon wages, and on the condition of the labourer, Your Committee have to observe, that as the pressure of foreign competition is heaviest on those articles in the production of which the rate of wages is lowest, so it is obvious, in a country exporting so largely as England does, that other advantages may more than compensate for an apparent advantage in the money price of labour. The countries in which the rate of wages is lowest are not always those which manufacture most successfully; and Your Committee are persuaded that the best service that could be rendered to the industrious classes of the community, would be to extend the field of labour, and of demand for labour, by an extension of our commerce; and that the supplanting the present system of protection and prohibition, by a moderate Tariff, would encourage and multiply most beneficially for the State and for the people our commercial transactions.

Your Committee further recommend, that as speedily as possible the whole system of differential duties and of all restrictions should be reconsidered, and that a change therein be effected in such a manner that existing interests may suffer as little as possible in the transaction to a more liberal and equitable state of things. Your Committee is persuaded that the difficulties of modifying the discriminating duties which favour the introduction of British colonial articles would be very much abated if the Colonies were themselves allowed the benefits of free trade with all the world.

Although, owing to the period of the Session at which the inquiry was begun, Your Committee have not been able to embrace all the several branches which come within the scope of their instructions, they have thought themselves warranted in reporting their strong conviction of the necessity of an immediate change in the Import Duties of the kingdom: and should Parliament sanction the views which Your Committee entertain on these most important matters, they are persuaded that by imposts on a small number of those articles which are now most productive, the amount of each impost being carefully considered with a view to the greatest consumption of the article, and thereby the greatest receipt to the Customs, no loss would occur to the revenue, but, on the contrary, a considerable augmentation might be confidently anticipated.

The simplification they recommend would not only vastly facilitate the transactions of commerce, and thereby benefit the revenue, but would at the same time greatly diminish the cost of collection, remove multitudinous sources of complaint and vexation, and give an example to the world at large, which, emanating from a community distinguished above all others for its capital, its enterprize, its intelligence, and the extent of its trading relations, could not but produce the happiest effects; and consolidate the great interests of peace and commerce by associating them intimately and permanently with the prosperity of the whole family of nations.

6 *August* 1840.

140. Sir Robert Peel's Budget speech (11 March 1842)

Hansard, 3/LXI/429–457.

. . . The House, then, will bear in mind, that in fulfilment of the duty I have undertaken, I present to them the deficit in this country for the current year to the amount of £2,350,000, with a certain prospect of a deficit for next year to the amount of at least £2,470,000, independently of the increase to be expected on account of China and Affghanistan, and that in India, that great portion of our empire, I show a deficit on the two last years which will probably not be less than £4,700,000. Sir, this is the amount of deficiency we have to meet (I mean, of course, only the part I have stated affecting this country); how shall that deficiency be supplied? We cannot escape the consideration of that question; and it is our duty, no doubt, before any proposition be made, to exhaust in consideration the modes by which that deficiency can be supplied. Shall we persevere in the system on which we have been acting for the last five years? Shall we, in time of peace, have resort to the miserable expedient of continued loans? Shall we try issues of Exchequer-bills? Shall we resort to saving-banks? Shall we have recourse to any of those expedients which, call them by what name you please, are neither more nor less than a permenant addition to the public debt? We have a deficiency of nearly £5,000,000 in two years; is there a prospect of reduced expenditure? Without entering into details, but looking at your extended empire, at the demands that are made for the protection of your commerce, and the general state of the world, and calling to mind the intelligence that has lately reached us, can you anticipate, for the year after the next, the possibility, consistent with the honour and safety of this country, of greatly reducing the public expense? I am bound to say I cannot calculate upon that. Is this a casual deficiency for which you have to provide a remedy? Is it a deficiency for the present year on account of extraordinary circumstances? Is it a deficiency for the last two years? Sir, it is not. This deficiency has existed for the last seven or eight years. It is not a casual deficiency. In the year ending the 5th of April, 1838, the deficiency was £1,428,000. In the year ending the 5th of April, 1839, the deficiency was £430,000. In 1840 it was £1,457,000. In 1841 the deficiency was £1,851,000; in 1842 I estimate the deficiency will be £2,334,030. The deficiency in these five years amounts to £7,502,000; and to that actual deficiency I must add the estimated deficiency for the year ending the 5th of April, 1843, £2,570,000, making an aggregate deficiency in six years of £10,072,000. I am sure I shall not be blamed for adhering to my resolution, in making a full and unreserved disclosure of our financial situation. I do it, as I said before, because I am deeply impressed with the conviction that a full knowledge of the truth is the first step to improvement; and because I have that confidence in the resources, in the energy, and the wisdom of Parliament, that I cannot consent to avail myself of that miserable subterfuge of withholding any knowledge I may be able to communicate with respect to the financial difficulties of the country. Well then, Sir, with this proof that it is not with an occasional or casual deficiency that we have to deal, will you, I ask, have recourse to the wretched expedient of continued loans? Sir, I cannot recommend such a step. It is impossible that I could be a party to a proceeding which I should think might, perhaps, have been justifiable at first, before you knew exactly the nature of your revenue and expenditure; but with these facts before me I should think I was disgracing the situation I hold if I could consent to such a paltry expedient as this. I can hardly think that Parliament will adopt a different view. I can hardly think that you, who inherit the debt that was contracted by your predecessors, when having a revenue they reduced the charges of the Post-office, and inserted in the preamble of the bill a declaration that the reduction of the revenue should be made good by increased taxation, will now refuse to make it good. The effort having been made, but the effort having failed, that pledge is still unredeemed. I advised you not to give that pledge; but if you regard the pledges of your predecessors, it is for you now to redeem them. If, however, you are not bound by the pledges of your predecessors you are bound, I apprehend, by the engagement which you yourselves have contracted. Almost the first vote you gave after the election of the present Parliament was the adoption of a resolution that it was impossible to permit that state of things to continue which presented constant deficits of revenue. Parliament assured the Crown that they would without delay apply themselves to the consideration of finance, and would adopt some measures for the purpose of equalizing revenue and expenditure. I apprehend, therefore, that with almost universal acquiescence I may abandon the thought of supplying the deficiency by the miserable device of fresh loans, or an issue of Exchequer-bills. Shall I then, if I must resort to taxation, levy that taxation upon the articles of consumption, upon those articles which may appear to some superfluities, but which are known to constitute almost the necessaries of life? I cannot consent to any proposal for increasing taxation on the great articles of consumption by the labouring classes of society. I say, moreover, I can give you conclusive proof that you have arrived at the limits of taxation on articles of consumption. I am speaking now of articles of luxury which might be supposed not to constitute the consumption of the laborious classes, and I advise you not to attempt taxation, even upon those articles, for you will be defeated in your expectations of revenue. The right hon. Gentleman opposite (Mr. F. Baring), attempting to redeem the pledge which had been given by Parliament to repair the deficiency which was caused by the defalcation of the Post-office revenue, proposed in 1840 that 5 per cent. additional duty should be laid on the articles of Customs and Excise, and 10 per cent. additional on the assessed taxes. [Noise.] I am much obliged to the House for the patience with which they listen to me, and feel sorry to trouble them with these details, but I do think them necessary parts of the statement I have to make. The net produce of the Customs and Excise, in the year ending the 5th January, 1840, after deducting drawbacks and repayments, was £37,911,000. And here I must observe, that I am now merely exhausting the different means by which men might contemplate the supplying of the deficiency, and trying to show that increased taxation upon any articles of consumption will not afford relief. I wish to carry your judgement along with me. I said that the net produce of the Customs and Excise in the year ending the 5th January, 1840, was £37,911,000, and the estimated increase in the Customs and Excise by the additional 5 per cent. was £1,895,000. Comparing, therefore, the income from Customs and Excise in 1840 with that in 1842–and I take 1842 in preference to 1841, because you can thus more fairly estimate the effect of the increased duty–I find while the estimated produce of the Customs and Excise was £39,807,000, the actual produce was only £38,118,000, the actual increase being, instead of £1,895,000, only £206,000; not 5 per cent. increase in the amount of revenue, but little more than one half per cent., realised in the attempt to impose 5 per cent. additional duty. In the depression of trade there may, undoubtedly, be circumstances sufficient to account for the expectations of the right hon. Gentleman not having been realised, but still, making every abatement for these causes of decrease, I think it impossible not to admit that 5 per cent. increase of duty on articles of consumption would not produce 5 per cent. in net amount to the revenue. At the same time the right hon. Gentleman's estimate with respect to the produce of the assessed taxes was fully realised. I know it may be said that full time has not been given for notifying the intention to discontinue some articles partaking of the nature of assessed taxes; but, on the whole, I think we may disregard that circumstance, for although the notice of such discontinuance may not have taken full effect, yet the inference, I think, may be fairly drawn, that the right hon. Gentleman did not overdraw his estimate. The net produce of assessed taxes in 1840 was £2,758,000, the 10 per cent. additional being £275,000, the estimated produce was £3,034,000; but the actual produce of the assessed taxes, including the additional 10 per cent. for the year ending the 5th January 1842, very far exceeded the right hon. Gentleman's estimate; for, instead of realising only £3,034,000, as he calculated, £3,500,000 was realised. From this perhaps I should make an abatement on account of the survey of windows. That new survey of windows produced an increase in the revenue of £430,000; consequently the increase in assessed taxes alone ought perhaps to be diminished to something like that amount; but still, if you make that abatement, you will find that the right hon. Gentleman's estimate was verified–there was an increase in the assessed taxes to the full amount he calculated, the increase being £311,000, or 11½ per cent. was produced by the nominal imposition of 10 per cent. additional duty. I compare these two results–I compare the complete failure of the taxes on consumption, and the complete justification of the taxes upon something analogous to property. I find in the one case the estimate was verified, I find in the other it was disappointed. These are the results I feel it my duty to bring before the committee; but my immediate object was to adduce a proof that you had arrived, for purposes of revenue, at the limits of taxation upon articles of consumption. Then I say, making abatements on account of the depression of trade, I do not think any man can resist the conclusion which I draw, that to lay 10 per cent. additional on Customs and Excise will end in nothing but failure and disappointment. I have now discarded the notions of supplying the deficiency by incurring fresh debt. I have attempted to carry your conviction with me, while I have endeavoured to show that I cannot look to taxation on articles of consumption. Now, it is possible to resort to other expedients. Shall I revive old taxes that have been abolished, or impose new ones? Shall I restore the old postage duties? I do feel it to be necessary that you should adhere, not to the contract you have entered into, but to observe the request I made at the commencement of my address–that you should suspend your judgment until you have heard the entire of my plan. I must deal with each of these questions step by step. What I ask is, that you should not condemn any individual proposition until you can judge of it in relation to the whole. Never doubting the social advantages of the reduction of the duty in postage, thinking that the duty as it existed was too high, and might fairly admit of reconsideration and reduction, I did nevertheless deprecate, in the then state of the finances, the reduction which took place to 1d. upon all letters.

I do believe, if it were necessary, I could show to you that from the post-office you do not receive one farthing of revenue. If you will add the charge of the packets to the other expenses of the post-office, the account which will be presented to you will show a deficit in the revenue of the post-office. But when I state that, I do not undervalue the importance of the reduction in a moral and social point of view. I will not say, speaking with that caution with which I am sometimes taunted, but which I find a great convenience–I will not say that the post-office ought not to be a source of revenue. I will not say that it may not fairly become the subject of discussion; but I will say this, that I do not think the recent measure has had a complete and full trial; and I am so sensible of the many advantages which result from it, that I cannot recommend that in the present year we should attempt to alter it. I say again, notwithstanding all the taunts to which I have been exposed during the last month in consequence of my proposal in respect to the Corn-laws, that no man can feel a more intimate conviction than I do, that whatever be your financial difficulties and necessities, you must so adapt and adjust your measures as not to bear on the comforts of the labouring classes of society. My conviction further is, that it would not be expedient with reference to the narrow interests of property, that that should be done. Well then, Sir, I must, with my sense of public duty, abandon the hope of realising in the present year any revenue from the post-office. Shall I revive the taxes which were laid upon great articles of consumption, and which were very productive? Shall I revive the taxes upon salt, upon leather, and upon beer? With respect to leather, for instance, I do not know that the reduction took place with perfect wisdom; I am very much afraid that the full amount of the reduction was not carried to the account of the consumer. I believe you omitted to take a step which you ought to have adopted concurrently with the reduction of the duty on leather–namely, to reduce the duty on the import of foreign hides. I am afraid you reduced the duty on leather in favour of a monopoly, and without benefit to the consumer. But the question is not now whether we shall reduce an existing duty; the question is whether we shall revive a duty that has been abolished, and on the faith of the abolition of which various contracts, numerous commercial and manufacturing arrangements, have been made. If I take the case of salt, for instance, I find that, since the reduction of duty, salt has been consumed in a variety of ways, in which its use was never before contemplated. On account of chemical discoveries and improvements, in consequence of the application of science to manufactures, salt now enters into a variety of products. The ground upon which the abolition of the duty was strongly urged was, the importance of facilitating the supply of salt to the working classes; but, independent of their consumption, in my opinion it would be unwise to revive the duty on this article, on account of its extensive use in manufactures. There might be a danger of interfering with manufacturing industry, which would greatly check its prosperity; there would be a necessary system of drawback on account of the salt consumed, which would lead to opportunities of evasion and fraud, and increase the necessity for larger excise establishments. I don't think, I need argue, therefore, against the revival of the duties on salt, leather, or beer. Shall I, then, resort to locomotion for the purpose of finding a substitute? Shall I increase the taxes on railways?

I confess nothing but a hard necessity would induce me to derive revenue from locomotion. In the present state of this country, when it is a great object to facilitate the transfer of labour, and to enable those to whom labour is capital to bring it to the best market–seeing the immense social advantages which result from the freedom of communication, not perhaps immediately visible, but still not the less real, I should contemplate with great reluctance and regret, the necessity of increased taxation upon railroads. Again, gas has been suggested as a proper object of taxation. I must say, I should be also unwilling to add to the taxes on gas. I range the taxes on locomotion and the taxes on gas-lights, on the same category with the taxes on salt–not that the same principle is exactly applicable; but I freely own, seeing the deficiency I have to supply, I should be unwilling to look for revenue either from locomotion or gas-lights. Shall I, then, look for any portion of this deficiency to any of those miserable dribblets of taxation which occupy the attention of provincial Chancellors of the Exchequer? There are those who seem to have nothing else to do but to suggest modes of taxation to men in office, and as I tried to discourage the applications to me for foreign consulships, and had thought of advertising with reference to Downing-street, I had no connection with the shop next door; I shall take this opportunity, with reference to these subjects of favourite occupation and amusement to those who in small communities turn their attention to financial affairs, and who fancy they have made some discovery that pretty nearly puts them on a level with Archimedes; when finding that piano-fortes, umbrellas, or such articles are not subject of taxation, they immediately suggest them to the Chancellor of the Exchequer, accompanied with a claim for a very large per centage on the ground of the novelty of their discovery and the certain success of its application,–I shall take this opportunity of discouraging all such suggestions by assuring these volunteer financiers that men who are spending eight or ten hours a day in consideration of matters of finance are at least as likely to form an accurate judgment on such matters as those who suggest such pitiful propositions. There is another source, which adopting this process of exhaustion, I must not forget, which was brought forward and urged upon the House by the late Government, and to which I feel it my duty to refer. Shall I then hope for the increase of revenue from diminished taxation? Before I apply myself to this point, let me remind you of the extent of your deficit, the amount of the sum to be provided for, and the proof I have offered you that it is not an occasional or casual deficiency you have to make good. No one has greater confidence than I have in the ultimate tendency of reduction in taxation on the great articles of consumption, if wisely managed; but after giving to this subject the fullest consideration, I have come to the complete conviction that it would be mere delusion to hope for supplying the deficiency by diminished taxation on articles of consumption. I have a firm confidence that such is the buoyancy of the consumptive powers of this country, that we may hope ultimately to realise increased revenue from diminished taxation; but a long period must elapse before this end is attained, and I feel confident that the adoption of any plan like that proposed by the late Government, or the adoption of any other plan for raising revenue by means of diminished taxation, would not afford any immediate relief, or provide any resources on which we might rely for supplying the deficiency of the revenue. I have looked with considerable attention to the effect produced by a reduction of taxation upon articles of considerable consumption, and I do perceive that in many cases that elasticity which gives, after the lapse of time, increased revenue, but in almost every instance–in all, I believe, without exception, the space of time which elapses, after reduction of taxation, before the same amount of revenue is realised, is very considerable. Let us take the case of wine. In 1825, the revenue derived from wine was £2,153,000. The duty was reduced from 9s. 1¼d. to 4s. 2¾d. the gallon; and in the next year after the reduction of the duty there was a falling-off of the duty from £2,100,000 to £1,400,000. In the next year, the duty amounted to £1,600,000; in the subsequent years to £1,700,000, £1,400,000, £1,500,000, and the duty has never since realised its former amount. Upon tobacco, the duty was reduced from 4s. per lb. to 3s. per lb. Previous to the reduction of the duty, the revenue derived from tobacco amounted to £3,378,000; and immediately after the reduction, there was a falling off. It fell from £3,300,000 to £2,600,000, then it rose to £2,800,000, and in the following years realised £2,700,000, £2,800,000, £2,900,000, and again, £2,900,000; but the duty on tobacco has never recovered its former amount. The case generally relied on as showing the advantage of a reduction of duty on articles of consumption, is that of coffee. The duty on coffee was diminished from 1s. per lb. to 6d. per lb. This was in 1824, when the revenue received from coffee amounted to £420,000. In the next year after the reduction the amount of duty fell to £336,000, then to £399,000, and in the third year the duty recovered itself, and has gone on advancing. Still, even in this instance of coffee, which is by far the most favourable case, a period of three years elapsed before the full amount of duty was realised. The duty on hemp was reduced from 9s. 2d. per cwt. to 4s. 8d. At the time of the reduction, the revenue derived from hemp was £236,000, and since then hemp has never yet paid but half that amount of duty. In the case of rum, there was an increase of revenue after the reduction of duty from 12s. 7d. per gallon to 8s. 6d. The duty on sugar was reduced from 27s. per cwt. to 24s. At the time of the reduction, the revenue derived from sugar amounted to £4,896,000; it then fell to £4,600,000, to £4,300,000, and then rose to £4,500,000, and it has never since paid the same amount of duty. I do not think I need go through the whole of the articles in detail in which a reduction of duty has taken place. In addition to tobacco, hemp, sugar, and the articles I have mentioned, the duty was also reduced on glass, beer, soap, paper, on newspapers and advertisements; but I think, I need not refer to all these articles in detail. In many of these cases, there has been no considerable reduction of the amount of duty, but, with the exception of coffee, which realised the full amount of duty in the third year after the reduction, and rum, there is not a single article the duty on which has recovered itself within a period of five or six years after a considerable reduction. Therefore, on this ground, I am led to believe, that with respect to the present deficiency of the revenue, which it is necessary to supply, you cannot look to that supply from a mere reduction of duty upon articles of consumption; and if you resort to that as the only means of supplying the deficiency, you must make up your mind to continue the system, which I thought you were ready to abjure, of having recourse to loans and those other devices I have before alluded to, for the purpose of making up the deficiency. I trust that I have–I will not say, convinced you that none of those measures ought to be adopted, but that, at any rate, I have clearly explained the grounds on which I cannot be a party to their adoption. I will now state what is the measure which I propose, under a sense of public duty, and a deep conviction that it is necessary for the public interest; and impressed at the same time, with an equal conviction that the present sacrifices which I call on you to make will be amply compensated ultimately in a pecuniary point of view, and much more than compensated by the effect they will have in maintaining public credit, and the ancient character of this country. Instead of looking to taxation on consumption,–instead of reviving the taxes on salt or on sugar,–it is my duty to make an earnest appeal to the possessors of property, for the purpose of repairing this mighty evil. I propose, for a time at least, (and I never had occasion to make a proposition with a more thorough conviction of its being one which the public interest of the country required)–I propose, that for a time to be limited, the income of this country should be called on to contribute a certain sum for the purpose of remedying this mighty and growing evil. I propose, that the income of this country should bear a charge not exceeding 7d. in the pound; which will not amount to 3 per cent., but speaking accurately, £2 18s. 4d. per cent.; for the purpose of not only supplying the deficiency in the revenue, but of enabling me with confidence and satisfaction to propose great commercial reforms, which will afford a hope of reviving commerce, and such an improvement in the manufacturing interests as will re-act on every other interest in the country; and, by diminishing the prices of the articles of consumption, and the cost of living, will, in a pecuniary point of view, compensate you for your present sacrifices; whilst you will be, at the same time, relieved from the contemplation of a great public evil. [Interruption, and cries of "Order!"] I hope hon. Gentlemen will allow me to make the statement I have yet to lay before the House uninterruptedly. In 1798, when the prospects of this country were gloomy, the Minister had the courage to propose, and the people had the fortitude to adopt, an income-tax of 10 per cent. The income-tax continued to the close of the war in 1802; and in 1803, after the rupture of the peace of Amiens, a duty of 5 per cent. was placed upon property. It was raised in 1805 to 6¼ per cent.; and so it continued to the end of the war. I propose that the duty to be laid on property shall not exceed 3 per cent., or, as I said before, exactly £2 18s. 4d., being 7d. in the pound. Under the former tax, all incomes below £60 were exempt from taxation, and on incomes between £60 and £150, the tax was at a reduced rate. I shall propose, that from the income-tax I now recommend all incomes under £150 shall be exempt. Under the former income-tax, the amount at which the occupying tenants were charged, was estimated at three-fourths of the rent. It is admitted, I believe, that to calculate the profits of the tenants at the three-fourths of the rent, was too high an estimate. I propose, therefore, that in respect of the occupying tenant, the occupation of land shall be charged at one-half, instead of three-fourths of the rent. I believe this to be a perfectly fair reduction, and it was contemplated in 1816, when Lord Bexley proposed the renewal of the income-tax. I believe it to be a perfectly fair reduction, inasmuch as rents have increased in reference to the value of land in a proportion to justify it. I propose, for

I see no ground for exemption, that all funded property, whether held by natives of this country or foreigners, should be subject to the same charge as unfunded property. This is the nature of the proposition which it is my intention, with the full and unanimous concurrence of my Colleagues, and with the deepest conviction on our parts that it is wise and necessary, to submit to the House. . . .

Now, Sir, having stated to the House all the new taxes I mean to propose, perhaps it may be convenient to the House that I should briefly review the total amount. Of course I am speaking of the year ending the 5th of April, 1843; as it is from the 5th of April, 1842, that I propose these taxes to commence with the exception of that on spirits, which (in order to avoid evasion) I must propose for adoption at the earliest possible period. Then, Sir, calculating with respect to the property-tax a receipt of £3,700,000 (dealing only, now, with round numbers)–from the stamp duties equalization £160,000, from the increase of spirit duties £250,000, and from the duty on the export of coal £200,000, I make the total £4,310,000 as the amount of annual estimated income derivable from the new imposts I propose. [MR. LABOUCHERE intimated across the Table that Sir Robert Peel had omitted an item of £70,000 to which the right hon. Baronet assenting, stated the amount then would be £4,380,000.] Now, Sir, I must deduct from this amount the estimated deficiency on actual votes, for which, of course, I must provide–that I take to be £2,570,000 leaving a surplus of £1,800,000. But then the House will bear in mind that this deficiency arises on votes for the current year, and that there must be added the excess of expenditure on the China expedition, &c., which I cannot estimate at less than £800,000. Whatever measures also it will be necessary for us to adopt in respect to India must be deducted from the estimate; but for the present, with these reserves, and subject to such additional deductions, I calculate on a surplus of £1,800,000 after providing for the excess of expenditure on actual votes. Having that surplus, then, Sir, in what way shall we apply it? I propose to apply it, namely, in a manner which I think will be most consonant with public feeling and opinion–by making great improvements in the commercial tariff of England, and in addition to these improvements to abate the duties on some great articles of consumption. Sir, I look to the tariff, and find that it comprises not less than 1,200 articles subject to various rates of duty. During the interval which I have been blamed for taking to consider the subject, I can only say, that each individual item in that tariff has been subjected to the most careful consideration of myself and colleagues. In the case of each article we have endeavoured to determine, as well as we can the proportion borne by the duty to the average price of the article, for the purpose of ascertaining to what extent it may be desirable to make reductions of the several duties; and the measure which I shall propose will contain a complete review, on general principles, of all the articles of the tariff, with a very great alteration of many of the duties. We have proceeded, Sir, on these principles (observe, that I am speaking of general views; there may be individual articles which should form exceptions, but I wish a general result); first, we desire to remove all prohibition, and the relaxation of duties of a prohibitory character; next, we wish to reduce the duties on raw materials for manufactures to a considerable extent–in some cases the duty we propose being merely nominal, for the purpose more of statistical than revenue objects; in no case, or scarcely any, exceeding, in the case of raw materials, 5 per cent. I speak of course in a general way. Then we propose that the duties on articles partly manufactured shall be materially reduced, never exceeding 12 per cent. Again, I say, I speak only as to general principles, and without reference to particular cases that may be excepted; while as to duties on articles wholly manufactured we propose that they shall never exceed 20 per cent. These are the general views of the Government as to the maximum duties to be imposed, not referring to certain commodities which I will mention subsequently. The course we have pursued, Sir, is this:–We have arranged the whole tariff under twenty heads. Under the first head, for instance, including live animals, and provisions of all kinds; under the second, articles considered as spices; under the third, seeds; under the fourth, wood for furniture; under the fifth, ores, and other materials for manufactures; and without, Sir, going through all the immense mass of detail, I propose forthwith to lay before the House the amended tariff scheme. It is all prepared, it is arranged as clearly as possible under the twenty different heads, classing as nearly as practicable articles of a similar nature, each schedule arranged under five columns–the first giving the names of the articles, the second the present rate of duty, the third the amount of duty actually received during the year 1840, taken from the Import Duties Committee Report, the fourth the proposed rate of duty to be levied on articles imported from foreign countries, fifthly the proposed rates of duty on the imports from British colonial possessions. Now, Sir, it appears that I could not lay before the House my project in any clearer way than in the one I intend. To attempt to go through all the provisions of my plan, at present, would increase my labour too much, and too greatly fatigue the House. Here, Sir, is the new tariff, arranged under the twenty different heads I mentioned; and on Monday morning all those engaged in commerce and manufactures throughout the country will have the opportunity of seeing what are the duties which the Government intend to propose. [The right hon. Baronet laid the paper on the Table.] Now, Sir, speaking generally, as I said before, I think that out of the 1,200 articles in the tariff, it is proposed to reduce the duty on 750–on all those articles which enter into manufactures as chief constituent materials. There remain about 450 articles on which it does not appear necessary for the interests of commerce and for the interests of consumers to make any deduction of duty. But on 750 duties out of 1,200 I do propose reductions, some of them most material. . . . I now address myself to the consideration of reductions in duties on great articles of consumption. Sir, the chief articles of consumption to which duties refer are (independently of wines, &c.) sugar, coffee, and tea. I wish I had it in my power to state to the House, that her Majesty's Government could propose to Parliament such an alteration in the duties on sugar as would be likely to afford a large measure of advantage to the consumer. I do not deny, that if we were wholly unembarrassed by the question of the slave-trade, that I should have felt it my duty to propose a considerable alteration on this subject; but, looking at our position with reference to our own West India colonies, and having due regard to our relations with foreign states, and bearing in mind the treaties into which we have entered, I confess I do not see how it would be possible for me with justice or with safety, to propose any modification of the duties now collected from sugar. . . . I now come to two articles of very general consumption–coffee and timber. With respect to both of those I trust that the propositions that I shall have to make will be more generally acceptable. I am sorry to say that though there has been an increase in the consumption of sugar, there has been a decrease in the consumption of coffee. In the year 1840 the home consumption of coffee was 2,870,000 lb. In 1841, it was 2,844,100 lb. The gross amount of duty received in the former year was £922,000, and in the latter £880,000. The duty on foreign coffee is 1s. 3d., while on coffee produced in British possessions the duty is only 6d., and the duty on coffee produced in territories comprehended within the limits of the East India Company's Charter is 9d. Will the House do me the favour to look for a moment at the effect of this condition of our fiscal regulations? Coffee the produce of Brazil and Hayti is conveyed to the Cape of Good Hope, and thence transferred to England, in order that it may come in at a duty of 9d. This, with 1d. for charges of freight, places foreign coffee under a burden of 10d., when coffee the produce of British possessions pays 6d. Now, it appears to me in this case the wisest, the fairest, and the best policy to make a reduction on great articles of consumption, instead of several of smaller amount on articles of minor importance. I desire to make the reduction considerable, and I desire at the same time to make it effectual, and the mode in which I propose to accomplish this is, by imposing two simple duties, and to get rid of the absurdity of sending coffee from Brazil and Hayti to take a voyage to the Cape of Good Hope before it comes to England. I thus appear to myself to get rid of the charges of freight, and to place the provisions respecting the importation of coffee upon a simple and intelligible basis. I intend that coffee the produce of British possessions shall come in at a duty of 4d., and that all foreign coffee shall pay 8d. I shall now proceed to calculate the probable loss to the revenue from this arrangement. In the year 1841 the quantity of coffee imported from our own possessions was 463,000 lb. The supply of foreign coffee during the same period was 10,849,000 lb. Now, with the altered duty I find, upon the most accurate estimate which can be made of the probable loss, that it will not exceed £171,000. The whole of the calculation into which I have entered stands thus:–

The Revenue for 1841, derived from the present duties, viz.	*Revenue* £
From British possessions, 17,571,884 lb. at 6d.	463,699
—— Foreign countries, 10,899,096 lb. at 9d., 1s. and 1s. 3d.	427,947
Revenue received in 1841 .	891,640
Assuming no increased consumption, the Revenue at the two duties of 4d. and 8d. would be–	£
From British possessions, 17,571,884 lb. at 4d. . . .	292,864
—— Foreign countries, 10,849,096 lb at 8d. . . .	361,636
Revenue for 1842–3 . .	654,500
Revenue for 1841 . .	891,646
Loss, assuming no increase of consumption	237,146
Assuming that the increase of consumption will be 10 per cent, *viz.* producing	65,450
Probable loss of revenue .	171,696

Adding this loss to that which I have already estimated will be incurred by the reduction of the duty on articles consumed in manufactures–namely, the sum of £270,000, it will show a total decrease of £441,000 in the revenue now obtained from the necessaries of life. The other great article to which it is necessary that I should now direct the attention of the House is the article of timber. I am anxious to begin by applying as much as possible of the surplus revenue to the reduction of the duty on timber, but here again I find myself considerably embarrassed by our relations with Canada. The present rate of duty on foreign timber is 55s. a load, but the duty on timber is now levied in a complicated and unfair way. And in taking the average amount of duty on foreign timber, including the duty on deals, staves, and laths, taking the whole together, the aggregate amount will not exceed 41s. a load. The duty on colonial timber is 10s. a load, and here also the average duty may be taken at 8s. or 9s. a load. It appears to me, that it would be of the utmost advantage, if you make a reduction in the duty on timber, to let it be such a reduction that the consumer should be certain of deriving some benefit from it, and then to make the reduction in such a way that, in the peculiar position of the Canadas, and knowing the importance attached by them to the timber trade, we should not suddenly, or indeed not at all, affect the interests of those colonies; and I think there can be a mode suggested if the House will consent to a considerable loss of present revenue, by which the object to which I have alluded may be attained. If I am correct in supposing that the amount of duty upon foreign timber does not exceed 41s. per load, the scope within which I can act is somewhat limited. There have been various measures proposed upon this subject. That measure which I must confess appeared to me to offer the greatest objection, was that proposed last year by Government, and which offered the slightest possible relief to the public. By the measure of last year, it was proposed to reduce the duty on foreign timber, but to increase that on Canadian timber. I am going to act on a totally different view. I wish to put all political considerations on one side. I am anxious to avoid, as far as possible, those paltry objects which sink into nothing when I consider the immense interests which are at stake. The measure of last year proposed no relief to the consumer, and no addition to the revenue. My object, having a surplus to deal with, is to consider how I can deal with it to the greatest advantage to the consumer–how, without inflicting any injury on Canada, I can secure the most substantial benefit to this country, to the manufacturing, to the commercial, and to the agricultural interests. It appears to me, that if there is one article more than any other, on which a great reduction of duty is likely to prove beneficial to the public, it is this. It may not offer such plausible promises as some other reductions that might be proposed. It may, for instance, be represented to the working classes that this is a reduction of duty from which they will derive no benefit. But that would be a very false and superficial view of the subject. The real way in which we can benefit the working and manufacturing classes is, unquestionably, by removing the burden that presses on the springs of manufactures and commerce. I should propose–as I believe the aggregate average duty upon foreign timber does not exceed 41s.–I should propose, in order that the reduction may be carried out to a sufficient extent to benefit the consumer, that for the present, the duty on foreign timber, as distinguished from deals, should be reduced to 30s. I should propose, that for the present year, that is to say, the year ending 5th April, 1843, the duties on deals should be reduced to 35s. But I propose to make a total change in the mode of collecting the duties, and to place all the ports of the Baltic on the same footing. I propose, that in future the duty shall be estimated by cubical measurement, instead of the cumbrous, injurious, and unfair mode by which the tax is at present levied. In the year after next I propose–for I am anxious to prevent the possibility of inflicting any injury on Canada; in the committee which sat in 1835, Lord Sydenham held out a distinct prospect to the Canadians, that no sudden measure should be adopted calculated to injure the timber trade of that country;–it is therefore the intention of her Majesty's Ministers to evince no disposition in the reduction which they should feel it their duty to make, to impose any disadvantage on the inhabitants of Canada. I stated last year, on the subject of the timber duties, that I should reserve my opinion with regard to them, until I should see how an alteration of them would affect our colonies, and particularly until I should consider its effect on our political relation with the important province of Canada. I still maintain, that the utmost caution should be exhibited in our relations with Canada, and that nothing should be rashly done that may be likely to affect injuriously the interests of its inhabitants. With this feeling I propose an alteration in the timber duties, and shall be anxious to benefit the Canadian as well as the British consumer. On these grounds I propose, that after the 5th of April, 1843, the duty on foreign timber should be reduced to 25s. a load; that the duty on deals be reduced to 2s. a load, and that the duty on lath-wood shall be reduced to 3s. a load. Now, I shall say at once that the adoption of this measure cannot fail to produce a great loss of revenue, but having made a reduction in the duty on articles that enter into the elements of manufactures, I cannot see any more beneficial reduction than a reduction of the duty levied upon timber. The total loss, in consequence of this reduction in the duty on timber, will, I estimate, amount to £600,000. If the House wish it I will go through the details of the calculations by which I arrive at this conclusion. I am ready to go into these details, but I own I should be glad to be spared them, as I shall be glad to spare the House the trouble of listening to them. There are two, and only two, other great reductions of duty to which I wish to call the attention of the House, and I cannot help thinking that on these I shall carry the unanimous opinion of the House with me. Sir, there are at present levied certain duties on the export of British manufactures–duties, Sir, which I think are contrary to a sound principle of legislation; and these duties I find amount to the sum of £108,000 a-year. Part of these duties arise from the export of woollens and of yarns which are exported to countries with which we have no reciprocity treaties.

I find the duty on woollen manufactures amounts annually to	£30,000
That on linen yarns to	4,000
On silks to	4,800
On manufactured iron to	24,000
On some other articles to	9,000
On earthenware to	8,000
On provisions to	5,200
Making altogether . .	£85,000

To these may be added for some minor articles about £20,000 giving a total of upwards of £100,000 a-year. Now, Sir, I propose to remit altogether the export duties on British manufactures, and thus there will be incurred a loss of revenue at £103,000 a-year. There is another and a different class of duties that I think unjust, and towards the removal of which I think a part of the surplus should be applied. In the first place, I will call your attention to the duty upon stage-coaches: and in dealing with this question you must consider the amount of competition which the proprietors of these coaches have to contend against, especially on those lines of road where railways have been established. To make that competition more difficult, you subject them to unjust taxation. As I said before, I am unwilling to place any new tax on locomotion; but I am anxious to propose the remission of existing encumbrances. At present, railways pay to the State only one-eighth of a penny a mile for every passenger, and, speaking of the present year, I do not propose any augmentation to this tax. I do not mean to say that these duties are too low; but, when the duty on stage-coaches is considered, I say stage-coaches pay a great deal too much. The rate of mileage imposed on stage-coaches, if licensed to carry not more than six persons, is one penny a mile; if licensed to carry not more than ten persons, three halfpence a mile; if not more than thirteen, twopence, and if not more than sixteen, threepence. Then, in addition to this, there is a license duty of 5s., besides the assessed taxes on coachmen and guards. On railroads, no corresponding taxes are imposed. I shall propose, that stage coaches be subjected to a uniform mileage of 1½d., that the license be reduced to 3s., and that the assessed taxes on coachmen and guards be taken off altogether. This proposition, if assented to by Parliament, will lead to a loss of revenue amounting to £61,000; but it is a loss which, I feel persuaded, can be vindicated on principles of strict and impartial justice. I also propose to take off the duty imposed upon persons who are in the habit of letting job carriages, and this will lead to a loss in the revenue of £9,000, making a total loss in the revenue of £70,000 on account of stage coaches. I will now shortly review the whole of the financial arrangements which I have detailed.

The estimated deficiency of this Year is . . .	£2,570,000
The reduction in the various articles of the tariff, to the number of 750, will not be more than . .	270,000
The loss on coffee I estimate at	170,000
That on timber at	600,000
The repeal of the export duty on British manufactures will occasion a loss of	100,000
And the reduction of the duties on stage coaches will lessen the revenue by	70,000
Making a total deficiency in the public income, in consequence of the proposed reductions of . .	£3,780,000

The loss of £3,780,000, deducted from the estimated revenue to be derived from the new taxes, and which is calculated at £4,300,000, will leave a surplus of £520,000 to meet the increased estimate which I may have to propose on account of India; to meet the increased charge which may be necessary to prosecute the war with China;

to meet any increased reduction of duty which it may be necessary to propose on account of the completion of commercial treaties with other countries. I believe I have now concluded the task I have undertaken. If I have been enabled clearly (which is all I have aimed at)–clearly and fully to develope the views of her Majesty's Government, I am greatly indebted for that success to the very kind and patient attention with which the House has listened to the exceedingly long, and, I am afraid, in some respects, tedious details with which I have been compelled to enter. I have laid before you, without reserve, the whole plan of the Government. I have given you a full, an explicit, and unreserved, but, I hope, an unexaggerated statement of the financial embarrassments in which we are placed. There are occasions when a Minister of the Crown may, consistently with honour and with good policy, pause before he presses upon the Legislature the adoption of measures which he believes to be abstractly right; he may have to encounter differences of opinion amongst Colleagues whom he esteems and respects; he may sincerely believe it to be for the public interest that the Government of which he is a Member should retain power, and that, therefore, he should not hazard its existence, by proposing a measure which might not ultimately succeed, and thereby endanger the safety and security of his Government; he may, on comparing the consequence of exciting and agitating the country by discussion upon a measure in which he may not ultimately succeed, think it possible that there is a disadvantage in proposing that which he believes to be abstractly right, for the evil of fruitless agitation may possibly countervail the enunciation of a right principle. But there are occasions, and this is one of them, upon which a Government can make no compromise–there are occasions, and this is one of them, upon which it is the bounden duty of a Government to give that counsel to the Legislature which it believes to be right–to undertake the responsibility of proposing those measures which it believes to be for the public advantage, and to devolve upon the Legislature the responsibility of adopting or rejecting these measures. I have performed on the part of her Majesty's Government my duty. I have proposed with the full weight and authority of the Government, that which I believe to be conducive to the public welfare. I now devolve upon you the duty, which properly belongs to you, of maturely considering and finally deciding on the adoption or rejection of the measures I propose. We live in an important era of human affairs. There may be a natural tendency to overrate the magnitude of the crisis in which we live, or those particular events with which we are ourselves conversant; but I think it is impossible to deny that the period in which our lot and the lot of our fathers has been cast–the period which has elapsed since the first outbreak of the first French revolution–has been one of the most memorable periods that the history of the world will afford. The course which England has pursued during that period will attract for ages to come the contemplation and, I trust, the admiration of posterity. That period may be divided into two parts of almost equal duration; a period of twenty-five years of continued conflict–the most momentous which ever engaged the energies of a nation–and twenty-five years, in which most of us have lived, of profound European peace, produced by the sacrifices made during the years of war. There will be a time when those countless millions that are sprung from our loins, occupying many parts of the globe, living under institutions derived from ours, speaking the same language in which we convey our thoughts and feelings–for such will be the ultimate results of our wide-spread colonisation–the time will come when those countless millions will view with pride and admiration the example of constancy and fortitude which our fathers set during the momentous period of war. They will view with admiration our previous achievements by land and sea, our determination to uphold the public credit, and all those qualities by the expedition of which we were enabled ultimately, by the example we set to foreign nations, to ensure the deliverance of Europe. In the review of the period, the conduct of our fathers during the years of war will be brought into close contrast with the conduct of those of us who have lived only during the years of peace. I am now addressing you after the duration of peace for twenty-five years. I am now exhibiting to you the financial difficulties and embarrassments in which you are placed; and my confident hope and belief is, that following the example of those who preceded you, you will look these difficulties in the face, and not refuse to make similar sacrifices to those which your fathers made for the purpose of upholding the public credit. You will bear in mind that this is no casual and occasional difficulty. You will bear in mind that there are indications amongst all the upper classes of society of increased comfort and enjoyment–of increased prosperity and wealth, and that concurrently with these indications there exists a mighty evil which has been growing up for the last seven years, and which you now are called upon to meet. If you have, as I believe you have, the fortitude and constancy of which you have been set the example, you will not consent with folded arms to view the annual growth of this mighty evil. You will not reconcile it to your consciences to hope for relief from diminished taxation. You will not adopt the miserable expedient of adding, during peace, and in the midst of these indications of wealth and of increasing prosperity, to the burdens which posterity will be called upon to bear. You will not permit this evil to gain such gigantic growth as ultimately to place it far beyond your power to check or control. If you do permit this evil to continue, you must expect the severe but just judgment of a reflecting and retrospective posterity. Your conduct will be contrasted with the conduct of your fathers, under difficulties infinitely less pressing than theirs. Your conduct will be contrasted with that of your fathers, who, with a mutiny at the Nore, a rebellion in Ireland, and disaster abroad, yet submitted, with buoyant vigour and universal applause (with the funds as low as 52), to a property-tax of 10 per cent. I believe that you will not subject yourselves to an injurious or an unworthy contrast. It is my firm belief that you will feel the necessity of preserving inviolate the public credit–that you will not throw away the means of maintaining the public credit by reducing in the most legitimate manner the burden of the public debt. My confident hope and belief is, that now, when I devolve the responsibility upon you, you will prove yourselves worthy of your mission–of your mission as the representatives of a mighty people; and that you will not tarnish the fame which it is your duty to cherish as the most glorious inheritance–that you will not impair the character for fortitude, for good faith, which, in proportion as the empire of opinion supersedes and predominates over the empire of physical force, constitutes for every people, but above all for the people of England–I speak of reputation and character–the main instrument by which a powerful people can repel hostile aggressions and maintain extended empire.

141. Cobden's protest against Peel's Corn Law (7 April 1842)

Hansard 3/LXII/75.

On the question that "This bill do pass."

MR. COBDEN said, he should be sorry to be present when the bill was passing without entering his protest against it. He ventured to denounce it as a robbery of the poor, without any compensation being given to them for the robbery. He ventured to predict that the people would not waste their time in future by petitioning that House for the repeal of the bread-tax; but that they would present their petitions, signed by millions, at the foot of the Throne, praying her Majesty to dismiss that House of Commons, and praying her to give the people an opportunity of giving an opinion as to this bread-tax. A system of promises, of chicanery, of trickery, and delusions, such as were never practised before, had led the electors to return members who would never be returned again; and he ventured to say, that the premier dared not take the sense of the people on this tax.

Bill passed.

House adjourned.

142. Gally Knight's speech on the Income Tax (11 April 1842)

Hansard, 3/LXII/224–231.

MR. H. GALLY KNIGHT: The hon. and learned Gentleman[1] who has just sat down will perhaps think, when he sees me rise immediately after him that he is not appreciated in Nottinghamshire as he deserves to be–for, if I remember right, the last time he went down to Nottingham, to agitate for the total repeal of the Corn-laws, he and his proposition were not treated in a very courteous manner, and, at this moment he may be under the impression that one of the representatives of that country is about to attack him again. But I am sure, Sir, after the speech which the learned Doctor has just delivered, I can have no disposition to show him any thing but the greatest civility–for, on the present occasion, he has spoken much more as a friend than as a foe. His speech was a beautiful struggle. He seemed to be longing to support the right hon. Baronet now at the head of the Government, and then he was dragged back by the recollection of former declarations. He approves of the general system of the right hon. Baronet, but he finds fault with some of the details–I shall take leave to advert, presently, to some of the learned Doctor's objections–but, Sir, I rose, principally, because, observing with how much vehemence, with how much animosity, the measures proposed by the right hon. Baronet are combated, hearing it asserted that some of his habitual supporters have taken the alarm, I could not bear to remain entirely silent, I could not resist my desire to express, in a very few words, the sentiments with which, as a landed proprietor, and country Gentleman. I regard the question which is now before the House. Sir, the noble Lord the

[1] Dr. John Bowring, M.P. for Bolton, and a founder of the Anti-Corn Law League.

Member for the City of London, would have the country believe, that the necessities of the moment are not so great as they have been represented, and that, even supposing the necessities to be great, his last year's budget would be preferable to the plan which has been brought forward by the right hon. Baronet. Sir, I am not surprised that the noble Lord should endeavour to make it believed that the necessities of the country are not so great as has been represented, because, whatever may be the amount of those necessities they are of his own creation; and, whatever taxes may be imposed, the country will never forget that they are the legacy of the last Administration. Sir, if it were not so serious a subject, I could represent to myself an amusing picture of "The Reading of the Will;" John Bull sitting by with a countenance getting more and more aghast every moment. *Imprimis*. We give and bequeath, to our beloved John Bull, a deficit of £5,000,000. *Item*, we give and bequeath to the aforesaid John Bull, a war in India. *Item*, a war in China. *Item*, an unsettled boundary in America. There are a good many codicils–but these I omit–Sir, with how much pleasure, with how much gratitude, may John Bull be supposed to listen to these last proofs of the care and the consideration of his departed rulers! No pressing necessity! Why Sir, we have not only to extricate ourselves from our present financial difficulties, not only to get our affairs into order, but also to provide the means of carrying on those operations which, now, must be carried on, however much we may regret that they were ever undertaken; one of which operations has led to consequences more calamitous than can be paralleled by any preceding passage of British history. Sir, as it appears to me, the necessities are so great as to render a vigorous exertion indispensable. And how have those necessities been produced? In two ways. First, by incurring extraordinary expenses through impolitic measures–secondly, by crippling our resources at the very time that those expenses were incurred. Of the first I adduce as a proof, the two wars into which this country has been unnecessarily plunged, the long mismanagement of Canada, finally producing a rebellion which it cost a large amount of blood and treasure to put down. Of the second, I adduce as a proof the taxes which have been recklessly abandoned for the sake of a brief popularity. Sir, I remember perfectly well that when the late Administration came into office, their Chancellor of the Exchequer said, that the Tories had done so much in the way of reduction of taxes, that little more could be attempted with safety. But the house-tax became unpopular–that very house-tax which Gentlemen opposite are now so fond of recommending–and, therefore, the house-tax was to be taken off. Lord Althorp said, that he was ashamed of taking it off, because it only pressed upon those who were able to bear it–that he could ill afford to give it up–but it had become unpopular–so, go it must. Sir, I might advert to the wretched practice of stopping up the gap with loans in the time of peace–but I will pass on to their last grand operation, the Penny-post–and, Sir, I must say that, however agreeable it may be to pay less for a thing than it is worth, it was unpardonable, in the then state of our finances to give up so large a source of revenue without redeeming the pledge which the late Ministry gave of substituting another tax in its stead. Sir, no doubt it is much more pleasant to take off taxes than to impose them–but, Sir, I say that a Ministry who, by taking off taxes inconsiderately, bring a country into the difficulties in which we find ourselves, are anything but the real friends of the people; and now, Sir, the noble Lord has ventured to accuse the right hon. Baronet of courting popularity. Does the right hon. Baronet court popularity by adopting a course the very opposite to that which was pursued by the late Administration? Does he court popularity by proposing a tax which is branded, on the opposite side of the House, with every opprobrious epithet? Does he court popularity by requiring from those upon whom he depends for political existence, the sacrifice of 50 per cent. of the protection which they have, hitherto, enjoyed? Sir, the right hon. Baronet has not courted popularity; and, therefore, I honour him. He has not sought to legislate for class-interests, but for all-interests–he has sought nothing but the good of the whole community. But then the noble Lord says, if there is a necessity, take my budget of last year. Now, what was the noble Lord's budget of last year? First, a revenue arising from imported corn, which could not be relied upon, for, should we happen to have the misfortune of a good harvest this year, the duty on imported corn would be small in amount, and, had the late Ministry remained in power, it would soon have been nothing, for the duty would not have been maintained. Second, an alteration in the timber-duties, not such an alteration as is now proposed by the right hon. Baronet, but such as would have been most injurious to the Canadas. Third, the admission of slave-grown sugar, to the complete destruction of the West-Indian planters, and in utter defiance of all the principles upon which the nation have been acting for years, and for the sake of which they have made so large a sacrifice. And, supposing this budget were to be adopted, and were to realise the most sanguine expectations of those who proposed it, what would it produce? Less than £2,000,000, according to the noble Lord's own showing, when more than £5,000,000 are wanted–how infinitely short is that of the existing necessity! Sir, I am astonished at the noble Lord's courage in bringing his damaged and rejected goods to market again. He may try to sell his stinking fish as much as he pleases, but they will not be taken off his hands. But then, Sir, the hon. and learned Member for Bolton[1] says that an Income-tax is so hateful that it must not be heard of. Sir, it is very easy to give a dog a bad name, and so get him hanged. But I must remain in the opinion, that if the money must be had, it could not be raised in a less objectionable manner. In the first place it spares the working classes–no slight recommendation. But then, it is unequal. Is there any tax that is not unequal? the tax on tea for instance–tea is become almost an article of necessity in the family of the labourer–the labourer pays the same amount of tax upon tea as is paid by the landlord–and it cannot be otherwise. But the hon. and learned Member cannot bear that professions should be touched, and the profits of commercial enterprise–yet even the noble Lord, the Member for the city of London, admitted that if you have recourse to an Income-tax, distinctions cannot be made. The hon. and learned Member for Dungarvon,[2] the other night, appealed to our feelings with imaginary pictures of extreme cases. I must be permitted to say, in passing, that as it appears to me, there cannot be a more unfair or deceptive mode of enforcing an argument, than dressing up cases of individual hardship in glowing colours, and endeavouring to break down the rule by the help of an exception which may, or

[1] Dr. John Bowring.

[2] R. L. Sheil.

may not, occur. But where would be the justice of taxing a yeoman whose little farm brings him in £200 a-year, and not taxing the physician, the lawyer, who is making his thousands a year? of taxing a country gentleman with a moderate fortune, who has no means of increasing his income, the whole of which he is expected to spend, and not taxing the merchant, the master-manufacturer, who is annually increasing his store, and is not found fault with, if he never opens his doors? But then the Income-tax is inquisitorial–but where is the danger of confiding the state of your affairs to commissioners who are sworn to secrecy? Nobody need be under apprehension, except those who intend to cheat their neighbours. As for me, Sir, it would only be to my advantage if the state of my affairs were published at Charing Cross–for it is notorious that every gentleman's income is doubled in the estimation of his neighbours–and every gentleman is expected to live up to those enormous calculations–to exercise hospitality accordingly, to subscribe accordingly, and so forth–whilst, if the exact truth were known, no more would be expected of him than he can conveniently afford. But the Income-tax is immoral; it leads to perjury. Sir, there is no surer way of making a man a rogue than letting him know that you think him one; and much more immorality will be caused by telling men you expect them to take false oaths, than would be caused by the tax itself. But, Sir, I will not entertain so base an opinion of my countrymen. I will not believe, that for the sake of escaping a tax, they will lay the sin of perjury to their souls. It would be odious indeed to legislate, upon any such supposition. I conclude, Sir, as I began, by repeating, that if the money must be had, an Income-tax is the least objectionable means. Sir, the tariff hardly forms a part of the present question; but neither is it fair, whilst we are discussing the burdens which are to be imposed, entirely to keep out of sight the relief to the commercial world, to the manufacturing classes, which the right hon. Baronet holds out by his proposed changes in the tariff. This is a part of his plan as much as the Income-tax, and the two should be considered together. Sir, I know that alarms have been excited by some of the proposed changes, and I do not pretend to say, that there are not individuals who will suffer, and that capital will not, in some instances, have to be taken out of one line, and transferred to another. No great changes–no breaking up of any monopolies –no adoption of a more liberal system can be carried out without these attendant consequences. But my belief is, that the fears of many are exaggerated, and that the community at large will derive a great advantage. I am aware that we landed proprietors shall be hit hard. First by the diminution of the protection on corn. Second by the tax on the tenantry, which eventually comes out of the pocket of the landlord. Third by the alteration of the duties on timber. His timber has hitherto been the landed proprietor's nest egg–he has hitherto had it to look to in case of any extraordinary expenditure–in case of any large agricultural improvements–perhaps his election year–perhaps a provision for a younger son. I fear he will find a great difference in this respect. I am aware we are hit hard–not so hard as some Gentlemen opposite would desire–yet, still, hard enough. But, Sir, we are content to suffer if the good of the country require it. I should indeed be sorry if mine were the only foot that was not pinched, when the country is in necessity. Neither has the right hon. Baronet ever said, that he will make no modifications. On the contrary, he has stated his willingness to listen to reasonable suggestions; and, I trust, that by those modifications, he will effectually remove any just cause of complaint. Sir, the hon. and learned Member for Dungarvon said the other night, wait till the tax comes into operation. Sir, I am willing to meet the hon. and learned Gentleman on his own ground. I say with him, wait till the measures of the right hon. Baronet come into operation–when they are in operation, I am persuaded that many will laugh at their fears, and some will blush, such as have not lost the power of blushing, at the opposition they have offered. I would only entreat Gentlemen opposite to allow the measures to come into operation, for every day's delay aggravates the distress of the manufacturing classes, with whom they sympathise so deeply, and so properly. It is perfectly well known, that at this moment there is a complete stagnation of trade–a stagnation in the towns, a panic in the country–merchants not knowing what to undertake, and farmers dreading the arrival of thousands of fat cattle, from countries which do not breed half what they want, and never yet produced such a beast as an English farmer would take to market, and all this will go on till these questions are settled. These are the evils which are occasioned by vexatious delays, nightly interposed for mere party purposes; but the eyes of the country are open; they see who are causing these delays, and they learn to esteem them accordingly. Sir, the noble Lord, the Member for the City of London, will, I know, consider it a matter of perfect indifference in what light this, or any other question appears to one of the heads of clay. He tells us, he thinks us agriculturists composed of the same clay with the acres which we cultivate, because we did not quite relish his mode of treatment. I thank him for the comparison; but I think we should, indeed, deserve the sarcasm were we to abandon those who are willing to give us a reasonable protection, and throw ourselves into the arms of those who would give us no protection at all. Sir, I am aware that some of us will have to undergo what will not be perfectly satisfactory; and when Gentlemen use the term satisfactory, or unsatisfactory, I believe they usually mean the having more, or less, money to spend. I am aware that we shall have less money to spend upon our pleasures, and something to give to the necessities of the country; but I believe, at the same time, that her Majesty's Ministers have given the best consideration in their power to these important subjects–with far superior means of obtaining information to those which any of us possess. I am convinced of the honesty of their intentions. I cannot doubt that they have brought forward such measures as will be for the permanent good of the country. I thank them for the bold and comprehensive plan which they have brought forward, and I beg to assure them of my cordial and willing support.

143. Chartism in the House of Commons (1842): Duncombe's speech introducing the Charter (2 May)

Hansard, 3/LXII/1373–1381.

MR. T. DUNCOMBE, in presenting it to the House, said,–Looking at the vast proportions of this petition–looking, too, at the importance attaching to it, not only from the matter it contains, but from the millions who have signed it, I am quite satisfied, that if I were to ask the House to relax the rules which it has laid down to govern the presentation of petitions, it would grant me the indulgence; but as I have given notice of a motion for to-morrow, that the petition should be taken into the serious consideration of the House, and that those who have signed it, should by their counsel and agents, be heard at the Bar of your House, in support of the allegations which the petition contains, I shall not ask the House to grant me that indulgence, but will keep myself strictly within the limits which have been laid down for the presentation of all petitions. I beg respectfully to offer to the acceptance of this House, a petition signed by 3,315,752 of the industrious classes of this country. The petition proceeds from those upon whose toil, upon whose industry, upon whose affection, and upon whose attachment, I may say, every institution, every law, nay, even the very Government, and the whole property and commerce of the country depend. These persons now most respectfully come before you, to state the manifold grievances under which they are suffering. They state those grievances at some length; I need not now go through them, because I mean to ask your Clerk to read them at the Table. I may state, however, that they attribute the manifold grievances and distresses, which they are now enduring, and have for a considerable length of time endured, to class-legislation and to the misrepresentation of their interests in this House. They state, that for a considerable length of time their interests have been grossly neglected, and that no interests beyond your own, have ever been thought of within your walls. They are ready to prove this at your Bar. In the first place, they ask you to hear them. They state in their prayer:–

> "That they cannot within the limits of this their petition, set forth even a tithe of the many grievances of which they may justly complain; but should your honourable House be pleased to grant your petitioners a hearing, by representatives at the Bar of your honourable House, your petitioners will be enabled to unfold a tale of wrong and suffering–of intolerable injustice–which will create utter astonishment in the minds of all benevolent and good men, that the people of Great Britain and Ireland, have so long quietly endured their wretched condition, brought upon them, as it has been, by unjust exclusion from political authority, and by the manifold corruptions of class legislation."

This petition proceeds, as I have stated, from 3,315,642 of the industrious classes. I have in my hand, a short analysis of the places in which the greater number of the signatures to the petition were obtained. The list of hamlets and towns from which less than 10,000 signatures were procured, is so very long, that I will not detain the House by reading it. I will name those towns only from which more than 10,000 have been obtained. They are these: Manchester, 99,680; Newcastle and districts, 92,000; Glasgow and Lanarkshire, 78,062; Halifax, 36,400; Nottingham, 40,000; Leeds, 41,000; Birmingham, 43,000; Norwich, 21,560; Bolton, 18,500; Leicester, 18,000; Rochdale, 19,600; Loughborough and districts, 10,000; Salford, 19,600; East Riding, Yorkshire, agricultural districts, 14,840; Worcester, 10,000; Merthyr Tydvil and districts, 13,900; Aberdeen, 17,600; Keithly, 11,000; Brighton, 12,700; Bristol, 12,800; Huddersfield, 23,180; Sheffield, 27,200; Scotland, West Midland districts, 18,000; Dunfermline, 16,000; Cheltenham, 10,400; Liverpool, 23,000; Staleybridge and districts, 10,000; Stockport, 14,000; Macclesfield and suburbs, 10,000; North Lancashire, 52,000; Oldham, 15,000; Ashton, 14,200; Bradford and district, Yorkshire, 45,100; Burnley and district, 14,000; Preston and district, 24,000; Wigan, 10,000; London and surburbs, 200,000; from 371 other towns, villages, &c. 2,154,807.–Total 3,315,752. I believe these to be every one of them *bona fide* signatures. The remedies that the petitioners suggest would be that they should have a voice in the election of representatives; that they should be represented in this House. They complain that at present they are totally and grossly misrepresented; and they pray that, after having heard them, if you should be satisfied with their arguments, you do immediately, without alteration, deduction, or addition, pass into a law the document entitled "The People's Charter;" which embraces the representation of male adults, vote by ballot, annual Parliaments, no property qualification, payment of members, and equal electoral districts. And your petitioners, desiring to promote the peace of the United Kingdom, security of property, and prosperity of commerce, seriously and earnestly press this their petition on the attention of your honourable House. I beg leave to move that this petition be brought up and read by the Clerk at the Table.

The petition was read by the Clerk, as follows:

"To the Honourable the Commons of Great Britain and Ireland, in Parliament assembled.

"The Petition of the undersigned people of the United Kingdom,

"Sheweth–That Government originated from, was designed to protect the freedom and promote the happiness of, and ought to be responsible to, the whole people.

"That the only authority on which any body of men can make laws and govern society, is delegation from the people.

"That as Government was designed for the benefit and protection of, and must be obeyed and supported by all, therefore all should be equally represented.

"That any form of Government which fails to effect the purposes for which it was designed, and does not fully and completely represent the whole people, who are compelled to pay taxes to its support and obey the laws resolved upon by it, is unconstitutional, tyrannical, and ought to be amended or resisted.

"That your honourable House, as at present constituted, has not been elected by, and acts irresponsibly of, the people; and hitherto has only represented parties, and benefitted the few, regardless of the miseries, grievances, and petitions of the many. Your honourable House has enacted laws contrary to the expressed wishes of the people, and by unconstitutional means enforced obedience to them, thereby creating an unbearable despotism on the one hand, and degrading slavery on the other.

"That if your honourable House is of opinion that the people of Great Britain and Ireland ought not to be fully represented, your petitioners pray that such opinion may be unequivocally made known, that the people may fully understand what they can or cannot expect from your honourable House: because if such be the decision of your honourable House, your petitioners are of opinion that where representation is denied, taxation ought to be resisted

"That your petitioners instance, in proof of their assertion, that your honourable House has not been elected by the people; that the population of Great Britain and Ireland is at the present time about twenty-six millions of persons; and that yet, out of this number, little more than nine hundred thousand have been permitted to vote in the recent election of representatives to make laws to govern the whole.

"That the existing state of representation is not only extremely limited and unjust, but unequally divided, and gives preponderating influence to the landed and monied interests to the utter ruin of the small-trading and labouring classes.

"That the borough of Guildford, with a population of 3,920 returns to Parliament as many members as the Tower Hamlets, with a population of 300,000; Evesham, with a population of 3,998, elects as many representatives as Manchester, with a population of 200,000; and Buckingham, Evesham, Totness, Guildford, Honiton, and Bridport, with a total population of 23,000, return as many representatives as Manchester, Finsbury, Tower Hamlets, Liverpool, Marylebone, and Lambeth, with a population of 1,400,000: these being but a very few instances of the enormous inequalities existing in what is called the representation of this country.

"That bribery, intimidation, corruption, perjury, and riot, prevail at all parliamentary elections, to an extent best understood by the Members of your honourable House.

"That your petitioners complain that they are enormously taxed to pay the interest of what is termed the national debt, a debt amounting at present to £800,000,000, being only a portion of the enormous amount expended in cruel and expensive wars for the suppression of all liberty, by men not authorised by the people, and who, consequently, had no right to tax posterity for the outrages committed by them upon mankind. And your petitioners loudly complain of the augmentation of that debt, after twenty-six years of almost uninterrupted peace, and whilst poverty and discontent rage over the land.

"That taxation, both general and local, is at this time too enormous to be borne; and in the opinion of your petitioners is contrary to the spirit of the Bill of Rights, wherein it is clearly expressed that no subject shall be compelled to contribute to any tax, talliage, or aid, unless imposed by common consent in Parliament.

"That in England, Ireland, Scotland, and Wales, thousands of people are dying from actual want; and your petitioners, whilst sensible that poverty is the great exciting cause of crime, view with mingled astonishment and alarm the ill provision made for the poor, the aged, and infirm; and likewise perceive, with feelings of indignation, the determination of your honourable House to continue the Poor-law Bill in operation, notwithstanding the many proofs which have been afforded by sad experience of the unconstitutional principle of that bill, of its unchristian character, and of the cruel and murderous effects produced upon the wages of working men, and the lives of the subjects of this realm.

"That your petitioners conceive that bill to be contrary to all previous statutes, opposed to the spirit of the constitution, and an actual violation of the precepts of the Christian religion; and, therefore, your petitioners look with apprehension to the results which may flow from its continuance.

"That your petitioners would direct the attention of your honourable House to the great disparity existing between the wages of the producing millions, and the salaries of those whose comparative usefulness ought to be questioned, where riches and luxury prevail amongst the rulers, and poverty and starvation amongst the ruled.

"That your petitioners, with all due respect and loyalty, would compare the daily income of the Sovereign Majesty with that of thousands of the working men of this nation; and whilst your petitioners have learned that her Majesty receives daily for her private use the sum of £164. 17s. 10d., they have also ascertained that many thousands of the families of the labourers are only in the receipt of 3¾d. per head per day.

"That your petitioners have also learned that his royal Highness Prince Albert receives each day the sum of £104. 2s., whilst thousands have to exist upon 3d. per head per day.

"That your petitioners have also heard with astonishment, that the King of Hanover daily receives £57. 10s. whilst thousands of the tax-payers of this empire live upon 2¾d. per head per day.

"That your petitioners have, with pain and regret, also learned that the Archbishop of Canterbury is daily in the receipt of £52. 10s. per day, whilst thousands of the poor have to maintain their families upon an income not exceeding 2d. per head per day.

"That notwithstanding the wretched and unparalleled condition of the people, your honourable House has manifested no disposition to curtail the expenses of the State, to diminish taxation, or promote general prosperity.

"That unless immediate remedial measures be adopted, your petitioners fear the increasing distress of the people will lead to results fearful to contemplate; because your petitioners can produce evidence of the gradual decline of wages, at the same time that the constant increase of the national burdens must be apparent to all.

"That your petitioners know that it is the undoubted constitutional right of the people, to meet freely, when, how, and where they choose, in public places, peaceably, in the day, to discuss their grievances, and political or other subjects, or for the purpose of framing, discussing, or passing any vote, petition, or remonstrance, upon any subject whatsoever.

"That your petitioners complain that the right has unconstitutionally been infringed; and 500 well disposed persons have been arrested, excessive bail demanded, tried by packed juries, sentenced to imprisonment, and treated as felons of the worst description.

"That an unconstitutional police force is distributed all over the country, at enormous cost, to prevent the due exercise of the people's rights. And your petitioners are of opinion that the Poor-law Bastiles and the police stations, being co-existent, have originated from the same cause, *viz.*, the increased desire on the part of the irresponsible few to oppress and starve the many.

"That a vast and unconstitutional army is upheld at the public expense, for the purpose of repressing public opinion in the three kingdoms, and likewise to intimidate the millions in the due exercise of those rights and privileges which ought to belong to them.

"That your petitioners complain that the hours of labour, particularly of the factory workers, are protracted beyond the limits of human endurance, and that the wages earned, after unnatural application to toil in heated and unhealthy workshops, are inadequate to sustain the bodily strength, and supply those comforts which are so imperative after an excessive waste of physical energy.

"That your petitioners also direct the attention of your honourable House to the starvation wages of the agricultural labourer, and view with horror and indignation the paltry income of those whose toil gives being to the staple food of this people.

"That your petitioners deeply deplore the existence of any kind of monopoly in this nation, and whilst they unequivocally condemn the levying of any tax upon the necessaries of life, and upon those articles principally required by the labouring classes, they are also sensible that the abolition of any one monopoly will never unshackle labour from its misery until the people possess that power under which all monopoly and oppression must cease; and your petitioners respectfully mention the existing monopolies of the suffrage, of paper money, of machinery, of land, of the public press, of religious privileges, of the means of travelling and transit, and of a host of other evils too numerous to mention, all arising from class legislation, but which your honourable House has always consistently endeavoured to increase instead of diminish.

"That your petitioners are sensible, from the numerous petitions presented to your honourable House, that your honourable House is fully acquainted with the grievances of the working men; and your petitioners pray that the rights and wrongs of labour may be considered, with a view to the protection of the one, and to the removal of the other; because your petitioners are of opinion that it is the worst species of legislation which leaves the grievances of society to be removed only by violence or revolution, both of which may be apprehended if complaints are unattended to and petitions despised.

"That your petitioners complain that upwards of nine millions of pounds per annum are unjustly abstracted from them to maintain a church establishment, from which they principally dissent; and beg to call the attention of your honourable House to the fact, that this enormous sum is equal to, if it does not exceed, the cost of upholding Christianity in all parts of the world beside. Your petitioners complain that it is unjust, and not in accordance with the Christian religion, to enforce compulsory support of religious creeds, and expensive church establishments, with which the people do not agree.

"That your petitioners believe all men have a right to worship God as may appear best to their consciences, and that no legislative enactments should interfere between man and his Creator.

"That your petitioners direct the attention of your honourable House to the enormous revenue annually swallowed up by the bishops and the clergy, and entreat you to contrast their deeds with the conduct of the founder of the Christian religion, who denounced worshippers of Mammon, and taught charity, meekness, and brotherly love.

"That your petitioners strongly complain that the people of this kingdom are subject to the rule of irresponsible law-makers, to whom they have given no authority, and are enormously taxed to uphold a corrupt system, to which they have never in person or by representation given their assent.

"That your petitioners maintain that it is the inherent, indubitable, and constitutional right, founded upon the ancient practice of the realm of England, and supported by well approved statutes, of every male inhabitant of the United Kingdom, he being of age and of sound mind, non-convict of crime, and not confined under any judicial process, to exercise the elective franchise in the choice of Members to serve in the Commons House of Parliament.

"That your petitioners can prove, that by the ancient customs and statutes of this realm, Parliament should be held once in each year.

"That your petitioners maintain that Members elected to serve in Parliament ought to be the servants of the people, and should, at short and stated intervals, return to their constituencies, to ascertain if their conduct is approved of, and to give the people power to reject all who have not acted honestly and justly.

"That your petitioners complain that possession of property is made the test of men's qualification to sit in Parliament.

"That your petitioners can give proof that such qualification is irrational, unnecessary, and not in accordance with the ancient usages of England.

"That your petitioners complain, that by influence, patronage, and intimidation, there is at present no purity of election; and your petitioners contend for the right of voting by ballot.

"That your petitioners complain that seats in your honourable House are sought for at a most extravagant rate of expense; which proves an enormous degree of fraud and corruption.

"That your petitioners, therefore, contend, that to put an end to secret political traffic, all representatives should be paid a limited amount for their services.

"That your petitioners complain of the many grievances borne by the people of Ireland, and contend that they are fully entitled to a repeal of the legislative union.

"That your petitioners have viewed with great indignation the partiality shown to the aristocracy in the courts of justice, and the cruelty of that system of law which deprived Frost, Williams, and Jones, of the benefit of their objection offered by Sir Frederick Pollock during the trial at Monmouth, and which was approved of by a large majority of the judges.

"That your petitioners beg to assure your honourable House that they cannot, within the limits of this their petition, set forth even a tithe of the many grievances of which they may justly complain; but should your honourable House be pleased to grant your petitioners a hearing by representatives at the Bar of your honourable House, your petitioners will be enabled to unfold a tale of wrong and suffering–of intolerable injustice–which will create utter astonishment in the minds of all benevolent and good men, that the people of Great Britain and Ireland have so long quietly endured their wretched condition, brought upon them as it has been by unjust exclusion from political authority, and by the manifold corruptions of class-legislation.

"That your petitioners, therefore, exercising their just constitutional right, demand that your honourable House do remedy the many gross and manifest evils of which your petitioners complain, do immediately, without alteration, deduction, or addition, pass into a law the document entitled 'The People's Charter,' which embraces the representation of male adults, vote by ballot, annual Parliaments, no property qualification, payment of Members, and equal electoral districts.

"And that your petitioners, desiring to promote the peace of the United Kingdom, security of property, and prosperity of commerce, seriously and earnestly press this, their petition, on the attention of your honourable House.

"And your petitioners, &c."

Petition to be printed.

144. Debate on the Charter (1842): Macaulay's speech (5 May)

Hansard, 3/LXXX/49–52.

. . . I have no more unkind feeling towards these petitioners than I have towards the sick man, who calls for a draught of cold water, although he is satisfied that it would be death to him; nor than I have for the poor Indians, whom I have seen collected round the granaries in India at a time of scarcity, praying that the doors might be thrown open, and the grain distributed; but I would not in the one case give the draught of water, nor would I in the other give the key of the granary; because I know that by doing so I shall only make a scarcity a famine, and by giving such relief, enormously increase the evil. No one can say that such a spoliation of property as these petitioners point at would be a relief to the evils of which they complain, and I believe that no one will deny, that it would be a great addition to the mischief which is proposed to be removed. But if such would be the result, why should such power be conferred upon the petitioners? That they should ask for it is not blameable; but on what principle is it that we, knowing that their views are entirely delusive, should put into their hands the irresistible power of doing all this evil to us and to themselves? The only argument which can be brought forward in favour of the proposition is, as it appears to me, that this course, which is demanded to be left open to the petitioners, will not be taken; that although the power is given, they will not, and do not intend to execute it. But surely this would be an extraordinary way of treating the prayer of the petition; and it would be somewhat singular to call upon the House to suppose that those who are seeking for a great concession put the object of their demand in a much higher manner than that which presented itself to their own minds. How is it possible that, according to the principles of human nature, if you give them this power, it would not be used to its fullest extent? There has been a constant and systematic attempt for years to represent the Government as being able to do, and as bound to attempt that which no Government ever attempted; and instead of the Government being represented, as is the truth, as being supported by the people, it has been treated as if the Government supported the people: it has been treated as if the Government possessed some mine of wealth –some extraordinary means of supplying the wants of the people; as if they could give them bread from the clouds–water from the rocks–to increase the bread and the fishes five thousandfold. Is it possible to believe that the moment you give them absolute, supreme, irresistible power, they will forget all this? You propose to give them supreme power; in every constituent body throughout the empire capital and accumulated property is to be placed absolutely at the foot of labour. How is it possible to doubt what the result will be? Suppose such men as the hon. Members for Bath[1] and Rochdale[2] being returned to sit in this House, who would, I believe, oppose such measures of extreme change as would involve a national bankruptcy. What would be the effect if their first answer to their constituents should be, "Justice, and the public good demand that this thirty millions a-year should be paid?" Then, with regard to land, supposing it should be determined that there should be no partition of land, and it is hardly possible to conceive that there are men to be found who would destroy all the means of creating and increasing wages, and of creating and increasing the trade and commerce of this country, which gives employment to so many! Is it possible that the three millions of people who have petitioned this House should insist on the prayer of their petition? I do not wish to say all that forces itself on my mind with regard to what might be the result of our granting the Charter. Let us, if we can, picture to ourselves the consequences of such a spoliation as it is proposed should take place. Would it end with one spoliation? How could it? That distress which is the motive now for calling on this House to interfere would be only doubled and trebled by the act; the measure of distress would become greater after that spoliation, and the bulwarks by which fresh acts of the same character would have been removed. The Government would rest upon spoliation–all the property which any man possessed would be supported by it, and is it possible to suppose that a new state of things would exist wherein every thing that was done would be right? What must be the effect of such a sweeping confiscation of property? No experience enables us to guess at it. All I can say is, that it seems to me to be something more horrid than can be imagined. A great community of human beings–a vast people would be called into existence in a new position; there would be a depression, if not an utter stoppage, of trade, and of all those vast engagements of the country by which our people were supported, and how is it possible to doubt that famine and pestilence would come before long to wind up the effects of such a system. The best thing which I can expect, and which I think every one must see as the result, is, that in some of the desperate struggles which must take place in such a state of things, some strong military despot must arise, and give some sort of protection–some security to the property which may remain. But if you flatter yourselves that after such an occurrence you would ever see again those institutions under which you have lived, you deceive yourselves: you would never see them again, and you would never deserve to see them. By all neighbouring nations you would be viewed with utter contempt, and that glory and prosperity which has been so envied would be sneered at, and your fate would thus be told: "England," it would be said, "had her institutions, imperfect

[1] J. A. Roebuck. [2] W. S. Crawford.

though they were, but which contained within themselves the means of remedying all imperfections. Those institutions were wantonly thrown away for no purpose whatever, but because she was asked to do so by persons who sought her ruin; her ruin was the consequence, and she deserves it." Believing this, I will oppose with every faculty which I possess the proposition for universal suffrage. The only question is, whether this motion should be agreed to. Now, if there is any Gentleman who is disposed to grant universal suffrage, with a full view of all its consequences, I think that he acts perfectly conscientiously in voting for this motion; but I must say, that it was with some surprise I heard the hon. Baronet the Member for Leicester,[1] agreeing with me as he does in the principles which I advocate, say, notwithstanding, that he is disposed to vote simply for the motion for permitting these petitioners to come to our Bar to speak in defence of their petition. [SIR J. EASTHOPE: To expound their opinion.] I conceive their opinions are quite sufficiently expounded. They are of such an extent that I cannot, I must confess, pretend to speak of them with much respect. I shall give on this occasion a perfectly conscientious vote against hearing the petitioners at the Bar; and it is my firm conviction that in doing so I am not only doing that which is best with respect to the State, but that I am really giving to the petitioners themselves much less reason for complaining than those who vote for their being heard now, but who will afterwards vote against their demand.

145. Sir Robert Peel's speech on the Second Reading of the Bill for the Repeal of the Corn Laws (16 February 1846)

Hansard, 3/LXXXIII/1003–1043.

Mr. Speaker, Two matters of great importance have occupied the attention of the House during this protracted debate–the one, the manner in which a party should be conducted; the other, the measures by which an imminent public calamity shall be mitigated, and the principles by which the commercial policy of a Great Empire shall for the future be governed. On the first point, the manner in which a party should be conducted, by far the greater part of this debate has turned. I do not undervalue its importance; but, great as it is, surely it is subordinate in the eyes of a people to that other question to which I have referred–the precautions to be taken against impending scarcity, and the principles by which your commercial policy shall hereafter be governed. On the party question I have little defence to make. Yes, Sir, these are I admit at once, the worst measures for party interests that could have been brought forward. I admit also that it is unfortunate that the conduct of this measure, so far as the Corns Laws are concerned, should be committed to my hands. It would, no doubt, have been far preferable, that those should have the credit, if credit there be, for an adjustment of the Corn Laws, who have been uniform and consistent opponents of those laws. That which prevented myself and those who concurred with me from committing it at once to other hands, was the firm conviction under which we laboured, that a part of this Empire was threatened with a great calamity. I did firmly believe, I do firmly believe, that there is impending over you a calamity that all will deplore. I did think that while there was that danger, and

[1] Sir John Easthope.

while I had the hopes of averting it, it would not be consistent with my duty to my Sovereign, or with the honour of a public man, to take that opportunity of shrinking from the heavy responsibilities which it imposed. While I retained the hope of acting with a united Administration, while I thought there was a prospect of bringing this question to a settlement, I determined to retain office and incur its responsibilities. When I was compelled to abandon that hope (my sense of the coming evil remaining the same), I took the earliest opportunity, consistent with a sense of duty and of public honour, of tendering my resignation to the Queen, and leaving Her Majesty the full opportunity of consulting other advisers. I offered no opinion as to the choice of a successor. That is almost the only act which is the personal act of the Sovereign; it is for the Sovereign to determine in whom Her confidence shall be placed. It was, indeed, my duty to ascertain, by the command of the Queen, whether those of my Colleagues who had dissented from me were either themselves prepared to form a Government, or to advise Her Majesty, if they themselves were not prepared, to commit to other hands the formation of a Government–a Government, I mean, to be composed of public men favourable to the maintenance of the existing Corn Law. Those from whom I differed, who had not concurred with me either as to the full extent of the danger to be apprehended, or as to the policy of altering the law, signified their opinion that it would not be for the public interests that they should form a Government; nor could they advise Her Majesty to resort to others for the formation of a Government founded on the maintenance of the existing Corn Law. Her Majesty determined to call upon the noble Lord (Lord J. Russell) to undertake the duty of forming an Administration. My firm belief was, that the noble Lord would have undertaken that duty; my firm persuasion was–the noble Lord will excuse me for saying so–that he would have succeeded if he had undertaken it. During the long course of my opposition to the noble Lord, I cannot charge myself with having ever said anything disrespectful of him. We have acted against each other for many years, and I don't recollect anything that ever passed between us likely to engender hostile or acrimonious feelings. But I must say, the noble Lord did disappoint me when he did not at once undertake the formation of a Government on the principle of adjusting this question. When my tender of resignation had been accepted, and when the noble Lord had been sent for by the Queen, I considered myself at perfect liberty to act in a private capacity on my own personal sense of the public interests, and my own feelings of public duty. I knew all the difficulties with which any man would have to contend who undertook the conduct of the Government. I knew there must be a great dislocation of parties. In the firm persuasion that the noble Lord would accept the office of First Minister, I felt it incumbent upon me, under the special circumstances under which he would have undertaken office, to diminish the difficulties with which he might have to contend in attempting a final settlement of the Corn Laws. I resolved, therefore, to give the noble Lord such assurances of support as it was in my power to give. In the explanation which I offered the other night, I limited myself to a detail of the facts which had preceded my retirement from office. The noble Lord's explanation commenced from that period. Of that explanation I have no complaint whatever to make. It was perfectly fair and candid on the part of the noble Lord. But there are additions to it which I am desirous of supplying, in the hope of being enabled to demonstrate that I had no wish to defraud others of the credit of adjusting the Corn Laws. My resignation of office was accepted by Her Majesty on the 6th of December last. On the 8th December, I addressed to Her Majesty the following communication, for the express purpose of enabling Her Majesty, by the knowledge of my views and intentions with regard to the Corn Laws, to diminish the difficulties of my successor:-

"Whitehall, Dec. 8, 1845.

"Sir Robert Peel presents his humble duty to Your Majesty, and, influenced by no other motive than the desire to contribute, if possible, to the relief of Your Majesty from embarrassment, and to the protection of the public interests from injury, is induced to make to Your Majesty this confidential communication explanatory of Sir Robert Peel's position and intentions with regard to the great question which is now agitating the public mind.

"Your Majesty can, if you think fit, make this communication known to the Minister who, as successor to Sir Robert Peel, may be honoured by Your Majesty's confidence.

"On the 1st of November last, Sir Robert Peel advised his Colleagues, on account of the alarming accounts from Ireland, and many districts in this country, as to the failure of the potato crop from disease, and for the purpose of guarding against contingencies, which in his opinion were not improbable, humbly to recommend to Your Majesty that the duties on the import of foreign grain should be suspended for a limited period, either by Order in Council or by Legislative Enactment; Parliament, in either case, being summoned without delay.

"Sir Robert Peel foresaw that this suspension, fully justified by the tenor of the report to which he has referred, would compel, during the interval of suspension, the reconsideration of the Corn Laws.

"If the opinions of his Colleagues had then been in concurrence with his own, he was fully prepared to take the responsibility of suspension-and of the necessary consequence of suspension, a comprehensive review of the laws imposing restrictions on the import of foreign grain and other articles of food, with a view to their gradual diminution and ultimate removal.

"He was disposed to recommend that any new laws to be enacted should contain within themselves the principle of gradual reduction and final repeal.

"Sir Robert Peel is prepared to support, in a private capacity, measures which may be in general conformity with those which he advised as a Minister.

"It would be unbecoming in Sir Robert Peel to make any reference to the details of such measures.

"Your Majesty has been good enough to inform Sir Robert Peel that it is your intention to propose to Lord John Russell to undertake the formation of a Government.

"The principle on which Sir Robert Peel was prepared to recommend the reconsideration of the laws affecting the import of the main articles of food was in general accordance with that referred to in the concluding paragraph of Lord John Russell's letter to the electors of the city of London.

"Sir Robert Peel wished to accompany the removal of restriction on the admission of such articles with relief to the land from any charges that may be unduly onerous, and with such other provisions as, in the terms of Lord John Russell's letter, 'caution and even scrupulous forbearance may suggest.'

"Sir Robert Peel will support measures founded on that general principle, and will exercise any influence he may possess to promote their success."

That was the assurance I conveyed to Her Majesty of my perfect readiness to support, if proposed by others, those measures which I had myself deemed necessary. I could not but forsee that in addition to all the other difficulties with which the noble Lord or any other Minister would have to contend, there would be some connected with the state of our revenue and expenditure. At the close of the present financial year there will probably be, as there has been in the years preceding, a considerable surplus of revenue after providing for the wants of the public service. In the coming year there must be increased estimates, reducing the future surplus, and I thought it right that my successor should not be exposed to the risk of an unfavourable contrast for which he could not be responsible. I added, therefore, to my assurance of support with respect to the Corn Laws this further assurance. It refers to points of great delicacy, but it is better to have no concealment or reserve.

"Sir Robert Peel feels it to be his duty to add that, should Your Majesty's future advisers, after consideration of the heavy demands made upon the army of this country for colonial service, of our relations with the United States, and of the bearing which steam navigation may have upon maritime warfare and the defence of the country, deem it advisable to propose an addition to the army and increased naval and military estimates, Sir Robert Peel will support the proposal – will do all that he can to prevent it from being considered as indicative of hostile or altered feelings towards France, and will assume, for the increase in question, any degree of responsibility, present or retrospective, which can fairly attach to him."

Now, when it is charged on me, that I am robbing others of the credit which is justly due to them, I hope that this explanation of the course I pursued, when I was acting under the firmest persuasion that the adjustment of this question would be committed to others, may tend to prove that I was not desirous of robbing others of the credit of settling this question, or of trying to embarrass their course. There were further communications made, and in the course of those communications it was proposed to put me in possession of the particular mode in which the noble Lord intended to arrange this question. I thought that it would be better that I should not be made acquainted with such details. I thought that my knowledge of them, or any appearance of concert between the noble Lord and myself, would have had the tendency rather to prejudice than promote the adjustment of this question. I, therefore, declined to receive the communication of those details; but I think that the noble Lord must have been satisfied that, though I declined to concert particular measures with him, yet it was my intention to give to the noble Lord, in his attempt to adjust this question according to his own views of public policy, that same cordial support which it is his boast he now intends to give me. I believe that must have been the impression of the noble Lord – [LORD J. RUSSELL: Hear, hear!] – because, after the communication with me, the noble Lord undertook the formation of a Government; and I am sure that the noble Lord will admit that no act of mine caused the failure of the noble Lord's attempt, and that I was in no way concerned in the reasons which induced the noble Lord finally to abandon it. I made no inquiry as to the persons who should constitute the new Government; I had no personal objections of any kind. My conviction was, that this question ought to be adjusted. I was prepared to facilitate its adjustment by others by my vote, and by the exercise of whatever influence I could command. So much for my conduct towards political opponents – better entitled than myself to undertake the repeal of the Corn Laws.

Now, Sir, with respect to the course which I have pursued towards those who so long have given me their support. I admit to them that it is but natural that they should withhold from me their confidence. I admit that the course which I am pursuing is at variance with the principles on which party is ordinarily conducted. But I do ask of them, whether it be probable that I would sacrifice their favourable opinion and their support unless I was influenced by urgent considerations of public duty – unless I was deeply impressed with the necessity of taking these precautions, and advising these measures. Notwithstanding that which may have passed in this debate – notwithstanding the asperity with which some have spoken, I will do that party (which has hitherto supported me) the justice they deserve. No person can fill the situation I fill without being aware of the motives by which a great party is influenced. I must have an opportunity of knowing what are the personal objects of those around me; and this I will say, notwithstanding the threatened forfeiture of their confidence, that I do not believe (speaking generally of the great body of the party) that there ever existed a party influenced by more honourable and disinterested feelings.

While I admit that a natural consequence of the course I have pursued, is to offend, probably to alienate, a great party, I am not the less convinced that any other course would have been ultimately injurious even to party interests. I know what would have conciliated temporary confidence. It would have been to underrate the danger in Ireland, to invite a united combination for the maintenance of the existing Corn Law, to talk about hoisting the flag of protection for native industry, to insist that agricultural protection should be maintained in all its integrity – by such a course I should have been sure to animate and please a party, and to gain for a time their cordial approbation. But the month of May will not arrive without demonstrating that I should thereby have abandoned my duty to my country – to my Sovereign – aye and to the Conservative party. I had, and have, the firm persuasion that the present temper of the public mind – the state of public feeling, and of public opinion, with respect to the Corn Laws – independent of all adventitious circumstances, make the defence of the Corn Laws a very difficult task. But with such a calamity as that which is impending in Ireland, it was utterly irreconcilable with my feelings to urge the landed interest to commit themselves to a conflict for the maintenance inviolate of a law which attaches at the present time a duty of 17s. to the quarter of wheat. What were the facts which came under the cognizance of my right hon. Friend the Secretary of State for the Home Department, charged with the responsibility of providing for the public peace, and rescuing millions from the calamity of starvation? We were assured in one part of this Empire there are 4,000,000 of the Queen's subjects dependent on a certain article of food for subsistence. We knew that on that article of food no reliance could be placed. It was difficult to say what was the extent of the danger –what would be the progress of the disease, and what the amount of deficiency in the supply of the article of food. But, surely, you will make allowances for those who were charged with the heaviest responsibility, if their worst anticipations should be realized by the event. We saw, in the distance, the gaunt forms of famine, and of disease following in the train of famine. Was it not our duty to the country, aye, our duty to the party that supported us, to avert the odious charge of indifference and neglect of timely precautions? It is absolutely necessary, before you come to a final decision on this question, that you should understand this Irish case. You must do so. The reading of letters may be distasteful to you; but you shall have no ground for imputing it to me that I left you in ignorance of a danger which I believe to be imminent. I may have lost your confidence–I will not try to regain it at the expense of truth. I can conciliate no favour by the expression of regret for the course I have taken. So far from it, I declare, in the face of this House that the day of my public life, which I look back on with the greatest satisfaction and pride, is that 1st of November last, when I offered to take the responsibility of issuing an Order in Council to open the ports, and to trust to you for approval and indemnity. I wished then, that by the first packet which sailed after the 1st of November, the news might have gone forth that the ports were open. The primary object of such a measure, of course, would have been to increase the supply of food, and to take precautions against famine, although other collateral advantages might have flowed from it. Had we opened the ports, and had our anticipations proved to be incorrect–had the result shown that we had formed a false estimate of this danger–I believe that the generosity of Parliament would have protected us from censure. [Hear, hear.] That would have been the case had our anticipations proved to be wrong; but what is the fact? During the latter part of December and January, there was a temporary suspension of alarm, after the opinions we had received from men eminent in science. I never shared in the sanguine hopes that there would be abundance of food, that the potato disease was exaggerated, and that we might safely trust to existing supplies. I felt that the time would arrive when the opinions of those individuals would be justified. And what is the fact? I will read to you some communications, not so much for the vindication of the Government as for the guidance of your own future course. It is not right that I should leave you in ignorance of the real facts of this case. [Hear, hear.] It is true the present proposition is not a suspension of the duties, but it is a virtual suspension. It comprehends the removal of the duty on maize and rice, and the reduction of the duty to a nominal amount on barley and oats, and the reduction of the duty on wheat from 17s. to 4s. Before you decide on rejecting or delaying this measure, hear and consider the reports which the last few days have brought from Ireland. You seemed to discredit the reports of official authorities; and some, I regret to say, countenanced the notion that public men were base enough to act in concert for the purpose of exaggeration. I will now read, therefore, no reports from the Lord Lieutenant. I will read letters which the last two mails have brought from Ireland, from men from whose statements you cannot have the pretence of withholding confidence. I will first read a communication from Sir David Roche, who was for some time Member for the city of Limerick. He was one of those who at first thought the apprehension of famine to be greatly exaggerated, and that extraordinary precautions were unnecessary. This day has brought me this letter from him, dated Carass, near Limerick, Feb. 11:–

> "No person was more disposed than I was to look with hope to that part of the potato crop in this country that appeared sound before Christmas. I thought it was quite safe and certain to keep in the usual way, and in my answer to the Lord Lieutenant's circular I stated that hope with great confidence, adding that the crop was so large, the sound portion would nearly feed the people." [This, then, is a disinterested authority.] "But I grieve to say, that every day convinces me of the error I was under; the potatoes that were apparently sound then, had more or less the disease in an incipient state, and the greater part is now obliged to be given to pigs and cattle, to save the owners from total loss. The Catholic clergy of several parishes have made this painful communication to me; my own experience as a landed proprietor and a practical farmer, holding in my possession large animal farms, in three different parts of this country, and also in the county Clare, entirely corresponds with their statements. I don't think by the 1st of May next, that out of one hundred acres of potatoes on my land, sound seed will be left me for next year's crop.
>
> "If the case is so bad with me, and it is nearly the same in the four districts I allude to, how much worse must it be with the poor, who have not the convenience and aid that large farming establishments, with substantial buildings, can command? In short, as one rides through the country, rotten potatoes are to be seen everywhere in large quantities by the side of the roads; pits, lately turned, in most cases smaller than the heaps of rotten potatoes alongside them; and those in the pits are certain, if not quickly consumed, to share in the general decay.
>
> "Such, Sir, is the state I may say of the entire country. No doubt for six or seven weeks, while the remains of the potatoes last, destitution will not be general; but I pray you, Sir, look to it in time."

There were some of us who did look to it in time, and I wish that our advice had been acted on. That is the Report from the county of Limerick. I now come to the Queen's County. The following is a copy of a Report, received February 12, 1846:–

> "Queen's County, Stradbally, Feb. 11, 1846.
>
> "With reference to the potato disease, I beg to state that I was requested by Sir Edward Walsh and Sir A. Weldon, two magistrates of this district, to make

a more searching inquiry into the state of the potatoes in the neighbourhood of the collieries than had hitherto been made. The instructions were, to make the examination by properties, and ruled forms were supplied by Sir A. Weldon, with such headings as he considered applicable to the case.

"On Monday morning, the 9th, I proceeded to Wolfhill, accompanied by the Rev. Mr. Emerson, the clergyman of the parish, and commenced with the property of Mr. Hovenden. Mr. Hovenden himself being with us, we examined every house on the property, took down the number of each family, the quantity of potatoes planted, and the quantity (from actual inspection) now remaining on lands, with the quantity of oats or other grain now in the possession of the family. On Tuesday, we went over the property of Sir Charles Coote, adjoining Mr. Hovenden's, and also over Mr. Carter's, and, so far as time would admit, examined a few families on the property of Mrs. Kavanagh, of Gracefield. Our inquiries extended to about 190 families altogether, and enable me with the most perfect accuracy to state the frightful extent to which the destruction of the potato crop has proceeded in that part of the country. Many families whom we visited, and who had planted sufficient for their ordinary wants, including the seed necessary for the ensuing season, have not had a potato of any kind for the last month."

Observe this is in the month of February, five months at least before there can be any supply from the natural bounty of Providence.

"Others have lost nearly all; and the few that still remain are totally unfit for human food. In every instance where we saw potatoes in pits in the fields we had them examined, and, with scarcely an exception, we found them to be a mass of putrefaction, perfectly disgusting, even to look at. We examined a few houses on the property of Sir Thomas Esmonde, where the land is of much better quality, but the result was in every case the same. There are literally no potatoes remaining in that part of the country.

"I understand the magistrates intend to meet on an early day, and make some representation, through the lieutenant of the county, on the above subject.

"W. W. HEMSWORTH,
"Sub-Inspector 1st Rate."

I pass on to Waterford. There are letters received within the last two days; one from the Lord Lieutenant of that county–Lord Stuart de Decies. It is dated the 10th February; I entreat the attention of the House to it. Lord Stuart de Decies is a person whose opinions must carry with them great authority. He says–

"His excellency will find in these statements an announcement of the alarming fact, that in two districts alone of the Union in question there are even at this early period of the year, no less than 300 persons whose stores of provisions are upon the point of becoming exhausted. In the meanwhile the rot is represented as making daily progress amongst the potatoes, which until lately it was hoped might have been preserved in a state of partial soundness for some time longer; and there is every reason, therefore, to anticipate that the distress now prevailing in certain localities will very speedily cause its pressure to be felt by the labouring classes throughout the Union. With this prospect in view, the probability is, that a rise in the price of all kinds of grain may be expected to take place in the course of the ensuing spring and summer months, although foreign supplies were to be admitted immediately duty free, and thus the facilities of providing food for the people in exchange for their labour be removed beyond the means which landed proprietors have at the present moment within their reach for this purpose. It is in these circumstances that I would venture respectfully to submit, as far as the interests of the county of Waterford are involved, that much good might be effected in keeping down prices by the establishment of Government corn stores from which grain might be purchased at first cost price in such towns as Youghal, Dungarvan, Waterford, Carrick, Clonmel, and, perhaps, Lismore. In all but the last mentioned of these towns, there is an adequate military force for the protection of such granaries, if established, and no part of the county would then be beyond twelve or fourteen miles distance from a depot, whence food on moderate terms might be drawn to those localities which stood in need of a supply."

The next I read is from Kerry, dated the 9th of February, from a gentleman whose statements I believe are entitled to the highest respect–Mr. Thomas Dillon:–

"I regret to have to report, for the information of Government, that serious ravages have been made latterly on the potatoes by the disease which, for the last two months, was supposed at least not to be progressive. Having gone round my district within the last ten days, I have had opportunities not only of hearing, but of witnessing the destruction which has been committed, and which is gaining ground rapidly, contrary to the hopes which have been for some time cherished, as to excite the utmost alarm among all classes: and for my own part I feel almost confounded at the difficulty that must exist in procuring a sufficiency of good seed for the ensuing crop."

Such is the report of Mr. Dillon, of Cahirciveen, resident magistrate. The House is aware that there has been sitting for some time past in Dublin a Commission, one of whose duties it has been to collect accurate information with respect to the extent of the deficiency in different localities. That Commission has lately made a report, which refers, I fear, to a period antecedent to that in which the disease has reappeared. I have here an official statement, from the highest authority, embracing almost every part of Ireland, every electoral district, with the exception of ninety-nine, having sent returns; and these are the facts reported by the Commissioners:–

"That in four electoral divisions the loss of potatoes has been nearly nine-tenths of the whole crop; in 93, between seven-tenths and eight-tenths; in 125, the loss approaches to seven-tenths of the whole crop; in 16, it approaches to six-tenths; in 596, nearly one-half of the crop is entirely destroyed; and in 582 divisions, nearly four-tenths of the crop are entirely destroyed."

Here are requisitions made to us, and we are acting upon them, to establish stores of corn for the people, to be retailed at cost prices, or given in remuneration for labour. [An hon. Member: It will be wanted for seed.] Yes; to get potatoes from foreign countries for the ensuing year is next to impossible. An eighth of the whole crop is required for seed; each acre of potatoes requires nearly a ton, three-fourths of a ton, at least, for seed; take the tonnage which it would require to bring in 10,000 tons of potatoes from any part of Europe where potatoes may still abound; it is impossible to supply the deficiency by foreign import. You must look for seed from the domestic supply–by making savings from the existing crop. And here is the danger, that when the pressure of famine is severe, the immediate craving of hunger will be supplied–the necessities of next year will be forgotten; the Government must interfere for the purpose of encouraging the saving of potatoes in sufficient quantities, in order to secure a supply of seed for next year. How are we to do this? By the substitution, I suppose, of some other articles of provision, to be given under wise regulations, for the purpose of preventing abuse. Suppose, now, that in April or May next, we shall be under the necessity of proposing votes of public money to cover past or future expenditure–will there be a cheerful acquiescence in those votes, if the Corn Law is to remain unaltered? We are now encouraging the resident proprietors, the clergy of the Established Church, and the clergy of the Roman Catholic persuasion, to make great exertions; we are telling them, "Individual charity in your localities must supply more than the Government can supply; you must give corn in exchange for seed potatoes, or for the sustenance of human life." Is it quite reasonable to make these demands on the private charity of those whose straitened means leave little disposable for charity, and at the same time to levy 17s. duty on the quarter of foreign wheat? Is the State to show no charity? For what is the duty to be levied? For Revenue? But we may have to spend public money in the purchase of corn–we may have to raise its price to the consumer by our unusual intervention. Surely it is a more becoming course to remit duty, than to buy heavily taxed corn! Shall we levy the 17s. for protection to domestic corn? What–when in 600 electoral divisions in Ireland only half the crop of potatoes has been saved, and in 600 more only three-fifths, while in some, nearly eight-tenths are gone? Do you believe that it would be for the credit and honour of the landed aristocracy of this country to say, "We throw upon the Government the responsibility of averting the evils of famine, but not one letter of the existing Corn Law shall be altered?" Would it be fidelity to the landed interest were I to counsel this? No; I believe that, whatever might have been the outward show of consistency, such a proposal would be the real 'treachery' which you impute to me, because I have thought it for your interest, and the interests of all, to relieve ourselves from the odium of stipulating for these restrictions on food in such a moment of pressure. What would have been said? Why, the pressure in Holland and in Belgium is not half so severe as it will be in Ireland; and see what the Government in those two countries did at an early period of the autumn. In Belgium, the Executive Government took upon itself the responsibility of opening the ports to every description of provisions. The Government of Holland exercised the power which it had to do this by ordinance. Belgium is an agricultural country; the Chambers (the Lords and Commons of a neighbouring State) assembled; the Government asked for indemnity, and for the continuance of open ports. Without a moment's hesitation, by acclamation as it were, without one dissentient voice, the representatives of the landed interest in Belgium gave the Government indemnity, and continued the permission freely to import every article of food. What, under similar circumstances, has been the course taken by the Parliament of this country? What has been the course taken by Parliaments as deeply interested as we can be in the welfare of agriculture? There have been times before the present when there has been the apprehension of scarcity in this country; what has been the remedy? What has been the remedy that the heart of every man suggested? What has been the remedy that legislative wisdom took? Why, in every case, without exception, the removal for a time of the duties upon foreign corn. [Cheers.] [An hon. Member: What was done at the end of the time?] I will come to that immediately. I rejoice in the cheer which I received from that quarter [looking to the Protection benches]; what is it but an assent–apparently a unanimous assent–["No!"] at any rate, a very general assent–that at a period of impending famine, the proper precaution to be taken is to encourage the free importation of food? I have a right to infer, that if that had been the proposal, namely, that existing duties upon corn and other articles of provision should be suspended for a time that proposal would have met with general assent. Then, if that be so, I ask you to expedite the passing of this Bill: either do that, or move as an Amendment that the duties upon all articles of provision shall forthwith be suspended.

I will not omit the other consideration–the course to be taken after you have suspended the law; I am trying now to convince you that I should have been unfaithful and treacherous to the landed interest, and to the party that protect the landed interest, if I had concealed the real pressure of this Irish case, and had called forth party cheers by talking about "hoisting the flag of protection"–or "rousing the British lion"–or "adhering to the true blue colour"–or steadfast maintenance of the Corn Laws "in all their integrity." I am trying to convince you, by fair reasoning, that that is a course which would not have been consistent either with the public interest, or with the credit of the landed aristocracy. That is all I am asking you now to admit. If you answer me, "We will readily consent to suspend this law until next harvest," I am rejoiced to have that admission from three-fourths of those by whom I shall be opposed, that it would but be wise to stipulate that for the present no alteration should be made in the Corn Law, that no maize should be admitted, at a reduced rate of duty, and that the duty upon wheat should be maintained at 17s.; I am rejoiced that I have established, to the satisfaction of the great majority, that that would not have been a prudent or a defensible course, I say it would not, because at all periods of our history the natural precaution that has been taken has been the admission, free of duty, of foreign corn in times of scarcity. I must quote some of those instances. In 1756, there was the apprehension of famine: Parliament was assembled: the first step taken was to prohibit, unwisely, in my opinion, the exportation of corn; the second was, to permit importation duty free. In 1767, you were again threatened with scarcity: the first act of the Parliament was, to admit provisions duty free. In 1791, Parliament altered the Corn Laws–they established a new Corn Law; in 1793, there was the apprehension of scarcity; notwithstanding the new Corn Law, one of the very first Acts upon the Statute Book of 1793 is to remove, for a time, all duties upon the importation of foreign corn. In 1795, there was an apprehension, not of famine, but of scarcity, severely pressing upon some classes of the community; and in that year, and again in 1796, the same remedy was adopted–the removal of all duty upon foreign corn. In 1799, the same course was pursued, and free importation allowed. Why then, I ask, with all these precedents–when the danger, in the case of some at least, was less than it is at present–would it have been wise for a Government to counsel that we should pursue a different course, refuse facilities for importation, and determine upon maintaining the existing law? Sir, I believe that course would have involved the Government and the Parliament in the greatest discredit; and so far from assisting us in maintaining the existing law, my firm belief is, that that law would have been encumbered with a degree of odium which would have made the defence of it impossible. It was upon these grounds that I acted. Seeing what had been done in neighbouring countries, and what had been uniformly done by your own Parliament, not when corn was at 100s. or 80s., but in periods when it was under 60s.–seeing that the acknowledged remedy for scarcity was opening the ports for the admission of foreign corn, I advised the suspension of the Corn Laws. Do not answer me by saying, "There was at the period to which you refer, a different Corn Law–there was no sliding-scale–there was no admission of foreign corn at a low duty when the price was high." It was exactly the reverse of this; during the whole of that period, when corn was above 54s. in price, it was admitted at a duty of 6d.; the law made provision for the free importation of corn with even moderate prices. And why did Parliament interfere? It was in order that the high duty should not attach on a reduction of price. When corn was below 54s., there was a duty of from 2s. 6d. to 24s. 3d.; when it was above 54s., the duty was 6d.; by the natural operation of the law, therefore, corn was admitted when prices were high; but there was a fear that, from a sudden importation from neighbouring ports, corn might fall below 54s., and the high duty might attach. To prevent that, and to give a guarantee to the foreign importer that he should be certain for a period of six months to have his corn admitted at a duty of 6d., Parliament interposed, and gave him that guarantee. If, then, we had refused to interfere, what a contrast might have been drawn between us and those Parliaments! Would refusal have been, or would it now be, for the credit either of Parliament or of Government? I think not. We advised, therefore–at least I advised, and three of my Colleagues concurred with me–the immediate suspension of the law. The question is, what shall we do now? The law is not suspended–Parliament is sitting. It would be disrespectful towards Parliament for the Executive to take any step; it is impossible for the Executive, by an Order of Council, to do that which might have been done by an extreme exercise of authority, when Parliament was not sitting; it would not be constitutional to do it. It may be true that the best time has passed away; that the 1st of November was a better period for doing this than the present. Yes, but admitting that, the necessity for acting with decision on the 16th February is only increased. True, the supplies of foreign corn might have been more ample, had the ports been opened on the 1st November; but you have six months yet before you–and what course do you suggest? If any one dissents from that course which we propose, let him propose another. You must make your choice. You must either maintain the existing law, or make some proposal for increasing the facilities of procuring foreign articles of food.

And now I come to that second consideration from which I said I would not shrink. After the suspension of the existing law, and the admission of foreign importation for a period of several months, how do you propose to deal with the existing Corn Laws? That is the question which a Minister was bound to consider who advised the suspension of the Corn Laws. Now, my conviction is so strong that it would be utterly impossible, after establishing perfect freedom of trade in corn for a period of seven or eight months, to give a guarantee that the existing Corn Law should come into operation at the end of that period, that I could not encourage the delusive hope of such a result. I know it may be said, that after a temporary suspension of the law, the law itself would revive by its own operation, that there would be no necessity for any special enactment to restore its vigour. But I think it is an utter misapprehension of the state of public opinion to suppose it possible that after this country, for eight months, should have tasted of freedom in the trade in corn, you could revive, either by the tacit operation of the law itself, or by new and special enactment, the existing Corn Law. Surely, the fact of suspension would be a condemnation of the law. It would demonstrate that the law, which professed by the total reduction of duty on corn when it had reached a certain price to provide security against scarcity, has failed in one of its essential parts. Yet you insist on the revival of this law. Now let me ask, would you revive the existing Corn Law in all its provisions? Would you refuse the admission of maize at lower duties?–at present the duty on maize is almost prohibitory. Do not suppose that those who advised suspension overlooked the consideration of the consequences of suspension–of the bearing it would have upon the state of the Corn Laws, and the question of future protection. At the expiration of suspension will you revive the existing law, or will you propose a new and modified Corn Law? If the existing law, every manifest defect must be preserved. By that law, the duty on maize varies inversely not with the price of maize, but with the price of barley. We want maize–the price of barley is falling, but we can get no maize, because there is a prohibitory duty on maize in consequence of the low price of barley. Oh, say some, we will have a little alteration of the law, we will provide for the case of maize. Now, do not disregard public feeling in matters of this kind. It is not right that mere feeling should overbear the deliberate conviction of reason; but depend upon it, that when questions of food are concerned, public feeling cannot safely be disregarded. In the course of last Session notice was given that maize should be imported duty free, because it was for the interest of the farmer to have maize for food for cattle. Do you think it possible to devise a new Corn Law, the leading principle of which should be that maize should come in duty free, because the admission of that article would enable the farmer to feed his cattle and pigs with it, but that there are certain other articles used for consumption by human beings–and in respect to them the law shall be maintained in all its force? Do you advise me to commit you to fight that battle? I am assuming now that the necessity for the suspension of the law has been established; that suspension having taken place, would you deliberately advise the Government, for the sake of the public interests, or for the sake of party interests, to give a pledge either that the existing Corn Law, at the expiration of that suspension should be revived unaltered –or that there should be some trumpery modification of it, for the special benefit of the feeders of pigs and cattle? Are you insensible to the real state of public opinion on this question? Are you insensible to the altered convictions of many of your own party? Could I safely rely upon your cordial and unanimous support, as a party, for the redemption of that pledge? Look to the change of opinion, not among politicians, which you are apt to attribute to some interested or corrupt motives; but look to the opinions that have been expressed–to the sincerity of which conclusive proofs have been given by some of the most honourable men that ever sat upon these benches. Did my noble Friend Lord Ashley vacate his seat for the county of Dorset from any interested or corrupt motive? Did Mr. Sturt, or Mr. W. Patten, avow their change of opinion from any interested or corrupt motives? Did Mr. Tatton Egerton offer to vacate his seat for Cheshire, or Lord Henniker his seat for Suffolk, from any other than a real change of opinion–from a conviction that the time was come for the adjustment of the question of the Corn Laws? Did Mr. Dawnay vacate his seat from such motive? Did a young Member of this House, Mr. Charteris, glowing with as high and honourable a spirit as ever animated the breast of an English gentleman–distinguished for great acuteness–great intelligence–great promise of future eminence –did he abandon his seat for Gloucestershire, and withdraw from this stirring conflict from any interested or corrupt motives? Surely these are proofs that that Minister who should suspend the law, and give a guarantee of the revival of it when the period of suspension expired, would have enormous difficulties to contend with.

But let us observe the course of the present debate, the admission and expressions of opinion of those who have been loudest in their condemnation of the Government. The first I notice is the hon. Member for Huntingdon.[1] Well, I confess I was surprised to hear from a gentleman of the name of Baring, some of the opinions introduced by him in regard to commerce and the Corn Laws. Would that hon. Gentleman follow me in the maintenance of the existing Corn Law after the suspension of it? So far from it, the hon. Gentleman thinks that this is just the time for a compromise on the subject. He then would abandon me, if, after the suspension, I had undertaken a guarantee to revive the existing law. He says this is just the time for a compromise. If ever there was an unfortunate moment for a compromise, it is the present. What is the meaning of a compromise? Clearly, a new Corn Law. Now, what would be the security for the permanence of that new Corn Law? [Cheers from the Protection benches.] You cheer; but what says every hon. Gentleman who has appeared on the part of the agriculturists? That what the agriculturist chiefly wishes for is, permanence as to the Corn Law. Would a modified Corn Law give that assurance of permanence? Is there, in truth, any choice between maintenance of the existing Corn Law and its repeal? . . .

This night, then–if on this night the debate shall close–you will have to decide

[1] Thomas Baring.

what are the principles by which your commercial policy is to be regulated. Most earnestly, from a deep conviction, founded not upon the limited experience of three years alone, but upon the experience of the results of every relaxation of restriction and prohibition, I counsel you to set the example of liberality to other countries. Act thus, and it will be in perfect consistency with the course you have hitherto taken. Act thus, and you will provide an additional guarantee for the continued contentment, and happiness, and well-being of the great body of the people. Act thus, and you will have done whatever human sagacity can do for the promotion of commercial prosperity.

You may fail. Your precautions may be unavailing. They may give no certain assurance that mercantile and manufacturing prosperity will continue without interruption. It seems to be incident to great prosperity that there shall be a reverse–that the time of depression shall follow the season of excitement and success. That time of depression must perhaps return; and its return may be coincident with scarcity caused by unfavourable seasons. Gloomy winters, like those of 1841 and 1842, may again set in. Are those winters effaced from your memory? From mine they never can be. Surely you cannot have forgotten with what earnestness and sincerity you re-echoed the deep feelings of a gracious Queen, when at the opening and at the close of each Session, She expressed the warmest sympathy with the sufferings of Her people, and the warmest admiration of their heroic fortitude.

These sad times may recur. "The years of plenteousness may have ended," and "the years of dearth may have come;" and again you may have to offer the unavailing expressions of sympathy, and the urgent exhortations to patient resignation.

Commune with your own hearts and answer me this question: will your assurances of sympathy be less consolatory–will your exhortations to patience be less impressive–if, with your willing consent, the Corn Laws shall have then ceased to exist? Will it be no satisfaction to you to reflect, that by your own act, you have been relieved from the grievous responsibility of regulating the supply of food? Will you not then cherish with delight the reflection that, in this the present hour of comparative prosperity, yielding to no clamour, impelled by no fear–except, indeed, that provident fear, which is the mother of safety–you had anticipated the evil day, and, long before its advent, had trampled on every impediment to the free circulation of the Creator's bounty?

When you are again exhorting a suffering people to fortitude under their privations, when you are telling them, "These are the chastenings of an all-wise and merciful Providence, sent for some inscrutable but just and beneficial purpose–it may be, to humble our pride, or to punish our unfaithfulness, or to impress us with the sense of our own nothingness and dependence on His mercy" when you are thus addressing your suffering fellow subjects, and encouraging them to bear without repining the dispensations of Providence, may God grant that by your decision of this night you may have laid in store for yourselves the consolation of reflecting that such calamities are, in truth, the dispensations of Providence–that they have not been caused, they have not been aggravated by laws of man restricting, in the hour of scarcity, the supply of food!

146. Disraeli's speech on the Third Reading of the Bill for the Repeal of the Corn Laws (15 May 1846)

Hansard, 3/LXXXVI/665–679.

. . . I say, then, assuming, as I have given you reason to assume, that the price of wheat, when this system is established, ranges in England at 35s. per quarter, and other grain in proportion, this is not a question of rent, but it is a question of displacing the labour of England that produces corn, in order, on an extensive and even universal scale, to permit the entrance into this country of foreign corn produced by foreign labour. Will that displaced labour find new employment? The Secretary of State says, that England is no longer an agricultural country; and the right hon. Gentleman, when reminded by the noble Lord the Member for Gloucestershire,[1] of his words, said, "No, I did not say that; but I said that England was no longer exclusively an agricultural country." Why, Sir, the commerce of England is not a creation of yesterday: it is more ancient than that of any other existing country. This is a novel assumption in the part of the Government to tell us that England has hitherto been a strictly agricultural country, and that now there is a change, and that it is passing into a commercial and manufacturing country. I doubt whether, in the first place, England is a greater commercial country now than she has been at other periods of her history. I do not mean to say that she has not now more commercial transactions, but that with reference to her population, and the population of the world, her commerce is not now greater than at other periods of her history; for example, when she had her great Levantine trade, when the riches of the world collected in the Mediterranean, when she had her great Turkey merchants, her flourishing Antilles, and her profitable, though in some degree surreptitious, trade with the Spanish main. But then it is also said that England has become a great manufacturing country. I believe, Sir, if you look to the general distribution of labour in England, you will find she may be less of a manufacturing country now than she has been. Well, I give you my argument; answer it if you can. I say, looking to the employment of the people, manufacturing industry was more scattered over the country a hundred years ago than it is now. Hon. Gentlemen have laid hold of a word uttered in the heat of speaking. I say manufacturing industry was more dispersed over the country then than now–there were more counties in which manufactures flourished then than at the present moment. For instance, in the west of England, manufactures were more flourishing, and your woollen manufacture bore a greater ratio in importance to the industrial skill of Europe 300 years ago than it does to the aggregate industry of Europe at the present moment. That manufacture might not have been absolutely more important; but as a development of the national industry, it bore a greater relative importance to the industry of Europe then than at the present moment. You had then considerable manufactures in various counties–manufactures a hundred years ago which are now obsolete, or but partially pursued. You have no doubt now a gigantic development of manufacturing skill in a particular county, which has been a great source of public wealth, a development of which Englishmen should be justly

[1] Hon. Grantley Berkeley.

proud. But, generally speaking, it is confined to one county; and now Ministers tell us we must change our whole system, because, forsooth, England has ceased to be an agricultural country, and has become a commercial and manufacturing one. That is to say, that we must change our whole system in favour of one particular county. Sir, that is an extremely dangerous principle to introduce. I have heard of a repeal of the Union, but we may live to hear of a revival of the Heptarchy, if Her Majesty's Ministers pursue this policy; if those portions of the country which are agricultural, or suffering under the remains of an old obsolete manufacturing population, are to be told that we must change our whole system because one county where there is a peculiar development of one branch of industry demands it. But what are the resources of this kind of industry to employ and support the people, supposing the great depression in agricultural produce occur which is feared–that this great revolution, as it has appropriately been called, takes place–that we cease to be an agricultural people–what are the resources that would furnish employment to two-thirds of the subverted agricultural population–in fact, from 3,500,000 to 4,000,000 of the people? Assume that the workshop of the world principle is carried into effect–assume that the attempt is made to maintain your system, both financial and domestic, on the resources of the cotton trade–assume that, in spite of hostile tariffs, that already gigantic industry is doubled–a bold assumption, even if there be no further improvements in machinery, further reducing the necessity of manual labour–you would only find increased employment for 300,000 of your population. Perhaps mechanical invention may reduce the number half, and those only women and children. What must be the consequence? I think we have pretty good grounds for anticipating social misery and political disaster. But, then, I am told, immense things are to be done for the agriculturist by the application of capital and skill. Let us test the soundness of this doctrine. When a man lends his capital, he looks to the security he is to have, and to what is to pay the interest. Is the complexion of these measures such as to render men more ready to lend money on landed estates? The mortgagee, when he advances money on land, looks to the margin in the shape of rent for his security. Will any man rise and maintain that the tendency of these measures is to increase that margin? But you are not only diminishing the opportunity of obtaining loans upon your own estates, but you are creating for capital an investment which will be more profitable for it in the estates of the foreigner. Look at the relations in which you will place the foreign merchant with his London correspondent. He has no longer to fear the capricious effects of the sliding-scale: he has got a certain market; he goes to his London banker with an increased security for an advance; he obtains his loan with ease; he makes his advances to the country dealers on the Continent as he makes his advance of English capital now in the foreign wool trade, before the clip and the great fairs; and thus, while you diminish the security of the landed proprietor, you are offering to the English capitalist a better and securer investment. But then you tell us of the aid to be had by the agriculturist from skill. It is not easy to argue on a phrase so indefinite as skill; but I think I can show you that the English agriculturist is far more advanced, in respect to skill, than even the English manufacturer. I don't mean to say that there are not English farmers who might cultivate their lands better and with more economy than they do; but the same may surely be said, in their respective pursuits, of many a manufacturer and many a miner, but what I mean to say is, that an English farmer produces more effectively and wastes less–is more industrious and more intelligent than the manufacturer. I will prove this by the evidence of a member of the Anti-Corn-Law League–Mr. Greg. Mr. Greg says, that the competition is so severe that he almost doubts the possibility of the English manufacturer long maintaining that competition with the Continental or American manufacturer, who approach them nearer every day in the completeness of their fabrics and the economy of their productions. But no such thing can be said of the English agriculturist, who, I have shown you, can produce much more per bushel than the French, Russian, or American agriculturist. So much, then, for the argument with respect to skill. There is one argument, or rather appeal, which I know has influenced opinion out of this House, and also within it. You bring before us the condition of the English peasant. It is too often a miserable condition. My hon. Friend the Member for Shaftesbury[1] has gained, and deserves, great credit for investigating the condition of the Dorsetshire labourer. He has introduced it into this discussion. Now, the condition of the Dorsetshire labourer is one of the reasons which induce me to support this law. It is very easy to say that the condition of the agricultural labourer, when compared with the general state of our civilization, is a miserable and depressed one, and that protection has produced it. If I cannot offer you reasons which may induce you to believe that protection has had nothing to do with it, I shall be perfectly ready to go to-night into the same lobby with Her Majesty's Ministers. I asked you the other night, if protection has produced the Dorsetshire labourer at 7s. per week, how is it that protection has produced the Lincolnshire labourer with double that sum? I do not say that is an argument. It is a suggestive question, which I will endeavour to follow up. Mr. Huskisson made an observation, in conversation with an acquaintance of mine, which has always struck me very forcibly. When Mr. Huskisson first settled in Sussex, his attention was naturally drawn to the extraordinary state of pauperism in that country; and after giving the subject all the meditation of his acute mind, he said that he traced it to the fact, that Sussex had formerly been the seat of a great iron trade, and that agriculture had never been able to absorb the manufacturing population. Now, apply that principle to the western counties, and don't you think it will throw some light upon their condition? They also have been the seats of manufactures–many of them obsolete, and many of them now only partially pursued. There, too, you will find that the manufacturing population has never been absorbed by the agricultural–that is, agriculture does not bear its ratio in its means of support to the amount of the population which it has to sustain, but which it did not create. And now go to Lincolnshire. I will rest our case on Lincolnshire. It is a new county; it is a protected county. Lincolnshire is to agriculture what Lancashire is to manufactures. The population there is produced by land and supported by land, in the same manner that the population of Lancashire has been produced and is supported by manufactures. Let us picture to ourselves for a moment that celebrated tower that looks over that city, which my gallant Friend and his

[1] R. B. Sheridan.

ancestors have represented since the time of the last Stuart. Let us picture him for a moment placing the arch-fiend of political economy in that befitting niche, and calling his attention to the surrounding landscape. To the north, extending to the Humber, an endless tract of wolds, rescued from the rabbits, once covered with furse and whins, and now with exuberant crops of grain: to the south, stretching for miles, is what was once Lincoln Heath, where in the memory of living men there used to be a lighthouse for the traveller, and which, even in the recollection of the middle-aged, was let to the warrener at 2s. 6d. an acre, now one of the best-farmed and most productive corn districts in the kingdom. Then turning from the wolds and the heaths eastward, reaching to the sea, he might behold a region of fens, the small ones drained by the steam-engine, with the East and West and Wildmere Fens, once more than half of the year under water, now cleared by large canals, and bearing magnificent wheats and oats; with the great Witham and Black Sluice drainage districts, one extending over 60,000 and the other 90,000 acres, admirably reclaimed and drained, and bearing and creating and well sustaining a large and industrious and thriving population. And all under the faith of Protective Acts of Parliament. I am told that it is the contiguity of manufactures that makes Lincolnshire so prosperous. But, Sir, the frontiers of Wilts are nearer that great manufacturing district of which Birmingham is the centre, than those of Lincolnshire are to Lancashire. Now, see what Lincolnshire has produced under protection. There you see the protective system fairly tested. But when you find the labourers in the western counties wretched and miserable, do not say that protection has been the cause of it, when protection is, perhaps, the reason why they exist at all; but see if you cannot find other causes for their poverty and means to counteract it. I must say, that nothing astonished me more than when the noble Lord the Member for Falkirk[1] asked the farmers in Newark market, "What has protection done for you?" Why, that market is supplied with the wheat of Lincoln Heath, the intrinsic poverty of whose soil is only sustained by the annual application of artificial manures, but which produces the finest corn in the kingdom. What has protection done for them? Why, if protection had never existed, Lincolnshire might still have been a wild wold, a barren heath, a plashy marsh. There are one or two points to which I could have wished to call the attention of the House, but which time will only permit me to glance at. I will not presume to discuss them. But you cannot decide this question without looking to your Colonies. I am not one of those who think it the inevitable lot of the people of Canada to become annexed to the United States. Canada has all the elements of a great and independent country, and is destined, I sometimes believe, to be the Russia of the new world. The hon. and learned Member for Bath,[2] in answering the speech of the noble Lord the Member for Lynn,[3] last night, treated our commerce with Canada very lightly, rather as a smuggling traffic than legitimate commerce. That is an argument for keeping the Canadas. I have no desire to see a smuggling trade if we can have any other. But I will ask the gentlemen of Manchester to consider what may become of the trans-Atlantic market for their manufactures, if the whole of that continent belong to one Power? But I must not dwell on the Colonies, and I shall

[1] Lord Dalmeny. [2] J. A. Roebuck. [3] Lord Brooke.

scarcely touch the case of Ireland. It is too terrible, especially if there be truth in the opinion of the noble Lord, whose conversion has been so much a matter of congratulation to the Government, that their measure must be fatal to small farmers. Why, Ireland is a nation of small farmers. There was, however, one observation made with respect to Ireland by the hon. Member for Stockport,[1] which, considering the effect it had, I cannot help noticing. The hon. Gentleman says, "Ireland an argument in favour of the Corn Laws! Of all countries in the world I never should have supposed that Ireland would have been brought forward in support of the Corn Laws." That is a saucy and gallant sally; but is it an argument? what does it prove? The population is reduced to the lowest sources of subsistence. Admitted; but how do they gain even their potatoes except by cultivating the soil, and by producing that wheat and those oats which they send to England? I should be very glad if that wheat and those oats remained in Ireland; but I ask, what will be the state of Ireland, if the effect of this measure on your markets be such as I have assumed? You say that capital will flow into the country, and manufactures will be established. What length of time will elapse before these manufactures are established? Perhaps before that time the iron trade will revive in Sussex, or we shall see the drooping energies of the Dorsetshire labourer revived by his receiving the same wages as are paid at Rochdale and Stockport. Believing that this measure would be fatal to our agricultural interests – believing that its tendency is to sap the elements and springs of our manufacturing prosperity – believing that in a merely financial point of view it will occasion a new distribution of the precious metals, which must induce the utmost social suffering in every class, I am obliged to ask myself, if the measure be so perilous, why is it produced? Sir, I need not ask what so many Gentlemen both in and out of this House have already asked, what was there in the circumstances of this country to authorize the change? If we are only a commercial and manufacturing people, all must admit that commerce was thriving and that manufactures flourished. Agriculture was also content; and even had it been suffering and depressed, what does it signify, since England has ceased to be an agricultural country? Obliged, then, to discover some cause for this social revolution, I find that a body of men have risen in this country, eminent for their eloquence, distinguished for their energy, but more distinguished, in my humble opinion, for their energy and their eloquence than for their knowledge of human nature, or for the extent of their political information. Sir, I am not one of those who, here or elsewhere, in public or in private, have spoken with that disrespect which some have done of that great commercial confederation which now exercises so great an influence in this country. Though I disapprove of their doctrines – though I believe from the bottom of my heart that their practice will eventually be as pernicious to the manufacturing interest as to the agricultural interests of this country, still I admire men of abilities who, convinced of a great truth, and proud of their energies, band themselves together for the purpose of supporting it, and come forward, devoting their lives to what they consider to be a great cause. Sir, this country can only exist by free discussion. If it is once supposed that opinions are to be put down by any other means, then, whatever may be our political forms, liberty

[1] R. Cobden.

vanishes. If we think the opinions of the Anti-Corn-Law League are dangerous–if we think their system is founded on error, and must lead to confusion–it is open in a free country like England for men who hold opposite views to resist them with the same earnestness, by all legitimate means–by the same active organization, and by all the intellectual power they command. But what happens in this country? A body of gentlemen, able and adroit men, come forward, and profess contrary doctrines to those of these new economists. They place themselves at the head of that great popular party who are adverse to the new ideas, and, professing their opinions, they climb and clamber into power by having accepted, or rather by having eagerly sought the trust. It follows that the body whom they represent, trusting in their leaders, not unnaturally slumber at their posts. They conclude that their opinions are represented in the State. It was not for us, or the millions out of the House, to come forward and organize a power, in order to meet the hostile movements of the hon. Member for Stockport. No, we trusted to others–to one who by accepting, or rather by seizing that post, obtained the greatest place in the country, and at this moment governs England. Well, Sir, what happens? The right hon. Gentleman, the First Minister, told his Friends that he had given them very significant hints of the change of his opinions. He said that even last year, Lord Grey had found him out, and he was surprised that we could have been so long deluded. Sir, none of the observations of the right hon. Gentleman applied to me. More than a year ago I rose in my place and said, that it appeared to me that protection was in about the same state as Protestantism was in 1828. I remember my Friends were very indignant with me for that assertion, but they have since been so kind as to observe that instead of being a calumny it was only a prophecy. But I am bound to say, from personal experience, that, with the very humble exception to which I have referred, I think the right hon. Baronet may congratulate himself on his complete success in having entirely deceived his party, for even the noble Lord, the Member for Lynn, himself, in a moment of frank conversation, assured me that he had not till the very last moment the slightest doubt of the right hon. Gentleman. The noble Lord, I suppose, like many others, thought that the right hon. Gentleman was, to use a very favourite phrase on these benches in 1842, "only making the best bargain" for the party. I want to know what Gentlemen think of their best bargain now? Suddenly, absolute as was the confidence in the right hon. Gentleman, the announcement was made that there was to be another change; that that was to occur under his auspices, which, only a few months before, he had aptly described as a "social revolution." And how was that announcement made? Were hon. Gentlemen called together, or had the influential Members of either House any intimation given to them of the nature of it? No, Sir. It was announced through the columns of a journal which is always careful never to insert important information except on the highest authority. Conceive the effect of that announcement on foreign countries, and on foreign Ministers. I can bear witness to it. I happened to be absent from England at the time, and I know of great potentates sending for English ambassadors, and demanding an explanation; and of English ambassadors waiting on great potentates, and officially declaring that there was not the slightest truth in the announcement. And all this time, too, Members of the

Government–I have some of them in my eye–were calling on other newspapers devoted to the Government, and instructing them to announce that the whole was an "infamous fabrication." How ingenuous was the conduct of Her Majesty's Government–or of that Minister who formed the omnipotent minority of the Cabinet, I leave the House to decide. But was it not strange that, after so much agitation, after all these schemes, after all these Machiavellian manœuvres, when the Minister at last met the House and his party, he acted as if we had deserted him, instead of his having left us? Who can forget those tones? Who can forget that indignant glance?

> "Vectabor humeris tunc ego inimicis eques;
> Meaeque terra cedet insolentiae;"

which means to say, "I, a protectionist Minister, mean to govern England by the aid of the Anti-Corn-Law League. And, as for the country Gentlemen, why, I snap my fingers in their face." Yet even then the right hon. Gentleman had no cause to complain of his party. It is very true that, on a subsequent occasion, 240 Gentlemen recorded their sense of his conduct. But then he might have remembered the considerable section of converts that he obtained even in the last hour. Why, what a compliment to a Minister–not only to vote for him, but to vote for him against your opinions, and in favour of opinions which he had always drilled you to distrust. That was a scene, I believe, unprecedented in the House of Commons. Indeed, I recollect nothing equal to it, unless it be the conversion of the Saxons by Charlemagne, which is the only historical incident that bears any parallel to that illustrious occasion. Ranged on the banks of the Rhine, the Saxons determined to resist any further movement on the part of the great Caesar; but when the Emperor appeared, instead of conquering he converted them. How were they converted? In battalions–the old chronicler informs us they were converted in battalions, and baptized in platoons. It was utterly impossible to bring these individuals from a state of reprobation to a state of grace with a celerity sufficiently quick. When I saw the hundred and twelve fall into rank and file, I was irresistibly reminded of that memorable incident on the banks of the Rhine. And now, Sir, I must say, in vindication of the right hon. Gentleman, that I think great injustice has been done to him throughout these debates. A perhaps justifiable mis-conception has universally prevailed. Sir, the right hon. Gentleman has been accused of foregone treachery–of long meditated deception–of a desire unworthy of a great statesman, even if an unprincipled one–of always having intended to abandon the opinions by professing which he rose to power. Sir, I entirely acquit the right hon. Gentleman of any such intention. I do it for this reason: that when I examine the career of this Minister, which has now filled a great space in the Parliamentary history of this country, I find that for between thirty and forty years, from the days of Mr. Horner to the days of the hon. Member for Stockport, that right hon. Gentleman has traded on the ideas and intelligence of others. His life has been one great appropriation clause. He is a burglar of others' intellect. Search the Index of Beatson, from the days of the Conqueror to the termination of the last reign, there is no statesman who has committed political petty larceny on so great a scale.

I believe, therefore, when the right hon. Gentleman undertook our cause on either side of the House, that he was perfectly sincere in his advocacy; but as, in the course of discussion, the conventionalisms which he received from us crumbled away in his grasp, feeling no creative power to sustain him with new arguments, feeling no spontaneous sentiments to force upon him conviction, the right hon. Gentleman, reduced at last to defending the noblest cause, one based on the most high and solemn principles, upon the "burdens peculiar to agriculture"–the right hon. Gentleman, faithful to the law of his nature, imbibed the new doctrines, the more vigorous, bustling, popular and progressive doctrines, as he had imbibed the doctrines of Mr. Horner–as he had imbibed the doctrines of every leading man in this country, for thirty or forty years, with the exception of the doctrine of Parliamentary reform, which the Whigs very wisely led the country upon, and did not allow to grow sufficiently mature to fall into the mouth of the right hon. Gentleman. Sir, the right hon. Gentleman tells us, that he does not feel humiliated. Sir, it is impossible for any one to know what are the feelings of another. Feeling depends upon temperament; it depends upon the idiosyncracy of the individual; it depends upon the organization of the animal that feels. But this I will tell the right hon. Gentleman, that though he may not feel humiliated, his country ought to feel humiliated. Is it so pleasing to the self-complacency of a great nation, is it so grateful to the pride of England, that one who, from the position he has contrived to occupy, must rank as her foremost citizen, is one of whom it may be said, as Dean Swift said of another Minister, that "he is a Gentleman who has the perpetual misfortune to be mistaken!" And, Sir, even now, in this last scene of the drama, when the party whom he unintentionally betrayed is to be unintentionally annihilated–even now, in this the last scene, the right hon. Gentleman, faithful to the law of his being, is going to pass a project which, I believe it is a matter of notoriety, is not of his own invention. It is one which may have been modified, but which I believe has been offered to another Government, and by that Government has been wisely rejected. Why, Sir, these are matters of general notoriety. After the day that the right hon. Gentleman made his first exposition of his scheme, a gentleman well known in this House, and learned in all the political secrets behind the scenes, met me, and said, "Well, what do you think of your chief's plan?" Not knowing exactly what to say; but, taking up a phrase which has been much used in the House, I observed, "Well, I suppose it's a 'great and comprehensive' plan." "Oh!" he replied, "we know all about it! It was offered to us! It is not his plan; it's Popkins's plan!" And is England to be governed by "Popkins's plan?" Will he go with it to that ancient and famous England that once was governed by statesmen–by Burleighs and by Walpoles; by a Chatham and a Canning–will he go to it with this fantastic scheming of some presumptuous pedant? I won't believe it. I have that confidence in the common sense, I will say the common spirit of our countrymen, that I believe they will not long endure this huckstering tyranny of the Treasury Bench–these political pedlars that bought their party in the cheapest market, and sold us in the dearest. I know, Sir, that there are many who believe that the time is gone by when one can appeal to those high and honest impulses that were once the mainstay and the main element of the English character. I know, Sir, that we appeal to a people debauched by public gambling–stimulated and encouraged by an inefficient and shortsighted Minister. I know that the public mind is polluted with economic fancies; a depraved desire that the rich may become richer without the interference of industry and toil. I know, Sir, that all confidence in public men is lost. But, Sir, I have faith in the primitive and enduring elements of the English character. It may be vain now, in the midnight of their intoxication, to tell them that there will be an awakening of bitterness; it may be idle now, in the spring-tide of their economic frenzy, to warn them that there may be an ebb of trouble. But the dark and inevitable hour will arrive. Then, when their spirit is softened by misfortune, they will recur to those principles that made England great, and which, in our belief, can alone keep England great. Then, too, perchance they may remember, not with unkindness, those who, betrayed and deserted, were neither ashamed nor afraid to struggle for the "good old cause"–the cause with which are associated principles the most popular, sentiments the most entirely national –the cause of labour–the cause of the people–the cause of England.

147. The Chartist Petition of 1848 in the House of Commons

Hansard, 3/XCVIII/284–301.

MR. THORNELY brought up a special report from the Select Committee on Public Petitions, which was read by the clerk at the table as follows:–

"The House, on the 26th of November last, directed your Committee, in all cases, to set forth the number of signatures to each petition; and also, having regard to the powers delegated to them, to report their opinion and observations thereupon to the House, and they have agreed to the following special report: That on the 10th of April last, a petition for universal suffrage, &c., from the inhabitants of the British Isles, and subjects of the British Crown, was presented to the House. Your Committee strongly feel the value of the right of petition, and they consider that the exercise of it is one of the most important privileges of the subjects of this realm. They feel the necessity of preserving the exercise of such a privilege from abuse; and having also due regard to the importance of the very numerously signed petition forming the subject of the present report, they feel bound to represent to the House, that in the matter of signatures there has been, in their opinion, a gross abuse of the privilege. The hon. Member for Nottingham[1] stated, on presenting the petition, that 5,706,000 names were attached to it; but upon the most careful examination of the number of signatures in the Committee-room, and at which examination thirteen law-stationers' clerks were engaged upwards of seventeen hours, with the person ordinarily employed in counting the numbers appended to petitions, under the superintendence of the clerk of your Committee, the number of signatures has been ascertained to be 1,975,496. It is further evident to your Committee, that on numerous consecutive sheets the signatures are in one and the same handwriting. Your Committee also observed the names of distinguished individuals attached to the petition, who can scarcely

[1] F. O'Connor.

be supposed to concur in its prayer: among which occurs the name of Her Majesty, as Victoria Rex, April 1st, F.M. Duke of Wellington, Sir Robert Peel, &c. &c. Your Committee have also observed in derogation of the value of such petition, the insertion of numbers of names which are obviously fictitious, such as "No Cheese," "Pug Nose," "Flat Nose." There are others included, which your Committee do not hazard offending the House and the dignity and decency of their own proceedings by reporting. It may be added that there are other signatures appended obviously belonging to the name of no human being."

On the question that the report do lie on the table,

MR. F. O'CONNOR said, he was happy to think that there had been unusual activity with respect to this petition. It was announced to him yesterday, about twelve o'clock, by a Member of the Government, that the petition had been examined, and that there were not above 1,900,000 signatures to it. He did not undertake to say, nor had he ever said, nor would it be possible for him to say, that there had not been some of the practices resorted to which the Committee had represented; but there was an old saying, "He who hides can find;" and he had no doubt that in a great national undertaking like that, something like the spy system had been had recourse to. He had, however, pretty strong collateral proof that the number of signatures to the petition had far exceeded what the Committee had reported; and, without wishing to cast the slightest blame upon the Committee on Petitions, he should move for a Committee to investigate that particular petition. He had himself received statements from parties who had been concerned in getting up that petition, and who, he was sure, would not lend themselves to anything of an improper kind, showing that in Manchester alone the petition had received 175,000 signatures, and in Birmingham 75,000; and he had other statements from England, Scotland, and Wales, from parties who had undertaken the petition, showing upwards of 4,800,000 signatures. He had presented a petition, praying for the introduction of the Land Company Bill, which contained 203,000 signatures. In that number there was no error, and he did himself lift that petition, and place it upon the table of that House. The petition which he presented on Monday, however, was on four rolls, and not a Member of that House could have lifted the largest of them. He did not impute anything to the Committee, but he did say, that if they left out absurdities, such as "Pugnose," "the Duke of Wellington," and so forth, he had no doubt but there would be left five million of legitimate signatures. He asserted, moreover, that thirteen clerks could not have counted 1,900,000 signatures in seventeen hours, nor could twenty have done it. He did not believe any such thing as that the petition was only signed by 1,900,000 persons; and if the House doubted his assertions, he would, ere long, present one with two or three times the amount.

MR. THORNELY, as Chairman of the Committee on Petitions, assured the hon. and learned Gentleman that the petition in question had been received with all the respect due to a petition so very numerously signed; and if he might take the liberty of speaking of an individual so humble as himself, he would say, that there were points which the petitioners urged for the consideration of that House – the ballot for instance–in which he entirely agreed with them. But the House would be aware–a fact of which the hon. and learned Gentleman was, perhaps, ignorant–that when the Committee on Petitions was appointed, at an early part of the Session, they were instructed to report to the House the number of signatures to each and every petition presented. It had been necessary to call in additional aid for that purpose in the case of the present petition; but he believed, and indeed he had no doubt that the number had been fairly ascertained. He should add that the petition had been weighed, and that its weight was 5¾ cwt. He had no more to say, except that the Committee was too well known to require any vindication by him.

. . . . .

MR. CRIPPS said, after what the hon. Gentleman had said, and the reflections he had made upon the Committee–[MR. F. O'CONNOR: I made no reflections upon the Committee.] If the hon. Gentleman did not mean to reflect upon the character of the Committee, he meant nothing at all. The Committee had taken every pains with this petition, that there should be no mistake. His attention was first called to the circumstance when the hon. Member made that audacious statement, that the petition was signed by 5,000,000 persons. He went from his place as soon as he heard that statement, and spent two hours and a half over that very interesting document, the Population Abstract for 1841; and he might state, that upon every calculation which he could make he came to the conclusion that the petition could not be signed by half that number. He certainly was not aware at that time that the petition was signed by women. He found, however, upon taking a number of sheets at random, that in every 100,000 names there were 8,200 women. The hon. Gentleman said the petition weighed five tons. They had weights and scales in the Committee-room, and found that it weighed little more than five hundred weight. Perhaps the hon. Member would say he meant five hundred weight. [MR. F. O'CONNOR: I never said so.] He would pledge his word of honour to the House, that the hon. Gentleman had said it weighed five tons. He had himself heard him say so. At any rate three crazy cabs brought it down to that House. He did not wish to throw ridicule and obloquy upon the petition, but he did throw ridicule and obloquy upon the hon. Gentleman who presented it.

MR. F. O'CONNOR: I rise, Sir, to order. The hon. Gentleman's observations require explanation.

MR. SPEAKER: If the hon. Gentleman wishes to make an explanation with regard to personal conduct, though he has no absolute right to speak upon the subject, I have no doubt the House will allow him. If the hon. Gentleman does not wish to explain personal conduct, he must not interrupt another hon. Member when he is addressing the House.

MR. CRIPPS continued: He would repeat the observation, and he would say that if ever any Member of that House had laid himself open to charges which ought to deprive him of every credence to which man is entitled, that Member was the hon. Member for Nottingham. He would say for himself, that he could never believe the hon. Member again; and he trusted that those deluded persons who had assembled on Kennington Common would also withdraw their confidence from him. Were such meetings to be allowed, bearing in their train robbery and the most notorious results; was another meeting to be held within a fortnight, for the purpose of concocting such a ribald mass of obscenity and impiety as was contained in the petition under consideration? Language the most disgusting pervaded the whole petition; there were words in it which the vilest strumpet in the street would blush to name. The Duke of Wellington's name occurred fifteen or sixteen times. The name of the hon. and gallant Member for Lincoln (Colonel Sibthorp) several times; and the names of the hon. Members for Manchester[1] and West Yorkshire[2] he did not know how many times. On one of the sheets he knew, and he believed on several of them, were written the words, "We could not get paid for any more today." He was thankful from the bottom of his heart, that he had not done what he was very nearly tempted to do. If he had only taken up a sheet of the petition, when it lay at the foot of the table, and had happened to have stumbled upon one of the ten or twelve sheets, he should have objected to the receipt of that petition; for he could have put sheets into the Speaker's hands, which he could never have read to the House. He deeply regretted that such blasphemy and obscenity should have caused the Government so much uneasiness, and have put them to so much expense. Now the hon. Gentleman said he could present a petition signed by three times as many persons. Why, the whole number of males in England above 15 years of age did not exceed 7,000,000 persons. He hoped the House would not cast a reflection upon the Committee on Public Petitions, by appointing another Committee to consider this particular petition.

Mr. O'Connor: There are three points on which I must give some explanation. I hope I shall do so without the excitement which the hon. Gentleman the Member for Cirencester[3] has displayed. The first point has relation to the House; the second to the Committee; and the third to myself personally. I stated at the outset that I attributed not the slightest blame–not even a sinister intention–to the Committee; but I said it was impossible for the number of clerks employed to have got through the work in double the time they were employed. With regard to the petition itself, I could not be supposed to be accountable for anything written in it. Was it possible for me, in the nature of things, to examine the different sheets? I never saw one of them till I saw them rolled up here. I am now told I had no business to present any petition the character of which I did not know. If such were the rule, that petition would never have been presented at all. As to my having forfeited my title to credence, in having presented a petition for which I am not responsible, with all respect to the House and the Committee, I shall have that explained elsewhere.

The hon. Member immediately left the House.

148. Paragraph of the queen's speech, dealing with commercial policy (1852)

Hansard, 3/CXXIII/19–20.

My Lords, and Gentlemen,

It gives Me Pleasure to be enabled, by the blessing of Providence, to congratulate you on the generally improved Condition of the Country, and especially of

[1] John Bright. [2] R. Cobden. [3] W. Cripps.

the Industrious Classes. If you should be of opinion that recent Legislation in contributing, with other Causes, to this happy Result, has at the same time inflicted unavoidable Injury on certain important Interests, I recommend you dispassionately to consider how far it may be practicable equitably to mitigate that Injury, and to enable the Industry of the Country to meet successfully that unrestricted Competition to which Parliament, in its Wisdom, has decided that it should be subjected.

149. Villiers' Free Trade Resolutions of 23 November 1852

Hansard, 3/cxxiii/351.

MR. VILLIERS rose, in pursuance of notice, to move the following Resolutions:–

"That it is the opinion of this House, that the improved condition of the Country, and particularly of the Industrious Classes, is mainly the result of recent Commercial Legislation, and especially of the Act of 1846, which established the free admission of Foreign Corn, and that that Act was a wise, just, and beneficial measure.

"That it is the opinion of this House, that the maintenance and further extension of the policy of Free Trade, as opposed to that of Protection, will best enable the property and industry of the Nation to bear the burthens to which they are exposed, and will most contribute to the general prosperity, welfare, and contentment of the people.

"That this House is ready to take into its consideration any measures consistent with the principles of these Resolutions which may be laid before it by Her Majesty's Ministers."

150. Resolutions on Commercial Policy adopted by the House of Commons (26 November 1852)

Hansard, 3/cxxiii/701–705.

That it is the opinion of this House, that the improved condition of the Country, and especially of the Industrious Classes, is mainly the result of recent Legislation, which has established the principle of unrestricted competition, has abolished Taxes imposed for the purposes of Protection, and has thereby diminished the cost and increased the abundance of the principal articles of the Food of the People.

. . . . .

That it is the opinion of this House, that this Policy, firmly maintained and prudently extended, will, without inflicting injury on any important Interest, best enable the Industry of the Country to bear its burthens, and will thereby most surely promote the welfare and contentment of the People.

Resolved–

That this House will be ready to take into consideration any measures, consistent with these principles, which, in pursuance of Her Majesty's gracious Speech and Recommendation, may be laid before it.

151. Gladstone's Budget speech (18 April 1853)

Hansard, 3/cxxxv/1359–1398.

. . . I now approach a very difficult portion of the task that I have to perform–the discussion of the Income Tax. The first question that this Committee has to consider is, whether or not it will make efforts to part with the income tax at once. I do not say that such an alternative is impossible. On the contrary, I believe that by the conjunction of three measures, one of which must be a tax upon land, houses, and other visible property, of perhaps 6d. in the pound; and another, a system of licences upon trade made universal, and averaging something like £7; and the third, a change in your system of legacy duties, it would be possible for you at once to part with the income tax. But Her Majesty's Government do not recommend such a course to the Committee. They do not recommend it because they believe, in the first place, that such a system would, upon the whole, be far more unequal and cause greater dissatisfaction than the income tax; they believe, likewise, that it would arrest other beneficial reforms of taxation; and they believe that it would raise that difficult question in regard to the taxation of the public funds of this country in a form the most inconvenient. I might dilate upon this subject, but it is needless to do so. I leave it to those, if such there be, who are prepared to recommend the immediate abandonment of the income tax. Such is not the recommendation of Her Majesty's Government.

Now, in regard to the income tax, I wish that I could possess the Committee with the impression that constant study has made upon my own mind, of the deep and vital importance of the subject. We are too apt to measure the importance of the subject by the simple fact, that we draw from this tax £5,500,000 of revenue. Sir, that sum is a large one, but the mention of it conveys no idea to the Committee of the immense amount and magnitude of the question. If you want to appreciate the income tax you must go back to the epoch of its birth; you must consider what it has done for you, in times of national peril and emergency; you must consider what, if you do not destroy it–and I will explain afterwards what I mean by 'destroy' –what it may do for you again, if it please God that those times shall return.

Sir, it was in the crisis of the revolutionary war that, when Mr. Pitt found the resources of taxation were failing under him, his mind fell back upon the conception of the income tax; and, when he proposed it to Parliament, that great man, possessed with his great idea, raised his eloquence to an unusual height and power.

There is a description of the speech of Mr. Pitt on that occasion, written by a foreigner, a well-known writer of the day–Mallet du Pan–which I may venture to read to the Committee; I believe, after the lapse of fifty-five years, it will be heard not wholly without interest. This is an account which, in a periodical that he edited, he gives of Mr. Pitt's speech, in 1798:–

> "From the time that deliberative assemblies have existed, I doubt whether any man ever heard a display of this nature, equally astonishing for its extent, its precision, and the talents of its author. It is not a speech spoken by the Minister; it is a complete course of public economy; a work, and one of the finest works,

upon practical and theoretical finance, that ever distinguished the pen of a philosopher and statesman. We may add this statement to the learned researches of such men as Adam Smith, Arthur Young, and Stuart, whom the Minister honoured with his quotations."

I do not know whether this Committee are aware how much the country owes to the former income tax; but, because I deem it to be of vital importance that you should fully appreciate the power of this colossal engine of finance, I will venture to place before you, in what I think an intelligible and striking form, the result which it once achieved. I will draw the comparison between the mode in which your burdens were met, during that period of the war when you had no income tax–during that period of the war when you had the income tax in a state of half-efficiency–and during the last and most arduous period of the war, when the income tax was in its full power.

From 1793 to 1798, a period of six years, there was no income tax; from 1799 to 1802, there was an income tax; but the provisions of the law made it far less effective, in proportion to its rate, than it is now; and from 1806 to 1815, a period of eleven years, you had the income tax in its full force. Now, every one of us is aware of the enormous weight and enormous mischief that have been entailed upon this country by the accumulation of our debt; but it is not too much to say, that it is demonstrated by the figures, that our debt need not at this moment to have existed, if there had been the resolution to submit to the income tax at an earlier period. . . .

. . . Sir, the general views of Her Majesty's Government with respect to the income tax are, that it is an engine of gigantic power for great national purposes, but at the same time that there are circumstances attending its operation which make it difficult, perhaps impossible, at any rate in our opinion not desirable, to maintain it as a portion of the permanent and ordinary finances of the country. The public feeling of its inequality is a fact most important in itself. The inquisition it entails is a most serious disadvantage. And the frauds to which it leads are an evil which it is not possible to characterise in terms too strong.

One thing I hope this House will never do, and that is, nibble at this great public question. Don't let them adopt the plan of reconstructing the income tax to-day, and saying, "If that does not work well, we'll try our hands at it again to-morrow." That is not the way in which the relations of classes brought into the nicest competition one with another under a scheme of direct taxation, are to be treated. Depend upon it, when you come to close quarters with this subject, when you come to measure and test the respective relations of intelligence and labour and property in all their myriad and complex forms, and when you come to represent those relations in arithmetical results, you are undertaking an operation of which I should say it was beyond the power of man to conduct it with satisfaction, but, at any rate, it is an operation to which you ought not constantly to recur; for if, as my noble Friend once said, with universal applause, this country cannot bear a revolution once a year, I will venture to say that it cannot bear a reconstruction of the income tax once a year.

Whatever you do in regard to the income tax, you must be bold, you must be intelligible, you must be decisive. You must not palter with it. If you do, I have striven at least to point out as well as my feeble powers will permit, the almost desecration I would say, certainly the gross breach of duty to your country, of which you will be guilty, in thus putting to hazard one of the most potent and effective among all its material resources. I believe it to be of vital importance, whether you keep this tax or whether you part with it, that you either should keep it, or should leave it in a state in which it will be fit for service on an emergency, and that it will be impossible to do if you break up the basis of your income tax.

Then you will ask me, "On what principle do you mean to proceed?–you have made an argument, so far as you have gone, to show that the tax cannot be reconstructed and cannot be amended; what will you do with it?"

What we wish to do, and what we shall aim at doing by the measure which I shall propose, is this:–We wish, in the first place, to put an end to the uncertainty respecting the income tax. We think it unfortunate that political circumstances have for the last two or three years led to a state of doubt in regard to the continuance of the tax, and have even begotten by degrees a feeling on the part of the public that the country is about to be entrapped unawares into its perpetuation. My belief is, that much of the uneasy feeling that prevails is traceable to that source, and I am very far from thinking that our merely asking of the Committee to renew this tax for a given term, in lieu of asking you to make it perpetual, would be sufficient to allay that anxiety or to remove that doubt.

There is a certain class of transactions with regard to which the uncertainty about the income tax operates most unfavourably–such as the terminable annuities, for example. It is very desirable that certainty should be restored on account of these transactions, and also on grounds more enlarged and general.

I think it also most desirable that effectual measures should be taken to mark this tax as a temporary tax. By this I do not mean merely, or chiefly, that I would commit the Government to an abstract opinion to be acted upon in future years. My own opinion is decidedly against the perpetuity of the tax as a permanent ordinary portion of our finances. But while I state the wish of the Government to propose it as a temporary tax, I do not ask you to rely on their words to bind them or yourselves, irrespectively of what may occur in the interim, as to what you will do under all circumstances at the expiration of the term which we propose to fix for its continuance now. I propose by positive enactment, by the measures which I shall invite you to adopt, to lay the ground for placing Parliament in such a position that at a given period it may, if it think fit, part with that tax.

Besides fixing on the tax a temporary character, we are most anxious to do what can be done, in order to meet the public feeling as to the inequality of the tax. For that public feeling we have not only respect, but sympathy, while we do not admit that it is our duty, as persons charged with the conduct of public affairs, to shape our measures according to any feeling or sentiment whatever, until we have examined the practical form which they are to take, and tried it by the light of our understanding. We propose, Sir, to introduce certain mitigations into the operation of the income tax. We propose to extend the principle of commutations, which is now applicable only to trades, to professions also. A more important mitigation which we propose to make is this: There is a general feeling that a man ought to have, at any rate, the opportunity of investing the savings he may make from his income without being liable to the income tax upon them. We do not think it possible to make provisions of that kind applicable to savings simply as such. All we can do is to say, "If you choose to invest your savings in the form of a deferred annuity or a life assurance, the premium which you may pay upon that deferred annuity or life assurance up to one-seventh of your income, shall not be chargeable to your income tax, but may be deducted from your income tax before it is charged." I am not at all prepared to say that we would stop at that point if it were possible to do more. At the same time, this plan has considerable recommendations. I do not say that it will completely meet the case of persons who, being afflicted with sickness, cannot, except under peculiar circumstances, insure their lives, because, unfortunately, cases of that sort it is beyond the power of the Legislature to meet. But what I do say is this–that it is a relief which will admit of very extensive application. I cannot reckon that the reduction from the receipts of the tax in consequence of it will be less–though, of course, this is a matter of uncertainty–when we look to the total amount of life assurance in this country, than £120,000 a year. It establishes, however, no invidious distinctions between one class and another. It is open to all those who choose to avail themselves of it; but while it is open to them all, we know that practically the classes who are in the habit of insuring their lives are just those very classes whom it is your main object to relieve by the reconstruction of the tax–namely, the classes of professional men and of persons who are dependent upon their own exertions.

I think it will be necessary, in conjunction with the proposal I have just named, to propose that Government should itself become insurers of life. If it is to undertake that charge, as will probably be the case, it will insure lives on the same principles as those on which it is now a vendor of life annuities.

But while I say that our object is to meet the public feeling as to the inequality of the tax, and while I specify these modes of going some way to effect that object, I have more to lay before you upon this subject. And pray understand me. Do not let me through my neglect be misapprehended, or fail to state clearly the position of the Government. What we understand to be the sentiment of the country, and what we ourselves, as a matter of feeling, are disposed to defer to, and to share in, is, that the income tax bears upon the whole too hard upon intelligence and skill, and not hard enough upon property as compared with intelligence and skill. This, I say, is the sentiment which, with whatever varieties of form, has been expressed through various organs, and has awakened an echo in the public mind. I hope that I here state with accuracy, not as yet the precise measures that we propose, but the object which the reconstructors of the income tax have in view. Well, if that be their object–if they think that at present skill and intelligence are too severely pressed, and that property under the income tax pays too little, let me remind them that they must not form their judgment of the condition of classes from one single tax or from another single tax, but that they must look to the general effect of the whole system of taxation. And all I implore of them in that respect at this moment is, that they will reserve their decision upon the question whether the Government proposition sufficiently meets the case of skill and intelligence as compared with property until they have heard me throughout, if their kindness will permit them still to extend to me their patience.

Our proposition, then, in regard to the income tax is this:–We propose to renew it for two years from April, 1853, at the rate of 7d. in the pound. The Committee will recollect that I said we thought it our duty to look the whole breadth of this difficulty in the face–not to endeavour to escape it, not to endeavour to attenuate, or to understate it, but to face and to settle, if the Committee would enable us, the whole question of the income tax. We propose, then, to re-enact it for two years, from April, 1853, to April, 1855, at the rate of 7d. in the pound. From April, 1855, to enact it for two more years at 6d. in the pound; and then, for three more years–I cannot wonder at the smile which I perceive that my words provoke–for three more years–from April, 1857, at 5d. Under this proposal, on the 5th of April, 1860, the income tax will expire.

Sir, we think it far better–far more in accordance with our obligations, and far more likely to advance the interests of the country–that we should present to you what we think–and I will tell you why we think so by and by–a real substantive plan, under which the income tax may, if Parliament should think fit, be got rid of, than that we should come to you with some paltry proposal to shirk the difficulty by re-enacting it for two years, or re-enacting it for one year, and thereby prolonging the public uncertainty and dissatisfaction, and giving rise not only to doubts as to the position of the tax, but even as to the perfect good faith of Parliament in its mode of dealing with the country. Now, Sir, we think that the descending rates which we have embodied in the proposal for the renewal of the tax will tend to show to Parliament and to the country that our intention to part with it, or, at all events, our intention to put Parliament in 1860 in a condition to part with it, is a real and a *bona fide* intention.

But you will say–and say justly–that that intention does not of itself put Parliament in a condition to part with the tax,–that it is very well to say that it shall,–that for two years, remain at 7d. in the pound, that for two years more it shall be 6d., and for three years more 5d.; but that when it comes to 5d. you may find that there is still a deficiency, and that you again want the 7d., or that when you come to the end of the period with the rate of 5d. in the pound, you may find you cannot part with it. With respect to this objection I have to say, that before the close of my present statement I shall endeavour to give you full satisfaction on that point; and I will further venture to say that, whatever you may think of the plan I have to propose, no Gentleman in the Committee shall leave his place to-night with the opinion that the Government are paltering with the House of Commons, or that I am not presenting a proposal which is at any rate substantive and intelligible.

I say, Sir, that our principles, with respect to the income tax (which is the cornerstone of our whole financial plan)–our principles with respect to the income tax required of us these things:–In the first place, to mark it effectually as a temporary tax; in the second place, to meet, in a way which we think good and effectual, the public feeling with respect to the inequality of the tax; and I will very shortly explain how we mean to attain this end. But, beyond this, I wish to ask–and this is the important question to which I seek to draw the attention of Parliament–if you determine to renew the income tax, will you make its early extinction your first and sole object, or will you, in order to bring to completion the noble work of commercial reform which is so far advanced, once more associate the income tax with a remission of duties, extensive in itself and beneficial to the community? We have considered fully these two alternatives; and we have decided deliberately in favour of the second.

While we propose to renew the income tax, we propose to associate it during the years which it has still to run with a great and beneficial remission of taxes. But the statement which I have already made with respect to the surplus, is one not altogether promising in this respect. He would be an ingenious Minister of Finance who should found an extensive remission of taxation on a surplus of £800,000, £200,000 or £300,000 of which he regards as accidental or uncertain. If we are to propose a remission of taxes, we must have funds out of which to make the remission. This is, of course, an elementary truth, but I am sorry to say that it is not wholly needless to impress it upon the House.

We have, therefore, to consider–and this, Sir, is the most invidious of all the portions of my task, upon which I am now about to enter–we have now to consider what are the means open to us, in consistency with justice, for creating a fund which, in conjunction with our present surplus, we can apply to an extensive and beneficial remission of taxes.

Now, the first question which is raised is this–if the income tax is to be continued, shall it also be extended? And the view of the Government is this–that the late Administration were right in stating that, if the income tax was to be continued, the exemptions under it should be narrowly considered; and therefore we are prepared to deal with the question of these exemptions.

What, in the first place, let me ask, is the case of persons enjoying incomes immediately below £150 per annum? There may be those who say that it is dangerous to attempt to levy the income tax on incomes below £150; but it is my opinion that the safety of that measure depends in a great degree–I may say mainly–on its justice; and if you can show that it is required by justice to other classes, and that it would be advantageous to the country, and even to the parties themselves who would be immediately affected by it, I am not afraid, with the confidence I entertain in the character of the English people, that there would be any danger attaching to such a measure. There were apprehensions, we know, entertained in 1842 that the imposition of the income tax in any shape would be found unpopular; but the sense of justice and enlightened prudence of the people, appreciating as they did the great benefit achieved by its instrumentality, divested it, if not of the unpopularity, certainly of the odious character which it was thought might generally have attached to it.

Well, now, what is the case of persons enjoying incomes below £150? It is well known that persons of that class have very largely benefited by the measures consequent on the income tax up to the present time. Twelve millions of taxes have been remitted, and they have enjoyed their full share of this, without the charge of one farthing. I don't propose that we should carry the tax down to the regions where it would trench on labour. To my view it is a right and expedient principle–taking it in connexion with all the circumstances of the case–that we should not trench upon what I would call the territory of labour. That territory will probably be defined sufficiently for my purpose by the figure of £100 a year; and what I am saying now has reference to the case of incomes between £100 and £150. Their case is, that they have enjoyed up to the present time the full benefit of the remission of the £12,000,000 of taxes to which I have referred. But that is not all. If we were going to continue the income tax for a short period without any compensating advantage, then, indeed, it might not be expedient that I should ask you to extend it to a lower amount than at present; but I am going, before I conclude, to ask you to support the Government in enacting a great and beneficial remission of taxes; and I say, before you confer that great additional benefit, let us consider how far the results of our plan can be distributed equitably among the various classes of the community.

I will present to the Committee what I think they will consider some interesting results with respect to the past operation of our recent legislative remissions. With a view to the decision of the question which I am now opening, it appeared to me a matter of extreme interest to collect a number of *bona fide* cases of the distribution of the expenditure of particular families receiving different rates of income, marking the proportion in which they had each profited by the adoption of the income tax, and the measures connected with it. My right hon. Friend the head of the Poor Law Board (Mr. Baines), kindly lent me his able and effective aid, and I have thus been enabled to collect a body of trustworthy information of the kind which I am now about to present to the Committee.

I shall not trouble you with the details, but merely give the general results of a few *bona fide* cases of actual expenditure, and I believe they are fair average cases, which will exhibit the actual savings which have been realised by persons whose incomes are below £150, and also by those whose incomes are above £150, in consequence of the adoption of the income tax, and of the remission of taxes, and the changes in our commercial system which were brought about through its medium. But it should be recollected that, in estimating the savings, I have taken credit for the further remissions which I am about to propose as well as for those which have already taken place.

I have collected six cases of incomes varying from £175 to £400 a year; and, after taking credit at moderate rates for the principal part of their savings, and carefully setting down the various items which go to make up their incomes, I find that their gross incomes amount to £1,359, and their gross savings to £63 1s. 3d., making a gain of above five per cent upon the gross amount of their incomes; and even if you deduct the income tax which they have paid, there will still remain a saving of £22. 16s. 6½d., or nearly two per cent upon their incomes. This, I think, is not an unsatisfactory result which I have presented to the Committee.

But I have likewise got four cases of the actual expenditure of persons with incomes between £100 and £150, and these, the Committee should understand, are not cases which have been selected for the purpose of arriving at a particular result, but are cases which have been fairly and honestly collected for the purpose of showing the actual distribution of expenditure of the two classes to which I have referred. One is the case of a country tradesman with £120 per annum; the second is the case of a retired Liverpool tradesman (having six children) with £120 per annum; the third is the case of a widow in the country, with an income from £120 to £150 (say £135 per annum); and the fourth is the case of a clerk in a country town, with £100 per annum; making a total income of £475, and their gain has been £29. 6s. 11d., or between 6 and 7 per cent. Deducting income tax at the rate of 5d. in the pound, the savings would amount to £19. 9s., or more than 4 per cent. So that you see clearly from this that the persons with incomes between £100 and £150, have apparently profited by the changes in our legislation to a considerably greater extent than those with incomes above £150.

I ought to say that in estimating the savings I have endeavoured to keep strictly within the bounds of moderation, and that I have no doubt that the results could easily have been swelled if I had chosen. Now, Sir, it appears to us that these facts offer a rather strong reason for considering whether, when we propose to renew the income tax in the case of persons with incomes above £150, it is not demanded by justice that we should expect that persons with incomes below £150 should, to some reasonable extent, become sharers in the burden. Her Majesty's Government think that in justice we ought to make this demand upon them.

What we propose is this–we propose so far to complicate the tax as to introduce a provision that incomes between £100 and £150 shall be liable at the rate of 5d. in the pound for the whole time during which the tax is levied, so that, for the first two years, incomes above £150 will pay 7d. in the pound, and incomes below £150, 5d.; for the next two years, the one will pay 6d., and the other 5d., and for the following three years both classes will alike pay at the rate of 5d. in the pound. I estimate that this tax of 5d. on incomes from £100 to £150 will produce £250,000; but as it will not be levied till the latter half of the current financial year, the sum of £125,000 only will come to credit in the financial year of 1853–54.

I now come to another great exemption–the exemption of Ireland. . . .

I will now give the Committee an account of the manner in which my estimate stands, as a whole, with respect to the income tax. The estimated produce of the tax, supposing there be no change in the existing system–is £5,550,000. Deduct life assurances (£120,000), of which one-half only comes to charge this year, namely, £60,000, there will be left £5,490,000. The extension below £150 we reckon at £125,000; and the extension to Ireland at £230,000; making the total for the year 1853–54, according to the proposed plan, £5,845,000.

I now come to another proposal for the augmentation of taxation, to which I invite the special attention of the Committee. It is one of great importance. It involves both economical and social considerations of the highest nature. I have stated to the Committee that we propose to enlarge our means by new taxation with a view to further beneficial changes in our fiscal system. That is one object we have in view.

Another object is–and it is likewise an important object–to meet the public feeling, which we recognise and share, that the operation of the income tax is severe upon intelligence and skill as compared with property. I frankly own my total inability to meet the feeling which has been excited upon the subject of the income tax, by any attempt to vary the rate of the tax according to the source of the income; and that I think I should be guilty of a high political offence if I attempted it. But let me now point out to you that if you think that intelligence and skill under our system of taxation pay too much, and property too little there are means of equalising the burdens of the two classes, in a manner which would be, on the whole, safe, honourable, and efficacious.

Sir, I refer to the question of the legacy duty–a question which it is perfectly plain cannot long be withheld from the consideration of the House. . . .

It is obvious, when we regard the burdens upon property in this country, that there is a great mass of taxation that attaches to property which may be roughly called–I do not know whether the term is capable of a strict legal construction, but it will best convey my meaning–rateable property, which includes, along with real property, a great amount of leasehold, copyhold, and so forth, which is not real property, but which is subject to the burdens of real property; which is subject to taxation by the income tax, which is subject to the land tax, though, as a whole, in a somewhat less degree than land itself, which is subject to the extra charges on the transfer of property, and which is subject generally to all the charges that affect visible property as contrasted with invisible property, and especially which is liable to the great weight of local taxation. There is, between these items, a sum of £14,000,000 or £15,000,000 of taxes in the three kingdoms laid entirely on rateable property, to which not real property only, not land only, but leasehold and copyhold property also are subjected. This property is now struck in both ways; it is subject to the legacy and probate duties, and it is also subject to all the burdens incident to real property.

The Government propose to amend the whole foundation of the law, by striking a new distinction, and by saying that whatever exemption or partial advantage shall be given to real property shall be given in conjunction with it to other property which is now subjected to similar special burdens. We propose, therefore, totally to abolish, for the purpose of legacy duty or succession tax, the effect of settlement, so that the person who succeeds to personal property will pay according to his interest. He will pay upon the capital, if he succeeds to the capital; and if he succeeds to a lesser interest, he will pay on the value of that lesser interest. The Government, then, thinking it just that a less amount shall be taken from rateable property than from property that does not pay these special burdens, have to ask in what way that distinction can best be struck. It has long been the policy of this country–the result, it may be, of measures accidentally taken, but not on that account the less beneficial –that visible and rateable property should be principally taxed in the form of an annual charge. Now, it would be obviously highly inconsistent, while we leave such property subject to its heavy annual burdens, to aggravate them by laying a heavy charge upon capital. For the Government would then force and accelerate, by the pressure of fiscal enactments, changes in the tenure of this property; and that acceleration would be, in my opinion, not only unjust, but most cruel and mischievous in a social point of view.

We think that if anything in the nature of a distinction is taken in the legacy duties in favour of rateable property as against the other descriptions of property, the fairest mode in the case of an estate would be found to be this – that the successor to real and rateable property should be in all cases taxed upon the life interest only, or on a minor interest, if he has only a minor interest. It is difficult for me to enter upon a full discussion of all the reasons that have led us to that conclusion. The question is very much connected with the great difficulty of any attempt to ascertain the capital values of real property. As a matter of fact, under the social arrangements of this country, our great estates are settled estates. Leaving this subject, however, for future discussion, it is our opinion that our proposal ought to include the legacy duties, but that some remission ought to be granted to property, which is now subject to a great weight of peculiar and exceptional taxation; and we think that the best mode of framing that provision would be to charge the succession of rateable property upon the life interest of the person succeeding in the net annual income after the deduction of encumbrances.

We propose that the duty should be leviable, as was proposed by Mr. Pitt, in eight half-yearly instalments. In cases where there is a succession to a life interest, our proposal would be that the unpaid residue of the tax should drop in the event of a new succession before the last instalment is payable; but in the case of a succession in fee the whole will be charged, and if death occurs before the remaining instalment is paid, the duty will become a debt of the Crown against the estate. That is our proposal with regard to the legacy duties. . . .

152. Gladstone's Budget speech (10 February 1860)

Hansard, 3/CLVI/812–872.

. . . There is a deficit of £9,400,000, the best means of providing for which it becomes our duty to consider; and we ought not, in my opinion, to face a question of such magnitude as is now before us, without having duly weighed the principles upon which we are to proceed, and the policy on which we mean to act. Now I have already indicated to you a summary budget which might have the effect of filling up the hiatus which I have mentioned. I have also shadowed out to you another and a more generous budget, which, providing you with an income tax of 1s. in the pound, would achieve the same object, and would enable you to relieve the consumers of tea and sugar to the extent of the remaining portions of the war duty; as well as that more niggardly budget, which would keep up the duties on tea and sugar, and would still leave the country liable to an income tax of 9d. in the pound. With what views, then, and upon what principles, are we to face this state of circumstances? I may at once venture to state frankly that I am not satisfied with the state of the public expenditure, and the rapid rate of its growth. I trust, therefore, that we mean in a great degree to retrace our steps. The process of retracing our steps in such a matter, however, even were it resolved upon and begun, is one which must necessarily be gradual; for, if it be not pursued with circumspection and with caution, it will serve but to aggravate the very evils which it may be intended to remove. I assume, therefore, whether the Committee concurs with the Government in the expediency of the Estimates which they have submitted, or are about to submit to the House, or whether it does not, that you can effect no radical change in the scale of that expenditure on which you have now, for a series of years, embarked–no radical change, I mean, applicable to the operations of the present year, or to the provision you will have to make for filling up the gap which yawns before you, and which is represented by the figures £9,400,000. The real question with which we have to deal is whether we ought upon this occasion to say our necessities are great, our means too narrow, to enable us to effect any commercial reforms. Such reforms are all very well, it may be contended, for fine weather, but they do not suit a period of pressure and alarm. That is, I know, a favourite doctrine with some classes, but against the justice of that doctrine I for one protest. And upon the part of the Government, I do not hesitate to say that, at an epoch so marked and signal in our financial history as the year 1860, it is their opinion that it is the duty of Parliament to take some steps in advance in that career of commercial improvement which, perhaps, more than any other cause, has contributed to confirm the prosperity of the country, and the security of its institutions, under the auspices of the Sovereign under whose rule it is our happiness to live.

There are in the present year special reasons why we should pursue such a policy as that to which I refer. The first of these I find in the cessation of the Long Annuities.[1] Are we to be told that when a sum of £2,000,000 and upwards annually, which we have hitherto been obliged to pay on the national debt, comes into our possession, it only remains for us to cast it into that great gulf of expenditure, there to be swallowed up and to disappear? That sum is a mighty engine for the purposes of relief, while for the purposes of expenditure, such as expenditure is now, it is comparatively unimportant. Applied to the purposes of relief, you may by its means shed a thousand blessings over the land; thrown into the scale of your expenditure it represents, after all, but the difference between the £13,000,000 which you have already added to that expenditure and the £11,000,000 which you might have added. The next of these reasons is to be found in the state of the tea and sugar duties. They have continued to be levied for three years at a rate exceeding that which was fixed for time of peace, and this even while the income tax was allowed to sink to 5d. I do not say that we are bound to choose these particular duties for reduction unless we find that a reduction of them will be the best of all the reductions that may be within our choice; but I do confidently urge that the position of these duties offers a strong reason why we should endeavour to afford on this occasion a considerable relief, and give attention to the claims of the people, as well as to the claims of trade, on which the prosperity of all classes mainly depends. There is yet another special reason. It is my intention before sitting down to propose to the Committee that they shall apply

[1] Terminable annuities, against which sums constituting part of the National Debt had been borrowed. - Ed.

in aid of the expenditure of the year a sum of not less than £1,400,000, which is no part of the proposed taxation of the year, but which will be obtained by rendering available another portion of the malt credit, and the credit usually given on hops. That may, under our present circumstances, be a salutary measure; but if we are employing in aid of the year extraordinary resources which form no part of its public burdens, that is a reason why we should also include in its arrangements special benefits, and make use of the means thus supplied for carrying forward the great work of public improvement.

But, Sir, I am not satisfied to place this duty on narrow grounds of whatever kind. It is not simply because annuities are falling in–it is not simply because we have considerable funds to be drawn from this source or that. We must look at the question from another point of view. We must take it for granted that for the present we have attained to what may be called a high level of public expenditure, and that we are likely to remain on that high level for some time at least. Is that a reason, or is it not, why we should arrest the process of reforming the commercial legislation of the country? I say that is no reason for stopping–I say more, it is a distinct reason for persevering in that process and carrying it boldly and readily to its completion. Let us, however, glance for a moment at our position. If we were, in the year 1860, to hold our hands, let us consider what aspect our procedure would bear. For seven years, under the pressure of war and of demands for increased expenditure, we have intermitted the course of commercial improvement on which we had entered: we have now arrived at a year of unexampled financial relief as regards the charge of the public debt, a year of which the Ways and Means will be enlarged by special resource, and a year which obliges us to reconsider the existing duties on tea and sugar. If, after such a period of years, we stop in 1860, will it not be supposed that we stop for ever? In truth, if this be not a fitting opportunity for endeavouring to give increased effect to the beneficial principles of your legislation, I, for one, must frankly own I know not when such an opportunity will arise. But, Sir, I come now to the broader view of the truth of the case. Our high taxation is not a reason for stopping short in our commercial reforms; it is a reason why we should persevere in them. For it is by means of these reforms that we are enabled to bear high taxation. What, I ask, has the country done during the last six months? It has paid an income tax, which, during the half-year, was at the rate of 1s. 1d. in the pound. Would that tax, so suddenly imposed, have been borne as it has been borne without discontent, but for the strength which the country has derived from the recent commercial legislation? In stating that this great and sudden augmentation of the income tax has been borne without discontent–[An hon. Member: Hear, hear!]–I speak in general terms. Indeed, I now remember that I myself had, about a fortnight ago, a letter addressed to me, complaining of the monstrous injustice and iniquity of the income tax, and proposing that, in consideration thereof, the Chancellor of the Exchequer should be publicly hanged. Of course I do not mean to say there has in no individual case been a murmur; but, upon the whole, speaking with the necessary latitude that must attach to general expressions, I am justified in saying that this high rate of taxation has been borne throughout the country with a most extraordinary, laudable, and honourable forbearance. It was, I think, Lord Londonderry who complained of the people of England as exhibiting an "ignorant impatience of taxation;" but I think, were he to rise from the dead and again take his place in this House, he would be very much more likely to describe them as distinguished by an ignorant patience of taxation.

I wish, however, Sir, to show more particularly the connection that subsists between commercial reforms, as affecting trade and industry, and the power to pay the high taxes you have imposed. These two subjects are inseparably locked the one in the other. You shall have the demonstration in figures. I again ask you for a moment to attend with me to the experience of two periods. I take the ten years from 1832, the crisis of the Reform Bill, down to 1841, during which our commercial legislation was, upon the whole, stationary; and I take the twelve years from 1842 to 1853, within the circuit of which are comprehended the beneficial changes that Parliament has made. In the ten years from 1832 to 1841 this was the state of things:–You imposed of Customs and Excise duties £2,067,000, and you remitted £3,385,000, exhibiting a balance remitted over and above what you imposed of £1,317,000, or at the rate of no more than £131,000 a year. Now, observe the effect on the state of the revenue. During these ten years the Customs and Excise increased by £170,000 a year; while the increase of the export trade was £15,156,000, or at the annual rate of £1,515,000. Let us next take the twelve years from 1842 to 1853. You remitted during that period of Customs and Excise £13,238,000, and imposed £1,029,000, presenting a balance remitted of £12,209,000, or an annual average of £1,017,000. What was the effect on the revenue? The Customs and Excise increased £2,656,000, or at an annual rate of £221,000. When you remitted practically nothing, your Customs revenue, in consequence of the increase of the population, grew at the rate of £170,000 per annum; and when you remitted £1,017,000 a-year, your Customs and Excise revenue grew faster than when you remitted nothing, or next to nothing at all. I ask, is not this a conclusive proof that it is the relaxation and reform of your commercial system which has given to the country the disposition to pay taxes along with the power also which it now possesses to support them? The foreign trade of the country, during the same period, instead of growing at the rate of £1,515,000 a year, grew at the rate of £4,304,000. I say, then, Sir, without hesitation, that it is the duty of the Legislature, both on account of the special circumstances of the juncture, and likewise, and still more, on the broad ground of general and comprehensive principle, at this time to make considerable remissions; and if that be so, the next question is on what principle you should make them.

When we have arrived at this stage of the question, the subject of the tea and sugar duties may naturally occur to the mind of every one as having a presumptive claim, at any rate, to the first consideration. I am bound, however, to say that these are not the subjects on which it has appeared to the Government that they might operate with the greatest advantage. No doubt the duties on tea and sugar are taxes most desirable to be reduced. They are harmless and beneficial articles–articles of universal consumption, and I trust the time may arrive, and arrive at no distant date, when we may be able to recur to our former standard in regard to these taxes. But, on the other hand, there never was a time when the people were so well able to pay these taxes as now. The increase in the consumption of these articles is regular, and the revenue is a growing revenue. If we are to have a very large scale of expenditure and a very high income tax, I cannot think, while the bulk of the burden should fall on the shoulders of those having property, that it is otherwise than desirable that the labouring classes should bear their share of the burden in a form in which it will be palpable and intelligible to them, rather than in forms in which it will be veiled from their eyes. But, Sir, I take my stand more especially on this consideration;–the duties on tea and sugar, whatever else they may be, are simply revenue duties. They entail no complexity in the system of Customs law; above all, they entail none of the evils that belong to differential duties; and I will by-and-by invite you to join the Government in adopting measures whereby you will be able to counteract and root out evils of that peculiar and aggravated kind, as well as to give relief in the price of commodities. But I do not hesitate to say that it is a mistake to suppose that the best mode of giving benefit to the labouring classes is simply to operate on the articles consumed by them. If you want to do them the *maximum* of good, you should rather operate on the articles which give them the *maximum* of employment. What is it that has brought about the great change in their position of late years? Not that you have legislated here and there, taking off 1d. or 2d. in the pound of some article consumed by the labouring classes. This is good as far as it goes, but it is not this which has been mainly operative in bettering their condition as it has been bettered during the last ten or fifteen years. It is that you have set more free the general course of trade; it is that you have put in action the process that gives them the wisest field and the highest rate of remuneration for their labour. Take the great change in the corn laws; it may even possibly be doubted whether up to this time you have given them cheaper bread–at best it is but a trifle cheaper than before; that change, however, is one comparatively immaterial; but you have created a regular and steady trade which may be stated at £15,000,000 a year; by that trade you have created a corresponding demand for the commodities of which they are the producers, their labour being an essential and principal element in their production, and it is the price their labour thus brings, not the price of cheapened commodities, that forms the main benefit they receive. That is the principle of a sound political economy applicable to commercial legislation, and that is the principle on which we will to-night invite you to proceed.

I may simply state, therefore, in passing, in regard to the tea and sugar duties, that we shall ask Parliament to renew them,–not to renew them for any lengthened period, but only for one year, with the further addition of three months till July, 1861; an addition for which we shall ask on the simple ground that the 1st of April is an inconvenient period, as it restricts too much the time within which Parliament has to consider the question.

SIR J. PAKINGTON: You propose to leave the duties as they are?

The CHANCELLOR of the EXCHEQUER: I mean to ask for the duties precisely as they now stand; that is, 1s. 5d. per pound on tea, and the duties on sugar, which are classified at various rates on the various descriptions, but which may be represented on the whole as being about 3s. the cwt. above the *minimum* point at which they stood fixed in 1853.

Having this far stated to the Committee the conviction of the Government that we ought to have remissions, and large remissions of duty–and further that we ought to have those particular remissions in reference to all others by which we may most effectually act upon the trade and commerce of the country, and upon the demand for the labour of the people–I come now to the question of the commercial treaty with France. And, Sir, I will confidently recommend the adoption of the treaty to the House, as fulfilling and satisfying all the conditions of the most beneficial kind of change in our commercial legislation. . . .

Part VI

LAW, PENAL SYSTEM, AND COURTS

LAW, PENAL SYSTEM, AND COURTS

Introduction

IT was to be anticipated that the Reform Act should bring with it an increasing demand for reform of the courts and the law. The middle classes to whom the Act extended power suffered in their business relations from the law's complexities and delays; the law was perhaps particularly the stronghold of the crusted brand of Toryism that had fought the Act to the last; and it was in the field of law reform that the genius of Bentham, the type and patron saint of middle-class intellectualism and reforming energy, had displayed itself first and on its most elaborate scale. But much had been started, and something achieved before the Act, and Professor Holdsworth, the great historian of English law, thinks it a fortunate circumstance that development was thus continuous. In criminal law, in particular, the labours of Romilly and McIntosh had culminated in the reforms of Peel, from 1826 onwards, which had relieved the law of many archaisms and drastically reduced the number of capital offences. The apparent vindictiveness of the older law was not wholly hard-heartedness; it was in large part a confession of weakness, a reflection of the lack of adequate police, which Peel began to rectify, and which was put right concurrently with later law reform.[1] Legislation had been driven to rely on terror; and the weapon broke short in its hands, for juries refused to convict when the penalty was both so harsh and so haphazard in its incidence. After 1833 the death penalty ceased to be more than exceptionally enforced except for murder. But the shadow of the gallows was still dark in the land; in 1836 there were nearly 500 condemnations to death, though only 34 people were actually hanged. In 1837 the death penalty was abolished for a further series of offences, and in 1861 six statutes, the product of a preceding labour of a number of years, consolidated and reformed large sections of criminal law. Executions continued to be public till 1868, and occasioned vast and often largely drunken gatherings, not always all drawn from the lower strata of society.

In 1828, in a great speech in the House of Commons, Brougham had elaborated a whole programme of legal reform. One of the obstacles to its carrying out began to be removed in 1830, with measures which, in a number of instances, substituted salaries for the fees by which court officials, and even judges, had hitherto been remunerated. This made procedural changes possible without undue hardship to individuals, and weakened an interest strongly opposed to reform. Brougham carried out a first simplification of the archaic mazes of the land law in 1833, and set up the Judicial Committee of the Privy Council as a court of appeal in colonial and ecclesiastical cases. He also worked with exemplary speed to reduce the arrears of Chancery decisions which Eldon, as fine a lawyer and hesitant a judge as he was a bad and bold politician, had left behind him. From the public point of view the outstanding grievances were the expense and delay of almost any civil actions, the centralization

[1] Part VIII.

in London of jurisdiction for any but the most trivial cases, and the separation between Equity and Chancery, and the Common Law and the Courts. The opportunities for evasion and delay,[1] and the difference between costs that the courts might award and the expenditure to which claimants in contested actions were put, were such as to make any attempt to enforce a small debt an adventure which might last months and even years, and cost many times the sum at stake. Equity offered many remedies which were not open to the common law courts. In complex cases interminable expense and delay might be occasioned by the necessity to recur from one to the other as the issues developed, or as the ingenuity of practitioners saw opportunities of obstruction or victory. In 1840 the Lords set up a select committee to inquire into the procedure and practice of Chancery and Exchequer Chambers. The extract from the evidence of a Chancery barrister at No. 157 illustrates a state of affairs which Jarndyce v. Jarndyce hardly parodied. After more than a decade of struggle, in which Brougham had been the chief protagonist, the County Court Act was carried in 1846.[2] The ancient county courts had been limited to £2 in their jurisdiction, and had largely ceased to function. In many places old Courts of Requests, or newer courts set up by recent statutes, did their best to meet local needs. In place of this patchwork the Act set up a uniform system of district courts all over the country. Primarily they were to deal with small debts and contracts, but it is noteworthy that a limited jurisdiction in equity, probate, and admiralty was also included in the courts' competence. Their business grew steadily and the Judicature Commission of 1867–1875 refers to the experiment as one that had so vindicated itself in public esteem as to make it impossible to go back on it.

In the 'fifties two Royal Commissions were at work concurrently on law reform, the one on the Common Law Courts and the other on Chancery. Legislation resulted from their Reports, and in its Third Report[3] the Commission on the Common Law Courts reported complacently that "the Technicalities which brought so much discredit on our jurisprudence" had now disappeared. This view was not generally accepted, however, and in particular the Judicature Commission of 1867–1875–set up as a result of action on the part of Roundell Palmer, afterwards Lord Selborne–emphasized the necessity of a single series of courts.[4] This was achieved by Selborne's Supreme Court of Judicature Act, 1873.[5] The case for the Act was expounded in the House of Commons by the Attorney-General, Sir J. D. Coleridge, and the intervention in the debate of Mr. C. M. Norwood "venturing to interrupt the flow of legal eloquence" expressed the strong approval of the business community. The original proposal had been that the new Court of Appeal should both supercede the Judicial Committee of the Privy Council, except on ecclesiastical matters, and take the place of the House of Lords as a final Court of Appeal. The first proposal was lost in debate, and before the second came into effect, amending legislation at the instance of Lord Cairns, Disraeli's Chancellor, restored the judicial power of the House of Lords. Provision was made, however, for the appointment of Lords of Appeal in Ordinary[6] to make sure that sufficient legal talent should be available in the House to make it an adequate and impressive tribunal. They were salaried, and sat in the House of Lords for life only. Amending legislation has added to or altered the detail of Lord Selborne's Act, but in substance the structure of the courts today is as it set them up. It is further noteworthy that the Act provided for annual meetings of the judges to consider current needs for reform.

[1] No. 162. [2] No. 160. [3] No. 162. [4] No. 163. [5] No. 167. [6] No. 168.

The blemishes that had made contact with the courts something that only the expert and the wily could with confidence essay, had thus been removed. In other, and even more fundamental aspects, the position of individuals was modified by legal reform in the period. A course of legislation, of which Acts of 1842[1] and 1869[2] are the most important, virtually did away with imprisonment for private debt. Thus the process, so familiar in Victorian fiction, and so frequent in fact in the lives of the improvident–the process that began with the bailiff's tap on the shoulder and ended in more or less squalor and splendour, for periods that might be weeks or might stretch into years, in the promiscuous yet not unordered society of a debtors' prison, passed from the scene. Another of the hazards that gave early Victorian life its melodramatic quality was eliminated. An Act of 1836[3] ended what had been, with few exceptions, the monopoly of the Established Church of the great stages of individual existence–baptism, marriage, and burial. Not only might the ceremonies now be performed in Dissenting places of worship, but it became possible to be married in purely secular fashion in a registrar's office. Divorce had always been possible, though, as Mr. Justice Maule's sentence on an unfortunate bigamist in 1845[4] shows, so difficult and costly as to be possible only exceptionally, and for the well-to-do. After a select committee of 1851–1853 had considered the issues, legislation in 1857 set up a regular and not impossibly expensive procedure by which divorce might be achieved.[5] Gladstone spoke against the Bill in the Commons a hundred times. Normally, at the time, a husband entered into complete control of his wife's property. With the aid of Chancery lawyers, where the property could stand the expense, it had been possible so to tie it up in a woman's name as to defeat this control. The Married Women's Property Act of 1870[6] made it possible for a woman, not necessarily well-to-do, to be a wife and still to preserve or acquire an economic independence of her husband. Legislation such as this entered into the texture of personal life. Still more, we can discover in it a movement away from a society based on institutions, and the status and consequence which these imply for individuals, to one in which institutions were judged, not so much by their place in the tradition and structure of society as a whole as by their immediate utility, and the fairness of their operation as between individual and individual.

Early prison reform, associated with the shining names of Howard and of Elizabeth Fry, had been primarily humanitarian. Bentham first directed the nation's thought to the consideration of penology as a science. An Act of Peel's, in 1824, obliged each county to have its jail and house of correction and to adopt some measure of classification of prisoners. Other reforming Acts were on the statute book: new prisons were built, and when there were warm-hearted and strong-willed individuals to lead, much was done to order and improve them. But not until Benthamite administrative machinery was brought to bear did progress on an equal front begin. A Lords Committee of 1835[7] sketches a programme; the institution of Prison Inspectors by an Act of the same year supplies the machinery. Extracts from their first Reports[8] illustrate on the one hand the administrative inertia that paralysed reform in many prisons and towns, and on the other the achievement in which the rising standard of justices' administration in the counties[9] had resulted. But prisons were still places of detention rather than punishment; debtors and the law's delay swelled and diversified their population; death and transportation were the principal

[1] No. 158. [2] No. 164. [3] No. 155. [4] No. 159. [5] No. 161.
[6] No. 165. [7] No. 153. [8] No. 154. [9] Part VIII.

punishments, and prevented, to some extent, the envisaging of the problem of a long-term prison population. It was on transportation that the attention of the 'thirties concentrated. When it was possible that the penalty for the theft of half a crown might be seven years' transportation, it can be seen how heavily its prospect might weigh on the labouring population. It was a sort of civil death, a severing of all the natural ties, though its defenders maintained that the heart-rending scenes which its imposition as a sentence occasioned in court were paralleled with the sailing of every emigrant ship. But as a punishment it was convenient; it seemed to offer society the chance of a permanent excision of the offending element, and it could be argued, not wholly without reason, that it gave the offenders a chance of a new start in a new country. It was also a method of plantation. New South Wales had become the principal place to which convicts were sent after the loss of the American colonies. With the growth of population, the social dislocation and crime of the early years of the century, and the numbers thus sent out, the problems raised could no longer be ignored. The Molesworth Report[1] is the classic discussion of them. Few state papers make more lurid and terrible reading. Yet it must not be forgotten that humanity kept breaking in. Many transported peasants and mechanics under kindlier masters, and such there were, though they do not figure largely in the Report, found their labour better appreciated and paid for than at home, and won their way finally to a position which might not otherwise have come within their reach. The instance of the emancipist who made an immense fortune–the original, no doubt, of Dickens's Magwitch–"No one has done as well as me–I am famous for it"–was exceptional, but neither unique nor wholly misleading. In 1841 the assignment system was done away with. But no subsequent inquiry, and there were several, reported against the system of transportation as a whole, and the pressure for its abolition came from Australia, not England, and then was not altogether unanimous. The last convict ship to Australia sailed in 1867.

Meanwhile reform proceeded in England. In the late 'thirties and 'forties more than forty new prisons were built. In 1853 the Penal Servitude Act began the organization of long-term imprisonment as a punishment. It was followed by others which organized remission for good conduct and created the ticket-of-leave system. The Parkhurst Prison Act of 1838 set this prison aside for juveniles. Reformatories began to be founded; a Youthful Offenders Act of 1854 gave powers to send to them; industrial schools followed, and between 1854 and 1867 thirty-six boys' and fourteen girls' reformatories were established. Here again the work of devoted individuals sowed the seed and watered the growing plants. In the discussions and papers on penology in the period, criticisms of flogging, except for whipping instead of prison, for juvenile first offenders; insistence on the 'separate' or even the 'silent' system to minimize the danger of evil communications; the value of work, preferably work that was in itself useful, but failing that the treadmill; the necessity of strict and uniform discipline, but the recognition, as well, that prisoners are accessible to hope and better feelings, are the predominant notes. In 1877 the prisons of the country were finally placed under Home Office control. The legislation of the century had achieved immense results, firstly in limiting prison as a punishment to those guilty of crime and not merely of misfortune or improvidence; secondly in humanizing and systematizing conditions in the prisons themselves. Rule and uniformity, justice, as men can understand it, had replaced variety, capriciousness, and even, no doubt, cruelty. These were

[1] No. 156.

important results, even if it is true that the spirit, even of criminals, is wayward, and finds its occasion as often in variety as in rule, and that the problem of making prison as little as may be a prison of the spirit as well as of the body, remained, as it still remains, a challenge to administration and administrators.

SELECT BIBLIOGRAPHY

The subjects of the present Part were not of sufficient party and political interest to attract many great parliamentary debates. The energy of Brougham and Cottenham was mainly responsible–after long efforts–for the County Court Act of 1846, and the speech of the latter on the Second Reading of the Bill gives a valuable historical summary of these efforts. The Divorce Act of 1857 occasioned violent parliamentary controversy, but perhaps generated more heat than light. The debates on the Supreme Court of Judicature Act, 1873, on the other hand, befitted their subject, and in both Houses were full and valuable.

Parliamentary Papers provide a mass of material. The *Report of the Lords Committee on the Administration of Justice* of 1840 (*Parlty. Papers*, 1840/xv) discusses, primarily, the shortcomings of Chancery and the Exchequer Courts. *Returns* of 1847–1848 (*Parlty. Papers*, 1847–1848/li) give figures of the early work of the county courts. A *Report of Commissioners on County Courts* in 1854 further examines their work and makes many suggestions for reform (*Parlty. Papers*, 1854–1855/xviii). In 1851, Commissioners were appointed to inquire into the Processes, Practice and Pleadings of the Superior Courts. Their successive *Reports* are in 1851, 1853, and 1860 (*Parlty. Papers*, 1851/xxii, 1852–1853/xl, 1857, sess. 2/xxi, and 1860/xxxi). At the same time a commission was sitting on Chancery, and reported at intervals (*Parlty. Papers*, 1852/xxi, 1854/xxiv, i, 1856/xxii, i, 1863/xv, 1866/xvii and 1867/xix). A Royal Commission on Divorce reported in 1853 (*Parlty. Papers*, 1852–1853/xl). Questions of the consolidation of statute law were very much to the fore in these discussions, and a commission was appointed in 1866 to consider a Digest of Law (*Parlty. Papers*, 1869/xix and 1870/xviii). Meanwhile a fresh commission–the Judicature Commission–had been appointed, and reported at intervals (*First Report*, *Parlty. Papers*, 1868–1869/xxv; *Second Report*, 1872/xx; *Third, Fourth and Fifth Reports*, 1874/xxiv). Its discussions thus overlapped the passing of the High Court of Judicature Act.

A. V. Dicey, *Law and Opinion in England* (London, 1920), is the classic and indispensable background. F. W. Maitland and F. C. Montague, *A Sketch of English Legal History* (London, 1915), and Edward Jenks, *A Short History of English Law* (London, 1912), afford no more than very general views of this period. The sketch by Mr. Justice C. S. C. Bowen, "The Administration of the Law, 1837–87", in *The Reign of Queen Victoria*, edited by T. H. Ward (London, 1887), is excellent; so, also, is J. Blake Odgers, *A Century of Law Reform* (London, 1903). But until Sir William Holdsworth's monumental *History of English Law* is completed (vols. 1–13, London, 1923–1952; vol. 13, ed. A. L. Goodhart and H. G. Hanbury, 1952; vol. 14 still to be issued), the historical student is ill-served in the secondary works on the subject. W. S. Holdsworth, *Dickens as a Legal Historian* (Yale, 1928), is a valuable study. Sir James Stephen, *History of Criminal Law* (3 vols., London, 1883), L. Radzinowicz, *History of English Criminal Law and its Administration from 1750*: vol. 1, *Movements for Reform* (London, 1948), and Sir T. Snagge, *Evolution of County Courts* (London, 1904), are valuable for their subjects.

On the state of prisons a Lords Committee of 1835 issued five *Reports*, supported by valuable evidence, including that of Samuel Hoare and Elizabeth Fry commending the reformatory schools for juveniles then privately established, and advocating wide reforms (*Parlty. Papers*, 1835/xi and xii). A select committee of the Commons in 1836 also advocated reforms (*Parlty. Papers*, 1836/xxi). The *First Report of the Inspectors of Prisons* appeared in 1836 (*Parlty. Papers*, 1836/xxxv). Thereafter *Reports* appear annually, though their historical interest diminishes as uniformity tended to establish itself. The classic paper on transportation is that of the Select Committee of 1836–1838 (the Molesworth Committee), a drastic *Report*, backed by a horrifying body of evidence (*Parlty. Papers*, 1836/xix and 1837–1838/xxii). But later *Reports* do not accept all its conclusions. Later important papers are the *Lords Select Committee on the Execution of the Criminal Law*, especially as regards juvenile offenders (*Parlty. Papers*, 1847/vii); the

Commons Select Committee on Prison Discipline (*Parlty. Papers*, 1850/xvii); the *Reports of the Lords and the Commons Select Committees on Transportation* (*Parlty. Papers*, 1856/xvii), a further *Select Committee on Transportation* (*Parlty. Papers*, 1861/xiii), a *Lords Select Committee on Prison Discipline* (*Parlty. Papers*, 1863/ix); and the *Report of the Commissioners on Penal Servitude* (the Grey Commission) (*Parlty. Papers*, 1863/xxi). The later *Report of the Penal Servitude Commissioners of 1868–9* (*Parlty. Papers*, 1878–1879/xxxvii and xxxviii), opens with a history of the subject, and contains a mass of evidence and an index.

S. and B. Webb, *English Prisons under Local Government* (London, 1922), and R. S. E. Hinde, *The British Penal System, 1773–1950* (London, 1951), are leading secondary authorities. G. Rusche and O. Kircheimer, *Punishment and the Social Structure* (New York, 1929), and Max Grunhüt, *Penal Reform* (Oxford, 1946), though primarily expository, contain also a great deal of historical material.

Sir William Holdsworth's *History of English Law* has reached vol. xvi (1966), the last three volumes dealing with the Victorian period.

L. Radzinowicz's *History of English Criminal Law and its Administration* has now reached vol. iv.

153. Second report of the Lords' Select Committee on Gaols and Houses of Correction (1835)

Parlty. Papers, 1835/xi–Conclusions.

1st. That it is expedient that One uniform System of Prison Discipline be established in every Gaol and House of Correction in England and Wales.

2nd. That, for the sake of securing Uniformity of Discipline, it is expedient that the Rules and Regulations of the Gaols shall in future be submitted to the Secretary of State for his Approval, instead of, as at present, to the Judges of Assize.

3rd. That Inspectors of Prisons be appointed to visit the Prisons from Time to Time, and to report to the Secretary of State.

4th. That entire Separation, except during the Hours of Labour and of Religious Worship, and Instruction, is absolutely necessary for preventing Contamination, and for securing a proper System of Prison Discipline.

5th. That Silence be enforced, so as to prevent all Communication between Prisoners both before and after Trial.

6th. That Persons whose Trials have been postponed, or who, having been tried, have been acquitted on the Ground of Insanity, shall not be Confined in the Gaols or Houses of Correction.

7th. That the Officers of the Prisons shall not be permitted to receive any Portion of the Prisoners Earnings.

8th. That the Earnings of convicted Prisoners shall be hereafter paid to the Fund out of which the Prison is maintained.

9th. That the Dietary of every Prison be subject to the Approval of the Secretary of State as a Part of the Prison Rules and Regulations, and that it is most desirable that convicted Prisoners should not be permitted to receive other than the Gaol Allowance; but if in any Case of very urgent and special Necessity the Surgeons should order any Increase of Diet to a Prisoner not in the Infirmary, he shall state in his Journal the Cause and Extent of such Order.

10th. That the Practice in some Prisons, and in certain Cases, of paying Money to the Prisoners in lieu of supplying them either wholly or in part with Food or Fuel, be declared to be illegal.

11th. That the Use of Tobacco in any shape by the Prisoners be prohibited in every Prison.

12th. That convicted Prisoners be not permitted to receive Visits or Letters from their Friends during the first Six Months of their Imprisonment, unless under peculiar and pressing Circumstances.

13th. That the Use of Day-rooms, as such, be discontinued.

14th. That no Wardsman, Monitor, Yardsman, or Prisoner be permitted to sell any thing whatever, or to let out to Hire any Article to any Person confined in the Prison.

15th. That where the Chaplain shall be appointed to a Prison or Prisons, and the Number of Prisoners, including Debtors, which it is calculated may be received therein shall not be less than Fifty, it is most desirable that the Time of such Chaplain should be devoted to the Duties of such Prison or Prisons, that he should not hold any other Preferment with Cure of Souls, and that he should reside as near as possible to the same.

16th. That in every Prison wherein the Number of Prisoners exceeds Fifty a Schoolmaster, not being one of the Prisoners, shall be appointed.

17th. That every Prison be provided with a certain Number of solitary Cells for the Punishment of refractory Prisoners.

18th. That in Cases where the Punishment of whipping is resorted to it is expedient that it should be defined as regards both the Extent to which it may be carried and the Instruments with which it may be inflicted.

19th. That at every Michaelmas Quarter Sessions Twelve specified Days be appointed, *viz.* Three in Each Quarter, and that on each of such Days the Visiting Justices do visit and inspect the Prison under their Charge, according to the Provisions of the Sixteenth and Seventeenth Sections of the Gaol Act.

154A -B. Prison Inspectors: First report (1836)

Parlty. Papers, 1836/xxv/pp. 16–20 and 271–272.

154A. Newgate

... We first visited that part of the prison called the Chapel Yard. To this are attached three rooms or wards, Nos. 10, 11, and 12, which the prisoners occupy by day, and in which they sleep at night. All the prisoners have access to the yard, and can go to all the rooms. In this yard there are at times 50 or 60 prisoners. When first visited by us the number was 20, of whom we found in room No. 10, eight; No. 11 six; and in No. 12, six.

Here were associated together the convicted and the untried, the felon and the misdemeanant, the sane and the insane, the old and young offender. In the Appendix to our Report will be found a return of the names, ages, offences, and date of admission, of all the prisoners in the above-mentioned wards on the day on which we first inspected them, together with the date of trial of such as had been convicted. By reference to this return, it will be seen that all the classes, which are required by the Gaol Act to be kept distinct, ("care being taken that prisoners of those classes do not intermix with each other,") are here confounded together; and, as if to increase the evil, and to show a greater contempt for the law, there is also added the insane.

In ward No. 10 we found that the wardsman, a convicted prisoner, owned all the bedding, the crockery ware, the knives, forks, kettles and saucepans for the use of which each prisoner pays him 2s. 6d. per week. The above-mentioned articles are purchased for the purpose by the wardsman, upon his appointment to his situation. —— who was wardsman until a few days ago in this ward (No. 10), paid, on his appointment, £3. 10s. The present wardsman, —— has as yet paid nothing; but if he continues in his situation he will do so, and will receive from the prisoners the usual weekly pay. In this ward, in consequence of the high demand of money for extra accommodations, such as are considered the most decent and respectable of the prisoners are usually placed; and it appeared to us, that as many as were able to pay the sum required, readily found admission into it.

There was a good supply of Bibles and Prayer-books, provided by the prison, together with other religious books, the gift of a Captain Brown. These books, particularly the Bibles, bore little appearance of having been used.

On examining the cupboards of this ward we discovered a pack of cards, apparently much used, a cribbage-board and pegs, and two draught-boards and men. We also found four tobacco pipes, in some of which the tobacco still remained; and a box with tobacco in it. These, though forbidden by the prison regulations, were quite exposed on the shelves of the cupboards, and must have been detected, on the most superficial inspection of the ward, by any officer of the prison.

We found also a bundle of newspapers, twelve in all; and, upon inquiring, we were informed that a daily paper is taken in, in this ward. The newsman who lives next door to the Giltspur-street Compter, and who is also a tobacconist, brings it regularly every day to his customers, the prisoners, to whom he has access, unattended by an officer. One of the principal turnkeys, who accompanied us, said that the daily papers were allowed by the governor, but that no Sunday paper was admitted; such papers, he said, were strictly forbidden. This he told us aloud, in the hearing of the prisoners. But we subsequently ascertained that Sunday papers were as publicly brought into the prison on the Sunday morning, as the other papers were during the rest of the week; that several of them were purchased by the prisoners in the different wards of the prison; that during the whole of Sunday they were openly used by the prisoners; that on Sunday evenings the turnkey above alluded to regularly borrowed the Sunday paper, The Dispatch, from a prisoner, and returned it to him on the Monday.

We found porter in a bottle on the shelf, though none could have been brought into the ward since one o'clock the day before.

The wardsman had a snuff-box and snuff, which he used continually and openly: there was also another snuff-box in the ward; and each prisoner, if he liked, might have had one.

We observed in the cupboard mince pies and cold provisions, any quantity of which may be brought in by the friends of the prisoners – to the untried three times, and to the convicted once a week; but, as these are indiscriminately mixed together, they assist one another in having a regular and abundant supply of provisions, which all, both untried and convicted, procure by means of money or friends.

We found two boxes, containing two or three strong files, four bradawls, several large iron spikes, screws, nails and knives; all of them instruments calculated to facilitate attempts at breaking out of prison, and capable of becoming most dangerous weapons in the hands of desperate and determined men.

We also found several books: amongst them Guthries' *Grammar*, a song book, the *Keepsake Annual* for 1836, and the —— by ——, 18 plates, published by Stockdale, 1827. This last is a book of a most disgusting nature, and the plates are obscene and indecent in the extreme. It was claimed as his property by a prisoner named ——, and was kept in the cupboard without any attempt at concealment. We also met with large bundles of papers, which on examination proved to be rough draughts of briefs for the use of prisoners' counsel; and were informed by one of the principal turnkeys, that the wardsman of No. 10, Chapel Yard, and also the wardsman of the Master's Side Yard, are permitted by the prison authorities to draw briefs for the defence of prisoners, both male and female, and to receive 5s. for each brief.

Last sessions ——, a prisoner, drew 11 briefs (eight for males, and three for females,) and received the money for the whole. One of the principal turnkeys informed us that he had known some sessions, and that not long ago, in which the wardsman had drawn from 20 to 30 briefs. The wardsman who draws the brief has the prisoner (if a male) brought to him, and from him he receives the particulars of his case. If the brief is for a female, the wardsman goes round to that part of the prison occupied by the females, and there converses with the female prisoner, separated from her only by open iron railings, not in the hearing, nor at all times in the sight, of any officer, male or female. Sometimes the female is admitted to the male side of the prison, and sees the wardsman who is to draw her brief in a room called the "Bread Room." Before the present Session the female prisoner was at these times unaccompanied by any female officer. Under the present regulations one of the matrons accompanies the female prisoner when admitted to the male side; but when the wardsman takes the statements of the female prisoner at the gate or visiting railings of the female prison, the interview is quite private. The facts upon which the brief is to be prepared are frequently stated aloud in the ward, and difficult points of a defence are occasionally discussed amongst the prisoners before the brief is drawn.

There were also in this cupboard several small blank paper books, which one of the ladies who visit Newgate had left with the prisoners, in order that they might write in them answers to Scripture questions given to them by her. The books were applied to different purposes; some contained the sentences, names, and residences of prisoners who had been in the ward, and accounts of debts owing by the prisoners to the wardsman. We learned that the wardsman supplied to the ward candles, blacking, paper, salt, newspapers, pens, ink, and paper, for which collections were made amongst the prisoners weekly; occasions on which the wardsman is enabled to make additional profits.

Visitors are admitted to the untried three days in each week (Monday, Thursday and Saturday); to the convicted but on one day weekly (Tuesday) from half past ten in the forenoon till two in the afternoon.

In this yard the visitors are admitted close to the prisoners, separated only by open iron railings, and rarely in the presence of an officer.

Though it is said that only one person is allowed by the prison regulations to visit any prisoner on the visiting days, yet, in addition to our having seen several friends at one time visiting the same prisoners, we found that there are several modes of evading this rule; for, as all the prisoners have access to the yard during the visiting hours, any one prisoner may see the friends of all the rest; and, under the pretence of seeing different prisoners, a number of friends may contrive to hold unrestricted intercourse with any one prisoner.

Visitors are searched at the outer lodge; men by a male officer, and women by a female, who are always in attendance for that purpose. But from the number of visitors, which on some days amounts to 100 or 150, the shortness of the time for the search of so many, the disagreeable nature of the duty, the impossibility of its being effectively performed, and the result of our inquiries among prisoners and officers, we are satisfied that various improper and dangerous articles, such as cards, tobacco, watch-spring saws and fine files, to aid attempts to escape, pocket fire-arms, powder and balls, might with ease be introduced to a considerable and alarming extent.

Cold provisions, in any quantity, are brought in; whole joints, meat pies, and almost any kind of delicacy, find their way unchallenged both to untried and convicted prisoners. Money, also, to any amount is admitted; and we have reason to know that individuals have had in their possession several sovereigns at one time.

When we visited the rooms, there was a comfortable fire in each of them, round which the prisoners were seated at their ease; and we noticed scarcely anything in the apartments that indicated the discomfort or privations of a place of penal confinement.

The untried and convicted were treated exactly alike. Of the latter, several pass the whole time of their sentence in the same room, and under the same treatment, with those who are awaiting their trial, and merely retained for safe custody. The convicted, by availing themselves of the good offices of the untried, (who are generally willing to aid their companions in every way,) are enabled to procure provisions and other comforts, as before their trial: so that the only additional privation to which their conviction subjects them is that nominal one which consists in a restriction as to the visits of their friends to one day in the week instead of three.

Visitors bring clean linen likewise, as no provision is made for washing the linen of the prisoners in the prison: and as scarcely sufficient soap is allowed to wash even a shirt, a prisoner who has no friends is in a manner constrained to use his foul linen.

Among the visitors, persons of notoriously bad character, prostitutes, and thieves, find admission. Many of the prostitutes are very young girls, sometimes not more than twelve or thirteen years of age: others have visited different men, yet are admitted under the name of wives and sisters. Several prisoners have informed us that such characters are common among the visitors; and the officers whom we have examined have acknowledged that though they use precautions to exclude bad characters, yet many such they know have daily ingress; and that they have the governor's permission to admit to a man who has no respectable friends, the woman or girl he has lived with, that she may supply him with provisions and clean linen: this permission extends both to the untried and to the convicted.

The beer-man comes into the prison every day from twelve till one, with four three-gallon cans: when they are empty, he sends his boy for more. Sometimes an officer is at the yard gate, who may be present at the distribution of the beer; but this is not generally the case.

The wardsman, a prisoner, usually receives the beer, and hands it to the prisoner. A pint only is allowed by the prison regulations to each prisoner daily, whether untried or convicted; But no steps are taken to limit the supply to the regulated quantity: no account is taken of the quantity brought into the prison, nor of the number of pints served to the different wards, nor of the prisoners who have received their allowance, who may and do often come twice or thrice; so that not only can those who have money obtain the pints which may be drawn for those who have none, but even a much larger quantity than a pint for every man confined in the ward may be, and constantly is, obtained.

We observed the beer-man distributing the beer, no officer being present to see that no more than the proper quantity of beer was received by the prisoners, who in fact might, unchecked, have obtained as much as they chose to purchase. And from our own observation, the statements of prisoners, and those of officers at present in the prison, we have no hesitation in expressing our belief, that almost any quantity of beer which the prisoners can afford to purchase may be brought into the wards.

In visiting No. 11 ward in Chapel Yard we found six prisoners. There are sometimes as many as sixteen or more confined in this room.

The wardsman, a prisoner under sentence of two years' imprisonment for conspiracy, had been nine months in confinement, during seven of which he had filled that office. He had no bedding to let out; but had a bed for himself, his own property. The crockery, tinware, knives, forks, and basons, also belonged to him; and for the use of these he is allowed to charge the prisoners 1s. per week, ward dues. Some paid, and some did not. He would not inform us what he paid, on his appointment, for his stock of goods, nor the amount of his weekly receipts. But his weekly profits must at times be considerable. He supplies the prisoners with salt, pepper, candles, blacking, hearthstone and whiting; and occasionally makes collections of a penny or more, according to the number, from each prisoner in this ward for these articles, and for the purchase of a newspaper on Sundays. The wardsman informed us, in the hearing of one of the principal turnkeys (by whom he was not contradicted), that the newsman regularly brought the Sunday newspapers about half-past eight on the Sunday morning; that the ward below always purchased one or more, and that most frequently his ward did the same, though they could not afford a daily paper. He added, that this paper was openly read in the ward, from the time it was received until the hour of Divine Service; and, after chapel was over, all the remainder of the day; and he stated that he never heard that the purchase or perusal on a Sunday of the Sunday papers was forbidden by the Governor or any officer. In this ward the prisoners sometimes borrowed the newspaper belonging to the ward below.

The prisoners sleep on rope mats, and have two rugs to cover them. The mats are laid upon the floor at night, and are rolled up and put by on a shelf, or are hung up against the walls during the day. These mats may be placed as close together as the prisoners choose; and on our visits at night to the wards, we found them sleeping, some by themselves, others two, three, and even four together, as close as bodies could possibly be placed.

All the other particulars of ward No. 10, as to provisions, visits of friends, money, and beer, are applicable to this and every other ward in the prison, except perhaps the cells, in some minor points.

The ward was well supplied with Bibles, Prayer-books, and other religious books; but they did not seem to have been much used. On the table was a volume of Mavor's *British Tourist.*

154B. Southern and Western Counties

London, 1 February, 1836.

My Lord,

I HAVE the honour to transmit to your Lordship the results of my first visit to the Southern and Western District, embracing certain portions of the Counties of Dorset, Gloucester, Hants, Hereford, Leicester, Northampton, Oxford, Salop, Somerset, Warwick and Worcester.

I have much gratification in stating to your Lordship the cordial reception which I have uniformly experienced on the part of the Visiting Magistrates, and, with scarcely an exception, from the officers of the prisons. The former gentlemen, instead of construing our mission into a possible interference with their own province, sought opportunities of meeting me, and most liberally facilitated my inquiries: and the latter often voluntarily pointed out defects, inconveniences and bad usages, expressing, at the same time, their satisfaction in this additional occasion of subjecting the details of their establishment to examination.

In all the County Gaols which I have entered, a remarkable degree of cleanliness and neatness has reigned throughout, equalling that which is usually maintained among the middle classes in England, and largely surpassing the standard which generally prevails in the most splendid residences of Continental Europe. This observation will not be considered trivial by those who appreciate the influence which these two qualities daily exercise over the health of the body, and the discipline of the mind. Among the Borough and Town Gaols, and those placed under local jurisdiction, these characteristics are far less prominent, and sometimes, indeed, are scarcely visible; but these blemishes appear to me, in the various shades in which they exist, to be derived rather from the narrow space and unsuitableness of the building, from the limited funds, the scanty salaries, and the insufficient service, than from wilful neglect on the part of the keepers, who, indeed, are often sensible of evils which they do not possess the power of remedying.

From the recent introduction of silence into some prisons I have not yet been able to trace a single instance of mischievous consequences. My conversations with prisoners, officers, surgeons, chaplains and magistrates, have not led to the discovery of any case in which disease, either of body or of mind, has been affirmed by any party to have grown out of this mode of discipline. The experiment, it is true, has not yet been practised for a long period; but I am bound to add, that all the persons most conversant with the interior of prisons, who have favoured me with their conclusions on this head, pronounce decidedly in its favour, and entertain an expectation of its probable efficacy in increasing the repugnance to incarceration.

In some few prisons I have noticed a scale of diet which has to me appeared insufficient. Such an opinion has not been forced upon me by any strong remonstrances on the part of the prisoners, nor by any symptoms of disease which seemed to be the result, nor by any alterations of physiognomy, but entirely by general considerations. A diet may be too small for the necessities of man, even although it does not produce a speedy and sensible change in the form and constitution: its effects may operate slowly and invisibly on his frame, and may reserve their complete development for a remote period of his life, entailing thus a future punishment which the well-intentioned advisers would be the last to desire or to anticipate.

The branch of my inquiries which has afforded me the most unmixed satisfaction is that which relates to the proportion of deaths which occurs in the principal gaols which I have visited. The rate of mortality is, in most of these abodes, so remarkably low, that I can confidently affirm, that in very few situations of life is an adult less likely to die than in a well-conducted English prison. A singular contrast is presented, in this respect, by the majority of foreign ones. In the prisons of Paris the annual mortality has been estimated at 1 in 23 annually; at the depot of Mendicity of St. Denis, at Paris, it has even amounted, according to Villerme, to nearly 1 in 3 annually. The yearly deaths in the principal prisons of the Netherlands were estimated, a few years since, by Quetelet, at 1 in 27. Similar facts might be cited from the prisons of Germany and of America.

Previously to any extension of the plan of confinement in separate cells during the day, it appears highly necessary to consider the various modes of warming the cells which may be most conveniently adopted in different prisons. This is a point which requires the immediate attention of those who may contemplate the introduction of any such system into the establishments which they superintend.

Several Magistrates have intimated to me their expectation that the Inspectors of Prisons will hereafter recommend certain general measures relating to the economy of prisons. So candid a disposition, on their part, to receive, renders it doubly incumbent that the utmost caution should be used in proposing; and I presume to offer my conviction, that it can only be after a far more extensive investigation, and after long and earnest deliberation, that an attempt can with safety be made to establish any general principles.

I have the honour to remain, my Lord,
Your Lordship's most obedient servant,
(BISSET HAWKINS.)

To the Right honourable the Secretary of State
for the Home Department.

155. Civil Marriage Act (1836)

Statutes of the Realm, 6 & 7 Wm. IV c 85.

Whereas it is expedient to amend the law of Marriages in England: Be it enacted by the King's most Excellent Majesty, by and with the Advice and Consent of the Lords Spiritual and Temporal, and Commons, in this present Parliament assembled, and by the Authority of the same, That after the First Day of March in the Year One thousand eight hundred and thirty-seven, notwithstanding any thing in this Act contained, all the Rules prescribed by the Rubrick concerning the solemnizing of Marriages shall continue to be duly observed by every Person in Holy Orders of the Church of England who shall solemnize any Marriage in England: Provided always, that where by any Law or Canon in force before the passing of this

Act it is provided that any Marriage may be solemnized after Publication of Banns, such Marriage may be solemnized in like Manner on Production of the Registrar's Certificate as herein-after provided; provided also, that nothing in this Act contained shall affect the Right of the Archbishop of Canterbury and his Successors, and his and their proper Officers, to grant Special Licenses to marry at any convenient Time and Place, or the Right of any Surrogate or other Person now having Authority to grant Licences for Marriages. . . .

18. And be it enacted, That any Proprietor or Trustee of a separate Building, certified according to Law as a Place of Religious Worship, may apply to the Superintendent Registrar of the District, in order that such Building may be registered for solemnizing Marriages therein, and in such Case shall deliver to the Superintendent Registrar a Certificate, signed in Duplicate by Twenty Householders at the least, that such Building has been used by them during One Year at the least as their usual Place of public Religious Worship, and that they are desirous that such Place should be registered as aforesaid, each of which Certificates shall be countersigned by the Proprietor or Trustee by whom the same shall be delivered; and the Superintendent Registrar shall send both Certificates to the Registrar General, who shall register such Building accordingly in a Book to be kept for that Purpose at the General Register Office; and the Registrar General shall indorse on both Certificates the Date of the Registry, and shall keep one Certificate with the other Records of the General Register Office, and shall return the other Certificate to the Superintendent Registrar, who shall keep the same with the other Records of his Office; and the Superintendent Registrar shall enter the Date of the Registry of such Building in a Book to be furnished to him for that Purpose by the Registrar General, and shall give a Certificate of such Registry under his Hand, on Parchment or Vellum, to the Proprietor or Trustee by whom the Certificates are countersigned, and shall give public Notice of the Registry thereof by Advertisement in some Newspaper circulating within the County, and in the *London Gazette*; and for every such Entry, Certificate, and Publication the Superintendent Registrar shall receive at the Time of the Delivery to him of the Certificates the Sum of Three Pounds. . . .

21. And be it enacted, That any Persons who shall object to marry under the Provisions of this Act in any such registered Building may, after due Notice and Certificate issued as aforesaid, contract and solemnize Marriage at the Office and in the Presence of the Superintendent Registrar and some Registrar of the District, and in the Presence of Two Witnesses, with open Doors, and between the Hours aforesaid, making the Declaration and using the Form of Words herein-before provided in the Case of Marriage in any such registered Building. . . .

156. Transportation: Molesworth report (1838)

Parlty. Papers, 1837–1838/XXII/pp. 5–21.

. . . After sentence of transportation has been passed, convicts are sent to the hulks or gaols, where they remain till the period of their departure arrives. On board convict vessels the convicts are under the sole control of the surgeon-superintendent, who is furnished with instructions, as to his conduct, from the Admiralty. The precautions, which have been taken against disease, and the better discipline now preserved in these ships, have applied an effectual remedy to the physical evils of the long voyage to Australia, and prevented the mortality amongst the prisoners, which prevailed to a fearful extent during the earlier periods of transportation. Little diminution, however, has taken place in those moral evils, which seem to be the necessary consequences of the close contact and communication between so many criminals, both during the period of confinement previous to embarkation, and during the weariness of a long voyage.

As soon as a convict vessel reaches its place of destination, a report is made by the surgeon-superintendent to the governor. A day is then appointed for the colonial secretary, or for his deputy, to go on board, to muster the convicts, and to hear their complaints if they have any to make. The male convicts are, subsequently, removed to the convict barracks; the females to the penitentiaries. In New South Wales, however, regulations have lately been established, by which, in most cases, female convicts are enabled to proceed at once from the ship to private service. It is the duty of an officer, called the principal superintendent of convicts, to classify the newly-arrived convicts; the greater portion of whom are distributed amongst the settlers as assigned servants; the remainder are either retained in the employment of the government, or some few of them are sent to the penal settlements.

In 1836 the number of assigned convicts in Van Diemen's Land was 6,475; in New South Wales in 1835 the number was 20,207. In the earlier periods of the colony of New South Wales the supply of convicts so much exceeded the demand for their services by the settlers, that the Government used to grant certain indulgences to those settlers, who were willing to maintain convicts. More recently, the demand has exceeded the supply; the obtaining convict labourers has become, therefore, to a certain degree a matter of favour, which has given rise to complaints of abuse in the distribution, especially of the more valuable convicts. All applications for convicts are now made to an officer, called the commissioner for the assignment of convict servants, who is guided in his distribution of them by certain Government regulations. Settlers, to whom convicts are assigned, are bound to send for them within a certain period of time, and to pay the sum of £1 a head for the clothing and bedding of each assigned convict. An assigned convict is entitled to a fixed amount of food and clothing, consisting, in New South Wales, of 12 lbs. of wheat, or of an equivalent in flour and maize meal, 7 lbs. of mutton or beef, or 4½ lbs. of salt pork, 2 oz. of salt, and 2 oz. of soap weekly; two frocks or jackets, three shirts, two pair of trousers, three pair of shoes, and a hat or cap, annually. Each man is likewise supplied with one good blanket, and a paliasse or wool mattress, which are considered the property of the master. Any articles, which the master may supply beyond these, are voluntary indulgences. The allowance in Van Diemen's Land differs in some particulars, and on the whole is more liberal.

Male assigned convicts may be classed under the various heads of field labourers, domestic servants, and mechanics: the services of the last class being of more value than those of the two former, are estimated in assignment as equal to those of two or more field labourers. In the assignment of convicts scarcely any distinction is made either on account of the period of the sentence, or on account of the age, the character, or the nature of the offence of the convict. The previous occupation of a convict in this country mainly determines his condition in the penal colonies. For instance, domestic servants, transported for any offence, are assigned as domestic servants in Australia: for the greater portion of such servants in those colonies, even in the establishments of the wealthiest classes, have hitherto been transported felons. They are well fed, well clothed, and receive wages from £10 to £15 a year, and are as well treated in respectable families, as similar descriptions of servants are in this country. In many instances, masters have even carried to an illegal extent their indulgences to their convict servants.

Convicts, who are mechanics, are as well, if not better, treated, than those, who are domestic servants; for as every kind of skilled labour is very scarce in New South Wales, a convict, who has been a blacksmith, carpenter, mason, cooper, wheelwright, or gardener, is a most valuable servant, worth three or four ordinary convicts; he is eagerly sought after, and great interest is made to obtain him. As a mechanic can scarcely be compelled by punishment to exert his skill, it is for the interest of the master to conciliate his convict mechanic in order to induce him to work well; in too many cases this is effected by granting to the skilled convict various indulgences; by paying him wages; by allotting to him task-work, and by permitting him, after the performance of the task, to work on his own account; and, lastly, by conniving at, or overlooking disorderly conduct; for the most skilful mechanics are generally the worst behaved, and most drunken.

The condition, however, of by far the most numerous class of convicts, those, who are employed, as shepherds or neatherds, (of whom in 1837 there were above 8,000 in New South Wales), and in agriculture generally, is undoubtedly inferior to that of a convict, who is either a domestic servant or a mechanic; they are, however, according to most of the witnesses better fed, than the generality of agricultural labourers in this country; most masters either pay them wages in money, or give them, instead of money, tea, sugar, tobacco, spirits, and other trifling indulgences.

On the whole, therefore, Your Committee may assert that, in the families of well-conducted and respectable settlers, the condition of assigned convicts is much the same, as the condition of similar descriptions of servants in this country; but this is by no means the case in the establishments of all settlers. As the lot of a slave depends upon the character of his master, so the condition of a convict depends upon the temper and disposition of the settler, to whom he is assigned. On this account Sir George Arthur, late Governor of Van Diemen's Land, likened the convict to a slave, and described him "as deprived of liberty, exposed to all the caprice of the family, to whose service he may happen to be assigned, and subject to the most summary laws;" "his condition (said Sir George) in no respect differs from that of the slave, except that his master cannot apply corporal punishment by his own hands, or those of his overseer, and has a property in him for a limited period. Idleness and insolence of expression, or of looks, anything betraying the insurgent spirit, subject him to the chaingang or the triangle, or hard labour on the roads." Sir R. Bourke, the late Governor of New South Wales, has designated as a slave code, the law which, in that colony, enables a magistrate, generally himself a master of convicts, to inflict 50 lashes on a convict for "drunkenness, disobedience of orders, neglect of work, absconding, abusive language to his master or overseer, or any other disorderly or dishonest conduct." For these offences the convict may likewise be punished by imprisonment, solitary confinement, and labour in irons on the roads. That this law is by no means inoperative, is proved by the fact that, in 1835, the number of summary convictions in New South Wales amounted to 22,000, though the number of convicts in the colony did not exceed 28,000; that in one month in 1833, 247 convicts were flogged in that colony, and 9,784 lashes inflicted, which would give for the year, 2,964 floggings, and above 108,000 lashes inflicted chiefly for insolence, insubordination, and neglect of work. In Van Diemen's Land the law, which determines the condition of a convict servant, is severer, and the number of summary convictions proportionately more numerous, than in New South Wales. In 1834 the number of convicts in Van Diemen's Land was about 15,000; the summary convictions amounted to about 15,000; and the number of lashes inflicted was about 50,000. On the other hand, a convict, if ill-treated, may complain of his master; and if he substantiate his charge, the master is deprived of his services; but for this purpose the convict must go before a bench, sometimes 100 miles distant, composed of magistrates, most of whom are owners of convict labour. Legal redress is therefore rarely sought for, and still more rarely obtained by the injured convict.

With regard to the general conduct of assigned convicts, Your Committee would observe, that the misconduct and licentiousness of convict mechanics, and of convict domestic servants in the towns were complained of by every witness connected with either penal colony. Mr. Burton, judge of the Supreme Court in New South Wales, in a charge delivered in 1835, attributed to convict servants the number of burglaries and robberies, which were committed in Sydney; and it was the opinion of most of the witnesses from New South Wales, that the assignment of convicts in towns should be immediately discontinued.

With regard to the general conduct of assigned agricultural labourers, there was a considerable diversity of opinion amongst the witnesses examined by Your Committee; convict labourers were said to behave ill or well, according as they were treated by their masters. The evidence, however, of Sir G. Arthur, appears to Your Committee to be conclusive on this point, with regard to which he wrote to the Secretary of State for the Colonies in the following terms:

> You cannot, my Lord, have an idea of the vexations, which accompany the employment of convicts, or of the vicissitudes attendant upon their assignment. Their crimes and misconduct involve the settlers in daily trouble, expense, and disappointment. The discipline and control of the convicts in Van Diemen's Land is carried, perhaps, to a higher degree, than could ever have been contemplated. Many of the convicts have been greatly reformed, when in the service of considerate and judicious masters; but, with all this abatement, there is so much peculation, so much insubordination, insolence, disobedience of lawful orders, and

so much drunkenness, that reference to the magisterial authority is constant, and always attended with loss of time and expense to the settlers. There can be no doubt, things appear better in the colony than they really are; for, in numberless instances, masters are known to submit to peculation rather than incur the additional expense of prosecuting their servants. Two hundred felons, after having been for a long time under confinement in the gaols or hulks of England, and subsequently pent up on board a transport, are placed in charge of the masters or their agents, to whom they have been assigned. The master has then to take the convict to his home (either to the other extremity of the island, a distance of 140 miles, or nearer, as the case may be); and well would it be, if he could get him quietly there, but the contrary is of too frequent occurrence. Whether with some money the convict has secreted, or from the bounty of some old acquaintance, the assigned servant, now relieved for the first time for some months from personal restraint, eludes the vigilance of his new master, finds his way into a public-house, and the first notice the settler has of his servant, for whom he has travelled to Hobart Town, for whose clothing he has paid the Government, for whose comfort he has, perhaps, made other little advances, is, that he is lodged in the watch-house with the loss of half his clothing, or committed to gaol for felony.

This is not in the slightest degree, an overdrawn picture, but a plain matter of every day occurrence. A settler, newly arrived, thinks it a vexation not to be endured; but he soon falls into compliance with difficulties, which are visited alike upon all; and, finding there is no escape from them, he is forced to participate in the common mischief, which he cannot avert.

From the preceding description of the condition of assigned convicts, the great inequality of that punishment must have been apparent; but on this subject Your Committee would now wish to direct the attention of the House to the written opinions of some of the highest authorities in the penal colonies. Amongst others to that of the late Governor of New South Wales, Sir R. Bourke, who stated that;

It is one of the most apparent and necessary results of the system of assignment to render the condition of convicts, so placed, extremely unequal, depending, as it must, on a variety of circumstances, over which the Government cannot possibly exercise any control. It would be quite impracticable to lay down regulations, sufficient to remedy this inequality. The temper, character, station in society of the master, the occupation in which it might be found convenient to employ their servant, and the degree of connexion or variance, that might happen to subsist between this and his previous habits, have an unmeasurable influence over his condition, both physical and mental, which no regulations whatever can anticipate or control.

. . . Assignment is the punishment for female, as well as for male convicts; the proportion of the former to the latter is about one to ten. In respectable families the condition of convict women, as respects their food, clothing, and indulgences, is much the same as that of women servants in this country. Their general conduct, according to the testimony of every witness, examined before Your Committee, is (to use the words of Sir E. Parry) "as bad as anything could well be;" he could "hardly conceive anything worse." At times they are excessively ferocious, and the tendency of assignment is to render them still more profligate; they are all of them, with scarcely an exception, drunken and abandoned prostitutes; and even were any of them inclined to be well-conducted, the disproportion of sexes in the penal colonies is so great, that they are exposed to irresistible temptations; for instance, in a private family, in the interior of either colony, a convict woman, frequently the only one in the service, perhaps in the neighbourhood, is surrounded by a number of depraved characters, to whom she becomes an object of constant pursuit and solicitation; she is generally obliged to select one man, as a paramour, to defend her from the importunities of the rest; she seldom remains long in the same place; she either commits some offence, for which she is returned to the Government; or she becomes pregnant, in which case she is sent to the factory, to be there confined at the expense of the Government; at the expiration of the period of confinement or punishment, she is reassigned, and again goes through the same course; such is too generally the career of convict women, even in respectable families. It can be easily imagined, what a pernicious effect must be produced upon the character of the rising generation of the Australian colonies, in consequence of the children of settlers being, too frequently, in their tenderest years, under the charge of such persons. Many respectable settlers are, however, unwilling to receive convict women as assigned servants, when they can possibly dispense with the services of females; and in many instances convict men-servants are preferred for those domestic occupations, which are performed in this country by women only. A considerable portion, therefore, of the female convicts are retained in the service of the lower description of settlers, by whom, it is notorious, that they are not uncommonly employed as public prostitutes.

Female convicts are allowed to marry free men, but they remain under the surveillance of the police, and are liable to be sent back to the factory in case of misconduct; marriages between female convicts and persons who have been convicts are encouraged; and the Government even permits the marriage of convicts in assigned service, provided that the permission of the master is obtained, and a security given by the master to the Government, that the offspring will not become chargeable to the state. From the female factory at Paramatta, most of the convicts, who are permitted to marry, obtain their wives. Such marriages among convicts rarely however turn out well; for the woman not unfrequently becomes the common property of the convict servants on the establishment; and gives rise to innumerable quarrels among the men, who purchase her favours generally by petty larcencies upon their masters.

In delineating the characteristic features and effects of the assignment system, Your Committee have abstained from dwelling upon the enormous and complicated abuses, which at times have existed, and which perhaps even now, in spite of the utmost efforts of the colonial authorities, exist in various parts of that system; those abuses may chiefly be summed up under the following heads. First, the assignment of convicts to their wives or other relations, that have followed them to the colony, with the proceeds of the offences, for which they were transported, and upon which they have set up a profitable business, have become wealthy, and thus have held out to their acquaintances in this country strong temptations to pursue a similar career of crime; second the employment of convicts as clerks in the various departments of Government, where they have had means of acquiring knowledge, of which the most corrupt and dangerous use has been made; third, the employment of convicts, as clerks to attornies, with free access to the gaols, which has given rise in the colony to an unparalleled system of bribery and connivance at crime; at one time even the clerk of the Attorney-general was a convict, and performed all the legal business of his master; and lastly, the entrusting to convicts of the education of youth in the various public seminaries; the connexion of convicts with the press; these and other abuses, of which mention is to be found in every page of the evidence, appear, to a greater or less degree, to be inherent in the system of assignment....

The convicts under the immediate charge of the Government in the Australian colonies, may be divided into those who are retained in the service of the Government merely because they are required as labourers, those who are returned by their masters as unfit for service, those who having suffered for some offence committed in the colony, are retained for a certain period of probation in the employment of the Government, and those who, for crimes committed in the colonies, are worked on the roads generally in irons, or are sent to the penal settlements.

To commence with a description of the first class of convicts, those who are retained in the service of the Government, not as an additional punishment. On the arrival of a convict vessel in the penal colonies of Australia, an application is made to the assignment commissioner from the proper authorities for the number of the convicts who are required for the service of the Government. These convicts are selected without reference to their past conduct, except that prisoners who are described to be of very depraved character are not usually assigned to settlers, and remain under the charge of the Government; in some few cases directions to this effect are sent out from England. In Van Diemen's Land all mechanics are retained in the service of the Government, and placed either in the engineer department or in the loan-gang; a few convicts likewise are selected out of every ship for the police. In the year 1835, out of 14,903 convicts in Van Diemen's Land there were in the road department, 1,687; engineer ditto, 516; miscellaneous, including marine survey, &c., 716; constables and field-police, 338; total, 3,257. There are no returns of a similar description with regard to New South Wales. It appears, however, that the number of convicts retained (not as punishment) on the public works in the latter colony, has of late years considerably decreased; and most of those works are now performed by contract.

Convicts in the employment of Government are generally worse off than those assigned as servants; they are employed chiefly on the public works of the colony; some of them are, however, in situations of comparative ease, such as clerks, messengers, constables in the police and so forth, in which services (Sir George Arthur says) it is a necessary evil to employ convicts. That it must be an enormous evil to employ convicts, or persons that have been convicts, in the police, especially in such communities as New South Wales and Van Diemen's Land, seems to Your Committee to be a self-evident proposition. Many of the convicts so employed appear to have been of the worse possible character; willing to take bribes; conniving at the offences of the convict population; when employed as scourgers, defeating the sentence of the law; sometimes bringing false accusations against innocent persons, other times screening the guilty from justice; committing outrages on female prisoners committed to their charge; and, in short, frequently defeating all the efforts of the Government to prevent crime. In the present state of Van Diemen's Land, Sir George Arthur thought it impossible to obtain a police of free emigrants: some three or four years ago he said that he took into the police a number of Chelsea pensioners and of free emigrants, but they proved worse than the convicts.

Large parties of convicts, called road-parties, are employed in making roads in New South Wales and Van Diemen's Land; these parties consist mostly of convicts who have been returned to Government by their masters as being unfit for service, and of convicts who, having been convicted of some offence in the colony, have been sent on the expiration of their sentence, to work for a certain period on the roads before they were re-assigned. The conduct of this description of convicts is described in the charge, already referred to, of Judge Burton:

> Judge Burton said, that "he had been induced, by what had been proved before him in that court, gravely to consider the subject of convicts working in gangs out of irons; it was, he felt convinced, one of the most fruitful sources of crime in the colony. He had before him a return, from which it appeared that the number of convicts at this time employed upon the roads is 2,240, of whom 1,104 are out of irons; and when the jury considered who these latter men were, and what they had been; placed under the guardianship of a convict overseer; that they left their huts in any number, armed or unarmed, as they pleased; in short, from the evidence he had upon his notes respecting the conduct of the road-parties of the colony, it would appear that those establishments were like bee-hives, the inhabitants busily pouring in and out, but with this difference, the one works by day, the other by night; the one goes forth to industry, the other to plunder. To the carelessness or worse conduct of overseers he did attribute a vast proportion of the burglaries and robberies that were committed in country districts."

As the charge of Judge Burton must of itself be considered the best possible evidence which can be adduced upon this subject, it is unnecessary, in order to confirm the facts therein stated, to refer in detail to the unanimous testimony of every witness who has been examined. Every one of those witnesses spoke in the strongest terms of the disorders, crimes, and demoralization which were occasioned in the colony of New South Wales by the road-parties. Composed entirely of criminals, some of them of the very worst character (all of them ultimately degraded and demoralized by associating together), these parties were dispersed over a wide extent of country, under a most incomplete and inefficient system of superintendence, with overseers most of whom had been convicts, and in many cases with convicts for the deputy overseers, to whose sole charge the road-parties were sometimes left for many days. Prisoners in the road-parties were sometimes in league with the convict servants of the neighbouring settlers, upon whose property they committed every description of depradation, the fruits of which were consumed in intoxication and other debauchery. The condition of convicts in the road-parties on the whole appears to have been a more disagreeable one than that of assigned servants; the former are subjected to a greater degree of restraint than assigned convicts. The nature of the work of convicts in road-parties, particularly that of breaking stones under a hot sun, was irksome, though the quantity of work which they performed was very slight. Nevertheless, the example of these parties had so demoralizing an effect upon convicts in private establishments, that an idle and worthless convict often preferred being in a road-party; and convicts, who disliked the masters to whom they were assigned, sometimes endeavoured to get themselves sent to a road-party, in hopes that, after the expiration of their punishment, they might be assigned to a better situation. Road-parties out of irons have been nearly discontinued in New South Wales; and the few, which have been kept up since January 1837, are placed under such regulations, as it is hoped will diminish, to a certain extent, some of the above-mentioned abuses. Many persons connected with that colony consider that, in its present state, the road-parties are a necessary evil, because, in their opinion, it would be impossible to obtain a sufficient supply of free labour to repair the roads, and free labourers would consider themselves degraded by an occupation that had been a punishment for convicts. Moreover, free labourers would not submit to the same degree of superintendence and discipline as convicts; and it is said they would probably, therefore, commit outrages as great, if not greater than those committed by convicts. General Bourke likewise observed, "that, great as the complaints are which are made by a certain portion of the colonists on account of the crimes committed by the road-parties, still greater is the demand for good roads; and if those parties were broken up, they would probably be regretted in the colony." . . .

Convicts, it has already been observed, are subjected to a particular code of laws, for neglect of convict discipline and other offences. Female convicts are punished by being sent to the penitentiaries, where, according to the nature of their offence, they are either placed in solitary confinement with bread and water, or employed in picking wool or in breaking stones; some few are sent to the penal settlements of Moreton Bay. The labour imposed on women in the factory at Paramatta in New South Wales is said to be very slight, and many convicts prefer being sent there to being assigned. Assigned convict women, who are with child, are generally returned to the factory when near their period of confinement; they are placed in a separate class, intermediate between the punishment class and that of the women who are waiting to be assigned. This class appears to be a very numerous one, as, out of 590 females in the factory at Paramatta in 1836, 108 were nursing children; what portion of the remainder were pregnant women is not stated; at the same time there were in the factory 136 children between the ages of one and three years, the illegitimate children of convicts. The factory at Paramatta is, therefore, in reality a lying-in hospital; it appears to have been, up to a very late period, under very inefficient superintendence; but this has recently been changed. In the penitentiaries at Hobart Town and Launceston, in Van Diemen's Land, the female convicts are employed in spinning, picking wool, and needlework; the punishment is said to be somewhat severe.

Your Committee will delay their examination into the nature and number of the offences committed by male convicts to a subsequent portion of their Report. They will now proceed to examine merely the nature of the punishments inflicted, which, says Captain Maconochie, "are severe, even to excessive cruelty. Besides corporal punishment to the extent of 50 to 75 lashes, and even, in some rare instances, 100 lashes, solitary confinement, and months, or even years, of hard labour in chains (on the roads or at a penal settlement) are lightly ordered for crimes in themselves of no deep dye; petty thefts (chiefly in order to obtain liquor), drunkenness, insolence, disobedience, desertion, quarrelling among themselves, and so forth."

Most convicts have a greater dread of flagellation than of hard work in the road-parties or in the chain-gangs. Settlers generally prefer flagellation as a punishment for their convict servants; for though it excites revengeful feelings in offenders, it occasions less interruption of work. In the Appendix of the First Report of Your Committee ample proofs are to be found of the severity with which this punishment is inflicted in New South Wales. The condition of the road-parties has already been described. In 1834 the number of convicts in the chain-gangs of New South Wales was about 1,000, and in those of Van Diemen's Land in 1837 about 700; this description of punishment is a very severe one. Sir G. Arthur said, "as severe a one as could be inflicted on man." Sir R. Bourke stated, "that the condition of the convicts in the chain-gangs was one of great privation and unhappiness." They are locked up from sunset to sunrise in the caravans or boxes used for this description of persons, which hold from 20 to 28 men, but in which the whole number can neither stand upright nor sit down at the same time (except with their legs at right angles to their bodies), and which, in some instances, do not allow more than 18 inches in width for each individual to lie down upon on the bare boards; they are kept to work under a strict military guard during the day, and liable to suffer flagellation for trifling offences, such as an exhibition of obstinacy, insolence, and the like; being in chains, discipline is more easily preserved amongst them, and escape more easily prevented than among the road-parties out of chains. This description of punishment belongs to a barbarous age, and merely tends to increase the desperation of the character of an offender. The nature of the duty imposed upon the military in guarding the chain-gangs has the worst effects upon the character and discipline of the soldiers. Colonel Breton, who commanded a regiment in New South Wales, stated to Your Committee, that it produced the greatest demoralization among the troops, and the men became reckless; the demoralization arose, he said, partly from drunkenness, of which there was much amongst the troops in that country; he had no less than 16 soldiers transported to Norfolk Island, all of them from being drunk on sentry; demoralization was likewise produced amongst the troops by their intercourse with the prison population, which could not be prevented, because many of the men found their fathers, brothers, and other relations, amongst the convicts. The same gentleman stated that a convict assigned to a good master is quite as well off as any servant in England, and better off than a soldier; and that two of the men in his regiment deserted in order to be transported.

For crimes of greater magnitude convicts are re-transported. The penal settlements of New South Wales are Norfolk Island and Moreton Bay; at the former, the number of convicts in 1837 were about 1,200; in the same year the number at Moreton Bay did not exceed 300, as the establishment there has been considerably diminished, and only offenders under short sentences were sent there. Moreton Bay is likewise a place of punishment for convict females, who are re-transported for offences committed in the colony. The number of convicts at the penal settlement of Van Diemen's Land, Port Arthur, was in 1835, 1,172. Norfolk Island is a small and most beautiful volcanic island, situated in the midst of the ocean, 1,000 miles from the eastern shores of Australia, and inaccessible, except in one place, to boats. Port Arthur is on a small and sterile peninsula, of about 100,000 acres, connected with Van Diemen's Land by a narrow neck of land, which is guarded, day and night, by soldiers, and by a line of fierce dogs. All communications, except of an official nature, between these places and the settled districts are strictly forbidden; the penal settlements of Norfolk Island and Port Arthur are inhabited solely by the convicts and their keepers. "The work appointed for the convicts," to use the expression of the chief superintendent of convicts in Van Diemen's Land, "is of the most incessant and galling description the settlement can produce; and any disobedience of orders, turbulence or other misconduct is instantaneously punished by the lash."

The condition of the convicts in these settlements has been shown to Your Committee to be one of unmitigated wretchedness. Sir Francis Forbes, chief-justice of Australia, stated, in a letter to Mr. Amos on the subject of transportation, that "The experience furnished by these penal settlements has proved that transportation is capable of being carried to an extent of suffering such as to render death desirable, and to induce many prisoners to seek it under its most appalling aspects." And the same gentleman, in his evidence before Your Committee, said, "that he had known many cases in which it appeared that convicts at Norfolk Island had committed crimes which subjected them to execution, for the mere purpose of being sent up to Sydney; and the cause of their desiring to be so sent was to avoid the state of endurance under which they were placed in Norfolk Island; that he thought, from the expressions they employed, that they contemplated the certainty of execution; that he believed they deliberately preferred death, because there was no chance of escape, and they stated they were weary of life, and would rather go to Sydney and be hanged." Sir Francis Forbes likewise mentioned the case of several men at Norfolk Island cutting the heads of their fellow prisoners with a hoe while at work, with a certainty of being detected, and with a certainty of being executed; and, according to him, they acted in this manner apparently without malice, and with very slight excitement, stating they knew they should be hanged, but it was better than being where they were. A similar case was mentioned by the Rev. Henry Stiles, in his Report to Sir Richard Bourke on the state of Norfolk Island. And Sir George Arthur assured Your Committee that similar cases had recently occurred at Port Arthur. Sir Francis Forbes was then asked, "What good do you think is produced by the infliction of so horrible a punishment in Norfolk Island; and upon whom do you think it produces good?" His answer was, "That he thought that it did not produce any good;" and that, "If it were to be put to himself, he should not hesitate to prefer death, under any form that it could be presented to him, rather than such a state of endurance as that of the convict at Norfolk Island." . . .

In order to complete the description of the various conditions, in which persons, who have been transported, are to be found in the penal colonies, Your Committee must mention those who have obtained a conditional or absolute pardon, or have become free by the expiration of their sentences: they are termed emancipists or expirees. In this class are to be found some individuals who are very wealthy, and have accumulated immense fortunes; one is said to have possessed as much as £40,000 a year. Every witness examined gave the same account of the mode in which these fortunes have been made. The emancipist who acquires wealth, in most cases commences his career by keeping a public-house, then lending money on mortgage; he then obtains landed property and large flocks, the latter frequently consisting of stolen cattle which he has purchased. As a case in point, Dr. Lang and Mr. Mudie mentioned that of the individual whom they stated to be in possession of £40,000 a year. This individual was transported, about the end of the last century, for stealing geese on the commons of Yorkshire. He began his career as a prisoner in the employment of Government, in building the gaol at Parramatta; at that time rum was occasionally allowed to convicts; he was, however, a very temperate man, and sold his rations of spirits; he thus accumulated some money, and was enabled, when he became free, to set up a public-house, and to keep a gig and horse for hire. On one occasion he was hired to drive to Parramatta, a female emancipist, who was likewise in possession of some property. This led to an acquaintance between them; he subsequently married her, and was enabled to increase his business considerably. At the period referred to, there was no regular market at Sydney. The farmers brought their loads of wheat and other produce to the town, and made exchanges with persons who paid them partly in money, partly in the commodities which they required. The farmers were chiefly emancipists, who, at the expiration of their sentence, had obtained grants of land near Windsor: an ignorant and dissolute set of people, totally unreformed by their punishment, and unable to resist any temptation. They mostly frequented the house of the emancipist above mentioned; there they would remain drunk for days, unconscious of what they had consumed or what they had given away. When recovered from the stupor of intoxication, they were frequently charged by their host for a sum far exceeding their means of payment. Credit was always given, on condition of signing warrants of attorney, which were at hand ready filled up. The instruments were drawn up by convicts, for in those days amongst that class only could persons be found qualified to perform the duties of the legal profession. When the farmers were once under the control of the individual, whose career Your Committee are describing, they were obliged to return to his house, till the amount of debt was such, that he feared lest it might surpass the value of their property. He then dispossessed them of their estates, and by this system of measures he had at one time obtained possession of a great proportion of the cultivated land in the colony of New South Wales. Such were the means, according to Dr. Lang, by which both the emancipist in question, and many others, have acquired great wealth. The greater portion, however, of this class are labourers and small shopkeepers; and if industrious, they have every facility for making an honest livelihood, but as, on the expiration of their sentence, they are exposed to every description of temptation, the greater portion of them retain the habits of profligacy which first led them into crime, and become still more worthless and dissipated. Of the numerous crimes committed in the colony, the greater portion are perpetrated by this class. Among the emancipists and ticket-of-leave men are to be found the cattle-stealers, receivers of stolen goods, keepers of illicit spirit-shops and squatters, of the number and extent of whose offences every witness spoke in the strongest terms. In Van Diemen's Land the number of expirees or emancipists probably does not exceed 3,000. Sir George Arthur described them as the worst class in the colony.

157. Chancery Delays: Lords' Select Committee on Administration of Justice 1840: evidence of Sutton Sharpe

Parlty. Papers, 1840/xv/pp. 182–191.

. . . Perhaps the Committee will allow me to mention three Causes which have come under my Observation lately which will illustrate what I have been saying; in Two of them I was personally concerned, the other has been furnished to me. One is the Cause of Bankes v. De Spencer. The Bill in this Case was filed in the Year 1832; the Cause was set down for hearing in Trinity Term 1834; as in this Stage it could be heard as a short Cause, it was heard in December 1834. A Reference was made to the Master to take certain Accounts; the Master made his Report on the 11th of June 1836, and the Cause was set down for hearing, on further Directions, in Michaelmas 1836. It did not get into the regular Paper for hearing till July 1839. During that Time an Event occurred, the Birth of a Child, which rendered it necessary for the Plaintiff to file a Supplemental Bill, which was filed in the Month of January 1838; this would not have been necessary if the Cause had been heard in Michaelmas Term 1836, when it was ready for hearing: this Supplemental Bill necessarily occasioned a considerable Expense. On the 30th of July 1839 the Cause was again on the Paper for hearing, as it was also on the 31st of that Month; it then went out of the Paper, and did not come in again before the Vacation. In Michaelmas Term 1839 a special Application was made to the Vice Chancellor to let the Cause stand at the Head of the Paper the First Day of Causes after Term, which was ordered; it accordingly stood on the Paper on the 3rd of December. It was in the Paper again on the 4th of December, and on the 5th; then it went out of the Paper, and did not come in again till the 18th of December; it was in the Paper again on the 29th of January, the 30th of January, the 12th of February, the 13th, the 15th, the 17th, the 18th, the 19th, the 20th, the 21st, the 24th, the 25th, the 26th, the 27th, the 28th, the 29th, the 2nd of March, the 3rd and 4th of March, without being touched, and on the 5th of March it was called on and partially heard, and again partially heard on the 6th; it came on again on the 9th, but was not then touched, and on the 10th it was finally heard and disposed of.

Q. Have the Solicitors a Fee upon each of those days that the Cause is in the Paper?

They have.

Q. Every Party?

Yes; besides the Refreshers that were given to Counsel each Term the Cause was in the Paper. Another of the Causes I mentioned above was the Cause of Jackson v. Pickering, which was heard before the Lord Chancellor. I believe it was one of the last original Causes the Lord Chancellor heard. The Bill in that Case was filed in the Year 1834; Evidence was gone into; and the Cause was not ready for hearing till February 1837, when it was set down. It did not come into the Paper till the 5th of June 1840, when it was heard, and a Decree made; it would not have come into the Paper then, but for the Circumstance of the Lord Chancellor taking original Causes. In 1838, during the Interval between the setting down, one of the Parties died, which rendered a Bill of Revivor and Supplement necessary; and again, in 1839, another Party became bankrupt, which occasioned a further Supplemental Bill. The Decree which has been made merely directs Inquiries as to Parties. When the Master has made his Report, the Cause will have to be heard again for further Directions, when, from the Nature of the Cause, Accounts only can be directed; so that it will have to be heard a Third Time before a final Decree can be made. There are a great many Parties, and it is therefore certain that if it has to wait Two Years again each Time between the setting down and the hearing, several more Bills of Revivor and Supplement will be necessary.

Q. You stated the Sum which you calculated as the Expense of every year's delay?

For Term Fees alone I calculated the Expense as above 8,600 l. a Year upon the 800 Causes waiting for hearing. I am unable to calculate the Expenses which are occasioned by Bills of Revivor and Supplement.

Q. So that in the Three Years the Expense for Term Fees is 25,800 l., for which the Suitor gets nothing?

Yes. The annual Expense which might be saved is 8,600 l. This does not, as far as I understand, pay the Solicitor any thing like the Interest of the Money that he is out of Pocket during that time. This, however, as I observed before, is a small Portion only of the Expense occasioned by the Delay; the Expenses occasioned by Bills of Revivor and Supplement are much greater. The Third Case I mentioned before was the Cause of Kidd v. North. I was not engaged in the Cause, but I believe it was a Suit to take the Opinion of the Court upon the Construction of some testamentary Papers. The Bill was filed in January 1836, so that it might have been heard within Seven or Eight Months after the Bill was filed, if there had been sufficient Power in the Court. It did not, however, come into the Paper for hearing till the 27th of June 1838; it then was in the Paper Two Days, the 27th of June and the 3rd of July. In the meantime one of the Parties died, and it was necessary, in March 1839, to file a Bill of Revivor. The Cause did not come into the Paper again till the 20th of February 1840; it was in the Paper the 20th, the 26th, the 27th and 29th of February; on the 2nd, the 3rd, the 4th, the 5th, the 9th, the 10th, the 11th, the 13th, the 14th, the 16th, the 17th, the 18th, the 19th, the 20th, of March; and it was not heard till the 21st of March 1840, when there was a simple Decree for Administration.

158. Insolvent Debtors' Act (1842)

Statutes of the Realm, 5 & 6 Vict. c. 116.

"Whereas it is expedient to protect from all Process against the Person such Persons as have become indebted without any Fraud or gross or culpable Negligence, so as nevertheless their Estates may be duly distributed among their Creditors:" Be it enacted by the Queen's Most Excellent Majesty, by and with the Advice and Consent of the Lords Spiritual and Temporal, and Commons, in this present Parliament assembled, and by the Authority of the same, That if any Person not being a Trader within the Meaning of the Statutes now in force relating to Bankrupts, or if any Person being such Trader, but owing Debts amounting in the whole to less than Three hundred Pounds, shall give Notice, according to the Schedule to this Act annexed, to One Fourth in Number and Value of his Creditors, and shall cause the same Notice to be inserted Twice in the London Gazette, and Twice in some Newspaper circulating within the County wherein he resides, he may present a Petition for Protection from Process to the Court of Bankruptcy, if he has resided Twelve Calendar Months in London or within the London District, or to the Commissioner of Bankruptcy in the Country within whose District he may have resided Twelve Calendar Months, which Petition shall have annexed to it a full and true Schedule of his Debts, with the Names of his Creditors, and the Dates of contracting the Debts, severally, the Nature of the Debt, and the Security (if any) given for the same, and also of the Nature and Amount of his Property, and of the Debts owing to him, with their Dates, and the Names of his Debtors, and the Nature of the Securities (if any) which he may have for such Debts, and which Petition shall also set forth any Proposal which he may have to make for the Payment, in whole or in part, of his Debts; and it shall thereupon be lawful for the Judge or Commissioner of the Court of Bankruptcy to whom, by any Order of the Court, as herein-after provided, the same shall be referred, or for the Commissioner in the Country to whom the Petition shall be presented, to give, upon the filing of such Petition, a Protection to the Petitioner from all Process whatever, either against his Person or his Property of every Description, which Protection shall continue in force, and all Process be stayed, until the Appearance of the Petitioner in Court, as herein-after provided; and upon the Presentation of any such Petition all the Estate and Effects of the Petitioner shall forthwith become vested in the Official Assignee who shall be nominated by the Commissioners acting in the Matter of the said Petition; and such Official Assignee shall and may forthwith take possession of so much thereof as can be reasonably obtained and possessed without Suit; and the said Official Assignee shall hold and stand possessed of the same in like Manner as Official Assignees hold and possess Estates and Effects under and by virtue of the Statute relating to Bankrupts. . . .

2. Provided always, and be it enacted, That nothing herein contained shall be held or construed to hinder or prevent the said Insolvent from being arrested or held

to Bail under the Authority of any Judge's Order for that Purpose, in like Manner as may now by Law be done, notwithstanding any Protection which may be granted under the Authority of this Act. . . .

4. And be it enacted, That the Commissioner so authorized, or the Commissioner in the Country, (as the Case may be,) shall, on the Day notified by such Notice as aforesaid, proceed to examine upon Oath the Petitioner, and any Creditor who may attend such Examination, and any Witness whom the Petitioner or any Creditor may call; and the said Commissioner may adjourn the Examination from Time to Time, and summon to be examined before him any Debtor of such Petitioner, or any Creditor of such Petitioner, or any other Person whose Evidence may appear necessary for the Purposes of the Enquiry; and if it shall appear to the said Commissioner that the Allegations in the Petition and the Matters in the Schedules are true, and that the Debts of the Petitioner were not contracted by any Manner of Fraud or Breach of Trust, or any Prosecution against the Petitioner whereby he had been convicted of any Offence, or without having at the Time of becoming indebted reasonable Assurance of being able to pay the Debts, and that such Debts were not contracted by reason of any Judgment in any Proceeding for Breach of the Revenue Laws, or in any Action for Breach of Promise of Marriage, Seduction, Criminal Conversation, Libel, Slander, Assault, Battery, malicious Arrest, malicious suing out a Fiat of Bankruptcy, or malicious Trespass, and that the Petitioner has made a full Discovery of his Estate, Effects, Debts, and Credits, and has not parted with any of his Property since the presenting of his Petition, it shall then be lawful for the said Commissioner to cause Notice to be given that on a certain Day, to be named therein, he will proceed to make an Order, unless Cause be shown to the contrary; which Order shall be called a Final Order, and shall be for the Protection of the Person of the Petitioner from all Process, and for the vesting of his Estate and Effects in an Official Assignee, to be named by such Commissioner, together with an Assignee to be chosen by the Majority in Number and Value of the Creditors who may attend before the Commissioner on such Day, or for the carrying into effect such Proposal as the Petitioner shall have set forth in his Petition, provided that the Consideration of such final Order may be adjourned from Time to Time by the Commissioner without any fresh Notice: Provided always, that it shall be lawful for the said Commissioner, if he shall think fit, to direct in such final Order some Allowance to be made for the Support of the Petitioner out of his Estate and Effects.

5. And be it enacted, That at the first Examination of the Petitioner it shall be lawful for the Commissioner to renew the Order for Protection, and to renew it from Time to Time until the final Order for Protection and Distribution. . . .

159. Divorce: sentence of Mr. Justice W. H. Maule in R. *v.* Thomas Hall (1845)

W. S. Holdsworth, *History of English Law*, x, pp. 623–624.

"Prisoner at the bar"–he said–"you have been convicted of the offence of bigamy, that is to say of marrying a woman while you have a wife still alive, though it is true she has deserted you, and is still living in adultery with another man. You have, therefore, committed a crime against the laws of your country, and you have also acted under a very serious misapprehension of the course which you ought to have pursued. You should have gone to the ecclesiastical court and there obtained against your wife a decree *a mensa et thoro*. You should then have brought an action in the courts of common law and recovered, as no doubt you would have recovered, damages against your wife's paramour. Armed with these decrees you should have approached the legislature, and obtained an Act of Parliament, which would have rendered you free, and legally competent to marry the person whom you have taken on yourself to marry with no such sanction. It is quite true that these proceedings would have cost you many hundreds of pounds, whereas you probably have not as many pence. But the law knows no distinction between rich and poor. The sentence of the court upon you therefore is that you be imprisoned for one day, which period has already been exceeded, as you have been in custody since the commencement of the assizes."

160. County Courts Act (1846)

Statutes of the Realm, 9 & 10 Vict. c. 95.

Whereas sundry Acts of Parliament have been passed from Time to Time for the more easy and speedy Recovery of Small Debts within certain Towns, Parishes, and Places in England: And whereas by an Act passed in the Eighth Year of the Reign of Her Majesty, intituled *An Act to amend the Laws of Insolvency, Bankruptcy, and Execution*, Arrest upon *Final* Process in Actions of Debt not exceeding Twenty Pounds was abolished, except as to certain Cases of Fraud and other Misconduct of the Debtors therein mentioned: And whereas by an Act passed in the Ninth Year of the Reign of Her said Majesty, intituled *An Act for the better securing the Payment of Small Debts*, further Remedies were given to Judgment Creditors, in respect of Debts not exceeding Twenty Pounds, for the Discovery of the Property of Debtors, and Punishment of Frauds committed by them: And whereas by the last-mentioned Act Her Majesty is enabled, with the Advice of Her Privy Council, to extend the Jurisdiction of certain Courts of Requests and other Courts for the Recovery of Small Debts to all Debts and Demands, and all Damages arising out of any express or implied Agreement, not exceeding Twenty Pounds, and also to enlarge and in certain Cases to contract the District of such Courts, and make certain other Alterations in the Practice of such Courts in manner in the now-reciting Act mentioned: and it is expedient that the Provisions of such Acts should be amended, and that One Rule and Manner of proceeding for the Recovery of Small Debts and Demands should prevail throughout England: And whereas the County Court is a Court of ancient Jurisdiction having Cognizance of all Pleas of Personal Actions to any Amount by virtue of a Writ of Justices issued in that Behalf: And whereas the Proceedings in the County Court are dilatory and expensive, and it is expedient to alter and regulate the Manner of proceeding in the said Courts for the Recovery of Small Debts and Demands, and that the Courts established under the recited Acts of Parliament, or such of them as ought to be continued, should be holden after the passing of this Act as Branches of the County Court under the Provisions of this Act, and that Power should be given to Her Majesty to effect these Changes at such Times and in such Manner as may be deemed expedient by Her Majesty, with the Advice of Her Privy Council: Be it enacted by the Queen's most Excellent Majesty, by and with the Advice and Consent of the Lords Spiritual and Temporal, and Commons, in this present Parliament assembled, and by the Authority of the same, That it shall be lawful for Her Majesty, with the Advice of Her Privy Council, from Time to Time to order that this Act shall be put in force in such County or Counties as to Her Majesty, with the Advice aforesaid, from Time to Time shall seem fit; and this Act shall extend to those Counties concerning which any such Order shall have been made, and not otherwise or elsewhere: Provided always, that no Court shall be established under this Act in the City of London.

2. And be it enacted, That it shall be lawful for Her Majesty, with the Advice aforesaid, to divide the whole or Part of any such County, including all Counties of Cities and Counties of Towns, Cities, Boroughs, Towns, Ports and Places, Liberties, and Franchises therein contained, or thereunto adjoining, into Districts, and to order that the County Court shall be holden for the Recovery of Debts and Demands under this Act in each of such Districts, and from Time to Time to alter such Districts as to Her Majesty with the Advice aforesaid, shall seem fit, and to order from Time to Time that the Number of Districts in and for which the Court shall be holden shall be increased until the whole of such County shall be within the Provisions of this Act, and with the Advice aforesaid to alter the Place of holding any such Court, or to order that the holding of any such Court be discontinued, or to consolidate any Two or more of such Districts, and from Time to Time, with the Advice aforesaid, to declare by what Name and in what Towns and Places the County Court shall be holden in each District; and if it shall appear to Her Majesty that any Part of any County, Liberty, City, Borough, or District may conveniently be declared within the Jurisdiction of the County Court of an adjoining County, it shall be lawful for Her Majesty, with the Advice aforesaid, to order that such Part shall be taken to be within the Jurisdiction of the County Court holden for the Purposes of this Act for such adjoining County in and for such District as Her Majesty shall order in like Manner as if it were Part of such adjoining County.

3. And be it enacted, That every Court to be holden under this Act shall have all the Jurisdiction and Powers of the County Court for the Recovery of Debts and Demands, as altered by this Act, throughout the whole District for which it is holden, and there shall be a Judge for each District to be created under this Act, and the County Court may be holden simultaneously in all or any of such Districts; and every Court holden under this Act shall be a Court of Record. . . .

161. Divorce Act (1857)

Statutes of the Realm, 20 & 21 Vict. c. 85.

"WHEREAS it is expedient to amend the Law relating to Divorce, and to constitute a Court with exclusive Jurisdiction in Matters Matrimonial in *England*, and with Authority in certain Cases to decree the Dissolution of a Marriage:" Be it therefore enacted by the Queen's most Excellent Majesty, by and with the Advice and Consent of the Lords Spiritual and Temporal, and Commons, in this present Parliament assembled, and by the Authority of the same, as follows:

I. This Act shall come into operation on such Day, not sooner than the First Day of *January* One thousand eight hundred and fifty-eight, as Her Majesty shall by Order in Council appoint, provided that such Order be made One Month at least previously to the Day so to be appointed.

II. As soon as this Act shall come into operation, all Jurisdiction now exerciseable by any Ecclesiastical Court in *England* in respect of Divorces *a Mensa et Thoro*, Suits of Nullity of Marriage, Suits of Jactitation of Marriage, Suits for Restitution of Conjugal Rights, and in all Causes, Suits, and Matters Matrimonial, shall cease to be so exerciseable, except so far as relates to the granting of Marriage Licenses, which may be granted as if this Act had not been passed. . . .

162. Progress of Procedural Reform: Third Report of Commissioners on Superior Courts of Law (1860)

Parlty. Papers, 1860/XXXI/pp. 345–346.

We, Your Majesty's Commissioners, appointed to inquire into the Process, Practice, and System of Pleading in the Superior Courts of Law at Westminster, the manner of conducting suits and other proceedings in such Courts and on the circuits, and the costs, charges, and expenses incidental thereto, the practice at the judges' chambers, and the duties of the several officers, clerks, and other persons of and connected with such Courts, circuits, and judges' chambers, humbly certify to Your Majesty that we have further proceeded to consider the matters thus committed to our investigation and We submit to Your Majesty this our Third and Final Report.

In the year 1850, Your Majesty was pleased to direct us and our late lamented colleague Sir John Jervis to inquire into and report upon the Process, Practice, and System of Pleading in the Superior Courts of Common Law at Westminster. At that time much dissatisfaction prevailed amongst the practitioners and suitors. It was complained, and with justice, that the proceedings in actions, though undefended, of which the great majority of cases consists, were unnecessarily tedious and costly. It was also a subject of deep and just dissatisfaction that the time of the Courts was frequently occupied, and expense and delay occasioned, by frivolous arguments and discussions upon points merely of technical form altogether irrelevant to the merits. Justice was frequently defeated in trials at Nisi Prius, in consequence of variances between the Pleadings and the Evidence; or of objections to the stamps upon documents; or from want of authority to adjourn the trial when an unforeseen difficulty arose; or from other circumstances which occasionally, after very great trouble and expense had been incurred, rendered the trial wholly fruitless, and left the real question in controversy between the parties undecided. To these and other causes of complaint we have referred in our former Reports.

Our First Report was presented in the year 1851. We discussed therein all the ordinary proceedings in an action, and made suggestions for their improvement by abolishing all unnecessary steps, by removing the possibility of a defeat of justice by mere technical objections, and by putting an end to the fictions which, as in outlawry and ejectment, had incumbered the law. We further recommended the payment of the officers of the Superior Courts by salaries instead of fees, and the abolition, or at least revision, of the various charges upon the suitors in respect of the proceedings in those Courts.

In consequence of that Report the Common Law Procedure Act of 1852 and the Nisi Prius Officers' Act (15 & 16 Vict. c. 73.) were enacted, and these Acts were followed by two sets of Rules made by the Judges in Hilary Term 1853.

In our Second Report (1853) we proceeded to deal with the following important subjects:–Trial by Jury, the instances in which it might be dispensed with, and the mode in which the constitution of Juries might be improved; the trial at Nisi Prius and the incidents, and the improvements necessary in that part of our Procedure for perfecting the administration of justice; the law of evidence, and the further alterations required to complete the course of improvement which modern legislation has introduced into this branch of the law; the expediency of an appellate jurisdiction in cases of New Trial, and of special cases stated by consent of parties. These, together with several other subjects of minor importance, fully considered and discussed in our Report, related to the existing Procedure of the Common Law Courts in Actions at Law.

In a second branch of our Second Report we considered the necessity of enlarging and extending the Procedure of these Courts, so as not only to invest them with powers previously exercised by Courts of Equity alone, by way of assistance to the Courts of Common Law in the progress of an action, called auxiliary Equity, but also to enable them to exercise the powers of Courts of Equity for the protection of legal, as distinguished from equitable rights, and for the enforcing of legal obligations.

We strongly urged that these powers should be conferred on the Courts of Common Law, on the ground that every Court ought to possess within itself the means of administering complete justice within the scope of its jurisdiction; and that the Courts of Common Law, to be able satisfactorily to administer justice, ought to possess in all matters within their jurisdiction, the power to give all the redress necessary to protect and vindicate common law rights, and to prevent wrongs, whether existing, or likely to happen unless prevented.

This Report was followed by the Common Law Procedure Act of 1854. By this Act the legislature gave effect, in substance, to all our recommendations contained in that Report relating to the existing Procedure in an action at law, with the exception of our recommendation as to the constitution of juries; this subject being reserved, as it was understood, for consideration at a future period when the law relating to this matter was to be generally revised. Effect also was given to our recommendations as to conferring on the Courts of Common Law the powers previously exercised by the Courts of Equity alone, as auxiliary to the Courts of Law. But the legislature abstained from enlarging the powers of the latter Courts, so as to enable them to protect common law rights from threatened invasion, or to enforce the specific performance of common law obligations.

The experience of the several years which have elapsed since the new system of

Procedure, with such great and varied improvements, has been in operation, enables us to express a confident opinion as to its working. We have delayed making this Report in order to have the advantage of this experience before we submitted to Your Majesty our final views on the important subjects upon which Your Majesty was pleased to command our services.

As regards the amendments and alterations in the Procedure in actions at law, we are happy to be able to report, that they have rendered the Procedure simple, economical, and speedy, and have had the effect of limiting the costs to the expenses of the necessary and essential steps in a cause.

The extent of the reform effected will be exemplified by the fact that in nine months of the years 1852–3 (the first during which the new system was partially introduced), as compared with the same period in the preceding year, by the abolition of proceedings of a formal character, all involving considerable expense, reported by us to be unnecessary, and thereupon abrogated, the Rules granted by the three Courts were during that time reduced in number from 38,009 to 3,081, and this notwithstanding an increase in the number of Writs issued.

The technicalities which brought so much discredit on our jurisprudence have now disappeared, and the Courts, owing to the improved system of Pleading and Procedure, and the large additional power of amendment, are occupied in adjudicating upon the substantial merits of the Cases in litigation, while, from the operation of the same causes, it very rarely occurs in trials at Nisi Prius that the real question in controversy is not decided by the jury.

Nevertheless, there are still a few suggestions which we think it necessary to make as to this branch of the subject, partly as to matters omitted in our former Reports, partly as to improvements which the practical working of the existing system has shown to be desirable. . . .

163. Need for further reform: First Report of the Judicature Commission (1868–1874)

Parlty. Papers, 1868–1869/xxv/pp. 5–10.

In commencing the inquiry which we were directed by Your Majesty to make, the first subject that naturally presents itself for consideration was the ancient division of the Courts, into the Courts of Common Law, and the Court of Chancery, founded on the well known distinction in our law between Common Law and Equity.

This distinction led to the establishment of two systems of Judicature, organized in different ways, and administering justice on different and sometimes opposite principles, using different methods of procedure, and applying different remedies. Large classes of rights, altogether ignored by the Courts of Common Law, were protected and enforced by the Court of Chancery, and recourse was had to the same Court for the purpose of obtaining a more adequate protection against the violation of Common Law rights, than the Courts of Common Law were competent to afford. The Common Law Courts were confined by their system of procedure in most actions, – not brought for recovering the possession of land, – to giving judgment for debt or damages, a remedy which has been found to be totally insufficient for the adjustment of the complicated disputes of modern society. The procedure at Common Law was founded on the trial by jury, and was framed on the supposition that every issue of fact was capable of being tried in that way; but experience has shown that supposition to be erroneous. A large number of important cases frequently occur in the practice of the Common Law Courts which cannot be conveniently adapted to that mode of trial; and ultimately those cases either find their way into the Court of Chancery, or the Suitors in the Courts of Common Law are obliged to have recourse to private arbitration in order to supply the defects of their inadequate procedure.

The evils of this double system of Judicature, and the confusion and conflict of jurisdiction to which it has led, have been long known and acknowledged.

The subject engaged the attention of the Commissioners appointed in 1851 to inquire into the constitution of the Court of Chancery. Those learned Commissioners, after pointing out some of the defects in the administration of justice arising out of the conflicting systems of procedure and modes of redress adopted by the Courts of Common Law and Equity respectively, state their opinion, that "a practical and effectual remedy for many of the evils in question may be found in such a transfer or blending of jurisdiction, coupled with such other practical amendments, as will render each Court competent to administer complete justice in the cases which fall under its cognizance."

In like manner the Commissioners appointed in 1850 to inquire into the constitution of the Common Law Courts make, in their Second Report, a very similar recommendation. They report that "it appeared to them that the Courts of Common Law, to be able satisfactorily to administer justice, ought to possess in all matters within their jurisdiction the power to give all the redress necessary to protect and vindicate Common Law Rights, and to prevent wrongs, whether existing or likely to happen unless prevented;" and further that "a consolidation of all the elements of a complete remedy in the same Court was obviously desirable, not to say imperatively necessary, to the establishment of a consistent and rational system of procedure."

In consequence of these Reports several Acts of Parliament have been passed for the purpose of carrying out to a limited extent the recommendations of the Commissioners. . . .

The alterations, to which we have referred, have no doubt introduced considerable improvements into the procedure both of the Common Law and Equity Courts; but, after a careful consideration of the subject, and judging now with the advantage of many years experience of the practical working of the systems actually in force, we are of opinion that "the transfer or blending of jurisdiction" attempted to be carried out by recent Acts of Parliament, even if it had been adopted to the full extent recommended by the Commissioners, is not a sufficient or adequate remedy for the evils complained of, and would at best have mitigated but not removed the most prominent of those evils.

The authority now possessed by the Court of Chancery to decide for itself all the questions of Common Law has no doubt worked beneficially. But the mode of taking evidence orally before an Examiner, instead of before the Judge who has to decide the case, has justly caused much dissatisfaction; and Trial by Jury, – whether from the reluctance of the Judge or of the Counsel to adopt such an innovation, or from the complexity of the issues generally involved in the suit, or because the proceedings in Chancery do not give rise to so many conflicts of evidence as proceedings in other Courts, – has been attempted in comparatively few cases.

In the Common Law Courts the power to compel discovery has been extensively used, and has proved most salutary; but the jurisdiction conferred on those Courts to grant injunctions and to allow equitable defences to be pleaded has been so limited and restricted, – the former extending only to cases where there has been an actual violation of the right, and the latter being confined to those equitable defences where the Court of Chancery would have granted a perpetual and unconditional injunction, – that these remedies have not been of much practical use at Common Law, and Suitors have consequently been obliged to resort to the Court of Chancery, as before, for the purpose of obtaining a complete remedy.

Much therefore, of the old mischief still remains, notwithstanding the changes which have been introduced; and the Court of Chancery necessarily continues to exercise the jurisdiction of restraining actions at law on equitable grounds, and even claims to exercise the jurisdiction in cases where an equitable defence might be properly pleaded at Common Law. . . .

The litigation arising out of Joint Stock Companies has constituted a very large proportion of the business which has engaged the attention of Courts of Law and Equity for some years. Directors of Joint Stock Companies fill the double character of agents and trustees for the companies and shareholders; and the effect of their acts and representations has frequently been brought into question in both jurisdictions, and sometimes with opposite results. The expense thus needlessly incurred has been so great, and the perplexity thereby occasioned in the conduct of business so considerable, as to convince most persons, who have followed the development of this branch of the law, of the necessity that exists for a tribunal invested with full power of dealing with all the complicated rights and obligations springing out of such transactions, and of administering complete and appropriate relief, no matter whether the rights and obligations involved are what are called legal or equitable. . . .

CONSTITUTION OF THE SUPREME COURT

We are of opinion that the defects above adverted to cannot be completely remedied by any mere transfer or blending of jurisdiction between the Courts as at present constituted; and that the first step towards meeting and surmounting the evils complained of will be the consolidation of all the Superior Courts of Law and Equity, together with the Courts of Probate, Divorce, and Admiralty, into one Court, to be called "Her Majesty's Supreme Court," in which Court shall be vested all the jurisdiction which is now exercisable by each and all the Courts so consolidated.

This consolidation would at once put an end to all conflicts of jurisdiction. No suitor could be defeated because he commenced his suit in the wrong Court, and sending the suitor from equity to law or from law to equity, to begin his suit over again in order to obtain redress, will be no longer possible.

164. Debtors' Act (1869)

Statutes of the Realm, 32 & 33 Vict. c. 62.

. . .

4. With the exceptions herein-after mentioned, no person shall, after the commencement of this Act, be arrested or imprisoned for making default in payment of a sum of money.

There shall be excepted from the operation of the above enactment:

1. Default in payment of a penalty, or sum in the nature of a penalty, other than a penalty in respect of any contract:
2. Default in payment of any sum recoverable summarily before a justice or justices of the peace:
3. Default by a trustee or person acting in a fiduciary capacity and ordered to pay by a court of equity any sum in his possession or under his control:
4. Default by an attorney or solicitor in payment of costs when ordered to pay costs for misconduct as such, or in payment of which any court having jurisdiction in bankruptcy is authorized to make an order:
5. Default in payment for the benefit of creditors of any portion of a salary or other income in respect of the payment of which any court having jurisdiction in bankruptcy is authorized to make an order:
6. Default in payment of sums in respect of the payment of which orders are in this Act authorized to be made:

Provided, first, that no person shall be imprisoned in any case excepted from the operation of this section for a longer period than one year; and, secondly, that nothing in this section shall alter the effect of any judgment or order of any court for payment of money except as regards the arrest and imprisonment of the person making default in paying such money.

5. Subject to the provisions herein-after mentioned, and to the prescribed rules, any court may commit to prison for a term not exceeding six weeks, or until payment of the sum due, any person who makes default in payment of any debt or instalment of any debt due from him in pursuance of any order or judgment of that or any other competent court.

Provided–(1) That the jurisdiction by this section given of committing a person to prison shall, in the case of any court other than the superior courts of law and equity, be exercised only subject to the following restrictions; that is to say,

(*a*) Be exercised only by a judge or his deputy, and by an order made in open court and showing on its face the ground on which it is issued:

(*b*) Be exercised only as respects a judgment of a superior court of law or equity, when such judgment does not exceed fifty pounds, exclusive of costs:

(*c*) Be exercised only as respects a judgment of a county court by a county court judge or his deputy.

(2) That such jurisdiction shall only be exercised where it is proved to the satisfaction of the court that the person making default either has or has had since the date of the order or judgment the means to pay the sum in respect of which he has made default, and has refused or neglected, or refuses or neglects, to pay the same.

Proof of the means of the person making default may be given in such manner as the court thinks just; and for the purposes of such proof the debtor and any witnesses may be summoned and examined on oath, according to the prescribed rules.

Any jurisdiction by this section given to the superior courts may be exercised by a judge sitting in chambers, or otherwise, in the prescribed manner.

For the purpose of this section any court may direct any debt due from any person in pursuance of any order or judgment of that or any other competent court to be paid by instalments, and may from time to time rescind or vary such order:

Persons committed under this section by a superior court may be committed to the prison in which they would have been confined if arrested on a writ of capias ad satisfaciendum, and every order of committal by any superior court shall, subject to the prescribed rules, be issued, obeyed, and executed in the like manner as such writ.

This section, so far as it relates to any county court, shall be deemed to be substituted for sections ninety-eight and ninety-nine of the County Court Act, 1846, and that Act and the Acts amending the same shall be construed accordingly, and shall extend to orders made by the county court with respect to sums due in pursuance of any order or judgment of any court other than a county court.

No imprisonment under this section shall operate as a satisfaction or extinguishment of any debt or demand or cause of action, or deprive any person of any right to take out execution against the lands, goods, or chattels of the person imprisoned, in the same manner as if such imprisonment had not taken place.

Any person imprisoned under this section shall be discharged out of custody upon a certificate signed in the prescribed manner to the effect that he has satisfied the debt or instalment of a debt in respect of which he was imprisoned, together with the prescribed costs (if any).

. . .

165. Married Women's Property Act (1870)

Statutes of the Realm, 33 & 34 Vict. c. 93.

1. The wages and earnings of any married woman acquired or gained by her after the passing of this Act in any employment, occupation, or trade in which she is engaged or which she carries on separately from her husband, and also any money or property so acquired by her through the exercise of any literary, artistic, or scientific skill, and all investments of such wages, earnings, money, or property, shall be deemed and taken to be property held and settled to her separate use, and her receipts alone shall be a good discharge for such wages, earnings, money, and property. . . .

166A–B. Debate on Supreme Court of Judicature Act (1873)

166A. Speech of the Attorney General, Sir J. D. Coleridge (9 June)

Hansard, 3/CCXVI/643–654.

. . . He would now proceed as briefly as he could to describe the general proposals of the measure. The great defect in the system was the conflict of jurisdiction that existed between the Courts of Law and the Courts of Equity. Most descriptions which were epigrammatic and antithetical were sure to be incorrect; and it was not correct to say, as he had heard it stated, that they had established one set of Courts for correcting the intolerable injustice which another set of Courts had committed. At the same time, that description contained truth. No doubt, the Courts of Common Law, without the ameliorating and softening hand of Equity, would have administered a system under which this country, with its various complicated relations, would have found it impossible to live. There had been an inconvenient contest between the Courts of Law and the Courts of Equity, and that would be put an end to at once if the Bill passed. There were Courts of Law and Courts of Equity, each of them separate and distinct, with co-ordinate jurisdiction, unable to interfere with each other, except as the Court of Chancery interfered with suits at Common Law. These defects were known both to lawyers and suitors; but the public at large were not interested in them, and therefore let things go on as they were. The first and main principle of the Bill was that there should be one Queen's Court–the Queen's Court of Supreme Jurisdiction; and in that Court perfect Law and perfect Equity should be together administered. That Supreme Court, into which all the existing Courts would be merged, would itself be divided into a High Court of Justice and an Appellate Court, of which the various Courts of Appeal and of First Instance would respectively form part. The Bill was not one for the fusion of Law and Equity. Law and Equity would remain, and for this reason–they were not the creatures of statute; an inherent distinction existed between them, and the subject-matter of Law and of Equity was not the same, and could not be made the same by Act of Parliament. The defect of our legal system was, not that Law and Equity existed, but that if a man went for relief to a Court of Law, and an equitable claim or an equitable defence arose, he must go to some other Court and begin afresh. Law and Equity, therefore, would remain if the Bill passed, but they would be administered concurrently, and no one would be sent to get in one Court the relief which another Court had refused to give. It seemed to him that that was the only intelligible way of dealing with the question. Great authorities had no doubt declared that Law and Equity might be fused by enactment; but in his opinion, to do so would be to decline to grapple with the real difficulty of the case. If an Act were passed doing no more than fuse Law and Equity, it would take 20 years of decisions and hecatombs of suitors to make out what Parliament meant and had not taken the trouble to define. It was more philosophical to admit the innate distinction between Law and Equity, which you could not get rid of by Act of Parliament, and to say, not that the distinction should not exist, but that the Courts should administer relief according to legal principles when these applied, or else according to equitable principles. That was what the Bill proposed, with the addition that, whenever the principles of Law and Equity conflicted, equitable principles should prevail. Few Common lawyers would deny that where the two principles differed Equity was right and Common Law wrong; and the Bill, therefore, did homage in such cases to the superior breadth and wisdom of Equity. Though the separate jurisdiction of the Courts would be merged in the one Supreme Court, it was more philosophical to recognise facts, and as for the general convenience, as it was impossible you could have 31 or 32 judges all sitting together, there must be

Divisions of the Court, the question arose–what shall they be called? Now, he thought it very important to preserve historical associations wherever you could do so. England was not the least great in its legal history and associations, and to destroy all those associations in the nomenclature of the Law Courts would be unwise. As the things remained it was well that the names also should remain. Instead, therefore, of calling these different Courts by names which were not only new but new-fangled, it was proposed to call them by the old names–the Chancery, Queen's Bench, Common Pleas, Exchequer, Bankruptcy Divisions, and so on. Further, as there must be a division of labour, and the Courts must consider criminal informations, election petitions, registration appeals, questions of real property, specific performance, winding-up cases, questions between husband and wife, the enforcement of trusts, and so on, it was far more convenient, while getting rid of any conflict of jurisdiction, that the work which the Courts now did they should continue to do, at all events in the first instance. Every Division of a Court would have the jurisdiction to hear any class of business; but if it were found that some kinds of business could be better decided by one Division than another, this business might be transferred, without cost or inconvenience to the suitor. He hoped that we should thus get rid of the scandals of our present procedure, and that, while preserving necessary and inevitable distinctions, we should not allow them to obstruct the process of substantial relief to suitors. That brought him face to face with the Amendment of his hon. and learned Friend the Member for Denbigh (Mr. Osborne Morgan), which ran thus–

> "That, in order to ensure the due administration of Law and Equity by the High Court of Justice as provided by this Bill, it is expedient that provision should be made for the appointment to each division of such Court of one or more Judge or Judges practically conversant with the principles and administration of Equity."

That hon. and learned Gentleman, in this matter, might be regarded as the spokesman of a number of distinguished men who had addressed the Lord Chancellor on the subject, and it was not unnatural that men who had grown up under a system such as that administered in the Court of Chancery should be anxious respecting the tendency of a Bill dealing with it. Although his (the Attorney General's) knowledge of Equity procedure was naturally imperfect, he could assure his hon. and learned Friend he would give very little support to a measure which would prevent the full operation and development of that admirable and beneficent system, whatever faults might be incidental to its working. But if his hon. and learned Friend thought him prejudiced in favour of Common Law he would probably recollect that the Lord Chancellor, who originally introduced this Bill to the notice of Parliament, was for many years the ornament of the Courts of Equity, and that he of all men would be the last to injure a system to which he owed, and which owed him, so much. His hon. and learned Friend the Solicitor General, also, was one of the most powerful among those who now practised in those Courts, and no one would suppose he would willingly impair a system he so thoroughly understood, and of which he was so great an ornament. Being himself a representative of what Lord Westbury had been pleased to describe as the degraded and baser parts of the law–a description which gave evidence of a not very accurate acquaintance with the subject with which the noble and learned Lord dealt–he could not hope that his professions of tenderness for Equity would have as much weight as the fact that the sympathies of the Lord Chancellor and the Solicitor General were distinctly in favour of it. The Judges, his hon. and learned Friend perhaps knew, had loudly called for help. In effect they had said–"If we are to be turned into Courts of Equity, for God's sake send us some men who understand Equity, and do not leave us a prey to distinguished Equity counsel" –such, perhaps, as my hon. and learned Friend. It was manifest, therefore, that in both the Equity and Common Law Courts there should be persons competent to give information on points respecting which the Judges, having been brought up under a different system, were naturally wanting. It would not do for the Bench to be inferior to the Bar. Of course, it must always be that some distinguished members of the Bar should be superior to some upon the Bench; but those were exceptional cases, and it could not be tolerated that the Bar as a body should be superior in knowledge to the Bench. It was, therefore, obvious that it would be impossible to work this Bill properly, unless some such thing as his hon. and learned Friend suggested was done. If the Fates were kind, and permitted the continuance of his noble and learned Friend in office, it was his intention that everything necessary and proper for the administration of the law under the Bill should be done. He was not authorized to speak in the name of hon. Gentlemen opposite, but he believed that what he had said of the Lord Chancellor could be said with equal truth of Lord Cairns, should he again fill the office he so worthily filled some years ago. In fact, it would be impossible to administer the Bill satisfactorily, except in the sense suggested by his hon. and learned Friend's Amendment. Still, that was a very different thing from enacting that such a course should be pursued; because to enact what his hon. and learned Friend's Amendment pointed to would be to stereotype on the face of an Act of Parliament that distinction between Law and Equity which it was the object of the Bill to destroy. Henceforth, if this Bill came into operation, all men practising in the Courts would soon be sufficiently accomplished to deal with the law on either side. Of course, a period of transition would occur, during which some difficulty would be experienced, but the transitional period would not be of long duration. Under the circumstances, therefore, he thought his hon. and learned Friend would see that it was most inexpedient to press his Amendment, and that he would be content with an assurance that his object should be carried out. So much for the High Court of Appeal. What could be more anomalous than the present state of the Courts of Appeal? As far as Common Law cases were concerned, there were two Courts of Appeal–first, the Exchequer Chamber, and then the House of Lords. In the Court of Chancery, speaking under correction he would say there was not always a reference to an intermediate Court of Appeal; in certain cases there might be an appeal to the House of Lords, without the intermediate appeal to the Lords Justices. Then there was the Judicial Committee of the Privy Council for appeals from the Colonies, Ecclesiastical and Admiralty cases. The Exchequer Chamber had almost every fault that a Court of Appeal could have. It was uncertain–he would speak tremblingly of the Judges in the presence of the right hon. and learned Gentleman (Dr. Ball); but they were men who had feelings, and he had known cases when a judgment of a particular Court, if there were any means of over-ruling it, was pretty sure to be over-ruled in the Exchequer Chamber. Then, there was no absolute necessity that the Exchequer Chamber should have a larger number of Judges than the Court which it overruled, and it had often happened that where the two Courts were divided, it was the opinion held by the minority of Judges which had prevailed. The Court sat, too, but for a very limited time, and that time was uncertain. The Lords Justices formed a much better Court of Appeal, and for a very long time had given satisfaction. The Privy Council, too, for something like 25 or 26 years was about as good a Court as this Empire contained; but it became exceedingly difficult to maintain it in that high state of efficiency, because, as it was until lately an entirely unpaid Court, it was almost entirely dependent on the services of unpaid Judges. At last it became almost impossible for it to continue its sittings. The Judicial Committee still remained an absolutely good Court; but that had happened which some predicted when the Bill for its improvement was before Parliament. It would be said that if we were to have paid and unpaid Judges on the tribunal, in a short time it would be the paid Judges only that would attend. It had not quite come to that, but very nearly so, and he could not help thinking that the sort of august character which the Privy Council possessed was in peril of being lowered and the Court brought to the condition simply of a well-officered and well-filled tribunal. As for the House of Lords, it was his duty, whatever hon. Gentlemen opposite might think, to say what he thought of it as a judicial institution. For his part, he would say that if this Bill did nothing else but get rid of the House of Lords as a judicial tribunal it would be worth while to pass it. He could not believe that if suitors had any power of combination the House of Lords would have lasted as a judicial institution to the present time, such were the expenses and delays of it. He was himself in a case which had been pending in the House of Lords for six or seven years. The utter irresponsibility of the Judges who composed it made it a perfectly indefensible institution. He did not know what would be said now of Chancery Appeals, but he did know that some time ago they used to be decided by a single Peer, and a caustic Lord Justice used to say that the way they were decided made him hold up his hands in respectful amazement. Practically, at present the Common Law Appeals were decided by a single Judge, for there was not a single Common Law Lord but one who attended the sittings of the House of Lords. Lord Penzance was too ill at present to attend, and before he generally was too busy. He recollected cases in which the unanimous opinion of the Court of Common Pleas and of the Court of Exchequer was overruled by this single Common Law Lord, the Judges not being summoned. Besides, the House of Lords now was not what it used to be in former times. Everyone knew that it was to the House of Lords, as a co-ordinate branch of the Legislature, and to the whole Peerage that the Constitution wisely, or unwisely, intrusted the declaration upon appeal of what was the law of England; the Judges were in those days habitually summoned as their advisers, and the House of Lords, in 99 cases out of 100, or even in a still larger proportion, followed the advice given by the Judges. It was perfectly true that

Lord Eldon said he had the right to overrule all the Judges in England, but that was a right which neither that noble and learned Lord nor the House of Lords itself had ever yet exercised. The House of Lords was at that time a convenient medium through which to ascertain the judgment of all the Judges; but that was not the case now. The whole character of the House of Lords was definitely changed in the famous case of *The Queen v. O'Connell.* The lay Members of the House attended in large numbers on that occasion, as they had done in former days; but the Duke of Wellington earnestly advised them to take no part in the decision. They acted upon his advice and abstained from voting, and the Law Lords divided according to their political sentiments. He had no doubt that they were perfectly honest in what they did, but the fact was that the noble and learned Lords who were opposed in opinion to O'Connell voted against him, and those who were in favour of his views voted for him. From that day to this an appeal to the House of Lords had really been an appeal to two or three Law Lords who happened to attend, for the rule of the House now was, that the Judges were not summoned unless both parties desired it. (*Dissent.*) He might be wrong about the rule, but, at all events, the Judges were very seldom summoned. Practically the Appellate Jurisdiction of the House of Lords was in different hands from what it used to be, and from what the constitution intended it should be, and he saw no reason for maintaining the new state of things for which there was no precedent, and which was found extremely inconvenient. That, indeed, might be said to be the opinion of the House of Lords itself, which had passed that Bill and sent it down to them with those provisions. Now, the Court of Appeal which it was proposed to create would consist of 12 or 14 persons. There would be five *ex officio* Members–the Lord Chancellor, the three Chief Judges of the Common Law Courts, the Master of the Rolls; the four paid Judges of the Privy Council–who took office with the understanding that they should be available for any reconstruction of the Court of Supreme Appeal–and three others–an ex-Lord Chancellor or Judge, and certain Scotch and Irish Judges, if they thought fit to come. The Court of Appeal would sit in two divisions all the year round, according to rules to be drawn up, and the present unintelligible and inconvenient distinction between Terms and Vacations would be abolished. Except an increase to the salary of the Judges of the Admiralty Court, as proposed by the House of Lords, and an increase of £1,000 a year to the salaries of the paid Members of the Court of Appeal other than the *ex officio* Members, the Bill did not create any additional charge to the country–or, at least, certainly no permanent additional charge. Speaking on these matters on the second reading, it would be understood that he spoke with entire reserve; that the whole of those matters were absolutely open, and that he was merely describing the Bill as it came from the other House. The Judges of the High Court would be reduced to the old standard at which they stood before the House of Commons transferred the Election Petition business to them, and made that a reason for adding three members to the Judicial Bench. Experience had shown that the Election Judges –those at least who had been added–had not their time fully occupied, and it was desirable that highly-paid persons should be fully employed. To the new Court of Appeal it was proposed to transfer the whole of the English appeals to the House of

Lords, and also the whole judicial business of the Privy Council, excepting the ecclesiastical appeals. The jurisdiction of the House of Lords would be kept alive for the hearing of Scotch and Irish appeals. If the Scotch and Irish people preferred that that should be so, they were entitled to have their preference, and as an Englishman he had no right to meddle with it. He had always thought the defect of the Judicial Committee of the Privy Council, if it had a defect, was in ecclesiastical matters, and that the presence of Bishops on that tribunal contributed nothing whatever to the weight of its decisions as legal decisions, while it affected to give them a sort of factitious spiritual influence which three Bishops who happened to be Privy Councillors could not possibly confer. He thought that questions of property and law, even as far as the interests of the Church herself were concerned, ought to be decided by lawyers. However, they had to deal with questions which were not strictly legal questions, and therefore the Judicial Committee would remain for the purpose of ecclesiastical appeals. As he had stated, there would be two Divisions of the Supreme Court, to one of which would be entrusted the cases now dealt with by the Judicial Committee. In that case, the whole jurisdiction and process being thus transferred to the Supreme Court, the decisions would still remain as the decisions of the Queen herself, Her Majesty being advised by the Judges of that Court, as she was now advised by the Judicial Committee. They would sit continuously all the year round, and as he had said before, the Terms and Vacations would be abolished. There would also be sittings in London and Middlesex. Another important provision in the Bill was the power of appointing official and regularly constituted referees. It was proposed that the judge in Chambers or the Court should be able at any stage of the case, if it clearly appeared not to be a case fit for trial in Court or for adjudication by a Judge and jury, to refer it by an Order. There would be attached to the Courts certain official referees, who would take those references as part of their regular duty. He hoped that portion of the Bill would be found satisfactory, and get rid, in working, of one of the justest causes of complaint that existed, at all events, on the Common Law side of the question. He did not mean to go at length into the Schedule of Procedure, which would be found exceedingly important. That was matter rather of discussion clause by clause in Committee than one which could usefully occupy the attention of the House at the present stage. In general, it was an attempt to initiate a more sensible and intelligible mode of procedure–to get rid, if possible, of the defects both of Chancery and Common Law procedure, and to produce something in the shape not of pleading, but procedure, that should be at once sensible and satisfactory. Such in outline was this measure which he had introduced–he knew how imperfectly–to the attention of the House. There were two subjects connected with the question of Law Reform–the Reform of the Law itself and the reform of the procedure by which the Law was administered; and they were very distinct. In some respects this Bill, in different portions of it, dealt with both these subjects; and he trusted it would be found to deal with them satisfactorily. At any rate, such as it was, he begged leave to recommend it to the attention of the House of Commons. So far as the Government were concerned, they did not aspire or pretend to any greater responsibility or merit in the question than having recognized the position of public opinion, and striven, as far as they could, to give effect to it. He asked the House to recollect that the Bill came to them with the sanction of the House of Lords–it came to them from the House of Lords, which had shown both great wisdom and patriotism in declining any longer to stand in the way of a great public advantage, for which there was a great public demand. The Government proposed to do no more than accept the will of Parliament, to become, in this respect, the ministers of its will and interpreters, as far as they understood them, of the wishes of the people–perfectly content, if they could conduct the Bill to a successful issue, to give credit when they found it was due to others for having by intelligent discussion brought about that state of public opinion and feeling which rendered that or any other measure possible. With regard to the Notice of the hon. Member for East Sussex (Mr. Gregory) to send the Bill to a Select Committee, that was a Motion contingent on the second reading, and could not come before them unless the second reading was carried. He would, therefore, say no more than this–Here was a large, important, and valuable contribution to Law Reform; they had waited for it long enough, too long–and he would be no party to any proceeding that had any tendency to imperil its success, or even, in any appreciable manner to delay its progress.

166B. Speech of Mr. C. M. Norwood[1] (12 June)

Hansard, 3/CCXVI/863.

MR. NORWOOD said, there was one unfortunate class of persons who had a deep interest in this question, though they were not lawyers, and he ventured to interrupt the flow of legal eloquence to say a few words on their behalf. They were the suitors, who suffered from the present extremely expensive, dilatory, and unsatisfactory arrangements of our legal procedure, upon which this Bill would effect a vast and important improvement. Sometimes commercial men had a difficulty in knowing which tribunal they ought to apply to in order to get their grievances redressed, and more frequently complete relief could not be obtained in a Court either of Law or Equity; but this Bill proposed that there should be only one portal through which suitors could enter, and afterwards they would find the proper division for the discussion and adjudication of their cases; he approved the Bill because it abolished all the arbitrary distinctions between Courts of Law and Equity; because it shortened and simplified the procedure; because it established one–and that an efficient–Court of Appeal; because it invested the Common Law Judges with equitable powers; because sittings were to be held during the vacation for hearing cases of immediate importance; and because the present system of Terms was to be abolished. As to the provision which enabled the Judges to send cases to referees, he, as a commercial man, thought it would prove a very beneficial one, as it would obviate the inconvenience of the present system, under which cases were frequently referred to arbitration after very considerable expense had been incurred. He also approved a clause which allowed a Judge to decide cases with the assistance of two assessors, instead of trying

[1] Kingston-upon-Hull.

them before a promiscuous jury. Many improvements might be effected which were not referred to in the Bill now under consideration. For example, local commercial Courts might be established; but as a layman, representing laymen, he heartily supported the measure, because it proceeded in a right direction, and he trusted the Law Officers of the Crown would not consent to its references to a Select Committee, especially if that Committee were to be composed, as the hon. and learned Member for Dungarvan (Mr. Matthews) had suggested, solely of gentlemen belonging to the legal profession.

167. Supreme Court of Judicature Act (1873)

Statutes of the Realm, 36 & 37 Vict. c. 66.

PART I

3 . . . From and after the time appointed for the commencement of this Act, the several Courts herein-after mentioned, (that is to say,) the High Court of Chancery of England, the Court of Queen's Bench, the Court of Common Pleas at Westminster, the Court of Exchequer, the High Court of Admiralty, the Court of Probate, the Court for Divorce and Matrimonial Causes, and the London Court of Bankruptcy, shall be united and consolidated together, and shall constitute, under and subject to the provisions of this Act, one Supreme Court of Judicature in England.

4 The said Supreme Court shall consist of two permanent Divisions, one of which, under the name of "Her Majesty's High Court of Justice," shall have and exercise original jurisdiction, with such appellate jurisdiction from inferior Courts as is herein-after mentioned, and the other of which, under the name of "Her Majesty's Court of Appeal," shall have and exercise appellate jurisdiction, with such original jurisdiction as herein-after mentioned as may be incident to the determination of any appeal.

5 Her Majesty's High Court of Justice shall be constituted as follows:–The first Judges thereof shall be the Lord Chancellor, the Lord Chief Justice of England, the Master of the Rolls, the Lord Chief Justice of the Common Pleas, the Lord Chief Baron of the Exchequer, the several Vice-Chancellors of the High Court of Chancery, the Judge of the Court of Probate and of the Court for Divorce and Matrimonial Causes, the several Puisne Justices of the Courts of Queen's Bench and Common Pleas respectively, the several Junior Barons of the Court of Exchequer, and the Judge of the High Court of Admiralty, except such, if any, of the aforesaid Judges as shall be appointed ordinary Judges of the Court of Appeal.

Subject to the Provisions herein-after contained, whenever the office of a Judge of the said High Court shall become vacant, a new Judge may be appointed thereto by Her Majesty, by Letters Patent. All persons to be hereinafter appointed to fill the places of the Lord Chief Justice of England, the Master of the Rolls, the Lord Chief Justice of the Common Pleas, and the Lord Chief Baron, and their successors respectively, shall continue to be appointed to the same respective offices, with the same precedence, and by the same respective titles, and in the same manner, respectively, as heretofore. Every Judge who shall be appointed to fill the place of any Judge of the said High Court of Justice shall be styled in his appointment, "Judge of Her Majesty's High Court of Justice," and shall be appointed in the same manner in which the Puisne Justices and Junior Barons of the Superior Courts of Common Law have been heretofore appointed: Provided always, that if at the commencement of this Act the number of Puisne Justices and Junior Barons who shall become Judges of the said High Court shall exceed twelve in the whole, no new Judge of the said High Court shall be appointed in the place of any such Puisne Justice or Junior Baron who shall die or resign while such whole number shall exceed twelve, it being intended that the permanent number of Judges of the said High Court shall not exceed twenty-one.

All the Judges of the said Court shall have in all respects, save as in this Act is otherwise expressly provided, equal power, authority, and jurisdiction; and shall be addressed in the manner which is now customary in addressing the Judges of the Superior Courts of Common Law.

The Lord Chief Justice of England for the time being shall be President of the said High Court of Justice in the absence of the Lord Chancellor.

6 Her Majesty's Court of Appeal shall be constituted as follows:–There shall be five *ex officio* Judges thereof, and also so many ordinary Judges (not exceeding nine at any one time) as Her Majesty shall from time to time appoint. The *ex officio* Judges shall be the Lord Chancellor, the Lord Chief Justice of England, the Master of the Rolls, the Lord Chief Justice of the Common Pleas, and the Lord Chief Baron of the Exchequer. The first ordinary Judges of the said Court shall be the existing Lords Justices of Appeal in Chancery, the existing salaried Judges of the Judicial Committee of Her Majesty's Privy Council, appointed under the "Judicial Committee Act, 1871," and such three other persons as Her Majesty may be pleased to appoint by Letters Patent; such appointment may be made either within one month before or at any time after the day appointed for the commencement of this Act, but if made before shall take effect at the commencement of this Act.

Besides the said *ex officio* Judges and ordinary Judges, it shall be lawful for Her Majesty (if she shall think fit) from time to time to appoint, under Her Royal Sign Manual as additional Judges of the Court of Appeal, any persons who having held in England the office of a Judge of the Superior Courts of Westminster hereby united and consolidated, or of Her Majesty's Supreme Court hereby constituted, or in Scotland the office of Lord Justice General or Lord Justice Clerk, or in Ireland the office of Lord Chancellor or Lord Justice of Appeal, or in India the office of Chief Justice of the High Court of Judicature at Fort William in Bengal, or Madras, or Bombay, shall respectively signify in writing their willingness to serve as such additional Judges in the Court of Appeal. No such additional Judge shall be deemed to have undertaken the duty of sitting in the Court of Appeal when prevented from so doing by attendance in the House of Lords, or on the discharge of any other public duty, or by any other reasonable impediment.

The ordinary and additional Judges of the Court of Appeal shall be styled Lords Justices of Appeal. All the Judges of the said Court shall have, in all respects, save as in this Act is otherwise expressly mentioned, equal power, authority, and jurisdiction.

Whenever the office of an ordinary Judge of the Court of Appeal becomes vacant, a new Judge may be appointed thereto by Her Majesty by Letters Patent.

The Lord Chancellor for the time being shall be President of the Court of Appeal. . . .

PART 2

16 The High Court of Justice shall be a Superior Court of Record, and, subject as in this Act mentioned, there shall be transferred to and vested in the said High Court of Justice the jurisdiction which, at the commencement of this Act, was vested in, or capable of being exercised by, all or any of the Courts following; (that is to say,)

(1) The High Court of Chancery, as a Common Law Court as well as a Court of Equity, including the jurisdiction of the Master of the Rolls, as a Judge or Master of the Court of Chancery, and any jurisdiction exercised by him in relation to the Court of Chancery as a Common Law Court;
(2) The Court of Queen's Bench;
(3) The Court of Common Pleas at Westminster;
(4) The Court of Exchequer, as a Court of Revenue, as well as a Common Law Court;
(5) The High Court of Admiralty;
(6) The Court of Probate;
(7) The Court for Divorce and Matrimonial Causes;
(8) The London Court of Bankruptcy;
(9) The Court of Common Pleas at Lancaster;
(10) The Court of Pleas at Durham;
(11) The Courts created by Commissioners of Assize, of Oyer and Terminer, and of Gaol Delivery, or any of such Commissions:

The jurisdiction by this Act transferred to the High Court of Justice shall include (subject to the exceptions herein-after contained) the jurisdiction which, at the commencement of this Act, was vested in, or capable of being exercised by, all or any one or more of the Judges of the said Courts, respectively, sitting in Court or Chambers, or elsewhere, when acting as Judges or a Judge, in pursuance of any statute, law, or custom, and all powers given to any such Court, or to any such Judges or Judge, by any statute; and also all ministerial powers, duties, and authorities, incident to any and every part of the jurisdictions so transferred.

17 There shall not be transferred to or vested in the said High Court of Justice, virtue of this Act,–

(1) Any appellate jurisdiction of the Court of Appeal in Chancery, or of the same Court sitting as a Court of Appeal in Bankruptcy:
(2) Any jurisdiction of the Court of Appeal in Chancery of the County Palatine of Lancaster:

(3) Any jurisdiction usually vested in the Lord Chancellor or in the Lords Justices of Appeal in Chancery, or either of them, in relation to the custody of the persons and estates of idiots, lunatics, and persons of unsound mind.

(4) Any jurisdiction vested in the Lord Chancellor in relation to grants of Letters Patent, or the issue of commissions or other writings, to be passed under the Great Seal of the United Kingdom:

(5) Any jurisdiction exercised by the Lord Chancellor in right of or on behalf of Her Majesty as visitor of any College, or of any charitable or other foundation:

(6) Any jurisdiction of the Master of the Rolls in relation to records in London or elsewhere in England.

18 The Court of Appeal established by this Act shall be a Superior Court of Record, and there shall be transferred to and vested in such Court all jurisdiction and powers of the Courts following: (that is to say,)

(1) All jurisdiction and powers of the Lord Chancellor and of the Court of Appeal in Chancery, in the exercise of his and its appellate jurisdiction, and of the same Court as a Court of Appeal in Bankruptcy:

(2) All jurisdiction and powers of the Court of Appeal in Chancery of the county palatine of Lancaster, and all jurisdiction and powers of the Chancellor of the duchy and county palatine of Lancaster when sitting alone or apart from the Lords Justices of Appeal in Chancery as a Judge of re-hearing or appeal from decrees or orders of the Court of Chancery of the county palatine of Lancaster:

(3) All jurisdiction and powers of the Court of the Lord Warden of the Stannaries assisted by his assessors, including all jurisdiction and powers of the said Lord Warden when sitting in his capacity of Judge:

(4) All jurisdiction and powers of the Court of Exchequer Chamber:

(5) All jurisdiction vested in or capable of being exercised by Her Majesty in Council, or the Judicial Committee of Her Majesty's Privy Council, upon appeal from any judgment or order of the High Court of Admiralty, or from any order in lunacy made by the Lord Chancellor, or any other person having jurisdiction in lunacy.

19 The said Court of Appeal shall have jurisdiction and power to hear and determine Appeals from any judgment or order, save as herein-after mentioned, of Her Majesty's High Court of Justice, or of any Judges or Judge thereof, subject to the provisions of this Act, and to such Rules and Orders of Court for regulating the terms and conditions on which such appeals shall be allowed, as may be made pursuant to this Act.

For all the purposes of and incidental to the hearing and determination of any Appeal within its jurisdiction, and the amendment, execution, and enforcement of any judgment or order made on any such appeal, and for the purpose of every other authority expressly given to the Court of Appeal by this Act, the said Court of

Appeal shall have all the power, authority, and jurisdiction by this Act vested in the High Court of Justice.

20 No error or appeal shall be brought from any judgment or order of the High Court of Justice, or of the Court of Appeal, nor from any judgment or order, subsequent to the commencement of this Act, of the Court of Chancery of the county palatine of Lancaster to the House of Lords or to the Judicial Committee of Her Majesty's Privy Council; but nothing in this Act shall prejudice any right existing at the commencement of this Act to prosecute any pending writ of error or appeal, or to bring error or appeal to the House of Lords or to Her Majesty in Council, or to the Judicial Committee of the Privy Council, from any prior judgment or order of any Court whose jurisdiction is hereby transferred to the High Court of Justice or to the Court of Appeal. . . .

Section 31

For the more convenient despatch of business in the said High Court of Justice (but not so as to prevent any Judge from sitting whenever required in any Divisional Court, or for any Judge of a different Division from his own,) there shall be in the said High Court five Divisions consisting of such number of Judges respectively as herein-after mentioned. Such five Divisions shall respectively include, immediately on the commencement of this Act, the several Judges following: (that is to say,)

(1) One Division shall consist of the following Judges; (that is to say,) The Lord Chancellor, who shall be President thereof, the Master of the Rolls, and the Vice-Chancellors of the Court of Chancery, or such of them as shall not be appointed ordinary Judges of the Court of Appeal:

(2) One other Division shall consist of the following Judges; (that is to say,) The Lord Chief Justice of England, who shall be President thereof, and such of the other Judges of the Court of Queen's Bench as shall not be appointed ordinary Judges of the Court of Appeal:

(3) One other Division shall consist of the following Judges; (that is to say,) The Lord Chief Justice of the Common Pleas, who shall be President thereof, and such of the other Judges of the Court of Common Pleas as shall not be appointed ordinary Judges of the Court of Appeal:

(4) One other Division shall consist of the following Judges; (that is to say,) The Lord Chief Baron of the Exchequer, who shall be President thereof, and such of the other Barons of the Court of Exchequer as shall not be appointed ordinary Judges of the Court of Appeal:

(5) One other Division shall consist of two Judges who, immediately on the commencement of this Act, shall be the existing Judge of the Court of Probate and of the Court for Divorce and Matrimonial Causes and the existing Judge of the High Court of Admiralty, unless either of them is appointed an ordinary Judge to the Court of Appeal. The existing Judge of the Court of Probate shall (unless so appointed) be the President of the said Division, and subject thereto the Senior Judge of the said Division, according to the order of Precedence under this Act, shall be President.

The said five Divisions shall be called respectively the Chancery Division, the Queen's Bench Division, the Common Pleas Division, the Exchequer Division, and the Probate, Divorce, and Admiralty Division.

168. Appellate Jurisdiction Act (1876)

Statutes of the Realm, 39 & 40 Vict. c. 59.

1. This Act may be cited for all purposes as "The Appellate Jurisdiction Act, 1876."

2. This Act shall, except where it is otherwise expressly provided, come into operation on the first day of November one thousand eight hundred and seventy-six, which day is herein-after referred to as the commencement of this Act.

3. Subject as in this Act mentioned an appeal shall lie to the House of Lords from any order or judgment of any of the courts following; that is to say,

(i) Of Her Majesty's Court of Appeal in England; and

(ii) Of any Court in Scotland from which error or an appeal at or immediately before the commencement of this Act lay to the House of Lords by common law or by statute; and

(iii) Of any Court in Ireland from which error or an appeal at or immediately before the commencement of this Act lay to the House of Lords by common law or by statute.

4. Every appeal shall be brought by way of petition to the House of Lords, praying that the matter of the order or judgment appealed against may be reviewed before Her Majesty the Queen in her Court of Parliament, in order that the said Court may determine what of right, and according to the law and custom of this realm, ought to be done in the subject-matter of such appeal.

5. An appeal shall not be heard and determined by the House of Lords unless there are present at such hearing and determination not less than three of the following persons, in this Act designated Lords of Appeal; that is to say,

(i) The Lord Chancellor of Great Britain for the time being; and

(ii) The Lords of Appeal in Ordinary to be appointed as in this Act mentioned; and

(iii) Such Peers of Parliament as are for the time being holding or have held any of the offices in this Act described as high judicial offices.

6. For the purpose of aiding the House of Lords in the hearing and determination of appeals, Her Majesty may, at any time after the passing of this Act, by letters patent appoint two qualified persons to be Lords of Appeal in Ordinary, but such appointment shall not take effect until the commencement of this Act.

A person shall not be qualified to be appointed by Her Majesty a Lord of Appeal in Ordinary unless he has been at or before the time of his appointment the holder for a period of not less than two years of some one or more of the offices in this Act described as high judicial offices, or has been at or before such time as aforesaid, for not less than fifteen years, a practising barrister in England or Ireland, or a practising advocate in Scotland.

Part VII

CENTRAL ADMINISTRATION

CENTRAL ADMINISTRATION

Introduction

THE overhaul of the administration, which is one of the achievements attributable to the Victorian voracity for reform, may be said to derive from three influences: the movement for Economical Reform, which began half a century earlier; Benthamite criticism and administrative doctrine; and the desire of an increasingly business-minded Parliament to see that public business was conducted with the same economy and efficiency as competition imposed upon private affairs. A supporting factor was the increasing conscientiousness which the spread of Evangelical and Anglican piety bred in the country at large, and particularly in the middle and upper classes. The Economical Reform movement had been political in object, directed to the reduction of the influence of the Crown; and a political aim, the elimination of the power of patronage in politics and of the influence of politics upon the efficiency of administration, continued to operate. This particular target was not big enough, in fact, to absorb all the arrows directed against it. But it served to draw attention to more deeply rooted problems.

As has been said,[1] the more valuable forms of government patronage had already largely been eliminated, and what remained was probably of less political significance than it seemed. It comprised numbers of small posts, largely under Customs and Excise. In 1820, Liverpool had handed over the patronage of Customs and Excise to the office itself, but since then Treasury had got a lot of it back. In most departments some of the initial patronage, and virtually all promotion,[2] was in the hands of the department itself. Many posts required professional qualifications; virtually all had fixed ages of entry; and the more important, *e.g.* the Foreign Office, had qualifying examinations. Most were subject to probation. Convention required that the sitting member of a constituency, if he were a supporter of the Government, should be consulted before any vacancy occurring in his constituency was filled. Candidates nursing opposition seats might also expect some consideration. Ministers dealing with patronage always complained that they had not nearly enough to meet demands, and most kept a waiting list of applicants. Similar complaints were made by members. In political circles generally, as is revealed by the debates on Administrative Reform in 1855, some disposition had grown up to regard patronage as hardly worth the trouble that it entailed. But in the 'fifties, as at every stage of the movement for Economical Reform, there were ministers who feared that the executive might be weakened too much, and party managers who were afraid of the effect upon discipline in the House and in constituencies. In 1853, Sir James Graham, despite his record of reform, held these views. This was among the factors that kept the reform movement of the decade in check. And it can be argued, perhaps, that in a matter so closely bound up with deep-rooted habits and expectations, the too precipitate expulsion of the devil of patronage might have opened the door to the entry of seven more.

[1] Part II, Introduction. [2] No. 169.

From the 'thirties onwards, some quiet reform improving the administrative efficiency of departments had been going on, notably at the Admiralty, under Sir James Graham.[1] A debate in 1848, on the estimates for civil contingencies, gave rise to a demand for economy, in which the Protectionists, still sore after their recent defeat, supported the Radicals, from whom such movements more normally came. This probably explains the series of departmental inquiries, initiated under Sir Charles Wood and Sir George Grey, Russell's Chancellor of the Exchequer and Home Secretary[2] in that year, and carried on by Disraeli and Gladstone, the succeeding chancellors. Extracts from the Report on the Treasury in 1849,[3] on the Colonial Office in the same year,[4] and on the Board of Ordnance in 1853[5] are printed. The Board of Ordnance was regarded as something of a model office at the time; the extracts from the Roebuck Report[6] illustrate the disarray into which it fell under the impact of war, and in the absence of a master-general. It is clear from these reports that from the administrative angle the dominant problem was not the quality of the intake but rather its effective use. This demanded the proper separation of the more routine tasks from those requiring experience and judgment, the proper training of those who would be carrying responsibility later, and, above all, promotion by merit rather than simply by seniority. Gladstone, in 1853, had the principle of competition very much in his mind. There had just been published the Report of the Royal Commission on Oxford University,[7] which had suggested the need, among other reforms, of opening elections to fellowships and scholarships to wider competition. On Gladstone was to fall the duty of piloting through the House the Bill on which the reform of the university was to be based. In March 1853 he instructed Sir Stafford Northcote and Sir Charles Trevelyan–who had been concerned in many of the earlier reports–to investigate the subject of civil service reform as a whole. The famous Northcote-Trevelyan Report–the foundation document, it may almost be called, of the modern Civil Service–was completed in November 1853, circulated fairly freely amongst educationalists and civil servants throughout the winter, and was published in February 1854. A fortnight before its publication an article in *The Times* contained a remarkable anticipation of its conclusions. The Report[8] contained a great deal of criticism of the personnel, methods, and organization of the service, and proposed to rectify the faults by the setting up of a single unified service, by the initiation of entry into it by competitive examination, by the separation of routine from responsible duties, and by greater insistence on promotion by merit. The aim was to secure to the service the cream of the youth of the country. Appended to the Report was a letter from Benjamin Jowett, the celebrated Balliol tutor, supporting the proposals, and more particularly emphasizing the value and the practicability of entrance by examination. The opinions of a number of other educationalists were obtained, and were almost unanimously in favour of the scheme, as likely to provide an invaluable stimulus to university studies, and through them to the schools. Other views were also sought and published; that of Sir James Stephen endorsed the criticisms, but rejected the remedies of the Report, and is so cogent and penetrating in the criticisms which it makes of its assumptions as to form its almost indispensable supplement. J. S. Mill was enthusiastically in support.[9] The opinions of senior Civil Servants themselves, asked for later, were neither uniform nor eulogistic, except about the presentation of the Report. Several expressed doubts whether the qualities and the outlook

[1] No. 169. [2] No. 180. [3] No. 170. [4] No. 171. [5] No. 172.
[6] No. 181. [7] Part XI, No. 243. [8] No. 173. [9] No. 174.

developed in competitive study were those best suited to the Civil Servant; others feared that promotion by merit might be regarded as a synonym for favouritism; many felt that to deprive heads of departments of their power of controlling entry would weaken their disciplinary authority; and not all were prepared to accept the view that, from the personnel point of view, it was practicable to fuse the departments in a single unified service. Even those who were prepared to accept, more or less, the proposals put forward by the Report condemned its strictures on the existing service as unfair. George Arbuthnot made himself the mouthpiece of this feeling,[1] and it cannot be said that the reply of the authors of the Report[2] was very convincing. Political opinion was sceptical. The queen feared that open competition would lower the character of the service; the Whig element in the Cabinet was unconvinced; and there were no immediate signs of enthusiasm in Parliament. Before Gladstone could bring the issue to decision, Aberdeen's Cabinet had fallen, and Gladstone himself was out of office.

George Cornewall Lewis, who became Chancellor of the Exchequer in Palmerston's Government, had been one of the critics of the Report. The Order in Council of 21 May 1855,[3] regulating entry to the Civil Service, was his work and represented the Whig view. Its great step was to set up the Civil Service Commissioners, with the duty of ascertaining that entrants to the Civil Service possessed the requisite qualifications. But what the qualifications were was to be settled, in the case of each department, with the head of that department. The Commission's first fight was to establish its control of all examinations. Not all departments had even entrance examinations at the start; nomination still prevailed, but the rule that gradually became general was limited competition amongst nominees, and in 1861, after the report of a Select Committee which had been critical of it, Palmerston imposed this in the case of all posts leading to positions of responsibility. Early correspondence of the Commissioners varies from that with the factory inspectors as to the qualifications to be required of candidates whose age was to be between twenty-five and forty and who were to undertake delicate and responsible duties from the start, to that with the General Register Office, as to the examination of messengers. In their second Report the Commissioners claim it as a merit that they had failed no candidate for history alone. The Commissioners themselves believed in open competition, and in their third, sixth, and thirteenth Annual Reports particularly, commended it strongly. Resolutions in favour of it were passed in the House of Commons in 1856 and 1857, but no Government action followed, and the subject was not pressed. In 1869 and 1870 Henry Fawcett raised the issue again, and on the second occasion Gladstone accepted the principle on behalf of his Government.[4] The resulting Order in Council of 4 June 1870[5] gave the Civil Service Commissioners the power at last - under Treasury control, and with specified exceptions, of which the Foreign Office was the most important - themselves to determine the qualifications of entrants, and this led to the institution of open competition.

The crucial phase of the question of Civil Service Reform was associated with a still wider attack on patronage resulting from the activities of the Administrative Reform Association, and the scandals arising from the Crimean War. The Administrative Reform Association had its occasion in some notorious malversations on the part of a Customs official named Everett, in 1851. Its political prominence was associated with the meteoric rise of A. H. Layard, the discoverer of Nineveh, Liberal member for Aylesbury in 1852, and in the same year made under-secretary for foreign affairs, and president of the Association in 1855. Layard was told in the House

[1] No. 175. [2] No. 176. [3] No. 177. [4] No. 187. [5] No. 188.

that in view of his own rise, without any private recommendation, the accusations he made sat ill in his mouth. The Crimean War, it must be remembered, resulted in considerable part from the pressure of Radical jingoism upon the Government. A generation had grown up which had forgotten the perils and strains of the Napoleonic wars, and what the price of victory had been. Government after Government, moreover, had won credit or evaded criticism by cutting the army down or starving the administrative machines on which it depended. Wellington had remained commander-in-chief–an office not for a considerable number of years subordinated to the secretary of state for war–until his death in 1852; Hardinge, one of his officers, succeeded him, and Raglan, another, was to command in the Crimea. The confidence of a great professional tradition had not been matched by adequate testing under actual strain, and much aristocratic amateurism, which the duke had known how to deal with in his professional prime, had crept in alongside of it. Finally, the Government which was to handle the war was a coalition hardly fully compacted, as yet, and containing no one, in a relevant position, possessing the drive, the instantaneous grasp of priorities in a rapidly changing position, and the capacity for an irreverent handling of precedent and tradition, which are essential in war. The campaigns were to provide a searing experience for the governing classes and the nation. Rightly, the first and the lasting impression was of the grandeur of the physical courage shown throughout–from the tenacious heroism of the infantry at Alma, through the magnificence of the insufferable Cardigan's ride, at the head of the Six Hundred without a backward glance at his troops, right into the Russian guns, to the bitter fighting of the actual assault on Sebastopol. But beyond that common thrill of pride, all was discomfiture, division, and rage. For the first time in war what actually was happening, week by week, was told to the public by a brilliant war correspondent who pulled no punches, Russell, of *The Times*. The remorseless Radical Roebuck–'Old Tear 'em'–insisted on dragging forth the tale of error.[1] The lassitude of political chiefs was matched by the improvidence and irresponsibility of military decisions. The prestige of the governing classes reached, perhaps, its nadir within the period. The administrative mistakes were typical Civil Service ones–those of an airless bureaucratic machine conditioned to its procedures but not to its responsibilities, and clinging in panic to its protocol. But it was starved of the man-power that it needed. The only thing well done, apart from sheer fighting and endurance, was the work of Florence Nightingale, and that was achieved in the face of every sort of official obstruction and delay.

It was in an air heavy with these revelations that the crucial debates on administrative and Civil Service reform took place. Parliament met, in 1855, on 28 January, under the threat of a motion by Roebuck for an inquiry into the situation of the army in the Crimea. Russell, who for some months had been unhappy with his colleagues, and concerned over the administration of the war but nevertheless shared with the rest of the Cabinet responsibility for what had been done and left undone, resigned the following day. After two days' debate on Roebuck's motion, Aberdeen's Government was defeated in an angry House by 305 to 147. Derby, to the dismay of Disraeli, declined the post of responsibility and honour. Russell, no one would serve. Ironically enough, in view of their recent relations,[2] it was to Palmerston that the queen turned, as the country had done already. Even his barque was nearly wrecked; the Roebuck motion had been directed against the previous Government, and it might have been thought that, at the crisis of a war, the fall of the Government

[1] No. 181. [2] Part I, Nos. 12–21.

would have satisfied its supporters. But it soon became clear that this was not so, and Palmerston had to abandon resistance to the inquiry. This cost him the support of Graham, Gladstone, and Herbert, within less than three weeks of the formation of his Government. They regarded the motion as directed against their Peelite associate, the duke of Newcastle, who had been Aberdeen's secretary for war. It was the refusal of Peelite support that had caused Derby to despair of the republic. Palmerston replaced his ministers and carried on. By courage and resilience that won the heart of Parliament and of the country, and by a plain sense of duty in war, Palmerston had saved his Government, and perhaps government in general from a deeper discredit. By the time the debates came on, and the Roebuck Report was ready for publication, the tide of war was perceptibly on the change; the great Autocrat of Russia had died discouraged in the spring, and the weight of allied reinforcements was beginning to tell. But the attack was nevertheless lively. Layard made it an attack on the aristocracy,[1] Bulwer Lytton drove it home against the 'Whig cousinage'. "Your Cabinets have been one colossal instance of family patronage. You trace your map of office as the Chinese trace a map of the world. The Chinese draw a square; into that square they describe a circle, which fills up all the space except four little corners. The circle is the Celestial Empire; the four little corners are assigned to the miserable remnants of mankind. So, when you come into power, you describe round Downing Street your circle; in that circle you place the sacred families of the Whigs–that is the Celestial Empire; and to the four little corners you banish the herd of your supporters." But Layard and Lytton were, after all, the lightweights of debate; referring to the Administrative Reform Association, the Annual Register of 1855 spoke of it as "unsupported by any names carrying any considerable intellectual weight or political influence, ... (it) had not gained any perceptible hold ... upon the sympathies of the masses, or the convictions of the intelligent portion of the community". The adhesion to the Association of a popular novelist of the name of Charles Dickens, a close associate of Layard, had not affected this verdict. Gladstone's measured vindication of aristocracy,[2] on the other hand, carried weight, the more for his reputation as a reformer, immensely enhanced by his Budget of 1853.[3] The debate–three weeks after the issue of the Order in Council of 21 May–was also the first full-dress debate on Civil Service reform. On this subject, Gladstone made clear his preference for open competition. Romilly, one of the early Civil Service reformers, but nevertheless an opponent of the Northcote-Trevelyan Report, had referred to the danger that it might lead to "a democratic civil service by the side of an aristocratic legislature". He was quoted in the debate. "This was just the spirit Gladstone loathed," writes his biographer, Morley. But it has been pointed out by Professor Hughes that Gladstone commended open competition to Russell on the ground that it would lead to a more aristocratic Civil Service, not to a democratic one. "I have a strong impression that the aristocracy in this country are even superior in natural gifts, on the average, to the mass; but it is plain that with their acquired advantages, their *insensible* education, apart from book-learning, they have an immense superiority. This applies, in its degree, to all who may be called gentlemen by birth and training; and it must be remembered that an essential part of any such plan as is now under discussion is the separation of work, wherever it can be made, into mechanical and intellectual, a separation which will open to the highly educated class a career and give them a command over all the higher parts of the civil service, which, up to this time, they

[1] No. 178. [2] No. 179. [3] Part V, Introduction and No. 151.

have never enjoyed." George Cornewall Lewis made the vote a question of confidence in the Government, and, on an amendment which Palmerston accepted, the Government triumphed by 349 to 356. A second debate on 10 July was on a motion for open competition, and its extension to the Diplomatic and Consular services. This was lost by 125 to 140. Meanwhile Roebuck had overplayed his hand on his committee. The draft report he had prepared was rejected in favour of one by Seymour. What Roebuck's would have been like may be surmised from the one actually accepted.[1] In the debate of 17 July upon it he made the same mistake, moving a motion of 'severe reprehension' on every member of the Cabinet responsible for conditions in the Crimea, and making a particular set at Palmerston. He gave the impression that having upset one Government, he was now determined to bring down another, and his speech was not a successful one. Russell described it as "showing the beak and talons of a bird of prey, but inside is nothing but straw". His motion was defeated by 289 to 182, and the minority was swollen by the fact that the division was taken on the previous motion, and some of those who voted for him were Peelites who felt in honour bound to challenge a direct vote on the issue. The Radical riot was over; so far as the Civil Service was concerned, the year's debates virtually decided that for the next fifteen years, without running the risk of Gladstone's somewhat schoolmasterly conception of aristocracy, its higher ranks should be the preserve of gentlemen; its tradition in years of important development was so formed; and the ease of social contact between its members and ministers, which was what Romilly had in mind, was thus preserved. Nor did competition, when it first came, in view of the emphasis in the examinations on classics, do much more than 'annex' the Civil Service to the universities. So far as politics were concerned, the 'Whig cousinage', enlarged to admit the commanding talents of a Gladstone or a Lowe, entered on its palmiest period, not broken, indeed, until the advent, in 1874, of Tory democracy. But the alert had been sharp. It is not fanciful, perhaps, to look on the crisis of the Crimea as completing the work of the Reform Act. As the latter had put the aristocracy on its mettle politically, so the Crimean crisis put it on its mettle in the army and in the administration. Its best might be the best that there was, but the warning had been issued that its best was required of it.

The Crimean War brought a clarification of political responsibilities for the army; in 1854 the secretaryship for war and the colonies had been divided into its component elements; and in 1855 the secretaryship-at-war, with mainly financial responsibilities, which Sidney Herbert had held, was united with the secretaryship of war, until its abolition in 1863. Miss Nightingale, authentically the Lady with the Lamp, the sainted succourer of death-beds, was also one of the ablest administrative brains of her day. Supported by the queen and Prince Albert, she applied her demonic power to the fine, but frailer, soul of Herbert, who had sent her to the Crimea, and drove him to the task of cleansing the Augean stables of the medical administration of the army, and of the application thereto of modern and scientific principles. Through heartbreaking disappointments and delays the work went on. Next, when Herbert became secretary of war in Palmerston's 1859 Cabinet, she drove him to the still more herculean task of the reform of War Office administration. She killed him; and War Office reform had to await the advent of Cardwell, another Peelite, in Gladstone's reforming ministry of 1868–1874. Under him a clear-cut division of the office into the departments of the commander-in-chief, now subordinated to the secretary of

[1] No. 181.

state, ordnance, and finance, was achieved; the purchase of commissions was abolished; and steps were taken to concentrate an effective striking force from detachments scattered in garrisons all over the Empire, and to create an effective reserve. But a more fundamental reform was initiated by Miss Nightingale. Out of the hell of her Crimean ordeal–it was her own phrase–had been born in her mind a profound and passionate sympathy for the British private soldier–Wellington's "scum of the earth, enlisted for pay". Her immense prestige and influence were used to force the authorities to think of him as a human being, deserving of human consideration, and humane conditions. Ultimately she succeeded. The long-run social consequences of this vindication of ultimate democracy in the context, in this country, least propitious to it, would require a lengthy consideration.

The third major trend of general historical consequence in the administrative history of the period is the steady elaboration of the instruments of public financial responsibility. Graham started it with his reorganization of Admiralty accounting in 1832.[1] In 1834 the Exchequer was reorganized; payments in were centralized in the Bank of England, and the comptroller-general was made responsible for all payments out. In 1836 a paymaster-general took all the services, including the Civil Service, within his scope. In 1846 Graham's appropriation audit was extended to the army departments, and between 1856 and 1858 to the War Office. The power to transfer surpluses from one head to another had been retained, but the audit made plain the fact of such transfer, and it could be debated by Parliament if it wanted. In 1858 parliamentary ratification of transfer was required. In 1857 the Select Committee on Public Monies recommended the systematic application of the appropriation audit throughout the whole range of public expenditure.[2] The setting up of the Committee of Public Accounts in 1861[3] provided for a parliamentary check on expenditure, after it had been incurred, on the way that money had been used, apart from the narrow question of the authority for its use. Finally the Exchequer and Audit Act of 1866[4] met the desire of the Select Committee on Public Monies by providing strong and uniform machinery to secure full parliamentary control over all expenditure of public money. The completion of this machinery was a technical accomplishment of considerable importance. It served to express the strong sense of parliamentary supremacy that was the heart of Victorian constitutionalism. It was an accepted maxim of the time that a good administration is always also an economical administration. In perfecting the machinery of parliamentary financial control, it was assumed that it would be the pleasure and the duty of Parliament, as it ought also to be within its power, to see that in all public contexts this maxim was given its fullest effect. A sense of the sacredness of public money, even down to the smallest sums, pervaded Victorian society, in strong contrast to the laxity it had inherited from Regency and eighteenth-century England. In a rich society this was not primarily a principle of stinginess; public money could be freely spent where it was properly spent. It derived rather from the deepened sense of public reponsibility: money was the sinews of public life, and the public servant owed it unremitting care. It expressed also the strong individualism of the period; public money was really private money, somebody's money appropriated from them for public ends. This strict sense of financial responsibility radiated from public through local and semi-public administration–that of Friendly Societies, for example[5]–into private life. It may have been narrow, in some respects, but it undoubtedly had a bracing effect.

[1] No. 169. [2] No. 182. [3] No. 183. [4] Nos. 184–186. [5] Part III, Introduction and No. 108.

SELECT BIBLIOGRAPHY

The *Parliamentary Debates* of June and July 1855 on Administrative Reform and on the Roebuck Report, of April 1856 on Admission to the Civil Service, and of July 1857 on the Extension of Competition are of primary importance. Those of 1869 and 1870, prior to Gladstone's acceptance of the competitive principle, are important, but not of the same interest.

The *Report on Inquiries into Civil Service Establishments* (including the *Northcote-Trevelyan Report*) (*Parlty. Papers*, 1854/xxvii), the *Papers on the Reorganisation of the Civil Service* (*Parlty. Papers*, 1854–1855/xx), the *Report on the Army before Sebastopol* (the *Roebuck Report*) (*Parlty. Papers*, 1854–1855/ix, Parts 1–3), are the capital papers of the critical years 1854–1855. The *Annual Report of the Civil Service Commissioners*–beginning in 1856 (*Parlty. Papers*, 1856/xxii), especially the earlier ones, illustrate the teething troubles of this central organ of nineteenth-century administrative reform. The *Third*, *Sixth*, and *Thirteenth Annual Reports* (*Parlty. Papers*, 1857–1858/xxv, 1861/xix, and 1867–1868/xxii), deal especially with the competitive principle. The *Report of the Select Committee on the Nomination and Examining of Candidates for Junior Posts in the Civil Service* (*Parlty. Papers*, 1860/ix), is an interim report, and the *Report of the Civil Service Enquiry Commission* (the *Playfair Report*) (*Parlty. Papers*, 1875/xxiii, 1876/xxii), sums up–though from a point of view not entirely accepted–the experience of the first generation of reform.

E. W. Cohen, *Growth of the British Civil Service, 1780–1939* (London, 1941), gives a connected account; see also H. Finer, *The British Civil Service* (London, 1927). C. S. Parker, *Life and Letters of Sir James Graham* (2 vols., London, 1907), R. E. Leader, *Life and Letters of J. A. Roebuck* (London, 1897), John Morley, *Life of W. E. Gladstone* (3 vols., London, 1903), and Sir G. O. Trevelyan, *Life and Letters of Lord Macaulay* (2 vols., London, 1876), throw special light on subjects of administrative reform. The best accounts of the question of Civil Service reform in the 'fifties are E. Hughes, "Sir Charles Trevelyan and Civil Service Reform", in *English Historical Review*, vol. xliv (1949), and "Civil Service Reform, 1853–5", in *History*, vol. xxvii (1942). R. H. Lewis, "Edwin Chadwick and Civil Service Reform", in *Birmingham University Historical Journal*, 2 (1951), should also be consulted.

On financial administration, the *Reports of the Select Committee on Public Monies* (*Parlty. Papers*, 1856/xv, and 1857, Sess. 2/ix) contain a great deal of information and discussion. A. J. V. Durell, *The Principles and Practice of the System of Control over Parliamentary Grants* (Portsmouth, 1917), is the standard authority. There is, unfortunately, no work devoted specifically to administrative history during the century, and the student must have recourse to the constitutional histories–D. L. Keir, *The Constitutional History of Modern Britain, 1485–1937* (London, 1938), K. B. Smellie, *A Hundred Years of English Government* (London, 1937), and A. B. Keith, *The Constitution of England from Queen Victoria to George VI* (2 vols., London, 1940). J. A. R. Marriott, *The Mechanism of the Modern State* (2 vols., London, 1927), may also be used. Sir R. Biddulph, *Cardwell at the War Office* (London, 1904), is a valuable study of the work of a great army reformer.

Olive Anderson, *A Liberal State at War* (1967) – problems, primarily administrative, of Crimean War; *The Janus-face of mid-nineteenth century Radicalism*, Victorian Studies vi (1965); Valerie Cromwell, *Interpretation of Nineteenth Century Administration – an Analysis*, Victorian Studies ix, 1966; Oliver McDonagh, *A Pattern of Government Growth: the Passenger Acts 1800–1860* (1962).

169A–B. Graham's reforms at the Admiralty (1830–1834)

169A. Patronage

Parker, *Life and Letters of Sir James Graham*, 1907, I, p. 163.

To ——, M.P.

Admiralty, September 25, 1832.

You cannot doubt my sincere and anxious wish to do everything fairly within my power to uphold your interest, and to give you efficient assistance and support. But I am not at liberty to set aside professional claims on account of political differences. In my opinion the Government is best served, and its real interests best supported, by perfect fairness and strict impartiality in the distribution of professional rewards.

All promotion in the Dockyard will henceforth be given as the reward of merit, on the recommendation of the Admiral Superintendent. As patronage I cease to exercise it, and I have made it over to the Board, with the intention of carefully watching its distribution.

169B. Financial reform

Parker, *op. cit.*, pp. 167–168.

Memorandum by Sir William Anderson

Sir James Graham's great talent for dealing with the most complicated details of business was remarkably displayed in the complete reform of the whole system of Naval accounts which he carried out immediately after his accession to office in 1830.

The great extension of the Naval Service during the protracted hostilities which terminated in 1815, and the complications which arose from the peculiar mode of meeting the demands of the naval charges during years of great financial pressure, had brought the accounts of the Naval Departments into a state of great confusion.

The fifteen years of peace which had succeeded had done little to place them on a systematic footing. There was little disposition on the part of Governments to give the country more information respecting their financial proceedings than they were obliged to furnish, and there was no earnest determination in Parliament to require it. It is due to Sir James Graham to state that he stimulated public opinion on this question, and initiated a reform of the National Accounts which is still in progress.

Sir James Graham felt that all his efforts to establish greater conformity between the actual expenditure and the votes of Parliament would be unavailing, unless he succeeded in restoring the proper constitutional control of the Legislature in this great branch of public expenditure, by establishing a system of account capable of reducing to order the vast and complicated details of Naval expenditure.

His first step was to present the estimates of the annual naval expenditure in a simple form, intelligible to the House of Commons and the country; he next ordered that the accounts should be kept upon the same system as those of the commercial world, being convinced that accounts which concerned all should be intelligible to all; and in order to secure the truth of these accounts, and to prevent the possibility of a relapse into the state of confusion from which he had succeeded in extricating them, he introduced a Bill into Parliament by which the Government became bound to present an annual account of the Naval Expenditure to the House of Commons audited by an independent Board of Commissioners, the Audit Board.

These regulations have now been thirty years in operation; the improvements of which he laid the solid foundation have stood the test of war; and although the Service has more than doubled, the system has continued to work admirably, and few Departments of the State can account with equal clearness and accuracy for the expenditure of the public money entrusted to their charge. When the complicated details of the Naval Expenditure, conducted in every part of the globe, in every description of currency, and through a multitude of subordinate agents, are considered, too much praise can scarcely be given to Sir James for the energy with which he pursued his task, and the early period at which he brought it to a successful issue.

But the benefit of his measures was not limited to the Department in which he introduced them; they have been extended to other Departments of the State with equally beneficial results. . . .

170. Committee of inquiry into Treasury establishments (2 March 1849)

Parlty. Papers, 1854/XXVII, pp. 42–43.

. . . It has for many years been fully established as the rule of the Office, that merit and qualification, and not seniority, should be the prevailing motives in selecting persons for promotion; and this principle was emphatically asserted on the last occasion of the revision of the Office in 1834, as follows:–

"My Lords consider this a fit opportunity for recording as an invariable regulation, that the under-named situations will be filled, as vacancies occur, by the promotion of the fittest person to be selected from the whole Office, and not by seniority, *viz.*:–

"The Principal Clerk Assistant to the Secretaries, who executes the duties now performed by Mr. Crafer in preparing minutes on ordinary papers.

"The five Chief Clerks.

"The five Senior Clerks.

"Also on a vacancy of Assistant Clerk, the first of the Junior Clerks will not be promoted as of course, but my Lords will promote the first on the list of Junior Clerks who may be deemed by their Lordships on due inquiry to be fully capable of executing in a proper manner all the duties of an Assistant Clerk, and to have so conducted himself as to satisfy the Board that he is entitled to promotion."

It is indispensable for the efficiency and character of the Office that those persons only should be promoted who feel an active interest in their duties, and take pains to qualify themselves for the higher employment of the Department; and we are of opinion that this principle should be acted upon with as much strictness in making promotions from the Junior as from the Senior ranks. The habits which make valuable public servants are generally formed in early life; and it is right that a young man should feel, from his first entering the Office, that his future advancement will entirely depend upon his own conduct.

We have no amendment to suggest in the existing rules which require that there should be an examination previously to admission, and a year's probation before the appointment is confirmed; and we recommend that they should be strictly acted upon, and that the superior officers of the Treasury should be enjoined, as well for the sake of the young men themselves, as on public grounds, to take immediate notice of any neglect of duty on the part of those serving under them.

171. Committee of inquiry into establishment and duties of the Colonial Office (15 December 1849)

Parlty. Papers, 1845/XXVII, pp. 81–83.

. . . The appointment of proper persons to fill the situations of permanent Under Secretary, Assistant Under Secretary, and Precis Writer, must be left to the conscience and the judgment of the Secretary of State; and it is so extremely important, both to the public interest and to the Secretary of State himself, that these offices should be effectively executed, that the best selection is likely always to be made of which circumstances admit.

But in providing a proper succession of Senior Clerks for the part which they have to perform, a great deal remains to be done. In this case the previous training, being entirely within the walls of the Office, depends upon the measures taken by the Government for the purpose; and as the field of selection is very limited, the preparation and instruction of the small number of persons from among whom the Senior Clerks must be appointed, is a matter of serious public importance. The training given to the Clerks in the Colonial Office is nevertheless at present of the most imperfect kind.

They generally receive their original appointments to the Establishment before their education is finished or their characters are developed; and the early age at which they become their own masters, the dry and distasteful nature of the duties assigned to them, and the various attractions of a London life, are very unfavourable to the formation of those habits which make good public servants.

As there is no examination previously to admission, there is no security that the persons admitted possess the talents and attainments which will render their services valuable on promotion to higher stations in the Office. The year's probation, although it answers useful purposes of its own, cannot supply the place of a preliminary examination, partly because the duties which are at present allotted to young men on first entering the Office are not such as furnish any test of fitness for the higher situations, and partly because a faithful report upon the conduct and qualifications of the probationer cannot easily be obtained after habits of personal intercourse have once been established.

The training which the present constitution of the body of the Establishment affords is by no means calculated to develop the talents required for the successful transaction of the serious business of the Office. While the functions of the Colonial Office are remarkable for their variety, importance and difficulty, and experience and ability of a high order are necessary for their proper performance, the official education partakes in a great degree of a mechanical character. Although there is a separate department of the Office in which persons on the footing of Law Stationers' Clerks are employed, under the superintendence of a Clerk, in copying official papers, the greater part of the work of this description is still done by the gentlemen on the Establishment. who are also charged with the duty of making up, directing, and sealing the despatches, and of keeping, arranging, and producing, as occasion requires, the current papers of the Office. The first years of official employment are those in which the knowledge, the self-confidence, and the aptitude for business required for the proper discharge of difficult and responsible duties should be obtained; and it is much to be regretted that persons likely to succeed to important situations in the public service should have occupations assigned to them at this critical period of life which are unimproving and unsuited to their education and prospects, and as such likely to give them a distaste for their profession. If, after ten or fifteen years spent in incessant copying and other routine work, the spirit, the mental activity, and the wide extent of acquired knowledge necessary for vigorous intellectual exertion in the transaction of business like that of the Colonial Office, are wanting, it is the fault of the system, and not of the individuals who have been placed in circumstances so unfavourable to them.

The honours and rewards of the Establishment are removed by so many gradations from a young man on this obscure labour before he can hope that his exertions will attract the notice of the Secretary of State, that the prizes of the Office have practically little influence on him. There must be something very defective in a system which does not hold out the usual motives to professional exertion, and fails to secure for the public service the zeal and activity of early manhood, because it does not offer any scope for a just and reasonable ambition.

According to the *theory* of the office, a Clerk can reach the first class only after he has been promoted three times on the ground of superior merit, the claims arising from length of service being provided for by the annual increase of salary within each class; but, practically, it has been found very difficult to enforce the principle of promotion according to merit, even in filling up vacancies in the senior class; while as regards the other classes of the office, the *habit* has been to promote everybody in his turn, without regard to comparative merit or qualification. In making this statement we must be understood only as describing what has been the general practice of the Office on a review of a series of years, for we are aware that there have been exceptions. When considerable changes took place in the Office while Lord Ripon was Secretary of State, the rule of seniority was altogether departed from; and when vacancies have occurred since Lord Grey has been Secretary of State, his Lordship has in each case called upon the permanent Under Secretary of State to report what member of the class below that in which the vacancy has occurred, he considered the fittest to succeed to it, distinctly stating that, except in cases of equality of merit, seniority was not the principle on which it was right that the selection should be made. We believe that it will be impossible to overcome this tendency, and to give to official promotion the stimulating influence it ought to have, while the Office is constituted as it is at present.

172. Committee of inquiry into establishment and functions of the Board of Ordnance (17 December 1853)

Parlty. Papers, 1854/XXVII, pp. 307–308.

. . . On commencing our inquiry into the establishment and functions of the Board of Ordnance, in accordance with the directions which we had received from the Lords of the Treasury, we found that the intentions of their Lordships had been already to some extent anticipated by the formation of a Committee within the Department itself, consisting of the Clerk of the Ordnance (Mr. Monsell), the Principal Storekeeper (Sir Thos. Hastings), and the Chief Clerks in the offices of the Master-General and Secretary (Messrs. Elliot and Wood). Mr. Anderson, the Assistant Paymaster General, and Mr. Hoffay, the Inspector in charge of Military and Naval Accounts at the Audit Office, assisted us in everything that related to the accounts of the Department.

The appointment of this Committee has not only materially lightened our labours in the conduct of the inquiry which has been intrusted to us, but has proved, as we believe, highly beneficial to the public interests. The business of the Ordnance Office is of a kind which peculiarly requires to be revised by persons thoroughly acquainted with its details, practically conversant with its daily working, and capable of forming an accurate judgment of the relative importance of its several parts. It consists chiefly of the management of an extensive system of accounts, with the details of which it is difficult for a stranger to the Office to interfere, except for the purpose of offering suggestions, but which is susceptible of continual and gradual improvements by those who are charged with its direction, and who have the power of making experiments with a view to its simplification, and to the economy of labour upon it, without endangering its completeness or its accuracy.

We are gratified by finding that the officers of the Board of Ordnance have for a long series of years been engaged in the work of self-reform; and that very important improvements have consequently been introduced into the Department. The Committee to which we have referred have carried those improvements further; and we confidently hope that the spirit which appears to prevail throughout the Office will continue to produce fresh efforts and fresh results of the same character.

173. The Northcote-Trevelyan Report on the Organization of the Permanent Civil Service (February 1854)

Parlty. Papers, 1854/XXVII, pp. 367–376.

. . . We now proceed to comply with that part of our instructions which states that, in connection with the inquiries which we were directed to make into each particular office, it is highly necessary that the conditions which are common to all the public establishments, such as the preliminary testimonials of character and bodily health to be required from candidates for public employment, the examination into their intellectual attainments, and the regulation of the promotions, should be carefully considered, so as to obtain full security for the public that none but qualified persons will be appointed, and that they will afterwards have every practicable inducement to the active discharge of their duties.

It cannot be necessary to enter into any lengthened argument for the purpose of showing the high importance of the Permanent Civil Service of the country in the present day. The great and increasing accumulation of public business, and the consequent pressure upon the Government, need only to be alluded to; and the inconveniences which are inseparable from the frequent changes which take place in the responsible administration are matters of sufficient notoriety. It may safely be asserted that, as matters now stand, the Government of the country could not be carried on without the aid of an efficient body of permanent officers, occupying a position duly subordinate to that of the Ministers who are directly responsible to the Crown and to Parliament, yet possessing sufficient independence, character, ability, and experience to be able to advise, assist, and, to some extent, influence, those who are from time to time set over them.

That the Permanent Civil Service, with all its defects, essentially contributes to the proper discharge of the functions of Government, has been repeatedly admitted by those who have successively been responsible for the conduct of our affairs. All, however, who have had occasion to examine its constitution with care, have felt that its organisation is far from perfect, and that its amendment is deserving of the most careful attention.

It would be natural to expect that so important a profession would attract into its ranks the ablest and the most ambitious of the youth of the country; that the keenest emulation would prevail among those who had entered it; and that such as were endowed with superior qualifications would rapidly rise to distinction and public eminence. Such, however, is by no means the case. Admission into the Civil Service is indeed eagerly sought after, but it is for the unambitious, and the indolent or incapable, that it is chiefly desired. Those whose abilities do not warrant an expectation that they will succeed in the open professions, where they must encounter the competition of their contemporaries, and those whom indolence of temperament or physical infirmities unfit for active exertions, are placed in the Civil Service, where they may obtain an honourable livelihood with little labour, and with no risk; where their success depends upon their simply avoiding any flagrant misconduct, and attending with moderate regularity to routine duties; and in which they are secured against the ordinary consequences of old age, or failing health, by an arrangement which provides them with the means of supporting themselves after they have become incapacitated.

It may be noticed in particular that the comparative lightness of the work, and the certainty of provision in case of retirement owing to bodily incapacity, furnish strong inducements to the parents and friends of sickly youths to endeavour to obtain for them employment in the service of the Government; and the extent to which the public are consequently burdened, first with the salaries of officers who are obliged to absent themselves from their duties on account of ill health, and afterwards with their pensions when they retire on the same plea, would hardly be credited by those who have not had opportunities of observing the operation of the system.

It is not our intention to suggest that all public servants entered the employment of the Government with such views as these; but we apprehend that as regards a large proportion of them, these motives more or less influenced those who acted for them in the choice of a profession; while, on the other hand, there are probably very few who have chosen this line of life with a view to raising themselves to public eminence.

The result naturally is, that the public service suffers both in internal efficiency and in public estimation. The character of the individuals influences the mass, and it is thus that we often hear complaints of official delays, official evasions of difficulty, and official indisposition to improvement.

There are, however, numerous honourable exceptions to these observations, and the trustworthiness of the entire body is unimpeached. They are much better than we have any right to expect from the system under which they are appointed and promoted.

The peculiar difficulties under which the Permanent Civil Service labours, in obtaining a good supply of men, as compared with other professions, are partly, natural and partly artificial.

Its natural difficulties are such as these:-

Those who enter it generally do so at an early age, when there has been no opportunity of trying their fitness for business, or forming a trustworthy estimate of their characters and abilities. This to a great extent is the case in other professions also, but those professions supply a corrective which is wanting in the Civil Service, for as a man's success in them depends upon his obtaining and retaining the confidence of the public, and as he is exposed to a sharp competition on the part of his contemporaries, those only can maintain a fair position who possess the requisite amount of ability and industry for the proper discharge of their duties. The able and energetic rise to the top; the dull and inefficient remain at the bottom. In the public establishments, on the contrary, the general rule is that all rise together. After a young man has been once appointed, the public have him for life; and if he is idle or inefficient, provided he does not grossly misconduct himself, we must either submit to have a portion of the public business inefficiently and discreditably performed, or must place the incompetent person on the retired list, with a pension, for the rest of his life. The feeling of security which this state of things necessarily engenders tends to encourage indolence, and thereby to depress the character of the Service. Again, those who are admitted into it at an early age are thereby relieved from the necessity of those struggles which for the most part fall to the lot of such as enter upon the open professions; their course is one of quiet, and generally of secluded, performance of routine duties, and they consequently have but limited opportunities of acquiring that varied experience of life which is so important to the development of character.

To these natural difficulties may be added others arising from what may be called artificial causes.

The character of the young men admitted to the public service depends chiefly upon the discretion with which the heads of departments, and others who are entrusted with the distribution of patronage, exercise that privilege. In those cases in which the patronage of departments belongs to their chief for the time being, the appointments which it commonly falls to his lot to make are either those of junior clerks, to whom no very important duties are in the first instance to be assigned, or of persons who are to fill responsible and highly paid situations above the rank of the ordinary clerkships. In the first case, as the character and abilities of the new junior clerk will produce but little immediate effect upon the office, the chief of the department is naturally led to regard the selection as a matter of small moment, and will probably bestow the office upon the son or dependant of some one having personal or political claims upon him, or perhaps upon the son of some meritorious public servant, without instituting any very minute inquiry into the merits of the young man himself. It is true that in many offices some kind of examination is prescribed, and that in almost all the person appointed is in the first instance nominated on probation; but, as will presently be pointed out, neither of these tests are at present very efficacious. The young man thus admitted is commonly employed upon duties of the merest routine. Many of the first years of his service are spent in copying papers, and other work of an almost mechanical character. In two or three years he is as good as he can be at such an employment. The remainder of his official life can only exercise a depressing influence on him, and renders the work of the office distasteful to him. Unlike the pupil in a conveyancer's or special pleader's office, he not only begins with mechanical labour as an introduction to labour of a higher kind, but often also ends with it. In the meantime his salary is gradually advancing till he reaches, by seniority, the top of his class, and on the occurrence of a vacancy in the class above him he is promoted to fill it, as a matter of course, and without any regard to his previous services or his qualifications. Thus, while no pains have been taken in the first instance to secure a good man for the office, nothing has been done after the clerk's appointment to turn his abilities, whatever they may be, to the best account. The result naturally is, that when the chief of the office has to make an appointment of visible and immediate importance to the efficiency of his department, he sometimes has difficulty in finding a clerk capable of filling it and he is not unfrequently obliged to go out of the office and to appoint some one of high standing in an open profession, or some one distinguished in other walks of life, over the heads of men who have been for many years in the public service. This is necessarily discouraging to the Civil Servants, and tends to strengthen in them the injurious conviction, that their success does not depend upon their own exertions, and that if they work hard, it will not advance them,–if they waste their time in idleness, it will not keep them back.

It is of course essential to the public service that men of the highest abilities should be selected for the highest posts; and it cannot be denied that there are a few situations in which such varied talent and such an amount of experience are required, that it is probable that under any circumstances it will occasionally be found necessary to fill them with persons who have distinguished themselves elsewhere than in the Civil Service. But the system of appointing strangers to the higher offices has been carried far beyond this. In several departments the clerks are regarded as having no claim whatever to what are called the staff appointments; and numerous instances might be given in which personal or political considerations have led to the appointment of men of very slender ability, and perhaps of questionable character, to situations of considerable emolument, over the heads of public servants of long standing and undoubted merit. Few public servants would feel the appointment of a barrister of known eminence and ability to some important position, like that of Under Secretary of State, as a slight, or a discouragement to themselves; but the case is otherwise when someone who has failed in other professions, and who has no recommendation but that of family or political interest, is appointed to a Librarianship, or some other such office, the duties of which would have been far better discharged by one who had been long in the department, and to whom the increased salary attached to the appointment would have been a fair reward for years of faithful service.

One more peculiarity in the Civil Service remains to be noticed. It is what may be called its fragmentary character.

Unlike the Military and Naval, the Medical, and the Commissariat Services, and unlike even the Indian Civil Service, the public establishments of this country, though comprising a body of not less than 16,000 persons, are regulated upon the principle of merely departmental promotion. Each man's experience, interests, hopes, and fears are limited to the special branch of service in which he is himself engaged. The effect naturally is, to cramp the energies of the whole body, to encourage the growth of narrow views and departmental prejudices, to limit the acquisition of experience, and to repress and almost extinguish the spirit of emulation and competition; besides which, considerable inconvenience results from the want of facilities for transferring strength from an office where the work is becoming slack to one in which it is increasing, and from the consequent necessity of sometimes keeping up particular departments on a scale beyond their actual requirements.

Having thus touched upon some of the difficulties with which the public service is beset, we come to the consideration of the problem, What is the best method of providing it with a supply of good men, and of making the most of them after they have been admitted?

The first question which here presents itself is, Whether it is better to train young men for the discharge of the duties which they will afterwards have to perform, or to take men of mature age, who have already acquired experience in other walks of life?

Our opinion is, that, as a general rule, it is decidedly best to train young men. Without laying too much stress on the experience which a long official life necessarily brings with it, we cannot but regard it as an advantage of some importance. In many offices, moreover, it is found that the superior docility of young men renders it much easier to make valuable public servants of them, than of those more advanced in life. This may not be the case in the higher class of offices, but is unquestionably so in those where the work consists chiefly of account business. The maintenance of discipline is also easier under such circumstances, and regular habits may be enforced, which it would be difficult to impose for the first time upon older men. To these advantages must be added the important one of being able, by proper regulations, to secure the services of fit persons on much more economical terms. A young man who has not made trial of any other profession will be induced to enter that of the Civil Service by a much more moderate remuneration than would suffice to attract him a few years later from the pursuit of one in which he had overcome the first difficulties and begun to achieve success; while to attempt to fill the ranks of the Civil Service with those who had failed elsewhere, and were on that account willing to accept a moderate salary, would be simply to bring it into discredit. It cannot be doubted that, even in the absence of proper precautions for securing good appointments, it is more probable that a fair proportion of eligible men will be found among a number taken at their entrance into life, particularly if pains be bestowed upon them after their appointment, than among an equal number taken after some years of unsuccessful efforts to open another line for themselves. The temptation to jobbing, and the danger of decidedly improper appointments being made, is also considerably less in the case of the selection of young men than in that of persons more advanced in life.

The general principle, then, which we advocate is, that the public service should be carried on by the admission into its lower ranks of a carefully selected body of young men, who should be employed from the first upon work suited to their capacities and their education, and should be made constantly to feel that their promotion and future prospects depend entirely on the industry and ability with which they discharge their duties, that with average abilities and reasonable application they may look forward confidently to a certain provision for their lives, that with superior powers they may rationally hope to attain to the highest prizes in the Service, while if they prove decidedly incompetent, or incurably indolent, they must expect to be removed from it.

The first step towards carrying this principle into effect should be, the establishment of a proper system of examination before appointment, which should be followed, as at present, by a short period of probation. The necessity of this has been so far admitted that some kind of examination does now take place before clerks are admitted into any of the following offices:–The Treasury, the Colonial Office, the Board of Trade, the Privy Council Office, the Poor Law Board, the War Office, the Ordnance Office, the Audit Office, the Paymaster General's Office, the Inland Revenue Office, the Emigration Office, and some others. These examinations vary in their character; in some offices more is required than in others, and in some cases what is required will be more rigidly enforced by one set of Examiners than by another.

The preliminary examination of candidates for civil employment, however, cannot be conducted in an effective and consistent manner throughout the Service, while it is left to each department to determine the nature of the examination and to examine the candidates. Some on whom the duty of examining devolves feel no interest in the subject; others, although disposed to do their best, are likely to entertain erroneous or imperfect conceptions of the standard of examination which ought to be fixed, and to be unable to apply it properly after it has been settled. The time and attention of the superior officers are fully occupied in disposing of the current business of their respective departments. To do this in a creditable manner will always be their primary object; and as the bearing of the subject under consideration upon the efficiency of their departments, although very important, is not of a direct or immediate kind, and is not likely to have much effect during their own tenure of office, what has to be done in reference to it will either be done by themselves in a hurried and imperfect manner, or will be left by them to their subordinate officers to be dealt with at their discretion. In a large department, in which numerous candidates have to be examined, want of time will prevent the superior officers from giving the subject the attention it deserves; and other matters, although of infinitely less real consequence, will have the precedence, because they press, and must be disposed of at the moment. Moreover, a large proportion of the persons appointed to a public department usually consists of young men in whose success the heads of the office or the principal clerks take a lively personal interest, owing to relationship or some other motive connected with their public or private position; and an independent opinion is hardly to be expected from an examiner who is acting under the orders of the one, and is in habits of daily intercourse with the other. A public officer ought not to be placed in a situation in which duty might require him to make an unfavourable report under such circumstances. Lastly, even supposing every other circumstance to be favourable, it is impossible that each department, acting for itself, can come to such just conclusions in regard to the nature of the preliminary examination, or can conduct it in such a fair, and effective, and consistent manner, as would persons having the advantage of a general view of the subject as it affects every public department, and who should have been selected for the duty on account of their experience in matters of this description.

We accordingly recommend that a central Board should be constituted for conducting the examination of all candidates for the public service whom it may be thought right to subject to such a test. Such board should be composed of men holding an independent position, and capable of commanding general confidence; it should have at its head an officer of the rank of Privy Councillor; and should either include, or have the means of obtaining the assistance of, persons experienced in the education of the youth of the upper and middle classes, and persons who are familiar with the conduct of official business. It should be made imperative upon candidates for admission to any appointment, (except in certain special cases which will presently be noticed,) to pass a proper examination before this Board, and obtain from them a certificate of having done so.

We are of opinion that this examination should be in all cases a competing literary examination. This ought not to exclude careful previous inquiry into the age, health, and moral fitness of the candidates. Where character and bodily activity are chiefly required, more, comparatively, will depend upon the testimony of those to whom the candidate is well known; but the selection from among the candidates who have satisfied these preliminary inquiries should still be made by a competing examination. This may be so conducted as to test the intelligence, as well as the mere attainments of the candidates. We see no other mode by which (in the case of inferior no less than of superior offices) the double object can be attained of selecting the fittest person, and of avoiding the evils of patronage.

For the superior situations endeavours should be made to secure the services of the most promising young men of the day, by a competing examination on a level with the highest description of education in this country. In this class of situations there is no limit to the demands which may ultimately be made upon the abilities of those who, entering them simply as junior clerks, gradually rise to the highest posts in them. To obtain first-rate men, it is obvious that recourse should be had to competition. It would be impossible to impose upon each candidate for a clerkship, as a positive test of his fitness for the appointment the necessity of passing an examination equal to that of first-class men at the universities; but if, on the occurrence of a vacancy it is found that a number of candidates present themselves, of whom some are capable of passing such an examination, there can be no reason why the public should not have the benefit of such men's services, in preference to those of persons of inferior merit. It may be repeated that no other means can be devised of avoiding the evils of patronage, which, if, in this case, less objectionable because of the comparatively small number of superior appointments, is much more objectionable in its effects on the public business of the country.

. . . . .

Upon a review of the recommendations contained in this paper it will be seen that the objects which we have principally in view are these:–

1. To provide, by a proper system of examination, for the supply of the public service with a thoroughly efficient class of men.

2. To encourage industry and foster merit, by teaching all public servants to look forward to promotion according to their deserts, and to expect the highest prizes in the service if they can qualify themselves for them.

3. To mitigate the evils which result from the fragmentary character of the Service, and to introduce into it some elements of unity by placing the first appointments upon an uniform footing, opening the way to the promotion of public officers to staff appointments in other departments than their own, and introducing into the lower ranks a body of men (the supplementary clerks) whose services may be made available at any time in any office whatever.

It remains for us to express our conviction that if any change of the importance of those which we have recommended is to be carried into effect, it can only be successfully done through the medium of an Act of Parliament. The existing system is supported by long usage and powerful interests; and were any Government to introduce material alterations into it, in consequence of their own convictions, without taking the precaution to give those alterations the force of law, it is almost certain that they would be imperceptibly, or perhaps avowedly, abandoned by their successors, if they were not even allowed to fall into disuse by the very Government which had originated them. A few clauses would accomplish all that is proposed in this paper, and it is our firm belief that a candid statement of the grounds of the measure would insure its success and popularity in the country, and would remove many misconceptions which are now prejudicial to the public service.

STAFFORD H. NORTHCOTE.

November 23, 1853. C. E. TREVELYAN.

174. The Northcote-Trevelyan Report: views of John Stuart Mill

Parlty. Papers, 1854–1855/xx, p. 94.

May 22nd. 1854

The proposal to select candidates for the Civil Service of Government by a competitive examination appears to me to be one of those great public improvements the adoption of which would form an era in history. The effects which it is calculated to produce in raising the character both of the public administration and of the people can scarcely be over-estimated.

It has equal claims to support from the disinterested and impartial among conservatives and among reformers. For its adoption would be the best vindication which could be made of existing political institutions, by showing that the classes who under the present constitution have the greatest influence in the government, do not desire any greater share of the profits derivable from it than their merits entitle them to, but are willing to take the chances of competition with ability in all ranks: while the plan offers to liberals, so far as the plan extends, the realization of the principal object which any honest reformer desires to effect by political changes, namely, that the administration of public affairs should be in the most competent hands; which, as regards the permanent part of the administrative body, would be ensured by the proposed plan, so far as it is possible for any human contrivance to secure it.

When we add to this consideration the extraordinary stimulus which would be given to mental cultivation in its most important branches, not solely by the hope of prizes to be obtained by means of it, but by the effect of the national recognition of it as the exclusive title to participation in the conduct of so large and conspicuous a portion of the national affairs; and when we further think of the great and salutary moral revolution, descending to the minds of almost the lowest classes, which would follow the knowledge that Government (to people in general the most trusted exponent of the ways of the world) would henceforth bestow its gifts according to merit, and not to favour; it is difficult to express in any language which would not appear exaggerated, the benefits which, as it appears to me, would ultimately be the consequences of the successful execution of the scheme. . . .

175. The Northcote-Trevelyan Report: views of G. Arbuthnot, auditor of the Civil List

Parlty. Papers, 1854–1855/xx, pp. 403–405.

Treasury Chambers, March 6th. 1854

A Report by Sir Stafford Northcote and Sir Charles Trevelyan, on the Organisation of the Permanent Civil Service, having been recently presented to Parliament, has become a public document, and is open to public comment.

In that Report there are expressions which appear to me to reflect strongly on the character of the individuals of whom the Civil Service is composed. It admits that "the Permanent Civil Service, with all its defects, contributes to the proper discharge of the functions of Government;" but it proceeds to state that admission into that Service is chiefly sought after "for the unambitious, the indolent, or incapable;" that "those whose abilities do not warrant that they will succeed in the open professions, where they must encounter the competition of their contemporaries, and those whom indolence of temperament and physical infirmities unfit for active exertions, are placed in the Civil Service, where they may obtain an honourable livelihood with little labour and no risk."

Such language, employed by gentlemen who had a solemn and responsible duty imposed on them by your Lordships, is calculated to convey a very unfavourable impression regarding the general characteristics of the Civil Service, and to create a very painful feeling in the minds of an honourable class of men, whose labours are little known, and who, from their position, have no opportunity of coming forward to justify themselves before the public.

It may appear irregular to refer, in connexion with this question, to observations in a public journal; but I cannot avoid allusion to an article in the *Times* newspaper, which appeared a short time previously to the presentation of the Report, and in which the same opinions were conveyed in expressions still more severe and offensive. It is impossible to disconnect the Report altogether from the article in the *Times*, because it was evident that the writer had access to information not then before the public; and I may refer to that article in proof of the impression which this journalist derived from the information communicated to him. I cannot conceal from your Lordships that the attack upon the Public Service, published in an influential journal, and bearing the appearance of authority, created a strong feeling of indignation in the minds of the Civil Servants, which had been confirmed and strengthened since they found the same opinion reiterated in a public and formal document.

I submit, my Lords, that charges so serious against the general body of the Public Servants ought not to be lightly put forth; and, as I trust that I shall be able to satisfy your Lordships that the imputations cast against that body are undeserved, I presume, as the senior in rank, or at any rate the nearest to your Board of the class of officers which is aggrieved, to approach you on their behalf, with an humble but most earnest remonstrance against the publication of such aspersions in the authentic form of a State Paper.

It is not easy to understand how a Service, if composed of the materials described in the Report, should deserve even the meed of praise which is accorded to it of "contributing essentially to the proper discharge of the functions of Government;" nor, if the motives which are said to influence those who seek admission to the Service should generally prevail, how "the trustworthiness of the entire body" should yet be "unimpeached."

These contradictions are so palpable that I should almost hope that the Report, though dated the 23d November 1853, and not presented to Parliament until nearly the end of February 1854, had been composed in haste, and that its writers were hardly aware of the force of the expressions which they have used. Yet that those expressions amount to a general charge against the body of Civil Servants cannot be denied. It is asserted distinctly that "the Public Service suffers both in internal efficiency and in public estimation" from the causes assigned; that "the character of the individuals influences the mass, and that it is thus that we often hear complaints of official delays, official evasions of difficulty, and official indisposition to improvement."

My Lords, I aver that these are unjust imputations. They are unfounded both in respect of alleged causes and effects. Even if the complaints alleged had a substantial existence, they could not be attributed to the causes from which they are said to proceed. I appeal from the authors of this Report to statesmen, high in the estimation of the public, who have had ample opportunities of ascertaining the qualities of the Civil Service, and who, though differing in political opinions, have agreed in their testimony to the general uprightness, the zeal and efficiency of the officers of whom it is composed, and to the willing and useful aid which is rendered by them to all administrations without reference to politics. I appeal from this Report to Sir Charles Trevelyan himself, if he still recollects the time when he first came to the Treasury, an entire stranger to the Service, and necessarily unacquainted with the forms of procedure, and even the principles which govern the routine of a public office in England. He once owned that at that period he found among the gentlemen of this office intelligence, activity, and that willing aid and co-operation, without which he could not have mastered the ordinary details of his duty. He has, on later occasions, when circumstances called forth some public acknowledgement of the merits of those officers, expressed a feeling of pride at being a member of that Service, which he now condemns as largely composed of "the unambitious, the indolent, and the incapable. . . ."

176. The Northcote-Trevelyan Report: reply of Sir Stafford Northcote and Sir Charles Trevelyan to Arbuthnot

Parlty. Papers, 1854–1855/xx, pp. 413–415.

Treasury, April 10th, 1854.

Your Lordships having been pleased to communicate to us some remarks addressed to your Honourable Board by the Auditor of the Civil List on the Report which we presented to your Lordships in November 1853, on the Organization of the Permanent Civil Service, and having invited us to offer any observations thereon, we beg leave to tender to your Lordships our thanks for the opportunity thus afforded to us of explaining ourselves on points upon which our meaning appears to have been misunderstood, and of removing, as we trust we shall be able to do, some of the objections which have been urged against the proposals which we have made.

The remarks of Mr. Arbuthnot relate first, to the statements which we have made as to the actual state of the Permanent Civil Service; and secondly, to the plan which we have proposed for its re-organization. We will, therefore, address ourselves to these points in the same order.

In the first place, we beg leave to express our sincere regret that the language of any portion of our Report should have been such as to create a painful feeling in the minds of the able and honourable body of men composing the Service to which we ourselves belong, and with which we cannot but feel it an honour to be connected. We gladly take this opportunity of adding our own testimony to that of the more eminent persons to whom Mr. Arbuthnot refers, with respect to "the general uprightness, the zeal and efficiency of the officers of which it is composed, and to the willing and useful aid which is rendered by them to all administrations, without reference to politics;" and Sir Charles Trevelyan particularly desires, in answer to the appeal especially made to him, to repeat in the most emphatic manner his acknowledgement of the kind, hearty, and able co-operation for which he has long been and still is so largely indebted to the officers with whom he has the honour of being connected in the department over which your Lordships preside.

We admit that, looking to the effect which the publication of our remarks was likely to have upon the minds of persons less well acquainted with the Civil Service than your Lordships, it was an error on our part that we did not more distinctly express the sense we entertain of its merits; and we regret that we failed to do so; although we cannot but observe that it was in strictness unnecessary for us to enter into any other questions than those which your Lordships had proposed to us, *viz.*, "the best mode of obtaining full security for the public that none but qualified persons would be appointed, and that they would afterwards have every practicable inducement to the active discharge of their duties." In the fulfilment of the task thus assigned to us, it became necessary for us to speak freely of the defects which we had observed in both these respects–defects which, as appears from the terms of the Minute which we have quoted, had already attracted your Lordships' attention, and the existence of which seems to us to be fully admitted in the remarks of Mr. Arbuthnot. The necessity thus imposed upon us was an irksome one; but a sense of duty forbade us to shrink from stating what we believed to be the truth. We endeavoured to make our remarks as little offensive as possible, and, before presenting our Report to your Lordships, we took the precaution of showing the draft of it to several eminent members of the Permanent Civil Service, who were kind enough to offer many valuable suggestions upon various points which we had dealt with.

With regard to the allusion which Mr. Arbuthnot has made to an article which appeared in the *Times* newspaper some time before the presentation of our Report to Parliament, we have only to say that we are in no way responsible for the language employed by the newspaper in question, that we are wholly ignorant of the authorship of the article which has been complained of, and that we are not aware that the writer possessed any other information on the subject than such as was to be obtained from a perusal of the Report, which, though not yet presented to Parliament, had been long since laid before your Lordships, and had been shown in a printed form to a considerable number of persons. . . .

177. Order in Council of 21 May 1855, on entry to the Civil Service

Parlty. Papers, 1856/XXII. First Report of Civil Service Commissioners, p. 363.

ORDER OF HER MAJESTY IN COUNCIL REGULATING THE ADMISSION OF PERSONS TO THE CIVIL SERVICE OF THE CROWN

At the Court at Buckingham Palace the 21st Day of May 1855;

Present,

THE QUEEN'S MOST EXCELLENT MAJESTY IN COUNCIL

WHEREAS it is expedient to make Provision for testing, according to fixed Rules, the Qualifications of the young Men who may from Time to Time be proposed to be appointed to the junior Situations in any of Her Majesty's Civil Establishments.

Now therefore, Her Majesty, by and with the Advice and Consent of Her Privy Council, doth order, and it is hereby ordered, that the Right Honourable Sir Edward Ryan, Assistant Comptroller General of the Exchequer, John George Shaw Lefevre, Esquire, Companion of the Bath, Clerk Assistant to the House of Lords, and Edward Romilly, Esquire, Chairman of the Board of Audit, or such other Persons as Her Majesty may from Time to Time approve in the Stead of them or any of them, shall be Commissioners for conducting the Examination of the Young Men so proposed to be appointed to any of the Junior Situations in the Civil Establishments as aforesaid, and shall hold their Offices during the Pleasure of Her Majesty, and shall have Power, subject to the Approval of the Commissioners of Her Majesty's Treasury, to appoint from Time to Time such Assistant Examiners and others as may be required to assist them in the Performance of the Duties herein-after assigned to them.

And it is hereby ordered, that the Commissioners of Her Majesty's Treasury do prepare and submit to Parliament an Estimate for the Remuneration of a Secretary to the said Commissioners, and of such Examiners and others as may be required to assist in the Performance of their Duties.

And it is hereby ordered, that all such young Men as may be proposed to be appointed to any Junior Situation in any Department of the Civil Service shall, before they are admitted to Probation, be examined by or under the Directions of the said Commissioners, and shall receive from them a Certificate of Qualification for such Situation.

And it shall be the Duty of the Commissioners in respect of every such Candidate, before granting any such Certificate as aforesaid,

1st. To ascertain that the Candidate is within the Limits of Age prescribed in the Department to which he desires to be admitted;

2d. To ascertain that the Candidate is free from any physical Defect or Disease which would be likely to interfere with the proper Discharge of his Duties;

3d. To ascertain that the Character of the Candidate is such as to qualify him for Public Employment; and,

4th. To ascertain that the Candidate possesses the requisite Knowledge and Ability for the proper Discharge of his official Duties.

The Rules applicable to each Department under each of the above Heads should be settled, with the Assistance of the Commissioners, according to the Discretion of the chief Authorities of the Department; but, except that Candidates for Admission to any of the Junior Situations in any Branch of the Civil Service will be required to obtain Certificates of Qualification as aforesaid, such Examining Board shall not make any Alteration in respect to the Nomination or Appointment of Candidates by those who are or may be charged with the Duty of Nomination and Appointment.

After the Candidate has passed his Examination, and received his Certificate of Qualification from the Commissioners, he shall enter on a Period of Probation, during which his Conduct and Capacity in the Transaction of Business shall be subjected to such Tests as may be determined by the Chief of the Department for which he is intended; and he shall not be finally appointed to the Public Service unless upon satisfactory Proofs of his Fitness being furnished to the Chief of the Department after Six Months' Probation.

And it is lastly hereby ordered, that in case the Chief of any Department considers it desirable to appoint to any Situation for which there are no prescribed Limits of Age a Person of mature Age having acquired special Qualifications for the Appointment in other Pursuits, such Person shall not in virtue of this Order be required to obtain any Certificate from the said Commissioners in order to obtain such Appointment, but the Chief of the Department shall cause the Appointment of any Person not previously examined to be formally recorded as having been made on account of special Qualifications.

(Signed) WM. L. BATHURST.

178. Commons debate on administrative reform (15–18 June 1855): Layard's resolution and speech

Hansard, 3/CXXXVIII/2040–2063.

MR. LAYARD rose to move the following Resolution–

> "That this House views with deep and increasing concern the state of the nation, and is of opinion that the manner in which merit and efficiency have been sacrificed, in public appointment, to party and family influences, and to a blind adherence to routine, has given rise to great misfortunes, and threatens to bring discredit upon the national character, and to involve the country in great disasters–

. . . There are three propositions in that Resolution, as I have already stated, and I shall endeavour to substantiate each of them. I will first take the proposition relating to the state of the nation. I have heard it said that these words are now uncalled for, because of the successes we have recently achieved. But I deny that; I intended my Resolution to have application only to the military operation of the war. I look upon the campaign in the Crimea as an episode; upon our failure as a witness, and to the Blue-books as evidence; but they form only a part, and but a small part, of the question which I propose to bring before the House. But if the Blue-books, that contain so much that must be painful to the House and to the country are to remain dead letters, then our cup of disgrace will be full indeed, and I hope that something will be done upon those Blue-books irrespective of my Motion. What I mean by the state of the nation is, that I am fully convinced that this country is becoming very distrustful of this House and is losing its confidence in public men; that the people begin to believe there are great defects in our administrative system, and that a remedy must be applied to those defects; that the Government of this country has become a class monopoly, and that the recent changes in the Government show that that monopoly does not go out of the hands of a few families; and that the Government do not sufficiently represent the feelings of the country at large. They see a liberal Government voting against every liberal measure that has been proposed this session, and voting in the lobby on all these questions with hon. Members sitting on the opposite sides of the House in contradistinction to the liberal party on this side of the House. They have also seen those who have hitherto been the leaders of the people, and the representatives of popular opinions, absorbed in the Government and remaining mute and silent on questions connected with the opinion of which they were once the advocates. Is it then astonishing that the confidence of the people has waned with regard to public men? They have been so often betrayed by public men that I am not surprised that confidence in them is so much shaken. The country think that the great offices of State are sacrificed to the interests of party, and that the public service has been neglected, and to this they trace the disasters that have taken place. Now, Sir, I ask whether that is not a state of the nation that is alarming, and whether it may not give rise to a state of feeling that may be dangerous? That is what I mean by the state of the nation; and I say, let us if possible remove these impressions. I propose to look into three departments–the army, as that branch to which is confided the honour and defence of the country; the diplomatic and consular service, to which the conduct of foreign affairs is entrusted; and the civil service, which has the conduct of national affairs at home.

Sir, to begin with the army. This is, undoubtedly, a very difficult and delicate question. I know that hon. and gallant Gentlemen in this House feel very indignant that a civilian should touch the army, but I ask the House whether any but a civilian can touch the army? Why, a military man dare not touch the army. There is no doubt I may be led into errors in dealing with the army. The rules and regulations that affect the army have for some time been a matter of study to me, but I may be pardoned for some misapprehensions when even very eminent military men are ignorant of some of the rules and their application–nay, even of the very existence of some of the regulations affecting the army. I hold in my hand a letter from a gentleman of some rank in the army, whose name the House will see I cannot mention, and I cannot, therefore, give my authority; but this letter expresses so fully my own feelings and the existing state of things, that I will read it to the House. He says:–

> "A civilian, undertaking as you have done, to attack military abuses so deeply rooted, and of such long standing, as those which disgrace our service, is (as you very justly remark) placed in a particularly difficult position; for unacquainted as you, perhaps, are with all the minor details and intricacies which sometimes even puzzle professional men, you are not able to receive open assistance and evidence, which would probably be the ruin of any military man who might volunteer to enact such a Curtian part; and many a man who might be indifferent to the consequences as regarded himself, might feel averse to sacrifice the prospects of some near relation, who might either be, or be intended to be, in the military profession, and whose future prospects might thus be prematurely blighted in the bud. Then, again, you will have against you all those military men of family connection and great interest who, having profited by a corrupt system, will strenuously oppose any reform or innovation in the same. All these circumstances combined render your task one of no ordinary difficulty; still I would not despair, for you have not only the spirit of the times and public opinion in your favour,

but also all that hard-working and ill-rewarded portion of the army, who have not sufficient interest or family connections to push them unfairly forwards. All such, if they dare not openly applaud, will look with secret pleasure on your undertaking, and I am sure. back it indirectly by any means which will not bring them under the influence of that inquisitorial tribunal which can more or less influence the fortunes of nearly every officer in the service, whatever may be his merits, in the same manner that it can by its fiat place men, most unfitted, in the highest and most responsible situations, which has unfortunately of late been so fully and fatally proved."

Sir, I believe that letter eminently expresses the whole truth of this question with regard to the army. But I have another letter from an eminent military man, whose name I am permitted to mention–Sir W. Napier. I have spared no pains to go to the best military authorities before I ventured to touch upon this subject. Sir William Napier's letter is most fair and proper, and although it tells against me in some respects, I will draw the attention of the House to it. He says:–

"The question of promotion from merit and promotion from favouritism I have never examined carefully, thinking the latter an inevitable consequence of human selfishness, and the former impossible to solve, except in a few instances. With respect to favouritism generally, however, it certainly pervades the British army to an inordinate degree, seeing that no officer of high or low rank, no man below the rank of an officer, no civilian related to or interested for an officer by relationship or friendship, or seeking himself to enter the army, but whose first thought and immediate course is not, very vehemently, to beseech some person privately to use influence to obtain by favour what is sought for. The universal constant prayer is, 'Let me have your interest.' Sometimes, indeed, some poor forlorn officer merely states his long and arduous services, his wounds, and the number of his relations who have died in action; but this only to sway the influential person addressed, not as grounds for acceding to his claim. Why is this? Surely because the absolute necessity of private interests, apart from merit, is universally felt to be dominant. Your purpose is to bring public opinion to bear on this system so strongly that an amelioration must take place, and I for one will not shrink from cheering you on in such a patriotic course. But while I do so on general principles, it would be ungenerous, ungrateful, and unjust not to state that I have had, I may say, hundreds of applications for officers and soldiers, who have had only their services to recommend them–favour without service I never asked for–and, while Lord Raglan was Military Secretary, in no instance did I ever fail of success, nor have I in the very few cases which I have brought before General Yorke, the present Military Secretary, found the least backwardness to aid deserving men."

If I were not addressing the House I should cheer that sentiment as much as any man; but, although that sentiment may tell against me, the fact as to the manner in which Sir William Napier states that his recommendations have been received, are an argument in support of my case. Sir William Napier is a great military authority. He has access to the Horse Guards. He can recommend persons. Fortunately, his soul abhors a job, and he would never recommend any one for promotion who is unworthy of it. If every promotion went in the same way I should not complain. If I saw promotions made upon the recommendation of such men as Sir W. Napier, or that gallant General who so much adorns this House (Sir De Lacy Evans), or any man equally distinguished and equally pure, I should have no doubt whatever of the propriety of those appointments. It is not such recommendations as these that we complain of, or are disposed to call in question. A curious word occurs in the regulations which affects the very commencement of every man's career in the army. That regulation is, that all recommendations for commissions shall certify the elegibility of the person recommended in respect to education, character, and "connections." I do not really understand what is the meaning of the word "connections," unless it be relationship to persons of a certain position. I shall be very happy if hon. Gentlemen will explain it. I have no wish to put a wrong construction upon it; I merely take the word as it stands. . . .

I come now to the diplomatic service, in which I am somewhat more at home, as I have had considerable personal experience of it, and have made it, too, a subject of study, and on which, therefore, I can speak with some confidence. I will divide it into two parts–diplomacy proper, and the consular service. Recent events have shown us of what importance our diplomatic service is, and what important questions are committed into its hands; and yet, if there is one service more than another which is made the vehicle of favouritism it is our diplomatic. Here is a little book published annually by the Foreign Office, which gives a list of those who are employed in our diplomatic service. I open it at random and I read–Hanover–Minister, the hon. John Duncan Bligh, C.B.; Secretary of Legation, hon. G. Edgcumbe; First Attaché, hon. W. Nassau Jocelyn. Then I go to Austria. There the Minister is the Earl of Westmoreland; the Secretary of Legation, hon. Henry G. Elliot; First paid Attaché, hon. Julian H. C. Fane. I turn to Berlin, and there I read–Minister, Lord Bloomfield; Secretary of Legation, Lord Augustus Loftus; First paid Attaché, hon. Lionel S. Sackville West; Second Attaché, hon. William G. C. Elliot; and so on throughout, showing what a complete monopoly the service is. From this little book I have made the following analysis of the composition of the service–Heads of Missions: 7 lords, 9 honourables, 2 baronets, 3 noble families; 7 gentlemen–nearly all small missions; 21 against 7. Secretaries of Legation–2 lords, 9 honourables, 1 baronet, 5 noble families; 7 gentlemen: 17 against 7. Paid Attachés–1 lord, 7 honourables, 6 noble families; 10 gentlemen: 14 against 10, but the 10 include Turkish or Persian Missions. Unpaid Attachés–2 lords, 5 honourables, 9 noble families; 17 gentlemen; 16 against 17. My hon. Friend the Member for Stafford (Mr. Wise) the other night mentioned the case of Mr. Stanley, who had been a précis-writer in the Foreign Office, and who, after six days' service as second attaché, was made first attaché; and, after three years' service as first attaché, was promoted to the post of secretary of legation. Certainly I should have thought that that family had had enough–two peerages and a bishopric, besides other things, ought to have sufficed for them. Then, on the other hand, there is the case of Mr. Alison–emphatically a man of genius–who has been kept in the embassy at Constantinople since 1839; an abler man does not exist; yet the Government, though they have made him Oriental Secretary, will not allow him to rank as a secretary of legation or to claim increase of pay; he is kept under such men as Mr. Stanley, and others who have been put over his head. What is the result of such a system as this? Why, honest, able, hard-working men give themselves up to despair, or get into a morbid state, and become unable to serve the public as they were wont to do. The system literally destroyed them. There are a great many other cases, all of which are equally bad; and let the House take my word for it–for I have been engaged in diplomacy and in the Foreign Office–there is nothing but favourtism in diplomacy. Yet the noble Lord (Viscount Palmerston) gets up and says that it is a great mistake to suppose that when vacancies occur in the higher offices the selections are not made with a view to efficiency. . . .

179. Commons debate on administrative reform (15–18 June 1855): Gladstone's speech

Hansard, 3/CXXXVIII/2105–2110.

. . . The hon. Member for Dudley (Sir S. Northcote) has scarcely done justice, I think, to the hon. Member for Aylesbury's[1] speech. It appears to me that, so far from having merely recapitulated the evils which he thought existed, without having any clear idea of how they were to be remedied, the hon. Member for Aylesbury stated distinctly that he had arrived at the conclusion that a free competitive examination must be adopted in order to any effectual good. I may, perhaps, be permitted to remind the hon. Gentleman and the House that this question is not now for the first time brought under public notice by the labours of the Administrative Reform Association. The efforts of all Governments for some time past, without distinction or party, have been directed to effecting some improvement in this respect. Immense good has been done from a pure love of right and justice, and an enlightened desire for the promotion of the public interests. In this way, and owing to no pressure from this House, have the revisions of official establishments to which I have alluded been regularly conducted from year to year. When I took office as Chancellor of the Exchequer I found that those revisions had been in steady and rapid progress under the right hon. Gentleman who preceded me. When they were brought to something like completeness, I, on the part of Lord Aberdeen's Government, requested Sir Charles Trevelyan and my hon. Friend (Sir. S. Northcote), who had taken a most important part in their detailed examination, to draw up a general Report on the state of the civil service, with a statement of remedies broader and larger in their nature than could conveniently be treated of in the separate Reports of each distinct establishment. The Government of Lord Aberdeen, without pledging itself to the particular details of the Report, advised the Crown to announce to Parliament its intention to make a great change in the system of admissions to the public service; and although, on account of the pressure of other affairs, I had not the opportunity of

[1] Sir Austin Henry Layard.

officially explaining that measure to this House, yet it was well understood that it involved the entire abandonment of what is called patronage in reference to civil appointments. And here I must say one word in behalf of the aristocracy; because, while I acquit my hon. Friend on this head, there is, nevertheless, a tendency out of doors to mix up the two ideas of corruption and weakness in the public service, and the prevalence of the aristocratic element. Now, I believe that no Cabinet could have been more aristocratically composed than that over which Lord Aberdeen presided. I myself was the only one of the fifteen noblemen and gentlemen who composed it who could not fairly be said to belong to that class, and I may, therefore, speak with more freedom. Yet that Cabinet, so composed and aristocratically formed, conceived and matured a plan for the total surrender of its patronage; and it so happens that while I was the only individual in it who could not be considered as in any manner connected with the aristocracy, I was also the only minister who had no possible claim to the merit of that proposal, for the very simple reason that I had no patronage at all to relinquish; the business of the Chancellor of the Exchequer, under a very wise arrangement, being to cut up other people's patronage–that term, in its ordinary acceptation, being inapplicable to the very responsible appointments which he has to make. It is impossible to say what reception this scheme might have met in this House had it been fairly introduced here for discussion, but our own consciences will, I think, tell us that it would not have been quite so easy to secure its adoption by the representatives of the people, among whom there is a large infusion of the democratic element, as it was to obtain for it the unanimous assent of a Government so constituted as was that of Lord Aberdeen. I believe the principle of patronage can never be wholly eradicated; but all that can be done in that direction the late Cabinet was quite ready to propose if this House should have been resolute enough to agree to it.

The country, I think, is in danger of being misled by a number of feeble and illusory remedies; and when asked what they mean, they generally state remedies of which each is more vague and illusory than the other. For example, it is asked, "Why don't you examine candidates for public employment as severely as you please?" but at the same time those who say this shrink from the principle of open competition. Now, you cannot examine rigidly without the application of competition. The practice of the Board of Inland Revenue shows the present system in its most favourable form. There the nominating power is lodged outside of the department, and within it lies the power of rejection. The Secretary of the Treasury receives with good humour the recommendations to appointments made by Members of Parliament in favour of their constituents, and then hands them over to the Inland Revenue Board; which, on its part, exercising a free discretion, and adopting the test of a stringent examination, very frequently rejects the candidates. This remark especially applies to that Board while it has been administered by the extremely able men who now sit upon it, than whom no better public servants could be found in this or any other country, be the system what it may, and, let you ransack any private or public establishment you please, I defy you to produce those who can beat them. However, when you have to deal with cases where the chiefs of departments nominate to appointments in their own offices, it is vain to talk of severely testing the qualifications of candidates, because no board of examiners you may name could ever assume such a responsibility. My hon. Friend said he doubted whether the Order in Council recently issued was likely on the whole to tend to the public interest with respect to admissions to the civil service. I rest its defence, in the first place, on the ground that it makes the examinations universally and publicly known. The departmental examinations which now take place, and which vary with the state of each public establishment at particular moments, inflict great hardship upon many individuals, because it it not known that the examinations have to be undergone; or, if known, it is generally supposed that they are not very strict; and if an unfortunate man under those circumstances happens to stumble upon a severe examination and is thrown over, he thinks it rather hard that he should have been entrapped unwarily. The future examinations, however, will be universally known, and will be conducted by persons independent of the department concerned; so that this measure has at least some elements of good, and though it may fall short of what the public has a right to require, I believe it will correct what may be fairly called bad appointments. But, further, the Order in Council opens the door to every further improvement. There is nothing in it which tends to stereotype the principle of nomination; on the contrary, I firmly believe that that principle will in some cases be materially relaxed by it, and in others altogether abolished. I feel bound to give in my full adhesion to the doctrine of the hon. Member (Mr. Layard), that the admission to the public service should be thrown open; and I do so, first, because I believe all the other remedies that have been suggested are perfectly futile. You have been told to dismiss inefficient men; but all experience, I think, proves that, under a Government like ours, dismissal from the civil service can only be resorted to with effect in cases of the most extreme, most flagrant, and scandalous inefficiency; and if you trust to the exercise of the mere power of dismissal, you will trust to that which is really no remedy for the evils of which we complain. The noble Lord the Member for Lynn (Lord Stanley) has given an indication of an opinion that public servants ought to have a right of appeal against the heads of departments, and the means of bringing their cases under some sort of judicial trial. If you wished to give the finishing stroke to the public service, and to destroy and utterly paralyse it by allowing those who hold offices to entertain the idea of a vested right being the tenure by which they hold them, you would most completely attain that object by adopting the suggestion of the noble Lord. We hear a great deal said of probation, of division into classes, and the advancement from one grade to another, as remedies for the evils which exist in the civil service. But these remedies are upon the surface alone–they do not touch the heart and depth of the matter, which is this:–you have human selfishness to deal with, you have to meet that principle which makes men attend to their own interest rather than that of the public, and next to their own interest to that of their families, connexions, friends, and constituents–in fact, to the interest of everybody except to that of the public, which they ought to attend to. That is the principle; and all your petty little peddling as to the details of probation and division into classes, is merely paltering with the question. The truth is that this division into classes has been already tried; and to those who have a genius for arithmetic nothing can present a more beautiful appearance than the office of a Secretary of State; when the whole establishment is divided into departments–every man rising from one place to the other by an increase of £5 or £10 a year–and all is arranged with a nicety and exactitude as if it has been done by the scales of a goldsmith. But all this is nonsense and delusion. The real question differs entirely from this. What is the object we ought really to have in view? I apprehend it is not the question of admission, which I agree is most important–but the real question is–how can you procure promotion by merit? Does it take place at present? It takes place in certain cases, but I am sorry to say that these may be one in fifty or one in a hundred, and are very rare cases indeed, and arise from one or two causes; the merit is either so signal, conspicuous, and undeniable that no man can make it a subject of cavil, or the chief of a department, having more than ordinary resolution and energy, sets his face against all difficulties, and brings his system of promotion by merit into operation. What you want, however, is a good general system; and, I appeal to those who have been and who are heads of departments, what is prejudicial to this? I say that the obstacle is in the opinion of the civil service itself–that the present tone of the civil service is not favourable to promotion by merit, but, on the contrary, is in favour of promotion by seniority. Promotion by merit is not believed in, but is looked upon with distrust, and regarded as a cover for jobbery; and this feeling gives rise to so much inconvenience, that no one hardly ever, and save in a few exceptional cases, attempts to act upon it. The consequence of this is that, although there are many excellent incomparable men in the service, yet a low tone pervades the public service; the quantity of duty performed is small; bad and middling men are overpaid, and therefore the good men are underpaid; and, with an unsatisfactory discharge of duty, you have a state of discontent in the civil service permanent and all but universal. The question, then, is, how can you bring into the civil service a different tone of opinion with respect to promotion by merit? I admit the difficulty of this question; but it seems to me that the indisposition to see men promoted by merit is mainly due to the present system of admission. Men now get into the service by favour, and it is difficult to make them understand that they are to be promoted by merit; but if you bring them in on merit, then, as a natural consequence, they will entertain the idea that they will get on by merit. But those who receive their appointment from one of twenty causes distinct from merit look upon what they have received, not as remuneration for their duty, but in the nature of a gift in which they have a vested right, and they watch it with the jealousy that men watch their vested rights, and they do not understand being put aside from succession to higher office on account of a man of greater merit, any more than a man would understand giving up his private property to his neighbour because he is a wiser and better man. You must throw open the civil service to all the world, you must obtain for it the best men as far as you can ascertain who the best men are by an examination and by the most rigid scrutiny, and then, whatever other evils you may incur, you give it to be understood that the men who come into the civil service do not receive their appointments by favour, and have not any other right to obtain or hold their places except the right which depends upon efficiency. You will thus change the basis of your system, and by doing so, I, for one, am sanguine that you will substitute for the present opinion that prevails in the civil service, adverse to promotion by merit, a totally different opinion. Men will come on merit and seek only to get on by merit. Then, when you have done your best, you will be far from perfection, but you will, I think, find you have obtained a better system than now prevails. . . .

180. Commons debate on administrative reform (15–18 June 1855): Chancellor of the Exchequer's (Sir G. Cornewall Lewis) speech

Hansard, 3/CXXXCIII/2131–2133.

. . .With the permission of the House, I will briefly call their attention to the steps which have already been taken for the revision of some of the principal departments of the Government. In the year 1848 a revision of the Home Department took place at the time my right hon. Friend, who is now Home Secretary (Sir G. Grey) was at the head of that department. I was myself Under Secretary for the department, and a revision took place after a careful examination, in which Sir Charles Trevelyan, then Assistant Secretary to the Treasury, assisted, and the result was the introduction of various reforms. In the year 1849 a revision of the department of the Treasury took place; after a careful examination, conducted by Sir Charles Trevelyan and Mr. Gibson Craig, certain reforms were introduced. In the same year a similar investigation was made into the Colonial Office with a similar result; and in 1852, under the Government of Lord Derby, an investigation was made with regard to the Chief Secretary's Office, Dublin; the Irish Office, London; the Privy Council Office, Dublin; and the Fines and Penalties Office, Dublin. Since that time there has been a revision of the War Office, of the Board of Trade, of the Poor Law Board, of the Privy Council Office, and of the Committee of Privy Council on Education; of the Colonial Land and Emigration Office, of the Copyhold Enclosure and Tithes Commission, of the Board of Ordnance, of the Office of Works, of the Post Office, and of the Office of the Registrar General. In all those cases extensive reforms have been the consequence. It will be in the recollection of the House that important reform has likewise taken place in the constitution of the Indian Service, and a change has been made in the examination of candidates for that service. A consolidation of the War Department has likewise been recently introduced. The examples which I have quoted show that although the adoption of the Amendment of the hon. Baronet is perfectly consistent with the course which not only the present but former Governments have pursued, it is not needed for the purpose of stimulating them to revise the public departments, but that, on the contrary, they have already, of their own free will, pursued the very course now pressed upon them. With regard to the institution of tests, I will refer to the Order in Council, the origin of which has been explained by my right hon. Friend the Member for the University, and the provisions of which have been canvassed by several Members who have addressed the House. It is not my purpose to discuss at present the question whether the plan which that Order embodies sufficiently remedies all the evils which are said to exist in the present system, or whether it will be desirable to introduce into this country for the first time a system of admitting an unlimited number of candidates without the nomination of the head of any department. I will only remark that this Order in Council provides a great additional security for merit in administrative appointments beyond that which now exists. A regular examination, conducted under the superintendence of a board of persons who are independent of each department and unconnected with the heads of those departments, affords a greater security than has ever hitherto existed for the exclusion of unfit persons from the service of the Crown. Whatever difference of opinion may exist as to ulterior measures which it may be thought prudent or wise to adopt, surely it cannot be denied that the provisions of the Order, which has recently been brought into force for the first time, afford a guarantee for the merit of persons appointed in the different public departments, inasmuch as by prescribing a certain amount of qualification they will prevent any one from entering the service of the Crown who does not possess that requisite degree of attainments. I cannot but think that the Order in Council to which I have referred gives a practical proof of the efforts made by Her Majesty's Government for securing the efficiency of administrative departments, and goes much further in that direction than any of the very general recommendations which are offered at meetings out of doors. . . .

181. The Roebuck Report on the Army before Sebastopol (18 June 1855)

Parlty. Papers, 1854–1855/IX.

The Condition of our Army before Sebastopol

An army encamped in a hostile country, at a distance of 3000 miles from England, and engaged during a severe winter in besieging a fortress which, from want of numbers, it could not invest, was necessarily placed in a situation where unremitting fatigue and hardship had to be endured. Your Committee are, however, of opinion that this amount of unavoidable suffering has been aggravated by causes hereafter enumerated, and which are mainly to be attributed to dilatory and insufficient arrangements for the supply of this army with necessaries indispensable to its healthy and effective condition. In arriving at this opinion, they have made allowance for the unexpected severity of the storm on the 14th. of November, and they have not been unmindful of the difficulties which a long period of peace must inevitably produce at the commencement of a campaign. . . .

From the 16th. of September, when the army landed in the Crimea, until the end of October, or, as some witnesses state, until the middle of November, the troops suffered from overwork and from dysentery, but were not, upon the whole, ill-provided with food: even at this period there was a want of clothing for the men in health, and a painful deficiency of all appliances for the proper treatment of the sick and wounded. . . .

From the middle of November this army was, during a period of many weeks, reduced to a condition which it is melancholy to contemplate, but which was endured, both by officers and men, with a fortitude and heroism unsurpassed in the annals of war. They were exposed, under single canvas, to all the sufferings and inconveniences of cold, rain, mud, and snow, on high ground, and in the depth of winter. They suffered from fatigue, exposure, want of clothing, insufficient supplies for the healthy, and imperfect accommodation for the sick. . . .

The Conduct of the Government at Home

. . . The general direction of the war was in the hands of the Duke of Newcastle, who, in the spring of 1854, held the office of Secretary of State for War and Colonies. In July these departments were divided, and the Duke, being relieved of colonial duties, undertook the immediate conduct of the war.

When this important change was effected, it does not appear that any Order in Council, Minute, or other document was prepared, defining the special duties of the War Department. The Duke, as Secretary of State, had undoubtedly, before as well as after the change, ample powers. . . . He states, however, that he felt his means to be insufficient for the due performance of his separate duties as Secretary of State for War; he considered the organisation of all the war departments and their relation to each other to be in an unsatisfactory state; but he felt it to be impossible, consistently with attention to pressing business, to attempt their re-organisation. . . .

At the date of the expedition to the East, no reserve was provided at home adequate to the undertaking. . . . The order to attack Sebastopol was sent to Lord Raglan on the 29th. of June: the formation of a reserve at Malta was not determined upon until early in November. . . .

. . . When the Duke of Newcastle informed Lord Raglan that he had 2,000 recruits to send him, he replied that "those last sent were so young, and unformed, that they fell victim to disease, and were swept away like flies. He preferred to wait."

In December the power of re-inforcing the army with efficient soldiers was so reduced that the Government thought it necessary to introduce a Foreign Enlistment Bill, for the purpose of raising a foreign legion. . . .

The Secretary of State for War

On accepting the Secretaryship for War, the Duke of Newcastle found himself in this disadvantageous position: he had no separate office for his department, no document prescribing his new duties, no precedents for his guidance, and his Under-Secretaries were new to the work. In this situation he undertook the superintendence of numerous departments, with whose internal organisation he was dissatisfied, and the management of a war urgently requiring prompt and vigorous operations.

The Duke was imperfectly acquainted with the best mode of exercising his authority over the subordinate departments, and these departments were not officially informed of their relative position, or of their new duties towards the Minister for War. His interference was sought for in matters of detail, wherein his time should not have been so occupied, and he was left unacquainted with transactions of which he should have received official cognisance. . . .

The evidence, moreover, shows that the Duke was long left in ignorance, or was misinformed respecting the progress of affairs in the East. He was not, until a late period, made acquainted with the state of the hospitals at Scutari, and the horrible mode in which the sick and wounded were conveyed from Balaclava to the Bosphorus. Lord Aberdeen has significantly observed, that the Government was left in ignorance, longer than they ought to have been, of the real state of matters in the East. The Ministers, he says, were informed of the condition of the army from public papers and private sources long before they heard it officially, and, not hearing it officially, they discredited the rumours around them. Thus, whilst the whole country was dismayed by the reports, and was eagerly looking for some gleam of official intelligence, the Cabinet, according to the statement of Ministers, was in darkness.

. . . The Duke sent a commission to inquire into the state of the hospitals at Scutari and in the Crimea. The commission was issued in October; it did not report until April. . . .

With the same benevolent intention, the Duke, through the channel of the Foreign Office, requested Lord Stratford de Redcliffe to take upon himself, in addition to his many onerous duties, a certain amount of supervision and assistance of these hospitals.

The clothing of the troops was not within the province of the Secretary of State. . . . The system of clothing the army was then, and still is, in a state of transition; whenever the existing contracts cease, the clothing will be supplied by the Ordnance, or by a clothing department.

The warm clothing was considered so important that, upon hearing of the loss of the 'Prince' steamer . . . Ambassadors, ministers, consuls, agents were applied to for assistance; money was profusely expended, and at a later period in the winter the troops must have received a supply far larger than was required for their reduced numbers.

The Secretary-at-War

. . . The division of the Secretaryship of War and Colonies, though technically it did not alter the position of the Secretary-at-War, yet practically diminished the exercise of his power, and tended to limit his functions to the original duties of his office, namely the financial business of the army. Even in these matters the authority of a Secretary of State, when exerted, must necessarily over-ride the control of a Secretary-at-War. Mr. Sidney Herbert, as Secretary-at-War, had no power to originate anything, but from praiseworthy motives, and with a view to relieve the Duke of Newcastle, he undertook to do a good deal which was not the business of his office. Thus, in December, having learnt, from private sources, the deplorable condition of the hospitals, he wrote to the commandant, to the chief medical officer, and to the purveyor, urging and authorising them to procure whatever might be wanted, assistants, supplies, or additional buildings; promising them his approbation for such outlay, and placing unlimited funds at their disposal.

While expenditure was thus encouraged, some financial regulations were still enforced, suitable to a time of peace, but inapplicable to a period of war, and operating unjustly on the soldiers who had been wounded, or afflicted with sickness in the Crimea. According to these regulations, every soldier coming into a hospital is obliged to bring with him his kit; but though the troops, upon landing in the Crimea, had been deprived of their knapsacks, which in many cases were never restored, yet no order had been issued to furnish another set in lieu of those articles which the soldier had been compelled to relinquish, and which are essential to his cleanliness and comfort. Again, upon leaving the hospital, men were exposed to a recurrence of sickness from insufficient clothing, and no proper arrangement had been made to furnish this supply. . . .

The Ordnance Department

. . . In April 1854 Lord Raglan, the Master-General of Ordnance, was appointed to the command of the Forces in the East, and shortly afterwards Sir Hew Ross was named Lieutenant-General of the Ordnance, an office which had been for many years abolished but which was now revived.

Lord Aberdeen, in making this appointment, had to some extent in view the abolition of the office of Master-General; this subject had not, however, been considered by the Cabinet, and in the meantime the Ministers believed that the Lieutenant-General would have all the authority of the Master-General.

The Lieutenant-General does not possess this power; he is only a Board Officer; and while in reference to military duties he exercises the authority of Master-General, yet as regards the civil functions of the Ordnance he acts only as a member of the Board.

. . . During the summer and autumn of 1854, a Board Officer, the Surveyor-General, was also employed abroad; so that during a period when the pressure of business was heavier, and when the expenditure of the department was larger than in any previous year, two officers were wanting whose functions the most economical administrations had been unable to dispense with in times of peace.

The Ordnance, even with its peculiar constitution, may work efficiently while under the supervision of a vigilant Master-General, who has supreme authority . . . but the substitution of a Lieutenant-General changes the whole system of the office; its duties are then divided amongst the members of the Board without any supervising authority. . . .

From the evidence it will be seen that a conflict of authority arose between the members of this Board. At a time when urgent business required their attention, they were engaged in disputes, in preparing statements, and in making appeals to the Secretary of State for War. . . . In noticing the unseemly conduct of this Board. . . . Your Committee observes with regret, that the public service has suffered from the want of judgment and temper on the part of officers who were entrusted during a critical period with important public duties.

. . . After perusing the evidence it will excite no surprise to find that the arrangements attempted by this office in reference to warm clothing, huts, and Minie rifles, were imperfect and dilatory. . . .

. . . . Your Committee must express their dissatisfaction with the administration of the contract system under this department. . . .

The tools supplied to the army are stated to be of bad quality. Under a recent order, the Ordnance furnishes all tools. . . . The Committee . . . feel bound, at the same time, to mention the admirable equipment of the corps of artillery attached to the army, and the testimony generally given to the efficient armament provided for the navy.

Transport Department at Home

... The mode in which ships were taken up is described by Captain Milne, and, considering the pressure of the public service, this duty seems to have been ably performed....

There is, it is said, an obvious error in comparing the transport service between England and the Crimea to a mercantile arrangement for the conveyance and delivery of a given amount of tonnage. The transports, when sent to the Crimea, could not deliver their stores and return; a large number were permanently detained from military considerations, and many others were kept at Balaclava, because there were no warehouses on shore to receive their cargo.

Many complaints were made to your Committee of the mode in which stores were sent to the East. . . . The chief complaints have arisen in reference to mixed cargoes. . . . Until December it appears that a cargo-book was not regularly kept. A Treasury Minute, dated 12th. December 1854, states, that some articles sent out to the Crimea have been taken back to England in the same vessels, and brought out again to the Crimea before they have been delivered. . . . Ships were also so loaded, that on arriving at the port to which part of the cargo was destined, the position of that part of the cargo was unknown, and the ship had to proceed on her voyage carrying with her things that ought to have been delivered at the intermediate port. Much suffering was the consequence of this faulty mode of proceeding, the sick at Scutari being in need of stores, which, in consequence of bad arrangements, were carried to Balaclava.

Your Committee inquired why ships for the conveyance of the sick and wounded had not been prepared at an early period of the war. . . . The unnecessary sufferings of the soldiers directly referable to this neglect form one of the most painful portions of the evidence; but on what department the blame should rest, whether on the office of the Commander-in-Chief, or of the Secretary-at-War, or of the Secretary of State for War, your Committee are unable to decide. . . .

Thus it appears that the preparation of ships for the conveyance of the sick and wounded was first forgotten, and subsequently neglected. When it is remembered that out of the limited number of the British Army, 13,800 were removed sick or wounded between the 30th. September and the 17th. of February, the dreadful consequences of this neglect may be imagined. . . .

The Transport Service in the Black Sea

. . . Sir James Graham said that the naval commander-in-chief, Vice-Admiral Dundas, had, under the Queen's regulations, authority over the whole of the transports. . . . Lord Raglan had a concurrent authority over this service.

Vice-Admiral Dundas, on the contrary, alleged that he had nothing to do with the transports. According to his assertions, they were entirely under the management of Lord Raglan, Rear-Admiral Boxer, and Captain Christie. . . .

In Balaclava there was a division of authority: the transports were under the immediate direction of Captain Christie; the harbour was under the management of another naval officer, and the shore was subject to military authority. . . .

The Commissariat in the East

It is the duty of the Commissariat to furnish the army, when in the field, with provisions for the men, forage for the animals, and land transport. . . .

The military system in this country affords the Commissariat no opportunity of becoming acquainted with the army, or of ministering to its wants; so that in a campaign the officers of this department find themselves called upon to furnish supplies in regard to which they have had no experience; while the officers and men, being often ignorant of the proper duties of the Commissariat, consider this department responsible for everything they may require.

Land Transport

From the first the system of the land transport was found to be imperfect. No adequate measures were adopted for its improvement, so that the army, when encamped before Sebastopol, depended for all its supplies upon a service defective in its organisation and in its superintendence. . . .

The Road

So much of the suffering of the troops has been ascribed to the wretched, or, as some witnesses state, the almost impassable condition of the seven miles between Balaclava and the camp, that your Committee endeavoured to ascertain who was responsible for the maintenance of the roads, and what insuperable obstacles impeded their repair.

When the army reached the heights above Sebastopol they found two principal roads from Balaclava to Sebastopol, one the fine government road called the Woronzoff road; the other, further to the left, a useful farm road. The army held the Woronzoff road up to the time of the battle of Balaclava, in October. Immediately after that action it became necessary to draw in the outposts, which lost to the army the use of that road: the other road, however, remained, and was available for all purposes until the rains commenced.

On the 13th. of November Commissary-General Filder wrote to the Quartermaster-General, expressing his apprehension, and calling attention to this important subject.

The duty of making and maintaining roads for the army falls upon the Department of the Quartermaster-General. This officer was about this time disabled by severe illness. Sir J. Burgoyne, the Chief Engineer Officer on the staff, and other military authorities, state that the soldiers could not be withdrawn from the trenches for the repair of the road; the men were already overtasked by military duties; they were growing weaker from day to day, while their difficulties were increasing. An attempt was made to employ Turkish troops on this work, but it was soon abandoned.

From the 14th. of November, the date of the hurricane, the land-transport was gradually reduced in strength, until it almost ceased to exist. The Commissary-General writes "The men and beasts perished owing to the fatigue they underwent in struggling through the deep mud with supplies, and from exposure to wet and cold." . . .

As far as the information obtained enables your Committee to form an opinion, it appears to them that in this matter there was a want of due foresight and decision. . . The probable failure of the communication was not, however, brought to the notice of the Duke of Newcastle until too late to enable him to take measures in England to prevent the serious calamities which subsequently arose.

Food for the Men

. . . The witnesses are not agreed as to the quantity of fresh meat supplied to the army. . . . Vegetables, which according to the intentions of the Government should have been issued gratuitously, were very scantily supplied; indeed several witnesses assert that none were ever seen in the camp. . . . Coffee, which had been ordered as an extra ration, was distributed to the troops in a green state, and (there being no means of roasting it) was of little use. . . .

Forage

When the army first encamped before Sebastopol, stacks of forage were found in the neighbourhood; these were soon consumed. . . . After the hurricane the supply of forage failed, and under the combined effects of work, exposure, and insufficient food, the cavalry gradually ceased to exist as an effective force.

To what extent the Commissariat is responsible for the deficiency in all these supplies, is a question to which it is not easy to give a definite answer.

Sir C. Trevelyan, speaking as the head of the Commissariat, and desirous of relieving the department of responsibility, affirms their conduct throughout to have been irreproachable, and ascribes blame to other persons. . . .

The Medical Department at Home

The medical Department of the Army and Ordnance is under a Director-General, who has an assistant to aid him in his multifarious duties. Dr. Smith, the Director-General, states that he was under the immediate authority of five different superiors – the Commander-in-Chief, the Secretary of State, the Secretary-at-War, the Master-General of the Ordnance, and the Board of Ordnance. . . . The entire failure of this corps, and the consequent suffering of the army are abundantly proved. . . .

The Medical Department in the East

The army, when sent to the East, had a greater number of medical men in proportion to the troops, than ever before accompanied a British army, and the witnesses generally concur in testifying to their zeal and efficiency; many of these were, however, disabled by sickness. . . . The condition of the tent-hospitals . . . was, from the 28th. of November to the 23rd. of January . . . so wretched and painful to hear that your Committee gladly avoid repeating these deplorable details. The medical men, it is said, were indefatigable in their attention; but so great was the want of the commonest necessaries, even of bedding, as well as of medicines and medical comforts, that they sorrowfully admitted their services to be of little avail. . . .

The Hospitals at Scutari

. . . Major Sillery was commandant, and had sole military charge of the hospitals. Dr. Menzies was superintendent of all the hospitals. . . . Dr. Hall, the Inspector-General of the Army was sent by Lord Raglan to inspect the hospitals in October. He remained at Scutari about three weeks, and then reported them "to be in as good a state as could reasonably be expected." . . . In justice to Dr. Menzies, it must be admitted that he was engaged in incessant and onerous duties. . . . The duties of Dr. Menzies were further obstructed by a conflict of authority with the purveyor, who claimed to act independently, under the instructions of the Secretary-at-War. . . . Your Committee must declare it to be their opinion, that blame attaches to Dr. Menzies, inasmuch as he did not report correctly the circumstances of the hospital. . . . When it is remembered that the insufficiency of these stores was a source of much suffering, if not of more fatal results, it must be observed, that heavy responsibility attaches to the Commander-in-chief of the Forces, who, acting on the representation of the Quartermaster-general, retained Mr. Ward in his office, after he had been pronounced unfit to discharge its duties. . . . The apothecary's department at Scutari was in no better condition. . . . When the quantities of hospital stores which were sent from England are contrasted with the scarcity, or rather the absolute dearth of them at Scutari; and when the state of the purveyor's accounts is remembered, it is impossible not to harbour a suspicion that some dishonesty had been practised in regard to these stores. . . .

In order to show the dreadful discomfort of the men, and the neglect on the part of the authorities, it may be sufficient to state, that in the barrack hospital of Scutari, during the month of November, while there were about 2000 patients in that hospital, the whole number of shirts washed was only six. . . . The want of an energetic governing authority, with an adequate staff to maintain constant inspection and efficient discipline, appears to your Committee to have been the chief cause of all the evils: 5,000 or 6,000 men, although in hospital, require the care, superintendence, and control of an efficient general officer as much as the same number in the field. Mr. Herbert says that "Major Sillery . . . worked very indefatigably in his department, according to his own light, but that he was not a man of the rank in the army and the weight which he ought to have had, to be at the head of an establishment of such a gigantic character." . . . It may not have been possible for Lord Raglan to have spared such an officer, with a sufficient staff for this service, in the pressing circumstances of his position in the Crimea. . . .

Your Committee, in conclusion, cannot but remark, that the first real improvements in the lamentable condition of the hospitals at Scutari, are to be attributed to private suggestions, private exertions, and private benevolence. Miss Nightingale, at the suggestion of the Secretary-at-War, with admirable devotion, organised a band of nurses, and undertook the care of the sick and wounded. A fund, raised by public subscription, was administered by the proprietors of the *Times* newspaper, through

Mr. M'Donald, an intelligent and zealous agent. The Hon. and Rev. Sidney Godolphin Osborne, Mr. Augustus Stafford, and the Hon. Josceline Percy, after a personal inspection of the hospitals, furnished valuable reports and suggestions to the Government. By these means much suffering was alleviated, the spirits of the men were raised, and many lives were saved. . . .

It appears that the sufferings of the army resulted mainly from the circumstances in which the expedition to the Crimea was undertaken and executed. The Administration which ordered the expedition had no adequate information as to the amount of force in the Crimea or Sebastopol. They were not acquainted with the strength of the fortresses to be attacked, or with the resources of the country to be invaded. They hoped and expected that the expedition would be immediately successful, and, as they did not foresee the probability of a protracted struggle, they made no provision for a winter campaign; what was planned and undertaken without sufficient information, was conducted without sufficient care or forethought. This conduct on the part of the Administration was the first and chief cause of the calamities which befel our army.

. . .

18th. June, 1855.

182. Select Committee on Public Monies (1856–1857)

Parlty. Papers, 1857/p. 500.

6. *Extension of the Appropriation Check, and Presentation of Audited Accounts to Parliament*

The concurrent audit, or appropriation check, first applied to the expenditure of the Grants for Naval Services in 1832, and subsequently extended to the several Army Grants, was a new security introduced for ensuring the strict appropriation of the Grants of Parliament. It was not intended to limit the discretion of the responsible departments of the Executive Government in which it was established, but to secure a revision of their accounts by an independent authority, invested with sufficient powers of investigation to detect any misapplication of the Votes, or any deviation from the appropriation sanctioned by Parliament. This check now applies to the Naval and Military Expenditure, and is regulated by the provisions of an Act (9 & 10 Vict. c. 92) passed in 1846; also to the expenditure of the Offices of Woods and Forests, and Public Works; and the Commissioners of Audit transmit annually to the Treasury, for presentation to the House of Commons, accounts of Naval and Military Expenditure, compared with the Grants, accompanied by Reports, in which they direct attention to every departure from the provisions of the Appropriation Act. Your Committee recommend that this important check upon the application of the public money be extended to the accounts of the Income and Expenditure kept at the Treasury, to the accounts of the Revenue Departments, and to the various accounts comprising the expenditure of the Votes for Civil Services, including Civil Contingencies. For the latter service two accounts should be presented; one showing the final payments charged against the Vote for Civil Contingencies, and the other showing a balanced account of the transactions of the year, including the outstanding advances at the close of the year, and the balance unissued brought down to the following year. These accounts to be presented for the past year along with the estimate for Civil Contingencies for the current year. Your Committee are also of opinion that the whole of these accounts, finally audited, should be presented to Parliament before the close of the year succeeding that to which they relate.

In order to strengthen the check upon the Government in regard to issues of money, for any service whatever in excess of the sum voted by Parliament, Your Committee recommend that all payments of the Paymaster-general shall be checked from day to day, in the departments in which they are authorised or made, by an officer to be appointed by the Commissioners of Audit: it will be the duty of this officer to follow from day to day the appropriation of every payment to its proper account, and to report immediately to the Commissioners any excess of the Vote sanctioned by Parliament, or other irregularity.

And Your Committee further recommend that these audited accounts be annually submitted to the revision of a Committee of the House of Commons, to be nominated by the Speaker. It is desirable that an annual account of all guaranteed loans, including the payments made, and the arrears, if any, due to the Consolidated Fund, shall be presented to this Committee, and that they do report thereon specially to The House.

Your Committee suggest that the Audit Board should no longer transmit through the Treasury those accounts which they are bound to lay before Parliament, but should communicate them direct, and that the appropriation and inspection of Army and Navy Accounts, the selection of officers for the respective duties, their removal or dismissal, should rest entirely with the Audit Board.

Your Committee has recommended a large extension of the duties and powers of the Board of Audit. If these suggestions be adopted, it will be necessary that the composition and relative position of this Board, as a great department of the State, should be reconsidered by the Executive Government. The Board of Audit is responsible to Parliament alone, and the station and emoluments of the person at the head of it should be equal to the importance of the duties to be performed, and not second in rank to any of the permanent officers presiding over other principal departments....

183. Setting up of Public Accounts Committee: Gladstone's motion of 9 April 1861

Hansard, 3/CLXII/318.

PUBLIC ACCOUNTS

SELECT COMMITTEE MOVED FOR

The CHANCELLOR of the EXCHEQUER, in moving for the appointment of a Select Committee on Public Accounts, said that the object of the Committee would be to revise the accounts of the public expenditure after they had gone through the regular process of examination in the hands of the executive Government. That was obviously the true completion of the duty of that House with regard to the public money. The Committee on Public Monies which sat two or three years ago had made this recommendation, and made it unanimously. He should, therefore, move that a Select Committee be appointed for the examination from year to year of the audited accounts of the public expenditure; and if that Motion was adopted, he would on a future day move that a Committee of that nature be appointed at the commencement of every Session; and, likewise, that the order for the appointment of that Committee be made a standing order of the House.

Motion *agreed to.*

Select Committee *appointed,* "for the examination from year to year of the Audited Accounts of the Public Expenditure."

184. Gladstone's speech introducing the Exchequer and Audit Act (9 February 1866)

Hansard, 3/CLXXXI/275–276.

The CHANCELLOR of the EXCHEQUER presented a Bill to consolidate the duties of the Exchequer and Audit Departments, to regulate the receipt, custody, and issue of public monies, and to provide for the audit of the accounts thereof. He said, the course he proposed to take with regard to the Bill was to introduce it that night, and in consideration of its importance to allow a fortnight to elapse before he moved the second reading. He should next propose to refer it to the Select Committee on Public Accounts; and, as it was a Bill almost entirely relating to public accounts, it would receive a more impartial, authoritative, and searching examination before that Committee than it would in any other way. The object of the Bill was, first of all, to consolidate the departments of Exchequer and Audit, while the personal functions of the Controller of the Exchequer would not be interfered with. The next object of the Bill was to apply to what was called the Exchequer check the principles of modification recommended by the very important Committee on Public Monies which sat some years ago, so as to preserve the constitutional form of the Exchequer check, but to introduce harmony into all proceedings subsequent to that operation so as to get rid of a greal deal of unnecessary and expensive book-keeping now carried on. The third and most important object was this. During the discussion which arose last year out of Mr. Edmunds' case, it became known to Parliament much more fully than had formerly been the case, that there were many branches of public receipt and expenditure that were not subjected to audit, and that the whole system of audit was in a most unsatisfactory state. Some of the expenditure was audited by the Audit Board, which was quite right; some of it by the Treasury, which was quite wrong, for the Treasury was a department for controlling and not auditing, the expenditure; and, lastly, a good deal of it was not audited at all. The Government proposed to substitute for that three-fold irregular and anomalous method of proceeding an uniform method, by which the whole of the expenditure should be audited by the proper department appointed for the purpose–namely, the Audit Board. The appropriation audit would therefore be carried throughout the whole of the public expenditure.

MR. BOUVERIE said, that the system of audit had hitherto not been satisfactory.

The ancient system had become obsolete, and lately had, in fact, been no check at all. Under these circumstances, he believed that the Bill now introduced would effect a very great improvement.

Motion *agreed to.*

Bill to consolidate the duties of the Exchequer and Audit Departments, to regulate the receipt, custody, and issue of Public Monies, and to provide for the audit of the accounts thereof, *ordered* to be brought in by Mr. Chancellor of the Exchequer and Mr. Childers.

Bill *presented*, and read the first time.

185. Special report of the Committee of Public Accounts on the Exchequer and Audit Act (March 1866)

Parlty. Papers, 1866/vii, p. 519.

The Committee of Public Accounts, to whom the Exchequer and Audit Departments Bill was referred:–have considered the said Bill, and taken Evidence thereon, which they have agreed to Report to the House; and have gone through the Bill, and made Amendments thereunto; and have agreed to the following special report:

Your Committee recommend that in the event of the said Bill becoming law, it should be made a Standing Order of this Honourable House, that all Reports on Appropriation and Consolidated Fund Accounts, and the Treasury Minutes prescribed in Schedule (B) of the said Bill, be referred to the Committee of Public Accounts.

15 March 1866

186. Exchequer and Audit Act (1866)

Statutes of the Realm, 29 & 30 Vict. c. 39.

3. At any Time within Twelve Months after the passing of this Act it shall be lawful for Her majesty, Her Heirs and Successors, by Letters Patent under the Great Seal of the United Kingdom to nominate and appoint the Person who shall at that Time hold the Office of Comptroller General of the Receipt and Issue of Her Majesty's Exchequer, and Chairman of the Commissioners for auditing the Public Accounts, to be Comptroller General of the Receipt Accounts, in this Act referred to as "Comptroller and Auditor General," and also to nominate and appoint One of the Persons who shall at that Time hold the Offices of Commissioners for auditing the Public Accounts to be "Assistant Comptroller and Auditor."

The said Comptroller and Auditor General and Assistant Comptroller and Auditor shall hold their Offices during good Behaviour, subject, however, to their Removal therefrom by Her Majesty, Her Heirs and Successors, on an Address from the Two Houses of Parliament; and they shall not be capable of holding their Offices together with any other Office to be held during Pleasure under the Crown, or under any Officer appointed by the Crown; nor shall they be capable while holding their

Offices of being elected or of sitting as Members of the House of Commons; nor shall any Peer of Parliament be capable of holding either of the said Offices.

. . . . .

21. The Treasury shall cause an Account to be prepared and transmitted to the Comptroller and Auditor General for Examination on or before the Thirtieth Day of September in every Year, showing the Issues made from the Consolidated Fund of Great Britain and Ireland in the Financial Year ended on the Thirty-first day of March preceding, for the Interest and Management of the Public Funded and Unfunded Debt, for the Civil List, and all other Issues in the Financial Year for Services charged directly on the said Fund; and the Comptroller and Auditor General shall certify and report upon the same with reference to the Acts of Parliament under the Authority of which such Issues may have been directed; and such Accounts and Reports shall be laid before the House of Commons by the Treasury on or before the Thirty-first Day of January in the following Year, if Parliament be then sitting, and if not sitting then within One Week after Parliament shall be next assembled.

22. On or before the Days specified in the respective Columns of Schedule A. annexed to this Act, Accounts of the Appropriation of the several Supply Grants comprised in the Appropriation Act of each Year shall be prepared by the several Departments, and be transmitted for Examination to the Comptroller and Auditor General and to the Treasury, and when certified and reported upon as herein-after directed they shall be laid before the House of Commons; and such Accounts shall be called the "Appropriation Accounts" of the Moneys expended for the Services to which they may respectively relate; and the Treasury shall determine by what Departments such Accounts shall be prepared and rendered to the Comptroller and Auditor General, and the Comptroller and Auditor General shall certify and report upon such Accounts as herein-after directed; and the Reports thereon shall be signed by the Comptroller and Auditor General: Provided always, and it is the Intention of this Act that the Treasury shall direct that the Department charged with the Expenditure of any Vote under the Authority of the Treasury shall prepare the Appropriation Account thereof: Provided also, that the Term "Department", when used in this Act in connexion with the Duty of preparing the said Appropriation Accounts, shall be construed as including any Public Officer or Officers to whom that Duty may be assigned by the Treasury.

. . . . .

26. Every Appropriation Account when rendered to the Comptroller and Auditor General shall be accompanied by an Explanation showing how the Balance or Balances on the Grant or Grants included in the previous Account have been adjusted, and shall also contain an explanatory Statement of any Excess of Expenditure over the Grant or Grants included in such Account, and such Statement as well as the Appropriation Account shall be signed by such Department.

27. Every Appropriation Account shall be examined by the Comptroller and Auditor General on behalf of the House of Commons; and in the Examination of such Accounts the Comptroller and Auditor General shall ascertain, first, whether

the Payments which the accounting Department has charged to the Grant are supported by Vouchers or Proofs of Payments, and, second, whether the Money expended has been applied to the Purpose or Purposes for which such Grant was intended to provide: Provided always, and it is hereby enacted, that whenever the said Comptroller and Auditor General shall be required by the Treasury to ascertain whether the Expenditure included or to be included in an Appropriation Account, or any Portion of such Expenditure, is supported by the Authority of the Treasury, the Comptroller and Auditor General shall examine such Expenditure with that Object, and shall report to the Treasury any Expenditure which may appear, upon such Examination, to have been incurred without such Authority; and if the Treasury should not thereupon see fit to sanction such unauthorized Expenditure, it shall be regarded as being not properly chargeable to a Parliamentary Grant, and shall be reported to the House of Commons in the Manner herein-after provided.

28. In order that such Examination may as far as possible proceed, *pari passu*, with the Cash Transactions of the several accounting Departments, the Comptroller and Auditor General shall have free Access, at all convenient Times, to the Books of Account and other Documents relating to the Accounts of such Departments, and may require the several Departments concerned to furnish him, from Time to Time, or at regular Periods, with Accounts of the Cash Transactions of such Departments respectively up to such Times or Periods.

187. Gladstone's acceptance of the competitive principle for entry to the Civil Service (25 February 1870)

Hansard, 3/CXIX/812.

... The administrative changes, as my hon. Friend defines them, are very considerable, although the principle upon which he proposes we should act in making them at first sight looks simple enough. The general idea which Members conceive is, that first appointments in the Civil Service are to be regulated by open competition–the correlative principle having been long ago established–namely, that promotions in the Civil Service are regulated by the Chiefs of Departments, and are understood and believed to be given–and, I am bound to say, are given–under the influence of merit and service alone. But when we pass beyond these general statements there are very important matters of detail to consider. There is that which of itself amounts to a complete reorganization of the Civil Service–the division proposed to be introduced and which I hope will be carried out as far as possible, and made as clear as possible, between duties which are mechanical and formal, and those duties which require high mental training. That is a question which cannot be decided by rule of thumb; it cannot be disposed of by laying down a strict and absolute principle for all the Departments, but it requires of necessity a careful examination into the circumstances of each Department; and the precise point at which the line is to be drawn is a matter that cannot be settled except in detail and after minute scrutiny. There are other matters to be considered in establishing the principle of open competition. For example, it will be necessary that the responsible officers of the Government should reserve in a very strict and clear manner, so as to preclude all possibility of mistake, the power of defining and determining, from time to time, what are those superior offices which are to be considered as Staff appointments, and to which persons may be introduced and appointed irrespective of any prior services they may have rendered in the Civil Departments. That is a matter of the utmost consequence, and one on which, when once open competition is established, it is necessary the clearest understanding should prevail; because those who come into the Civil Service upon the basis of open competition, determined only by merit, may be disposed to rate highly, and perhaps justly so, their own claims to the fulfilment of what they may consider a covenant with respect to prospective advancement. We must, therefore, consider carefully the terms of that covenant, so as to reserve in the hands of the Government that discretion with respect to the higher appointments which it is absolutely necessary for the public service they should retain. Both, therefore, with respect to the limit, upwards, of those offices the first appointments to which need not be, and could not be, the subject of open competition; and, again, with respect to the limit, downwards, of all that class of offices with regard to which a test examination applies, and a rate of pay governed by what the market requires, much has to be considered. . . . I will not say that our plan is quite complete, but communications have been held between the Treasury and the other Departments of the State; and though I cannot at the present moment undertake to state whether it would be in our power within a short time to establish in every public office a system of open competition, I can venture to say, unless our present expectations are very much disappointed, it will be within a limited period in our power to announce the establishment of a system of open competition upon an extended scale, a scale quite sufficient, even if there should be exceptions, to enable the public to test its principle in a perfect scale, and determine upon the propriety of applying it to any cases that may remain with greater advantage than we may be said to possess at this moment. . . .

188. Order in Council of 4 June 1870, on entry to the Civil Service

Parlty. Papers, 1876/XXII, pp. 17–19.

At the Court at Balmoral, the 4th day of June 1870

PRESENT:

THE QUEEN'S MOST EXCELLENT MAJESTY IN COUNCIL

WHEREAS it is expedient to continue, with certain amendments, the existing provision for testing according to fixed rules the qualifications of persons who may from time to time be proposed to be appointed, either premanently or temporarily, to any situation or employment in any of Her Majesty's Civil Establishments, except as herein-after mentioned;

. . . . .

V. Except as herein-after is excepted, all appointments which it may be necessary to make, after the 31st day of August next, to any of the situations included or to be included in Schedule A. to this Order annexed, shall be made by means of competitive examinations, according to regulations to be from time to time framed by the said Civil Service Commissioners, and approved by the Commissioners of Her Majesty's Treasury, open to all Persons (of the requisite age, health, character, and other qualifications prescribed in the said regulations) who may be desirous of attending the same, subject to the payment of such fees as the said Civil Service Commissioners, with the consent of the said Commissioners of Her Majesty's Treasury, may from time to time require; such examinations to be held at such periods, and for such situations, or groups of situations in the same or different departments, as the said Civil Service Commissioners, with the approval of the said Commissioners of Her Majesty's Treasury, shall from time to time determine, and to have reference either to the vacancies existing at the time of the examinations respectively, or to the number which may be estimated to occur within any period not exceeding six months after the commencement of the examinations, as the said Civil Service Commissioners, after consultation with the chief authorities of the various departments, and with the approval of the said Commissioners of Her Majesty's Treasury may deem expedient.

. . . . .

Part VIII
LOCAL GOVERNMENT

LOCAL GOVERNMENT

Introduction

ENGLAND faced the nineteenth century with a machinery of local government that was Elizabethan in its main structure, and medieval in many of its forms. Drastic reconstruction was inevitable. The county authorities were the Justices of the Peace, collectively responsible, in Quarter Sessions, for the affairs of the county as a whole, and collectively and individually exercising supervision over parish administration. The judicial forms of medieval administration were still largely preserved; that is to say that the normal method of dealing with whatever required to be done was for the Grand Jury, High Constables of Hundreds, or local Justices to make a 'presentment' on the subject to Quarter Sessions, followed by an order of the court. There was little or no professional staff with a continuing responsibility for supervision and action. There were approximately two hundred and fifty boroughs administered under charters derived from the Crown or from manorial lords. Their government had, in most cases, originally been reasonably representative of the active and responsible elements in their towns. But in many cases the towns themselves had decayed, while none of the towns that had sprung into importance in the last century had acquired corporate status. In the course of time and, as the Municipal Commissioners of 1835 report,[1] in the case of those that sent members to Parliament, largely in order to bring their electorates under control, the popular basis of the corporations had narrowed, and they had become oligarchies whose responsibility for the conduct of the local interests entrusted to them, and often of considerable corporate property, was subject to little control but that of their own sense of duty. This was not invariably ineffective, but was mostly so, particularly where the oligarchy was a fairly wide one, dominated by the shopkeeping class. A number of boroughs derived their charters from manorial grant, and in many places–Manchester among them–manorial machinery, court baron and court leet, still played an important part in local government. It was attendance at the court leet of the Moseley owners of the manor on which Manchester stood that drove Cobden to say, in 1837, that he "would put an end to this thing". Many urban districts had to cope with their problems through the machinery of parish administration. In its typical rural form the parish, in the language of Mr. and Mrs. Webb, was a 'unit of obligation'; its churchwardens, overseers, surveyors of roads, and constables, were annually chosen from among the parishioners, the more substantial of whom, at any rate, had all to take their turns of office, under the supervision of the local justices. They were responsible for the maintenance of the church fabric and of local roads and bridges, for the care of the parish poor, for repressing crime and disorder, and for whatever they might choose to deal with, which was normally little or nothing, under the compendious law of nuisance, which comprised practically all that the country had in the way of a code of public health. The little scope that this framework of administration offered for

[1] No. 190.

dealing with the problems of a country in the throes of an economic and social transformation was, in instances, admirably exploited, but the failures were naturally more conspicuous than the successes. What new ground had been broken administratively was mainly in connexion with Statutory Authorities, set up under special Acts of Parliament. These fell broadly into the four classes of Sewer Authorities, Incorporations of the Poor, Turnpike Authorities, and Improvement Commissioners under various titles, such as Streets Commissioners, Lighting and Paving Commissioners, Police Commissioners, and so on. Sewer Authorities dated back, in most instances, to legislation of Henry VIII, and were originally drainage authorities, rather than sewer authorities in the modern sense. Administratively, and in point of the areas with which they dealt, they were in few cases abreast of the problems with which they had to deal. Their deficiencies belong rather to the subject of Public Health,[1] and need not detain us here. Poor Law Incorporations similarly belong to Poor Law History.[2] Turnpike Authorities, for a while, dealt effectively with a small but important part of the nation's roads, and their history, in our period, has been glanced at in the Introduction to Part III. Improvement Commissioners arose from the initiative of groups of local residents of the better-to-do classes; their constitutional structure was generally oligarchic; they were not bound to the traditional forms of administration, and usually employed professional staffs; and in many towns most of what was effective in the coping with the problems of increased population and size was due to them. But in many instances their areas and powers were limited; initiative depended on the continued supply of men of energy and public spirit; and in any case there was a great deal of overlapping with other authorities. Nor was there, in the case of any of these authorities, any means of enforcing responsibility or action except through appeal to a higher court: Quarter Sessions in the case of a parish, or King's Bench, through a *mandamus* or *certiorari*, in the case of the other authorities.

Reform, and a more exacting sense of public duty, had already begun to send up the county rate from about the last quarter of the eighteenth century. The Select Committee on County Rates of 1834[3] enumerated, among the elements of this rising expenditure, the increased costs of criminal prosecution, which, until 1752, had fallen on the prosecutor, and, from that date onwards, had become increasingly reimbursable by the County Treasurer; rising costs of the transportation of prisoners to jail; prison building and improvement, in response to the humanitarian campaigns of Howard, the efficacy of which is evidenced by the report of the first prison inspectors,[4] and the growing costs of county bridges in an age of increasing traffic, and particularly wheeled traffic. From the ratepayers' point of view, even more serious was the rising poor rate, levied by the parish, but under the sanction of justices.[5] Under the pressure of this increasing business, the forms of county administration were gradually being altered. Court and County days at Quarter Sessions were tending to become distinct, and most of the administrative business was transacted in what was virtually committee, behind closed doors, only the formal decisions being announced in court. Much work, such as on county buildings, or bridge reconstruction and maintenance, was contracted out; and in many counties the nucleus of a professional staff was growing up. The effect of increased cost and decreased publicity, in an increasingly disrespectful age, however, was to create the suspicion of jobbery and waste. Devon pioneered in setting up a standing finance committee, to keep a constant eye on expenditure. The example was followed by what were generally regarded as the

[1] Part X. [2] Part IX. [3] No. 189. [4] Part VI, No. 154B. [5] Part IX and Part III, No. 91.

model administrations of Gloucestershire and the West Riding, and was commended by the Committee of 1834 to the other counties.[1] An Act of 1836 (3 & 4 Wm. IV. c. 48) required estimates and appropriations to be approved in open court. Whether thanks to the work of the Finance Committee, or for other reasons, the peak of the county expenditure in the 'twenties, in Devon, at any rate, was considerably reduced in the 'thirties. In 1836 half the costs of prosecutions, and in 1846 the whole, were transferred to the national account.

The greatest innovation in nineteenth-century local government was the Poor Law of 1834, which touches, however, so many, and such fundamental issues as to require a part to itself.[2] Here it may be noted that much of its popularity with Whigs and Radicals lay in its transfer of responsibility for poor law administration from the justices to primarily elected boards of guardians, of which justices were only *ex officio* members; that it introduced within its special sphere a greater measure of central supervision and control of local government than had existed in England since the seventeenth century; and that it represented the principle of specific administrative machinery for specific jobs as against the range of responsibilities of boroughs and Quarter Sessions, a principle which is repeated in the health boards of the 1848 Public Health Act and the school boards of the 1871 Education Act. It may be added that the method and precision of poor law administration almost certainly exercised a beneficent influence on local government generally. The prestige of the new model stood so high in its early years that the Commissioners on County Rates of 1836 speak with approval of the campaign which Joseph Hume had inaugurated to introduce representation of the unions into county administration, at any rate on the financial side. This is the connexion in which we first begin to hear of county councils.[3] Hume's Bill was counted out in 1836, and lost on second reading on its re-introduction[4] in 1837, and lost again in 1839. Hume and T. Milner Gibson returned to the charge in the late 'forties and early 'fifties, and, at different times, won some measure of approval both from Peel and from Russell. But by that time the question had become rather an academic one, interesting few but Radicals. The standard of administration in the counties was probably higher than anywhere else in the field of local government. Economy had been what its earlier critics had cared about most, and economy, according to the Select Committee of 1850 on County Rates and Expenditure,[5] the justices had given them. The County Rates Bill of 1852 recognized implicitly that there was a measure of anomaly in taxation without representation by imposing further standardization of financial procedure, a greater publicity of accounts, and a more rigid audit upon the counties, but did not seek to go any further. A Select Committee of 1867 on County Financial Arrangements[6] again gave the justices a clean bill of health as regards the purity and public spirit of their administration. But by this time ideas of democratic reform were in the ascendant again, and the report disinterred the proposals of 1836. They were not wholly to disappear from view till they were transmuted into the great County Councils Act of 1888.

The Report of the Commissioners on Municipal Corporations has been described by Mr. and Mrs. Webb as a "violent political pamphlet". Its criticisms of the old corporations[7] contain nothing that is not true, but little that is generally true, and the strictures of Sir Francis Palgrave on the haste and bias of his colleagues' work–from which he dissented–have much to be said for them. But in spite of their exaggerations, the situation described by the commissioners was one which could not be allowed to

[1] No. 189. [2] Part IX. [3] No. 192. [4] No. 193. [5] No. 198. [6] No. 203. [7] No. 190.

endure, as Peel recognized. The Act of 1835,[1] which dealt with it, was a compromise, or, more properly, a diagonal of forces. In the Commons the Whig majority, hounded on by the Radicals, forced the Government's proposals through relentlessly. In the Lords, Lyndhurst led an opposition that had much in it that was factious and obstructive. Melbourne, on 3 August, in what was, perhaps, the tautest and most impressive statement of the case for the Bill, protested against the Lords' decision to hear counsel for the corporations. The proceeding threatened to be endless, and finally wore out the patience even of their supporters. When the Bill came back to the Commons, Russell and Peel rallied the moderates for a compromise. But the Lords had forced significant changes, and changes for the better. The insistence on a property qualification for councillors was a wise measure at the time; the provisions for the election of aldermen, and for the retirement of a third of the council each year, were calculated to improve it as an instrument of local business, if not of local politics. For the conception of the Act had been predominantly political. Its Radical supporters had been primarily interested in overthrowing the borough oligarchies, which were mainly Tory, and substituting a government elected by the ratepayers, which was likely to be predominantly Radical or Whig, a 'shopocracy', as Manchester Tories came later to call it. The three-year residential qualification for voters excluded most of the working classes; in Manchester, for many years, the municipal constituency was smaller than the parliamentary one, based on a £10 householding qualification, but with only a year's residence. The Act applied only to the 178 boroughs which held charters from the Crown, though it provided a procedure through which new towns could apply for corporate status. In a number of cases where the town had outgrown its original boundaries, these were extended. Where Improvement Commissioners existed, they were to continue to function, though provision was made for voluntary fusion with the corporations, where this was desired. The significant exception was with regard to police and lighting powers. Every corporate borough was placed under the explicit obligation to set up a watch committee, and, under it, a borough police, which was to take the place of any existing police. Similarly, the Act conveyed a general power to light the whole of the borough, or to compel Lighting Commissioners to do so, where the corporation judged this to be necessary from a police point of view. Lighting was regarded as a police rather than as an amenity measure. In his speech of 4 August in the Lords, it was on the importance of the Bill from the point of view of public order that Melbourne laid his chief stress, with a significant glance at the Reform riots in Bristol. The point was calculated to impress his Tory hearers.

So far as the newer problems of urban government were concerned, the Act went little way towards solving them. In smaller boroughs in which petty graft had been dominant it is doubtful if it brought about more than a change of its practitioners. The new electorate, the 'shopocracy', cared, in general, more for economy than for municipal progress. In Liverpool the old corporation had managed the great docks' undertakings with vision and public spirit, and had carried out important public works. Its successor, representing Whig and Radical opposition to the old ascendancy –Liverpool had been the seat of Canning and Huskisson–achieved little beyond the organization of the police, and it was not till the Tory victory in the municipal elections of 1842–the beginnings of a forty years' Tory ascendancy–that the forward march of the town was decisively renewed. Manchester, Birmingham, and Bolton

[1] No. 191.

applied for incorporation soon after the Act had been passed. Unfortunately, departures were made from the statutory form of application, with the result that the legality of the Orders in Council incorporating the towns was challenged, and they began their corporate history with a humiliating period of suspended animation, while the question was being settled. Ultimately, court decisions and fresh legislation at the hands of Peel in 1842 confirmed the corporations' position. The Birmingham Street Commissioners had a fine record of improvement, and continued in being and in activity for a decade after the corporation had got into its stride. They had been responsible for fine market buildings, and a town hall which, until the Chamberlain epoch, was the main focus of civic pride. In discussion with the railway companies they planned the layout of railway stations in Birmingham; they initiated a large sewage plan in 1842; and they began the policy of buying up sites in the centre of the town which provided the starting-point for the civic-centre scheme of the Chamberlain epoch. The occasion of their junction with the corporation–for which some of the commissioners had been preparing for a decade–was common opposition to the threats of centralized control implicit in the Public Health Bills under discussion from 1845 to 1848.[1] The commissioners had been negotiating with ministers to obtain powers over the whole drainage area of Birmingham, and on the corporation's accepting their policy they agreed to hand over the whole of their powers and properties to it. But in the next ten years 'economists' won the upper hand in the council, wrecked most of the commissioners' policies, and quarrelled with and dismissed the commission's brilliant and energetic surveyor, Piggott Smith. Birmingham, which had been one of the healthiest, became one of the sickliest of British cities, and, as late as 1873, held the record in England for diseases that come from dirt and pollution. Manchester's history was more fortunate. The Police Commissioners had supplied the town with gas since 1807, and had devoted the considerable profits to town improvement. The union with the borough came earlier in this case, in 1843, and the Manchester Police Act of 1844 gave very wide powers to the new reinforced corporation. In public health, the town, like Birmingham, secured itself a special position, and even the fearless Chadwick adopted the policy of not crossing the corporation in Manchester health matters. By the end of the decade, Manchester, according to the historian of its local government, had built up "one of the earliest local sanitary codes", and was "giving a lead to most of the other large towns in the country". The sense of civic duty and pride, when it began effectively to function, found its roots as much in the traditions of the older oligarchies as in the newer elective forms of government.

Peel's magnificent experiment with the Metropolitan Police passed through a difficult decade in the 'thirties, and owed more of its successful emergence to the patience and high sense of duty of its first commissioners, Colonel Rowan and Richard Mayne, than to political or popular support. Melbourne and Duncannon, at the Home Office in the early 'thirties, were niggardly and unsympathetic in the treatment of widows, and of men injured in the course of their duties, and consistently refused a distinctive uniform and recognition of their public status to the commissioners. The metropolitan magistrates, who had themselves controlled the police before the institution of the force, were unhelpful, and, in instances, definitely antagonistic. London Radicalism, with the signal exception of Francis Place, was bitterly hostile to a force which threatened its power of dominating the streets, and it was

[1] Part X.

patronized, in its unceasing campaign of vilification against the police, by some who should have known better, such as J. A. Roebuck. A London jury, after the Radical demonstration at Coldbath Fields in 1833, in which Constable Culley was stabbed to death with a knife, returned a verdict of 'justifiable homicide' at his inquest. But a select committee of 1834 vindicated the force from the grosser of the popular charges brought against it, and recorded its high approbation of the aims and achievements of Rowan and Mayne. It also recommended the transfer to the commissioners of the horse patrol, set up in the days of highwaymen, and hitherto under independent control. Russell effected this in 1836. The reputation which the force had acquired in circles better able and more disposed to pass disinterested judgment upon it is evidenced by the increasing demand from watch committees in the provinces for Metropolitan officers to head and train their forces, and from private associations such as the Barnet Association, which undertook so large a part of the police responsibility of the period, for men. Russell proved a more appreciative home secretary than his predecessors; legislation in 1839 and 1840 strengthened and clarified the legal position of the police in some important particulars, and added further large districts to the area under its control. The decade of difficulty of the force was now over, and its high reputation established.

The commissioners on county rates of 1836 had pointed out that the improvements in the Metropolitan and borough police had had the effect of driving crime into the country, where the half-hearted and amateur efforts of the parish constables were totally unable to deal with it.[1] To investigate this problem a Commission on the Constabulary Forces was set up, consisting of Shaw Lefevre, Edwin Chadwick, now almost automatically included in such inquiries, and Rowan. It reported in 1839,[2] in one of the most instructive and entertaining papers of a period rich in such literature, almost a guide to current crime. The commissioners rejected the commonly accepted view that poverty and distress were the great sources of crime, and referred its ubiquity and persistence rather to the prospect of a long run of immunity from apprehension that the lack of an effective police afforded to criminals. The most striking characteristic of contemporary crime was the menace represented by 'travellers', *i.e.* tramps. They roamed the country in large numbers, often on a regular circuit of race-meetings and fairs, sometimes in twos and threes, sometimes in relatively large bands. Much of their danger was due to the facilities afforded to them by the completely unregulated tramps' lodging-houses, of which there were an astonishing number. Chester, for example, had between one hundred and fifty and two hundred, and nearly every village and small town had at least its two or three. The tramps' lodging-house, according to the commissioners, was "the place of resort of the mendicant, the flash house of the rural district, the receiving house for stolen goods, the most extensively established school for juvenile delinquency, and commonly, at the same time, the most infamous brothel of the district". One of the most notorious was that run by 'Tiger-faced Sal' at Wisbech. Isolated houses had to shutter and arm against attack, farm crops were subject to constant depredation, lonely roads were unsafe at all times, and no one was wise to travel after dark. The only cure for this state of affairs was a professional 'preventive police', constantly on the job, able to build up a body of knowledge of the habits and personalities of criminals, and unremittingly on their trail. The commissioners adopt the view, of which current amendments in the criminal law were a reflection,[3] that it is not the

[1] No. 192. [2] No. 195. [3] Part VI.

severity, but the certainty of punishment that constitutes the real deterrent to crime. The effectiveness of a properly organized police had been demonstrated not only in the metropolis and in the boroughs, the commissioners argue, but in rural districts as well, such as Barnet and Stow-on-the-Wold, where preventive associations, enlisting professional help, had completely transformed local conditions, and even in the smaller areas of parishes that had adopted the Lighting and Watching Act of 1834 (3 & 4 Wm. IV, c. 90). But to deal with the problem as a whole, and not merely locally, professional control and unified forces acting over considerable areas were necessary. These were metropolitan principles, as distinct from the magisterial control which was the established tradition of the countryside, as it had been in London and the boroughs as well. Peel's administrative prescience had looked beyond the metropolitan problem, and in 1829 he had supported a Cheshire Act which had provided for the payment of full-time constables, to act under magisterial control in the different districts of the county, and give professional stiffening and supervision to the work of the parish constables. This experiment naturally challenged the commissioners' attention, and they gave it lengthy consideration, condemning it unhesitatingly on the double ground that only a unified force, acting over a considerable area, could cope with the itinerancy which was a feature of current crime, and avoid the local entanglements which the 1836 commissioners had criticized in the case of the parish constable,[1] and that it was constitutionally improper that the magistrate who, as local head of the police, virtually initiated prosecution, should also be the judge. They recommended that the metropolitan force should act as a training centre from which counties, on petition from Quarter Sessions, should be enabled to draw the men they required. County forces were to be under Quarter Sessions control–as distinct from that of individual magistrates–but under general supervision from the metropolitan commissioners and the home secretary. This would have meant a fairly high degree of centralization, and Russell pronounced against it. His proposal was that counties should be enabled to set up unified forces, under Quarter Sessions control, subject only to Home Office approval of the regulations under which they operated. Even this met with a good deal of criticism, before it reached the statute book.[2] The immediate political context was the threat from the Physical Force Chartists,[3] and the legal difficulties with the Manchester, Preston, and Birmingham charters, which imposed on these towns the humiliating necessity of having their police under the temporary control of Home Office commissioners. There was thus some plausible ground for the fears of 'centralization' and a 'french police', which were expressed. But in fact control of their forces was handed back to the corporations in question as soon as the legal position had been cleared, and their damaged prestige was restored and consolidated.

The 1839 Act came to be adopted in just over half of the counties. In the others it was deemed too costly. One of the most successful of county chief constables, Captain McCarthy, R.N., of Essex, had to meet a proposal, made at Quarter Sessions in 1850, that the wages of his men should be reduced in accordance with a recent fall in the price of corn. He prepared a balance-sheet of the cost of the force against the savings to the county that resulted from its activities, and estimated that the net cost of a vastly improved state of public order was just over £80. An Act of 1842,[4] which Maitland has described as a "gallant attempt to put new life into the old constabulary", regularized the method of appointment of parish constables, and made

[1] No. 192. [2] No. 196. [3] Part V. [4] No. 197.

provisions for parish lock-ups, and the appointment of superintending constables on the Cheshire model. A number of counties adopted this system. Northumberland, for example, had twelve mounted superintending constables who patrolled the whole county, and was otherwise dependent on parish constables. Other counties did nothing, like Somerset, which attained an unenviable notoriety with the judges for the length and seriousness of its criminal calendar. The next great inquiry was the Select Committee of 1852–1853.[1] It had no hesitation in pronouncing in favour of the 1839 system for the counties. The other problem before it was that of the inefficiency of the forces in some of the smaller municipalities. Romsey, for example, was described by a witness as a 'sort of Alsatia'. Part of it, Romsey Extra, fell into the county, and about this there was no complaint. But in the borough itself beer-house influences dominated the watch committee, and a mayor known to be a reformer was not summoned to its meetings. Palmerston headed a petition of residents for the fusion of the borough police with the county, a step which had met with marked success in the comparable town of Andover. But a counter petition was organized in the beer-houses and defeated the move. Legislation followed the committee's report in due course. The Act of 1856[2] made it compulsory for all counties to raise and organize a police force on the lines laid down in 1839. Further, the Act provided for the inspection, by inspectors sent down by the Home Office, of all forces in the country, and for the payment of a grant to those forces reported as efficient. The grant was not to be payable to the corporations of towns with a population of less than 5,000, which were therefore virtually compelled to place themselves for police purposes in the hands of their county. The Act completed the police revolution of the century, not the least important of the many revolutions of the time in its political and social effects. The standard of public order was greatly improved as the result of the organization of an effective police all over the country; tension between classes lost some of its uglier features; and individuals came to know a freedom of movement about the country and in the streets of towns, and a security in their homes which had been absent in the earlier and sterner years of the century. At the same time, the compromise between central and local control preserved contact between the police and the population, and made it possible for the police to be not only a force but also an influence on the side of respect for the law and the principles of constitutional freedom.

The character of the unique problem set by London is indicated in the Second Report of the Commissioners on Municipal Corporations in 1837.[3] It affords a further illustration of the indisposition of the commissioners to look beyond purely political problems that, on the score of the complexity of the issues involved, and of the popular and satisfactory character of the city corporation (which was responsible for only a tiny fraction of the metropolitan area), they made no recommendations on the subject. Yet sanitary and housing conditions in London were as bad as, if not worse than, anywhere else in the country. They began to be tackled in a serious fashion when the unified Metropolitan Sewers Commission was set up in 1847. But the history of the commission was a stormy one.[4] A Royal Commission on the Corporation of London, reporting in 1854, recommended the maintenance of the corporation much as it was, but proposed the setting up of municipal bodies in the other districts of London, and of a Metropolitan Board of Works to deal with the common problems of the area.[5] The latter suggestion was carried out by the

[1] No. 199. [2] No. 202. [3] No. 194. [4] Part X. [5] No. 200.

Metropolis Local Management Act of 1855.[1] A board of representatives of the larger parishes and of groups of the smaller ones was set up, under a paid, full-time chairman, and the vestries were made uniformly elective. Responsibility for drainage, paving, scavenging, and the repression of nuisances was divided between the board and the parishes, the board controlling the general pattern and undertaking the larger works, under the sanction of the commissioner for works, and, in the case of those calling for very large expenditure, of Parliament itself. The Metropolitan Board never succeeding in catching the imagination of Londoners or of the country. But under its rule the back of the major problems of urban living in London was broken. The report that the board issued in 1889[2] as a sort of funeral salute over its own grave, as it yielded place to the London County Council, illustrates not only the sort of job that London had needed but the problems that, on a lesser scale, had faced every big town in the country.

At the end of the period things were ripening for a change. The main consideration of reformers at the beginning had been to get things done, or at any rate started, and the administrative means had been chosen without much thought of the pattern they would finally make. The pattern that by this time had emerged has been described as "chaos of areas, a chaos of authorities, and a chaos of rates". There were in England and Wales, "52 counties, 239 municipal boroughs, 70 Improvement Act districts; 1,006 urban sanitary districts, 41 port sanitary authorities, and 577 rural sanitary districts; 2,051 school board districts, 424 highway districts, 853 burial board districts, 649 unions, 194 lighting and watching districts, 14,946 poor law parishes, 5,064 highway parishes not included in urban or highway districts, and about 13,000 ecclesiastical parishes. The total number of local authorities who taxed the English ratepayer was 27,069, and they taxed him by means of 18 different kinds of rates." The setting up of the Local Government Board in 1871 had seemed to promise a larger envisaging of problems. But the hope had turned out delusively.[3] Dramatically, however, in the closing years of the period, Birmingham, under Chamberlain, had advertised what civic pride and corporate enterprise could do to regenerate a community, and Disraeli's Government had responded with appropriate legislation, Radical mayor and Tory premier running a race to make the crooked places of the land straight, and its stinking places sweet. Meanwhile the Goschen Report on Local Taxation[4] had turned its attention to the distribution of the burden of rates between town and country, and owner and occupier, and had hinted at the economic outlook of the future. Rate expenditure might be looked upon not as a burden but as an investment in health and happiness. Issues other than local government were to take immediate priority in the politics of the country, but within twenty years the administrative instruments of the new faith were to be fashioned.

[1] No. 201. [2] No. 205. [3] Part X, Introduction. [4] No. 204.

SELECT BIBLIOGRAPHY

Among the *Parliamentary Debates*, that on the Municipal Corporations Bill in 1835 is of primary importance, and, on metropolitan government, that on the Metropolitan Local Management Act of 1855. On county government, the debates of 1836, 1837, 1849, 1850, and 1852 on the various Bills for setting up county boards and again in 1866 and 1870 on abortive proposals of a similar kind are valuable.

The *Reports* of the Commons and Lords *Select Committees on County Rates* (*Parlty. Papers*, 1834/XIV and 1835/XIV), and the *Report of the Royal Commission on County Rates* (*Parlty. Papers*, 1835/VI and 1836/XXVII), provide the fundamental discussion in public papers on the subject of county government. The *Report of the Royal Commission on Municipal Corporations* (*Parlty. Papers*, 1835/XXIII–XL), though described by S. and B. WEBB as "a violent political pamphlet . . . issued as a judicial report", occupies, nevertheless, the same position in relation to municipal government, and the *Reports* of the assistant commissioners on the individual boroughs are of great value to the local historian. The criticism of the commissioners' *Report* by SIR FRANCIS PALGRAVE is in the last of the volumes cited. The *Second Report* of the commission (*Parlty. Papers*, 1837/XXV) deals with London. The *Report of the Select Committee on the County Rates Expenditure Bill* (*Parlty. Papers*, 1850/XIII), the *Report of the Royal Commission on the Corporation of London* (*Parlty. Papers*, 1854/XXVI), those on *Metropolitan Local Taxation* (*Parlty. Papers*, 1861/VIII), the *Reports of the Select Committee on the Local Government and Taxation of the Metropolis* (*Parlty. Papers*, 1866/XIII and 1867/XII), the *Report of the Select Committee on County Financial Arrangements* (*Parlty. Papers*, 1867–1868/IX), the *Report of the Select Committee on Local Taxation* (*Parlty. Papers*, 1870/VIII), and the *Goschen Report on Local Taxation* (*Parlty. Papers*, 1870/LV), continue the public discussion. There are also a number of inquiries into and reports upon specific projects of metropolitan improvements. The *Report of the Metropolitan Board of Works* on the eve of its expiry (*Parlty. Papers*, 1899/LXVI), contains an elaborate review of the work of the board since its institution in 1855.

On police subjects the most informing *Parliamentary Debates* are those on the County and District Constables Bill, and on the Manchester and Birmingham Police Bills, in 1839, and on the Police in Counties and Boroughs Bill in 1856. The *Reports of the Select Committee on the Police of the Metropolis* (*Parlty. Papers*, 1833/XIII and 1834/XVI), dealing with popular charges against the police; the *Report of the Royal Commission on the Constabulary Force* (*Parlty. Papers*, 1839/XIX); and that of the *Select Committee on Police* (*Parlty. Papers*, 1852–1853/XXXVI) are the principal public papers.

Of secondary authorities, S. and B. WEBB, *English Local Government* (London, 1906–1931), especially vol. 1, *Parish and County*, vols. 2 and 3, *Manor and Borough*, vol. 4, *Statutory Authorities for Special Purposes*, and vol. 6, *The King's Highway*, deal primarily with pre-reform conditions, but are indispensable for background. J. REDLICH and H. W. HIRST, *Local Government in England* (2 vols., London, 1903); H. J. LASKI, W. I. JENNINGS and W. A. ROBSON (eds.), *A Century of Municipal Progress* (London, 1935); K. B. SMELLIE, *A History of Local Government in England* (London, 1946); H. FINER, *English Local Government* (London, 1936), are general histories. W. I. JENNINGS, *Principles of Local Government Law* (London, 1931), and B. KEITH LUCAS, *History of the Franchise in English Local Government* (Oxford, 1951), are also of high general value. J. TOULMIN SMITH, *Local Self Government and Centralisation* (London, 1851), J. S. MILL, *Representative Government* (London, 1861), and COBDEN CLUB, *Essays on Local Government* (London, 1875), may be consulted for varying influential views. L. W. GRICE, *National and Local Finance* (London, 1910), and E. CANNAN, *A History of Local Rates in England* (London, 1912), should be consulted. F. CLIFFORD, *A History of Private Bill Legislation* (London, 1885), and P. ORLO WILLIAMS, *Private Bill Legislation* (2 vols., London, 1948), are valuable for an aspect of parliamentary procedure of high importance to the development of local government.

F. W. Maitland, *Justice and Police* (London, 1885), is a masterly small treatment, and W. Melville Lee, *History of Police and Prisons in England* (London, 1901), Charles Reith, *The British Police and the Democratic Ideal* (Oxford, 1948), Jennifer Hart, "The Reform of Borough Police, 1835–56", in *English Historical Review*, vol. lxx (1955), deal more generally with police history. The importance of studies of local history and government in the nineteenth century is being increasingly realized; among those of special value may be mentioned A. Redford, *History of Local Government in Manchester* (3 vols., Manchester, 1939); S. D. Simon, *A Century of City Government* (Manchester) (London, 1938); B. D. White, *History of the Corporation of Liverpool, 1835–1914* (Liverpool, 1951); C. Gill and A. Briggs, *History of Birmingham*, (2 vols. Oxford, 1952).

Asa Briggs, *Victorian Cities* (1963); R. Newton, *Victorian Exeter* (1968) – social, political history; H. J. Dyos, *Victorian Suburb, Camberwell* (1961) – study of London sprawl and its problems; *The Growth of Cities in the nineteenth century, a review of some recent writing*, Victorian Studies ix, 1966.

189. Select Committee on county rates (1834)

Parlty. Papers, 1834/XIV, pp. 3–11.

THE SELECT COMMITTEE appointed to inquire into the COUNTY RATES and HIGHWAY RATES, in England and Wales, and to Report their Opinion whether any and what Regulations may be adopted to diminish their Pressure upon the Owners and Occupiers of Land; and who were empowered to Report the MINUTES of the EVIDENCE taken before them to The House;—HAVE considered and inquired into the Matters to them referred, and have agreed upon the following REPORT:

On the general subject of County Rates, the following recommendation is made in the Report of the Committee on the State of Agriculture of last Year:

Your Committee has already glanced at the increase of certain outgoings borne by the Farmer, which, it is clearly established in Evidence, have not been compensated by a corresponding reduction of his fixed Money Payments; on the contrary, while the profitable returns from Land have generally decreased, the burthens to which it is subject have been augmented. The Poor Rate is heavier, the County Rate is heavier, the Highway Rate has increased; and the Evidence would lead to the conclusion, that the outgoings of the Farmer are generally larger than he can afford to pay during the present prices of agricultural produce, without a sacrifice of the Profit on his Capital which he is entitled to realize; those outgoings, however, which the Law does not impose, are placed beyond the control of the Legislature, are private bargains, open from time to time, and regulated by competition; and where Parliament cannot interfere, any recommendation or opinion pronounced by Your Committee would certainly be inefficacious for good, perhaps even productive of evil. Who are to judge what Profit, Rent and Wages ought to be? Certainly no legislative authority; for these are matters of convention, dictated by the reciprocal convenience of the parties, and silently indeed, but surely, adjusted by their reciprocal necessities.

In proportion as both Rent and Wages are excluded from the cognizance and the control of the Legislature, it becomes important that Parliament should watch with jealousy those burthens which are imposed by law on Land, and which it is within their competency to revise and modify.

The whole subject of the County Rate is particularly worthy of a separate consideration. The improved arrangement of the Gaols, admitting of the classification and separation of Criminals; the payment of the Costs of Prosecutions, both at the Assizes and Quarter Sessions, not only of Felonies but of Misdemeanors, whereby the want of a public prosecutor in England is now supplied; the vast expenditure on Bridges for the improvement of the great inland lines of communication, an object of national importance; all these are growing charges imposed by Law, levied by County Rate, and borne principally by Land; anomalous, from the circumstance that purposes of general utility are thus defrayed by Local Taxation, subject to abuse, because placed under the control of authorities not personally responsible; and requiring, therefore, in the opinion of Your Committee, the early and deliberate attention of the Legislature. . . .

FINANCE

It appears by a Paper laid on the Table of the House of Commons, that the total money levied by assessment for Poor Rate and County Rate, in the year ending 25 March 1833, was 8,606,501 l.; that of this sum 5,434,890 l. was levied directly from Land; while 3,171,611 l. was the total levied from Dwelling-houses, Mills, Factories, Navigations and Manorial Profits. Thus the proportion levied from Land was to all other sources as 100 to 58, or nearly as 10 to 6; so that five-eighths of the whole were levied from Land. The proportion in County Rates, taken alone, would be somewhat, but not materially, different. On the other hand, it must be remarked that a large proportion of the sum levied on Dwelling-houses is paid by the owners of Land.

The following Table shows the amount received at the respective periods by Treasurers for Counties, and applied to such purposes as come more immediately under the head of County Rate: this amount, for the two first dates, is as near an approximation as can be given, the Returns being faulty.

Date	*Amount received by County Treasurer*
	£
Years ending 25 March 1793 . . .	184,080
" " " " 1803 . . .	235,844
" " " " 1813 . . .	510,730
" " " " 1823 . . .	571,108
" " " " 1833 . . .	757,238

The very large increase of County Rate may be accounted for in various ways. The great improvement in the means of communication; the system of classification and discipline adopted in our prisons; and the payment of the costs of prosecutions, appear to be the three great sources of increased expense. . . .

GENERAL EXPENDITURE

The complaints made by the Agricultural Districts in the West Riding of the County of York, of the enormous and rapid increase of the County Rates, led to the appointment, in 1831, of a Finance Committee. The Committee are now annually appointed at the Pontefract Sessions, held at Easter, and make their report at the ensuing Easter. To enable them to do this, the Accounts are closed on the 31st of December; and between that period and Easter the Chairman has ample time to look over the Accounts with the Treasurer, and obtain his explanation. The Committee meet on the Monday in the Sessions week, and make their report to the Magistrates on the Wednesday. The results of this Committee have been: First, to bring the Accounts from a state of confusion into a state of clearness and order. Secondly, so far to control the Expenditure, that in the Year 1833 the Rates were nearly 4,000 l.

less than in 1826, notwithstanding the increase of crime, and the addition of several new burthens. It does not appear that any rule is laid down for the appointment of the Committee, but the business has now got into such a train, that only one meeting of the Committee takes place prior to the Sessions.

In Devonshire, the greatest advantages have been derived from a similar Committee. Captain Buller states, that he was appointed Chairman of the Committee of Accounts in 1828; that in that year the County Expenses, exclusive of 3,839 l. for new Buildings, amounted to 20,216 l. In the year ending Michaelmas 1832, those expenses were reduced to 14,969 l. The reduction was effected in the following manner. In the conveyance of felons a reduction of 1,059 l. was effected, by making a contract for their conveyance; and by a further arrangement, the expense of conveying felons from the hundred of Roborough will be reduced from 1,553 l. in 1828, to 350 l., the sum agreed for by the present contract. The reduction of expense in the repair of County Buildings, by adopting the system of contract, is from an average of 1,200 l. a year to 500 l. Other expenses have been greatly reduced by the system of contract by tender, a strict attention to economy, and the discussion of every question in open Court. In the County of Devon, it is the practice of the Committee of Accounts to report every Quarter, giving a comparison of the Expenses of that Quarter with the corresponding Quarter of the former Year, and offering any suggestion that may occur to them. The Treasurer reports next, stating how many Rates are required; and lastly, the County Surveyor states the number of Bridges that want repair, and the Sums required.

Your Committee suggest, that in every County a Finance Committee should be appointed to regulate and control the Expenditure. That the Finance Committee should be appointed annually, at such times and in such manner as the Magistrates in Quarter Sessions should direct. That the Estimates for every year should be submitted by the Treasurer of the County to the Finance Committee; and, after the inspection and approbation of such Committee, published in one or more of the County Papers of the largest circulation four weeks at least previous to the Quarter Sessions, at which orders authorizing any General Expenses should be made. That the discussion of Estimates for future Expenses should always take place in open Court. That the Magistrates should, if they think proper, direct the same process to be gone through Half-Yearly or Quarterly instead of Yearly. That all orders of individual Magistrates should be under the control of the General Quarter Sessions. That the Accounts of the Treasurer and his Vouchers should be submitted to the Finance Committee previously to the audit by the Magistrates.

190. Royal Commission on Municipal Corporations (1835)

Defects in Constitutions of Municipal Corporations, according to Commissioners of 1835

First Report

Parlty. Papers, 1835/XXIII.

71. . . . The most common and most striking defect in the constitution of the Municipal Corporations of England and Wales is, that the corporate bodies exist

independently of the communities among which they are found. The Corporations look upon themselves, and are considered by the inhabitants, as separate and exclusive bodies; they have powers and privileges within the towns and cities from which they are named, but in most places all identity of interest between the Corporation and the inhabitants has disappeared. This is the case even where the Corporation includes a large body of inhabitant freemen: it appears in a more striking degree, as the powers of the Corporation have been restricted to smaller numbers of the resident population, and still more glaringly, when the local privileges have been conferred on non-resident freemen, to the exclusion of the inhabitants to whom they rightfully ought to belong.

. . . . .

73. The importance which the privilege of electing Members of Parliament has conferred upon Corporate Towns, or rather upon the governing bodies there, and the rewards for political services, which are brought within the reach of the ruling corporators, have caused this function to be considered in many places as the sole object of their institution. In some Boroughs this right has survived all other traces of municipal authority. The custom of keeping the number of corporators as low as possible may be referred to this cause, rather than to the desire of monopolizing the municipal authority, which has been coveted only as the means of securing the other and more highly prized privilege.

Hence a great number of Corporations have been preserved solely as political engines, and the towns to which they belong derive no benefit, but often much injury, from their existence. To maintain the political ascendancy of a party, or the political influence of a family, has been the one end and object for which the powers intrusted to a numerous class of these bodies have been exercised. This object has been systematically pursued in the admission of freemen, resident or non-resident; in the selection of municipal functionaries for the council and the magistracy; in the appointment of subordinate officers and the local police; in the administration of charities entrusted to the municipal authorities; in the expenditure of the corporate revenues, and in the management of the corporate property. The most flagrant abuses have arisen from this perversion of municipal privileges to political objects. The Commissioners have generally found that those Corporations which have not possessed the Parliamentary franchise, have most faithfully discharged the duties of town government, and have acquired, more than others, the confidence and good-will of the communities to which they belong. This has been the case in some, even where the ruling bodies are strictly self-elected, and where the general character of their constitutions is open to the objections common to the great majority of Corporations. Very few large corporate towns were without Members of Parliament, even before the Reform Act, so that many instances cannot be given from among them. The Corporations of Leeds, Lynn and Doncaster may be cited as turning their attention to their municipal duties more sedulously than the majority. Among the small towns, deserving the same character, we refer to the Corporations of Louth, Bideford, Maidenhead, Beccles, South Molton and Stratford-upon-Avon.

. . . . .

77. In the few boroughs in which the powers of local government are vested in a numerous body of freemen, the general character of the governing body is vitiated by the defects of its organization, which have already been pointed out. The exclusive and party spirit which belongs to the whole corporate body, appears in a still more marked manner in the councils by which in most cases it is governed. It has been stated that the members of these councils are usually self-elected, and hold their offices for life. They are commonly of one political party, and their proceedings are mainly directed to secure and perpetuate the ascendency of the party to which they belong. Individuals of adverse political opinions are, in most cases, systematically excluded from the governing body. Since the repeal of the Corporation and Test Acts, and the removal of the civil disabilities of the Catholics, very few instances occur in which either Catholics or Dissenters, who often form a numerous, respectable and wealthy portion of the inhabitants, have been chosen into the governing body of the corporation. These councils, which embody the opinions of a single party, are entrusted with the nomination of magistrates, of the civil and criminal judges, often of the superintendents of police, and are or ought to be the leaders in every measure that concerns the interests and prosperity of the town. So far from being the representatives either of the population or of the property of the town, they do not represent even the privileged class of freemen; and being elected for life, their proceedings are unchecked by any feeling of responsibility. The discharge of the functions with which they are entrusted, is rendered difficult by the dislike and suspicion which the manner of their election inevitably entails upon them.

78. To this system may be traced the carelessness often observed in the execution of their duties; and persons well qualified for the council are excluded, sometimes for want of vacancies, sometimes through the rejection of the electing body, sometimes through the refusal of such persons to identify themselves with a system of which they disapprove. The common council of the city of London presents a striking exception to the system of self-election for life, and it affords a remarkable instance of the absence of those evils which we refer to it. The common councilmen of this city are annually elected by a numerous constituency, yet changes seldom happen among them. The important requisites of experience in the functionary, and the power of control in the electors, are there effectually united, and produce that efficiency and confidence which are wanting in most other corporate towns. The history of the common council of London is that of a body which has watched vigilantly over the interests of its constituents, and for a long series of years has studied to improve the corporate institutions with great earnestness, unremitting caution, and scrupulous justice.

79. It is part of the general system of close Corporations that all their affairs should be managed with the strictest secrecy, sometimes secured by oaths administered to the members of the common council. The inhabitants who are subject to the authority of the Corporation, have frequently very imperfect information, as to its nature and extent; they are ignorant whether it derives its sanction from prescription, from charters, or from bye-laws; and the only mode by which they can obtain information is often through the troublesome and expensive process of an application for a

mandamus or *quo warranto*. The bye-laws which are made, as well as those which are repealed, are seldom published, and the public is generally unacquainted with their provisions, except from common rumour. This ignorance is sometimes shared by the members of the Corporation. Hence violations of the charters and bye-laws have been often made with impunity.

. . . . .

83. In some cases the duties of the mayor have been totally neglected, either from want of capacity or from want of will; occasionally from non-residence. At Hartlepool, where the mayor is chosen in rotation from the capital burgesses, many of whom are non-resident, it sometimes happens that the mayor never attends even to be sworn into office. At Winchester, the present high steward was chosen mayor during an important litigation in which the Corporation was involved. He was the son of the patron, and was admitted a freeman the year before his election as mayor. The mayor was *ex officio* a member of the committee for conducting the litigation; but he appointed a deputy, and entered on the records of the Corporation a protest of his ignorance of all relating to it. At Durham, the mayor of the year 1831–2 refused to render the usual account of receipts to the common council. The mayor of Grampound left the borough upon its disfranchisement, and the corporation books and accounts have not been found since. No new mayor was elected after the disfranchisement, until the year in which the present Commission issued. In some boroughs, the same mayor is continued from year to year; and in others, as at Cambridge and Tenby, it has been the custom to elect two or three persons in rotation. The effect of entrusting the election to the freemen, constituted as those freemen now generally are, is to degrade the office in the estimation of the persons to be governed. At Maidstone, the election is merely a struggle to try the strength of opposing parties without any personal preference, and bribes are given by persons wishing to avoid being elected.

84. The method of appointing the Recorder is often very objectionable. At Newport, in the Isle of Wight, the recorder is appointed formally by the Crown on the nomination of the whole corporation, but practically on the dictation of the patron. On one occasion, a nobleman was chosen recorder there, whose connexion with the Corporation consisted in his being a trustee for the managing the property of a deceased patron. At Woodstock, the recorder's office has been vacant for several years, because the patron's nominee was opposed. The Recorders of some boroughs are elected by a constituency of freemen, such as we have already characterised. At Berwick-upon-Tweed, a Recorder so chosen, tries capital felonies. This officer also unites functions in some cases, which are improperly joined. This occurs, when he lives in the neighbourhood, and discharges the duties of a resident magistrate, at the same time that he is by virtue of his office, the presiding judge of the Criminal Court. In many instances he performs no duties whatever, and his nominal connexion with the borough is only a form through which he exercises over it an unwarrantable control.

The charters have often empowered the Recorder to appoint a deputy. The exercise of this power is occasionally useful; but the practice of appointing a deputy permanently to discharge all the duties of the Recorder is very mischievous. Not only is the appointment placed in the hands of an irresponsible individual, but the difficulty of finding qualified persons to fill the situation is increased. Many persons would accept the office of principal, who would decline the office of deputy.

. . . . .

89. The party spirit which pervades the Municipal councils, extends itself to the magistracy, which is appointed by those bodies, and from their members. The magistrates are usually chosen from the aldermen, and the aldermen are generally political partisans. Hence, even in those cases in which injustice is not absolutely committed, a strong suspicion of it is excited, and the local tribunals cease to inspire respect. The corporate Magistrates, generally speaking, are not looked upon by the inhabitants with favour or respect, and are often regarded with positive distrust and dislike.

90. The corporate magistrates are often selected from a class incompetent to the discharge of judicial functions, and the consequence has been a great defect in the administration of justice. At East Retford, a respectable witness, who had been clerk to the magistrates, declared that one of the magistrates was in the habit of conversing familiarly with the culprits brought before him, and endeavoured to impress them with the idea that he was performing an unwilling office. On one occasion he saw the magistrate fighting with a prisoner, and struggling with him on the floor. At Malmesbury, the magistrates are often unable to write or read. At Wenlock blank warrants have been signed by the magistrates: in one case a blank warrant of commitment was granted by mistake, instead of one of apprehension, and the constable had it in his possession for several weeks before he executed it. The jurisdiction of the borough magistrates at Wenlock is exclusive; it extends over 17 parishes, and contains a population exceeding 17,000 persons.

Even when the corporate magistrates belong to a superior class, they are often selected from the senior aldermen only, who, from age and infirmities, soon become incapable of performing the functions of their office, while a mistaken notion of dignity keeps them from resigning it.

. . . . .

92. The evils resulting from the ignorance and inefficiency of the borough magistrates, are heightened by gross defects in other parts of the judicial system. The juries of the borough courts are often exclusively taken from the freemen, who, besides being composed of an inferior class, are strongly tainted with party feelings. Northampton furnishes a strong instance of this. At Carmarthen, verdicts are frequently given against justice, from party bias. The population of that town is 10,000, but the jurors are chosen from a small body of 178 burgesses. At the spring assizes of 1833, a true bill was found by the grand jury of the borough for a capital felony. The grand jury consisted of 20 burgesses; of these, 17 belonged to the Corporation party, and the foreman was the committing magistrate. The panel of the petty jury contained 46 persons belonging to the Corporation party, 12 of the defendants' party, and only two neutrals. An application was made to the Judge, to order the indictment

to be tried in Carmarthenshire. The trial took place there, and the defendants were acquitted. The only answer to this statement was given by one of the sheriffs, who said that there was not a sufficient number of respectable persons of the defendants' party, to enable him to summon a grand jury equally from both sides, and that the petty jury was summoned from those burgesses who had not attended the previous assizes. At Haverford West, where none but burgesses can serve on the juries, there are only 141 burgesses, and not 50 who are fit to serve on them: the juries there have been openly reprimanded by judges and magistrates for improper acquittals of burgesses upon criminal prosecutions; the practice has not been checked by such reprimands, and the general opinion is, that it is "impossible to convict a burgess."

. . . . .

102. The police belonging to Municipal Corporations is for the most part very insufficient, and for supplying the deficiency, resort is had to local Acts. The superintendence of the police, and the powers necessary for watching, paving, lighting, cleaning and supplying the towns with water, instead of being entrusted to the municipal authorities, are for the most part committed by these Acts to various independent bodies; although none of these towns are too extensive to be embraced by one system of municipal government; for instance, every quarter of the town of Bath is under the care of a separate board, except one, which is totally unprotected. Much confusion results from this divided authority. The powers of local taxation, and the superintendence of matters so closely connected with the comfort and well-being of the inhabitants, which are now exercised by these bodies, appear to belong precisely to that class of objects for which corporate authority was originally conferred; but great dissatisfaction would prevail among the inhabitants, if these powers were entrusted to the Municipal Corporations as at present constituted. In several towns much apathy is now shown by the inhabitants with respect to the municipal benefits conferred by these Acts; in Southampton, where the consent of the inhabitants is required to bring them within the powers of a local Act, nearly half of the town has refused the benefit of it. Great jealousy often exists between the officers of police, acting under the Corporation and those under the Commissioners of these local Acts, and the corporate body seldom takes any active share in the duties of the board, of which its members form a part. At Bristol, a notoriously ineffective police cannot be improved, chiefly in consequence of the jealousy with which the Corporation is regarded by the inhabitants. At Hull, in consequence of the disunion between the governing body and the inhabitants, chiefly arising out of a dispute about the tolls and duties, only seven persons attended to suppress a riot, out of 1,000 who had been sworn in as special constables, and on another similar occasion none attended. At Coventry, serious riots and disturbances frequently occur, and the officers of police, being usually selected from one political party, are often active in fomenting them. In some instances, the separate and conflicting authority of the Commissioners is avowedly used as a check and counterbalance to the political influence of the Corporation. At Leeds, no persons are elected Commissioners of Police whose political principles are not opposed to those of the Corporation.

An ineffectual attempt to obviate the evils resulting from the want of a well-organized system is made in some towns by subscriptions for private watchmen. At Winchester, after a local Act had been obtained, its powers were found to be insufficient, and the town is now watched by private subscription, to which the commissioners contribute £100 from the rate.

The superintendence of the paving and lighting, &c., of the various towns is in the same unsatisfactory state, but, in this branch of police, the want of a single presiding authority leads perhaps to less evil and inconvenience.

. . . . .

110. In general, the corporate funds are but partially applied to municipal purposes, such as the preservation of the peace by an efficient police, or in watching or lighting the town, &c.; but they are frequently expended in feasting, and in paying the salaries of unimportant officers. In some cases, in which the funds are expended on public purposes, such as building public works, or other objects of local improvement, an expense has been incurred much beyond what would be necessary if due care had been taken. This had happened at Exeter, in consequence of the plan of avoiding public contract, and of proceeding without adequate estimates. These abuses often originate in the negligence of the corporate bodies, but more frequently in the opportunity afforded to them of obliging members of their own body, or the friends and relations of such members.

111. Some Corporations consider that their property has been vested in them solely as trustees for the public; but, in most cases, this truth is acknowledged only when forced on their attention, is received with difficulty and qualification, and is continually forgotten. Few Corporations admit any positive obligation to expend the surplus of their income for objects of public advantage. Such expenditure is regarded as a spontaneous act of private generosity, rather than a well-considered application of the public revenue, and the credit to which the Corporation, in such a case, generally considers itself entitled, is not that of judicious administrators, but of liberal benefactors. Even in these cases, party and sectarian purposes often prevail in its application.

112. From this erroneous but strongly rooted opinion, that the property of the Corporations is held in trust for the benefit of the corporate body only, distinguishing that body from the community with which it is locally connected, the transition is not difficult to the opinion that individual corporators may justifiably derive a personal benefit from that property. At Cambridge, the practice of turning the Corporation property to the profit of individuals was avowed and defended by a member of the council.

. . . . .

In conclusion, we report to YOUR MAJESTY that there prevails amongst the inhabitants of a great majority of the incorporated towns a general, and, in our opinion, a just dissatisfaction with their Municipal Institutions; a distrust of the self-elected Municipal Councils, whose powers are subject to no popular control, and whose acts and proceedings being secret, are unchecked by the influence of public opinion; a distrust of the Municipal Magistracy, tainting with suspicion the local administration of justice, and often accompanied with contempt of the persons by whom the law is administered; a discontent under the burthens of Local Taxation, while revenues that ought to be applied for the public advantage are diverted from their legitimate use, and are sometimes wastefully bestowed for the benefit of individuals, sometimes squandered for purposes injurious to the character and morals of the people. We therefore feel it to be our duty to represent to YOUR MAJESTY that the existing Municipal Corporations of England and Wales neither possess nor deserve the confidence or respect of YOUR MAJESTY's subjects, and that a thorough reform must be effected, before they can become, what we humbly submit to YOUR MAJESTY they ought to be, useful and efficient instruments of local government.

We humbly submit this our Report to YOUR MAJESTY's Royal Consideration.

191. Municipal Corporations Act (1835)

Statutes of the Realm, 5 & 6 Wm. IV, c. 76.

IX. . . . And be it enacted, That every Male Person of full Age who on the last Day of August in any Year shall have occupied any House, Warehouse, Counting-house, or Shop within any Borough during that Year and the whole of each of the Two preceding Years, and also during the Time of such Occupation shall have been an Inhabitant Householder within the said Borough, or within Seven Miles of the said Borough, shall, if duly enrolled in that Year according to the Provisions herein-after contained, be a Burgess of such Borough and Member of the Body Corporate of the Mayor, Aldermen, and Burgesses of such Borough: Provided always, that no such Person shall be so enrolled in any Year, unless he shall have been rated in respect of such Premises so occupied by him within the Borough to all Rates made for the Relief of the Poor of the Parish wherein such Premises are situated during the Time of his Occupation as aforesaid, and unless he shall have paid on or before the last Day of August as aforesaid all such Rates, including therein all Borough Rates, if any, directed to be paid under the Provisions of this Act, as shall have become payable by him in respect of the said Premises, except such as shall become payable within Six Calendar Months next before the said last Day of August: Provided also, that the Premises in respect of the Occupation of which any Person shall have been so rated need not be the same Premises or in the same Parish, but may be different Premises in the same Parish or in Different Parishes: Provided also, that no Person being an Alien shall be so enrolled in any Year and that no Person shall be so enrolled in any Year who within Twelve Calendar Months next before the said last Day of August shall have received Parochial Relief or other Alms, or any Pension or charitable Allowance from any Fund intrusted to the charitable Trustees of such Borough herein-after mentioned: Provided that in every Case provided in this Act the Distance of Seven Miles shall be computed by the nearest public Road or Way by Land or Water. . . .

XIV. And whereas in divers Cities, Towns, and Boroughs a certain Custom hath prevailed, and certain Bye Laws have been made, that no Person, not being free of a City, Town, or Borough, or of certain Guilds, Mysteries, or Trading Companies within the same, or some or one of them, shall keep any Shop or Place for putting to Show or Sale any or certain Wares or Merchandize by way of Retail or otherwise, or use any or certain Trades, Occupations, Mysteries, or Handicrafts for Hire, Gain, or Sale within the same; be it enacted, That notwithstanding any such Custom or Bye Law, every Person in any Borough may keep any Shop for the Sale of all lawful Wares and Merchandizes by Wholesale or Retail, and use every lawful Trade, Occupation, Mystery, and Handicraft, for Hire, Gain, Sale or otherwise, within any Borough. . . .

XXV. And be it enacted, That in every Borough shall be elected, at the Time and in the Manner herein-after mentioned, One fit Person, who shall be and be called 'The Mayor' of such Borough; and a certain Number of fit Persons, who shall be and be called 'Aldermen' of such Borough; and a certain Number of other fit Persons, who shall be and be called 'The Councillors' of such Borough; and such Mayor, Aldermen, and Councillors for the Time being shall be and be called 'The Council' of such Borough; and the Number of Persons so to be elected Councillors of such Borough shall be the Number of Persons in that Behalf mentioned in conjunction with the Name of such Borough in the Schedules (A.) and (B.) to this Act annexed; and the Number of Persons so to be elected Aldermen shall be One Third of the Number of Persons so to be elected Councillors; and on the Ninth Day of November in this present Year the Councillors first to be elected, under the Provisions of this Act, and on the Ninth Day of November in the Year One thousand eight hundred and thirty-eight, and in every Third succeeding Year, the Council for the Time being of every Borough shall elect from the Councillors, or from the Persons qualified to be Councillors, the Aldermen of such Borough, or so many as shall be needed to supply the Places of those who shall then go out of Office according to the Provisions herein-after contained; and that upon the Ninth Day of November in the Year One thousand eight hundred and thirty-eight, and in every Third succeeding Year, One Half of the Number appointed as aforesaid to be the Whole Number of the Aldermen of every Borough shall go out of Office; and the Councillors immediately after the first Election of Aldermen shall appoint who shall be the Aldermen who shall go out of Office in the Year One thousand eight hundred and thirty-eight, and thereafter those who shall go out of Office shall always be those who have been Aldermen for the longest Time without Re-election: Provided always, that any Aldermen so going out of Office may be forthwith re-elected, if then qualified as herein provided; provided also, that the Aldermen so going out of Office shall not be entitled to vote in the Election of a new Alderman. . . .

XXXI. And be it enacted, That upon the First Day of November One thousand eight hundred and thirty-six, and in every succeeding year, One Third Part of the Number appointed as aforesaid to be the whole Number of the Councillors of every Borough shall go out of Office; and in the said Year 1836 those who shall go out of Office shall be the Councillors who were elected under the Provisions of this Act by the smallest Number of Votes in this Present Year, and in the next Year 1837 those who shall go out of Office shall be the Councillors who were elected under the Provisions of this Act with the next smallest number of Votes in this Present Year. . . .

LXXV. And whereas it may be expedient that the Powers now vested in the Trustees appointed under sundry Acts of Parliament for paving, lighting, cleansing, watching, regulating, supplying with Water, and improving certain Boroughs, or certain Parts thereof, should be transferred to and vested in the Councils of such Boroughs respectively; be it enacted, That the Trustees appointed by virtue of any such Act of Parliament as last aforesaid, wherein the Trustees, or the Persons whose Trustees they may be, are not beneficially interested, may, if it shall seem to them expedient, at a Meeting to be called for that Purpose, transfer in Writing under their Hands and Seals all the Powers vested in them as such Trustees by any such Act or Acts of Parliament as aforesaid to the said Body Corporate of such Borough and the said Body Corporate of such Borough shall thenceforth be Trustee for executing by the Council of such Borough the several Powers and Provisions of any such Act or Acts of Parliament, and the Members of the Council shall have the same Powers and be subject to the same Duties as if their Names had been originally inserted in such Act or Acts, or as if they had been elected under the Provisions of any such Act or Acts as such Trustees respectively: Provided always, that no such Transfer as aforesaid shall be made of the Powers vested by virtue of the Acts mentioned in Schedule (E.) which relate to the Town of Cambridge, without the Consent of the Chancellor, Masters, and Scholars of the University of Cambridge.

LXXVI. And be it enacted, That the Council to be elected for any Borough shall, immediately after their First Election, and so from Time to Time thereafter as they shall deem expedient, appoint, for such Time as they may think proper, a sufficient Number of their own Body, who, together with the Mayor of the Borough for the Time being, shall be and be called the Watch Committee for such Borough; and all the Powers herein-after given to such Committee may be executed by the Majority of those who shall be present at any Meeting of such Committee, the whole Number present at such Meeting being not less than Three; and such Watch Committee shall, within Three Weeks as Occasion shall require, appoint a sufficient Number of fit Men, who shall be sworn in before some Justice of the Peace having Jurisdiction within the Borough to act as Constables for preserving the Peace by Day and by Night, and preventing Robberies and other Felonies, and apprehending Offenders against the Peace; and the Men so sworn shall not only within such Borough, but also within the County in which such Borough or Part thereof shall be situated, and also within every County being within Seven Miles of any Part of such Borough, and also within all Liberties in any such County, have all such Powers and Privileges, and be liable to all such Duties and Responsibilities, as any Constable duly appointed now has or hereinafter may have within his Constablewick by virtue of the Common Law of this Realm, or of any Statutes made or to be made, and shall obey all such lawful Commands as they may from Time to Time receive from any of the Justices of the Peace having Jurisdiction within such Borough, or within any County in which they shall be called on to act as Constables, for conducting themselves in the Execution of their Office. . . .

XC. And be it enacted, That it shall be lawful for the Council of any Borough to make such Bye Laws as to them shall seem meet for the good Rule and Government of the Borough, and for Prevention and Suppression of all such Nuisances as are not already punishable in a summary Manner by virtue of any Act in force throughout such Borough, and to appoint by such Bye Laws such Fines as they shall deem necessary for the Prevention and Suppression of such Offences; provided that no Fine so to be appointed shall exceed the Sum of Five Pounds, and that no such Bye Law shall be made unless at least Two Thirds of the whole Number of the Council shall be present; provided that no such Bye Law shall be of any Force until the Expiration of Forty Days after the same or a Copy thereof shall have been sent, sealed with the Seal of the said Borough, to One of His Majesty's Principal Secretaries of State, and shall have been affixed on the outer Door of the Town Hall or in some other public Place within such Borough; and if at any Time within the said Period of Forty Days His Majesty, with the Advice of His Privy Council, shall disallow the same Bye Law or any Part thereof, such Bye Law or the Part thereof disallowed shall not come into operation: Provided also, that it shall be lawful for His Majesty, if He shall think fit, at any Time within the said Period of Forty Days, to enlarge the Time within which such Bye Law, if disallowed, shall not come into force; and no such Bye Law shall in that Case come into force until after the Expiration of such enlarged time.

192. Royal Commission on county rates (1836)

Parlty. Papers, 1836/xxvii.

Upon mature consideration of the facts brought before us in the course of our inquiry, we have no doubt that the most operative, and the only constant cause of increase in the charge for prosecutions, has been the continued multiplication of crime, occasioned, of course, in part by the advance of population, but resulting also in a great measure from the influence of other causes, upon which it does not fall within our province to dilate.

For this, as well as for other reasons, the greatest attention is due to the suggestions addressed from various quarters to the Commission as to the expediency of establishing an improved rural police.

The police establishment for the country (so far as ordinary purposes are concerned) consists in general of a constable for each parish or township, elected to serve for the year. He is most commonly an uneducated person from the class of petty tradesmen or mechanics, and in practice is usually nominated by his predecessor on going out of office. No inquiry takes place into his qualifications or fitness for the office, and indeed he is said to be often the person in the parish the most likely to break the peace. So common is it for the constable to be unable to write or read, that an improper fee is often charged upon that ground by the magistrate's clerk:– "*for making out the constable's bill for conveyance to gaol.*"

"The manner of appointing constables, in my opinion, might be advantageously altered," says a correspondent, "for the court leet jury and steward being irresponsible parties, and the jurymen not liking the burden themselves, often appoint persons of bad character, and sometimes for the purpose of keeping them off the parish."

If respectable persons are sometimes chosen at the leet, they "find substitutes for a small sum, and these deputies blunder through the year, and when they are most wanted are never to be found."

Entirely ignorant of his duties when first appointed, the parish constable is often displaced at the end of the year, when his acquaintance with them is, perhaps, beginning to improve. Even when suited in other respects to the employment, his efficiency is always in a great measure impaired by the nature of his position with regard to those among whom he is called upon to act. Belonging entirely to their class, and brought into constant contact with them by his ordinary occupations, he is embarrassed in the discharge of his duty by considerations of personal safety, interest, or feeling, and by an anxiety to retain the good will of his neighbours.

When all these circumstances are considered, it would be surprising if the constables were found to render satisfactory service. In point of fact they are deficient in zeal and activity to a degree which it is difficult to exaggerate, and it may be said, without undue severity, that they are in all respects utterly unfit for the duties to which they are appointed.

The accuracy of this statement we believe will be generally admitted by those who have opportunities of becoming acquainted with the subject by personal observation. It is at all events fully supported by the evidence before us; and is indeed little more than a summary of the complaints which we have received from various quarters relative to the state of the parochial police. "No person can be aware," says the Treasurer of the West Riding of Yorkshire, "of the reluctance shown by the parish constables in apprehending felons, particularly since the disposition shown by the lower orders to retaliate by committing destruction on their property. There is not a single constable," he afterwards adds, "who dares move, nor has he any encouragement to move; and if he does moves, he is quite incompetent."

"We cannot go on in the country," says another witness, "with our present police. When there is the least danger we are obliged immediately to call out the special constables." "The present system of police," says another, "is unsound. The present parochial police consists of a constable in each parish, who is annually elected; who, as soon as he knows his business, is liable to be removed, and frequently is removed; who is in a situation of equality and fellowship, &c., and has very often to make his election between violating his duty as a constable, and forfeiting the regard and affection of his neighbours." "The great end of police is to prevent crime," is the remark of another gentleman of great experience on this subject: "who ever heard of this being the object of the present force? They are worse than useless."

It is the deliberate opinion of a very valuable correspondent, that our constabulary system has greatly promoted the increase of crime; that no useful improvement can be introduced into the present miserable system of attempting to exercise police through parish constables annually elected. "Our constable system is so absurd and unjust that I really do not think it fair or equitable to blame or deride the unfortunate conscripts who are compelled to be tithingmen; if I did, I could compose a farce with the anecdotes to be collected of petty occurrences in the warfare with offences in this neighbourhood,–neglect of duty, forgetfulness, ignorance, blunders, cowardice without excuse, supineness, &c."

Opinions similar to these are expressed by many other competent witnesses whose communications are inserted in the Appendix to this Report. Indeed the current of evidence as to the decayed and worn out state of the parish constabulary force, is irresistibly strong.

The defects of the present constabulary force are the more striking when viewed in contrast with the improved system of an organized and permanent police as established in the metropolis, and in some other parts of the kingdom. Not only in London and Westminster, but in several other places where that method has been adopted, it has been attended with the most satisfactory results, and we are not aware of a single exception to the remark. Its effect in the case of the Barnet Association, established in 1813, is fully described in the course of one of the examinations taken under this Commission. After stating that it extends over eight entire parishes, and partially over five more, the Secretary of the Association declares that after a trial of 22 years he "can speak of its success most completely," and says, that "it has fully answered its end; so much so, that the subscription increases every year, and there are not now many persons above the rank of yeomen who are not members of it in that extensive circle." He also states that "the Association is very popular, that neighbouring parishes seek to be admitted into it, and that it is taken as a model by others." Of the Cheshire Constabulary Act another witness states that "though the system was not liked by the rate-payers at first, on account of the expense, it has now worked itself into favour, and been found most efficient." Another correspondent, a magistrate of Oxfordshire, states, "It is in contemplation to establish a regular police in this district by subscription, similar to that established at Stow-in-the-Wold, which has been productive of the best results." But the most striking testimony as to the salutary operation of a regular system of police in the particular districts where it is established, is borne by those who describe its effect upon other parts of the country not enjoying the same advantage. "The police of London," says the Treasurer of the West Riding of Yorkshire, in his examination before the Commissioners, "has driven all the rogues into the country. We are inundated with them. The police not being uniform for the whole country, but more active in some parts than others, has driven them down to the rural districts." Another gentleman, a magistrate of the Riding, observes, "We cannot go on in the country with our present police. The thieves are driven now out of the great towns which have effective police, and it is impossible for us to go on with parish constables." "I have heard," says another witness, "that a great many vagabonds are driven away from Barnet into the neighbouring parishes, and that the neighbouring parishes have suffered in consequence." "The activity of the Metropolitan Police," observes another, "causes increased depredations to be committed within a circle of from five to ten miles beyond their precincts."

"The vigilance of the police in cities and large towns," observes a Worcestershire magistrate, "has driven the worst characters to infest small towns and villages, where I am sorry to say, there is a total want of police or protection to property. In the market town of Pershore the police force consists of two drunken cobblers, being the deputies of two nominal constables annually elected from the class of shopkeepers."

"Systems of police," says our Hampshire correspondent, "are rapidly and happily starting up in the large towns, in imitation of London; but in the country there is no other known and legal means but that of the parish constable or tithing-man; and yet in that institution, whatever it may have been formerly, in very different times, there is not one principle of vitality or exertion. Whilst there has been everything to increase crime in Great Britain, from increase of luxury, fluctuation of employment in manufacturing districts, increase of wealth, and incredibly increased facilities of motion and communication, we, by continuing to oppose Alfred's tithing-men to offence, in its incalculably augmented power and means, have marvellously favoured its progress."

It seems, therefore, upon the whole, unquestionable, that the establishment throughout the kingdom of an improved police, to act in lieu of the present parochial constables and other local officers of the peace, would tend very powerfully to the more effectual prevention of crime. We believe too that there is no other measure by which that great object could be so effectually promoted. It would not perhaps be *essential* to a plan of this description that the new police agents should be appointed by Your Majesty's Government, or that they should compose a collective force, the different branches of which should co-operate with each other, as occasionally required, or that they should be subject to the regulation of a central board. It is obvious, however, that any given number of persons so organized would act with incomparably better effect than if distributed into separate parochial or district establishments, each acting exclusively for a particular place, and subject to a distinct local regulation.

It may appear, upon the first impression, that any plan for improvement in the general police, whether upon the local or central principle, would be attended with too much expense to be advantageously adopted. But in order to ascertain the true value of that objection, we must take into the account the heavy charges which now result from the want of proper regulation on the subject in question. By giving great encouragement and facility to crime, it proportionably swells the expenditure, and that not only under the head of prosecutions, but of gaols and maintenance also, which amounted, in the year 1834, to no less a sum than £222,786. It is obvious, indeed, that its effect must be felt under all the heads of charge connected with the prosecution of crime, and these collectively comprise (as already stated) more than half the entire expenditure from the County Rate. To the inefficiency of the present police are also to be attributed many charges on that fund for damages from tumultuous assemblies, and for damages sustained at elections; and many of the expenses incurred by individuals in procuring the assistance of a police officer from the metropolitan or from some other establishment, to detect offenders; in employing watchmen or guards to secure their property from depredation, and in subscribing to voluntary associations for the prevention or prosecution of crime.

But the present system is not only expensive from its incompetency to its proper object–it is in itself of a very costly character. In this remark we principally refer to the manner in which the constables are remunerated. The payments made to them under the County Rate appear on the face of the accounts to be comprised under the different heads of "High and Special Constables," and "Conveyance to Gaol." Under these heads respectively the charge was,

	In 1792	*In 1832*	*Increase per cent.*
Constables	£659	£26,688	£4,338
Conveyance	£4,865	£25,201	£525

Under the same heads collectively the charge amounted, in 1834, to the sum of £45,036. But the receipts of constables are in fact of much larger amount, and a great portion of them are derived from funds unconnected with the County Rate. They receive remuneration from four different sources—from Government, (in the shape of rewards and the expenses of search and apprehension under 7 Geo. IV. c. 64) from the County Rate, from parishes, and from individuals. . . .

. . . It was impossible to enter thus largely into the various charges imposed upon a particular fund, without being led to some consideration of the nature of the fund itself, and the method under which it is raised; and the rather as complaints are constantly made of the present mode of levying and administering the County Rate.

The principle of the rate seems open to serious objections, upon the ground that the charge is imposed by persons not chosen by the rate payers. No other tax of such magnitude is laid upon the subject, except by his representatives. The possibility of improving the present system in this particular, will be a subject for subsequent remark.

Another objection is, that though a great portion of the fund is applied to the protection of personal property, it is levied exclusively upon the realty. It is clear, however, that personal property could not be subjected to effectual taxation to the County Rate, and no alteration of the system on this point could be practicable. But the consideration that there is an undue pressure (as there certainly appears to be,) upon the landed interest, leads to the inference that it ought to be relieved from some of the existing burthens. If Parliament were now for the first time to be making provision for the safe custody of criminals, and the repair of the main roads and the bridges upon them, it would not be thought reasonable to throw the expense of these national concerns upon a local fund raised exclusively upon the occupiers of lands and houses. It seems just, therefore, that these charges, or a part of them, should be taken off from the County Rate and transferred to the public revenue; a fund to which every species of property contributes its share.

There appears to be reasonable ground of objection also as respects,

1st, The valuation for the rate.

2nd, The collection.

3rd, The appropriation.

4th, The audit.

Supposing a general valuation of any county for the purpose of the County Rate to be once correctly made, it is nevertheless subject to rapid derangement. The value or rateable ability of each parish fluctuates from time to time by the creation, extinction, improvement, or deterioration of properties, and particularly by the effect of inclosures. Considerable changes of this description are said to be usually perceptible in the course of seven years. Under such circumstances, supposing the general valuation to remain uncorrected, the pressure of the charge as between the different parishes in the county will become unequal. The general valuations should therefore be frequently renewed; but in most parts of the kingdom they are allowed to remain for long periods of time without alteration. From a statement annexed to the Report of the Select Committee of the House of Commons on County Rate, it seems that there are only nine counties in which a valuation has been made within the last seven years; in eight, the date of the existing valuation is not known; in five, it appears to be about 100 years old. In Dorset it appears that in the year 1834, the valuation had not virtually altered since 1672, (26 Chas. II.) a period of more than 160 years, though 50 inclosures had taken place in that county, even since the 27th Geo. III., and property nearly to the amount of £300,000 per annum had been created in the county, of which not one fragment is assessed to the County Rate. In 18 counties the assessment to the property tax is adopted as the valuation for the County Rate. In seven counties of Wales there is no valuation; but the assessment is according to an apportionment to each hundred, made from 40 to 90 years ago. In one of these counties it is stated, that many thousand acres of land have been inclosed since the period of valuation, but that no alteration has been made in consequence of such inclosures.

Valuations have been recently made in the West Riding of York and in the county of Lancaster at a moderate expense, but with a degree of correctness which appears to have given general satisfaction. Their effect has been to make the large towns contribute in a more just proportion, and greatly to relieve the agricultural interests. Though in other counties the results might probably be less striking, we have no doubt that a similar course would be attended with advantage in most other parts of the kingdom; and that in every instance the expense of the valuation would be more than compensated by the amount of benefit derived. We think the measure of periodical valuations should be made imperative, for it is obvious that those who have the advantage of being rated too low under the existing valuations, will always be opposed to their revision.

2. The present mode of collecting the County Rate is not satisfactory. The high constable receives and pays over moneys in a loose and irregular manner, giving, in general, no security to the county and no voucher to the overseers, and making long journeys in person to carry moneys to the treasurer.

The expense of collection, *per se*, no where appears, but it is no doubt very considerable, and it is to be observed that in some counties it forms a separate charge upon the parishes and is in addition to the amount which they are called upon to pay for County Rate.

"In stating the amount of the County Rate," was the observation of a magistrate of great experience, Mr. Becher, "it may be well to bear in recollection, that there are several charges resulting from the mode of collection, such as the fees paid to the chief constables, and the allowances made to the petty constables as a compensation for their time and trouble, which, although not appearing on the account, yet do in fact make a very considerable addition to the expenses on the landed interest." He then mentions a parish (Thurgaston,) in which the payment for the Poor Rate in the then three last years was £52, and the County Rates and constables' bills were £54.

3. The management of the county funds is regarded with some distrust. The salaries given to county officers have been considered as extravagant, and the holders of the offices as sometimes ill-qualified, as well as overpaid. Improper prices are sometimes thought to be paid and immoderate fees and charges allowed. Whatever ground there may be for these imputations, it is at least natural that they should be made, while the fund is administered by persons over whose proceedings there is no effectual control.

4. There seems to be no efficient Audit of the county accounts. No prospective estimates are presented of probable expenditure, nor is any abstract of the accounts supplied to render them intelligible. The only material check is that afforded by the recent Act, 3 and 4 Will. IV. c. 48, providing that the business shall be transacted in open court, and that appears to be insufficient. To make the control complete, more time and opportunity should be allowed for examination of the accounts.

It is impossible not to admit that the persons who contribute to the County Rate have little control over its expenditure. The administration of this fund is the exercise of an irresponsible power, entrusted to a fluctuating body. A magistrate of Somersetshire who is, with reason, "averse to any measure having a tendency to lessen the character and influence of the magistracy," nevertheless expresses himself upon this subject, in a document placed in our hands, with great distinctness. "I cannot," he says, "avoid remarking the objections to giving that respectable, but very varying body, the court of quarter sessions, the authority to raise, expend, and audit the accounts of large and indefinite sums of money, without any effectual responsibility; and I doubt also the advantage of giving the quarter sessions the patronage of offices, together with the power to fix the emoluments thereof. It is a temptation to magistrates to make interest for these offices, and then to increase the salaries for the sake of the holders. When the quarter sessions of a county are held at different places, different sets of magistrates attend; and though this may be unobjectionable, for the purposes of the original institution of the court, it is ill-suited to any systematic attention to the duties of the pecuniary administration lately imposed upon them."

One of the topics adverted to in this communication is the objection to the authority under which the fund is raised. Some of those by whom that objection is advanced are of opinion that the rate-payers should be entitled to elect the magistrates by whom the rate is imposed, but we think that course of proceeding clearly inexpedient. A popular election of magistrates, having any judicial duties to perform, is, in our judgment, greatly to be deprecated.

It is, on the other hand, proposed by a member of the legislature, that the whole financial concerns of a county should be taken from the magistrates and lodged in a responsible board. We confess, however, that we should much disapprove the exclusion of the magistrates from all participation in the financial concerns of the county, and we decidedly give the preference to the view taken by another gentleman, who has much considered the subject, and who suggests the formation of a central county board of representatives from the boards of guardians, at which central board the magistrates, or a part of them, should have *ex officio* seats.

This plan of applying the machinery of the new Poor-Law Unions to the controlling the county expenditure appears to us not undeserving of attention. The guardians are already elected to represent parishes. They meet and transact business of local finance, at their own board, with the neighbouring magistrates. It is represented to us that they are found to proceed very harmoniously with the magistrates at those boards; and no reason is apparent why persons elected by boards of guardians should not satisfactorily conduct the affairs of the county in conjunction with a limited number of the magistrates. "I am disposed to think," says the witness referred to, "that though the magistrates would be unwilling to concede the whole of the control to the rate-payers, they would not object to a concurrent control on the part of the rate-payers with themselves."

It is a question for the decision of the legislature, whether a county council cannot be in this manner conveniently formed, to regulate the imposition of the local charge, or whether the audit is the fitter season for letting in a moderate infusion of popular control. Auditors are always elected in boroughs to control the expenditure of rates, in the nature of a County Rate, and it seems fitting that a board of audit should be constituted for the supervision of the County Rate itself.

Upon the course and method of local taxation we do not feel ourselves called upon by the nature of our Commission to suggest specific improvements, but we may be permitted to state generally, that we think the subject deserves greater attention than it has hitherto received. A negligent and, in some instances, a corrupt administration of parochial funds has been clearly established; and we think sufficient appears upon the face of this Report, to prove the possibility of introducing an improved management of the financial concerns of a county at large, and a consequent reduction of the general burthen.

All which matters in this our Report contained, we humbly submit to Your Majesty's most gracious consideration.

193. Hume's speech introducing his County Boards Bill (10 February 1837)

Hansard, 3/xxxvi/415–416.

Mr. Hume rose to ask leave to bring in a Bill which he had introduced last Session, for the appointment of County Boards, to superintend the financial department in each county. The late period at which the Bill had been introduced last Session, prevented its getting farther than the first reading. Since, then, however, the country had been made acquainted with its provisions and its objects, for he had sent a copy of the Bill to the clerk of the peace in each county. Perhaps he might be told by some persons that this was a very gratuitious act, but he conceived he had only done his duty. A Bill brought in by the hon. Member for Stroud,[1] and passed at the end of

[1] Lord John Russell.

last Session, had rendered most of the enactments, which the Bill he formerly introduced contained, useless. The one he now sought to introduce made a complete distinction between the financial and the judicial business of the county. It was limited to the financial department only–the judicial, he thought, ought to remain with the representatives of his Majesty. Much misconception had gone abroad on the subject of the present Bill, and he thought it necessary to state its principle and its object. It was intended that a council should be elected in each county by the rate-payers in the county for the management of the finances. By the previous Bill it was provided that all divisions of the counties were to be made by commissioners to be named under the Bill. Some suggestions had been made to him on this point, and it was now intended that the divisions made by the Poor Law Commissioners should be adopted where that was found advantageous. He therefore proposed that the Commissioners should have a discretionary power to adopt divisions already existing, and to make them where it was necessary; and he had no doubt that if the council were once established, they would, in a few years, be able to point out the exact limit of every division. It was proposed, also, that an election should take place in every parish, the votes to be taken by proper officers, and the returns to be sent to the officer of the union. The Bill also appoints auditors, to be elected by the rate-payers, and all officers under the Bill, from the secretary to the servant, were to be paid a certain fixed salary, but to be entitled to no fees. The Bill also proposed the establishment of a system of police under the direction of the county board. They would thus obtain throughout the country one uniform and systematic body of police, which he believed would prevent a great many offences, and he was sure that the expense of such a system of efficient police would not exceed the sum expended on the present inefficient body. The Bill went to assimilate the counties to the burghs, and to give to rate-payers the management and control over their finances. It was also proposed that the unions should have the power of recommending individuals to be appointed by his Majesty as justices of the peace. This was a point which he was aware was considered of very great difficulty, but he deemed it essential to the well-working of the system, and hoped it would meet with no opposition. He was anxious to see a responsible magistracy, as it appeared to him the country stood greatly in need of it. He moved that leave be given to bring in a Bill for placing the finances of counties under a County Board, to be elected by the rate-payers.

194. Royal Commission on Municipal Corporations on London (1837)

Parlty. Papers, 1837/xxv.

. . . The course followed by the Legislature in the Statute 5 & 6 Will. 4. c. 76. (commonly called the Municipal Corporation Reform Act), so far as relates to those Towns included within its provisions, was to bring all that would popularly be termed the Town within the scope of the same municipal authority. In many of those Towns the additions so made were inconsiderable; in others they bore a considerable proportion to the ancient Borough; as, for instance, in the City of Bristol, where the population has been increased by such additions from 59,000 to 104,000; and in the Borough of Liverpool, where it has been raised from 165,000 to 206,000. But in all these cases it was assumed, not only that the nucleus of the Town, consisting of the old Municipal Borough, was the most important part of the whole united district, but also that the utmost extension thus given to the limits of the Borough was still not sufficient to overpower and destroy its primary importance in the new community formed by the union of it with all its suburbs.

It appears, from the foregoing statements, that this assumption cannot be made in the case of the Metropolis. Nevertheless, we do not find any argument on which the course pursued with regard to other Towns could be justified, which would not apply with the same force to London, unless the magnitude of the change in this case should be considered as converting that which would otherwise be only a practical difficulty into an objection of principle.

We have pointed out how small a proportion of the Metropolis is comprehended within the Municipal Boundary. We are unable to discover any circumstance justifying the present distinction of this particular district from the rest, except that in fact it is, and has long been, so distinguished. It is evident that any reasoning, founded on the assumption that questions respecting the Corporation relate to the whole Town of London, will be entirely fallacious; and this necessarily introduces much perplexity into all discussions on the corporate system, owing to the great difficulty which there is in preventing such an assumption from being made.

We hardly anticipate that it will be suggested, for the purpose of removing the appearance of singularity, that the other quarters of the Town should be formed into independent and isolated communities, if indeed the multifarious relations to which their proximity compels them would permit them to be isolated and independent. This plan would, as it seems to us, in getting rid of an anomaly, tend to multiply and perpetuate an evil.

If we consider the several parts of the whole Metropolis merely with regard to their population and extent, the City of Westminster is a most important quarter of the Town. The circumstance that it is also the seat of Your Majesty's Government, and the place where Parliament usually meets, gives a new and distinctive character to it, with reference to some of the foregoing circumstances.

By the Corporation Reform Act, the principal power over the details of local government has been entrusted, in a great number of the provincial towns of Great Britain, to bodies chosen by the inhabitants, reserving for the Central Government those means of communication, and of general superintendence, which are necessary to secure uniformity of action throughout Your Majesty's Dominions of Great Britain, and to maintain those local municipalities in a state of due subordination to Your Majesty's supreme authority. A new and very important question, as it appears to us, must necessarily arise, in a Town which is the seat of the Legislature and supreme executive power of the State, with respect to the proper division of municipal authority between the Officers of Government and a municipal body which might be established in the Metropolis for the same, or for some of the same, purposes as elsewhere. We do not take upon ourselves to give any opinion upon this question, conceiving that it will be sufficient thus to indicate it.

In one particular, and that a most important and practical one, the opinion of

Parliament has been already declared by the establishment of a Metropolitan Police, under the orders of Commissioners appointed by, and immediately dependent upon, Your Majesty's Executive Government. We scarcely anticipate that any argument can be brought forward to show that this system can be partially right. We can see no middle course for the establishment of an efficient Police throughout the Metropolis, between placing the whole under a Metropolitan Municipality, and entrusting the whole to Commissioners, or other similar officers under the immediate control of Your Majesty's Government.

Other topics suggest similar conclusions, as the paving, sewage and lighting of the streets, which, as it seems to us, can never be so economically and efficiently performed in one town as when superintended by an undivided authority; and the only real point for consideration is, how far these duties for the whole Metropolis could be placed in the hands of a Metropolitan Municipality, or how far they should be entrusted to the Officers of Your Majesty's Government. With respect to sewage, indeed, there is an obvious absurdity in placing the City, and any large district which drains into it from a higher level, under different superintendence.

The navigation of the river Thames, to which the empire owes so much of its greatness, raises another most important question. In the first place, the inhabitants of every quarter of the Town might reasonably require that the privileges of ownership and conservancy, as they are called, should not continue to be confined to one district, to which they were granted when it, in fact, constituted the whole Metropolis; but, further, it is plain that the proper management of the port and river is not a matter which concerns solely the inhabitants of the Metropolis. The inhabitants of other parts of Your Majesty's dominions have a right to ask whether these functions, the due performance of which is of vital importance to all, are properly within the province of any local Municipality, however extended; and why they should not be under the direct control of the general executive Government of the country.

Premising these observations on those points which naturally arise out of the consideration of the City of London viewed only as a part of the Metropolis, we now proceed to the examination of matters relating to the constitution of London considered by itself, with subsidiary reference only to such questions as those to which we have thus cursorily alluded.

195. Royal Commission on Constabulary Forces (1839)

Parlty. Papers, 1839/XIX.

We now beg leave to recapitulate the chief conclusions which we have endeavoured to set forth in this our Report.

I. Having, with a view to judge of the extent of any requisite remedy by means of a paid constabulary force, made a general investigation as well as to the state of crime as to the present state of the unpaid constabulary, we find in respect to the state of crime:

1. That the public information as to the number of crimes committed, inferred from the extent of crimes judicially pursued and punished, is widely erroneous.

2. That there is an average of upwards of 100,000 commitments annually to the gaols of the able-bodied population of England and Wales for Criminal offences.

3. That there are from 11,000 to 20,000 persons constantly in the criminal gaols; of which number a large proportion are persons known as living wholly by habitual depredation; and from inquiries made in a large number of the individual cases of prisoners confined for thefts in these gaols, we find that on the average such prisoners in the rural districts, where there is no trained constabulary, have been at large living by depredation during average periods upwards of five years; and that the criminal prisoners in the gaols in the towns, where there is a paid and trained force, have not been able to pursue their depredations more than half that time. But that nevertheless in either districts, prisoners are liberated with the prospect and the temptation of a career of unknown but long duration for the future, before permanent removal by process of law or by natural causes.

4. That with relation to the particular crimes committed by such habitual depredators, no information is possessed by the unpaid constables.

5. That it results from a special investigation of the habits of the classes of habitual depredators; that a large proportion of them are migratory; that they migrate from town to town, and from the towns where they harbour, and where there are distinct houses maintained for their accommodation, they issue forth and commit depredations upon the surrounding rural districts; the metropolis being the chief centre from which they migrate: and that they harbour in provincial towns in proportion to their magnitude, and in proportion to the facilities for plunder or to the absence of protection in the surrounding districts.

6. That judging from particular cases in which we have made inquiries, a large proportion, if not always the majority, of prisoners in the county gaols for offences committed within the rural districts, are persons who have migrated from the towns to the rural districts.

7. That from the impunity enjoyed by the classes of depredators, migrant or resident, property is rendered insecure; in some places so much so on the part of the labouring classes as greatly to impair the value of property to them, and their motives to industry and frugality.

8. That in the rural districts agricultural produce is subjected to extensive depredation which often interferes with the most advantageous course of production.

9. That a large proportion of the highways are left without any protection whatsoever from any constabulary or other civil force.

10. That on the highways of a large part of the country, commercial travellers and strangers who travel singly, otherwise than by public conveyances, and carry money about them, abstain from travelling after dark, from fear of robbery and violence; and that farmers return from market in company, from the like fear, after dark.

11. That the products of commercial industry *in transitu* on the highways being almost entirely without protection from any civil force, are subject to extensive and systematic depredation.

12. That in the absence of due protection, property carried by sea in ships which are wrecked on those parts of the coast where shipwrecks occasionally or frequently

occur, is subject to extensive habitual depredation, and life is endangered or lost, under circumstances of barbarity disgraceful to a civilized nation.

II. Having investigated the general causes of depredation, of vagrancy, and mendicancy, as developed by examinations of the previous lives of criminals or vagrants in the gaols, we find that in scarcely any cases is it ascribable to the pressure of unavoidable want or destitution; and that in the great mass of cases it arises from the temptation of obtaining property with a less degree of labour than by regular industry, which they are enabled to do by the impunity occasioned by the absence of the proper constitutional protection to the subject.

III. Having specially examined the state of public security against breaches of the peace in the manufacturing districts, we find,

1. That the free investment of capital and employment of labourers, and the progress of manufacturing industry is impeded and endangered, and combinations carried on by violent and unlawful means; that murder has been resorted to, and that threats of murder, and arson, and personal violence are resorted to by such combiners as means to effect their objects.

2. That for the prevention of the disturbances peculiar to such districts, as well as for the prevention of the more ordinary breaches of the peace, amidst the new and increasing population, no other efficient force than a military force is provided.

3. That such force is inadequate for the purpose of the prevention of disorders, and that from the reluctance which is felt in having recourse to it for the purpose of repression, it is rarely used until considerable evil has been occasioned.

4. And we further find that from the want of an efficient preventive force, the peace and manufacturing prosperity of the country are exposed to considerable danger.

IV. Having specially investigated the state of the constabulary force, and the execution of the constitutional principles of penal administration connected with that force, we find,

1. That the early constitutional principles of local responsibility for offences committed, by compensation to the sufferers, or by amercements to the Crown, has been impaired; and that there does not exist an adequate local interest to ensure the adoption of efficient means for the prevention of crimes, especially of crimes committed against the persons of strangers, travellers, or wayfarers.

2. That in the majority of instances, the courts leet, or other functionaries charged with the duty of appointing fit and proper persons to act as constables, do not appoint persons who possess the requisite legal qualifications in respect of intelligence, substance, character, and connexions.

3. That the modes of carrying out the early constitutional principles of action of a constabulary force, of seeking information of offences, felonies, or misdemeanours committed, and of instituting quick and fresh pursuit for the apprehension of the offenders, have fallen into desuetude, and that no new modes adapted to the present circumstances of society have been introduced.

4. That offenders, after having committed extensive depredations in one district, have recourse to another; the people in which, having received no warning, are enabled to take no measures of prevention; and that until detected and pursued by some private individuals, usually at their own private cost, the depredators proceed without interruption by any public officers from district to district.

5. That the criminal law is often extensively dispensed with, and its execution left to the discretion of private and unauthorized individuals.

6. That in consequence of the extensive dereliction of the constitutional principles of penal administration, self-protection is extensively resorted to by private individuals separately, as well as by individuals associating together for mutual protection.

7. That there are upwards of 500 private or voluntary associations for self-protection in different parts of the country, by the payment of rewards for the apprehension of felons and the expenses of their prosecution, independently of a large number of associations for self-protection by subscription for the maintenance of private watchmen; and of other private associations for the removal of various evils, such as the suppression of vagrancy and mendicancy, which it is the business of the Government to prevent or repress.

8. That the protection obtained by such associations is in proportion to the cost extremely inadequate, and that the practice of investing private hands with public powers for their own use, is fraught with much inconvenience, and some danger of mischief to the public by large associations.

9. That the proper performance of the legal duties of constables in the present state of the law and circumstances of the community would require from persons otherwise properly qualified in respect to substance and character, a sacrifice of time and labour which would render the compulsory service of the office grievously burthensome, and that within the time allowed for such service the requisite information and experience for its proper performance could not ordinarily be obtained.

10. That it is essential to the proper performance of the duties in question that they should be performed by an agency specially trained, paid, and appointed, during good behaviour, for the purpose, and subjected to the control of superior and trained officers, who are themselves specially qualified and subjected to effective responsibility.

V. Having specially investigated the cases of the trial of paid constables, we find in the case of the trial of a paid constabulary force appointed and controlled, according to an Act of Parliament for the county of Chester, by the magistrates at quarter and petty sessions, we find

1. That the appointment and management of a paid constabulary force in separate divisions, separately managed at the discretion of the justices at the petty sessions of those divisions, is an arrangement of itself incompatible with any efficient and economical system for the prevention of crime.

2. That such a mode of appointment and separate management in separate divisions does not comprehend any adequate local interest or proper security for the due protection of property or persons unconnected with the vicinity on the Queen's highways, or the constitutional responsibilities in that behalf to the sovereign authority.

3. That any less scale of administration of a paid constabulary than for a whole county, does not comprehend a sufficiently wide basis for ultimate and complete efficiency and economy, either as to the county regarded separately, or in its general relation to the rest of the kingdom.

4. That the appointment and executive control of any paid constabulary force for the conservation of the peace are proved to be incompatible with the due and impartial discharge of the functions of the justice of the peace, with the maintenance of proper respect for the office, or the efficient direction and control of the force itself, or the avoidance of party or local animosities, or the jealousies arising on the part of the labouring classes from the relation of employer and workmen.

VI. Having examined the effects and tendencies of the other paid constabulary forces, separately organized and directed in towns, we find–

1. That whilst the paid forces which have been instituted on the model of the Metropolitan Police force, in many of the municipal towns, have rendered considerable benefits to the inhabitants of those towns, they have not gained these benefits by preventing or suppressing the whole of the evils from which they are freed, but by shifting a portion of it, or driving depredators into adjacent districts.

2. That a considerable proportion of the habitual depredators in the rural districts harbour in the towns, where since they do not, unless under safe opportunities, pursue their practices, they receive no molestation.

3. That, in consequence of the absence of a proper constabulary force and the want of due protection in the rural districts, the towns are subject to the occasional escapes of delinquents, and are obliged to maintain a stronger or more expensive constabulary force than would otherwise be necessary to guard against criminals who subsist chiefly by depredations in the surrounding country.

4. That the like results must be produced by separate or uncombined arrangements for the prevention of crime.

VII. Having investigated the most favourable instances of the trial of a paid and well appointed constabulary force in the rural districts, we find–

1. That by means of such force the habitual depredations of resident delinquents have been prevented, and that they have been reformed or constrained to courses of honest industry.

2. That the districts in which such force has acted have been kept free from vagrants and mendicants, and from migratory depredators; and that habitual depredations on agricultural produce and crimes in general against property have been prevented.

3. That the disorders in beer-shops and ill-regulated houses of public resort, and other sources of temptation and causes of domestic distress and immorality, have been repressed.

4. That for a time, and during the continuance of the full efficiency of the force, the public peace, the efficiency of the laws, and the authority of the magistrates have been restored or increased as regards riotous or individual infractions, and a state of

order produced, such as to leave but little immediate anxiety in the minds of the peaceable and well-disposed of the population for further amendment.

VIII. Having inquired into the services other than in the prevention or repression of crime which a paid and well-appointed constabulary force may render, we find–

1. That they may render extensive public service in the prevention of the loss of life, and destruction of property, and in the diminution of the feelings of alarm arising from calamities by fire or other causes.

2. That they may render various local, civil, and administrative services, as in reporting on the state of the roads, and in maintaining the free transit of persons and goods.

3. That they may aid the public service of administrative departments of the Government; and especially that they may to an important extent prevent the infraction of the laws of the Excise and Customs, and thereby increase the revenue.

IX. Having inquired as to the mode in which such a force should be appointed, and the probable expense, we find–

1. That it is essential for the efficiency and attainment of all compatible services from a constabulary force,–first, that the constables should be trained, or appointed from a trained force, secondly, that neither by appointment nor otherwise should they be privately connected with the district in which they act, thirdly, that they should at periods be changed from district to district, fourthly, that whilst they should act under local direction for the performance of various local and administrative duties, for the repression of the practices of migratory depredators, vagrancy, and offences which concern the community at large more than the particular locality, they must act under general rules and principles, and in subordination to general directions from one general and responsible executive authority.

2. That such a trained and moveable force, under general and responsible direction, will produce greater advantages than at least double the number of untrained, irremoveable constables, acting more expensively under separate, independent, and voluntary, or untrained and irresponsible direction.

3. That the expense of a general and uniform force, which we believe would be adequate to the attainment of these objects, would be under half a million sterling per annum.

4. That the saving from the services of such a force would be considerable; that, independently of the saving to individuals of the greater proportion of the money or produce now taken by habitual depredators, there would be much saving effected on upwards of two millions of money, now expended chiefly in the cost of repression and of punishment in various ways, amongst others in the maintenance of delinquents in gaols, in transports, and in the penal colonies, as well as in the prevention of frauds upon the revenue.

5. That much time, which we cannot accurately determine, would be required to obtain proper persons and fit them by training for the proper discharge of their duties, and to organize an efficient trained force.

6. That the only available district or trained force that can at present be obtained is the new Metropolitan Police force.

7. That the great majority of instances, or nearly all, of the successful trial of a paid constabulary force, have been instances where trained men have been obtained from the Metropolitan Police force, comprehending about 200 instances in towns and rural districts.

We therefore propose–

I. That as a primary remedy for the evils set forth, a paid constabulary force should be trained, appointed, and organized on the principles of management recognized by the legislature in the appointment of the new metropolitan police force.

II. That for this purpose on application in writing, under the hands and seals of a majority of the justices assembled at any quarter sessions of the peace for the county, setting forth the insecurity of person and property, and the want of paid constables, the commissioners of police shall, with the approbation of the Secretary of State for the Home Department, direct a sufficient number of constables and such officers as may, upon such examination as the said commissioners shall make or direct, be by them deemed adequate for the due protection of life or protection of life or property within the county.

III. That force shall be paid one-fourth from the consolidated fund and three-fourths from the county rates, as a part of the general expenses of the whole county.

IV. That the constables so appointed shall report their proceedings to the magistrates of the quarter and petty sessions where they are stationed.

V. That the superintendents shall be subject to dismissal upon the representation of the justices of the peace in quarter sessions, and that the serjeants and constables shall be subject to dismissal upon the representation of the justices of the peace in petty sessions.

VI. That the magistrates shall frame rules and regulations for the service of process and attendance at petty or quarter sessions of such force, which rules shall be submitted to the Secretary of State, and, if approved by him, shall be binding.

VII. That the commissioners shall frame rules and regulations for the general management of the police, which rules shall, on the approbation of the Secretary of State, be binding.

The principles embodied in our recommendations being based on extensive experience, we feel confident that however they may for a time be impeded by adverse interests, these interests and the prejudices engendered by them will yield before the light of future experience which will lead to the ultimate adoption of measures on the principles of those we propose. If one uniform and trained force be efficiently directed to the prevention or repression of crime we cannot doubt of success.

We can find no solid grounds for the supposition often entertained that a large amount of crime is a necessary evil incidental to the present condition of society, and that the most ignorant and base of the community may defeat the exertions of a well appointed agency instituted for the repression of their crimes.

The appointment of a proper force for the prevention or repression of crimes has sometimes been viewed with apprehension on the supposition that such a force might be used to impair the political liberty of the subject.

If we were to admit that a diminution instead of an increase of the political liberty of the subject were the probable consequence of the establishment of an efficient constabulary force, we should nevertheless be prepared to show that the evils we have found in existence in some districts and the abject subjection of the population to fears which may be termed a state of slavery, which the objectors would endure from a groundless fear of loss of liberty, form a condition much worse in all respects than any condition that could be imposed by any government that could exist in the present state of society in this country. We do not believe that in this country any government could possibly exist which subjected the people to domiciliary attacks and to have their houses broken open and plundered, and their lives endangered at night, or which caused a large proportion of the population to abstain from travelling singly after dark for fear of being put in danger of their lives and stripped of their property by armed men,–which allowed its agents to pillage or maltreat the unfortunate people wrecked on the coasts, or which generally inflicted such evils as are now inflicted by upwards of 40,000 thieves, robbers, or marauding hordes of various descriptions, against whom the honest in almost every part of the country have been driven to associate for self-defence. Neither do we see any motives which could induce any government in these times to impose political restraints so oppressive or so mischievous on any industrious community as we find imposed by illegal means on the manufacturing population of the city of Norwich and other parts of the kingdom; nor do we believe that by any form of the abuse of the powers of a government it could use any agency such as secret committees have employed in the manufacturing districts to coerce the honest and industrious, but peaceable, to purposes injurious to them, by actual murder or the fear of life or maiming, or the threats of such fire and pillage as were displayed in the burning of the city of Bristol.

The apprehensions expressed of danger to the liberty of the subject from the institution of a preventive police are usually supported by reference to institutions having that name on the continent; but we believe it will be found that the notions prevalent as to the state and operations of such institutions are even more erroneous than those we have found prevalent on the state of the penal administration in this country. We believe it will be found that the police force in a neighbouring country, which has been referred to as a preventive police, is in no proper sense in sound theory or in actual practice preventive; and that it has had none of the chief effects popularly attributed to it. Although organized for political purposes, to the neglect, as we believe, of the main purposes of a preventive police–the protection of private individuals in the enjoyment of their rights against infractions by depredators or others,–it has not saved the various governments which have depended on it, if any have; and in all large movements by the whole of the community it has been disregarded or thrown aside as of no serious account. The trained force which we propose is of little more than one constable to 2,000 inhabitants;–a force three or four times more numerous than that we propose were absurd as a means of constraining the whole community to any course which they felt to be inimical to them.

What such a force might do with the tacit consent of the community, and what we believe to be most important for the liberty of the subject it should do, is to enforce the laws for the suppression of conspiracies, riots, or dangerous violences, by which ignorant or fanatical, or rapacious minorities may seek their ends. Without the assent or aid of the community, that is to say, without information from the people, a police or constabulary force cannot perform properly even its ordinary duties.

The safe course for maintaining the freedom of the subject appears to us to be, not to render the authorities impotent, but to make them strictly responsible for the use of the power with which they may be invested for the public service. The securities respecting which the greatest anxiety should be manifested, are the securities that the power which the Legislature may confer for the general advantage shall be fully used. The great mass of evil indicated in our Report is ascribable not to the abuse, but to the neglect and disuse of beneficial powers. The chief and proper objection, as we conceive, to the police forces abroad are, that they act on powers which are arbitrary: the force which we propose could only act on powers which are legal, and for which they would be responsible to the courts of law, and ultimately to the Parliament.

What has been done partially in particular places, may be done generally and more completely throughout the country, by the more efficient application of the like means. If a constabulary force were well appointed and trained on a uniform system, and were placed under trained and responsible direction for the whole county, it would, we are assured, soon enable Your Majesty's subjects to sleep under a feeling of security from midnight plunder and violence; it would give protection to the industrious classes in the enjoyment of property, and by enhancing its value create additional motives to industry and frugality; it would give freedom and security to travellers on the roads, and humane succour to natives, and hospitality to strangers thrown by shipwreck on our coasts; it would free the country from mendicancy and vagrancy, and the various evils that follow in their course; it would free the industry of the manufacturing labourers and increase the inducements to the investment of capital by protecting them from lawless violence; it would tend to secure the people from the alarms and dangers of riotous disturbances of the peace, by affording a powerful means of repressing them without the risk of military execution and bloodshed, without putting hostile parties in array against each other, without endangering animosities by arming neighbour to conflict with neighbour, and master with servant; all this, and much more beneficent service it might be made to render at an immediate expense of less than one-fourth of the sum recently saved by one amendment in local administration; or, as we feel confident, all these great objects may be accomplished with an ultimate saving of the whole expense from upwards of two millions of money, now chiefly expended on what have been proved before Committees of both Houses of Parliament, and pronounced by them to be, ineffective or demoralizing systems of punishment.

All which we now humbly certify to Your Majesty.

(Signed) (L.S.) CHARLES SHAW LEFEVRE.

Whitehall Place, (L.S.) CHARLES ROWAN.

March 27, 1839. (L.S.) EDWIN CHADWICK.

196. County and District Constabulary Act (1839)

Statutes of the Realm, 2 & 3 Vict. c. 93.

. . . In all Cases where it should be made to appear to any Two or more Justices of the Peace of any County, Riding, or Division having a separate Commission of the Peace, or to any Two or more Justices of the Peace of any Liberty, Franchise, City, or Town in England or Wales, upon the Oath of any credible Witness, that any Tumult, Riot, or Felony had taken place or might be reasonably apprehended in any Parish, Township, or Place situate within the Division or Limits for which the said respective Justices usually act, and such Justices should be of opinion that the ordinary Officers appointed for preserving the Peace are not sufficient for the Protection of the Inhabitants and the Security of the Property in any such Parish, Township, or Place as aforesaid, then and in every such Case such Justices, or any Two or more Justices acting for the same Division or Limits, are thereby authorized to nominate and appoint, by Precept in Writing under their Hands, so many as they should think fit of the Householders or other Persons (not legally exempt from serving the Office of Constable) residing in such Parish, Township, or Place as aforesaid, or in the Neighbourhood thereof, to act as Special Constables for such Time and in such Manner as to the said Justices respectively should seem fit and necessary, for the Preservation of the Public Peace, and for the Protection of the Inhabitants, and the Security of the Property in such Parish, Township, or Place: And whereas the Powers of Justices of the Peace for making such Appointments as aforesaid were enlarged by an Act passed in the Sixth Year of the same Reign, intituled *An Act for enlarging the Powers of Magistrates in the Appointment of Special Constables*: And whereas it is expedient that the Powers of the said Justices for appointing Constables be further enlarged, and that Powers be given for charging the Expences of paying such Constables upon the several Divisions in which they shall be appointed: Be it therefore enacted by the Queen's most Excellent Majesty, by and with the Advice and Consent of the Lords Spiritual and Temporal, and Commons, in this present Parliament assembled, and by the Authority of the same, That in all Cases where it shall be made to appear to the Justices of the Peace of any County in England or Wales in General or Quarter Sessions assembled, or at any Adjournment thereof, that the ordinary Officers appointed for preserving the Peace are not sufficient for the Preservation of the Peace, and for the Protection of the Inhabitants, and for the Security of Property within the County, it shall be lawful for them to set forth the same, by a Report in Writing under the Hands of the Majority of the Justices there present, and to declare how many Constables are needed in their Opinion to be appointed within their County for the Purposes aforesaid, and the Rates of Payment which it would be expedient to pay to the chief and other Constables; and every such Report shall be sent to one of Her Majesty's Principal Secretaries of State. . . .

3. And whereas it is expedient that the Rules for the Government, Pay, Clothing, and Accoutrements and Necessaries of such Constables as may be appointed under this Act be uniform, as nearly as may be; be it enacted, That such Rules shall be from Time to Time made by one of Her Majesty's Principal Secretaries of State, but not

so as to increase the Number of Men proposed to be appointed; and the Rules so made shall be sent to the Clerk of the Peace for each County in which or in any Division of which this Act shall be in operation; and it shall be lawful for the Secretary of State, upon the Representation of the Justices of the County, setting forth any special Reasons, to amend or add to such Rules so as to make them applicable to the special Circumstances of such County; and all such Rules shall be binding on all Persons whom they may concern; and Copies of all such Rules shall be laid before both Houses of Parliament within Six Weeks after the making thereof, if Parliament is then sitting, and if Parliament is not sitting then within Six Weeks after the next meeting of Parliament.

4. And be it enacted, That as soon as any such Rules, as finally settled, shall have been received from the Secretary of State, the Justices of the County in General or Quarter Session assembled, or at any Adjournment thereof, shall, subject to the Approval of the Secretary of State, appoint a Person duly qualified according to the Rules to be Chief Constable of the County, and in every Case of Vacancy of the Office shall, subject to the like Approval, appoint another fit Person in his Room; and every Chief Constable so to be appointed may hold his Office until dismissed by the Justices in General or Quarter Session assembled, or at any Adjournment thereof: Provided always, that when any County shall have been divided for the Purpose of returning Members to serve in Parliament for each Division, it shall be lawful to appoint Two Chief Constables for such County, if the Justices of such County shall think fit: Provided also, that it shall be lawful to appoint the same Chief Constable for Two or more adjoining Counties or Parts of Counties, if the Justices of such Counties in General or Quarter Session assembled shall mutually agree to join in such Appointment. . . .

6. And be it enacted, That, subject to the Approval of Two or more of the Justices of the County in Petty Sessions assembled, the Chief Constable shall appoint the other Constables to be appointed for the County, and a Superintendent to be at the Head of the Constables in each Division of the County, and at his Pleasure may dismiss all or any of them, and shall have the general Disposition and Government of all the Constables so to be appointed, subject to such lawful Orders as he may receive from the Justices in General or Quarter Session assembled, or at any Adjournment thereof, and to the Rules established for the Government of the Force. . . .

10. And be it enacted, That all chief or other Constables appointed under this Act shall be restrained from employing themselves in any Office or Employment for Hire or Gain other than in the Execution of their Duties under this Act, and shall be exempt from being returned and from serving upon any Juries or Inquests whatsoever, or in the Militia, nor shall they be inserted in any Jury Lists while they shall continue to be such Constables. . . .

17. And be it enacted, That every Chief Constable, unless prevented by sufficient Cause, shall attend every General and Quarter Session of the Justices of the County, and at every Adjournment thereof, and shall make quarterly Reports to the Justices of all Matters which they shall require of him concerning the Police of the County, and shall obey all lawful Orders and Warrants of the said Justices in the Execution of

his Duty; and that the Superintendents of Divisions shall in like Manner attend every Session of the Justices holden for their respective Divisions, and shall make the like Reports to the Justices of such Divisions.

197. Parish Constables Act (1842)

Statutes of the Realm, 5 & 6 Vict. c. 109.

"Whereas it will increase the Security of Persons and Property if further Provision be made for the Appointment of fit Persons to act as Constables in the several Parishes of England, and if Power be given to pay them for the Performance of their Duties;" be it therefore enacted by the Queen's most Excellent Majesty, by and with the Advice and Consent of the Lords Spiritual and Temporal, and Commons, in this present Parliament assembled, and by the Authority of the same, That after the Expiration of Eighty Days and before the Expiration of One hundred Days next after the passing of this Act, and on some Day after the Twenty-fourth Day of March and before the Ninth Day of April in each following Year, the Justices of the Peace of every County in England shall hold a Special Petty Session of the Peace in their several Divisions for the Appointment of Parochial Constables, of which Session due Notice shall be given to every Justice usually acting in that Division.

2. And be it enacted, That the Justices shall, within Thirty Days next after the passing of this Act, and within the first Seven Days of February in each following Year, issue a Precept, under the Hands of any Two of them, to the Overseers of each Parish within the Division, requiring them to make out and return, within Eighty Days next after the passing of this Act and before the Twenty-fourth Day of March in each following Year, a List in Writing of a competent Number of Men within their respective Parishes qualified and liable to serve as Constables, and also to perform all other Requisitions in the said Precepts contained; and with the said Precept shall be given Notice to the said Overseers of the Time and Place where such Special Session of the Peace as aforesaid will be holden.

3. And be it enacted, That the Overseers of every Parish, upon the Receipt of such Precept, shall summon a Meeting of the Inhabitants in Vestry to be holden within Fourteen Days after the Receipt of the said Precept; and the Vestry at such Meeting shall make out a List in Writing of such Number as shall be named in the Precept of Men residing within their Parish who shall be qualified and liable to serve as Constables, with the Christian Name and Surname, and with the true Place of Abode, the Title, Quality, Calling, or Business of each, written at full Length: Provided also, that it shall be lawful for the Vestry to annex to the said Return the Names of any Number of Men willing to serve the Office of Constable, and whom the Vestry will recommend to be appointed, although not having the Qualification herein-after mentioned. . . .

5. And be it enacted, That every able-bodied Man resident within the said Parish, between the Ages of Twenty-five Years and Fifty-five Years, rated to the Relief of the Poor, or to the County Rate, on any Tenements of the net yearly Value of Four Pounds or upwards, except such Persons as shall be exempt or disqualified as herein-after mentioned, shall be qualified and liable to serve as Constable of that Parish. . . .

11. And be it enacted, That when any List shall have been allowed the Justices shall choose from the allowed List the Names of such Number of Persons as they shall deem necessary (having regard to the Extent and Population of the Parish) to act as Constables within the Parish during the Year then next following, and until other Constables shall be chosen and sworn to act in their Stead as Constables for such Parish: Provided always, that where any Person shall have been chosen to serve, and shall have served, the Office of Constable, either in Person or by Substitute, as herein-after provided, he shall not be liable to be again chosen until every other Person in the Parish liable and qualified to serve shall have also served the Office of Constable, either in Person or by Substitute. . . .

18. And be it enacted, That it shall be lawful for the Vestry assembled for the Purpose of making such Return as aforesaid to resolve that one or more paid Constables shall be appointed for their Parish; and if the Vestry shall so resolve a Copy of the Resolution, and of the Amount of Salary which the Vestry shall resolve on paying to such Constable or Constables, shall be sent by the Overseers to the Justices, with the Return herein-before mentioned.

19. And be it enacted, That the Justices at the Session of the Peace holden for the Appointment of Constables, upon receiving from any Parish a Copy of any such Resolution as aforesaid, if they shall be satisfied with the Amount of Salary agreed to be paid, shall appoint so many paid Constables to act for the Parish as shall be agreed to by the Resolution, or if the same Resolution shall have been agreed to by more Parishes than one adjoining each other, may, if they shall think fit, appoint the same paid Constable to act conjointly for all such last-named Parishes; and in every Parish in which a paid Constable shall be appointed under this Act, the Justices, if they shall think fit, need not appoint any unpaid Constable, or may appoint a smaller number of unpaid Constables than they had otherwise resolved on appointing for that Parish; and every such Constable shall hold his appointment till he shall resign or be dismissed for misconduct by the Justices of the Division in Petty Sessions assembled, or until the Vestry shall rescind the Resolution for his appointment at any Meeting of the Vestry holden for making such return as aforesaid.

20. And be it enacted, That the amount of the Salary to every such paid Constable shall be paid by the Overseers out of any Monies in their hands collected for the Relief of the Poor. . . .

22. And be it enacted, That it shall be lawful for the Justices of the Peace in any County in General or Quarter Sessions assembled, if they shall think fit, to order that Lock-up Houses for the temporary Confinement of Persons taken into Custody by the Constable, and not yet committed for Trial, or in Execution of any Sentence, shall be provided in such Places within the County as the Justices shall think fit . . . or instead of providing new Lock-up Houses, to order that the Lock-up Houses, Strong Rooms, or Cages belonging to any Parish be appropriated for the Purposes of this Act, and if necessary be enlarged or improved, and the Expense of building, hiring, or otherwise providing, repairing and furnishing such Lock-up Houses shall be defrayed out of the County Rates: Provided always . . . that no such Lock-up House shall be built or otherwise provided enlarged or improved, except upon such Place as shall be

approved by one of Her Majesty's Principal Secretaries of State; Provided also that every such Lock-up shall be within the inspection of Her Majesty's Inspectors of Prisons.

23. And be it enacted, That whenever the Justices shall have provided a Lock-up House under this Act, they shall also appoint a Superintending Constable to have the Charge thereof, who shall have all the Powers and Immunities of a Parish Constable under this Act, and shall have the Superintendance of the Parish Constables appointed in such Parishes as shall be ordered by the Said Justices, and under such Regulations as they shall make; and every such Superintending Constable shall be entitled to hold his Office until dismissed by the Justices in General or Quarter Sessions assembled, and shall receive such Salary out of the County Rates as the Justices assembled as aforesaid shall order.

198. Select Committee on County Rates and Expenditure Bill (1850)

Parlty. Papers, 1850/XIII.

THE SELECT COMMITTEE to whom the COUNTY RATES AND EXPENDITURE BILL was referred, and who were empowered to Report their Opinion, together with the Minutes of Evidence taken before them, to The House:–HAVE considered the said Bill, and have taken some evidence thereon.

The Committee have agreed that the first Clause should stand part of the Bill, which Clause is as follows:

"Be it enacted by the Queen's Most Excellent Majesty, by and with the Advice and Consent of the Lords Spiritual and Temporal, and Commons, in this present Parliament assembled, and by the Authority of the same, as follows, That a County Financial Board, for the purposes hereinafter mentioned, shall be established in every County throughout England and Wales, and every County Financial Board shall consist of such number of Members as is hereinafter directed to be elected, and such Members shall be elected at the times and in the manner hereinafter prescribed: Provided always, that each of the three Ridings of the County of York, and each of the Parts or Divisions of Lindsey and Kesteven and Holland in the County of Lincoln, shall, for the purposes of electing such County Financial Board, and for the other purposes of this Act, be deemed to be a distinct and separate County."

The Committee have negatived all the subsequent Clauses of the Bill, and have not provided any mode in which County Financial Boards are to be constituted, and have not invested such Boards with any of the Financial Powers now exercised by County Magistrates.

The Committee have also negatived the Preamble of the Bill.

The Committee have, further, to Report the following RESOLUTIONS to the House.

Resolved,–

1. THAT the Evidence which has been given before this Committee has tended to prove that the Financial Affairs of Counties have been conducted by the Courts of Quarter Sessions, generally, with proper attention to economy, with just regard to the public interests, and with all the publicity required by law.

2. THAT in those Counties in which the conduct of the Magistrates in the administration of Financial business has been proved to have caused dissatisfaction, that feeling

appears principally to have arisen either from the adoption of the Rural Police, in which case further experience of the utility of that force has either mitigated or removed the disposition to complain; or, from the cost of erecting or enlarging Gaols and Lunatic Asylums, in which cases the Magistrates have necessarily increased for a time the pressure of County Rates, only in the fulfilment of public duties, prescribed by Acts of the Legislature.

3. THAT, although forms of petition appear to have been sent to every Board of Guardians for their adoption, and that at a time when the circumstances of the country have rendered Rate-payers in rural districts peculiarly sensible of the burden of local taxation, the number of Petitions to the Legislature in favour of the Bill does not appear to this Committee to have been such as to prove that any general desire prevails in the country for this measure.

4. THAT the effect of the Bill would be to exclude a numerous body of gentlemen in every county in England, from the transaction of Financial business in which as Magistrates and Proprietors, they have immediate and extensive interest, and which, under the authority of successive Statutes, they and their predecessors have conducted for a long period of time to the advantage, and generally to the satisfaction of the public, and to substitute for them a small and fluctuating body of men, who would in many cases be less fitted for the discharge of such duties, and who would individually have a much less degree of pecuniary interest in the counties in which they live.

5. THAT this Committee is of opinion, that if the management of County Finances were transferred to Boards so constituted, there would be serious risk of injury and impediment to the public service, without any equivalent advantage.

6. THAT this Committee cannot recommend The House to adopt a Bill which they consider to be open to such grave objections.

7. THAT if it should be thought desirable to give a more popular constitution to the authority by which County Finances are administered, there is so much difficulty in determining the best mode of effecting that object, the details which it involves are so complicated, and the interests concerned are so important, that, in the opinion of this Committee, the arrangement of such a change ought to be undertaken by Her Majesty's Government.

8. THAT the Evidence which this Committee has received, has led them to the conclusion, that improvements might be effected in the present mode of transacting the Financial business of Counties, some of which would require Legislative Enactments.

9. THAT economy of County Rates would be promoted, if Clerks of the Peace were remunerated for their services by fixed Salaries instead of by Fees, and the duties of their office would in such case be as well, if not better discharged.

10. THAT notices of the Financial and other business to be transacted at each Quarter Sessions for Counties, ought to be previously advertised in the County Newspapers for two or more weeks, for the information of the Rate-payers at large, and copies of Annual Financial statements ought to be distributed to every Union within each County, for circulation.

11. THAT the Financial Accounts of Counties ought to be annually audited by

some efficient and responsible officer, and the right of inspecting all Vouchers and Accounts of Public Expenditure ought, under regulations, to be given to the Ratepayers.

20 June 1850.

199. Select Committee on Police in Counties and Boroughs (1852–1853)

Parlty. Papers, 1852–1853/xxxvi.
Second Report of the Committee, pp. 163–164.

THE SELECT COMMITTEE appointed to consider the expediency of adopting a more Uniform System of Police in England and Wales, and in Scotland, and who were empowered to report their Opinion, together with the Minutes of Evidence taken before them, to the House;–HAVE further considered the Matters to them referred, and have agreed to report the following RESOLUTIONS, together with MINUTES of EVIDENCE.

Resolved, 1. THAT the Acts for the appointment of District Constables (2 & 3 Vict. c. 93, and 3 & 4 Vict. c. 88), commonly called the Rural Police Act, has (from the permissive character of its enactments), failed to provide such a general and uniform Constabulary Force as, in the opinion of Your Committee, is essentially required for the prevention of crime and security of property.

Resolved, 2. That in the districts in which the Rural Police Act has been adopted, its efficiency for the prevention of crime, by rendering the detection and apprehension of offenders more prompt and certain, has been proved to the satisfaction of Your Committee; that it has tended to the maintenance of order, and the improved habits of the population; that vagrancy has greatly decreased, and, more especially in combination with the casual relief order of the Poor Law Board, has been, in some places, almost entirely suppressed; and the effectual protection afforded to property peculiarly exposed to depredation, has, in the opinion of owners and holders of land, rendered its occupation more desirable. The adoption of the Rural Police, therefore, in the opinion of Your Committee, has proved highly advantageous to those districts, whether tested by moral, social or economical considerations.

Resolved, 3. That the Superintending Constables appointed under the 5th & 6th Vict. c. 109, have proved useful as Police Officers, to the extent of their individual exertions and services within their respective divisions, but that the appointment of a Superintending Constable in each petty sessional division provides no remedy for the inefficiency of Parochial Constables; and it is the opinion of Your Committee that any system of Police mainly dependent on the aid of Parochial Constables, must prove ineffectual for the protection of property, more especially that of the poorer classes, for the prompt detection and pursuit of offenders, the maintenance of order, and other duties of a Police Force, for which their necessary avocations and local connexions entirely disqualify them.

Resolved, 4. That the actual cost of the Rural Police Force is ascertainable by the ratepayers, while the great aggregate saving effected by it is not so generally known or appreciated. That it is, on the other hand, difficult to ascertain the full extent of the indirect and undefined expense of the Parochial Constables: it has, however, been proved to Your Committee, that it greatly exceeds the amount at which it is generally estimated.

Resolved, 5. That where the population of separate districts within the same county differs in amount and in the character of its employments, and consequently in its requirements for a Police Force, an equitable adjustment of the Police rate to meet those cases should be provided for by enactment, and that such an arrangement would tend to remove the objections now partially entertained against the adoption of the Rural Police Act.

Resolved, 6. That the efficiency of all existing Police Forces is materially impaired by the want of co-operation between the Rural Constabulary and the Police under the control of the authorities of boroughs, or other local jurisdictions. That, in order to secure that co-operation which uniformity can alone afford, Your Committee are of opinion, that the smaller boroughs should be consolidated with districts or counties for Police purposes, and that the Police in the larger boroughs should be under a similar system of management and control to that of the adjoining district or county, and (where practicable) under the same superintendence, by which arrangement a considerable saving would be effected in the general expenditure.

Resolved, 7. That, taking into consideration the aid afforded (hitherto partially and gratuitously) by the Rural Police for the protection of the revenue, the valuable services it has rendered for the maintenance of order, and in promoting the observance of the laws, in reducing the cost of prosecutions, and the effectual protection it gives to life and property of every description, by which the holders of a large amount of property not contributing to the Police Rate are greatly benefited, it is the opinion of Your Committee that it is a matter worthy of the consideration of The House whether some aid should not be afforded by the Government towards defraying the cost of an improved and extended system of Police, without essentially interfering with the local management of that Force.

Resolved, 8. That it is the opinion of Your Committee, that it is most desirable that legislative measures should be introduced without delay by Her Majesty's Government, rendering the adoption of an efficient Police Force on a uniform principle imperative throughout Great Britain.

5 July 1853.

200. Royal Commission on the Corporation of London (1854)

Parlty. Papers, 1854/XXVI.

Now, as the City of London is not enumerated in the schedules to the Municipal Corporations Act, neither its internal constitution, nor its boundaries have been affected by the provision of that Act. The position of the Corporation of London is indeed so peculiar as to render its comprehension in a general measure of municipal regulation a matter of extreme difficulty, and to point it out as a fit subject for special and separate legislation. The antiquity, extent, and importance of its privileges, the long series of its charters, the large amount of its revenues, its metropolitan position, and its historical associations, combine to give it a character different from that of any other municipal borough. It may be added that the continued predominance of the popular element in the formation of its governing body furnished a reason in 1835 for excepting it from the Municipal Corporations Act; seeing that one of the principal defects which that Act was intended to remedy, was the practical exclusion of the principle of popular election from the government of the borough, and the accumulation of power in the hands of a small body of persons. The Commissioners state in their general report of 1835, "The most common and most striking defect in the constitution of the municipal corporations of England and Wales, is that the corporate bodies exist independently of the communities among which they are found. The corporations look upon themselves, and are considered by the inhabitants, as separate and exclusive bodies; they have powers and privileges within the towns and cities from which they are named, but in most places all identity of interest between the corporation and the inhabitants has disappeared." From the defect described in this passage the Corporation of London has for many years been exempt. The manner in which the Common Council is elected has produced to a great extent an identity of interests between the governing municipal body and the existing municipal community, and has secured to the latter a council representing their general opinions and feelings. The Municipal Commissioners particularly advert to the Common Council of London as distinguishing that Corporation from the close corporations which then prevailed throughout the country. . . .

The Municipal Corporations Act has now been the law of the land for nearly twenty years; all the important municipal corporations in England are subject to its provisions, and it appears on the whole to have been attended with beneficial effects, and to have given satisfaction to the country. Upon a consideration of these facts, we have come to the conclusion that, in revising the constitution of the Corporation of London, it will be advisable to apply to it the leading provisions of that statute, making, at the same time, due allowance for those peculiar circumstances already adverted to, which distinguish the London Corporation from other corporations, and which render a difference of institutions, in certain respects, expedient.

In laying down this principle, however, for our guidance, we are desirous of limiting its application to the constitution of the Corporation. That portion of the Municipal Corporations Act which consists in an extension of the boundaries of the borough so as to comprehend all portions of the town and its suburbs lying beyond the old limits, seems to us inapplicable to the case of the metropolis. If the procedure of the legislature in the Municipal Corporations Act were taken as a precedent, absolutely and without discrimination, in reforming the London Corporation, it would be necessary, not only to alter its constitution but to advance the present boundaries of the City until they surrounded the entire metropolis; a process by which an area of 723 acres would be converted into an area of 78,029 acres, – by which a population of 129,128 would be converted into a population of 2,362,236, – and an assessment of 953,110 l. would be converted into an assessment of 9,964,348 l. A change of this magnitude would not only alter the whole character of the City

Corporation, but it would, as it seems to us, defeat the main purpose of municipal institutions. London, taken in its full extent, is (as it has with literal truth been called) a province covered with houses; its diameter from north to south and from east to west is so great that the persons living at its furthest extremities have few interests in common; its area is so large that each inhabitant is in general acquainted only with his own quarter, and has no minute knowledge of other parts of the town. Hence the two first conditions for municipal government, minute local knowledge and community of interests, would be wanting, if the whole of London were, by an extension of the present boundaries of the City, placed under a single municipal corporation. The enormous numbers of the population and the vast magnitude of the interests which would be under the care of the municipal body would likewise render its administration a work of great difficulty. It may be added that the bisection of London by the Thames furnishes an additional reason for not placing the whole town under a single municipal corporation. All roads, streets, sewers, gas-pipes, and water pipes, in short, all means of superficial or subterraneous communication which run in continuous lines from north to south, are necessarily stopped by the river. Many of these are directly or indirectly the subjects of municipal control; and therefore a municipal body which governed the metropolis both north and south of the Thames would find that the continuity of its operations was, in many respects, broken off by natural circumstances. These considerations appear to us decisive against the expediency of placing the whole of the metropolis under a single municipal corporation, without adverting to those more general questions of public policy which naturally suggest themselves in connexion with the subject. . . .

With the single exception of London, the local government of every considerable town in the United Kingdom is vested in a municipal corporation. This government is not confined to a portion of the town, but, since the recent statutory reforms, comprehends its entire circuit. In London, however, as we have already seen, the municipal government extends over only a small portion of the entire town, whether measured by area or by population. If it were held that municipal institutions were not suited to a metropolitan city, no reason could be found, except its antiquity and existence, for maintaining the Corporation of London, even with its present limited area. It appears to us, however, that a metropolitan city requires, for its own local purposes, municipal institutions not less than other towns. We believe, indeed, that the utility of municipal institutions is greater, and their want more felt, in a large, populous, opulent, and crowded metropolis, than in a country town of less size, population, and wealth. Those functions of local government, moreover, which in other towns are performed by the municipal authorities, are, in the metropolis, actually discharged by parochial functionaries, or by boards created by local acts, though they may be discharged in a less uniform and efficient manner. In some cases, indeed, in the parishes on the outskirts of the metropolis, they may, from a want of powers in the general law, be left for a time altogether unprovided for, to the serious inconvenience of the inhabitants, and to the permanent injury of the owners of property within the district. We may refer to the evidence of a deputation of the vestry of St. Pancras, appended to our Report, as illustrating the evils which now arise in large parishes where new building is in progress on a large scale, from the absence of an efficient municipal organization, applicable to new portions of the town as they successively spring into existence.

Although the City of London is the only part of the metropolis which possesses a municipal organization, there are at present within the metropolitan district seven Parliamentary boroughs, each of which, with the exception of Greenwich, contains a larger number of inhabited houses, and a larger population than the City, as appears from the subjoined statement.

HOUSES AND POPULATION IN 1851 IN THE METROPOLITAN BOROUGHS

Boroughs	*Inhabited houses*	*Population*
Finsbury	37,427	323,772
Marylebone	40,513	370,957
Tower Hamlets . . .	75,710	539,111
Westminster	24,755	241,611
Lambeth	39,154	251,345
Southwark	23,751	172,863
Greenwich	15,401	105,784

	Inhabited houses	*Population*
City of London . . .	14,693	109,128

Of those seven boroughs five received the right of returning members to Parliament under the Reform Act of 1832, and we concur in the opinion expressed by the Lord Mayor, in his evidence given before our Commission, that "as the legislature has already decided to enfranchise other portions of the metropolis as Parliamentary boroughs, the legislature ought to complete the work by enfranchising them for municipal purposes also" (Question 7,196). We think, indeed, that if an attempt were made to give a municipal organization to the entire metropolis, by a wider extension of the present boundaries of the City, the utility of the present Corporation, as an institution suited to its present limited area, would be destroyed; while, at the same time, a municipal administration of an excessive magnitude, and therefore ill adapted to the wants of the other parts of the metropolis, would be created. But we see no reason why the benefit of municipal institutions should not be extended to the rest of the metropolis, by its division into municipal districts, each possessing a municipal government of its own. What the form of this government should be, and what should be the number or extent of the districts, are questions not lying within the scope of our Commission, and upon which we are not competent to express any opinion. We recommend, at the same time, that the slight municipal connexion which now subsists between Southwark and the City of London be dissevered; and that some small spaces included within the external boundaries of the City, but not forming a part of it, be annexed to it. . . .

Recommendations: . . .

27. That the external boundaries of the City remain unchanged; but that the municipal connexion, between the Corporation of London and a part of the borough of Southwark be abolished.

28. That the rest of the metropolis be divided into districts for municipal purposes.

29. That in the event of such division being made, a Metropolitan Board of Works be created, composed of members deputed to it from the council of each metropolitan municipal body, including the Common Council of the City.

30. That the coal duties now collected by the Corporation of London, so long as they remain in force, be under the administration of this Board; and that in case the coal duties which expire in 1862 should not be renewed, the 4d. duty now levied on behalf of the City should cease at the same time.

31. That this Board be empowered to levy a rate, limited to a fixed poundage, for public works of general metropolitan utility, over the metropolitan district.

32. That no works be executed by the Board unless the plans have been approved by a Committee of the Privy Council.

We have thus endeavoured, in obedience to Your Majesty's commands, to express our opinion of the present state of the Corporation of London, and of the changes in the existing system which appear to be required by considerations of public advantage. We desire to state that, although we have found much which in our judgment calls for amendment, yet we have discovered nothing which can affect injuriously the honour and integrity of the officers to whom the affairs of this great Corporation have been confided.

Some of the alterations which we have recommended will reduce the income of the Corporation, but others will, at the same time, relieve its burdens and diminish its expenditure. Again, some of the reforms which we have suggested will curtail its powers and privileges; but they will at the same time remove mischievous restraints upon trade and industry, and will abolish other institutions unsuited to our modern legislation. We trust that the changes in the constitution of the Corporation which we have indicated, and which are founded upon the recognized policy of the country with respect to municipal boroughs, will place it on a more solid and enlarged basis; and that the Corporation will continue, under an amended system, to possess abundant means not only for purposes of public usefulness, but also for the exercise of a decent hospitality and splendour. We may be permitted to add that, while we have abstained from recommending an extension of the boundaries of the City, by which it would include the entire metropolis, we have proposed such an arrangement as will enable the Corporation to form a part of a general metropolitan system.

201. Metropolis Local Management Act (1855)

Statutes of the Realm, 18 & 19 Vict. c. 120.

. . . A Board, to be called "The Metropolitan Board of Works," shall be constituted as herein-after mentioned, and such Board shall by such Name be a Body Corporate, and have perpetual Succession and a Common Seal, and sue and be sued, and have Power and Authority (without any Licence in Mortmain) to take, purchase, and hold Land for the Purposes of this Act. . . .

The Metropolitan Board of Works shall have Power to make, widen, or improve any Streets, Roads, or Ways, for facilitating the Passage and Traffic between different Parts of the Metropolis, or to contribute and join with any Persons in any such Improvements as aforesaid, and to take, by Agreement or by Gift, any Land, Rights in Land, or Property, for the Purposes aforesaid (or otherwise) for the Improvement of the Metropolis, on such Terms and Conditions as they may think fit; and such Board, where it appears to them that further Powers are required for the Purpose of any Work for the Improvement of the Metropolis or public Benefit of the Inhabitants thereof, may make Applications to Parliament for that Purpose, and the Expenses of such Application may be defrayed as other Expenses of the said Board: Provided always, that before the Metropolitan Board of Works commence any such Works, the estimated Expense whereof shall exceed Fifty thousand Pounds, the Plan of such Works, together with an Estimate of the Cost of carrying the same into execution, shall be submitted by such Board to the Commissioners of Her Majesty's Works and Public Buildings; and no such Plan shall be carried into effect until the same has been approved by such Commissioners; and no such Works shall be commenced in Cases where the Expense thereof shall exceed the Sum of One hundred thousand Pounds, without the previous Sanction of Parliament.

202. Police in Counties and Boroughs Act (1856)

Statutes of the Realm, 19 & 20 Vict. c. 69.

. . . In every County in which a Constabulary has not been already established for the whole of such County under the said Acts of the Second and Third and Third and Fourth Years of Her Majesty, or either of them, the Justices of such County at the General or Quarter Sessions holden next after the First Day of December One thousand eight hundred and fifty-six, shall proceed to establish a sufficient Police Force for the whole of such County, or where a Constabulary is already established in Part of such County then for the Residue of such County, and for that Purpose shall declare the Number of Constables they propose should be appointed, and the Rates of Pay which it would be expedient to pay to the Chief and other Constables, and shall report such their Proceedings to One of Her Majesty's Principal Secretaries of State; and upon the Receipt from the Secretary of State of such Rules as are mentioned in Section Three of the said Act of the Second and Third Years of Her Majesty, all the Provisions of the said Acts of the Second and Third and Third and Fourth Years of Her Majesty shall take effect and be applicable in relation to such County, in like Manner as by the said Acts provided, upon the Adoption of such Acts for any County by the Justices thereof, and the Receipt of such Rules as aforesaid from the Secretary of State, subject nevertheless to the Amendments contained in this Act. . . .

3. In any County where, after the Establishment, under the said Acts of Her Majesty or either of them, of a Constabulary for any Division or Divisions thereof, Constables have been or shall be appointed under such Acts and this Act, or any of them, for the Residue of the County, or for Divisions constituting together such Residue, there shall be One General County Police Establishment, and any Divisional Police Establishment or Establishments which may have been constituted in such County shall be consolidated with and form Part thereof, and a Chief Constable shall be appointed for such County, in like Manner and with the like Powers as in any Case where a Police Force is Established for the whole County in the first instance. . . .

15. It shall be lawful for Her Majesty, by Warrant under Her Royal Sign Manual, to appoint during Her Majesty's Pleasure Three Persons as Inspectors under this Act, to visit and inquire into the State and the Efficiency of the Police appointed for every County and Borough, and whether the Provisions of the Acts under which such Police are appointed are duly observed and carried into effect, and also into the State of the Police Stations, Charge Rooms, Cells, or Lock-ups, or other Premises occupied for the Use of such Police; and each of the Inspectors so appointed shall report generally upon such Matters to one of Her Majesty's Principal Secretaries of State, who shall cause such Reports to be laid before Parliament; and such Inspectors shall be paid, out of such Money as may be provided by Parliament for the Purpose, such Salaries and Allowances as shall be determined by the Commissioners of Her Majesty's Treasury.

16. Upon the Certificate of One of Her Majesty's Principal Secretaries of State, that the Police of any County or Borough established under the Provisions of the said Acts and this Act, or any of them, has been maintained in a State of Efficiency in point of Numbers and Discipline for the Year ending on the Twenty-ninth of September then last past, it shall be lawful for the Commissioners of Her Majesty's Treasury to pay from Time to Time, out of the Monies provided by Parliament for the Purpose, such Sum towards the Expenses of such Police for the Year mentioned in such Certificate as shall not exceed One Fourth of the Charge for their Pay and Clothing, but such Payment shall not extend to any additional Constables appointed under the Nineteenth Section of the said Act of the Third and Fourth Years of Her Majesty; provided that before any such Certificate shall be finally withheld in respect of the Police of any County or Borough, the Report of the Inspector relating to the Police of such County or Borough shall be sent to the Justices of such County, or to the Watch Committee of such Borough, who may address any Statement relating thereto to the Secretary of State; and in every Case in which such Certificate is withheld, a Statement of the Grounds on which the Secretary of State has withheld such Certificate, together with any such Statement of the Justices of Watch Committee as aforesaid, shall be laid before Parliament.

17. No such Sum as aforesaid shall be paid towards the Pay and Clothing of the Police of any Borough, not being consolidated with the Police of a County under the said Act of the Third and Fourth Years of Her Majesty, or this Act, the Population of which Borough according to the last Parliamentary Enumeration for the Time being does not exceed Five thousand.

203. Select Committee on County Financial Arrangements (1867–1868)

Parlty. Papers, 1867–1868/IX.

THE SELECT COMMITTEE appointed to inquire into the present mode of conducting the FINANCIAL ARRANGEMENTS of the COUNTIES in ENGLAND and WALES, and whether any Alteration ought to be made either in the Persons by whom, or the Manner in which, such Arrangements are now Conducted;–HAVE considered the matters to them referred, and have come to the following RESOLUTIONS, which they have agreed to Report to the House–

THAT it is the opinion of this Committee–

1. That it appears by the evidence given before the Committee, by persons residing in various counties of England,–

1st. That the administration of the financial business of Counties has been hitherto conducted by the magistrates with a general regard to economy.

2nd. That, nevertheless, a desire prevails on the part of county rate-payers to place the County Finance more directly under their own control, by means of elected representatives to be associated with the magistrates in the expenditure of the rate.

3rd. That this desire appears to arise generally from considerations of public policy, but also, in some instances, from a want of sufficiently detailed information as to county expenditure.

2. That this Committee, judging from the general tenour of the evidence, believes that a system of financial control, of which the following shall form the principal provisions, would be satisfactory to the rate-payers:

1st. That the Boards of Guardians in counties should elect representatives, who should be admitted to take part in and vote at all meetings of magistrates held in such counties for the consideration of questions of the county expenditure.

2nd. That in cases where a Poor Law Union is situated in more than one county, a representative may be elected in each county where there are at least six parishes or townships; and that where there is a less number, the parishes or townships should be added to the adjoining union for the purposes of election.

3rd. That committees appointed for the purpose of managing the finances of separate departments, should consist of an equal number of magistrates and representatives, each body electing its own members of such committees.

3. That this Committee is of opinion that the mode of keeping the public accounts should be uniform in all counties; that a detailed statement of them should be published in some newspaper of the county at least once in each year, and be forwarded to each Board of Guardians; and that some officer should be appointed for the Audit of Public Accounts.

4. That the clerk of the peace of every county shall be elected by the court of quarter sessions.

13 July 1868.

204. Goschen Report on local taxation (1870)

Parlty. Papers, 1870/LV.

. . . The investigation which I have undertaken appears to lead to the following general results:–

1. The increase in Local Taxation in England and Wales has been very great–less than in other countries, but, nevertheless, so considerable as to justify the especial attention which it has aroused.

2. Speaking broadly, the increase in Direct Local Taxes has been from 8,000,000 l. to 16,000,000 l.

3. The greater portion of this increase, at least 6,500,000 l., has fallen upon Urban, not upon Rural districts.

4. Of the total increase, 2,000,000 l. are due to the Poor Rate, 5,000,000 l. to Town Improvement Rates, and 1,000,000 l. to Police and Miscellaneous purposes.

5. The increase in Rateable Value has during the same period been extraordinarily great, and has followed to a certain extent the course of the increase of Local Taxation, being greater in the Urban and Manufacturing than in the Agricultural districts. Nevertheless the increase of Rates has approached more nearly to the increase in the Rateable Value in the four counties, Middlesex, Surrey, Lancashire, and West Riding, taken together, than in the remaining counties of England.

6. The statistics of separate counties, the division of the country between Urban and Rural Unions, the analysis of various kinds of Rates, the comparison of the imposts on Houses in England with corresponding burdens in other countries, the mode of valuation in England as compared with that followed elsewhere, all point to the conclusion that House Property in England is very heavily taxed.

7. An historical retrospect seems to prove that, as regards the burdens on Lands, they are not heavier than they have been at various periods of this century, nor as heavy as they are in most foreign countries, the increase in the special Rates falling on Lands, such as County and Highway Rates, having been insignificant as compared with the increase in Urban Rates. As regards the Poor Rate, the burden on Lands in the country generally, whatever may be the case in special districts, has increased very slightly in amount, and not at all as regards the Rate in the £.

8. The Poor Rate as regards Towns has undoubtedly increased, and caused new burdens in many places. In those Rural districts where the Poor Rate is now high, it has, with few exceptions, always been high, and constitutes an hereditary burden which has at all times been heavy, but which has gradually been lightened by the transfer of a portion of it to other kinds of Property.

9. The consideration of the increase in the burden of Local Taxation must be viewed in connection with results obtained by the Expenditure incurred. Of the average increase of 8,000,000 l., that portion which is due to the Poor Rate, *i.e.* 2,000,000 l. may be regarded as a lamentable increase of burden, except so far as it represents, not an increase in pauperism, but the more humane and at the same time more costly treatment of the helpless, the sick, and the insane. For the increase in the item of County Police, amounting to upwards of 500,000 l., it may be said that a

distinct equivalent in value is secured. As regards the increase in Miscellaneous Purposes, amounting to about 500,000 l., spent on Registration, Vaccination, Burial Boards, and on some of the objects to which the County Rate is applied, the same principle would apply. A small portion only of this sum is analogous to the Poor Rate, which is a burden imposed on Taxpayers from which they may be said themselves to derive no benefit.

There remain the 5,000,000 l. of Urban Rates, on which it has been necessary so often to dwell. This sum represents the Municipal Expenditure of our Towns, the Lighting and Paving of the Street, Sanitary Improvements of every kind, and Public Works of various descriptions, from vast enterprises like the Thames Embankment, the Main Drainage of the Metropolis, and the many important works undertaken at a large outlay by Liverpool, Manchester, and the other large growing Towns of the North of England, to the smaller but innumerable operations which have been instituted by the seven hundred Local Boards established during the last ten years. A great portion of the outlay on these purposes must be regarded as remunerative in many senses, and as being not so much a burden as an investment.

I submit that no review of Local Taxation in England and Wales can be fairly conducted, unless full weight is given to the distinctions which have been indicated.

205. Metropolitan Board of Works' review of its own work (1889)

Parlty. Papers, 1889/LXVI.

(i) *Problem facing the Board in 1855*

Thirty-three years have elapsed since the Metropolitan Board of Works was called into existence by Sir Benjamin Hall's "Act for the better Local Management of the Metropolis," and the year just closed is the last during which the Board will have jurisdiction, or be able to give an account of the way in which it has performed the duties and discharged the responsibilities cast upon it by the Legislature. The Board, it is true, remains in existence three months longer, that is to say, until 31st March 1889; but, as its annual Reports and accounts are required to be made up to the end of December in each year, there will be no further opportunity of giving to the Legislature and to the inhabitants of London an account of its stewardship. On 1st April next, according to the Local Government Act passed in the last Session of Parliament, all the powers, duties, and liabilities of the Board will (unless the Local Government Board shall previously fix some other date) pass to the County Council of London to be constituted under the provisions of that Act, and the Board will no longer exist.

In view of the impending change, it seems desirable that the Board, in its last annual Report, should not confine itself to a simple record of the year's proceedings, but by briefly describing the condition of London in 1855, and by tracing the alterations and improvements effected since that date, endeavour to bring home to the mind of the Londoner of 1888 how much more favourable are the conditions under which he lives, in point of health, comfort and convenience of every kind, than were those of the generation which witnessed the passing of the Metropolis Management Act. The better state of things is due, no doubt, in part to the social, political, and financial reforms of the last 30 or 40 years; but, after making full allowance for these, it will be seen to how great an extent the improved conditions of life in London are to be attributed to the works of the Board and of the subsidiary local bodies created by the Act of 1855.

The Londoner of to-day, accustomed to the unity of management which he sees continually exemplified in the great drainage system, the fire brigade, the embankments of the Thames, the new main thoroughfares running through different districts and connecting one part of the town with another, finds it difficult, if indeed he ever makes the attempt, to realise that so recently as the beginning of the second half of this century such unity of management was altogether unknown, and that there was no single representative body to care for or attend to those important branches of municipal administration which concern the great city as a whole, and which can only be efficiently dealt with by treating it as a whole. At that time the only part of the metropolis which had a complete organisation for even local purposes was the City of London proper, containing an area of little more than one square mile. This, no doubt, had been for several centuries the extent of the urban area, and, as buildings and population extended beyond these limits, there had been no adjustment or extension of the boundaries so as to include within the City the whole of the urban population. The consequence was that until the passing of the Metropolis Management Act in 1855 the large and populous districts of London outside the City had no general system of local government, and were for the most part wholly unconnected with each other. Each parish had its own method of parochial administration, some having a representative constitution, others being under the control of self-elected bodies to a great extent irresponsible to the ratepayers, and many of them being governed by local statutes presenting great diversity in their objects and provisions.

The 'Times,' writing on the subject of 20th March 1855, used these words:-

> "We may really say that there is no such place as London at all, the huge city passing under this title being rent into an infinity of divisions, districts, and areas. . . . Within the metropolitan limits the local administration is carried on by no fewer than 300 different bodies, deriving powers from about 250 different local Acts, independent of general Acts. The number of Commissioners employed, though not precisely ascertainable, Sir Benjamin Hall estimates by his own computation at about 15,000."

The necessary consequence of this want of connection between the different districts was, there was no co-operation or conjoint action, and that the needs of London as a whole, needs common to every great city, received very little attention. . . .

(ii) *Powers and Functions of Board*

Since the Act of 1855 many other Acts of Parliament have been passed, conferring powers and imposing obligations upon the Board as the central municipal authority of the metropolis. Indeed, as the necessity has arisen from time to time for the performance of some municipal duty concerning London as a whole, the Legislature has looked to the Board as the body to which the duty must necessarily be entrusted.

A summary of all the Statutes conferring powers upon the Board will be found in the Appendix No. 1 to this Report; and the functions which at the present date devolve upon the Board, and which under the recent Act are about to pass, with others, to the new County Council of London, may be shortly stated as follows:–

(1.) The maintenance of the main sewers, the interception of sewage from the Thames, its conveyance to a distance from London, and its purification before being discharged into the river.

(2.) The prevention of floods from the Thames.

(3.) The formation of new main thoroughfares through crowded districts, and the carrying out of other great improvements.

(4.) The control over the formation of new streets, and over the erection of buildings, and the construction of local sewers. The naming of streets and numbering of houses.

(5.) The construction and maintenance of highways across the Thames, whether in the form of bridges, tunnels, or ferries.

(6.) The formation and maintenance of parks and gardens, and the preservation of commons and open spaces.

(7.) The demolition of houses in areas condemned as unhealthy under the Artizans' and Labourers' Dwellings Improvement Acts, and the sale or letting of the land for the erection of improved habitations.

(8.) The maintenance of a fire brigade for the extinction of fires and the saving of life and property in case of fire.

(9.) The supervision of the structural arrangements of theatres and music-halls, with special reference to the safety of persons frequenting them.

(10.) The sanctioning of tramways.

(11.) The control over the construction of railway bridges.

(12.) The supervision to a limited extent of the gas and water supply.

(13.) The control over the sale and storage of explosives, petroleum, and other inflammable substances.

(14.) The supervision of slaughter-houses and various offensive businesses; also of cowsheds, dairies, and milk-shops; and the prevention of the spread of contagious diseases among cattle, horses, and dogs.

(15.) The supervision and control of what is known as baby-farming; and other matters of detail incidental to municipal government.

. . .

(iii) *Sewerage*

In the summer of 1858 which was unusually hot, the condition of the river became exceedingly bad, the continual stench being such as to cause considerable apprehension and alarm among the inhabitants of London. The palace of the Legislature, being close to the river, was invaded night and day by the offensive effluvium, and it was suggested that the comfort and even the safety of the legislators required that their place of meeting should be elsewhere. The following extracts from the 'Times' newspaper graphically describe the state of things at that time:-

> On 11th June, in the House of Commons, "Mr. Brady wished to ask whether the noble Lord had taken any means to mitigate the effluvium from the Thames. Hon. Members, sitting in the committee-rooms and library were scarcely able to bear it." – ('Times,' 12th June, 1858).
>
> On 18th June, "Mr. Mangles said," in the House of Commons, "that when he was a young man Thames salmon were celebrated. The salmon, wiser than Members of Parliament, had avoided the pollution, and he was informed that cartloads of fish were taken out of the Thames which had died in consequence of the state of the river. A noble mansion was prepared for the right honourable gentleman who occupied the chair, but could any honourable gentleman expect the Speaker to live in an atmosphere into which they would not put their worst enemy? They had built on the banks of the Thames a magnificent palace for the Legislature, but how could they direct the attention of any foreigner to it when he would be welcomed by a stench which was overpowering? – ('Times,' 19th June 1858).
>
> "What a pity it is that the thermometer fell ten degrees yesterday. Parliament was all but compelled to legislate upon the great London nuisance by the force of sheer stench. The intense heat had driven our legislators from those portions of their buildings which overlook the river. A few Members, indeed, bent upon investigating the subject to its very depth, ventured into the library, but they were instantaneously driven to retreat, each man with a handkerchief to his nose. We are heartily glad of it. It is right that our legislators should be made to feel in health and comfort the consequences of their own disregard of the public welfare . . . As long as the nuisance did not directly affect themselves, noble Lords and honourable gentlemen could afford to disregard the safety and comfort of London; but now that they are fairly driven from their libraries and committee-rooms – or, better still, forced to remain in them with a putrid atmosphere around them – they may perhaps spare a thought for the Londoners." – (Leading article in 'The Times,' 18 June 1858.)
>
> "I am one of those unfortunate lawyers who 'hug the festering shore,' and festering it is indeed with a vengeance. The stench in the Temple to-day is sickening and nauseous in the extreme; we are enveloped in the foul miasma which spreads on either side of this repository of the filth of nigh three millions of human beings, and day and night every breath of air which we draw for the sustenance of life is tainted with its poisonous exhalations." – (Letter signed T.S., in 'The Times' of 18th June 1858.)

Thus, in consequence of Sir Benjamin Hall and the Legislature failing in the first instance to place reliance on the body they had called into existence, much valuable time was lost. Eventually, however, the Government was driven to the conclusion that the Board must be freed from the restriction which was the cause of the dead-lock, and be allowed to proceed with the sewerage works according to the plan of its own engineer. This solution was facilitated by a change of Administration which took place in February 1858, the Earl of Derby having succeeded Viscount Palmerston as Prime Minister, and Lord John Manners having become First Commissioner of Works in place of Sir Benjamin Hall. In July the Government introduced into the House of Commons a Bill, which on the 2nd of August following was passed under the title of "An Act to alter and amend the Metropolis Management Act, 1855, and to extend the powers of the Metropolitan Board of Works for the purification of the Thames and the main drainage of the metropolis." The Act repealed the 136th section of the Act of 1855, which required the Board to obtain the consent of the First Commissioner of Works before intercepting the sewage from the Thames. It empowered the Board to borrow the amount of 3,000,000 l. for the purpose of the works, which were to be completed by the end of the year 1863, and the guarantee of Her Majesty's Treasury was given for the payment of the principal and interest. To provide for these payments the Board was required to raise a rate equivalent to 3d. in the pound during 40 years from the passing of the Act. By a subsequent Act, passed in the year 1863, the borrowing power was increased by a further sum of 1,200,000 l., and the time for the completion of the works was extended to 31st December 1866.

The Board, thus set free from outside control, and armed with all necessary powers, proceeded to carry into effect its plan for intercepting the sewage from the Thames in its course through London. For this purpose three main intercepting sewers were constructed, on each side of the river, termed respectively the high-level, the middle-level, and the low-level. The high and middle-level sewers discharged by gravitation, and the low-level discharged only by the aid of pumping. The three intercepting sewers on the north side of the Thames were made to converge and unite at Abbey Mills, West Ham; where the contents of the low-level sewers are pumped up to the higher level, and the aggregate stream of sewage flows through the northern outfall sewer, which is carried on a concrete embankment across the marshes to Barking Creek, and there flows into the river by gravitation. On the south side of the Thames the three intercepting sewers were made to unite at Deptford Creek. Here the sewage from the low level is pumped up to a higher level, and the united streams of sewage flow in one channel, through Woolwich, to Crossness, where it is pumped up into a reservoir and discharged into the river.

The greater part of the new sewerage works, including the reservoir at Barking Creek, was completed by the year 1864, in which year sewage began to be discharged at Barking. In the same year the Deptford pumping-station was also opened; and in April 1865 the sewerage works on the south side of the river, including the reservoir at Crossness, being practically completed, the Crossness pumping-station was formally opened by H.R.H. the Prince of Wales, in the presence of a numerous and distinguished assemblage, consisting of members of the Legislature, and representatives of all the scientific and learned bodies of London. The low-level sewer, part of which it has been determined to form in connection with the Embankment of the Thames between Westminster and Blackfriars, was completed a few years later; and the sewage of Fulham, Hammersmith, and the western suburbs of London was subsequently brought into the main channel formed in connection with the Chelsea Embankment, near the termination of which, in Grosvenor-road, the sewage is raised by pumping to a higher level, and continues its course eastward through the main low-level sewer.

The following statistics will convey some idea of the magnitude of the main drainage works:-

NORTH SIDE OF THE THAMES

	Length	Diameter
Northern High Level Sewer .	7½ miles	From 4 ft. to 9½ by 12 ft.
Northern Middle Level Sewer .	9½ "	" 4½ ft. by 3 ft. to 10½ ft.
Piccadilly Branches . .	2¾ "	
Northern Low Level Sewer .	8¼ "	" 6¾ ft. to 10¼ ft.
Hackney Branch . .	2½ "	
Isle of Dogs Branch . .	1⅞ "	
Western Sewers–Main Line .	5⅛ "	" 4 ft. by 2 ft. to 5 ft.
Fulham Branch . . .	1⅓ "	
Acton Line . . .	1⅜ "	
Northern Outfall Sewer . .	5½ "	Two culverts, each of 9 ft. diameter.

Abbey Mills Pumping Station.–Eight engines, each of 142 horse-power, capable of raising 15,000 cubic feet of sewage per minute to a height of 36 feet.

Western Pumping Station at Pimlico.–Four engines, each of 90 horse-power, with a supplementary engine of 120 horse-power, capable of raising 6,000 cubic feet of sewage per minute to a height of 18 feet.

Reservoir at Barking Creek.–Area of 9½ acres.

SOUTH SIDE OF THE THAMES

	Length	Diameter
Southern High Level Sewer .	5⅜ miles	From 4½ by 3 ft. to 10½ ft.
Effra Branches ditto . .	7¼ "	" 7 ft. to 10½ ft.
Southern Low Level Sewer .	9½ "	" 4 ft. to two culverts, each of 7 ft.
Bermondsey Branch . .	2¾ "	" 5 ft. to 5½ ft.
Southern Outfall Sewer . .	7½ "	" 11½ ft.

Deptford Pumping Station.–Four engines, each of 125 horse-power, capable of raising 13,000 feet of sewage per minute to a height of 18 feet.

Crossness Pumping Station.–Four engines, each of 125 horse-power, capable of raising 17,000 cubic feet of sewage per minute to a height of 10 to 30 feet.

Crossness Reservoir.–Area of 6½ acres.

The total length of the main intercepting sewers is about 82 miles; they are capable of intercepting daily 63 million cubic feet, or nearly 400 million gallons of sewage, and the total cost of the works has been about 4,600,000 l. The average daily quantity of sewage discharged is about 160 million gallons.

To make the great work of diverting the sewage from the Thames in London more complete and efficient, the Board has virtually reconstructed all the old main sewers, which formerly, under the care of the Metropolitan Commissioners, were by the Act of 1855 transferred to the Board. These sewers, often spoken of as the old valley lines, consisted for the most part, originally, of open water-courses, which, rising in the highest parts of the London district, found their way circuitously into the Thames. The abolition of cesspools had the effect of bringing these water-courses into general use as sewers, and the Board found it necessary to cover such of them as remained open, and in most cases to straighten and deepen them so as to afford good outlets for the sewage into the new intercepting sewers. The total length of the main sewers transferred to the Board in 1855 was about 165 miles, and about one-fifth of them, at the time of their coming under the Board's control, were offensive open sewers, while many of the covered ones were of defective design, and out of repair. Nearly three-quarters of a million sterling was spent in reconstructing these sewers in an effective and permanent manner, and fitting them for connection with the new system.

The intercepting sewers were, it has already been said, designed to carry off with the sewage so much of the rainfall as could *reasonably* be provided for; that is to say the sewers were of sufficient capacity to take ordinary quantities of rain. It was manifestly impracticable to make them so large that, no matter how heavy or copious the fall of rain, it should all be immediately carried away without the sewers being at any time overcharged. Exceptional storms had, however, to be provided for, and this was done by constructing overflow weirs at the junctions of the intercepting sewers with the main valley lines. When rain is falling in great abundance, the ordinary contents of the sewers are, of course, largely diluted with fresh water, and, as soon as the intercepting sewers are full, the water flows over the weirs, and along the original channels into the Thames. A few years ago it was found that, in consequence of the remarkable growth of London, and the gradual conversion into streets and paved surfaces of what had before been pervious soil, the provision for the escape of the storm-waters was insufficient, and that some of the populous suburbs were liable to flooding when the fall of rain was unusually heavy. The Board thereupon resolved to construct a number of additional sewers, principally in the northern, eastern, and southern districts, for the express purpose of receiving and carrying quickly away the great volumes of water produced by a heavy fall of rain. These storm-water sewers, begun in the year 1880, and completed a year or two ago, at a cost of nearly 700,000 l., have effectually relieved nearly all the localities which were formerly subject to flooding. . . .

Sewer Cleansing.–The cleansing of the main and intercepting sewers (in all about 250 miles in length) is done by a special staff of men employed by the Board for the purpose. The number of men employed is 124, of whom 18 are foremen or gangers, and the annual cost of the work is about 15,000 l.

Local Sewerage and Drainage.–Whilst the Board was engaged in diverting the sewage, in reconstructing the main sewers, and in the other works above-mentioned, the vestries and district boards also were actively occupied in improving the local sewerage of their respective districts. Many of the old local sewers were shallow and otherwise imperfect, and it was necessary to reconstruct them with better gradients to correspond with the improved main sewers made by the Board. More than 1,100 miles of new sewers have been laid by the local bodies since 1855, the plans for which were all submitted to and examined by the Board, in order that it might be ascertained that they were in harmony with the general system. By section 69 of the Metropolis Management Act the Board's approval is required before any new sewer can be made. . . .

(iv) *Thames Embankment*

The idea of embanking the Thames between Westminster and the City of London had long been an object of contemplation with persons interested in the improvement and embellishment of the capital. Sir Christopher Wren first propounded the idea when the plans for rebuilding the City after the Great Fire were under consideration. Nearly two centuries passed, however, before anything practical was done towards realising the conception. Several schemes had, it is true, been in the meantime proposed, the most worthy of note being that of Sir Frederick Trench in the third decade of this century, and a few years later that of Mr. John Martin, the well-known painter, who with remarkable foresight combined with his design of an embankment a scheme for intercepting the sewage from the river. In 1840 Mr. James Walker prepared a plan for the City Corporation, and this was succeeded at different times by several other projects.

It was in the year 1860 that the idea first assumed practical form and shape, under the influence of the strong desire felt by the public and the Legislature to see the offensive mudbanks and the mean and unsightly buildings which disfigured the shores of the river, particularly between Westminster and Waterloo Bridges, give way to something better and more worthy of the first city of the kingdom. In that year a Select Committee of the House of Commons, which had been appointed to consider the subject, recommended that the Middlesex shore of the river between Westminster and Blackfriars should be embanked. The Committee further recommended that, as the Legislature had already entrusted to the Board the main drainage of London, and given it powers to deal with the foreshore of the river in connection therewith, the construction of the embankment should also be confided to the Board. In the following year a Royal Commission was appointed to examine the various proposals for carrying out the work. The Commissioners, of whom the then Lord Mayor (W. Cubitt) was Chairman, recommended a solid embankment between Westminster Bridge and the east side of the Temple Gardens, and an embankment with a dock from thence to Blackfriars Bridge, together with a road throughout the whole length; the road to be 100 feet in width from the Clock Tower of the Houses of Parliament to the east end of the Temple Gardens, and beyond that point 70 feet. It was mentioned that such an embankment would supply three *desiderata*: (1) a convenient site for a low-level sewer; (2) improved navigation; (3) relief to the thoroughfare from the east to the west end of London, and especially to the Houses of Parliament. The Commissioners, however, upon one important point, the question of the body which should carry out the work, came to a conclusion different from that of the Select Committee of the previous year. They suggested that, in view of the magnitude of the work, the important and varied interests affected by it, and the necessity for its early completion, the undertaking should be entrusted to a body of Special Commissioners.

The Board, through its Chairman, pointed out to the Government the inexpediency of calling into existence a new and non-representative body to carry out a work of this kind, seeing that one of the principal objects of the Legislature in creating the Board had been that the Board should take in hand such public improvements as were needed, and seeing also that the low-level sewer which it was suggested should be formed in connection with the embankment was a work the responsibility for which already devolved upon the Board. The Government admitted the justice of the Board's view, and in the year 1862 introduced a Bill which, after further inquiry by a Select Committee of the House of Commons, was passed, and which imposed upon the Board the duty of embanking the Thames between Westminster and Blackfriars as proposed.

Many difficulties were encountered during the progress of the work, that which entailed the most delay being the arrangement, authorised by the Metropolitan District Railway Act, 1864, for the construction of the railroad in connection with the embankment. The railway company's works proceeded very slowly in consequence of the difficulty of raising sufficient capital, and the Board had frequently to urge upon the company the necessity for greater expedition.

It should here be mentioned that in the year 1868 the Board obtained from Parliament power to modify the original design for the eastern end of the embankment. The Act of 1862 provided, in accordance with the recommendation of the Royal Commissioners, for a solid embankment with a road 100 feet wide between Westminster Bridge and the east side of the Temple Gardens, and for an embankment with dock openings and a road 70 feet wide between the last-mentioned point and Blackfriars, it having been deemed necessary to preserve access to the Whitefriars Dock and to the works of the City of London Gas Company, which were then on the river bank. By the Metropolitan District Railway Act, 1864, it was enacted that the eastern end of the embankment should be so constructed as to best suit the formation of the railway as well as the convenience of the gasworks and docks. Accordingly, after much negotiation with the railway company and the other parties, it was agreed in the year 1868 between the Board and the company that the eastern end of the embankment should be, like the rest, a solid embankment with a road 100 feet wide, and this agreement was in the same year ratified by the Legislature. After this the conjoint works proceeded more rapidly, and by the middle of the year 1870 were completed. On the 13th of July in that year the new thoroughfare from Westminster to Blackfriars was opened in state by His Royal Highness the Prince of Wales, on behalf and by command of Her Majesty the Queen, who had originally intended to be present in person, but who was subsequently, owing to indisposition, under the necessity of relinquishing her gracious intention. The Board thought it appropriate that Her Majesty's name should be associated with the accomplishment of a work of construction which, in the opinion of all, Englishmen and foreigners alike, was one of the finest of which any city could boast, and accordingly gave to it the name Victoria Embankment.

The total area of ground reclaimed from the river, and previously covered with offensive mudbanks, was 37¼ acres. Of this area the carriageway and footway occupy 19 acres. A space of about 10 acres is covered by gardens and ornamental grounds devoted to the public use, and the remainder became, in accordance with the Act of Parliament, the property of the Crown, of the Societies of the Inner and Middle Temple, and of other adjacent landowners. The net cost of the embankment, and of the works connected with it, was 1,156,981 l. . . .

(v) *Parks*

Among the subjects to which the Board early directed its attention was that of providing public parks for the inhabitants of parts of London in which such places of recreation did not already exist. The 144th section of the Metropolis Management Act authorised the Board to apply to Parliament whenever it was of opinion that further powers were required for the purpose of any work for the improvement of the metropolis or the public benefit of the inhabitants. It was accordingly proposed that the Board should apply to Parliament for power to make a park in the north of London. Doubt was, however, felt, as doubt has often since been felt, how far the authority to apply to Parliament given by the statute extended. To remove all question so far as public parks were concerned, a clause was inserted in an amending Act of the year 1856, in which it was declared that the powers given to the Board by the 144th section of the Act of 1855 did extend to applications to Parliament for the purpose of providing parks, pleasure grounds, and open spaces. Thus fortified, the Board, in the year 1857, applied for and obtained power to provide a park for the benefit of the inhabitants of the then Parliamentary Division of Finsbury, which included the thickly-populated parishes of Saint Luke and Clerkenwell, and other districts in the centre of London. A fine piece of ground on the northern outskirts of London, in the parish of Hornsey, was acquired for the purpose; and the park, having been formed, inclosed, and laid out, was opened to the public in August 1869. Finsbury Park, as it is called, has year by year been growing in attractiveness and popular favour, and the Board has neglected nothing which could contribute to make it a place of healthy recreation and intelligent enjoyment for all classes. Its value for these purposes has continually increased; for, whereas when it was first laid out there was open ground on every side of it, the town has of late years so extended that the park is now nearly surrounded with streets and houses.

In 1864 the Board obtained from Parliament power to provide a park for the south-eastern district of London, to be called Southwark Park. A suitable piece of ground, 63 acres in extent, in the parish of Rotherhithe, was acquired for the purpose, and the park was opened to the public in June 1869. At the time of its formation the park was to a great extent surrounded by open ground used as market gardens, but it is now in the midst of a large working population, and is of much value as a place of resort. The same care is bestowed upon it as upon Finsbury Park, although, owing to less favourable conditions of site and surroundings, it may not present so attractive an appearance. . . .

(vi) *Open Spaces*

It has been a great advantage to London to have on its outskirts a number of commons and other tracts of open ground available for public resort. Previously to the year 1866 the inhabitants of London had no legal rights in connection with these places. They were, like other common land in England, open to the public by custom, but the only legal rights were those of the lords of the manors and of the copyholders and commoners in each case. Thus it came about that portions of the commons had from time to time been taken for the formation of railways, and other considerable portions had, as in the case of Wandsworth Common, been appropriated to other purposes. Railway companies, finding that common land could be acquired at a much less price than other land, were always ready to carry a line across a common. The consequence is that some of the finest commons in the neighbourhood of London, such as those of Tooting and Wandsworth, are intersected by railways in various directions, and, instead of presenting an unbroken extent of ground, the commons are divided into small and almost separate areas. This process would probably have continued, had it not been for the action of the Board, and the aid afforded by a number of public-spirited persons, who saw that London as well as other parts of the country was in danger of losing its open spaces, which were being encroached upon year by year.

The Board resolutely opposed any further alienation of ground forming part of a common or open space within the limits of its jurisdiction. This action, and the persistent efforts of the persons here spoken of, who were alive to the danger of the people of London losing what they had long enjoyed, and which by reason of the increase of their numbers they would have still more need of in the future, led to the House of Commons, in 1865, appointing a Select Committee to inquire into the best means of preserving for the public use the forests, commons, and open spaces in and around London. The Committee, after a long inquiry, recommended, among other things, that the Act 20 Hen. 3, c. 4, commonly called the Statute of Merton, which enabled the lord of a manor to inclose, without either the assent of the commoners or the sanction of Parliament, should be repealed, and that no inclosure should take place under the provisions of the Inclosure Acts within the metropolitan area. They further recommended the appointment of a body of trustees for the preservation of commons and open spaces within the area.

In the following year the Government introduced a Bill, which, after a good deal of discussion and alteration, became law, under the title of the Metropolitan Commons Act, 1866, and which, whilst not quite following the lines suggested by the Select Committee, prescribed a mode of procedure under which the commons in the neighbourhood of London could be permanently secured for the people. This Act of Parliament, supplemented by others subsequently passed, has enabled the Board to acquire all the commons and open spaces on the outskirts of London, within the limits of the Board's jurisdiction, and these places are now secured for the perpetual use and enjoyment of the public. The circumstances connected with them differed in almost every case, and the proceedings which had to be taken and the sums of money paid for acquiring and preserving them have been various. In the case of Blackheath, one of the first commons preserved, the Earl of Dartmouth, lord of the manor in which the greater part of the common is situated, generously refrained from making any claim with respect to his manorial rights, and gave all the assistance necessary to enable the inclosure Commissioners, or, as they are now called, the Land Commissioners, to settle a scheme for the management of the common. In other cases the Board has had to purchase the manorial rights, sometimes for large sums of money, and has also had to compensate copyholders for the surrender of their interests. The contrast in some cases is striking. Whereas, for instance, Blackheath, the largest and one of the finest commons in the neighbourhood of London, containing 267 acres, has been secured to the public without any payment for manorial or other rights and interests, the commons at Hackney, consisting of Hackney Downs, London Fields, the two Mill Fields, and a few other areas, amounting in all to about 150 acres, have only been permanently secured, after many years' efforts and some litigation, upon payment of large sums of money. No less than 90,000 l. has been paid for the various rights and interests in the common lands of Hackney, which, at the time of their being placed under the Board's control, were, beyond the grazing of a few animals, yielding no profit to anyone. . . .

(vii) *Bills in Parliament*

One of the disadvantages under which the inhabitants of London lay before the creation of the Board was the absence of any representative authority competent to protect their local interests when assailed by the promoters of undertakings in Parliament: in such matters, for instance, as the making of railways across the suburban commons, encroachments of various kinds on the public way, and other acts of aggression formerly regarded as quite legitimate and proper. This point was not specifically dealt with or referred to in Sir Benjamin Hall's Act. It is probable that power to protect the public interests was considered as implied in the constitution of the Board as the central representative authority of London. However that may be, the disadvantage was so manifest that in the year 1861 a Select Committee of the House of Commons, appointed to inquire into the local taxation of the metropolis, drew attention to it. In the Third Report made by the Committee to the House of Commons in that year these words occur: "There appears to be no authority charged with the responsibility of watching over schemes for the construction of railways within the metropolis and protecting the interests of the inhabitants;" and the Committee suggested that the Board should be empowered, when sufficient grounds existed, to appear by counsel before Select Committees of the Houses of Parliament, and to pay out of the rates the expenses thus incurred.

To enable the Board to act upon this suggestion, Standing Orders were made by both Houses of Parliament, requiring, with respect to any future undertakings to which the sanction of Parliament might be sought, that, if any portion of the proposed works were to be within the limits of the metropolis, a copy of the plans and sections relating to such portion of the works should be deposited at the office of the Board on or before the 30th of November in each year, and that a copy of the Bill by which the works were to be authorised should be deposited with the Board on or before the 21st of December following. Another Standing Order of the House of Commons says that it shall be competent to the Referees on Private Bills to admit petitioners, being the municipal or other authority having the local management of the metropolis or of any town, or the inhabitants of any town or district alleged to be injuriously affected by a Bill, to be heard against such Bill, if they shall think fit. Since these Standing Orders were made it has been the regular practice of the Board to examine carefully the plans of every proposed work or undertaking in the metropolis, and to present petitions and appear by counsel and witnesses before Select Committees in opposition to any scheme which appeared to interfere in any way with the public property or the rights and interests of the inhabitants of London. The Board's action has frequently resulted in important modifications being made in the plans and proposals submitted to Parliament; and sometimes, when the proposals have been such as to call for strenuous resistance, has resulted in their defeat or abandonment. It has, however, occasionally happened that Committees of Parliament have sanctioned proposals made by promoters of railway and other undertakings against which the Board has earnestly contended. A notable instance of this occurred a few years ago, when notwithstanding the determined resistance offered by the Board before Select Committees of both Houses, the Metropolitan District Railway Company was allowed to put ventilating shafts in the Victoria Embankment, Queen Victoria Street, and other prominent public thoroughfares. That the opposition of the Board was amply justified was proved by the loud outcry made by the public and by all the organs of public opinion, when the actual construction of the ventilating shafts was begun. This confirmation of the Board's action, however, which would have been valuable and perhaps effective if it had been given, while the scheme was before Parliament, came too late to stop the mischief. . . .

(viii) *Fire Brigade*

In the brief review of the state of London in the year 1855, with which this Report begins, it is mentioned that at that time the only public provision for extinguishing fires was, that the churchwardens and overseers of every parish were required by law to keep a fire-engine for putting out fires in the parish. This obligation was imposed by an Act of the year 1774, the purpose of which was stated to be the further and better regulation of buildings and party walls, and the more effectual preventing of mischiefs by fire within the cities of London and Westminster, and other parishes and places. The utter inadequacy of the parochial machinery led the principal fire insurance companies of London to establish firemen and fire-engines of their own; and in the year 1832 the companies owning fire-engines united to form a single fire-engine establishment, the money required for its maintenance being contributed by most of the leading insurance offices in London. The fire offices' establishment, though far superior in efficiency to the parochial machinery for extinguishing fires, was yet not adequate to the continually increasing requirements of London. Many years elapsed, however, before it was enacted by the Legislature that there should be a single fire brigade under the control of a public authority.

In June 1861 occurred the great fire in Tooley-street, perhaps the largest and most destructive with which the fire-engine establishment of the insurance companies had been called upon to deal, and at which Mr. Braidwood, the superintendent, lost his life. On the 10th of February 1862 the House of Commons, on the motion of Mr. Thomson Hankey, appointed a Select Committee to inquire into the arrangements for the protection of life and property against fire in the metropolis; and on the 21st of the same month a representative committee of the insurance companies addressed a letter to the Secretary of State for the Home Department, intimating the wish and intention of the companies to give up their fire-engine establishment at as early a date as might be consistent with the formation of a new and efficient organisation. In May the Select Committee made a report, recommending that a fire brigade should be formed, under the superintendence of the Commissioner of Police of the Metropolis, which should form part of the general police establishment, and that the Act of Parliament requiring parishes to maintain fire-engines should be repealed.

The idea of making the fire brigade in London an adjunct of the police organisation does not seem to have met with favour from the Government, for in the year 1863 Sir George Grey, then Secretary of State for the Home Department, opened a correspondence with the Board and with a representative committee of the insurance companies, with a view to the establishment by the Board of a fire brigade, towards the cost of which the fire offices and the Government should contribute. The negotiations between the Home Department, the Board, and the fire offices were somewhat protracted, and were concerned mainly with the question of the cost of the proposed fire brigade, and the relation which the contributions of the companies should bear to the amount to be drawn from the ratepayers. The companies were anxious that the total amount to be contributed by them should not exceed 30 per cent. of the amount to be raised by rate. This limitation was, however, not adopted; and it was settled that their contributions should be at the rate of £35 per million of the amount insured. In a letter to the Board from the Home Department on the 27th March 1865 it was stated that the Secretary of State (Sir George Grey) had "satisfied himself that a fire brigade could be instituted at an annual cost of 50,000 l. of sufficient strength to provide adequate protection to the district under the management of the Metropolitan Board." It was further stated that the Government would propose to Parliament an annual contribution of 10,000 l. in aid of the proposed brigade; that the fire insurance companies had agreed to transfer to the brigade the plant, stock, staff, and stations of their fire-engine establishment, subject to existing liabilities, and to contribute annually a sum equal to £35 per million on their insurances, which, calculated upon their business for 1863, would amount to 10,156 l.; and that the sum of about 30,000 l. remaining to be provided could be raised by a rate of a halfpenny in the pound. The Board was asked whether it concurred in the general arrangement proposed; and, as the conditions appeared equitable, the contributions of the fire offices being about a third of what would have to be raised from the ratepayers, the Board intimated its concurrence.

The arrangement was sanctioned by Parliament in an Act passed the same year, which declared that on and after the 1st of January 1866 the duty of extinguishing fires and of protecting life and property in case of fire in London should devolve upon the Board, and repealed the obligation under which the parochial authorities had hitherto lain to maintain fire-engines for use in their respective parishes. On the appointed day the whole body of firemen, 130 in number (including Captain Shaw, the superintendent, who had succeeded Mr. Braidwood), together with all the stations, engines, plant and appliances of the old fire-engine establishment, passed into the service of the Board. The fire-engine stations of the insurance companies, 17 in number, were all in the central parts of London; and, as the parochial authorities ceased to maintain fire-engines, measures had at once to be taken to extend the new organisation, so as to afford protection to all parts of London. This was a task attended with some difficulty, but one which was eventually accomplished.

The Fire Brigade Act provided that the Board should undertake not only the extinction of fires and the protection of property, but also the protection of life in case of fire. The saving of life from fire had for many years been undertaken by an incorporated society called the Royal Society for the Protection of Life from Fire, which had begun its operations about the year 1844. The society, which was supported by voluntary contributions, had at the time of the passing of the Fire Brigade Act about 85 fire-escapes stationed at well-known places in the principal parts of London, each under the charge of a trained man. No arrangement was made previously to the passing of the Act for relieving this society of its beneficent labours, and it was not until the Act had been in operation a year and a half, and the fire brigade organisation had been considerably extended, that the Board was in a position to undertake the saving of life from fire. On the 1st of July 1867 as the result of negotiations with the society, all the fire-escapes and the staff of attendants (with the exception of a few men who were getting too old for the work, and who received suitable compensation) were transferred to the Board, and since that date the extinguishing of fires and the saving of life from fire have been carried on together as parts of the same organisation. . . .

Part IX

THE POOR LAW

THE POOR LAW

Introduction

THE Poor Law was one of the most intractable problems facing the outset of the Victorian Age, and at the same time the seed-plot of some of its most important initiatives and influences. The structure of Poor Law administration before the 1834 Act was still, in the main, that set up by the famous statute of Elizabeth (43 Eliz. I, c. 2), which made the parish the unit of relief, and overseers of the poor, chosen in each parish and acting under the supervision of the local justices, responsible for its administration. Here and there changes had been made in the pattern. A number of towns, such as Bristol and Exeter and Liverpool, had obtained local Acts setting up corporations of the poor, with a responsibility extending over a number of their urban parishes. Certain metropolitan and other parishes had acquired extended and more flexible powers through the same process. Some country districts had availed themselves of the clauses of Gilbert's Act (22 Geo. III, c. 83) to form unions of parishes, not always, since union was by agreement, on any very intelligible geographical plan. There was little in the way of prescribed administrative standards, and no central administrative control. Even in parishes there was the greatest variety of practice; in some the utmost laxity prevailed; in others, where a vigorous lead had been given by energetic and public-spirited individuals, reforms had been introduced. But, as in eighteenth-century local administration generally, there was no machinery for transmuting reforming impulses into general administrative practice, nor enough professional element in the general administration to give steadiness and continuity to amateur impulse. As a result the aspect and accent of the problem varied from town to town, and from parish to parish.[1]

But the side of the question that caused most contemporary heart-searching was what is now known as the Speenhamland system, and was then usually called the 'allowance system'. As a general practice over the southern half of the country this dated from 1795, from the decision of the Berkshire Justices, meeting at the Pelican Inn at Speenhamland, on the outskirts of Newbury, to supplement wages from the rates. The year was one of great distress, and of a sharp increase in the price of bread. As the war and the bad years continued, what had originally been an expedient designed to tide over an emergency hardened into a system, and was copied elsewhere. Details varied, but the general principle was that the allowance varied with the number in the family, and with the price of bread. The system has been defended as having averted widespread starvation and probable revolution in the dark years of the war. But its survival into peace involved a heavy burden on the rates,[2] and was held to be destroying the independence, the industry, and the morals of the rural workers, the last because the possession of children, whether legitimate or illegitimate, constituted a title to extra relief. From 1817 onwards, Select Committees of the House had several times examined the problem and had recognized its gravity, but had seen

[1] No. 210. [2] No. 206A and Part III, No. 91.

no way of dealing with it except by abolishing the Poor Law, a course which Malthusian principles supported, indeed, but which was generally felt to be impracticable.

It was therefore a decision of some courage, on the part of the Whigs, to undertake to tackle the subject while they were still deep in the struggle for the Reform Bill. Two accidents, as they may not improperly be called, helped them to break out from the circle which had bounded the efforts of their predecessors. The first was the suggestion made by one junior minister–Hyde Villiers–to another, Lord Howick, the son of the Prime Minister, that a Royal Commission should be appointed to analyse the situation, make proposals for dealing with it, and so prepare public opinion for the necessary legislation. The Cabinet adopted the idea, and the success that attended its carrying into practice established it as the proper preliminary approach to legislation dealing with complex social questions. A strong Commission was appointed, with Bishop Blomfield, of London, as its chairman, and Bishop Sumner, of Chester, Sturges Bourne, Frankland Lewis, and Nassau Senior among its members. The two bishops had taken part in previous examinations of the question; Sturges Bourne and Frankland Lewis were Canningite and Tory politicians respectively, united by an interest in social questions; and Senior was the recently retired Drummond Professor of Political Economy at Oxford. The second fateful accident was the friendship between Senior and Edwin Chadwick, the secretary and confidant of Bentham in the sage's later years. Senior persuaded Chadwick to accept nomination as an Assistant Commissioner. Chadwick's energy and power of social analysis soon won him rank as a Commissioner; he provided the most important constructive proposals in the Report; and he won and kept, for twenty tempestuous years, a position for himself and for the Benthamite administrative gospel that he represented, in the inner advisory circles of government. Again the event was decisive for much more than the Poor Law. Chadwick's career may almost be said to constitute the bridge between the eighteenth century and the modern conceptions of government.

The conclusions and recommendations of the Commissioners[1] were supported in the text of the Report by numerous examples and a considerable body of evidence, and behind them stood the voluminous reports of the Assistant Commissioners, each of whom had been given an area to report upon. Many historians have tended to look on the Report of 1834 from the standpoint of the Minority Report on the Poor Law of 1909, and of the great *History of the Poor Law* by Mr. and Mrs. Webb, which was written to elaborate its theses. But to look at the Report of 1834 in the light of the administrative experience and powers of social analysis gained in the succeeding three-quarters of a century–not a little as a result of the foundations that the Report laid down–is unhistorical. It is from the standpoint of the problems and the prepossessions of its own time that the Report should be regarded. Senior and Chadwick–its chief authors–have been criticized for concentrating on the evils of the allowance system and neglecting industrial unemployment. This they undoubtedly did. But the allowance system was the problem primarily before them–defined by the earlier inquiries, recognized by public opinion, and resulting, in the general view, from definite mistakes of public policy. It had taken root in the country within the lifetime of the generation then living, and its potentialities for evil were still, in the Commissioners' view,[2] unexhausted. At the moment it was more or less confined to the

[1] No. 206. [2] No. 206A.

agricultural counties. But it was capable of extension to industry with greater advantage to the employer, perhaps, than with farming, for the problem of supervision was more manageable in a factory than in the scattered fields of a farm. If the evil were not checked, the Commissioners saw a prospect that "whole branches of manufacture might follow the course, not of coal mines, or of streams, but of pauperism", and a semi-slave population be created in the towns, as well as in the countryside. Industrial unemployment, on the other hand–serious, and even catastrophic, as it might be from time to time–called in the contemporary conception for quite other remedies than the Poor Law could supply–for Free Trade, especially;[1] nor, in an age which still largely accepted the conception of the economic system as a self-adjusting mechanism, had its nature and causes received the attention and analysis they were later to attract. Its 'hard core'–the hand loom weavers–were to be the subject of an almost continuous separate inquiry from 1834 to 1841.[2]

From the contemporary point of view the Report succeeded in putting the problem with which it dealt both in a new intellectual light, and into manageable practical form. It broke with the Malthusian principles which had been the intellectual staple of earlier discussion, and asserted that if the productive efficiency of the worker, which the allowance system was destroying, were to be restored, more capital would be attracted to the land, and there would be plenty of work for all. It cited the example of parishes which had restored the will to work by a strict administration of relief, and adopted, as its central recommendation, the principle on which these parishes had worked, that the conditions of relief should, in general, be 'less eligible' than that of the independent labourer. From this, for the able-bodied, followed the workhouse test, the refusal of any relief except within the workhouse. On the basis of these principles the Commissioners were confident that the Poor Law could be taken out of normal economic life and confined to the function of rescuing its casualties. To a Poor Law thus restored to its proper character, the Commissioners were prepared to give an unqualified blessing. So reinvigorated, it should be able to look after the aged, the sick, and the truly indigent much better than before; and the Commissioners recommended, for these purposes, a 'break-up' of its immediate administration, the strict segregation of the different classes of paupers, and the care of them, preferably, in different institutions.[3] Further, they strongly asserted that the cessation of the subsidization of wages would drive up their general level.[4] The assertion is constantly and confidently repeated in later annual reports, and though, in the 'thirties and 'forties–an unpropitious time for agriculture–the prophecy received little substantiation, it came true in the 'fifties,[5] and there is no ground to dispute either its reasonableness or its sincerity. The proposals for administrative reorganization represented an even more drastic breach with the past. They were largely embodied in the Act of 1834, which will be summarized below, and may be said to have resulted in the setting up of the first modern administrative machine in the century. Before the publication of the Report a volume of *Excerpts of Evidence* was published and put on sale, and the Report itself was widely distributed, and, in a popular octavo form, even more widely sold. The deliberate search for the widest possible publicity was the policy of Chadwick, and reflected the modernity of his outlook. It paid handsome dividends; the Report was widely attacked, as was inevitable in view of the drastic nature of its recommendations, as well as widely approved,

[1] Parts III and V. [2] Part XII, Introduction and No. 252. [3] No. 206H.
[4] No. 206C. [5] Part III, Introduction.

but there can be no question that it convinced all but a minority of the reflecting minds of its generation, and it takes its place not only as the fundamental document of its subject but as a fundamental document of Victorianism.

The Poor Law Amendment Act of 1834 (4 & 5 Wm. IV, c. 76) is too long and detailed to reproduce. Primarily, it set up a Commission of three to supervise the local authorities on whom would fall the task of the detailed administration of relief. The Commission was not to be under direct ministerial control, and neither the Commissioners themselves nor any of their Assistant Commissioners might sit in Parliament. It was thus completely extra-Parliamentary. It was given a wide power of issuing orders and of making rules and regulations with the force of law. Orders to individual unions could be issued on the Commission's own responsibility. General Orders had to be submitted to the Secretary of State and by him laid before Parliament for forty days, before they came into effect. Commissioners, and Assistant Commissioners acting with delegated authority, might call for papers from any of the authorities under their control, summon witnesses, and conduct examinations on oath. The Commission was required to submit to the Secretary of State an annual report of its proceedings, and might be called upon by him to submit to him a special report on any topic within its competence on which he might desire information. The detailed administration of relief was to be conducted within unions of parishes, and the duty of dividing the country into unions was laid on the Commissioners. They might not, however, include in the unions they set up parishes already formed into unions under Gilbert's Act, or those enjoying a special position under local Acts of Parliament, nor did the form of government prescribed for the ordinary unions apply to these. Parishes were to continue to be responsible for the costs of Poor Law administration, contributing to their unions on the basis of a three years' average of their number of chargeable paupers. Unions were to be controlled by boards of guardians elected on a rate-paying franchise, with plural voting according to the amount of rates paid. Resident justices were *ex officio* guardians. The Commissioners could lay down the qualifications to be required of administrative officers appointed by the guardians, and exercised some control over their dismissal. They had very considerable powers of direction and of veto over the actions of unions, but they might not order relief in individual cases, and their power of directing expenditure on the building of workhouses was limited in amount. Provision was made by the Act for the keeping by guardians of proper minutes, records, and accounts, and the accounts had to be audited regularly.

The Act contained little provision as to the policy that was to be followed. It was understood that the principles of the 1834 Report would be put into force, but, in accordance with the recommendations of the Report itself, a large measure of discretion was left as to the time and mode of their application. The Commissioners appointed were George Nicholls (who had won a reputation for himself by anticipating the principles of the Report in a successful administration of Southwell), Frankland Lewis, and J. G. Shaw-Lefevre. Chadwick, to his bitter and justified disappointment, was not Commissioner, but only Secretary. There is a long tale of reversionary promises made to him by Melbourne, and never carried out, and of assurances of a special position meanwhile, which has been disentangled by Professor S. Finer, which goes far to explain Chadwick's dominance in the early days of the Commission, and the Commissioners' quarrel with him later.

The Commission set rapidly about its work, and in the space of a couple of years it had organized the greater part of the country into unions. It met with a good deal of opposition, to be expected, as it observed, in the case of measures which disturbed the distribution of nearly £7,000,000 of relief *per annum*, and affected the source from which a large part of the population derived a good deal of its subsistence,[1] but it claimed that its success showed that it had the co-operation of the responsible elements of society. Aided by a couple of good harvests, it had also introduced its Prohibitory Order,[2] applying the workhouse test to able-bodied applicants for relief, in a large part of the South. The Commission's view of its own proceedings is given in its Second Report.[3] When, however, it turned to deal with the Midlands and the North, it met difficulties of a far different order. In the first place, the break of economic luck was this time against it. In the autumn of 1836 a crisis hit the trade and industry of the country from which they did not fully recover until the early 'forties.[4] In Nottingham, in which the union had just been organized, and the Prohibitory Order applied, a large part of the population was out of work. Workhouse accommodation soon became inadequate, and to build enough to cope with the crisis would have been impossible, as well as clearly uneconomic. A large, privately raised fund to aid the distressed helped at the start. Meanwhile the Commissioners had been keeping closely in touch with the situation, and, when it became necessary, authorized the union to issue outdoor relief to the able-bodied on condition of their working on a road which the union undertook to build for the benefit of the town.[5] Clearly, the workhouse test had proved its unsuitability to the circumstances of major industrial crisis. But the Outdoor Labour Test Order issued to the Nottingham Union took its place thenceforth in the regular repertoire of the Commission's administrative expedients, serving for exceptional unemployment as the workhouse test served in normal conditions. The Commissioners claimed that their own supervision, and the improved administrative machinery of the Act, enabled the expedient to be resorted to, where necessary, without the old risks of abuse,[6] and in their Report on the subject, proffered their Nottingham experience as a proof that "the system established under the Poor Law Amendment Act was peculiarly applicable to the case of a manufacturing district in a period of distress". The 1837–1838 Select Committee also spoke of it as "vindicating the flexibility" of the law.

In the North, the allowance system had gained little hold, and relief was resorted to, in the main, only in times of industrial distress. The Registration Act of 1836[7] had provided for clerks to guardians acting as Registrars for births, deaths, and marriages,[8] and made it essential that unions should be set up promptly. But the Commissioners' initial moves in this direction not only coincided with the onset of industrial distress, but came shortly after the Short Time movement had been brought into renewed activity in the attempt to defeat Poulett Thompson's Bill to lower the age of protection to children under the 1833 Factory Act.[9] Richard Oastler, the 'Factory King', threw himself with all the warmth of his patriarchal Toryism into the fight that shortly began against the New Poor Law, and was supported not only by his lieutenants in the Factory Act agitation, and the tumultuous eloquence of J. R. Stephens, and later of Feargus O'Connor, but also by a number of Tory magistrates. The opposition not only determined to make the Act unenforceable in the North but demanded its repeal for the whole of the country. In Huddersfield, intimidation made it impossible for the union to act effectively for nearly two years.[10] In

[1] No. 207A. [2] No. 213. [3] No. 207. [4] Part III, Introduction and No. 94.
[5] No. 208A. [6] No. 208A. [7] Part X, Introduction. [8] No. 208B. [9] Part XII. [10] No. 208B.

Todmorden, John Fielden, the factory-owner paladin of the Ten Hours' movement, used his mill-bell to summon his hands when the emissaries of the Commissioners made their appearance, and police were stripped naked and driven from the parish. In Bradford, metropolitan police and considerable bodies of troops had to be called in to quell the disturbances. The Commissioners persisted, however; the Government stood firm behind them; and the onset of Chartism[1] resulted in the absorption of the protests into the wider movement. This was by no means an advantage to the immediate objective, for it substituted visionary for practical and limited aims, and alienated Tory sympathies. The machinery of the Act was finally set up throughout the North, but for a long time the Commissioners left unions very much to their own devices, and the Prohibitory Order, in particular, was very sparingly applied, in the main only to rural districts.

These events brought the whole principle of the Act again into discussion in Parliament. Apart from the popular movement, there was plenty of material for opposition. Humanitarian sentiment, and much Christian feeling, was shocked by the harsh economic philosophy of the Act. Chadwick's hand had been ungentle with jobbers and vested interests, of which there had been plenty under the old régime. Magistrates who found themselves reduced to sharing power with an elected board where they had once reigned supreme, and to obeying rules where they had been accustomed to making them, were not indisposed to feel that the people's rights were in jeopardy. *The Quarterly Review* had criticized the original Report unfavourably; the Tory Press was critical; and, above all, the great influence of *The Times* and the voice of its proprietor, John Walter, Member for Berkshire, were cast unhesitatingly in a sustained campaign against the Act. Some of the agitation was not very scrupulous. Committees, both of the Lords and of the Commons, found that the Rev. Stringer Bull, one of Oastler's lieutenants, had been guilty of gross misrepresentation and exaggeration in allegations he had brought of heartless administration under the Act. John Walter, giving notice in the House for a motion for a committee of inquiry, refused to give either the Government or the Commissioners notice of the cases that he intended to raise–"the rakings of *The Times* for the last twelve-months", as Hume scornfully called them–so that they, on their side, might investigate the facts. But Hume freely admitted that there were many instances of harshness and hardship, nor was it likely that an extreme laxity of administration, in which sentimentality and popular blackmail had played a considerable part, could be corrected without giving plenty of opportunity for harshness, stinginess, and cant to rush into their places. The degree of centralization involved in the Act, and the independent position of the Commissioners, alarmed a good many. Walter did not exaggerate when he said that not since Star Chamber had an irresponsible public body possessed such power. The Act–or perhaps the popular agitation against it–had brought Poor Law administration much more into politics. The abuses of the past, when only a parish could be attacked, were politically not worth gunning for. But the position was different when it was possible to hold a single Commission responsible for everything that went on, and, behind the Commission, to attack the Government.[2] There had been relatively little debate when the Act was first passed, though a small minority had fought it hard. There was to be plenty now–indeed an almost continuous debate and investigation, from Walter's motion for a committee of inquiry in February 1837 till Peel obtained a further five years' life for the Commission

[1] Part V. [2] Nos. 210, 211.

in 1842. Walter's committee was appointed; and later in the year, after the General Election occasioned by the accession of Queen Victoria, a further one was set up to continue its work. The Lords also appointed a committee of inquiry. In 1839 and 1840 the powers of the Commissioners were extended for a further year, and in 1841 there was considerable debate on Russell's proposal to extend them, first, for ten years, and then, in an amended Bill, for five. This was strongly opposed, and overtaken finally by the defeat of his Government. Peel's measure for a provisional extension for six months, brought forward on his accession to power, was also opposed. In 1838 John Fielden introduced a Bill for the repeal of the Act. There were also a number of debates, in both Houses, on petitions–for the printing of which there existed a central office in London–and on allegations of abuses in individual unions. Apart from the Commissioners' annual reports a number of papers were issued dealing with these. There can be no doubt that a deep and genuine concern existed in the political country about the harshnesses and injustices that were said to exist. The main pressure was to give a larger discretion to guardians, but the Commissioners, or rather Chadwick behind them, saw in this the beginning of a return to the old administrative anarchy; nor were all guardians anxious to forgo the shelter against local pressure that the Commission's authority provided for them. Despite the half-sympathy of the Commons' Select Committee of 1837–1838, and a vote of the House, which was, however, indirectly rescinded, the Commissioners had their way. Russell and the Government stood firmly for the Act and behind them were Peel, Graham, and Wellington.[1] No one could defend the state of affairs before the Act; and no one could suggest anything effective to put in the Commission's place. Nor could anyone, even among the critics of the Act, impugn the high character and the purity of intention of the Commissioners. The inquiries of the committees vindicated them, and, by and large, vindicated the administration of the Act. Chadwick and his associates, though warily unresponsive to popular agitation, and unsentimental to a degree, had a nose for real abuses. Some of the worst of these occurred in Private Act Incorporations and Gilbert unions, which, on the ground that the Commissioners were not empowered to alter their structure, claimed to be independent of their administrative control as well. In several instances the Commissioners had to force London incorporations to recognize their duty to homeless unfortunates.[2] But not till their authority had been upheld in test cases in the courts in the 'forties did the Commissioners, in face of the outcry in the country against centralization, venture fully to assert the control over all bodies administering the Poor Law which the Act of 1834 had given to them. The segregation of the sexes in the workhouses was one of the subjects of the bitterest popular outcry; it had, in fact, been enforced in a number of the better-administered workhouses before the Act. Senior's and Chadwick's programme in their Report had envisaged the supersession of the old 'mixed general workhouse'. This was not achieved, in face of local inertia and political difficulty, but few of the new Bastilles reached the standard of promiscuity of the old poor-houses. A number of speakers in the debates, and the Committee of 1837–1838, reported that the standard of care of the aged, the sick, and the children was considerably improved. Gradually, as the debates went on, the House rallied to the opinion of Cripps, the Member for Cirencester, who, after investigation, reported that "not one tenth" of the allegations so freely made against the Commissioners "had been brought home to them". Russell, in March 1841, roundly accused

[1] No. 210. [2] No. 212.

Wakley, Member for Finsbury (one of the new metropolitan constituencies) and one of the most venomous of the critics, of the demagogic activity that Tory critics of the Reform Act had prophesied would result from the erection of constituencies without organic unity or political tradition. Opinion hardened, and the enemies of the Act were left more and more to an unsupported battle. After prolonged consideration of all that they could say, the political country accepted the Act.

Confidence had not been established, however, for more than a few years, when it was upset again by a first-class scandal. Bone-crushing had been decided on as a workhouse task after a good deal of inquiry and hesitation, and then with the proviso that 'dry' and not 'green' bones should be used. The combination of a disregard of this injuction, a bad workhouse master, a slack board of guardians, an overworked Assistant Commissioner who failed to give adequate supervision, with arbitrary handling by the Commissioners, produced the Andover Bones Scandal–starving paupers scrambling for the gristle from the bones. Almost as disturbing was the incidental revelation, in evidence before the Select Committee of Inquiry, that Chadwick, in consequence of quarrels, had practically been extruded from his office, and was violently critical of what he regarded as the slovenly and unimaginative administration of the Commission. He returned to the theme before the Select Committee of 1847 on Settlement and Poor Removal.[1] The Commissioners had no effective defence; clearly their heads had wanted knocking together; and the game of the enemies of the Commission's independence was won. The Act of 1847 (10 and 11 Vict. c. 109) changed its personnel and turned it into the Poor Law Board, under a Parliamentary chief, thus making it like any other government department. The change made for peace; it is not so sure that it made for energy and efficiency. In its palmy days the Commission had been conscious of its vulnerability to criticism and convinced that it had a job to do; it had sought to carry the public with it by vigorous initiative and by courting publicity. The political chiefs of minor departments are not normally encouraged to go in for adventurous administration; unpopular policies threatened the safety of the Government, and, on the other hand, criticism by outside persons of administrative details brought the protective forces of party solidarity into play. On the Board, the torpor of industrious, unheroic days descended. Major changes of policy were few; in some directions, notably in the treatment of casuals, administration was tightened; in others relaxed and humanized. In the early 'sixties, in connexion with the sharp distress of the winter of 1860–1861, the general principles of Poor Law administration were challenged once more.[2] The Select Committee of Inquiry vindicated them. But its Report left no doubt that whether unavoidably or not, or whether as the result of the long hostile campaign, the price of preventing exploitation had been a deep alienation of the population from the machinery of official relief.

One result of the Act of 1834 was to put squarely before the public problems which could not have been disentangled before, or envisaged in identifiable and manageable form. Among these were pauper education, and the medical care of the poor. Few workhouses, before 1834, made any pretence of giving child inmates any education. In too many cases they were shipped off to mill or mine as pauper apprentices at a very tender age. This abuse the Commissioners soon brought under control. As early as 1837 Russell was claiming among the advantages of the Act that workhouse children now had schoolmasters and schoolmistresses to look after them. The

[1] No. 217A. [2] No. 218A.

Commissioners early favoured the farming out of pauper children to schools such as Aubin's, at Norwood, the scene of the early experiments of Dr. Kay, afterwards Sir James Kay-Shuttleworth.[1] Later they supported the plan of 'district schools', to be run and paid for by groups of unions and to receive all their child paupers. A clause in the Poor Law Act of 1844 (7 & 8 Vict. c. 101, s. 40) gave statutory facilities for this, but guardians responded slowly, and workhouse schools remained the rule. In 1846 Peel's Government made them eligible for grants from the funds of the Committee of Council for Education on the usual condition of receiving the council's inspectors. This produced a continuous, if slow, improvement in the quality of their work. The Newcastle Report of 1861 reported adversely on them, but not all those with a knowledge of their work took the same view.[2]

Arrangements for the medical treatment of the poor before 1834 were sometimes good, more often bad, in any case haphazard. Under the Commissioners every union had to appoint its medical officer. The practice of many unions at the beginning, though one frowned upon by the Commissioners, was to invite tenders for the post, the terms of which usually included the provision of at any rate routine medicines by the doctor himself. From the beginning there was a sharp conflict between the determination of most guardians, supported by the Commissioners, that the standard of medical attention for paupers should not be higher than the independent labourer could afford, and the desire of most doctors to do their job properly, and get paid for doing a proper job. This and some of the larger ideas that began to take shape within the framework of the Act are illustrated by the Report of the Select Committee on Medical Relief of 1844.[3] The Commissioners had issued a General Order on Medical Relief in 1841. In 1854 the Poor Law Board forbade the practice of tendering for medical services. Many guardians continued, however, to appoint their medical officers by the year, the better to be able to curb any tendencies to extravagance that they might show. But, despite their reluctance, publicity and the influence of regular and responsible administrative control forced the standard of care upwards.

A problem remaining from the pre-1834 system was that of the Law of Settlement, modified in 1834, but still a potent influence. The principle was that the pauper was entitled to relief only in the parish of his 'settlement'. Under the 'allowance system' there had been a strong inducement to prevent labourers from acquiring a settlement in parishes to which they might become chargeable, and the law powerfully restricted mobility. Under the 1834 Act a settlement became easier to obtain; relief could not be obtained by the able-bodied until they were destitute, and could not then be refused to them, though ultimately they might be charged or even removed to their parish; and within the relatively larger unit of the union–a wide enough limit, anyway, for the ordinary labourer's mobility–charges could be arranged between parishes without necessarily moving the pauper. Thus the continued shipping about of miserable paupers which had once been such a feature of rural life diminished considerably. But influxes of Irish and Highland labourers after the potato famine of 1846–1847 raised the problem again, and led to some not very successful attempts in the 'fifties to simplify and humanize the law on the subject. The problem ultimately raised was that of parish, as against union, chargeability. The basis of parish chargeability adopted in 1834 made it to the interest of parishes to restrict settlement where they could, and some were small enough, and sufficiently dominated by a few large landowners, for such a policy to be practicable. The evil

[1] Part XI. [2] No. 218B. [3] No. 216.

social effects of this and of settlement legislation generally are analysed in the Report of 1847 on the subject,[1] and in the special reports which the Poor Law Board called for from its inspectors in 1850. In 1865 the Union Chargeability Act was passed.[2] In terms of social history the result of increasing the size of the unit of charge and of settlement was to make the restriction of settlement virtually impossible, and so to cut the nerve of one of the hoariest of the incidental abuses of the Poor Law.

A different problem was posed by the unemployment in the cotton districts resulting from the American Civil War. Here was a population, diligent and disciplined, thrown out of work not only by no fault of its own, but as a result of events unconnected with the normal working of the economic system, which the thought of the time still looked on as self-adjusting but for incidental rubs with which individuals must make their own reckoning. Thus it fell within none of the Board's normal categories. It called forth an immense charitable effort, both in the suffering county itself and in the country as a whole. Ordinary relief was, of course, available. But it is to the credit of the board that it took special steps with the double object both of seizing some advantage from the catastrophe and of preserving the self-respect of the unemployed by finding relief work for them of a permanently constructive value. By the Union Relief Act of 1863 (25 & 26 Vict. c. 100) and the Public Works Act of 1865 (26 & 27 Vict. c. 110) unions in the areas affected were given considerably increased borrowing powers for the purpose of carrying out drainage and paving works as measures of relief. The contribution to the relief of unemployment was perhaps limited, as the study by Mr. W. O. Henderson of the subject has suggested, but at any rate something considerable was done for the health and amenity of the county, and the effect on morale is less easy to measure. We shall probably not be wrong in assuming that the new attitude shown to industrial casualties, though in special circumstances, helped generally to sweeten industrial relations and to prepare the way for humaner and less rigid theories.

When all its shortcomings of insight and defects of temper are reckoned against it, the Poor Law Amendment Act remains the most important administrative revolution of its time. Counties, and even the reformed municipalities, pursued their courses little troubled by central stimulus or control,[3] but in the sphere of the Poor Law something of that vigorous interaction of local and central that had characterized Tudor government was restored, with the addition of modern administrative techniques and machinery. It was too good a machinery not to be used. The organization of public vaccination[4] and the registration of births, marriages, and deaths were early added to its jobs. Joseph Hume would have had representatives of the guardians sit with the justices on County Financial Boards.[5] After the Public Health Act of 1848, sanitary duties began to descend on the unions.[6] The Select Committee on Agricultural Statistics of 1853 found in the clerks to the guardians the most reliable available machinery for the collection of the statistics that they needed. Earlier inquiries had had to rely on the amateur, and sometimes amateurish, efforts of country parsons. Under the Workshops Act of 1867[7] unions became responsible in many places for duties of factory inspection. The value of a machinery of administration at once uniform, locally controlled, and centrally directed, was clearly becoming increasingly evident, and in this way the Act of 1834 prepared the way for the revolution in local government and administration that marks the last quarter of the century.

[1] No. 217B. [2] Nos. 219, 220. [3] Part VIII. [4] Part X, Introduction.
[5] Part VIII, Introduction and Nos. 192, 193, 203. [6] Part X. [7] Part XII.

In its own sphere the achievements of the Act, if qualified, were not less outstanding and important. Local parsimony and inertia, the cessation of political pressure, the hamstringing of the central administrative drive through the quarrels between Chadwick and the Commissioners, prevented the full development of the services for the necessitous which the Report of 1834 had envisaged. Harshness may have been used, but harshness was initially necessary; and in the end the harshness particularly complained of, the workhouse test, was relatively sparingly applied. The vast bulk of those relieved, the bulk even of the able-bodied, continued to receive relief out-of-doors. The decline of rates which had marked the early years of the Commission was reversed, though it may be said that the population was increasing throughout the period, and that better value was obtained for the money. Less was achieved and less changed in many directions in which the Commission had set out with the highest hopes. But few initiatives that have hands and feet to get anywhere in history, get precisely where they had hoped to get. There is no doubt that a new standard in administration was set, and this was in itself a major revolution. And in the main task to which it addressed itself, the Commission and its successors can claim almost unqualified success. There can be no manner of doubt that the allowance system, as it was in being in 1834, went to the root of national well-being. In checking it, and in restoring the threatened spirit of independence and industry, the Commission preserved, if they did not in part create, the Victorian doctrine of work on which the most characteristic achievements of the age depended.

SELECT BIBLIOGRAPHY

The *Parliamentary Debates* on the original passing of the Poor Law Amendment Act were relatively slight; the thorough Parliamentary discussion begins with John Walter's motion in February 1837 for a Select Committee to inquire into the Poor Laws. From then till the end of the 1842 Session every aspect of Poor Law Administration was thoroughly discussed in a series of debates on Select Committees, petitions, and Bills for the renewal of the Commissioners' powers. The debate on the incidents connected with the Andover Union in 1846, and on the change from the Commission to the Poor Law Board in 1847, are of less general interest. A more widely ranging debate took place in 1867, on the Metropolitan Poor Bill of that year.

A preliminary sketch of the evidence and views of the Poor Law Commission was published in 1833, as *Extracts of Information from the Reports of Assistant Commissioners on the Poor Law*. The *Report on the Administration and Practical Operation of the Poor Laws* (*Report*+12 vols., *Parlty. Papers*, 1834/xxvii–xxxix–*Report* in 1834/xxvii, followed by Assistant Commissioners' *Reports*) came the following year and the *Report* itself–the fundamental document of the subject–was published in octavo (London, 1834). Thereafter came a flood of public papers. The *Annual Reports of the Poor Law Commissioners* touch, in turn, on every topic of Poor Law administration, and are essential for the history of its first few years. The *Reports of the Select Committee on the Administration of the Poor Laws* (*Parlty. Papers*, 1837–1838/xviii, Parts 1–3, and 1837–1838/xix, Parts 1 and 2), cover every aspect of the problem and should be used in conjunction with the *Debates* of 1837–1838. In 1839 the Commissioners were asked themselves to report on the *Administration of the Poor Laws* (*Parlty. Papers*, 1840/xvii). Apart from the regular flow of *Reports*, a number of special papers and returns on administrative scandals–most of which are also referred to in the *Annual Reports*–were called for in the 'forties. Reference has been made, in the *Bibliography* to Part V, to *Reports* by Poor Law officials on distress in various towns. On special topics, the *Report of the Select Committee on Medical Relief* (*Parlty. Papers*, 1844/xi) discusses the situation in this respect, both generally, and with a number of local illustrations. A further *Select Committee on Medical Relief*, ten years later (*Parlty. Papers*, 1854/xii), contains, *inter alia*, evidence from Charles Kingsley. *Reports* of 1844 and 1845 deal with *Gilbert Unions* (*Parlty. Papers*, 1844/x, 1845/xiii). The *Report on the Andover Union* (*Parlty. Papers*, 1846/v, Parts 1 and 3), deals with the scandal that precipitated the end of the Commission, and in connexion with it *Parlty. Papers*, 1846/xxxvi, dealing with bone-crushing as a pauper task, should be studied. The mid-century problem of *Removal of the Poor*–exacerbated by Scotch-Irish immigration due to the potato famine–is discussed in a series of papers (*Parlty. Papers*, 1847/xi, 1854/xvii, 1857–1858/xiii; see also *Second Report of Poor Law Board* (*Parlty. Papers*, 1850/xxviii). The major inquiry of the 'sixties is in the *Report of the Select Committee on Poor Relief* (*Parlty. Papers*, 1861/ix, 1862/x, 1863/vii, 1864/ix). Besides general questions of administration, this deals with medical relief, pauper education, the classification of paupers, and the pressing question of the incidence of costs. On the Lancashire Cotton Famine and the consequent distress, the *Fifteenth*, *Sixteenth*, *Seventeenth* and *Nineteenth Annual Reports of the Poor Law Board* (*Parlty. Papers*, 1863/xxii, 1864/xxv, 1865/xxii, 1867–1868/xxiii) contain valuable information.

The standard histories of the subject are G. Nicholls and T. Mackay, *History of the English Poor Law* (3 vols., London, 1854 and 1899), and S. and B. Webb, *English Poor Law History*, vols. vii–ix of *English Local Government* (3 vols., London, 1927–1929). S. and B. Webb, *English Poor Law Policy* (London, 1910), is an earlier discussion of the issues involved, in connexion with the great Poor Law Enquiry of 1911. Gilbert Slater, *Poverty and the State* (London, 1930), covers a wide period, but has chapters devoted to special aspects of Poor Law administration. S. E. Finer, *The Life and Times of Sir Edwin Chadwick* (London, 1952), with an elaborate classified bibliography, is indispensable. Marian Bowley, *Nassau Senior and Classical Economics* (London, 1937), should be consulted for the views of one of the framers of the *Report* of 1834 and critics of later developments, and LIONEL ROBBINS, *The Theory of Economic Policy in English Classical Political Economy* (London, 1952), for a more general discussion of the theories underlying the Poor Law. Articles on "The New Poor Law", in *Quarterly Review*, vols. LIII and LIV (1834 and 1835), and on "The Principles and Progress of the Poor Law Amendment Act" (by EDWIN CHADWICK), in *Edinburgh Review*, 63 (1836), may also be referred to. C. DRIVER, *Tory Radical: the Life of Richard Oastler* (Oxford, 1946), deals with one of the most formidable critics of the new administration; D. HUDSON, *Life of Thomas Barnes* (Cambridge, 1943), with the editor responsible for *The Times* during the period, and the *History of the Times*, vol. I, *The Thunderer in the Making, 1765–1841* (London, 1945), with the newspaper that J. A. ROEBUCK described as "the great parent of all this opposition to the Poor Law". G. LEWIS, *Letters of George Cornewall Lewis* (London, 1870), throws light on the leading figure among the Commissioners in the last period of the Commission. HUMPHRY HOUSE, *The Dickens World* (Cambridge, 1941), CECIL WOODHAM SMITH, *Florence Nightingale* (London, 1950), and S. SQUIRE SPRIGGE, *Life and Times of Thomas Wakley* (London, 1897), touch Poor Law administration at various points.

DAVID ROBERTS, *How Cruel was the Victorian Poor Law*, Hist. J. vi., 1963; MARK BLAUG, *Myth of the Old Poor Law and Making of the New*, J. Ec. Hist. xxiii, 1963; *Poor Law Report re-examined*, J. E. Hist. xxiv, 1963; R. A. LEWIS, *William Day and the Poor Law Commissioners*, Univ. Birm. Hist. J. ix, 1964 – a Misfit in the bureaucracy.

206A–I. Report from His Majesty's Commissioners for inquiring into the Administration and Practical Operation of the Poor Laws (1834)

Published by Authority, London, Fellowes, 1834.

206A. Progressive character of burdens and evils associated with the existing law

op. cit., p. 54.

It is with still further regret that we state our conviction that the abuses of which we have given a short outline, though checked in some instances by the extra-ordinary energy and wisdom of individuals, are, on the whole, steadily and rapidly progressive.

It is true, that by the last Parliamentary Return (that for the year ending the 25th. March 1832) the total amount of the money expended for the relief of the poor, though higher than for any year since the year 1820, appears to fall short of the expenditure of the year ending the 25th. March, 1818; the expenditure of that year having been £7,890,014, and that for the year ending the 25th. March, 1832, £7,036,968. But it is to be remembered, 1st., That the year ending the 25th. of March, 1818, was a period of extraordinary distress among the labouring classes, especially in the manufacturing districts, in consequence of the high price of provisions, unaccompanied by a corresponding advance in wages; 2ndly, That in the year ending the 25th. March, 1832, the price of corn was lower by about one-third than in 1818, and that of clothes and of the other necessaries of life lower in a still greater proportion, so that, after allowing for an increase of population of one-fifth, the actual amount of relief given in 1832 was much larger in proportion to the population than even that given in 1818, which has generally been considered as the year in which it attained its highest amount; and, 3rdly, That the statement of the mere amount expended, whether estimated in money or in kind, affords a very inadequate measure of the loss sustained by those who supply it. A great part of the expense is incurred, not by direct payment out of the rates, but by the purchase of unprofitable labour. Where rate-payers are the immediate employers of workpeople, they often keep down the rates, either by employing more labour than they actually want, or by employing parishioners, when better labourers could be obtained. The progressive deterioration of the labourers in the pauperised districts, and the increasing anxiety of the principal rate-payers, as their burthen becomes more oppressive, to shift it in some way, either on the inhabitants of neighbouring parishes, or on the portion of their fellow-parishioners who can make the least resistance; and the apparent sanction given to this conduct by the 2 and 3 William IV c. 96,[1] appear to have greatly increased this source of indirect and unrecorded loss. . . .

206B. Principles of a sound system

op. cit., pp. 227–228.

The most pressing of the evils which we have described are those connected with the relief of the Able-bodied. They are the evils, therefore, for which we shall first propose remedies.

[1] A temporary Act of 1832, empowering parishes to employ their poor.

If we believed the evils stated in the previous part of the Report, or evils resembling, or even approaching them, to be necessarily incidental to the compulsory relief of the able-bodied, we should not hesitate in recommending its entire abolition. But we do not believe these evils to be its necessary consequences. We believe that, under strict regulations, adequately enforced, such relief may be afforded safely, and even beneficially.

In all extensive communities, circumstances will occur in which an individual, by the failure of his means of subsistence, will be exposed to the danger of perishing. To refuse relief, and at the same time to punish mendicity when it cannot be proved that the offender could have obtained subsistence by labour, is repugnant to the common sentiments of mankind; it is repugnant to them to punish even depredation, apparently committed as the only resource against want.

In all extensive civilised communities, therefore, the occurrence of extreme necessity is prevented by alms-giving, by public institutions supported by endowments or voluntary contributions, or by a provision partly voluntary and partly compulsory, or by a provision entirely compulsory, which may exclude the pretext of mendicancy.

But in no part of Europe except England has it been thought fit that the provision, whether compulsory or voluntary, should be applied to more than the relief of *indigence*, the state of a person unable to labour, or unable to obtain, in return for his labour, the means of subsistence. It has never been deemed expedient that the provision should extend to the relief of *poverty*; that is the state of one, who, in order to obtain a mere subsistence, is forced to have recourse to labour.

From the evidence collected under this Commission, we are induced to believe that a compulsory provision for the relief of the indigent can be generally administered on a sound and well-defined principle; and that under the operation of this principle, the assurance that no one need perish from want may be rendered more complete than at present, and the mendicant and vagrant repressed by disarming them of their weapon – the plea of impending starvation.

It may be assumed, that in the administration of relief, the public is warranted in imposing such conditions on the individual relieved, as are conducive to the benefit either of the invididual himself, or of the country at large, at whose expense he is to be relieved.

The first and most essential of all conditions, a principle which we find universally admitted, even by those whose practice is at variance with it, is, that his situation on the whole shall not be made really or apparently as eligible as the situation of the independent labourer of the lowest class. Throughout the evidence it is shown, that in proportion as the condition of any pauper class is elevated above the condition of independent labourers, the condition of the independent class is depressed; their industry is impaired, their employment becomes unsteady, and its remuneration in wages is diminished. Such persons, therefore, are under the strongest inducements to quit the less eligible class of labourers, and enter the more eligible class of paupers. The converse is the effect when the pauper class is placed in its proper position, below the condition of the independent labourer. Every penny bestowed, that tends to render the position of the pauper more eligible than that of the independent labourer, is a bounty on indolence and vice. We have found, that as the poor's-rates are at present administered, they operate as bounties of this description, to the amount of several millions annually.

The standard, therefore, to which reference must be made in fixing the condition of those who are to be maintained by the public, is the condition of those who are maintained by their own exertions. But the evidence shows how loosely and imperfectly the situation of the independent labourer has been inquired into, and how little is really known of it by those who award or distribute relief. It shows also that so little has their situation been made a standard for the supply of commodities, that the diet of the workhouse almost always exceeds that of the cottage, and the diet of the gaol is generally more profuse than even that of the workhouse. It shows also, that this standard has been so little referred to in the exaction of labour, that commonly the work required from the pauper is inferior to that performed by the labourers and servants of those who have prescribed it: so much, and so generally inferior as to create a prevalent notion among the agricultural paupers that they have a right to be exempted from the amount of work which is performed, and indeed sought for by the independent labourer. . . .

206C. Effect of the reform on wages

op. cit., p. 339.

Before the experiment was made, it might fairly have been anticipated that the discontinuance of parochial allowances would effect little or no improvement in wages unless a similar change were made in the neighbouring parishes. When a considerable proportion of the labourers who had been entirely dependent upon the parish were driven to rely on their own industry, it might have been anticipated that the wages of the entire body of labourers within the parish would have been injuriously affected by their competition. And this certainly would have been the case if they had added nothing to the fund out of which their wages came. That fund is, in fact, periodically consumed and reproduced by the labourer, assisted by the land and the farmer's capital, and, all other things remaining the same, the amount of that fund, and consequently his share of it, or, in other words, the amount of his wages, depends on his industry and skill. If all the labourers in a parish cease to work, they no longer produce any fund for their own subsistence, and must either starve or be supported, as they were at Cholesbury,[1] by rates in aid. A single person who has no property and is supported without working, bears the same relation to the labourers who do work as the parishioners of Cholesbury bore to the neighbouring parishes. He is supported by a sort of rate in aid on their industry. His conversion from a pauper, wholly or partially supported by the labour of others, into an independent labourer producing his own subsistence, and in addition to that, a profit to his employer, so far from injuring his fellow workmen, produces on them the same effects, as the enabling the inhabitants of Cholesbury to support themselves has produced on the parishes which had to supply them with rates in aid. This has been

[1] A small Buckinghamshire parish where the owners and occupiers of the land had renounced interest in it; neighbouring parishes helped to support it (*Report*, p. 64).

perceived by some of our witnesses. A farmer of considerable intelligence, who had resided in Cookham, and observed the effects of the change in that parish, declared his conviction that if such a change could be generally introduced, the money saved in poor's-rates would almost immediately be paid in wages. The withdrawal of relief in aid of wages appears to be succeeded by effects in the following order:–First, the labourer becomes more steady and diligent; next, the more efficient labour makes the return to the farmer's capital larger, and the consequent increase of the fund for the employment of labour enables and induces the capitalist to give better wages. . . .

206D. Effect of dispauperization on morals and content of labourer

op. cit., pp. 240–241.

The next class of specific effects which have followed the application of the principle of keeping the condition of the pauper inferior to that of the independent labourer, is, that it has arrested the increase of population, which the evidence shows to be produced by the present state of the law and of its administration. . . . In the Report from Cookham, it is stated, that "some very striking consequences have resulted from the operation of the present system. In the eight years preceding the operation of the new system, the increase of population was very rapid; for the eight years subsequent there was, as compared with the eight years preceding, a positive diminution. Improvident marriages are less frequent." In the Report from Swallowfield, it is stated, that, "the number of improvident marriages is diminished about one half." In Bingham, the diminution of improvident marriages was about one-half; and yet, in all these parishes, illegitimate births, instead of having been promoted by the diminution of marriages, have been repressed still more effectually, and in the last, almost extinguished. . . .

Whatever impels any class into courses of sustained industry must necessarily diminish crime; and we find that one characteristic of the dispauperised parishes is the comparative absence of crime. In Bingham, before the change of system took place, scarcely a night passed without mischief; and during the two years preceding 1818, seven men of the parish were transported for felonies; now there is scarcely any disorder in the place. In Uley and Southwell parishes crime has similarly ceased.

In almost every instance the content of the labourers increased with their industry. . . .

206E. Results of offering work instead of allowance

op. cit., pp. 257–261.

The circumstances of a rural parish being, to a considerable degree, an independent community, separated by the barriers of the law of settlement from other parochial communities, and the general knowledge possessed by the witnesses of the principal circumstances of all or most of the individuals of its labouring population, give a very high value to the results of the experiment made in each of the rural parishes which we have mentioned. The uniform success of the principle, and the remarkable similarity of its incidents, in different parishes, in different parts of the country, and under different circumstances, appear to us to prove its correctness, and to leave no doubt that it would be productive of similar effects throughout the country.

Further evidence of the beneficial operation of the principle on which the improvements described in the preceding statements were founded, is afforded in almost every pauperised district; first, by the comparative character of those resident labourers who, having a distant settlement, can only claim temporary relief, and that subject to an order of removal to their own parishes; and, secondly, by the condition of that part of the labouring population which still remains independent of parochial aid. We have already stated that in every district the conditions of this class is found to be strikingly distinguishable from that of the pauper, and superior to it, though the independent labourers are commonly maintained upon less money.

. . . . .

If, while the general administration of the Poor-Laws were allowed to remain on its present footing, such occasional or partial relief as that which is available to the settled labourer of a parish were rendered equally available to the unsettled labourers, we cannot doubt that such a proceeding would demoralise and depress this respectable and valuable class to the level of the settled and pauperised labourers. This is ample reason against assimilating the condition of the unsettled to that of the settled labourers, but none against placing the settled on the same footing as the unsettled. The present practice as to unsettled labourers, is almost exactly that which we propose to make the rule for all classes, both settled and unsettled.

. . . . .

We attach much importance to the general superiority of the conduct and the condition of the non-parishioners, the unsettled labourers. Although the evidence afforded from the dispauperised parishes appears to us to be conclusive as to the effects which may be anticipated from a similar change of system throughout the country, it is still liable to the objection, however unreasonable, that these parishes are individual and scattered instances too few to establish a general conclusion; but the evidence afforded by the character and condition of the unsettled labourers pervades the whole country. Every body of labourers resident and labouring within a parish of which they are not parishioners, and where the distance of their own parishes, and the administration of the poor's-rates does not render partial relief available, may be referred to in proof of the general effects which would follow an improved system of administering relief. These labourers make no complaint of their having no right to partial relief, and we have not met with an instance of their having suffered from the want of it. The fact of the non-settled labourers maintaining an independent condition, whilst they have a right by law to return at the public expense to their own parishes, and claim parochial aid, proves that they themselves consider their present condition more advantageous than that of paupers, and that so considering it, they are anxious to retain it.

From the above evidence it appears, that wherever the principle which we have thus stated has been carried into effect, either wholly or partially, its introduction has been beneficial to the class for whose benefit Poor-Laws exist. We have seen that in every instance in which the able-bodied labourers have been rendered independent of partial relief, or of relief otherwise than in a well-regulated workhouse–

1. Their industry has been restored and improved.
2. Frugal habits have been created or strengthened.
3. The permanent demand for their labour has increased.
4. And the increase has been such, that their wages, so far from being depressed by the increased amount of labour in the market, have in general advanced.
5. The number of improvident and wretched marriages has diminished.
6. Their discontent has been abated, and their moral and social condition in every way improved.

. . .

206F. Proposed abolition of outdoor relief to able-bodied

op. cit., pp. 261–262.

We therefore submit, as the general principle of legislation on this subject, in the present condition of the country:–

That those modes of administering relief which have been tried wholly or partially, and have produced beneficial results in some districts, be introduced, with modifications according to local circumstances, and carried into complete execution in all.

The chief specific measures which we recommend for effecting these purposes are–

First, that except as to medical attendance, and subject to the exception respecting apprenticeship herein-after stated, all relief whatever to able-bodied persons or to their families, otherwise than in well-regulated workhouses (*i.e.* places where they may be set to work according to the spirit and intention of the 43rd. of Elizabeth) shall be declared unlawful, and shall cease, in manner and at periods hereafter specified; and that all relief afforded in respect of children under the age of 16 shall be considered as afforded to their parents. . . .

206G. Need of central supervision

op. cit., pp. 294–297.

Witnesses, when speaking of the necessity of withdrawing all discretionary power from the distributors, in their own parishes, usually express a hope that the relief may be fixed, and to the "smallest detail unalterably prescribed by the legislature". The evidence, however, proves that little more reliance can be placed on the voluntary execution by the present agency of any regulations, than on their correct execution of any general principle of management prescribed to them.

It appears, too, that the actual condition of the pauperised districts does not admit of legislation in detail. The differences in administering the law in different districts have produced habits and conditions of the population equally different. The best-informed witnesses have represented that the measures applicable to adjacent districts are totally inapplicable to their own; and it appears to us, that measures which might be safely and beneficially introduced into the majority of parishes in a district might, if immediately introduced, be productive of suffering and disorder to the remainder. Even if the simultaneous and complete execution of so great a change of system throughout the country were practicable, we consider it desirable to avoid it.

It must be remembered that the pauperised labourers were not the authors of the abusive system, and ought not to be made responsible for its consequences. We cannot, therefore recommend that they should be otherwise than gradually subjected to regulations which, though undoubtedly beneficial to themselves, may, by any sudden application, inflict unnecessary severity. The abuses have grown up in detail, and it appears from our evidence that the most safe course will be to remove them in detail. We deem uniformity essential; but, in the first instance, it is only an approximation to uniformity that can be expected, and it appears that it must be obtained by gradations in detail, according to local circumstances. And although uniformity in the amount of relief may be requisite, it may not be requisite that the relief should be invariably the same in kind. In Cumberland, and some others of the northern counties, milk is generally used where beer is used in the southern counties. The requisite equality in diet would probably be obtainable without forcing any class of the inmates of the workhouses in the northern counties to take beer, or those of the southern counties to take milk. . . .

By many it is considered that the only means by which the system can be effectually amended, is the management of the whole Poor-law administration as a branch of the general government. The advocates of a national rate, and those who are willing and desirous that the Government should take upon itself the whole distribution of the funds for the relief of the poor, do not appear to have considered the expense and difficulties in the way of obtaining such an agency throughout the country.

We have received no definite plan for the purpose, and have prepared none. We trust that immediate measures for the correction of the evils in question may be carried into effect by a comparatively small and cheap agency, which may assist the parochial or district officers, wherever their management is in conformity to the intention of the legislature; and control them wherever their management is at variance with it. Subject also to this control, we propose that the management, the collection of the rates, and the entire supervision of the expenditure, under increased securities against profusion and malversation, shall continue in the officers appointed immediately by the rate-payers. This course, we believe, will be the most easily practicable, and will best accord with the recommendations of the majority of the witnesses, and with the prevalent expectation of the country.

The course of proceedings which we recommend for adoption, is in principle that which the legislature adopted for the management of the savings' banks, the friendly societies, and the annuity societies throughout the country. Having prescribed the outline and general principles on which those institutions should be conducted, a special agency (which, in this instance, was constituted by one barrister only) was appointed to see that their rules and detailed regulations conformed to the intention of the law. This agency, we believe, has accomplished the object effectually. From magistrates and clergymen, who act as trustees and managers of savings' banks, we have learned that it is found to work satisfactorily to them and to the members at large, because they are aware that the decision by which any regulation is established or disallowed is made on extended information derived from all similar institutions throughout the kingdom, instead of being made only on such as the neighbourhood might chance to afford. We believe that the control has also been found beneficial by the members of friendly societies and has put a stop to many which were founded, either ignorantly or dishonestly, on principles fraught with ruin to the contributors. Since the adoption of this measure, there has been only one appeal against the barrister's decision, and that appeal was disallowed.

We recommend, therefore, the appointment of a Central Board to control the administration of the Poor-Laws, with such Assistant Commissioners as may be found requisite; and that the Commissioners be empowered and directed to frame and enforce regulations for the government of workhouses, and as to the nature and amount of the relief to be given and the labour to be exacted in them, and that such regulations shall, as far as may be practicable, be uniform throughout the country....

206H. Segregation in workhouses

op. cit., pp. 306–314.

Even in the larger workhouses internal subdivisions do not afford the means of classification, where the inmates dine in the same rooms, or meet or see each other in the ordinary business of the place. In the largest houses, containing from eight hundred to a thousand inmates, where there is comparatively good order, and, in many respects, superior management, it is almost impossible to prevent the formation and extension of vicious connexions. One part of a class of adults often so closely resembles a part of another class, as to make any distinction in treatment appear arbitrary and capricious to those who are placed in the inferior class, and to create discontents, which the existing authority is too feeble to suppress, and so much complexity as to render the object attainable only by great additional expense and remarkable skill. Much, however, has been accomplished in some of the existing houses, but much more it appears to us, may be effected, and at a less expense by the measures that we proceed to suggest.

At least four classes are necessary:–1. The aged and really impotent; 2. The children; 3. The able-bodied females; 4. The able-bodied males. Of whom we trust that the two latter will be the least numerous classes. It appears to us that both the requisite classification and the requisite superintendence may be better obtained in separate buildings than under a single roof. If effected in the latter mode, large buildings must be erected, since few of the existing buildings are of the requisite size or arrangement, and as very different qualities, both moral and intellectual, are required for the management of such dissimilar classes, each class must have its separate superintendent. Nothing would be saved, therefore, in superintendence, and much expense must be incurred in buildings. . . .

Although such is the general tenor of the evidence, we cannot state that there may not be some districts where new workhouses would be found requisite, but we have no doubt that where this does occur, the erection of appropriate edifices, though apparently expensive, would ultimately be found economical. Under a system of district management the workhouses might be supplied under one contract at wholesale prices. Mr. Mott states that if 500 persons cost £10 per head, or £5,000; 1,000 persons would cost only £9 per head, or £9,000. He also states, that there would be no more difficulty in managing five or six combined workhouses than five or six separate wards or rooms in one house. Considerable economy would also be practicable in combined workhouses, by varying the nature of the supplies. In the smaller workhouses the children receive nearly the same diet as the adults; if they were separated they might receive a diet both cheaper and more wholesome.

To effect these purposes we recommend that the Central Board be empowered to cause any number of parishes that they may think convenient to be incorporated for the purpose of workhouse management, and for providing new workhouses where necessary, to declare their workhouses to be the common workhouses of the incorporated district, and to assign to those workhouses separate classes of poor, though composed of the poor of distinct parishes, each distinct parish paying to the support of the permanent workhouse establishment, in proportion to the average amount of the expense incurred for the relief of its poor, for the three previous years, and paying separately for the food and clothing of its own paupers. . . .

2061. Further recommendations

op. cit., pp. 319–357.

We recommend, therefore, that the Central Board be empowered and required to take measures for the general adoption of a complete, clear, and, as far as may be practicable, uniform system of accounts. . . .

We further recommend, therefore, that the Central Board be empowered to incorporate parishes for the purpose of appointing and paying permanent officers, and for the execution of works of public labour. . . .

We recommend, therefore, that the Central Board be directed to state the general qualifications which shall be necessary to candidates for paid offices connected with the relief of the poor, to recommend to parishes and incorporations proper persons to act as paid officers, and to remove any paid officers whom they shall think unfit for their situations. . . .

We recommend that the Central Board be empowered to direct the parochial consumption to be supplied by tender and contract, and to provide that the competition be perfectly free. . . .

We therefore recommend, that under regulations to be framed by the Central Board, parishes be empowered to treat any relief afforded to the able-bodied, or to their families, and any expenditure in the workhouses, or otherwise incurred on their account, as a loan, and recoverable not only by the means given by the 29th. section of the 59th. Geo. III. c. 12,[1] but also by attachment of their subsequent wages, in a mode resembling that pointed out in the 30th., 31st., and 32nd., sections of that Act. . . .

We recommend, therefore, that the Central Board be empowered to make such

[1] Act to Amend Laws for the Relief of the Poor, 1819. It empowered overseers to such relief by loan, and facilitated the attachment of wages and pensions.

regulations as they shall think fit respecting the relief to be afforded by apprenticing children, and that at a future period, when the effect of the proposed alterations shall have been seen, the Central Board be required to make a special inquiry into the operation of the laws respecting the apprenticing children at the expense of parishes, and into the operation of the regulations in that respect which the Board shall have enforced. . . .

We recommend that the Central Board be empowered and directed to frame and enforce regulations as to the relief to be afforded to vagrants and discharged prisoners. . . .

We recommend, therefore, that the Board be required to submit a Report annually, to one of Your Majesty's Principal Secretaries of State, containing–1. An Account of their Proceedings; 2. Any further amendments which they may think it advisable to suggest; 3. The Evidence on which the suggestions are founded; 4. Bills carrying those amendments (if any) into effect, which Bills the Board shall be empowered to prepare with professional assistance. . . .

We recommend that the Central Board be empowered to appoint and remove their Assistants and all their subordinate officers. . . .

We recommend, therefore, that settlement by hiring and service, apprenticeship, purchasing or renting a tenement, estate, paying rates, or serving in an office, be abolished. . . .

We recommend, therefore, that (subject to the obvious exceptions of persons born in prisons, hospitals, and workhouses) the settlement of every legitimate child born after the passing of the intended Act, follow that of the parents, or surviving parent: and that at the age of sixteen years, or the death of its surviving parent, such child shall be considered settled in the place in which it was born. . . .

And to afford further facilities to the proof of a birth settlement,–We recommend that whenever there shall be any question regarding the settlement by birth of a person, whether legitimate or illegitimate, and whether born before or after the passing of the intended Act, the place where such person shall have been first known by the evidence of such person, by the register of his or her birth or baptism or otherwise, to have existed, shall be presumed to have been the place of his or her birth, until the contrary shall be proved. . . .

We recommend that the general rule shall be followed, as far as it is possible, and that every illegitimate child born after the passing of the Act, shall, until it attain the age of sixteen, follow its mother's settlement. . . .

Secondly, with respect to the Mother.–As a further step towards the natural state of things, we recommend that the mother of an illegitimate child born after the passing of the Act, be required to support it, and that any relief occasioned by the wants of the child be considered relief afforded to the parent. . . .

We recommend that the same liability be extended to her husband. . . .

On the other hand, we recommend the repeal of that part of the 35 Geo. III. c. 101, s. 6, which makes an unmarried pregnant woman removable, and the 50 Geo. III. c. 51, s. 2; which authorises the committal of the mother of a chargeable bastard to the House of Correction.

We recommend, therefore, that the vestry of each parish be empowered to order the payment out of the rates raised for the relief of the poor, of the expenses of the emigration of any persons having settlements within such parish, who may be willing to emigrate; provided, that the expense of each emigration be raised and paid, within a period to be mentioned in the Act.

207A–D. Second Annual Report of the Poor Law Commission

Parlty. Papers, 1836/xxix.

207A. Unpopularity of the Act

loc. cit., p. 5.

. . . It could not be expected, that an Act which so materially disturbed the distribution of as large a sum of money as £7,000,000 per annum, which of necessity changed the source from which a large portion of the inhabitants of the country derived their customary means of subsistence, and which in so doing opposed itself not only to the interests, the prejudices, and the fears of a large portion of the population, but pressed hardly on the sincere though mistaken notions of charity, which were established in the breasts of others, could possibly be carried into effect without difficulty and resistance. Your Lordship, therefore, will learn without surprise that the powers of the Act, and our means of carrying it into operation, have been put to the proof by every means which ingenuity could devise. That the pauper labourers themselves, whose interests were to be so greatly affected, should adopt this course was naturally to be anticipated. It is due, however, to the good sense and acuteness of this class of persons to say, that they very quickly understood the true bearing of the Act; and that in many districts they set themselves, without much delay, fairly and honestly to seek a livelihood by their own industry. Many striking instances of the revival of this feeling amongst that portion of the working classes will be found in the Reports of our Assistant Commissioners. In other places, where a reliance on the poor-rate had become engrafted in the manners and habits of the labouring population, every method has been resorted to for the purpose of impeding the operation of the law. Partial riots have occurred in different counties; but by the aid of small parties of the Metropolitan police (who, by the provisions of a most useful Act of the last session, can now be sworn in and paid as special constables in any county of England and Wales), occasionally aided by the support of a military force, these disturbances have been put down without any considerable injury to property. . . .

207B. Effects of the new law

loc. cit., pp. 23–24.

We now proceed to explain the effects which have been produced by the operation of the new law upon the manners, comfort and general condition of the labouring classes, and as it has affected the ratepayers.

With respect to the first, and, as we think, by far the most important and interesting branch of the subject, the accounts are from all quarters alike gratifying and conclusive. We do not undertake to deny that cases of individual suffering may have occurred. We know of no state of human society which ever did, or, as we believe, ever can exist, in which such cases may not occur. We have abundant proof that they did occur far more frequently under the old system of Poor Law Administration, than under that which we have been commissioned to establish; and we think that those persons are in error who suppose that, because an alleged case of distress and suffering is brought forward, it is to be taken as a conclusive argument against the policy of the new system. Many such complaints have reached us; almost all of them on inquiry have proved to be greatly exaggerated, or else utterly destitute of foundation. Still we do not deny that disease, accident, ignorance or neglect may have occasioned suffering which could not in all possible cases have been instantly provided for; but we assert that such cases will be far less frequent than heretofore. The guardians, relieving officers and medical officers are active, watchful and efficient; and in addition to these (which may be partly considered as newly created powers), the powers of the magistrates and overseers of the poor, as to all cases of sudden and real emergency, remain in operation as heretofore. It is from ignorance and misapprehension as to the real nature of the change which is taking place, that doubts and distrust as to its tendency are found still to prevail in some instances. That these doubts and misapprehensions will soon be dispelled we cannot but believe. That the public is rapidly acquiring a correct view of the change which has taken place among the labouring classes, we think we shall be able to demonstrate; and for this purpose we shall extract from some of the numerous letters which have been addressed to our Assistant Commissioners, passages which will carry with them a weight of authority which no statement of ours could equally impart. . . .

207C. Financial results

loc. cit., pp. 29–30.

Our Assistant Commissioners, on entering new districts, are frequently met with assurances that our instructional letters have been acted upon with as much promptitude and exactness as if they had been orders; and the state of the administration, especially in the progressive substitution of relief in kind for relief in money, and the check put to the extension or continuance of out-door relief, wherever there is a workhouse, verify these assurances. Another motive frequently impels the adoption of this course, namely, that of meeting investigation and preparing for the approaching change, by reducing the future averages of contribution to the expenses of the Union establishment. The Returns from the united parishes contain numerous announcements that these preparatory proceedings have been successfully adopted. The extensive effect of the impulse given by the change of the law, and the wide promulgation of its principles by means of the Reports which His Majesty's Government have caused to be published, as well as the correspondence, admonitory and instructional, of this office, is shown in the reduction of the rates in those parishes which have not yet been placed under the control of Boards of Guardians. Amongst the reductions which are general, must be included the reductions of the expense of litigation. The effect of the new machinery is however marked by the fact, that whilst the reductions in the best managed of the separate parishes generally average about 20 per cent., the reductions in the new Unions, which have been for more than half a year in operation, average about 43 per cent., often including expenses for furniture, and alterations, constituting a portion of the expenses of the first outlay.

We are not aware of any parish, distinguished for its improved management previously to its being included in a Union, where the ratepayers have not participated in the advantages of management on a larger scale. So far as the Returns have yet been received, it appears that in the best managed parishes, those in some of which petitions were preferred against being included in the new Unions, setting forth, as the grounds of exemption, their former good management, and that they could sustain nothing but loss from the Union, a reduction has nevertheless taken place. In one of the best managed parishes in the kingdom, the rural parish of Cookham, in Berks, a parish where the poor-rates at one time amounted to nearly £4,000 per annum, it appears that the expenditure for 1834–5 was £700; for 1835–6, £580; the average expenditure for three years preceding the Union was £852. The average expenditure for the present year, formed on an estimate of the two last quarters, is £560.

In the parish of Hitchin, in Hertfordshire, another well-managed parish, where an increase was confidently predicted, the poor-rates in 1835, before the formation of the Union, amounted to £1,716; after the Union they were reduced to £496.

The parish of Swallowfield, in the Wokingham Union, expended annually an average sum of £540, for the relief of the poor in 1833, 1834, 1835; during the year ended March 1836, the sum so expended was £231.

The rates of the parish of Uley, in Gloucestershire, now included in the Dursley Union, were, before the Union, £1,408; the rate of expenditure for the last year was £428.

In a parish from whence petitions were presented to both Houses of Parliament, protesting that their own good management could not be exceeded, the parish of Stoke Pogis, in Buckinghamshire, the expenditure has been reduced, from £853, in 1834–5, to £490 in 1835–6.

We have already stated, that we have added other parishes to some of the existing Unions as originally constituted; and the experience already obtained under the Commission indicates that the direction of future alterations of Unions will be in the addition of other parishes. The extent of many of the Unions was regulated by emergencies at the time of their formation, and some doubts as to the local capabilities for management on a larger scale. With reference to any opposition to the extension of the field of management, it may be satisfactory to your Lordship to be informed, that the principles upon which that extension was determined are fully borne out, not only by a comparison of the progress of the parishes in Union with the progress of the parishes ununited, but by a comparison of the progress of the larger with the smaller Unions. Thus, if of the 110 Unions which we have specified as having been in operation more than 12 months, we take the 43 largest, and compare the results with the 24 positively smallest, and the 27 intermediate, in area, population, and rates we find that the savings effected in these Unions are in the following proportions:

43 largest Unions, rate of saving 46 per cent.
24 smallest Unions, rate of saving 29 per cent.
26 intermediate Unions, rate of saving 42 per cent.

So, if of the 64 Unions that have been in operation six months and upwards, we compare the 22 largest with the 15 smallest and 27 intermediate sized Unions, the reductions have been, in the

22 largest Unions, 41 per cent.
15 smallest Unions, 28 per cent.
27 intermediate Unions, 36 per cent.

207D. Workhouse dietaries

loc. cit., pp. 56–59.

Men only quoted.

1. Breakfasts – 6 ozs. bread and 1½ ozs. cheese. Dinners – Sundays, 5 ozs. meat and ½ lb. potatoes. Tuesdays and Thursdays, ditto. Other days 1½ pints soup. Supper – days on which there was meat for dinner, 6 ozs. bread and 1½ pints broth; other days, 6 ozs. bread and 2 ozs. cheese.
2. Breakfasts–6 ozs. bread and 1 oz. cheese. Dinners–Sundays, 16 ozs. of meat pudding plus vegetables; Monday, 7 ozs. bread and 1 oz. cheese; Tuesdays and Fridays, 16 ozs. suet pudding plus vegetables; other days, bread and cheese as Mondays. Supper – 6 ozs. bread and 1 oz. cheese.
3. Breakfasts – 8 ozs. bread and 1½ pints gruel. Dinners – Sundays, 7 ozs. bread, 2 ozs. cheese; Mondays, ditto; Tuesdays, 8 ozs. cooked meat, ¾ lb. potatoes; Wednesdays, as Sundays; Thursdays, 1½ pints soup and 6 ozs. bread; Fridays, bread and cheese, as Sundays; Saturdays, 5 ozs. bacon, ¾ lb. potatoes. Suppers, 6 ozs. bread 1½ ozs. cheese.
4. Breakfasts – 8 ozs. bread and 1½ pints gruel; Dinners, Sundays, Tuesdays, and Fridays, 2 pints soup and 6 ozs. bread; Wednesdays, 6 ozs. pickled pork plus vegetables; Mondays and Thursdays, 12 ozs. rice or suet pudding with vegetables. Suppers – 6 ozs. bread and 2 ozs. cheese.
5. Breakfasts – 7 ozs. bread, 1½ pints gruel or porridge. Dinners – Sundays, 5 ozs. meat and ¾ lb. vegetables; Thursdays, ditto; Mondays, 1½ pints soup and 7 ozs. vegetables; Fridays, ditto; Tuesdays, 14 ozs. rice or suet pudding; Wednesdays, 7 ozs. bread and 2 ozs. cheese. Suppers – Sundays, Tuesdays and Thursdays, 7 ozs. bread and 2 ozs. cheese. Other nights, ¾ lb. potatoes.
6. Breakfasts – 6 ozs. bread, 1 oz. cheese. Dinners – Sundays, 16 ozs. suet pudding; Mondays, 6 ozs. bread, 1 oz. cheese; Tuesdays and Thursdays, 4 ozs. meat and ¾ lb. potatoes; yeast dumpling; Wednesdays and Saturdays, bread and cheese, as Mondays; Fridays, 11 ozs. meat dumpling. Supper, 6 ozs. bread, 1 oz. cheese, 1 pint broth.

208A–B. Third Annual Report of the Poor Law Commission

Parlty. Papers, 1837/XXXI.

208A. Unemployment at Nottingham

In their Fourth Report, in the following year (1837–1838/XXVIII) the Commissioners note the intensification of the distress. By August 1837, charitable subscriptions were no longer able to cope with it, and the Commission permitted outdoor relief of the able-bodied in return for task work. The situation continued to worsen until October, by which time a good deal of further workhouse accommodation had been added, and a food kitchen opened. By the following April it eased, and in June outdoor relief and employment were brought to an end.

The greater part of the important manufacturing counties of Stafford, Nottingham and Leicester, was arranged in Unions before the close of the last parochial year (25th March, 1837). . . . In these Unions the administration of relief by the Boards of Guardians had hardly been undertaken before the interruption of the American trade produced a cessation in the demand for labour, more sudden in its approach and more extensive in its operation than has been known on any former occasion, Your Lordship is aware that an opinion has prevailed with many persons, that the provisions of the Poor Law Amendment Act, though useful in the agricultural districts of the south and east of England, are both uncalled for and inapplicable in the populous manufacturing districts of the north. We hold ourselves prepared to show that these views and opinions are unfounded, but it is a matter of deep regret to us that the new system was so imperfectly organized and established in the central manufacturing districts when the pressure of distress and difficulty arose, as to render it impossible for us to show all the benefits which might have been effected under it, if its organization had been complete and mature. . . .

It is, however, to the proceedings in Nottingham that we are chiefly desirous of drawing your Lordship's attention, as they appear to throw considerable light on the working of the Act in a manufacturing district, under circumstances as trying and difficult as can at any time be expected to occur.

This Union, which consists of the three parishes constituting the town of Nottingham, and containing an aggregate population amounting to 50,000 was formed in July, 1836. It was distinguished at the outset by this peculiarity, that the rule prohibiting out-door relief to able-bodied male paupers was issued at once on the formation of the Union. Our object in at once establishing this rule was to make the administration of relief to the poor conform to the practice already established in the parish of St. Mary (the principal and most populous parish in the Union), in which, for three years previous to the formation of the Union, no relief had been given to able-bodied males, excepting in the workhouse.

Under the operation of this rule our attention could not fail to be specially drawn to the working of this Union, when in the early part of the spring the pressure of commercial distress and the suspension of employment caused the manufacturers to discharge a large proportion of their workmen; and we directed our Assistant Commissioner, Mr. Gulson, to give as large a portion of his time and attention as could be spared from the rest of his extensive district to the Nottingham Union, and to aid the Board of Guardians to the utmost with his advice and assistance.

We knew that the Union was very inadequately provided with workhouse accommodation. It was possessed of an old workhouse capable of containing about 520 persons, but not admitting of that arrangement and classification which is found practically to be so essential to good order in such establishments. As the applications for relief increased, it was satisfactory to us to find that the Guardians took steps to increase the workhouse accommodation by occupying certain premises belonging to the parish as nurseries for children and as houses for old men, and finally by using a workhouse belonging to the parish of St. Nicholas as a hospital for the sick. They were by these means enabled to provide room for nearly 700 persons within their houses.

A constant communication was kept up with the Board of Guardians, from whom we received a weekly report, as well as with our Assistant Commissioner; and it soon became evident that a necessity would speedily arise for relieving more persons than could be provided for within the walls of the workhouses, and after full consideration we felt it to be our duty to authorize Mr. Gulson to assure the Guardians that the rule which prohibited them from giving relief to able-bodied male persons excepting in the workhouse should be suspended whenever they should find the pressure such as that, in their opinion, there existed a necessity for so doing. Preparation was thus made for placing the Guardians in a situation to meet the whole difficulty, (whatever might be its extent,) of affording the necessary relief to such destitute persons as might be unable to maintain themselves when thrown out of work.

At this stage of our proceedings it was determined by the principal inhabitants of the town to resort to a subscription for the purpose of relieving the unemployed operatives, this being considered a better mode of affording them support than by having recourse to the poor-rate. The kind feeling and praiseworthy benevolence of the principal persons in the town and its neighbourhood succeeded in raising about £4000 for this purpose, and a committee of the inhabitants was formed to superintend the application of the money.

Bearing in mind the important question which has been pressed upon us, namely, in what way could the necessities of the working classes in the manufacturing districts be provided for in so sudden and so unforseen an emergency, if no such subscription existed, as in the case of Nottingham, and if the relief of the necessitous poor should have to be provided for out of the poor-rate only, we think that the experience of what has occurred, and is still occurring in Nottingham, enables us confidently to state that the Union authorities would be enabled to meet any exigencies which might arise in the manufacturing districts out of a distressed state of trade or other contingency, notwithstanding there should be no fund subscribed, or other means for the support and employment of those operatives who might be suddenly thrown out of work; and we entertain no doubt that in Nottingham, if the subscribed funds shall be exhausted before the distress ceases, the Board of Guardians will be able to meet the pressure out of the funds placed by law at their disposal.

In attempting clearly to exhibit to your Lordship the grounds of this opinion, we think it right to state that it has not been the custom in Nottingham to give relief to able-bodied individuals when the usual amount of employment prevailed, and that the practice of resorting to out-door labour as a medium of relief is adopted only when there is a pressure on the workhouse beyond what could conveniently be managed. Assuming therefore that the rule prohibiting out-door relief to able-bodied male persons has been put in force in any Union comprising a manufacturing population before the access of pressure from commercial distress shall have arrived, we have shown by the course pursued in Nottingham, that whenever a necessity for relaxing that rule shall have arisen, such relaxation may forthwith be made, and, further, that the rules under which relief should then be administered might at once be adapted to local circumstances, and to the emergency, however sudden or urgent it might be.

It is needless for us to undertake to prove the superior efficacy of an elected Board of Guardians, consisting of men chosen by the rate payers on account of their habits of business, firmness of character, and knowledge of the law, and the advantage which could not fail to be derived from their superintendence under such an emergency as is here adverted to, as compared with that of annual parochial overseers, or even with a select vestry elected under Sturges Bourne's Act; and still less do we think it necessary to show that subordinate officers who could efficiently carry the directions of the Guardians into effect, would be much more easily provided under the new system than the old; but what we are desirous of pointing out to your Lordship is, that by adopting an out-door labour test in addition to the in-door workhouse test, and applying it according to sound rules similar to those which have been generally adhered to by the Committee superintending the distribution of the subscribed funds in Nottingham, that almost any conceivable amount of pressure might be met and adequately provided for. It must be admitted that in-door relief is more certain, simple, and easy in its application; but the out-door labour test is the same in principle. In both cases a man's time is taken in exchange for his maintenance, and he must be withdrawn from other modes of gaining subsistence in order to test the reality of his present want and destitution.

In providing the description of work necessary to meet an extensive pressure of the description alluded to, it was correctly held at Nottingham that it should be of permanent and public utility, and of a description which would not otherwise be undertaken. In conformity with these principles the Committee of Management resolved to construct a road through some property belonging to the corporation.

No doubt appears to be entertained on the part of those best informed upon the subject, that on the recurrence of such emergencies some such work may always be found if it be diligently sought for.

The persons employed were paid by the piece, and vigilantly superintended. In spite of such precautions, however, some men of bad character appear to have conducted themselves in so improper a manner as to make it doubtful whether the subscription may not thereby be discouraged.

Nothing appears to have been more clearly proved in the experience of such cases as this of Nottingham, than that no payment should be made, either from subscribed funds, or from the poor-rates, in the shape of allowances to make up wages:–an error of this kind was committed during a period of commercial distress which occurred a little before the close of the late war, when a number of parishes commenced manufacturing hosiery in order to employ the framework-knitters, although stockings were already sold at such low prices as to be ruinous to those who made them. As this example is both curious and pregnant with instruction, we think it right to give it in detail.

It was thought right by the parish authorities to employ the paupers at their own trades: the parish purchased cotton, and manufactured goods which they afterwards sold at a loss of 50 per cent. or more. These goods being brought into the market necessarily reduced the price of labour for that description of article, and the consequence was that it immediately effected a large reduction in the men's wages. In the framework-knitting trade it is customary for the master workmen to take from the hosier or other manufacturer a number of frames, for which they pay a weekly rent. In times of depression of trade it is the interest of the hosier to keep the frames going, and he will give a partial employment to the workers of these frames. If the workman can obtain the aid of parish allowance, his employer will obtain his frame-rent, and thus be enabled to keep his workmen together at the expense of the parish.

The efforts which were thus made to relieve the distress had the evident tendency to increase the cause of it, namely, production beyond the demand, and in this manner both to prolong its duration and aggravate its intensity. . . .

208B. Resistance to the Act at Huddersfield

The Fourth Report (1837–1838/XXVIII) notes that the Huddersfield Union had been set up in tranquillity. But it did not begin to function effectively till March 1839.

Report from the Commissioners to the Right Honourable Lord John Russell, relative to proceedings in the Huddersfield Union.

Poor Law Commission Office, Somerset House,
21st June, 1837.

My Lord,

We have recently issued under our hands and seal, as the Poor Law Commissioners for England and Wales, certain orders relating to thirty-three townships in the upper division of the Wapentake of Aghigg, in the West Riding of York, and in the execution of those orders circumstances have arisen which we deem it our duty to report for the information of your Lordship, as her Majesty's Secretary of State for the Home Department.

By orders, of the dates 21st January and 26th January respectively, the townships in question were, under the 26th section of the Poor Law Amendment Act, declared a Union for the administration of relief to the poor, under the title of the Huddersfield Union, and the Guardians of the poor of that Union were directed by the original order of the 21st January, to hold their first meeting at the George Inn, Huddersfield, on the 15th February, and to proceed thereat or as soon thereafter as conveniently might be, to the election of their clerk, and to the exercise of the functions assigned them, by an Act, entitled "An Act for the Registration of Births, Deaths, and Marriages."

By the same order, the Guardians were directed not to assume the administration of relief to the poor until the averages of the several townships of the Union should be ascertained, and until further orders should be issued by ourselves in that behalf.

At the first meeting of the Guardians, held on the 15th of February, in pursuance of this order, a motion was made by Joseph Armitage, Esquire, of Mills Bridge, an *ex-officio* Guardian, seconded by Mr. Thomas Leigh, of Almonbury, in the following terms:–"That as there is in the House of Commons a Bill to amend the Poor Law Bill–it is believed that an allusion was intended by these words in the Bill for amending the Registration Act–since passed into a law–that as Honley is not represented, and three or four other Guardians have not produced their authority to act, this meeting be adjourned to Monday the 3rd day of April, at eleven o'clock, at this house, then and there to meet for the purposes of this Act, and the Act for the Registering Births, Deaths and Marriages."

By way of amendment to this motion, it was proposed "That the Board proceed to the election of a Clerk," and on a division the amendment was lost, and the original motion carried by a majority of 18 to 14.

It is material to observe, that the effect of this adjournment was to postpone all proceedings in execution of the order of Union until the election of a new Board of Guardians, which had been directed to take place on the Monday next following the 25th March.

In the interval which thus occurred between the first meeting of the 15th February and the time for electing a new Board, exertions of an extraordinary nature appear to have been made to excite a spirit of hostility to the provisions of the Poor Law Amendment Act throughout the several townships of the Union, with the distinct and avowed object of defeating the operation of the law. Amongst the various means by which individuals interested to effect this object endeavoured to obtain their end, was the publication in writing as well as by harangues, of false and inflammatory statements regarding the mode of administering relief to the poor intended to be introduced under the authority of our Commission, and the excitement thereby produced among the lower classes of operatives was openly directed by the leading parties engaged in this system of agitation against the persons and property of any who should dare to undertake the office of Guardian in a spirit friendly to the operation of the law. We regret to say that these proceedings were successful to the extent of causing Guardians to be elected for some of the townships whose disposition was known to be unfriendly to the introduction of the new law, and who were understood at the time of their election to be disposed to pursue in a hostile spirit that system of adjourning the proceedings which had been commenced in the first instance under the sanction of the *ex-officio* Guardians at the meeting of the 15th of February.

In pursuance of the adjournment above mentioned, the new Board of Guardians met on the 3rd of April. This meeting was intruded upon by a large number of persons who demanded to be present at the proceedings, and who refused to withdraw from the room where the Guardians were assembled. The meeting was in consequence adjourned for one hour, and on the re-assembling of the Guardians the exclusion of all strangers from the place of meeting was effected by a number of special constables, acting under the direction of those magistrates who attended the meeting as *ex-officio* Guardians, *viz.*, J. Armitage, Esq., B.R.N. Battye, Esq., and W. H. Battye, Esq.

At this meeting several motions for adjournment were proposed, the effect of which would have been to postpone any proceedings under the order, until after the 1st July, by which the due operation of the "Act for Registering Births, Deaths, and Marriages" would have been defeated. It appeared, however, that a majority of the Guardians were not prepared at this time to act so directly in contravention of the law, since on the representation of the Assistant Commissioner that any such adjournment would be a direct breach of the law, an adjournment to the 5th of June was brought forward by way of amendment, and supported by many Guardians on the Ground that it was expedient to avoid the expense of a clerk as long as possible.

Ultimately a division took place on a motion to proceed to the election of a clerk, when there appeared to be 18 Guardians in favour of that motion and 21 against it, the three *ex-officio* Guardians voting in the minority. Subsequently the proposed adjournment to the 5th of June was carried by a majority of 19 to 10, the three *ex-officio* Guardians again voting in the minority, and several of the elected Guardians declining to vote altogether.

Previously to the 5th of June, the day on which the adjourned meeting was to be held, a letter was addressed by us to the Board of Guardians, of which the following is a copy:–

"Poor Law Commission Office, Somerset House,
3rd June, 1837.

"Gentlemen,

"The Poor Law Commissioners for England and Wales have had under their consideration the proceedings which took place at the first meeting of the Board of Guardians of the Huddersfield Union, and also those which occurred at the subsequent meeting of the 3rd of April last.

"The Commissioners perceive with regret, that on both those occasions the Guardians declined proceeding to the election of a Clerk of the Union, and to the exercise of their functions under the 'Act for the Registration of Births, Deaths, and Marriages,' and that instead of proceeding therein, the Guardians adjourned their meeting on both those occasions to a subsequent period.

"The Commissioners now call the attention of the Board of Guardians to the circumstances that the 'Act for the Registration of Births, Deaths, and Marriages,' is to take effect from the 1st of July next, before which time it will be necessary that the Guardians should have not only appointed their clerk, who by virtue of his office will become Superintendent Registrar of the Union, but should also have divided the Union into districts, and have appointed a registrar to each of those districts, and the Commissioners have to express their earnest desire that the Guardians will no longer delay the execution of the powers and functions assigned to them by the Act above mentioned.

"The Commissioners also think it their duty to acquaint the Guardians, that if the Provisions of the Registration Act should fail of being carried into effect through their default, they will alone become responsible for defeating the intentions of the Legislature; and the Commissioners have to state it as their opinion, that any further postponement of the necessary proceedings will be a direct contravention not only of the Order of Union, but of that section of the Registration Act which requires the Guardians to exercise the powers in question.

"Signed by order of the Board,
(Signed) "*E. Chadwick*, Secretary."

"To the Board of Guardians of the Huddersfield Union."

At this meeting we have reason to believe, from information supplied to us through various sources, that a considerable majority of the whole number of Guardians were prepared to proceed to the election of a clerk, and to execute the functions assigned them under the provisions of the Registration Act, and that the law failed of being carried into effect on this occasion in consequence of the personal intimidation of the parties who were called upon to act in that behalf.

It appears that on the morning of the 5th of June, about one hour before the meeting of the Guardians, which had been appointed to take place at the workhouse, Huddersfield, at eleven o'clock, a large assemblage of persons collected in front of the Druid's Arms Inn, and were addressed in violent and inflammatory language by Mr. Oastler and other persons; that at the hour appointed for the meeting of the Guardians, this assemblage proceeded under the exhortation and direction of the speakers to the workhouse, where the Guardians were about to assemble; that on arriving at the workhouse the outer gates were immediately forced, and the yard and entrances to the building filled with persons in a state of great excitement; that the Guardians having adjourned their meeting to the Albion Hotel, on their way thither were insulted, threatened with violence, and actually assaulted in several instances by the accompanying crowd; that the chairman of the Guardians was at this time preserved with great difficulty from violence of a serious nature, and the police officers and special constables engaged in protecting his person, and the persons of the other Guardians, underwent many personal injuries themselves from the violence of the crowd; that the Guardians, having with difficulty obtained possession of the room provided for them at the Albion Hotel, were during the whole time of their meeting beset by a crowd of persons who several times attempted to force their way into the building; that their proceedings were interrupted by stones being thrown into the room in which they were assembled; and that ultimately the meeting broke up prematurely under the dread of violence from those assembled without.

We are informed from sources in which we place confidence, that it was under the influence of intimidation thus exercised that a majority of the Guardians on this occasion declined to proceed to the election of a clerk; a resolution to that effect having been negatived by a majority of the Guardians present. By another resolution the meeting was adjourned to meet again on Monday the 12th of June following, at the Albion Hotel.

On receiving full intelligence of these occurrences, a verbal communication on the subject was immediately made by us to the Under Secretary of State for the Home Department, and the following letter was despatched by the post of Saturday the 10th instant, addressed to the Board of Guardians of the Huddersfield Union.

"To the Guardians of the Huddersfield Union.
Poor Law Office, London, 10th June, 1837.

"Gentlemen,

"The Poor Law Commissioners for England and Wales have received from your chairman an official report of the resolutions passed at your recent meeting of the 5th June instant.

"It appears from that report that a majority of the Guardians have declined to proceed to the election of a clerk, and that the appointment of a superintendent registrar is contemplated in lieu thereof, and may probably take place at the next meeting of your Board.

"The Commissioners are therefore desirous of stating for your immediate information, that they are fully of opinion that your Board has no authority to proceed to the appointment of a superintendent registrar, under the present circumstances of the Huddersfield Union, but that the only legal course by which the Guardians can proceed to make the necessary arrangements under the Registration Act, is to elect their clerk, who will by virtue of his office become superintendent registrar of the Union, provided he chooses to accept that situation; it is only in case of his refusal to accept that situation, that the Guardians can appoint any other person than their clerk to be the superintendent registrar of the Union.

"The Commissioners desire also to point out to the Board of Guardians, that no act or resolution of a majority of their body, which is in direct contravention of the law, can be of any force or validity to prevent such portion of the Board as may be willing to act in execution of the law from proceeding effectually therein, provided that three Guardians be willing so to act, which number is sufficient to constitute a quorum under the 38th section of the Poor Law Amendment Act.

"The Commissioners entertain an anxious hope that the above explanation of the actual state of the law will induce a sufficient number of the *ex-officio* and elected Guardians of the Union to proceed in execution of the functions which have been distinctly assigned to them by the Legislature.

" Signed by order of the Board,
(Signed) "*E. Chadwick*, Secretary."

A copy of the above communication was forwarded to each of the *ex-officio* Guardians of the Union, together with a circular letter in the following terms:–

"Poor Law Office, London, 10th June, 1837.

"Sir,

"I am directed by the Poor Law Commissioners for England and Wales to forward to you, as an *ex-officio* Guardian of the Huddersfield Union, the accompanying copy of a letter addressed by them to the Board of Guardians of that Union, and to request the favour of your attendance at the meeting of the Board, which will take place at the Albion Hotel, Huddersfield, on Monday next the 12th instant, when it is hoped that that part of the order of the Commissioners of the date 21st January last, which relates to the appointment of a clerk of the Union, will be carried into effect by the *ex-officio* Guardians, and such portion of the elected Guardians as may be induced to act in execution of the law.

"I am, Sir, your obedient servant,
(Signed) "*E. Chadwick*, Secretary."

Of the proceedings which took place at the meeting of the 12th of June we have received information to the following effect:–that several of the Guardians disposed to act in execution of the law were prevented by fear of violence from attending the meeting; that on the assembling of some of the Guardians in pursuance of the adjournment, several persons, not being Guardians, intruded themselves upon the meeting, asserting their right to be present at, and to witness the proceedings; that in the presence of these persons the Guardians proceeded to business; that although there were 25 Guardians present at the meeting, of whom it appeared that only 16 were opposed to the election of a clerk, yet no election of a clerk did in fact take place and that a further adjournment to the 11th of September next was subsequently proposed and carried.

It appears further from our information that no *ex-officio* Guardian attended this meeting. From Joseph Armitage, Esq., one of the *ex-officio* Guardians, we have received the following letters, which appear to have been written–the former in the morning of Monday the 12th of June, and previously to the meeting–and the latter in the afternoon of the same day and subsequently to the meeting.

"Huddersfield, 12th June, 1837.

"Sir,

"In reply to your letter of the 10th, I regret that we did not receive it on Saturday, there having been on that day a bench of magistrates, and I might have had an opportunity of conferring with them thereon.

"Yesterday being Sunday I did not send for my letters, and consequently your communication was not delivered to me till this morning.

"With regard to my attendance as an *ex-officio* Guardian at the Board this day, I fear I shall be unable to be present, as I am called on by the Secretary of State to keep the peace of the town, and my services will be required elsewhere.

"Should any other magistrates attend, your communication shall be laid before them, and if I can be spared so as to assist the Guardians in carrying the law into effect, I will do so. I will write to you again after the meeting.

"I have the honour to be, Sir,
"Your most obedient servant,
(Signed) "*Joseph Armitage*."

"Sir,

"I had the honour of writing to you this morning, and now beg to inform you that the meeting of Guardians was held at the Albion Hotel, agreeable to adjournment. It was quite out of my power to attend as an *ex-officio* Guardian, as no other magistrate came into the town during the day. I, therefore, felt that the peace and safety of the town was intrusted to my care, and I remained at the George Inn, in communication with the civil and military authorities. I am informed the Guardians resolved not to elect a clerk; and adjourned the meeting for three months.

"I am, Sir, your most obedient servant,
(Signed) "*Joseph Armitage.*"

"Milnsbridge House, June 12, 1837.
"To Mr. Chadwick."

From the four other *ex-officio* Guardians, *viz.*–Joseph Walker, Esq., Sir John Lister Kay, Bart., B. R. N. Battye, Esq., and W. W. Battle, Esq.,–to whom our letters of the 10th June were addressed, we have received no communication.

209. Report of the Select Committee of Commons on Poor Laws (1837–1838)

Your Committee have agreed to the following Resolutions, on various points connected with the present state of the law and its administration, to the most important of which they have thought it their duty to invite the particular attention of The House in the course of their Report:–

1.–That, in the important duties committed to them the Commissioners have evinced zeal, ability and great discrimination; and the Committee recommend the continuance of their power, in preference to any system which, by leaving the administration of the Poor Laws without the control and superintendence of a Central Board, might cause the recurrence of those abuses which existed in many counties previously to the passing of the Poor Law Amendment Act.

2.–That the Evidence taken before the Committee proves that the practice of confining relief to the able-bodied male paupers to the workhouse, has been in many districts established by the Guardians in the discretion left to them by the Commissioners, and that where this practice has been enforced by an order of the Commissioners, such order has in several instances been issued at the suggestion of the Guardians. That the Committee are convinced, that the utmost benefit has resulted from the general adoption of this system of relief, and they strongly recommend that it should in future be adhered to, subject to such occasional departures from the ordinary rule, under the pressure of special circumstances, as it appears that the local boards have been ready to adopt, and the Commissioners to sanction, in cases of real necessity.

3.–That a power should be continued to the Boards of Guardians, taking into consideration the character of the parties, to relieve, out of the workhouse, widows with young children left dependent upon them for support.

4.–THAT it appears that relief to the aged and infirm has been generally given out of the workhouse, and that the allowances to this class of paupers have been rather increased than diminished since the passing of the existing law; the Committee approve of this mode of administering the law. . . .

210. Speech of the Duke of Wellington on the petition presented by Earl Stanhope, alleging abuses in the administration of the Poor Law (7 June 1839)

Hansard, 3/XLVI/189–190.

. . . (before the Act of 1834) The real truth of the matter was that in every parish in the country there existed abuses, he would venture to say a hundred times greater than any of those which the noble Earl had brought forward. . . . In every parish, he repeated, there were abuses, and in each abuses upon a different principle from those in the neighbouring parish, so that no law could be produced to remedy them, for the law which should apply to Parish A, instead of removing the abuses existing in Parish B would only tend to aggravate them and render them intolerable. At length the Administration of which the noble Viscount (Melbourne) was a member took up the matter. There was a very general and searching inquiry into the whole state of the administration of the Poor Laws, as a result of which it was, and of the experience of the various attempts to amend these laws, the present measure was arranged and brought into Parliament. It passed both Houses in a very short space of time, and looking to the importance of the subject, with an extra-ordinary degree of unanimity, for he believed on the principle there was no division whatever, and hardly a difference of opinion in that House: he believed there was none in the other House of Parliament and very little difference upon any part of the details. With respect to the administration of the law, he had observed it in different parts of the country, and he must say that its administration had been entirely satisfactory, and most particularly to those parties who were likely to become its more immediate objects. That part of the law of which the noble Earl, and the noble Baron behind complained most–namely the existence of the Poor Law Commissioners–was, in his opinion, the most important part of it. The truth of the matter was, that the abuses in the administration of the Poor Laws were so numerous, so various, and at the same time so inveterate, that it was absolutely impossible to get the better of them without the constitution of some central authority which should superintend the execution of the law, taking care that it was duly administered, and that those intrusted with its execution in the country did not infringe its provisions. Such, he believed, was the object of the institution of the Boards of Guardians and the Commissioners. Every measure had been adopted to secure the publicity of the reports, to enable Parliament to acquire a knowledge at any time of all their transactions, upon any particular subject: and he must say it was this part of the noble Earl's conduct that astonished him the most, for while he ought to know that at any time he could have the means of ascertaining the conduct of those authorities upon any point, particularly that comprised in the petition he had read three or four times to their Lordships, instead of moving for the production of the papers and the correspondence, and ascertaining precisely what the real facts were, he went into detail of all the allegations in the petition, producing exaggerated statements on the subject, and was thus guilty of all the injustice of doing an injury to the reputations of those persons whom he traduced. . . .

211. Speech of Lord John Russell on the second reading of the Bill to renew powers of Poor Law Commissioners (15 July 1839)

Hansard, 3/XLIX/363–364.

. . . There might be abuses under the present Act, but every case was magnified to a great degree, and the evidence by which it was supported was very much exaggerated, and brought to tell against the Crown and the Government; while under the old system, if, in a parish work-house the paupers were ill-treated, or jobbing was carried on to the greatest possible degree, it was a mere local affair; it concerned only a few parish authorities, and it was the interest of no-one to bring the case forward, either in the public prints or in Parliament, nor would he be listened to who did bring it forward. But when a case was to be made against the Crown, or against a Secretary of State, it then became a matter of great importance and paramount interest. . . .

212. Case of Jane Coffee: Commissioners' remonstrances and directions to guardians of St. Luke's, Middlesex (1840)

Parlty. Papers, 1841/XXI.

This is one of several cases in which the Commissioners reprimanded the St. Luke's Guardians for failure to relieve destitution. The Metropolitan Police, through the Commissioner, Richard Mayne, had earlier represented that the police still found cases of extreme destitution at large in the streets, and the Commissioners had replied that it was the duty of relieving officers in all cases to admit them. The language of Dr. Kay, Assistant Commissioner, in the case of Martin Molloy, in which the authorities of St. Luke's and Holborn were concerned, was equally uncompromising. In the case of Jane Coffee the relieving officer's objection to receiving her had been that she was a syphilitic prostitute. St. Luke's, as a Local Act Incorporation, had claimed not to be subject to the Commissioners' regulations.

The Poor Law Commissioners desire that the Guardians will charge their officers that the condition of the pauper is the sole ground on which they are to determine applications for relief, and disease enhances the claim of a destitute person for relief. . . . The relief of destitution is not to depend on the applicant's presenting evidence of good character and conduct, but is secured by the law, for all persons who are in need; independently of such considerations, destitute persons are not to be permitted to perish from want, whether their necessity arises from imprudence, or want.

213. General order regulating outdoor relief (1841)

Parlty. Papers, 1842/XIX, pp. 42–43.

To THE GUARDIANS OF THE POOR of the several Unions named in the Schedule hereunto annexed;

To the Churchwardens and Overseers of the several Parishes and Places comprised within the said Unions;

To the Clerk or Clerks of the Justices of the Petty Sessions held for the Division or Divisions in which the Parishes and Places comprised within the said Unions are situate: and to all others whom it may concern.

We, the Poor Law Commissioners, in pursuance of the authorities vested in Us by an Act passed in the fifth year of the reign of His late Majesty King William the Fourth, intituled "*An Act for the Amendment and better Administration of the Laws relating to the Poor in England and Wales,*" do hereby rescind so much of any order or orders heretofore issued by the Poor Law Commissioners as relates to the administration of relief to be given to able-bodied poor persons, and to poor persons not resident in their parish or Union, in the several Unions named in the Schedule hereunto annexed.

And We do hereby order, direct, and declare, with respect to each and every of the Unions named in the said Schedule, as follows:-

Article 1. Every able-bodied person, male or female, requiring relief from any parish within any of the said Unions, shall be relieved wholly in the workhouse of the Union, together with such of the family of every such able-bodied person as may be resident with him or her, and may not be in employment, and together with the wife of every such able-bodied male person, if he be a married man, and if she be resident with him; save and except in the following cases:-

1st. Where such person shall require relief on account of sudden and urgent necessity.

2nd. Where such person shall require relief on account of any sickness, accident, or bodily or mental infirmity affecting such person, or any of his or her family.

3rd. Where such person shall require relief for the purpose of defraying the expenses, either wholly or in part, of the burial of any of his or her family.

4th. Where such person, being a widow, shall be in the first six months of her widowhood.

5th. Where such person shall be a widow and have a legitimate child or legitimate children dependent upon her, and incapable of earning his, her, or their livelihood, and no illegitimate child born after the commencement of her widowhood.

6th. Where such person shall be confined in any gaol or place of safe custody.

7th. Where the relief shall be required by the wife, child, or children of any able-bodied man who shall be in the service of Her Majesty as a soldier, sailor, or marine.

8th. Where any able-bodied person, not being a soldier, sailor, or marine, shall not reside within the Union, but the wife, child, or children of such person shall reside within the same, the Board of Guardians of the Union, according to their discretion, may afford relief in the workhouse to such wife, child, or children, or may allow out-door relief for any such child or children being within the age of nurture, and resident with the mother within the Union.

Article 2. In every case in which out-door relief shall be given on account of sickness, accident, or infirmity, to any able-bodied male person resident within any of the said Unions, or to any member of the family of any able-bodied male person, an extract from the medical officer's weekly report (if any such officer shall have attended the case), stating the nature of such sickness, accident, or infirmity, shall be specially entered in the minutes of the proceedings of the Board of Guardians of the day on which the relief is ordered or subsequently allowed.

But if the Board of Guardians shall think fit, a certificate under the hand of a medical officer of the Union, or of the medical practitioner in attendance on the party, shall be laid before the Board, stating the nature of such sickness, accident, or infirmity, and a copy of the same shall be in like manner entered in the minutes.

Article 3. No relief shall be given from the poor-rates of any parish comprised in any of the said Unions, to any person who does not reside in some place within the Union, save and except in the following cases:–

1st. Where such person, being casually within such parish, shall become destitute.

2nd. Where such person shall require relief on account of any sickness, accident, or bodily or mental infirmity, affecting such person, or any of his or her family.

3rd. Where such person shall be entitled to receive relief from any parish in which he may not be resident, under any order which justices may by law be authorised to make.

4th. Where such person, being a widow, shall be in the first six months of her widowhood.

5th. Where the relief shall be allowed for a child under the age of 16 maintained in a workhouse or establishment for the education of pauper children not situate within the Union.

6th. Where any person, not being able-bodied, shall not reside within the Union, and the wife, child, or children of such person shall reside within the same, relief may be afforded to such wife, child, or children, by the Guardians of the Union, as they shall think fit.

7th. Where such person shall, at some time within the twelve calendar months next preceding the date of this Order, have been in receipt of relief from some parish in the Union, being settled in such parish, and not being resident therein.

Article 4. Provided always, that in case the Guardians of any of the said Unions shall depart in any particular instance from any of the regulations hereinbefore contained, and shall, within 15 days after such departure, report the same and the grounds thereof to the Poor Law Commissioners, and if the Poor Law Commissioners shall approve of such departure, then the relief granted in such particular instance shall, if otherwise lawful, not be deemed to be unlawful, or be subject to be disallowed.

Article 5. No relief which shall be contrary to any regulation in this Order shall be given by way of loan; and every relief which may be given to or on account of any person above the age of 21, or to his wife or any part of his family under the age of 16, under Article 1., or any of the exceptions thereto, or under any of the exceptions to Article 3, or under the proviso in Article 4, may, if the Guardians shall think fit, be given by way of loan.

214. Extract from general order on workhouse rules (1841)

loc. cit., pp. 47–53.

Any pauper who shall neglect to observe such of the regulations herein contained as are applicable to and binding on him;–

Or who shall make any noise when silence is ordered to be kept;
Or shall use obscene or profane language;
Or shall by word or deed insult or revile any person;
Or shall threaten to strike or to assault any person;
Or shall not duly cleanse his person;
Or shall refuse or neglect to work, after having been required to do so;
Or shall pretend sickness;
Or shall play at cards or other games of chance;
Or shall enter or attempt to enter, without permission, the ward or yard appropriated to any class of paupers other than that to which he belongs;
Or shall misbehave in going to, at, or returning from public worship out of the workhouse, or at prayers in the workhouse;
Or shall return after the appointed time of absence, when allowed to quit the workhouse temporarily;
Or shall wilfully disobey any lawful order of any officer of the workhouse;

Shall be deemed DISORDERLY.

Any pauper who shall, within seven days, repeat any one or commit more than one of the offences specified in Article 34;

Or who shall by word or deed insult or revile the master or matron, or any other officer of the workhouse, or any of the Guardians;
Or shall wilfully disobey any lawful order of the master or matron after such order shall have been repeated;
Or shall unlawfully strike or otherwise unlawfully assault any person;
Or shall wilfully or mischievously damage or soil any property whatsoever belonging to the Guardians;
Or shall wilfully waste or spoil any provisions, stock, tools, or materials for work, belonging to the Guardians;
Or shall be drunk;
Or shall commit any act of indecency;
Or shall wilfully disturb the other inmates during prayers or divine worship;

Shall be deemed REFRACTORY.

It shall be lawful for the master of the workhouse, with or without the direction of the Board of Guardians, to punish any *disorderly* pauper by substituting, during a time not greater than forty-eight hours, for his or her dinner, as prescribed by the dietary, a meal consisting of eight ounces of bread, or one pound of cooked potatoes, and also by withholding from him during the same period, all butter, cheese, tea, sugar, or broth, which such pauper would otherwise receive, at any meal during the time aforesaid.

And it shall be lawful for the Board of Guardians, by a special direction to be entered on their minutes, to order any *refractory* pauper to be punished by confinement in a separate room, with or without an alteration of diet, similar in kind and duration to that prescribed in Art. 36 for *disorderly* paupers; but no pauper shall be so confined for a longer period than twenty-four hours, or, if it be deemed right that such pauper should be carried before a justice of the peace, and if such period of twenty-four hours should be insufficient for that purpose, then for such further time as may be necessary for such purpose.

It shall be lawful for the Board of Guardians, by any special or general order, to direct that a dress different from that of the other inmates shall be worn by *disorderly or refractory* paupers, during a period of not more than forty-eight hours, jointly with, or in lieu of the alteration of diet to which any such pauper might be subjected by the regulations herein contained; but it shall not be lawful for the Board of Guardians to cause any penal dress or distinguishing mark of disgrace to be worn by any adult pauper or class of adult paupers, unless such pauper or paupers shall be disorderly or refractory within the meaning of Article 34 or Article 35, of this order.

215. Commissioners' explanatory letter on outdoor labour test, accompanying General Order of 1841

Parlty. Papers, 1842/XIX, pp. 105–106.

It was the custom of the Commissioners to accompany a General Order with a long letter explaining its effect. In this case the letter gives a clearer and shorter account of the Commission's policy than the Order itself conveys.

SIR,

THE Poor Law Commissioners have thought it expedient to issue to certain Unions in the Northern counties, to which no regulations concerning the out-door relief of the able-bodied have been hitherto issued, an Order prescribing an out-door labour-test for able-bodied males.

It appeared to the Commissioners that, although the circumstances of these Unions were such as rendered it impracticable or inexpedient for the Commissioners to include them in their General Prohibitory Order of the 2nd of August last, it was nevertheless advisable, for the prevention of abuses inseparable from the out-door relief of the able-bodied, to issue to these Unions some regulations on the subject.

The following are the principal abuses which the Order is intended to prevent:–

1. The payment of the wages of able-bodied persons wholly or partially out of the Poor Rate, or in other words the affording of relief to able-bodied persons whilst they are in the employment of private individuals and in the receipt of wages.
2. Imposture on the part of able-bodied paupers who may continue chargeable to the rates whilst able to maintain themselves by proper exertion.
3. The payment of rents from the Poor Rates.

Against these abuses, to arrest which is the interest of the poor themselves as much as of the rate-payers, the provisions of the Poor Law Amendment Act were mainly directed. That statute evidently contemplates, under ordinary circumstances, the adoption of the workhouse as the most effectual remedy for the evils in question; but in cases where the Guardians have not provided adequate workhouse accommodation, or where large numbers of able-bodied persons are often suddenly thrown out of employment by the fluctuations of manufactures, the Commissioners may, if they think fit, exercise the power conferred on them by Sec. 52 of the Poor Law Amendment Act, of prescribing other conditions for the relief of the able-bodied than admission into the workhouse.

The following are the provisions of the Order:–

Article 1 provides that half the relief is to be in kind, and that no able-bodied person shall receive relief whilst in employment for any other person, but shall be set to work by the Guardians.

The advantages of this mode of relief, and its tendency to prevent misapplication by the man of what is furnished for the use of his wife and family, have already been often pointed out by the Commissioners, and will be evident to all who have witnessed its employment on a large scale. The articles given should be those of first necessity, such as bread or potatoes.

It is to be observed that this Article applies only to able-bodied men who are not relieved in the workhouse, and therefore that, so far as the workhouse may serve, the Guardians may, if they think fit, admit into it any able-bodied applicant for relief.

Article 2 makes it necessary for the Guardians to report the mode of employment (such, for instance, as stone-breaking, removing earth, picking oakum, or labour at a hand-mill), together with the place and time of work, and any other regulations, to the Poor Law Commissioners. This report must be made within fourteen days after the Order comes into force; and the arrangements, if varied afterwards, must be reported in the same manner.

With reference to the mode of payment, the Commissioners think that it is always expedient to treat whatever is given as *relief*, and not as *wages*.

The Guardians should consider what is sufficient for the wants of the man and his family, or the man alone, if he be single. This sum they should order (half at least of which is to be in kind) as *relief* to be given on condition that the man performs a certain task of work to the satisfaction of the Superintendent.

It is presumed that the task required will be carefully fixed at what it is reasonable for an able-bodied man of average strength to perform. If the pauper should refuse to perform this task, he should be told that inasmuch as he is able *partly* to maintain his family by giving the Guardians the benefit of that quantity of work in return for the relief, and if he refuses or neglects so to do, he will subject himself to punishment under Section 3 of the Vagrant Act, 5 Geo. IV., c. 83.

Thus the misconduct of the man will not interrupt the relief to his wife and children, whilst he himself will be punished for his misconduct.

Article 3 requires the appointment of one or more officers to superintend the labour. Unless this be done the whole system will fail to answer its end; and though the first abuse of payment of wages out of rates may not occur, the second, *viz.*, of wilful and fraudulent chargeability on the part of the pauper will defeat all the endeavours of the Guardians to protect the rate-payers. The rate will be relied on as a means of enabling workmen to continue and hold out against offers of reasonable wages, or will deter them from seeking for employment elsewhere.

On the due selection of the Superintendent, and the vigilant performance of his duties much will depend.

Articles 4 to 10 relate to the appointment, salary, and continuance in office of the Superintendent.

Article 11 contains the exceptions to Article 1. That is to say, the able-bodied cases in which the Guardians may afford relief without requiring labour, and without affording one-half in kind. These exceptions are, in great measure, identical with those in Article 1 of the Order of 2nd August, 1841, prohibiting the out-door relief of the able-bodied; and the Commissioners believe that the Guardians will find the discretion thus remaining in their hands sufficient to meet all ordinary instances of hardship. The Order of 2nd August, however, included able-bodied females as well as males; and as the present Order includes only males, the exceptions relating to widows in that Order are here omitted. The Guardians will remark that as the Order is confined to able-bodied persons, and therefore does not comprehend the aged and infirm, the latter class are not excepted in this Article, or adverted to in any of the observations in this Letter.

Article 12 requires a medical certificate as the proof of illness, when such illness is the ground of an exception to the Order.

Article 13 prohibits the payment of rent; but it will be seen that if a case of sudden urgency occurs, or if an idiot is found in a destitute state, the Board of Guardians, or even the Relieving Officer or Overseers will in no way be prevented from procuring temporary lodgings to meet the urgency of the case. This proviso, however, will not authorize the continuance of such charge for lodging longer than is sufficient to meet the case, or if the lodging be procured by the Officers, to bring it before the next meeting of the Board of Guardians. It is scarcely necessary to add, that if a destitute person is too ill to be removed, a medical man's certificate to that effect would justify the Relieving Officer in retaining the lodging in which such person had been placed, until his state should allow of his removal to the workhouse, or he should cease to be chargeable; but the authority of the Guardians should always be obtained on the first practicable occasion, and should be renewed from time to time as opportunity may offer.

Article 14 empowers the Commissioners to sanction any particular instance not coming within the exceptions in Article 11, if reported by the Guardians within fifteen days.

Article 15 makes any relief which is contrary to the Order if given absolutely, equally contrary to it if given by way of loan, but authorizes the Guardians to make relief given in conformity with the Order a loan to the pauper, and thus brings such relief within Section 58 of the Poor Law Amendment Act.

Signed by order of the Board,

The Clerk to the Guardians. EDWIN CHADWICK, *Secretary*.

216A–B. Select Committee on Medical Relief (1844)

Parlty. Papers, 1844/IX.

216A. From evidence of G. J. Guthrie, F.R.S., President of the Royal College of Surgeons

loc. cit., pp. 373–374, *qq.* 3812–3813.

You stated that you would make the unions consist of not more than 15,000?–No, I think not; it does not so much matter how many people there are in a union, provided it is of such reasonable dimensions that the union-house is not more than eight or 10 miles from its most distant part. I have an objection to the extent of a medical district being beyond three miles from the centre of the district of parish, but I have said nothing about the number of districts in a union. I have mentioned that wherever there is in a village a duly-qualified practitioner, I would employ him; but I would not let a man have more than 10,000 persons under his care, nor half so many, if I could help it. With regard to my position here, I beg to state, that I am here nominally as an evidence or a witness; but that, in fact, I am neither evidence nor witness. I am only an advocate for the sick poor and the poor medical men. I have little personal knowledge of any of the facts I have stated, except from the hundreds of communications I have received; but I have made such inquiries, that I am able to say I can prove every important fact I have mentioned.

Lord R. *Grosvenor*: In the course of the attention you have given to this subject, have you at all compared the medical relief to the poor previous to the passing of the new poor law with what it was before?–I think I have said, that there is a very essential difference. The relief is infinitely greater than it was before; it is given to a much greater number of people. The Commissioners deserve great credit for it: the point upon which they do not deserve credit is, that they do not insist on its being paid for in a reasonable manner.

216B. From the evidence of H. Wyldbore Rumsey, of Gloucester, giving evidence for Provincial Medical and Surgical Association

loc. cit., pp. 689–690, *qq.* 9361–9363.

Would not the loss thus sustained by the community be more effectually prevented by improving the social condition of the working classes, their houses, and the drainage and sewerage of towns?–I am aware that a large proportion of this extra sickness and mortality might be effectually prevented by such improvements, and it is highly desirable that they should be made compulsory; but what I am desirous of urging is, that sanatory regulations cannot be complete and efficient without the active co-operation of the medical profession. The duty of the district medical officer, as I have before said, should be to prevent as much as to cure disease. He should constantly represent to some properly constituted authority the removable causes of disease, the sources of endemic disorders, and malaria. As far as his power extends, he should be, everywhere, the district vaccinator; he should visit the habitations of the working classes, and report their condition from time to time. It would be both his duty and interest, and, I may add, a high gratification to him, to advise the poor respecting their physical management, and to suggest such domestic improvements as come within their own power to effect for themselves. The aid of engineers, architects, and surveyors, is also very necessary in their respective departments; but the great reform which is needed in the sanatory state of our town populations cannot be worked out without medical assistance cordially given.

To what local executive authority would you commit the sanatory management of the town or district?–The direction of sanatory measures, and the superintendence of the public dispensaries, should, in our opinion, be vested in local Boards of Health. It has been objected by Mr. Chadwick that while such Boards have often been recommended, it has only been in general terms, without specifying what shall be their power and extent of action: we agree with him that a Board whose powers are merely suggestive can now be of no practical advantage where the evils are so well known, and the general nature of the remedies so clearly pointed out; but we entertain very strong objections to vesting in Boards of Guardians the powers required to carry into effect sanatory improvements. There are many reasons why such powers should be committed to corporate authorities to be established for the express purpose of protecting the public health. The responsibilities are too great and important to be entrusted to individuals acting without the sanction and aid of bodies of intelligent persons in every locality. Such a Board might be formed in every large town, and it should be composed of persons whose education, station, and freedom from sordid views, would fit them for the direction of such important affairs. I would specify the magistrates, the clergy, the chairman and vice chairman of the Board of Guardians, and the honorary physicians and surgeons of the medical charities. Some arrangement might also be made to obtain the voluntary co-operation of some two or more leading members of the legal profession, and the principal architects and engineers residing in the locality. Here would be a properly constituted body, not merely for the government of the public dispensary, but for the execution of all sanatory measures. This Board should appoint one paid medical referee, one of the principal practitioners in the locality, whose duties would be to attend its meetings, give advice and assistance in the execution of sanatory improvements, and form the medium of communication between the district medical officers and the Board. It might also be expedient to appoint a civil engineer or surveyor to be constantly present at the meetings of the Board. Mr. Baker of Leeds has suggested Boards of this kind, though not, I think, so complete as they should be in their constitution. He would call them Boards of Civil Control, and he mentions a number of objects to which their attention might be advantageously directed. I need not enumerate the principal objects which would occupy the attention of a Board of Health: they would occur obviously to any one. But there are a few points, not generally mentioned, which have always appeared to me of great importance: 1st, the provision of public baths, under proper regulations, for the working classes; 2d, the supply of well-trained nurses and properly educated midwives to attend the poor; and, 3dly, the examination of the mortuary registers, and the direction of the vaccination of the district, which have, in the absence of more competent authorities, been committed to the Poor Law Boards.

I have already mentioned the superintendence of the public dispensaries. I say nothing of infirmaries, because it appears to me that the in-patients of those noble institutions are already in very good hands; and with regard to out-patients (except such as were made so after being in the hospital) I assume that this class would greatly diminish under a good dispensary system. The infirmaries should, however, be induced to send periodical reports of the sickness and mortality within their walls. The Board of Health should sit weekly, and the periodical reports of the district medical officers should be submitted to this Board, as well as to the proposed medical inspector. These Boards would be in communication with the medical inspector, who should be an *ex-officio* member of all the Boards in his district. Each Board should be co-extensive in its sphere of action with the Board of Guardians. The two bodies would co-operate for the benefit of the poor: but all the medical and sanatory superintendence of the union should be vested in the Board of Health.

What are your objections to these sanatory functions being committed to Boards of Guardians?–First, because I think the other duties and functions of the guardians are incompatible with that close attention to this important subject which it demands. Secondly, because it is their business as guardians of the poor-rates to retrench all expenditure; and this main principle of action unfits them to a certain extent for measures of a more enlarged character, which though entailing expense, are yet based on a prudential economy. Thirdly, because many of the elected guardians are deficient in that intelligence and information essential to dealing properly with questions of this nature. All the *ex-officio* guardians would, as magistrates, be members of the Board of Health, where according to my proposition they would meet colleagues possessing like themselves all the requisite qualifications for these important duties.

217A–B. Criticism of poor law administration: from evidence before the Select Committee on Settlement and Poor Removal (1847)

Parlty. Papers, 1847/XI.

217A. From the evidence of Edwin Chadwick

loc. cit., pp. 229–250.

Are the Committee to understand that your opinion is that the remedy for the evils of parochial settlement which you have described is to be found in union settlement?–What I should recommend would be union settlement and union rating in the first instance, and afterwards, on the experience of that, when the steady administration of the system and the equalization of the burthen has removed prejudice and given confidence, to go a step further, to the total abolition of settlement altogether.

Would you contemplate that the total abolition of settlement should be accompanied by a national rate?–No; by a union or district charge, and a district rate.

Then is it your notion that the ultimate object to which legislation on this subject should tend would be union chargeability and a total abolition of settlement?–Undoubtedly.

But that in the meantime, as a first step, you would have union chargeability and union settlement?–Yes, with contribution, in the first instance, on the present averages.

Will you describe to the Committee in what mode you would propose to raise the rates during the period of union settlement and union chargeability?–During the first period I would let the parishes contribute in the proportion of their present contribution as to establishment charges.

. . . . .

Do you consider there is as much pauperism now, induced by lax administration of the law, as there used to be at the time of the first inquiry into the operation of the law?–It is very unequal. In some districts there appears yet to be a combination of allowances on the roads, with indirect evasions of the law, and where, I am afraid, the evasion is now nearly as great as it was at the time of our inquiry. I had not an opportunity of going down to make local inquiry, but, from the information I got, I believe that the track of fires in Norfolk and Suffolk, in 1844, was a chequered track of returned abuses. It was not to be seen at the union, but in the working of the highway rate, and in various other modes. In some 700 parishes of Norfolk and Suffolk I was informed the old distinction between married and single was maintained, and I believe it is now maintained to the amount of 3s. a week in wages.

Is this owing to the discretion that it still allowed to Boards of Guardians in awarding relief?–To a very large extent it is; I attribute it to that part of the present poor-law which throws the burthen upon the occupiers of a narrow area, who endeavour (if it be not too strong an expression) to get back by fraud what is imposed upon them by force. In various ways they try to get relief, or sometimes by throwing their labourers on the highway rates, sometimes by subscription rates; and in various other ways the old abuse does prevail very largely, even in those comparatively well-conditioned agricultural districts of Norfolk and Suffolk.

But this is with the knowledge of the guardians at the union Board?–I believe so.

. . . . .

Is it part of your scheme that the boundaries of unions should be revised?–Yes.

While this parochial contribution is to form part of the scheme, do you mean that you would alter the unions, supposing you were to commence the scheme?–In some cases; you might very frequently in some cases of small unions consider the union as a district for relief, and have union contributions, much in the same way as has been proposed for various purposes, district audits, and district appointment of auditors.

The formation of the present unions was perfectly arbitrary, was not it; they were not formed from any connexion between the property and people, were they?–I cannot say that it was perfectly arbitrary; the Assistant Commissioners did the best that they could under the then existing circumstances. A great deal of opposition arose from not understanding the law. It was my understanding that the first arrangement was an arrangement which would subsequently require revision; or if there were any principle at all, my view was to take the market town as the centre of a union, comprehending within that union all the parishes the people of which habitually resorted to, and from the market town. That might be taken as comprehending very generally a convenient administrative area; in my view the first were adopted as provisional arrangements. There are towns, such as Sheffield, and places like Gravesend and Milton, which are cut in half; several other towns I might instance, where they might be formed into one union, and not only be one within themselves, but, very conveniently for the future administration of relief, include large portions of the suburbs.

By including large portions of the suburbs would not you mix up an agricultural with the town population?–I think you would very frequently include a town population; that is to say, a population who transact their business within the town, but who now escape rates, and get rid of any concern with the place where their business is conducted by going to reside in the suburbs.

Take the instance of Manchester; if you were to throw a large agricultural suburb into Manchester, would that be fair upon the rural parish?–Very generally I think it would. In that very instance of Manchester, if I remember rightly, a very important suburb occupied by manufacturers is excluded from Manchester, and the agricultural portion of it is really only a few cow fields and market gardens for the supply of the town. The land there is certainly of very increased value from its proximity to the town, and it ought, on many accounts, to be included. There are various portions of towns, some portions of London, for instance, like the City, which, consisting of warehouses and places of business and manufactories, are left by the occupiers. The workmen and servants, and other people connected with them, reside not in the city itself, the place of their work, but in a suburb just beyond, and outside that suburb are the suburban residences of the city merchants and tradesmen; so that in London, people who work in the city of London are thrown upon poor places, like St. George's, for instance, while the tradesmen residing in Camberwell or beyond it escape the burden in both places, the intermediate suburban parish having to bear all the burden, often very unfairly; and those inequalities in various towns where they are extending in the shape of suburbs, must greatly increase. Persons renting only a warehouse with a counting-house, doing all their business there, their workmen being located in another place, almost entirely escape contribution, and that contribution falls upon the places where the workmen reside, which in a very large proportion of cases are not at all the places where they work.

Then in justice to the ratepayers generally, you think if a union settlement and rating were adopted, it would be necessary to remodel some of the unions?–Yes, I think the benefit would be extended by remodelling them; I think you would increase the benefit of the abrogation of the law of settlement by extending the area as far as you can.

217B. From the evidence of the Hon. and Rev. Sidney Godolphin Osborne, rector of Durweston and Bryanston, Dorset

loc. cit., pp. 569–578.

. . . I honestly confess, that two years ago, if I had been asked whether I would have held up my hand to do away the law of settlement, I would have held up both hands against it. I now honestly confess, that as far as my will is concerned, I wish the law of settlement did not continue one day longer, for I have become convinced, not only of the evils which result necessarily from it, but that it has been made again in the hands of others to produce worse evils. At the same time, I am most fully convinced of the immense importance of keeping up some local tie. I admit the difficulty; but I still do say that it is of essential importance that this should be done. Our population are altering in character daily. There was a time,–when I first took orders, and lived much amongst the poor,–when they scarcely knew the village beyond them, or two villages off: for one letter that they ever wrote, I am satisfied that they write 20 now; for one letter I had to read, I am satisfied that I should have to read 40 now, excepting that they can read themselves. With regard to the difficulty of getting children out to service, the rapidity of communication, the mere fact that a letter, worded in a way that we might perhaps find fault with, but still carrying some simple message from the mother to the child, can, for one penny, reach that child, and receive as simple an answer back, I am convinced has had a great effect upon the poor. I recollect the time when I never knew an instance of a poor man making a will; I now have to do it for them. Within the last 10 days a case occurred, in which the man's sole bequest was his great coat to another man, and to secure the rest of his few things to his widow. We are now progressing towards a state in which, it must have followed that all settlement would be done away with; at the same time, I must say that I do fear that there is very great danger in doing away with settlement, in any way which shall tend to entirely sever the connexion between the parochial authorities or the upper orders, and the lower, but I do not see that this necessarily follows. I think settlement may be done away with; and I think still that a good deal of this wholesome influence may be yet kept up.

Do you think that the law of settlement is at all necessary to establish a tie between the landlord or occupier and his dependent?–Yes, I think it is, to this degree; as it is now, there are very few parishes in England belonging to any proprietor, who is looked up to at all in the world, which have not certain charities and certain means of education more or less good. There is an established connexion, not merely between a clergyman and his flock, but between the flock and the squire, through the clergyman. There are no end of ties existing now, which I think of the greatest possible use. Take this last winter that is just past; submit any itinerant population to the sufferings and trials that have been gone through in the south-western districts; and I assert that there would have been disturbance; but for the extent of private charity this year, and the extent of private influence, and the extraordinary efforts that have been made to find work, and particularly that personal influence which landlords and tenants have over men whose fathers worked for them before, and whose children are still working for them, and who have been Christmas after Christmas, or whatever the time may be, in the habit of receiving one or other kindness from them, we should have had mischief. I say that this influence is one which if it is to be destroyed by doing away with settlement, however great the evils of it, I would be against it; but I do not see why much of this may not be yet kept up and settlement be repealed. There are of course enormous difficulties in the way, and it would be presumption in me to lay any plan before the Committee, and to say that I think that would be the best. I can only give an opinion.

You have mentioned as one of the general evils that have resulted from the present law, that the labourers are exceedingly ill-housed for the want of cottages; from your experience, are you of opinion that the distance which labourers sometimes have to go to their work is a serious evil?–Undoubtedly. I cannot enter into those great niceties of calculation, that the man or the work is deteriorated, but that there is an evil in it I have no doubt so far as regards the farmer. I have no doubt there is an evil, but a far greater evil in the tendency of it to drive the poor into the country towns.

You have stated that you partly attribute to the present law the great hardship upon the labourer when he is subjected to removal, that you attribute to it also the not building cottages, and letting them fall down, the labourers being badly housed to the great detriment of their morality and comfort; their being driven to a distance from their work, and their being congregated together in small country towns, and you mentioned other evils which you partly ascribe to the present law of settlement, do you not think that all those tend, if that is the effect of the law of settlement, to weaken the ties of attachment between the upper and labouring classes in the country? –I cannot quite arrive at that conclusion, and for this reason. The law of settlement brings every person either in distress or sickness in the parish necessarily before a great number of individuals directly more or less connected with him from time to time. Every additional case of sickness in the parish in all probability brings the clergyman and occasionally the overseer, or brings the farmer himself, in contact with his men, and gives the farmer an opportunity, which many of them have taken advantage of, I am happy to say, of doing little kindnesses to their men; in these times there is no end of circumstances of this kind, more easily known than described.

Suppose you had a poor law, and suppose a man to be entitled to relief in the place where he resides, would he not be equally brought into contact with the higher orders under those contingencies?–I believe the law of settlement can be repealed and those ties kept up. If I did not feel that, I should be the first to cry out against the repeal.

• • • • •

As far as regards the poor man, the workhouse being the test of destitution, it has failed entirely in Dorsetshire?–Not entirely; I think it will act upon some characters; upon an impertinent man, for instance, a man who gives himself airs with his master. The threat to him of the workhouse is of great service. So far as any means of raising wages it does fail.

Still you are convinced that means are used from the way-rate and from private subscriptions, so as to enable the poor man, not upon his wages, but upon his wages and that rating upon the parish, to subsist?–Undoubtedly. If you ask me whether wages are not paid to a certain extent out of the rate, I admit the fact. I think an honourable Member of this House, the chairman of a Board of Guardians in Oxfordshire, told me himself, that by private subscriptions they have a regular bread allowance throughout all the large families there.

Your impression is, that not only has the Poor-law Amendment Act failed in raising the general rate of wages, but it has failed in rooting out the allowance system?–Undoubtedly.

218A–B. Select Committee on the Administration of Relief of the Poor (1864)

Parlty. Papers, 1864/IX.

218A. Distress in the metropolis (1860–1861)

loc. cit., pp. 189–193.

METROPOLITAN DISTRESS IN 1860 AND 1861

The few weeks of unusually severe weather which preceded the first meeting of Your Committee on the 1st of March 1861, had deprived large numbers of persons in the Metropolis of their usual employment, and had, in several parts of it, occasioned a considerable amount of distress. Nearly the whole of the labourers in and about the London Docks, and along the banks of the river, were thrown out of work by the severe frost which set in on the 17th of December, and, with two slight intermissions lasted until the 19th of January: and their numbers were largely increased by the necessary cessation of all market-garden operations around the Metropolis. For the relief of the persons thus deprived of their ordinary means of support, considerable sums of money, voluntarily contributed, were placed at the disposal of the police magistrates, and of the clergymen and others, in the several localities in which the distress existed. It appeared to have been generally assumed that the machinery of the Poor Law was inadequate to meet the prevailing distress; and that not only the rules and regulations under which parochial and union relief was administered required to be modified, but that the funds placed at the disposal of the guardians were insufficient for such an emergency. Several public writers and speakers alleged that the Poor Law had "broken down," and, on the assembling of Your Committee, we found that such an impression very generally prevailed. Your Committee, under these circumstances, deemed it expedient, in the first instance, to inquire into the then recent metropolitan distress, with the view of ascertaining how far the law, in its ordinary mode of operation, was able to bear the strain of such an emergency. Although it was sufficiently clear that the localities of the distress were chiefly parts of the City of London, Bethnal Green, Lambeth, Greenwich, and Poplar, Your Committee had considerable difficulty in obtaining any authentic evidence as to either its extent or intensity. The statistics of pauperism enable Your Committee to state with accuracy the numbers chargeable in each week, and the amount expended for their relief. But the numbers relieved through the agency of police magistrates, or of voluntary committees, can only be vaguely conjectured. The amount of money distributed may be stated with tolerable precision.

It appears that the average pauperism of the Metropolis is 96,752. The addition to this number, during the five weeks of the frost, was,–

1st week	6,648
2d "	14,735
3d "	31,567
4th "	38,637
5th "	28,664

For the five weeks, therefore, the pauperism was raised from the average of 96,752 to 135,389.

Of the numbers relieved by voluntary agency no statements were presented to Your Committee, nor indeed do the accounts of the numbers appear to have been kept either by the magistrates or by the local committee who were the agents of the distribution. It is not possible to approximate with any degree of accuracy the numbers relieved by voluntary agency.

Still less is it possible to estimate satisfactorily the character of the distress that was actually relieved. By far the greater number of cases were relieved without any investigation into the circumstances, and in those cases in which inquiry is alleged to have been made it was not of such a nature as to elicit the facts of the actual condition of the applicants. Mr. Farnall, the Poor Law Inspector of the metropolitan district, was of opinion that the distress "scarcely ought to bear the name of a crisis." And he supported this opinion by the striking statement that relief, subject to the usual conditions, was offered to 15,463 men, of whom "1,003 came into the workhouse, and 4,230 accepted the stone yard out of the whole 15,463, therefore there were only 5,233 who accepted the test at all;" and he added, "The rest were never heard of again."

A different estimate of the nature of the emergency was, however, formed by other witnesses. Mr. Southgate, Chairman of the Board of Guardians of Shoreditch, speaks of it as having been a time of "extraordinary pressure." Mr. Yardley, the police magistrate, designates it as "an extreme case of distress." Mr. Bromley states that a single Refuge was called upon to relieve 14,000 cases during the winter. Mr. Howard, Chairman of the Bethnal-green Board of Guardians, is of opinion that but for charitable subscriptions "there would have been a fearful loss of life from starvation." The Rev. Mr. M'Gill, speaking from his own observation, describes the period as one of "unparalleled misery." The Rev. C. H. Carr, of St. John's Church, Limehouse, states that there was an entire cessation of work for almost the whole of his population. Mr. Selfe, the police magistrate, describes the period as one of "extreme distress;" and adds, "I think the distress was terrible; the amount to which the pawn-shops were filled with the absolute necessaries of the home, as it is called, and the way in which it was stripped to support bare life, was terrible." The language of Mr. Knox, the police magistrate, at Worship-street, is still more emphatic: "As we walked round to visit the district, I certainly saw sights of the most extreme and awful misery; there was no doubt about it; their articles of furniture were gone from the house; the frame of a bedstead would be remaining, and the sacking gone; there were a man and his wife and six children lying upon shavings in the room; they would show you a bundle of pawn-tickets, with nothing remaining in the room; and I beheld sights such as you would not suppose it possible to witness in London."

The mode in which the relief of this distress, whatever may have been its extent and character, was provided for, was, firstly, through the usual agency of Boards of Guardians, and, secondly, through voluntary contributions administered by the police magistrates, and by various benevolent societies.

There can be no doubt that the machinery of Poor Law administration was adequate to the occasion, and that the guardians possessed the requisite powers for raising the funds necessary for the relief of the distress. The administrators of the law were not hampered by the rules or regulations of the Central Board, and the clerks and chairmen of the several unions, and the Poor Law Inspector of the metropolitan district, expressed strongly their opinions that the whole of the distress which existed during the period of the frost could have been provided for through the agency of the Boards of Guardians. Mr. Bowring, clerk to the City of London Union, and a gentleman of great experience "had not the slightest doubt that the 5,000 persons who were relieved at the Mansion House and the Guildhall could have been relieved by the City Union." Mr. Richard Cobbett, who has been chairman of the Board of Guardians of the parish of St. Martin-in-the-Fields for 21 years, having been asked "If there had been a great number of persons applying to you for relief, would you have considered that the parish was incapable of giving the relief?" replied, "I should have considered that our parish was quite equal to meet the relief." "If the pressure had been very great, the probability is that about Christmas we should have been compelled to increase the rate." "There would have been no difficulty whatever in getting the rate." Mr. Alderman Sheriff Abbiss, who has been for several years chairman of the City of London Union, "Entirely concurred in the opinion of Mr. Bowring, that there were ample means of supplying any number of applications for relief, and that there was neither any difficulty in making a rate or collecting a rate, nor in finding agents or relieving officers to distribute it, supposing that an extraordinary number of applications had been made." "All the applications that were made to the City of London Union were relieved, and we found no difficulty whatever; and I believe that there would have been no difficulty in relieving the whole number who applied at the different police offices." Mr. G. A. Farr, clerk to the guardians of the Whitechapel Union, who has been connected with union and parochial administration for upwards of 20 years, informed Your Committee, that although there was a vast increase in the number of cases relieved, being in the fourth week of the Lady-day quarter, 2,862 above the average, yet the guardians found no difficulty at all in meeting this exigency. Mr. W. Southgate, chairman of the Board of Guardians of Shoreditch, was "confident that the guardians could have relieved all that came to them." "The Poor Law Board do not interfere with us in giving relief; as to distribution of relief, we have nothing to complain of." "I think if they had not got anything from Worship-street (police office), the poor would have been attended to (by the guardians), but of course they would not have got the amount of relief which they got there." Mr. S. R. Stockton, one of the directors of the poor of the parish of St. Pancras, stated that the directors "had not the least difficulty in relieving the applications that were made to them; their machinery was complete:" "they had relieving officers enough;" they "could have relieved in a humane and adequate manner the whole number applying." They "did not require the assistance of the voluntary subscriptions of benevolent people." "The Poor Law did not break down in our parish." "The Poor Law Board did not in any way interfere with us during the late distress; we got on very well; the machinery was in good order, and

I am of opinion that we worked it satisfactorily." Mr. William Turner, one of the directors of the Poor of St. Pancras, was decidedly of opinion "that the arrangements were sufficient to relieve the poor under the Poor Law, without the poor resorting to private charity." Mr. Edward Collinson, Chairman of the Board of Guardians of St. George the Martyr, stated that the guardians "had a great many applications during the frost, but they did not find any difficulty in providing for their relief." "There was decidedly no occasion for the indiscriminate relief given at the police offices"; had it been necessary the parish "could have relieved as many again." Mr. Legg, Chairman of the Board of Guardians of the parish of Bermondsey, detailed the extent of distress and the mode of relieving it, and stated that in that parish there was no "breakdown of the Poor Law; we could have done more if there had been any necessity for it." It appeared to Your Committee that as a general rule the guardians of the several unions and parishes felt that very little restraint, if any, was imposed upon them by any rule or regulation of the Poor Law Board. During this emergency, relief appears to have been administered by these bodies very much at their own discretion. Although the order known as the "prohibitory order" is not in force in the Metropolis, yet the guardians felt that as a protection against imposture it was necessary, in the cases of able-bodied men, to enforce the test of the workhouse. Some evidence was offered to Your Committee that this operated virtually as a refusal of relief, so great was the reluctance of the poor to accept relief in this form. Mr. William Howard, Chairman of the Board of Guardians of Bethnal Green parish, was of opinion that so great was the reluctance of the poor to enter into the workhouse, that if they had not been relieved by voluntary contributions "there would have been a fearful loss of life through starvation." Where the workhouse was not applied, some other test, such as stone-breaking, or oakum-picking, appears to have been generally adopted. It appeared, however, that a very small proportion of the applicants to whom relief under this test was offered, accepted it. In St. Pancras, for example, of 700 people to whom relief under the test was offered, 400 refused it. Although some witnesses expressed an opinion that this reluctance to accept relief upon such conditions showed that the test was applied with harshness, yet a very considerable amount of evidence went to prove that it arose from the great facility with which the relief voluntarily contributed could be obtained. The indiscriminate way in which these contributions were distributed, and the want of concert and organization in the arrangements for the distribution, may be seen from the evidence of the Metropolitan police magistrates. Mr. Henry S. Selfe, magistrate of the Thames police court, stated that his colleague and himself differed so much as to the expediency of receiving the sums subscribed, and as to the mode in which they should be distributed, that they agreed to divide the joint fund, and act independently of one another in distributing it. The total amount sent to the court was about £4,000, and of the £2,000 that he received he had disposed of £1,600; £400 was distributed by himself, *propria manu*, and the remaining £1,200 was given to persons who undertook to furnish him with the particulars of the mode in which it was distributed. There was a considerable balance in hand. He gave no money where he had not the pledged word of some one known to himself that the applicant was worthy of relief. The persons who were relieved by him were almost exclusively persons of good character, and the greater part of them had never received parish relief. The persons who signed the papers recommending applicants for relief were clergymen, district visitors, Roman Catholic priests, and others residing in the district. Although the distress was so great, during the whole period that he had been a magistrate crime was never less; he accounted for it by supposing that the poor having a knowledge that so much was being done for them to alleviate their distress, abstained from the commission of crime. He would not himself discourage the receipt of money at the police courts in times of great distress. The distribution of relief, he was bound to say, was foreign to the duties of the magistrates; but he did not think it interfered with the performance of them. He considered it necessary as a condition for relief that a test of work or strict inquiry should be applied. If there were no discrimination as to relief, and undeserving persons were relieved, it doubtless tended to demoralize those who were struggling to be independent. He had no communication with the guardians during the pressure. He believed them to be humane, and to have a desire to perform their duty; and in the main he was disposed to agree with Mr. Yardley, that there was hardly a complaint against a parochial authority which was not found to be groundless. As a whole, the officers, in his judgement, discharged their duties well and efficiently. At the same time, there were a number of cases which the Poor Law never could touch; and he did not conceive it possible that a thoroughly official system, paid for by compulsory contributions, could be without some kind of hardship to the poor. The workhouse test, or the labour test, which no doubt was properly applied in the case of the sturdy vagrant or the idle, was wholly unfit, in his judgement, to be applied to a vast number of those who were destitute. In the eastern district of the Metropolis there were numbers of the most deserving poor who would never go near the poorhouse; they would sooner die. He was anxious, therefore, that nothing should be done to interfere with those who were willing to do what they could in a subsidiary way, by relieving distress which the Poor Law could not touch. No system of Poor Law relief, if devised by angels, inasmuch as it would have to be administered by men, could ever prevent the necessity for voluntary exertion, and the more of the latter the better, provided that it was conducted wisely. He considered that it was not desirable that the police magistrates should themselves distribute the contributions, but they had means which those who contributed the funds had not, of knowing trustworthy channels through which it might be distributed. Three-fourths of the sums entrusted to him were distributed by the clergymen of the Established Church, dissenting ministers of different denominations, Roman Catholic priests, district visitors, and medical men. No Poor Law on earth could have removed the necessity for charity during the pressure. He had heard persons, whose opinions were entitled to respect, say that the distribution had a very beneficial effect, not only as to general feeling among the poor, but actually in preventing bread riots. At a recent meeting of the police magistrates, Mr. Hall, the chief magistrate, made a communication from the Home Office. He intimated that it was thought inexpedient to make the police courts places where crowds should assemble, and that it was desirable to check that mode of relief. It was then attempted to lay down rules as to how relief should be administered for the future; but a proposal to that effect was negatived by a large majority. It was then unanimously resolved that the magistrates should endeavour to give effect to the views expressed by the authority by which they were bound.

Your Committee also examined Mr. Yardley, who said that he was the magistrate at the Thames police court during the severe part of the same winter, and that his district included the Stepney and Poplar Unions and part of the Whitechapel Union. A very large sum was contributed to the poor-box of the court. The money was distributed among the dock labourers and those who were employed in casual work generally about the banks of the river and the wharves. In such a winter as the last it was impossible to carry out inquiries into the character or circumstances of applicants, and, in fact, it was not attempted. The course adopted was this: there was generally a large number of persons, sometimes about 2,000, collected around the court. Between the court and the police-station was a large open space, to which, at a certain hour, the persons were admitted; and after having been kept there for two or three hours, they passed as quickly as possible through a passage leading by the side of the court, whilst officers stationed there distributed silver to each one as he passed. As much as £120 was given away in silver in one day, but the amount ordinarily given was £80 or £90 a day. Generally speaking, a question or two was asked, and the hands of the people were looked at, to ascertain whether their calling was that of extreme hard work. This was the only test that they could apply. He had all along been of opinion that police magistrates were very improper persons to distribute funds in the way in which they were called upon to distribute them during the pressure: it was impossible that they could use that discretion which was desirable. He had no reason to suppose that there was any neglect whatever on the part of the relieving officers in the district. During the 14 years that he had been at the court, not a day passed but some complaint was made to him against a relieving officer. He always investigated those complaints, and invariably found that they were groundless. He had no reason to believe that there was either inability or unwillingness on the part of the relieving officers, on the occasion of the frost, to distribute the relief which they were bound to give to the poor. On the contrary, he had always seen the greatest good-feeling and zeal evinced by them. He did not suppose that any of the persons who applied to him for relief would have been refused parochial relief had they gone to the relieving officers. He felt that the relief afforded by the parish might be sufficient to keep body and soul together, and prevent extreme distress, but that it was not sufficient to keep a working man in that condition in which he should be when he returned to hard work. He did not communicate with the parish authorities on the subject of the funds at his disposal. He considered that they should be administered quite independently of parochial relief, and that the money distributed should be in addition to the parish allowance. The best mode of administering relief was, as a general rule, the giving of money. If a person were relieved in kind, and were inclined to be improvident, he would take the articles and sell them for an inadequate value. He was sorry to say that he had heard, and he had reason to believe it, that there was a particular public-house in his district where any amount of bread could have been obtained at 4d. per quartern-loaf; in fact, the bread which was given in relief was taken there and exchanged for beer, and then sold by the publican at a reduced rate. He was well aware that there were flocks of people going about the streets crying that they were snowed out; many of them, no doubt, were gross impostors. If they had presented themselves to him and had the appearance of hardworking men, he had no doubt but that he should have relieved them. The amount sent to the Thames Police Court for distribution during the pressure was £4,000, a sum equal to that which had been sent during the eight preceding years. He had refused considerable sums of money, and had returned as much as he possibly could. He was afraid that the public, in consequence of recent exposures, had felt some doubt and hesitation about relying upon charitable institutions. People were eager to apply their money to the relief of distress, and went to the magistrates for want of, as they considered, better means.

218B. Pauper education

loc. cit., 216–218.

Whatever may have been the state of education in workhouses previously to 1847, there can be no doubt that since that period it has made remarkable progress. The starting point of this improvement was the payment of the salaries of teachers out of the Parliamentary grant, and the consequent examination of workhouse schools by the Inspectors of the Committee of Council for Education. All the witnesses examined by Your Committee concur in attributing to these measures the great change for the better which since that time appears to have taken place in the condition of workhouse schools. The opinion expressed by Mr. Tufnell is in accordance with that given by all the other witnesses:–"The Parliamentary grant has been beneficial; it has very much improved the children in all the workhouses, and it has given a very superior class of masters and mistresses to those who existed under the former system, before that grant was made by Parliament." The effect of this change was strongly insisted on by the witnesses, as shown–

1st. In the improved intellectual education of the children.
2nd. Their improved industrial training.
3rd. The success of Boards of Guardians in placing the children in service.

"In most workhouses," Mr. Tufnell says, "the intellectual education of the children is extremely good." Mr. Lambert, one of the Poor Law Inspectors, is decidedly of opinion that the intellectual education of children in workhouses is better than that of the same class out of the workhouse. Mr. Doyle, another of the Poor Law Inspectors, stated to Your Committee, that "in 1847 the Committee of Council, through their Inspectors, made it almost a condition of giving a grant to a school that an efficient system of industrial training should be introduced into the schools everywhere. There was hardly a union in my district in which the means of industrial training were not provided for boys and girls. Land was taken for boys; men were employed to teach them shoemaking and tailoring; wash-houses were built for girls, and industrial trainers appointed and paid by the Committee of Council on Education. There is no department of the Poor Law administration in which so great and so beneficial a change has taken place as in the industrial training of the children in workhouse schools. The whole of the evidence of the school inspectors appears to me to be as conclusive upon that as upon any other point referred to in their reports." Mr. Hawley, Poor Law Inspector, stated that "with respect to industrial training, I believe that that portion of the education of the children has been pushed as far as it can be in the workhouse schools. With regard to the girls they are taught everything that is useful to them in after-life; all sorts of household work, sewing, and making and mending their own clothes; and lately, washhouses and laundries have been introduced into most of the workhouses, which have been the means of getting a great many girls into situations which they otherwise, perhaps, would not have obtained. With regard to the boys, I am afraid that industrial training has not been pushed so far with them as with the girls, simply for the reason that the guardians have not had it in their power to extend it." "Generally," says Sir J. Walsham, "the schools now are doing all that I apprehend the schools could be required to do. There is scarcely a rural union in my district in which they have not land for the boys, and in which some industrial training is not followed for the girls."

In the annual reports of the Inspectors of the Committee of Council there are frequent references to the progress of industrial training. In 1854, Mr. Ruddock reports: "There has been a gratifying increase in the number of unions giving the special industrial instruction to children in field labour. This improvement has been greatly facilitated by the consent of the Treasury to allow the salary of the labour superintendents to be repaid out of the Parliamentary grant." In 1859 he reports: "In very many cases land to an extent varying from one to twelve acres has been rented for the especial instruction of the children, and agricultural superintendents engaged. In other branches pauper workmen have been removed from the shops, and the boys have been employed under a respectable paid trade-master instead of being dependent upon the casual instruction of some pauper who might happen to know the trade. The girls have been instructed in washing and ironing in many more workhouses than has hitherto been the case, and, in the majority of them, under a respectable paid laundress." In the following year he says: "Greater attention is to be noticed in the industrial training of the children during the past year than I have been able to report previously. . . . There is a continuous increase of out-door industrial employment for the boys, by means of renting land and of employing paid agricultural superintendents." In 1849, Mr. Symons, another of the School Inspectors, reports: "I trace a great increase of effort to give employment with the spade. The proportion of boys thus employed has risen from 12 per cent in 1848 to 22·23 per cent in 1849, and it is still increasing. . . . For girls industrial employment exists much oftener than for boys." In the following year he says: "To a much greater extent than I ventured to hope, means for industrial training have been taken by the different Boards of Guardians; and in 21 spade husbandry has been commenced with various degrees of completeness." Still later, in 1855, Mr. Symons writes: "Needlework is, with very few exceptions, taught very fairly everywhere, and in some schools admirably. . . . I never now encounter fancy work. That which is done consists of making and mending the commonest garments for daily use. Precisely that sort of industry is taught to girls which will be of service to the wives of labouring men and domestic farm servants. . . . The school work prospers beyond my expectations."

The effect of this combination of industrial with intellectual education is described in the Reports of Mr. Hedley, Mr. Fraser, and Mr. Hare, three of the Assistant Commissioners who were appointed by the Royal Commission to inquire in several parts of the kingdom into the state of the popular education. The attention of Your Committee was drawn by witnesses, Mr. Coode, Mr. Doyle, and Mr. Lambert, to passages in those Reports which had been presented to the Royal Commission, speaking of the good effects of the industrial training which had been introduced into workhouse schools and the general improvement of those schools.

Mr. Fraser says:–

"While upon this part of my subject, I ought not to omit to notice the very satisfactory condition of many of the Workhouse Schools. I may particularly specify those at Dorchester, Cerne, Yeovil, Hereford, and Ledbury. Not only the intelligence and knowledge, but the healthy cheerful air of the children's faces and manners, impressed itself upon me very vividly. The instruction given is not ambitious in its range, but thoroughly sound of its kind, the writing, almost without exception, good; and the reading of the girls in the Hereford Workhouse, the best for articulation and freedom from provincialism that I heard in the country. It struck me that the condition of the Workhouse Schools very nearly approached the ideal of what elementary education in this country, under our confessedly difficult social circumstances, ought to be,–perfectly unassuming, and perfectly in keeping with what the children's future career is likely to be.

The teachers are rarely persons of what would be called high attainments, have not often been trained; but the mistresses generally are motherly people of mature age, and they are all, in the instances I have quoted, evidently of strong common sense, and thoroughly understand what is possible in their schools, and what is not. I would point to the mistresses at Dorchester, Cerne, Yeovil, and Hereford, as types of the sort of teacher in whose hands our mixed rural schools would be certain to succeed.

I attribute the efficiency of Workhouse Schools chiefly to the operation of the following causes:–

1. The regularity of the attendance of the children. Every child in the house, unless sick, is certain to be in school.
2. The adequacy of the teaching power. The schools that I saw were all small, and without pupil teachers, but in no case with more than 20 children to the single instructor.
3. The unambitious character of the instruction given, which gives time for what is taught being taught thoroughly.
4. The mixture of industrial with mental work, the advantages of which I fully admit where the combination is possible. These children rarely receive more than three hours' culture a day.

5. The constant intercourse between the children and their teachers. They are thus out of the reach of (what are too often) the vulgarising and demoralising influences of home; hence, the pronunciation in the Workhouse Schools is very rarely provincial; and in most cases you can hardly believe, as you look on their happy trustful faces, that you have before you a set of pauper children, whose portion, both present and future, is generally assumed to be of all men the most miserable." – *Report of Assistant Commissioners*, vol. 2, pp. 89–90.

219. Union Chargeability Act (1865)

Statutes of the Realm, 28 & 29 Vict. c. 79.

WHEREAS it is expedient to make Provision for the better Distribution of the charge for the Relief of the Poor in Unions than is by Law now established:" Be it therefore enacted by the Queen's most Excellent Majesty, by and with the Advice and Consent of the Lords Spiritual and Temporal, and Commons, in this present Parliament assembled, and by the Authority of the same, as follows:

1. From and after the Twenty-fifth Day of *March* One thousand eight hundred and sixty-six, so much of the Twenty-sixth Section of the Fourth and Fifth *William* the Fourth, Chapter Seventy-six, as requires that each of the Parishes in a Union formed under the Authority of that Act shall be separately chargeable with and liable to defray the Expense of its own Poor, whether relieved in or out of the Workhouse of such Union, shall be repealed; and all the Cost of the Relief to the Poor, and the Expenses of the Burial of the dead Body of any poor Person under the Direction of the Guardians, or any of their Officers duly authorized, in such Union thenceforth incurred, and all Charges thenceforth incurred by the Guardians of such Union in respect of Vaccination and Registration Fees and Expenses, shall be charged upon the Common Fund thereof.

2. When any Pauper relieved in any such Union shall be settled in any Parish situated in another Union or subject to a Board of Guardians, and shall not be exempt from Removal by reason of any Provision of the Law, the Guardians of the Union to which such Pauper shall be chargeable may obtain an Order of Removal addressed to the Guardians of the Union or Parish, or the Overseers of the Parish, as the Case may require, in which such Pauper shall be settled, and the Guardians of such last-mentioned Union or Parish shall receive such Pauper in like Manner and subject to the like Incidents and Consequences as in the Case of Orders of Removals heretofore obtained by Overseers, with such Modifications as may be necessary to meet the Circumstances of the Chargeability to the Union instead of the Parish.

3. The Guardians obtaining such Order may defend the same, and the Guardians upon whom it shall be made may appeal against the same, in like Manner and with the like Incidents and Consequences as in the Case of Orders obtained or appealed against by Overseers. . . .

8. From and after the Twenty-fifth Day of *March* One thousand eight hundred and sixty-six, the Period of One Year shall be substituted for that of Three Years

specified in the First Section of the Statute Twenty-fourth and Twenty-fifth of Victoria, Chapter Fifty-five. . . .

10. For the Purposes of the Burial of any poor Person dying in the Workhouse of any Union, such Workhouse shall be considered as situated in the Parish in the Union where such poor Person resided last, previously to his Removal to the Workhouse.

220. Poor Law Board's letter to guardians on Union Chargeability Act (18 April 1866)

Parlty. Papers, 1866/xxxv, pp. 28–29.

Poor Law Board, Whitehall, S.W.,
6th April 1866.

Sir,

I am directed by the Poor Law Board to communicate again with the Guardians on the subject of that part of the Union Chargeability Act of 1865 which relates to the removal of paupers.

That Act having put an end to Parochial Chargeability in the Union has transferred the power of obtaining orders of removal to the Board of Guardians. This power may in some few instances be properly exercised for the benefit of the pauper removed, and in others for that of the ratepayers of the Union; but the Board think that any general and indiscriminate exercise of the power on the part of the Guardians is calculated to cause suffering, expense, and other inconvenience, without ensuring any corresponding benefit. They strongly recommend to Boards of Guardians the exercise, as far as practicable, of a spirit of mutual forbearance in regard to the removal of paupers who may be removable.

They deem it advisable to recall to the attention of the Guardians a consideration of the limits which have been imposed upon their power in this matter by the Legislature.

No person who has resided for one whole year in the Union, whether in one or in several parts of it, without interruption and without relief, can be removed from it. Periods of relief do not operate as an interruption of the residence, but are only not to be calculated as part of the time of residence.

Moreover, periods of residence, under certain specific circumstances, both in and out of the Union, are prevented from being computed in the calculation of the time of residence, or from operating as an interruption of the residence.

No widow residing with her husband at the time of his death can be removed within the first year of her widowhood.

Deserted wives also, after a residence of one year from the time of their desertion, without relief, are exempt from removal.

Children cannot be removed from their parents or some other relatives with whom they may be residing, and orphans derive from their parents the exemption which the latter had acquired at their death.

Lastly, no person whose chargeability arises in respect of relief made necessary by sickness or accident which will not produce permanent disability can be lawfully removed.

When all these large classes have been excluded the number of removable paupers will probably be far from considerable. This number, again, will be further reduced by excluding those who, by reason of the trivial cost of their relief or from other causes, may not, in the opinion of the Guardians, be fit subjects of an order of removal.

The Board, therefore, do not think it can be necessary that the Guardians should forthwith provide any additional officers or assistants, or set on foot an elaborate arrangement for dealing with this subject as one requiring extensive operations.

They recommend the Guardians to appoint from themselves a small committee, to whom shall be referred the subject of the removability of the poor persons in receipt of relief from the Union. The committee may by a few inquiries instituted through the Relieving Officers or through members of the Board of Guardians readily obtain the requisite information to enable them to report upon the subject from time to time, so as to ascertain and distinguish the classes of irremovable and removable poor, and in the case of the latter to point out when they recommend that orders of removal should be taken out, or that application should be made for the removal without an Order in the manner provided for by the 6th section of the recent Act.

It will rest with the Board of Guardians to adopt these recommendations or not as they shall consider most expedient, and if they determine upon the removal of any pauper they must direct their clerk to take the requisite steps in the matter.

If, as the Board anticipate, there will be few occasions for the exercise of this power, the labour of that officer will be insignificant; but if there should be a considerable number of removals, and consequently a large increase of the demands upon his time and labour, it will become proper that either his salary should be increased, or additional assistance should be given to him.

Upon this point, however, nothing can be decided until there has been some reasonable amount of experience as to the working of the new law.

I am, &c.

W. G. Lumley,

Assistant Secretary.

To

The Clerk of the Guardians.

Part X
PUBLIC HEALTH

PUBLIC HEALTH

Introduction

"THE first writers who established satisfactorily the high mortality of cities," wrote William Farr, in a public paper[1] which itself marked an epoch in the subject, "took a gloomy and perhaps fanatical view of the subject. Cities were declared vortices of vice, misery, disease and death; they were proclaimed the 'graves of mankind.' The population of the country, it was said, was drawn to them to be sacrificed; and those who entered left all hope behind, for no prospect of health in cities was beheld." In the decade in which Farr wrote, the whole future of England, with the commanding position she had won for herself in Europe, her immensely expanding wealth, and her increasingly urban civilization seemed to lie under the doom to which he referred; it was like a canker at the core of her prosperity, and on the possibility of its removal her survival and the oecumenical significance of the new techniques of civilization that she had introduced seemed largely to depend. In the eighteenth and early nineteenth centuries, remarkable as it may seem in the light of what we know of conditions in them, the health of towns had improved. But in the 'thirties the rate of urban expansion outran scientific and administrative control, and in a number of large towns a significant deterioration took place. In the light of this position the visitations of the cholera, which first came to the country in 1831–1832, may be regarded almost as a blessing in disguise. They had a spectacular and a monitory character which the calculations of the statisticians lacked. It is true that within a few years of the first crisis little remained of the Board of Health hastily set up to deal with it save a memory and a name, and in a few towns a stimulus towards piecemeal and rather dilatory reforms. But at least the memory remained, and when, in 1847, the scourge became imminent again, the threat of it provided, at a decisive moment, the dynamic to drive through more lasting measures of reform.

The continuous history of the Public Health agitation dates from 1838; the impulse that launched a movement which did more, perhaps, than any other in the century to humanize the conditions under which the working classes lived came from the hated Poor Law Commission, and the occasion of its initiation was an auditor's surcharge. Overseers, before the Poor Law Amendment Act of 1834, had had the power of dealing with nuisances. The Act had not continued this power in the guardians. Nevertheless, the Shoreditch guardians, under pressure from epidemic influenza and typhus, insisted on trying to improve the sanitary conditions in the union which they believed to be largely responsible. Their auditor objected to the charges that they thus incurred, and Chadwick, always interested in preventible disease, got authority to have an investigation made, with the immediate object of making out a case for the restoration of their sanitary powers to the Poor Law authorities. The persons he chose for the inquiry were Dr. Kay, afterwards Kay-Shuttleworth, well known for the researches he had undertaken for the Manchester

[1] No. 223.

Statistical Society into health and housing in Manchester; Dr. Neil Arnott, who had experience in similar inquiries; and Dr. Southwood Smith, the physician of the London Fever Hospital. A description of the sanitary conditions in certain parts of the East End of London[1] and an analysis of the social effects of epidemic fever[2] formed part of their reports. In presenting their case to the public they emphasized that the neglect of sanitary precautions was defeating the purpose of the recent, and still bitterly controversial, Poor Law Amendment Act. The aim of that measure had been to create conditions in which the frugal and industrious working man could prosper by his own endeavours, without being dragged down by the weight of diffused pauperism all round him. Individually, working men could not control the bad sanitary conditions in which so many of them lived, nor could they, in the majority of cases, avoid their effects; they had to live where they could. The all-too-frequent result was that for all their efforts, they were pushed down again into the abyss from which the Poor Law Amendment Act had sought to raise them.

Meanwhile another of Chadwick's initiatives was about to come to fruition. In 1836, as a result of the demand of Dissenters for marriage facilities in their own chapels, a system of State registration of births, deaths, and marriages had been initiated, with clerks to boards of guardians acting as district registrars, reporting to a central Registrar-General's office. Material from which vital statistics for the country could be compiled thus became centrally available. Chadwick had been instrumental in securing that the causes of death should be amongst the facts recorded. He had also obtained the appointment of William Farr as the Registrar-General's Compiler of Abstracts. Farr's annual reports to his chief inaugurated, in the words of Sir John Simon, "a new branch of medical literature"; his "statistical nosology"[3] was the indispensable scientific instrument for the analysis of the problems of Public Health and for pin-pointing black spots.

A decade of public agitation and inquiry was inaugurated by Chadwick's action, and out of it a new science and a new legislation were to spring. Bishop Blomfield, of London, who had been chairman of the Poor Law Inquiry Commission, and had thus been enabled to appreciate Chadwick's calibre, moved in the House of Lords that Chadwick should be called upon to undertake an inquiry covering the whole of the country. Out of this came, in 1842, Chadwick's Report on the Sanitary Condition of the Labouring Classes,[4] intellectually the most searching and the most comprehensive of the many reports of the time. In the House of Commons, R. A. Slaney moved for a Select Committee on the Health of Towns. This took a great deal of valuable evidence, and though later its researches and analyses were to be surpassed, its recommendations may be regarded as the programme of the whole movement of the decade, the expression of its glad confident morning, before the complexity of the problems to be tackled, and the ferocity of the opposition to be met, had been fully realized. In Joseph Fletcher's evidence before it, there was indication of the maze of legislative provisions and administrative arrangements that had to be sorted out before effective action could be obtained. At this stage the point on which reformers chiefly insisted was the necessity of an Act to prescribe standards of building, and this had Chadwick's authority behind it.[5] When Chadwick's own recommendations came to be made, however, in his 1842 Report,[6] he had leapt far ahead. In the interval he had formulated the whole of his sanitary doctrine. This comprised sewers, pipe drainage, universal water-closets, and abundant water supplies

[1] No. 221. [2] No. 222. [3] No. 223. [4] No. 224. [5] Cf. No. 224H for his later views. [6] No. 224.

for every purpose, including washing the streets and flushing the sewers. The items of his programme locked together and could not be applied piecemeal; they had to be accepted altogether, or not at all. Chadwick also disagreed with the recommendation of the Health of Towns Committee that local boards of health should be set up. He proposed, instead, to centre sanitary administration round boards of guardians and their medical officers, on the ground that their responsibility for pauperism gave them a more active and continuing interest in sanitary problems than purely advisory or supervisory boards could have. He also had in mind that the boards of guardians were in being, and that they constituted the only machinery of local government in the country which was, at the same time, under adequate central supervision. But it was natural that his critics should remember that he was Secretary of the Poor Law Commission. Other reports of these years were those of a Select Committee on the Building Regulation Bill of 1842–a measure which was lost–which is remarkable for the number of petitions received by the committee from towns giving reasons why, in their particular cases, the Act was unnecessary, and of a Committee on Burials in Towns, dealing with the overcrowding of the dead. The latter is one of the most nauseating public documents in the whole of the period, though it can be paralleled by G. A. Walker's *Gatherings from Graveyards*. In both, the description of the conditions in which grave-diggers worked make it fully comprehensible that it was a professional necessity for them to be constantly drunk on raw spirits. Chadwick was also asked for a report on the same subject, and brought forward the arguments for the regulation of funeral charges and the municipalization of cemeteries, which were to be put into action in London nearly a decade later. There followed, within the next few years, the Buccleugh Commission on the Health of Large Towns, 1845–1847, and the Grosvenor Commission on the Health of the Metropolis, 1847–1848. The general themes are the same; the immense tax that sanitary neglect entailed on the nation's resources, the impossibility of dealing with it under existing law, the need for the enactment of new and more rigid compulsory standards, above all, the need everywhere for expert initiative and control, and for the consolidation of the inchoate fragments of sanitary administration of the country into an effective, centrally controlled machine. A new authoritarianism had been formulated, and largely at the hands of the leading disciple of Benthamism in the country; for openly or behind the scenes Chadwick had played a leading part in all these inquiries.

The same years saw the formation of a number of voluntary associations for propaganda on health matters, or for the initiation, at private expense, of ameliorative measures of one sort or another. The most influential of these was the Health of Towns Association, founded in 1844. Its chairman was Lord Normanby; its chairman of committees Lord Ashley; and among the founder members were the Bishop of London, Lord Fortescue, Lord Robert Grosvenor, Lord John Manners, Benjamin D'Israeli, R. A. Slaney, the Rev. C. Girdlestone, John Simon, James Smith of Deanston, Dr. Southwood Smith, Tom Taylor, and Thomas Tooke. The roll of names shows that the movement transcended party and political sects; its paladins were men to whom the sanitary cause seemed an overwhelming call of conscience or of common sense, compelling them, for the moment, out of their cabals and coteries into its service.

Legislation lingered, however, not on account of lack of zeal on the part of its promoters, or of the strength of the opposition, though that was considerable, but rather because of the complexity of the issues involved, and also because the break of political luck was against it. The major Bills matured for consideration just as the Irish famine and the Corn Law crisis broke on the country. In 1840 and 1841 Acts were passed for free vaccination. Administration was through the Poor Law machinery, but acceptance of the benefit did not carry with it the disqualification from voting which, in those austerer times, was the normal concomitant of Poor Law relief. These, however, were measures to put to rout a foe that had already been substantially defeated in the eighteenth century. Building Bills were introduced in 1841 and 1843, but failed, Chadwick's change of front on the subject causing hesitation and some irritation in Government circles. Lord Lincoln, Peel's Commissioner of Woods and Forests, introduced a major Health of Towns Bill in 1845, but withdrew it till the next session for further consideration by the Government and the House, and in the next session the Government fell. In 1846 a Baths and Wash-houses Act was passed, sponsored by the Association for Promoting Cleanliness among the Poor, and also a Nuisances Removal Act, a temporary Act, giving guardians the powers for which Chadwick had asked in 1839. In 1847, thanks mainly to the initiative of Joseph Hume, an important series of Clauses Acts was passed. These provided models of private Bill legislation on a number of police and sanitary topics, based not only on the best of current practice but also on the needs which recent inquiries had revealed. Their effect was to simplify and cheapen the acquisition of new powers by Corporations and Improvement Commissioners,[1] and also to make for uniformity, since the clauses could be included by reference in private Acts, and adherence to the model facilitated uncontroversial passage. Lord Morpeth, Lord Lincoln's successor in Russell's Government, took up his predecessor's task, and introduced a Health of Towns Bill in 1847. It was criticized especially for its inclusion of London within the authority of the General Board of Health that it proposed to set up, and Morpeth withdrew it. Much evidence before the various inquiries had already demonstrated the inefficiency of the ancient Sewer Commissions of the Metropolis. But London local politics was a dangerous subject to touch, because of the power of the metropolitan borough Members of Parliament, and the political activity of the vestries. Morpeth determined that a further high-powered inquiry, specifically into the subject, would facilitate his tasks. This decision coincided with a crisis in Chadwick's career. For some years his unhappy relations with the Commissioners,[2] and especially with George Cornewall Lewis, appointed in 1839 and related by marriage to half Russell's Cabinet, had rendered his office as Secretary to the Poor Law Commission practically a nullity. In 1847, in consequence of revelations of dissension and inefficiency in the administration of the Commission, Russell determined to supersede it by a politically controlled board.[3] Chadwick had cleared himself from personal responsibility at these inquiries, but at the cost of further antagonizing Lewis and the powerful Villiers clan, his wife's family. Russell decided not to appoint him to the new Poor Law administration. Chadwick, however, made it clear that he would not accept any slur on his public reputation, and was prepared to go over to the attack on the Whig Cabinet and its protégés, if necessary. At the same time his now immense reputation in health matters made it impossible to overlook him in any public health administration which might be set up. The combination of these factors resulted in his being given unprecedented responsibilities. He was appointed to the Grosvenor Commission on the Health of the Metropolis, which Morpeth was setting up. Before the inquiry was over, Morpeth determined to dismiss the existing Commissions of Sewers, and

[1] Part VIII, Introduction. [2] Part IX, Introduction. [3] Part IX, Introduction.

constitute a new and unified one for the whole of the metropolis. Chadwick was not only appointed to this, but also allowed to choose a large number of the members. In 1848 Morpeth passed his Public Health Act, which now excluded the metropolis from its purview. It set up a General Board of Health of three members–Morpeth himself, as the ministerial representative, Chadwick, as the paid official, and a third unpaid member, who was to be Lord Shaftesbury. For Morpeth's combination of a genuine devotion to duty with outstanding tact and powers of handling men, the qualities he himself lacked, Chadwick developed the deepest admiration; and he and Shaftesbury, the representatives respectively of Benthamite atheism and evangelical fundamentalism, found enduring ties in their common social enthusiasms. Chadwick had never been so happy before in his relations with colleagues, and the Whig Government deserves some credit for matching his powers with congenial and complementary team-mates. Events were to add further to his responsibilities. Cholera was threatening. To avoid complicating his already overburdened Health Bill, Morpeth had passed a further Nuisances Removal Bill, which renewed the Act of 1846 and also put upon the Board of Health the responsibility for dealing with cholera, when the presence of the disease should be notified. In September 1848 cholera was proclaimed.

The cholera emergency at first overshadowed everything else. The Board's Report of 1849[1] illustrates at once the devouring energy of its activity, the slackness of the response, and the weight of the obstruction that it met with. Neither machinery nor powers for really concerted action had in fact been created. The jumble of overlapping and often conflicting local authorities had not been straightened out, and the Board's proposal to set up joint committees in each area, with pooled powers, was ruled by its legal advisers to be beyond its competence. The Board found itself with the authority to issue directions, but with no practical means of enforcing them. Self-satisfied bumbledom, in town and parish, incapable of grasping the implications of the crisis, cried out aloud against centralization. What was done in the countryside as a whole, was done in the main, in fact, on the initiative of devoted individuals and groups, rather than on the impulsion of the Board. In London alone, Chadwick's position on the Commission of Sewers enabled him to achieve action in some degree commensurate to his plans. Millions of gallons of water were forced through the sewers, 'elongated cess-pools', as Chadwick had called them. In common with most people of his time, Chadwick thought that the transmission of cholera was due to the miasma of filth; he knew that a large part of the population of London drew their drinking water from the Thames, but was satisfied that the filth he was forcing into the river would bear little relation in bulk to the volume of the river's flow, and was better in it than in the drains. It is now known that cholera is an intestinal infection, carried in excrement, and particularly active in water, though the activity is then quickly exhausted. *The Times*, in general a supporter of Chadwick's campaigns, protested violently that he was poisoning London's drinking water. In the late summer of 1849 the cholera became water-borne; deaths in London rose from 246 in June to 1,952 in July, 4,251 in August, and 6,644 in September. Meanwhile Parliament agreed to an amended Nuisance Act, which slightly increased the Board's power, and the Treasury allowed it an increase of a couple of inspectors in its establishment. In the autumn the epidemic died slowly down, and by November it had passed.

London affairs, generally, were going badly for Chadwick. In the Commission of

[1] No. 225.

Sewers an unscrupulous opposition from friends of the dispossessed older authorities, and from enemies of Chadwick's sweeping plans and domineering methods, delayed business, caused dissension in the staff, and frustrated the experiments Chadwick was intent on carrying out. The Metropolitan Sewers Act of 1848 put the unification of the Commissions on a statutory basis, and made the appointment of a new Metropolitan Commission necessary. Chadwick was again the leading figure, but the dissensions and uproars continued, and at the end of the cholera epidemic, when Chadwick himself was ill and prostrated by his enormous labours, ministers decided that a totally new Commission was necessary, from which Chadwick's name must be omitted. Even Morpeth agreed and undertook to break the news to Chadwick.

Still the indomitable man refused to accept defeat. The cholera mortality had brought the question of overcrowded graveyards into prominence again. Chadwick and Shaftesbury persuaded an incautious Government to pass the Metropolitan Burials Act of 1850. This gave power to the General Board of Health to purchase the metropolitan cemeteries, to close such of them as it thought fit, and also to contract with undertakers for the conduct of funerals at the cemeteries under its control. In principle this gave it authority to regulate the charges and conduct of funerals throughout the metropolis. There were abuses enough that called for regulation, but the cure was a drastic one. It was in connexion with this Act that a new medical member was added to the Board, Dr. Southwood Smith; later this gave rise to the description of the Board as consisting of "two lords and a barrister to preserve the health of the living, and then, after a year or two of doubtful success, a physician to bury the dead". It also created a situation in which the Civil Service members of the Board could, and did, outvote the minister sitting upon it as a representative of the Government. This ambitious experiment in centralization was expected to pay its own way, and its practical prospects depended on the rapid acquisition of cemeteries. The borrowing powers allowed for this purpose proved to be inadequate; Treasury was unsympathetic, and application had to be made to Parliament. By this time Goverment and the House realized what they had done, and an Act of 1852 brought the scheme to an end, though out of the débâcle were saved powers for the Secretary of State to close burial grounds by Order in Council, and extended borrowing powers for parishes to enable them to acquire new ones. Concurrently, Chadwick had been fighting another battle to win back his London empire. He had long meditated the problem of the London water supply. The cholera epidemic, and his own policy of flushing the sewers, had drawn renewed attention to it. The Board of Health had no *locus standi* in the matter, but Chadwick revived the moribund Grosvenor Commission in order to put forward an ambitious scheme for drawing water from the Surrey hills. If it had been accepted, it would have been necessary to reconstruct the Metropolitan Sewer Commission, and Chadwick hoped that he might thus win his way back to the original scene of his London authority. He came within measurable distance of success, but other schemes were also in the field, and his enemies, and the water companies, were too much for him. Under the measure adopted, the water companies were reprieved for another fifty years, though with securities for the gradual improvement of their supplies.

In the Government's original plan, the Board of Health was to be Chadwick's primary field of operation; his other activities were to be provisional and subordinate. To the Board he was now reduced. It had attracted him less, because London was, after all, the problem that offered the greatest scope for the grandiose planning and large-scale administration that were Chadwick's passion, and several of the larger cities had already contracted out of the board's sphere of control[1] by private Act. The Public Health Act, on which the powers and duties of the Board were based, can only be summarized. In the first place it set up the General Board, as has been described. Secondly, it provided for the setting up of local boards of health. The process of establishing these might be initiated in two ways: on the petition of a tenth of the inhabitants of the area, or by the action of the General Board, where the death-rate exceeded 23 in the thousand. The average for the country was 21, covering a range of 15/16 in the best districts to 30/31 in the worst. The next stage involved an elaborate series of inquiries, conducted by the General Board. If the Board was then satisfied that the setting up of a local Board was desirable, it could proceed to do so by Order in Council where the boundaries of the area did not cross those of existing local government areas and by Provisional Order, requiring the sanction of Parliament, where the Board took the view that existing boundaries were not suitable for purposes of sanitary administration. In corporate towns, the town council became the local board. In non-incorporated districts the local board members were elected by the ratepayers, with plural voting for every £50 of rate assessment, up to a maximum of six votes for any one individual. There were special provisions for areas partly within and partly without corporate boundaries. Local boards might appoint surveyors and medical officers, but could not dismiss them without the consent of the General Board. They were given powers to enforce drainage, provide and maintain sewers, and compel the provision of privies. They could pave and cleanse streets, and provide a scavenging service. They dealt with nuisances, offensive trades, and meat inspection. They were empowered to inspect and regulate common lodging-houses.[2] Under certain limitations they could close burial grounds, provide or control water supplies, and provide public parks. They could raise a rate, and were given borrowing powers for the construction of works, subject to the General Board's approval of the plans. The last was a provision for which Chadwick had had to fight; it was the principal sanction through which the General Board's control of local boards' sanitary policy could be enforced.

In the five years of its work under Chadwick's impulsion, the General Board, despite the restricted field of its influence, achieved, as its final Report[3] shows, no inconsiderable measure of success. But even where its work was most valuable, the procedure under the Act left a good deal of dissatisfaction behind. Where the initiative in setting up a local board was taken by petition, the names of petitioners were not disclosed; there was no provision for a counter-petition; and the General Board, if scrupulous that no representation should be unheard, and no fact that might be of importance to its decision be suppressed, yet made its decision on its own view of the sanitary facts, and was quite prepared to accept the position of working with a minority of the ratepayers–the enlightened minority, it chose to assume–on behalf of the majority of the residents, that is the unenfranchised working classes. The General Board's power of virtual veto over local board works of which it did not approve was ruthlessly exercised. Chadwick took an engineering administrator's view of public health, not a medical one. He was a fanatical enemy of filth, and rode roughshod over medical views that ventured to suggest that its peremptory removal was not the first step to be taken in all circumstances. Despite his confident dogmatism,

[1] Part IX, Introduction. [2] Part VIII. [3] No. 226.

his medical views were not always right, as in his diagnosis of cholera, and consequent flushing of the London sewers. His biographer, Professor Finer, has expressed the view that most of the measures taken, or recommended, by the General Board in the cholera epidemic, though they may have done a great deal of general good, did good only incidentally, as far as the cholera was concerned, and may well have sacrificed lives in doing it. Doctors did not know any more than Chadwick–it was not till some time later that the proper diagnosis of the causes of cholera was made–but doctors do not take kindly to lay dogmatism even when they do not know the answers themselves. Thus, although Chadwick had many doctors fighting on his side, he had many angry opponents among them. Even in sanitary engineering he belonged to a school of his own. It was largely due to him that the new invention of glazed earthenware pipes came into general use for drainage. Sir John Simon has spoken of this as the most valuable sanitary contrivance which had been introduced since Roman times. The older practice had been to make use of brick tunnels, made large enough for men to get in them and clean them out. It was clogged sewers of this type that Chadwick had described as 'elongated cess-pools'. Because of their glaze, their smaller size, and the consequent quicker movement of sewage through them, pipe drains were less likely to clog, and Chadwick maintained that by frequent flushing, which could be achieved by storm water, and by street washing in dry weather, they could be kept entirely free. They were also considerably cheaper than tunnel sewers, and Chadwick could claim that the Board's practice, which was that which he recommended, saved the public a great deal of money. But many engineers were attached by conservative habit to the older practice, and the railway engineers, the "folk heroes" of the time, as Professor Finer has so aptly called them, ranged themselves on this side. Some incidental failures of pipe drainage were ruthlessly exploited against Chadwick, and, again, his claim to stand for expert scientific opinion was challenged by other eminent experts. In the Metropolitan Sewer Commission the influence of the railway engineers had been thrown decisively against him, and had played a large part in his extrusion. The supporters of tunnel schemes had had their way, and some disastrous mistakes resulted, though any general scheme of London drainage could not but be an advance on the chaos that had previously existed. In the country, through the General Board, Chadwick's authority was greater. Orthodox engineers found contracts over which the Board had control going to new and comparatively unknown men, who had accepted Chadwick's views. As a result a large part of the engineering profession was in outcry against him.

Thus, what Palmerston was later to call the war of the clean and dirty parties grew up, and shook not only London but the country as a whole. The issues ran deep, as well as wide. Economic individualism, in the hour of its triumph over the Corn Laws, found itself challenged by a sanitary doctrine that involved innumerable interferences with private property, often in fields in which it was strongly and profitably entrenched. The power of consumer-demand to secure the provision of proper and adequate housing, drainage, water-supply, and burying grounds was sharply questioned. It was proposed to burden the suppliers of these commodities with specific and often onerous obligations, and to lay upon the body of property-owners generally, in their capacity as ratepayers, the cost of providing, superintending and administering services which, in the popular economic conception, competition automatically secured. The challenge to political preconceptions was equally sharp. Many of the most fruitful private initiatives in housing and sanitary reform, as Chadwick amply recognized,[1] came from large landowners and capitalists, and the same classes, in which habits of responsibility and practical experience were combined, provided many of the local leaders in the sanitary struggle. Radicalism, on the other hand, though claiming to be the friend of the masses, was frequently hostile. Chadwick himself had clearly moved far from the primal simplicities of the Benthamite conception of representative government–everyone to count for one, and nobody to count for more than one–as the infallible cure for popular ills. He expected nothing from the working classes, though he laboured constantly for them, and less than nothing from the ratepayer democracy, which was, indeed, his principal foe. He cared more about the ends he had in mind than about the constitutional processes through which they had to be achieved, and showed little regard to the ethics of constitutionalism. The sanitary struggle was not without general political bearings. Much of the scientific and innovating enthusiasm which had found its way in the 'thirties into Radical ranks is absorbed in it, and the Radicalism of the 'fifties and early 'sixties wears a less vigorous and buoyant, if not a slightly old-fashioned, air in consequence. On the other hand, the older governing classes, which had been so bitterly assailed in the earlier period, found themselves, locally at any rate, in the position in which the tangible interests of the working classes seemed safer in their hands than in those of their professed political friends, and they began to recover both self-confidence and political prestige. An empirical and practical criticism of constitutional democracy grew up in place of old-fashioned Toryism; the question with which J. S. Mill opens the discussion of his *Representative Government* (1860)–whether an efficient despotism might not be better than constitutional liberty–became a common topic of debate in the 'fifties. Finally, the categories of religious thought did not escape wholly unshaken. The dominant piety of the time, like its economic doctrine, was an individualist one. The Christian's duty was to accept the order of the world as he found it, to do his own duty in the station in which he found himself, to help his neighbour as an individual in need of help, and to promote the work of saving souls; but inequalities of station were to be accepted as part of the providential discipline of life: they were not in themselves a proper object of Christian concern nor were they in any real sense a hindrance in the Christian's way to God. Against such views as these, Report after Report emphasized the wanton cruelty and destruction of the fabric of decent living involved in sanitary neglect, the virtual impossibility in some of the conditions it created of a sober and self-respecting life. Not a few parsons played a vigorous part in the sanitary struggles of their parishes. To these, the abandonment of the traditional political quietism, if not Conservatism, of their cloth, and the embarking on the turbulent and often muddy waters of controversy, cannot, in a number of cases, have been an easy decision. It was in some ways a prophetic one.

In 1854 the five years' term of the General Board under the 1848 Act came to an end, and fresh Parliamentary sanction was necessary to renew it. All the interests which Chadwick had offended combined to oppose it–the professional interests he had flouted, the economic interests which his doctrines threatened, the politicians whom he had fought, the mass of local interests-vestrymen, officials, the "Hectors and Memnons of intramural muck", as *The Quarterly Review* called them-over whom he had ridden roughshod. Palmerston and Russell fought valiantly for him, but he had, in truth, made it very difficult to defend him in Parliament. The hostile speech of Seymour–who, as Commissioner of Woods and Forests, had found himself

[1] No. 224G.

outvoted and disregarded in the Board of Health–voiced not only his personal resentment but that of the thousands of critics whose opposition had been pushed brusquely aside. Chadwick had to be sacrificed if public health administration was to be saved, and the greatest practical reformer of his age was summarily retired on a pension. But it is a question whether his work was not, in fact, done. With all his failures, and with all the opposition he had aroused, he had put the sanitary idea on the map, and perhaps no one less dogmatic and determined could have done so much in so short a time. But he was born rather to be the minister of an enlightened despot than the civil servant of a constitutional State. He was an instinctive believer in centralization. The deepest criticism of his work is that of his greatest disciple, Sir John Simon, who wrote that to despair of local energies for local purposes was to despair of the purposes themselves.

The major change in the new set-up parallels that in Poor Law administration in 1847. By the Public Health Act of 1854 the Board of Health was subordinated to the President and Vice-President of the Council. By the Local Government Act of 1858 the Board was abolished, its medical duties being transferred to the Privy Council, where John Simon became the medical officer, and exercised a great influence in a small office. Its administrative duties went to the Home Office. A small local government department was set up in the latter department to deal with applications on the part of localities for the setting up of local boards–the procedure still being on the lines of the Act of 1848–and to supervise and assist in the financing of their public works. The new spirit in the administration was expressed in a paper which Tom Taylor, the secretary of the department, read in 1857 to the Birmingham Congress of the Social Science Association, on *Central and Local Action in Town Improvement*. The annual reports of the department showed a steady spread of sewage and water schemes throughout the country, proof that the sanitary idea now had hands and feet. In 1858 a Medical Practitioners Act carried to a successful issue efforts which Sir James Graham had first made in 1844-1845 to set up a Medical Register, and so gave the public and profession their first real protection against quacks. A Select Committee on the Adulteration of Food in 1855–1856 resulted in a Food Adulteration Act in 1860. A new form of census return in 1864 brought the statistical instrument to bear more closely on public health problems. The great work of Florence Nightingale in the Crimea marked an epoch in the administration of military hospitals, and civilian hospitals benefited from the impulse. Yet it marks the scientific novelty of sanitary doctrine that the *Practical Hygiene* of Dr. E. A. Parkes, Professor of Hygiene at the Netley Military Hospital, published in 1864, is described by Sir John Simon as the "earliest systematic work of its kind in the English language". In 1866 a Sanitary Act increased the powers of local authorities, and gave ratepayers the right to appeal to the Secretary of State if they were not doing their duty. The cause was still not without its zealots. William Cowper, Palmerston's son-in-law, and Robert Lowe, as successive Vice-Presidents of the Council, played distinguished parts in seconding the work and ideas of John Simon. But by the 'sixties the time for consolidation had come. Public health administration was suffering from the "chaos of authorities"[1] and conflict of responsibilities that was affecting the whole field of local government. A thorough and authoritative survey was carried out between 1869 and 1871 by the Adderley Commission, appointed under Derby, and continued by Gladstone. Most of the creative work arising from its Report belongs to the period of the next Part

[1] Part VIII, Introduction.

of this volume. But its review of the existing sanitary state of the country[1] rounds off the story with which we have been concerned. One of its recommendations was carried out at once–the uniting of sanitary and Poor Law administration under a single head, the Local Government Board, set up in 1871. Consolidation was desirable, but the immediate results were unsatisfactory from the public health point of view. The more elaborate administration of the Poor Law Board became the framework of the new department. Its officials were placed in the control of finance, and the traditions of a department brought into being to check the expenditure of money were applied in contexts where it needed to be spent. The public health officials–even Simon–found themselves reduced to the role of consultants and expert advisers, without full control over policy. The enthusiasm and knowledge necessary to the proper care of public health had been created in the earlier years of the century; an administrative machine for the carrying out of policy was now to hand, but the harmonious marrying of the two was still to come.

[1] No. 227.

SELECT BIBLIOGRAPHY

Among the *Parliamentary Debates*, those on the Public Health Bills of 1847, 1848, and 1854 are the capital ones, that of 1854 affording a particularly illuminating view of the animosities that the Board of Health succeeded in arousing.

Among public papers the *Appendices* to the *Fourth and Fifth Annual Reports of the Poor Law Commissioners* (*Parlty. Papers*, 1837–1838/xxviii and 1837/xx), are important. The *Annual Reports of the Registrar General*, beginning with the 1839 series of *Parliamentary Papers*, are valuable, especially the earlier ones, from a general historical point of view, and in them, particularly, the *Letters to Registrar General*–reports within reports–of William Farr, the Compiler of Abstracts to the Registrar-General. Farr published an article on "Vital Statistics" in J. R. McCulloch's *Statistical Account of the British Empire*, revised edn. (2 vols., London, 1839), and a collection of his papers was published by the Statistical Society, and edited by Noel Humphrey, under the title of *Vital Statistics* (London, 1885). The more important of the great series of inquiries of the 'forties are those of the *Select Committee on the Health of Towns* (*Parlty. Papers*, 1840/xi); *Select Committee on the Health of Towns: Interment of Bodies* (*Parlty. Papers*, 1842/x); *Select Committee on the Regulation of Buildings* (*Parlty. Papers*, 1842/x); Edwin Chadwick, *The Sanitary Condition of the Labouring Population*, published by the Poor Law Commission (London, 1842); *Report by Edwin Chadwick on Intramural Interment* (*Parlty. Papers*, 1843/xii); *The Royal Commission on the Health of Great Towns* (the Buccleugh Commission) (*Parlty. Papers*, 1844/xvii and 1845/xviii); the *Select Committee on Private Bills* (*Parlty. Papers*, 1846/xii); the *Metropolitan Sanitary Commission* (the Grosvenor Commission) (*Parlty. Papers*, 1847–1848/xxxii). The *Reports of the Select Committee of 1840* and of the *Buccleugh Commission*, in particular, contains much material dealing with particular localities, and are important to the local historian. The *Reports of the Board of Health*, particularly that for 1849 (*Parlty. Papers*, 1849/xxiv), covering the cholera, and the final *Report* of the Chadwickian phase (*Parlty. Papers*, 1854–1855/viii), covering the years 1848 to 1854, are extremely valuable. Among the papers dealing with the inspection of Common Lodging Houses (see also *Introduction* to Part VIII and *Parlty. Papers*, 1839/xix–*Report of Royal Commission on an Efficient Constabulary*, for police aspects), are *Reports on the Condition of Common Lodging Houses and the Operation of the Common Lodging House Act* (*Parlty. Papers*, 1852–1853/lxxviii), dealing with the metropolis, and also certain provincial towns; *Second Report by Captain Hay* on the same subject (*Parlty. Papers*, 1854/xxxv), and *Reports received by the Board of Health* (*Parlty. Papers*, 1857, sess. 2/xli); *Reports on the Adulteration of Food* contain much valuable and startling information (*Parlty. Papers*, 1854–1855/viii, 1856/viii), to which the curious may wish to add *Report on the Adulteration of Port Wine* (*Parlty. Papers*, 1854–1855/i). The work of the Local Government Department set up under the Act of 1858 may be studied in the *Annual Reports of the Local Government Department*. Sir John Simon, *Public Health Reports* (2 vols., London, 1887), are the collected annual reports of the Medical Officer of the Privy Council at the time. The *Report of the Royal Commission on Sanitary Inspection* (the Adderley Commission) (*Parlty. Papers*, 1868–1869/xxxii and 1871/xxxv), is an exhaustive survey of the whole state of the public health question; the *Second Report* (in the second of the two volumes cited above) has a history of the subject. The story is continued after 1871, in the *Annual Reports of the Local Government Board*. The *First Report* (*Parlty. Papers*, 1872/xxviii), contains a retrospective review by Tom Taylor, the Secretary of the Local Government Department from its inception, of the activities of that Department, which was mainly concerned with health.

Among contemporary articles illustrating opinion may be singled out John Austin, "Centralisation", in *Edinburgh Review*, vol. 86 (1847); F. O. Ward, "Sanitary Consolidation", in *Quarterly Review*, vol. lxxxviii (1851); and Tom Taylor, *Central and Local Action in relation to Town Improvement* (Report of National Association for Promoting Social Science, Birmingham

Meeting, 1857). A valuable collection of contemporary pamphlets, many of them dealing with health, is in the *Forster Collection* at the South Kensington Museum.

The standard, and still indispensable, secondary authority is SIR JOHN SIMON, *English Sanitary Institutions*, 2nd edn. (London, 1897), to which his *Personal Recollections* (London, 1898), may be added. R. L. HUTCHINS, *The Public Health Agitation, 1833–48* (London, 1909), and J. H. H. WILLIAMS, *A Century of Public Health* (London, 1931), are more recent accounts. CHADWICK–so long neglected, except for the still indispensable B. W. RICHARDSON, *Health of Nations* (2 vols., London, 1887)–has now received some of his meed in D. D. JONES, *Edwin Chadwick and the Early Public Health Movement* (Iowa, 1931); A. LEWIS, *Edwin Chadwick and Public Health Administration* (London, 1951); and above all in S. FINER, *Life and Times of Edwin Chadwick* (London, 1952), with full bibliographies, both of CHADWICK's writings and of other contemporary and modern relevant literature; and A. JEPHSON, *Sanitary Evolution of London* (London, 1907). Biographies of other figures important in the movement are EDWIN HODDER, *Life and Work of the Seventh Earl of Shaftesbury* (3 vols., London, 1887); J. L. and BARBARA HAMMOND, *Lord Shaftesbury*, revised edn. (London, 1936); and C. WOODHAM SMITH, *Florence Nightingale* (London, 1950).

E. CHADWICK, *Sanitary Conditions of the Working Classes in 1842*, ed. M. W. FLINN (1965) – most valuable reprint with introduction; ROYSTON LAMBERT, *Sir John Simon and English Social Administration* (1963); C. S. NEWMAN, *Evolution of Medical Education in the Nineteenth Century* (1957); BRIAN ABEL SMITH, *The Hospitals, 1800–1948* (1960); J. E. O. NEIL, *Finding a Policy for the Sick and the Poor* – Victorian Studies vii (1964).

221. Public cost of sanitary neglect: fourth Report of the Poor Law Commissioners (1838)

Appendix A 1, Report relative to certain charges disallowed by the auditors, to Fourth Report of the Poor Law Commissioners.

Parlty. Papers, 1837/8/xxxviii, pp. 211–213.

In general, all epidemics and all infectious diseases are attended with charges immediate and ultimate, on the poor-rates. Labourers are suddenly thrown, by infectious disease, into a state of destitution, for which immediate relief must be given. In the case of death, the widow and the children are thrown as paupers on the parish. The amount of burthens thus produced is frequently so great as to render it good economy on the part of the administrators of the poor laws to incur the charges for preventing the evils, where they are ascribable to physical causes, which there are no other means of removing. The more frequent course has been, where the causes of disease are nuisances, for the parish officers to indict the parties for nuisance, and to defray the expenses from the poor-rates.

During the last two years the public has suffered severely from epidemics. At the present time, fever prevails to an unusually alarming extent in the metropolis, and the pressure of the claims for relief in the rural Unions, on the ground of destitution caused by sickness, have recently been extremely severe; but, in the course of the investigations of the claims for relief arising from the prevalent sickness, extensive and constantly acting physical causes of sickness and destitution have been disclosed and rendered fearfully manifest. With reference to the claims for relief on the ground of sickness, in the metropolis, we have directed special inquiries to be made of the medical officers of the new Unions. We have also directed local examinations to be made, in parts of the metropolis where fever was stated to be the most prevalent, by Dr. Arnott, by Dr. Southwood Smith (the chief physician of the London Fever Hospital), and by Dr. Kay, our Assistant Commissioner. The more important communications of the medical officers are comprehended in the medical report prepared by Dr. Kay, with the concurrence of Dr. Arnott. We have given their opinions in a Supplement to this Report, and also the report made to us by Dr. Southwood Smith, on the sanatory condition of the districts comprehended by Bethnal Green and Whitechapel. From this last report we select the following instances of the condition in which several neighbourhoods, densely populated by the labouring classes, have been found:–

"*Lamb's Fields.*–An open area, of about 700 feet in length and 300 feet in breadth. Of this space about 300 feet are constantly covered by stagnant water in winter and summer. In the part thus submerged there is always a quantity of putrefying animal and vegetable matter, the odour of which, at the present moment, is most offensive. An open filthy ditch encircles this place, which, at the western extremity, is from 8 to 10 feet wide. Into this part of the ditch the privies of all the houses of a street called North-street open: these privies are completely uncovered, and the soil from them is allowed to accumulate in the open ditch. Nothing can be conceived more disgusting than the appearance of this ditch for an extent of from 300 feet to 400 feet, and the odour of the effluvia from it is at this moment most offensive.

Lamb's Fields is the fruitful source of fever to the houses which immediately surround it, and to the small streets which branch off from it. Particular houses were pointed out to me, from which entire families have been swept away; and, from several of the streets, fever is never absent. In several houses in Collingwood-street, fever of the most severe and fatal character has been raging for several months. Part of the street called Duke-street is often completely under water: this street consists of about 40 houses; in 12 of them all the members of the families residing in them have been attacked with fever, one after another, and many have died.

"*Virginia-row.*–In the centre of this street there is a gutter, into which potato parings, the refuse of vegetable and animal matter of all kinds, the dirty water from the washing of clothes and of the houses are all poured, and there they stagnate and putrefy. In a direct line from Virginia-row to Shoreditch, a mile in extent, all the lanes, courts, and alleys in the neighbourhood pour their contents into the centre of the main street, where they stagnate and putrefy. Families live in the cellars and kitchens of these undrained houses, dark and extremely damp. In some or other of these houses fever is always prevalent. 'My assistance here,' said the medical officer who was attending me, 'is always required: I am never without cases of fever here.'"

An instance of other prevalent causes is stated in the communication of Mr. Tensh, the medical officer to the Hackney Board of Guardians:–

"In my district, comprising Homerton and Mare-street, of the Hackney Union, I am seldom without cases of a typhoid character, and have carefully searched through my register of sickness from Lady-day 1837 to Lady-day 1838, and find there have been 24 cases of severe typhus, of which four were fatal; 15 of the number were, in one locality named Silkmill-row and Wick-street, attributable, I think, to an obstruction by a dam to a mill, which allows a large accumulation of decaying and other matter of deleterious nature, likely to cause an atmosphere not at all congenial to health, which aided by, I am sorry to say, the innate want of cleanliness and care on the part of the poor, frequently gives rise to fevers of this description, notwithstanding my very urgent and strenuous endeavours to inculcate their importance to their own welfare and comfort. There are two or three other places where the drainage is not so good as it might be: Cross-street and College-street, Homerton; Wood's-yard and Wells-street. These are, I believe, private property. As to that previously mentioned, it has been the subject of litigation between, I believe, the parochial authorities and the party to whom it belongs."

Several officers have fallen victims to the prevalent disease. The excuse from one Union, for answers being only given by one medical officer is, that the other officer had fallen a victim to typhus fever, caught in the course of the performance of his duties in the infected neighbourhoods. In one Union, two of the relieving Officers have, within a short time, been carried off by fever, caught in a similar manner. The extent of the pressure upon the rates, in many instances arising from the causes specified, may be judged of from the following return from the parish of Bethnal Green, which has a population of 62,018:–

"St. Matthew, Bethnal Green.

FEVER REPORT.

"Numbers of fever cases attended by the medical officers of this parish, for one quarter ending 25th March 1838.

Mr. Taylor, out-door surgeon	256 cases.
Mr. Goodwin, ditto	136
Mr. Ager, house surgeon	129
Total .	521

"The cost of in-door cases is at least 5s. weekly, averaging 20s. for each case, before the patient is sufficiently recovered.

"Twenty-six cases were admitted into the London Fever Hospital, at the cost of £27. 6s. to the parish for the last quarter, in addition to the number above reported."

It is stated that the number of fever cases which have been attended by the medical officers in the parish of Whitechapel, within one year, is upwards of 2,000.

All the evidence is strongly expressive of the want of immediate legislative measures to check the evil against which the Boards of Guardians have made such exertions as were within their power. The guardians of Camberwell state that they have made representations to the Commissioners of Sewers, from which we extract the following, of the date of the 18th ultimo:-

"They, the guardians, beg to represent that a proper drainage is extremely essential to a great part of this parish, on account of its exceedingly low level, while it is comparatively easy of attainment by reason of the gravelly nature of its soil.

"They beg to remind the Commissioners that an attempt to drain the village of Peckham was made some years since, but this drain has been left in an unfinished and imperfect state, and the guardians wish to impress on the Commissioners the necessity of its immediate completion.

"The guardians have been given to understand that this completion has been hitherto delayed by the want of funds; but they cannot admit this to be a valid excuse, when it consists with their own knowledge that a great number of the inhabitants are rated to the sewers, which, as far as they, the inhabitants, are concerned, have no existence, and from which, of course, they can derive no benefit.

"The guardians therefore earnestly request the Commissioners to take this matter into their immediate and most serious consideration; and they press it more earnestly at the present time, because, in addition to the ordinary nuisances, the pond on the green, which is situate in the very heart of the village, has, ever since the frost, sent forth such a terrible effluvia as to render the front rooms of the houses around it scarcely habitable, and to fill the whole neighbourhood with alarm at the probable consequences when the hot weather shall arrive."

Mr. Bowling, a medical officer of the Kensington Union, states,-

"We have always had, at certain seasons of the year, fever prevailing to a great extent among the poor, attributable in a great measure to miasma, produced by a quantity of water which has been left stagnant on the surface of the earth after brick-making, and which, in process of time, had become full of vegetable matter. Some years ago this evil had become so alarming that the inhabitants, influenced by the respectable medical men in the neighbourhood, agreed to adopt measures for improving the drainage, and the parish expended considerable sums in so doing; but we have still several places, inhabited by paupers, without any drainage at all, or what there is so very insufficient that a great quantity of filth of all descriptions is constantly lying on the surface.

"It appears, by the register of sickness and mortality, that we have had 104 cases of fever from the 29th of September to the 25th of March, and the greater part of these are certainly to be attributed to causes that might be removed by improved drainage or greater cleanliness. These are independent of small-pox and other diseases, the malignancy of which must be increased by the above circumstances."

Mr. Wagstaffe, one of the medical officers of Lambeth, represents that not only the existence of disease, but of particular diseases, may be inferred from obvious physical and removable causes:–

"According to the district or situation, so you will have the different degrees of fever, such as ague, typhus in all its stages, yellow, and many other kinds."

We have eagerly availed ourselves of the opportunity of making the present Report to submit to your Lordship the urgent necessity of applying to the Legislature for immediate measures for the removal of these constantly acting causes of destitution and death. All delay must be attended with extensive misery, and we would urge the consideration of the fact, that in a large proportion of cases the labouring classes, though aware of the surrounding causes of evil, have few or no means of avoiding them, and little or no choice of their dwellings. The Boards of Guardians have now the services of an efficient body of officers, including experienced medical officers, to guide them in the application of sanatory measures more efficiently than was practicable by the overseers of single parishes under the old system. Until more complete measures could be obtained, and even as a temporary measure, we should recommend that the guardians should be empowered to exercise the like powers that have heretofore been exercised, and incur the like charges that have heretofore been irregularly incurred by parish officers; that they should be empowered to indict parties responsible for such nuisances as those described, and to make arrangements with the owners of property, or take other measures, according to circumstances, for the removal of the causes of disease in cases where there is no ostensible party who can be required to perform that duty. So extreme has been the social disorder, and so abject is the poverty of some of the places which are now the seats of disease, that great numbers of the dwellings have been entirely abandoned by the leaseholders.

222. Fever and pauperism: fifth report of the Poor Law Commissioners (1839)

Appendix C 2, by Dr. Southwood Smith, of Fifth Report to the Poor Law Commissioners. *Parlty. Papers*, 1839/xx, p. 118.

There is no disease which brings so much affliction into a poor man's family as fever. From the ages which the preceding Table shows to be peculiarly predisposed to this malady, it is obvious that it most commonly attacks the heads of the family, those upon whose daily labour the subsistence of the family depends. The present returns afford melancholy evidence of the pauperizing influence of this prevalent and fatal disease. They show that out of the total number of persons in London who received parochial relief during the last year, more than one-fifth were the subjects of fever. In Bethnal-green the proportion was one-third, in Whitechapel it was nearly one-half, and in St. George the Martyr it was 1,276 out of 1,467. Placing out of consideration the suffering of the individual attacked with fever, which is one of the most painful maladies to which the human being is subject, placing out of view also the distress brought upon all the members of the family of the sick, it is plain that this disease is one of the main causes of pressure upon the poor rates. That pressure must continue, and the same large sums of money must be expended year after year for the support of families afflicted with fever, as long as those dreadful sources of fever which encompass the habitations of the poor are allowed to remain. They would not be allowed to remain if their nature were really understood, and if the ease with which the most urgent of them might be removed were known.

While systematic efforts, on a large scale, have been made to widen the streets, to remove obstructions to the circulation of free currents of air, to extend and perfect the drainage and sewerage, and to prevent the accumulation of putrefying vegetable and animal substances in the places in which the wealthier classes reside, nothing whatever has been done to improve the condition of the districts inhabited by the poor. These neglected places are out of view and are not thought of; their condition is known only to the parish officers and the medical men whose duties oblige them to visit the inhabitants to relieve their necessities, and to attend the sick; and even these services are not to be performed without danger. Such is the filthy, close and crowded state of the houses, and the poisonous condition of the localities in which the greater part of the houses are situated, from the total want of drainage, and the masses of putrefying matters of all sorts which are allowed to remain and accumulate indefinitely, that during the last year, in several of the parishes, both relieving officers and medical men lost their lives in consequence of the brief stay in these places which they were obliged to make in the performance of their duties. Yet in these pestilential places the industrious poor are obliged to take up their abode; they have no choice; they must live in what houses they can get nearest the places where they find employment. By no prudence or forethought on their part can they avoid the dreadful evils of this class to which they are thus exposed. No returns can show the amount of suffering which they have had to endure from causes of this kind during the last year; but the present returns indicate some of the final results of that suffering; they show that out of 77,000 persons 14,000 have been attacked with fever, one-fifth part of the whole; and that out of the 14,000 attacked nearly 1,300 have died. The public, meantime, have suffered to a far greater extent than they are aware of, from this appalling amount of wretchedness, sickness and mortality. Independently of the large amount of money which they have had to pay in the support of the sick, and of the families of the sick, pauperized in consequence of the heads of those families having become unable to pursue their occupations, they have suffered more seriously from the spread of fever to their own habitations and families. It is notorious that this disease has been very prevalent during the last year among the industrious classes who have never received parochial relief, and that it has found its way even into the dwellings of the rich, where it has proved extremely mortal. Generated in Bethnal Green, in Whitechapel, in St. George the Martyr, in Lambeth, in Holborn, &c., it has spread to the better streets in the immediate neighbourhood of these and similar places, and thence to still wider and more airy streets at a greater distance, and ultimately to the most remote streets and the great squares. There can be no security against the constant recurrence of this calamity, but the adoption of measures adequate to diminish very materially, if not entirely to prevent, the generation of the febrile poison in every district. This might be done to a large extent by an amendment of the Building Act; by carrying into the districts of the poor improvements similar to those already completed, or now in progress, in the places inhabited by the wealthier classes; by removing as far as practicable the obstacles to a free circulation of air in the closest and most densely populated neighbourhoods; by the construction of underground sewers, with effectual surface-drainage into them, and by the immediate removal of refuse animal and vegetable matters by an efficient body of scavengers. The expenditure necessary to the adoption and maintenance of these measures of prevention, would ultimately amount to less than the cost of the disease now constantly engendered. The most pestilential of these places, when once put into a wholesome condition, could be maintained in that state at a comparatively small expense; whereas as long as they are allowed to remain in their present condition, the results must continue the same; it follows, that the prevention of the evil, rather than the mitigation of the consequences of it, is not only the most beneficent but the most economical course.

I am, &c.

(Signed) SOUTHWOOD SMITH.

223. Use of vital statistics: Farr's letter to the Registrar-General; Registrar-General's report

William Farr's Letter to the Registrar-General: Appendix to Registrar-General's Second Report, 1840.

Parlty. Papers, 1840/XVII, pp. 39–47.

Sir,

The abstract which I have the honour to submit to you comprises 342,529 deaths registered in the year 1838. The causes were assigned in 330,559 instances. Your First Report contained abstracts of the causes of 141,607 deaths, with which the present facts will afford the materials for an interesting comparison.The fatality of different diseases in the year 1838, and their effects in the half-year preceding, will be shown; and the combined observations, presenting a more extensive series than has ever before been published in this or in any other country, will serve as the basis of well-grounded deductions. A careful analysis of the results will show the common causes of death in England.

In arranging the facts which the returns contain, the fatal diseases have been referred to as many distinct heads as could be advantageously distinguished in the present state of medical science, and in this early stage of registration. The diseases have been grouped according to their mode of prevalence, and according to the systems of organs principally involved; the relative extent to which the sexes have suffered from each cause and class of causes is exhibited; the causes of deaths in the several districts, counties, and large divisions of the country, are displayed in an extensive series of tables; and the observations have been thrown into various combinations, calculated to demonstrate the influence of the principal springs either of health or mortality. The nature of the classification was explained in your First Report: it was shown there that several classifications of diseases had been proposed; that medical writers were divided in opinion as to the absolute merits of existing classifications; that the superiority of a classification could only be established by the number of facts which it generalized, or the practical results to which it led; that more arrangements of the facts than one may be useful, but that the main object in view should regulate its principle; and finally, that a *statistical nosology*, to throw the clearest light upon the health of a nation, should be founded upon the mode in which diseases affect the population.

The classification which was proposed last year has been put to the test; and, as I hope to be able to show that the principal anticipations held out have been realized, no sufficient reason can be alleged for changing the frame-work of the arrangement, whatever improvements may be made in its details. At the same time it is freely admitted, that the facts themselves constitute the lasting, staple value of the abstracts; and that, within certain limits, the more extensive the list of causes the better, as it will always be easy to combine, and may be difficult to separate, distinct diseases referred in the report to one head. The list of causes has, on these grounds, been slightly extended.

The facts in the Appendix are published in sufficient detail to be available in the study of special causes; and physicians all over the country will find at their disposal the materials for investigating the various forms of fatal diseases in their own neighbourhood, and the means of comparing them with the diseases of other localities. The intelligence and sagacity of all the members of the medical profession will thus be brought to bear upon the facts in the Report; and it may be confidently anticipated that, in the lapse of time, innumerable results will be elicited of the highest interest to medical science and to humanity. . . .

Is the excessive mortality of cities inevitable? It has not long been established to the public satisfaction that the mortality in dense populations is excessive. The simple process of comparing the deaths in a given time out of a given number living is a modern discovery; and as some individuals died at all ages in the healthiest, or attained the highest ages in the unhealthiest classes, and epidemics desolated the country as well as towns, though to less extent, the unaided reason was baffled in its attempts to unravel the intricate facts, and to draw conclusions which could justify or stimulate public interference. If the law of nature had been, that all the inhabitants of an unhealthy place attained the age of forty years, and of a healthy place the age of fifty years, and then invariably died, the difference would have been perceived in two or three generations: but the law of nature was different; in both cases infants died at the breast, men perished in the prime of life, and old men grew grey with age; the proportions only varied, and the difference was in the average duration of life, which varied from twenty to fifty years, and yet remained undetermined. It was probably not generally known before the publication of your First Report, that the mean duration of life was from 25 to 30 years in the east districts, and from 40 to 50 years in the north and west districts of the metropolis; it is not therefore surprising, that the relative mortality of remote districts remained so long undiscovered.

The first writers who established satisfactorily the high mortality of cities took a gloomy and perhaps fanatical view of the question. Cities were declared vortices of vice, misery, disease and death; they were proclaimed "the graves of mankind." The population of the country, it was said, was drawn to them to be sacrificed; and those who entered left all hope behind, for no prospect of health in cities was beheld. Happily the further application of the methods which those eminent writers employed, and the facts which the registers furnish, enable us to analyse the causes of death in cities; and to show that while the mortality is increased as much as they stated, the apprehensions into which they were betrayed were ill-founded when applied to the future. There is reason to believe that the aggregation of mankind in towns is not inevitably disastrous. Health and life may be preserved in a dense population provided the density be not carried beyond certain limits. Of this the nature of the causes to which the mortality is due, as well as the rapid improvement in the health of London within the last two centuries, is presumptive proof; and the favorable condition of several districts of the metropolis leaves little room for doubt on the subject.

224A–J. Chadwick's Report on the Sanitary Condition of the Labouring Population (1842)

London: W. Clowes and Sons . . . . for Her Majesty's Stationery Office, 1842.

224A. Gas and water socialism

op. cit., pp. 74–77.

. . . Bath, however, is supplied with water under the authority of the local Act of 6 Geo. III (c. 70), for paving etc. which, after reciting that there was a scarcity of water within the city and precincts, and that there were in the neighbourhood of the said city several springs of water belonging to the corporation, enacts that the corporation shall have full power to cause water to be conveyed to the said city from such springs, and gives them authority to enter upon and break up the soil of any public highway, or common, or waste ground, and the soil of any private grounds within two miles of the city, and the soil or pavement of any street within the city, in order to drain and collect the water of the springs, and to make reservoirs sufficient for keeping such water, and to erect conduits, water-houses, and engines necessary for distributing it, and to lay under ground aqueducts and pipes most convenient for the same purpose. The Act vests the right and property of all water-courses leading from the said springs to the city, and also of all reservoirs, conduits, water-houses, and engines, erected or used for the purpose, in the mayor, aldermen, and citizens of Bath. The following extract from a communication from the Rev. Whitwell Elwin, who has closely investigated the economy of the poorest classes in that city, thus describes the present state of the supply:–

"Bath is surrounded by hills which pour down a vast quantity of water into reservoirs. Pipes are laid from these reservoirs to every part of Bath, and as the springs from which the water originally rises are as high up on the hills as the roofs of the houses, water can be carried into the attics without the application of a forcing pump: thus no machinery is employed. The only water-works are the pipes which convey the water.

"These reservoirs are the property of different persons, and there are five distinct parties by which particular districts in Bath are supplied. They are the Bath Corporation, the Freemen's Company, the Circus Company, the Duke of Cleveland, and Captain Gunning. There can scarcely be said to be any competition, because the possession of a spring in a particular locality gives a monopoly of the surrounding neighbourhood. But wherever there is room for selection, the supply of the corporation is always preferred. It is often resorted to even where the distance is much greater than to other springs; the supply being more regular, more abundant, and cheaper than the rest, with the exception of that of the Duke of Cleveland, who only provides his own tenants. The corporation supplies more than three parts of the town. There are at present 2184 persons paying water-rates, but the number of houses furnished with water is considerably greater, because courts and rows of cottages have frequently a common cistern. Where this is the case each cottage making use of the cistern pays a rent of 10s. a-year, and where the house has a cistern of its own, 20s. a-year. The charge for the water is in proportion to the rent of the house. The quantity of water supplied is about a hogshead a-day. In summer, when the springs are low, the quantity is not so great. The laying down and repair of the feather, that is the pipe which branches from the main pipe, is at the cost of the tenant.

"In addition to these private supplies the corporation provides five public pumps, which are open to all the inhabitants free of expense.

"The greater part of the cottages in the town itself, but not in the suburbs, make use of the water-works. There is generally a pump in addition, which yields water too hard and bad for domestic purposes.

"The water rents of the corporation for the last year were 3,233 l. 2s., the expenses (including salaries, rent for springs, repairs of pipes) 449 l. 3s. 3d. thus leaving a profit of 2,783 l. 18s. 9d. This sum is applied to the reduction of the borough rate.

"The advantages of this system over private companies appear to me great and incontestable. Here are no expenses for solicitors, or litigation between rival concerns; no collusion between coalescing companies to raise the charges to the utmost amount that the inhabitants will bear; no exorbitant salaries to the variety of officers, which every separate establishment demands. A few watermen, whose united salaries are only 114 l. 8s. per annum, is the sole addition to the ordinary corporation machinery. When to this we add that all the profits are for the benefit of the town and not for individuals–that the sum paid in water-rate is thus pretty nearly deducted from the borough rate–we can hardly hesitate to strike the balance. The corporation management, here at least, gives unlimited satisfaction. They are under the direct control of the rate-payers, properly desirous to conciliate their opinion, and are sure to hear of any incivility, which, as they have no interest in protecting it, they are always ready to redress."

In this instance, however, it is to be observed that the real cost of the water to the corporation is not more than one-seventh their charge to the consumer; consequently, the charge for a supply out of the house may be said to be less than 1s. 6d. per annum; and it will admit of little doubt that if the water were lifted by steam power and carried into every tenement, as it might be, the actual expense need not be doubled; six-sevenths then of the charge, which is about the same as the ordinary charges of water companies, is to be considered as a borough rate, levied in the shape of a water rate, applied doubtless to some other proper public services.

An example is presented in Manchester of the practicability of obtaining supplies for the common benefit of a town without the agency of private companies. In that town gas has for some years past been supplied from works erected and conducted not by the municipality but by a body appointed under a local Act by an elected committee of the ratepayers. This mode of supplying the town was, it appears, violently opposed by private interests; but I am informed that the supplies of gas are of as good or even of a better quality, and cheaper than those obtained from private companies in adjacent towns; that improvements in the manufacture of the gas are more speedily adopted than in private associations, and the profits are reserved as a public fund for the improvement of the town. Out of this fund a fine Town Hall has been erected, whole streets have been widened, and various large improvements have been made; and the income now available for the further improvement of the town exceeds 10,000 l. per annum, after providing for the expense of management and the interest of the sinking fund on the money borrowed. There are now in the same districts in the metropolis no less than three immense capitals sunk in competition, – three sets of gas-pipes passing through the same streets, three expensive sets of principal and subordinate officers where one would suffice, comparatively high charges for gas to the consumers, and low dividends to the shareholders of the companies in competition. Where a scientific and trustworthy agency can be obtained for the public, manifest opportunities present themselves for considerable economy on such modes of obtaining supplies. A proposal was made in Manchester to obtain supplies of water for the town in the same manner as the supplies of gas, but the owners of the private pumps, who it is stated, have the monopoly of the convenient springs, and exact double the charge for which even private companies are ready to convey supplies into the houses, made a compact and effectual opposition to the proposal, contending that the supplies of rain-water (which are sometimes absolutely black with the soot held in suspension), together with that from the springs was sufficient, and the proposal was defeated. These petty interests could not, however, avail against the more powerful interest of a joint-stock company, which was established to procure supplies for the middle and wealthier classes of the town.

There appears to be no reason to doubt that the mode of supplying water to Bath and gas to the town of Manchester might be generally adopted in supplying water to the population. Powers would be required to enter into the lands adjacent to the towns on a reasonable compensation to the owners to obtain supplies of water; and as the management of water-works requires appropriate skill, it would be necessary to appoint an officer with special qualifications for their superintendence. Ordinary service may be obtained for the public, if recourse be had to the ordinary motives by which such service is engaged in private companies. It is not mentioned invidiously, but as a matter of fact, that the majority, not to say the whole, of such undertakings by joint-stock companies, are, in the first instance, moved by a solicitor, or engineer, or other person, for the sake of the office of manager of the works, and that the directors and shareholders, and the inducement of profit to them, through the benefit undoubtedly to the public, are only the machinery to the attainment of the object for which the undertaking is primarily moved. If competent officers be appointed and adequately remunerated for the service, there can be little doubt that the public may, as at Bath and Manchester, be saved the expense of the management by the occasional attendance of unskilled directors, and that they may save the expense of dividends, or apply the profits to public improvements, as at Manchester, and moreover avoid the inconveniences and obstructions undoubtedly belonging to the supply of a commodity so essential to the public health, comfort, and economy by a private monopoly. Bad supplies of water would, I apprehend, generally be less tolerated by the influential local inhabitants of all parties from a public municipal agency than from a private company. . . .

224B. Fever a dirt, not a destitution disease

loc. cit., pp. 133–134.

. . . Mr. Baker, in his report on the condition of the population, after giving an instance of the contrast presented by the working-people living in better dwellings, situated in better cleansed neighbourhoods (to which I shall advert when submitting the evidence in respect to preventive measures), describes the population living in houses–

"With broken panes in every window-frame, and filth and vermin in every nook. With the walls unwhitewashed for years, black with the smoke of foul chimneys, without water, with corded bed-stocks for beds, and sacking for bed-clothing, with floors unwashed from year to year, without out-offices, . . . while without, there are streets, elevated a foot, sometimes two, above the level of the causeway, by the accumulation of years, and stagnant puddles here and there, with their foetid exhalations, causeways broken and dangerous, ash-places choked up with filth, and excrementitious deposits on all sides as a consequence, undrained, unpaved, unventilated, uncared-for by any authority but the landlord, who weekly collects his miserable rents from his miserable tenants.

"Can we wonder that such places are the hot-beds of disease, or that it obtains, upon constitutions thus liberally predisposed to receive it, and forms the mortality which Leeds exhibits. Adult life, exposed to such miasmata, gives way. How much more then infant life, when ushered into, and attempted to be reared in, such obnoxious atmospheres. On the moral habits similar effects are produced. An inattention on the part of the local authorities to the state of the streets diminishes year by year the respectability of their occupiers. None dwell in such localities but those to whom propinquity to employment is absolutely essential. Those who might advocate a better state of things, depart; and of those who remain, the one-half, by repeated exhibitions of indecency and vulgarity, and indeed by the mere fact of neighbourship, sink into the moral degradation which is natural to the other, and vicious habits and criminal propensities precede the death which these combinations prepare."

No education as yet commonly given appears to have availed against such demoralizing circumstances as those described; but the cases of moral improvement of a population, by cleansing, draining, and the improvement of the internal and external conditions of the dwellings, of which instances will be presented, are more numerous and decided, though there still occur instances of persons in whom the love of ardent spirits has gained such entire possession as to have withstood all such means of retrieving them. The most experienced public officers acquainted with the condition of the inferior population of the towns would agree in giving the first place in efficiency and importance to the removal of what may be termed the physical barriers to improvement, and that as against such barriers moral agencies have but a remote chance of success.

A gentleman who has had considerable experience in the management of large numbers of the manufacturing population stated to me that in every case of personal and moral improvement the successful step was made by the removal of the party from the ill-conditioned neighbourhood in which he had been brought up. When a young workman married, he interfered to get him a better residence apart from the rest; and when this was done important alterations followed; but if he took up his abode in the old neighbourhood, the condition of the wife was soon brought down to the common level, and the marriage became a source of wretchedness.

Benevolent persons, viewing the bare aspect of some of the most afflicted neighbourhoods, have raised subscriptions for the purchase of furniture, bedding, and blankets, for the relief of the inmates, but by this pecuniary aid they have only added fuel to the flame; that is, they have enabled the inmates to purchase more ardent spirits. The force of the habit, which is aggravated by misdirected charity, is indicated in the following instances, of which one was mentioned to me by the Rev. Whitwell Elwin:–

"I was lately informed by a master tailor of Bath that one of his men, who had earned £3 a-week at piece-work for years, had never within his knowledge possessed table, chairs, or bedding. I found the statement on examination to be strictly true. Some straw on which he slept, a square block of wood, a low three-legged stool, and an old tea-caddy, are the complete inventory of the articles of a room, the occupier of which, with only himself and his wife to maintain, was wealthier than many in the station of gentlemen. He had frequently excited lively compassion in benevolent individuals, who, supposing that he was struggling for very existence, furnished him with a variety of household goods, which were regularly pawned before a week was out, and afforded to the superficial observer fresh evidence of the extremity of his distress. The cause of all this is quickly told: the wife was to be seen going to and fro several times a-day with a cream-jug of gin, and to gratify this appetite, they had voluntarily reduced themselves to the condition of savages. I could add numerous instances of a similar kind. Indeed, were a stranger to go through the town, and judge only from the appearance of things, I am convinced that he would select his examples of greatest privation not from the really poor, but from men who were in the receipt of more than 30s. a-week. Charity, which when prompted by pure motives, always blesses him that gives, does not always bless him that takes. I am afraid that the indiscriminate adoption of dirt and rags as a test of poverty, especially in a town like Bath, where private charity prevails on an extensive scale, operates as a premium upon ill habits, and as a discouragement to cleanliness, and leads many to affect a vice which was not habitual to them." . . .

224C. Comparative chances of life in urban and rural districts, and in different classes of the community

loc. cit., pp. 155–160.

. . . To compare the chances of life between a crowded manufacturing population and a less crowded rural population, I selected the county of Rutland, because it had been selected as an average agricultural district for a comparison as to its general condition by the members of the Statistical Society of Manchester, and they deputed their agent, Mr. J. R. Wood, to make inquiries on an examination from house to house. The following are portions of his examination:–

"Amidst what population have you inquired from house to house?–Amidst a portion of the population of Manchester, *viz.* Pendleton, having a population of about 10,000; I visited every house. In like manner I went through Branstoun, Egleton, and Hambleton, in Rutlandshire, being a rural population of upwards of 1,000, and Hull, having a population of nearly 40,000 exclusive of Sculcoates, Ashton, and Dukinfield. I also went over for the purpose of checking an inquiry into the state of the population of those towns, which had been previously made by another party. In Liverpool I did not go from house to house; I went into a considerable number of the houses amidst the poorer districts. In certain districts of Manchester, though not for the Statistical Society, I did the same. In Birmingham I made many memoranda, and, as far as my limited time would permit, I visited a portion of the population. In York, containing a population of 26,000, I went into every street and court, visiting occasionally, to obtain a general idea of the condition of the inhabitants. York included 23 parishes of small extent, all which I visited.

"What did you find to be the condition of the tenements in the rural districts as compared with the towns you examined?–In Branstoun, Egleton, and Hambleton, being in a rural district, the houses are low, never exceeding two stories; many of them are thatched, and nearly all are built of stone. To each a garden is attached which is generally of sufficient dimensions to supply the family with vegetables. As there are no cellars, most of the houses have a small dairy or store-room attached, which, however, has not been counted in reckoning the number of rooms in each house. Forty-one per cent. of the dwellings in Branstoun, and 51 per cent. in Egleton and Hambleton I found to be 'wellfurnished.' In Manchester and Salford 52 per cent., and in the Dukinfield district 61 per cent., had that character. The proportion reported to be *comfortable* in each district were:–

In Branstoun	50 per cent.
Egleton and Hambleton	65 "
Manchester, &c.	72 "
Dukinfield	95 "

"The word '*comfortable*' must always be a vague and varying epithet, nor is it possible to attach any precise definition to it. In filling up this column I was guided by observing the condition of the dwelling, apart from any consideration of order, cleanliness, and furniture. If I considered it capable of being made comfortable for the tenant, I set it down accordingly; if it were damp, the flooring bad, and the walls ill-conditioned, I reported it uncomfortable. The general appearance of the interior of the houses (in Rutlandshire) indicated thrifty poverty, and instances of the squalid misery so frequent in large towns were here extremely rare. In comparing the physical condition of the people in the three parishes, Egleton and Hambleton appeared to have some slight advantage over Branstoun, while 31 per cent. of the houses in the former parishes contained four rooms only; 17 per cent. in the latter had this advantage. In its amount of sleeping accommodation, also Branstoun is inferior to the neighbouring parishes.

"From a comparison of the tables with those in a former Report, it appeared that in Egleton, &c., 14 per cent. of the families have more than three persons to a bed; Branstoun, 19 ditto; Dukinfield, 33 ditto; and Bury, 35 ditto.

"The rents of the houses in Rutlandshire would appear to be very low compared with those in large manufacturing towns. Not only is the average cost of the former less than half of the latter, but for that diminished cost the dimensions of the houses are double those in large towns, with comforts and conveniences which the latter never can possess.

	£	s.	d.
Egleton, &c., average yearly rent . .	2	17	3
Branstoun	3	0	0
Dukinfield, &c.	6	14	0
Manchester, &c.	7	11	8"

But moral causes, inducing habits of sobriety, appear from the report of the Manchester Society to contribute to the general result of the superior condition of the Rutland population, in which the duration of life amongst the lowest classes appears to be nearly as high as amongst the highest classes in Manchester. Wages in Lancashire, it must be premised, were then (in 1837), and, as I am well informed from the payers of several thousand labourers, are now at least double what they are in Rutlandshire. The Society state in their report that it appears–

"That the people do nearly as much for themselves in Rutlandshire as they do in Manchester, notwithstanding the more extensive endowment of their schools.

"In a separate examination of three parishes in Rutlandshire, carried on from house to house, the larger attendance of children at school in that county was confirmed, and it also appeared that the average time of their remaining at day schools was greater than in Lancashire. In Pendleton, near Manchester, one third only of the children appeared to remain at school above five years, and one third remained less than three years; while, in the three parishes of Rutlandshire which were visited, it was found that, of the children who had left school, one half had remained there above five years.

"The teachers generally bear irreproachable characters, which had doubtless much influence on the character and deportment of the population, whose manners appeared exceedingly orderly and respectful.

"In the dame schools it was very gratifying to observe the marked difference in general appearance and order, as compared with schools of a similar class in large towns. The mistresses are almost invariably persons of good moral character, of quiet orderly habits, cleanly in their habitations, decent in their personal appearance, and of respectful deportment. The scholars, too, except in one or two instances, were found clean and tidy, however mean their attire, and generally remained orderly and quiet during the visit. The rod or cane is much less in use than in the towns formerly examined, though it usually forms part of the furniture of the school. The girls were generally found sewing or knitting, and in many schools the boys learn to knit.

"A society for the promotion of industry, supported by subscriptions, exists in the country; and prizes are given to those children, who, according to their age, have performed the most work during the year. This excites a great competition as to which village shall produce the queen of the knitters, or the queen of the sewers, and many ladies in the county consider the Society to have great influence in inducing habits of diligence and order. The moral effect is no doubt good, and a greater interest in the lower class of schools is also thereby created amongst the gentry.

"In conclusion, we may observe that the visitation of the houses of the labouring poor in Rutlandshire, and the observation of their language, manners, and habits, leave a favourable impression with regard to their moral condition. Swearing and drunkenness are far from common, and the general conduct of the people is marked by sobriety, frugality, and industry."

Mr. Wood was asked–

"You have seen the following returns of the average ages of death amongst the different classes of people in Manchester and Rutlandshire:–

	Average age of death	
	In Manchester Years	In Rutlandshire Years
Professional persons and gentry, and their families	38	52
Tradesmen and their families, (in Rutlandshire, farmers and graziers are included with shopkeepers)	20	41
Mechanics, labourers, and their families .	17	38

Bearing in mind the fact that wages are nearly double in Manchester to the average of wages in Rutlandshire, though rents are higher in Manchester: are the different chances of life amongst each class of the population to the extent they are indicated by the returns, conformable to what you would have anticipated from your personal examinations of the houses and observations of the condition of the inhabitants?–They are decidedly conformable to my anticipation in the general results. I apprehend, however, that some allowance must perhaps be made for the very high average age in Rutlandshire, from the circumstance that many of the children or young people migrate from thence to manufacturing neighbourhoods for employment. These would certainly have passed the age at which the greatest mortality takes place amongst children; but we may expect that their migration, as it is a constant migration, might to some extent increase the average age of death or apparent duration of life in Rutlandshire, though not very materially. On the other hand, there is, perhaps, a larger proportion of children in Manchester. The results certainly correspond with my own impressions as to the relative condition of the different classes in the different neighbourhoods."

In the union comprehending the adjacent manufacturing district of Bolton, the proportions of deaths in the several classes as returned by the superintendent-registrar were as follows in the year 1839:-

No. of deaths	*Bolton Union*	*Average age of deceased*
103	Gentlemen and persons engaged in professions, and their families	34 years
381	Tradesmen and their families	23
2,232	Mechanics, servants, labourers, and their families .	18

It is proper to observe, that so far as I was informed upon the evidence received in the Factory Inquiry, and more recently on the cases of children of migrant families, that opinion is erroneous which ascribes greater sickness and mortality to the children employed in factories than amongst the children who remain in such homes as these towns afford to the labouring classes. However defective the ventilation of many of the factories may yet be, they are all of them drier and more equably warm than the residence of the parent; and we had proof that weakly children have been put into the better-managed factories as healthier places for them than their own homes. It is an appalling fact that, of all who are born of the labouring classes in Manchester, more than 57 per cent. die before they attain five years of age; that is, before they can be engaged in factory labour, or in any other labour whatsoever.

Of 4,629 deaths of persons of the labouring classes who died in the year 1840 in Manchester, the numbers who died were at the several periods as follows:-

Under 5 years of age	2,649 or 1 in 17
Above 5 and under 10	215 or 1 in 22
Above 10 and under 15	107 or 1 in 43
Above 15 and under 20	135 or 1 in 34

At seven, eight, or nine years of age the children of the working classes begin to enter into employment in the cotton and other factories. It appears that at the period between 5 and 10 years of age the proportions of deaths which occur amongst the labouring classes, as indicated by these returns, are not so great as the proportions of deaths which occur amongst the children of the middle classes who are not so engaged. Allowing for the circumstance that some of the weakest of the labourers' children will have been swept away in the first stage, the effect of employment is not shown to be injurious in any increase of the proportion who die in the second stage.

In a return obtained from a district differently situated (Bethnal Green, where the manufactory is chiefly domestic) it appears that of 1,268 deaths amongst the labouring classes in the year 1839, no less than 782, or 1 in 14, died at their own residences under 5 years of age. One in 15 of the deaths occurred between 5 and 10, the age when employment commences. The proportion of deaths which occurred between 10 and 15, the period at which full employment usually takes place, is 1 in 60 only.

In that district the average age of deaths in the year 1839 was as follows, in the several classes, from a population of 62,018:-

No. of deaths	*Bethnal Green*	*Average age of deceased*
101	Gentlemen and persons engaged in professions, and their families	45 years
273	Tradesmen and their families	26
1,258	Mechanics, servants, and labourers, and their families	16

The mean chances of life amongst the several classes in Leeds appear from the returns to the Registrar-general generally to correspond with the anticipations raised by the descriptions given of the condition of the labouring population.

No. of deaths	*Leeds Borough*	*Average age of deceased*
79	Gentlemen and persons engaged in professions, and their families	44 years
824	Tradesmen, farmers, and their families	27
3,395	Operatives, labourers, and their families . .	19

But in Liverpool (which is a commercial and not a manufacturing town) where, however, the condition of the dwellings are reported to be the worst, where, according to the report of Dr. Duncan, 40,000 of the population live in cellars, where 1 in 25 of the population are annually attacked with fever,-there the mean chances of life appear from the returns to the Registrar-general to be still lower than in Manchester, Leeds, or amongst the silk weavers in Bethnal Green. During the year 1840, the deaths, distinguishable in classes, were as follows:-

No. of deaths	*Liverpool, 1840*	*Average age of deceased*
137	Gentry and professional persons, &c. . . .	35 years
1,738	Tradesmen and their families	22
5,597	Labourers, mechanics, and servants, &c. . . .	15

Of the deaths which occurred amongst the labouring classes, it appears that no less than 62 per cent. of the total number were deaths under five years of age. Even amongst those entered as shopkeepers and tradesmen, no less than 50 per cent. died before they attained that period. The proportion of mortality for Birmingham, where there are many insalubrious manufactories, but where the drainage of the town and the general condition of the inhabitants is comparatively good, was, in 1838, 1 in 40; whilst in Liverpool it was 1 in 31. . . .

224D. Misery not a check to the pressure of population on subsistence

loc. cit., pp. 176–177.

An impression of an undefined optimism is frequently entertained by persons who are aware of the wretched condition of a large portion of the labouring population; and this impression is more frequently entertained than expressed, as the ground of inaction for the relief of the prevalent misery from disease, that its ravages form the natural or positive check, or, as Dr. Short terms it, a "terrible corrective" to the pressure of population on the means of subsistence.

In the more crowded districts, which have been the subject of the present inquiry, the facts do not justify this impression; they show that the theory is inapplicable to the present circumstances of the population. How erroneous the inferences are in their unrestrained generality, which assume that the poverty or the privation which is sometimes the consequence, is always the cause, of the disease, will have been seen from such evidence as that adduced from Glasgow and Spitalfields, proving that the greater proportion of those attacked by disease are in full work at the time; and the evidence from the fever hospitals, that the greatest proportion of the patients are received in high bodily condition. If wages be taken as the test of the means of subsistence, it may be asked how are such facts to be reconciled as these, that at a time when wages in Manchester were 10s. per head weekly on all employed in the manufactories, including children or young persons in the average, so that if three or four members of a family were employed, the wages of a family would be 30s. or 40s. weekly, the average chances of life to all of the labouring classes were only 17 years; whilst in the whole of Rutlandshire, where the wages were certainly not one half that amount, we find the mean chances of life to every individual of the lowest class were 37 years? Or, to take another instance, that whilst in Leeds, where, according to Mr. Baker's report, the wages of the families of the worst-conditioned workers were upwards of £1. 1s. per week, and the chances of life amongst the whole labouring population of the borough were only 19 years; whilst in the county of Wilts, where the labourer's family would not receive much more than half that amount ot wages in money, and perhaps not two-thirds of money's worth in money and produce together, we find the average chances of life to the labouring classes 32 years?

If, in the most crowded districts, the inference is found to be erroneous, that the extent of sickness and mortality is indicative of the pressure of population on the means of subsistence, so is the inference that the ravages act to the extent supposed, as a positive check to the increase of the numbers of the population. In such districts the fact is observable, that where the mortality is the highest, the number of births are more than sufficient to replace the deaths, however numerous they may be. . . .

224E. Social effect of age composition of the population

loc. cit., pp. 200–203.

. . . . Whenever the adult population of a physically depressed district, such as Manchester, is brought out on any public occasion, the preponderance of youth in the crowd and the small proportion of aged, or even of the middle aged, amongst them is apt to strike those who have seen assemblages of the working population of other districts more favourably situated.

In the course of some inquiries under the Constabulary Force Commission as to the proportions of a paid force that would apparently be requisite for the protection of the peace in the manufacturing districts, reference was made to the meetings held by torchlight in the neighbourhood of Manchester. It was reported to us, on close observation by peace-officers, that the bulk of the assemblages consisted of mere boys, and that there were scarcely any men of mature age and experience, who, it was stated, generally disapproved of the proceedings of the meetings as injurious to the working classes themselves. These older men, we were assured by their employers, were intelligent, and perceived that capital, and large capital, was not the means of their depression, but of their steady and abundant support. They were generally described as being above the influence of the anarchical fallacies which appeared to sway those wild and really dangerous assemblages. The inquiry which arose upon such statements was how it happened that the men of mature age, feeling their own best interest injured by the proceedings of the younger portion of the working classes, how they, the elders, did not exercise a restraining influence upon their less experienced fellow-workmen? On enquiring of the owner of some extensive manufacturing property, on which between 1000 and 2000 persons were maintained at wages yielding 40s. per week per family, whether he could rely on the aid of the men of mature age for the protection of the capital which furnished them the means of subistence? he stated he could rely on them confidently. But on ascertaining the numbers qualified for service as special constables, the gloomy fact became apparent, that the proportion of men of strength and of mature age for such service were but as a small group against a large crowd, and that for any social influence they were equally weak. The disappearance by premature deaths of the heads of families and the older workmen at such ages as those recorded in the returns of dependent widowhood and orphanage, must to some extent practically involve the necessity of supplying the lapse of staid influence amidst a young population by one description or other of precautionary force.

On expostulating on other occasions with middle-aged and experienced workmen on the folly as well as the injustice of their trade unions, by which the public peace was compromised by the violences of strike after strike, without regard to the experiences of the suffering from the continued failures of their exertions for objects the attainment of which would have been most injurious to themselves, the workmen of the class remonstrated with, invariably disclaimed connexion with the proceedings, and showed that they abstained from attendance at the meetings. The common expression was, they would not attend to be borne down by "mere boys," who were furious, and knew not what they were about. The predominance of a young and violent majority was general.

In the metropolis the experience is similar. The mobs against which the police have to guard come from the most depressed districts; and the constant report of the superintendents is, that scarcely any old men are to be seen amongst them. In general they appear to consist of persons between 16 and 25 years of age. The mobs from such districts as Bethnal Green are proportionately conspicuous for a deficiency of bodily strength, without, however, being from that cause proportionately the less dangerously mischievous. I was informed by peace officers that the great havoc at Bristol was committed by mere boys. . . .

. . . The facts indicated will suffice to show the importance of the moral and political considerations, *viz.*, that the noxious physical agencies depress the health and bodily condition of the population, and act as obstacles to education and to moral culture; that in abridging the duration of the adult life of the working classes they check the growth of productive skill, and abridge the amount of social experience and steady moral habits in the community: that they substitute for a population that accumulates and preserves instruction and is steadily progressive, a population that is young, inexperienced, ignorant, credulous, irritable, passionate, and dangerous, having a perpetual tendency to moral as well as physical deterioration. . . .

224F. Inability of workmen to improve their own condition

loc. cit., pp. 231–233.

I may assume that it has been proved that the labouring classes do possess the means of purchasing the comforts of superior dwellings, and also that they are not benefited by exemptions from the immediate charges wherever requisite to defray the expense of those superior comforts.

I shall now show how little it is in the power of these classes voluntarily to obtain these improvements,–setting aside entirely the consideration of the obstacles arising from depraved habits already formed.

The workman's "location," as it is termed, is generally governed by his work, near which he must reside. The sort of house, and often the particular house, may be said to be, and usually is, a monopoly. On arriving at manhood in a crowded neighbourhood, if he wishes to have a house, he must avail himself of the first vacancy that presents itself; if there happen to be more houses vacant than one, the houses being usually of the same class, little range of choice is thereby presented to him. In particular neighbourhoods near Manchester, and in other parts of the county of Lancaster, in some other manufacturing and in some rural districts, instances occur of the erection of improved ranges of larger and better constructed houses for the labouring classes; and, making deduction for the occasional misuse of the increased space by sub-dividing them and overcrowding them with lodgers, the extent to which these improved tenements are sought, and the manner in which an improved rent is paid, afford gratifying evidence of an increasing disposition prevalent amongst artisans to avail themselves of such improvements. These opportunities, however, are comparatively few, and occur in districts where multitudes continue in the most depressed condition, apparently without any power of emerging from it.

The individual labourer has little or no power over the internal structure and economy of the dwelling which has fallen to his lot. If the water be not laid on in the other houses in the street, or if it be unprovided with proper receptacles for refuse, it is not in the power of any individual workman who may perceive the advantages of such accommodations to procure them. He has as little control over the external economy of his residence as of the structure of the street before it, whether it shall be paved or unpaved, drained, or undrained. It may be said that he might cleanse the street before his own door. By some local acts the obligation to do so is imposed on the individual inhabitants. By those inhabitants who have servants this duty may be and is performed, but the labourer has no servant; all of his family who are capable of labour are out a-field, or in the manufactory or the workshop, at daybreak, and return only at nightfall, and this regulation therefore is unavoidably neglected.

Under the slavery of the existing habits of labourers, it is found that the faculty of perceiving the advantage of a change is so obliterated as to render them incapable of using, or indifferent to the use of, the means of improvement which may happen to come within their reach. The sense of smell, for instance, which generally gives certain warning of the presence of malaria or gases noxious to the health, appears often to be obliterated in the labourer by his employment. He appears to be insensible to anything but changes of temperature, and there is scarcely any stench which is not endured to avoid slight cold.

It would have been matter of sincere congratulation to have met with more extensive evidence of spontaneous improvement amongst the classes in receipt of high wages, but nearly all the beneficial changes found in progress throughout the country are changes that have arisen from the efforts of persons of the superior classes. Inquiries have been made for plans of improved tenements, but none have been found which can be presented as improvements, originating with the class intended to be accommodated. In the rural districts, the worst of the new cottages are those erected on the borders of commons by the labourers themselves. In the manufacturing districts, the tenements erected by building clubs and by speculating builders of the class of the workmen, are frequently the subject of complaint, as being the least substantial and the most destitute of proper accommodation. The only conspicuous instances of improved residences of the labouring classes found in the rural districts are those which have been erected by opulent and benevolent landlords for the accommodation of the labourers on their own estates; and in the manufacturing districts, those erected by wealthy manufacturers for the accommodation of their own workpeople.

224G. Advantages to employers and employed of better housing

loc. cit., pp. 233–236.

Preparatory to the exposition of the means of protection of the public health provided by the existing law, and of the modifications that appear to be requisite for the attainment of the object in question, I would submit for consideration practical examples of its partial attainment by means of improved dwellings; combined with examples of other improvements effected in the moral condition of the labouring classes, by the judicious exercise of the influence possessed by their superiors in condition.

Throughout the country examples are found of a desire, on the part of persons of the higher class, to improve the condition of the poorer classes by the erection of dwellings of a superior order for their accommodation. These, however, are generally at a cost beyond any return to be expected in the present state of the habits of the people in the shape of rent, or any return in money for an outlay on an ordinary investment of capital. But the instances about to be noticed, though generally originating in benevolence, and without the expectation of a return, do, in the results, prove that in money and money's worth, the erection of good tenements affords the inducement of a fair remuneration to the employers of labour to provide improved accommodation for their own labourers.

Wherever it has been brought under observation, the connexion of the labourer's residence with his employment as part of the farm, or of the estate, or of the manufactory on which he is employed, and as part of the inducement to service, appears to be mutually advantageous to the employer and the employed. The first advantages are to the person employed.

We everywhere find (in contradiction to statements frequently made in popular declamations) that the labourer gains by his connexion with large capital: in the instances presented in the course of this inquiry, of residences held from the employer, we find that the labourer gains by the expenditure for the external appearance of that which is known to be part of the property,–an expenditure that is generally accompanied by corresponding internal comforts; he gains by all the surrounding advantages of good roads and drainage, and by more sustained and powerful care to maintain them; he gains by the closer proximity to his work attendant on such an arrangement, and he thus avoids all the attacks of disease, occasioned by exposure to wet and cold, and the additional fatigue in traversing long distances to and from his home to the place of work, in the damp of early morning or of nightfall. The exposure to weather, after leaving the place of work, is one prolific cause of disease, especially to the young. When the home is near to the place of work, the labourer is enabled to take his dinner with his family instead of at the beer-shop.

The wife and family generally gain, by proximity to the employer or the employer's family, in motives to neatness and cleanliness by their being known and being under observation; as a general rule, the whole economy of the cottages in bye-lanes and out-of-the-way places appears to be below those exposed to observation. In connexion with property or large capital, the labourer gains in the stability of employment, and the regularity of income incidental to operations on a large scale; there is a mutual benefit also in the wages for service being given in the shape of buildings or permanent and assured comforts; that is, in what would be the best application of wages, rather than wholly in money wages.

In the manufacturing districts there is a mutual and large gain by the diminution of the labour of the collection of rents, the avoidance of the risks of non-payment, and also in the power of control for the prevention of disturbances, and the removal of tenants of bad character and conduct.

Surprise is frequently expressed at the enormous rents ranging up to and beyond 20 per cent. on the outlay, exacted by the building speculators in the towns. But when the experience of these descriptions of tenements is examined, it is found that the labour of collecting the rents, and the labour of protecting the property itself against waste from unprincipled tenants, is such as to prove that accommodation given to the disorderly and vicious is scarcely remunerative at any price. The tenants are loosely attached, and large numbers migratory, partly from the nature of their work; and having little or no goods or furniture, they have no obstacles to removal; they frequently, before absconding, commit every description of waste; they often burn shelves and cupboard-doors, and the door itself, and all timber that can be got at for the purpose. An objection frequently made against laying on the water in houses inhabited by a population addicted to drinking is, that they would sell the receptacles and destroy the pipe, and let the water run to waste, for the sake of the lead. The expense and delay of legal remedies precludes redress for such injuries.

In some of the worst neighbourhoods in Manchester, the whole population of a street have risen to resist the service of legal process by the civil officers. In the course of the Constabulary Inquiry I was informed by the superintendent of the old police of that town, that one of the most dangerous services for a small force was attending to enforce ejectments. This they had often to do, cutlass in hand, and were frequently driven off by showers of bricks from the mobs. The collection of the rents weekly in such neighbourhoods is always a disagreeable service, requiring high payment. This, and the frequent running away of the tenant, and the waste, greatly reduce the apparently enormous rent obtainable from this poorer class of tenants. For all these vices, risks, and defaults of others, the frugal and well-conducted workman who has no choice of habitation, is compelled to pay in the shape of an increased rent; he is most largely taxed in the increased rent, necessary as an insurance for the risks and losses occasioned by the defective state of legal remedies.

All these risks the employer is enabled to diminish or avoid, by selecting his own tenants, and he has the best means of doing so; by reservations of rent on the payment of wages, he saves the labour and risks of collection; nor will the vicious workman so readily commit waste in the house belonging to his employer as in one belonging to a poorer and unconnected owner. The employer has, moreover, the most direct interest in the health and strength of his workpeople.

It is not supposed that these are arrangements which can be universal, or readily made the subject of legislation. At the commencement of some manufactures, the additional outlay may not be practicable. But those manufactures have generally had the greatest success where good accommodation for the workpeople was comprehended in the first arrangements. When, however, a manufactory has been once established and brought into systematic operation, when the first uncertainties have been overcome and the employer has time to look about him, there appears to be no position from which so extensive and certain a beneficial influence may be exercised as that of the capitalist who stands in the double relation of landlord and employer. He will find that whilst an unhealthy and vicious population is an expensive as well as a dangerous one, all improvements in the condition of the population have their compensation. In one instance, of a large outlay on improved tenements, and in provision for the moral improvement of the rising generation of workpeople, by an expensive provision for schools, the proprietor acknowledged to me that although he made the improvements from motives of a desire to improve the condition of his workpeople, or what might be termed the satisfaction derived from the improvements as a "hobby," he was surprised by a pecuniary gain found in the superior order and efficiency of his establishment, in the regularity and trustworthiness of his workpeople, which gave even pecuniary compensation for the outlay of capital and labour bestowed upon them. He stated that he would not, for £7000, change the entire set of workpeople on whom care had been bestowed for the promiscuous assemblage of workpeople engaged in the same description of manufactures. . . .

224H. Difficulties of a Building Act

loc. cit., pp. 282–288.

All the information as to the actual condition of the most crowded districts is corroborative of the apprehensions entertained by witnesses of practical experience, such as Mr. Thomas Cubitt and other builders, who are favourable to measures for the improvement of the condition of the labouring classes, that anything of the nature of a Building Act that is not equally and skilfully administered will aggravate the evils intended to be remedied. To whatever districts regulations are confined, the effect proved to be likely to follow will be, that the builder of tenements which stand most in need of regulation will be driven over the boundary, and will run up his habitations before measures can be taken to include them. The condition of the workman will be aggravated by the increased fatigue and exposure to weather in traversing greater distances to sleep in a badly-built, thin, and damp house. An increase of distance from his place of work will have the more serious effect upon his habits by rendering it impracticable to take his dinner with his family, compelling him either to take it in some shed or at the beer shop. It is also apprehended that anything that may be done to increase unnecessarily or seriously the cost of new buildings, or discourage their erection, will aggravate the horrors of the overcrowding of the older tenements; at the same time, the certain effect of an immediate and unprepared dislodgement of a cellar population, would be to overcrowd the upper portions of the houses where they reside. It would indeed often be practicable to make those cellars as habitable as are the cellars inhabited by servants in the houses of the middle and higher classes of society. The difficulties which beset such regulations do not arise from the want of means to pay any necessary increase of rents for increased accommodation, but in the very habits which afford evidence of the existence of the sufficiency of the means of payment.

For practical legislation on the subject of increased charges on tenements, the labourers must be considered to be in a state of penury, and ready to shift from bad to worse for the avoidance of the slightest charges, and therefore to be approached with the greatest caution. . . .

The most important immediate general measure of the nature of a Building Act, subsidiary to measures for drainage, would be a measure for regulating the increments of towns, and preventing the continued reproduction in new districts of the evils which have depressed the health and the condition of whole generations in the older districts. Regulations of the *sites* of town buildings have comparatively little effect on the cost of construction, and it may in general be said that a Building Act would effect what any enlightened owner of a district would effect for himself, if laying it out with a view to the most permanent advantage; or what the separate owners would effect for themselves if they had the power of co-operation, or if each piece of work were governed by enlarged public and private views. Had Sir Christopher Wren been permitted to carry out his plan for the rebuilding of London after the great fire, there is little doubt that it would have been the most advantageous arrangement for rendering the whole space more productive, as a property to the great mass of the separate interests, by whom the improvement was defeated. The most successful improvements effected in the metropolis by opening new lines of street, and the greater number of the openings projected are approximations at an enormous expense to the plan which he laid down. The larger towns present instances of obstructions of the free current of air even through the principal streets, and of deteriorations which a little foresight and the exercise of an impartial authority would have prevented. In one increasing town, a builder made a successful money speculation by purchasing such plots of ground as would enable him to erect impediments and extort compensation for their removal from the path of improvements in buildings. The improvements affecting whole towns are also frequently frustrated by the active jealousies of the occupants of rival streets. It would appear to be possible to provide an impartial authority to obtain and, on consultation with the parties locally interested, to settle plans for regulating the future growth of towns, by laying down the most advantageous lines for occupation with due protection of the landowners' interest. The most serious omissions in the building of common houses are so frequently oversights as to make it probable, that if it were required that a plan of any proposed building should be deposited with a trustworthy officer, with a specification of the arrangements intended for the attainment of the essential objects, such as cleansing and ventilation, the mere preparation of the document would of itself frequently lead to the detection of grievous defects. An examination of Mr. Loudon's specification of the requisites of cottages will show that a large proportion of the most important of these are independent of the cost of construction. . . .

2241. Need of expert scientific direction in sanitary matters

loc. cit., pp. 322–323.

. . . But however the charge may be diffused, and to whatever extent opposition on the part of the smaller owners may be obviated by care, it cannot safely be overlooked that in the poorest districts where it is most important that the works should be well executed, the superior direction of such expenditure will, in the ordinary course, fall into the hands of the owners of the worst-conditioned tenements, who have the greatest dread of immediate expenses, and who are under the strongest influence of petty jealousies; for in such districts it is precisely the class of persons who cannot agree to profitable measures of private drainage, who are the owners of the worst tenements, who, having leisure during the intervals of their weekly collections, and from other causes, are most frequently found in honorary offices for the direction of local expenditure. One officer, when asked how it was that in a district where fever had been rife nothing had been done under the authority of the law, which authorized its being cleansed? replied, that the Board had made precisely the same objections that were made when the cholera appeared; when it was proposed to cleanse the district, the answer made at the Board was, that "they did not believe it would do any good:" and those of the officers who were landlords of the weekly tenements said, "Why should we disturb and drive away our tenants?" and those who were shop-keepers said, "Why should we frighten away our customers by representing the neighbourhood as unhealthy?" consequently nothing was done.

The legislature, in making demands for such honorary services, has usually proceeded on the theory which views all those who may be called upon to render them, as persons qualified to understand the whole subject intuitively, and having no other interest or views than to perform the services zealously for the common weal; whereas, in the locality they are viewed in a totally different light, not as public officers, but in their private capacities, as owners or tradesmen, competitors for advantages of various kinds. However unjust this impression may frequently be, it is the impression that commonly prevails; and since all of one class cannot have a share in the administration of such funds, others of the same class, whether owners or tradesmen, view the persons exercising the power as rivals, and distrust their administration accordingly. As an owner, one member of a local Board is strongly indisposed to any line of operations that will apparently improve the property of another; and as an owner, too, he is under the strongest jealousy if he proposes or does anything which may appear to benefit his own property at the public expense.

Neither is such distrust as to trustworthiness from skill and adverse private interests confined to the administration of the public works of sewerage and drainage; it is fortified by the example of the local administration of the works of road construction and repair, a branch of administration so inseparably connected with drainage operations, as to justify and require a joint consideration with them.

Witnesses of the most extensive practical experience lay the greatest stress on the necessity of lifting these important branches of administration out of the influence of petty and sinister interests, and of doing so by securing the appointment of officers of superior scientific attainments, who (subject to a proper local as well as general control) may be made responsible for directing any new expenditure on a scale of efficiency as well as of economy. A competent, scientific, and efficient management, let it be applied to what part of these works it may, can scarcely fail to be immediately as well as ultimately the most economical management. But it will be found on examination that the consolidation of all the structural arrangements, comprising under-drainage and surface-drainage, road structure and repair, under one service, is most required for the sake of efficiency. Division of labour in the arts derives its efficiency from combination, adaptation, and subordination to direction to one end; but that which appears to be a division of labour in local administration is, in fact, an insubordinate separation, weakening the means of procuring adequate skill and power, occasioning obstructions and defective execution, and enhancing expense. Were pins or machines made as sewers and roads are constructed; shafts of pins would be made without reference to heads,–in machinery screws would be made without sockets, and, it may be confidently stated, there would not be a safe or perfect and well-working machine in the whole country....

224J. Recapitulation and conclusions

loc. cit., pp. 369–372.

After as careful an examination of the evidence collected as I have been enabled to make, I beg leave to recapitulate the chief conclusions which that evidence appears to me to establish.

First, as to the extent and operation of the evils which are the subject of the inquiry:–

That the various forms of epidemic, endemic, and other disease caused, or aggravated, or propagated chiefly amongst the labouring classes by atmospheric impurities produced by decomposing animal and vegetable substances, by damp and filth, and close and overcrowded dwellings prevail amongst the population in every part of the kingdom, whether dwelling in separate houses, in rural villages, in small towns, in the larger towns–as they have been found to prevail in the lowest districts of the metropolis.

That such disease, wherever its attacks are frequent, is always found in connexion with the physical circumstances above specified, and that where those circumstances are removed by drainage, proper cleansing, better ventilation, and other means of diminishing atmospheric impurity, the frequency and intensity of such disease is abated; and where the removal of the noxious agencies appears to be complete, such disease almost entirely disappears.

That high prosperity in respect to employment and wages, and various and abundant food, have afforded to the labouring classes no exemptions from attacks of epidemic disease, which have been as frequent and as fatal in periods of commercial and manufacturing prosperity as in any others.

That the formation of all habits of cleanliness is obstructed by defective supplies of water.

That the annual loss of life from filth and bad ventilation are greater than the loss from death or wounds in any wars in which the country has been engaged in modern times.

That of the 43,000 cases of widowhood, and 112,000 cases of destitute orphanage relieved from the poor's rates in England and Wales alone, it appears that the greatest proportion of deaths of the heads of families occurred from the above specified and other removable causes; that their ages were under 45 years; that is to say, 13 years below the natural probabilities of life as shown by the experience of the whole population of Sweden.

That the public loss from the premature deaths of the heads of families is greater than can be represented by any enumeration of the pecuniary burdens consequent upon their sickness and death.

That, measuring the loss of working ability amongst large classes by the instances of gain, even from incomplete arrangements for the removal of noxious influences from places of work or from abodes, that this loss cannot be less than eight or ten years.

That the ravages of epidemics and other diseases do not diminish but tend to increase the pressure of population.

That in the districts where the mortality is the greatest the births are not only sufficient to replace the numbers removed by death, but to add to the population.

That the younger population, bred up under noxious physical agencies, is inferior in physical organization and general health to a population preserved from the presence of such agencies.

That the population so exposed is less susceptible of moral influences, and the effects of education are more transient than with a healthy population.

That these adverse circumstances tend to produce an adult population short-lived, improvident, reckless, and intemperate, and with habitual avidity for sensual gratifications.

That these habits lead to the abandonment of all the conveniences and decencies of life, and especially lead to the overcrowding of their homes, which is destructive to the morality as well as the health of large classes of both sexes.

That defective town cleansing fosters habits of the most abject degradation and tends to the demoralization of large numbers of human beings, who subsist by means of what they find amidst the noxious filth accumulated in neglected streets and bye-places.

That the expenses of local public works are in general unequally and unfairly assessed, oppressively and uneconomically collected, by separate collections, wastefully expended in separate and inefficient operations by unskilled and practically irresponsible officers.

That the existing law for the protection of the public health and the constitutional machinery for reclaiming its execution, such as the Courts Leet, have fallen into desuetude, and are in the state indicated by the prevalence of the evils they were intended to prevent.

Secondly. As to the means by which the present sanitary condition of the labouring classes may be improved:–

The primary and most important measures, and at the same time the most practicable, and within the recognized province of public administration, are drainage, the removal of all refuse of habitations, streets, and roads, and the improvement of the supplies of water.

That the chief obstacles to the immediate removal of decomposing refuse of towns and habitations have been the expense and annoyance of the hand labour and cartage requisite for the purpose.

That this expense may be reduced to one-twentieth or to one-thirtieth, or rendered inconsiderable, by the use of water and self-acting means of removal by improved and cheaper sewers and drains.

That refuse when thus held in suspension in water may be most cheaply and innoxiously conveyed to any distance out of towns, and also in the best form for productive use, and that the loss and injury by the pollution of natural streams may be avoided.

That for all these purposes, as well as for domestic use, better supplies of water are absolutely necessary.

That for successful and economical drainage the adoption of geological areas as the basis of operations is requisite.

That appropriate scientific arrangements for public drainage would afford important facilities for private land-drainage, which is important for the health as well as sustenance of the labouring classes.

That the expense of public drainage, of supplies of water laid on in houses, and of means of improved cleansing would be a pecuniary gain, by diminishing the existing charges attendant on sickness and premature mortality.

That for the protection of the labouring classes and of the ratepayers against inefficiency and waste in all new structural arrangements for the protection of the public health, and to ensure public confidence that the expenditure will be beneficial, securities should be taken that all new local public works are devised and conducted by responsible officers qualified by the possession of the science and skill of civil engineers.

That the oppressiveness and injustice of levies for the whole immediate outlay on such works upon persons who have only short interests in the benefits may be avoided by care in spreading the expense over periods coincident with the benefits.

That by appropriate arrangements, 10 or 15 per cent. on the ordinary outlay for drainage might be saved, which on an estimate of the expense of the necessary structural alterations of one-third only of the existing tenements would be a saving of one million and a half sterling, besides the reduction of the future expenses of management.

That for the prevention of the disease occasioned by defective ventilation, and other causes of impurity in places of work and other places where large numbers are assembled, and for the general promotion of the means necessary to prevent disease, that it would be good economy to appoint a district medical officer independent of private practice, and with the securities of special qualifications and responsibilities to initiate sanitary measures and reclaim the execution of the law.

That by the combinations of all these arrangements, it is probable that the full ensurable period of life indicated by the Swedish tables; that is, an increase of 13 years at least, may be extended to the whole of the labouring classes.

That the attainment of these and the other collateral advantages of reducing existing charges and expenditure are within the power of the legislature, and are dependent mainly on the securities taken for the application of practical science, skill and economy in the direction of local public works.

And that the removal of noxious physical circumstances, and the promotion of civic, household, and personal cleanliness, are necessary to the improvement of the moral condition of the population; for that sound morality and refinement in manners and health are not long found co-existent with filthy habits amongst any class of the community.

225A–C. General Board of Health and 1848 cholera: report of the Board of Health, July, 1849

Parlty. Papers, 1849/XXIV.

225A. Regulations issued by the Board of Health

loc. cit., pp. 83–87.

To the Guardians of the Poor of the several Unions and Parishes named in the Schedules hereunto annexed;

To the Councils and other Governing Bodies of Cities and Boroughs, Commissioners under Local Acts, the Surveyors of Highways, their Deputies and Assistants, The Trustees, County Surveyors and others, by Law intrusted with the Care and Management of the Streets and Public Ways and Places within the said Unions and Parishes;

To the Owners and Occupiers of Houses, Dwellings, Churches, Buildings, and Places of Assembly within the said Unions and Parishes, and others having the Care and Ordering thereof;

And to all to whom it may concern.

Whereas by the provisions of the "Nuisances Removal and Diseases Prevention Act, 1848," for the prevention of epidemic, endemic, and contagious diseases, and by virtue of an order of the Lords of Her Majesty's Most Honourable Privy Council, bearing date the 28th day of September, 1848, directing that the said provisions of the said Act be put in force throughout the whole of Great Britain, We, the General Board of Health, are authorized to issue such directions and regulations as the said Board shall think fit for the prevention (as far as possible) or mitigation of epidemic, endemic, or contagious diseases; and whereas by the said Act it is provided that the directions and regulations to be issued as aforesaid shall extend to all parts or places in which the said provisions of the said Act shall for the time being be in force, under the order of Her Majesty's Privy Council, unless such directions or regulations shall be expressly confined to some of such parts or places, and then to such parts or places as in such directions and regulations shall be specified.

Now in exercise of the authority vested in us as aforesaid, we, the General Board of Health, do issue the directions and regulations hereinafter contained, to extend to all parts and places within the several unions and parishes named in the schedules hereunto annexed, and to all extra-parochial places adjoining to such unions and parishes, *viz.*:–

I. We direct that all councils and other governing bodies of cities and boroughs, commissioners under local acts, surveyors, and district or assistant surveyors of highways, trustees, county surveyors, and others, by law intrusted with the care and management of the streets, and public ways and places within the parts or places to which these directions and regulations extend, shall once at least in every twenty-four hours effectually cleanse all such of the streets, rows, lanes, mews, courts, alleys, and passages, and public ways and places, under their respective care and management, as by the medical officer of the guardians, or others authorized to superintend the execution of this direction and regulation, shall be certified in writing to be in a state dangerous to health, or to require frequent and effectual cleansing by way of precaution against disease, and shall remove all filth, ordure, and nuisance therefrom.

II. And where any such streets, rows, lanes, mews, courts, alleys, and any passages, public ways, or places, to which any houses or tenements adjoin, which have not been intrusted by law to the care or management of any council, commissioners, surveyors, trustees, or others, have been certified in writing, by such medical officers as aforesaid, to be in a state dangerous to health, or to require such frequent and effectual cleansing, we direct that every occupier of a house or tenement so adjoining shall keep or cause to be kept sufficiently cleansed, at least once in every twenty-four hours, such part of the street, row, lane, mews, court, alley, or passage, way, or place as adjoins the house or tenement occupied by him.

And we direct that all such works of cleansing and removal of filth, ordure, and nuisances as are required by these directions and regulations shall be done in such manner by effectual washing or otherwise, and with the use of such fluids or substances for preventing the escape of noxious effluvia during the operation as the medical officer of the guardians or others authorized to superintend the execution of these directions and regulations shall think necessary and shall direct.

III. We do hereby authorize and require the guardians of the said unions and parishes, by themselves or by their officers or persons employed under them in the administration of the laws for the relief of the poor, or by officers or persons specially appointed in this behalf, to superintend and see to the execution of the foregoing directions and regulations within their respective unions and parishes, and in any extra-parochial places adjoining thereto respectively.

IV. And, further, where it shall appear that by want or neglect of the council of any city, or borough, commissioners, surveyors, trustees, or others intrusted with the care and management as aforesaid, or by reason of poverty of the occupiers or otherwise, there may be any default or delay in the cleansing of or removing nuisances from any street, row, lane, mews, court, alley, passage, or public way, or place certified as aforesaid, within any of the said unions and parishes, or any extra-parochial place adjoining thereto, we authorize and require the guardians of such union or parish to cause such street, row, lane, mews, court, alley, passage, way, or place to be effectually cleansed, and all nuisances to be removed therefrom, and to do all acts, matters, and things necessary for that purpose.

V. We also direct as follows:-

That,

When and so often as any dwelling-house in any part or place to which these directions and regulations extend is in such a filthy and unwholesome condition as to be a nuisance to, or injurious to the health of any person; or

Where upon any premises, or any part or place as aforesaid, there is any foul and offensive drain, ditch, gutter, privy, cesspool or ashpit, or any drain, ditch, gutter, privy, cesspool or ashpit, kept or constructed so as to be a nuisance to or injurious to the health of any person; or

Where upon any such premises swine or any accumulation of dung, manure, offal, filth, refuse, or other matter or thing is kept so as to be a nuisance to or injurious to the health of any person; or

Where upon any such premises (being a building used wholly or in part as a dwelling-house), or being premises underneath any such building, any animal is kept so as to be a nuisance or injurious to the health of any person;

In each of the above-recited cases the owner or occupier, and persons having the care or ordering of such dwelling-house, or of the premises where the nuisance or matter injurious to health may be, shall cleanse, whitewash, or otherwise purify, as the case may require, such dwelling-house or building; or abate or remove the nuisance or matter injurious to health as aforesaid; with all reasonable speed after the publication of these our directions and regulations, or after the nuisance or matter injurious to health shall have arisen.

VI. In case, by reason of poverty or otherwise, the occupier of any such dwelling-house or premises is unable to perform any works required by these directions or regulations, such occupier shall give notice of such his inability to the guardians of the union or parish comprising the place wherein the premises shall be situated.

VII. We authorize and require the guardians aforesaid, by themselves or by officers by them authorized in this behalf,

To see to the execution of the directions hereinbefore contained for the cleansing and purifying of dwelling-houses, and for the abatement and removal of nuisances and matters injurious to health, in every case in which there shall not be a council or other governing body of a city or borough, or commissioners having jurisdiction for the removal of nuisances, or where such council, governing body, or commissioners shall not cause to be effectually executed such directions.

VIII. And in every case in which, from the poverty of occupiers or otherwise, there may be default or delay in the cleansing or purifying of any such dwelling-house, or in the abatement or removal of any such nuisance or matter injurious to health, and the medical officer, or other person duly authorized as aforesaid, shall certify that the same requires immediate attention,

We authorize and require such guardians to cause such dwelling-houses to be cleansed and purified, and such drain, ditch, watercourse, or gutter, to be frequently and effectually cleansed, and such nuisance or matter injurious to health to be abated and removed respectively, and to do all acts and provide all matters and things necessary for that purpose.

IX. And we do further authorize and require the guardians to direct their clerk to make out from the register of deaths, or from the district medical relief books, and from any public books or other sources from which information may be obtained within the union or parish, a list of places where epidemic, endemic, and contagious diseases have of late been frequent.

X. And we authorize and require such guardians to cause the medical officers employed by them, or specially appointed for the purpose, to visit the places of which a list shall be made out as aforesaid, and all such neighbouring and other places within such union, as shall appear to such medical officers (from being under like circumstances with the places included in such list or otherwise) to require visitation or examination.

XI. And each such medical officer shall, where it may be necessary, certify in writing to the board of guardians, and to the surveyors, trustees, occupiers, or others required to execute these directions and regulations, all such places as are in a state dangerous to health, or need frequent and effectual cleansing by way of preservation against disease, and such dwelling-houses as are in a filthy and unwholesome condition, and all such nuisances and matters injurious to health as ought to be abated, cleansed, and removed under these regulations.

XII. And each such medical officer shall forthwith, upon any case of Cholera, or of typhus, or other epidemic, endemic, and contagious diseases becoming known to him within the parish, union, or district under his visitation, report the same to the board of guardians.

XIII. And we do hereby authorize and direct the said guardians, where it may appear needful, to appoint such additional medical officers, and also to appoint such other officers as may be necessary to execute and superintend the execution of these regulations, and to publish and circulate, by printed hand bills or other means, notices of the provisions of the said Act for the prevention of nuisances, and of our regulations and instructions, or of such part of any of them as it may appear desirable to make publicly known.

XIV. And we hereby direct that in these directions and regulations, the words "guardians of the poor" shall mean the guardians, directors, wardens, governors, or other like officers having the management of the poor for any union, parish, or place, where the matter requiring the cognizance of any such officers arises; and the word "parish" shall include every place where the relief of the poor is administered by a board of guardians for such place.

225B. Board's account of resistance to its orders

loc. cit., pp. 22–36.

When we first proceeded to put in force the powers of the Nuisances Removal and Diseases Prevention Act, we found the parochial bodies, the authorities charged with the local execution of the law, generally unprepared for the exercise of their duties, in some cases entirely ignorant of them, and in others from the dread of expense, very reluctant to perform them.

In the first place in which we were called upon directly to interfere, at Dumfries, the parochial Board allowed a period of 20 days to elapse with a steadily progressive and alarming increase of the disease, without adopting a single efficient measure of precaution. On the first outbreak of the epidemic, indeed, a system of medical relief, apparently well adapted for meeting it, was agreed to; but this was broken up on the following day, by order of the parochial Board, on the alleged ground of expense. Though the attention of the local authorities had been specially called to our regulations, they had, up to this period, taken no steps with reference to operations of cleansing, to providing a house of refuge, or to organizing a proper system of medical relief. "I arrived in Dumfries," reported Dr. Sutherland, "on the 6th December; "up to that time, I believe, that no fewer than 147 persons had already been buried, "after having been struck down by the epidemic, and that without an effort to save "them although the power had been placed in the hands of the parochial Board for "the express purpose of being exercised. Precious time was wasted in mere petty "squabbles; the town has been clothed in mourning in consequence. Not a moment "was lost by me. I collected a staff as quickly as possible, arranged the districts, and "put everything in motion; but this process required further time, equally precious "with that which had been irretrievably lost; and it appears from our returns, that "it was not till the 13th of December that any material effect was produced, and by "that day 250 people had been consigned to the grave."

The local powers for the execution of the law were found to be extremely defective; the authorities for executing them, commonly not less so; with divided responsibility frequently conflicting, and wanting in the unity requisite to carry out prompt remedial measures, even when tolerable information existed with reference to them.

The separation of local administrative bodies in respect to the execution and control of works; the separation of the works for the water supply from the works for sewerage; the separation of the works for sewerage from those for house drainage, and of the whole from those for surface cleansing; the separation of the surface cleansing from the cleansing of sewers and drains, and even, as is sometimes the case, the separation of the cleansing of the main streets from that of courts and alleys; the separation of these and other services, for the consolidation and combination of which the Legislature has provided in the Public Health Act, have seriously impeded the execution of the Diseases Prevention Act.

The Legislature contemplates the Poor-Law Union in England and Wales with its medical officers, its Union house with its new fever wards, and its provision for medical relief, as the chief local administrative body by which preventive measures could be best carried out; and, in general, it is the most eligible for the purpose. But, in towns, there are also Commissioners of Pavements under Local Acts, who are charged with the duty of surface-cleansing as well as paving, who act independently, and who were frequently found to be unwilling to receive directions from the Boards of Guardians or the medical officers appointed by them. The Municipal Town Councils, have in some instances, the control over the road-ways, and they have also under their direction a body of police, whose services are of great importance, in the execution of orders, especially where it is requisite immediately to carry out combined regulations. Even where there is a fair and liberal desire to co-operate, on the part of these separate authorities, there has been a serious loss of time in the service of notices, and in framing expositions of the grounds of requests from one to the other. Added to these impediments, the separation affords the means of shifting responsibility from the one to the other.

Adopting a large remedial interpretation of the terms of the Act, "for taking measures of precaution with promptitude according to the exigency of the case," we had contemplated the issuing of regulations for carrying these provisions into effect, as we believe the Legislature would have done, had there been laid before it the special circumstances of the case, by forming Special Boards of Health, composed of members of the Town Councils, of the Boards of Guardians, and of the Paving Boards, who might give united directions to their officers. The law officers, however, were of opinion, that the general terms of the statute could not be so construed as to authorise a combination of the local authorities, with a view to bring their united powers to bear in the manner we proposed. The regulations were therefore carried out, chiefly by the separate powers of the Boards of Guardians, with the voluntary co-operation of the municipal or other authorities; but, at the best, with the inconveniences of delay from the separate action. Had it been possible to combine the various authorities, as at first contemplated, a far greater unity and efficiency would have been ensured both in England and Scotland.

In the metropolis, the multiplicity of the Paving Boards, some parochial and others not, charged with the duty of surface cleansing, and the removal of refuse, has also been productive of considerable inconvenience, since it has prevented answers being given or directions issued, until these Acts could be sought out and the powers and duties provided under them ascertained.

The following reply from the General Board of Health to an inquiry from the Rev. W. Dodsworth, the incumbent of Christ Church, Regent's-park, as to "what he should do in order to effect the cleansing and draining of his parish," in other words, what was the local law under which the parishioners were living, is illustrative of a very common obstacle to prompt, efficient, and economical local administration.

> "The General Board take the opportunity to state, that they have received applications similar to your own from householders, inquiring what steps they may take to obtain the removal of refuse, or to enforce proper cleansing, and what is the actual law and the state of its administration for sanitary purposes within their respective parishes, and what they, as householders, may do for its enforcement or aid. The General Board have been prevented giving early replies, as well as eventually satisfactory ones, by the excessive variety of the provisions of the numerous local Acts by which the objects have been sought to be attained.
>
> "The work of surface cleansing is, in many cases, performed by bodies of various descriptions, under the authority of local Acts. The jurisdiction of the authorities constituted under these Acts are as various as their powers. It is one of the Topics of the local inquiries, directed by the Legislature to be instituted under the Public Health Act, to ascertain upon the spot what the local Acts are, what are the bodies constituted under them, and how the powers so conferred are executed. Unless the General Board itself is informed upon these points, it is unable either to apply its own orders with the particularity which is requisite, or to give such information as that which is now sought.
>
> "The number, condition, and action of the bodies constituted by the local Acts is one object of investigation by the Metropolitan Sanitary Commissioners, and they have been hitherto unable to complete that inquiry.

"There appear to be upwards of 120 local Acts for the more dense portions of the Metropolis, for the management of upwards of 80 distinct local jurisdictions, many of which coincide neither with parish, nor Union, nor police district, nor any other recognized division. When a householder, who gives his address in a particular street, applies to know how he may proceed–if the local Act be sought out, and the provision in relation to the matter in question be also sought out–he cannot always be safely answered, inasmuch as streets are frequently divided, sometimes longitudinally, and paved and cleansed at different times, under different jurisdictions. At present no public maps are known to exist by which the area of the jurisdiction could in any such cases be ascertained correctly.

"In the parish of St. Pancras, where you reside, there are no less than 16 separate Paving Boards, acting under 29 Acts of Parliament, which would require to be consulted before an opinion could be safely pronounced as to what it might be practicable to do for the effectual cleansing of the parish as a whole.

"The General Board of Health can only state in answer to such applications, that the information sought can be obtained by no other means than local inquiry; and they hope that this will be done on behalf of householders, by the Parochial Board acting under the general directions of the Board of Health now issued."

The following extract from a letter by Mr. Payne, the coroner of the City of London, displays the general consequences of these defects; and the inconveniences and evils here represented will, we hope, be diminished by the consolidations provided for by the Public Health Act–

"The first child was attacked 10 days ago, and died last Sunday; the second was attacked on Tuesday morning last, and died in the afternoon; and the third since then; and two more were very ill from the same cause.

"The father of two of the children had not complained to anybody except his landlord, because *he said he did not know the state of the law*. The medical officer reported it to the clerk of the Board of Guardians on Saturday last; and Mr. Simon, the Officer of Health, said that no report had been made to the Guardians till Thursday morning last, which he thought a great neglect in the clerk to the Board.

"I found that the police constable, whose attention was drawn to the nuisance on Tuesday, reported it to his sergeant, the sergeant to the inspector, the inspector to the Commissioner of Police, and the latter to the Commissioners of Sewers.

"All this roundabout mode of doing business I deprecated as injudicious, and suggested that it would be desirable if the inmates of the courts and alleys were informed that they might complain *directly* to the Inspector of Nuisances for the district, whose duty it would be in such case to see to it immediately.

"There is every reason to believe that some of these lives would have been saved if the matter had been properly made known in the first instance."

Theoretically, it is supposed, that all the inhabitants are best acquainted with the state of their local law, and take an interest and part in its administration. Practically, their knowledge of it, in busy towns, is generally found to be such as that displayed in the above extracts; and resistance to local consolidation and simplification arises from the active canvassings of office-bearers, and persons pecuniarily interested in the administration, rather than from any spontaneous desire on the part of the great body of the population. The advantages, for the sake of efficiency and despatch, of uniform local procedure and administrative arrangements, have been pointed out before, but they are strongly re-enforced by the disastrous delays recently experienced.

The law gives to this Board no power to originate prosecutions for neglect or violation of its orders and regulations, and therefore we have no direct control over Guardians, whatever course they may adopt with reference to the orders of the Board, in consequence of which those orders have been, to a considerable extent, deprived of the authority which it was the intention of the Legislature to give to them, and which they must possess to accomplish that object fully.

The Guardians indeed incur a serious responsibility if any fatal consequence should be proved, by the verdict of a coroner's inquest, to result from their unlawful omission of the orders of the General Board of Health; but however important and necessary the investigation may sometimes be, to be able to fix responsibility only by the indirect and uncertain result of a coroner's inquest, appears to be a fundamental defect.

Examplifications of the impunity with which some Boards of Guardians consider they may disregard orders made under the authority of the Legislature, with the view of carrying out its provisions, have been afforded by the course adopted by the Guardians of the Whitechapel Union, by some of the Boards of Guardians connected with the Tooting children, and, more recently, by the select vestry of the borough of Liverpool.

At a time when deaths had already occurred from cholera, under extremely painful circumstances, and when there was reason to apprehend a serious outbreak of the disease, the Guardians of the Whitechapel Union entered on their Minutes the following resolution:-

> "That it is the opinion of the Guardians that, at present, the order of the Board of Health, of the 18th of November last, need not be acted on in this Union."

It appears that this deliberate act of disregard to the orders of the Board of Health was resolved upon on the same evening when the medical officers of the Union presented to the Guardians a written statement to the effect that malignant cholera had broken out in some parts of the district.

Here is an instance of a Board, composed for the most part of persons engaged in the daily routine of trade, not having in general, it must be presumed, the means of judging from any large observation or experience of the matter on which they decide, deliberately acting on a medical question against the opinion of their own medical officers, and in direct opposition to regulations framed on the largest experience, not only of this country, but of the whole of Europe–regulations so framed for the purpose of carrying out the express provisions of the Legislature.

It further appears, that on the 21st of November the Clerk of this Union having in conformity with the order of the Board of Health, laid before the Guardians returns from the four medical officers, and from some of the registrars of births and deaths, of those places in the Union where epidemic, endemic, and contagious diseases have of late been prevalent, the Guardians came to the following resolution:–

> "That the Clerk forward such particulars to the various Local Boards in the Union, but that the medical officers be *not* called upon to visit the places in question."

It must be borne in mind that this resolution was adopted by the Guardians at a time when cholera was not only actually prevailing in the district, but was spreading there under circumstances of so painful a nature, as to attract the attention of one of the coroners of Middlesex, Mr. Baker, who, on the 24th of November, addressed a letter of expostulation to them on the neglect of the measures which the circumstances of the time obviously required.

On the 14th of December the coroner again addressed a letter to the Clerk of the Union, in which he says:–

> "My attention as coroner has this day been called to several cases of sudden death in the parish of St. Mary, Whitechapel, of a most awful and appalling character, and I cannot but feel that a very heavy responsibility rests not only upon my shoulders, but upon those also of the Board of Guardians of the Whitechapel Union, in reference to these and all such cases, it appearing that there have been no less than 16 under the care of the medical officer lately.
>
> "I have this day been engaged in an inquiry into some of the deaths, more particularly alluded to in that letter, in Hairbrain-court, Rosemary-lane, and have myself viewed this evening the dead bodies of no fewer than three persons, but have been witness also to the most agonizing and appalling situation of others in a dying state in the same locality (within a few yards of the former), who were found by me to be in a state of distress and misery, which could not but be most afflicting to my mind, being surrounded by the most foetid and unwholesome vapours from privies and bad drainage, and filthiness, and much overcrowded; and allow me to say, in such a state as I could scarcely have deemed it possible to have existed, after the publication of the documents to which I have above alluded."...

... Yet more recently the Guardians of the parish of Liverpool appear to have pursued the following course. The affairs connected with the relief of the poor in the parish of Liverpool, are under the control of a Select Vestry, who here exercise the duties ordinarily performed by Guardians. The Select Vestry has nominated out of its own members, a "Medical Relief Committee," to which the direction of what concerns the medical relief is committed; and in order to facilitate the carrying into operation the Act for the Removal of Nuisances and Prevention of Contagious

Diseases, a "Joint Committee" has been constituted, consisting of a certain number of members selected from the Health Committee of the Town Council, from the Medical Relief Committee of the Select Vestry, and from the West Derby Board of Guardians; the object of this Joint Committee being to consider the measures necessary to promote the health of the town, and to communicate the results to the other bodies.

Liverpool has the further advantage of having an Officer of Health who so long since as August 9, 1848, in anticipation of the probable re-appearance of cholera in England, reported to the Health Committee of the Town Council, that in the event of the return of cholera, besides greater activity in the general measures of cleansing, scavenging, supply of water, &c., it would be necessary to make an addition to the parochial medical staff, and to that of the dispensaries, in order that immediate assistance might be given in the early stage of the disease, and to provide hospitals in different quarters of the town for the accommodation of the destitute, whom it might be inexpedient to treat at their own dwellings. A copy of this Report was sent to the Select Vestry.

The Joint Committee was appointed in the month of October, 1848. One of its earliest steps was to ascertain what measures were proposed by the Select Vestry, to afford medical attendance and medicines in the event of the re-appearance of cholera in Liverpool. In reply to inquiries made on this subject, the Chairman reported at a meeting held on December 12, 1848, that the Select Vestry had made preparations for appointing additional medical officers over and above the permanent staff of 13 employed by the Select Vestry; for providing dispensaries in every district of the parish, with hospitals attached to the same; and for opening of houses of refuge. The impression produced by this statement on the mind of the Officer of Health was, that all the measures requisite to meet an outbreak of cholera were in such a state of forwardness that they could be completed in a few days whenever the necessity arose; and he says that this being his conviction, he took no farther steps at that time.

On the 9th February, 1849, the Select Vestry did open a cholera hospital, and appointed two medical officers to take charge of it; but they chose it in a situation so remote and inconvenient, that the Medical Officer of Health thought it necessary on the 29th of March, to make to the Health Committee the following statement:-

> "The Medical Officer of Health begs to represent, that in the event of cholera becoming epidemic in Liverpool, the present cholera hospital in Queen Anne Street, will be found to be placed at an inconvenient distance from the localities where the disease is likely chiefly to prevail.
>
> "On the Sunday last, a woman who was removed from Henry Edward Street, in the state of collapse was found to be dead on her arrival at the hospital."

A copy of this Report was forwarded to the Medical Relief Committee.

On the 5th April, cholera still advancing, and no change having been made in the situation of the hospital, nor any steps, as far as could be ascertained, having been taken to provide a house of refuge, the Joint Committee again requested the Select

Vestry to inform them what provision had been made for treating cholera cases among the poor.

On the 30th of April, cholera still advancing, and nothing having as yet been done, the Medical Officer of Health again addressed a letter to the Chairman of the Medical Relief Committee, stating his belief that lives had been lost in consequence of the non-removal of the hospital, and that the opening of a house of refuge was urgently required. To this representation the Officer of Health received a reply from the Chairman, stating, that his letter was read to the Committee and entered on their Minutes, but that it did not appear to change their plans materially. "For myself," he adds, "I may say that I would gladly have been guided by your advice."

By this time the increase of cholera being very alarming, and finding that none of the measures recommended by him were adopted, the Medical Officer of Health next, that is, on the 30th of May, addressed the Joint Committee, calling their attention to the fact of the rapid increase of cholera, and stating that the great majority of the cases still continued to occur in a district remote from the hospital; that immediate steps should be taken to provide hospital accommodation in the locality where the disease prevails; that instances having occurred, in which several persons had been attacked in succession in the same house, a house of refuge ought to be opened without delay, in order that where deemed advisable, the healthy inmates of houses in which cholera appears may be removed for a few days, until the infected dwellings have been thoroughly cleansed and purified; and that as attacks of cholera generally take place in the night, stations should be appointed in the affected districts, where a medical practitioner being in attendance during the night might be ready to give immediate aid when called upon by the poorer inhabitants.

On the following day (June the 1st) the Joint Committee, in consequence of this communication, passed resolutions, recommending the Select Vestry to adopt forthwith the several measures here recommended.

But instead of adopting these measures the Select Vestry merely called upon the regular medical officers of the parish, to give their attention to their patients by night as well as by day; and appointed two additional medical officers for one week, to make a house-to-house visitation in two streets.

The Joint Committee not satisfied with these proceedings of the Medical Relief Committee, on the 7th of June again called the attention of the Select Vestry to their recommendations and requested to be informed what arrangements had been made for carrying them out.

During these discussions and delays, cholera had increased from 16 in the week ending the 19th of May, to 27 on the following week; 67 on the next week; 145 on the week following, and 187 on the week ending the 16th of June.

Though we were not at that time cognizant of the proceedings of the Select Vestry above described, yet, observing the progressive increase of cholera in this populous city, not perceiving any preparations for carrying the regulations under the Act into effect, and being constantly told in the Reports forwarded to us, that with cholera daily extending, there was no appearance of premonitory diarrhoea, an event which, if true, would have been an exception to the experience of every other place, both in this country and in Europe; we directed one of our Medical Inspectors (Mr. Grainger) to obtain authentic information on all the circumstances connected with this dangerous outbreak.

From Mr. Grainger's report, it appears, that no lists such as are required by the regulations of the General Board of Health had been made out; that no adequate medical relief had been provided; that no systematic plan for detecting and treating premonitory diarrhoea had been adopted; that no stations or depots had been opened, for affording assistance to the poorer classes in the night, and that no houses of refuge, and no sufficient hospital accommodation had been afforded.

Up to this time the Select Vestry, as well as all the authorities of Liverpool, were ignorant of the existence in any part of the town of any unusual prevalence of bowel complaint, and positively denied the fact, though, for a fortnight previously, at least, these disorders had increased to such an extent in the affected districts, that the inhabitants were in a state of alarm, and one of the witnesses examined said, that for the eight or ten days previously he had had many applications for medicine for bowel complaints, amounting to as many as 20 in a day; while another stated, that in consequence of the great increase of these attacks he had been detained for some nights preceding till half-past 11 or 12 o'clock at night, though his usual custom was to leave his shop for his residence at half-past nine.

From this and other evidence which we received, we issued on the 18th of June a Special Order requiring the Select Vestry to adopt the several measures which our Inspector represented to be necessary, and in the necessity of which the Officer of Health for Liverpool co-incided; the first of which regulations was, that the Board of Guardians forthwith appoint 12 extra medical officers, who should make house-to-house visitations once each day at the least, &c. On the reception of this Order, the Select Vestry thought proper to decide that no extra medical officers should be appointed, as required by our Order, and separated without making any preparation for carrying into effect the other regulations contained in the Order.

The body which thus deliberately violated the law, had neglected the discharge of their duties for at least a period of two months, in spite of repeated warnings by the Officer of Health of their own borough, and the earnest remonstrances of a Committee consisting partly of their own members, and that at a time when between 30 and 40 fresh attacks of cholera were occurring in their city daily; a neglect of duty which is described as inflicting much suffering and sacrifice of life.

We submit that the protection of the poor and helpless from preventible sickness, suffering, and premature disablement, and death, is a duty of the highest importance, and that negligence or omission in relation to it is a grave offence. The examples we have now received show that if measures for the prevention of these evils are placed on the footing of mere recommendations no attention will be paid to them. Such evils can be abated only by the exercise of powers adequate to enforce the measures which are required for their suppression. When it is intended that the operations of a law shall be efficient, the power of prosecuting for disobedience, as well as of laying down executive regulations are placed not in separate but the same hands; and the experience of the working of this Act shows that its provisions cannot be carried out, and consequently that the intentions of the Legislature cannot be realized, unless a power be given to the General Board of Health, similar to that given to other Boards, such as the Lunacy Commission, to originate prosecutions for the neglect or violation of its regulations.

The powers conferred for the prevention of epidemic diseases must, to accomplish their object, necessarily be summary; but if the orders made by one department can be enforced only by application to another department, delay must be incurred where promptitude is essential. On these grounds, and under the conviction that the object of the Legislature cannot be otherwise attained, we submit that this Board should be entrusted with the power of prosecuting for the neglect of its regulations.

225C. Comparison of cholera in this and other countries

loc. cit., pp. 44–45.

Whilst we represent, as it is our duty to represent, the negligences and omissions which have occasioned sickness and loss of life; yet it is right to present the evidence of the fact, which we believe to be conclusive, that the measures of precaution which have been adopted, that the cleansings which have taken place, and which have been carried to a greater extent than they ever were before, have been attended with proportionate benefits. We state these facts amidst a serious increase of the epidemic. We cannot venture to say what may be the extent of its further visitation; but as far as it has proceeded it has been light as compared with its course in other countries. In St. Petersburg, where little sanitary improvement has been effected, there have been officially reported, during the recent outbreak, nearly 25,000 attacks and 14,000 deaths; but it is believed that there have really been upwards of 20,000 deaths. In Paris, where, as far as we have been able to learn, little warning has been taken of the steady approach of the pestilence, and little preparation made against its invasion, the visitation has been more severe than it was formerly. We have received from the President of the Department of the Public Health of Paris returns, from which it appears that in 1832 the deaths in Paris were 14,503, while in 1848–9 the deaths have been 15,196, and the epidemic has not yet entirely subsided. In Paris, besides bad drainage, there is over-crowding to an extent of which some conception may be formed from the fact, that a population of nearly 1,000,000 of souls is crowded into little more than 40,000 houses; whilst the 2,000,000 of people in London are distributed amongst upwards of 280,000 houses; the average number of persons in each house being in Paris 25, and in London 7. On comparing the mortality in Paris during the recent outbreak of cholera, as stated in the official returns, with the mortality in London during the recent outbreak, as given in the Registrar-General's Returns, it appears, that whereas in Paris, out of a population, say of 10,000 souls, 144 persons have died, in London, out of a population of 10,000 souls, six persons have died.

But that the epidemic force in London is stronger than would be represented by this general result, is we think to be inferred from the severity of the visitation in other parts of the country where there has been an unusual degree of negligence, and where, consequently, the conditions have been more than commonly favourable for the localization of the disease. Under these circumstances the mortality has been as high, and even somewhat higher than at Paris. In some of the towns in Wales, the attacks in proportion to the population have been as 1 in 19, and the deaths in proportion to the attacks, as 1 in 3½. If the mortality of Paris had been at the same rate the deaths would have amounted to 15,261, instead of 15,186.

We cannot but lament, that in the towns and villages of our own country, where the causes tending to localize the disease were the most apparent, we have not been able to do more for their removal or mitigation. The obstacles to even a limited and temporary relief have been already stated. But if, by any means at our disposal, we had been able to diminish those evils to a far greater extent than we have found practicable, the relief thus afforded whatever its amount, would have been only palliative and temporary, and wholly inadequate to meet the permanent yet removablė causes of disease which exist in a greater or less degree in every town and village which has been brought under our notice. Until the whole of these removable causes have ceased to exist, the object of the legislature which we are charged with the duty of carrying out as far as may be practicable, will not have been accomplished. These causes can be effectually removed only by the practical application of the principles recognized in the Public Health Act, and the proceedings which we have taken, up to the present time, with reference to the execution of this latter Act, we now propose to describe.

226A–B. Report of the Board of Health on its work, 1848–1854

Parlty. Papers, 184/xxxv.

226A. Summary of its work

loc. cit., pp. 13–16.

. . . But for these extraordinary demands on our time and attention we might now have had the satisfaction of reporting a greater number of towns in the enjoyment of the powers and privileges of the Public Health Act, and these in a state of greater forwardness with their works; yet, considering that the labour in which we have been engaged is the first attempt to carry into practice a principle of legislation entirely novel, and that the staff of superintending inspectors to conduct the preliminary inquiries has never exceeded seven, and during the greater part of the time has been limited to five, we submit that as great a degree of progress has been made in the application of the Act as could have been reasonably anticipated.

We have now to state 284 towns have memorialized and petitioned in form for the application of the Act. Of these, up to the 31st December 1853, the requisite forms and proceedings prescribed by the Act, have been complied with in 182, including nine in which the Act has been incorporated with local Acts, comprising altogether a total population, according to the census of 1851, of upwards of two millions –(2,100,000.)

Within the last three months we have had petitions for the application of the Act from upwards of twenty towns.

Though in many of the 182 towns, the application of the Act has been comparatively recent, yet, in one hundred and twenty-six cases, surveys with a view of carrying the Act into operation have been completed or are in progress.

In seventy, plans of new works founded on the surveys have been laid out.

In thirty-one, including the cities of Gloucester, Salisbury, and Ely, and the towns of Dover, Preston, Lancaster, Penzance, Wigan, and Chelmsford, plans of combined works for water supply and drainage have been submitted to the Board for examination, and have been approved; mortgages of rates for the execution of these works have been sanctioned to the amount of upwards of £467,000, and the works are now, for the most part, in progress.

Besides the above sum for works entirely new, plans have been examined by the Board's inspectors for works of drainage to combine with waterworks already existing; for the extension of waterworks, and for other improvements contemplated by the Act, such as the paving and widening of streets, the opening of thoroughfares, the removal of obstructions to ventilation, &c. Plans having reference to works of this description, have been examined and approved for thirty-nine towns; and sanctions for the execution of these plans have been given to the amount of £589,000, making a total sum, for which mortgages of rates have been sanctioned, of upwards of one million, *viz.* £1,056,000.

In thirteen towns, including Rugby, Tottenham, Alnwick, Morpeth, Hitchin, Ormskirk, Barnard Castle, St. Thomas, Exeter, Ottery st. Mary, Ashby-de-la-Zouch, and Launceston, the whole of the public works for water supply and drainage are completed, and reported to be in full action; while the private portion, or that which connects the house drainage and water supply with the public works, is in rapid course of execution. With one exception (that of Croydon, to which we shall subsequently advert), these works are reported to be working satisfactorily:–that is to say, the main drainage works and the house drainage works, as far as they have been properly executed, are completely self-cleansing.

It is expected that in about thirty-five other towns combined public works will be completed, and in full action, in less than a year.

There will be further required an examination of surveys for fifty-seven towns, and of plans of works for one hundred and twelve towns.

Supposing the cost of the execution of such plans, after examination and approval, to be at the same rate as the cost for similar works in the thirty-one towns for which sanctions have already been given, according to the closest proximate estimate that can be formed, there will be required for the public works in these towns £3,643,156, and for their private works, at least £1,190,826, making altogether a total sum of £4,833,980. The rise in the price of labour and materials since those sanctions were given, will however, if they should continue at the present rates, augment the total expenditure to upwards of £6,000,000.

This estimate has respect only to the sum which will probably be required for town and house drainage, and water supply; being, for water supply brought to every house, an average of a penny halfpenny (1½d.) a house per week, and for main drainage or sewer drainage brought to the house, of 1d. per house per week. The average expense at which the works within the houses of the poorer classes have been executed under private improvement rates, for introducing a service pipe, putting down a sink, filling up the cesspool, and substituting a water-closet and self-cleansing house drains, and the construction of a dust bin, has been 1d. per week, being a total average cost of one halfpenny a day.

This amount does not include what may ultimately be found needful for collateral improvements, such as those already adverted to, – the formation of public walks, the opening of spaces for light and air, and the widening of thoroughfares.

One of the most important practical results of the Act has been, the facility which it has afforded for its general adoption by the diminution of expense, in relation both to its application and to works executed under it.

The great diminution of expense in the application of the Act, has arisen from the improvements included in its form of procedure. The diminution of the expense of works has been effected by a closer examination of their nature, and by the appointment of a class of engineering inspectors, who having devoted exclusive attention to this description of works, have made themselves acquainted with their specialities, and have learned the most efficient and economical modes of executing them. . . .

226B. Antagonisms aroused

loc. cit., pp. 48–54.

. . . We are aware that, in the discharge of the duties which have devolved upon us, we have unavoidably interfered with powerful interests, which have the immediate means of making themselves heard by members of Government and of Parliament.

Provisional orders which supersede Local Acts have interfered extremely with the professional emoluments of parliamentary and other agents.

With preceding Commissioners of Inquiry we have been under the necessity of stating facts with relation to the inefficiency and waste of former works, and their effect in aggravating existing evil. These expositions, required for the protection of the public against the extension of like works, amounted to the condemnation of the professional practice concerned in them, and militated also against the interests of contractors for their maintenance and execution. Where large amounts of money had been invested in such works, as in those for the supply of water, and for cemeteries, the hostility of trading companies, of directors, and of shareholders has been induced, and their hostility, coming from persons holding a public position and whose direct interest was unexplained, appeared to have been based on public grounds.

The scheme we proposed for improved and economical extra-mural burial endangered the emoluments of cemetery companies and the entire body of trading undertakers.

The demands on their time and energy which, for the saving of life, we were obliged to make on boards of guardians during the prevalence of cholera, excited in numerous instances loud complaints. We have already stated the general and favourable change which has taken place in the opinion of boards of guardians and other local authorities with reference to our proceedings on that occasion.

The report in condemnation of the present sources and works for the supply of water to the metropolis, necessarily excited the hostility of existing water companies, as well as of those who were before Parliament with plans for the extension of similarly constructed works from similar sources.

The requisition in accordance with the Act and with the recommendations of the Commissioners for improving the Health of Towns, that surveys should be completed in detail before any new works were undertaken, scrutinies into the efficiency and economy of the plans for town drainage and water supply, caused the active hostility of professional engineers who were unaccustomed to such checks, and who were now called upon to change their principles and practice of construction, and at the same time to reduce in particular cases their emoluments, (always proportioned to the amount of expenditure,) to extents such as are set forth in the instances before given.

These hostilities have been indicated both by the circulation throughout the country of misrepresentations of facts, and by suppression of facts, and in some instances, as has been already stated, by organized opposition.

To carry the provisions of the Public Health Act into extensive operation, the reduction of expense, as well as the improvement of works, was indispensable. It was foreseen that the attempt to reduce scales of charges and professional emoluments would be met by powerful opposition; that opposition has been encountered, and has been strengthened by the opposition of parliamentary agents and of others interested in the passing of local Acts.

The engineering opposition has been thus conducted. Instances of negligences and defects in the local execution of new works, causing partial failures in portions of them, have been collected, printed, and circulated, as examplifying the operation of the system recommended by the General Board, and have been sent to all Local Boards.

Thus a group of common lodging-houses occupied by the lowest order of Irish, in some instances as many as forty in one house, was selected; and the facts of that single case propagated as the metropolitan experience of the "unsuccessful results of the system of pipe drainage;" the fact being kept back that only in a small proportion of the cases where water-closets and pipe drains had been laid down had there been any proper supply of water; while at the same time, in the metropolis, in a number of other blocks of buildings, and upwards of 20,000 single houses, the pipe drains were working satisfactorily; the demand for them increasing at a rate with which the manufacturers had difficulty in keeping pace.

Accounts of particular stoppages of pipe sewers were promulgated without any reference to the circumstances which showed that they might have been expected to stop; without any notice of the large proportion of good work executed where nothing of the kind had occurred, or any allusion to the expenses of cleansing, the failures, and the cost of maintenance, as well as the sanitary evils of the old works. At Croydon some of the works had been constructed on erroneous principles against express instructions, and had been carelessly and negligently executed, and the natural failure of such faulty works has been pertinaciously represented to be the failure of the system.

A proportion (about six per cent.) of the house-drains had been badly laid, chiefly by private bricklayers without superintendence. The inlets both to the house-drains and the public sewers had been left unguarded; stoppages had occurred, in the proportion of about one-sixth of a mile to seventeen miles of pipe sewerage. The stoppages had been caused, not in consequence of the sewers being too small, but as appeared, on subsequent examination, from the inlets being too large. No provision in the specifications having been made for the thickness and strength of the pipes, the makers competed with each other in making them as thin as possible, and it is matter of surprise that there had been so little breakage, not amounting to more than one hundred and fifty yards in an unusually deep cutting. There being, in the then state of the market, no pipes readily obtainable which could be relied upon for the particular purpose, the expedient of a relieving arch of brick over the pipe was used for the length of the deep cutting. Notwithstanding the decisive proof of success with more than sixteen miles of sewer, statements were promulgated that the system of works had proved a total failure, and that it had been necessary to return to the use of brick culverts on the old system. In spite of the fact, that with the exception of the stoppages in question, the whole of the pipe sewers in the streets were self-cleansing in an extraordinary and unexampled degree, and had never been filled, conclusions were reported and promulgated, as from actual experience, that it had been found absolutely necessary to return to brick sewers of deposit, large enough for men to enter and cleanse away the accumulations of noxious deposit.

While the new works were in progress and approaching completion, an extraordinary epidemic which has prevailed in different parts of the country, in places where there are no new works whatsoever, attacked the higher class of houses in Croydon, those with old as well as those with new works. The disease was immediately ascribed to the operation of the new drainage works, although the first and most severe visitation of the epidemic was at the distance of upwards of three-quarters of a mile from the places where the works were going on. After the prevalence of the disease elsewhere had been shown, it was still alleged that the works at Croydon had aggravated it, notwithstanding the fact, that if the deaths had been in the same ratio as at Oxted, in the same county, which was deemed well situated, but undrained, they would have been one-third more numerous; or if they had been in the same proportion as at Sawbridgeworth, where the localizing causes were greater, they would have been more than doubled; or if they had been in the same rate as at Sheriff Hutton, where the localizing causes were still more aggravated, they would have been increased six-fold. The alleged causes of the epidemic at Croydon, the defective works, continued, but the disease itself has disappeared.

It was alleged that the works which were testified to have introduced good water, and to have removed foul smells from the poorest class of habitations, were a calamity; yet, such was the local appreciation of them, that the greater proportion were adopted voluntarily, and builders undertook, after hearing all that was promulgated against them, to pay the expense of the branch sewers themselves, that their houses might be connected with the system of tubular drainage out of their turn.

Some judgment may be formed of the ground of the opposition on the part of persons profiting by the preparation of private and local Acts, and by the works sanctioned by them, when it is considered that, by the method of modifying and incorporating local Acts with provisional orders, between two and three hundred thousand pounds have been already saved to the local administration of the country, compared with what would have been the expense of private Acts.

According to the lowest return of the average expense of Local Improvement Acts, *viz.*;–£1,627, there will have been saved £214,000 of expenses, or, according to another average, £380,000. There is reason to believe that this is a low comparative average, inasmuch as the Local Acts referred to are usually for single objects, as for water alone, or for paving and lighting alone.

Extensive opposition has been raised to the application of the Public Health Act, and hostility created against the members of the Board, and the new works promoted by them, originating apparently in the view that there has been an interference with professional emoluments, to the extent of the clear reduction of these expenses, whereas the interference which would have been justifiable in every case, could really have extended to very few cases; for if the former rates of expense had continued, they would have operated as complete barriers to the improvement works now in progress under the Public Health Act, and in the great majority of instances, to any applications whatsoever to obtain legislative sanction in the usual form.

We may further state one illustrative example of the nature of the opposition we have encountered. Under the Nuisances Removal and Diseases Prevention Amendmend Act, the scheme for a new cemetery costs £70 instead of from £800 to £2,000, which would have been spent in proceeding for a private Act. On this occasion, an intimation was received by our officers from parliamentary agents, that the course adopted by the Board was an interference with their professional emoluments, which would render it necessary on their part to raise opposition against the continuance of the Board itself.

One course adopted by those who are interested in opposing the economies and securities afforded by the Public Health Act, is to recommend the substitution of a sanitary measure which shall be compulsory on all towns, without any profusion or control with respect to the expenditure. This is the course of opposition selected by engineers. It is unnecessary to observe, that if this recommendation were adopted, it would increase the evil of wasteful and inefficient works, the burthen of which already presses on many of the most important towns and districts so heavily as to occasion an insuperable obstacle, at least for the time, to urgently-needed improvements.

With respect to the important trust imposed upon us, of examining works before sanctioning mortgages of rates, in order to ensure that such works shall be of value equal to the outlay, for a period co-extensive with the term of the mortgages, it is to be observed that the practice of the Treasury has been to cause notice to be given in the locality that it was proposed to undertake such and such new works; and if no local objection were raised, to issue the consent. Information has been communicated to us respecting cases where consent has been given, under circumstances which prove the entire insufficiency of this procedure to insure the protection intended,–where, for instance, the towns-people have been wholly unaware of the nature and expense of the works in question which competent inquiry must have elicited. We are satisfied, from our experience, that the examination of plans for works ought to be extended rather than diminished, and both the responsibility under which it is done and the power of doing it increased.

Notwithstanding the obstruction to the working of the Act, we are aware of only six, out of 182 Local Boards, which are in a state of antagonism with the General Board.

Two of these hostile boards, under the influence of small owners of the description of property requiring amendment, manifested their determination not to execute the Act, by an attempt to dismiss their surveyors, with a view to the entire breaking up of the boards, an attempt which we were bound to resist, because we could not sanction the removal of those officers without just and legal cause. With reference to two other hostile boards, plans of works were proposed which we could not sanction, on the grounds that the works themselves were not the most efficient, and that they were unduly expensive. On our withholding our sanction to these works, the parties interested in them made loud complaints of uncalled-for interference. In another town, in which the engineer employed has been at variance with the General Board, it was found necessary, on examination of the proposed works, to insist on a reduction of 24 per cent. on the gross sum, for which the sanction for a mortgage of the rates was sought. The performance of this duty was followed on the part of the engineer and others by Parliamentary opposition and complaint.

We are aware of no instance in which we have experienced hostility, but on some similar ground.

227. Report of the Adderley Commission on Sanitary Laws (1869–1871): present sanitary government in various places

Second Report: *Parlty. Papers*, 1871/xxxv/pp. 371–377.

Present Sanitary Government in Various Places

First, we state the result of our inquiries as to the general sanitary condition of various places under the existing state of things.

Most of the principal cities have Acts of their own for purposes of local Government. Some have anticipated, and most of them include the principal provisions of the public Acts. The powers under those Acts are exercised either by Town Councils or Commissioners.

In about seven hundred towns and districts in England the powers of the general Public Health and Local Government Acts are in force, and are exercised by Town Councils, or Commissioners, or elected Boards.

Still a considerable part of the country has no Local Government for sanitary purposes beyond that provided everywhere by the more recent Acts for the "removal of nuisances," construction of sewers, supply of water, and other purposes before enumerated.

Upon the whole, therefore, taking the country generally, there are, firstly, boroughs, large and small, not under the Local Government Acts, and boroughs, large and small, which have adopted those Acts.

There are, secondly, non-corporate towns not under those Acts, and many, both large and small, under the provision of those Acts.

There are, lastly, semi-rural districts formed under those Acts, while the greater part of the country remains under no Sanitary Authority, except such as the more recent Acts give to Vestries or Boards of Guardians.

Comparative condition of places under and not under the Public Health and Local Government Acts

We proceed first to collect the evidence showing the generally improving condition of various kinds of towns and places under the general Public Health and Local Government Acts, as contrasted with that of the same kind of places not under those general Acts. In the first category of *large boroughs*, those not under the general Local Government Acts will be found in most cases to have Local Acts, giving them equivalent powers, and therefore to offer no such contrast of inactivity with improvement.

General condition of large boroughs not under the Public Health and Local Government Acts

Liverpool, Manchester, and Birmingham are the most conspicuous examples of boroughs almost metropolitan in wealth and population, where the Local Government is entirely administrated through their Corporations acting under Local Acts, without any interference from the central government except such as all local government is subject to under the later general Acts.

All of them have carried out some system of cleansing and of water supply, and have medical and inspecting officers, and are furnished with many sanitary appliances.

The town clerk of Liverpool states that the Town Council efficiently administer the powers of local Government, which Local Acts give them at least as largely as the general Acts would. He attributes the somewhat high death-rate, though lower than that of Manchester, to the number of poor Irish and emigrants among the inhabitants, and only suggests that greater power should be given for the particular purposes of widening streets, and spreading a too crowded population. Sir. W. Denison also remarks on the overcrowding and want of water. A provision of one of the early Metropolitan Acts relating to smoke has been adopted into their Local Acts.

The health officer of Liverpool states that since the Act of 1866 made it imperative on the Local Authorities to take action against nuisances, 14,993 privies have been converted into water-closets, the Council assisting the poorer owners, who were the greater number, towards the cost, from the surplus funds of the borough. Cellar dwellings are regulated by Local Acts nearly on the same terms as by the general Act of 1848, and 424 unfit houses have been demolished, the Corporation paying full compensation. It was found extremely difficult to prevent the re-inhabitation of condemned cellars by any means short of actually filling them up.

A plan of sewage utilization has been commenced.

A very complete system of inspection is maintained in districts which was at first assisted by the police, but has since worked better as a separate service of its own.

The Corporation have taken former pumping works into their own hands from companies, and have carried out on a great scale their own water supply.

In short, the evidence about Liverpool shows that the sanitary requirements of this great town are fairly supplied under its Local Acts.

The town clerk of Manchester states that 22 Local Acts are in force in that city, many of which contain provisions similar to the General Sanitary Acts; some of them, indeed claiming to have been the models on which they were drawn. These include Waterworks and Improvement Acts, and a Burial Board Act.

That the Town Council, which is the governing body, is applying largely the Artizans and Labourers Dwelling Act, which puts the responsibility of making dwellings fit for human habitation on the owners.

Whenever they find the provisions of the public Acts superior to their own, they use them, as, for instance, in section 19 of the Sanitary Act of 1866, relating to smoke.

The death-rate is high, but chiefly among infants.

The medical officer of health is assisted by a health committee, and the police are employed as inspectors, being directed to give information of nuisances seen by them in the rounds of their duty. There is also in Manchester and Salford a sanitary association, which Dr. Trench describes as doing the work which he does in Liverpool.

The rivers are described as reaching Manchester so foul, that their additional pollution by this city scarcely makes them perceptibly worse.

The ashpit system is retained, and put in its best form.

They have recently obtained from Parliament further provisions against offensive trades.

The town clerk of Birmingham, describes the local administration of that midland metropolis as under the Municipal Corporation Act and two Improvement Acts of 1851 and 1861, with which some of the general Acts are incorporated, and under some general Acts besides. A section of one of their Local Acts limits their aggregate rate for improvements to 2s. in the pound and the street rate to 2s. 6d., neither of which can be exceeded without the consent of the ratepayers, which never can be got. Birmingham, however, is healthy, and well looked after, and great works are on foot both for water supply by company, and for sewerage, and sewage utilization by the corporation itself. There is also an admirable system of inspection of nuisances throughout the whole borough.

We may add the evidence received as to the general condition of Newcastle-upon-Tyne, which is the only large maritime borough not under the Local Government Act.

The Local Acts were repealed and consolidated in 1837, and amending Acts have passed in 1841, 1846, 1850, 1853, 1855, and 1865.

Great sanitary defects exist here, arising from the old-fashioned narrow streets or 'chares' in the lower part of the town, on the river, near the Castle.

The cholera has raged here with peculiar virulence in all its visitations of this country, and attached itself to the lower town.

Even in the new town demolition and re-construction have been so ill regulated that it is described as "an accumulation of unfinished streets."

The clerk to the Sanitary Committee of the Corporation, states that that committee, which is the Local Authority, have done much to remodel the town, and to make owners complete their undertakings. Where such works have been carried out, mortality has sensibly diminished. The ash-pit system is chiefly adopted here, as in Manchester.

The sewerage has been improved since 1853, upwards of 60 miles of main drainage having been made in the town, but they are still allowed to discharge by seven outfalls into the Tyne, the tide flowing beyond the town. There is some talk of intercepting and utilizing the sewage. The water and gas supply is undertaken by a private company.

The Corporation have established baths and wash-houses, and the Common Lodging House Act is efficiently carried out. Hospitals are provided for epidemics.

Newcastle is a large market for the north, and a complete system of inspection is maintained, both of every kind of market, and of lodging-houses, and of nuisances throughout the town.

In the south of England there are no large boroughs not under the Local Government Act.

General condition of large boroughs under the Public Health and Local Government Acts

To *compare* with this evidence on the condition of large boroughs under Local Acts, the condition of *large boroughs which have adopted* the provisions of the General Acts, we may take, as a fair example, the case of Bradford.

The town clerk of Bradford, in his written answers, states that the population of Bradford has increased from 66,000 to 106,000 in 1861; the estimate in 1869 being 138,000.

It had, in 1847, a charter granted, and by an Improvement Act in 1850, the Council were constituted the Local Board of Health, and adopted most of the powers of the public Acts. They have provided baths and wash-houses, and fairs and markets.

By a Corporation Waterworks Act, in 1854, amended in 1858, 1862, 1868, and 1869, they have supplied themselves with water, which gravitates down from large reservoirs, one being at a distance of nearly 30 miles. Mountain streams are impounded; springs of great purity are made use of; rainfall from extensive gathering grounds is collected, and an abundant supply for the outlying districts as well as the town is thus secured, at a cost on permanent works, which already reaches £800,000.

Public sewerage and drainage is being vigorously proceeded with, the only difficulty being that of outfall.

They have been ordered by the Court of Chancery to defoecate their sewage before 11th January, 1872.

The Clerk of the Guardians presents to the Sanitary Committee a return showing the localities where the deaths have occurred, and thus guides them to particular spots. When information of a serious character, indicating the presence of epidemic disease, is obtained, members of the Council institute a house-to-house visitation, the whole borough being arranged in districts for the purpose.

The building byelaws have, after very considerable discussion, been modified to facilitate the erection of cottage property.

Bristol is a large city, with 154,093 inhabitants, (by census, 1861) having a Local Improvement Act, under which, and using the powers of the Sanitary Act, it has carried out great improvements. It is an illustration of the good condition into which the whole country might be brought if the Local Authorities exercised their functions properly, and its improvements have been a great pecuniary bargain. Sewerage and drainage have been very much improved, floods have been much reduced, and disease thereby largely diminished, but the flagrant evil of a discharge into a tidal river still remains; but Dr. Budd, a resident physician, who is our witness, gives much credit to Bristol for its measures for preventing disease. A very able and energetic health officer attends every morning at the board of health, where he meets a staff of inspectors, each having a district under his charge. They furnish reports, and the health officer proceeds to the infected localities. A remarkable abatement of prevalent diseases has resulted and at no great expense, richly repaid. A considerable reduction of poor rates has followed, and of mortality from 31 to 22 per 1,000. Disinfection by anticipation has been the secret of Bristol's unexampled success, and is easier than suppression.

A year ago 100 cases of typhoid occurred in Bristol workhouse, and were found to come from vicious and abominable sanitary arrangements. Mr. Heaven, the Clerk to the Local Board, in his answers to circular questions, says that the Public Health Act, 1848, was applied by Provisional Order in August 1851; that the Improvement Acts of 1840 and 1847 relate to the construction of buildings and lines of streets; that the only byelaws made are for regulating lodging and slaughter-houses.

In Gloucester the adoption of the Acts has resulted in large combined works of water supply and sewerage, which have reduced the mortality from 24 in 1,000 (which was the rate in 1849) to 20½ in 1868, to which rate deaths in the county hospital contribute; £85,000, or more than one year's rateable value, has been expended on water supply, and £100,000 borrowed for sewerage and other public works. Only five per cent of the houses are unsupplied with water-closets. The drainage, however, is still into the Severn, though a net profit is made from the remaining scavenging. They have a surveyor, inspector, and assistant. Three adjoining local Boards imperfectly exercise their powers, and have a proportionately higher death-rate.

In Great Yarmouth, a great maritime borough, there was strong opposition to the introduction of the Public Health Act, from fear of heavy rates, but since its introduction in 1851 it has worked satisfactorily, and led to extensive drainage and sewerage operations. Considerable outlay has been also made for street improvements. Water has been supplied by a company, brackish and undrinkable water having before been drank. Defective drainage led to the first petition for the Act. The cholera had been very fatal in 1849, and from other causes the death-rate was always high. Complete sewerage is now carried out, but utilization of sewage is only under discussion.

The present Local Board, which is the Town Council, acts efficiently in sanitary matters.

Three adjoining places, parts of the borough, adopted the Local Government Act so lately as 1869, and their former government is already beginning to improve.

Oldham is a borough of 83,000 inhabitants (with a Local Act of 1826) which (in order to obtain a loan under the Public Works (Manufacturing Districts) Act, 1863), adopted for limited purposes the Local Government Act. But experiencing great complication in the working of their Act of 1826, in connexion with the part adoption of the public Acts, the Town Council in 1865 found it necessary to obtain a special Act for the local government of their borough, and thereby have with great convenience to the population consolidated and amended the provisions under which they had been previously governed. Since 1863 20 miles of main drainage have been constructed within the borough, costing nearly £20,000 and 16,500 lineal yards of paved streets through which the main sewers run, and a vast amount of connecting drainage, which, however, is still allowed to discharge into the streams. There are seven constables employed in visiting the whole town to enforce sanitary regulations, and upwards of 2,000 nuisances have been abated.

Swansea has a population of 60,000, and Mr. Richards, M.P., one of our colleagues, says of it, "Perhaps there is no town in England or Wales where sanitary works "have been more fully carried out." The readiness of the large ratepayers, owners of large smelting works, to encourage sanitary improvement, has been the cause. The water supply is very perfect, and town drainage, which, however, discharges into the sea. The cost has been large, but there is a very marked improvement in the health of the place.

Lincoln is a borough of 25,000 inhabitants, which in 1865 was induced to adopt the Act from the prevalence of fever and deficiency of water, and the inability of the old Commissioners to make a remedy. Buildings have been improved. The cesspool system is not yet abolished, the opposition to the expense of sewerage on such a scale as to render utilization possible being still unsubdued. No more drains are allowed to go into the river, but builders of new houses are allowed to make cesspools. The Corporation has shown extreme reluctance to execute the powers of the adopted Acts; certain of their members who were most active, having been excluded.

Monmouth is governed by its Town Council and Commissioners under a Local Act, 58 Geo. III. It does not give such large powers as the general Acts, and is full of obsolete enactments, and many of difficult construction. Old main drains discharge into the river. There are cesspools, and no regular cleansing of them. In the neighbouring country, wherever there is a stream, people build privies over it. There are waterworks made by a company. If the streams and springs were kept pure, there would be no need of artificial water supply. Some of the well water is very bad, corrupted by soakage of drains and cesspools.

General condition of small boroughs not under the Public Health and Local Government Acts

Stafford shows a confusion of old jurisdictions. The old borough is under Improvement Commissioners, while a district within the present municipality, called Newtown, remains without local government. The inhabitants outside the old borough are very desirous of obtaining the benefit of the Local Government Acts, especially with respect to the drainage of their houses, greatly needed; but every attempt has been frustrated upon a division of the council. The Corporation and Commissioners act separately, and often clash. Neither body has power to borrow money for improvements. There is an inspector of nuisances at a salary of £10 but no health officer. In a recent small-pox epidemic, the Authorities could not interfere. The Guardians have failed in attempts to improve the grossly-neglected condition of the town. Consumption and rheumatism prevail from the dampness of the soil, owing to dammed-up water, and scarlet and typhoid fever frequently recur. There is only surface drainage. Pigs are kept to consume the offal of slaughter-houses in the town, and cattle fairs are held in the streets. The water is contaminated by soakage. No control is exercised over the erection of houses, and fever arises from the poverty and abominable construction of workmen's dwellings. The Council defeated (on plea of expense) an attempt to adopt the general Acts.

Tiverton is an old borough, with a lace manufacture, and 10,447 inhabitants. The town clerk, who is also a clerk to the Board of Guardians of the Tiverton Union, states that the mayor, aldermen, and burgesses are the Local Authority, being *ex-officio* Commissioners under two Local Improvement Acts, 1794 and 1822, for lighting, paving, cleansing &c. They have made byelaws under the Municipal Corporation Act, and, of course, have the general powers and duties given by the Sanitary Acts. The adoption of the Local Government Act would simplify and complete the powers they want.

They have an abundant supply of good water from neighbouring hills, which a reservoir would make perfect, but they assume that they have no power to make one. This water runs into the town in an open course, and is fouled by every sort of refuse. The byelaws under the Municipal Corporation Act against such a nuisance are not enforced. Some outlay has been made on sewers, which are still imperfect, and have their outfall into the Exe.

Many other public works, most desirable and even inexpensive, their Local Acts give them no power to undertake. There is a reluctance to use the powers they have.

A new cemetery has been made, but the vaults in the old burial places, though found by medical men unfit, are not closed. Dilapidated houses are reported, but not repaired. The Guardians do not see to the Vaccination Act being enforced.

Mortality has been reduced where the sewerage is carried out.

Basingstoke, with a population of 4,640, is drained partly into a river of the purest water above the town, and partly into a canal. Soakage of sewage gets into the wells. The Local Government Acts have not been adopted from fear of expense, small cottage ratepayers having outvoted it at public meetings, and in 1865, when the matter was brought before the Corporation, it failed of the required two-thirds majority by one vote. Sanitary concerns are neglected.

Of Chichester there has been formal complaint to the Local Government Act Office, and a report made by the inspector. Its population is 9,000. No sanitary works have been constructed. An Act has been obtained for removing the complained-of cattle market from the streets. The relieving officer for the city is nuisance inspector. The Guardians do not consider they have any sanitary functions.

Street regulation is under a paving commission.

Seaford is an ancient borough, part of the cinque port of Rye, one of the old unreformed charter corporations. Its population is 1,150.

The governing body under the charter consists of a High Bailiff, Recorder, and Jurats. The Vestry is the Sewer Authority, and acts by a committee. The Corporation govern the borough, and in the Recorder's opinion are the Nuisance Authority, but the Home Office decided that the Vestry were the Nuisance Authority, and the Corporation do not so act. What little corporate property they have, after paying one or two servants, they seem to share among themselves.

Many houses are so dilapidated as to be unfit for decent people to live in.

They would not adopt the Local Government Act for fear of too much power getting into one or two hands, such as the agent of the chief landowner.

On complaint being made under the 49th section of the Sanitary Act of the state of the town, the Local Government Act Officer sent down an inspector, on whose recommendation £2,800 raised on a rateable value of £7,000 has been spent on drains, with an outfall into the sea.

They have removed a pestilential cesspool, into which all the filth of the place formerly entered.

A better water supply is wanted; the well water being good, but fouled.

They are shy of the expence, and want to pay off their sewer debt, and are afraid of their houses being interfered with. Nuisances are duly reported, but it is conceived that no power is given by the Acts as to dungheaps and pig-sties.

The rate of mortality is only 14 in 1,000.

General condition of small boroughs under the Public Health and Local Government Acts

A somewhat complicated case is Banbury borough, with its neighbouring townships of Neithrop in Oxfordshire, and Grimsbury in Northamptonshire. These were made a district under a Local Board in 1852, and considerable inconvenience is occasioned by each of these three portions being under different magisterial jurisdiction.

The board consists of 13; 6 for the borough, 6 for the townships, and the Mayor. Part of the district being outside the borough, separate rates and separate accounts are necessitated. Differing limits on rating have been only partly adjusted by provisional orders.

Drainage works were commenced immediately after the adoption of the Act; and complaints having been made by owners and occupiers on the stream into which they discharged, a farm has been taken for sewage utilization, which is now in full operation. Water-closets have been introduced throughout the town; a private company supply water. Byelaws, based on the Home Office model, have been adopted.

The death-rate has been reduced from 26 to 18 per 1,000, and the inhabitants attribute great additional comfort, as well as health and cleanliness, to their new system of drainage.

Knaresborough, an old borough, got an Improvement Commission 50 years ago, but adopted the Local Government Act last year, to prevent their being over-ridden by a Bill which was introduced by the Harrogate Water Company, the company for supplying Harrogate (three miles off) having proposed to take power to extend their works to Knaresborough. Drainage has been done by the Commissioners, and the town was consequently healthier. A retired sergeant of police is employed as inspector of nuisances and of lodging houses. The new Board is allowed to be a great improvement on the old Commission, though constituted of the same men.

Llanelly, having a population of 13,000, on an application emanating from a local Chamber of Commerce in 1850, applied the Public Health Act, 1848, and changed its old government under a Portreeve and Burgess for a Local Board of 12.

Considerable sewer and water works are in progress.

Considerably more than its rateable value has been borrowed, chiefly from the Public Loan Commissioners, for water, which has been hitherto deficient. And when the reservoir was low was very bad.

The Local Board have an inspector, who also acts as surveyor, with an assistant, but no officer of health.

General condition of non-corporate towns not under the Public Health and Local Government Acts

Tunbridge is a town of 7,000 inhabitants. There was no action by the Vestry in sanitary matters till, in 1866, it formed a Committee of its members to carry out the Sanitary Acts. They appointed two local surveyors, who reported that for want of sufficient fall it was impossible to drain the town. An engineer, however, made a plan, which was referred to Mr. Rawlinson, and approved by him, and the sanction of the Home Office was obtained to borrow the estimated cost of £6,000. The ratepayers, upon this, expressed such dissatisfaction as caused the Committee to resign, and so further proceedings were stopped. Another Committee was appointed to attend to certain nuisances, and the Vestry are in conference with the Local Government Acts Office about plans. Meanwhile the drainage of the lower parts of the town is very bad, and low fever at times hangs about those parts. A company supply water from the Medway, but not enough to flush drains. A tradesman in the town is paid £20 a year to inspect nuisances and lodging-houses. A main sewer runs through the town, made many years ago by private subscription.

Stow-in-the-Wold is a town of 1,000 inhabitants, with no local government but its Vestry, which has delegated its powers to a Committee of 15, but through internal dissension a portion resigned, and the number got reduced to 9. The most necessary works have since been stopped by litigation. Though the town stands on a hill, the drainage is far from satisfactory. The people dig till they get to a 'swilley,' or fissure in the rock, into which the sewage can run, and from which it oozes into the wells. There is no inspector of nuisances, which abound without ever being removed. The vestry accounts are never audited. The Clerk to the Committee says that the expenditure having been objected to, the Committee declined to have that question decided by an auditor instead of in a court of law. There is no law compelling any audit of a Vestry's sanitary expenditure.

Dorking is a town of 6,000 inhabitants, not under local government, wholly undrained. The sewage runs into the surface drains with the rain, and fever and disease are prevalent. The witness attributes the fever to cesspools. The water supply is very bad.

Ulverstone (on the evidence of Mr. Brogden, M.P.), has a population of nearly 8,000. In 1852, in consequence of the excess in the returns of the death-rate, Mr. Rawlinson inspected and reported, "Neither proper sewers nor drains, cesspools "crowded among cottages, prevalence of fever, and no local governing body with "sufficient power;" he recommended, however "no further proceedings (!) unless "on requisition from the ratepayers;" and nothing was accordingly done till 1858, when the mortality was again very heavy, and an ineffectual attempt was made to adopt the Local Government Act. In 1864, the death-rate being then over 35 per 1,000, Dr. Lankester was brought down to lecture, and he also made a report of the general unsanitary condition of the place. There were no sewers or drains, except of dry rubble for removing surface water. Street and yard channels were filled with liquid refuse. Cesspools were crowded amongst the cottages, and fever was chronic in the houses of the poor. The adoption of the Act was still opposed, at a great expense, by the majority of small ratepayers. A Board of Surveyors under the old Highway Act incurred some expense for drainage at their own risk. It was disputed whether they or the Board of Guardians were responsible for removing nuisances, and none are removed. The adoption of the Act was at length carried, but an appeal to the Secretary of State was immediately lodged against it on the ground of informality. By a compromise of dispute, a Committee of Guardians made some outlay on urgent improvements. Just enough has been done to frustrate the interference of the Secretary of State, and avoid local improvement.

Surbiton, with population of 7,000, was put under Improvement Commissioners by a local Act, 1855, incorporating the Towns Clauses, chiefly with a view to drainage, and with other powers. It is a district of 1,800 acres, one-third built on, adjoining Kingston-on-Thames. In four years the Commissioners have completely succeeded in curing a filthy condition, "purifying the air, and making the place habitable." In their endeavours to comply with the Thames Navigation Act, 1866, forbidding the discharge of sewage into the Thames after a given date, they have experienced considerable difficulty. The Metropolitan Board of Works have refused to admit the sewage of Surbiton, &c. at Putney. The Sewage Utilization Act, 1865, contained certain clauses intended, among other purposes, to benefit such places as Kingston, Surbiton, and Richmond. Under them the Local Authorities were enabled to take land compulsorily for making sewage farms, and to combine and make one joint scheme. The value of the land desired and the opposition from residents on the one hand, and the fear of expense among the Commissioners themselves on the other hand, defeated this scheme. The Chairman of the Commissioners would *enforce* combination and carry the sewage by pumping to a purely rural district at Bagshot Heath, at a distance of 12 or 13 miles.

Epping is a case of a small town of 2,000 inhabitants. On the passing of the Acts of 1866 and 1868, the Guardians discontinued their former Nuisance Committee, being advised that their powers determined.

An active medical officer of the Union, who is our witness, did his utmost to set the law in motion in vain. A special drainage district was formed in January 1868, but in order to defeat action the members of the Board resigned; since which there has been neither committee, nor inspector, nor any sanitary officer in the whole district. The Home Secretary is about to exert his powers under the 49th section of the Sanitary Act, but the locality hitherto has managed to evade his action. The sanitary condition of the place is very bad, the mortality greater than in any other part of Essex. Typhoid fever has prevailed from the want of drainage and of good water.

General condition of non-corporate towns under the Public Health and Local Government Acts

Croydon is stated by the Chairman of its Local Board to have been the first place to which the Public Health Act of 1848 was applied. Its rateable value being £210,000, it has spent £200,000 on sewage utilization, and the outlay has more than repaid itself, and £70,000 on supplying itself with water. The rate of mortality has fallen from 62 to 18 per 10,000.

Every householder is obliged to conform with the general system, and connect his house with the mains. There are two nuisance inspectors, and three house inspectors; no medical officer, but two physicians are members of the board. Money borrowed on mortgage of the rates at five per cent. is being paid off in 30 years.

Merthyr Tydvil is a district with a population of 55,000, under a Local Board, part of which has become overcrowded by increasing colliery works, and so subject to typhus. The medical officer states that several hundred workmen's houses are being run up in a neighbouring valley without system or drainage; the Board had, therefore, to use the powers of the Act against great difficulties. Merthyr Tydvil has spent £82,000 in collecting water from the hills around, and £30,000 on sewers, and can distinctly trace to such sanitary provisions a reduction of the death-rate from 30 to 20 per 1,000 within 19 years. The reduction of infant mortality has been peculiarly remarkable. The Artizans and Labourers Dwellings Act, 1869, has been put in operation, and regulations under the Diseases Prevention Act, 1855, worked successfully in suppressing a cholera epidemic in 1866.

Byelaws have prevented improper buildings, and enforced drainage, and there has been a complete registration of houses.

General condition of rural and semi-rural places not under the Public Health and Local Government Acts

East Bridgford is a parish of 460 inhabitants, where fever is constantly recurring from bad drainage, and the guardians have utterly failed even to put the powers which they have in force. There is excellent natural drainage, and the place ought to be very healthy. The people drink the water of the Trent after it has received the sewage of Nottingham. The wells are deep, but the soil is porous, and the drainage poured into holes called dry wells finds its way into them.

Terling is a country parish of 900 population, where a deadly fever once prevailed, the Board of Guardians having wholly neglected their sanitary duties. The Privy Council sent down an inspector, Dr. Thorne, and the Vestry, convinced of their duty, proceeded under his superintendence to construct waterworks. The Secretary of State, under the 96th section of the Sanitary Act, has employed the police to institute proceedings, and nuisances have since been effectually removed. The Vestry have since spent £1,700 in the supply of water. The drains from the houses go into the fields.

Biggleswade is a small town in Essex in a filthy condition, where the small rate-payers out-vote all propositions for adopting the Local Government Acts. (*See* evidence at length.)

Saxmundham is a rural parish of 1,200 population in Suffolk, whose Vestry formed a Committee for sanitary purposes under the Sanitary Act, the Guardians, of course, being the Nuisance Authority. The drains running into a brook created a nuisance, of which complaint at last came to the Home Secretary. Long discussion and correspondence with the Local Government Act Office ended at length in an order for abatement, and works are planned. Disputes still continue as to the comparative merits of rival schemes. Some cottages are stated to be unfit for habitation. There are several inspectors of nuisances in the union, usually relieving officers, receiving extra salaries of £10.

Mr. Field, a land agent near Oxford, states that the villages want public drains; they have insufficient water to drink. He gives a single instance of a parish, Fenny Compton, forming a water company. There are cottages, especially those of squatters, scarcely fit for a pig to live in. He knows cases of two whole families living all in one room. Inspectors of nuisances often work well, but are ill paid, and are very partial in the orders they give.

The Rev. W. Beckett, rector of Ingoldsthorpe, gives a bad account of all his large union, with the exception of one parish. Inspectors of nuisances are badly paid, with such salaries as £12, and are wholly inefficient. Nuisances prevail, and ill health is the consequence. Privies drain into open ditches, which extend through the marshes for two miles to the sea. Drinking water is fouled by soakage. Vile cottages abound, placed in unhealthy situations: keeping bodies of persons who have died from infectious diseases in small cottages is a great cause of complaint. The Highway Act, after adoption, has been abandoned as a failure.

Mr. Read, M.P. for South Norfolk, says the rural districts are generally well supplied with water and drainage; that privy accommodation has been much increased of late; and what they most complain of is water dammed up for mills and navigation. No use is generally made of village sewage. A few industrious cottagers may be found collecting house and pigstye refuse for their gardens, but most of the manure from labourers' dwellings fertilizes only the air with disease.

Lord Egerton says of the rural districts of Lancashire that in some places Local Boards and Guardians exercise a very proper jurisdiction, but other places are perfectly neglected. It depends on individual activity. Many such districts in that county suddenly become urban, and rapidly outgrow the powers of Rural Authorities. The transition state is a source of much difficulty. Vestries they have nothing to do with; they have no such thing in their rural districts.

Mr. Winn, M.P. for North Lincolnshire, and Chairman of Glanford Brigg Board of Guardians, gives a better account of the action of inspectors there. Improvements are going on in cottages. In North Lincolnshire generally they all have spring water close on the spot, but the drinking water is in cases polluted from privies and pigsties. But large works are not wanted; the cure would be within each parish. There is a Court of Sewers for surface drainage of the land discharging into the Trent. Relieving officers frequently act as inspectors of nuisances at extra salaries of from £5 to £10.

Mr. R. Clutton, a surveyor and land agent near Reigate, states that the Board of Guardians to which he belongs have a fairly good inspector of nuisances, paid £60, though he knows that in other unions they are much more efficient and worse paid. The Vestries usually get into the hands of inferior persons. There is much need of improvement in the privy and water supply of cottages, and great inertness in sanitary progress.

Mr. Huskinson, who is agent for large estates in Nottinghamshire, Leicestershire, Lincolnshire, Derbyshire and Suffolk, and has for many years been an inspector under the Inclosure Commissioners, states generally that in rural districts there is no application of sanitary laws, and that the state of rural parishes is as bad as possible. There are, he says, some parishes belonging to large proprietors where a good deal has been done with regard to sanitary matters, but they form a very small part of the whole, and as to the great bulk really nothing has been done at all. The state of the villages generally he describes to be this, that there are scarcely any house drains, and as a rule no street drains, or in but very few instances; there are open cesspools, very ill-constructed privies, and open and offensive ditches in many places, and those things of course have a serious effect, as he believes, on the health and comfort of the inhabitants. In many parishes the water supply is extremely defective. He says, that as a rule there is neither proper drainage nor water supply. As a rule, neither towns nor counties utilize sewage. Even the best-drained towns discharge into rivers or sea, and many are having chancery proceedings taken against them in consequence. *See* Nottingham. There is practically no acting authority.

Mr. Snowball, chief agent to the Duke of Northumberland, having experience in Durham, says, country villages within his knowledge are in general drained very badly, and ill supplied with water, and the same may be said of Bucks. Cottages were very bad, but are greatly improving; they are generally attached to farms, paying no rent, but not so in Durham and Yorkshire.

Lord Penrhyn gives a good account of a large Union in North Wales, in the management of which he takes part, and the more populous parts of which are under the Local Government Act.

General condition of semi-rural districts under the Public Health and Local Government Acts

Harrow obtained a Local Board in 1850 by provisional order, its district being 1,000 acres, (which includes the hamlet of Roxeth), and the rest of the parish, about 9,000 acres, being a special drainage district. The whole is a parish in the Hendon Union, the relieving officer of which is the Guardians' inspector of nuisances. All classes of inhabitants, including the highest, serve on the Board, and with such good-will that considerable sanitary works, interfering to a large extent with private property, have been executed with little cost in the way of compensation. The parish, being partly under the Act and partly not, has caused some difficulties. The clerk of the Board, states that works for utilizing the discharged sewage are in preparation. Land is already bought for irrigation, under the powers of the Lands Clauses Act. The inspector of nuisances is also surveyor and collector for the district, and though there is not a medical officer, there has always been a medical man on the Board.

Ottery St. Mary is a Devonshire parish of 9,944 acres, and 4,340 population, 2,500 of these being in the town, which obtained, by Order in Council, 1850, a Board consisting of nine, under the Public Health Act of 1848. A special district rate had been levied on the town for sewerage and water supply, but ceased on the adoption of the Local Government Act. Sewerage and water supply have been effected, and former ill health has diminished. The discharge of drains, however, is still into a stream, but removed below the town. An inspector of nuisances and surveyor have been appointed. Local government works satisfactorily, and former Vestry squabbles have ceased.

Aldershot presents a special case, where the establishment of a camp has brought an influx of nearly 8,000 population on a wild country, and government nominees are called upon to act as members of a Local Board. The district of the Local Board is drained into the Blackwater; water and gas are supplied by companies; a sanitary officer is appointed and a surveyor also is inspector of nuisances. Sewage utilization has been carried out for the camp.

Districts of the Forest of Dean, rapidly covered by a coal mining population, adopted the Act in 1866, and has thus partly mitigated the evils incidental to such hasty crowding.

So much for the comparative condition of various kinds of places under Local Acts, the general "Local Government" Acts, or no Acts for local government beyond the "Nuisance Removal," "Sewage Utilization," and "Sanitary" Acts.

. . . . .

Part XI
EDUCATION

EDUCATION

Introduction

THE strength and weaknesses of Victorian society are perhaps nowhere more fully displayed than in the field of education. Where popular education was concerned there was little to build on. There were good grammar schools scattered up and down the land, and through these, and through private patronage, lads of parts had been able to rise to the top, in law, in scholarship, and in the Church. So long as the routines of field and craft had bounded the horizon for the masses of the population, providing an ordered prospect and a discipline of life, schools had not seemed to matter much. But with the economic transformation, with the aggregation of masses of people in towns where there were neither the means nor the tradition of coherent social living, the situation wore another aspect. It was on the Christian conscience that its first serious impact was made. In 1807 and 1811 two societies had been founded with the development of popular education specifically in view: the British and Foreign Society, which included Churchmen and Nonconformists, and the National Society, which was exclusively Church. Very considerable progress had been made on these initiatives,[1] although, particularly in the larger towns, achievement was still far short of any reasonable standard.[2] Sunday schools as well played an important social role at this epoch, their crowded classrooms frequently offering to their inmates the only brief and broken glimpse they got of any humaner tradition of life than that of the factory and the slum, or of any destiny for man beyond that of the brutes that perish.

In the political world the Radical wing of the Whigs provided the chief sponsors of educational progress and reform. Whitbread, in 1806, Brougham, in 1820, and Roebuck, in 1833, brought forward Bills for creating a rate-aided system of national education. They all failed; and Brougham gave up hopes of achieving anything along compulsory lines. But his presence in Grey's Government played its part in the decision to make a State grant of £20,000 to the two societies, the first acceptance by the State of responsibility for popular education. Roebuck's activities were primarily responsible for the series of inquiries into the Education of the Poorer Classes that followed–the Select Committees of 1834, 1835, and 1837–1838. Russell later assumed the honourable role of the interpreter of this Radical tradition; the increased grant of 1839 and the administrative machinery that he set up[3] provided the bases of advance for the next generation, and in each subsequent advance he played an important part. Lord Stanley and Gladstone, however–the latter still in that phase of his career in which he was the hope of the unbending Tories–opposed Russell's policy as an intrusion of the State into the spiritual sphere.

The State helped only those who were prepared to help themselves. Where a responsible and suitable body or person could find two-thirds of the capital cost of a school, the State found the rest, subject to its right to inspect the school. A

[1] No. 228. [2] No. 229. [3] No. 232.

Committee of Council was set up to administer the grant,[1] and Dr. James Kay, later Kay-Shuttleworth, became its secretary. He had made his first reputation by a study of Manchester health and housing, and later became an Assistant Poor Law Commissioner, interesting himself particularly in pauper education. It was in Poor Law schools that the first experiments with pupil teachers were made. Kay was a firm believer in confessional schools, although with rigid guarantees for toleration. It fell to him to negotiate what became known as the 'Concordats', the arrangements with the different churches and controlling bodies by which the relations of government inspection to confessional control were to be regulated. It was conceded from the beginning to the Established Churches of England and Scotland that the inspectors appointed to their schools should be persons acceptable to them.[2] None the less Kay had a tussle with Dr. John Allen, the first Church Schools Inspector, as to whether his reports should be made, in the first instance, to his Archbishop or to the Committee of Council. Kay won. The British and Foreign Society had been content, at first, with less definite rights of consultation. But a report of Seymour Tremenheere's, the inspector appointed to its schools, gave it offence, and Tremenheere was ultimately withdrawn to begin a new and distinguished career as the first Inspector of Mines.[3] There followed a brief struggle between the Society and the Lord President of the Council, as a result of which the Society established its claim to parity of treatment.[4] The change in attitude is of the greatest significance. In effect it meant that Dissent was no longer content to accept toleration but demanded equality. In substance this was a denial of the principle of establishment. Alongside it went an increasing indisposition to accept or even to comprehend the Church's view that religious training was an integral part of education–indeed its foundation–not something that could be provided separately from it. To Churchmen this principle constituted the difference between a Christian and a pagan view of society–between the avowal and the mere tolerance of Christianity. But a religious education in this sense would tend, throughout the country at large, to be a Church education, and to Dissenters was merely another form of the Church's instinctive demand for privilege. These differences–not little ones–were to prove the greatest stumbling-block to educational progress in the century, and it is perhaps Kay's strongest claim to the title of founder of popular education in this country, which Matthew Arnold gave to him, that in this and later instances he produced formulae of compromise which enabled the work of school-building to go forward with the powerful stimulus of the State's support. The instructions drawn up for the inspectors[5] emphasized that, in their relations with school managers and teachers, their primary duty was to help, to place at their disposal the fruits of their own wider experience and knowledge, and that assistance was in no sense to be treated as implying control.

The method by which much of the earlier instruction had been carried on was the monitorial system, of which both Lancaster and Bell, the experts of the two societies, claimed to be the inventors. By this method, simple lessons were taught to a group of children, each of whom became, in turn, the instructor of another group. It could deal with only the simplest of lessons; but it made it possible to tackle large numbers, and in the absence of a corps of professional teachers it served its time. Brougham, in the grandiloquent way characteristic of him, and not uncharacteristic of the acclaim with which his generation was wont to welcome new inventions and simplifications of life, had called it the "steam-engine of the moral world". But its deficiencies were

[1] No. 232. [2] Nos. 233, 234. [3] Part XII. [4] No. 236. [5] No. 235.

recognized. A witness before the 1834 Select Committee said, "No merely mechanical arrangement can make up for the want of a lively interest in every part of the instruction of the school in the master himself. I have heard it observed that it is the excellency of Dr. Bell's system that 1,000 children may be under a process of mutual instruction, while the master merely supervises. The possibility of such a state of things is, I think, the great deficiency of that system."

The first purpose for which the increased grant of 1839 was intended was the foundation of a Normal College for the training of teachers. It proved impossible, however, to reach an agreement between the different Church interests as to a system of religious training acceptable to them all, and the project of a central, combined training college had to be abandoned. Kay and Carleton Tufnell, the Factory Inspector, founded the Battersea Training College with private funds, largely their own, and ran it, at the start, more or less on the lines of a religious community, with Kay himself in residence. The Borough Road College, for the British and Foreign Society, St. Mark's, Chelsea, for the National Society, and various diocesan colleges followed hard on its heels, helped by the Government grant. The Education Minutes of 1846[1] may be said to have consolidated the organization of a profession of teaching. Payments were provided for teachers who undertook the training of pupil teachers; a system of scholarships to training colleges was initiated, by which the more brilliant of the pupil teachers might win the proud title and frugal emoluments of Queen's Scholars; Government supplements to the salaries of certificated teachers were promised, and arrangements were made for pensioning teachers no longer capable of service. The minutes thus established the pupil teacher system, which Matthew Arnold was to call the "sinews of our popular education". In 1853, in the context of a Bill for rate-aided education in towns, which failed, Russell gave a capitation grant to rural schools, and this was extended a few years later to urban schools. Various minor grants for special purposes were added at different times, but those mentioned provided the principal channels of State aid to education.

Meanwhile, in another context and on a restricted scale, what was known as the 'Prussian principle', that is, compulsion, had in fact been introduced. The 1833 Factory Act[2] provided that children working in factories must attend school two hours a day. They must produce each Monday, as they presented themselves for work, certificates that they had attended school during the previous week, and the factory inspectors were empowered to invalidate the certificates if they were not satisfied that the schooling was efficient. But the power to compel employers to contribute towards efficient schooling was struck out of the Bill in the Lords. Its quality depended, therefore, on local opportunity, and more particularly on the sense of responsibility of the millowners, since children coming straight from the factory, and attending only two hours a day, were not suitable pupils for ordinary schools, even when such existed. In some cases the factory school was the stokehole, or some odd unoccupied corner, and the teacher a superannuated or incapacitated employee. The inspectors tended to look on the educational provisions of the Act more as a security that the children were not working beyond the statutory hours, than as a means of educating them, and, to a man, they were in favour of the compulsory provision of schools. But there were instances[3] in which employers took their responsibility to their child employees with great seriousness, and the inspectors, by assiduous commendation of these examples, were able to do something to generalize them.

[1] No. 240. [2] Part XII. [3] No. 230.

In 1843, Sir James Graham proposed so to reduce the hours of work of children that they would have either the morning or the afternoon free, and to provide for the setting up of schools, under bodies of trustees, and with provision for their part-maintenance out of rates, wherever the needs of the child population working in factories seemed to warrant it. As he pointed out, in the speech of great feeling and power[1] with which he introduced the Bill, the grant system, by its stipulation that the locality must make its own effort to become eligible for assistance from the State, failed, very often, to touch just those districts which needed assistance most. But it was his proposal–as it had been that of Whitbread and Brougham, his Whig predecessors, though not of Roebuck–that the new schools should be substantially under Church control, although with every security for freedom of conscience. The trustees he proposed were the parish clergyman, two of the churchwardens nominated by him, and four further persons, two of them millowners, to be nominated by the local magistrates in special session. It was improbable that one, at least, of the nominated trustees would not side with the clerical *bloc*, and so give it a permanent majority. The opposition of the enemies in principle of factory legislation was to be expected. But what was apparently unanticipated was the storm of criticism from Dissenters outside Parliament, in which the Wesleyans, hitherto rather for than against the Church in education matters, joined.[2] The provision that the schoolmaster should be a Churchman was also criticized by Russell, a reluctant opponent, as the revival of the defunct Test Act. Graham brought forward new proposals in an effort to placate the opposition;[3] the trustees were now to be the incumbent, a nominee of his, a representative of the more substantial donors to the school fund, and four elected representatives of ratepayers assessed at £10 and more. He also proposed that while the appointment of the headmaster should be subject to the bishop's veto, the appointment of other teachers should be made by the trustees. It is to be noted that the Bill did not abandon the voluntary system, so far as concerned the provision of schools; it was still to be necessary for the locality to subscribe a third of the capital cost, and on this condition a further third was to be lent by the State, and the remainder granted. Moreover, rate aid was not to be called on till an auditor's scrutiny had proved it necessary. But Graham's concessions, and his eloquent plea for the Bill, proved unavailing; the education clauses had to be jettisoned. Ashley, speaking with the authority that his position as a leading Evangelical and the chief public friend of the factory children[4] gave to him, pronounced a verdict on the tragedy of their sacrifice to sectarian differences from which there can be little dissent.[5]

Despite this check, by the 'fifties and 'sixties schools were covering the ground. The chief agency in this process was, without any doubt, the parson. To run a school had become almost as much a part of his accepted duty as his weekly sermons; wife and daughters were called in to help; and the Newcastle Report testifies to the financial sacrifice, out of proportion to their means, which parsons all over the country made in the cause. The description by one of the inspectors of the efforts of some of them in the North as 'heroic' is by no means exaggerated. According to the measure of their opportunities other religious bodies were not less active. A strong party, cohering round Congregationalism, for a long time refused any State aid, and notwithstanding this achieved a considerable result. Elsewhere schemes of rate aid were pressed, and a Manchester and Salford Bill on these lines, based on an agreement of the leading religious bodies, was barely defeated in the House of Commons in 1854.

[1] No. 237. [2] Part IV, No. 119. [3] No. 238. [4] Part XII. [5] No. 239.

Another group agitated for publicly provided secular education, with access to the schools for ministers of the various denominations at stated times, so that they might provide the religious instruction of their respective flocks.

In 1858 the Newcastle Commission was appointed to inquire into the present state of popular education in England. It reported in 1861. In one aspect it was a tale of considerable achievement that it had to record. The voluntary principle had succeeded in getting nearly as high a proportion of the eligible children into schools as the compulsory principle in Prussia, and a higher proportion than in Holland or France.[1] One of the Assistant Commissioners had failed to find "a moderately respectable man, making 12*s*. a week and upwards" who did not send his children to school. This was while the children's pence provided roughly a third of the maintenance cost of State-aided schools – approximately £1,600,000 – voluntary subscription and the State sharing the other two-thirds. The State-aided schools, so far as popular education was concerned, were better than the purely private ones; but the general standard of the education imparted by them, the regularity and length of period of attendance, and the availability of schools in some of the districts most needing them – the point to which Graham's Bill had been directed – all left very much to be desired. Fraser, one of the Assistant Commissioners, afterwards bishop of Manchester, gave, as his standard of adequacy in rural districts, "reading, writing, and spelling, so as to be able to write a letter, sufficient knowledge to be able to attach a reasonably accurate idea to mention he may hear of foreign parts, enough knowledge of scripture to follow a plain sermon, and sufficient recollection of the catechism to guide his conduct". This had, in general, to be obtained before the age of ten, as the lad or girl might then very probably begin work. In consequence the standard was very often not attained. The effect of employment, not always, despite the extension of the Factory Acts, entailing obligatory school attendance, is much emphasized as a cause of bad attendance and early school-leaving. But the general conclusion of the Commission that barely a quarter of the children attending school left with an adequate elementary education was hotly contested by the inspectors on whose reports it purported to be based, and Lowe, the Vice-President of the Council, had later to disavow it. The inspectors equally repudiated the suggestion that they had sacrificed the more elementary part of education to the more advanced stages which special grants had enabled many schools to build up. The Report also commented on the amount of office work entailed by the complications of the grants. It recommended against compulsion, a principle that in its view was losing ground, but proposed that in future grants should come from two sources: from the State, based on attendance and the general efficiency of the school, and from the county and borough rates, based on the results of an examination in reading, writing, and arithmetic. Special local boards of education were to be set up to conduct the examinations with the assistance of the inspectors.

The plan of rate support of schools without ratepayer control won nobody's suffrage. The same was not true of the suggestion of payment by results. This was embodied by Lowe in the Revised Code of 1862. The speech of Lord Granville, Lowe's chief, is the most temperate official statement of the policy behind it;[2] Lowe, in the House of Commons, spoke of the régime of bounties and protection which had hitherto prevailed in the educational world, and of the desirability of introducing a little Free Trade into it. In a later speech he promised that the new system "if not

[1] No. 244. [2] No. 245.

cheap, would be efficient, and if not efficient, it should be cheap". It was cheap; the education estimates went down, and despite a more flexible Tory code in 1867 did not rise to their 1861 level until 1870. Substantially the new code cut away, or cut down, building grants, salary grants, grants for the training of pupil teachers, payments to training colleges, teachers' pensions, and the various special grants. In their place it substituted a single grant payable on attendance and on the results of examinations in reading, writing, and arithmetic. Its publication raised a terrific storm; school and training college managers and authorities, on the one hand and teachers on the other, regarded it as a breach of the public undertakings on the faith of which they had embarked, the one their personal credit and contributions, the other their talent and industry; the bulk of the inspectors were notoriously opposed to what they regarded as the destruction of their professional work, and to the transformation of themselves–for on them would fall the interminable examining–into a species of educational excisemen; the revered voice of Kay-Shuttleworth was raised against it; the bulk of informed opinion thought that the changes would lead to the sacrifice of higher educational values–including religious training–to the scramble to make ends meet by pushing as many youngsters as possible through the examination machine. Lowe had twice to re-revise his code; but to the qualities of the academic politician–confidence in superior education and brains combined with defective human contacts–he allied those of a bonny fighter, and substantially he carried it. Within the narrow aims it set, it raised the standard of efficiency.

Lowe had grasped the nettle, but he had grasped the wrong nettle. The problem which called for immediate attention was that at which Graham's Bill had been aimed, and which the Newcastle Commission's scheme of education boards had been intended to solve, the problem, namely, of the urban districts in which there were neither enough schools nor enough wealth and public spirit in alliance to provide them under the voluntary system as it operated in the rest of the country. The Reform Act of 1867 gave the classes and districts thus situated the power to compel attention to their plight, and the problem could no longer be burked. For its peaceful solution every ounce of the goodwill built up in a generation of successful effort–which Lowe had so rashly emperilled–was to be necessary. Already, to the demand for the extreme Dissenting solution–secular (or, as it was now decided to call it, non-sectarian) education in the schools, with permission for ministers to come into the schools for the purposes of separate religious instruction–there was added the new and strident voice of Joseph Chamberlain, carrying with him the weight of Birmingham Radicalism, the best organized and most purposeful in the country. Gladstone's Vice-President of the Council in his 1868 Ministry was W. E. Forster, a Quaker who had left the Society on his marriage to the daughter of Dr. Arnold, committed, therefore, both to tolerance and to education. The speech in which he introduced his Education Bill of 1870[1] nearly carried the House by its warmth and humanity, till the impression it had created was checked by the acid incisiveness of Winterbotham, a Congregationalist, and the advanced Liberal member for Stroud. Forster had proposed to divide the country into school districts; to hold an inquiry into the provision of schools in each of them; if it was inadequate, to leave a period in which it might be made good by voluntary effort; and in default of this to charge a school board, elected for the district, to make the necessary provision at the public expense. Thus he built on the voluntary system, and afforded it a further opportunity, to which a

[1] No. 248.

remarkable response was made. In the five months' "period of grace" sixteen hundred successful applications for building grants were made, and two-thirds of the million and a half new school places created between 1870 and 1876 were owing to voluntary rather than to public initiative. Forster had provided a stringent conscience clause to be imposed on all schools in receipt of public aid, but he had proposed to allow school boards themselves to decide the religious complexion of their schools, and also whether to compel attendance. Liberal and Nonconformist opposition to the Bill increased, and the Government was forced to accept the Cowper-Temple clause, under which "no religious catechism or religious formulary which is distinctive of any particular denomination" was to be taught in board schools. But undenominational Bible teaching was permitted; Forster declared that he would sooner cut off his right hand than be a party to banishing the Bible from the schools. The Government had also to make other concessions; school boards were not to be entitled to contribute to the maintenance of denominational schools out of rates, although, in part compensation, the national contribution to them was increased; and boards were to be directly elected by ratepayers, thus opening the way to what was to become, in some districts, a very active form of local politics. The Bill was carried finally as much by Conservative as by Liberal votes; it was, in fact, a characteristic achievement of that central opinion in politics which party extremes so easily misportray. Nonconformist resentment in the Liberal ranks took long to die down, and played a considerable part in the weakening of Gladstone's Government and his defeat in 1874.

That the first Education Act should have been so largely a recognition and regulation of the work of private agencies epitomizes much in Victorian society. To see the defects of what had thus been created is easy; more difficult is it to see how else, without the gravest risk of social disruption, anything commensurable could have been accomplished. To have rushed in where Peel and Graham quailed might have been more than courage. It is easy, too, to criticize the narrowness of sect. But within that narrow frame there grew a practical social generosity and ardour to which it is difficult to find a parallel. One achievement of voluntarism was at any rate indispensable. By its demand upon individual conscience and effort, through the medium of the Churches, it gave the whole country the consciousness of the importance of education.

Even before the Elementary Education Act had passed, however, the problem it dealt with was slipping to the second rank in point of national importance. Matthew Arnold had already urged on the Newcastle Commission that the dominant problem of the time was to "organize your secondary education". Outside the newer public schools, some proprietary schools for the middle classes such as Failand in Somerset and West Buckland in Devon, and private schools, the provision for secondary education depended almost entirely on ancient endowments. Private schools commanded wide support, in an age that readily believed that you only got what was worth paying for by paying for it. But if they were good, as the Taunton Commission remarked, the tendency was for them to seek to rise in the social scale; and if they were bad, they might be nearly as bad as Dotheboys Hall. Ancient educational endowments were mostly for grammar schools, and Lord Eldon had laid it down, in 1805, that grammar schools were schools in which Greek and Latin were taught. Not till the Grammar Schools Act of 1840 was some flexibility in their teaching permitted. The provisions of a great many educational trusts were completely out of touch with modern conditions. In the majority of cases their terms might be varied by application through a Master in Chancery, but what this might mean in expense and delay is illustrated in Part VI.[1] In 1818, largely at Brougham's instance, Commissioners for Charitable Trusts had been appointed. They sat almost continuously till 1837, producing thirty-eight volumes of reports.[2] The resulting publicity led to a more scrupulous management of many trusts, and ultimately to the appointment of permanent Charity Commissioners, under Acts of 1853 and 1860, with powers to amend or rescind impracticable provisions. This aided many schools, but produced only piecemeal progress, so far as the provision for secondary education was concerned.

In 1864 the Taunton Commission was set up to inquire into endowed schools. It reported in 1867. It stated the national need, and drew up a plan of requirements for schools in three grades, corresponding roughly to upper, middle, and lower classes, with the emphasis on modern and commercial subjects increasing down the scale.[3] There is a noteworthy vindication of the need of women's education, which reminds us that those great ladies, Miss Buss and Miss Beale, had already begun, in North London and Cheltenham, their work of demonstrating that, in point of intellectual achievement and discipline, girls' schools need lag no whit behind boys'. The Commissioners proposed that the powers of the Charity Commissioners to deal with school trusts should be enlarged; that they should have a representative in all regions or counties, who should be a member of all school trusts; and that with the help of local nominees, or where the interest in education was active enough, possibly of local representatives, they should attempt to plan the resources of the region according to its needs. Parishes and towns were to be permitted to rate themselves for support of schools of the third grade, and, in conjunction, for those of the second. They also recommended a system of regular inspection and examination, of which private schools should be allowed to avail themselves if they wished. It was an imaginative plan, but before its time, on a subject on which the consciousness of the nation had only begun to be stirred. The Endowed Schools Act of 1869, which Forster piloted through the House of Commons, enlarged the powers of the Charity Commissioners to deal with educational trusts, but did no more than accelerate processes of reform already in operation.

The greater public schools had their own Commission and Act. It is perhaps not too much to say that earlier in the century their teaching had reduced itself to an endless conning of the minutiae of the grammer and versification of the classical tongues, and their discipline to a savage rule of the rod, interspersing an anarchy in which elder boys tyrannized over younger, and stronger over weaker, with all the unimaginative brutality of the natural boy. Butler, at Shrewsbury (1798–1836), had begun the reformation of the curriculum by restoring the emphasis more to the classical literatures themselves, with the result that Shrewsbury boys swept the prize and scholarship boards at the universities; and he also recognized and contained the authority of the elder boys by making them the instruments of his own discipline as *praeposters*. Arnold, at Rugby (1827–1842), carried the same tendencies further, introducing modern subjects, while preserving the classical staple of the teaching; enlarging prefect rule, and concentrating his own influence on his Sixth and on the Chapel, whence, Jehovah-like in his wisdom and kindness, and severity where needful, he ruled the school. He radiated an influence which, as Provost Hawkins of Oriel had prophesied of him in recommending his appointment, did not cease of its effect, despite his premature death, until he had changed the face of education in England.

[1] Part VI, Introduction and No. 157. [2] Nos. 231, 247. [3] No. 247.

The Clarendon Commission on the Public Schools, appointed in 1861 and reporting in 1864, had to face the facts that the schools they were reporting on had affirmed their place as the educational instruments of the governing class–including large sections of the middle class which had won its way to power–that their example was being imitated in new foundations, such as Cheltenham, Marlborough, and Wellington, and that with all their faults they represented the liveliest growing-point in English education, a fruit, and a source of nourishment to the English social and political tradition. They had, in the first place, to deal with the problems raised by the trust deeds of the foundations. Harrow, Rugby, and Shrewsbury were originally local foundations, with privileges for local residents which led to an influx into their towns of parents anxious to share them for their sons. The Commissioners decided[1] that the schools had become national institutions, and that local privileges ought to be progressively widened till they became national scholarships. It is impossible not to feel some sympathy with the Harrow tradesman, who, before a later inquiry, in reply to the question whether the strictly classical education of the school was the education Harrow tradesmen wanted for their sons, said, "Yes: they see great statesmen and great financiers at the head of the government rise out of a classical education, and they think this is the education their sons ought to have." The Commission had a little more difficulty in deciding that the references to "poor and indigent scholars" in foundation deeds required to be glossed with the social circumstances of the sixteenth and seventeenth centuries in mind, and that the endowments were intended for education rather than for poverty. They found many provisions for the government of schools which were not in touch with contemporary needs, and recommended a general pattern which left the headmaster responsible for the internal government of the school, with its broad policy and finances controlled by governors. They received evidence from the universities of the unsatisfactoriness of much of the classical teaching, though its best was the best that the country provided; and they themselves criticized the absence of history, modern languages, and science from the curricula. But on its intrinsic merits, in the interests of maintaining a single and intelligible standard of achievement, and, indeed, one universe of intellectual discourse, they vindicated the classical curriculum as the centre of the teaching. They also took note of the remnants still remaining of barbarous discipline, and barbarous subordination of the little boys to the great, as well of the humanization that had taken place; and they paid a tribute to the part that self-government in school played in preparing boys for leadership in the larger world. Substantially, the Report was a vindication of the better elements of the public-school tradition as it had taken shape in the century. The Public Schools Act of 1868 provided for the reform of trust deeds, and prepared the way for the progressive implementation of the Commission's recommendations, without subjecting the schools to further external control.

In the universities more of the dead hand of the past was apparent than of its sustaining influence. Signs of reform there were; in both universities written examinations were superseding the moribund disputations inherited from the past, and the institution of class lists had provided a new incentive to intellectual exertion among the undergraduates. But the number who took pass degrees, and spent the bulk of their time in hunting and drinking was still considerable. The story is told that some undergraduates of Magdalen wished to stay up over Christmas, ostensibly for reading, in reality to hunt. President Routh put up a notice that there would be compulsory

[1] No. 246.

chapel every day, and no dinner in Hall for the period, with the remark that "This sort goeth not out save by prayer and fasting." Already, earlier in the century, the scholarship in their chosen fields, classics and mathematics, and the teaching and organization of the universities had been attacked in a series of articles in the *Edinburgh Review*. Between 1831 and 1836, Sir William Hamilton, an ex-Snell Exhibitioner of Balliol, renewed the attack from the same quarter. To Hamilton, Oxford was at once the most imperfect and the most perfectible of academic institutions. The root of the trouble lay, in his view, in the virtual supercession of the university by the colleges; the university was in suspense; a knot of Heads of Houses, themselves chosen by Fellows elected under statutes that gave local or kinship preferences, inhibited the development of the professorial system and kept teaching within the colleges under the so-called 'tutorial system', which was really a system of advanced class instruction. The cure lay in Royal or Parliamentary intervention, in the remodelling of statutes, the resumption by the university of its teaching functions, and the opening of new Halls of Residence, to which Dissenters could be admitted. As things were, undergraduates could not be admitted to Oxford, and at Cambridge they could not take degrees, without subscribing to the Thirty-nine Articles. Hamilton's criticisms laid down the lines of division between reformers and conservatives for the next generation. A sharp attack on the Anglican monopoly, launched on the crest of the Radical wave of the 'thirties, resulted in the passing of a Bill for the admission of Dissenters through the Commons in 1834, but it was lost in the Lords. Meanwhile University College, London, with its brilliant professoriate, its medical school and hospital in 1834, was growing in strength, and knew no religious tests. King's College, its Anglican counterpart, got off to a slower start, but in 1836 London University was created as a degree-granting body, and in 1858 was empowered to grant degrees, except in medicine, to students not attending its colleges. A different, more popular, and more strictly intellectual conception of university education was being illustrated.

Wellington, as Chancellor of Oxford, had promised in 1837 that the university should reform itself. But both in Oxford, and to a lesser extent in Cambridge, the stranglehold of the Heads of Houses on the Hebdomadal Board and Senatus respectively caused progress to be slow. In the 'thirties and 'forties religious controversy[1] convulsed the life of Oxford, and the revival of historic Anglicanism provided new motives for attachment to the university's Laudian statutes and its traditional standards. The Oxford Movement, no doubt, gave a seriousness and idealism to undergraduate life which acted as a corrective to the older boisterousness, though university teachers giving evidence before the Clarendon Commission[2] stressed, in this respect, the influence of Arnold's pupils, and the spread of his ideals to the other public schools. At the date of the Report about a third of Oxford undergraduates came from the nine larger schools; at Cambridge just over a fifth. In other respects university life was changing; the rise of the Union from 1825 in Oxford, the first varsity cricket match in 1827, and the first boat race in 1829 both, within the period, to become annual events, provided newer, cheaper, and more popular fields for extra-academic distinction. Some broadening of teaching took place; in Cambridge it was still necessary for students who wished to achieve honours to take the Mathematical Tripos and in Oxford the Classical School, but Triposes in Mental and in Natural Science had been added at Cambridge, and Schools of Law and History and of Natural Science at Oxford, which could be taken additionally. Each university had earlier

[1] Part IV. [2] No. 246.

recognized the importance of the other's special field of study by setting up additional examinations in it. The Double First that Peel and Keble and Gladstone took at Oxford was in Classics and Mathematics.

In 1850 Lord John Russell announced[1] the Government's intention to set up a Commission of Inquiry into the Universities. Official Oxford protested[2] and refused to co-operate, though a strong body within the university had favoured the move and gave it every assistance. The Commissioners were graduates of the respective universities, and, for Oxford, included Arthur Stanley, Arnold's biographer, and the future dean of Westminster, as its secretary; Tait, ex-senior tutor of Balliol, headmaster of Rugby, and the future archbishop; and Liddell, headmaster of Westminster, and future dean of Christ Church. The Report,[3] published in 1852, was described by Viscount Canning as "one of the most able papers ever laid before either House". It was drastic both in criticism and in proposals for reform. Cambridge received its Commissioners more kindly, and was more kindly entreated. Both Reports proposed legislation to free the universities from the trammels of their ancient statutes, and to remodel their governments, and both proposed the setting up of an administrative Commission for each to carry through the details of reform. The Oxford University Act of 1854 and the Cambridge University Act of 1856 carried out these intentions, though Parliament and the Commissions in turn were reluctant to impose more than the minimum of reform from outside, and much that was contemplated in the Commissions' Reports was left to the slower processes of internal reform to achieve. But in both universities government was placed in the hands of bodies representative of Heads of Houses, professors, and resident tutors, with ratification of major measures by the body of resident masters. Dissenters were admitted to first degrees, that is to the teaching, but not to offices of government in the universities. In both, in the following period, professorial teaching developed, the range of studies and of examination was broadened, and the competition for fellowships and scholarships more widely opened. But proposals for non-collegiate Halls of Residence developed more slowly. Colleges continued to play the predominant part in teaching, and to be the effective centres of social life, and a modified tutorial system–personal rather than public teaching–to be the distinctive mark of the older universities as compared with the Scottish and London traditions. Newman's *Idea of a University* provided in 1852 a matchless vindication of the traditional English view that a coherent education requires the full life of a society dedicated to its purpose.

The 1850 Commissions provide the crucial moment of university history. In drawing power from widening sections of society, in size, in intellectual energy, in impact upon the nation, they thereafter steadily increased. They became fully national institutions. Much that was precious in association and idea was, no doubt, thereby sacrificed. In 1871, by the Religious Tests Act, Dissenters were admitted to all degrees except in Divinity, and to all offices, except those statutorily reserved for Anglicans. All but the traces of the Anglican monopoly disappeared, but in return, in the university atmosphere, sectarian animosities were mollified. Moreover, in their national role, it became possible for the older universities to play their part in the creating and shaping of the new, which in numbers, if not perhaps in influence, were shortly to outgrow them.

By 1871 Victorian education had reached its full expression. Its system, or lack of system, had many shortcomings, but on the other hand it had the virtues of variety

[1] No. 241. [2] No. 242. [3] No. 243.

and of conformity to the national character. When its products and output were compared with the erudition and technical accomplishment that resulted from the contemporary German system, or with the intellectual sophistication bred into the still marrowy bones of the growing French youth, they bore an inexpert and perhaps a slightly provincial air. But looking over the backward and abysm of time that separates our age from that, and calling to mind what the Victorians most sought to avoid – an excess of State centralization and an education directed solely to the mind, without care for the disciplines of religion and character – we can find reason, perhaps, not to be ashamed of the comparison.

SELECT BIBLIOGRAPHY

Of the *Parliamentary Debates* on primary education, the first that warms up to the subject is that on the Government's proposals to establish the Committee of Council for Education, and to set up a Normal School in 1839. The arguments and fears and prejudices involved in the issue were even more fully displayed in the debate on the education clauses of Graham's Factories Act Amendment Bill of 1843. Again, in 1847, on the Education Minutes of 1846, there were important debates in both Houses: on the Manchester and Salford Bill of 1853, in the Commons; on the Newcastle Report in 1861; on the Revised Code in 1862; and, at great length, on the Education Act of 1870. The question of the admission of Dissenters to Oxford and Cambridge was debated at some length in 1834, on the Petition from Members of the Senatus at Cambridge, and again on Wood's Bill to admit Dissenters. The crucial debates are, however, that of 1850 on Heywood's motion for the appointment of a Commission of Inquiry into the Universities, and that of 1854 on the Oxford University Bill. The debate on the parallel Cambridge University Bill was shorter and more amicable. There was a series of debates, not of major importance, on various Bills in the 'sixties to limit or abolish religious tests.

Among public papers, the *Reports of the Select Committee on Education of 1834*, and the *Select Committee on the Education of the Poorer Classes* (1835), and the similar *Committee* of 1837 (*Parlty. Papers*, 1834/IX, 1835/VII and 1837–1838/VII), provide the primary analyses of the problem. *Correspondence with reference to the setting up of the Committee of Council for Education* (*Parlty. Papers*, 1839/XLI) also contains a *Memorial on a System of General Education* submitted to Russell by the Committee of the British and Foreign School Society. The *Minutes of the Committee of Council for Education* were published among the *Parliamentary Papers*, but were also more conveniently issued separately in octavo (32 vols., London 1841–1869). They cover, primarily, the appointment of inspectors, the instructions given them, correspondence with the Churches and school societies, and the growth of the system of grants in aid, first of school building, and then of the training, salaries and superannuation of teachers, and the maintenance of schools. They contain also a great deal of material on the development of training colleges, and the reports of the inspectors, often of the highest value as documents both of general social history and of local history, including reports on special schools, such as that for the sons of Yeomen at Failand and the King's Somborne, Hants, school, on which Inspectors Allen, Moseley and Brookfield report at length between 1844 and 1854. A *Special Report by the Inspectors of Factories on Education under the Factory Acts* (*Parlty. Papers*, 1839/XLII) deals with a subject often referred to, as well, in their regular *Reports*. The subject of pauper education is dealt with in the *Reports of the Select Committee on the Administration of the Poor Laws* (*Parlty. Papers*, 1837–1838/VII), and a *Select Committee on the Education of Destitute Children* (*Parlty. Papers*, 1861/VII), and another on *Pauper Education* (*Parlty. Papers*, 1862/XLIX), are also important for this subject. They deal, *inter alia*, with Lord Shaftesbury's Ragged Schools movement. *The Royal Commission on the State of Popular Education in England* (the Newcastle Commission) covers the whole of these fields in an exhaustive *Report*, with five volumes of *Reports* from Assistant Commissioners (*Parlty. Papers*, 1861/XXI, Parts 1–6). Its conclusions were by no means universally accepted; Sir James Kay-Shuttleworth and Seymour Tremenheere defended the voluntary system in correspondence printed in a volume of Accounts and Papers (*Parlty. Papers*, 1861/XLVIII); its view of Pauper Education was challenged in the Select Committee referred to above and in another volume of Accounts and Papers containing papers from Poor Law inspectors (*Parlty. Papers*, 1862/XLIX), and the majority of the school inspectors impugned the accuracy of its account of the efficiency of current popular education in *Correspondence on Education* (*Parlty. Papers*, 1862/XLIII). These criticisms are reflected in the *Parliamentary Debates* referred to above. For the *Education Code of 1860*, see *Parlty. Papers*, 1860/LIII; the *Revised Code* in its various forms, and correspondence from Kay-Shuttleworth and Edwin Chadwick, together with memoranda from a variety of other interested authorities, is in *Parlty. Papers*, 1862/XLI. The modified *Code* of 1864 is in *Parlty. Papers*, 1864/XLIV.

On the Public Schools, the *Report of the Royal Commission on the Public Schools* (the Clarendon Report) (*Parlty. Papers*, 1864/XX and XXI), is a general *Report* with special accounts of each of the nine schools considered. Also valuable–and in some of its evidence amusing–is the *Report of the Lords Select Committee on the Public Schools Bill* (*Parlty. Papers*, 1865/X)–a committee of which Clarendon was chairman, and on which the Prince of Wales sat. An Appendix contains *Memoranda on Science in Education* by HUXLEY and TINDAL.

On Endowed Schools earlier sources of information are the *Report of the Select Committee on Charitable Trusts* (*Parlty. Papers*, 1835/VII), and a later *Digest of Educational Charities*, giving particulars county by county (*Parlty. Papers*, 1843/XVIII). The great authority is, however, the *Report of the Schools Inquiry Commission* (the Taunton Commission) (*Parlty. Papers*, 1867–1868/XXVIII, Parts 1–28). The *Reports* of Assistant Commissioners contained in the later parts summarize the condition and history of virtually all the endowed schools in the country, and contain also a *Report* by MATTHEW ARNOLD on middle-class education in Europe, and by the REV. JAMES FRAZER on middle-class education in America.

The *Report of the Royal Commission on Oxford University* (*Parlty. Papers*, 1852/XXII), the *Report of the Royal Commission on Cambridge University* (*Parlty. Papers*, 1852–1853/XLIV), and the *Report of the Select Committee on Oxford and Cambridge*–evidence only, but nevertheless valuable–(*Parlty. Papers*, 1867/XIII), are the principal public papers on university education.

Of secondary works, J. W. ADAMSON, *English Education, 1789–1902* (London, 1930) and H. C. BARNARD, *A Short History of English Education, 1760–1944* (London, 1947), R. J. ARCHER, *Secondary Education in England* (Cambridge, 1921), C. BIRCHENOUGH, *A History of Elementary Education in England and Wales* (London, 1914), F. SMITH, *A History of English Elementary Education* (London, 1931), and F. LEESE, *Personalities and Power in English Education* (Oxford, 1951), deal generally with the subject. J. E. G. DE MONTMORENCY, *State Intervention in English Education* (Cambridge, 1902), is valuable. SIR J. KAY-SHUTTLEWORTH, *Four Periods of English Education* (London, 1862), gives the views of the man who may claim to be the founder of elementary education, and F. SMITH, *Life and Works of Sir James Kay-Shuttleworth* (London, 1923), details and discusses his career and work. MATTHEW ARNOLD, *Report on Elementary Education, 1852–82* (ed. F. MARVIN, London, 1908), claims attention as the work of the most distinguished inspector of schools. SARAH AUSTIN (translator), *Cousin's Report on Education in Prussia* (London, 1842), exercised a good deal of influence as an account of the feared and admired "Prussian system". A. P. STANLEY, *Life and Correspondence of Thomas Arnold*, 12th edn. (London, 1881), J. J. FINDLAY, *Arnold of Rugby* (London, 1897), SIR J. OTTER, *Nathaniel Woodward, a Memoir of his Life* (London, 1925), illustrate movements in public school education. E. C. MACK, *Public Schools and British Opinion* (2 vols., New York, 1938 and 1941), is more general in scope. DOROTHEA BEALE, *The Education of Girls* (Cheltenham, 1869), B. A. CLOUGH, *A Memoir of A. J. Clough* (London, 1897), E. DAVIES, *Thoughts on Some Questions relating to Women, 1860–1908*, ed. E. E. C. JONES (London, 1910), and E. RAIKES, *Dorothea Beale of Cheltenham* (London, 1908), bear on the education of women.

C. E. MALLET, *History of the University of Oxford*, vol. III, *Modern Oxford* (London, 1927), has superseded earlier works, and Cambridge has been fortunate in D. H. W. WINSTANLEY as its historian, in *Unreformed Cambridge* (Cambridge, 1935), *Early Victorian Cambridge* (Cambridge, 1940), and *Late Victorian Cambridge* (Cambridge, 1947). A. I. TILLYARD, *History of University Reform from 1800* (Cambridge, 1913), offers a view of the reform movement. SIR WILLIAM HAMILTON's sustained onslaughts on the English universities in the *Edinburgh Review* are collected in his *Discussions*–together with some remarks on the Oxford University Commission–2nd edn. (London, 1853). MARK PATTISON, *Memoirs* (London, 1883), and E. ABBOT and LEWIS CAMPBELL, *Life and Letters of Benjamin Jowett*, 3rd edn. (2 vols., London, 1897), paint both a period and personalities. MARK PATTISON, *Oxford Studies* (London, 1855), and *Suggestions for Academical Reform* (London, 1868), W. WHEWELL, *Liberal Education, with especial Reference to Cambridge* (London, 1850), and J. H. NEWMAN, *The Idea of a University* (Dublin, 1852), expound the views, conservative and reforming, of the time. J. A. FROUDE, *The Oxford Counter-Reformation* in *Short Studies in Great Subjects*, vol. IV (4 vols., London, 1893), and WALTER BAGEHOT, *Oxford* (1882), republished in *Literary Studies*, vol. III (London, 1895), should perhaps not be neglected. H. H. BELLOT, *University College, London, 1826–1926* (London, 1929), and F. HEARNSHAW, *Centenary History of King's College, London* (London, 1929), celebrate the two great foundations from which London University has sprung.

ASHER TROPP, *The School Teachers* (1957) – position and struggles of elementary school teachers; BRIAN SIMON, *Studies in the History of Education 1780–1870* (1960); H. J. BURGESS, *Enterprise in Education* (1958) – work of Church in education; JAMES MURPHY, *The Religious Problem in English Education: The Crucial Experiment* (1959) – early Liverpool experiment in secular education; V. H. H. GREEN, *An Oxford Common Room* (1957) Lincoln College; JOHN SPARROW, *Mark Pattison and the Idea of a University* (1967); GEOFFREY FABER, *Jowett* (1957); W. R. WARD, *Victorian Oxford* (1965); D. NEWSOME, *History of Wellington College* (1959); L. P. WEHNAM, *Letters of James Tate* (1966) – country school to St. Paul's; J. P. T. BURY, *Romilly's Cambridge Diary 1832–42* (1967).

228. The position in the 'thirties: William Cotton on the work of the National Society

Parlty. Papers, 1834/IX, *qq.* 1876–1878.

What progress has the society made during the 23 years it has existed, and what is the extent of its connexion at present?–I have been endeavouring to refresh my memory with what has been done by the society, and I have made extracts from the Reports. In 1813 there were 230 schools in union, containing 40,484 children: such were the effects of the first operations of the society. There have been returns made since from the different schools in union, and also from those acting upon the same principle. For I should observe there are many schools acting precisely upon the same principle as the National Society, which are not in union with it, and from which schools a return has been obtained of the number of children under education. From the return, which comes down to 1831, it appears there were 10,965 schools in union and acting upon the same principle, having in them under education 740,000 children; but as no returns were received from many places, it was considered requisite to add to the above number an estimate of the number educated in those places, by which the number of children educated under the Church of England was brought up to 900,000. We now consider that the total number of children under education amounts to 1,000,000, and that more than 500,000 of them are educating in schools in union with the National Society, 3,500 places having now schools in union with the National Society.

Will you have the goodness to put in these Returns?–

(*The Witness delivered in the same, which are as follows:–*)

[See Table on page 846]

PROGRESS OF NATIONAL SCHOOLS

In 1813 (two years after the formation of the society) there were 230 schools in union, containing 40,484 children. In 1817 (when the society was incorporated) the statement made was, schools 725, scholars 117,000; and in 1820 (the period at which the last account was published, previous to that from which this corrected estimate was formed) there were 1,614 schools, and rather more (than) 200,000 scholars. These totals are now, in 1830, carried up to 2,609 places, containing about 3,670 schools, with about 346,000 scholars.

Progress of the Religions Education of the Poor in *England* and *Wales*, ascertained from the results of three Inquiries in 1819, 1826 and 1831. (Extracted from the Annual Report of the National Society for 1832.)

FIRST RESULT IN 1819

Obtained by means of Circulars addressed to the Clergy of the Established Church, by Order of Parliament.
N.B.–The Population of England and Wales in the preceding Census of 1811, was 10,150,615.

	England				Wales			
	Schools endowed wholly or partially		*Unendowed schools*		*Schools endowed wholly or partially*		*Unendowed schools*	
	Schools	*Scholars*	*Schools*	*Scholars*	*Schools*	*Scholars*	*Schools*	*Scholars*
On the new System of Mutual Instruction	302	39,590	820	105,582	10	990	41	4,480
Ordinary Schools on the old System	3,865	125,843	10,360	319,643	199	6,635	458	16,873
	4,167	165,433	11,180	425,225	209	7,625	499	21,353
Endowed Schools	—	—	4,167	165,433	—	—	209	7,625
			15,347	590,658			708	28,978
		Schools &c. in England		. .	. .	. . .	15,347	590,658
		Grand Total	. .	. .	. .	. . .	16,055	619,636

THIRD RESULT IN JANUARY 1832

Obtained by means of Circulars as on the National Society's previous Inquiry in 1826.
N.B.–The Population of England and Wales in the Preceding Census of 1831 was 13,894,574.

N.B.–This is the state of education in January 1831; the circulars by which the result was obtained were all dated for the 1st January 1831, and were issued in December 1830 and January 1831. The Returns in the Report give the number of schools and scholars, &c.

Can you state the present number?–The Report now in the press states the number of places in which there are schools in union with the society at upwards of 3,500, such schools educating above 500,000 children; and, including schools acting upon the same principle, though not immediately in connexion, 1,000,000 of children are educating in them.

SUNDAY SCHOOLS

	England		Wales	
	Schools	*Scholars*	*Schools*	*Scholars*
On the new System of Mutual Instruction	404	50,979	8	713
Ordinary Schools on the old System .	4,758	401,838	293	23,695
Total Sunday Schools 5,463; Scholars 477,225	5,162	452,817	301	24,408

SECOND RESULT IN 1826

Obtained by means of Circulars addressed by the National Society to the Clergy of the Established Church, under favour of a free cover granted by His Majesty's Government. N.B.–The Population of England and Wales in the preceding Census of 1821 was 11,978,875.

DIOCESE	*Schools*	*Scholars*	DIOCESE	*Schools*	*Scholars*
Bangor . . .	46	2,248	Lincoln . .	852	46,977
Bristol . . .	213	13,921	Lichfield & Coventry	574	37,098
Bath and Wells .	292	16,925	Llandaff . .	59	2,793
Canterbury . .	227	12,992	Norwich . .	706	32,125
Carlisle . . .	79	4,056	Oxford . . .	161	7,689
Chichester . .	141	8,114	Peterboro' . .	249	13,624
Chester . . .	466	57,619	Rochester . .	80	5,610
Durham . . .	167	10,133	Salisbury . .	329	18,437
Ely . . .	80	7,123	St. David's . .	136	8,431
Exeter . . .	411	23,557	St. Asaph . .	61	3,700
Gloucester . .	274	14,312	Winchester . .	333	21,464
Hereford . .	155	8,699	Worcester . .	170	11,308
London . . .	536	34,780	York . . .	679	51,201
TOTAL	3,087	214,479	TOTAL	4,388	260,449
				3,087	214,479
Returns in which the Schools, &c. are accurately given .				7,475	474,928
410 Schools entered, the Children of which were omitted .					20,500
Calculation upon the returns not received				924	55,000
			TOTAL	8,399	550,428

229. Education in large towns: report of the Select Committee on the Education of the Poorer Classes (1837–1838)

Parlty. Papers, 1837–1838/VII/pp. VII–IX.

Your committee now turn to the state of Education in the large manufacturing and seaport towns, where the population has rapidly increased within the present century; they refer for particulars to the Evidence taken before them, which appears to bear out the following results:

1st. That the kind of education given to the children of the working classes is lamentably deficient.

2nd. That it extends (bad as it is) to but a small proportion of those who ought to receive it.

3rd. That without some strenuous and persevering efforts be made on the part of Government, the greatest evils to all classes may follow from this neglect.

PLACE	*Population*	*Children of working classes at Daily schools, viz.*		TOTAL
		Day and Dame schools Very indifferent	*Other better schools*	
1836 Liverpool	230,000	11,336	14,024	25,000
1834 Manchester	200,000	11,520	5,680	17,100
1835 Salford	50,810	3,340	2,015	5,350
— Bury	20,000	1,648	803	2,451
1835 {Ashton, Duckenfield, Staley Bridge}	47,800	—	—	2,496
1837 Birmingham	180,000	8,180	4,697	12,877
1837 Bristol	112,438	. . . not including scholars in private schools . . .	5 to 15	4,135
			Total	5,254
1838 Brighton {B. & F.	40,634	1,367	3,053	4,400
National}	in 1831	863	3,247	4,110
1837 West Bromwich	—	. . . of 6,375 children under 14 years old	—	1,554
1838 Leeds (B. & F.)	123,393 in 1831	. . . no return of Dame or Day, but only Public schools	2,971	—
1838 Sheffield	96,692 in 1831	3,359	5,905	9,314
Northampton {B. & F.	20,000	1,011	1,215	2,226
National}		996	1,202	2,198
Reading (B. & F.)	15,595 in 1831	297	962	1,259
Exeter	28,242 in 1831	2,045	1,830 including evening	3,875
1836 York	25,359 in 1831	1,494	2,697	4,191

Note.–The general result of all these towns is, that about one in 12 receives some sort of daily instruction, but only about one in 24 an education likely to be useful. In Leeds, only one in 41; in Birmingham, one in 38; in Manchester, one in 35.

Your Committee do not propose in this place to enter into more detail on this subject, but refer to the Evidence taken before them; they would especially beg to refer to the Evidence of Dr. Kay, Mr. Riddall Wood, Mr. Corrie, and Mr. Buxton. These gentlemen describe in strong terms the misery and crime likely to arise from the neglected education of the children of the working classes in populous places.

Your Committee are fully persuaded that to this cause (embracing the want of religious and moral training) is to be chiefly attributed the great increase of criminals and consequently of cost to the country.

With regard to the numbers of children attending Sunday Schools, Your Committee do not think it necessary to enter into any long details, but refer to the Evidence on this point; they consider the instruction there given as of great advantage, by implanting feelings of religion and giving habits of order; but as imperfect without daily instruction also. They subjoin a short abstract of the numbers of children attending Sunday Schools in some of the larger towns.

CHILDREN IN SUNDAY SCHOOLS

Place	*Established Church*	*Dissenters*	*Catholics*
Manchester	10,284	19,932	3,812
Salford	2,741	6,250	613
Liverpool	6,318	8,350	700
Birmingham	4,500	11,830	338
Bristol	2,631	8,477	—
Brighton	870	1,820	—
Sheffield, B. & F.	2,687	8,705	—
Leeds, B. & F.	4,130	11,886	—
Wakefield, National	500	1,384	—
Northampton	{1,091 N[l] Ret[n] 788 B. & F.}	1,288	—
Exeter {National	2,470	1,193	—
Exeter {B. & F.	2,115	1,208	—
Reading	1,000	509	—
Westminster, 5 parishes	683	872	—
York	1,708	1,655	—

230. Education under the Factory Act: reports of inspectors of factories (1839)

Parlty. Papers, 1839/XLII/p. 357.

. . . But there is one factory school so superior to the rest, and so deserving of being held up as an example, to be imitated as closely as circumstances will allow, that I cannot refrain from mentioning it especially; and if the rest of the owners named in the list were to visit this school, they would, I am sure, at once admit that they have each something to do to bring their own to an equal degree of excellence. The school to which I allude is that established in the factory of Messrs. M'Connel & Co., of Manchester. They have provided a large, well-warmed and well-ventilated room, suitably and substantially furnished; they have engaged a competent and zealous master and mistress; reading, writing and arithmetic are taught to the children of both sexes; the girls are instructed in different kinds of needlework, and excellent maps are provided, and preparations are now making for teaching geography. Religious and moral training and habits of order, good breeding, and cleanliness and attention to neatness in dress have been objects of constant attention from the commencement, and the owners have it now under consideration to introduce a more special religious instruction, but which shall, at the same time, in no degree interfere with the conscientious scruples of the parents of the children, who, it will readily be supposed, in such a place as Manchester, must belong to various sects. The children are employed in the mill six hours a day, and attend school three hours. The school is opened in the evening for the benefit of those above thirteen years of age, who wish to avail themselves of its advantages when the day's work is over; and it is at present attended by forty-six voluntary scholars of this description from the mill. Six of the adult operatives have been selected as a visiting committee, an arrangement which is attended with many and great advantages. It secures a superintendence in aid of that of the proprietors, and the schoolmaster has the satisfaction of knowing that his exertions will be appreciated by those whose good opinion must be of great service to him. It is, besides, a link of good feeling and sympathy between the master and his work-people, the want of which is, I am persuaded, the main source of most of the evils that have been sometimes found to arise out of the unions and other combinations of the work-people. All my experience and all my inquiries have led me to the conviction, that the disposition of the working classes is to look up with respect and regard to their superiors, when they are kindly and considerately dealt with by them. But when there is an entire estrangement, when the proprietor of the factory never utters a word of friendly inquiry about them and their families, when he does not even know the faces of his work-people, but leaves all intercourse with them to subordinate agents, as is often the case in great towns, is it to be wondered at that they should believe the interest of the employer and the employed to be opposed, and that they should seek for advice any where rather than from their master? Mr. Heathcote, the superintendent of the Manchester division, in a late weekly report, states, "On Christmas-day I attended an examination of the children at Messrs. M'Connel's mills, by invitation. The examination did infinite credit to the children and their teachers, and reflects the highest honour upon the worthy proprietors." ...

231A–B. Endowed Schools: Select Committee on Charities (1835)

Parlty. Papers, 1835/VII.

231A. Berkhampstead

loc. cit., p. 645.

... Your Committee desire to invite attention to the case of the Berkhampstead Grammar School, as, apart from its own peculiar circumstances, it serves to illustrate the nature of the defects which pervade, in very many instances, similar institutions throughout the country, where, even though superintended by a Special Visitor, and administered under the Court of Equity, the Master of the School is practically beyond any existing control, and the funds of the endowment are wasted by the costs and delay inseparable from legal proceedings.

In this case Your Committee find that a valuable institution, with large funds and appropriate premises, adequate to the free education of a great number of children, and the liberal maintenance of the necessary instructors, with a surplus fund which, rightly administered according to the design of the benevolent founder, would afford comfortable provision to many deserving objects, in all material circumstances the reverse of what it ought to be. Your Committee find a Master and Usher, the latter the son of the Master, and appointed by him when a minor, the incorporated Trustees of the charity property, receiving to their own use considerable stipends, the school-house dilapidated, no boys on the foundation, and the surplus revenue so exhausted by law and other expenses as to leave an uncertain trifle for the relief of the poor. . . .

231B. State of grammar schools: Evidence of W. Grant, Stipendiary Commissioner

loc. cit., p. 660.

Would you say generally that the number of grammar schools is greater than required for the advantage of those for whom they were intended?—I think the foundations in some particular instances are useless ones from change of circumstances, but I should be very sorry to apply any general observation to all of them; in many places they supply a convenient house and residence, to tempt a scholar to settle in and take pupils, making the instruction of youth his profession and calling, and by the means of these endowments many opportunities are afforded, that would not otherwise be given, of opening classical schools.

Do they not in many instances afford the lowest class of society the power of educating their sons, and by means of a classical education to rise to the highest ranks of professions?—No doubt such instances occur frequently; in many cases the schools are connected with endowments of colleges; there is one at Bromsgrove, in Worcestershire, which is connected with Worcester college, Oxford, where the scholars have considerable advantages. As these schools throw open to every class of persons the means of advancing themselves in life, I think we should hesitate before we put an end to these opportunities, because we find in any particular instance a school that is useless. . . .

232. Setting up of Committee of Council for Education: Lord John Russell's letter to Lord Lansdowne (4 February 1839)

Parlty. Papers, 1839/XLI/pp. 255–257.

Whitehall, 4 February 1839.

My Lord,

I HAVE received Her Majesty's Commands to make a communication to your Lordship on a subject of the greatest importance. Her Majesty has observed with deep concern the want of instruction which is still observable among the poorer classes of Her subjects. All the inquiries which have been made show a deficiency in the general Education of the People which is not in accordance with the character of a Civilized and Christian Nation.

The reports of the chaplains of gaols show that to a large number of unfortunate prisoners a knowledge of the fundamental truths of natural and revealed Religion has never been imparted.

It is some consolation to Her Majesty to perceive that of late years the zeal for popular education has increased, that the Established Church has made great efforts to promote the building of schools, and that the National and British and Foreign School Societies have actively endeavoured to stimulate the liberality of the benevolent and enlightened friends of general Education.

Still much remains to be done; and among the chief defects yet subsisting may be reckoned the insufficient number of qualified schoolmasters, the imperfect mode of teaching which prevails in perhaps the greater number of the schools, the absence of any sufficient inspection of the schools, and examination of the nature of the instruction given, the want of a Model School which might serve for the example of those societies and committees which anxiously seek to improve their own methods of teaching, and, finally, the neglect of this great subject among the enactments of our voluminous Legislation.

Some of these defects appear to admit of an immediate remedy, and I am directed by Her Majesty to desire, in the first place, that your Lordship, with four other of the Queen's Servants, should form a Board or Committee, for the consideration of all matters affecting the Education of the People.

For the present it is thought advisable that this Board should consist of:

The Lord President of the Council.
The Lord Privy Seal.
The Chancellor of the Exchequer.
The Secretary of State for the Home Department, and
The Master of the Mint.

It is proposed that the Board should be entrusted with the application of any sums which may be voted by Parliament for the purposes of Education in England and Wales.

Among the first objects to which any grant may be applied will be the establishment of a Normal School.

In such a school a body of schoolmasters may be formed, competent to assume the management of similar institutions in all parts of the country. In such a school likewise the best modes of teaching may be introduced, and those who wish to improve the schools of their neighbourhood may have an opportunity of observing their results.

The Board will consider whether it may not be advisable for some years to apply a sum of money annually in aid of the Normal Schools of the National and of the British and Foreign School Societies.

They will likewise determine whether their measures will allow them to afford gratuities to deserving schoolmasters; there is no class of men whose rewards are so disproportionate to their usefulness to the community.

In any Normal or Model School to be established by the Board, four principal objects should be kept in view, *viz.*

1. Religious Instruction.
2. General Instruction.
3. Moral Training.
4. Habits of Industry.

Of these four I need only allude to the first; with respect to Religious Instruction there is, as your Lordship is aware, a wide or apparently wide difference of opinion among those who have been most forward in promoting education.

The National Society, supported by the Established Church, contend that the schoolmaster should be invariably a Churchman; that the Church Catechism should be taught in the school to all the scholars; that all should be required to attend Church on Sundays, and that the schools should be in every case under the superintendence of the clergyman of the parish.

The British and Foreign School Society, on the other hand, admit Churchmen and Dissenters equally as schoolmasters, require that the Bible should be taught in their schools, but insist that no Catechism should be admitted.

Others again contend that secular instruction should be the business of the school, and that the ministers of different persuasions should each instruct separately the children of their own followers.

In the midst of these conflicting opinions there is not practically that exclusiveness among the Church Societies, nor that indifference to Religion among those who exclude dogmatic instruction from the school, which their mutual accusations would lead bystanders to suppose.

Much therefore may be effected by a temperate attention to the fair claims of the Established Church, and the religious freedom sanctioned by law.

On this subject I need only say that it is Her Majesty's wish that the youth of this kingdom should be religiously brought up, and that the right of conscience should be respected.

Moreover, there is a large class of children who may be fitted to be good members of society without injury or offence to any party–I mean pauper orphans, children deserted by their parents, and the offspring of criminals and their associates.

It is from this class that the thieves and housebreakers of society are continually recruited. It is this class likewise which has filled the workhouses with ignorant and idle inmates.

The Poor Law Commissioners have very properly undertaken to amend the vicious system which has hitherto prevailed, and in the neighbourhood of the metropolis much has been already done under their auspices.

It is in this direction likewise that certain good can be accomplished. It sometimes happens that the training which the child of poor but virtuous parents receives at home, is but ill exchanged for the imperfect or faulty instruction which he receives at school debased by vicious association; but for those whose parents are dead, or who have no home but one of habitual vice, there can be no such danger.

In all such instances, by combining moral training with general instruction, the young may be saved from the temptations to crime, and the whole community receive indisputable benefit.

These and other considerations will, I am persuaded, receive from your Lordship the most careful attention. I need not enter, at present, into any further plans in contemplation for the extension of the blessings of sound and religious education.

I have, &c.

(signed) *J. RUSSELL.*

The Lord President of the Council,

&c. &c. &c.

233. Correspondence with the Education Committee of the Scotch Church Assembly (January 1840)

Parlty. Papers, 1839/XLI/pp. 385–386.

Committee of Council on Education
Council Office, Whitehall,
4 January 1840.

Sir,

I AM directed by the Committee of Council on Education to acknowledge the receipt of your letter, dated December 19th.

I am also to acknowledge the receipt of the report made by the Education Committee of the General Assembly "on the returns from Presbyteries regarding the examination of schools in the year 1839," which my Lords have perused with great interest and satisfaction.

The Committee of Council direct me to inform you, in reply to your inquiries, that the inspectors of schools aided by public grants are appointed by Her Majesty in Council, on the recommendation of the Committee of Council on Education; and, in order to afford you the fullest information respecting the duties of the inspectors, my Lords direct me to transmit the enclosed copy of instructions addressed to the inspectors for England and Wales. Instructions framed on the same principles, but modified so as to render them applicable to any peculiar circumstances in Scotland, will be issued to the inspectors for that country. With respect to such modifications, my Lords will be glad to receive any observations from the Committee of the General Assembly.

In these documents you will perceive that the inspection of schools is intended to be a means of co-operation between the Government and the ministers, local committees and trustees of schools, for the improvement and extension of elementary education; and my Lords embrace the opportunity of expressing their intention to co-operate with the Church of Scotland for the attainment of these results, as regards the schools which are placed by law, or by the condition of their endowments or constitution, under the superintendence of the Church of Scotland.

In further reply to your inquiry, my Lords direct me to assure you, that with respect to these schools, my Lords will at all times feel it their duty to communicate and co-operate with the Education Committee of the General Assembly, and will direct copies of their inspectors' reports to be transmitted to the Committee from time to time.

My Lords conceive this co-operation may best be promoted by selecting for the inspection of such schools gentlemen who possess the confidence of the Church of Scotland, while their acquaintance with all the technical details of elementary instruction, and their zeal for the education of the poorer classes, will afford a guarantee that they are fit agents for promoting the improvement and extension of such elementary education as may secure the religious and moral improvement of the children of the poor.

The Committee of Council consider that much advantage will arise from their Lordships having the opportunity of consulting the Education Committee of the General Assembly with respect to the selection of the inspectors of such schools; before, therefore, a recommendation of any gentleman for this office is made to Her Majesty in Council, my Lords will communicate the name to the Committee of the General Assembly for their observations.

I have, &c.
(signed) *J. P. KAY.*

John Gordon, Esq.,
Secretary to the Education Committee of
The General Assembly of the Church of Scotland.

234. Minute of 15 July 1840, on reference to the archbishops in appointment of inspectors to national schools

Parlty. Papers, 1840/XL/pp. 386–387.

THE Lord President having called the attention of the Committee to their previous Minutes relating to the appointment of inspectors of schools in connexion with the Church of England, their Lordships deliberated thereon, and resolved, that a report be presented to Her Majesty in Council, embodying the following recommendations: 1. That before any person is recommended to the Queen in Council to be appointed to inspect schools receiving aid from the public, the promoters of which state themselves to be in connexion with the National Society, or the Church of England, the Archbishops of Canterbury and York be consulted by the Committee of Privy Council, each with regard to his own province; and that they be at liberty to suggest any person or persons for the office of inspector, and that no person be appointed without their concurrence.

2. That the inspectors of such schools shall be appointed during pleasure, and that it shall be in the power of each Archbishop, at all times, with regard to his own province, to withdraw his concurrence in such appointment, whereupon the authority of the inspector shall cease, and a fresh appointment take place.

3. That the instructions to the inspectors with regard to religious instruction shall be framed by the Archbishops, and form part of the general instructions to the

inspectors of such schools, and that the general instructions shall be communicated to the Archbishops before they are finally sanctioned.

That each inspector at the same time that he presents any report relating to the said schools to the Committee of the Privy Council, shall transmit a duplicate thereof to the Archbishop, and shall also send a copy to the Bishop of the diocese in which the school is situate, for his information.

4. That the grants of money be in proportion to the number of children educated, and the amount of money raised by private contribution, with the power of making exceptions in certain cases, the grounds of which will be stated in the annual Returns to Parliament.

235. Instructions to inspectors (August 1840)

Minutes of Committee of Council for Education, 1840

Committee of Council on Education.
Council Office, Whitehall, Aug. 1840.

SIR,

1. Her Majesty having been graciously pleased, on the recommendation of the Committee of Council, to appoint you one of the Inspectors of Schools, the Committee request your attention to the enclosed paper of instructions, with the documents thereto annexed, for your guidance in the discharge of the duties which will devolve on you.

2. While an important part of these duties will consist in visiting, from time to time, schools aided by grants of public money made by the authority of the Committee, in order to ascertain that the grant has in each case been duly applied, and to enable you to furnish accurate information as to the discipline, management, and methods of instruction pursued in your schools, your appointment is intended to embrace a more comprehensive sphere of duty.

3. In superintending the application of the Parliamentary grant for public education in Great Britain, my Lords have in view the encouragement of local efforts for the improvement and extension of elementary education, whether made by voluntary associations or by private individuals. The employment of Inspectors is therefore intended to advance this object, by affording to the promoters of schools an opportunity of ascertaining, at the periodical visits of inspection, what improvements in the apparatus and internal arrangements of schools, in school management and discipline, and in the methods of teaching, have been sanctioned by the most extensive experience.

4. The inspection of schools aided by public grants, is, in this respect, a means of co-operation between the Government and the committees and superintendents of schools, by which information respecting all remarkable improvements may be diffused whenever it is sought; you will therefore be careful, at visits of inspection, to communicate with the [parochial clergyman, or other minister of religion,] connected with the school, and with the school committee, or, in the absence of a school committee, with the chief promoters of the school, and will explain to them that one main object of your visit is to afford them your assistance in all efforts for

improvement in which they may desire your aid; but that you are in no respect to interfere with the instruction, management, or discipline of the school, or to press upon them any suggestions which they may be disinclined to receive.

5. A clear and comprehensive view of these main duties of your office is at all times important; but when a system of inspection of schools aided by public grants is for the first time brought into operation, it is of the utmost consequence you should bear in mind that this inspection is not intended as a means of exercising control, but of affording assistance; that it is not to be regarded as operating for the restraint of local efforts, but for their encouragement; and that its chief objects will not be attained without the co-operation of the school committees;–the Inspector having no power to interfere, and not being instructed to offer any advice or information excepting where it is invited.

6. . . . In submitting the route of your visits of inspection for the approval of this Committee, my Lords request you to include these schools in your arrangements. When engaged in the inspection of a school aided by a public grant, a requisition may be presented to you from the promoters of some school, in the same town or village, not aided by a public grant, requesting you to visit their school. Whenever the special requirements of the public service permit your compliance with this request, my Lords are of opinion it is desirable that you should visit the school, and should convey to the parochial clergyman, the school committee, or chief promoters (whenever solicited to do so) the results of your experience in school management and education. You will specially report any such application to this Committee.

7. Acting on the principle of assisting local exertions, the Committee of Council have prepared a series of plans of school-houses for small parishes, villages, and towns, in which are exhibited those improvements which are suggested by an extensive comparison of the results of experience, and which they intend to render available to the promoters of schools, by furnishing them with an explanation of each plan in detail, together with specifications, working drawings, and estimates, and with forms for making contracts with builders, &c.

8. Their Lordships are strongly of opinion that no plan of education ought to be encouraged in which intellectual instruction is not subordinate to the regulation of the thoughts and habits of the children by the doctrines and precepts of revealed religion.

9. The Reports of the Inspectors are intended to convey such further information, respecting the state of elementary education in Great Britain, as to enable Parliament to determine in what mode the sums voted for the education of the poorer classes can be most usefully applied. With this view, reports on the state of particular districts may be required to ascertain the state of education in such districts, and how far the interference of Government or of Parliament can be beneficially exerted, by providing additional means of education. Your reports will be made to the Committee, but it is intended that they shall be laid before both Houses of Parliament.

The Committee doubt not you are duly impressed with the weight of the responsibility resting upon you, and they repose full confidence in the judgment and discretion with which your duties will be performed.

My Lords are persuaded that you will meet with much cordial co-operation in the prosecution of the important object involved in your appointment; and they are equally satisfied that your general bearing and conduct, and the careful avoidance of whatever could impair the just influence or authority of the promoters of schools, or of the teachers over their scholars, will conciliate the confidence and good-will of those with whom you will have to communicate; you will thus best fulfil the purposes of your appointment, and prove yourself a fit agent to assist in the execution of Her Majesty's desire, that the youth of this kingdom should be religiously brought up, and that the rights of conscience should be respected.

By order of the
Committee of Council on Education,
JAMES PHILLIPS KAY.

236A–B. Correspondence with the British and Foreign Society (1843)

Minutes of Committee of Council for Education, 1842–3.

236A. Lord Wharncliffe's letter of 13 January

loc. cit., p. 523.

... I will now close this letter by briefly stating that, 1st. The Committee of Council cannot consent to exempt from inspection by Government inspectors any schools whatever which have received or may hereafter receive aid from the Parliamentary grant.

2nd. The Committee of Council, whenever an occasion may arise for the appointment of an inspector, to be employed to inspect the schools connected with the British and Foreign School Society, will endeavour to make such an appointment as will inspire a confidence that such inspection will be conducted with every friendly feeling towards that society, but at the same time with a due sense of the independence of the inspectors. The Committee, however, cannot consent to the exercise of any control over such an appointment by the British and Foreign School Society.

3rd. The Committee of Council are prepared to consider any suggestions which the Committee of the British and Foreign School Society may make with regard to the mode in which the inspector shall perform his duty, with a view to remove such objections as that society have made to the mode in which that duty has been hitherto performed.

I have, &c.,
(signed) WHARNCLIFFE.

Henry Dunn, Esq.,
Secretary to the British and Foreign School Society.

236B. Lord Wharncliffe's letter of 30 November

loc. cit., p. 537.

Wortley Hall, Sheffield,
Nov. 30, 1843.

MY DEAR SIR,

Upon further consideration of what passed between Mr. Forster and you and myself, on Monday last, I think it desirable that you should be able, at your meeting with your Committee, to state to them exactly what the course is, which the Committee of Council propose to pursue, with regard to the appointment of Inspector of Schools connected with the British and Foreign School Society. I therefore, for this purpose, refer you to pages 19 and 20 of the volume of the Committee of Council's reports for 1839–40, containing a letter from Mr. Gordon, Secretary to the Education Committee of the Church of Scotland, and the answer of the Committee of Council upon the subject of the appointment of Inspectors for the schools, in connection with that Church. Those are the precise grounds upon which we are desirous of placing the appointment of Inspectors for your schools, and no Inspector for them will be appointed without the full concurrence of your Committee.

I earnestly hope that that Committee will be convinced, by the proposal of the Committee of Council to adopt that course, of their anxious wish to do every thing they can, consistently with their duty, to satisfy the British and Foreign School Society upon this important subject.

I am, &c.

(Signed) WHARNCLIFFE.

Henry Dunn, Esq.

237. Education clauses of Sir James Graham's Factory Bill (1843): Graham's speech announcing proposals (28 February)

Hansard, 3/LXVII/ 77–88.

. . . All the material powers of this nation have been developed and improved in the most remarkable manner–the entire people individually and collectively, appear to have been engrossed with this grand object; and the moral condition of the multitude has, as it seems to me, been most lamentably neglected. It is with peculiar grief and mortification that I say this; but I cannot but bear in mind, that while all the other governments of Europe, warned by the melancholy events which darkened the latter years of the last century–warned by those sad lessons, directed their earnest, their unceasing attention to the moral training and religious education of their people, England alone, Protestant Christian England, neglected this all-important duty of giving her people that training, that education, which so intimately concerns not only their temporal, but their eternal welfare. It may safely be asserted that this most important subject has been neglected in this country to a greater degree than in any other civilised nation. I must say that I think recent events in the manufacturing districts are pregnant with solemn warning. I quite agree with my noble Friend in what he has stated to the House on this topic. The law, it is true, has been triumphant, everything like violence has been subdued; and, in justice to the people of this country, I must add, that though their sufferings, their privations, their disappointments, have been great, yet even in those cases where there has been a breach of the law committed, that breach has not been accompanied by acts of cruelty or of remarkable outrage. The police and the soldiers have done their duty, the time is arrived when moral and religious instructors must go forth to reclaim the people from the errors of their ways. The harvest is abundant, but the labourers are few; it is time that the good work should be begun in earnest; it is time that a better seed, the seed of sound morality and Christian truth should be sown in the hearts of the people; and it must be the care of the nation–of the Government, with a view to the future peace, the future destinies of this country, to take this most serious subject into their anxious consideration. I can truly say that I have directed my thoughts to this question more anxiously than to any other. I know well the difficulties of it, and if I can but induce the House, in the temper which at this moment pervades it, on this one subject, to lay aside all party feelings, all religious differences, to endeavour to find out some neutral ground on which we can build something approaching to a scheme of national education, with a due regard to the just wishes of the established church on the one hand, and studious attention to the honest scruples of the dissenters on the other; in my judgment we shall be conferring a greater benefit on the people whom we represent than by any course of policy which can be adopted; and, for myself, I will say, that all party, all personal considerations will I gladly lay aside could I but hope that I might be made the humble instrument of proposing to the House anything approaching to a scheme which should lead to the happy consummation I desire with the sanction of the Legislature. . . .

Parliament has dealt with the subject of education as regards factory children, but in so imperfect and unsatisfactory a manner, as almost to render nugatory the measures which have been adopted. The Legislature has imposed upon manufacturers the necessity of giving the children in their employment some education, but it has been omitted to make any provision with regard to the quality or the degree of that education. This brings me to the second branch of the subject, to which I invite the attention of the House. No children under eight years of age are allowed to work in a factory; children between the ages of eight and thirteen may work in factories for eight hours a-day; but it is a condition of their so working, that they shall attend school for at least two hours each day. It must have been owing to negligence, for I cannot believe it to have been the intention of the Legislature, that no proper regulations were framed for the purpose of carrying into effect the proposed object of the act. Be that as it may, I will state what is the practical working of the act as it stands. A Roman Catholic master of a factory may have attached to his factory a school, with a Roman Catholic for schoolmaster, and may impose it as a condition on the children of Protestant parents, that to obtain work in his factory, they shall attend his school where the Roman Catholic version of the Scriptures is taught, and where they shall be trained in the Roman Catholic religion. I mention this as a proof of the little care and attention which has been bestowed upon the details of the enactment for the compulsory education of factory children. I do not think it right that the quality of the education should be thus neglected. I, therefore, purpose to deal with the quality of the education as well as other essential particulars. It appears to me that if children of this tender age, after being worked eight hours a-day, are sent to school, worn out with toil, without the opportunity of obtaining refreshment and relaxation, it is unlikely they will derive much benefit from any system of education, even the best, which may be administered to them. It is my intention to propose that children between the ages of eight and thirteen, employed in factories, shall not work more than six hours and a half in any one day; that if they work in the forenoon they shall not work in the afternoon, or if they work in the afternoon, they shall not work in the forenoon; but that day by day, either in the forenoon or the afternoon, they shall attend school for at least three hours. I have no reason to believe that the master manufacturers will be opposed to any such regulation. It certainly will be necessary for them, under such an arrangement, to have two sets of children to carry on their work; but I am satisfied that the humane feelings of the manufacturers, and the earnest desire, which I have every reason to believe they entertain to co-operate cordially with Parliament in improving the education of the rising youth of this nation, will induce them to acquiesce cheerfully in any measures which are necessary for effecting this paramount object. Having obtained three hours in each working day for the education of the children, the question next arises–how shall we provide for them a better education than they can obtain at present? Under the law, as it now stands, no master manufacturer can employ a child between the ages specified, unless the child can produce a certificate of its attending a school. I propose that, in every district, with respect to factory schools, certificates shall be granted, as at present, by any school in connexion with the National Society, or the British and Foreign School Society, and by any Roman Catholic school, on condition, however, that such school be open to the visits of the inspector appointed by the Privy Council on education; the inspector, of course, not being at liberty to interfere with the scheme of religious instruction given to Roman Catholic children; but taking care that no children of Protestant parents are educated in the tenets of the Roman Catholics. Thus, then, I provide for certificates being granted by schools in connexion with the National Society, and by the British and Foreign School Society, and also by Roman Catholic schools under the inspection I have stated. But the House will observe, that as might have been anticipated, the greatest want of education exists in the poorest districts. Now, the principle hitherto enforced by the Committee of Education in distributing the sum annually placed at their disposal by Parliament, has been to make no advance of money for the building of a school, unless two-thirds of the whole sum required for that purpose should previously have been raised by private subscription. In some cases, I believe, the rule has been relaxed, and grants have been made when half the whole sum required has been raised by subscription; but, beyond that, the Committee on Education have in no instance gone. I think it is most desirable to call forth local exertions for founding and maintaining schools, and that, it would be far from advantageous to throw the whole burden upon the public purse. It, therefore, appears to me indisputably necessary to adhere to the principle of making advances from the public fund only in proportion to some given amount raised by private subscription; but, at the same time, I am bound to declare, that as regards the poorer districts, some relaxation of the existing rule of proportion is imperatively called for. I propose, therefore, that in any districts where the regulations with respect to the education of factory children shall be in force, and in which local subscriptions, aided by public grants, may be inadequate to the erection of schools, the inhabitants shall be enabled to procure a loan, to the extent of one-third of the cost of the building, on the following conditions:–First, that one-third of the cost of the school-house shall be raised on the principle of local efforts; secondly, that a memorial shall be presented by certain of the inhabitants to the Committee of Council, praying for a grant of one-third of the expense of the building from the public fund, and for the loan of one-third. The Committee of Council will make inquiry as to the representation contained in the memorial, and refer the memorial and statement to the justices of the division, who will examine into the facts, and declare whether a school is necessary. If the justices declare a school-building necessary, the Committee of Council will make a grant of one-third of the cost of the building, and may empower commissioners to issue Exchequer-bills for one-third of the amount, repayment of which is to be obtained out of the poor-rates in a period of ten years. That is the mode in which I provide for the erection of the school. Then comes a matter of equal importance; namely, the support of the school. I propose to deal with it in this way:–I shall propose that trustees shall be appointed, who shall make quarterly examinations into the accounts and into the education given in the school. I shall have it provided, that out of the wages of the child shall be kept back by his master for his education a sum never exceeding 3d. per week, or more than a twelfth of the child's earnings. This will be in the nature of quarter pence paid by the child, and will provide a certain fund. The Committee of Council will enable the trustees to procure from the poor-rate of their district a sufficiency for the maintenance of the school provided that the cost of maintenance shall in no case exceed 3d. in the pound on the existing poor-rate. This I anticipate will provide an ample fund. Then comes a matter of great importance, which is the formation of districts for these schools, and these must be varied in reference to the different localities. I propose that these districts shall be formed in one of four ways–either of one entire parish or township, or of an ecclesiastical district, or of two or more ecclesiastical districts or parts of them. I propose to give the formation of these districts to the Committee of Council on Education. Then comes the question, "How are these district schools to be managed?" I propose that they shall be managed by trusts; and the composition of these trusts I will now state to the House. I propose that the trust shall contain seven individuals, and that an officiating clergyman of the district shall be one; if the district contains only one officiating clergyman, then such clergyman shall be a trustee *ex officio*. If the district contain more than one clergyman, or where the school shall be intended for two or more, or parts of two or more ecclesiastical, districts, I then propose to give the bishop of the diocese the power of selecting a clergyman to be such trustee. I propose that two of the churchwardens for the year shall be chosen by the clerical trustee, and added as trustees. I then propose a property qualification for all who are not thus *ex officio* trustees, and that the remaining four shall be appointed by the magistrates in a special session assembled for that purpose out of persons assessed to the poor-rate at a certain rate; and I further propose that two out of the four chosen trustees shall be mill-owners. I am unwilling to weary the House by entering into details, but considering the importance of the motion of my noble Friend, I am anxious to explain the views which the Government now seek to carry into effect with respect to this subject. I have provided in the manner pointed out for the erection and maintenance of schools, for the districts in which they are to be established, and for the trusts by which they are to be managed; and, now, I will state shortly the plan for the government of the schools. The general management of the schools will be under the control of the trustees; they will have the power of appointing the master, subject to the approval of the bishop of the diocese as to his competency to give religious instruction to members of the Established Church. The Holy Scriptures are to be taught daily, but no child will be required to receive instruction in the Catechism of the Church of England or to attend the Established Church whose parents object on religious grounds. . . .

238. Education clauses of Sir James Graham's Factory Bill (1843): Graham's speech on the Amended Bill (1 May)

Hansard, 3/LXVIII/1104–1118.

SIR JAMES GRAHAM: I have to thank the hon. Member for Dumfries for the courtesy with which he has acceded to my request, and I must be allowed to accept it as an omen that the temper in which this measure was discussed upon the evening on which I had the honour of first bringing it under the notice of the House, will prevail also on the present occasion, and that there will be manifested by the House, that earnest desire which characterised its former proceedings upon the subject–to deliberate with calmness and with patience upon a question of so much importance as the one which I have again to bring before it. I cannot dissemble for myself that although that spirit of calm forbearance prevails within these walls which is worthy of a deliberative assembly, much heat and excitement have arisen out of doors upon this very subject. The petitions which have been presented against those clauses of the Factories Bill to which I am about to advert have been numerous almost without a parallel. I might, if I thought it worth while, make some observations respecting the manner in which, in particular places, some of these petitions have been got up; I might point out the very gross misrepresentations which have been made out of doors, with respect to the scope, the objects, and the intentions of this measure; I might remark upon the means, that have been used to excite and stimulate opposition to it; but I shall abstain from all this. It is enough for me to know that these petitions are numerous, and have received the signatures of so many parties, that they are entitled to the utmost respect and attention from this House. I am at once ready to admit, that amongst the great Dissenting bodies of this country there does prevail at the present moment a very unanimous feeling against the educational clauses in this bill. Instead, therefore, of addressing to the House any observations such as those I have glanced at I think that it is the duty of Her Majesty's Government fairly to meet the question at issue; and I can assure the House, that I and my Colleagues have applied ourselves honestly and patiently to a consideration of the objections made to the measure, with an earnest desire, as far as it was consistent with the principles which I announced upon the occasion of my first bringing forward the bill–to apply particular remedies to these objections, so as to obtain as much chance as possible of ultimately arriving at a satisfactory conclusion. . . . I am obliged to the House for the patience and attention with which it has listened to the explanations

I have offered. I have endeavoured, in the most calm and dispassionate manner, to make intelligible to the House, as far as I am able, the precise nature, scope and extent of the alterations which I seek to make in the measure now before the House. Those alterations, I humbly contend, are in strict conformity with the principles which I originally laid down when I introduced the measure. I feel that I am justified in saying that these alterations have been framed with the respect which is due from Her Majesty's Government to the Church established in this country, and, at the same time, with the respect which is due to that perfect liberty of conscience and those tolerant principles which are no less established by law. I have stated to the House, not more warmly and deeply than I feel it, that the necessity of some such measure as this is urgent. It is my belief that imminent danger would result from its postponement. I may be wrong, but I feel intimately persuaded that if this measure, modified as it now is–a measure treated with signal forbearance by the political opponents of the Government, and with respect to which an earnest desire has been manifested to arrive, if possible, at a conciliatory adjustment–if a measure so proposed, so supported, and so treated in Parliament, shall fail to effect the great object of a combined system of education, from this time all further attempts to attain that end will be hopeless, and henceforth we must expect nothing but a system of education conducted on adverse principles, and in an antagonist spirit, which, I say it with deference, instead of producing a feeling of unity and good will amongst all classes of her Majesty's subjects, will but aggravate the bitter spirit which now exists; and I venture to predict that the most fatal consequences will ensue. I am really unwilling to touch upon these topics, yet the gravity of the question we are now discussing impels me to test the sincerity of some of the opposition which has been raised to this measure. No man in this House can more strongly deprecate the introduction of religious topics into our debates than I do; but yet I feel that the difficulties which the present measure has to contend against in this House, are connected with honest religious differences. How is it, however, that in England, the pride of Christendom,–England the mistress of the seas, that sends forth her commerce, her language, her manners, her arts, and, more than all these, her missionaries and her religion, to the utmost parts of the earth–how is it that in the heart of this very country, in this fair England, so great a mass of ignorance and infidelity–infidelity arising not from the perversion of the reasoning powers, but from want of knowing the saving truths of the Gospel–should be found? And how is it too, that at the same time such strife, such anger should be exhibited in the name of religion? Is it any mark of sincerity, either in Churchmen or Dissenters, that they should mingle with religion bitter and angry controversy? I say that the great Author of the Christian faith has left mankind, to the latest day, a test by which the sincerity of his followers may be tried. He has said, "By this shall all men know whether ye are my disciples: if ye love one another." In the early time, when the small band of Christians, with all its privations and its wants, was exposed to every species of suffering, extending even to martyrdom, the distinguishing characteristics to which I have referred attracted the notice of the Heathen and they exclaimed,–"See, how these Christians love one another." In these later days, the sceptic may point with scorn and derision at professing Christians, and observe–"See how these Christians hate and despise each other." Alas! these are the difficulties with which we have to contend; but I ask the House to continue to manifest the spirit in which it received what I before addressed to it, as well as what I have ventured to state on this occasion, and I say, let us elevate our hearts and minds, let us act the part of Christian Legislators, and evince that we are worthy of our high vocation. I am aware–for the symptoms are but too evident–that upon this question the waters of strife have overflowed, and now cover the land. This [here the right hon. Baronet placed the modified bill upon the Table]–this is my olive branch. I tender it in the hope that the harbinger of peace, ere long, may return with the glad tidings that the waters have subsided. On the part of the Government I tender this peace-offering in the spirit of concord, and of Christian charity and good-will. I will not yet abandon the hope that if it be received, at least in this House, in a corresponding spirit, it will still be possible to effect an object which concerns, in the highest degree, not only the temporal, but the eternal welfare of a great body of our fellow subjects, and which, if accomplished, will redound to the lasting renown of this House.

239. Education clauses of Sir James Graham's Factory Bill (1843): Lord Ashley's speech on the withdrawal of the proposals (19 June)

Hansard, 3/LXX/94–95.

Lord Ashley said, although he deeply regretted the loss of the educational clauses, he, for the sake of the rest of the bill, approved of the resolution the Government had come to. Even had it been possible for the Government to have carried the measure in that House, he did not think it would have met with that cordial sympathy and co-operation from the different classes affected by it, without which it could not have been effectually carried out. It should be borne in mind, that the Church, with a view to conciliation, were ready to make the very largest concessions, larger certainly than it had ever made before, but concessions made in the hope of conciliation and peace. But when the Church found that the terms which it proposed, so far from leading to conciliation and peace, only led to greater disunion and almost to effectual war, it had no alternative but to stop, at all events, at the point to which it had already advanced. Somewhere or other, however, a very great and deep responsibility did lie; it was not for him to point out who were the parties really responsible for the position at which they had now arrived. He certainly must say that the Government had shown their readiness to act. He saw the Church prepared to make concessions for the sake of conciliation and peace, and on the other hand he saw the great body of Dissenters rejoicing that they had been successful in their efforts to defeat the measure. Where-ever the fault lay one thing was quite clear–that the really suffering parties were the vast body of neglected children, who, as present appearances went, were now consigned to an eternity of ignorance. While he deplored the result to which the measure had come, he must be allowed to express his satisfaction at the manner in which it had been received and entertained in the first instance, and at the absence of all violence with which it had been received by the Dissenters in that

House. That reception did certainly afford some ground for hoping that hereafter something might effectually be done to arrest the further progress of vice, ignorance, and immorality in the country by means of some system of education. At present, however, it appeared that if united education were to become hereafter possible, the question was at present involved in the greatest difficulty, and it was one that had already produced the greatest agitation in the country. He for one, therefore, was prepared to say that unless a very mighty change should take place in the mutual temper of both parties, he would never be a party to any system, the object of which was, by mutual concession, to bring antagonist parties to act together in the same general plan. Once more, he desired to express his gratitude for the manner in which the proposition had been first received, and since entertained, and also to state his cordial hope and prayer that the time was not far distant when some means might be discovered whereby the men and women of this country in future generations might be put into that state which would fit them to be good subjects, and above all Christians, and extend to them the fruits of a religious education, by preparing them to share in a blessed immortality.

240A–B. Minutes of Committee of Council (August and December 1846)

Parlty. Papers, 1847/XLV/p. 1.

240A. Apprenticeship of pupil teachers

COUNCIL CHAMBER, WHITEHALL, 25th August, 1846.
By the Right Honourable the Lords of the Committee of Council on Education.

General Minute.

Their Lordships had under their consideration the sufficiency of the present numbers of Inspectors of Schools for the duties they have to perform, and

Resolved, – That it would be highly expedient that all the schools which are under the inspection of the Privy Council should be visited at least once in each year: that the existing number of Inspectors appears to be insufficient, as, notwithstanding their constant assiduity in the discharge of the duties intrusted to them, it is found impossible to make arrangements for the inspection of schools oftener than once in two years.

Their Lordships are, however, unwilling to make so considerable an addition at once to the number of Inspectors as would be necessary for an annual visit to each school, but will recommend the appointment of three new Inspectors this year, reserving for consideration hereafter any further appointments which may be required.

Their Lordships had further under their consideration the Report of the Inspectors of Schools, memorials from certain Boards of Education, and letters from the clergy and others, representing the very early age at which the children acting as assistants to schoolmasters are withdrawn from school to manual labour, and the advantages which would arise if such scholars as might be distinguished by proficiency and good conduct were apprenticed to skilful masters, to be instructed and trained, so as to be prepared to complete their education as schoolmasters in a Normal School.

Resolved, – That the Lord President cause Regulations to be framed defining the qualifications of the schoolmaster; the condition of instruction in the school; and the local contributions to be required as conditions on which annual grants of money may be made towards the stipends of apprentices in elementary schools; and further, cause indentures of apprenticeship to be prepared, declaring the duties of the apprentice and the nature of the instruction he is to receive; the periods of examination by the Inspectors of Schools, and the circumstances under which the indenture may be dissolved, in order that stipends increasing in each year of the apprenticeship may be granted in aid of local contribution.

It was further Resolved, – That as the masters having charge of the instruction and training of school apprentices will be selected for their character and skill; and as the education of the apprentices will increase the labour and responsibilities of such masters, it is expedient that the successful performance of these duties be rewarded by annual grants in aid of their stipends, according to the number of apprentices trained by each master.

It was further Resolved, – That it is expedient to make provision in certain cases, by a retiring pension, for schoolmasters and mistresses who, after a certain length of service, may appear entitled to such provision.

That the Lord President cause Regulations to be framed respecting the grants of such retiring pensions.

That it is expedient for the further encouragement of deserving schoolmasters, that small gratuities be annually distributed, under the authority of the Lord President, to schoolmasters whose zeal and success in teaching may, on the Report of the Inspector, appear to entitle them to such encouragement; and that Regulations be framed with reference to the distribution of such gratuities.

240B. Regulations on normal schools, education of schoolmasters, and grants in aid of their salaries

Parlty. Papers, 1847/XLV/pp. 5–6.

SUPPORT OF NORMAL SCHOOLS

Education of Schoolmasters and Mistresses, and Grants in aid of their Salaries

Exhibitions on behalf of successful Pupil Teachers to Normal Schools – Employment of certain of them in the Public Service. Grants in aid of Expenses of Normal Schools, and of the Salaries of Masters and Mistresses educated therein.

THE Committee of Council on Education had under their consideration their Lordships' Minutes as to the apprenticeship of pupil teachers in elementary schools.

It appeared further expedient to their Lordships, that the Lord President should authorize one or more of Her Majesty's Inspectors, together with the Principal of a normal school under inspection, to submit to his Lordship, from among the pupil teachers who had successfully terminated their apprenticeship, a certain number of those who, upon competition in a public examination, to be annually held by such Inspectors and Principals in each Inspector's district, might be found most proficient in their studies and skilful in the art of teaching, and concerning whose character and zeal for the office of teachers the Inspector of the district could give the most favourable report.

That the Committee of Council on Education, on comparison of the testimonials and examination papers of these apprentices, should award, for as many as they might think fit, an exhibition of £20 or £25 to one of the normal schools under the inspection of Her Majesty's Inspectors.

That the pupil teachers to whom such exhibitions should be awarded, should be thenceforth denominated "Queen's Scholars."

That the exhibition should be liable to be withdrawn if the Principal of the training school should be dissatisfied with the conduct, attainments, or skill of the "Queen's Scholar."

Their Lordships were also of opinion, that it might be useful to offer further incentives to exertion and good conduct among the pupil teachers, by opening to such of them as might not display the highest qualifications for the office of schoolmaster, but whose conduct and attainments were satisfactory, an opportunity of obtaining employment in the public service, under such regulations as may be hereafter adopted.

Their Lordships hope that the grant of an exhibition of £20 or £25 to the most proficient pupil teachers, to enable them to enter a normal school, may diminish the difficulty, experienced by the trustees and managers of such institutions, of maintaining them in efficiency. In order still further to reduce the burden of such establishments, their Lordships will award to every normal school subject to inspection a grant for every student trained therein, concerning whose character and conduct the Principal shall give a favourable report, and concerning whose attainments, skill in teaching, and general aptitude for the vocation of a schoolmaster, it shall appear to the Lord President, at the close of each of three years of training from the report of one or more of Her Majesty's Inspectors, and from the examination papers, that a certain standard of merit has been attained. Such grants shall be £20 at the close of the first year, £25 at the close of the second, and £30 at the close of the third year's course of instruction. This standard of acquirement shall not be so ordered as to interfere with the studies pursued in any normal school, but shall be adapted to those studies, so, however, as to apply impartially to all such normal schools an equal incentive to exertion, by requiring efficiency in a sufficient number of the studies pursued in them.

Their Lordships will further grant, in aid of the salary of every schoolmaster appointed to a school under their inspection, and who has had one year's training in a normal school under their inspection, £15 or £20 per annum; and in aid of the salary of every such schoolmaster who has had two years of such training, £20 or

£25 per annum; and of every such schoolmaster who has had three years of such training £25 or £30 per annum; provided he has upon examination, obtained the proper certificate of merit in each year, on the following conditions:–

1. That the trustees and managers of the school provide the master with a house rent-free, and a further salary, equal at least to twice the amount of this grant.

2. That the trustees and managers annually certify that his character, conduct, and attention to his duties are satisfactory.

3. That the Inspector report that his school is efficient in its organization, discipline, and instruction.

On the same conditions their Lordships will grant, in aid of the salaries of schoolmistresses appointed to schools under their inspection, who obtain similar certificates in a Normal School, two-thirds of the sums to be awarded to schoolmasters for each year's certificate of merit.

Retiring Pensions to Schoolmasters and Mistresses for long and efficient Services

That a retiring pension may be granted by the Committee of Council to any schoolmaster or schoolmistress who shall be rendered incapable by age or infirmity of continuing to teach a school efficiently.

Provided that no such pension shall be granted to any schoolmaster or schoolmistress who shall not have conducted a Normal or Elementary school for fifteen years, during seven at least of which such school shall have been under inspection.

That in all cases of application for pensions a report shall be required from the Inspector, and from the Trustees and Managers of the schools as to the character and conduct of the applicants, and the manner in which the education of the pupils under their charge has been carried on.

The amount of the pension shall be determined according to such report, but shall in no case exceed two-thirds of the average amount of the salary and emoluments annually received by the applicant during the period that the school has been under inspection.

A minute of the grant of every such pension, and of the grounds on which it has been awarded, shall be published in their Lordships' Minutes.

241. Lord John Russell's letter to the Duke of Wellington, Chancellor of the University of Oxford, announcing the intention to set up a Commission of Inquiry (8 May 1850)

Parlty. Papers, 1852/XXII/App. A, p. 2.

My Lord Duke,

Having announced in my place in Parliament the intention of Her Majesty's Ministers to advise that a Royal Commission should be appointed to inquire into the state and revenues of the Universities of Oxford and Cambridge; into the provisions of the statutes by which the said universities and their several colleges are governed; and to report their opinions whether any measures can be adopted by the

Crown or by Parliament by which the interests of religion and sound learning may be promoted in the conduct of education in the said universities, I am anxious to explain to Your Grace the views of Her Majesty's confidential servants in recommending this measure for Her Majesty's approbation.

I will not enter here into the question of the legality of such a commission. Had it been proposed to exercise powers going beyond inquiry and report, such a question might enter into consideration. But the present commission will be a commission to receive evidence and report opinions, without powers to determine any question, or to prescribe any course. It becomes the more expedient that the views which are entertained on the subject should be explained.

No one will deny that in the course of three centuries the increase of general knowledge, the growth of modern literature, the discoveries of physical and chymical science have rendered changes in the course of study at our national universities highly expedient. The universities themselves have acknowledged this expediency, and very large reforms of this nature have been adopted both at Oxford and Cambridge. These improvements, so wisely conceived, reflect the highest credit on those learned bodies.

The object of the proposed commission is not to interfere with these changes, but to facilitate their progress; not to reverse the decisions of the Universities by an authority *ab extra*, but to bring the aid of the Crown, and if necessary, of Parliament, to assist in their completion.

This can be done in two ways:–First, by ascertaining and recording, for the information of the Queen and the two Houses of Parliament, the new regulations which have been promulgated, and the mode in which those regulations are expected to take effect.

Secondly, by obtaining a knowledge of the obstacles which are interposed by the wills of founders, the retention of customs, and the decision of competent authority to the full development of that large and improved system of study which the Universities have sought to establish.

I will explain the nature of the obstacles to which I allude.

In many cases the advantages and emoluments of the separate colleges are limited by the wills of the founders, either to the natives of some particular county or district, or to the scholars educated in a particular school, or in some instances to the descendants of the founder and his family. Such restrictions cannot fail to be injurious, and to be injurious in proportion as the field of choice is narrowed by the particular condition annexed to the advantages of the college. In other instances the directions of the founder's will cannot be complied with under the existing law, and in such instances it might fairly be considered whether the interests of learning and the wants of the country may not be better considered by an expansion of the governing statutes.

Matters of this nature, however, require deliberate and calm inquiry. Commissioners conversant with the state of our Universities, and versed in a knowledge of the general policy of our law, will be of essential service, as well in pointing out the path of safe improvement as in marking the dangers of heedless innovation.

Various questions may and must arise in the course of this inquiry. For instance, has the school which has the privilege of commanding fellowships or other advantages in any particular college fallen off or increased in numbers and consequence since the bequest was made? Has the family of the founder left few or many descendants to enjoy his bounty? In the case of religious services prescribed by the founder, but now prohibited by law, does it appear to be the wish of the founder that in case no such religious service could be performed the foundation was, or was not, to aid in the purposes of education? In the case of Royal foundations how far has the Crown the power of consulting the good of the University in the application of endowment of a former Sovereign? These and similar questions require care for their investigation and prudence in their solution. For this purpose the utmost care will be taken in selecting commissioners who may not only be well qualified for their important task, but who may inspire respect and confidence by their character and position.

I have the honour to be, my Lord Duke,
Your faithful and obedient servant,
J. Russell.

May 8th.,
His Grace the Duke of Wellington.

242. Protest of the Hebdomadal Board of the University of Oxford against the proposed Commission

Parlty. Papers, 1852/xxii/App. pp. 3–5 (p. 309).

The Board of Heads of Houses and Proctors present their most respectful acknowledgements to his Grace the Chancellor of the University for his communication to them of the 11th inst. through the Vice-Chancellor, inclosing a copy of a letter from Lord John Russell of the 8th inst., respecting the intended appointment of a Royal Commission to inquire into the state, revenues, and statutes of the Universities of Oxford and Cambridge, and of their respective colleges; and the Board proceed, according to his Grace's desire, to report to his Grace upon this important subject.

They gladly recognise on the part of Her Majesty's Ministers their earnest desire to promote the interests of religious and sound learning, as well as to advance the cause of education; their approbation, also, of the reforms and improvements adopted by the University, and their wish and intention not to interfere with those changes, but to facilitate their progress, and to bring the aid of the Crown, and if necessary of Parliament, to assist in their completion.

This is the declared object of the proposed commission, and this, it is further stated, can be effected in two ways:–First, by ascertaining and recording, for the information of the Queen the mode in which those new regulations are expected to take effect.

Secondly.–By obtaining a knowledge of the obstacles which are interposed by the wills of founders, the retention of customs, and the decisions of competent authority, to the full development of that large and improved system of study which the universities have sought to establish.

We beg most respectfully to submit to your Grace that whilst a Royal Commission, such as has been suggested, would in our opinion lead to many injurious consequences contrary to the intentions of Her Majesty's Ministers, it is also unnecessary in either of the purposes above specified.

As to the first of those purposes, the Sovereign or the Parliament can at any time obtain from your Grace, through your Vice-Chancellor, or from the printed University statutes, ample information respecting all the new regulations, and the mode in which they are expected to take effect.

And as to the second purpose, respecting supposed obstacles from the wills of founders, or other similar causes, to the full development of that large and improved system of study which the Universities have sought to establish, we believe (confining ourselves of course to this University), that if the supposed obstacles anywhere exist, they produce no material effect upon the general academical system.

For your Grace does not need to be informed that all our junior students are members at once of the University and of some college or hall. If they belong to any hall (the halls at Oxford being only places of study, not incorporated societies), then they are solely under the statutes of the University; but if they are members of colleges, which are all of them distinct corporations independent of one another, and in many respects independent of the University, still their studies, nevertheless, are regulated by the statutes of the University, and they receive instruction partly from the public professors, partly from tutors, appointed indeed within the colleges, but recognised also and controlled by the general statutes of the University.

This combination of professorial and collegiate instruction is most important and beneficial, and some of the late changes in our system have been designed to restore this combined instruction to greater efficiency, when it had suffered some temporary interruption from the unforseen and unintended effects of earlier measures of reform. But experience proves that there is no reason to apprehend any obstacle to the full development of the University system, as to the instruction of the younger students, arising from any of the collegiate customs or statutes.

The recent regulations are only the latest of several successive measures of academic reform. The studies of this place have not continued, as would appear to be assumed in Lord John Russell's letter of the 8th inst., the same, or nearly the same, during the last three centuries; nor is it only of late that they have been altered or enlarged.

Two centuries ago–in 1636–the University revised the whole body of its statutes, and the academic system of study was admirably arranged at a time when not only the nature and faculties of the human mind were exactly what they are still, and must of course remain, but the principles also of sound and enlarged intellectual culture were far from imperfectly understood.

In process of time further changes and improvements became requisite, and the University has for the last half century, since the year 1800, been continually engaged in a series of academic reforms, designed to adapt the system to altered circumstances, or to the advanced state of science in some departments of knowledge; and if these reforms, however well designed, have not always so completely answered the expectations of their authors, or if they have not always met the wishes of all the members of the academic legislature, still from no quarter whatsoever has any obstacle or obstruction been opposed to the full development of the system of the University, and it cannot justly be said that our reformers have ever failed to produce their full effect through the supineness, indifference, or incompetency of the public instructors of our youth, whether the professors of the University or the tutors of colleges.

So far, then, as respects the University, its institutions, and its recent regulations, whether with reference to the University itself or to the aid derived to its institutions from the colleges, we humbly submit that a Royal Commission will obstruct, instead of assisting, the natural progress and improvement of the academical system; and this is the declared, indeed, the only declared object for the appointment of such a commission.

Various suggestions, indeed, are subsequently thrown out, and various questions raised, in Lord John Russell's letter to your Grace, bearing upon the state and wellbeing of the separate colleges, but only indirectly affecting the welfare of the University.

The several colleges in Oxford have been founded at various times from one to six centuries ago, in some few instances by Royal, but chiefly by private munificence. They have exercised an important and very salutary influence upon the discipline and the education of the University. But it should be observed that they have not been usually founded, or in all cases endowed, by subsequent benefactors directly for the education of youth, but for higher purposes.

The education of youth has, in most instances, been superadded to their other duties by the heads and fellows of colleges, of their own free will, to the great advantage of the community.

It may very well be that modern founders and benefactors might, in some instances, improve upon the ancient regulations if they were creating colleges anew of their own bounty; but it does not follow that the former foundations and endowments, when they are in no instance injurious to the community at large, often highly beneficial, ought therefore to be disturbed. If the restrictions upon the elections to fellowships, for example, might in some cases be advantageously modified or removed, still their removal would not to any considerable extent benefit the cause of education or sound learning, and the nature and amount of the existing restrictions, moreover, have been greatly exaggerated.

Fellowships are not commonly restricted to particular schools, but only scholarships, or probationary fellowships from which there is a subsequent election to the actual fellowships. The schools in question are for the most part our great public schools. The districts, again, from which confined fellowships are filled up often comprise several populous counties. It is not often, if ever, that the mere lineal descendants of founders have a claim to these, but the kindred of the founders traced collaterally, and also beyond the founder to his remote ancestors, and embracing therefore very many families, and opening a wide field of choice. The degree of preference, moreover, is often so slight, that what are called confined fellowships may be, and sometimes are, filled up from other districts besides what are prescribed.

If the colleges themselves would sometimes gain by the removal of such restrictions, the University at large, and the general course of education, would be but little affected by the change.

Tutors of colleges are not necessarily appointed from the fellows on close foundations, or from the fellows of colleges at all. Even the colleges themselves are sometimes benefited by the various provisions under which their fellows are elected. One uniform principle of election, or one kind of qualification or standard of merit, would be prejudicial to the general interests of the several societies, and through them to the country.

But it should be especially recollected that in all instances trusts and vested rights have been created and have been sanctioned by the Crown or by Parliament, which could not now be generally abrogated without great detriment to the future interests of charity, and great injustice to the persons and families and districts interested in these endowments.

Similar remarks would apply to the statutes of colleges, which have also been supposed to require alterations through the aid of a Royal Commission.

In many instances there already exists some power to revise and alter ancient statutes, vested either in the Colleges or their visitors. Wherever such powers are felt to be wanting or insufficient, and the colleges and their visitors desire additional powers of alteration, we do not doubt that the Legislature, upon a proper application made to them, would not be indisposed to confer such powers upon them. But for none of these purposes does the appointment of a Royal Commission appear to be requisite or desirable.

Thc preceding observations apply to the objects of the proposed Royal Commission with reference to the University and to the colleges separately, and to the connexion between the colleges and the University in respect of Education. In each of these relations the Commission would appear, we respectfully submit, to be uncalled for, if not positively injurious.

And, generally, we would take the liberty of expressing our conviction, that such a commission would entail several injurious effects upon the University, by no means contemplated by Her Majesty's Ministers.

However friendly their intentions towards the Universities and colleges, the appointment of such a commission, immediately succeeding the attacks repeatedly made by persons very inadequately acquainted with these bodies, would be commonly and naturally regarded as even designed to continue and to sanction these attacks.

It would obviously tend, also, not only to interrupt our labours and studies, but to check and obstruct the natural and healthy progress of improvement which has of late years proceeded as rapidly as is consistent with the proper working of the academical system.

And without entering into the question of the legality of a Commission appointed only to inquire and report, it is obvious that it would be of the nature of an unconstitutional proceeding, since it would seek to attain indirectly what could not be directly attained without an open violation of the constitution and of the rights and privileges of Her Majesty's subjects. And we respectfully submit that Her Majesty's dutiful and loyal subjects ought not to be exposed to the painful alternative of either withholding evidence from a Commission so appointed, lest they should betray their trusts and sanction a proceeding apparently unconstitutional, or of allowing Her Majesty's commissioners to listen only to imperfect information and partial statements upon subjects of great importance both to the Universities and the community at large.

Signed on behalf of the Board of Heads of Houses and Proctors,

F. C. PLUMPTRE, *Vice-Chancellor.*

Oxford, May 16.

243A–1. Report of the Royal Commission on the University of Oxford

Parlty. Papers, 1852/XXII.

243A. Narrowness of the university's role in national education

loc. cit., pp. 18–19.

. . . The total number of members of the University on the 31st of December, 1850, was 6060. The number of Undergraduates on the books, resident and non-resident, was 1402. The number of Members of Convocation was 3294. The remaining 1364 members were either Graduates who had not yet acquired the franchise, or Graduates who, having once lost it by removing their names from the books, have not yet recovered it by the statutable means. The number of Graduates of all ranks residing in Oxford does not, we believe, exceed 300.

These results may appear small when we remember the large endowments belonging to the Colleges. All feel it to be desirable that the benefits offered by the English Universities should be extended far more widely, and that, if possible, the most able and promising of the youth of the whole Empire should be attracted to these great Institutions.

There are several causes which tend to limit the number of Students at Oxford.

The education imparted there is not such as to conduce to the advancement in life of many persons, except those intended for the ministry of the Established Church. Many are now called to the Bar, and raised to the highest judicial functions, who have not been members of any University; and a large proportion of those Barristers who have received an academical education are said to be Cambridge men. Few Physicians are now educated at Oxford. Nor do many persons take a Degree with a view to enter into the legal profession as Solicitors, though the Legislature has given to Graduates an advantage as regards the duration of their articles.

The great bulk, we repeat, of those who actually resort to Oxford are destined for the ministry of the Church; and, so long as a Degree is required for Ordination, a considerable number of persons will repair to the University, be the education what it may, and though the expenses should remain what they are now. But the number of Students intended for Holy Orders would, we believe, become much greater if the expenses were considerably reduced. Indeed, the foundation of such institutions as Durham, Lampeter, and St. Bees, is probably owing in part at least to the great cost of an Oxford or Cambridge education.

The number of Students at Cambridge is greater than at Oxford, though at Cambridge the accommodation within College walls is more limited, and the endowments are much less considerable. This may be owing in part to the greater facilities for admission into a good or a popular College at Cambridge, together with the greater advantages there offered by open Fellowships and Scholarships; and another reason may be that the Examinations in that University can be more easily passed by persons who have not received a classical education. The absence also of a religious test at Matriculation, may sometimes cause a preference to be given to the sister University. But however it may be accounted for, the fact of such a superiority in numbers proves that Oxford, which has more Colleges and ampler revenues than Cambridge, ought to send forth a larger number of Students than at present.

While, however, we entertain a strong hope that the benefits of the University may be more widely extended, we limit our expectations by the circumstances and exigencies of modern times. It would be vain to look for the almost fabulous multitudes, which are said to have resorted to Oxford in the reign of King Henry III. At that time the University of Oxford was, we may almost say, the chief charity-school for the poor, and the chief grammar-school in England, as well as the great place of education for Students of Theology, of Law, and of Medicine. The oldest of the great Public Schools was not yet founded. The Inns of Court and the Schools of Medicine had no existence, and many students from foreign Universities thought their education incomplete until they had visited the most celebrated seat of English learning. There is, however, much to encourage the belief, that many impediments to the greatness of Oxford may be removed by the University or the Legislature, and that large classes, at present excluded, may in future generations, and even in our own, be attracted by the ample rewards, and the excellent education which Oxford may easily be enabled to offer. We shall hereafter show on the authority of the highest names, that it is possible to render Oxford a place of preparatory education both for Law and Medicine. Professional knowledge, in the strict sense, cannot be given in a provincial town. It must be acquired where the Professions are practised, that is, in Chambers and Courts of Law, and in the Hospitals of great cities. But young men intended for the higher branches of both Professions might, with advantage, spend the three or four years after seventeen in Oxford, provided that, besides the general training of the place, they were enabled and required to master the principles of those branches of knowledge which they must afterwards study in detail. The changes which are taking place in the administration of justice seem to render it necessary that persons in all grades of the Legal profession should receive an Academical education. It is certainly desirable that the manufacturing and mercantile, which has arisen by the side of the landed aristocracy, and which is exercising a great influence on the public counsels, should seek to have its sons brought up where so many emiment statesmen of past and present times have been trained; and that the Universities should not cease to send forth a succession of persons qualified to serve God in the State as well as in the Church. . . .

243B. Discipline

loc. cit., pp. 22–24.

. . . It is satisfactory to find, when we compare the discipline, the order, and the morals of the University with what they are reported to have been even within the memory of living men, that a decided reform has taken place. The venerable Mr. Philip Duncan says, "I have resided within the walls of New College for above "60 years, and have had great satisfaction in witnessing many admirable improve- "ments in discipline, morals, and education in the University." For some of the gravest charges formerly brought against both the authorities and the students of the University there appears now to be little or no ground. In the account of Oxford, given by Dr. Vicesimus Knox, towards the close of the last century, the Proctors are accused of attending chiefly to "vexatious formalities," and "passing unnoticed," or but slightly correcting, for the sake of appearance, "drunkenness and debauchery;" the Deans of Colleges are said "seldom to choose to incur the odium of being "disciplinarians, and of inspecting, with any peculiar vigilance, the conduct of the "juniors;" of "being often very attentive to court the favour of the young men "who are to succeed to Fellowships, and who may afterwards reward the negligence "of the Dean by Conferring upon him the honourable and profitable office of a "Principal." The Fellows of Colleges are said to "employ their attention and time "in the pursuit of vulgar enjoyments, such as the uneducated chiefly delight in–in "the bottle and in the joys of the chase." "In no places of education are young men "more extravagant: in none do they catch the contagion of admiring hounds and "horses to so violent a degree; in none do they more effectually shake off the fine "sensibilities of shame, and learn to glory in debauchery; in none do they learn more "extravagantly to dissipate their fortunes; in none do they earlier acquire a contempt "for their parents; in none do they learn so much to ridicule all that is serious and "sacred; in none do they run greater danger of ruining their health, fortune, character "and peace of mind; in none can they be less soberly brought up to the sacred "function, or to any other useful or honourable employment. Much of the corruption "of morals and unbelief of religion, which is now visible throughout the nation, is "derived from the ignorance, carelessness, and vice of Clergymen trained in the "Universities of England. . . . If the most unbounded libertinism of sentiment and "practice is a qualification for a Senator, then let him be educated in an English "University as now constituted." This description, running as it does so completely counter to the eulogy pronounced by Dr. Johnson on the Oxford College system, was probably too strong even for that time. But Johnson could see no defect in what he loved; and language like that of Dr. Knox could hardly have been used without some ground.

In all the points here mentioned the University and the Colleges have, under the influence of the general improvement of society, made a great advance. The grosser exhibitions of vice, such as drunkenness and riot, have, in Oxford, as in the higher classes generally, become rare. The intercourse of the Undergraduates with their Tutors has, in many cases, become more confidential and more frequent. The influence of the senior on the junior part of the University has increased, and is, for the most part, exercised for good. Greater attention is given to theological instruction; greater reverence is observed in the performance of Divine service. A religious Student is not now an object of persecution or scorn, but, as a general rule, of respect and confidence.

There still remains, however, much to be done towards the attainment of such excellence in Discipline as may be fairly expected; and the improvement which we have noticed in the University, and in the better Colleges especially, may warrant a hope that the amelioration will be progressive, and that all the parts of the system may be raised more nearly to the same level.

Of existing evils the most obvious are sensual vice, gambling in its various forms, and extravagant expenditure.

Little can be done by direct enactments to restrain the two first of these evils. External decency, on the whole, is well preserved in the town of Oxford. The amount of temptation to the unwary, however, is such as might, by increased vigilance on the part of the Proctors, be still considerably reduced. But in the villages round Oxford, and in places still more remote from the Proctor's jurisdiction, the opportunities to vice are too abundant. The Metropolis itself is not beyond the reach of ill-disposed or weak young men, who, as we have shown, may often have the whole day at their command.

Gambling is carried on in the University, as elsewhere, in such a manner as to make it extremely difficult of detection. When discovered it is always severely punished. At times, within the last twenty years, it has reached a great height. It is usually introduced into a College by one or two individuals, who bring the practice from without. A fashion thus springs up in the circle of their immediate acquaintance, which, indeed, often dies out when that one generation of Students has passed away, but which is very fatal in the mean time, since, from the nature of the case, it can be discovered only by accident. A system of espionage would be wholly uncongenial to the spirit of the place.

The habit of extravagant expenditure is more widely extended than either of the evils just mentioned. But flagrant instances of misconduct in this respect, such as come before the courts, and raise the indignation of the public, are less frequent than formerly; and a large number of Undergraduates are disposed to practise as strict an economy as their position admits. This is attested by the fact, that nearly one-half of the Students deal for grocery with a tradesman who refuses credit in all cases. But between the small class which is guilty of disgraceful extravagance, and the larger body which is prudent, there is still a considerable number of young men who spend far more than they have any right to spend.

Two or three specific forms of extravagance may be mentioned, some of them petty indeed in themselves, but which all help to swell a young man's aggregate expenditure. The power of the authorities may do something towards diminishing these; timely warning and good sense will do more.

One such point is alluded to by Professor Browne. "The debts," he observes, "into which Undergraduates are led, by the growing taste for furniture and decorations, totally unsuitable, are ruinous." This language is strong but the evil to which it points is very serious. We cannot forbear from alluding also to the excessive habit of smoking, which is now prevalent. Tobacconists' bills have, and that not in solitary instances, amounted to £40 a-year. A third cause of expense is the practice of dining at inns, taverns, and clubs, in or about Oxford, a practice which may be checked, as has been proved, under the administration of active Proctors. The Evidence of Mr. Jelf shows at considerable length the great evils hence arising, and the mode in which the practice may be, and has at times been, effectually repressed.

Driving, riding, and hunting are also causes of great expense. The University regulation, which imposes a heavy fine on those who are found driving, unless they have obtained permission from an officer of their College and one of the Proctors, is more or less enforced, and restrains the practice to some extent. Undergraduates are forbidden by Statute to keep horses without the sanction of the Head of their College; a rule which, however, is only partially enforced, and may be easily evaded by the use of hired horses. Of these amusements the most expensive is hunting. It seldom costs less than four guineas a day. Some of those who indulge in it are accustomed to it at home, and can afford it; and on this ground, as well as on the supposition that it often takes the place of worse pursuits, it is in several Colleges overlooked or permitted. It is, however, a matter which ought to be under strict control. A moderate indulgence in it has in some cases been compatible with serious study and academical distinction. But the present license ought to be repressed; and hunting ought at least never to be permitted by the College authorities without the express sanction of parents. In such cases, the temptation held out by the example of those who can afford the amusement to those who cannot, should always be taken into consideration.

These are some of the chief forms of extravagance in Oxford. They are attributable in some measure to a want of determination on the part of the authorities, but in a greater measure to the easy credit given by tradesmen to the Students. What a parent allows his son is too often expended in foolish or vicious indulgence, and the youth is enabled to obtain necessaries on trust. It is credit, then, which fosters the worst evils; but credit will be given as long as tradesmen are eager to sell. This is a subject which has often been discussed in the University, and out of it, and the Evidence laid before us contains several suggestions for meeting the evil, though more in the way of palliation than of cure. Many such propositions have been made and rejected after consideration, either from the practical impossibility of carrying them into effect, or because it was thought that if carried into effect they would encourage rather than check the evil. . . .

243C. Distinction of rank within the university

loc. cit., pp. 28–29.

. . . This, perhaps, is the most convenient place to offer some remarks on a subject not unconnected with that of which we have been treating.

Several of those who have given us evidence lay stress on the bad effect caused by the distinctions of rank and wealth which the University still retains among the

Students. Young noblemen wear a distinctive academical dress, take precedence of their academical superiors, are permitted to take Degrees at an earlier period than other Students, and in general are treated in a way that seems to indicate too great a deference to rank in a place of education. The sons of Baronets and Knights are also permitted to graduate earlier. This is a relic of a past state of things, when the different orders of society were much more widely separated than they are at present. Among the Fellows and Tutors of Colleges, whatever may be their birth, their fortune, or their social position out of the University, a perfect equality subsists. This is very beneficial, and among the junior members of the University it might at least be expected that there should be nothing in the institutions of the place to encourage an opposite feeling.

If distinctions of birth, even where they are in some measure warranted by the law of the land, are objectionable in a place of education, those made on the ground of mere wealth are still more objectionable; and the distinction between Gentlemen-Commoners, as they are called, and Commoners, rests on no other ground. We are here, however, bound to note the argument by which Archbishop Whately has defended the existing usage:–

"I am not for abolishing the distinction (or something amounting to it), between Commoners and Gentlemen-Commoners. If restrictions as to expense are laid down, such as are suitable to men who can only afford to spend from £100 to £200 per annum, or even considerably less, it can hardly be expected that these will be conformed to by men of ten or twenty times that income. Why should a man not be allowed a valet, or a horse, who has been always used to such luxuries, and to whom they are not more extravagant luxuries than shoes and stockings are to his fellow-students? And if restrictions are laid down, whch are in great measure evaded, or their violation connived at, there is more danger of others being drawn into expensive habits (which they can ill afford, and would fain avoid) if they belong to the same class which indulges in those habits.

All sumptuary laws made allowance for differences of expenditure in men of different classes. Their failure arose from the impossibility of classifying property in the whole common-wealth, and of keeping men in the classes laid down, which in a College may easily be effected.

If you can afford such and such luxuries, and wish for them, you must wear a silk gown, and be rated as Gentlemen-Commoners. If you decline this, you must be subject to the restrictions on Commoners."

This argument is, in our opinion, answered by the consideration, that practically the class of Gentlemen-Commoners is, as such, liable to the most serious disadvantages, as have been pointed out in various parts of the Evidence. A Gentleman-Commoner is well known to be marked out for every kind of imposition. He is usually courted by the worse amongst his equals: he receives less instruction and is subjected to a less careful discipline; and thus both the College and the individual suffer from the continuance of the system.

"This class may be regarded, taken collectively," says Professor Daubeny, "as the worst educated portion of the Undergraduates, and at the same time the one least inclined for study. If the qualification were even that of rank or station, something might be said in its defence; but it is notoriously only that of wealth; and if it be alleged in its behalf that its existence tends to set up a wholesome line of separation between those who can afford to indulge in expensive luxuries and those who cannot, and thus to diminish the chance of rivalry between the two, with respect to their habits of living, it may be replied, that in the largest and more aristocratical Colleges it fails in effecting this, now that so many wealthy parents are wise enough to enrol their sons in them merely as Commoners, whilst it might be expected that if the class of Gentleman-Commoners were abolished there would be then no inducement for men of fortune to resort elsewhere, excepting it were to secure the advantage of superior tuition, or more careful discipline; and hence that the remaining societies would either consist wholly of youths of moderate means, or that, if they contained an intermixture of young men of wealth, the latter would consist of such as were studious in their habits, and disinclined to extravagance."

We may add, that parents generally seem to concur in disapproval of the distinction spoken of. Young men of the best families, and of great wealth or expectations, are frequently entered as Commoners. The practice of taking Gentlemen-Commoners has been discontinued in several Colleges from a sense of its inexpediency. At Corpus Christi College it has been abolished since the issuing of Your Majesty's Commission. . . .

243D. Expenses

loc. cit., pp. 32–33.

. . . The following calculations, based on the Evidence, will convey a general notion of the expenses incurred by College Students:–

In Pembroke College we find that the average College battels, including tuition, washing, coals, and entertainments, besides the ordinary expenses of food, room rent, &c., amount to £271 for the 84 weeks. We add a moderate allowance for other expenses, including University and College fees, servants, books, groceries, and lights, with loss on furniture, and estimate the whole sum at about £370, as what ought to be the average cost of a Degree at Pembroke College.

Mr. Temple has given us an account of the expenses of an economical Undergraduate at Balliol; from which we calculate that, with great frugality, a young man at that College may take his Degree for about £370. This includes the items mentioned in the case of Pembroke, though not to the same extent as regards entertainments. The evidence of the Bursars of Balliol shows that the average expenses of that College are much higher than those stated by Mr. Temple.

A calculation, based on the evidence of Mr. Conybeare, and including the same items, gives about £360 as a fair estimate of the expenses required from a young man during his academical course at Christ Church.

In University College, taking the average amount of the Battels, and making the same calculation for other necessary items as in Pembroke, Balliol, and Christ Church, we estimate the average expenses of graduation to be about £430.

It is to be observed that none of these calculations include caution-money, travelling, clothes, wine, desserts, or amusements.

Mr. Eaton, one of the Tutors of Merton College, states the sum of £150 to be the lowest yearly sum for which he has known an Undergraduate to live in that Society. We understand Mr. Eaton to include in this sum expenses of every kind, such as are excluded in the former calculation. His statement of the average Battels leads us to infer that this is much below the usual cost of living in that College.

At St. Edmond Hall, Mr. Hill, the Vice-Principal, informs us that one or two members who have recently graduated, have not exceeded £240 in the amount of their College Bills, during the four years of their residence, inclusive of caution money, admission fees, furniture of rooms, and fees on taking the Degree. Several have defrayed the whole of their academic expenses from matriculation to graduation, comprehending both College bills and private expenses, with the exception of clothes and journeys, for £380.

In every College, wine-parties with desserts, are common. Such entertainments are very costly, even where the bounds of moderation are not exceeded. There are also various amusements, of which even the cheapest kinds involve considerable expense.

We have not thought it necessary to describe at length the accounts received from Lincoln, Corpus, Wadham, St. John's, Jesus, Worcester, Magdalen Hall, and St. Alban Hall, which appear in the Evidence. They lead to the same conclusions as the statements which we have made.

On the whole, we believe that a parent, who, after supplying his son with clothes and supporting him at home during the vacations, has paid for him during his University course not more than £600, and is not called upon to discharge debts at its close, has reason to congratulate himself. Those who allow their sons a private Tutor should add proportionately to their estimate. Private Tutors usually charge £10 a term, or £30 a year, for three hours a-week; £17 10s. a term, or £50 a-year, for six hours a-week. Private Tutors of high standing expect £20 a term: £30 is usually paid by young men who join a reading party during the vacation. . . .

243E. Means of enlarging the class from which the university draws

loc. cit., pp. 35–36.

. . . Having thus stated, so far as we are able, the actual expenses according to the present College system, we now proceed to consider whether the University may not be opened to a much larger and poorer class than that from which the Students are at present almost entirely taken.

With the view of obtaining a full discussion and detailed information on this important subject, we specified in the heads of inquiry submitted to eminent persons connected with the University various modes by which it appeared to us that such extension could be accomplished.

We have received in reply a mass of Evidence, of which the extent sufficiently indicates the interest felt in the matter by Members of the University. And that this interest is not confined to those who have now supplied us with Evidence is clear from the fact that an address was sent to the Hebdomadal Board in 1845 by many noblemen and gentlemen, both lay and clerical, among whom were Lord Sandon, Lord Ashley, Mr. Gladstone, and others of great name, praying them to adopt measures for the admission of a poorer class to the University. Their earnestness was evinced by the readiness which they expressed to furnish pecuniary assistance to such a scheme. Pamphlets to recommend a measure of this kind have also been written by Members of the University, who have declined to answer the questions addressed to them by Your Majesty's Commissioners. From these circumstances it is evident that many members of the University, both resident and non-resident, are deeply impressed with the need of some movement in this direction and are willing to incur the risks and to make the changes which it would involve.

The means for accomplishing this design, suggested by us in our printed paper of questions, were as follows:–

The establishment of new Halls, whether as independent Societies or in connexion with Colleges.

Permission to Undergraduates to lodge in private houses more generally than at present.

Permission to Students to become Members of the University, and to be educated in Oxford under due superintendence, without subjecting them to the expenses incident to connexion with a College or Hall.

Admission of persons to Professorial Lectures, to whom the Professors should be authorised to grant certificates of attendance without requiring any further connexion with the University.

No other scheme has been proposed to us for increasing the number of Students resident within the University; and each of the first three at least of these schemes has been strongly recommended in some part of the Evidence.

We would remark at the outset before discussing these plans in detail, that the first requisite for the adoption of any of them, must be to give to the University, to its Colleges, and to private beneficence, all possible freedom of action. Each plan is strenuously and exclusively supported by able and earnest persons; and it appears to us that it is only by actual experiment that the University can satisfy itself as to which is the best, and that the simultaneous operation of all, so far from preventing, might promote the success of each.

On this point Mr. Pattison's remarks appear to us to merit consideration.

"Instead of guessing in the dark at the probable effect of these plans, let us make the experiment. . . . What is urged is not the creation of any new machinery . . . but that an oppressive restriction should be removed, and the field thrown open to private enterprize and energy. When free, this will speedily run into the best channels. Let us leave Halls and Colleges, old and new, all with unlimited liberty of admission to work together, and trust to the power of self-adjustment in things, which will bring to the surface the capabilities of the several methods. . . . It is incumbent indeed on a University to be cautious and deliberate in all its proceedings. But experiments are not necessarily rash–there are wise ones–there are even wise experiments in legislation which do not answer, and then to desist from them involves no disgrace. . . . We in Oxford, are weary of scheming, suggesting, and pamphleteering. Give us leave to be doing something. Untie our hands and open our gates, and let us at least try if we can attract here, and can usefully deal with that larger circle of youth whom we are told we ought to have here. If only a little relaxation is given us, and if then our numbers do not increase, it will be impossible to avoid ascribing that to the usual abortiveness of half measures. But, indeed, the utmost that is now asked for is truly little. The ideal of a national University is that it should be co-extensive with the nation–it should be the common source of the whole of the higher (or secondary) instruction for the country; but the proposed measure would, after all, only go part of the way towards making it co-extensive with that part of the nation which supports the established Church. If we can only draft in 500, say 300 students (additional), from a class whose education has hitherto terminated with the national school or the commercial academy, the good that would be effected by acting even on this moderate scale cannot be represented by figures. It would be the beginning of a system by which the University would strike its roots freely into the subsoil of society, and draw from it new elements of life, and sustenance of mental and moral power."

The restrictions on the energies of the University of which Mr. Pattison here complains are, like many others which we have had occasion to mention, imposed by the Laudian Code. By the provisions of that Code no Student can be a Member of the University without being a Member of a College or Hall, in which he is constantly to take his meals, and to lodge at night. No College is permitted to lodge its Members in buildings adjacent to the College unless they be so situated as to have no entrance except through the common gate. Since the days of Laud, two Halls (Gloucester Hall and Hart Hall) have been turned into Colleges. The latter of these has, however, become extinct. No new places of education have since been created; nor is there, so far as appears, any provision in the University Statutes for establishing a new College or Hall without the assistance of the Crown or of the Legislature.

Whatever plan, therefore, be thought worthy of adoption, the first step must be to annul these restrictions of the Laudian Code. . . .

243F. Purposes of university reform

loc. cit., pp. 67–68.

. . . It is not surprising that men zealous in the cause of education, accustomed to see Fellowships bestowed for the most part like prizes in a lottery, and regarded as mere sinecures, should desire to apply the revenues which support them to the execution of a great and useful purpose. And, if these Fellowships must, as long as they exist, be given away by accident, and cannot be made means of rewarding past merit, of securing the future services of able men, or of remunerating actual teachers, any change might well be thought a gain.

Doubtless, Colleges were eleemosynary foundations, but their sole object was not, like that of an almshouse, to relieve indigence. They were intended no doubt to maintain scholars who were poor; and in an age when learning was regarded as ignoble by the great, and when nearly all but the great were poor, persons willing to enter the University as Students could hardly be found except among the poor. If, in modern days, those who impart or seek education in the Universities are not indigent, it must not be thought, therefore, that the poor have been robbed of their birthright. Rather the Universities, among other agencies, have so raised the condition of society, and mental cultivation is now so differently regarded, that persons intended for the learned professions are at present found only amongst the comparatively wealthy. Such persons, if elected for their merit to Fellowships and Scholarships would most faithfully fulfil the main objects of Founders, namely, the promotion of religion and learning.

We have no wish to encourage "poor scholars" to come to the University merely because they are poor. If we look to the wants of the country and the Church, we must believe that what is needed is not a philanthropic scheme for counterbalancing the inequalities of fortune, but rather enactments which will provide that neither the rich nor the poor, if they have the necessary qualifications, shall be deterred or debarred from following the course in which they can be most useful. What is needed is justice, directed to the removal of every impediment, every unnecessary expense; not charity, designed to produce, under artificial stimulants, a large class of Students without vocation or special aptitude for a learned profession. What is needed is encouragement to merit and industry; so that every promising youth, however poor, shall be able to command assistance to support him in the University. We hope that such encouragement will be amply provided, as it can easily be, and that Colleges will be so regulated as to enable all young men who may have gained a Scholarship to go through the Oxford course with as little expense as would be incurred in affiliated Halls, even according to the estimate of their warmest supporters. We also hope that the measures which we shall recommend will bring the expense of a University education within so moderate a compass, that few or none of those who have received the previous training indispensable for an Academical career will be excluded from its benefits; and that those who are poor, whether they can obtain a Scholarship or not, will find it possible to arrive at a Degree even more cheaply than is contemplated by the supporters of the Halls in question. . . .

243G. Fellowships

loc. cit., pp. 149–150.

. . . Of the changes required, perhaps the most important is that of removing restrictions on the Elections to Fellowships.

These restrictions are, as we have seen, of various kinds. The most injurious are those which confine the Fellowships to natives of particular localities, to members of particular families, and to those who are, or have been, Scholars in the College.

The result of these various limitations, whether imposed by Statutes or the practice of Colleges, is, that, of five hundred and forty Fellowships, there are scarcely twenty which are open to general competition; and of these, few, if any, can be considered as absolutely free from statutable restrictions.

Every other recommendation we propose depends in a greater or less degree on the removal of these restrictions. The extent of the evil, and the paramount necessity of removing it, are well stated in the words of Mr. Temple:–

"The system of election to Fellowships is, above all other defects at Oxford, that whose remedy is most needed and most important. The Fellows are so completely the governing body of the University, that, if no other change were made than to throw all the Fellowships open, and secure that the elections were honest, all other reforms would follow spontaneously. A body of men elected in the interest of learning would be sure, in course of time, to adapt everything to the needs of learning.

It is now too late to wait for the results of such a process; but the reform of the election to Fellowships still remains by far the most important of all the reforms that can be made in Oxford.

There are in Oxford 542 Fellowships. This does not include the Demyships at Magdalen, but it does include all the Fellowships at St. Johns and New College, and all the Studentships at Christ Church, which differ from Fellowships elsewhere in being tenable, and to some extent actually held, by Undergraduates.

From this body of men has to be supplied all the studying and all the educating power of the University–all the Professors, all the Tutors, all those who pursue learning for its own sake, and beyond the needs of practical life.

Out of this number, only 22 are in such a sense open that a young man, on first coming up, sees his way clear towards them with no other bar than may arise from his own want of talents or diligence.

The rest are almost all restricted to–

1. Persons born in particular localities.
2. Founders' kin.
3. Persons educated in particular schools.

The only Fellowships not so restricted are 10 at Balliol, 12 at Oriel, and 61 at Christchurch; and the latter are practically close, being in the gift of the Canons in rotation, who treat them very much as private property." . . .

Of all the reforms to be made at Oxford, this appears to me the vital one. Without a thorough reform here, all other reforms are as likely as not to be mischievous, for the skill to use them will be wanting. With a thorough reform here, all others become of less importance, for they are sure at last to follow. No corporate body is thoroughly reformed till its ablest men are put at the head of it. The Fellows have become the Heads of the University, and cannot be dislodged. The nation is bound to see that they are the ablest men that the University can supply. When this is done, there will be some meaning in the cry for "internal reform;" till then, any real reformation from within is impossible.

We will first show the evils arising from the system of close Fellowships. They are well stated in the following Evidence:–

"The effect of these restrictions," says Mr. Temple, "is most mischievous. Men who are naturally well fitted to be country Clergymen are bribed, because they are born in some parish in Rutland, to remain in Oxford as Fellows, until they are not only unfit for that, but for everything else. The interests of learning are entrusted to those who have neither talents nor inclination for the subject. The Fellowships are looked upon and used as mere stepping-stones to a living. A large number of the Fellows live away from the place, and thus in reality convert the emoluments to a purpose quite alien from that for which they were intended. On the other hand, the Undergraduates suffer a double loss; first, in being deprived of the legitimate stimulus to study, and, secondly, in having their instruction entrusted to an inferior body of men."

"The effects of the existing limitations of Fellowships to counties and dioceses," says Mr. Hayward Cox, "are undoubtedly the reverse of those contemplated by the Founders, whether the advancement of learning or of piety be understood to have been their object. They crowd the Colleges with inferior men, often without either the power or the inclination to promote the interests of education, withdraw many who might be useful in their appropriate spheres, hold out incentives to indolence, selfishness, and self-indulgence, and engage persons in the work of instruction who are without zeal in the pursuit, adopting it simply as a means supplied to them by their Collegiate position of enhancing their income temporarily until they succeed by rotation to those parochial duties and emoluments which are the ultimate objects of far the greater number. . . ."

243H. Scholarships

loc. cit., pp. 173–174.

. . . Hitherto we have spoken only or chiefly of the changes to be made in the Revenues of Colleges, so far as regards Students who have completed their course of Academic study. The recommendations which we have laid before Your Majesty would, we believe, effectually convert them into stimulants and rewards for the Students who have already become members of the University, and thus give greatly increased effect to its system of instruction. But we must not forget that the University is nearly as deeply interested in the excellence of the Schools throughout the country as in the excellence of the Colleges of Oxford, and that the endowments of Colleges may be used to mould and incite the Schools by encouragements in the form of Scholarships, as completely as the system and the character of the Colleges would be influenced if such measures as we have hitherto recommended should be carried into effect.

We have shown that the original object of Foundations was to support poor Students in their education at the University. These Students in the older Colleges entirely, and in all the Colleges to a great extent, consisted of the Fellows. But in more recent times, to these older Scholars or Fellows was added a class of younger Students, to whom the name of Scholar has since been exclusively applied, and who are now the chief representatives of the body of learners for which the College endowments were originally given. These Scholarships, whether part of the first

Foundations, or endowed by subsequent benefactions, have not, generally speaking, increased in value in the same ratio as Fellowships in the same College.

We are of opinion that it is a matter of the highest importance that Scholarships should be augmented where they are of inconsiderable value, and that they should also be greatly increased in number.

This would be really to act in accordance with the spirit of Collegiate Foundations, so far as it can be done in our times. It would be impracticable, as we have said more than once, to give a University education to poor persons who are not qualified to receive it. It would be an evil to do so in the present day, even if it were practicable. We have no wish to see in the Colleges an appendage of members on an inferior footing, such as we have spoken of as existing in them formerly. What the State and the Church require, as we have observed, is not poor men, but good and able men, whether poor or rich. The great resources of the Colleges render it easy for them to bring to the University those who are best fitted for a learned profession from almost every class in the country; and to enable many to live there as all Students receiving a liberal education should be supported. These resources would thus promote what were the paramount objects of Founders, or, at least, what were the paramount objects of the State in permitting the Founders to create perpetuities,–namely, the advancement of the higher branches of religious and secular knowledge. Fellowships are now for the most part obtained when men have ceased to be Students, and on the eve of leaving the University. A considerable part of the Revenues of Colleges may thus be devoted to the endowment of open Scholarships, so that in the great Schools, which now discharge a large share of the duties formerly devolving on the University, the beneficial effect may be produced, which may be expected in the University itself if all Students of real diligence and fair abilities shall be enabled to compete successfully for open Fellowships. . . .

2431. Professorships

loc. cit. pp. 173–181.

. . . The original object of College Foundations was, as we have seen, to encourage and reward learners; and this must always remain their principal object. Yet, for a long time past, the Colleges have undertaken the task of teaching, and Fellowships have formed a considerable portion of the income of College Tutors. This is not unreasonable. The Colleges absorbed the University; so that, practically, they shut up its Schools, and silenced its Professors. Therefore they made themselves responsible for that Instruction, which they had taken out of the hands of the larger and older Corporation. But, as we have shown in a previous section of our Report, Tutorial teaching is not sufficient for the wants of the University. In small Colleges, one or two Tutors are expected to teach everything; and in these, as well as in the larger Colleges, where the Tutors are more numerous, a College living tempts almost every man to quit his post on the first opportunity that offers. A Tutor has often more to do than one man can do, and abandons the work in despair; and those who have a more limited task do not consider it as a permanent occupation. The nature of the office, under present circumstances, often makes it unsatisfactory to men of high capacity

This state of things would not be materially altered, if the restriction of celibacy remained in full force, even though all others were removed. The remark of Adam Smith is true, that "when Church benefices . . . are many of them very considerable, the Church naturally draws from the Universities the greater part of their eminent men of letters. In this case (he adds), we are likely to find few eminent men among them, and those few amongst the youngest members of the Society, who are likely, too, to be drained away from it before they can have acquired experience and knowledge enough to be of much use to it." Since Adam Smith wrote, the Schools for the education of the middle and higher classes have become more numerous and more lucrative throughout the country; and, as these offer higher emoluments than College Tutorships without the restriction of celibacy, the result is that Colleges have less hold than ever upon their Tutors; and there is little hope that the University will ever possess a permanent body of eminent Teachers and learned men, so long as it is subject to this restriction.

It may be said, indeed, that the Halls, which have no Fellowships, obtain able Tutors, and keep them for a longer time than the Colleges can retain theirs. Tutors of Colleges who have received permission to marry, also remain a considerable time in the University. But we have already shown that, in Colleges generally, it would be inexpedient to grant this permission to more than one Tutor, and that in small Colleges it could hardly be granted at all. Besides, what the University wants is something more than what is commonly understood by a Tutor. It wants men who, after going through the course of study common to all, have devoted themselves chiefly to one branch of knowledge, and are prepared to devote their whole lives to its cultivation. It wants the ablest men in all departments, such as have been described in that portion of our Report in which we spoke of the Professors; men who would adopt learning as their profession, and give an European renown to Oxford. The little town of Giessen has been made illustrious by the presence of a single man: sovereigns contend for the possession of Leibig, but Giessen retains him, conscious that, with him would depart all her fame. What, in Germany, is done by grants from the public purse, must be done at Oxford by the revenues of the University, or rather of the Colleges, which have made themselves the University.

The illustrious men who founded the great Colleges of Oxford, in some instances, have themselves left proof that the purpose to which we propose to apply a portion of the College Revenues, was not alien from their thoughts. Bishop Fox, the Founder of Corpus Christi College, founded three Lectureships for Divinity, Latin, and Greek, in his College for the use of the whole University. The Lecturers were to be chosen solely in consideration of their fitness for the office. Foreigners, if more learned, were to be preferred to Englishmen, a provision which was acted upon in at least one case that we are acquainted with, by the choice of Ludovicus Vives, a Spaniard, in the year 1517, to fill the Greek Lectureship. They were to be excused from taking the oath demanded from other members of the Society. They were to have all the emoluments of Fellows, and a yearly stipend in addition, which stipend might be doubled in order to obtain the services of the best men. In this case it would have amounted to the same sum that was allowed to the President of the College.

So far as appears from the Statute, they were to be also exempt from the obligation to take Orders. All these liberal provisions have fallen into neglect. These Lectureships exist only in name, and are given as perquisites to College Tutors or Officers, who receive still the same annual payment fixed in the Statutes, which through the change of money is now of little value. At Magdalen, Waynflete also had previously founded three similar Lectureships for Divinity, Moral Philosophy, and Natural Philosophy, to which Fellowships were assigned free from all local restrictions, the Lecturers were to be the fittest men to be found in the whole University. The provisions also have fallen into disuse. We have, therefore, some means of judging, from the injunctions of Waynflete and Fox, how great Founders would have acted in our times. They threw off all restrictions when it became necessary to obtain eminent Teachers, and the stipends which they offered in order to attract such men, were such as must have placed them nearly on a level with the Head of the College.

In Cardinal College Wolsey founded six Professorships of Divinity, Canon Law, Civil Law, Medicine, Liberal Arts, and Latin, for the instruction of the whole University. These Professorships fell with him. But the Chairs of Divinity and Hebrew which King Henry VIII had established in the University, were endowed by King James I and King Charles I, with Canonries of Christchurch. The Margaret Professorship of Divinity and the two new Chairs of Pastoral Theology and Ecclesiastical History have been endowed in like manner by Your Majesty.

The Visitors sent by King Henry VIII order the Colleges of Merton, Queen's, New College, All Souls, and Magdalen, to furnish Instructors of the same kind for the general service of the University. It is true that these provisions were not carried into effect. But the fact of their being issued shows the view which, at the time of the Reformation, was taken of the duties of Colleges, and of the reasonableness of requiring them to contribute to the instruction of Students generally.

These ancient examples, and the five Collegiate Professorships at Christchurch, furnish the model which we desire to see followed in other Colleges. This course is also indicated in several parts of the Evidence.

We are of opinion that we shall be justified in calling on some of the Colleges to aid in the endowment of Professorships. Here we must observe, that these grants should not involve any obligation of celibacy; otherwise, as we have above shown, the alteration would be nugatory. The Colleges which we shall select for this purpose are those which have revenues larger than can be required for the purpose of educating their own members.

. . . . .

The Professor-Fellows should possess the same rights and privileges as the other Fellows; but we think, to adopt an expression of Mr. Wall's, that they should not be Professors because they are Fellows, but Fellows because they are Professors. The Fellowship would therefore follow the nomination of the Professorships; otherwise, the office would probably be filled up as the Headships of Colleges too often are now; and the Professorships might become as useless as the Readerships of Waynflete and Fox. This would be no greater hardship on the Colleges than the nomination of the Dean of Christchurch and its Canon-Professors by the Crown is on that Society;

while the advantages which the presence of an eminent Professor would confer on the College which would thus become his Academical home, are too obvious to need stating. It may be added, that the early history of Colleges furnishes precedents for such an amalgamation of Fellowships. In some instances the suppression of Fellowships, to increase the value of those which remain, is permitted by the Statutes; in others, new Fellowships have been united with those on the old Foundation for the same purpose; and in many Colleges, as we have seen, the value of the Fellowships has been augmented by keeping them at their original number instead of adding new Fellowships, as the Statutes enjoin, with the increase of the College property.

Several of the Professorships which we desire to see connected with Colleges have already some endowments. These might be applied to augment the stipends of the Professor-Fellows in case the Fellowships appropriated to them should be inadequate, or to found Professorships for new branches of learning independently of the Colleges, otherwise they might remain as affording a useful endowment, when it was thought well to have several Professors in the same department of knowledge.

But this is not all that the Colleges can do for literature and the University as a place of education. We have before stated that we are of opinion that it is necessary that a subordinate class of Professors, under the name of Lecturers or Readers, should be trained up in each School. Such an institution would supply the Members of the University generally with Instructors devoted to some one branch of learning, as well as retain superior men in Oxford, and supply a large choice of eminent candidates for the Professorships. It would doubtless be desirable that independent endowments should be formed for these Lecturers; but, if this shall be found to be impracticable, the object might be accomplished by allowing Fellows of Colleges, when appointed University Lecturers, to retain their Fellowships, so long as they held the office and resided in Oxford, and that without any obligation to remain unmarried, to take Holy Orders, or to vacate their Fellowships on succeeding to Property. The Fellowship would be their endowment, but they would find, in the necessity of obtaining a larger income, incentives to exertion which are often wanting to the present Instructors of the University.

The Lecturers would, naturally, become the substitutes of Professors incapacitated by illness or infirmity. . . .

244. The Newcastle Report on popular education (1861)

Parlty. Papers, 1861/XXI/pp. 293–328.

. . . In the foregoing chapters we have stated, in considerable detail, the facts, furnished by the evidence collected by us, which illustrate the present state of popular education in England and Wales. We come now to the most difficult part of the undertaking with which we have been intrusted–the suggestion of the measures best fitted, in our judgment, to extend and improve the elementary education of the poor. As any suitable plan for this object must necessarily take into account the actual state of the case as now existing, we think a rapid summary of the broadest facts which our inquiry has elicited may fitly precede a statement of our proposals.

The whole population of England and Wales, as estimated by the Registrar-General in the summer of 1858, amounted to 19,523,103. The number of children whose names ought, at the same date, to have been on the school books, in order that all might receive some education, was 2,655,767. The number we found to be actually on the books was 2,535,462, thus leaving 120,305 children without any school instruction whatever. The proportion, therefore, of scholars in week-day schools of all kinds to the entire population was 1 in 7·7 or 12·99 per cent. Of these 321,768 are estimated to have been above the condition of such as are commonly comprehended in the expression "poorer classes," and hence are beyond the range of our present inquiry. Deducting these from the whole number of children on the books of some school, we find that 2,213,694 children belonging to the poorer classes were, when our statistics were collected and compiled, receiving elementary instruction in day schools. Looking, therefore, at mere numbers as indicating the state of popular education in England and Wales, the proportion of children receiving instruction to the whole population is, in our opinion, nearly as high as can be reasonably expected. In Prussia, where it is compulsory, 1 in 6·27; in England and Wales it is, as we have seen, 1 in 7·7; in Holland it is 1 in 8·11; in France it is 1 in 9·0.

Before passing on to a much less pleasing aspect of the case, we should scarcely be doing it justice without adverting briefly to the surprisingly rapid progress of elementary education in this country since the beginning of the century. The Committee of the House of Commons, of which Lord Brougham, then Mr. Brougham, was chairman, and which was appointed in 1818 to inquire into the education of the people, obtained returns from the parochial clergy of all the day schools existing at that date, distinguishing those which had been established since 1803. Similar returns were obtained by a Committee of the House of Commons in 1833, presided over by the Earl of Kerry. Since then, in 1851, a complete educational census has been taken. The first two returns were probably defective, but they must have been sufficiently near the truth to show with tolerable accuracy the rapid pace at which day-school education has been advancing in this country. In 1803 the number of day scholars was estimated at 524,241, or one in 17½ of the whole population at that date. In 1818 the numbers were 674,883, or 1 in 17¼. In 1833 they were 1,276,947, or 1 in 11¼. In 1851 they were 2,144,378, or 1 in 8·36; while in 1858, according to our own returns and estimate, they have risen to 2,535,462, or 1 in 7·7. These statistics prove the great and steady progress which has been made since the early part of the century, both in the extent of the provision made for the education of the poorer classes, and in their appreciation of its worth.

We are bound to observe, however, that a very delusive estimate of the state of education must result from confining attention to the mere amount of numbers under day-school instruction. We have seen that less than three years ago there were in elementary day schools 2,213,694 children of the poorer classes. But of this number, 573,536 were attending private schools, which, as our evidence uniformly shows, are, for the most part, inferior as schools for the poor, and ill-calculated to give to the children an education which shall be serviceable to them in after-life. Of the 1,549,312 children whose names are on the books of public elementary day schools belonging to the religious denominations, only 19·3 per cent. were in their 12th year or upwards, and only that proportion, therefore, can be regarded as educated up to the standard suited to their stations. As many as 786,202 attend for less than 100 days in the year and can therefore hardly receive a serviceable amount of education, while our evidence goes to prove that a large proportion, even of those whose attendance is more regular, fail in obtaining it on account of inefficient teaching. Much, therefore, still remains to be done to bring up the state of elementary education in England and Wales to the degree of usefulness which we all regard as attainable and desirable.

The aid rendered by the Committee of Council in this important work our evidence shows to have been extremely valuable. But for obvious reasons, the plan on which it has been given has produced results falling far short of what is required. In the first place, very few of the smaller schools, in comparison of the larger, have been able to fulfil the conditions on which alone they could avail themselves of it; and secondly, as a consequence, assistance has not reached those which stand in greatest need of it. At the date of our statistical inquiries, it assisted 6,897 schools, containing 917,255 scholars; but it left unassisted 15,750 denominational schools, and about 317 Birkbeck, Ragged, and Factory Schools, containing altogether 671,393 scholars, while the whole of the private schools, in which 573,536 children attended, were entirely passed over. It may be fairly assumed that even the unassisted schools have profited to some extent by the stimulus indirectly applied to them by the aid rendered to the assisted, owing to which aid the standard of elementary education has been generally raised; but the facts which we have stated above show that the system has not effected, and we have reason to believe that it is not adapted to effect, a general diffusion of sound elementary education amongst all classes of the poor.

One other point deserves attention; it relates rather to the kind than to the amount of the instruction given in our public elementary schools to the children attending them. The children do not, in fact, receive the kind of education they require. We have just noticed the extravagant disproportion between those who receive some education and those who receive a sufficient education. We know that the uninspected schools are in this respect far below the inspected; but even with regard to the inspected, we have seen overwhelming evidence from Her Majesty's Inspectors, to the effect that not more than one-fourth of the children receive a good education. So great a failure in the teaching demanded the closest investigation; and as the result of it we have been obliged to come to the conclusion that the instruction given is commonly both too ambitious and too superficial in its character, that (except in the very best schools) it has been too exclusively adapted to the elder scholars to the neglect of the younger ones, and that it often omits to secure a thorough *grounding* in the simplest but most essential parts of instruction. We have shown that the present system has never completely met this serious difficulty in elementary teaching; that inspection looks chiefly to the upper classes and to the general condition of the school, and cannot profess to examine carefully individual scholars; and that a main object of the schools is defeated in respect of every child who, having attended for a considerable time, leaves without the power of reading, writing, and cyphering in an intelligent manner.

The foregoing review discloses to us the main defects in the existing state of popular education which any practical recommendations should aim to correct. Passing over all the minor changes which may be usefully adopted, mention of which will be found in other parts of this Report, we are agreed that our recommendations should tend to secure the following results. First, that all the children who attend the elementary day schools of the country should be induced to attend with sufficient regularity to enable them, within a reasonable period, to obtain a mastery over the indispensable elements of knowledge, reading, writing, and the primary rules of arithmetic; secondly, that all the schools in the country at which the children of the poor attend should be qualified and induced to put this amount of instruction within reach of their pupils; and, thirdly, that this should be done in such a way as not to lower the general standard of elementary instruction to this its lowest level of usefulness. How best to do these things appears to us to be the problem we have to solve, and the measures we have agreed to recommend have been framed with a view to its solution.

Before entering upon the fuller consideration of the measures by which we propose to attain these objects, it may be desirable to review the plans which from time to time have been proposed for the improvement of popular education, whether by extending the present system or by substituting another in its place. These will be best considered under the three heads of, first, proposals for leaving education to be provided by the voluntary contributions of parents or of charitable persons; secondly, proposals for the opposite plan of a compulsory State education; thirdly, proposals for substituting a system of rating for the present system adopted by Government. It is true that in theory the two latter proposals might be combined, but practically they have been kept separate. We shall then state the merits and defects of the present system, and propose means for its modification and extension. . . .

It has often been considered that the poor would be able to educate their children successfully without any further assistance than that of charitable persons; and this course has been recommended by many of those who are interested in popular education, who believe that the interference of Government with education is objectionable on political and religious grounds, and that it retards educational progress. It is right here to state, in speaking on this subject, that there exists among the members of the Commission, as among the nation at large, deeply seated differences of opinion with regard to the duty of Government in this country towards education.

The greater portion of the members of the Commission are of opinion that the course pursued by the Government in 1839, in recommending a grant of public money for the assistance of education, was wise; that the methods adopted to carry out that object have proved successful; and that while it is expedient to make considerable alterations in the form in which this public assistance is given, it would not be desirable either to withdraw it or largely to diminish its amount. Without entering into general considerations of the duty of a State with regard to the education of the poorer classes of a community, they think it sufficient to refer to the fact that all the principal nations of Europe, and the United States of America, as well as British

North America, have felt it necessary to provide for the education of the people by public taxation; and to express their own belief that, when the grant to education was first begun, the education of the greater portion of the labouring classes had long been in a neglected state that the parents were insensible to its advantages, and were (and still continue to be) in most cases incapable from poverty of providing it for their children, and that religious and charitable persons, interested in the condition of the poor, had not the power to supply the main cost of an education which, to be good, must always be expensive. They are further of opinion that, although the advance of education during the last 20 years has led to a wider and more just sense of its advantages, the principal reasons which originally rendered the assistance of Government desirable still form a valid ground for its continuance, partly because large portions of the country have been unable to obtain a due share in the advantages of the Grant, and in the improvements in education which have resulted from its operation, partly because there is still no prospect that the poor will be able by the assistance of charitable persons to meet the expense of giving an education to their children. They believe, therefore, that a withdrawal to any considerable extent of the public grant would have a tendency to check the general advance of education, and to give up much of the ground which has been won; and while they think that the present method of distributing the grant has many disadvantages, they believe them to consist in the manner in which the principle of giving public aid is applied and carried out, and not in the principle itself. Upon these grounds they have endeavoured in various parts of their report to indicate the points in which improvements are necessary, and the manner in which they may be most effectually introduced.

The minority admit that the responsibilities and functions of Government may be enlarged by special circumstances, and in cases where political disasters have retarded the natural progress of society. But they hold that in a country situated politically and socially as England is, Government has, ordinarily speaking, no educational duties, except towards those whom destitution, vagrancy, or crime casts upon its hands. They make no attempt at this distance of time to estimate the urgency of the circumstances which originally led the Government of this country to interfere in popular education. They fully admit that much good has been done by means of the grant; though they think it not unlikely that more solid and lasting good would have been done, that waste would have been avoided, that the different wants of various classes and districts would have been more suitably supplied, that some sharpening of religious divisions in the matter of education would have been spared, and that the indirect effects upon the character of the nation, and the relations between class and class would have been better, had the Government abstained from interference, and given free course to the sense of duty and the benevolence which, since the mind of the nation has been turned from foreign war to domestic improvement, have spontaneously achieved great results in other directions.

These members of the Commission desire that, a good type of schools and teachers having now been extensively introduced, the benefits of popular education having been manifested, and public interest in the subject having been thoroughly awakened, Government should abstain from making further grants, except grants for the building of schools, to which the public assistance was originally confined, and the continuance of which will be fair towards the parishes which have hitherto received no assistance; that the annual grants which are now made should be gradually withdrawn; and that Government should confine its action to the improvement of union schools, reformatories, and schools connected with public establishments, at the same time developing to the utmost the resources of the public charities, which either are or may be made applicable to popular education, and affording every facility which legislation can give to private munificence in building and endowing schools for the poor. It appears to them that if the State proceeds further in its present course, and adopts as definitive the system which has hitherto been provisional, it will be difficult hereafter to induce parental and social duty to undertake the burden which it ought to bear, or to escape from the position, neither just in itself nor socially expedient, that large and ill-defined classes of the people are entitled, without reference to individual need, or to the natural claims which any of them may possess on the assistance of masters and employers, to have their education paid for, in part at least, out of the public taxes. Nor do they feel confident that Government will ever be able to control the growing expenditure and multiplying appointments of a department, the operations of which are regulated by the increasing and varying demands of philanthropists rather than by the definite requirements of the public service.

They have felt it their duty, however, to regard the question as it stands after twenty-nine years of a policy opposed to their own; and on the rejection of their own view, they cordially adopt, in the second resort, the scheme of assistance approved by the majority of their colleagues, which they regard as better in every respect, and above all as a far nearer approach to justice, than the present extremely partial system.

We have thought fit to state the differences existing among us on this important point. It must not be inferred that this is the only matter on which we differ. In a subject involving so many statements, so many inferences, so many general principles, and so many executive details, universal concurrence was not to be expected, and has not in fact been obtained. . . .

Our review of the existing system has led us to the following conclusions:–We have seen that its leading principles have been to proportion public aid to private subscriptions, and to raise the standard of education by improving the general character of the schools throughout the country; that it has enlisted, in the promotion of education, a large amount of religious activity, and that, avoiding all unnecessary interference with opinion, it has practically left the management of the schools in the hands of the different religious denominations. In these respects it has been most successful. But we find that it demands, as a condition of aid, an amount of voluntary subscriptions which many schools placed under disadvantageous circumstances can scarcely be expected to raise; that it enlists in many places too little of local support and interest; that its teaching is deficient in the more elementary branches, and in its bearing on the younger pupils; and that while the necessity of referring many arrangements in every school to the central office embarrasses the Committee of Council with a mass of detail, the difficulty of investigating minute and distant claims threatens to become an element at once of expense and of dispute. We find further that Lord John Russell, one of its leading supporters, asserted in Parliament that "it was not intended by those who in 1839 commenced the system that its plan should be such as to pervade the whole country;" we see that it has been found necessary to break in upon its original principle of proportioning aid to subscription, and that this leads to a vast increase of expense, and we therefore conclude that if the system is to become national prompt means should be taken to remedy defects which threaten to injure its success in proportion to its extension, and to involve the revenue in an excessive expenditure. We now, therefore, proceed, in accordance with Your Majesty's instructions, to suggest the further measures which, in our opinion, "are required for the extension of sound and cheap elementary instruction to all classes of the people." We shall propose means by which, *in the first place*, the present system may be made applicable to the poorer no less than the richer districts throughout the whole country; *secondly*, by which the present expenditure may be controlled and regulated; *thirdly*, by which the complication of business in the office may be checked; *fourthly*, by which greater local activity and interest in education may be encouraged; *fifthly*, by which the general attainment of a greater degree of elementary knowledge may be secured than is acquired at present. . . .

245. Lord Granville's speech in the House of Lords, on the Revised Code (13 February 1862)

Hansard, 3/CLXV/172–176.

. . . Your Lordships are, no doubt, aware that the State now assists the schools by means of annual grants of various kinds. There is the capitation grant, there are payments to teachers, payments for teaching drawing, payments for pupil-teachers, payments for teaching pupil-teachers, for assistant teachers, for books, for apparatus, an industrial grant, and a small one made in certain cases where the master knows Welsh or Gaelic, and capitation grants according to the number of scholars. All these grants will be swept away by the new scheme, and the assistance which it is now proposed to give consists of one capitation grant, depending on certain conditions, such as the state of the school premises, and a satisfactory report of the Inspector upon the discipline and the religious instruction of the school; and then the managers of schools to claim one penny per scholar for every attendance after the first 100 at the morning or afternoon meetings of the school, and after the first twelve of the evening meetings. One third, however, of the sum thus claimable is forfeited if the scholar fails to satisfy the Inspector in reading, one-third, if in writing, and one-third if in arithmetic. For the purposes of examination, the children will be grouped according to age, and their failure in any one of these subjects will render the school liable to lose one-third of the allowance, and, if they fail in all, the State will contribute nothing towards the maintenance of the school. The course we have taken will, I think, meet to a great extent the objections which were raised against that portion of the existing system which has been condemned by the Commissioners. With regard to payments, those interested in the old system, no doubt, cry out against the new. All the memorials we have received agree in crying out as to the reduced amount of assistance which will be rendered to the schools under the Revised Code; but some of their arguments seem to be hardly consistent one with another. On the one hand they dispute the *data* on which the Report is founded, and deny that so few of the school children would be able to pass this elementary examination; while, on the other hand, they say that the number who could pass it is so small that the receipts of the schools must be materially reduced under the new system. Now, I do not wish to enter into an estimate of the expense, which must necessarily be contingent on a variety of circumstances. But the matter has been gone into over and over again, and the general result seems to be this:–If no improvement takes place in the instruction given, and if the defects pointed out by the Commissioners continue, a great public economy will be effected. On the contrary, if these defects are removed, I believe that the allowance to the schools will amount, after a very little time, to almost as much as at present. That result, however, will be contemporaneous with enormously increased efficiency in the schools, and with a great increase in the amount of useful instruction received by the children. . . . I am not going to enter into all the objections which have been advanced, but will deal only with some of the more prominent. The most serious one is the tendency of the new Code to disturb the progress of religious combined with secular instruction. At first the memorialists attacked the Committee of Council for what they declared to be a deliberate intention to injure the cause of religious education; but I am very happy to say that since then their tone has become more moderate, and they only now allege that the working of the scheme will necessarily have this effect. Now, nobody can read the history of this country without being aware how important a part has been played in it by the panic cry "Religion is in danger!" That panic has at times had mischievous results, and at other times it has had a most salutary influence upon the political conduct of the nation. It is also satisfactory to know that there exists such sensitiveness among the people on this subject that the cry always produces some effect. But I am persuaded that in the present instance this cry has been raised somewhat lightly and without any real foundation. We were once told by a venerable and learned Lord who always delights the House by his addresses, which are marked by the absence of a single superfluous word, that one of the great difficulties which lawyers experience in Parliament is that while in court they may use all their arguments, in Parliament they are only able to use their good arguments. Now, I cannot help thinking that the memorialists have adopted the legal rather than the Parliamentary way of stating their objections. As to this particular objection, I have been told an anecdote, for the truth of which I will not vouch, which seems to show that, unintentionally, some of these memorialists have put forward the religious question without themselves attaching much importance to it. A diocesan board met, I believe in a midland county, and unanimously agreed to seventeen resolutions against this unfortunate Code. The first of these resolutions embodied the religious objection. A Conservative Gentleman, and a distinguished Member of Parliament, afterwards–insidiously, I think–asked whether if, instead of the penny, a twopenny capitation grant was conceded their objections would be obviated? The board consulted again, and were–again unanimously–of opinion that that concession would remove all objections. My Lords, I really think that if you will look into this matter you will be of opinion that the religious objection is unfounded. The Revised Code makes no alteration whatever in the religious operation of the educational system as it existed under the old Code. The Order in Council of August, 1840, remains exactly as it was, and is not at all affected by the new Minutes; and therefore, technically, I may say that the new Code does not make the slightest alteration. . . .

246. Clarendon Report on the public schools (1864)

Parlty. Papers, 1864/xx/pp. 22–66.

. . . From the evidence of which we have here given a brief account, the following conclusions appear to follow:–

That boys who have capacity and industry enough to work for distinction, are, on the whole, well taught, in the article of classical scholarship, at the public schools;

But that they occasionally show a want of accuracy in elementary knowledge, either from not having been well grounded, or from having been suffered to forget what they have learnt;

That the average of classical knowledge among young men leaving school for college is low;

That in arithmetic and mathematics, in general information, and in English, the average is lower still, but is improving;

That of the time spent at school by the generality of boys, much is absolutely thrown away as regards intellectual progress, either from ineffective teaching, from the continued teaching of subjects in which they cannot advance, or from idleness, or from a combination of these causes;

That in arithmetic and mathematics the public schools are specially defective and that this observation is not to be confined to any particular class of boys. . . .

We shall now state generally the opinions we have formed respecting the course and subjects of instruction proper for these schools.

We believe that for the instruction of boys, especially when collected in a large school, it is material that there should be some one principal branch of study, invested with a recognized and, if possible, a traditional importance, to which the principal weight should be assigned, and the largest share of time and attention given.

We believe that this is necessary in order to concentrate attention, to stimulate industry, to supply to the whole school a common ground of literary interest and a common path of promotion.

The study of the classical languages and literature at present occupies this position in all the great English schools. It has, as we have already observed, the advantage of long possession, an advantage so great that we should certainly hesitate to advise the dethronement of it, even if we were prepared to recommend a successor.

It is not, however, without reason that the foremost place has in fact been assigned to this study. Grammar is the logic of common speech, and there are few educated men who are not sensible of the advantages they gained as boys from the steady practice of composition and translation, and from their introduction to etymology.

The study of literature is the study, not indeed of the physical, but of the intellectual and moral world we live in, and of the thoughts, lives, and characters of those men whose writings or whose memories succeeding generations have thought it worth while to preserve.

We are equally convinced that the best materials available to Englishmen for these studies are furnished by the languages and literature of Greece and Rome. From the regular structure of these languages, from their logical accuracy of expression, from the comparative ease with which their etymology is traced and reduced to general laws, from their severe canons of taste and style, from the very fact that they are "dead," and have been handed down to us directly from the periods of their highest perfection, comparatively untouched by the inevitable process of degeneration and decay, they are, beyond all doubt, the finest and most serviceable models we have for the study of language. As literature they supply the most graceful and some of the noblest poetry, the finest eloquence, the deepest philosophy, the wisest historical writing; and these excellences are such as to be appreciated keenly, though inadequately, by young minds, and to leave, as in fact they do, a lasting impression. Beside this, it is at least a reasonable opinion that this literature has had a powerful effect in moulding and animating the statesmanship and political life of England. Nor is it to be forgotten that the whole civilization of modern Europe is really built upon the foundations laid two thousand years ago by two highly civilized nations on the shores of the Mediterranean; that their languages supply the key to our modern tongues; their poetry, history, philosophy, and law, to the poetry and history, the philosophy and jurisprudence, of modern times; that this key can seldom be acquired except in youth, and that the possession of it, as daily experience proves, and as those who have it not will most readily acknowledge, is very far from being merely a literary advantage. . . .

Assuming, therefore, for the present at least, that the course of study is to run mainly–we do not say undeviatingly–in one track, we are of opinion that the classical languages and literature should continue to hold, as they now do, the principal place in public school education. We are equally convinced that they ought not to be studied solely and exclusively. To enter fully into this subject would require a lengthened dissertation. We may content ourselves with saying that it is the office of education, not only to discipline some of the faculties, but to awaken, call out, and exercise them all so far as this can be usefully done in boyhood; to awaken tastes that may be developed in after life; to impart early habits of reading, thought, and observation; and to furnish the mind with such knowledge as is wanted at the outset of life. A young man is not well educated–and indeed is not educated at all–who cannot reason or observe or express himself easily and correctly, and who is unable to bear his part in cultivated society from ignorance of things which all who mix in it are assumed to be acquainted with. He is not well educated if all his information is shut up within one narrow circle, and he has not been taught at least that beyond what he has been able to acquire lie great and varied fields of knowledge, some of which he may afterwards explore if he has inclination and opportunity to do so. The kind of knowledge which is necessary or useful, and the best way of exercising and disciplining the faculties, must vary, of course, with the habits and requirements of the age and the society in which his life is to be spent. Thus, when Latin was the common language of educated men, it was of primary importance to be able to speak and write Latin; so long as French is, though in a different manner and degree, a common channel of communication among educated persons in Europe, a man can hardly be called well educated who is ignorant of French. The mental faculties of men remain the same but the subjects on which, and the circumstances in which, they are to be exerted, vary considerably. The best form of discipline, therefore, may not be the same in the 19th as it was in the 16th century, and the information which will be serviceable in life is sure to be very different. Hence, no system of instruction can be framed, which will not require modification from time to time. The highest and most useful office of education is certainly to train and discipline; but it is not the only office. And we cannot but remark that while in the busy world too great a value perhaps is sometimes set upon the actual acquisition of knowledge, and too little upon that mental discipline which enables men to acquire and turn it to the best account, there is also a tendency which is exactly the reverse of this, and which is among the besetting temptations of the ablest schoolmasters; and that if very superficial men may be produced by one of these influences, very ignorant men are sometimes produced by the other.

The objections which have been commonly made to any extension of the old course of study are of a more or less practical character. It is said that many things which ought to be learnt ought not to be learnt at school, and are best acquired before going thither, or after leaving it; that they cannot be imparted there effectively nor without injury to more important studies, without dissipating the attention and overloading the mind; that the capacity for learning which an average boy possesses is after all, very limited, and his capacity for forgetting very great; that ability is rare and industry not very common; that if the apparent results are small, they do not quite represent the real benefit received; and that the actual results, such as they are, are the best which in practice it is possible to obtain.

There is truth in this, but not enough to support the conclusions it has often been used to establish. These arguments, in fact, have been employed against all the improvements which have been already introduced into our great schools, and introduced with proved success.

It is quite true that much less, generally speaking, can be mastered and retained by a young mind than theorists might suppose; and true that it is not easy to win steady attention from a high-spirited English lad, who has the restless activity and love of play that belong to youth and health, who, like his elders, thinks somewhat slowly, and does not express himself readily, and to whom mental effort is troublesome.

But these are difficulties which it is the business of the schoolmaster to contend with, and which careful and skilful teaching may to some extent overcome. If a youth, after four or five years spent at school, quits it at 19, unable to construe an easy bit of Latin or Greek without the help of a dictionary or to write Latin grammatically, almost ignorant of geography and of the history of his own country, unacquainted with any modern language but his own, and hardly competent to write English correctly, to do a simple sum, or stumble through an easy proposition of Euclid, a total stranger to the laws which govern the physical world and to its structure, with an eye and hand unpractised in drawing and without knowing a note of music, with an uncultivated mind and no taste for reading or observation, his intellectual education must certainly be accounted a failure, though there may be no fault to find with his principles, character, or manners. We by no means intend to represent this as a type of the ordinary product of English public-school education; but speaking both from the evidence we have received and from opportunities of observation open to all, we must say that it is a type much more common than it ought to be, making ample allowance for the difficulties before referred to, and that the proportion of failures is therefore unduly large. . . .

Natural science, with such slight exceptions as have been noticed above, is practically excluded from the education of the higher classes in England. Education with us is, in this respect, narrower than it was three centuries ago, whilst science has prodigiously extended her empire, has explored immense tracts, divided them into provinces, introduced into them order and method, and made them accessible to all. This exclusion is, in our view, a plain defect and a great practical evil. It narrows unduly and injuriously the mental training of the young, and the knowledge, interests, and pursuits of men in maturer life. Of the large number of men who have little aptitude or taste for literature, there are many who have an aptitude for science, especially for science which deals, not with abstractions, but with external and sensible objects; how many such there are can never be known, as long as the only education given at schools is purely literary; but that such cases are not rare or exceptional can hardly be doubted by any one who has observed either boys or men. Nor would it be an answer, were it true, to say, that such persons are sure to find their vocation, sooner or later. But this is not true. We believe that many pass through life without useful mental employment, and without the wholesome interest of a favourite study, for want of an early introduction to one for which they are really fit. It is not, however, for such cases only, that an early introduction to natural science is desirable. It is desirable, surely, though not necessary, for all educated men. Sir Charles Lyell has remarked on the advantage which the men of literature in Germany enjoy over our own, in the general acquaintance which the former possess with what is passing in the scientific world; an advantage due to the fact that natural science to a greater or less extent is taught in all the German schools. To clergymen and others who pass most of their lives in the country, or who, in country or town, are brought much into contact with the middle and lower classes, an elementary knowledge of the subject, early gained, has its particular uses; and we believe that its value, as a means of opening the mind and disciplining the faculties, is recognized by all who have taken the trouble to acquire it, whether men of business or of leisure. It quickens and cultivates directly the faculty of observation, which in very many persons lies almost dormant through life, the power of accurate and rapid generalization, and the mental habit of method and arrangement; it accustoms young persons to trace the sequence of cause and effect; it familiarises them with a kind of reasoning which interests them, and which they can promptly comprehend; and it is perhaps the best corrective for that indolence which is the vice of half-awakened minds, and which shrinks from any exertion that is not, like an effort of memory, merely mechanical. With sincere respect for the opinions of the eminent Schoolmasters who differ from us in this matter, we are convinced that the introduction of the elements of natural science into the regular course of study is desirable, and we see no sufficient reason to doubt that it is practicable. . . .

On the general results of public-school education as an instrument for the training of character, we can speak with much confidence. Like most English institutions–for it deserves to rank among English institutions–it is not framed upon a preconceived plan, but has grown up gradually. It is by degrees that bodies of several hundred boys have come to be congregated together in a small space, constantly associated with one another in work and in play; and it is by degrees that methods of discipline and internal government have been worked out by their Masters and by themselves, and that channels of influence have been discovered and turned to account. The organization of monitors or prefects, the system of boarding-houses, and the relation of tutor and pupil have arisen and been developed by degrees. The magnitude and the freedom of these schools make each of them, for a boy of from 12 to 18, a little world, calculated to give his character an education of the same kind as it is destined afterwards to undergo in the great world of business and society. Eton, Harrow, and Rugby are the *proscholia* in this respect of Oxford and Cambridge, as Oxford and Cambridge, with their larger, but still limited freedom, are for the training of adult life. The liberty, however, which is suited for a boy is a liberty regulated by definite restraints; and his world, the chief temptations of which arise from thoughtlessness, must be a world pervaded by powerful disciplinary influences, and in which rewards as well as punishments are both prompt and certain. The principle of governing boys mainly through their own sense of what is right and honourable is undoubtedly the only true principle; but it requires much watchfulness, and a firm, temperate, and judicious administration, to keep up the tone and standard of opinion, which are very liable to fluctuate, and the decline of which speedily turns a good school into a bad one. The system, we may add, is one which is adapted for boys, and not for children, and which should not be entered upon, as a general rule, till the age of childhood is past; neither, perhaps, is it universally wholesome for boys of every temperament and character, though we believe that the cases to which it is unsuited are not very numerous. But we are satisfied, on the whole, both that it has been eminently successful, and that it has been greatly improved during the last 30 or 40 years, partly by causes of a general kind, partly by the personal influence and exertions of Dr. Arnold and other great schoolmasters. The changes which it has undergone for the better are, we believe, visible in the young men whom it has formed during that period. The great schools–which, it must be observed, train for the most part the Masters who are placed at the head of the smaller schools, and thus exercise not only a direct but a wide indirect influence over education–may certainly claim, as Mr. Hedley says, a large share of the credit due for the improved moral tone of the Universities, as to which we have strong concurrent testimony.

"I think there has been a great improvement in the moral training and character of the young men who have come to the University of late years. The schools deserve much of the credit for it, though there is a great difference in schools in this respect; much of the change is due, no doubt, to the influence of public opinion."

The Master of Balliol says:-

"I have the very great satisfaction of expressing my conviction that a very marked improvement has taken place in the moral training and character of the young men who have come to the University, within the period of my remembrance. In this respect I make no distinction between public schools and other modes of education: but my opportunities of observation have been more extensive in reference to pupils of public schools."

Mr. Rawlinson, of Exeter, says:-

"I think that there has been a considerable improvement in the moral training and character of our young men from public, and even from private, schools within the period over which my experience extends. The change dates from the time when Arnold's pupils began to come up to Oxford, which was just about the time when I myself entered the University. It gradually progressed for some 15 or 20 years, as school after school passed into fresh hands. I doubt, however, if there has been any improvement recently; and I think great watchfulness is needed at all the public and other large schools to prevent a deterioration in this important respect."

Mr. Mayor, of St. John's College, Cambridge, writes:-

"In many respects there has certainly been an improvement of late years, especially in men coming up from the larger schools. There is less of roughness and more manliness. The Masters see more of the boys than they used, and exert a more powerful influence over them. I do not think that there has been the same change in the case of boys coming from home or from the smaller schools."

There is, we rejoice to find, a general agreement on this point, even among witnesses who differ widely in their estimate of the intellectual education which these schools afford. . . .

It remains for us to discharge the pleasantest part of our task, by recapitulating in a few words the advances which these schools have made during the last quarter of a century, and in the second place by noticing briefly the obligations which England owes to them,-obligations which, were their defects far greater than they are, would entitle them to be treated with the utmost tenderness and respect.

That important progress has been made even in those particulars in which the schools are still deficient, is plain from the short review contained in the foregoing pages, and will appear still more clearly from the more detailed statements in the Second Part. The proportion of masters to boys has been increased; the quantity of work exacted is greater than it was, though still in too many cases less than it ought to be. At the same time the advance in moral and religious training has more than kept pace with that which has been made in intellectual discipline. The old roughness of manners has in a great measure disappeared, and with it the petty tyranny and thoughtless cruelty which were formerly too common, and which used indeed to be thought inseparable from the life of a public school. The boys are better lodged and cared for, and more attention is paid to their health and comfort.

Among the services which they have rendered is undoubtedly to be reckoned the maintenance of classical literature as the staple of English education, a service which far outweighs the error of having clung to these studies too exclusively. A second, and a greater still, is the creation of a system of government and discipline for boys, the excellence of which has been universally recognized, and which is admitted to have been most important in its effects on national character and social life. It is not easy to estimate the degree in which the English people are indebted to these schools for the qualities on which they pique themselves most–for their capacity to govern others and control themselves, their aptitude for combining freedom with order, their public spirit, their vigour and manliness of character, their strong but not slavish respect for public opinion, their love of healthy sports and exercise. These schools have been the chief nurseries of our statesmen; in them, and in schools modelled after them, men of all the various classes that make up English society, destined for every profession and career, have been brought up on a footing of social equality, and have contracted the most enduring friendships, and some of the ruling habits, of their lives; and they have had perhaps the largest share in moulding the character of an English Gentleman. The system, like other systems, has had its blots and imperfections; there have been times when it was at once too lax and too severe–severe in its punishments, but lax in superintendence and prevention; it has permitted, if not encouraged, some roughness, tyranny, and licence; but these defects have not seriously marred its wholesome operation, and it appears to have gradually purged itself from them in a remarkable degree. Its growth, no doubt, is largely due to those very qualities in our national character which it has itself contributed to form; but justice bids us add that it is due likewise to the wise munificence which founded the institutions under whose shelter it has been enabled to take root, and to the good sense, temper, and ability of the men by whom during successive generations they have been governed.

247. Taunton Report on endowed schools (1867–1868)

Parlty. Papers, 1867–1868/XXVIII/pp. 78–88, 546–661.

... The most urgent educational need of the country is that of good schools of the third grade, that is, of those which shall carry education up to the age of 14 or 15. It is just here that the endowed schools appear most signally to fail, while nothing else takes their place. There may be a few good schools of the sort here and there, such for instance as the Bristol Trade School, and Hele's School at Exeter, and some others; but such schools are unquestionably not numerous nor well distributed. And the private schools cannot be relied on to fill up the gap; for as soon as a master is thoroughly successful in a school of this sort, there is everything to induce him to raise his terms, and to fill his school with boys of a higher social class; and thus the need still remains unsupplied. The evidence is almost unanimous that just here is our most conspicuous deficiency, and that the artizans, the small shopkeepers, the smaller farmers are in many places without any convenient means of educating their children at all, and still more often have no security that what education they do get is good.

When it is considered how very large a proportion of the population is included in these classes, it is evident that no other deficiency in our provision for education could well be more important. It is not only the case, however, that the number concerned is larger than that of any other class except the lowest, but that the wealth and prosperity of the country depend to so great a degree on the industry, and that industry on the intelligence, of those who are left thus uneducated. We have already made a special report on the statements made to us regarding the inferior rate of progress said to be visible in British manufacturers, when some of the productions of this country are compared with those that were sent by other nations to the Exhibition at Paris. This is ascribed in some measure to a want of technical instruction in our artisans, as well as in their employers and foremen. Such a want, however, would be a far less serious matter, if it stood alone. But we are bound to add that our evidence appears to show that our industrial classes have not even that basis of sound general education on which alone technical instruction can rest. It would not be difficult, if our artizans were otherwise well educated, to establish schools for technical instruction of whatever kind might be needed. But even if such schools were generally established among us, there is reason to fear that they would fail to produce any valuable results for want of the essential material, namely, disciplined faculties and sound elementary knowledge in the learners. In fact, our deficiency is not merely a deficiency in technical instruction, but, as Mr. Arnold indicates, in general intelligence, and unless we remedy this want we shall gradually but surely find that our undeniable superiority in wealth and perhaps in energy will not save us from decline. If we could provide good schools for our artizans up to the age of 14, then those who showed aptitude for special industrial pursuits would be in a fit condition to enter on the needed special study. But our first object should be to enable the whole of this large population, whose education we are now considering, to cultivate their children's understandings and make them really intelligent men. We need schools that shall provide good instruction for the whole of the lowest portion of what is commonly called the middle class, and we cannot overstate our sense of the importance of the need. These are the schools that we have called Schools of the Third Grade. . . .

The general character of the instruction to be given in schools of the second grade is determined by the fact that it is to cease at about 16. After that the boys are not supposed to go to the universities, but either to employments or to special preparation for employments. These schools would prepare youths for business, for several professions, for manufactures, for the army, for many departments of the civil service. Many of the farmers, many of the richer shopkeepers, many professional men, all but the wealthier gentry, would probably wish to have their sons educated in schools of this sort, if the education were thoroughly good of its kind.

We have already expressed our opinion that in such schools Greek should not be included, except as an extra and under special regulations. The shortness of the education would not allow such a knowledge of Greek to be acquired as could introduce the learner to Greek literature, and the time would be wanted for other subjects. But Latin would be a necessity in all but a very few of these schools, since most of the occupations presuppose it in some degree, and many of the examinations prescribe it. To Latin one modern language ought to be added and thoroughly well taught; and in some of the schools two modern languages, according to the general character of the place and the usual destination of the scholars. English literature and the elements of political economy should not be neglected. The mathematics in these schools ought to be at once strictly scientific and yet of a practical cast; not aiming at subtle refinements, but at practical applications. It would be by no means expedient that mere rough and empirical methods should be substituted for strict mathematical reasoning; but the minds of the learners should be perpetually brought back to concrete examples instead of being perpetually exercised in abstractions. It would be possible to put algebra, geometry, and trigonometry within the reach of many of the boys, and to go even further with a few. Lastly, these are especially the schools in which it would often be worth while to lay great stress on practical mechanics and other branches of natural science. Many of these schools would correspond to the *Realschulen* of Prussia, to the schools of industry of Zurich. In them would be educated many of the employers of skilled labour, to whom a knowledge of such science would be of the highest value. The *elite* also of the boys in the third grade schools would be often transferred here to be our accomplished workmen, our highest and most skilful artizans. . . .

Most of the schools of the first grade would make it their chief aim to prepare for the Universities. Not that all their scholars, nor perhaps in most cases more than a fourth or a fifth, would go to a University, but, as a rule, those who went would be the ablest and the most advanced; and their education would almost of necessity govern that of the rest. It is not therefore possible to prescribe a course of instruction for these schools without reference to what the Universities require. The schools would therefore be generally classical schools. But besides the classics it would now be generally admitted that English literature and the elements of political economy, modern languages, mathematics, and natural science ought to find a place in such schools as these, and that even if they be considered subordinate subjects they should be made a serious part of the business of the school; the masters who taught them should be put on a perfect footing of equality with the other masters; the time allotted to them should prove that they were valued; the marks assigned to them in promotions, the prizes given for proficiency in them, the care taken in examining the boys' progress, should be such as to stimulate the learners and prevent all suspicion, that, while classics were a reality, all other studies were a mere concession to popular clamour. . . .

The education given in schools of the First Grade marks the limit of our province. It is not our duty to discuss what should be the studies or the regulations of the Universities; but we think it our duty at this point to remark, that the organization of the education given in schools can never be complete, unless the Universities co-operate to make it so, by giving encouragement in due measure to every kind of study which the country needs. If any studies get no recognition at the Universities, or if no room is made for them, it is impossible for those studies to flourish in the schools. If science has an unpractical character at the Universities, it will be very difficult for the schools to give it a practical turn. If the Universities cut themselves off from the needs of the country, they make it much more difficult for the school to supply those needs. We cannot but consider it the duty of the Universities, placed as they are at the head of English education, to study carefully the requirements of the country, and to take their part in supplying them. . . .

The general deficiency in girls' education is stated with the utmost confidence, and with entire agreement, with whatever difference of words, by many witnesses of authority. Want of thoroughness and foundation; want of system; slovenliness and showy superficiality; inattention to rudiments; undue time given to accomplishments, and those not taught intelligently or in any scientific manner; want of organization,–these may sufficiently indicate the character of the complaints we have received, in their most general aspect. It is needless to observe that the same complaints apply to a great extent to boys' education. But on the whole the evidence is clear that, not as they might be but as they are, the Girls' Schools are inferior in this view to the Boys' Schools. . . .

The whole field which we have traversed is beset with questions which have been made matter of eager controversy, and we cannot hope that the conclusions at which we have arrived with regard to them will escape animadversion and dissent. But we have endeavoured to meet difficulties fairly, and to deal with them in such a manner as appeared to be most likely to promote the great objects we had in view, and most in accordance with the wants and disposition of the country.

With regard to educational endowments (to which our attention was more especially called by Your Majesty's commands), we have desired to maintain them, so far as they could be rendered really and adequately useful, for the great purposes for which they were intended; but to provide a complete and durable remedy for those wide-spread abuses which have been abundantly proved to exist in these institutions. It is true that the principle itself of educational endowments has sometimes been questioned on high authority, and we are disposed to admit that, unless they shall be so re-organized as to aid, they will positively obstruct the improvement of education; but, besides the fact that we find them in existence, we are of opinion that however liable they may be to perversion without vigilant and constant supervision, yet that they often give a character of dignity and permanence to schools which produces the most beneficial effect on the minds both of instructors and of scholars. We have also desired in various ways to encourage the systematic improvement of private schools, and the establishment of others of a more public character throughout the country, by the instrumentality of local bodies, without interfering unduly with that freedom of private action which is so wisely valued by Englishmen, and for the absence of which we believe that no exertions on the part of the State could adequately make up.

We have thought it desirable to give a good deal of elasticity at the outset to the system which we suggest, in order that it may be capable of subsequent adaptation, if necessary, to the advancing requirements and wishes of the community. We cannot conclude without expressing an earnest hope that whatever errors or deficiencies may be found in this Report, the subject to which it relates may receive from the Legislature that early attention which is alike urged upon us by the great and successful efforts now making in foreign countries to improve education, as well as by the circumstances of our own.

The result of our inquiry has been to show that there are very many English parents who, though they are willing to pay the fair price of their children's education, yet have no suitable schools within their reach where they can be sure of efficient teaching, and that consequently great numbers of the youth of the middle class, and especially of its lower divisions, are insufficiently prepared for the duties of life, or for the ready and intelligent acquisition of that technical instruction, the want of which is alleged to threaten such injurious consequences to some of our great industrial interests. We were of opinion that the subject either of technical or of professional education of any kind did not properly come within the scope of our inquiry, but, as it was brought incidentally before us, we considered it of so much consequence as applied to the arts of industry in this country that we thought it right to call special attention to it in a Report which we have already presented to Your Majesty.

We believe that schools, above most other institutions, require thorough concert among themselves for their requisite efficiency; but there is in this country neither organization, nor supervision, nor even effective tests to distinguish the incompetent from the truly successful; and we cannot but regard this state of things as alike unjust to all good schools and schoolmasters, and discreditable and injurious to the country itself. . . .

We have thought it our duty to inquire separately into the subject of Girls' Schools, and we have devoted this Chapter to that branch of the question.

On the gravity of it, it is needless to dwell. In our notice of Christ's Hospital we have quoted the authority of Mr. Hare in support of the opinion that an educated mother is even of more importance to the family than an educated father; and no one of reflection will controvert these words of Mr. Lingen: "If one looks to the enormous number of unmarried women in the middle class who have to earn their own bread, at the great drain of the male population of this country for the army, for India, and for the colonies, at the expensiveness of living here, and consequent lateness of marriage, it seems to me that the instruction of the girls of a middle-class family for any one who thinks much of it, is important to the very last degree." Mr. Fraser quotes a weighty opinion of Tocqueville, that the chief cause of the prosperity of the United States is the superiority of their women.

It is true that this conviction, as relating to the Middle Classes, may be looked on as recent and still growing, and as one which still greatly needs to be inculcated on and accepted by parents of that class. We have had much evidence showing the general indifference of parents to girls' education, both in itself and as compared to that of boys. It leads to a less immediate and tangible pecuniary result; there is a long-established and inveterate prejudice, though it may not often be distinctly expressed, that girls are less capable of mental cultivation, and less in need of it, than boys; that accomplishments, and what is showy and superficially attractive, are what is really essential for them; and in particular, that as regards their relations to the other sex and the probabilities of marriage, more solid attainments are actually disadvantageous rather than the reverse.

These considerations will not affect the character of the recommendations we shall offer. But it must be fully admitted that such ideas as we have referred to have a very strong root in human nature, and that with respect to the average, nay to the great majority of mankind, it would be idle to suppose that they would ever cease to have a powerful operation. Parents who have daughters will always look to their being provided for in marriage, will always believe that the gentler graces and winning qualities of character will be their best passports to marriage, and will always expect their husbands to take on themselves the intellectual toil and the active exertions needed for the support of the family. "The ideal presented to a young girl," says an able writer, Miss Davies, "is to be amiable, inoffensive, always ready to give pleasure and to be pleased." The statement may be exaggerated, but that the feeling it describes will ever cease to be extensively prevalent, can hardly be expected. A similar feeling, though not just the same, is reported by Mr. Stanton as that of "many excellent ladies, who would make all schools places of moral rather than intellectual training." In our Returns the girls' school is often spoken of as intended to be more a home than a school. The general feeling is illustrated by a singular rule which we have found in the Returns of one of the proprietary schools, that if a girl "found herself unhappy," due pains must be taken to remove that feeling; failing which it is directed that she be removed.

We have expressed these views thus early in this Chapter, because they belong to the whole subject-matter. The far-sighted and enlightened views about the education of girls, expressed by the many able and experienced ladies and other authorities whom we have consulted, we have no doubt, will meet with ever-increasing acceptance in this country; but we believe their advocates must be content to expect, even ultimately, a proportion of failures somewhat larger than must be reckoned on in most such attempts, and distinctly more than is probable in the corresponding work of the education of boys.

We cannot, however, say this without pointing out, though it may almost appear a truism, that the popular feeling to which we have referred, on one most important subject, that of the married life of women, is founded on a grave and radical misconception–a misconception especially, though by no means only, injurious to the Middle Class, and increasingly so in these days. The most material service may be rendered to the husband, in the conduct of his business and the most serious branches of his domestic affairs, by a wife trained and habituated to a life altogether different from that of mere gentleness and amiability of which we have spoken; a life of no slight intellectual proficiency and capacity for many functions too commonly thought to be reserved for the male sex. Mr. Bryce, too, has well dwelt on the greater amount of leisure possessed by the women in a mercantile community, if, indeed, it should not rather be said, that it is possessed by them alone; and remarked that we must, therefore, look to them for the maintenance of a higher and more cultivated tone in society.

248. W. E. Forster's speech on the motion for leave to introduce the Education Bill (17 February 1870)

Hansard, 3/CXCIX/440–466.

I am not going to detain the House with any long statement of facts, and still less do I intend to weary you with statistics; but there are two great categories of facts which I would beg you to bear in mind. The first is the broad fact of what we have existing at this moment in regard to primary education. I shall confine myself to that, respecting which we are pretty accurately informed, because it relates to the schools to which we vote Government money. Last year I moved the Education Estimate, and in addition to the money required for the central office, for Inspectors, and for normal schools, I asked for an annual grant of about £415,000 for primary schools in England and Wales. Of those schools about 11,000 were day schools and 2,000 night schools. The number of children upon the registers of those schools was about 1,450,000, and the average attendance about 1,000,000, representing, therefore, the education more or less imperfect of nearly 1,500,000 children. I say the education, according to these Returns, is very imperfect, because the attendance is very irregular, nevertheless the figures I have just referred to represent also a great amount of voluntary zeal, and much willingness on the part of parents to send their children to school. Now, while alluding to voluntary zeal, I must be allowed to state that I think no one could occupy my office without being fully aware of what the country owes to the managers of the schools at present in receipt of Government grants. Both before and during my tenure of that office I have had many opportunities of seeing those gentlemen at work, particularly ministers of religion of all denominations, though perhaps it has been my lot to see more of the clergy of the Church of England than of others. I have seen them at their work, and tried to help them occasionally; I know the sacrifices they have made, and not for a moment do I believe it possible that anyone who considers this question will disregard what they have already done, or will wish to do without their aid in the future. I sometimes hear it objected that they gain great influence by their efforts in promoting education. I believe they have not worked in order to attain that object, though far distant be the time when, in England, self-denying exertions, such as many of these gentlemen have made, will not give them influence!

Having alluded to what we already have, I will now ask–"What is it that we have not?" More or less imperfectly about 1,500,000 children are educated in the schools that we help–that is, they are simply on the registers. But, as I had the honour of stating last year, only two-fifths of the children of the working classes between the ages of six and ten years are on the registers of the Government schools, and only one-third of those between the ages of ten and twelve. Consequently, of those between six and ten, we have helped about 700,000, more or less, but we have left unhelped 1,000,000; while of those between ten and twelve, we have helped 250,000, and left unhelped at least 500,000. Some hon. Members will think I daresay, that I leave out of consideration the unaided schools. I do not, however, leave them out of consideration; but it so happens–and we cannot blame them for it–that the schools which do not receive Government assistance are, generally speaking, the worst schools, and those least fitted to give a good education to the children of the working classes. That is the effect of the present system. Exceptions, no doubt, may be picked out; but speaking generally, my assertion is borne out by the Reports presented annually by our Department, and particularly by the Report of last Session. I may also refer to the Report which will be speedily in the hands of hon. Members in consequence of the Motion made last year by the hon. Member for Stoke (Mr. Melly), concerning the educational condition of four great towns–Liverpool, Manchester, Leeds, and Birmingham. That Report, I have reason to believe, will abundantly confirm my statement that we cannot depend upon the unaided and uninspected schools. I have not myself had the opportunity of reading that Report, for I was so anxious that it should be laid before the House with the least possible delay that I did not keep it in my hands for a single hour. But I have had the privilege of corresponding with the two gentlemen who conducted the inquiries; and therefore I believe I can give pretty correctly the figures with regard, at all events, to Liverpool, and they are figures which may well alarm us. It is calculated that in Liverpool the number of children between five and thirteen who ought to receive an elementary education is 80,000; but, as far as we can ascertain, 20,000 of them attend no school whatever, while at least another 20,000 attend schools where they get an education not worth having. In Manchester–that is, in the borough of Manchester, not including Salford, there are about 65,000 children who might be at school, and of this number about 16,000 go to no school at all. I must, however, add that Manchester appears to be better than Liverpool in one respect, that there are fewer schools where the education is not worth having. As a Yorkshireman, I am sorry to say that, from what I hear, Leeds appears to be as bad as Liverpool; and so also, I fear, is Birmingham. . . .

Now, I will at once proceed to the main principles that run through all our clauses for securing efficient school provision. They are two in number. Legal enactment, that there shall be efficient schools everywhere throughout the kingdom. Compulsory provision of such schools if and where needed, but not unless proved to be needed. These being the principles, I now come to the actual provisions.

The first provision that would probably suggest itself to the minds of all hon. Members would be a system of organization throughout the country. We take care that the country shall be properly mapped and divided, so that its wants may be duly ascertained. For this, we take present known divisions, and declare them to be school districts, so that upon the passing of this Bill there will be no portion of England or Wales not included in one school district or another. I think it would be convenient if I at once state what these districts would be, although the grounds upon which we have proceeded I will, with the permission of hon. Members, allude to hereafter. We have taken the boundaries of boroughs as regards towns, and parishes as regards the country, and when I say parish, I mean the civil parish and not the ecclesiastical district. With regard to the metropolis, the difficulties of which, from its peculiar position, defy almost all attempts at legislation, we shall be guided very much by the counsel and advice of the Metropolitan Members; but after the greatest possible inquiry, we have come to the conclusion that the best districts we can take in the metropolis are, where they exist, the school districts already formed for workhouse schools, and where they do not exist, the boundaries of the vestries. If, then, we get all England and Wales divided into districts, our next duty is to ascertain their educational condition, and for that purpose we take powers to collect Returns which will show us what in each district is the number of schools, of scholars, and of children requiring education. We also take power to send down Inspectors and officers to test the quality of the schools, and find out what education is given. Then, I may at once state that if in any one of these districts we find the elementary education to be sufficient, efficient, and suitable, we leave that district alone. By sufficient, I mean if we find that there are enough schools; by efficient, I mean schools which give a reasonable amount of secular instruction; and by suitable, I mean schools to which, from the absence of religious or other restrictions, parents cannot reasonably object; and I may add that for the purpose of ascertaining the condition of these districts, we count all schools that will receive our Inspectors, whether private or public, whether aided or unaided by Government assistance, whether secular or denominational. If we find the district adequately supplied, we let it alone so long as it continues in that state, retaining for ourselves the power to renew the examination from time to time. It would, however, be vain for us not to suppose that we shall find a vast number of districts–I am afraid the enormous majority throughout the area of the country –where the educational provision is insufficient, and where that is so, as it is by public inquiry that that insufficiency must be ascertained, so it is by public provision that that need must be supplied. . . .

We have said that we must have provision for public elementary schools. The first question then is, by whom is it to be made? Now here for a time we shall test the voluntary zeal of the district. Not only do we not neglect voluntary help, but on condition of respecting the rights of parents and the rights of conscience, we welcome it. To see, then, whether voluntary help will be forthcoming we give a year. We think we ought to give enough of time to test the zeal and willingness of any volunteers who may be disposed to help; but we ought not to give longer time, because we cannot afford to wait. If that zeal, if that willingness, does not come forward to supply the schools that are required, then the children must no longer remain untaught, and the State must step in.

Now, then, we come at last to what will undoubtedly be looked upon as the most important part of the Bill–namely, the compulsory provision where it is wanted. I have said that there will be compulsory provision where it is wanted, but not otherwise. We come now to the machinery for its application where it is proved to be wanted. How do we propose to apply it? By school Boards elected by the district. We have already got the district; we have found out the educational want existing in it–we see that the district must be supplied–we have waited in the hope that some persons would supply it; they have not done so. We, therefore, say that it must be supplied; but by whom? It would be possible for the Government to attempt to supply it by defraying the expenses from the taxes; and I believe that one or two hon. Gentlemen think that would be the best way. No doubt it would be possible for the Government to try to do this; but I believe it would be impossible for them to effect it. I believe it is not in the power of any central Department to undertake such a duty throughout the kingdom. Consider also the enormous power it would give the central administration. Well, then, if Government cannot do it itself by central action, we must still rely upon local agency. Voluntary local agency has failed, therefore our hope is to invoke the help of municipal organization. Therefore, where we have proved the educational need we supply it by local administration–that is, by means of rates aided by money voted by Parliament, with central inspection and control. I wish to be frank with the House, and I therefore say that undoubtedly this proposal will affect a large portion of the kingdom. I believe it will affect almost all the towns, and a great part of the country. . . .

I now come to another part of the subject–to that part to which I referred at the beginning of my remarks when I said that the country would expect that we should secure, if possible, the attendance of the children. This attendance question is a difficult question, but we must face it. To leave it alone is to leave the children untaught, and to force the taxpayers to pay for useless schools. I shall at once state what I expect may surprise the House. It is that, after much thought upon the matter, the Government has permitted me to put before the House the principle of direct compulsion. This may seem to be a startling principle; but, although I feel that I have already occupied the House much longer than I should have wished to do, it is a principle of the Bill which I feel I cannot quickly pass over. It has only been within the last few months that thought on the matter has brought me to the conclusion that the principle of direct compulsion ought to be adopted. . . .

We must not delay. Upon the speedy provision of elementary education depends our industrial prosperity. It is of no use trying to give technical teaching to our artizans without elementary education; uneducated labourers–and many of our labourers are utterly uneducated–are, for the most part, unskilled labourers, and if we leave our workfolk any longer unskilled, notwithstanding their strong sinews and determined energy, they will become over-matched in the competition of the world. Upon this speedy provision depends also, I fully believe, the good, the safe working of our constitutional system. To its honour, Parliament has lately decided that England shall in future be governed by popular government. I am one of those who would not wait until the people were educated before I would trust them with political power. If we had thus waited we might have waited long for education; but now that we have given them political power we must not wait any longer to give them education. There are questions demanding answers, problems which must be solved, which ignorant constituencies are ill-fitted to solve. Upon this speedy provision of education depends also our national power. Civilized communities throughout the world are massing themselves together, each mass being measured by its force; and if we are to hold our position among men of our own race or among the nations of the world we must make up the smallness of our numbers by increasing the intellectual force of the individual.

But there are many men, I doubt not many Members of this House–and these not the least earnest to do their duty, or the least able to help their fellows–who are swayed not so much by these general considerations as by the condition of the individuals around them. Well, then, to these gentlemen let me say one word–I am not a fanatic in this matter of education, I know well that knowledge is not virtue –that no education, much less elementary education, gives power to resist temptation–is a safeguard against calamity; but we all know that want of education–that ignorance is weakness, and that weakness in this hard struggling world generally brings misfortune–often leads to vice. Let us then each of us think of our own homes, of the villages in which we have to live, of the towns in which it is our lot to be busy; and do we not know child after child–boys or girls–growing up to probable crime, to still more probable misery, because badly taught or utterly untaught? Dare we then take on ourselves the responsibility of allowing this ignorance and this weakness to continue one year longer than we can help? . . .

Part XII

INDUSTRIAL CONDITIONS AND LEGISLATION

INDUSTRIAL CONDITIONS AND LEGISLATION

Introduction

INDUSTRIAL conditions in early Victorian England were a chaos which it became the business of the epoch gradually to order. The very vigour, many-sidedness, and experimental character of industrial development bore the primary responsibility for this. Factories started up in adapted houses, or in an odd shed or so, built on to their premises, transferred to new ones in the suburbs, crept, and sometimes flooded out to moor and hill-side as circumstances and the resources of their promoters dictated. These came themselves largely from the ranks; working men who had graduated as foremen and had managed to lay their hands on a little capital or credit, the younger sons of tradesmen and farmers. Railways had not yet created the technical conditions of labour mobility, yet it flowed in, or coagulated from the surrounding countryside as it was required. Much of it was necessarily 'green' labour, and throughout the early part of the period, at any rate, it was relatively easy, in face of labour troubles, to replace existing labour with fresh. Improvisation, the need to make small resources go a long way, desperate hard work, and the rough and even brutal standards of working-class life marked the beginnings of many of the large enterprises and substantial fortunes of a later date. The large factory, planned for a considerable body of labour, and entailing heavy capital expenditure, is the exception rather than the rule. Only such enterprises could house and look after the workers that industry summoned together as by a magician's wand;[1] otherwise their need was catered to by those who could make a profit out of it–letters of garrets and cellars, the speculative builders of shacks. That such development ought to be regulated and controlled was an idea that had no roots in the assumptions of the times, and employers themselves, for the most part, accustomed to a harsh life, were little likely to worry about it. That working men should work the whole of their time, and women and children when and where they could, was, on the other hand, the age-old tradition of farm and domestic manufacture, and probably the rule of life of most of the employers themselves. The energy, the enterprise, the success in expanding industry and extending employment involved in this sort of spontaneous development were plain for contemporaries to see; where, beyond all this, it was leading, what it would sum up to in social terms, was not easily foreseeable, and could be exactly known only after the event, and even then, in view of the novelty of the techniques of social investigation, only after a considerable time-lag. As late as the debates on the 1844 Factory Act, Charles Buller, the most perceptive mind among the younger Radicals, pleaded for a new legislation appropriate to a new age, and was castigated by Sir James Graham, the promoter of the Bill, for advocating a "Jack Cade course of legislation". The dominant outlook of the time accepted as a

[1] Nos. 250C and 262.

matter of course that wages must rise and fall not only with the general prosperity of an industry, but also with its shorter range fluctuations. The idea that State or trade-union action might smooth out fluctuations is only exceptionally considered in governing circles,[1] and only spasmodically put forward and acted on by the working men themselves. Trade unionism, liberated in 1824–1825 from the trammels of statutory illegality, was undergoing a phase of rapid but short-lived expansion at the opening of the period, buoyed up by hopes of large-scale expropriation and of the organization of an Owenite paradise. Loose organization and discipline, permitting defeat in detail by the employers, the notorious repression of the Dorchester labourers, with which should be contrasted, however, the humane and even kindly treatment of the Exeter labourers, in a parallel case a month or so later, burst the iridescent bubble. Trade unionism fell back for twenty years, except for one or two sporadic bursts of wider activity, on the craft and local unions which had provided its continuous history for the previous half-century.

Three major attitudes shape the course of development in the field of industrial conditions and relations. The business attitude was dominated by the relatively modern theory of competitive individualism, the most important English expression of the mood of confident theorization that dominated the period of the French Revolution. Historically, it was the legacy of several generations of the frustrating struggle of commercial and industrial development against a decadent mercantilism; further, it reflected the comprehensible, if sometimes crude, self-confidence and self-satisfaction of men who could point to the new world growing up round them as their own creation; and it came to be reinforced by the sense that a body of doctrine from Adam Smith to Ricardo–only half understood, no doubt, as regards its reservations and underlying assumptions, but understood as supporting it, and speaking with the very voice of reason and science–gave approval of it. It was thus felt as warranting the ready assumption of the owning and employing classes that if others were like themselves, energetic, self-denying, and adaptable, squalor and distress could be reduced to understandable and tolerable proportions. In assessing this attitude we must not read back into early Victorian times the sense of assured industrial supremacy that belongs to mid-Victorianism. This stake was still being played for; not till after the turning-point of the century could capital and initiative be tolerably sure of commanding reward. In the earlier years–years of fluctuating markets and widespread recurrent crises[2]–risk was a reality, and ruin not merely an abstract possibility to millowner and merchant, but the lurking companion of all his enterprises, perpetually waiting to take advantage of overconfidence, of mistakes of judgment, or even just of bad luck. The success stories of the period reared their monuments to posterity; the failures disappeared, for the most part, into oblivion. A further point that must not be overlooked is that competitive individualism, with a sincerity not wholly self-interested, stood for an equalitarian, as opposed to the traditional hierarchical conception of society; in its own view of itself it was genuinely emancipatory. This had other aspects than the protest against privilege. It was one of the consequences of the stringency with which the creed was applied that social benevolence was relegated to the sphere of private duty–a duty that was between a man and his conscience rather than between him and his fellows, or between him and the State as representing his fellows. The alternative view was held to involve the claim to manage a man's life for him, which it was his right, as well as his duty, to manage himself. The

[1] No. 252. [2] Part III.

business man's protest against interference was often quite sincerely in the name of other men's rights as well as his own, the rights of those who would never stand on their feet till they fell on them. And the private duty of benevolence was often splendidly discharged.

A great part of the country felt, and thought, however, in terms of an older pattern of duty. Consciously or not, the model in its mind was the well-regulated village–still frequently to be met with throughout the century–where squire and parson ruled without question, and as unquestioningly took responsibility for everyone's welfare. Workers came from backgrounds where this conception of social duty defined the standard of well-being and well-doing; millowners, in many cases, looked forward to founding a family which would inherit and practise its obligations. The effort of these patriarchal ideals to find an intelligible role in the greater society that industrialism was creating is one of the most important factors in nineteenth-century social history. They formed the core of Oastler's and Sadler's Toryism;[1] they found natural support in the Church; Disraeli and Young England sought to capture Conservatism for them; and they provide a more charitable explanation than Roebuck's–"the manufacturers have troubled us in our dominions; we will put a torch to their factories"–of the continuing sympathy that the landed interest showed with the factory worker. But their most effective work was in the industrial field itself. The role of the good employer in Victorian social reform has been little emphasized in modern works on the subject, though hardly a Report from Factory or Mines Inspectors but dwells on it. To the 1833 Factory Commissioners, the problem of factory conditions was that of bringing the smaller and less responsible factory-owners up to the standards set by the best.[2] To the factory inspectors it was that of protecting good employers–and good intentions in the less firm of purpose–from the competition of the unscrupulous.[3] When the inspectors were called on to report on the feasibility of legislation to prevent accident, it was to the better employers that they applied for advice, and on their practice that they based their report.[4] In his great speech introducing the Bill of 1842 to prohibit the underground labour of women and children in mines, Ashley paid tribute to "the great coalowners of the North; had they been the only parties with whom we had to deal" the Bill would not have been necessary. In the same speech he refers to "instances of generous and paternal care, of willing and profuse expenditure for the benefit of their people" among the millowners. It is among the bigger capitalists that care for factory conditions and the housing and amenities of the workers is most often found.[5] The smaller ones had necessarily more restricted opportunities, and probably more restricted sympathies, though it is not to be presumed that even with them personal friendliness and sympathy with their workers did not often mitigate the sense of the necessity of getting the utmost, and giving the least possible, for which the competitive rage and the economic insecurity of the time gave ostensible reason. Most of the literature from which our knowledge is derived has a reforming purpose, and consequently emphasizes abuses more than conditions which did not call for corrective action. Welfare measures, moreover, particularly in the case of mines or factories opening up in hitherto unindustrialized country, had their economic justification.[6] But, by itself, patriarchalism was not adequate to the problems of great industrial society. Its limitations are perhaps best exposed in the case of the Flockton mine of Messrs.

[1] No. 249. [2] No. 250. [3] No. 253.
[4] No. 257. [5] Nos. 250 and 262. [6] No. 262 and Part X, No. 224G.

Stansfield and Briggs, so sympathetically described by J. C. Symons, one of the Assistant Commissioners under the Children's Employment Commission of 1842. Flockton was a thin seam pit of some of the best coal in Yorkshire, in a district which drew forth some of the Commissioners' sharpest animadversions. Its owners and the 'ladies of the manor' ran Sunday schools, recreation clubs, and a sports ground for their workers, and in the evidence of the mine-workers themselves, devoted themselves unstintingly to their welfare. Yet the same evidence–particularly that of the women and children–reveals conditions in their pits at once indefensible and impossible for the individual owner, faced with competition, to do away with himself. Only standards imposed by legislation on the willing and the unwilling alike could protect the well-disposed from the competition of the less scrupulous, and prevent the connivance of the workers themselves in many of the worst of the abuses. But if patriarchal ideas could not cover the necessary ground, they provided the example, the sympathy, and the understanding, without which legislation might not have been tried, and certainly could hardly have succeeded.[1]

Supplementing, and to a large extent bridging the gap between the two contrasting attitudes that have been described, was Benthamite administrative Radicalism. Earlier legislation, in 1802, 1819, and 1829, had sought to deal with the abuses of child and female labour in the textile factories, but had never solved the administrative problems of enforcement. A popular campaign in the North, under the field leadership of Richard Oastler, and the Parliamentary leadership of Michael Sadler,[2] and after his death of Lord Ashley, attained enormous dimensions and demanded a Ten Hours Bill to restrict the working of factories to a ten-hours' day. Sadler brought forward a Bill, and a Select Committee on it had heard evidence from the leaders of the agitation, and from workpeople. At this point, and before the factory-owners could be heard, Parliament was dissolved. In the new Parliament the Government–and the House, by the barest of majorities–decided to appoint a Commission to investigate and report on the subject, and not to continue the Select Committee of the previous Parliament. The aim was to get an expert, expeditious, and impartial report, rather than prolong the controversy to which the appalling evidence produced before the Select Committee had led. Tooke, Chadwick, and Southwood Smith, the Commissioners appointed, shared the assumptions of the economic science of their time. It would have been difficult, indeed, to have found men capable of doing their job who did not. But they had, as well, a regard for facts, and a capacity for social analysis which made the Report they produced[3] a landmark in the history of the problem they were investigating. The earlier legislation had followed the Elizabethan tradition in relying upon the part-time and amateur–and often interested–Justices of the Peace for a task of enforcement which essentially needed expert and continuous attention. The administrative crux of the Report, and of the Act which followed,[4] was therefore the provision for the appointment of whole-time inspectors with wide powers of making regulations and prosecuting for breaches of the Act. A further provision for regular reports from them to the Government provided an increasing body of expert and impartial information which was to prove of inestimable value in the guidance of Government and public opinion on the subject.

Throughout the 'thirties the principle of the Act remained in dispute. The case of its critics was that it was impractical, unenforceable, and unfair. The Government was hesitant, and both the parties were divided. In 1836, Poulett Thomson, President

[1] No. 253. [2] No. 249. [3] No. 250. [4] No. 251.

of the Board of Trade, introduced a Bill to reduce from thirteen to twelve the age at which hours of labour, under the Act, were limited to eight a day. This was widely interpreted as the beginning of a movement of surrender. The Bill was fiercely debated, and only withdrawn after the majority for it fell to two. Meanwhile Ashley pressed continuously, and even bitterly, for amending legislation to meet the administrative defects that experience had revealed in the Act. He had much Tory support, though Peel, in 1836, as in 1844, was hesitant, accepting the principle of the Act, but disliking the general idea of imposing restrictions upon industry, and feeling the invidiousness of legislating for the textile factories while evils as gross, and even worse, remained untouched in other branches of industry. Radical opinion ranged from the hostility of Hume and Roebuck, to the passionate championship of the millowner, Fielden. Slowly, as their resentment at the attacks on them died down, and as experience showed that restriction did not necessarily involve impracticable interference in their management of the mills, the millowners' opposition grew less.[1] Probably the turning-point in the public debate was the Select Committee of 1839–1841, which Ashley persuaded the House to set up, and which issued a series of six reports. The inspectors gave evidence, and were able to argue that with a certain number of amendments the Act could be made not only enforceable, but enforceable without any serious friction or large apparatus of bureaucracy, and without the power of making regulations which the Act had given to them, and to which much exception had been taken. For various reasons the amending legislation which was now generally agreed to be necessary was delayed until 1844, when the last great pitched Parliamentary battle on the subject was fought. The individualist opposition was strengthened by the accession of the Anti-Corn Law Leaguers, notably John Bright, Ashley's doughtiest opponent in these years. Peel and Graham were determined not to risk any undue disturbance of industry, just recovering from depression under their fostering care.[2] They refused in consequence to go as far as the Ten Hours advocates, despite pressure from their supporters, and a vote of the House in favour of a Ten Hours Amendment of Ashley's which they compelled it virtually to rescind. The Report of the Royal Commission on the labour of children in other industries and in agriculture, consequent on the famous Report on the Labour of Women and Children in Mines, had just been published, and Peel was able to illustrate his thesis that the evil ran through the whole of industry and employment. Interruptions showed that he did not shake the House's desire to hit it where it could be hit. Nevertheless the 1844 Act was a great measure, the 'logical outcome', a recent historian of Factory Legislation has said, of the garnered administrative experience of the previous decade, in a field in which the finding of a smoothly working administrative pattern was essential for success. It also extended protection to women, introduced the half-time system for children, thus facilitating their schooling, and in its provisions for the fencing of machinery, etc., and for the reporting of accidents, laid the foundations on which the code of safety regulations was in course of time to be reared. The Ten Hours men had to wait only till 1847 for their triumph. The collapse of Peel's control over his party, and a slump in which many mills would have been glad to have had ten hours' work a day, secured Fielden's Act,[3] the foundation charter of working-class leisure,[4] a relatively easy passage. Acts of 1850 and 1853 dealt with enforcement difficulties by establishing limits of hours, a 'normal working day', within which alone protected persons could be employed, thus vindicating in substance a further

[1] No. 253. [2] Part III. [3] No. 260. [4] No. 261.

contention of the Ten Hours movement–for if protected persons did not work, in general the others did not–that it was essential to enforcement to 'limit the motive power'.

A problem of the textile industries to which no solution was found was that of the hand-loom weavers. Called for in increasing numbers, at an earlier period, by the invention of power spinning, they were cast on the industrial scrap-heap when power weaving followed. The occupation was not difficult to learn, the loom itself not expensive, and the independence of working at home a further element of attraction. But the consequent isolation was an element of weakness in the weavers' bargaining position. Their agony was a protracted one; employers did not put capital into power looms until competition compelled them to, and continued to call on hand-loom weavers in times of expanding markets, or in particular branches of the trade. But the hand-loom weavers were the first to be stood off in slack times, and in times of distress the whole body of them was likely to be virtually workless and penniless. Wherever, in the worst years, instances of the extremest distress in the cotton towns are quoted, it is probable that the persons concerned will be hand-loom weavers and their families; it is noted as an exceptional feature of the intense distress in Stockport in 1842 that only a small proportion in the town were hand-loom weavers. The problem engaged the attention of a Select Committee in 1834–1835,[1] and was the subject of a prolonged inquiry, equipped with travelling Assistant Commissioners, and under Commissioners including Nassau Senior and Samuel Jones Loyd, in 1839–1841. The categories of the accepted political economy were seriously strained, and as an example in the applied economics of the time the Final Report of the Commissioners forms an invaluable supplement to the Poor Law Report of 1834. A variety of contributory factors to the predicament of the wretched weavers was recognized: the deflationary policy pursued in the 'twenties, and associated with the name of Peel, restrictions on the mobility of labour arising from the Settlement Laws,[2] trade-union restrictions on entry into alternative industries,[3] lack of education, and particularly education in design. Regulation of wages was proposed by John Fielden, and the establishment of trade boards considered. But there was no disguising the predominant facts that hand-loom weaving was on the way out, and the weavers themselves too many. More general reforms, in the free-trade direction, were among the recommendations; the 'forties, faced with wider problems on an almost equally distressing scale, were not disposed to consider palliatives for the situation of an outmoded industry; and, in general, the hand-loom weavers were left to die off, or drift off, which, by the midway mark of the century, most of them had done.

In 1842 the textile trades lost the monopoly of public attention that they had resented so much. Ashley secured the appointment of a Royal Commission on the Labour of Women and Children in Mines and Factories. The first Report,[4] dealing with mines, was appalling enough to enable him to drive a Bill through Parliament prohibiting the labour of women and children underground in less than four months. Miners were not unprosperous[5] and were not, as the factory workers often were, under an absolute economic need to work their women, as they did in a minority of districts, and their children, as they did in all. But socially they were a neglected population, and standards of life, save, as the Reports of the Assistant Commissioners bring out, where employers or resident gentry gave a lead, or religion–most often Methodism–took a hand, were brutal and crude. An incidental result of the Mines

[1] No. 252. [2] Part IX. [3] No. 254. [4] No. 258. [5] Nos. 255 and 256.

and Collieries Bill of 1842 was the creation of the post of Commissioner for Mines and Mining Populations, which gave an opportunity for the transfer thereto of Seymour Tremenheere, the Inspector of British and Foreign Society Schools.[1] Tremenheere emphasized, in season and out, the value of social care, the little of it there was, and the duty owed by those who took money from coal to those who laboured underground to earn it. There is ample evidence that generous effort met with a generous response. Two Acts of 1850 and 1860 laid the foundations of safety legislation, and together with that of 1842 constitute the chief contribution of the State to making the employment itself less brutalizing.

Conditions in a host of other industries were dealt with in the Second Report of the Commission, to which, as has been said, Peel made extensive reference in his speech in 1844. His emphasis was on the unfairness of piecemeal treatment of the problem, and the administrative difficulties of dealing with it as a whole. This deterred further important action till a new Children's Employment Commission of 1861–1868 found conditions in many of the trades much as they had been in 1842. There was, however, the important difference that in many of them the demand for legislative action now came from the masters themselves. A passage from these reports dealt with the wide prevalence of an abuse of almost classic notoriety–the use of climbing boys for chimney-sweeping–which had had the attention of a series of Acts of Parliament, but not the benefit of the administrative techniques worked out in connexion with the textile industries. In 1864 and 1867 further industries were brought within the scope of the Acts. But, as had been the case with textiles and mines, the worst abuses were found in the smaller undertakings–where the conditions approached most nearly to the family industry of which Oastler had been in the habit of drawing a somewhat idealized picture. To deal with this, the Workshops Act of 1867 brought a number of establishments employing less than fifty persons–hitherto exempt–under legislative control. Local authorities were made responsible for inspection, under the supervision of the Factories Department. The Inspectors' Reports[2] show both the iniquity of the conditions prevailing in many of the smaller industries and the lack of a sense of responsibility and of administrative capacity in many of the local authorities. In 1871 the responsibility was given entirely to the Factory Department.

Factory legislation represented the action of the State, exercised, directly, in protection of women and children, indirectly of the whole working class. The achievement of a satisfactory code resulted from the synthesis of patriarchal traditions with a newer science of social analysis and administration, assisted by devoted Parliamentary leadership. Trade unionism, the organized effort of the working classes to protect themselves, and particularly their wage standards, met with a less fortunate historical fate. Factory legislation represented a particular application of a legislative tradition, which, if abandoned in the eighteenth and early nineteenth centuries, went back to Tudor times. It could build on history. But the same legislative tradition, as a corollary of its general assumption of responsibility for welfare, had treated trade-union activity as an illegitimate interference with the functions of the State. Much of the flavour of conspiratorial activity continued to cling to trade unionism even after the Combination Acts had been repealed (1824–1825). The practice of swearing to secrecy and of elaborate initiation ceremonies tended to die out after the Dorchester labourers case. But secret intimidation, often of a violent and dastardly kind,

[1] Part XI, Introduction. [2] No. 267.

continued to mark the activities of some of the unions to the end of the period. The strikes in Glasgow which led to the Select Committee of Inquiry of 1837–1838[1] were marked by acts of violence, including murder and vitriol throwing, and the existence of a secret committee of the Spinners Union, responsible for acts of violent intimidation, was stoutly averred by Sheriff Alison in evidence before it. Five spinners were transported, after a protracted trial, and trade-union sympathy was as strong for them as it had been for the Dorchester labourers. Legally unobjectionable means of intimidation were open to trade unions in numerous other ways, and it is probably true to say that at no time were they scrupulous in their respect for the freedom of dissentient members of their own class. A further objection to them that was felt with a good deal of force at a time of rapid industrial change, and of considerable distress amongst the less skilled workers, was the attempt on the part of the unions–representing, at this time, the skilled minorities of the working class–to restrict the competition of their particular labour markets by limiting the number of apprentices, and, on occasion, by objecting to the employment of non-union men and the use of new machines, or of improved processes.

The employer who prided himself on a responsible attitude to his workpeople–and we have seen that there were many such–resented trade unions as coming between him and his men. To the up-and-coming competitive-minded employer, on the other hand, they tended to appeal simply as trying to rig the labour market in their own favour, and dictate to him the conduct of his business. There were many tributes in the period to the splendid quality of the British workman, and the asset that his skill and trained powers of application represented to the nation. But that the preservation of such an asset demanded concerted action, even that the offer and payment of wages below a reasonable minimum was an anti-social act, received only sporadic and incomplete recognition. The general assumption was that such matters were regulated by supply and demand, were the subject of inevitable laws.[2] It is not true that the current economics regarded labour simply as a factor in production, and ignored its human claims. The economists were, almost without exception, reformers with wide human sympathies and ideals. But the conditions of the industrial labour market, in a time of such rapid change, with its main recruits coming from the ranks of the agricultural labourers, used to low cash earnings and a family wage, and from Irish and Highland immigrants with even lower standards of life, were such as to make the problem of introducing any coherence or stability into it wellnigh an insuperable one. As has been mentioned, a prolonged study of the most intractable instance, that of the hand-loom weavers, had failed to produce any acceptable concrete suggestion. Moreover there was enough of hard drinking and riotous living among the industrial population, whenever circumstances permitted, to lend force to the contemptuous assertion of many employers–often risen from the ranks themselves and speaking with first-hand knowledge–that anything above the barest subsistence wage went to the pot-house, and reacted adversely on industrial discipline. No general regulatory force, compatible with the continued progress of industry, suggested itself therefore to the economists save the crude operation of supply and demand in a chaotic market, no issue from the instability of the labourers' condition save, individually, by prudence, sobriety, and thrift, conferring a power of surmounting temporary misfortune and of waiting for a favourable market, and, generally by education, and, above all, by later marriage and the restriction of births, so diminishing, in the long run, the flood of

[1] No. 254. [2] No. 264.

labour arriving on the market. In this last, all of them, up to and including John Stuart Mill, saw the principal hope. Substantially, for the feckless, improvident, and intemperate labourer who was all too common a type, they saw little prospect till he amended his ways. In such a context, trade-union action, representing largely the defence of their monopoly advantages by an aristocracy of labour, seemed to have little to commend it. It is perhaps not altogether certain that the economists' priorities were wrong–that a higher standard of personal discipline and personal self-respect among the labouring classes was not a prerequisite of any considerable improvement of their material condition, rather than vice versa. Be that as it may, it became generally understood that economics was against trade unions, and in an age in which, perhaps, too many people thought that they understood economics, this was enough to confirm their bad name.

To the working man, on the other hand, the assumption that a contract between himself and his employer was in all cases one between a willing buyer and a willing seller was an arrant sophistry; he was conscious only of having to sell his labour as quickly and continuously as he could, or starve. To him, therefore, his trade union, if he had one, was his only means of putting himself on something like a basis of equality in bargaining with his employer. Exceptionally,[1] but only exceptionally, this function of trade unions was recognized outside of working-class ranks themselves. The practices to which exception was taken–attempts to regulate the entry into skilled trades, to check recourse to overtime, to preserve trade demarcations and prevent the substitution of mechanical machine-tending for skilled craft work–were regarded by trade unionists as a legitimate defence of the capital of skill they had built up, often through the course of a long apprenticeship. As a means of preserving the tradition of craftsmanship and highly developed industrial skill, which was of such value to the economy of the country, such arrests to the levelling flood of competition were not without their economic justification. A trade unionism of this character was naturally conservative, from a point of view of immediate technical progress in industry. Trade-union organization constitutes economic power, as much as the control of a large industrial capital, and equally was subject to abuse. It was not to be expected therefore that groups of favoured workpeople should not on occasion put the preservation of their own position before all other interests together. The point at which the protection of a tradition of industrial skill, and the respect for acquired rights, could no longer be allowed to weigh against the general advantages of the introduction of new processes, and of the opening of opportunities to unskilled workers, though impossible to define in advance, was not impossible to discern in the event. As the total civilizing influences of the epoch came gradually to bear, it began to be appreciated on both sides that the ultimate arbiter in a prolonged strike was likely to be public opinion,[2] and that neither claims of right, of which both sides might be convinced, nor the exercise of the last ounce of power, was as likely to weigh with its judgment as its view of the concrete issues at stake. On the working-class side, as on the employers', special factors delayed the recognition of the other side's point of view. If there was a popularized conception of economics which, to the employers, seemed to justify very nearly all that they wanted to do, there was a working-class mythology–deriving from similar intellectual sources, but adapted for different consumption–which served to entrench working men in their own circle of ideas. From Locke, ultimately, through Adam Smith and Ricardo and the British

[1] No. 254. [2] No. 264.

socialist school of the early part of the century came the view that labour was the source of value, and, as its corollary, the conception of the Right of the working man to the Whole Produce of Labour–the view, particularly difficult of acceptance in an age in which entrepreneurial initiative had transformed the whole conception of production, that the real creators of the new wealth springing up round them, with a moral title, in consequence, to the whole of it, were the hands who had come when they were bidden, and done what they were told. Further, there had developed the idea that it was only necessary for a group of working men to accumulate a little capital for them to be able to carry on co-operative production successfully, in competitive conditions, dispensing with an employing class. This theory received a good deal of well-intentioned middle-class patronage, including that of John Stuart Mill. As late as 1852 the engineers solaced the bitterness of defeat by the determination to apply their union funds henceforth to the founding of co-operative enterprises in which they would be their own employers, and could give themselves all that they wanted. The middle years of the century saw, in fact, a number of attempts at co-operative production, almost uniformly failures. The Owenite and Chartist phases of trade unionism had given considerable currency to such ideas, and in the years of depression they had become associated with a deeply rooted class bitterness. Their effect on industrial relations was frequently that concessions made out of a sense of fair play, and advantages conceded out of a sense of social duty by employers, might be looked on as instalments on account of a good deal more that was due. The finding of common ground with those who might have done most to promote stabler industrial conditions and relations, the more responsible of the employers, was thus rendered correspondingly more difficult.

Chartism generated a good deal of strike activity among the cotton workers and the miners of the North and of Staffordshire, though trade unionism generally stood aloof. The muddle of issues in one Staffordshire miner's mind–subjected, in that year of 1842, to varied and intensive propaganda–is illustrated by his remark, at a meeting of owners and men presided over by the earl of Dartmouth, that nothing effective could be done till there was a "total repeal of the butties". Attempts at larger-scale organization of the northern coalfields culminated in an obstinate and unsuccessful strike in 1844.[1] By about 1850 the attempt was temporarily abandoned, to be revived at the end of the decade, and lead to the foundation of the Miners Association of Great Britain in 1863, under the leadership of Alexander Macdonald. The Association did not, however, secure the allegiance of the Lancashire and Welsh miners. Meanwhile the cotton spinners union had secured, in 1853, the first of the general price-lists for piece-work which were to play so large a part in their union history. But the most important new ground was broken by the formation, in 1850, after several years of activity, principally on the part of William Allan and William Newton, of the Amalgamated Society of Engineers, a union of several of the older and solider craft unions. It was some years before the amalgamation equalled, in numerical strength, the largest of the unions which, by a majority, had thrown in their lot together. The features of the new organization were its heavy subscription of 1*s.* a week; its combination of Friendly Society and trade-union functions, which gave it exceptional stability and financial resources; its thorough organization, and its strong central control of trade policy. The progress of the amalgamation aroused apprehensions among the employers, which were accentuated by successful piecemeal attacks upon some of

[1] No. 262.

them, and brought to a head by the issue, by the union, of a circular in December 1851, announcing its objection to piece-work and overtime. This precipitated a prolonged struggle in which the engineers received a good deal of support from other unions and supporters outside their own class. The importance of public opinion was recognized on both sides, but the powerful influence of *The Times* was cast decisively against the workers,[1] and not only had they ultimately to withdraw their objection to piece-work and overtime, but a large number of them were compelled by the employers to sign the notorious *Document*, renouncing their union, before they were allowed to work again. But the union took the view that signature was under duress, and allowed signatories to remain secretly members, and actually the membership of the union grew rather than declined. Thus, on the extremer stands they had taken, both sides were substantially defeated. The 'New Model' of the engineers' organization was copied by other craft unions, notably the carpenters, and a London building strike in 1859, for a nine-hours' day, in which again the union was momentarily defeated, and the *Document* imposed, with a like lack of ultimate success, demonstrated both the toughness of the new unionism and its power, where its objectives were moderate, to command a considerable volume of public support. The temper of the dominant trade unionism began to change. Though delegates were sent to the Marxist International at Brussels in 1864, the group of London leaders–the 'Junta'–addressed themselves more and more to middle class and especially Liberal opinion. They welcomed the efforts of Gladstone to encourage working-class thrift;[2] they swelled, if they did not largely constitute, the rising Radical demand for further franchise reform. Alexander Macdonald led the miners on similar lines, and obtained, in 1871, recognition from the owners for his union. In 1874, with his colleague Thomas Burt, he was to become a Liberal Member of Parliament, forging the first link of the chain which was to lead, ultimately, to the Labour Party.

Meanwhile a recrudescence of intimidation among small unions in Sheffield, and building unions in Manchester, and the discovery that the whole legal position of unionism was unsound, brought a crisis in trade-union history which led to the inquiry of the Royal Commission of 1867–1868. Trade unions had found legal protection for their corporate activity and funds in Friendly Society legislation. In 1867 a judicial decision laid it down that they were not entitled to such protection. The question of trade-union status and powers, and the linked issues of the legal relations of employer and employee, lap over the period of this volume, and their settlement forms one of the major achievements of Disraeli's second ministry, 1874–1880. The Majority Report of the Royal Commission[3] had retrospective, rather than prospective, interest. Its legislative proposals were disregarded, and the Minority Report of Lord Lichfield, Thomas Hughes, and Frederic Harrison, friends of the unions, is more important in this respect. If it does not open the new epoch in trade-union history, the Majority Report closes the old one. It did not mince its words about the illegality and violence, indeed, of much of the trade-union activity of the past, and of many smaller unions at the time, but it recognized the responsibility of outlook of the larger unions. It found ground for deploring the effect of trade unionism on the character and outlook of many working men, and the effect of the rigidities it introduced both on the old patriarchal relations of employers and men, in the best circumstances, and on the free development of industry in competitive conditions. These were Victorian attitudes. But it recognized that the trade unions had come to command,

[1] Nos. 263, 264. [2] Part II, No. 64. [3] No. 268.

by whatever means, the allegiance of the artisan, and that in a world in which Disraeli was presenting him with household suffrage the old patriarchal relationships were ceasing to have any very obvious place. The artisan preferred an organization for his own defence to reliance on either the market or on the integrity and generosity of his employer; the trade union had come to stay.

In the years since the middle of the century the workman's position had improved considerably. Sir John Clapham has calculated that, between 1850 and 1882, wages rose 30 per cent for the man who stayed in the same job, and 50 per cent as an average, reflecting the fact that there were more better-paid jobs available. Taxation had increased 10 per cent for the richer classes, and diminished 5 per cent for the poorer. Where, in 1842, the working man paid 16 per cent of his wages in taxes, in 1882 he was paying only 7½ per cent. Hours were tending to a 54 or 54½ average–other industries approximating to the regulated ones–as against a 63-hour week common enough in the earlier period. These are solid improvements. There were still many black spots, neglected populations, and industries in which neither State nor trade union had stepped in to prevent exploitation. There was still, also, much brutality, drunkenness, and profligacy among sections of the working population, without apparent overriding economic cause.[1] The Victorian economy had opted for the strong. It had sought to preserve freedom, flexibility, the opportunity for initiative, and cared more for encouraging industry and thrift than for helping those who did not help themselves–whether from lack of discipline, or lack of opportunity. If, in the succeeding period, the emphasis steadily shifted to helping the weak as weak, rather than helping them to be strong, the position that the economy had won, and the attitudes it had inculcated, were not without a part in helping the experiment to success.

[1] No. 266.

SELECT BIBLIOGRAPHY

In the *Parliamentary Debates* the great tourneys, in which the issues at stake in industrial legislation were most fully displayed, were the debates on Ashley's Ten Hours Bill, which afterwards became Althorp's Bill, in 1833; those on Poulett Thompson's Bill in 1836, and perhaps most instructive of all, those on Graham's Bill of 1844. There were important debates on the Ten Hours Bill in 1846 and 1847.

Amongst the public papers, the three great inquests on working conditions in the country call for first mention–the *Report of the Commissioners on Conditions in Factories* (*Parlty. Papers*, 1833/xx), the *Report of the Commissioners on the Labour of Women and Children in Mines and Factories*, the first *Reports* of which were the famous ones on conditions primarily in coal-mines (*Parlty. Papers*, 1842/xv, *Report*, and 1842/xvi–xvii, *Evidence* and *Report of Assistant Commissioners*), followed by a *Report on the Employment of Women and Children in Agriculture* (*Parlty. Papers*, 1843/xii), and the *Second Report of the Commissioners on the Labour of Women and Children in Factories* (*Parlty. Papers*, 1843/xiii, *Report*, 1843/xiv and xv, *Reports of Assistant Commissioners*), dealing chiefly with non-textile factories, and finally the *Reports of the Children's Employment Commission*, 1862–1867 (*Parlty. Papers*, 1863/xviii, 1864/xxii, 1865/xx, 1866/xxiv, and 1867/xvi). This last survey deals entirely with industries not subject to regulation, and therefore to regular report, and the final *Report* deals with agriculture. The *Report of the Select Committee on the Factories Bill* (Sadler's Committee) (*Parlty. Papers*, 1831–1832/xv), together with the report on Mines, referred to above, is the chief source of horror stories. From 1834 onwards the *Reports of the Factory Inspectors*, appearing in the annual series, form the prime source not only of expert and impartial information on working conditions in factories, but incidentally of much other economic information, and of information and comments on the education of factory children. The principal papers dealing with the plight of the hand loom weavers are the *Report of the Select Committee on Hand Loom Weavers* (*Parlty. Papers*, 1835/xiii), and the *Reports of the Commissioners on Hand Loom Weavers* (*Reports of Assistant Commissioners*, *Parlty. Papers*, 1839/xlii, 1840/xxiii and xxiv; *Report of Commissioners*, 1841/x). These *Reports* are of great value not only for the issues of economic policy involved, but also for local historians. The early reports of the schools inspectors (see *Bibliography* to Part XI) contain valuable accounts of social conditions, especially in mining districts. The *Report of the Midland Mining Commission* (Tancred's Report) (*Parlty. Papers*, 1843/xiii) is a classic. As with the textile industries, mining, after the Act of 1842 prohibiting the underground labour of women and children, is the subject of regular *Annual Reports of the Commissioner for Mines and Mining Populations*. The Commissioner was Seymour Tremenheere, and the *Reports* deal widely with social conditions, including trade unionism and strikes. On Trade Unions, *Parlty. Papers*, 1835/xlvi, contain the *Indictment of the Dorchester Labourers* (Dorchester Unionists) and 1837/xlvi, *Correspondence* with reference to their Pardon. The *Report of the Commissioners on Combinations of Workmen* (*Parlty. Papers*, 1837–1838/viii) contains a mass of information on contemporary trade-union practice and problems. Views critical of the effect of trade unionism in Norwich and a proposal to appoint stipendiary magistrates for trade disputes may be found in the *Report of the Commissioners on an Efficient Constabulary* (*Parlty. Papers*, 1839/xix). The *Report of the Select Committee on Masters and Apprentices* (*Parlty. Papers*, 1856/xiii) deals with the proposal of Councils of Conciliation. *Reports* on *Intimidation at Sheffield* (*Parlty. Papers*, 1867/xxxii), and on *Outrages at Manchester* (*ibid.*, 1867–1868/xxxix), were offshoots of the inquiries of the *Royal Commission on the Rules and Organisation of Trade Unions*, whose *Reports* (*Parlty. Papers*, 1867–1868/xxxix and 1868–1869/xxxi), survey the past and provide the principal material for the contemporary discussion of the future of trade unionism.

Of secondary sources, much valuable material will be found in the general economic histories listed in the *Bibliography* to Part III, more particularly in J. H. Clapham's magisterial survey. G. D. H. COLE, *A Short History of the British Working Class Movement* (London, 1947), G. D. H. COLE and A. W. FILSON, *British Working Class Movements Select Documents, 1789–1875*, (London, 1951), MAX BEER, *A History of British Socialism* (London, 1921), and LIONEL ROBBINS, *The Theory of Economic Policy in English Classical Political Economy* (London, 1952) are valuable general works. S. KYDD ('Alfred'), *History of the Factory Movement* (London, 1857), is the virtually contemporary history of the struggle; B. L. HUTCHINS and A. HARRISON, *A History of Factory Legislation* (London, 1926), and N. W. THOMAS, *The Early Factory Legislation* (London, 1951), are admirable modern accounts. C. DRIVER, *Tory Radical: the Life of Richard Oastler* (Oxford, 1946), and S. FINER, *Life and Times of Sir Edwin Chadwick* (London, 1952), both with extensive bibliographies, are indispensable. E. HODDER, *Life and Letters of the Seventh Earl of Shaftesbury* (3 vols., London, 1887), J. L. and B. HAMMOND, *Lord Shaftesbury* (London, 1921), and *The Bleak Age* (London, 1934) are valuable; the first two for a leading actor in the factory movement, and the last for a view of the age in which it took place. J. WESLEY BREADY, *Lord Shaftesbury and Social-Industrial Progress* (London, 1926), may be added. S. and B. WEBB, *The History of Trade Unionism* (London, 1921), is the standard work. It may be supplemented by S. and B. WEBB, *The Story of the Durham Miners 1662–1921* (London, 1921); N. EDWARDS, *The History of the South Wales Miners* (London, 1926); R. W. POSTGATE, *The Builders' History* (London, 1923); W. MILNE BAILEY, *Trade Union Documents* (London, 1921); and R. Y. HEDGES and A. WINTERBOTHAM, *A Legal History of Trade Unionism* (London, 1930). An article on "Strikes", in *Quarterly Review*, vol. CVI (1859), may be referred to for a responsible contemporary view. JOSEPH ARCH, *Autobiography* (London, 1898), describes the conditions out of which the effort to found an Agricultural Workers Union came. A. L. BOWLEY, *Wages in the United Kingdom in the Nineteenth Century* (London, 1900), and *Wages and Income in the United Kingdom since 1860* (London, 1937), are the result of statistical inquiry and analysis; A. REDFORD, *Labour Migration in England, 1800–1850* (Manchester, 1926), is the standard work on an important factor in labour conditions. F. ENGELS, *The Condition of the Working Class in England* (tr. London, 1892), is perhaps rather an essay in Marxian historiography than an objective account, but does not suppress the worst; similarly, P. MAYHEW, *London Life and Labour and the London Poor* (3 vols., London, 1864), deals with the seamy side of London life. GERTRUDE WEBB, "The Education of a Factory Child", in *Economic History*, vol. III (1934–1937); R. K. WEBB, "Working Class Readers in Early Victorian England", in *English Historical Review*, vol. LXV (1950), and T. P. THOFSEN, "The Artisan and the Culture of Early Victorian England", in *Birmingham University Historical Journal*, vol. V (1954), are valuable articles attempting estimates of the cultural outlook of sections of the working classes.

J. T. WARD, *The Factory Movement 1830–1855* (1962); J. C. GILL, *Parson Bull of Byerley* (1963); B. C. ROBERTS, *The Trade Union Congress, 1868–1921* (1958); G. F. A. BEST, *Shaftesbury* (1964); ASA BRIGGS and JOHN SAVILLE, *Essays in Labour History in Memory of G. D. H. Cole* (1960); S. POLLARD, *History of Labour in Sheffield* (1959); DAVID ROBERTS, *Victorian Origins of the Welfare State* (1960); MAURICE BRUCE, *The Coming of the Welfare State* (1966); W. H. OLIVER, "Consolidated Trade Union of 1834" *Ec. Hist. Review* xvii (1964).

249. Speech of Michael Sadler in the House of Commons, on the second reading of Factories Regulation Bill (13 March 1832)

Hansard, 3/II/342–345.

. . . Sir, the Bill which I now proceed to implore the House to sanction by its authority, has, for its purpose, to liberate children and other young persons employed in the mills and factories of the kingdom, from that over exertion and confinement which common sense, as well as long experience has shown to be utterly inconsistent with the improvement of their minds, the preservation of their morals, or the protection of their health: in a word, to rescue them from a state of suffering and degradation which, it is conceived, the children of the industrious classes in hardly any other country endure, or ever have experienced, and which cannot be much longer tolerated. Sir, I am aware that some Gentlemen profess, upon principle, a great reluctance to legislate upon these matters, holding such interference to be an evil. So, I reply, is all legislation–upon whatever subject–an evil only to be tolerated for the purpose of preventing some greater evil; and I shall, therefore, content myself with meeting this objection, common as it is, by simply challenging those who urge it to show us a case which has stronger claims for the interposition of the law, whether we regard the evil to be abated in regard to the suffering individuals, to society at large, to posterity, or to the utter helplessness of those on whose behalf we are called on to interfere; or, lastly, the fact–which experience has left no longer in doubt–that if the law does not, there is no other power that can or will adequately protect them. But, I apprehend, the strongest objection that will be offered on this occasion will be grounded upon the pretence that the very principle of the Bill is an improper interference between the employer and the employed, and an attempt to regulate by law the market of labour. Were that market supplied by free agents, properly so denominated, I should fully participate in those objections. Theoretically, indeed, such is the case, but practically, I fear the fact is far otherwise, even regarding those who are of mature age; and the boasted freedom of our labourers in many pursuits will, on a just view of their condition, be found little more than nominal. Those who argue the question upon mere abstract principles seem, in my apprehension, too much to forget the condition of society, the unequal division of property, or rather its total monopoly by the few, leaving the many nothing whatever but what they can obtain from their daily labour; which very labour cannot become available for the purpose of daily subsistence, without the consent of those who own the property of the community, all the materials, elements, call them what you please, on which labour is to be bestowed, being in their possession. Hence it is clear that, excepting in a state of things where the demand for labour fully equals the supply (which it would be absurdly false to say exists in this country), the employer and the employed do not meet on equal terms in the market of labour; on the contrary, the latter, whatever be his age, and call him as free as you please, is often almost entirely at the mercy of the former: he would be wholly so were it not for the operation of the Poor-laws, which are a palpable interference with the market of labour, and condemned as such by their opponents. Hence it is, that labour is so imperfectly distributed, and so inadequately remunerated, that one part of the community is over-worked, while another is wholly without employment; evils which operate reciprocally upon each other, till a country which might afford a sufficiency of moderate employment for all, exhibits at one and the same time part of its inhabitants reduced to the condition of slaves by over exertion, and another to that of paupers by involuntary idleness. In a word, wealth, still more than knowledge, is power, and power, liable to abuse whenever vested, is least of all free from tyrannical exercise, when it owes its existence to a sordid source. Hence have all laws, human or divine, attempted to protect the labourer from the injustice and cruelty which are too often practised upon him. Our Statute-book contains many proofs of this, and especially in its provision for the poor. . . .

250A–G. Report of Commissioners on the employment of children in factories (1833)

Parlty. Papers, 1833/xx.

250A. Hours

loc. cit., pp. 11–12.

. . . In England, in the north-eastern district, in a few factories, the regular hours of labour do not exceed eleven. In general, both at Leicester and Nottingham, they are not less than twelve. "Eleven hours is called a day at Leeds;" but it is seldom that in this district the hours are really less than twelve, while occasionally they are thirteen. In Manchester the regular hours of work are twelve. There are many places in the western district, as at Coventry and Birmingham, in which the regular hours of labour do not exceed ten; while it appears that some of the workpeople labour upon an average not more than nine hours daily. In these towns indeed there is no factory labour properly so called, for the operatives, with few exceptions, work at their own houses. But in some of the factories in the great clothing district the hours of labour are the same; seldom if ever exceeding ten. In general, however, they are somewhat longer; both in the carpet and in the clothing factories they are seldom less than eleven and scarcely ever more than twelve; this is the average; for there is considerable irregularity in both; in the carpet factory, partly on account "of the dissipated habits of many of the weavers who remain idle for two or three days, and make up their lost time by working extra hours to finish their piece on Saturday," and partly because "the weaver has often to wait for material from the master manufacturer where particular shades of colour may have to be died for the carpet he is weaving; while the clothing factories, being for the most part worked by water power, cannot of course be carried on with regularity". One of the witnesses, a proprietor, states that owing to the want of a due supply of water the workpeople sometimes cannot work more than three hours a day in summer; and that on an average they do not, in the summer season, work more than six hours a day. Another witness, an operative, deposes that his children in the factory in general go away after nine hours work, and that they play so much that he does not think they really work above four or six hours. And a third witness, a proprietor, (chairman of the woollen manufacturers of Gloucestershire,) deposes that in his own factory, in those parts in which children are employed, the regular hours are from nine in the morning until four in the evening, deducting an hour for dinner; and that for the last three years the children have worked only seven hours daily. In all the districts these hours are exclusive of the time allowed for meals, and of time lost from the machinery going wrong, and from holidays.

In some factories, in the several districts, there is no intermission of the work day or night. In such cases two sets of workpeople are employed, each set commonly working twelve hours. Occasionally there are three sets, and then each set works eight hours. . . .

250B. Complicity of parents

loc. cit., p. 1418.

. . . From the causes already assigned, namely the irregularity with which the operative is supplied with material for his work, the irregularity of the power by which the machinery is driven, and the dissipated habits of the workers, favoured, if not induced, by the occasional idleness growing out of the two first causes, it appears that in the carpet factories it is the constant practice, and in the clothing district the frequent practice, to work extra hours:–"It is very much the case with some sort of men to go idle part of the week and to work extra hours the rest. In such cases I have known men to work from three o'clock in the morning till ten o'clock at night; the drawers must work the same hours; they must always go together; they can't do without one another." "It is the practice for the weavers to be idle and dissipated part of the week and to work extra hours the rest. We abound with that evil; we witness it every week round; even the regular workman must often be idle part of the week, from the irregularity of the work coming in. It is very oppressive indeed to the children." "I have known instances, in the depth of winter, of drawers being called up to work by four o'clock in the morning, and earlier. I believe it is the common practice for the idle weavers to place their draw-boys in the looms, and to employ younger boys or girls as drawers, to make up for their own laziness or dissipation. The weavers are in general idle the early part of the week, and they afterwards work from eighteen to twenty hours to make up their lost time, during which the draw-boy or draw-girl must attend them. I have known frequent instances of their commencing work at two or three o'clock in the morning."

In the clothing district both workmen and masters agree in stating that if extra work for extra pay were refused when a press of business comes, the workmen so refusing would lose their situations; both also concur in the statement, that it is the constant practice for parents, and even for children themselves, to apply to the masters for extra work for additional wages, and cases have been detailed in which children have worked upwards of fourteen hours.

It appears that parents encourage their children to make the extraordinary efforts, of which we have given some examples, by leading them to consider the wages which they thus earn as peculiarly their own, although a cheat is often practised upon them even with regard to these extra wages. While all the witnesses agree in the statement, that whatever the child earns by its regular hours of labour is uniformly appropriated by the parent, it appears that a large portion of the additional wages earned by extra hours is also taken by the latter. . . .

250C. Variety in working conditions

loc. cit., pp. 19–21.

. . . The present inquiry has likewise brought together a large body of evidence relative to those various circumstances connected with the state of factories which concur with the nature of the employment in exerting an important influence on the health of the workpeople, whether children or adults, but which more especially affects the health of the former. Such concurrent circumstances are, the situation of the factory, the state of the drainage about the building, the size and height of the workrooms, the perfect or imperfect ventilation, the degree of temperature, the nature and quantity of the effluvia evolved, whether necessarily or not necessarily, in the different processes of manufacture, the conveniences afforded to the work-people for washing, and changing their clothes, on leaving the factory, and the habitual state both of the factory and of the operatives as to cleanliness. Details, which place in a striking point of view, on the one hand, the conservative influence of careful and judicious attention to such concurrent causes in the general arrangements of the establishment, and on the other, the pernicious consequences that result from inattention to them, will be found in the account given of the state of individual factories in most of the Reports of Sir David Barry, in the Reports from Scotland in general, and in many parts of the Reports from Leicester, Nottingham, and the western district. In relation to all those circumstances, the Reports of the Commissioners agree in showing that the large factories, and those recently built, have a prodigious advantage over the old and small mills. The working-rooms in the large and modern buildings are, without exception, more spacious and lofty; the buildings are better drained; more effectual expedients are adopted to secure free ventilation and to maintain a more equable and moderate temperature.

It is of the old and small mills that the report pretty uniformly is–"dirty; low-roofed; ill-ventilated; ill-drained; no conveniences for washing or dressing; no contrivance for carrying off dust and other effluvia; machinery not boxed in; passages so narrow that they can hardly be defined; some of the flats so low that it is scarcely possible to stand upright in the centre of the rooms;" while the account of the recent structures and the large establishments in general is–"infinitely better managed in respect to ventilation, height of roofs, and freedom from danger to the workers near the machinery, by the greater width of the passages in the working-rooms, and by the more effectual boxing in of the machinery, than those on a small scale." There are not wanting establishments in which every advantage of this kind is combined in an almost perfect degree, of which the following may be cited as examples:

Deanston Cotton-mill Factory, near Doune in Perthshire.—"This is one of those beautifully situated and admirably regulated great manufacturing establishments which it is a pleasure to see, on account of the general arrangements of every department of this extensive work, as well as the happiness which a numerous population engaged in the pursuits of industry apparently enjoy. The apartments in the mill first erected are not equal in height nor in other respects to those of the works lately erected; but the whole are clean, well ventilated, and have the machinery well fenced. The preparing-rooms in the lately erected part of the work are, owing to the superior construction of the fanners, which blow the whole of the dust to the open-air, more thoroughly freed from the impurities generally prevailing in the preparation-rooms than those in any factory where we have hitherto been. Indeed, I ought more properly to have said, which was literally the case, that there was no appearance of dust nor of impure air in those preparing-rooms. Even in the web-dressing-room a fanner is most usefully employed in dissipating the noxious heat and moisture. It seems strange that those fanners have not yet found their way into the flax-spinning establishments which we have seen, and where they are so very requisite on account of the quantity of dust and refuse of the material floating in the room, to such an extent as almost to obscure the nearest objects. The windows, instead of being constructed in the usual way in many of the mills which we have seen, so that only a single pane of glass in each window can be opened, are so hung that the whole of the upper part of each window may be let down from the top, and a free current of air admitted. The general heat of the apartments is from 65° to 70°. A greater degree of warmth is never required, excepting in the web-dressing-room, where the thermometer to-day stood at 80°. The temperature of the atmosphere yesterday in the shade, at the period of our inspection, varied from 65° to 68°. There are here apartments for the females to dress and undress in, and a pipe of water in each story, and every arrangement is adopted throughout the work that tends to the convenience and accommodation of the persons employed. The workers live at the distance of about a mile from the works, with the exception of about a hundred of them, for whom the company have built houses, let to them. I can hardly say whether the construction of those houses, or the ingenious contrivances with a view to the convenience of the people which Mr. Smith has put in execution, or the cleanness and neatness with which the interiors of those nice cottages are kept by the workers, are most to be admired. There are bits of garden ground attached to each of the houses, and a drain has been constructed for carrying off every sort of filth. The whole arrangements about this extensive factory, at which cotton-spinning, power-weaving, iron-founding, and machine-making are carried on, are obviously made with a view, as far as possible, to the substantial comfort of the people; and a more cheerful, happy-looking set of industrious men and women, and of young people, is seldom, if I am not mistaken, to be found. There is abundance of room throughout the whole work; no appearance of human beings crowded on each other in any part of it. There are forty spinners in an apartment eighty-two feet long by fifty-two in breadth."

"The rooms are ventilated in the old mill by means of windows, and in the new mill by means of openings between the windows into chimneys, in addition to windows opening up and down. The drainage is perfect. The water-closets have water-traps fitting into moveable receptacles, which are removed every morning. Rooms with water-cocks, for washing and dressing, are being prepared in the new mill. The general atmosphere of the rooms is clear and well ventilated. There are no offensive smells. Dust fans are employed, revolving in large tubes, which draw up all the dust with considerable force, and keep the atmosphere of the rooms light, fresh, and agreeable. These machines are highly worthy of general adoption in all manufactories." . . .

250D. Treatment of children

loc. cit., pp. 22–29.

It will appear from the evidence annexed to this report that the Commissioners have everywhere investigated with the utmost care the treatment to which children are subjected while engaged in the labour of the factory. These inquiries have obtained from the children themselves, from their parents, from operatives, overlookers, proprietors, medical practitioners, and magistrates, such statements amongst others as the following:–"When she was a child too little to put on her ain claithes the overlooker used to beat her till she screamed again."–"Gets many a good beating and swearing. They are all very ill used. The overseer carries a strap." "Has been licked four or five times." "The boys are often severely strapped; the girls sometimes get a clout. The mothers often complain of this. Has seen the boys have black and blue marks after strapping." "Three weeks ago the overseer struck him in the eye with his clenched fist so as to force him to be absent two days; another overseer used to beat him with his fist, striking him so that his arm was black and blue." "Has often seen the workers beat cruelly. Has seen the girls strapped; but the boys were beat so that they fell to the floor in the course of the beating, with a rope with four tails, called a cat. Has seen the boys black and blue, crying for mercy.

"The other night a little girl came home cruelly beaten; wished to go before a magistrate, but was advised not. That man is always strapping the children." "The boys are badly used. They are whipped with a strap till they cry out and shed tears; has seen the managers kick and strike them. Has suffered much from the slubbers' ill-treatment. It is the practice of the slubbers to go out and amuse themselves for an hour or so, and then make up their work in the same time, which is a great fatigue to the pieceners, keeping them 'on the run' for an hour and a half together, besides kicking and beating them for doing it badly, when they were so much tired." "The slubbers are all brutes to the children; they get intoxicated, and then kick them about; they are all alike." "Never complained to the master; did once to his mother and she gave him a halfpenny not to mind it, to go back to work like a good boy. Sometimes he used to be surly, and would not go, and then she always had that tale about the halfpenny; sometimes he got the halfpenny, and sometimes not. He has seen the other children beaten. The little girls standing at the drawing-head. They would run home to fetch their mothers sometimes." . . .

It appears in evidence that in Scotland, and in the eastern district of England, where the harshest treatment of children has taken place, the greatest number of bad cases occur in the small obscure mills belonging to the smallest proprietors, and that the bad treatment is inflicted by violent and dissipated workmen, often the very men who raise the loudest outcry about the cruelties to which the children are subject in factories. . . .

Reports of factories in which corporal punishment is strictly forbidden, and, as is proved by the testimony of all classes of witnesses is never inflicted, will be found also in Mr. Mackintosh's Report at pages 3. 14. 15. 17. 18. 19. 20. 21. 27. 28. 32. 33. 34. 36. 37. 40. 41. 42. 43. 45. By all classes of witnesses it is stated, that "strapping was more customary in former times than it is now;" "that the usage of the children is very different; they are not now beat;" "that he has seen boys severely beat when he was a young man, but not for a number of years;" "that he does not use a strap now, though he did formerly." . . .

Statements to the same effect are made by the other commissioners for Scotland, Mr. Mackintosh and Sir David Barry. "Whatever may be thought of the nature or duration of the work to be performed by children, the general tenor of the whole body of evidence will be allowed sufficiently to disprove the existence of any system of corporal punishment as a stimulus to exact it, some very conclusive admissions (Mr. Steele, p. 67; Mr. Henderson, p. 81), negativing satisfactorily the existence of any thing which can be called habitual cruelty practised upon children." These admissions are made by men who have had extensive experience of the whole interior management of factories, and their avowed predilections would not lead them to conceal any deformities in the system. We had, I believe, during our progress no one intimation, even anonymously, to direct our inquiries to any quarter where any habitual ill-usage of children was insinuated to exist at present. The facts which come nearest to such treatment will be found, with one exception, to be of some years standing. Of the whole number of children I have seen only one, a little girl, had a mark of a blow visible, and that, upon inquiry, was inflicted by her own father.

In like manner, from the statements and depositions obtained under the present inquiry in the several districts in England, and from all classes of witnesses, it appears that in the great majority of cases, corporal punishment is prohibited by the proprietors, while it is proved on oath by several witnesses that operatives and overlookers have been suspended and even dismissed from their employment for disobeying this command. It is impossible to read the evidence from Leeds, Manchester, and the western district without being satisfied that a great improvement has taken place within the last few years in the treatment of children. What ill-treatment still exists is found chiefly in the small and obscure factories, while both in the large and small factories in England it is inflicted by workmen over children whom they themselves hire and pay, and who are completely under their control. In Scotland, personal chastisement when inflicted is inflicted by the overlooker; in England, by the workpeople. Among the indications of a desire on the part of the proprietors to promote the comfort and health of the workers in general and of the young people in particular, we cannot help referring to the medical examination by Dr. Hawkins of the factory at Belper and Milford, belonging to the Messrs. Strutt, in which two thousand workpeople are employed; it is stated that a man who is a good swimmer is employed by the proprietors twice a day in summer to a pond appropriated to their use for the purpose of bathing; and of a factory belonging to Mr. William Newton at Cresbrook mills, Tideswell, remarkable for the large number of apprentices which it contains, there is the followng statement; Mr. Newton receives nothing with the children, and gives them nothing more than board, lodging, washing, and raiment, and a monthly allowance of pocket money to each apprentice, which varies from 6d. to 1s. 6d. Mr. Newton provides two individuals who act as Sunday schoolmasters. They do not go to church because the nearest church is three miles off, but prayers are read to them twice on the Sunday. "I must state," adds Dr. Hawkins, "to the honour of Mr. Newton, that after a very minute and unexpected examination of his establishment, and of the apprentices in private, I could ascertain no point in their treatment that savoured of niggardliness nor of harshness. The remoteness of the situation, the distance from public opinion, the absence of parents and relations, all afford an opportunity for abuse; but that opportunity is not seized. I particularly questioned the children separately, and obtained from them the following particulars of their diet. Their breakfast is of milk porridge and bread, as much as they please; their supper is the same. They have meat six days in the week for dinner, and as much as they choose, with potatoes and broth. There are separate eating as well as sleeping rooms for the boys and girls. The girls also have a separate piece of ground to play in. They have clean sheets once a fortnight, and clean shirts and shifts once a week. The beds are clean and neat, and not too many in a room; three little ones sleep in one bed, and two of the older in one bed. The greater part remain and marry in this establishment. Mr. N. affirms that during the last twenty-four years only one of his apprentice girls has been pregnant before marriage, and that during the same period only four such cases have occurred in the whole of his mill." . . .

250E. Effects of labour on children

loc. cit., pp. 35–36.

From the whole of the evidence laid before us of which we have thus endeavoured to exhibit the material points we find–

1st. That the children employed in all the principal branches of manufacture throughout the kingdom work during the same number of hours as the adults.

2nd. That the effects of labour during such hours are, in a great number of cases,

Permanent deterioration of the physical constitution:

The production of disease often wholly irremediable: and

The partial or entire exclusion (by reason of excessive fatigue) from the means of obtaining adequate education and acquiring useful habits, or of profiting by those means when afforded.

3rd. That at the age when children suffer these injuries from the labour they undergo, they are not free agents, but are let out to hire, the wages they earn being received and appropriated by their parents and guardians.

We are therefore of opinion that a case is made out for the interference of the Legislature in behalf of the children employed in factories.

4th. In regard to morals, we find that though the statements and depositions of the different witnesses that have been examined are to a considerable degree conflicting, yet there is no evidence to show that vice and immorality are more prevalent amongst these people, considered as a class, than amongst any other portion of the community in the same station, and with the same limited means of information. Distinguished from other classes by being collected together (both sexes, young and old,) in large numbers, the language and behaviour common to uneducated people, under such circumstances, is found to be checked in no inconsiderable degree by the presence of fathers, mothers, and brothers; and for any evil of this kind which may nevertheless exist, the proper remedy seems to be a more general and careful education of the young people.

5th. In regard to the inquiry "in what respect the laws made for the protection of such children have been found insufficient for such purpose;" we find that in country situations the existing law is seldom or never attempted to be enforced, that in several principal manufacturing towns it is openly disregarded, that in others its operation is extremely partial and incomplete, and that even in Manchester, where the leading manufacturers felt an interest in carrying the act into execution as against the evasion practised by the small mill-owners, the attempt to enforce its provisions through the agency of a committee of masters has for some time back been given up. On the whole we find that the present law has been almost entirely inoperative with respect to the legitimate objects contemplated by it, and has only had the semblance of efficiency under circumstances in which it conformed to the state of things already in existence, or in which that part of its provisions which are adopted in some places would have equally been adopted without legislative interference, as there is reason for presuming, if we advert to the fact, that such provisions have actually been adopted in the progress of improvement in other branches of manufacture unrestricted by law. On the other hand the large classes of workpeople, who come within the provisions of the recent as of all former Acts, have been familiarized with contempt of the law, and with the practice of fraud, evasion, and perjury.

250F. The Ten Hours' agitation

loc. cit., pp. 37–49.

Having defined the evil arising from the present employment of children in factories, we have proceeded to investigate what measures admit of being taken for their future protection. In this stage of the inquiry we have found the attention of the public, as well as of the parties concerned, so powerfully directed to the plan for the regulation of labour in factories, known under the title of the Ten Hour Bill, that a large body of evidence has necessarily come before us as to the probable operation of such provisions of the proposed plan as have become matter of public speculation. We proceed to submit some portions of that evidence, having first stated as our conclusions formed on a view of its whole tenor:–

1. That this bill does not accomplish the object at which it purports to aim. Its professed object is the protection of children; but it does not protect children. For the same evidence which shows that the legislative protection of children is necessary shows that the restriction of the labour of children to ten hours a day is not an adequate protection. . . .

2. This bill, making no provision for the occupation of any part of the time of children for their own benefit, either before or after their hours of labour, and taking no charge of their education, elementary or moral, leaves the removal of a most important portion of the evil under which children suffer unattempted.

3. While this bill does and attempts to do so little for children, its operation, if it could be carried into effect, would be to restrict the labour of adults, as well as that of children, to ten hours.

Independently of the objection which there appears to be in principle to any compulsory interference with the hours or terms of adult labour, we find reason to anticipate very serious practical evils from imposing any such arbitrary restriction on the operations of so large a proportion of the manufacturing industry of the country.

The most direct and undisputed consequence of the passing of the Ten Hour Bill would be the general limitation of the labour of adults within the same hours as those assigned to children and adolescents. We are spared the labour of weighing conflicting testimony on this point, as it is generally admitted or assumed on both sides of the question. On the part of the manufacturers it is generally taken for granted that such will be the first effect of the measure under discussion, and that assumption is made the basis of reasoning as to its ultimate issue. With the operatives the same assumption is prominently put forward in the arguments of most of the leading advocates of the measure, and is generally dwelt upon as forming a principal item amongst the benefits which they expect to derive from the passing of the measure. It may be sufficient to adduce instances of explicit statement of this expectation, in which the conflicting parties are agreed, before proceeding to those ulterior consequences on which their views are naturally opposite. . . .

It is deserving of attention, that while the protection due to children is sought to be extended to persons of eighteen and of twenty-one, the topics which have been constantly urged to engage the public sympathies in favour of the above-mentioned measure have borne exclusive reference to the claims of children, properly so called. There is not one of the motives of persuasion which have been commonly urged by the friends of the Ten Hour Bill which affords a colourable plea for extending the protection of the Legislature to the labour of adults or adolescents. It might be sufficient to establish the correctness of this observation if we simply referred to the general impression which is felt by the public with regard to the proper objects of compulsory interference as described by the supporters of the Ten Hour Bill. The language held in every place where popular excitement has been directed against the sober investigation of this subject shows clearly, that, whatever may be the real views of those parties who have made themselves most prominent in agitating the question, they knew how to select the ground where the real strength of their case lay when it came to be pleaded before the public tribunal. Accordingly, peculiar stress was laid upon such instances as those, which appear not wholly unknown in the west riding of Yorkshire, of parents carrying their children to mills in the morning on their backs, and carrying them back at night. The deficiency of time for education and of time for play, and the cruelty of immuring children of tender age in factories, have been principally dwelt upon as the hardships of the present system. Processions of children, and studied compositions presented by children, have been in all cases the machinery employed to divert public attention from the true state of the question.

We should not feel ourselves warranted in suppressing our conviction that the interests of the children, which alone supply materials for popular excitement on the subject of the proposed measure, are, of all other considerations, that which appears to enter least into the councils of the operative agitators for that measure.

It ought to be remarked, in the first place, that such acts of severity and cruelty towards children employed in factories as are still found of occasional occurrence, are for the most part chargeable neither on the masters nor on the overlookers, but on the spinners or the slubbers themselves. It is the practice of these latter parties to engage the children who work under them, and corporal punishment, when it is inflicted at all in factories, is administered to a child by the hands of a parent, or at least on the child of a working-man by a working-man, in most cases himself the parent of children in like circumstances. It farther appears in evidence, that sometimes the sole consideration by which parents are influenced in making choice of a person under whom to place their children is the amount of wages, not the mode of treatment to be secured to them. . . .

250G. Elements of an effective Bill

loc. cit., pp. 68–75.

The short time which has been allowed us by the constant accessions of evidence to consider and define the leading principles which we have recommended as a basis for legislation on this subject has not permitted us to enter, with any degree of completeness which would satisfy ourselves, into the detail of the measures which may be found requisite for carrying those principles into practical operation.

The measures for consideration, with reference to this object, are, first, those to be framed for the provision of securities with regard to the age of the parties taken into employment in factories, and next, those which relate to the duration of their daily labour.

Any measures by which the enforcement of the law shall be made chiefly dependent on those who have an interest in breaking it may be expected to prove as inefficient as the provisions of the existing law. On the part of the parent, who, under the existing law, is called upon to give the certificate of the age of the child, (which certificate forms at present the main security against evasion on this point,) we find a strong interest in the commission of fraud, amounting sometimes almost to a necessity; on the part of the immediate agents or overlookers, probably the friends of the parent, a willingness to connive at it; and on the part of the masters no especial motive to exert vigilance. This state of interests in opposition to the law is only met by the occasional attempts of informers, or of persons engaged specially for that purpose without the mills, to obtain information and evidence of what is passing within.

Thomas Worsley, a witness who had considerable experience as agent for the masters at Manchester, and for the operatives at Stockport, states amongst the difficulties of obtaining a prosecution, that under the existing law "you have got to produce the parents to prove the actual age of the child" (which proof, we would observe, is to disqualify him for employment); "then you have to produce a person who worked near the child in the same room, to prove that on the day named in the information the child worked more than the legal hours; all this has to be proved in the first instance: then, with reference to Sir John C. Hobhouse's Bill, if you lay the information against the master, the overlooker or manager can still depose that he received orders from the master not to work children more than is allowed by the act, and his oath to this effect is still sufficient to cause the information to be quashed, notwithstanding you may have succeeded in proving the former part of your case." . . .

On the consideration of the difficulties displayed in the testimony of these witnesses, we are prepared to recommend, that it should be declared unlawful to employ any child of the prescribed age without a certificate from a surgeon or medical man resident in the township where the mill or factory is situated, who shall certify, on inspection of the child, that he believes it to be of the full growth and usual condition of a child of the age prescribed by the legislature, and fitted for employment in a manufactory. This certificate should be given in the presence of a magistrate, by whom it should be countersigned, provided that he also were satisfied that the child was of the average condition of a child of the prescribed age. The age would be fixed by the legislature, as one of the means of determining the phsyical condition, which alone is the proper qualification for employment. Unless a discretion of this nature were given to the parties certifying they might feel themselves bound to certify to the age of the child, on the production of copies of baptismal registers which are easily forged, or on the evidence of parents who would be under temptations to perjure themselves, such as have already been described.

The duties performed in this instance by the parties certifying are similar in their nature to those performed by two magistrates in binding parish apprentices. If the medical certificate alone were required, it is to be apprehended that in many neighbourhoods practitioners would be found whose practice is dependent on the labouring classes, and who would sometimes find a difficulty in refusing certificates to children below the proper standard as to age or condition.

The most important period for the exercise of vigilance is however that of admission to the period of full work. We propose that it should be guarded by a similar but a more special examination and certificate or indenture, to be given by an inspector who should also certify, on examination, that the child examined has received an elementary education of the nature which may be hereafter prescribed. This last provision may be made to serve as a check against evasions of such regulations as may be adopted with regard to attendance at schools, or misapplications of the previous time allowed by the reduced labour.

We shall not at present treat of the collateral securities and penalties with which it might be requisite to accompany the foregoing regulations.

As one security against children being worked beyond the time prescribed, we propose that the proprietor of a mill shall be liable to a penalty on proof of a child having been within the mill more than eight hours; one half the penalty should be paid to the informer, the other half we propose should be applied to the use of the school where the child went, unless it were a school attached to the mill. This provision we consider would obviate many technical difficulties, and the necessity of obtaining the evidence of workmen in the mill, or of parties interested, and we conceive, would facilitate conviction. As we propose that the only facts which it shall be requisite to prove to support the information shall be, that the child was seen to enter and was seen to leave the mill at a distance of time from the hour of entrance exceeding the time allowed by law, the onus should be thrown on the mill-owner of proving that any of the children or young persons in his employment are duly certificated.

Several eminent manufacturers have represented to us, that the only certain method of ensuring obedience to any legislative measures on this subject would be by the appointment of officers charged with the powers and duties requisite to enforce their execution. The necessity of some appointments of this nature has indeed been urged from all parts of the country.

In general it is conceived that the officer ought to be resident, and should be charged with exclusive jurisdiction of complaints relating to the infraction of legislative regulations of manufactories. The prominent objection to such an establishment of resident officers is chiefly the expence; for the manufactories being spread all over the country, such officers must necessarily be very numerous and expensive, if they are adequately paid for their services. We consider that by giving to the magistrates a concurrent jurisdiction on complaints made before them, a comparatively small agency would suffice.

The necessity of the appointment of inspectors has been most urgently stated by those manufacturers who have had chiefly in view the restriction of the hours of labour in other factories to the level of their own. The greater necessity of the appointment of some special agency for the enforcement of the measures we have recommended must be admitted, when it is recollected that they relate solely to the children, and are not directly conducive to the immediate interests either of the master manufacturers, or of the operatives, or of any powerful class, and are not therefore likely to receive continuous voluntary support. On the whole, we recommend the appointment by the Government of three inspectors to go circuits of the chief manufacturing districts, at intervals as short as may be practicable, and exercise the functions with which they may be invested for carrying the law into force. For this purpose each inspector should have the right of entering all manufactories where children are employed, and of ordering machinery to be fenced off, and directing arrangements of a sanitary nature, compatible with the execution of the manufacturing processes; and he should also have cognizance of the arrangements for the education of the children employed. He should have power to hear and determine all complaints of infraction of the provisions of the law, to give directions with relation to them to peace officers, and fine for neglect. It should be the duty of the inspectors to meet as a board, to report periodically to the Government for the use of the Legislature as to their proceedings and as to any amendments for the law which they might find requisite or which might be called for. For this purpose they should be invested with the power of examining witnesses on oath, and of compelling their attendance.

In several of the most important manufacturing districts the resident magistrates are manufacturers; and the appointment of officers of the character and the concurrent jurisdiction we have recommended would enable a complainant to reserve his complaint, if he thought proper, until the period of the visit of the inspectors. Some mills are so remotely situated in solitary places apart from towns that it would be impracticable to visit them with the same frequency. But in these places the difficulty of finding a magistrate who was not a manufacturer, before whom a complaint might be made, probably would not exist.

We consider that the performance of the function of reporting periodically to the Government, by persons whose duty it should be to examine the evidence on which allegations of abuse were founded, and to whom all complaints might be referred for examination, would be attended with considerable advantages, in the security it would give against the occurrence of practices inconsistent with humanity, and in the protection which on the other hand it would extend to the master-manufacturers against groundless complaints. . . .

Since the whole of our recommendations have for their object the care and benefit of the children, we have been desirous of devising means for securing the occupation of a portion of the time abridged from their hours of labour to their own advantage. We think the best mode of accomplishing this object will be the occupation, suppose of three (or four) hours of every day in education; and we are the more disposed to recommend this, since it will secure two ulterior objects of considerable importance: first, it will be the best means of preventing the employment of the same child in two different factories on the same day, or in any other kind of labour likely to be injurious to its health; and secondly, it will better qualify the persons so educated to adapt themselves to other employments, if in after life the vicissitudes of trade or other causes should render it desirable that they should find other means of support.

As a means of securing that the prescribed portion of every day should be devoted to the purpose of education, we recommend that every child on entering a factory be required to produce a ticket certifying that such portion of time has been spent in school; the afternoon set certifying that they have been at school during the prescribed number of hours on the forenoon of the same day; and the morning set that they have been at school during the same number of hours in the afternoon of the preceding day. And we further recommend, that the inspector be required and empowered to direct the execution of such regulations and securities, adapted to local circumstances, as he may deem requisite for the accomplishment of this object.

From the evidence collected it appears that in many of the mills numerous accidents of a grievous nature do occur to the workpeople. It appears also that these accidents may be prevented, since in some mills where more care of the workpeople is in general displayed they are prevented. It appears further that whilst some manufacturers liberally contribute to the relief of the sufferers, many other manufacturers leave them to obtain relief from public bounty or as they may.

The refusal to contribute to the expence of the cure of those who have been maimed, is usually founded on the assertion that the accident was occasioned by culpable heedlessness or temerity. In the cases of the children of tender years we do not consider this a valid defence against the claim for contribution from the employer. We cannot suppose an obligation to perpetual caution and discretion imposed on children at an age when those qualities do not usually exist. The indiscretion of children must, we consider, be presumed, and guarded against as a thing that must necessarily, and to a greater or less extent, be manifested by all of them.

But the accidents which occur to the adults are of themselves evidence (unless they were wilfully incurred in a state of delirium) that the individual used all the caution of which he is capable; as it may be presumed that the loss of life or limb, or the infliction of severe pain, would rarely be wantonly incurred.

Some of the manufacturers have proposed that the inspectors, who they think ought to be appointed to ensure compliance with any legislative regulation, should have power to inspect the factories, and direct what parts of the machinery should be fenced off, and that after such directions have been complied with, the manufacturer should be relieved from further responsibility.

We concur in the proposition for giving such power to inspectors, but we do not concur in the proposal to relieve the manufacturer from responsibility.

We apprehend that no inspector would probably be so fully conversant with all the uses of every variety of machinery as to be acquainted with all the dangers which may be provided against; and also, that whilst there is much machinery which does not from its nature admit of being boxed off, there is much that could not be made entirely safe without the reconstruction of whole manufactories.

Excluding from consideration the cases of culpable temerity on the part of the adults, and assuming that the aid to be given when accidents do occur shall afford no bounty on carelessness, the cases which remain for provision are those of adults which may be considered purely accidental. Taking a case of this class where mischief has occurred in the performance of the joint business of the labourer and his employer; the question is by which of these parties the pecuniary consequences of such mischief shall be sustained.

We conceive that it may be stated as a principle of jurisprudence applicable to the cases of evils arising from causes which ordinary prudence cannot avert that responsibility should be concentrated, or as closely as possible apportioned on those who have the best means of preventing the mischief. Unless we are to impose on the workman the obligation of perpetual care and apprehension of danger, the nature of the injuries inflicted are of themselves evidence that all the care which can be taken by individuals attending to their work is taken by them; it is only the proprietor of the machinery who has the most effectual means of guarding against the dangers attendant upon its use.

If such an extent of pecuniary responsibility for the accidents which are incidental to the use of the machines is imposed upon him, those consequences will be more likely to be taken into account, and to be guarded against at the time of the erection of the machinery. The workmen are not prone to regard many of the immediate dangers which are remote and contingent, and many of the accidents are of a nature apparently too uncertain to form data for insurance. It could hardly be expected that a workman in entering a manufactory should object that any portion of the machinery is dangerous, and that it ought to be boxed off. But the proprietor of the machine is necessarily the person who can best forsee all the consequences incidental to its use, and can best guard against them. By throwing upon him a portion of the pecuniary responsibility for those mischiefs, we combine interest with duty, and add to the efficiency of both.

If the pecuniary consequences from unavoidable accidents were considerable, the imposition of the proposed responsibility may be met by the master, or by a deduction from the wages. Considering the defective nature of most existing modes of provision against sickness and casualties by benefit or friendly societies, and also unhappily the large proportion of those who from improvidence do not take advantage of these or other means (of which some portion of the working class avail themselves in so examplary and admirable a manner), if we were to devise a form of insurance against the casualties in question, available to all classes, we should recommend that measures should be taken to secure from the master the regular deductions of the amount of the contribution of the persons employed.

We propose that in the case of all accidents whatsoever from machinery occurring to children under fourteen years of age, the proprietor of the machinery shall pay for the medical attendance on the child, and all the expences of the cure, until medical attendance is no longer required; and also during the same period shall continue to pay wages at the rate of half the wages enjoyed by the individual in question at the time of the occurrence of the accident.

We are of opinion that persons above that age, in all cases where the injury was received from accidents in the ordinary course of business, where there was no culpable temerity, should receive similar treatment at the expence of the employer, and should also be allowed half wages until the period of cure, as we believe that an allowance of full wages would occasion considerable fraud in the protraction of that period, especially in the cases of accidents of a less serious nature.

We think that the remedy should be given on complaint before a magistrate or the inspector.

With regard to fatal injuries occasioned by wilful negligence, we have at present no new remedies to suggest as substitutes to those at present afforded by the common law.

We trust that in consideration of the extremely short period to which we have been limited in the performance of the task assigned to us, allowances will be made for the unavoidable imperfection of the Report which we now respectfully submit.

(L.S.) THOMAS TOOKE.
(L.S.) EDWIN CHADWICK.
(L.S.) THOMAS SOUTHWOOD SMITH.

25th June 1833.

251. Factories Regulation Act (1833)

Statutes of the Realm, 3 & 4 Wm. IV, c. 103.

1. WHEREAS it is necessary that the Hours of Labour of Children and young Persons employed in Mills and Factories should be regulated, inasmuch as there are great Numbers of Children and young Persons now employed in Mills and Factories, and their Hours of Labour are longer than is desirable, due Regard being had to their Health and Means of Education; be it therefore enacted by the King's most Excellent Majesty, by and with the Advice and Consent of the Lords Spiritual and Temporal, and Commons, in this present Parliament assembled, and by the Authority of the same, That from and after the First Day of January One thousand eight hundred and thirty-four no Person under Eighteen Years of Age shall be allowed to work in the Night, (that is to say,) between the Hours of Half past Eight o'clock in the Evening and Half past Five o'clock in the Morning, except as herein-after provided, in or about any Cotton, Woollen, Worsted, Hemp, Flax, Tow, Linen, or Silk Mill or Factory wherein Steam or Water or any other mechanical Power is or shall be used to propel or work the Machinery in such Mill or Factory, either in scutching, carding, roving, spinning, piecing, twisting, winding, throwing, doubling, netting, making Thread, dressing or weaving of Cotton, Wool, Worsted, Hemp, Flax, Tow, or Silk, either separately or mixed, in any such Mill or Factory situate in any Part of the United Kingdom of Great Britain and Ireland: Provided always, that nothing in this Act shall apply or extend to the working of any Steam or other Engine, Water-wheel, or other Power in or belonging to any Mill or Building or Machinery when used in that Part of the Process or Work commonly called fulling, roughing, or boiling of Woollens, nor to any Apprentices or other Persons employed therein, nor to the Labour of young Persons above the Age of Thirteen Years when employed in packing Goods in any Warehouse or Place attached to any Mill, and not used for any Manufacturing Process; provided also, that nothing in this Act shall apply or extend to any Mill or Factory used solely for the Manufacture of Lace. . . .

6. . . . And be it further enacted, That there shall be allowed in the Course of every Day not less than One and a Half Hours for Meals to every such Person restricted as herein-before provided to the Performance of Twelve Hours Daily Work.

7. And be it enacted, That from and after the First Day of January One thousand eight hundred and thirty-four it shall not be lawful for any Person whatsoever to employ in any Factory or Mill as aforesaid, except in Mills for the Manufacture of Silk, any Child who shall not have completed his or her Ninth Year of Age.

8. And be it further enacted, That from and after the Expiration of Six Months after the passing of this Act it shall not be lawful for any Person whatsoever to employ, keep, or allow to remain in any Factory or Mill as aforesaid for a longer Time than Forty-eight Hours in any One Week, nor for a longer Time than Nine Hours in any One Day, except as herein provided, any Child who shall not have completed his or her Eleventh Year of Age, or after the Expiration of Eighteen Months from the passing of this Act any Child who shall not have completed his or her Twelfth Year of Age, or after the Expiration of Thirty Months from the passing of this Act any Child who shall not have completed his or her Thirteenth Year of Age: Provided nevertheless, that in Mills for the Manufacture of Silk, Children under the Age of Thirteen Years shall be allowed to work Ten Hours in any One Day. . . .

11. And be it further enacted, That from and after the Expiration of Six Months after the passing of this Act it shall not be lawful for any Person to employ, keep, or allow to remain in any Factory or Mill any Child who shall not have completed his or her Eleventh Year of Age without such Certificate as is herein-after mentioned, certifying such Child to be of the ordinary Strength and Appearance of a Child of the Age of Nine Years, nor from and after the Expiration of Eighteen Months after the passing of this Act any Child who shall not have completed his or her Twelfth Year of Age, without a Certificate of the same Form, nor from and after the Expiration of Thirty Months after the passing of this Act any Child who shall not have completed his or her Thirteenth Year of Age, without a Certificate of the same Form, which Certificate shall be taken to be sufficient Evidence of the Ages respectively certified therein.

12. And be it further enacted, That for the Purpose of obtaining the Certificate herein-before required, in the Case of Children under the age of Eleven, Twelve, or Thirteen Years respectively, the Child shall personally appear before some Surgeon or Physician of the Place or Neighbourhood of its Residence, and shall submit itself to his Examination; and unless the Surgeon or Physician before whom the Child has so appeared shall certify his having had a personal Examination or Inspection of such Child, and also that such Child is of the ordinary Strength and Appearance of Children of or exceeding the Age of Nine Years, and unless also such Certificate shall within Three Months of its Date be countersigned by some Inspector or Justice, or in that Part of the United Kingdom called Scotland by some Inspector or Justice or Burgh Magistrate, such Child shall not be employed in any Factory or Mill. . . .

17. "And whereas by an Act, intituled *An Act for the Preservation of the Health and*

Morals of Apprentices and others employed in Cotton and other Mills and Cotton and other Factories, passed in the Forty-second Year of the Reign of His late Majesty George the Third, it was amongst other things provided, that the Justices of the Peace for every County or Place in which such Mill was situated should appoint yearly Two Persons not interested in or in any way connected with such Mills or Factories in such County to be Visitors of such Mills or Factories, which Visitors so appointed were empowered and required by the aforesaid Act to enter such Factories at any Time they might think fit, and examine and report in Writing whether the same were conducted according to the Laws of the Realm, and also to direct the Adoption of such Sanitory Regulations as they might, on Advice, think proper: And whereas it appears that the Provisions of the said Act with Relation to the Appointment of Inspectors were not duly carried into execution, and that the Laws for the Regulation of the Labour of Children in Factories have been evaded, partly in consequence of the Want of the Appointment of proper Visitors or Officers whose special Duty it was to enforce their Execution;" be it therefore enacted, That upon the passing of this Act it shall be lawful for His Majesty by Warrant under His Sign Manual to appoint during His Majesty's Pleasure Four Persons to be Inspectors of Factories and Places where the Labour of Children and young Persons under Eighteen Years of Age is employed, and in the Case of the Death or Dismissal of any of them to appoint another in the Place of Such deceased Inspector, which said several Inspectors shall carry into effect the Powers, Authorities, and Provisions of the present Act; and such Inspectors or any of them are hereby empowered to enter any Factory or Mill, and any School attached or belonging thereto, at all Times and Seasons, by Day or by Night, when such Mills or Factories are at work, and having so entered to examine therein the Children and any other Person or Persons employed therein, and to make Inquiry respecting their Condition, Employment, and Education; and such Inspectors or any of them are hereby empowered to take or call to their Aid in such Examination and Inquiry such Persons as they may choose, and to summon and require any Person upon the Spot or elsewhere to give Evidence upon such Examinations and Inquiry, and to administer to such Person an Oath.

18. And be it further enacted, That the said Inspectors or any of them shall have Power and are hereby required to make all such Rules, Regulations, and Orders as may be necessary for the due Execution of this Act, which Rules, Regulations, and Orders shall be binding on all Persons subject to the Provisions of this Act; and such Inspectors are also hereby authorized and required to enforce the Attendance at School of Children employed in Factories according to the Provisions of this Act, and to order Tickets or such other Means as they may think fit for Vouchers of Attendance at such Schools; and such Inspectors are also hereby required to regulate the Custody of such Tickets or Vouchers, and such Inspectors may require a Register of them to be kept in every School and Factory; and such Inspectors are also hereby authorized and required to order a Register of the Children employed in any Factory and of their Sex and Hours of Attendance, and of their Absence on account of Sickness, to be kept in such Factory; and all Registers, Books, Entries, Accounts, and Papers kept in pursuance of this Act shall at all Times be open to such Inspectors, and

such Inspectors may take or cause to be taken for their own Use such Copy as they may think proper: and such Inspectors shall also make such Regulations as may be proper to continue in force any Certificates, Tickets, or Vouchers required by this Act, and such Certificates, Tickets, or Vouchers so continued in force shall have the same Operation and Effect as new Certificates, Tickets, or Vouchers; and such Inspector shall order and is hereby authorized to order the Occupier of any Factory or Mill to register or cause to be registered any Information with relation to the Performance of any Labour in such Mill or Factory, if such Inspector deem such Information necessary to facilitate the due Enforcement of any of the Provisions of this Act or of any of the Regulations which he may make under the Authority of this Act; and such Inspector is hereby authorized to order such Occupier of any Mill or Factory to transmit, in such Manner as may be directed in such Order, any Information with relation to the Persons employed or the Labour performed in such Mill or Factory that such Inspector may deem requisite to facilitate the Performance of his Duties or any inquiry made under the Authority of this Act. . . .

20. And be it further enacted, That from and after the Expiration of Six Months from the passing of this Act every Child herein-before restricted to the Performance of Forty-eight Hours of Labour in any One Week shall, so long as such Child shall be within the said restricted Age, attend some School to be chosen by the Parents or Guardians of such Child, or such School as may be appointed by any Inspector in case the Parents or Guardians of such Child shall omit to appoint any School, or in case such Child shall be without Parents or Guardians; and it shall and may be lawful, in such last-mentioned Case, for any Inspector to order the Employer of any such Child to make a Deduction from the weekly Wages of such Child as the same shall become due, not exceeding the Rate of One Penny in every Shilling, to pay for the Schooling of such Child; and such Employer is hereby required to pay the Sum so deducted according to the Order and Direction of such Inspector. . . .

252. Report of the Select Committee on hand loom weavers (1834–1835)

Parlty. Papers, 1835/XIII/pp. XI–XII.

Having now gone through a cursory digest of the case of the Hand-Loom Weavers, as it was submitted to them in Evidence, and expressed their sentiments on the remedy to which their attention was called, Your Committee venture to lay before the House their opinion as to the general causes of this lamentable state of things.

Of the combination of causes to which the reduction of wages and consequent distress of the Weaver may be attributed, the following appear to be the most prominent:–

1st. Increase of machinery propelled by steam.
2nd. Heavy and oppressive taxation, occasioned by the war.
3rd. Increased pressure thereof, from operations on the currency and contractions of the circulating medium in 1816, 1826, and 1829.

4th. The exportation of British yarn, and foreign competition created thereby, from the increase of rival manufactures abroad.

5th. The impulse given by low wages and low profits to longer hours of work.

On these causes Your Committee beg to submit the following observations:

With respect to the first, *viz*. "Increase of machinery propelled by steam". It would appear from the Evidence, that although the Power-Loom has been now for some years past in operation, yet that it has but very lately, in comparison, been brought into direct competition with the Hand-Loom; that at this very moment, even, there are branches of the Hand-Loom business in which there is no immediate prospect of the Power-Loom interfering with them, but which are, notwithstanding, more or less in the same state of wretchedness and destitution described in the foregoing pages; while the general fall in wages, and consequent distress of the Hand-Loom Weavers, has been rapidly progressive ever since the termination of the late war; and especially marked at the stated periods of 1816, 1826, and 1829.

This decline in the circumstances of the Weavers, Your Committee cannot attribute to the mere transition from a state of war to that of peace, supposed by some to have destroyed a monopoly possessed by this country in the foreign market during the war, because the quantity of British produce and manufactures exported, measured by the official value, has been exactly doubled since the war. Your Committee has therefore turned their attention to other probable causes, which may have affected the Weavers' condition. And in comparing his condition with that of other producers, in other branches of industry, they find, whether in the produce of the land, or of the Power-Loom, or of articles affected neither by seasons or machinery, a tremendous fall has taken place since 1814. Neither can Your Committee attribute this fall in the value of every commodity to such assigned transition from war to peace; because, in addition to the reason before stated, in all the wars of the last century, save one, prices fell during the war, and rose on the return of peace.

Looking, on the other hand, to the constant co-incidence, during the late war, of a rise in all prices, simultaneously, with an increase of the Bank of England and country note circulation; and looking also to the fall in all prices concurrently with the preparation for payment, by the Bank of England, of its notes in gold on the return of peace; looking, moreover, to the rise in all prices at the two distinct intervals of 1817, 1818, and 1823, 1824, and 1825, when the resumption of cash payments was either deferred or modified, and the Bank of England was again induced to increase its circulation; and lastly, looking to the fall in all prices, when the issues of the Bank of England were again withdrawn in 1819 and 1826; and the extinction of one pound notes in 1829; looking at all these circumstances in conjunction, Your Committee cannot withhold their conviction that the Bill of 1819, commonly called Mr. Peel's Bill (the preparation for, and completion of which has just been described,) has been the main cause of the great pressure on industry resulting from the fall in prices.

That some branches of industry have been better able to stand this pressure than others, appears to Your Committee undeniable; especially in cases where they have been assisted by external circumstances. For instance, that part of the export trade which consists of yarn, the produce altogether of machinery propelled by power, has been stimulated by the increased demand of yarn for foreign Weavers. The home trade, depending for the most part, or entirely, for its support on the well-being of the agricultural interest, and that interest having suffered to such an extent from the fall in the price of its produce; the result, from this adversity in the home-trade, has been to double any disadvantage which might have befallen the Hand-Loom Weaver from the introduction of the Power-Loom. His condition has been as if half his market were taken away from him at the very moment that twice the number of Weavers (in the shape of the Power Loom) were brought to contend against each other for work.

Your Committee are not in the least disposed to deny the influence the Power Loom has had upon the condition of the Hand-Loom Weaver; but they cannot help lamenting that such should have been the course of our legislation, that instead of breaking the force (at its commencement) of this almost necessary evil on the Hand-Loom Weaver, and instead of causing it to be as gradual as possible, it has actually gone out of its way to quicken its progress, and to aggravate, to an inconceivable extent, the burden and the pressure of it. As an instance of this, the distress and disemployment of agricultural and other labourers, in consequence of the fall in prices resulting from Mr. Peel's Bill, has prevented the absorption of the Weavers in agriculture and other pursuits, as they gradually might become supernumerary. This would have been the natural process; it is the mode of relief suggested by Dr. Adam Smith in such an emergency; but Parliament has effectually interfered to prevent their taking advantage of it; thus giving the Weavers an unexceptionable plea for demanding Parliamentary protection, if it is to be found, at the present moment.

In all changes, such as have been described, the most ingenious and the most dexterous will, of course, suffer the least. Machinery propelled by steam, producing goods at less trouble and cost than even the most ingenious artisan, may thus be looked on in the light of the most dexterous workman, and of course has experienced in proportion a smaller share of difficulty, especially under the circumstances of less taxation falling upon it. Again the graduation of operatives having suffered more or less in proportion to their skill, strength, and ability; in struggles of this kind the weakest will go to the wall; and this is equally true whether applied to land or manufactures. The poor soil (as respects the cost of production) may be termed the less dexterous manufacturer of corn, as the Hand-Loom Weaver, in the same sense, is the less expert manufacturer of goods.

In addition to the Hand-Loom Weaver being the weakest party in the contest going on, they have had (what they consider) a disadvantage of another kind compared with some, *viz.* living and working in their own houses, being spread over large districts of country, and detached from their brethren working in the same line: this has thrown difficulties in the way of their combinations to prevent the reduction of wages, which of late years have so frequently taken place among the operatives employed in masses in factories and other trades. In stating this, Your Committee would be understood to be far from expressing any approbation of such systems of combination; because whatever is extracted unduly out of the capital of the employer in the shape of wages, must eventually react on the condition of the employed. It was also stated by several witnesses, that the fear of being finally reduced to the destitute condition of the Hand-Loom Weavers, had induced other trades to combine to prevent it.

Concluding their observations on the subject of the Power-Loom, Your Committee beg again, to be distinctly understood that nothing can be further from their opinion than that the Hand-Loom Weavers, in certain branches of their trade, can ultimately resist the effects produced by the introduction of the Power-Loom. All they have contended for, and that is supported by the evidence before them, is that the Power Loom itself would never have been the cause of such immediate wide-spread misery and distress, as that of which the Hand-Loom Weavers now so reasonably complain. They report the opinion, that other causes, wholly apart and distinct from the Power Looms, have tended to aggravate their difficulties; and that if they had to contend with the Power-Loom alone, the difficulties, though they might have been sufficiently apparent, would have been greatly mitigated.

With respect to the second cause operating on the condition of the Weaver, *viz.* "Heavy and oppressive taxation occasioned by the war", no comment appears to be necessary.

With respect to the third cause, *viz.* "Increased pressure thereof, from operations on the currency, and contractions of the circulating medium in 1816, 1826, and 1829," it may be useful to show the feelings of the Weavers themselves on the subject, as exhibited before Your Committee in an answer by *Hugh Mackenzie*, a most intelligent Weaver, from Glasgow:

"985. Do you ascribe your distress to what is called the Corn Bill?–With respect to the Corn Bill, there are many different opinions upon it; but as relates to us as Weavers, we are persuaded that though the Corn Bill were off to-morrow, such is the nature of our manufactures, and the disposition for cheapness, that they would reduce us just exactly proportionately to the fall of corn.

"986. Do you suppose that what is called Peel's Bill has been instrumental in affecting either your employment or your wages; do you know what is called Peel's Bill for reducing the quantity of money?–Yes, I have heard tell of Peel's Bill; what I understand by it is this, that it has been a means of contracting the currency. Now, under such circumstances as that, there is nothing more clear than that it must be a general evil to the country. I shall illustrate this to you just now. The higher the circulation of money in this country is, so much the better; for we stand on artificial ground in comparison with that of the rest of the surrounding nations of Europe. This becomes necessary on account of the very great burthen of the National Debt. If the country has an artificial burthen to bear, it becomes absolutely necessary that it should have artificial means of support. If the circulation of the country (that is the value of labour) be 200,000,000£ yearly, and the taxation 50,000,000£, it is clear that there is one-fourth of it in taxation, paid out of this 200,000,000£. We shall suppose, then, by Peel's Bill, or any other measure, the currency is restricted to 100,000,000£, being still the yearly value of labour. If we pay still 50,000,000£ of taxation, it makes the burthen double; and I might add that if the income of all other classes, productive and unproductive, was reduced proportionably as the Weavers are, it would be impossible to pay the taxation, and a national bankruptcy would be the consequence."

With respect to the fourth cause, *viz.* "The exportation of British yarn, and foreign competition created thereby from the increase of rival manufactures abroad", Your Committee cannot but lament that any temporary pressure in the manufacturing interest, subsequent to 1815, should have led to so great an increase in the export of yarn: because, however individually profitable in the first instance, nothing can be more certain than that, by encouraging weaving abroad, we allow the foreigner to get between the British manufacturer and the market, and so cut off a lasting source of profitable employment to our fellow countrymen. That this encouragement to foreign weaving by the export of yarn has added to the disadvantageous circumstances operating on the condition of the Hand-Loom Weaver, Your Committee sees little reason to doubt.

With respect to the fifth cause, *viz.* "The impulse given by low wages, and low profits, to longer hours of work". These longer hours of work, as it appears from the Evidence, proceed from a hope in the minds both of masters and men, that increased exertion will compensate for the fall in profits and wages; but the result of this system is, that goods are produced more than commensurate with the demand; and the ultimate effect, consequently, is an injurious reaction on those engaged in it; and it has become, in fact, the fruitful source of that "ruinous home competition" which the Weavers make one of the principal grounds of their complaint.

These appear to Your Committee to be the efficient causes, remote and immediate, of the suffering, demoralisation, and discontent of the Hand-Loom Weaver.

To the above enumeration of causes, Your Committee beg to add the subjoined suggestions from one of the witnesses, Mr. *James Jenkins*, many of which appear to be valuable:–

"I beg leave to add the following suggestions on the advantages to be derived from the establishment of local boards of trade in Coventry:–

"It could decide differences between masters and workmen, and between masters and apprentices.

"It might put into operation the *livret* system of France, which would enable workmen leaving their homes for want of employment to obtain it in places where they were unknown, and by which the losses of manufacturers by embezzlements would be diminished.

"It would establish a school of art, the principal thing wanted to put the English manufacturer on a level with the French.

"It would stimulate mechanical invention and skill, by distributing rewards and honours.

"It could facilitate the introduction of the best machinery used in other places, and improved modes of manufacture.

"It could collect statistical information, and prevent the continual necessity of Parliamentary inquiries.

"It would be instrumental in introducing new branches of industry to take up the surplus labour of a place.

"It would enable workmen to obtain the full market price for their labour, and when the state of the demand justified it, would facilitate their obtaining advances in wages.

"It could counteract the present practice of weavers bringing up their children to branches of trade already overstocked with workmen, and assist their introduction into other trades where labour was wanting."

Dr. Bowring also furnished Your Committee with very valuable information respecting industrial institutions in France (similar in their nature and objects to the above) of which he has had much recent experience, and for which information Your Committee beg to refer to the Evidence.

Your Committee would also add the following suggestions from the Evidence, as worthy of adoption:

1st. A more exact specification of the length and breadth of the pieces of goods to be manufactured:

2nd. A cheaper legal form of indenture of apprentices, and a reduction of the stamp duty to 5s.

And 3rd. A more summary and effectual protection against embezzlement of weaving materials.

Your Committee cannot conclude this Report without pointing out to Your Honourable House the very great disadvantages to which the Hand-Loom Weaver is exposed by reason of such taxes as those on malt, hops, sugar, and soap, which, by raising the price of articles of the first necessity, renders him either less able to consume the production of Great Britain and her Colonies, or causes him to be a more costly instrument of production than he would otherwise be to the Manufacturer: who has thus an additional inducement to substitute mechanical for manual labour.

1 July 1835.

253. Horner's report of 1837 on the changing attitude of millowners

Parlty. Papers, 1837/XXXI/pp. 92–94.

. . . Although there have been many instances of transgressions of the law, the greater number of which have been proceeded against, I see a decided change for the better within the last three months; for the strong dislike to the Act, which existed among a large number of the most respectable mill-owners, has greatly subsided. From what I have seen, and from the opinions I have heard expressed by them and their work-people, there is evidently an increased conviction on the minds of both that an effective interference of the Legislature, for the protection of the children employed in factories, is necessary, and that it is just in principle; although there is still an impression with many that the restrictions have been carried further than the case required. Operatives, especially when they were themselves parents, very frequently of late have said to me that they are satisfied that the limitation of hours, and the obligation to attend school, must produce great and lasting benefits to the children. The expressions of contentment with the principle of the law, as it stands, appear to me to have become more frequent, from three causes; first, because it is more clearly seen that a restriction of the hours of infant labour in factories is necessary to satisfy the wishes of the country; secondly, because the apprehended difficulties of carrying the provisions of the present Act into practice have been found upon trial, in most situations, to have existed more in imagination than in reality, or, at least, they have been far more easily got the better of than was believed to be possible; and, lastly, because it does not interfere with adult labour.

The hostility to the Act, to which I have alluded, and which has in many instances considerably impeded its operation hitherto, was evidently created, not so much by the interference itself, as by indignant feelings in the minds of many of the most extensive and respectable mill-owners, arising from the great injustice with which they have been treated in the various discussions and publications to which the factory question has given rise; where accusations of the most discreditable conduct and motives have been unsparingly brought forward against mill-owners, as a body, without distinction. That there were some whose conduct had been such as to merit the terms of reprobation employed was unfortunately too clearly proved by the evidence laid before Parliament; and that there are still many who appear to be indifferent either to the health or moral state of the children they employ, and to view them in no other light than as tools let out to hire, is too clearly proved by the prosecutions which have taken place in my district in the last half-year, and by the little disposition evinced by them to forward the humane objects of the Act by a small sacrifice of trouble and expense. But, that instances of cruelty and oppression are common, or occur in a greater proportion among mill-owners than other classes, or that there is among them a smaller proportion of benevolent good men, may be most confidently denied. Indeed I know of no description of persons of whom so many instances may be brought forward of active benevolent exertions and large pecuniary sacrifices to promote the welfare of the people they employ. To this I bear the most willing testimony from very ample opportunities of observation.

It is very difficult for the mill-owners to come forward in their own defence to repel those unjust attacks upon the general character of their body; for they have no association or standing committee, whose duty it would be to watch over their common interests, and refute the calumnies; and if the task were undertaken by a single individual among them his statements, however trustworthy, would be liable to be undervalued or disregarded, as coming from an interested person; but, as I do not stand in that last-mentioned position, and as I have, in the discharge of my functions as Commissioner of Inquiry and Inspector, in the course of the last three years, visited as great a number of factories as perhaps any other individual, possessing authority to inquire, has done, I deem it an act of public duty and of justice (considering the relation in which I stand to the mill-owners, and as reference is so constantly made to the factories in my district) to take this occasion of my official Report to your Lordship most unequivocally to deny the truth of those general accusations against the masters so freely indulged in of late, and of those pictures of oppression, debilitated health, and suffering, represented to be characteristic of factory employment. I feel the more urgently called upon thus to express my firm conviction at the present time, because statements, recently made on different occasions, and calculated to make a great impression upon the public mind, have been giving fresh currency to very erroneous representations of the condition of the factory-workers, and are fostering prejudices, the most unjust, against a large and respectable portion of the community. The instances brought forward are, it is true, extracted from Parliamentary documents; but these were proved, by other evidence laid before Parliament by the Factory Commissioners, to be far from being applicable to factories generally; and they belong, moreover, to a state of things that existed more than three years ago; no notice whatever being taken of the great extent to which the evils have been remedied by the operation of the present Act.

When I have been visiting those establishments (of which I could draw out a long list) where order, cleanliness, and an attention on the part of the master to the comfort and welfare of his workpeople are conspicuous, I have often wished that those who so thoughtlessly believe and give currency to tales of the miseries of the factory-workers, and of the cruelty and hard-heartedness of their masters, would go to some of the mills to which I could send them, and judge for themselves. They would then see how greatly they have erred in their general condemnation of what they term the *factory system*, and how much virtue, intelligence, comfort, and happiness are to be found among the workers in a well-regulated mill. The statements as to the unhealthiness of factory employment are also exceedingly erroneous, inasmuch as a part, and comparatively a small part, is unfairly held out as a representation of the general condition. To be convinced of this, one has only to see the young women and lads coming out from a great power-loom shed, even in the heart of a great town like Manchester or Stockport, with all their disadvantages, and still more in the smaller towns and rural districts; or to see the workers in the woollen and worsted factories in the West Riding of Yorkshire. I am satisfied that what may then be seen would lead any unprejudiced observer to the conclusion that no collection of the working classes, in other occupations in this country, can possibly exhibit a larger proportion of well-fed, well-clothed, healthy, and cheerful-looking people. It seems, besides, to be entirely overlooked by those who represent the condition of the workpeople in factories in so unfavourable a light, that the question can, in fairness, be only considered as one of comparison between them and those engaged in other occupations, (all trades being accompanied, more or less, with disadvantages,) and whether evils equally great, both as regards the health and the morals of the people, as any of those which exist in the worst parts of the worst-managed factories, do not prevail, in an equal or greater degree, in many other trades. That such is the case, no one is ignorant who has paid the least attention to the subject, and particularly as regards children. That the factory system, even in the best-regulated establishments, was defective, in so far as young children laboured 12 hours a-day, there can be no doubt; for no arrangements of the best-intentioned master could prevent the evils that were inherent in a system which deprived children of that fair proportion of air and exercise natural to their time of life, and without which their chance of growing up in full health and strength must at least have been considerably diminished, and which cut them off from all opportunity of being properly educated. But this objection does not apply to the factories subject to this Act only; the interposition of the law, for the protection of children employed in many other factories and trades, is no less necessary; and so long as children can be sent to other occupations, where the hours of work are unlimited, and where no obligation to attend school exists, the cotton, woollen, and flax mill-owners will be placed in an unfair position; and the plans for improving the condition of those factory children, which are contemplated by the present Act, will be materially interfered with. . . .

254. Trade unionism in the later 'thirties: evidence of Sheriff (afterwards Sir Archibald) Alison before the Select Committee on Combinations of Workmen (1837–1838)

Parlty. Papers, 1837–1838/VIII.

1954. Mr *O'Connell.* Then the result of such a combination as that of the cotton-spinners is, to help to diminish their education and industry?–The tendency in practice clearly is to establish a monopoly of skilled against the efforts of unskilled industry, and to fence in the monopoly of skilled labour by a power of intimidation to which the working classes find it impossible to make any resistance.

1955. But if the means of intimidation, or the possibility of intimidation were taken away, then the evil effects of such a combination would not be much felt?–If you could only establish this state of things, that the workmen combine, and that they then give that liberty to others which they take to themselves, that is to say, that they keep their hands off their neighbours, I should be the greatest possible friend to combinations; and if we could once see that elysium established, I, for one, would give them my most entire support. Let them combine, but let them keep their hands off their neighbours; but unhappily that has never taken place yet, at least in that part of Scotland with which I am acquainted.

1956. In fact, that could not take place without their efforts being crippled to a great extent?–I know the opinion of all combinations is, and particularly the cotton-spinners, that, without intimidating the new hands who might interfere with their monopoly, their illegal efforts, of course, must prove nugatory. Their combination, I think, might have a very beneficial effect in their own favour, if it was limited merely to legal acts. I think, for example, that it is a very good thing for the cotton-spinners, as well as every other class of labour, to combine, because it enables numbers, to a certain degree, to compensate and to enter with equality into the lists with capital, and therefore I think that combinations are essential to support the rights of labour in the competition with capital; but then what I desiderate is, a means for the civil magistrate of separating the outrage and intimidation which hitherto, notwithstanding the change in the Combination Laws by Mr Hume's Act, has been invariably the concomitant of every strike, not only of every strike, but of every trades' union during the whole of its existence, because the actual occasions of strike which come under the notice of the civil magistrate, and which attract the attention of the public, are but a small part of the operation of the trades' union. The trades' union is permanent in its operations. Every trades' union, including that of the cotton-spinners, is exercising a continual control, in subordinate matters, upon the masters in whose employment the men are. And occasionally strikes are going on between isolated individual masters and their own workmen, in consequence, not of a general contest about wages, but of some quarrel with the individual, such as about an unpopular manager, or their having admitted hands not members of the union, or their having admitted too many apprentices, or something of that kind. In consequence of that the trades' union is exercising a continual control over the masters and over the other workmen engaged in the business; and the pressure of that continual control is felt permanently by persons in other trades who are wishing to get their sons into the cotton-spinning line.

2116. Mr. *O'Connell.* Is there any connexion in your opinion between the combination of the cotton-spinners and the distress of the hand-loom weavers?–I gave some evidence on that subject in a former examination, in answer to the questions of my Lord Ashley; but I am strongly impressed with the effect it has had upon the circumstances of the hand-loom weavers, and I was so much aware of it that I recommended to Mr Symons, the Government commissioner who is now investigating the state of the hand-loom weavers of Glasgow, to turn his attention particularly to that subject; but he told me just before I left Glasgow, that such was the terror of the witnesses in the hand-loom line on the subject of strikes, that out of the first 20 he had examined, he had only been able to get one who would utter the words "unions" and "strikes" but in the twenty-first witness he did stumble upon one who was less alarmed, and he gave important evidence on that subject. I am perfectly convinced that the distress of the hand-loom weavers is mainly and almost entirely to be ascribed to the exclusive monopoly established by the forcible conduct of the trades in all other lines, which prevents their sons getting into any other line.

2117. Preventing the free circulation of labour?–Preventing the free circulation of labour; every trade is fenced round by prohibitions, which render it impossible for a person to get into it, except a son or a brother, or some relation of an already existing member; in short, it is the old spirit of monopoly revived in the persons of the skilled labourers, with this difference, that it is not a few merchants, but a few hundred or thousand workmen, who exclude a hundred thousand of unskilled workmen.

2118. Who operate tyrannically upon all those who would wish to dispose of their labour freely and without the influence of those unions?–Who operate so tyrannically that the lower orders find it impossible to oppose any resistance to it. I am convinced that if a sufficiently vigorous and powerful government were established in the manufacturing districts to restore the freedom of labour, the immediate effect would be a great increase in the persons brought to trial for those offences, because in the transition from the present state, which is one of unlimited despotism on the part of the skilled trades, to one of freedom on the part of the unskilled trades, there would probably be a great contest. The present tranquillity arises from the comparatively irresistible power of the skilled trades, which nobody thinks of resisting, any more than they would think here of resisting the Queen's guards.

2119. Mr *Milnes*. In fact, it is a complete system of castes?–It is a complete system of castes, which are operating to exclude all persons from those particular lines, except the favoured connexions of the skilled trades; it throws down all the others to the lowest point of depression.

2120. Mr *O'Connell*. Thus making a species of aristocratic class amongst the labouring population?–Exactly; I have long been convinced that the system is just a system of the aristocracy of skilled labour against the general mass of unskilled labour; and I think the question is far more one between one class of workmen and another, than between the workmen and the masters; for the real sufferers are not the masters so much as the other workmen who are excluded. I am quite sure that for one complaint which I have received from the masters, I have received 50 from the workmen suffering under the system.

2121. By "skilled", do you not mean skilful?–By "skilled labour", I mean the labour of those peculiarly difficult trades to learn, which have got an organization of trades' unions, such as cotton-spinners, iron-moulders, colliers, iron-miners, and so on; and by "unskilled labour", I mean the labour that is easily learned without an apprenticeship, such as the labour of a ploughman, a hand-loom-weaver, or a scavenger.

2122. Do you foresee any injury to the general interests of trade and commerce from these combinations?–I think that the system of combination, if it goes on as it has done, will undoubtedly ruin the manufacturing industry of the country, and that in more than one way. I do not think it is conceivable that the manufacturers will submit to the present system of coercion and ruin imposed upon them by the workmen; and if they find by experience that it cannot be arrested, I think they will either migrate with their capital to other States, as they have done already, or that they will contrive machinery which will supersede altogether the hand of man in manufactories. That effect has already taken place in a great degree in the cotton-spinners' line. There is the self-adjusting mule, which had been known, but it had not spread to any great degree in Glasgow; but since the late strike of the spinners in 1837, the number of persons who have given orders for self-acting mules, or for double wheels, which reduces the number of spinners to one half, is so great, that already it has had a very serious effect in throwing the cotton-spinners out of employment; and I therefore think it very probable that in five or seven years the cotton-spinners will be reduced to the same destitution as the hand-loom weavers are now. The destitute situation of the hand-loom weavers is in a great measure to be ascribed to the previous combinations of that trade. About 15 or 20 years ago, almost all the serious combinations were on the part of the weavers; the consequence was this, that the attention of the masters was turned in a most serious manner to the application of machinery to supersede the human hand in that department, and the consequence was the discovery of the power-loom weaving, which has brought machinery to compete with the human hand to such a degree in the hand-loom weaving line, as has, coupled with the combinations of other skilled trades, reduced them to their present deplorable condition; and I anticipate a similar result for the cotton-spinners, and all other trades in which the system of combination, accompanied by outrage, has taken strong root, at least in all those trades where the application of machinery is possible; because, where it is not possible, I anticipate the total destruction of the trade from the continuance of the system, and that the capital will leave the country. I know more than one instance of great mercantile establishments which have been decidedly ruined by strikes among the workmen; they calculated their strikes at the time when they knew there were heavy bills running against their employers, and by holding out a series of months they entirely ruined them.

2407. You stated that you thought the hours of employment, of work, should be peremptorily fixed at ten hours a day. In that answer, have you taken into consideration the power of receiving education, or of attending to religious observances, which would be conferred upon the workmen if the number of hours which they work were reduced?–I had in view that as one of the principal reasons; I think that would be one beneficial effect; and that another would be, that they would have more time for really useful education, for reading books worth reading, and that they would be less tempted to habitual indulgence in drinking spirits, which arises from the excess of labour, and from the undue command of money arising from high wages.

2408. Lord *Ashley*. Then you treat with contempt the argument often urged, that if the working classes had a little more time they would spend that time in a pothouse?–I think that if the working classes had more time, a considerable proportion of them would take to useful reading. In short, I think that the working classes are just like ourselves. In the House of Peers, or in the House of Commons, a certain portion of the Members are good men, who will read; a certain portion of them are indifferent characters, who will take to dissipation; and I think that the working classes are just the same; I do not think they are a bit worse than we are; and I am sure that we, in the same situation, would do just as they do.

2409. Then your opinion is, that if more time were allowed to the working classes, it would tend to promote their moral and spiritual improvement?–I think it would have a considerable effect in adding to it.

2410. And that it would have a considerable effect in adding to the general prosperity of the state, and consequently to the safety of the country?–Certainly; in short, I think a diminution of the hours of labour is an indispensable preliminary. I am quite certain that if any person will consider the number of hours they work and the heat, and also the severity of the labour, they will find that it would require an intellect as gigantic as that of Sir Isaac Newton or of Lord Bacon, to come back after that and take to intellectual exertion; they require the excitement of ardent spirits.

255. Seymour Tremenheere's account of the miners and iron workers of Bedwelty and Merthyr Tydvil in 1839: Report to the Committee of Council for Education

Parlty. Papers, 1840/XL/pp. 208–213.

The parishes which were the focus of the insurrectionary movement, and to which I therefore confined my attention, were those of Bedwelty, Aberystwyth, Mynnyddyslwynn, and Trevethin, in the county of Monmouth; and Merthyr-Tidvil in Glamorganshire, adjoining Bedwelty on the west. The four first-named of these furnished the body of men who marched down the valleys in three divisions from three different points, to the attack of Newport, on the night of Sunday, the 3rd of November, while it is generally believed that the Merthyr men were held in reserve to act immediately on the first attack proving successful.

A glance at the physical aspect of this district, and at the manner in which its population is distributed, made it evident, that a mere inquiry into the state of education would leave untouched many subjects tending to illustrate the peculiarities most prominent in the condition of the society which had grown up in those remote valleys. These subjects I did not decline whenever they arose naturally out of the inquiry into the state of education, and seemed to connect themselves with the moral and intellectual condition of the people. At the same time I did not fail to impress upon all persons with whom I came into communication, that my instructions only directed me to investigate the state of education, and that, in seeking for information on collateral topics, I was endeavouring to satisfy my own mind on questions suggested by the educational inquiry, with the view of submitting to my Lords the Committee of Council such observations on the moral and social habits of the people in this portion of the hill district, as might seem not unworthy of their attention with reference to the main subject of the elementary education of the labouring classes. The information so obtained was committed to notes made at the time; and from these notes this report has been compiled.

The parishes to which the inquiry refers are situated in the north-eastern angle of that mineral mountain range which extends across a large part of South Wales. They comprise a tract of country about 20 miles east and west, and 10 miles north and south, forming an irregular triangle, having Merthyr-Tidvil and a point a few miles west of Abergavenny for the base, and a point a little to the west of Risca for the apex. From the northern boundary-line of this district, or the base of the triangle, six parallel valleys run off in the direction of north and south. Towards the heads of these valleys most of the largest iron-works, with the population clustered around them, may be marked on the map by dark spots where the highest points of the valleys run up towards the summits of the central ridge. The valleys have there attained a high elevation; are susceptible of but scanty culture; and are separated from each other by tracts of cheerless moorland. The people are for the most part collected together in masses of from 4,000 to 10,000. Their houses are ranged round the works in rows, sometimes two to five deep, sometimes three stories high. They rarely contain less than from one to six lodgers in addition to the members of the family, and afford most scanty accommodation for so many inmates. It is not unusual to find that 10 individuals of various age and sex occupy three beds in two small rooms. Far worse instances might be given. The surface of the soil around is frequently blackened with coal, or covered with high mounds of refuse from the mines and the furnaces. The road between the rows is so imperfectly made as to be often, in wet weather, ankle deep in black mud. Flat pavement is rarely seen, except in some new works now erecting. Volumes of smoke from the furnaces, the rolling-mills, and the coke-hearths, are driven past, according to the direction of the wind. Gardens are few, and almost entirely neglected. Due attention to sewerage is also overlooked. The house of the master or resident director stands conspicuous amidst a small group of stunted and blackened trees. About a dozen other houses of decent exterior may be seen, inhabited by the surgeon, the agents, and other officers belonging to the works. These 10 or 20 superior members of the establishment, a few small shopkeepers, and many thousand people depending on daily labour, constitute for the most part the respective divisions of society among these colonies in the desert. The population congregated in the lower part of the parish of Bedwelty, and in Mynnyddyslwynn, towards the apex of this triangular district, forming a small proportion of the whole, is differently distributed. About two-thirds are engaged in numerous small collieries, employing from 50 to 150 men each, and are scattered in detached cottages among an agricultural population. The valleys have there expanded, the hills declined in height, and become susceptible of cultivation, and are covered with neat farms and cottages, each with its garden. There is, however, the same marked deficiency in the number of every other class except that which is dependent on daily labour.

The entire population of these five parishes, according to the lowest estimate given by persons most conversant with each, amounts to 85,000.

In some few instances, a portion of the population attached to the works within these parishes is located beyond their boundaries. Their condition differs in no respect from the rest, and the general results of the inquiry can be very slightly affected by their omission.

DAY SCHOOLS

The following Table shows the number of Common Day and Dame Schools in each of these Parishes respectively; the Number of Children frequenting them, and the proportion they bear to the whole Population.

PARISHES	*Common Day Schools for the Elementary Education of the Working Classes*	*Dame Schools and Schools for Children of from Two to Five Years of Age*	*Total Children attending Day and Dame Schools*	*Total Population*
Merthyr . . .	15	8	1,322	34,000
Bedwelty . . .	13	10	825	20,000
Aberystwyth . .	2	4	300	8,000
Trevethin . . .	13	7	638	16,000
Mynnyddyslwynn. .	4	4	223	7,000
	47	33	3,308	85,000

. . . Inquiry was made among the clergy, the ministers of dissenting congregations, the teachers of Sunday-schools, agents at the different works, secretaries of benefit clubs, schoolmasters, and other individuals whose occupations give them opportunities of forming an opinion, as to the degree of intellectual cultivation prevailing among the labouring classes of the hills. The result of the general testimony appeared to be, that of the adult working population a large proportion could neither read nor write; that very many had only acquired the art of knowing the letters and words; and that very few could read with ease to themselves, and with understanding. Wherever books were found in any cottage, the Bible was among them. It was also found in many in which the inmates confessed that they could not read it. In one part of the district in which inquiries were made, in 1,448 houses, three-fourths were found provided with Bibles, and one-fourth without. Where the inmates could read, song-books, hymn-books and religious tracts were the usual store. In about 200 cottages in different parts of the district, in which the question was asked, 10 only, exclusive of those belonging to superior engineers, were found to contain any book of general literature. . . .

An extensive result of this deficiency of education among the working-classes of this district, and of the means of obtaining general information through the medium of the language with which they are chiefly familiar, is an insensibility to the value of instruction, and an indisposition to procure it for their children. Many other causes combine to encourage this feeling. Their occupations are such, that in general the absence of any previous mental culture is no obstacle to their obtaining good employment. Success in their calling being the result of mechanical skill, rather than, as in some other mining operations, of careful judgment and previous calculation, the higher qualities of the mind are called into play in a comparatively small degree. Even those individuals among them who are appointed to situations of responsibility, possess in general very slight attainments. It occurred recently in one of the largest works, that, out of 11 competitors for a situation of that nature, only one could write. Their employments have but a slight tendency to impress upon them the value of intellectual proficiency. The great majority, therefore, are content to remain without any instruction. In the entire district, the number of adults attending evening-schools was about 90. Of the few who have learned to read at all, a large proportion confine themselves to the restricted literature of their own language. It is perceived by them that their children are sure of being able to gain an ample livelihood at an early age, without the aid of "learning." The parents are, therefore, apt to believe that their superiors are actuated by some selfish motive in endeavouring to induce them to send their children to school. They are averse to the trouble of making their children clean every day, in cases where they are sent to schools in which cleanliness is enforced. If the children object to go to school, the parents not unfrequently abstain from insisting upon it. If they send them at all, it is seldom for many months at a time. They are taken away whenever the father has not earned as much as usual, or has spent more. They think instruction of any kind very little necessary for the girls, whose assistance at home they are unwilling to dispense with. The boys are taken into the coal or iron mine at eight or nine years old, often earlier. The value of the labour of the youngest is about 6d. a-day. Their occupation consists in opening and shutting air-doors, in throwing small pieces of coal or ironstone into the trams, or in handing implements to the men at work. A boy thus learns early to become a good miner. It is not improbable, however, that not much skill in that respect would be lost by his beginning somewhat later; and it is certain, that from the time he enters the mine, he learns nothing else. A mother stated that her husband wanted to take one of her boys, then only seven years old, into the mine. She said, "that her others had gone there young enough at eight; and after they once went there, they turned stupid and blind-like, and would not learn any thing, and did not know what was right; and now they were like the rest, they went to the public-houses like men." The following statement of the wages of boys at one of the works may be taken as an average of the whole:-

	Per week
Boys, from 7 to 9 years of age	3s. to 5s.
„ „ 9 to 16 „ „ „	6s. to 12s.

They leave their homes at an early age, if they find they can be boarded cheaper elsewhere, and they spend the surplus of their wages in smoking, drinking and gambling. Boys of 13 will not unfrequently boast that they have taken to smoking before they were 12. All parental control is soon lost. Shortly after the age of 16 they begin to earn men's wages. Early marriages are very frequent. They take their wives from the coke-hearths, the mine and coal-yards, or other employments about the works, in which they have been engaged from 16 years or earlier; having had no opportunities of acquiring any better principles or improved habits of domestic economy, and being in all other respects less instructed than their husbands.

It cannot be said that poverty is in this district the cause of the deficiency of education. The steady demand for labour, and the rates of wages, for the last seven years, have been such that the earnings of children of a very early age can rarely have been absolutely necessary to the father of a family. In order to arrive at an approximation to the proportion of persons earning the different rates, it is necessary to analyse the various grades of workmen employed by one furnace. According to information derived from several iron-masters, the number of men, women and children, to which one furnace gives employment, may be stated at 280. They may be thus divided, according to their denominations and the rates earned:-

Labourers	*Parts in 100*	DENOMINATIONS	*Rates per Week clear of all deductions*
70	25	Furnace and mill-men	25 to 60s.
100	35·7	Miners and colliers	21 „ 25s.
40	14·3	Artisans	18 „ 24s.
35	12·5	Labourers	12 „ 18s.
35	12·5	Boys, women, old men, and inferior workmen	3 „ 12s.
280	100		

The above rates are formed from a comparison of various statements received from the masters; from inspection of their books in some instances; and from statements of the men themselves in various parts of the district. Each description of labourer has frequent opportunities of earning considerably more than the rates here given; and those who have begun with the lower rates have of late years been able very soon to rise permanently to the higher. Steady miners and colliers are generally able to approach the higher rate; and the abundant store of provisions, the substantial and costly furniture, generally seen in their cottages, together with the ample supply of good clothing with which themselves and their families are furnished, afford, among other circumstances, sufficient proof that the receipts of workmen of those grades are at least as high as they are here represented. Steady men, at one of the largest works, were raising, as appeared by the books, between 70 and 80 tons of coal per month, at 2s. per ton; others were only raising between 40 and 50 tons. The manager of the works stated that there was nothing in the state of the work at the mine which prevented the last-mentioned workmen from earning as much as the former.

The clear receipts of those employed about the mills and furnaces, amounting in numbers to one-fourth of the whole, are, as appears by the table of rates, such as are obtained by few classes of labourers in this or any other country. An additional proof that inability on the part of the parents to pay the cost is not the cause of so few children being sent to school, is found in the fact, to which schoolmasters and others interested in the subject bear testimony, that the attendance of children is quite as great when wages are low as when they are high, and generally more regular. The pecuniary obstacle, if any there be, arises from a cause admitted by none more readily than by the majority of the workmen themselves; from the habit of devoting to objects of immediate and sensual enjoyment almost the whole of their earnings not required for their actual subsistence. . . .

256. Dr. John Allen on the mining population in Northumberland and Durham in 1840: Report to the Committee of Council for Education

Parlty. Papers, 1841/xx/pp. 159–161.

. . . As far as regards their outward circumstances, perhaps few classes among our labouring population are in a better condition than the colliers of the northern district. After working for eight or ten hours in the pit, they come home to wash themselves thoroughly, and sit down to a plentiful meal.

Their houses are in general clean, roomy, and well furnished. You can scarcely enter one which does not contain a good four-post bedstead, a mahogany chest of drawers, and a clock. Each householder lives rent-free, paying only 3d per week for the leading of his coal. A small plot of ground for potatoes is commonly attached to each dwelling; and large families, if provident, make a bargain with their employers for grass for a cow. . . .

The pitmen have hitherto been little influenced by political agitations. Reading rooms do not prosper among them; and although some sale for worthless and seditious papers is doubtless found amongst them, the publications chiefly circulated are books of piety and devotion. In one cottage I noticed Adam Clarke's Bible,

Wesley's Sermons, Milner's Church History, and Leighton's Works. Those who have any deep religious feelings are ordinarily Methodists. The parishes are extensive, and the great tithes are not often in the hands of the incumbents. On the winning of a colliery, a large population is suddenly located in a district which may very probably be some miles distant from the church, the pastor of which may find his charge increased within a few months by some thousands, the families being sometimes brought into the parish by carts, to the number of 500 in a day. The church is almost unavoidably slow in her operations; it requires considerable exertion to raise a consecrated place for worship within three years; but in this time the people must in a great measure have formed their habits, and such as are disposed to listen to teachers will have found them for themselves. An instance was pointed out to me where, in a few weeks, a population of 3000 had risen up at the distance of three miles from the parish church, the incumbent having to provide additional spiritual attendance and the means of locomotion, out of an income of £75 per annum. A person well acquainted with the district, mentioned 6000 or 7000 as the average number of persons which, in the thickly populated parishes, fell to the charge of a single clergyman–a disproportion which is greatly increased when we take into account that, out of every 100 clergymen, probably 20 at least, from some cause or other, will not be effective among a population so difficult of access.

Within the last 16 years the attention of the clergy has been visibly drawn to the necessity for raising school-houses and unconsecrated buildings for public worship contemporaneously with the introduction of this shifting population into remote neighbourhoods. The owners of collieries are, in most cases, willing to provide their labourers with a room which may be used as a day and night-school during the week, and on the Sunday is opened to one or two sects (and in some instances three) in succession, for the purposes of public worship. But in very few cases does it seem to have occurred to those who derive such large revenues from the soil, that, for a man to be in any sense the spiritual pastor of the people, he must be with them as their adviser and friend during the week as well as a preacher to them on the Sunday. . . .

In the present state of things Sunday-schools are an institution to which the serious-minded will look with the deepest interest. It is true that the instruction given at such schools must be very limited, and the teachers are often very little fitted, by their age and their habits of thought, to dig into the minds of others. In many places pious poor may be found, but what these have, they commonly are not able (through deficiency of training) to impart to others. But may we not hope that persons of a higher range of understanding, of more thought, information, and experience, will gradually be induced to give their services to the amelioration of the condition of those beneath them? Are not the upper classes becoming daily more sensible of their identity of interest with those whose faculties of labour are their sole inheritance? Are there no signs of a growing sense of the responsibilities men are laid under by superior rank and education? The great want felt through the whole district is that of schoolmasters, men who may be better educated and more systematically trained, but above all, men who may in some degree be sensible of the great trust reposed in them when a parent confides to them the education of his children.

257. Factory inspectors' special reports on the practicability of legislation for the prevention of accidents: Horner's views

Parlty. Papers, 1841/x/pp. 206–208.

LONDON, 2nd April 1841

MY LORD,

In obedience to the directions contained in the letter of the Hon. Fox Maule, of the 2nd of March last, I have now the honour to lay before your Lordships the following Report upon the subjects referred to in that letter.

I shall begin by stating the sources from which I have obtained the information upon which the conclusions I have come to are founded.

The subject had for some time previously engaged my attention, for I had been long struck with the recklessness with which dangerous parts of machinery are left exposed in some mills, which in others are guarded with the utmost care. I saw that to correct the evil entirely by legislative interference would be attended with much difficulty; but it was evident that if no more were required than that those same parts which are boxed off in some mills should be made equally secure in others, the circumstances of both being alike, the risk of accidents would be very greatly diminished. I began therefore to collect facts and opinions, in order to endeavour to arrive at some practical conclusions, by conversing with mill-owners and their over-lookers, and with the makers of machinery; and the first documents which I have now to refer to are two letters (Nos. 1 and 2 in the Appendix), which I received last May.

Having heard that the subject had been taken up by the Select Committee on Factories, and that recommendations on the subject would be contained in their Report, I thought it not unlikely that I might be called upon for an opinion as to the practicability of a remedy for such serious evils, and I resumed my enquiries. I again applied to Mr. Fothergill, and received from him in February the letter No. 3. Remembering the admirable manner in which the machinery is guarded in a cotton factory belonging to Messrs. Horrocks, Miller, and Co., of Preston, I requested Mr. Ewings, the superintendent in that part of my district, to visit that factory, and to give me a detailed account of what had been done. The letter No. 4 is the reply which I received from Mr. Ewings; and it was followed by another (No. 5), giving me the result of an enquiry I had asked him to make in some well-regulated flax spinning factory. I shortly afterwards had an opportunity of conversing with Mr. Walker, the managing partner in the firm of Wood and Walker, of Bradford, proprietors of one of the largest and best managed worsted mills in the kingdom, and which was for some time under my inspection; having understood that Mr. Walker held very decided opinions as to the possibility of guarding against accidents, without any call upon the mill-owner beyond what is just and reasonable. I shortly afterwards received from him the letter No. 6.

Upon receipt of your Lordship's directions, conveyed to me in the letter of Mr. Maule, of the 2nd of March, I took measures for obtaining further information through the medium of the superintendents, by sending to each a copy of that letter, and requesting them to make enquiries at the best sources to which they could find access. The results of their investigations are contained in their respective reports, which I annex (Nos. 7, 8, 9 and 10). After I had received them, I went to Manchester, and conversed with some mill-owners, overlookers, and operatives, and also with some makers of machinery. Some notes which I made of these conversations will be found under No. 11. I then went to Bradford in Yorkshire, to meet, by appointment, my colleague Mr. Saunders, who had been engaged in a careful investigation of the subject, assisted by the superintendent of his district, especially Mr. Baker, of Leeds, and who, at the request of Mr. Saunders, met us at Bradford. After carefully considering the additional information which Mr. Saunders and Mr. Baker communicated to me, and after going over with them the evidence which I had myself obtained, I came to the conclusions which I have now the honour to lay before your Lordship.

It is proved, I think, by a great preponderance of evidence, that without going beyond what has been already done spontaneously in many factories, and without proposing any thing beyond that which mill-occupiers and the makers of machinery pronounce to be both reasonable and practicable, it is very possible to frame and to enforce enactments, prohibiting the cleaning of dangerous machinery while in rapid motion, and requiring the dangerous parts of machinery to be fenced off, which would very greatly lessen the risk of accidents; in other words, that it is both reasonable and practicable to require that the example of humane and considerate mill-occupiers shall be followed by those who have hitherto been, or may hereafter be, culpably negligent, in not taking those precautions for the safety of their work-people, which it is a clear and obvious duty in them to do. The kind of enactments that are called for, and are considered capable of being carried into effect, I will now proceed to state. . . .

258. Report of the Commission on the labour of women and children in mines (1842)

Parlty. Papers, 1842/XIII.

(a) *First Report. Tables of Proportion of Children and Young People employed in different Districts*

TABLE NO. I.–ENGLAND

Districts	*Adults*		*13 to 18*		*Under 13*		*Total of children and young persons to 1000 adult males*	*Proportion of children and young persons in the whole number employed*	*Proportion of children in the whole number under 18*
	Males	*Fem.*	*Males*	*Fem.*	*Males*	*Fem.*			
Leicestershire . .	1000	—	227	—	180	—	407	Two-sevenths.	Much more than one-third.
Derbyshire . . .	1000	—	240	—	167	—	407	Two-sevenths.	Much more than one-third.
Yorkshire . . .	1000	22	352	36	246	41	675	Upwards of one-third.	Much more than one-third.
Lancashire . . .	1000	86	352	79	195	27	653	Upwards of one-third.	Upwards of one-third.
South Durham . .	1000	—	226	—	184	—	410	Two-sevenths.	Much more than one-third.
Northumberland and North Durham .	1000	—	266	—	186	—	452	Nearly one-third.	Much more than one-third.

TABLE NO. IV.–WALES

Districts	*Adults*		*13 to 18*		*Under 13*		*Total of children and young persons to 1000 adult males*	*Proportion of children and young persons in the whole number employed*	*Proportion of children in the whole number under 18*
	Males	*Fem.*	*Males*	*Fem.*	*Males*	*Fem.*			
Monmouthshire . .	1000	—	302	—	154	—	456	Nearly one-third.	One-third.
Glamorganshire . .	1000	19	239	19	157	12	427	Approaching one-third.	Much more than one-third.
Pembrokeshire . .	1000	424	366	119	196	19	700	One-third.	More than one-third.

Proportion (nearly) of Females to adult Males, and of Females under age to Males under age.

Districts	*Adults*	*From 13 to 18*	*Under 13*
Yorkshire . . .	1 to 45	1 to 28	1 to 25
Lancashire . . .	1 to 12	1 to 13	1 to 37
EAST OF SCOTLAND:			
Mid Lothian . . .	1 to 3	1 to 5½	1 to 20
East Lothian . . .	1 to 3	1 to 3½	1 to 10
West Lothian . . .	1 to 5	1 to 7	1 to 10
Stirlingshire . . .	1 to 4½	1 to 8	1 to 10
Clackmannanshire . .	1 to 5	1 to 5	1 to 11½
Fifeshire	1 to 5½	1 to 10	1 to 30
WALES:			
Glamorganshire . .	1 to 53	1 to 53	1 to 83
Pembrokeshire . .	1 to 2½	1 to 8½	1 to 53

(*b*) *First Report: Conclusions*

From the whole of the Evidence which has been collected, and of which we have thus endeavoured to give a digest, we find,–

In regard to COAL MINES–

1. That instances occur in which Children are taken into these mines to work as early as four years of age, sometimes at five, and between five and six, not unfrequently between six and seven, and often from seven to eight, while from eight to nine is the ordinary age at which employment in these mines commences.
2. That a very large proportion of the persons employed in carrying on the work of these mines is under thirteen years of age; and a still larger proportion between thirteen and eighteen.
3. That in several districts female Children begin to work in these mines at the same early ages as the males.
4. That the great body of the Children and Young Persons employed in these mines are of the families of the adult workpeople engaged in the pits, or belong to the poorest population in the neighbourhood, and are hired and paid in some districts by the workpeople, but in others by the proprietors or contractors.
5. That there are in some districts also a small number of parish apprentices, who are bound to serve their masters until twenty-one years of age, in an employment in which there is nothing deserving the name of skill to be acquired, under circumstances of frequent ill-treatment, and under the oppressive condition that they shall receive only food and clothing, while their free companions may be obtaining a man's wages.
6. That in many instances much that skill and capital can effect to render the place of work unoppressive, healthy, and safe, is done, often with complete success,

as far as regards the healthfulness and comfort of the mines; but that to render them perfectly safe does not appear to be practicable by any means yet known; while in great numbers of instances their condition in regard both to ventilation and drainage is lamentably defective.

7. That the nature of the employment which is assigned to the youngest Children, generally that of "trapping", requires that they should be in the pit as soon as the work of the day commences, and, according to the present system, that they should not leave the pit before the work of the day is at an end.

8. That although this employment scarcely deserves the name of labour, yet as the Children engaged in it are commonly excluded from light and are always without companions, it would, were it not for the passing and repassing of the coal carriages, amount to solitary confinement of the worst order.

9. That in those districts in which the seams of coal are so thick that horses go direct to the workings, or in which the side passages from the workings to the horseways are not of any great length, the lights in the main ways render the situation of these Children comparatively less cheerless, dull, and stupifying; but that in some districts they remain in solitude and darkness during the whole time they are in the pit, and, according to their own account, many of them never see the light of day for weeks together during the greater part of the winter season, excepting on those days in the week when work is not going on, and on the Sundays.

10. That at different ages, from six years old and upwards, the hard work of pushing and dragging the carriages of coal from the workings to the main ways, or to the foot of the shaft, begins; a labour which all classes of witnesses concur in stating requires the unremitting exertion of all the physical power which the young workers possess.

11. That, in the districts in which females are taken down into the coal mines, both sexes are employed together in precisely the same kind of labour, and work for the same number of hours; that the girls and boys, and the young men and young women, and even married women and women with child, commonly work almost naked, and the men, in many mines, quite naked; and that all classes of witnesses bear testimony to the demoralizing influence of the employment of females underground.

12. That, in the East of Scotland, a much larger proportion of Children and Young Persons are employed in these mines than in other districts, many of whom are girls; and that the chief part of their labour consists in carrying the coals on their backs up steep ladders.

13. That when the workpeople are in full employment, the regular hours of work for Children and Young Persons are rarely less than eleven; more often they are twelve; in some districts they are thirteen; and in one district they are generally fourteen and upwards.

14. That in the great majority of these mines night-work is a part of the ordinary system of labour, more or less regularly carried on according to the demand for coals, and one which the whole body of evidence shows to act most

injuriously both on the physical and moral condition of the workpeople, and more especially on that of the Children and Young Persons.

15. That the labour performed daily for this number of hours, though it cannot strictly be said to be continuous, because, from the nature of the employment, intervals of a few minutes necessarily occur during which the muscles are not in active exertion, is neverthless generally uninterrupted by any regular time set apart for rest and refreshment; what food is taken in the pit being eaten as best it may while the labour continues.

16. That in well-regulated mines, in which in general the hours of work are the shortest, and in some few of which from half an hour to an hour is regularly set apart for meals, little or no fatigue is complained of after an ordinary day's work, when the Children are ten years old and upwards; but in other instances great complaint is made of the feeling of fatigue, and the workpeople are never without this feeling, often in an extremely painful degree.

17. That in many cases the Children and Young Persons have little cause of complaint in regard to the treatment they receive from the persons in authority in the mine, or from the colliers; but that in general the younger Children are roughly used by their older companions; while in many mines the conduct of the adult colliers to the Children and Young Persons who assist them is harsh and cruel; the persons in authority in these mines, who must be cognizant of this ill-usage, never interfering to prevent it, and some of them distinctly stating that they do not conceive that they have any right to do so.

18. That, with some exceptions, little interest is taken by the coal owners in the Children and Young Persons employed in their works after the daily labour is over; at least little is done to afford them the means of enjoying innocent amusement and healthful recreation.

19. That in all the coal-fields accidents of a fearful nature are extremely frequent; and that the returns made to our own queries, as well as the registry tables, prove that of the workpeople who perish by such accidents, the proportion of Children and Young Persons sometimes equals and rarely falls much below that of adults.

20. That one of the most frequent causes of accidents in these mines is the want of superintendence by overlookers or otherwise to see to the security of the machinery for letting down and bringing up the work-people, the restriction of the number of persons that ascend and descend at a time, the state of the mine as to the quantity of noxious gas in it, the efficiency of the ventilation, the exactness with which the air-door keepers perform their duty, the places into which it is safe or unsafe to go with a naked lighted candle, and the security of the proppings to uphold the roof, &c.

21. That another frequent cause of fatal accidents in coal mines is the almost universal practice of intrusting the closing of the air-doors to very young Children.

22. That there are many mines in which the most ordinary precautions to guard against accidents are neglected, and in which no money appears to be expended with a view to secure the safety, much less the comfort, of the workpeople.

23. That there are moreover two practices peculiar to a few districts which deserve the highest reprobation, namely,–first, the practice not unknown in some of the smaller mines in Yorkshire, and common in Lancashire, of employing ropes that are unsafe for letting down and drawing up the workpeople; and second, the practice, occasionally met with in Yorkshire, and common in Derbyshire and Lancashire, of employing boys at the steam-engines for letting down and drawing up the workpeople.
24. That in general the Children and Young Persons who work in these mines have sufficient food, and, when above ground, decent and comfortable clothing, their usually high rate of wages securing to them these advantages; but in many cases, more especially in some parts of Yorkshire, in Derbyshire, in South Gloucestershire, and very generally in the East of Scotland, the food is poor in quality, and insufficient in quantity; the Children themselves say that they have not enough to eat; and the Sub-Commissioners describe them as covered with rags, and state that the common excuse they make for confining themselves to their homes on the Sundays, instead of taking recreation in the fresh air, or attending a place of worship, is that they have no clothes to go in; so that in these cases, notwithstanding the intense labour performed by these Children, they do not procure even sufficient food and rainment; in general, however, the Children who are in this unhappy case are the Children of idle and dissolute parents, who spend the hard-earned wages of their offspring at the public house.
25. That the employment in these mines commonly produces in the first instance an extraordinary degree of muscular development accompanied by a corresponding degree of muscular strength; this preternatural development and strength being acquired at the expense of the other organs, as is shown by the general stunted growth of the body.
26. That partly by the severity of the labour and the long hours of work, and partly through the unhealthy state of the place of work, this employment, as at present carried on in all the districts, deteriorates the physical constitution; in the thin-seam mines, more especially, the limbs become crippled and the body distorted; and in general the muscular powers give way, and the workpeople are incapable of following their occupation, at an earlier period of life than is common in other branches of industry.
27. That by the same causes the seeds of painful and mortal diseases are very often sown in childhood and youth; these, slowly but steadily developing themselves, assume a formidable character between the ages of thirty and forty; and each generation of this class of the population is commonly extinct soon after fifty.

When we consider the extent of this branch of industry, the vast amount of capital embarked on it, and the intimate connexion in which it stands with almost all the other great branches of trade and manufacture, as a main source of our national wealth and greatness, it is satisfactory to have established, by indubitable evidence, the two following conclusions:–

1. That the coal mine, when properly ventilated and drained, and when both the main and the side passages are of tolerable height, is not only not unhealthy, but, the temperature being moderate and very uniform, it is considered as a place of work, more salubrious and even agreeable than that in which many kinds of labour are carried on above ground.
2. That the labour in which Children and Young Persons are chiefly employed in coal mines, namely, in pushing the loaded carriages of coals from the workings to the mainways or to the foot of the shaft, so far from being in itself an unhealthy employment, is a description of exercise which, while it greatly develops the muscles of the arms, shoulders, chest, back, and legs, without confining any part of the body in an unnatural and constrained posture, might, but for the abuse of it, afford an equally healthful excitement to all the other organs; the physical injuries produced by it, as it is at present carried on, independently of those which are caused by imperfect ventilation and drainage, being chiefly attributable to the early age at which it commences, and to the length of time during which it is continued.

There is, however, one case of peculiar difficulty, *viz.* that in which all the subterranean roadways, and especially the side passages, are below a certain height: by the Evidence collected under this Commission, it is proved that there are coal mines at present in work in which these passages are so small, that even the youngest Children cannot move along them without crawling on their hands and feet, in which unnatural and constrained posture they drag the loaded carriages after them; and yet as it is impossible, by any outlay compatible with a profitable return, to render such coal mines, happily not numerous nor of great extent, fit for human beings to work in, they never will be placed in such a condition, and consequently they never can be worked without inflicting great and irreparable injury on the health of the Children.

In regard to IRONSTONE MINES, we find–

That on account of the greater weight of the material to be removed, the labour in these mines, which are worked on a system similar to that of the coal mines, is still more severe than that in the latter, and renders the employment of older and stronger Children a matter of absolute necessity; while the ironstone pits are in general less perfectly ventilated and drained than the coal mines, and are, therefore, still more unhealthy, producing the same physical deterioration and the same diseases, but in a more intense degree.

In regard to BLAST FURNACES, for reducing the ores of iron, we find–

That the operations connected with these works involve the absolute necessity of night work; that Children and Young Persons invariably work at night with the adults; that the universal practice is for one set of workpeople to work one week during the day, and the same set to work the following week during the night; and that there is, moreover, in addition to the evil of alternate weeks of night work, a custom bearing with extreme hardship upon Children and Young Persons, namely, that of continuing the work without any interruption whatever during the Sunday, and thus rendering every alternate Sunday the day during which the labour of one set of workpeople is continued for twenty-four hours in succession; a custom which still prevails, notwithstanding that a considerable proportion of the proprietors have dispensed with the attendance of the workpeople during a certain number of hours on the Sunday without disadvantage to their works.

In regard to UNDERGROUND LABOUR IN TIN, COPPER, LEAD, AND ZINC MINES, we find–

1. That very few Children are employed in any kind of underground work in these mines before they are twelve years old, and that in many cases even the young men do not commence underground work until they are eighteen years of age and upwards.
2. That there is no instance in the whole kingdom of any girl or woman being employed in underground work in these mines.
3. That it is in the Cornish district alone that Children and Young Persons of any age are constantly employed under ground in considerable numbers.
4. That, in general, the Children and Young Persons employed in these mines have sufficient food, and decent and comfortable clothing.
5. That employment in these mines does not, in general, produce any apparent injury to the young worker during the period of boyhood and adolescence, but that his employment is essentially, and in every mode in which it has hitherto been carried on, necessarily injurious in after life.
6. That the very general and early deterioration and failure of the health and strength of those who have followed this occupation from boyhood and youth, is increased by certain circumstances which are not necessarily connected with the nature of the employment; among these may be reckoned the practice, almost universal in these mines, of associating the Young Persons in partnership with the adult miners, by which the former are stimulated to exertions greatly beyond their age and powers; and though these Young People, thus excited, work with spirit and without apparent injury for some time, yet in a few years it is proved by experience that they have expended the whole capital of their constitution.
7. That this result is materially hastened by the fatigue of climbing the ladders; these being, with few exceptions, the only means by which the miners can go to and return from their places of work.
8. That these, however, are only the accessory causes of the general and rapid deterioration of the health and strength of the miners; since the primary and ever active agent which principally produces this result is the noxious air of the places in which the work is carried on; the difficulties connected with the purification and renovation of this air, and with the whole subject of ventilation, being incomparably greater in the mines in question than in coal mines.

9. That the ultimate effect of the disadvantageous circumstances under which the miner is obliged to pursue his laborious occupation, is the production of certain diseases (seated chiefly in the organs of respiration), by which he is rendered incapable of following his work, and by which his existence is terminated at an earlier period than is common in other branches of industry, not excepting even that of the collier.

With regard to the surface employments connected with DRESSING THE ORES OF TIN, COPPER, LEAD, AND ZINC, we find–

That these employments, though entered into at very early ages, and in the Cornish district by great numbers of girls as well as boys, are wholly free from the evils connected with underground work; that, with the exception of a very injurious exposure to the inclemency of the weather, which might be obviated by a small expenditure in providing shelter, and with the exception of two or three occupations, such as those of "bucking" and "jigging", for the manual labour of which the substitution of machinery is gradually taking place, there is nothing in this branch of mining industry injurious, oppressive, or incompatible with the maintenance even of robust health, which indeed is described as the general condition of the workpeople; the Children and Young Persons thus employed having commonly sufficient food, and warm and decent clothing, being subjected to no harsh or tyrannical treatment, and enjoying an almost complete immunity from any serious danger.

With regard to the works for SMELTING ORES OF TIN, COPPER, LEAD, AND ZINC, we find–

That in smelting the ores of lead, near the places at which they are raised, no Children and very few Young Persons are engaged, while those employed in the tin works will require a separate notice in treating of manufactures; but that in the copper works of South Wales, in which the Cornish ores are smelted, and in those of North Wales, which reduce the ores raised in their vicinity, a number of Children and Young Persons are employed, from nine years of age and upwards (in South Wales girls as well as boys), of whom those engaged at the calcining furnaces regularly work with the men twenty-four hours consecutively, on alternate days, without excepting the Sunday; a term of work which is some-times extended to thirty-six hours, and even to forty-eight hours, when, as in South Wales, the "long watch" includes the Sunday.

We have thus endeavoured to present a faithful account of the "actual state, condition and treatment" of the Children and Young Persons employed in the "Collieries and Mines" of the United Kingdom, and "of the effects of such employment on their Bodily Health": the effects of this employment on their "Morals", it appears to us, will best be shown by bringing them into view in our next Report, in connexion with the intellectual, moral, and religious state of the whole of that portion of the working population which is included under the terms of our Commission.

All which we humbly certify to Your Majesty.

THOS. TOOKE.
T. SOUTHWOOD SMITH.
LEONARD HORNER.
ROBT. J. SAUNDERS.

Westminster, April 21, 1842.

259. The economy of shorter hours: letter from Gardner's of Preston, to the chairman of meeting in Corn Exchange, Manchester (22 April 1845), reported by Horner

Parlty. Papers, 1845/xxv/ pp. 456–457.

SIR,–It was my intention to have been with you this evening, but a severe cold makes it quite unsafe for me to venture out. As I believe some opinion or expression of feeling will be expected from me, as to the conclusions I may have come to from the working of my Preston mill, for the past 12 months, 11 instead of 12 hours each day, as previously, I therefore avail myself of the present opportunity of stating that I am quite satisfied that both as much yarn and power-loom cloth may be produced at quite as low a cost in 11 as in 12 hours per day; at least, that it has been so the last 12 months, in my mills at Preston. So fully satisfied am I on this point, that if it should please God to spare my life to the season of the present year when we light up again, it is my present intention to make a further reduction of time to 10½ hours, without the slightest fear of suffering loss by it. I find the hands work with greater energy and spirit; they are more cheerful, and apparently more happy. All the arguments I have heard in favour of long time appear based on an arithmetical question,–if 11 produce so much, what will 12, 13, or even 15 hours produce? This is correct, as far as the steam-engine is concerned; whatever it will produce in 11 hours, it will produce double the quantity in 22. But try this on the animal horse, and you will soon find he cannot compete with the engine, as he requires both time to rest and feed.

My much respected manager and friend, Mr. Heaton, tells me he has passed all the grades of a mill, and has worked 11, 12, 13, and even 14 hours per day, and was daily exhausted; but he says they knew their hours, and worked accordingly–that he would have done more and better work in less time. It is, I believe, a fact not questioned, that there is more bad work made the last one or two hours of the day than the whole of the first nine or ten hours. There can be no doubt but 11 hours are quite sufficient for any one to exhaust the whole of his or her strength in any one occupation, situation, or atmosphere, although the work is not laborious.

It can be no small gratification to any employer of a large number of hands to see them healthy and happy, with an opportunity of improving their minds. I am satisfied those mills that work short hours will have a choice of hands, and then individual interest will accomplish what is necessary, without the intervention of the Legislature. I beg to state that, about 20 years ago, we had many orders for a style of goods much wanted. At the time we had about 30 young women, none under 20 or over 40 years of age, winding coloured yarn in our Manchester warehouse; the principal part was at Bolton and Preston. To increase the quantity of the work, I requested they would work (instead of 11) 12 hours. At the end of the week, I found they had got a mere trifle more work done; but, supposing there was some incidental cause for this, I requested they would work 13 hours the following week, at the end of which they had produced less instead of more work. The overlooker told me the hours were too long, and invited me to be in the room with them the last hour of the day. I saw they were exhausted, drowsy, and making bad work and little of it; I therefore reduced their time two hours, as before. Since that time I have been an advocate for shorter hours of labour.

–ROBERT GARDNER.

April 22nd, 1845.

260. Fielden's Ten Hours' Act (1847)

Statutes of the Realm, 10 & 11 Vict. c. 29.

WHEREAS an Act was passed in the Fourth Year of the Reign of His late Majesty, intituled *An Act to regulate the Labour of Children and young Persons in the Mills and Factories of the United Kingdom*; and another Act was passed in the Session of Parliament held in the Seventh and Eighth Years of the Reign of Her present Majesty, intituled *An Act to amend the Laws relating to Labour in Factories*; and by the said first-mentioned Act it was provided, that no Person under the Age of Eighteen Years should be employed in any such Mill or Factory as in the said Act is mentioned, in any such Description of Work as therein-before specified, more than Twelve Hours in any One Day, nor more than Sixty-nine Hours in any One Week, except as therein-after is provided; and by the said last-mentioned Act it was provided, that no Female above the Age of Eighteen Years should be employed in any Factory as defined by the said Act, save for the same Time and in the same Manner as young Persons (by the said Act defined to be Persons of the Age of Thirteen Years and under the Age of Eighteen Years) might be employed in factories: And whereas it is expedient to alter the said Acts for the Purpose of further restricting the Hours of Labour of young Persons and Females in Factories:" Be it enacted by the Queen's most Excellent Majesty, by and with the Advice and Consent of the Lords Spiritual and Temporal, and Commons, in this present Parliament assembled, and by the Authority of the same, That, notwithstanding any thing in the said Acts contained, from the First Day of July One thousand eight hundred and forty-seven no Person under the Age of Eighteen Years shall be employed in any such Mill or Factory, in such Description of Work as in the said first-mentioned Act is specified, for more than Eleven Hours in any One Day, nor for more than Sixty-three Hours in any

One Week, except as in the said Act is provided; and that from the said First Day of July One Thousand eight hundred and forty-seven the said Two Acts before mentioned shall in all respects be construed as if the Provision in the Provision in the said first-mentioned Act contained, as to Persons under the Age of Eighteen Years working in Mills and Factories, has been confined to Eleven Hours instead of Twelve Hours in any One Day, and to Sixty-three Hours in any One Week instead of Sixty-nine Hours.

II. And be it enacted, That from the First Day of May One thousand eight hundred and forty-eight no Person under the Age of Eighteen Years shall be employed in any such Mill or Factory, in such Description of Work as in the said first-mentioned Act is specified, for more than Ten Hours in any One Day nor more than Fifty-eight Hours in any One Week, except as in the said Act is provided; and that from the First Day of May One thousand eight hundred and forty-eight the said Two Acts shall in all respects be construed as if the Provision in the said first-mentioned Act contained, as to Persons under the Age of Eighteen Years working in Mills and Factories, had been confined to Ten Hours instead of Twelve Hours in any One Day and Fifty-eight Hours in any One Week instead of Sixty-nine Hours.

III. And be it enacted, That the Restrictions respectively by this Act imposed as regards the working of Persons under the Age of Eighteen Years shall extend to Females above the Age of Eighteen Years.

IV. And be it enacted, That the said Two herein-before mentioned Acts as amended by this Act, and this Act, shall be construed together as one Act.

V. And be it enacted, That this Act may be amended or repealed by any Act to be passed in this present Session of Parliament.

261. The old factory weaver: effect of Ten Hours' Act on the domestic life of workers, reported by R. J. Saunders, factory inspector

Parlty. Papers, 1850/XXIII/pp. 308–309.

In coming home one night, after being in a distant allotment, I called in to see an old factory weaver; it was very interesting and delightful to behold the old man sitting with his youngest son; they had a basket of potatoes between them, and were cutting the potatoes for sets, and both seemed at a loss, being new gardeners, but were very glad to have an opportunity of learning; he had three daughters, and two young women lodgers, very busy sewing and knitting, and all teaching each other. The old mother was preparing supper and breakfast for the next morning, as all have to be carried out. I asked the old mother how she liked the Ten-hour Bill, she said very well, she did not know how she must do if the girls worked any longer, they assisted her all they could, and were learning to do household work, and could sew and knit better than she could, and could read very nicely too; they could not do with any more than ten hours. The old father said it was a grand thing the Ten-hours Bill, he was learning to be a gardener, and would not like to have to give it up, which he would have to do if they worked any more hours.

262. Report of Seymour Tremenheere, commissioner for mines and mining populations, on strike trouble in Northumberland (1849–1850)

Parlty. Papers, 1850/XXIII/pp. 624–628.

. . . In this same parish a better spirit had lately shown itself in regard to the restriction of labour and the question of strikes at most of the other collieries. Those under the management of Mr. Charles Carr had previously given much trouble; but Mr. Carr informed me that at the large colliery of Seghill, employing upwards of 700 men and boys, the men had come to see their real interest in working steadily and doing a full day's work, instead of obliging him to employ more hands. They had lately resisted the threats of the Seaton-Delaval men, and informed Mr. Carr that, if any attempt was made by those men to interfere with them, they would fight their own battle. They are now earning 4s. 4d. a-day on an average, and working eleven days per fortnight. Mr. Carr added, that he never had a set of men more willing to exert themselves on a pressure of trade. They had said to him, "that they would do more work rather than that he should increase the number of men, and overburden them with too many hands."

This proof of improved intelligence since the serious disturbances of 1844 is probably owing, in great part, to the personal exertions of Mr. Carr in reasoning with the most intelligent of the men on their previous conduct; also, probably, in no small degree to the fact that, for the last three years, a most intelligent and zealous clergyman has resided close to them as minister of the newly formed district of this parish, and who has lost no opportunity of setting their minds right on the various topics that concern their real welfare in every relation of life. That gentleman, together with Mr. Carr and some of the most intelligent among his men, have lately exerted themselves to revive the lending library, the failure of which I mentioned in a former report. It now consists of between 700 and 800 volumes: the room appropriated to it is open two nights in the week, and, in addition to the books, there are many of the best London papers, 'The Times,' &c., and some of the most instructive magazines and other periodicals.

In this parish (Earsdon), the state of which I have more fully described in my Report of 1846, and which until three years ago had only one clergyman, with a salary of less than £100 a-year, for the superintendence of upwards of 10,000 souls – a parish which, according to the statement of some of the principal agents, returned to its landowners, without cost or risk on their part, not less than £30,000 a-year in mine-royalties and "way-leaves," and in which an immense capital had been engaged by other parties in the commercial speculation of raising coal – it has been observed that the spread of infidelity had become considerable, and especially among many of the working men who were the greatest readers. It is also notorious that still a considerable proportion of the young men are members of no religious body, and are growing up with very slight notions of religion in any form, with minds pre-occupied, if they read at all, by the slanderous, unsound, and superficial cheap publications which I have above described, and obscured by all the erroneous views of their own interests which have led to so many of those strikes and combinations which occasion such loss of capital and disturbance of trade in this district. It is not, therefore, surprising to find it to be the general opinion that the present apparent improvement of feeling or conduct in the pitmen of any particular colliery is not to be depended upon, and that, although it is the common impression among the masters that the rate of wages is higher than can be long sustained, a general strike will ensue the moment an attempt is made to reduce them. Such is the penalty paid for the loss of authority and the domination of error.

I have described in my Reports for 1846 and 1849 the very different principles that have prevailed in the setting on foot and management of the extensive works of the Derwent Iron Company (mentioned in those Reports as the Consett Iron-works), in the county of Durham. These works are among the largest in the kingdom. They were commenced in 1841; and in the course of little more than four years from that time there were erected 14 blast-furnaces, rolling-mills &c., capable of turning out 900 tons of bar-iron per week, 12 refineries, 22 steam-engines to turn machinery, and 35 coal and iron pits to supply materials; and there were collected on a high tract of moorland a population of about 15,000 souls. Even if no sense of moral responsibility towards these 15,000 people had actuated the gentlemen who embarked in this great commercial enterprise, the lowest motives of calculation would have induced them as men of business not to expose such a vast capital without taking some security, as far as was possible, against the ignorance or misconduct of their work-people. I know no great iron-work or other field of industry in the kingdom where so strict and conscientious a regard has been shown by the employers to the duties of their position, or where a more earnest and personal care has been devoted to everything that could contribute to the health, comfort, and well-being, in every respect, of the labouring population. The cottages are of the best kind, ample gardens are attached, covered drains laid down, good roads and pathways made, good order maintained by a sufficient body of police and by strict control over the public-houses, excellent schools established, libraries and other means of information and amusement encouraged, clergymen appointed, churches built, ample opportunities afforded for the religious worship of the various dissenting sects, who are always ready to organize their congregations as soon as the population begins to collect in a new spot. The rates of wages and other details of employment are arranged on the fairest and most liberal terms, and the principles of management, as they have been on various occasions explained to me, have appeared to me to be based on a most equitable consideration for what is due to the labouring man, and to be carried into effect with strict integrity and unbending firmness.

I know no place where such an occurrence as a strike seemed so little probable, or where it could be so little justified.

A general strike, therefore, last autumn, of all the colliers employed at these works was a circumstance calculated to excite no little surprise throughout these two counties.

At that time, the delegates of the "union" had succeeded in their policy of causing strikes at individual collieries, and, emboldened by their success in several instances, they avowed their intention of endeavouring to "win" at the Consett works also.

Accordingly one of their principal men came and obtained employment at these works, and drew the colliers by degrees into his plans. These were, to set up several small grievances, and under cover of those to reduce the quantity of work, lower the earnings, and make that a pretext for a demand of a higher rate of wages. The decision and firmness of the manager, Mr. William Cargill, baffled this policy; and several offenders were sent off to Durham Gaol for deserting their work and for violent assaults, in one of which a policeman received very serious injuries. Nevertheless, a general strike of the colliers ensued. The pretexts which they put forward were personally and minutely examined into at the time by the editor of a local paper, well disposed to the interests of the colliers, the 'Durham Chronicle,' and pronounced by him to be altogether unfounded. The "coal-measures" which they complained of were ascertained to be the ordinary coal-measures of the trade; the roadways, which had been asserted to be wet, were proved not to be so; the "fines" complained of turned out on inquiry to have been most light, many of the leaders confessing that they had not been fined more than a few pence since the works began, and others not at all; and the least able colliers were earning throughout the year from 20s. to 22s. per week, while the best workmen were earning 30s. by six and a half to seven hours' work with house and fire-coal free. Mr. Cargill favoured me with a list of the actual earnings of the whole of the colliers in his employ at the time of the strike, which is most accurately drawn up, and conclusive as to the above assertions.

As soon as the men began to depart from the agreement under which they were hired, and to restrict their earnings, Mr. Cargill, in addition to sending some of the leaders to prison, immediately, with his usual decision, placed such an additional number of men in the pits that the union men were unable to earn even the sum they had restricted themselves to. On the general strike of the "union colliers" thereupon occurring, Mr. Cargill had no difficulty in filling the pits with miners, common labourers, and others, thrown out of work in consequence of the strike of the colliers.

> "Numbers," Mr. Cargill says, "flocked into the collieries most readily, and, although not practised at the work, soon gained more than their usual earnings at other labour, and we accordingly never worked fewer coals during the strike than the usual quantity. The best men we have as colliers are countrymen whom we have trained ourselves. The strength of the strike did not last three weeks. We diminished our make of iron for a month or six weeks; three furnaces were merely kept hot, and a very small one blown out, which we were glad of the opportunity of repairing. After six weeks the union gradually dissolved. We discharged from 80 to 90 men, chiefly young men from 20 to 23 years of age, brought up in other parts of the district, and lately taken into our employ. Not a single man wished to go; they would have stayed most readily, and earnestly begged to be allowed to resume work on the terms of their bond. They all admitted that they had nothing really to complain of, and that they had been thoroughly contented and satisfied with our employment, and expressed regret at having yielded to the agitation of the delegates."

Mr. Cargill added, that, unexpected and vexatious as was this occurrence, he conceives that, in bringing forth the good feeling of the great mass of the people in their employ, who supported them so readily in their struggle with the colliers, it has shown that, putting out of view for the moment all higher motives, even in the lowest sense of pecuniary gain they have been amply repaid for all they have expended with a view to the moral and intellectual improvement of their population. Had they not been so supported, but on the contrary had any ill-founded sympathy been shown by the miners, labourers, and others, with the misguided colliers, it is probable that the strike might have lasted many months instead of a few weeks, and that it might have obliged them to put out furnaces and discontinue other parts of their works, a proceeding which would have cost them probably five times as much as they have spent towards raising the intelligence, securing the comfort, and promoting the good morals and religious training of their people.

All, therefore, that has resulted from this unprovoked and ill-advised struggle is, that some 80 or 90 young men have been dismissed from a place of work, a more desirable one than which they will not easily find, and that the delegates who fomented it have been obliged to seek other localities in which to employ themselves as they have done here.

From the accounts I heard of the strikes at particular collieries in other parts of these two counties, I believe I have given sufficient particulars to illustrate the principles on which they proceeded.

I inquired whether any active measures had been adopted during and since the prevalence of the cholera to add to the means of cleanliness and external comfort of the houses in the large colliery villages. I was informed that numerous under-drains had been laid down, and better arrangements made in many instances for the more frequent removal of the ashes and other refuse from before the doors. The habits, however, of the colliers have been formed under a system of neglect in these and many other important particulars, which it will require many years of enlightened attention and perseverance to amend. The consequences of that neglect have long since recoiled with no little force on their employers.

263. *The Times* and the engineering lock-out (January–April 1852): editorial of 12 January 1852

This morning 36 firms in one of our most important trades close their works, and 10,000 ingenious operatives will be reduced for their daily subsistence to the alms of others or the forestalment of a fund provided against more genuine necessities. The masters maintain their conditions, and the working engineers refuse to give up their demands. This state of things concerns not only the welfare of thousands, but the immediate interests of commerce and society. Carried to these extremes the dispute must cause the ruin of one party, if not of both, and it may destroy the iron trade of these islands for ever. Again, therefore, we address ourselves to the workmen, and request their earnest attention to observations which their own sense will tell them are both well meant and true.

The dispute can only be arranged by the men's withdrawing the notices served by their Council on the masters, or by the masters' relinquishing their demand for such withdrawal, or by a compromise between the two conditions. We will state in plain language why the masters cannot give way. They cannot give way, because by so doing they would admit and receive the notices before mentioned, requiring the abolition of overtime and piecework. If they admit these notices, one of two things must happen – either the notices are to remain a dead letter, or the demands they contain will be enforced. Of course the first of these suppositions is absurd, as it would be ridiculous for men to make such a stand in behalf of a circular which they never intended to come into operation. The Amalgamated Society, therefore, if its notices are allowed to remain unwithdrawn, will proceed at the fittest opportunity to employ its best means of coercion in bringing its desires to pass. These means have hitherto consisted in "advising" the men to "withdraw" from the firm refusing to yield; and as this, however disguised, is nothing more or less than a "strike," the masters, after giving way for a month or two, would find themselves just where they are now. Clearly, this course would never answer.

But there is a second course – that, namely, of assenting, when the pressure arrives, to the society's demands, and *conceding* "the abolition of overtime and piecework." Why should not the masters do this? We can give an answer in a very few words. They cannot do so, because by such an act they would forfeit the indispensable rights of employers to make their own terms for labour in an open market. If a master is forbidden to employ such men as best suit him, on such conditions as he can get accepted, it is absolutely impossible that he can maintain a remunerative trade. He is subject to competition as well as his men, and if the natural effects of competition are felt in the sale of the article while they are not permitted to make themselves felt in the cost of its production, the consequences, as every workman must see, will be the speedy ruin of the business. The known and natural value of labour regulates the value of the manufactured commodity in the markets of the world. To keep this latter value at an artificial height is a plain impossibility, and as it is from this fund alone that labour can be paid, it is a piece of manifest folly to think that wages can be maintained while manufactures are exposed to depreciation. Yet this is what the Amalgamated Society demand. They say to their employers, "You shall not execute your orders with 20 men if the work can be so arranged as to provide wages for 30. You shall get a job done by the piece instead of parcelling it out in day work, for though both you and the man whom you select may be gainers by such a bargain, those shut out from the mob would lose." This is the real meaning of the resolution for the discontinuance of "overtime and piecework." If the masters accepted such terms they must infallibly become bankrupt in the end, and they cannot fare worse by holding out now. *This* course, therefore, would answer no better than the other.

Having explained why the masters must needs be firm, we will now state why the men should yield. They should yield because their objects are absolutely impracticable, and wholly inconsistent with the natural laws of society. They wish to secure the engineering trade from all the drawbacks to which every trade is liable as science advances and population increases. Increasing population brings more hands into the market; advancing science makes the call for them less. "Planing, slotting, and shaping machines" are instruments for superseding skilled labour in "shaping," "slotting," and "planing." Unskilled hands are enabled to do that for which skilled hands were formerly required, and skilled labour falls accordingly in demand and value. Besides this, as new generations spring up, and more mouths every day are looking out for bread, the labour market becomes more largely supplied, and the supply therefore fetches a smaller price. Now, all these irresistible operations of social laws the Amalgamated Society is attempting to withstand. To keep the available supply of labour as low as possible, they insist that none but "skilled hands" shall be employed even where unskilled hands would suffice; to keep the skilled hands few in number, they insist that an "apprenticeship" shall be first served, and by way of damming up the source from which the market could be fed, they actually restrict within arbitrary limits the number of apprentices who shall be permitted to enter the trade. Not satisfied with this, they forbid that one skilled hand should sell more of his labour than another, either by working overtime for his master, or at his own time for himself. The general aim and scope of the society is first to keep the trade of working engineers as small and exclusive as possible, and next to secure every working engineer in an equal share of the employment which has been thus monopolized.

These objects may dazzle the eyes of operatives, but they can never be obtained. The demands of the men *cannot* be granted if the masters were ever so compliant, and they ought not to be granted if they could be. Neither working engineers nor any other class of workmen have any right to exclude their fellow countrymen from following their trade in just such numbers as they think fit. No smith or machinist possesses the smallest title to say who shall or who shall not be employed at machinists' work. An agricultural labourer might as well demand that no person should be permitted to emigrate who has not passed seven years at the plough. Is there any one of the men now out upon strike who would not consider himself at perfect liberty to become a butcher or a gardener or a glazier to-morrow, if he saw his way to a livelihood by such pursuits? Yet at the very last meeting of these engineers we find it actually alleged as an "injury and grievance," that Messrs. Hibbert and Platt were endeavouring to teach "labourers" to do machinists' work "by a new machine." Why, if they and all employers in this and every other trade did not do so, neither our commerce nor our prosperity would be where they are. It is the proper object of every producer to lessen the cost of production and his success becomes the benefit of consumers at large. Every master machinist or millwright has a most undoubted right both to substitute cheap labour for dear or to supercede both by machinery as far as he can. The cry of these intelligent engineers is merely the cry of the handloom weavers—a cry against inevitable and irresistible laws. They cannot possibly gain their ends, because no master by so conducting trade could find the wherewithal to pay them; and they cannot count upon public sympathy, because their purposes are directly destructive of public freedom. If engineering labour is beaten down in the market by the increase of hands, engineers must share the lot of their fellow men. They cannot keep their trade select while every other trade is crowded. We must all fare alike; nor can any possible good be done by attempts to "organize" one kind of "labour" to the prejudice of all others.

As regards the withdrawal of the notices, there is no room for meeting half way. Mr. Newton's folly must be at once and unconditionally repudiated. We see the men are publishing "resolutions" in defence of their intentions. Let them simply, by withdrawing the notices in question, abandon their project of organizing labour in other forms than that which it naturally takes. This much is all that is needed to remove obstacles otherwise insuperable. *Then*, having made their sensible disclaimer, let them represent to their employers–what the employers are quite prepared to acknowledge–the good effects of regular hours and such an arrangement of business as would leave the workman with a reasonable leisure in the evenings. It must necessarily be the interest of the masters to keep their men healthy, cheerful, and willing, and with these views they might make some sacrifice or agree together upon some general understanding. In such requests as these the workmen would have the support of the country at large, whereas now, unfortunately, they are so committed, through the delusions of their leaders, to impracticable objects, that opinion is wholly on the side of those who are driven to resistance. Already, we are happy to say, there is some sign of awakening sense. The Birmingham and Bristol men have shown themselves superior to the follies of the "council," and we can hardly doubt but that many members of an intelligent body must at heart be repenting their course. Let them make amends for their error by returning at once from ruinous idleness to honest employment.

264. *The Times* and the engineering lock-out (January–April 1852): editorial of 30 April 1852

The Executive Council of the Amalgamated Society of Engineers have enlightened the country by a detailed exposition of their own discomfiture and humiliation. In this document, which we published in our paper of yesterday, an inevitable confession of folly was blended with a preposterous assertion of right. The "Council" at length acknowledges in plain language that "hostile resistance of labour against capital is not calculated to enhance the condition of the labourer," and it recommends, therefore, the discontinuance of the struggle by general submission. These resolutions, however, are accompanied by "a few words of comment," in which the Council takes credit for the best of causes no less than of conduct, and characterises the result of the dispute as the oppression of "right unsupported by strength," by "rich, strong-handed wrong." We can hardly persuade ourselves that there is much occasion for any repetition of the truth on this notorious question; but, in taking our leave of the controversy, we may as well compress the great moral of the story into a few plain paragraphs.

It is quite true that the operatives have been beaten by the immediate pressure of want. It is quite true, in this sense, that capital has out-starved labour, or in other words, that money has got the better of industry. But this consequence, as we warned the operatives at the first rupture, was absolutely inevitable. If labour and capital are ever brought into collision under such conditions of society as exist among us, capital must needs work its will with labour. In extraordinary circumstances, such, for instance, as are now reported from Australia, labour may command a positive mastery over capital; but the relative power of these two possessions must be determined by social conditions, and cannot possibly be decided by ordinance or law. It was the great error of the misguided operatives that they actually compelled a collision which they should have done their utmost to obviate. No statute or enactment could give labour the ascendancy over capital, but the operations of capital might be modified by judicious management, and controlled to a large extent by the influence of public opinion. In other words, it required an impulse from the labourers' side to drive the employers into effective combination, and it further required manifest misconduct in the same parties to furnish such combination with external support. The history of this very contest shows how long it was before the masters could be forced into united action. Firm after firm had been reduced to submission on one point after another, and less than six months ago the Amalgamated Society were thoroughly convinced that the victory was going to be their own. All these hopes the Executive Council destroyed. So unscrupulously did they frame their projects, and so boldly did they avow their designs, that the employers were driven into combination for their very existence. Capital had not overpowered labour at Messrs. HIBBERT and PLATTS': nor at Messrs. PARR, CURTIS, and MADELEY'S. Mr. NEWTON exercised in June last, on behalf of his "Council," an oppression as severe as his own side experiences now. It was not until labour had been "organised" for the very subjugation of capital that capital put itself on fair ground by an "organisation" of its own; but when this had once been done there was no escaping the result. The operatives were beaten because the Masters' combination was made as strong as their own, and this occurred because the masters were forced into resolute action. It is idle for Mr. NEWTON to denounce the victory of capital over labour; this victory is the result of an irreversible law, and its consequences are ascribable to those only who forced these elements of production into such deadly collision.

The Executive Council not only precipitated a hopeless battle, but took post on untenable ground. As the standard of their principles they demanded the abolition of overtime and piecework. Overtime and piecework, it was perfectly true, had been suggestive of many abuses, but the Executive Council had actually struck the ground from under their own feet by avowing that these abuses constituted no substantial part of their objections. Moreover they had declared in plain terms that these demands were but preliminaries to a general assertion of dominion over the "destinies of trade," so that they actually pitted labour against capital on a question which deprived the weaker side of all support and armed the stronger with the energy of desperation. Mr. NEWTON engaged his fellow-workmen in a battle which could only be won at the cost of the original stake. If they could have vanquished the employers, the consequence would have been not that the employers' capital would have been at the disposal of the labourers' association, but that it would have turned into other channels altogether. When the destinies of the trade had fallen into Mr. NEWTON's hands the trade itself would have ceased to exist.

But though the actual struggle of labour against capital was thus hopeless–hopeless not from any accidental circumstances of advantage or disadvantage, but from the operation of irresistible laws–the result might have been materially modified by the influence of public opinion. It was in the power, indeed, of the press to secure either party in the substantial fruits of victory. For want of this external support, it is perfectly true, as stated by the Executive Council, that the Society failed, but monstrously false that such support was withheld through the agency of money. "Our opponents," says the manifesto of the expiring Council, "great in the world of wealth, were enabled to command the most influential portion of the press." Mr. NEWTON's own hand may be recognised in this audacious assertion. None know better than the engineers themselves that they had every possible fair play, that they had even an instinctive sympathy of the public in their favour, and that it was from their own mouths entirely that their judgment was given. They appealed to arbitration–and disregarded the friendly advice of their own selected arbiter. They mustered their aristocratic patrons–and these patrons after volunteering to defend their cause were compelled, from the very emptiness of the case, to be defaulters. What they had to fight against was not money nor combination, but truth. They had to deny their own spoken words, to retract their own printed opinions, and to obtain credit for principles which they had never pretended to recognise before. In this attempt they failed, and the victory remained with their opponents.

Mr. NEWTON had been anxious to involve operatives of all trades in the mischief of his own making; we hope, at any rate, that they will all take warning by the example. One maxim to be drawn from this story is that combinations of labourers must always become weak exactly at the point of their greatest apparent strength, for it is the development of this very strength which alarms capital into effectual exertion. The little trades' unions of the mechanics were often successful in their efforts against particular employers. It was only when Mr. NEWTON had "amalgamated" their forces for conquest that they proved wholly inferior. In the next place, the assent of public opinion is clearly indispensable to the winners in struggles like these. Opinion, to which the capitalist is even more amenable than the labourer, would have driven the employers to a compromise if their case had not been constituted in such invincible strength by the manifest weakness of their opponents. The Amalgamated Society rendered it impossible to do otherwise than support those who resisted such extravagant designs. It cannot now be disguised that the masters are stronger than before, but this consequence is due to the Executive Council alone. They forced on a life and death struggle between capital and labour by serving their circular notices on the several firms of employers. By refusing to withdraw these notices they produced a strike. By persisting in this strike with obstinate tenacity they suggested still further reprisals, and at length gave occasion to a "declaration" levelled against all such contingencies for the future. There is nothing done which has not been the immediate work of Mr. NEWTON and his colleagues. In making this acknowledgment, however, we must once more impress on the employers the expediency of conciliatory courses. They have won the day and can afford to be victorious; nor will anything so effectually complete the destruction of

"Amalgamated Societies" as the disuse of practices invidiously exemplifying the advantages of capital over labour.

265. A golden year: Horner on the prosperity of workers (1852)

Parlty. Papers, 1852–1853/XL/p. 553.

. . . I believe the workpeople never were so well off as they are at present; constant employment, good wages, cheap food, and cheap clothing; many cheap, innocent, and elevating amusements brought within their reach; and, thanks to the last Factory Act, the greater proportion of all the operatives in mills have at length time for some mental improvement, healthful recreation, and enjoyment of their families and friends.

266. R. Baker, factory inspector, on conditions in the Potteries in 1865

Parlty. Papers, 1865/XX/pp. 519–524.

. . . Thus, Mr. Palmer, of Longton, writes–

"The provident institutions established in the town have contributed largely to its improvement. Some of the earliest of these institutions were identified with the Sabbath school system, and were called 'The Children's Saving Fund,' established for the laudable object of enabling parents to provide for the clothing of their children, and to secure other household comforts. In this fund, parents and children were allowed to accumulate their savings without interest. And to show the extent to which they were made use of, from one of these funds, £400 was invested in one year by upwards of 700 depositors. Since saving banks and other facilities for depositing money at interest have arisen in the town, these societies have diminished in extent and importance. They continue to exist, however, though in a limited degree. In three schools from which I have obtained returns £304. 10s. 4d. was saved during the first year by 553 depositors; and it is due, no doubt, to these commencements of savings, that in hundreds of instances the germ of provident habits has been fostered and brought to maturity.

"In addition to these savings banks, there are insurance societies, and sick and friendly societies, eminently calculated to benefit the working classes. Last, though not least, I would notice another institution which has yielded a giant power for good, and borne a very important share in improving, re-organizing, and remodelling the town, and in elevating its social status: I allude to building societies. These have taught fresh practical lessons in life, which will long be remembered with pride and gratitude. They have effected reforms in character, improved positions, elevated and enlarged conceptions, and with many, have changed the very objects of life. They have incited to industry, economy, and forethought. A man can plant his foot on his own little spot of earth, and with honest pride, call it his own.

"There had been several building societies in Longton before 1850, but it was not till then that the Longton Freehold Society commenced its operations, and purchased estates. Amongst others, what is called the Dresden Estate was purchased for £6,259. 4s. 1½d., and divided into 190 lots containing nearly 600 yards each, amongst 101 shareholders. Sutherland Road Estate was purchased at a cost of £1,346. 2s. 3d., and divided into 41 lots among 29 members. Bridge Street Estate was purchased at a cost of £2,850., and divided into 98 lots among 41 shareholders. Thus, by means of this society, building land at a first cost of £10,455. 17s. 1½d. has been purchased and divided at the same cost into 329 lots, amongst 171 shareholders. But even these figures do not represent the numbers of persons among whom the land has been divided. The fact, that the allotments were too large for many of the original allottees, has led to divisions and subdivisions of them in great abundance; and, in some cases, land allotted by this society at an original cost of 1s. 1d. per yard, has been re-sold at 10s. per yard, and the average price at which it now sells is 7s. per yard. The land thus procured, together with other land brought into the market at a comparatively low price, created a necessity for building funds. Industrious thoughtful men began to see how much by care and economy they could accomplish, and to apply themselves in real earnest; and, as the result of their intelligent enterprise, we have as it were, three separate new towns created, and a fourth, now in course of erection. Dresden contains 505 houses, owned by 168 individuals, estimated at an annual rental of £6,000. Eastvale contains 270 houses, two manufactories, and two mills, together owned by 102 individuals at an estimated rental of £3,161. 6s. 9d., with a population of 1,500 persons. Bridge Street contains 95 houses, owned by 27 individuals, at an estimated rental of £665, besides Woodhouse, Anchor Ground, Ashwood, and other places in which no erections have been made. At present there is scarcely a foot of building land to be obtained at any price within the precincts of the town proper.

"The extent of these building society operations may be guessed at from the following statistics:–

	£	s.	d.
"They have advanced upon mortgage securities .	211,640	16	3
"Paid on completed or withdrawn shares . .	40,925	18	1
	£252,566	14	4

"The number of shareholders by whom this amount has been paid is 1,914, and the number of the shares 47,898½. These transactions, too, are totally independent of the land society's operations, and of the building societies in existence before 1850. Besides all this, the enormous sum of £131,797. 12s. 8d. has been invested in these societies by way of deposits, which further proves, that members of building societies are not the only provident people in the district. There are now, in fact, more than 1,400 subscribing members to building societies in the town, looking anxiously forward to the day when their own homes will repay their prudence and economy."

The simple fact of these savings being effected, and of these houses being erected, by the will of working men, is an immensely significant one. All these owners of houses are freeholders; and every man has earned his own freehold from a desire to possess it. Whilst in the same locality, employed at the same work, earning the same wages, and without any extraordinary drawback, a vast number of those who possess no such properties, live on from day to day, regardless of every enjoyment which is not sensual; exhibiting no desire for an elevation of character amongst their fellow men, wasting their money in profitless pursuits, or in degrading pastimes, and being for ever unprepared for the commonest vicissitudes, which bring such misery in their train.

Then Mr. Palmer, after presenting the bright side of the picture, very fairly shows the other side also:–

"To attempt to set up the dogma that we are all provident people, would be a glaring fallacy. Wherever there is excess of any kind, there will be found improvidence; and in Longton, it must be honestly admitted, that improvidence developes itself in many forms. Amongst a large class of men, whose facilities for personal, domestic, and social elevation are great, there is a strong vitiated tendency. Whilst their weekly means hold out, they revel in excess. They freely eat, drink, and take their pleasure. Very often they earn their money like slaves, and spend it in the most lavish manner. When they get hold of it, they are in an intense hurry to dispose of it. They appear to have no conception of its value, except so far as it may secure their present gratifications, and never dream of providing for future contingencies. They leave that department of social science for the special consideration of parish officials. They neither understand the theory nor the practice of economy. Their lifelong creed is 'sufficient into the day is the evil thereof.' So there exists a class of men, of whose virtues we can say but little, but of whose want of virtue, volumes might be spoken. The tattered, sallow, begrimed aspect of these men, the forlorn condition of their poorly clad wives and half-naked and half-starved children, and the abject wretchedness of their filthy and ill-furnished homes, are features peculiar to this type of humanity, which excite both pity and disgust.

"Towards these deplorable evils, it is to be feared, that a portion of the female community contributes. Amongst the class to which we refer, there is a glaring neglect or ignorance of home duties, and utter incapacity to manage well their household affairs. Dirt, disorder, and discord are everywhere present. The husband finds no comfort in his home, and little or nothing to enlist his sympathies, and consequently seeks pleasures and comfort elsewhere. Home becomes gradually neglected, forsaken, hated. Excesses creep upon him, and, at last, an odious reputation attaches to him which shuts him out from the companionship of respectable associates.

"In ameliorating the condition, and improving the moral, mental, and social position of this class, there is a wide field for the united co-operation of all Christian men of every creed. Very much doubtless has been done, but there is a greater work yet to be done; and, I may add, that there never existed a greater influence for good than now.

"Drunkenness is at this time, perhaps, the most generally demoralizing form of Longton depravity. From robbery and violence we are well protected by a vigilant police, under most excellent management and supervision.

"Prostitution, as compared with some other places, is scarcely known here, for it is stated by one, very well informed on the subject, that there are but sixteen known prostitutes among us, and some of these not wholly dependent upon their nefarious trade for a living."

This is what Mr. Palmer writes of Longton in 1864, and though we may not absolutely say of the other towns "*ab uno disce omnes,*" yet much of what has been written of Longton applies not only to the Potteries, but to much of South Staffordshire also, of which I shall say a few words before I close my report.

What strikes one most forcibly, is the great lack of any middle class of workmen, between those who appear to be utterly improvident and wasteful, and the "careful," prudent, and energetic men, of whom Mr. Palmer has spoken with so much force, who thrive well in business, and to whose thrift is owing mainly the great number of freeholds round about. The men appear to be all thriving and saving, or else in want, except immediately on the receipt of their wages; and it is to this latter class to which a considerable number of the wage population belongs. To use the expressive language of a workman, to whom I was speaking on the subject, "there is no set of workmen among the potters who will wash and dress themselves after a day's labour, go out and smoke a pipe, have one glass and no more, and then go home. They are all either thoroughly for home, or all against home." How many excuses do the drunkards make for the holydays which they keep. Saint Monday has hitherto been a very patron amongst them, and is, by some, absolutely idolized. On his day occur all the weekly rabbit races, dog races, and hop-step-and-jump matches, for sums which to an agricultural labourer, would be a year's maintenance for his whole family. If they hire at Martinmas, an old-fashioned condition of labour which is still retained in the Potteries, they "wet the bargain" till it is drenched through and through. If there is a "wake," they keep it for a week. In short, whatever can be converted into an excuse for a break off, is adopted as a matter of course.

Under these circumstances, the homes of such people, what are they? "What I should call a comfortable and well furnished house," says an informant who is in the habit of visiting them regularly,–

"Is scarcely ever to be found amongst this class. The furniture above and below stairs is, generally, of the poorest kind. The women, from going early to work, have had but few opportunities afforded them of becoming acquainted with home duties before they marry; and in consequence, their homes are deserted by the men for the public house.

"In those parts of England with which I am familiar, I have never met with girls and women who knew so little of the common use of the needle, as in Longton. Hence the rags which disgrace the children, and the great waste of money which is caused by the want of a few stitches in time. Even the children's under-clothing is often bought ready made, and worn till it will no longer hold together.

"The same waste and extravagance goes on with the food. At the beginning of the week I have seen often, meat, fish, spirits and beer, where, three days afterwards, there was only bread and water. A full stomach during the early part of the week, and an empty one at the end of it, is a very common rule.

"Education I consider, to be at a very low ebb amongst them; rather better amongst the women than the men. But, in most cases, even the simplest reading and writing is most imperfect. Any person, however incompetent, who has opened a 'cottage school' as it is called, is blindly trusted by the parents with the all-important first few years of a child's life. What little it learns too, is soon forgotten when it goes to work; its only chance of seeing a book usually being at the Sunday School.

"Unchastity, so far as I can judge, is not a common vice amongst the potters. Drunkenness and ignorance, which latter is more a misfortune than a fault, are the present great evils of which society has to complain, for neither of them are considered a disgrace, even in these days of progress."

Rags and comfortless homes certainly stand everywhere in prominent relief, in many of the wealthiest districts both of North and South Staffordshire, where the wages of the family of ten amount to £3, £4, and £5 a week. I have been told of an instance, in South Staffordshire, where the family wages were as high as £6 a week, and where a prepayment of them was necessary, in consequence of extravagance, before the Saturday night.

Then, as to the effect of such examples upon the children, of whom, perhaps, as many as 90 per cent. never go to school, and do not know what instruction or discipline is. We know what that must be, and how the condition of life in which they are brought up, is continued and exaggerated with their growth into man and womanhood! Need I then say any more to show, what work lies in the future for the regeneration of districts such as these. Here are desolate homes, destitute though rich, where there are incomes, not only sufficient to bring up, but to train the families of educated men who pay poor rates for the maintenance of such wasteful people, when dissipation has done its work. Here are women who do not know what women's duties are, and who bring no attractions to the domestic hearth, whereby to draw the husband from other scenes, and from habits of dissipation. Here are men, who might be so well and comfortably off in life that want might be a word unknown; and here are children, with the spark of intelligence ready to be struck, but with so few kindly hands to strike it, that it remains unlit for ever. And so it appears to me that the Potteries have been but another unit in the mischief which arises out of the absorption of all the labourer's time in the production of that wealth by which we are to become commercially great, at the cost of nearly every religious, moral and intellectual obligation which the possession of it should only the more strengthen us to foster and uphold.

267A–B. Conditions under the Workshops Regulation Act of 1867

Parlty. Papers, 1870/xv.

267A. Sheffield: Reported by Robert Redgrave

loc. cit., pp. 155–161.

. . . There are a vast number of workshops in Sheffield, which, indeed, of all the towns in my district, would seem most to require the intervention of an authority to regulate excessive labour; nothing has been done, and the mayor and corporation have refused even to inquire into complaints forwarded to them. Mr. Gould reports thus:–

"In compliance with your instructions of 17th July last, I beg to report upon the reception accorded to the 'Workshops Act, 1867,' in the various districts of the Sheffield subdivision.

"The towns governed by either a corporate body or a local board, in those portions of Yorkshire, Nottinghamshire, Lincolnshire, and Derbyshire which are comprised in the subdivisions in question, are,

		Population about
Yorkshire.	Sheffield	230,000
	Rotherham . . .	26,000
	Doncaster	17,500
Notts.	Worksop	8,000
	Retford	10,000
Lincs.	Brigg	3,500
	Gainsborough . . .	8,000
Derbyshire	Chesterfield . . .	14,000

"There are also several villages in the district, governed by neither local board nor any tangible authority, wherein children, young persons, and women are employed in various trades, and which the 'Workshops Act,' as at present formed, is powerless to touch.

"Of the towns above-named, the only one in which the carrying out of the 'Workshops Act' would seem to present any difficulty, is Sheffield.

"In the other seven, situated as they are, for the most part, in purely agricultural districts, and having no staple trades of their own, there are very few establishments, except those of milliners, dressmakers, and clothiers, which are not provided for by the Factory Acts.

"I may therefore for the moment dismiss them, merely saying that the greatest courtesy has been shown me by the local authorities in each, who express themselves as ready and willing to carry out any instructions they may receive.

"With respect to Sheffield, I am sorry to be compelled to report a totally different feeling on the part of the local authorities. From interviews I have on various occasions held with these gentlemen (commencing in January 1868), and reported to you, as well as from your personal experience of their views, you are aware that a disinclination, in the first instance, to act, has been followed by a distinct refusal to move in the matter at all. The real reasons for such refusal are very palpable, but are entirely beside the purpose of this report. The alleged reasons for such refusal are (1) the inefficacy of the Act to compel them to carry it out, and, (2) that superior powers are conveyed to the Inspectors of Factories, who, says the chairman of the board, 'are the individuals intended to put the Act in force, and paid for that special purpose.'

"The result is, that since the local authorities repudiate their responsibility, nothing has been done in Sheffield to diminish the immense amount of discontent arising from the inequality of the privileges accorded respectively to those who work in factories and workshops.

"In Sheffield alone, exclusive of the villages referred to above, where a large amount of work incidental to the staple trades of the district is carried on, there are, roughly, about 2,500 workshops, in which are employed variously from 49 down to two or three hands; and from the total absence of supervision on the part of the local authorities, and the consequent facilities afforded for employing young hands, and working them any hours, the occupiers of these workshops are enabled to compete at a very great advantage with the occupiers of the factories.

"The difference is most severely felt in the silver plating, electro, and Britannia metal works.

"I have in a former report to you strongly recommended that some special trades, at present exclusively carried on in 'workshops,' should be included among those subject to the provisions of the Factory Acts; such as, wood turning, horn, bone, ivory cutting, &c, because they are principally carried on in buildings the greater part of which are devoted to trades already under the Factory Acts, and are intimately connected with such trades. Therefore, by doing away with the contrast at present existing in the treatment of the two cases, the thorough working of the Factory Acts will be greatly facilitated; but whether you endorse my recommendation or not, it will be utterly impossible to carry out the Factory Acts in Sheffield satisfactorily, unless either the local authorities are compelled to carry out in their entirety the provisions of the 'Workshops Act,' or a completely new arrangement be made.

"I beg, then, most distinctly to state,–

> "(1) That no reason can be alleged by the local authorities of Sheffield for declining to bring the Act in question into operation which cannot be urged with equal or even greater force by the local authorities of other towns where the Act is in full vigour.
>
> "(2) That the character of the Sheffield trades generally would render such local supervision, if possible, more efficacious than in most other places.
>
> "(3) That the utility of the Factory Acts, as regards Sheffield, is greatly impaired, and its administration neutralized, by the present state of affairs, and by the attitude of antagonism assumed by the local authorities. . . ."

266B. Birmingham: Reported by Robert Baker

loc. cit., pp. 411–413.

. . . But since my last Report this Act, imperfect as it is, has become either much more popular with certain local authorities, or else the notice which Colonel Akroyd gave for ascertaining the number of those bodies who had and had not applied the law to their respective jurisdictions has roused them into activity. Many Inspectors have been appointed with full power to carry the Act into effect. Unfortunately, there is one simple reason why even this first step will not be effectual without a second being also taken. Several of these Inspectors have been appointed without salaries, and others with salaries so inadequate that it is utterly impossible to devote the time to the duties which the Act requires. This is one of the reasons why I have before recommended that, whilst the local authorities should appoint the Inspector, the Secretary of State should settle the scale of payment.

I was happy to think, when I first saw the subjoined correspondence, that the corporation of Birmingham had at last arrived at the determination to enforce the

Act even as it is, which they might have done quite as easily as at Leek or any other place; and with an immense advantage to the children employed, and to the employers also, in destroying in part, if not altogether, the competition between workshops and factories which is now so prevalent.

The town clerk of Birmingham, it appears, recently wrote to Mr. Farrow, wishing for information "as to the operation of the Workshops Regulation Act, 1867, and requesting the favour of his replies to the annexed inquiries so far as related to Leek":-

Question 1.-Had any officer been appointed under the Workshops Regulation Act?

Answer.-Mr. R. Farrow, the sanitary inspector of this district, has been appointed ever since the Act came into operation.

Question 2.-If so, what appointments have been made, and at what annual cost?

Answer.-To administer the law without favour or affection, and report monthly to Mr. Baker, the chief Inspector of Factories.

Question 3.-Is the result satisfactory or otherwise?

Answer.-Very satisfactory, considering the defects in the Act.

Subsequently Mr. councillor Chamberlain wrote to Mr. Farrow as follows:-

"It is probable the town council of Birmingham will shortly have again under discussion the propriety of putting the Workshops Act in force in their borough. Many members of the council appear averse to this step, not because they dispute the principles of the Act, but because they are so faulty in construction that no good purpose will be served by them, and that their amendment should precede their application.

"Knowing that the Acts are in force in your district, I venture to trouble you for your opinion on the matter, and especially to ask you to define (and, if possible to give some illustration of) the advantages that have accrued to the working population of the district in consequence of the enforcement of the Act.

"I understand it is specially to the sanitary arrangements that your attention has been called. I have also written to Capt. May at Stoke, for information.

"Apologising for,' &c.

Mr. Farrow's answer was as follows:-

"Public Offices, Leek.

"Sir,

"In reply to your note of the 27th inst., I may state that, as sanitary inspector my instructions are to report upon the existence of any evil which is known to depreciate the value of life in the district. In any matter in which the sanitary authority cannot direct me to deal with the evil, I urge the subject upon the attention of the proper authority.

"My experience is that the due administration of factory law is an element of the highest importance to a local government in promoting the physical and social wellbeing of the general population within its jurisdiction; consequently it has been to our interest that I should report every irregularity of this kind to Mr. Baker in the same manner as I should do were I under his direct control. Indeed, I may say that every important improvement made in factory legislation forms a kind of landmark in our vital statistical record. The Workshops Regulation Act (notwithstanding all its glaring defects) is of much more importance to the well-being of this district than all the Factory Acts put together. If necessary, I could give many practical illustrations of this. Large factories you know, as a rule, are managed by intelligent men of business who are conscious of their moral responsibilities. The class of persons who manage small workshops are, as a rule, very different. As a rule I find factory law much more needed in small establishments than in large ones.

"During the first three months after the Workshops Act came into operation we increased the number of half-timers at school 2,000 per cent.

"The enclosed printed reports will give you a general idea as to the good results obtained.

"The various difficulties with which I have to contend, and opinions as to the amendments of the law, and other matters, will be found in Mr. Baker's printed report for the half-year ending October 1868 (pages 320 to 334).

"I am fully convinced that no local authority can afford to allow Factory and Workshops Acts to remain a dead letter within its district, and that the only effectual manner by which they can be satisfactorily carried out is by similar arrangements to those made by Mr. Baker and the local authority of this district.

"I enclose you a copy of our abstract and register, also a copy of the several forms used, which are provided at the cost of the local authority. Form No. 1 cost the parents 1s. filling up, and will from time to time, as the child changes its employer, serve to prove its age.

"No. 2 are supplied by me to the several schools; the teacher weekly gives each child its own certificate, the child hands it to the employer, who places it on a separate file, and keeps it in the room or place where the child works, and I examine and affix my initials to them monthly. Nos. 3 & 4 will be understood. No. 5 is the form on which I report monthly to Mr. Baker and the local authority.

"I am, Sir.
"Yours faithfully,
"ROBERT FARROW."

268. Report of the Royal Commission on Trade Unions (1867–1869): Majority Report

Parlty. Papers, 1868–1869/XXXI, Eleventh Report.

OBJECTS OF TRADES UNIONS AND METHOD OF ATTAINMENT

26. The objects of trades unions are in general of a twofold character:–

I. *First.* Those of an ordinary friendly or benefit society–*viz.*, to afford relief to the members of the union when incapacitated from work by accident or sickness; to allow a sum for the funeral expenses of the members and their wives; and sometimes to provide superannuation allowances for members incapacitated by old age.

II. *Secondly*. Those of a trade society proper–*viz*., to watch over and promote the interests of the working classes in the several trades, and especially to protect them against the undue advantage which the command of a large capital is supposed by them to give to the employers of labour.

27. The objects last referred to are, in the great majority of the existing trades unions, the main objects of the members in associating together. It is, however, found desirable by the promoters of trades unions to combine with these objects the functions of a friendly or benefit society. Additional members and additional funds are thus obtained; and the hold which the society has over its members is strengthened by the consideration that any member who should subject himself to expulsion for disobedience to the orders of the union, issued in what it deems the interests of trade, would thereby forfeit the superannuation and other benefits to which he would be entitled, it may be, from a long course of subscription continued with the very object of securing to himself those benefits.

28. With respect to the trade purposes of the unions, one of the most constant objects is to obtain for the members the best rate of wages which they can command, and to reduce the number of hours in which the wages are earned. A further object is to bring about a more equal division of work among the members of the trade, and its distribution among a greater number of workmen, than would prevail under the influence of unrestrained competition; and this object is sought by attempting to establish a uniform minimum rate of wages.

29. The agency through which the trades unions endeavour to effect these purposes is of two kinds–direct and indirect. The direct agency is by means of what is termed a "strike"–a simultaneous cessation from work on the part of the workmen. The strike is the ultimate sanction, as between the workmen and the employer, of all the demands insisted upon by the union. It is usually preceded by an intimation that if the concession required be not granted the men will quit work in a body. If this intimation fails to produce the desired effect, the case is ordinarily brought before the governing body of the union; and if the proposed proceeding is approved, the strike is organized and the men are called off work.

30. The policy and conduct of strikes would seem to constitute an important part of the duties of the council of a union. In the case of the *Amalgamated Society of Carpenters and Joiners*, Mr Applegarth, the secretary, informed us (qu. 54) that the number of strikes involving a large number of men are about 12 in a year. Speaking of the success which had attended the establishment of a branch union at Bradford in raising wages and shortening hours, he says (qu. 145): "Our men were continually agitating in a very businesslike manner with their employers, and the result has been, as here stated, that they have got their hours reduced and the wages increased." Their general policy is to take advantage of a brisk trade to insist on a rise of wages, and when trade is slack they resist a fall (Applegarth, qu. 95; Allan, qu. 857–861). It appears, however, in evidence that in many cases leaders of unions fail to consider whether the circumstances of the trade are such as to call for or admit of a rise of wages. It is with them rather a question of the relative strength of the two parties.

31. It does not appear to be borne out by the evidence that the disposition to

strike on the part of workmen is in itself the creation of unionism, or that the frequency of strikes increases in proportion to the strength of the union. It is, indeed, affirmed by the leaders of unions that the effect of the established societies is to diminish the frequency, and certainly the disorder, of strikes, and to guarantee a regularity of wages and hours rather than to engage in constant endeavours to improve them. But supposing such results to follow, as stated, from the establishment and action of a powerful trades union in any trade or district, it is not unreasonable to assume that the diminished frequency of strikes may arise not from any want of disposition to strike on the part of the members of the union, but from the fact that its organization is so powerful as, in most cases, to obtain the concession demanded without recourse to a strike. The effect of a very powerful and rich union organization in moderating the disposition to strike is shown in the evidence of Messrs Allan (qu. 814–844), Applegarth (135–137), W. Macdonald (2289), Harnott (1054), Coulson (1417–1424), A. Macdonald (15,592–15,594, 15,620), Pickard (15,830, etc.), Wilkinson (18,743), Self (19,804), Mundella (19,691), and Cooper (14,201–14,210).

32. The indirect agency above referred to is of a more complex nature; but it will be found to resolve itself into–

1. An attempt to limit the number of workmen to be employed in any branch of industry, and so to create a monopoly of labour with its attendant power to command a higher rate of wages.

2. To repress competition among the workmen themselves.

33. It is said by some advocates of trades unions that men, if left to independent action, will, in the struggle for employment, by competition with each other lower the rate of wages at which they are willing to work; and will, also, be tempted by the love of gain to injure themselves by working long hours and overtaxing their strength, thereby compelling others to follow their example. It is deemed more for their interest, therefore, that they should by arrangement together refuse to accept less than a certain rate of wages or to work more than a limited number of hours, and should also resort to other expedients for distributing the work equally amongst them, and making it go as far as possible in furnishing them a moderate amount of employment.

34. The monopoly of labour is attempted to be effected by means of rules, or by a practice tacitly adopted among the members of the unions, limiting the number of apprentices to be allowed in a trade, and excluding from work as far as practicable workmen not belonging to the union. The limitation of the number of apprentices is not insisted on by all the unions, but it is a matter to which some of them attach the greatest importance. The question, and the question of the employment of boys to do work which it is urged by the unionists ought to be done by men, have led to many disputes. Mr Allan, the secretary of the *Amalgamated Society of Engineers*, one of the largest unions in the United Kingdom, and every way one of the most considerable, says (qu. 841) that the disputes with employers during the last 10 years have "principally arisen from piecework and the large number of boys employed."

35. The right to limit the supply of labour in a given trade, and so to raise the rate of wages, is distinctly claimed by some of the unionists. Mr Wilkinson, the

secretary of the *National Flint Glassmakers' Friendly Society*, says (qu. 18,717): "The limitation of apprentices is simply because we consider that as working men who have been brought up in the trade and devoted a number of years to learn it . . . we have a right in a certain measure to limit the supply in accordance with what the demand may be." And Mr Shreeve, the secretary of the *Printers' Machine Managers' Trade Society*, says (qu. 19,949): "The way in which we look at this apprentice question is simply this–that we have served our time to a business and we wish to get a respectable living by it. We know that if there are four men to do two men's work the wages must come down."

36. On the same ground, objection is sometimes made to the employment of women in certain kinds of work. A union of warpers in Manchester refused to allow the wife and sisters of one of their members to warp. "It was against their rules," they said, "to allow women to warp, for if women were introduced into their market the wages of the men would be reduced."*

37. Sometimes the monopoly of the work of a district has been attempted. A society of brickmakers in Manchester, as stated in the report of the Examiners into that district, "claim an extent of four miles round Manchester in every direction, an area of 120 square miles, as their peculiar district, within the limits of which they permit no bricks to be made except by Manchester union men, nor any bricks to be used except those made within the district. They accomplish the latter object by means of an alliance with the Manchester Bricklayers' Union, the members of which will not set any bricks not made within the above-named district. Levenshulme is claimed by both the Manchester and Stockport Unions, and is a kind of debateable ground between them."†

38. The chief expedients for repressing competition among the workmen are rules, or a tacit understanding, prescribing a *minimum* rate of wages, to be accepted and a *maximum* number of hours to be worked by the members of the union, and prohibiting them from working overtime or taking piecework. The opponents of overtime and piecework appear to us to hold that the man who works overtime takes so much from the common stock of labour, and thus injures the rest; and that the man who takes piecework, besides that he gets more than his share of the common stock of work, is apt to show what may be done by skill and industry, and so raises the standard of expectation on the part of the employer.

39. The opponents of piecework further attempt to justify the rules against it on the grounds that piecework, where quick despatch becomes the main consideration of the workman, is apt to lead men to hurry over their work in a slatternly manner, and so results in inferior workmanship, which, when finished, the employer has no means of checking or testing. It is in the interest, therefore, as they allege, of the employers and the public, not less than that of the workmen, that they object to piecework. The employers, however, by no means accede to this view. Their opinion is almost universally in favour of piecework wherever the circumstances of the work admit of its adoption. Mr Robinson, the engineer of the *Atlas Works* at Manchester, in commenting on the statement of Mr Allan, the secretary of the *Amalgamated*

* *Report of the Manchester Examiners*, p. xxi. † *Ibid.*, p. ix.

Society of Engineers (qu. 678) that "as a general rule" piecework "is inferior", and (qu. 19,088) that in "places where piecework is worked there is a tendency on the part of the working men to slide over the work," says (qu. 19,089): "The plan of doing piecework in an establishment like ours and in Whitworth's and Beyer's, has led to such a reputation for our work that we can get a higher price than other firms;" and (qu. 19,090) that "it is far easier to check the quality of work done in a properly organized establishment than it is to check the amount of the work."

40. Other expedients of a minor character, and having the same object in view, are rules, or a tacit understanding existing in some unions, confining each class of workmen strictly to their own division of labour–*e.g.*, restricting the mason from on any occasion setting or displacing a brick, or the bricklayer a stone, or either of them from doing any portion of the work which belongs to a plasterer; and rules against what is called "chasing"–*i.e.*, prohibiting the leading man, where several workmen are working in line, from proceeding at more than a moderate rate; and rules limiting the number of bricks to be carried in a hod, and prohibiting the carrying of bricks in a wheelbarrow, and prohibiting the working of stone at the quarry, and the like; matters which, although they may have the appearance of being of minor importance, are vexatious and harassing to the employers, and are sometimes attended with great inconvenience and loss.

41. Some of the instances brought under our notice, in which the rules of trades unions interfere with employers in the mode of conducting their business, are of a more extravagant character. Such, for instance, are the following: a union of bricklayers at Manchester interfered to insist that a Manchester builder, constructing a railway station at Bury, should take at least half the men from Manchester (qu. 3454); the *National Association of Operative Plasterers* interfered to require an employer, whose head office was at Manchester, although he had a branch office at Bolton, to pay Manchester wages for a job at Bolton (qu. 3416).

42. It is not pretended that in framing the rules of the union any regard is had to the convenience of the employer. The rules, says Mr Conolly, a member of the *Operative Society of Stonemasons*, and a leading man among unionists, "are made for men, not for masters; we do not take masters into the account at all in the arrangement of the matter; we merely look upon them as men who step in with their capital and who want to get the greatest profit they can out of their capital, while we want to get the greatest profit we can out of our labour; and we find that by an arrangement of this sort, without depriving society of the advantage of the skill of its members, we can gain our object" (qu. 1349). . . .

EFFECTS OF TRADES UNIONS ON THE CHARACTER OF WORKING MEN, AND ON THEIR RELATIONS WITH THEIR EMPLOYERS

45. That trades unions have had certain injurious effects on the character of the working men, as well as on the relations between them and their employers, seems not to admit of doubt. Thus much the evidence which we have collected appears to us to establish. But in respect to the special character and extent of those effects, there

is, as might be expected, great discrepancy between the witnesses. The employers complain that trades unions have fostered a spirit of antagonism between themselves and their workmen which formerly did not exist. There is no longer, they say, the cordial and friendly feeling which used to be common between the two classes. The workmen, looking rather to the approval of their unions than to that of their employers, are less anxious than of yore to stand well with the latter; and the employers on their part no longer feel under the same obligation to look after the interests of their workmen and to assist them in periods of difficulty. Misunderstandings which often would be readily settled if there were free and friendly intercourse between them, are exasperated and prolonged. Such are the allegations of the employers. Nor can it be said that they are materially shaken, or even strongly denied, on the part of the unionists. These, in general, seem rather to regard those sentiments of which the employers regret the decline, as founded on mistaken notions of inferiority on the one hand and patronage on the other.

46. But many statements will be found in the evidence implying a deterioration in the character of the workmen in more material respects than these. It is said that the better class among them are losing, under the influence of the trades unions, the character of self-reliance and independence by which they used to be distinguished. The desire of the workman to excel, to do the best in his power to give satisfaction to his employer, to improve himself, and if possible to rise in the world, is damped by the thraldom in which he is held to the rules of his union, and by the systematic disapproval on the part of his fellow unionists of all efforts to go beyond that average level of exertion which it is the aim of the unions to maintain.

47. To this it is replied on the part of the unions, that their real tendency, considered in a wider and more equitable view, is to raise, not depress, the character of the workman, by making him feel that he is not an insulated agent, subject to oppression, or at all events to accidents over which he can exercise no control, but a member of a strong united body, capable at once of defending his rights and of ensuring him a resource in case of temporary need. It is maintained also that the practice of having a code of working rules agreed to between employers and workmen, such as the better unions seek to establish, embracing a book of wages, of laws, and of trade rules, is attended with the best results; that it tends to diminish and usually to extinguish the occurrence of strikes, and to establish a spirit of co-operation between masters and workmen.

48. It is no necessary part of our duty to pronounce authoritatively between these conflicting assertions. We can only hope that the body of evidence which we have collected will be of service to those who may wish to study for themselves some of the most difficult and momentous questions with which society has now to deal. Thus much only we will intimate as the apparent result of our enquiries: that, whether the circumstance is to be regretted or not, the habitual code of sentiment which prevailed between employers and workmen in the times when the former were regarded by both law and usage as the governing class is now greatly relaxed, and cannot be revived. A substitute has now to be found for it, arising from the feelings of equity, and enlightened self interest, and mutual forbearance, which should exist

between contracting parties who can best promote their several chances of advantage by aiding and accommodating each other.

49. With regard to the coercion occasionally practised by the majority over the minority in the unions, and to the more habitual coercion which they are apt to exercise, and of which many of their defenders seek to justify the exercise, over their fellow workmen who do not belong to the union, we need not enter here into any detailed statements, because the abundant evidence relating to this subject tells its own story without the aid of any summary. To how great an extent this system has been carried in the case of some unions may be seen at large in the Reports of the Examiners into certain proceedings of some of the trades unions of Sheffield and Manchester. In many of the trades unions in those neighbourhoods crime and outrage have been the habitual methods of enforcing the trade laws of the union. "Rattening", one of the mildest of these methods–*viz.*, the abstraction of the workman's tools, so as to prevent him from working for his livelihood until he has obeyed the arbitrary orders of the union–they look upon (according to one of their advocates and apologists) as little if at all worse than distraining for rent by a landlord. According to another of their advocates and apologists, they regard workmen who stand aloof from the union with a feeling akin to that which defenders of their country have towards a citizen who deserts to the invaders for the sake of better pay. Here is manifest, on the testimony of their friends, an utter perversion of all sense of law and duty. And it is to be observed that the discreditable proceedings to which we refer have by no means been confined to the lower class of workmen. With regard to the outrages at Manchester and in the neighbourhood, the Examiners report as follows on the brickmakers' and other unions into which they made enquiry: "The outrages which we have related, and which rendered life and property insecure, were, in our opinion, all of them instigated and sanctioned by the several unions in the districts in which they were respectively committed. They were all deliberately planned and executed in the furtherance of a system, which had for its object the subjection of both masters and men to the rules of the union, and the destruction of the freedom of labour."*

50. One observation, however, we feel it necessary to make. Leaving out of the question grosser cases of outrage, and confining ourselves to the more ordinary cases of vexatious interference with the workmen's liberty which have been brought before us, it must be noticed that very nearly the whole of these instances rest on the testimony of the employers; the workmen themselves, those on whom the alleged tyranny actually presses, have not come forward in any numbers in answer to our general invitation, to substantiate them. As far as the workmen are concerned–if we except the evidence of members of the *Free Labour Registration Society*, a body organised for the particular purpose of counteracting the trades unions–few complaints of the present influence of trades unions, and no suggestion for the curtailment of their power, have been brought before us. No independent and insulated workmen have volunteered to express themselves in that sense. This may be interpreted, either as implying that the labouring classes in general are not discontented with the restrictions which the trades unions appear to impose on industry, or (as we believe)

* *Report of the Manchester Examiners*, p. xxv.

as implying that the influence of those unions is so very extensive, and their ramifications so minute, and the general dislike to oppose an established class feeling so strong, that the real sentiments of the workmen opposed to unions have been, to a great extent, withheld from us.

EFFECT OF TRADES UNIONS ON THE TRADE AND INDUSTRY OF THE COUNTRY

51. The effect which unions have had in impeding the development of trade, whether by simply raising prices, or by diverting trade from certain districts or from this country abroad, is a matter excessively difficult to determine. That unionism frequently occurs with a declining trade is sufficiently plain: that they stand in relation of cause and effect is another thing. It is obvious that many points in a very complex chain of reasoning have to be determined before this can be proved. It must first be shown what is the actual as well as the relative diminution in production. It must then be determined how far this represents a general diminution in demand, and how far it stands for production of other markets. Then, if a distinct case is made out that the trade has gone into other channels, it remains to be shown to which of the possible causes this is due.

52. There are many rules and practices of trades unions of which it must be predicted that their effect, in so far as they are really effective, must of necessity be to enhance the price of commodities by raising or artificially keeping up the cost of production. But whether such rules and practices are really sufficient for that object – whether they are not either far less effectual than is commonly supposed, or liable to be counteracted by other causes operating in a contrary direction – is a question incapable of solution without an investigation extending to a great variety of subjects besides that directly submitted to us.

53. The industries on which trades unions may be supposed to have had an effect must be divided into two classes – those in which foreign competition cannot, and those in which it can, materially interfere with the productive industry of the country.

54. In the first case, there is nothing *a priori* to prevent the operation of trades unions from raising the cost of commodities until the rise is checked by the diminution of consumption. Such an instance is afforded by the various trades engaged in building; in these, unionism extensively prevails, and to its history much of the early part of our Inquiry was directed. Referring to the evidence which we have received with respect to those trades as containing our sources of information, and expressing no positive opinion on an extremely intricate question, we are disposed to think that the operation of trades unions may have tended to enhance in these trades of late years the cost of production, and that houses and other buildings might have been somewhat better and cheaper at the present time had not trades unions interfered so extensively and so vexatiously with the proceedings of the employers. It does not necessarily follow that they have raised wages in those trades and improved thereby the condition of the workmen; the contrary, in the long run, is more probable.

55. The other classes of trades – that class in which production may be interfered

with by foreign competition–is far more important, since it may be truly said that on the power of this country to produce her staple commodities better and more cheaply than the rivals with whom she has to compete, her commercial prosperity mainly depends. Accordingly, we have not failed to give our special consideration to every fact which has been brought before us relating to so essential a part of our Inquiry. But we are compelled to admit that we have been unable to arrive at any very definite solution of the problem, whether or not trades unions have had of late years a mischievous operation in this direction. It will, no doubt, be found that our evidence contains many statements on the part of masters to the effect that under the prevalence of trades unions their own special business has been in their belief interfered with by foreign competition, or (more commonly) that they have reasonable grounds for apprehending such interference. But, as we have said, even where the fact of a decline of production is admitted, it by no means follows that we have arrived at the cause; and, taking the more general evidence afforded by the returns of our export trade for the last few years, we cannot state that we have traced any distinct connexion between its fluctuations in particular employments and the prevalence of trades unions in those employments.

269. The changed attitude to factory legislation: report of Robert Redgrave, factory inspector

Parlty. Papers, 1871/XIV/p. 533.

. . . I continue to receive from the sub-inspectors excellent accounts of the observance of the various regulations which we have to enforce. The harmonious co-operation of employers of all classes, and the increasing feeling that the interests of employers and employed are bound together, have greatly contributed to this end.

Nothing can shew in stronger light the great change that has taken place in the acceptance and observance of the Factory Regulations, than the recommendations in the reports of the factory inspectors 25 years since, contrasted with those which I have frequently felt it my duty to submit.

My former colleagues, hampered by opposition and obstructed on every side, filled their reports with urgent recommendations for increased power, for more stringent regulations, and more certain penalties.

It has been my good fortune to be able to demonstrate, as I trust I have done with sufficient justification, that useless and annoying regulations may be removed, and that a yet readier and more cheerful observance of the law will follow the removal of rules which now serve no useful purpose. . . .

INDEX TO TEXTS

The figures refer to the numbered documents, not to the pages